Lecture Notes in Computer Science 2348
Edited by G. Goos, J. Hartmanis, and J. van Leeuwen

Springer
Berlin
Heidelberg
New York
Barcelona
Hong Kong
London
Milan
Paris
Tokyo

Anne Banks Pidduck   John Mylopoulos
Carson C. Woo   M. Tamer Ozsu (Eds.)

Advanced Information Systems Engineering

14th International Conference, CAiSE 2002
Toronto, Canada, May 27-31, 2002
Proceedings

Springer

Series Editors

Gerhard Goos, Karlsruhe University, Germany
Juris Hartmanis, Cornell University, NY, USA
Jan van Leeuwen, Utrecht University, The Netherlands

Volume Editors

Anne Banks Pidduck
M. Tamer Ozsu
University of Waterloo, School of Computer Science
200 University Avenue West, Waterloo, Ontario, Canada, N2L 3G1
E-mail: {apidduck/tozsu}@uwaterloo.ca

John Mylopoulos
University of Toronto, Pratt Building
6 King's College Road, Toronto, Ontario, Canada, M5S 3H5
E-mail: jm@cs.toronto.edu

Carson C. Woo
University of British Columbia, Faculty of Commerce and Business Administration
2053 Main Mall, Vancouver, B.C. Canada V6T 1Z2
E-mail: Carson.Woo@ubc.ca

Cataloging-in-Publication Data applied for

Die Deutsche Bibliothek - CIP-Einheitsaufnahme

Advanced information systems engineering : 14th international conference ;
proceedings / CAiSE 2002, Toronto, Canada, May 27 - 31, 2002. Anne Banks
Pidduck ... (ed.). - Berlin ; Heidelberg ; New York ; Barcelona ; Hong Kong ;
London ; Milan ; Paris ; Tokyo : Springer, 2002
 (Lecture notes in computer science ; Vol. 2348)
 ISBN 3-540-43738-X

CR Subject Classification (1998): H.2, H.4-5, H.3, J.1, K.4.3-4, K.6, D.2, I.2.11

ISSN 0302-9743
ISBN 3-540-43738-X Springer-Verlag Berlin Heidelberg New York

This work is subject to copyright. All rights are reserved, whether the whole or part of the material is
concerned, specifically the rights of translation, reprinting, re-use of illustrations, recitation, broadcasting,
reproduction on microfilms or in any other way, and storage in data banks. Duplication of this publication
or parts thereof is permitted only under the provisions of the German Copyright Law of September 9, 1965,
in its current version, and permission for use must always be obtained from Springer-Verlag. Violations are
liable for prosecution under the German Copyright Law.

Springer-Verlag Berlin Heidelberg New York
a member of BertelsmannSpringer Science+Business Media GmbH

http://www.springer.de

© Springer-Verlag Berlin Heidelberg 2002
Printed in Germany

Typesetting: Camera-ready by author, data conversion by DA-TeX Gerd Blumenstein
Printed on acid-free paper   SPIN 10870009   06/3142   5 4 3 2 1 0

Preface

The explosive growth of the Internet and the Web have created an ever-growing demand for information systems, and ever-growing challenges for Information Systems Engineering. The series of Conferences on Advanced Information Systems Engineering (CAiSE) was launched in Scandinavia by Janis Bubenko and Arne Solvberg in 1989, became an important European conference, and was held annually in major European sites throughout the 1990s. Now, in its 14th year, CAiSE was held for the first time outside Europe, showcasing international research on information systems and their engineering.

Not surprisingly, this year the conference enjoyed unprecedented attention. In total, the conference received 173 paper submissions, the highest number ever for a CAiSE conference. Of those, 42 were accepted as regular papers and 26 as short (poster) papers. In addition, the conference received 12 proposals for workshops of which 8 were approved, while 4 tutorials were selected from 15 submissions.

The technical program was put together by an international committee of 81 experts. In total, 505 reviews were submitted, with every member of the committee contributing. Decisions on all submissions were reached at a program committee meeting in Toronto on January 26-27,2002. Workshop and tutorial proposals were handled separately by committees chaired by Patrick Martin (workshops), and Jarek Gryz and Richard Paige (tutorials).

We wish to extend a great "THANK YOU!" to all members of the program and organizing committees for their volunteer contributions of time and expertise. The fact that so many busy (and famous!) people took the trouble to help us with the organization of this conference and the formation of its technical program speaks well for the future of CAiSE and the field of Information Systems Engineering.

May 2002

Anne Banks Pidduck
John Mylopoulos
Carson Woo
Tamer Özsu

Organization

CAiSE 2002 was organized by the Department of Computer Science, University of Waterloo, and the Department of Computer Science, University of Toronto.

Organizing Committee

General Chair:	Tamer Özsu (University of Waterloo, Canada)
Program Committee Chairs:	John Mylopoulos (University of Toronto)
	Carson Woo (University of British Columbia)
Panel and Tutorial Chairs:	Jarek Gryz (York University, Canada)
	Rich Paige (York University, Canada)
Local and Publicity Chair:	Manuel Kolp (University of Louvain, Belgium)
Workshop and Poster Chair:	Patrick Martin (Queen's University, Kingston, Canada)
Proceedings Chair:	Anne Banks Pidduck (University of Waterloo)

Local Arrangements Committee

Luiz-Marcio Cysneiros
Linda Liu
Patricia Rodriguez-Gianolli

Manuel Kolp (Chair)
Jianguo Lu

Donors

IBM Center for Advanced Studies
Institute for Computer Research
Bell University Laboratories

Academic Supporters

University of Waterloo, Department of Computer Science
University of Toronto, Department of Computer Science
University of Louvain, IAG School of Management
University of British Columbia, Commerce and Business Administration
York University, Department of Computer Science
Queen's University, Kingston, Department of Computing and Information Science

Program Committee

Ken Barker (Canada)
Daniel Berry (Canada)
Alex Borgida (USA)
Paul Bowen (USA)
Sjaak Brinkkemper (The Netherlands)
Michael Brodie (USA)
Christoph Bussler (USA)
Silvana Castano (Italy)
Jan Dietz (The Netherlands)
Johan Eder (Austria)
Marcel Franckson (France)
Mariagrazia Fugini (Italy)
Antonio Furtado (Brazil)
Andreas Geppert (Switzerland)
Paolo Giorgini (Italy)
Martin Glinz (Switzerland)
Sol Greenspan (USA)
Alan Hevner (USA)
Juhani Iivari (Finland)
Sushil Jajodia (USA)
Keith Jeffery (UK)
Manfred Jeusfeld (The Netherlands)
Hermann Kaindl (Austria)
Hannu Kangassalo (Finland)
Gerti Kappel (Austria)
Steven Kimbrough (USA)
Kostas Kontogiannis (Canada)
Manolis Koubarakis (Greece)
Alberto Laender (Brazil)
Julio Leite (Brazil)
Maurizio Lenzerini (Italy)
Michel Leonard (Switzerland)
Chin Li (China)
Marin Litoiu (Canada)
Peri Loucopoulos (UK)
Kalle Lyytinen (Finland)
Neil Maiden (UK)
Sal March (USA)
Pat Martin (Canada)
Nancy Mead (USA)
Misha Missikoff (Italy)

David Monarchi (USA)
Hausi Müller (Canada)
Oscar Nierstrasz (Switzerland)
Andreas Oberweis (Germany)
Antoni Olivé (Spain)
Andreas Opdahl (Norway)
Maria Orlowska (Australia)
Maurizio Panti (Italy)
Mike Papazoglou (The Netherlands)
Jeff Parsons (Canada)
Oscar Pastor (Spain)
Barbara Pernici (Italy)
Alain Pirotte (Belgium)
Dimitris Plexousakis (Greece)
Klaus Pohl (Germany)
Radhakrishnan.T (Canada)
Sudha Ram (USA)
Bill Robinson (USA)
Colette Rolland (France)
Michel Scholl (France)
Michael Schrefl (Austria)
Timos Sellis (Greece)
Mike Shaw (USA)
Olivia Sheng (USA)
Keng Siau (USA)
Jacob Slonim (Canada)
Arne Solvberg (Norway)
Veda Storey (USA)
Eleni Stroulia (Canada)
Alistair Sutcliffe (UK)
Mohan Tanniru (USA)
Bernhard Thalheim (Germany)
Costantino Thanos (Italy)
Aphrodite Tsalgatidou (Greece)
Yannis Vassiliou (Greece)
Yair Wand (Canada)
Benkt Wangler (Sweden)
Tony Wasserman (USA)
Christopher Welty (USA)
Roel Wieringa (The Netherlands)
Eric Yu (Canada)

Tutorials

Fact-Oriented Modeling
Presenter: Terry Halpin, Microsoft Corporation

The Application of Workflow Management Technology in Process-Based B2B Integration
Presenter: Christoph Bussler, Oracle Corporation

The Web-Services Phenomenon: Concepts, Technologies, Current Trends, and Research Directions
Presenter: Michael P. Papazoglou, Tilburg University, The Netherlands

Publish/Subscribe: Applications, Concepts, and Algorithms
Presenter: H-Arno Jacobsen, University of Toronto, Canada

Workshops

Agent-Oriented Information Systems (AOIS 2002)
Organizers: P. Giorgini, Y. Lesperance, G. Wagner, E. Yu

Goal-Oriented Business Process Modeling (GBPM 2002)
Organizers: I. Bider, P. Johannesson

2nd Workshop on Data Integration over the Web (DIWeb 2002)
Organizers: Z. Bellahsene, Z. Lacroix

Workshop on E-Services and E-Business Technology
Organizers: M. Orlowska, C. Bussler, J. Yang, B. Pernici

Design and Management of Data Warehouses (DMDW 2002)
Organizers: J. Hammer, M. Jeusfeld, I. Song, M. Staudt, D. Theodoratos

Evaluation and Modeling Methods in Systems Analysis and Design (EMMSAD 2002)
Organizers: T. Halpin, K, Siau, J. Krogstie

E-Services and the Semantic Web (ESSW 2002)
Organizers: R. Hull, S. McIlraith

Doctoral Consortium
Organizers: A. Hinze, J. Kotlarsky

Table of Contents

Invited Presentations

The Grand Challenge in Information Technology and
the Illusion of Validity 1
Michael L. Brodie

Metadata and Cooperative Knowledge Management 2
Matthias Jarke

Ontology-Driven Conceptual Modeling 3
Christopher Welty

Metadata and Cooperative Knowledge Management 4
Matthias Jarke and Ralf Klamma

Web Component: A Substrate for Web Service Reuse and Composition 21
Jian Yang and Mike. P. Papazoglou

Developing Web Applications

Designing Web-Based Systems in Social Context:
A Goal and Scenario Based Approach 37
Lin Liu and Eric Yu

A State Machine Based Approach for a Process Driven Development
of Web-Applications 52
Rakesh Mohan, Mitchell A. Cohen, and Josef Schiefer

Knowledge Management

Supporting Dimension Updates in an OLAP Server 67
*Alejandro A. Vaisman, Alberto O. Mendelzon, Walter Ruaro,
and Sergio G. Cymerman*

The COMET Metamodel for Temporal Data Warehouses 83
Johann Eder, Christian Koncilia, and Tadeusz Morzy

Exploring RDF for Expertise Matching within
an Organizational Memory 100
Ping Liu, Jayne Curson, and Peter Dew

Deployment Issues

Describing and Communicating Software Architecture in Practice:
Observations on Stakeholders and Rationale 117
Kari Smolander and Tero Päivärinta

The Individual Deployment of Systems Development Methodologies 134
Magda Huisman and Juhani Iivari

Supporting the Deployment of Object-Oriented Frameworks 151
Daqing Hou, H. James Hoover, and Eleni Stroulia

Semantics of Information

A Conceptual Modeling Approach to Semantic Document Retrieval 167
Terje Brasethvik and Jon Atle Gulla

Multidimensional Semistructured Data:
Representing Context-Dependent Information on the Web 183
Yannis Stavrakas and Manolis Gergatsoulis

The Role of Semantic Relevance in Dynamic User Community
Management and the Formulation of Recommendations 200
Nick Papadopoulos and Dimitris Plexousakis

System Qualities

Can We Ever Build Survivable Systems from COTS Components? 216
Howard F. Lipson, Nancy R. Mead, and Andrew P. Moore

Towards a Data Model for Quality Management Web Services:
An Ontology of Measurement for Enterprise Modeling 230
Henry M. Kim and Mark S. Fox

A Modelling Approach to the Realisation
of Modular Information Spaces 245
Moira C. Norrie and Alexios Palinginis

Integration Issues

Data Integration under Integrity Constraints 262
*Andrea Calì, Diego Calvanese, Giuseppe De Giacomo,
and Maurizio Lenzerini*

Babel: An XML-Based Application Integration Framework 280
Huaxin Zhang and Eleni Stroulia

Integrating and Rapid-Prototyping UML Structural
and Behavioural Diagrams Using Rewriting Logic 296
Nasreddine Aoumeur and Gunter Saake

Analysis and Adaptation

Verification of Payment Protocols via MultiAgent Model Checking 311
M. Benerecetti, M. Panti, L. Spalazzi, and S. Tacconi

SNet: A Modeling and Simulation Environment
for Agent Networks Based on i* and ConGolog 328
Günter Gans, Gerhard Lakemeyer, Matthias Jarke, and Thomas Vits

Usage–Centric Adaptation of Dynamic E–Catalogs 344
Hye-young Paik, Boualem Benatallah, and Rachid Hamadi

Retrieval and Performance

Reengineering of Database Applications to EJB Based Architecture 361
Jianguo Lu

Efficient Similarity Search for Time Series Data Based on the Minimum
Distance 377
Sangjun Lee, Dongseop Kwon, and Sukho Lee

A High-Performance Data Structure for Mobile Information Systems 392
John N. Wilson

Requirements Issues

External Requirements Validation for Component-Based Systems 404
Andreas Leicher and Felix Bübl

Using Business Rules in EXtreme Requirements 420
Maria Carmen Leonardi and Julio Cesar Sampaio do Prado Leite

Evaluating CM3: Problem Management 436
Mira Kajko-Mattsson

Schema Matching and Evolution

Database Schema Matching Using Machine Learning
with Feature Selection 452
Jacob Berlin and Amihai Motro

Evolving Partitions in Conceptual Schemas in the UML 467
Cristina Gómez and Antoni Olivé

Schema Evolution in Heterogeneous Database Architectures –
A Schema Transformation Approach 484
Peter Mc. Brien and Alexandra Poulovassilis

Workflows

Serviceflow Beyond Workflow? Concepts and Architectures
for Supporting Inter-organizational Service Processes 500
Ingrid Wetzel and Ralf Klischewski

Design for Change: Evolving Workflow Specifications in ULTRAflow 516
Alfred Fent, Herbert Reiter, and Burkhard Freitag

An Alternative Way to Analyze Workflow Graphs 535
W. M. P. van der Aalst, A. Hirnschall, and H. M. W. Verbeek

Semantics and Logical Representations

Auditing Interval-Based Inference 553
Yingjiu Li, Lingyu Wang, X. Sean Wang, and Sushil Jajodia

A Logical Foundation for XML 568
Mengchi Liu

Providing the Semantic Layer for WIS Design 584
Richard Vdovjak and Geert-Jan Houben

Understanding and Using Methods

Towards a Framework for Comparing Process Modelling Languages 600
*Eva Söderström, Birger Andersson, Paul Johannesson, Erik Perjons,
and Benkt Wangler*

Generic Models for Engineering Methods of Diverse Domains 612
N. Prakash and M. P. S. Bhatia

Role of Model Transformation in Method Engineering 626
Motoshi Saeki

Modeling Objects and Relationships

A Generic Role Model for Dynamic Objects 643
Mohamed Dahchour, Alain Pirotte, and Esteban Zimányi

Understanding Redundancy in UML Models
for Object-Oriented Analysis 659
Dolors Costal, Maria-Ribera Sancho, and Ernest Teniente

Representation of Generic Relationship Types in Conceptual Modeling 675
Antoni Olivé

Short Papers

Building Spatio-Temporal Presentations Warehouses
from Heterogeneous Multimedia Web Servers 692
Michel Adiba and José-Luis Zechinelli-Martini

A Practical Agent-Based Method to Extract Semantic Information
from the Web 697
J. L. Arjona, R. Corchuelo, A. Ruiz, and M. Toro

Process Inheritance 701
Christoph Bussler

Addressing Performance Requirements Using a Goal
and Scenario-Oriented Approach 706
Zhiming Cai and Eric Yu

Querying Data with Multiple Temporal Dimensions 711
Carlo Combi and Angelo Montanari

Query Explorativeness for Integrated Search
in Heterogeneous Data Sources 715
Ruxandra Domenig and Klaus R. Dittrich

Using Nested Tables for Representing
and Querying Semistructured Web Data 719
*Irna M.R. Evangelista Filha, Altigran S. da Silva,
Alberto H. F. Laender, and David W. Embley*

Defining and Validating Measures for Conceptual Data Model Quality 724
Marcela Genero, Geert Poels, and Mario Piattini

An Architecture for Building Multi-device Thin-Client Web
User Interfaces 728
John Grundy and Wenjing Zou

A Framework for Tool–Independent Modeling
of Data Acquisition Processes for Data Warehousing 733
Arne Harren and Heiko Tapken

Managing Complexity of Designing Routing Protocols
Using a Middleware Approach 737
Cosmina Ivan, Vasile Dadarlat, and Kalman Pusztai

Deferred Incremental Refresh of XML Materialized Views 742
Hyunchul Kang and JaeGuk Lim

Requirements for Hypermedia Development Methods:
A Survey of Outstanding Methods 747
Susana Montero, Paloma Díaz, and Ignacio Aedo

An Approach for Synergically Carrying out Intensional
and Extensional Integration of Data Sources Having Different Formats ... 752
Luigi Pontieri, Domenico Ursino, and Ester Zumpano

DSQL – An SQL for Structured Documents (Extended Abstract) 757
Arijit Sengupta and Mehmet Dalkilic

A Comparative Study of Ontology Languages and Tools 761
Xiaomeng Su and Lars Ilebrekke

Life Cycle Based Approach for Knowledge Management:
A Knowledge Organization Case Study 766
Vijayan Sugumaran and Mohan Tanniru

Parallel Query Processing Algorithms for Semi-structured Data 770
Wenjun Sun and Kevin Lü

Domain-Specific Instance Models in UML 774
Marco Torchiano and Giorgio Bruno

Extended Faceted Ontologies 778
*Yannis Tzitzikas, Nicolas Spyratos,
and Panos Constantopoulos and Anastasia Analyti*

On the Logical Modeling of ETL Processes 782
Panos Vassiliadis, Alkis Simitsis, and Spiros Skiadopoulos

Intelligent Agent Supported Flexible Workflow Monitoring System 787
Minhong Wang and Huaiqing Wang

A Meeting Scheduling System Based on Open Constraint Programming ... 792
Kenny Qili Zhu and Andrew E. Santosa

Author Index 797

The Grand Challenge in Information Technology and the Illusion of Validity

Michael L. Brodie

Verizon Communications Information Technology
Boston, MA, USA
michael.brodie@verizon.com

Abstract

Rather than progressing in revolutionary, paradigm-shifting steps, Computer Science and Information Technology (IT) follow the much more mundane path called Normal Science by Thomas S. Kuhn in "The Structure of Scientific Revolutions." Scientific and Industrial Revolutions arise only in rare circumstances. The path so often projected by the Industrial IT and Computer Science communities is of revolutions and paradigm shifts. Notwithstanding the Illusion of Validity, the belief in the visions and the claims based on proponent provided justifications, the track record suggests that most claims for emerging technologies are simply false. What should responsible computer scientists and information technologists do when faced with evaluating claims for purported technical advances and new directions? What is a likely outcome of a hot new technology? For example, when will Cooperative Information Systems (CoopISs) come into being? Will we see the claims for Web Services and the Semantic Web realized? Barring rare Nobel Prize-worthy contributions and genuine revolutions the answer is a qualified no - not as claimed and not in the proposed timeframes. Why? Because at their heart is the Grand Challenge of Computer Science: automatically dealing with the "semantics" of data and of computation, e.g., semantic heterogeneity, on which there has been little progress in decades.

This talk looks at the history of claims for emerging technologies, particularly those that contain the Grand Challenge. It reviews some seldom-applied formal and informal methods that can be used to evaluate the potential success of such claims and asks questions such as: What can we expect from Web Services? and How should national funding agencies invest in these areas? The talk concludes after suggesting practical but not novel steps towards making progress, by announcing the next killer app!

Metadata and Cooperative Knowledge Management

Matthias Jarke[1,2]

[1] Fraunhofer FIT
Schloß Birlinghoven, 53754 Sankt Augustin, Germany
[2] RWTH Aachen, Informatik V
Ahornstr. 55, 52072 Aachen, Germany
jarke@cs.rwth-aachen.de

Abstract

Cooperative knowledge management refers to the work practice or culture facet of information systems engineering; it plays a key role especially in engineering and consulting domains. However, in comparison to technology-centered and business-process-centered meta modeling approaches (exemplified by UML and ERP), this aspect has received significantly less attention in research and is much less mature in terms of international standardization. We claim that additional interdisciplinary research effort is needed in this direction, and discuss different points of attack, largely in terms of their implications for better metadata management and meta modeling.

Ontology-Driven Conceptual Modeling

Christopher Welty

IBM Watson Research Center
Hawthorne, New York, USA
welty@us.ibm.com

Abstract

Ontology is a discipline of Philosophy concerned with what is, of the kinds and structures of objects, properties, events, processes and relations in every area of reality. The first recognition that the work of this philosophical field was relevant to designing and creating computer systems was made by John McCarthy in 1980, who claimed that one must first "list everything that exists – creating an ontology of our world." The computer science use of the term "ontology" has since undergone some evolution, and today it is normally taken as synonymous with knowledge engineering in AI, conceptual modeling in databases, and domain modeling in object-oriented design. This is not, however, simply a new word for something computer scientists have been doing for 20-30 years; Ontology is hundreds, if not thousands, of years old. We have been working for some time on adapting fundamental notions from this centuries-old field to the younger discipline of conceptual modeling, as the core of a formal (that is, domain independent) methodology for developing ontologies and evaluating ontological decisions. Among other things, we use our methodology to clean taxonomies by exposing inappropriate and inconsistent subsumption relations.

Metadata and Cooperative Knowledge Management

Matthias Jarke[1, 2] and Ralf Klamma[2]

[1] Fraunhofer FIT
Schloß Birlinghoven, 53754 Sankt Augustin, Germany
[2] RWTH Aachen, Informatik V
Ahornstr. 55, 52072 Aachen, Germany
jarke@cs.rwth-aachen.de

Abstract. Cooperative knowledge management refers to the work practice or culture facet of information systems engineering; it plays a key role especially in engineering and consulting domains. However, in comparison to technology-centered and business-process-centered meta modeling approaches (exemplified by UML and ERP), this aspect has received significantly less attention in research and is much less mature in terms of international standardization. We claim that additional interdisciplinary research effort is needed in this direction, and discuss different points of attack, largely in terms of their implications for better metadata management and meta modeling.

1 Conceptual Modeling and Meta Modeling

Since its invention in the mid-1970s until relatively recently, conceptual modeling was a manual documentation exercise, at best supported with some drawing tools, sometimes with syntactic correctness checks of the models, sometimes with 'automated' transformation to code frames of usually doubtful quality. Only 20 years later the efforts of standardization organizations and research groups to provide formalizations of conceptual modeling techniques and 'intelligent' tools for supporting these formalizations resulted in reasonably powerful metadata repositories which cannot only store and manipulate such models but have a reasonable formal foundation to explain why and how these models are related to each other by using meta models.

An early example has been the ConceptBase system developed in our group since the late 1980's. ConceptBase was originally developed as a repository for lifecycle-wide metadata management in information systems engineering [Jarke and Rose 1988]. Its formal basis has been a version of the Telos meta modeling language [Mylopoulos et al. 1990] which was re-axiomatized in terms of Datalog with stratified negation [Jeusfeld 1992], thus enabling reuse of all the results on query optimization, integrity checking, and incremental view maintenance developed in the logic and object database communities [Jarke et al. 1995].

On the other hand, Telos itself was an abstraction of the pioneering formalization of the widely used structured methods by [Greenspan 1984]. These methods (and this has not changed in their object-oriented successors such as UML) offer multiple modeling viewpoints, perspectives or contexts [Motschnig 1995]. Managing the relationships among these viewpoints has been a central design issue in ConceptBase and its applications. The key feature Telos provides for this purpose is an unlimited instantiation hierarchy with rules and constraints for defining formal semantics across multiple levels (so-called meta formulas). This allows the full range of data, metadata, meta models, meta meta models, etc. to be managed with full querying, deduction and integrity checking facilities within a single repository.

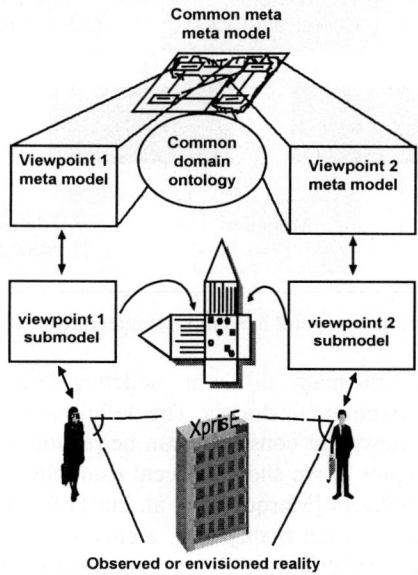

Fig. 1. Integration of heterogeneous model viewpoints via a shared meta meta model

The viewpoint resolution strategy shown in figure 1 [Nissen and Jarke 1999] focusses on the cooperative analysis of an observed or envisioned reality from multiple, interrelated viewpoints. In contrast to traditional design methods which aim at orthogonality of modeling concepts, it emphasizes judicious use of viewpoint overlaps and conflicts at all levels of instantiation for quality control and knowledge elicitation:

A shared meta meta model provides a small core ontology of the domain, similar to the ones used in engineering product and process modeling standard approaches such as STEP. The difference here is that our meta meta model comes with a fairly rich definition of meta meta concept semantics through meta-formulas which constrain the relationships of objects within and across meta models, models, or even data (the optimization of these meta-formulas efficiently constituted the key advance in the ConceptBase implementation [Jeusfeld 1992, Staudt and Jarke 2001]).

Relationships between meta models (i.e. between the constructs of different modeling formalisms used for representing heterogeneous viewpoints) was originally managed indirectly by defining each modeling construct as an instance of a specific meta meta model concept and then automatically specializing the associated meta-formulas.

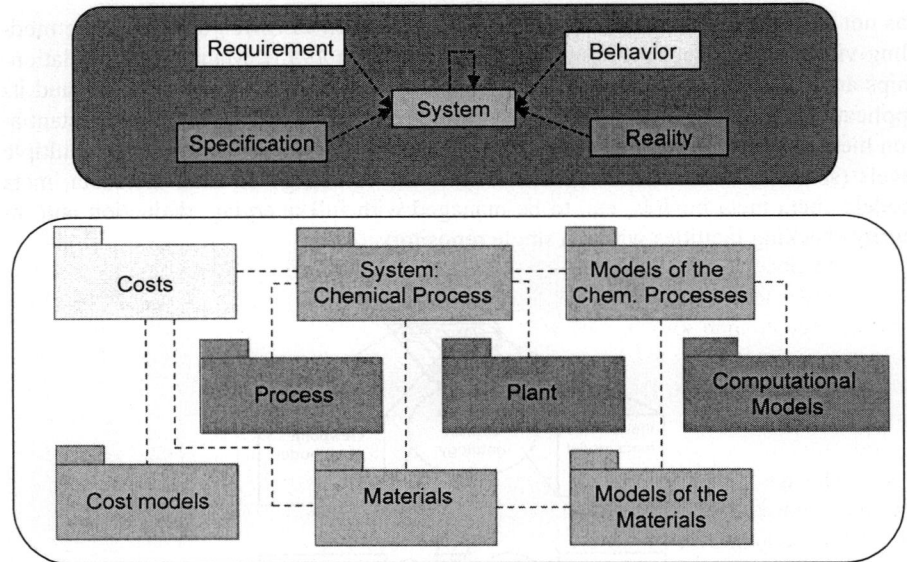

Fig. 2. Chemical engineering viewpoint meta models integrated via shared meta meta model

In complex domains with many different modeling formalisms, this leaves too many options for inter-viewpoint constraints. The definition of more elaborate domain ontologies to which the viewpoint constructs can be related is a fashionable solution [Staab et al. 2001]. In figure 2, we show a recent example from an interdisciplinary project with chemical engineers [Marquardt et al. 2001]. It illustrates the complexity of co-managing information about reality (e.g. a chemical plant and the materials it works with and produces), specified behavior (processes operating on these plants), observations of actual behavior with respect to requirements (e.g. costs), and highly complex mathematical models and simulation tools for the analysis of all the above. Under the shown system-theory inspired basic meta meta model, a rich ontology of several hundred concepts has been developed in order to facilitate modeling and cross-viewpoint analysis at a sufficiently fine-grained level. Some details about this so-called process data warehousing approach can be found in [Jarke et al. 2000].

In cases such as this one, this ontology-enriched approach can be technically supported by linking more expressive special-purpose reasoners (e.g. from description logics [Horrocks 1999]) to ConceptBase which keep the ontologies internally consistent and well-organized. On the other hand, none of these special-purpose reasoning mechanism can currently replace the initial Datalog-based optimization because they do not provide the infinite instantiation capabilities (cf. also [Calvanese et al. 2001]).

In a specific modeling process, further specialization of the inter-viewpoint analysis can be derived from the meta formulas. But again, this requires at least the identification and documentation of which model objects in the different viewpoints refer to the same phenomena in reality. Thus, as figure 1 shows, the models need not only be related through the shared meta meta model but also by a shared grounding in reality. This grounding is, in short, provided by scenario-based approaches as discussed later.

The resulting relationships can be documented using practice-proven matrix-based representations such as the 'house of quality' from quality function deployment.

The above approach proved quite useful in applications such as business process analysis under varying theories of what constitutes good or bad business practice [Nissen and Jarke 1999], cooperation process analysis [Kethers 2002], re-engineering of both large-scale database schemas and application codes [Jeusfeld and Johnen 1995], organization of multimedia teaching materials [Dhraief et al. 2001], and the structured tracing of large-scale engineering processes [Ramesh and Jarke 2001].

While ConceptBase and a few other semi-commercial research prototypes (such as the MetaEdit which emphasizes the management of relationships between graphical notations rather than logical concepts [Kelly et al. 1996] but otherwise has a similar philosophy) created some individual early success stories, metamodeling has become mainstream only due to the rising need for metadata facilities for heterogeneous information integration, and the provisioning of relatively cheap metamodeling facilities in widespread products such as the Microsoft Meta Data Engine [Bernstein et al. 1999]. This has paved the way to information model standardization efforts in several domain research and vendor communities. But even nowadays, key questions such as a high-level algebra for manipulating large sets of complex interrelated models remain largely unanswered [Bernstein 2001]. Maybe as a consequence, even the mainstream commercial tools tend to be under-utilized with respect to their potential.

In the remainder of this paper, we focus on one particularly challenging application domain for improved metamodeling and metadata management facilities: cooperative knowledge management. In section 2, we explain the meaning of this term by contrasting it with the more established UML and ERP approaches. In section 3, we review recent theories from cultural science, organizational behavior, and engineering how successful cooperative knowledge management could operate, and discuss the implications for enhanced metadata management based on experimental solutions in a number of domains. These theories also provide some additional evidence for the importance of scenario-based approaches, not only in conceptual modeling and requirements engineering, but also in knowledge delivery and teaching. Finally, we summarize our observations and the resulting research challenges.

2 The Culture Gap in Information Systems Engineering

The last few years have seen major breakthroughs in the use of conceptual modeling and meta modeling in information systems engineering [Mylopoulos 1999]. The breakthrough was achieved via two different avenues.

On the one hand, starting from the successes of object-oriented programming in the late 1980's, numerous object-oriented design and analysis methodologies were proposed during the early 1990's and finally converged in the Unified Modeling Language (UML) [Rumbaugh et al. 1999]. UML basically generalizes proven programming technologies to analysis and design. Not surprisingly, the main usage of UML nowadays is in late design.

On the other hand, starting from best practice analyses in various branches of business, ERP researchers and vendors have developed standard software for the administrative processes of enterprise resource planning (production planning and scheduling, human resources, accounting/ financials), culminating in comprehensive software packages such as SAP or Oracle Financials. These systems and models basically encode proven business practices, at the modeling level by software tools such as ARIS [Scheer 1994] or INCOME [Oberweis et al. 1994]. Coming from an organizational viewpoint, the key success factor is significantly reduced domain analysis effort, combined with the cost and risk reduction involved with using parameterized off-the-shelf software systems compared to developing software from scratch.

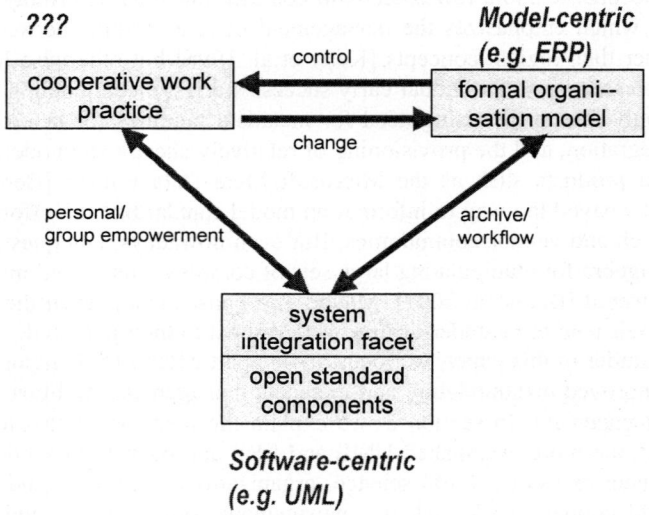

Fig. 3. The culture gap in the cooperative information systems landscape

Proponents of these two approaches see limited relevance in each others' work. For OO proponents, ERP research is some domain ontology standardization work in OMG subgroups that clearly comes in importance after having the UML itself. For ERP leaders, UML is yet another notation, 'nice-to-have' but not mission-critical; many tools focus on older notations such as ER diagrams or Petri nets. Moreover, as sketched in figure 3, neither of the approaches deeply considers work practice communities [Wenger 1998] in the core competence areas of companies. But this is exactly is where knowledge management – the creation, combination, and dissemination of knowledge within and across organizations – is most needed.

As observed by numerous researchers and practitioners [Ulich 1992] and detailed for the case of information systems engineering in [deMichelis et al. 1998], successful information systems require a flexible balance among formal organization, cooperative work practice (often also called organizational culture), and the information system technology in use. This balance is clearly missing in either of the mentioned approaches due to their lack of interaction with the organizational work practice.

The three-tier client-server architecture of ERP systems can historically be understood as bringing standardized business processes back into the once chaotic PC usage landscape [Laudon 1986]. The difficulties SAP faced to integrate the cooperation-oriented customer-relationship management (CRM) into their process-oriented ERP software [Plattner 1999] illustrates the point. This is despite the fact that this kind of external service-oriented collaboration (cf. [Schäl 1996]) is much more structured than internal project-oriented collaboration and knowledge management e.g. in engineering departments. Engineering, not accidentally, happen to be the one area where most businesses have not managed to implant their ERP solutions well.

Similarly, UML offers only one (albeit innovative and important) feature related to work practice: use cases of systems interaction. However, considerations of work practice are crucial not just in the requirements phase but throughout the whole systems lifecycle including actual usage. Methods for systematic use-case oriented testing, selling, user documentation, and operations management are still immature.

Within the work practice support community (e.g. CSCW), many solutions have been tried out with varying success, but no standard modeling techniques of the kind described above have emerged. Partially, this may be due to the negative attitude that many CSCW researchers have towards modeling itself, especially towards process modeling and workflows which they consider too restrictive. Instead, somewhat reminiscent of the database field, many approaches within this community focus on offering information and communication technology as a *medium* for cooperation. The usage of such systems evolves by successful experiences in a grass-root manner -- provided the learning effort is low, there are practical win-win situations at each step of adoption, and the formal organization does not prevent it.

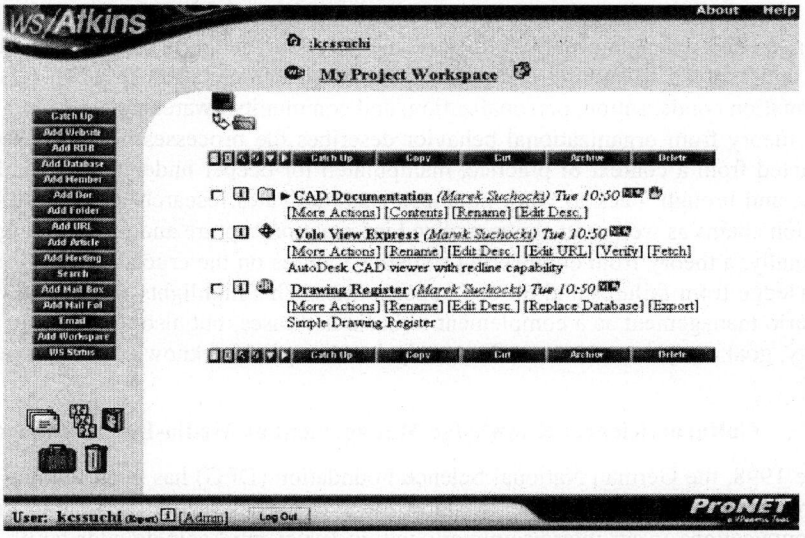

Fig. 4. The BSCW shared workspace environment

As a prototypical example, consider the grass-root diffusion of the Basic Support for Cooperative Work (BSCW) system developed at Fraunhofer FIT [Appelt 1999] in a large British civil engineering firm. The BSCW (cf. the screendump in figure 4) provides an internet-based open workspace environment organized in a folder hierarchy of multimedia documents. Users can invite other users to share their workspaces with certain access rights and a defined level of version management, can define how to get notified or made visually aware of changes others have made in documents, etc.

In the civil engineering firm, this system was initially adopted by a small group of engineers to manage the documented knowledge created during their participation in a European project. Recognizing and advertising the usefulness, system usage rapidly spread into many internal engineering projects throughout the company. In a next step, the system began to be used by engineering groups in joint efforts with the company's customers. Only after departments already offered this collaboration service to customers as an Application Service Provider (ASP), the formal organization finally took notice of this work practice innovation and placed it under information management within the company! Clearly, knowledge management should be able to deal more proactively with such cooperative work practice innovations.

3 Perspectives on Cooperative Knowledge Management

The creation and management of knowledge in heterogeneous communities of practice [Wenger 98] has fascinated researchers at least since Socrates. Of course, depending on the disciplinary viewpoint, the understanding of the involved processes and tools varies widely, even when the focus is on information systems support.

Among the many proposals, we review three theories we have found useful for our own knowledge management research. Briefly, a theory from the cultural sciences discusses how changing media influence the way knowledge is represented, distributed and evolved in cultural discourses. This motivates metadata research related to information condensation, personalization, and community awareness.

A theory from organizational behavior describes the processes how knowledge is extracted from a context of practice, manipulated for deeper understanding and creativity, and brought back to work practice. This motivates research in information escalation chains as well as in contextualized information capture and provisioning.

Finally, a theory from engineering statistics focuses on the crucial issue of refining knowledge from failures and missed opportunities. This highlights the critical role of scenario management as a complement to basic use cases, but also the need for traceability, goal analysis and cause-effect analysis in cooperative knowledge management.

3.1 Cultural Science: Knowledge Management as Media-Enabled Discourse

Since 1998, the German National Science Foundation (DFG) has been funding a major research center in Cologne to study the interplay between media and cultural communications in an interdisciplinary setting (www.uni-koeln.de/inter-fak/fk-427/). The theoretical basis of this effort [Jäger 2001] interprets knowledge creation and management as a cultural discourse in which the inter-medial transcription of concepts and the addressing of the created media objects within the culture play a central role. The basic idea is illustrated in figure 5.

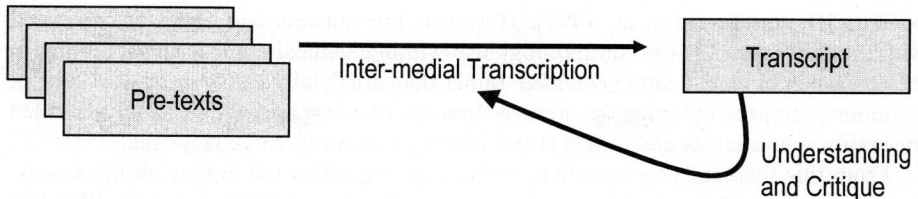

Fig. 5. Transcription creates interpretations of media in media

The key point is simple: it is impossible to develop and debate concepts separately from the media through which they are communicated. Empirical studies [Daft and Lengel 1986, Grote and Klamma 2000] show that even the mental maps of people strongly depend on the media through which they communicate effectively. This appears to argue strongly against the possibility of purely abstract conceptual modeling or ontology building, without explicit consideration how these models/ontologies are captured and communicated via media. Similar claims have incidentally been made concerning the advantages of scenario-based analysis techniques over pure conceptual modeling (for an overview cf. [Jarke et al. 1998]).

New concepts are, according to [Jäger 2001], developed by making selections from an initially unstructured set of media-based 'pre-texts' and converting them through a process called intra- or *inter-medial transcription* into a so-called transcript, a media object describing the new concept.

Transcription and targeted dissemination have a number of consequences:

1. It condenses and structures the set of pre-texts in terms of designate some of them as evidences, counter-examples, or points of critique, while de-emphasizing others.
2. It thus enables a new reading of the pre-texts where the kind of readership is determined by the media through which the transcript is prepared and communicated. Well-designed transcripts can significantly increase the community of practice for a certain piece of knowledge, or may intentionally focus on specific 'insiders'.
3. Thus, transcription does not only change the status of passive understanding by others but it also enables further cooperative knowledge creation by stimulating debate about the selected pre-texts and about the transcription itself.

As a prototypical example [Jäger 2001], consider a historical narrative which sheds provocative new light on the almost infinite set of historical records, thus causing a debate including criticisms of both the chosen sources and the chosen transcription.

As an engineering knowledge management example of critiquing a transcript through another one, consider a large set of natural language use cases arranged in organized in BSCW folders according to their supposed relevance to architecture components. Now we run a text mining system over the same document collection which automatically clusters the use cases according to their similarity and visually compares these clusters with the folder organization. In a multi-country software standardization project in the chemical industries, this approach served to detect errors in the placement of use cases or the relevance of use cases to multiple architectural components [Braunschweig et al. 1999]. However, this success was strongly correlated with the fairly standardized terminology use within chemical engineering (pointing to the relevance of *empirically grounded* rather than artificially constructed ontologies); a similar attempt to optimize the archive structure of newspaper articles analysis failed miserably -- journalists are trained to use inventive, non-repetitive language!

From this theoretical perspective, meta modeling offers the unique ability to custom-tailor media, thus allowing community-specific or even person-specific [Riecken 2000] transcription and addressing. Language plays a special role because it is best suited for *intra*-medial transcriptions, i.e. meta-discourses about itself. Thus, despite the fact that such meta-discourses tend to become overly abstract and detached from practice, metadata in computer-tractable language can play a key role to drive the tailoring of transcription and addressing media; of course, extensible instantiation hierarchies such as offered by Telos, or reflexive object-oriented formalisms can be particularly useful in this context

Transcriptions in constructed media can radically change the knowledge community. As an (admittedly not very commercial) example, a Judaistic hypothesis of how knowledge was encoded within Talmudic tractates over its development history of several centuries, has been the basis for a transcription of the traditional Mishna and Gemara rolls into a structured and annotated multi-lingual hypertext using XML-oriented metadata management [Hollender et al. 2001]. This transcript, for example, supports switching between languages such as English, German, and Hebrew while maintaining the knowledge structure through e.g. color highlighting and annotations. Such features make these texts –formerly readable only by a few rabbinic specialists – accessible to beginning students and other interested parties with limited knowledge in both Hebrew and Judaistic concepts. This re-addressing has rapidly created a worldwide teaching and learning community (of course including heated debates about the adequacy of the underlying theory itself).

At a broader albeit simpler level, the full transcription and re-targeting process is supported by information brokering frameworks such as the Broker's Lounge developed in Fraunhofer FIT ([Jarke et al. 2001], see figure 6). The Broker's Lounge supports, in an interoperable way, a range of possible brokering processes – each involving particular ways of collecting and selecting pre-texts (sources, typically extacted from document management systems or the Internet), their analysis with respect to a given transcript expressed through categorization (metamodel) and conceptualization (ontology), and their selective dissemination and personalization.

However, only in much more limited and well-managed settings such as data warehousing, current transcription mechanisms involve rich semantic or media transformations, powerful quality checks, and the like. Case studies show that, in these latter cases, even nowadays organizations accept the need to manage extremely complex multi-perspective metadata at conceptual, logical, and physical levels to achieve organization-critical data quality needs [Schäfer et al. 2000].

3.2 Business View: Knowledge as Information in a Context of Action

While cultural scientists may see knowledge creation and management as a value in itself, knowledge for business has value only in the context of organizational action

[Mandl and Gerstenmaier 2000]. Probably the best-known theory along these lines was proposed by [Nonaka and Takeuchi 1995]. As the mapping of their process model into our framework in figure 7 shows, Nonaka and Takeuchi see knowledge creation and management mostly as an exercise of transferring knowledge from one context of work practice to another context of work practice.

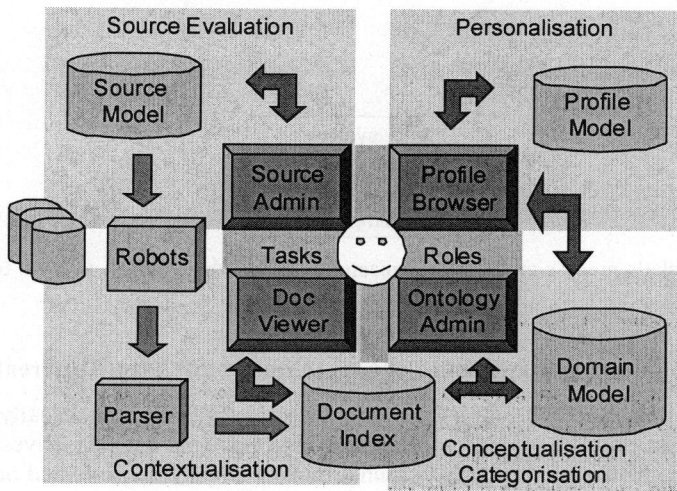

Fig. 6. The Broker's Lounge environment for adaptable information brokering

This transfer can either be handled implicitly by being aware of what other people in the culture do; this is called *socialization*. It is interesting to note that the CSCW community has, in the last few years, placed great emphasis on supporting awareness in geographically and temporally distributed work settings to enable this kind of transfer [Gross and Specht 2001]. Relevant metadata include interest and attention models, privacy models, models of space, time, and task settings, all with a goal to make awareness as informative and unobtrusive as possible in comparison to the same-place same-time setting. Such metadata can, for example, be employed in some kind of event server which resolves which events in a distributed setting should be captured and how to broker them to interested parties [Prinz 1999].

Alternatively, knowledge transfer can go through an explicit de-contextualization and memorization step (called *externalization*), followed by formal manipulation of the resulting (media) artifacts (called *combination*) and by the re-contextualization into the same or an alternative work practice context (called *internalization*). Most computer science work in knowledge management, including approaches from case-based reasoning (drawing analogies from past practice cases to new practice cases), from data/text mining (finding general patterns in large data or case sets), and even the media-enabled transcription approach discussed above relates to the conversion and connection tasks related to the combination step [O'Leary 1998]. In contrast, broad information systems support for the full cycle in figure 3 remains a major challenge.

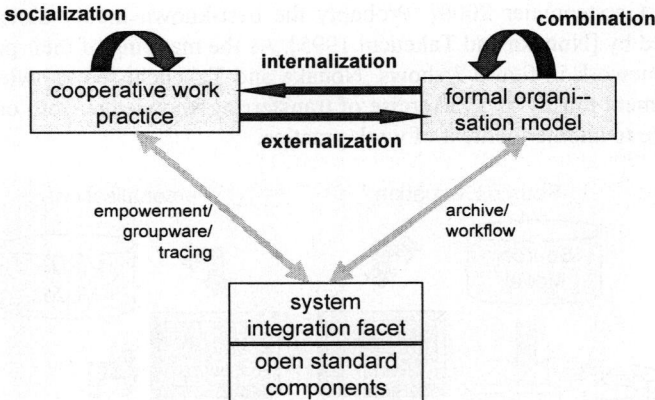

Fig. 7. Nonaka's process model of organizational knowledge creation adapted to our framework

3.3 Engineering View: Knowledge is Defined by What Is Different or Wrong

Another critical success factor is how knowledge management can actually stimulate a community of practice to engage in this process, i.e. what actually drives the knowledge management cycle. An answer found in many engineering-oriented organizations and communities is: recognized failures and missed opportunities. A typical quotation from a senior engineering manager in the automotive industry: 'we judge our engineers by how well they deviate from the textbook'.

Starting from statistical test theory, [Dhar 1998] has argued that organizations recognize failures of attempted action (type I errors) relatively easily and therefore have a natural tendency towards increasing caution and bureaucracy. However, it is equally important not to miss opportunities (avoid type II errors), e.g. by creating autonomy for (real or simulated) experiments as well as enabling their sharing.

The sources for such innovative ideas can be everywhere in work practice, including the usage practice of customers. *Helpdesk systems* are becoming an important way to achieve this. The traditional way of looking at these systems is that they form sub-communities organized in escalation chains such that, if the knowledge of the first-line helpdesk people is insufficient to answer a call, it can be escalated to second-line service specialists, and – in the worst case – back all the way into design-level product quality circles (cf. figure 8). The driving force of all this (and in some sense the source of the knowledge!) is the customer who complains or asks for help.

In such escalation chains, knowledge creation happens in two directions. The obvious one, realized in many products on the market, is a gradual improvement of service quality by transferring knowledge from designers to the helpdesk personnel.

The less obvious one – where most organizations still have severe problems – is the mining of the complaint and solution experiences for improving design and servicability within and across product families. Besides the combination techniques required for representing and generalizing such experiences, the transcription of this knowledge for use in the design communities and the targeting to the places where it is most relevant for organizational improvement prove to be critical [Klamma and Jarke 1998]. Metadata include escalation workflows, competence networks, and organizational principles of how the content of the organizational memory is structured and linked to situated process models along the lines discussed, e.g. in [Rolland 1998].

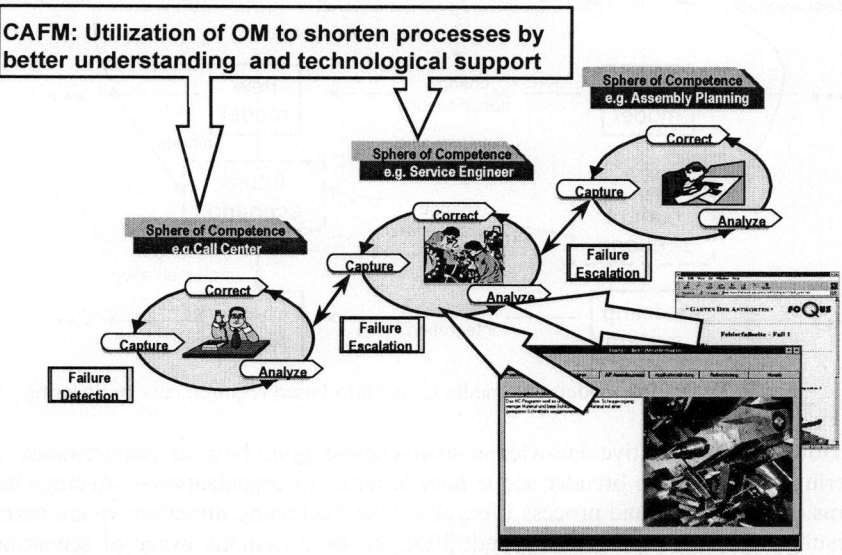

Fig. 8. Failure-driven knowledge creation: escalation chains in complaint management

4 Implications for Knowledge Modeling and Management

When we link the three theoretical approaches sketched for cooperative knowledge management to the discussion of metadata in the first part of this paper, the lessons can be summarized as follows. The theories

emphasize the careful design of media in addition to underlying formalism, including attention focussing by suitable transcription techniques

emphasize the linkage of knowledge to action, with the implication of seamless de-contextualization from action, re-contextualization into action, and careful design of communications networks in distributed work practice

emphasize the need to accept the full richness of reality in a knowledge management system, including the learning from product and process errors as well as from opportunities recognized by customers.

It is interesting to note that many of these arguments reflect similar discussions on scenario-based design where scenarios are seen as middle-ground abstractions for organizational memory, because (1) they delay commitment while encouraging participation, (2) they focus on use and differences, and (3) improve memorization and reuse (cf. [Jarke et al. 1998] for more details). Indeed, the CREWS framework shown in figure 9 in a certain sense already reflects the circular nature of goal discovery and observation focus discussed in the transcriptivity theory of [Jäger 2001], and its goal orientation reflects the need to handle exceptions systematically [Sutcliffe et al. 1998].

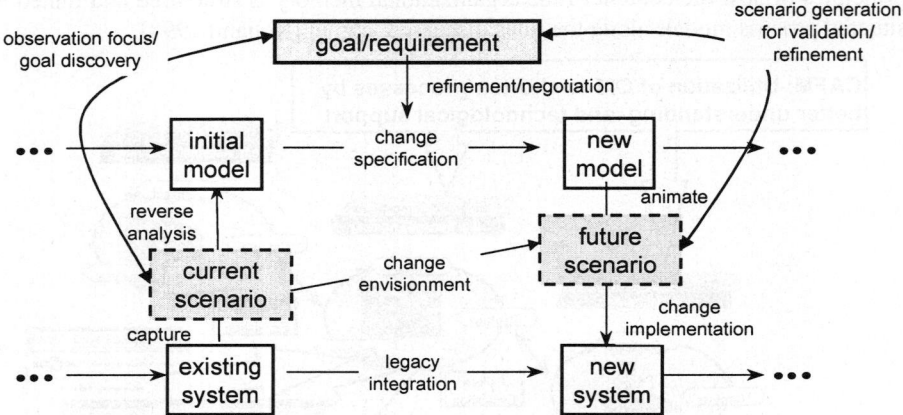

Fig. 9. Integrating models and media in scenario-based requirements engineering

However, cooperative knowledge management goes beyond requirements engineering because of its broader scope both in terms of organizational coverage and in terms of the product and process lifecycles. One interesting direction we are currently pursuing with a group at MIT [Fendt 2001] is the systematic usage of scenarios organized around meta models for knowledge dissemination via eLearning.

As a final example, figure 10 shows a prototype Virtual Entrepreneurship Lab [Klamma et al. 2001] in which collections of video clip scenarios (taken mostly from interviews with well-known international entrepreneurs, venture capitalists, and the like) are arranged according to a conceptual meta model derived from a suitable underlying theory which, however, is never formally shown to the students. Only the base categories of the domain meta meta model are shown to the students as dimensions of interest (cf. vertically arranged buttons on the right of figure 10). Selecting one or more such dimensions creates a thumbnail gallery of scenarios arranged around a larger viewing window to which the student can drag and play a video of interest. Based on this choice, the video gallery can then re-arrange itself according to the meta models; but the student can also create his or her own view in the lower left part of the figure. Initial tests in a high-tech entrepreneurship class at RWTH Aachen show very encouraging results compared with traditional teaching techniques.

A crucial success factor of the Virtual Entrepreneurship Lab is the availability of the MPEG-7 ISO standard for multimedia metadata [Avaro and Salembier 2001] which make this integration of media and models no longer an exotic adventure. In this manner, the requirements for advanced metadata and meta modeling identified in this paper are actually beginning to be addressed by standards which give hope that our quest for a maturity of cooperative knowledge management similar to UML or ERP approaches may actually make significant advances in the next few years.

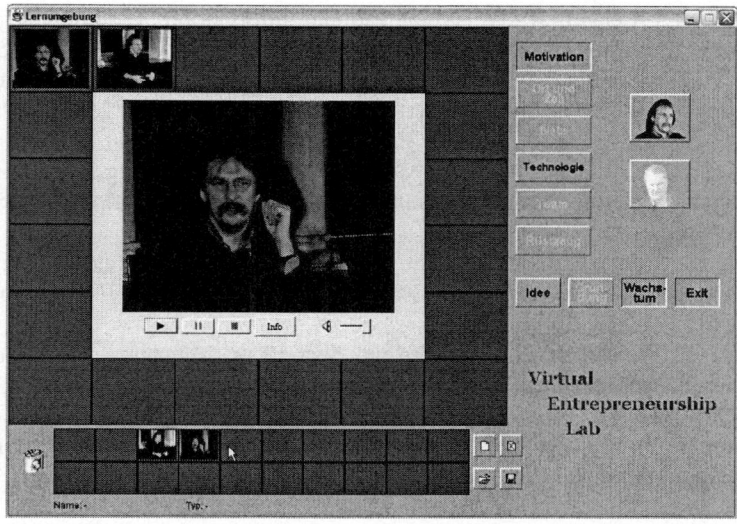

Fig. 10. Scenario-based approach to knowledge delivery: The virtual entrepreneurship lab

Acknowledgements

This work was supported by German National Science Foundation (DFG) within the collaborative research centers SFB/FK 427 "Media and cultural communication" and SFB 476 "IMPROVE". We like to thank Roland Klemke and Wolfgang Prinz for the fruitful discussions.

References

1. Appelt, W.: WWW Based Collaboration with the BSCW System. Proc. SOFSEM'99, Milovy, Czech Republic, LNCS 1725 (1999), 66-78.
2. Avaro, O., Salembier, P.: MPEG-7 Systems: overview, IEEE Transactions on Circuits and Systems for Video Technology 11, 6 (2001): 760-764.
3. Bernstein, P. A.: Generic model management – a database infrastructure for schema management. Proc. CoopIS 01, Trento, Italy, LNCS 2172, Springer 2001, 1-6.
4. Bernstein, P. A., Bergstraesser, T., Carlson, J., Pal, S., Sanders, P., Shutt, D.: Microsoft repository version 2 and the open information model. Inform. Systems 24, 2 (1999):71-98.
5. Braunschweig, B., Jarke, M., Becks, A., Köller, J., Tresp, C.: Designing standards for open simulation environments: a computer-supported use case approach. Proc. 9th Intl. Symposium on Systems Engineering (INCOSE 99), Brighton, UK, vol. 2, 69-76.
6. Calvanese, D., De Giacomo, G., Lenzerini, M., Nardi, D., Rosati, R.: Data integration in data warehousing. Intl. J. Cooperative Information Systems, spring 2001.

7. Daft, R. L., Lengel, R. H.: Organizational Information Requirements, Media Richness and Structural Design, Management Science, 32, 5 (1986): 554-571.
8. Dhar,V. Data mining in finance: using counterfactuals to generate knowledge from organizational information systems. Information Systems 23, 7 (1998): 423-437
9. Dhraief, H., Nejdl, W., Wolf, B., Wolpers, M.: Open Learning Repositories and Metadata Modeling, Proc. 1st Semantic Web Working Symposium, Stanford 2001, 495-514.
10. Fendt, K.: Contextualizing content. In Knecht, M., v. Hammerstein, K. (eds.): Languages across the curriculum. National East Asian Language Ctr., Columbus, Oh 2001, 201-223.
11. Ghezzi, C., Nuseibeh, B., eds. Special Section on Managing Inconsistency in Software Development. IEEE Trans. Software Engineering 24, 11 (1998), and 25, 6 (1999).
12. Greenspan, S.: Requirements modeling – a knowledge representation approach to software requirements definition. Ph.D. Thesis, Computer Science Dept., Toronto 1994.
13. Grote, K., Klamma, R.: Media and Semantic Relations. Comparison of Individual and Organizational Knowledge Structures. Dagstuhl Seminar "Knowledge Management. An Interdisciplinary Approach", Schloss Dagstuhl, Germany, 09.07.2000 – 14.07.2000.
14. Gross, T., Specht, M. Awareness in context-aware information systems. Proc. Mensch & Computer 01, Bonn 2001.
15. Hollender, E., Klamma, R., Börner-Klein, D., Jarke, M. A comprehensive study environment for a Talmudic tractate., Dutch Studies by Foundation for Near Eastern Languages and Literatures (DS-NELL) (in print).
16. Horrocks, I.: FaCT and iFaCT. Proc. International Workshop on Description Logics (DL'99), Linköping, Sweden, CEUR-WS 22, 133-135.
17. Jarke, M., Bui, X. T., Carroll, J. M. Scenario management: an interdisciplinary approach. Requirements Eng. 3, 3-4 (1998): 155-173.
18. Jarke, M., R. Gallersdörfer, M. A. Jeusfeld, M. Staudt and S. Eherer (1995). ConceptBase - a deductive object base for meta data management. Intell. Inform. S. 4, 2 (1995): 167-192.
19. Jarke, M., Klemke, R., Nick, A. Broker's Lounge – an environment for multi-dimensional user-adaptive knowledge management. Proc. HICSS 34, Wailea, Hw, 2001.
20. Jarke, M., List, T., Köller, J.: The challenge of process data warehousing. Proc. 26th Intl. Conf. Very Large Databases, Cairo 2000, 473-483.
21. Jarke, M., Rose, T.: Managing the evolution of information systems. Proc. SIGMOD 1988, Chicago, IL.
22. Jeusfeld, M.: Änderungskontrolle in deduktiven Objektbanken. DISKI 19, infix Publ. Bad Honnef, Germany, 1992 (Diss. Univ. Passau 1992).
23. Jeusfeld, M., Johnen, U.: An executable meta model for re-engineering database schemas, Intl. J. Cooperative Information Systems 4, 2-3 (1995): 237-258.

24. Kelly, S., Lyytinen, K., Rossi, M.: MetaEdit+ – a fully configurable multi-user and multi-tool CASE and CAME environment. Proc. CAiSE 96, Heraklion, Greece, 1996, 1-21.
25. Kethers, S.: Capturing, formalising, and analysing cooperation processes – a case study. Proc. ECIS 2002, Gdansk, Poland (to appear).
26. Klamma, R., Jarke, M. Driving the organizational learning cycle: the case of computer-aided failure management. Proc. 6th ECIS Conf. (Aix-en-Provence 1998), 378-392.
27. Klamma, R., Moog, P., Wulf, V.: How to start a company? The Virtual Entrepreneurship Lab (VEL) as a teaching aid and training instrument for potential start-ups (in German). Proc. G-Forum Jahreskonferenz, Lüneburg/Germany 2001.
28. Laudon, K.: From PCs to managerial workstations: organizational environment and management policy in the financial industry. In Jarke, M. (ed.): Managers, Micros, and Mainframes – Integrating Systems for End Users. John Wiley & Sons 1986.
29. Mandl, H., Gerstenmaier, J. (ed.): Die Kluft zwischen Wissen und Handeln. Hogrefe 2000.
30. Marquardt, W.; von Wedel, L.; Bayer, B.: Perspectives on lifecycle process modeling. Proc. Foundations of Computer-Aided Process Design, AIChE Symposium Series 323, Vol. 96 (2000), 192-214.
31. deMichelis, G., Dubois, E., Jarke, M., Matthes, F., Mylopoulos, J., Papazoglou, M., Schmidt, J.W., Woo, C., Yu, E. A three-faceted view of information systems: the challenge of change. Comm. ACM 41, 12 (1998): 64-70.
32. Motschnig-Pitrik, R. An integrating view on the viewing abstraction – contexts and perspectives in software development. Journal of Systems Integration 5, 1 (1995): 23-60.
33. Mylopoulos, J. Information modeling in the time of the revolution. Information Systems 23, 3-4 (1998): 127-156.
34. Mylopoulos, J., Borgida, A., Jarke, M., Koubarakis, M.: Telos – a language for managing knowledge about information systems. ACM Trans. Inform. Systems 8, 4 (1990): 327-362.
35. Nissen, H. W., Jarke, M. Repository support for multi-perspective requirements engineering. Information Systems 24, 2 (1999), 131-158.
36. Nonaka, I., Takeuchi, H. The Knowledge-Creating Company, Oxford Univ. Press, 1995.
37. Oberweis, A., Scherrer, G., Stucky, W.: INCOME/STAR – methodology and tools for the development of distributed information systems. Inform. Systems 19, 8 (1994):643-660.
38. O'Leary, D. Knowledge management systems: converting and connecting. IEEE Intelligent Systems 1998(5):30-33.
39. Papazoglou, M. P., Schlageter, G. (eds.). Cooperative Information Systems: Trends and Directions. Academic Press, 1998.
40. Plattner, H.: Customer relationship management. In Scheer, A.-W., Nüttgens, M. (eds.): Electronic Business Engineering Proc. WI 99, Saarbrücken), Physica 1999, 1-12.

41. Prinz, W. NESSIE: An Awareness Environment for Cooperative Settings. Proc. ECSCW'99: 6th European Conference on Computer Supported Cooperative Work,, Copenhagen 1999, Kluwer Academic Publishers, 391-410.
42. Ramesh, B., Jarke, M.: Towards reference models for requirements traceability. IEEE Trans. Software Eng. 27,1 (2001): 58-93.
43. Riecken, D. (Hrsg.): Special Issue on Personalization. Comm. ACM 43, 8 (2000).
44. Rolland, C.: A comprehensive view of process engineering. Proc. CAiSE 98 (Pisa), 1-24.
45. Rumbaugh, J., Jacobson, I., Booch, G. The Unified Modeling Language Reference Manual. Addison-Wesley 1999.
46. Schäfer, E., Becker, J.-D., Jarke, M. DB-Prism – integrated data warehouses and knowledge networks for bank controlling. Proc. 26th VLDB Conf., Cairo, Egypt, 715-718.
47. Schäl, Th. Workflow management systems for process organizations. Springer 1996.
48. Scheer, A.-W. Business Process Engineering. Springer 1994.
49. Staab, S. Schnurr, H.-P., Studer, R., Sure, Y.: Knowledge processes and ontologies. IEEE Intelligent Systems 16, 1 (2001).
50. Staudt, M., Jarke, M.: View management support in advanced knowledge base servers. Intelligent Information Systems 15, 3 (2000): 253-285.
51. Sutcliffe, A., Maiden. N., Minocha, S., Manuel, D.:Supporting scenario-based requirements engineering. IEEE Trans. Software Eng. 24, 12 (1998).
52. Ulich, E. Arbeitspsychologie. Stuttgart: Schäffer-Pöschel 1992.
53. Wenger, E.: Communities of Practice – Learning, Meaning, and Identiy, Cambridge University Press, Cambridge, UK, 1998.

Web Component: A Substrate for Web Service Reuse and Composition

Jian Yang and Mike. P. Papazoglou

Tilburg University, Infolab
PO Box 90153, 5000 LE, Tilburg, Netherlands
{jian,mikep}@kub.nl

Abstract. Web services are becoming the prominent paradigm for distributed computing and electronic business. This has raised the opportunity for service providers and application developers to develop value-added services by combining existing web services. Emerging web service standards and web service composition solutions have not addressed the issues of service re-use and extension yet. In this paper we propose the concept of *web component* that packages together elementary or complex services and presents their interfaces and operations in a consistent and uniform manner in the form of a class definition. Web components are internally synthesized out of reused, specialized, or extended elementary or complex web services. They are published externally as normal web services and can thus be employed by any web-based application.

1 Introduction

The Web has become the means for organizations to deliver goods and services and for customers to discover services that match their needs. By web service, we mean a self-contained, internet-enabled applications capable not only of performing business activities on its own, but also possessing the ability to engage other web services in order to complete higher-order business transactions. Examples of such services include catalogue browsing, ordering products, making payments and so on. The platform neutral nature of the web services creates the opportunity for building *composite services* by using existing elementary or complex services possibly offered by different enterprises. For example, a `travel plan` service can be developed by combining several elementary services such as `hotel reservation`, `ticket booking`, `car rental`, `sightseeing package`, etc., based on their WSDL description [13]. Web services that are used by a composite service are called *constituent services*.

Web service design and composition is a distributed programming activity. It requires software engineering principles and technology support for service reuse, specialization and extension such as those used, for example, in component based software development. Although web service provides the possibility for offering new services by specialization and extension instead of designing them from scratch, to this date there is little research initiative in this context. In this paper we introduce the concept of *web component* to facilitate this very idea of web service reuse, specialization and extension.

Web components are a packaging mechanism for developing web-based distributed applications in terms of combining existing (published) web services. Web components have a recursive nature in that they can be composed of published web services while in turn they are also considered to be themselves web services (albeit complex in nature). Once a web component class is defined, it can be reused, specialized, and extended. The same principle applies to service composition activities if we view a composite service as a special web service, which contains composition constructs and logic.

Normally, composite services are developed by hard-coding business logic in application programs. However, the development of business applications would be greatly facilitated if methodologies and tools for supporting the development and delivery of composite services in a co-ordinated and effectively reusable manner were to be devised. Some preliminary work has been conducted in the area of service composition, mostly in aspects of workflow-like service integration [3], service conversation [7], and B2B protocol definition [1]. However, these approaches are either not flexible or too limited as they lack proper support for reusability and extensibility.

Services should be capable of combination at different levels of granularity, while composite services should be synthesized and orchestrated by reusing or specializing their constituent services. Therefore, before complex applications can be built on simple services or composite services, we need to look at a fundamental aspect of composition: *composition logic*. Composition logic dictates how the component services can be combined, synchronised, and co-ordinated. Composite logic is beyond conversation logic (which is modeled as a sequence of interactions between two services) and forms a sound basis for expressing the business logic that underlies business applications.

We use the concept of web component as a means to encapsulate the composition logic and the construction scripts which oversee the combination of existing web services. These constructs are private (non-externally visible) to a web component. The public interface definition provided by a web component can be published and then searched, discovered, and used in applications as any other normal web service. Web components can also serve as building blocks to construct complex applications on the basis of reuse and extension.

In this paper we will concentrate on how web components are used for composite service planning, definition and construction. The contribution of this paper is three-fold:

- it proposes the concept of a web component for creating composite services and web service re-use, specilization, and extension;
- it also proposes a light-weight service composition language that can be used as the script for controlling the execution sequence of service compositions. Since this language is expressed in XML it can be exchanged easily across the network;

– Finally, it provides a complete framework for web service composition so that composite web services can be planned, defined, and invoked on the basis of web components.

The paper is organized as follows. Section 2 presents a framework for service composition. Section 3 discusses different forms of service composition so that basic composition logic can be derived, and introduces the Service Composition Specification Language (SCSL) that defines a web component and provides implementation scripts. Section 4 outlines the features of the Service Composition Planning Language (SCPL) and Service Composition Execution Graphs (SCEG). In section 5 we demonstrate how SCSL, SCPL, and SCEG work together to fulfill the tasks of planning, design, implementation, and execution of composite web services. Section 6 presents related work and summarizes our main contributions. Finally, section 7 concludes the paper.

2 Service Composition: Technical Challenges

In this section we will first analyze the nature of service composition, provide a framework for service composition and application development based on web services. Subsequently, we illustrate the characteristics of composition logic which lays the foundation for creating web components.

2.1 A Framework for Service Composition

The real challenge in service composition lies in how to provide a complete solution. This means to develop a tool that supports the entire life cycle of service composition, i.e., discovery, consistency checking and composition in terms of re-use and extendibility. This comes in contrast to the solutions provided by classical workflow integration practices, where service composition is pre-planned, pre-specified, has narrow applicability and is almost impossible to specialise and extend.

Service composition spans three phases: (1) planning, (2) definition, and (3) implementation. By *planning*, we mean the candidate services (elementary or composite) that are discovered and checked for composability and conformance. During this phase alternative composition plans may be generated and proposed to the application developer. The outcome of this phase is the synthesis of a composite service out of desirable or potentially available/matching constituent services. At the *definition* phase, the actual composition structure is generated. The output of this phase is the specification of service composition. Finally, the *implementation* phase implements the composite service bindings based on the service composition specification. The following types of service composition are used throughout these phases:

– *Explorative composition*: service composition is generated on the fly based on a customer (application developer's) request. The customer describes the

desired service, the service broker then compares the desired composite service features with potentially matching published constituent service specifications and may generate feasible (alternative) service composition plans. These plans result in alternative service compositions that can be ranked or chosen by service customers depending a criteria such as availability, cost and performance. This type of service composition is specified on the fly and requires dynamically structuring and co-ordination of constituent services.
- *Semi-fixed composition:* Here some of the actual service bindings are decided at run time. When a composite service is invoked, the actual composition plan will be generated based on a matching between the constituent services specified in the composition and the possible available services. In this case, the definition of the composite service is registered in an e-marketplace, and it can be used just as any other normal service, i.e., it can be searched, selected, and combined with other services.
- *Fixed composition:* a fixed composite service synthesizes fixed (pre-specified) constituent services. The composition structure and the component services are statically bound. Requests to such composite services are performed by sending sub-requests to constituent services.

We can conclude that the following main elements are needed to develop a complete solution for service composition: (1) service request description, (2) service matching and compatibility checking, (3) description of service composition, and (4) service execution monitoring and coordination. In this paper we shall concentrate on the first three items in some detail.

2.2 Composition Logic

Composition logic we refer to the way a composite service is constructed in terms of its constituent services. Here, we assume that all publicly available services are described in WSDL. Composite logic has the following two features:
- *Composition type:* this signifies the nature of the composition and can take two forms:
    - *Order:* indicates whether the constituent services in a composition are executed in a serial or parallel fashion.
    - *Alternative service execution:* indicates whether alternative services can be invoked in a service composition. Alternative services can be tried out either in a sequential or in a parallel manner until one succeeds.
- *Message dependency:* indicates whether there is message dependency among the parameters of the constituent services and those of the composite service. We distinguish between three types of necessary message dependency handling routines in a composition:
    - *message synthesis:* this construct combines the output messages of constituent services to form the output message of the composite service.
    - *message decomposition:* this construct decomposes the input message of the composite service to generate the input messages of the constituent services;

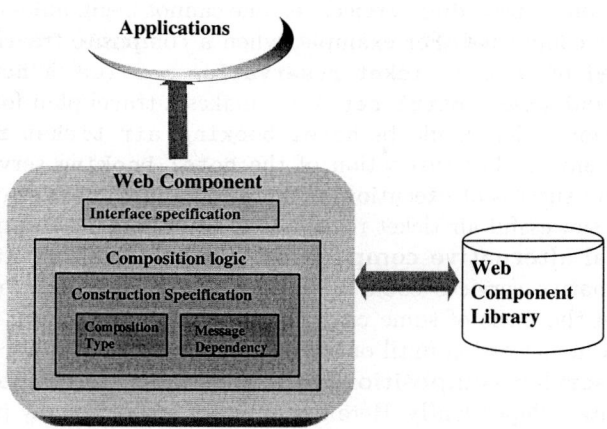

Fig. 1. Web component ingredients

- *message mapping:* it specifies the mappings between the inputs and outputs of the constituent services. For example, the output message of one component service is the input message of another service.

Examples of message dependency are given in Section 3.3 and Figure 3. The composition types together with message dependency constructs form the basis of composition logic, which is specified in web components. Figure 1 depicts the ingredients of a web component. It illustrates that a web component presents a single *public interface* to the outside world in terms of a uniform representation of the futures and exported functionality of its constituent services. It also internally specifies its *composition logic* in terms of *composition type* and *message dependency* constructs. The process of web service composition design becomes a matter of reusing, specializing, and extending the available web components. This enables a great deal of flexibility and reusability of service compositions.

3 Creation of Web Components

In this section, we first present the basic constructs for expressing composition logic, then we demonstrate how web components are specified in SCSL and in terms of web component classes.

3.1 Basic Constructs for Service Composition

The following constructs have been identified to serve as the basis for compositions [12]:

1. **Sequential service composition (sequ).** In this case, the constituent services are invoked successively. The execution of a constituent service is

dependant on its preceding service, i.e., one cannot begin unless its preceding service has committed. For example, when a composite travel plan service - composed of an `air ticket reservation service`, a `hotel booking service`, and a `car rental service` - makes a travel plan for a customer, the execution order should be `hotel booking`, `air ticket reservation`, and `car rental`. The invocation of the `hotel booking` service is dependent on the successful execution of the `air ticket reservation` because without a successful air ticket reservation, hotel booking can not go ahead.
2. **Sequential alternative composition (seqAlt).** This situation indicates that alternative services could be part of the composition and these are ordered on the basis of some criterion (e.g., cost, time, etc). They will be attempted in succession until one service succeeds.
3. **Parallel service composition.** In this case, all the component services may execute independently. Here two types of scenarios may prevail:
   (a) **Parallel with result syncronization (paraWithSyn).** This situation arises when the constituent services can run concurrently, however, the results of their execution need to be combined. For example, purchasing a PC may involve sending inquiries to different companies which manufacture its parts. These inquires may run in parallel, however, they all need to execute to completion in order to obtain the total configuration and price.
   (b) **Parallel alternative composition (paraAlt).** In this situation alternative services are pursued in parallel until one service is chosen. As soon as one service succeeds the remainder are discarded.

Although these constructs represent the most common cases of service composition, to make the composition logic complete, we also need to introduce two additional control constructs: **condition** and **while_do**. The former is used to decide which execution path to take, while the latter is a conventional iteration construct.

The various composition types may result in different message dependencies and therefore require different message handling constructs. Table 1 summarizes the message dependency handling constructs required for different types of service composition.

The basic composition types together with message dependency handling constructs provide a sound basis for forming the composition logic in a web component.

Similar basic routing mechanisms such as *sequential* and *parallel* for use in distributed computations and workflows can be found in [9,10]. The main difference between this work and ours is that they provide basic constructs for control flow execution, whereas we use them as part of the abstraction mechanism for defining web service interfaces and the composition logic for building composite services.

Table 1. Message handling used in different types of composition

	messageSynthesis	messageDecomposition	messageMapping
sequ	X	X	X
seqAlt			X
paraWithSyn	X	X	X
paraAlt			X
condition			X
while_do			X

3.2 The Web Component Class Library

Web component classes are abstract classes used as a mechanism for packaging, reusing, specializing, extending and versioning web services by converting a published WSDL specification into an equivalent object-oriented notation. Any kind of web service (composite or not) can be seen as a web component class provided by an organization and can be used in the development of distributed applications.

The web component class library is a collection of general purpose and specialized classes implementing the primitives and constructs discussed in the previous section. Classes in the web component library act as abstract data types i.e., they cannot be instantiated. They provide basic constructs and functionality that can be further specialized depending on the needs of an application. A distributed web application can be build by re-using, specializing, and extending the web component library classes. The web component library classes can be categorized as follows:

- *web service construction class:* this abstract class is used for creating definitions out of WSDL specifications. This construction class will generate a web component class for a registered web service defined in WSDL, i.e., the service messages, interface and implementation.
- *web component class:* this class represents all elementary or composite web services. There are six subclasses in this category which implement the composition constructs discussed in the previous section (see Table-1).
- *application program class:* this class is used to develop application programs by using the web component classes. Since application program classes are web components, they also can be reused, specialized, and extended.

Figure 2 the web component class definition for a `travelPlan` service. We assume that a travel plan is a composite service which combines the two services `hotelBooking` and `ticketReservation` which are published by the two service providers `Paradise` and `DisneyLand`, respectively. In this figure, class `TravelPlan` is defined as a subclass of class `sequ` which provides the basic operations for the sequential type of composition and message dependency handling. The TripOrderMessage in the travelPlan interface includes such information as the dates, the type of rooms, the location, and the preferred airline for the trip. These are the combined input messages from the WSDL specification of the `hotelBooking` and `ticketReservation` web services. In the construction specification of the `travelPlan` service the TripOrderMessage is shown to be decomposed to its constituent messages `Paradise.HotelBookingMsg` and `DisneyLand.TicketResMsg` which need to be executed at the `Paradise` and `DisneyLand` service provider sites, respectively.

```
class TravelPlan is sequ {
  public   TripOrderMessage tripOrderMsg;
  public   TripResultMessage tripResDetails;
  public   travelPlanning(TripOrderMessage) -> TripResultMessage;
  private  void compose(Paradise.makeBooking, DisneyLand.makeRes);
  private  void messageDecomposition(TravelPlan.TripOrderMsg,
                                     Paradise.HotelBookingMsg,
                                     DisneyLand.TicketResMsg);
  private  void messageSynthesis(TravelPlan.TripResDetails,
                                 Paradise.HotelBookingDetails,
                                 DisneyLand.E-ticket);
}
```

Fig. 2. Web component class definition for travelPlan service

A web component is specified in two isomorphic forms: a class definition (discussed above), and an XML specification in terms of a Service Composition Specification Language (SCSL). Interacting web components and services (across the network) can only communicate on the basis of exchanging XML Web service specifications and SOAP messages. Thus although web component classes serve as a means for specification and reusability they need to be converted to an equivalent XML representation in order to be transmitted across the network. For this purpose we use the SCSL.

3.3 Web Component Specification in XML

There are two parts in SCSL: the interface of the composite service specified in its `defn` part and the construction of the composition logic is specified in its `construct` part, (see Figure 3). These are isomorphic to the interface and construction parts of a web component shown in Figure 2. The `construct` part of an SCSL specification consists of a `compositionType`, a series of activities, and message handling constructs. Activities are internal (non-visible) elementary tasks that need to be performed to achieve a certain web component operation. These are executed remotely in the web sites hosting the web service constituents. The composition type in SCSL specifies the nature of activity execution according to the discussion in section 3.1, while message handling specifies how service and activity messages are processed.

```
<webService name="travelPlan">
<!--== Message definition ==-->
  <definition>
    <message name="tripOrderMsg">
      <part name="hotelBookingMsg" element="hotelBookingMsg"/>
      <part name="ticketResMsg" element="ticketResMsg"/>
    </message>
    <message name="tripResDetails">
      <part name="hotelBookingDetails" element="hotelBookingDetails"/>
      <part name="e-ticket" element="e-ticket"/>
    </message>
  </definition>
<!--== The composite service interface definition ==-->
  <defn>
    <portType name="travelPlaner">
      <operation name="travelPlanning">
        <input message="tripOrderMsg"/>
        <output message="tripResDetails"/>
      </operation>
    </portType>
  </defn>
<!--== The composite service implementation details ==-->
  <construct>
    <composition type="sequ">
      <activity name="hotelBooking">
        <input message="hotelBookingMsg"/>
        <output message="hotelBookingDetails"/>
        <performedBy serviceProvider="Paradise"/>
        <use portType="hotelBookingHandler" operation="makeBooking"/>
      </activity>
      <activity name="ticketReservation">
        <input message="ticketResMsg"/>
        <output message="e-ticket"/>
        <performedBy serviceProvider="Disney Land"/>
        <use portType="ticketResHandler" operation="makeRes"/>
      </activity>
      <messageHandling>
        <messageDecomposition>
          <source message="tripOrderMsg"/>
          <target message="hotelBookingMsg"/>
          <target message="ticketResMsg"/>
        </messageDecomposition>
        <messageSynthesis>
          <source message="hotelBookingDetails"/>
          <source message="e-ticket"/>
          <target message="tripResDetails"/>
        </messageSynthesis>
      </messageHandling>
    </composition>
  </construct>
</webService>
```

Fig. 3. Service Composition Specification Language (SCSL)

In SCSL we adopt the same convention as WSDL [13], i.e., the `portType` is used for grouping `operations`. Operations represent a single unit of work for the service being described. The example of `travelPlan` illustrated in Figreu 3 corresponds to the web component class isslustrated in Figure2 and provides a single `portType` named `travelPlaner` with one operation `travelPlanning`. The activity `hotelBooking` uses the operation `makeBooking` of port type `hotelBookingHandler`. The activity `ticketReservation` uses the operation `makeRes` of port type `ticketResHandler`.

We also specify how input and output messages of constituent services operations are linked from (to) those of the composite service. Here we rely on the three types message handling: (1) message synthesis, (2) message decomposition, and (3) message mapping described in section 2.2. For example, the output message `hotelBookingDetails` of the constituent operation `makeBooking` and the output message `e-ticket` of the constituent operation `makeRes` are composed into the output message `tripResDetails` of the composite service `travelPlan` in the `messageSynthesis` part. The input message of the composite service `travelPlan` called `tripOrderMsg` is decomposed into two messages: the input message `hotelBookingMsg` of constituent operation of `makeBooking` and input message `ticketResMsg` of constituent operation `makeRes`.

Although the above example is meant for sequential compositions, the other types of composition can be specified in a similar fashion. Note Figure 3 is a much simplifier version of the SCSL for illustrative purposes. The binding specifications are not included in this figure.

The XML schema of SCSL is not provided for reasons of brevity.

4 Service Composition Planning and Composition Execution Languages

As discussed in section 2, service composition should be planned and generated according to service developer's request. With this in mind, we are developing a **Service Composition Planning Language (SCPL)** that specifies how a composite service is built up in terms of the relationships among constituent services such as execution order and dependency. The resulting specification combines services from the web component library and presents them in the form of web component classes as described in the previous. These specifications will subsequently generate a service execution structure in the form of a **Service Composition Execution Graph (SCEG)**. When the SGEC is executed it invokes the corresponding services at remote site and co-ordinates them. In the following, we will first introduce the concepts of SCPL and SCPG by means of a simple example then we will present their formal specifications.

Figure 4 illustrates how a composite service called `HolidayPlan` can be planed in SCPL by combining three component services `restaurantBooking`, `hotelReservation`, and `sightseeing`. In this example, we specify that `restaurantBooking` and `hotelReservation` have to run sequentially, and there is data dependency between them, i.e., the location of the hotel determines the

```
Composition holidayPlanning
  C1: sequ (hotelReservation, restaurantBooking)
      mapping (hotelBooking.location = restaurantBooking.location)
  C2: paraWithSyn (C1, sightseeing)
```

Fig. 4. Specification of a service composition plan

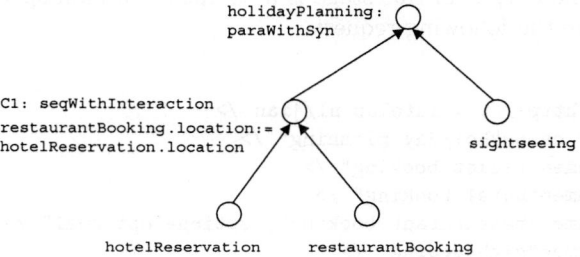

Fig. 5. The service composition execution graph

location of the restaurant, while Sightseeing can run in parallel with the other two services.

There are two aspects of SCPL which make it flexible and extensible: (1) a labelling system which can be used to label any composition. The labels can be used in any place where services (operations) are required. We can build a composition plan recursively by labelling existing composition plans. (2) plan variables and macros which can be used in the place where the service (operation) and composition types (such as sequential, paraWithSyn etc) are required. This second aspect is not discussed in this paper due to space limitations. SCPL provides a simple light-weight but powerful mechanism for service composition nesting and substitution, composition extension, and dynamic service selection.

A Service Composition Execution Graph (SCEG) is generated on the basis of an SCPL specification. Figure 5 illustrates the SCEG corresponding to the SCPL specification in Figure 4 .

Formally an SCEG is a labelled DAG $P = <N, A, spe>$ where N is a set of vertices, A is a set of arcs over N, such that

- for every operand and label in a statement in SCPL, create a vertex;
- for $v \in V$, $spe(v)$ represents the type of composition and the mapping specification;
- if u is used in v for composition, introduce an arc $u \to v$.

The service composition execution graph is used for coordinating constituent service execution at remote sites and run time service selection based on the user requirement specifications. These issues are further discussed in the next section.

5 Service Composition: A Complete Picture

In this section, we explain how the SCSL, the SCPL and the SCEG work together to create service compositions. Recall that as already explained in section 2, there are three stages of service composition: planning, definition, and implementation. We address these in the following.

The *planning* stage involves service discovery, composability and compatibility checking. The output of this stage is a composition plan specified in SCPL. Assume we have the following request:

```
<request>
  <from src="http://www.infolab.nl/jian />
  <vocabulary name="holiday planning" />
  <service name="ticket booking" />
  <service name="hotel booking" />
  <service name="restarurant booking", option="optional" />
  <service name="sightseeing" />
  <result> $serviceInfo </result>
  <condition condition="ticketBooking.date=hotelBooking.date">
  <condition condition="restarurantBooking.loc=hotelBooking.place"
</request>
```

This request can be satisfied if we find the services which match the required constituent services either completely or partially. For service discovery, it is important to find an appropriate service with the right capability. Service discovery relies on the following steps:

- Semantic relatedness: during this step, the requested service is compared against the service description in the repository in terms of service contents to decide how closely related they are. Services with a high degree of relatedness will be selected as relevant services for further capability checking.
- Capability analysis: the capabilities of the services selected from the previous step are checked in terms of the functions they provide to determine whether they can accomplish completely or partially the tasks of the requested service.
- Syntactic analysis: "capable" services have their syntax of their interfaces checked to determine how they can be combined to achieve the requested higher-order service.

We can view a web service (S) as a triple: $< C, A, P >$ where C, A, P stand for contents, activities (capabilities), and properties respectively. Contents refer to what the service is about. Activities are a set of operations the service provides. Properties refer to some end point information about the service such as payment methods, cost, etc. C is used in conjunction with semantic relatedness checks, A is used in capability and syntax check, while P is used for selecting alternative composition plans.

We can identify two types of checking depending on the nature of composition: *compatibility checking* and *conformance checking*. Service $S1$ is compatible with $S2$ when $S1$ is at least as capable as $S2$ and $S1$ can substitute $S2$. Service S conforms to S' when S and S' can be combined in a way that the output of S can be taken as the input of S'. Here, we introduce two symbols: $\diamond$ for "compatibility" and $\triangleright$ for "conformance". As P does not play an important role in service discovery, we only consider C and A for the purpose of semantic and syntactic checking.

Service $S = <C, A, P>$, where $\forall a \in A$, we define $a = <op, I, O>$, where op, I, and O stand for operation, inputs and outputs respectively. For input, we have $I = <p_1, \ldots, p_m>$, and for output, we have $O = <q_1, \ldots, q_n>$., where every p_i ($i = 1\ldots m$) and q_j ($j = 1\ldots n$), takes the form $<name>:<type>$.

Definition 1. *Service S' is compatible with S ($S' \diamond S$) if the contents of S are a subset those of S' ($S.C \subset S'.C$) and the operations of S' are compatible with those of S ($S'.A \diamond S.A$).*

Definition 2. *Activities in Service S' are compatible with the activities in service S ($S'.A \diamond S.A$) when $\forall a \in S.A$, if we can find an operation $a' \in S'.A$ such that $a' \diamond a$.*

Definition 3. *Operations $a' \diamond a$ if*
(1) the pre-condition and the post-condition of $a'.op$ are equivalent to $a.op$,
(2) the inputs $a'.I \diamond a.I$ and
(3) the outputs $a'.O \diamond a.O$.

Definition 4. *S' conforms to S ($S' \triangleright S$) if:*
(1) the the contents $S'C$ and $S.C$ are overlapping and
(2) $\exists a' \in S'.A, \exists a \in S.A$ such that $a'.O \diamond a.I$.

There is still a lot of research that needs to be done in the area of compatibility and conformity checking. However this is beyond the scope of this paper. Some primary research results can be found in [11,8].

To exemplify these issues, we use the above service request holidayPlanning as an example and assume we have a choice between the following two plans specified in SCPL after semantic and capability checking:

```
CompositionPlan1 holidayPlanning
C1: sequential (ticketBooking, hotelBooking, restaurantBooking)
    Mapping (ticketBooking.arrive_date=hotelBooking.date,
            RestarurantBooking.loc=hotelBooking.place)
C2: paraWithSyn (C1, sightseeing)
   Sythesizing (holidayPlanning.schedule=C1.schedule+sightseeing.schedule)

CompositionPlan2 holidayPlanning
C1: sequential (travelPlan, restaurantBooking)
    Mapping (RestarurantBooking.loc=hotelBooking.place)
C2: paraWithSyn (c1, sightseeing)
   Sythesizing (holidayPlanning.schedule=C1.schedule+sightseeing.schedule)
```

`CompositionPlan1` contains three services and defines two mappings. The first mapping indicates that the arrival date must be the same as the hotel check-in date. The second mapping indicates that the restaurant and the hotel must be located at the same place. `CompositionPlan2` contains two services one of which is a composite service defined and constructed in Figure3. The mapping `ticketBooking.arrive_date=hotelBooking.date` is assumed to be accomplished by the composite service `travelPlan`.

To choose among alternative composition plans generated by the planning stage, we need look at the properties of the candidate constituent end point services (such as cost, performance, binding requirements). Suppose that `CompositionPlan1` is selected, we can then use the `sequ` and `paraWithSyn` web component classes to *define* and *construct* the plan in an incremental fashion. We first generate C1 by using the web component class `sequ` as a super-class and further extend it with new message types and operations. Then we use the web component class `paraWithSyn` as a super-class to construct an application program class `holidayPlanning` by linking C1 together with another service `sightseeing` and specifying the appropriate message dependency handlings. The final class definition then can be transformed into SCSL. The code in Figure 6 illustrates how the web component class `holidayPlanning` is defined.

To *execute* a composite service, an SCEG graph is generated. As already stated in Section 4, the SCEG is a labelled DAG. Every node in this graph is a composite service with its children representing constituent services. The root node is the application we want to build. The type of composition and the message dependency is indicated in the label of the node. The node in the SCEG bind to and execute web services at different sites while the overall control is situated at the site which launches the application. The algorithm for SCEG execution has been developed on basis of the *depth-first search*.

```
class C1 is sequential {
  public TravelSchedule travelSchedule;
  ... //public operations
  private void compose(TicketBooking, HotelBooking, RestaurantBooking);
  private void messageMapping(TicketBooking.date, HotelBooking.date);
  private void messageMapping(RestaurantBooking.location,
                              HotelBooking.location);
}
class HolidayPlanning is paraWithSyn {
  public HolidaySchedule holidaySchedule;
  ... //public operations
  private void compose(C1, Sightseeing);
  private void messageSynthesizing(HolidayPlanning.holidaySchedule,
              C1.TravelSchedule, Sightseeing.Schedule);
}
```

Fig. 6. An application program class HolidayPlanning

6 Related Work

Most of the work in service composition has focussed on using work flows either as a engine for distributed activity coordination or as a tool to model and define service composition. Representative work is described in [2] where the authors discuss the development of a platform specifying and enacting composite services in the context of a workflow engine. The eFlow system provides a number of features that support service specification and management, including a simple composition language, events and exception handling.

The workflow community has recently paid attention to configurable or extensible workflow. The approach described in [6] allows for automatic process adaptation. The authors present a workflow model that contains a placeholder activity, which is an abstract activity replaced at run-time with a concrete activity type. This concrete activity must have the same input and output parameter types as those defined as part of the placeholder. In addition, the model allows to specify a selection policy to indicate which activity should be executed.

The work presented in [5] proposes some interesting ideas in workflow interoperation. It provides infrastructure to support dynamic aspects in planning, scheduling, and execution by introducing workflow schema templates. Reuse of existing workflow schema and templates can be achieved by schema splicing. However how this approach can be used in service composition is not clear.

The workflow approaches provide some basic mechanisms that can be used for supporting dynamic service co-ordination and composition. However as the authors pointed out in [1,4], workflow systems do not cater for the dynamic and distributed nature of service composition for two reasons: (1) a common workflow modelling and management environment is impossible to achieve especially across different enterprises since no WFMS vendor shares the same workflow syntax and semantics; (2) workflow systems do not offer facilities such as changing flow definitions which is a fundamental requirement for service composition. Therefore, these solutions may work only for semi-fixed and fixed compositions, however, they do not work well with explorative composition which requires the service composition structure to be generated on the fly and the composition itself to be changeable. Moreover, they do not support parameterization, reuse, specialization, and nesting of service compositions.

Our approach differs from the above in the following ways:

- in this paper we propose an integrated approach towards service composition, which includes composition planning, specification, implementation and execution.
- The concept of web component is introduced for web service reuse, specialization, and extension.
- At the planning stage, variables and macros can be introduced in the SCPL which can be used for service substitution.
- Unlike workflow schemas SCSL is a light-weight specification language in XML which can be executed in different organizational settings without too much implementation overhead.

7 Conclusion

It is obvious that service composition is not just an interoperability problem. The real challenge in service composition is how to provide a complete solution in terms of tools that support the entire cycle of service composition, i.e., discovery, consistency checking, composition, re-use, and extendibility.

In this paper, we presented a framework to discuss the different forms of service composition and their essential characteristics. Based on this framework, we presented an approach for composition planning, definition, implementation, and execution. In order to support the need for flexible, scalable, extensible service composition, we introduced the concept of web component that packages together elementary or complex services and presents their interfaces and operations in a consistent and uniform manner in the form of class definitions. This approach is light weight, flexible, and leads to reusable web components when compared with current popular workflow solutions.

References

1. C. Bussler. The Role of B2B Protocols in Inter-Enterprise Process Execution. Proc. Of the 2nd VLDB-TES Workshop, Rome, 2001.
2. F. Casati, S. Ilnicki, L. Jin, V. Krishnamoorthy, M. C. Shan. Adaptive and Dynamic Service Composition in eFlow, *HP Lab. Techn. Report, HPL-2000-39* .
3. F. Casati and Ming-Chien Shan. Dynamic and adaptive composition of e-services, *Information Systems*, 26(2001), page 143-163, 2001.
4. F. Casati, M. Sayal, and M. C. Shan Developing E-Services for Composing E-Services. Proc. Of the 13th CAiSE conference, Switzerland, 2001
5. V. Christophides, R. Hull, A. Kumar, and J. Simeon Workflow Mediation using VorteXML. Bulletin of the IEEE Computer Society Technical Committee on Data Engineering, 2000.
6. D. Georgakopoulos, H. Schuster, D. Baker, and A. Cichocki. Managing Escalation of Collaboration Processes in Crisis Mitigation Situations. Proceedings of ICDE 2000, San Diego, CA, USA, 2000.
7. H. Kuno, M. Lemon, A. Karp, and D. Beringer. Conversations + Interface = Business Logic. Proc. Of the 2nd VLDB-TES Workshop, Rome, 2001.
8. M. Mecella, B. Pernici, and P. Craca. Compatibility of e-Services in a Cooperative Multi-platform Environment. Proc. Of the 2nd VLDB-TES Workshop, Rome, 2001.
9. M. P. Papazoglou, A. Delis, A. Bouguettaya, M. Haghjoo. "Class Library Support for Workflow Environments and Applications". IEEE Transactions on Computer Systems , vol. 46, no.6, June 1997.
10. W. M. P. van der Aalst and A. Kumar. XML Based Schema Definition for Support of Inter-organizational Workflow. Information System Research (accepted)
11. W-J Van Heuvel, J. Yang, and M. P. Papazoglou. Service Representation, Discovery, and Composition for E-Marketplaces, *Proc. Of International Conference on Cooperative Information Systems (cooPIS01)*, Sep, 2001.
12. J. Yang, M. P. Papazoglou, and W-J Van Heuvel. Tackling the Challenges of Service Composition. Proc. of ICDE-RIDE workshop, San Jose, 2002.
13. Web Service Definition Language. http://www.w3.org/TR/wsdl.

Designing Web-Based Systems in Social Context: A Goal and Scenario Based Approach

Lin Liu and Eric Yu

Faculty of Information Studies, University of Toronto
{liu,yu}@fis.utoronto.ca

Abstract. In order to design a better web-based system, a designer would like to have notations to visualize how design experts' know-how can be applied according to one's specific social and technology situation. We propose the combined use of a goal-oriented language GRL and a scenarios-oriented notation UCM for representing design knowledge of web-based systems and information systems in general. Goals are used to depict business objectives, functional and non-functional system requirements. Tasks are used in the exploration of alternative technologies and their operationalizations into system constructs. Actors are used to do role-based analysis on social relationships. Scenarios are used to describe elaborated business processes or workflow. The approach is illustrated with an example of designing a web-based training system.

1 Introduction

In the context of requirements engineering and system design, goal-driven and scenario-based approaches have proven useful [9]. In order to overcome some of the deficiencies and limitations of these approaches when used separately, proposals have been made to couple goal, scenario and agent concepts together to guide the system design process. As there are both overlaps and gaps between these approaches, their interactions can be complex and highly dynamic.

In general, goals describe the objectives that the system should achieve through the cooperation of agents in the software-to-be and in the environment [14]. It captures „why" the data and functions are there, and whether they are sufficient for achieving the high-level objectives that arises naturally in the requirements engineering process. The incorporation of explicit goal representations in requirement models provides a criterion for requirements completeness, i.e., the requirements can be judged as complete if they are sufficient to establish the goals they are refining.

Scenarios present possible ways in which a system can be used to accomplish some desired functions or implicit purpose. Typically, it is a temporal sequence of interaction events between the intended software and its environment (composed of other systems or humans). A scenario could be expressed in forms such as narrative text, structured text, images, animation or simulations, charts, maps, etc. The content of a scenario could describe either system-environment interactions or events inside a system. Purpose and usage of scenarios also varies greatly. It could be used as means to elicit or validate system requirements, as concretization of use-oriented system descriptions, or as basis for test cases. Scenarios have also become popular in other fields, notably human-computer interaction and strategic planning [2].

A successful design relies on the clarity of user requirements and the close matching of requirements and the adopted technologies. In this paper, we explore the combined use of a goal-oriented notation GRL [5] and a scenario-based notation UCM [1] in early requirements engineering and system design. The GRL language is used to support goal and agent-oriented modelling and reasoning, providing guidance to the design process. The scenario orientation of the UCM notation allows the behavioral aspects of the designed system to be visualized at varying degrees of abstraction and levels of detail. Combining the two notations makes it possible to evaluate technical solutions according to their contributions to the objectives of different stakeholders, guiding the design towards viable solutions.

Information system design is a knowledge-intensive process. It involves domain-specific knowledge, generic software design knowledge and knowledge about the specific situations of the current design. GRL and UCM together provide an ontology for expressing such knowledge. For example, domain-specific know-how on picking a lesson structure is represented as UCM scenarios of common lesson structures. Generic software design knowledge on the possible collaboration mechanisms for a web-based system is depicted as a GRL means-ends structure that connects the possible mechanisms (e-mail, newsgroup, chat, screen-sharing and audio/video conferencing) to the goal „Determine Collaboration Mechanism".

In the next section, basic concepts of GRL and UCM are introduced. In section 3, we summarize our approach of using GRL and UCM together to incrementally modelling requirements and design. In section 4, a case study in the e-training domain is used to illustrate the proposed approach. In section 5, related work is discussed. Conclusions and future work are in section 6.

2 Modelling Notations

2.1 GRL

The Goal-oriented Requirements Language (GRL) [5] is a language for supporting goal and agent oriented modelling and reasoning about requirements, especially for dealing with non-functional requirements (NFRs)[3][14]. It provides constructs for expressing various types of concepts that appear during the requirements and high-level design process. There are three main categories of concepts: intentional elements, intentional links, and actors. GRL elements and links are intentional in that they are used in models that answer questions about intents, motivations and rationales, such as:

- Why particular behaviors, information and structures are chosen to be included in the system requirements?
- What alternatives are considered?

- What criteria are used to deliberate among alternative options?
- What are the reasons for choosing one alternative over others?

A GRL model can either be composed of a global goal model, or a series of goal models distributed amongst several actors. If a goal model includes more than one actor, then the intentional dependency relationships between actors can also be represented and reasoned about.

The intentional elements in GRL are goal, task, softgoal, resource and belief. A *goal* is a condition or state of affairs in the world that the stakeholders would like to achieve. In general, how the goal is to be achieved is not specified, allowing alternatives to be considered. A goal can be either a business goal or a system goal. Business goals are about the business or state of the business affairs the individual or organization wishes to achieve. System goals are about what the target system should achieve, which, generally, describe the functional requirements of the target information system. In GRL graphical representation, goals are represented as a rounded rectangle with the goal name inside.

A *softgoal* is typically a quality (or non-functional) attribute on one of the other intentional elements. A softgoal is similar to a (hard) goal except the criteria for whether a softgoal is achieved is not clear-cut. It is up to the developer to judge whether a particular state of affairs in fact sufficiently achieves the stated softgoal. Non-functional requirements (NFRs), such as performance, security, accuracy, reusability, interoperability, time to market and cost are often crucial for the success of an information system. In GRL, non-functional requirements are represented as softgoals and addressed as early as possible in the software lifecycle, and be properly reflected in design decisions before a commitment is made to a specific implementation. In the GRL graphical representation, a softgoal, which is „soft" in nature, is shown as an irregular curvilinear shape with the softgoal name inside.

A *task* specifies a particular way of doing something. It may consist of subgoals, subtasks, resources and softgoals. These sub-components specify a particular course of action while still allowing some freedom. Tasks are used to incrementally specify and refine solutions in the target system. They are used to achieve goals or to "operationalize" softgoals. These solutions provide operations, processes, data representations, structuring, constraints and agents in the target system to meet the needs stated in the goals and softgoals. In GRL graphical representation, tasks are represented as a hexagon with the task name inside.

A *resource* is a (physical or informational) entity, about which the main concern is whether it is available. Resources are shown as rectangles in GRL graphical representation.

Belief is used to represent design assumptions and environmental conditions. Beliefs make it possible for domain characteristics to be considered and properly reflected in the decision making process, hence facilitating later review, justification and change of the system, as well as enhancing traceability. Beliefs are shown as ellipses in GRL graphical representation.

Intentional links in GRL include means-ends, decomposition, contribution, correlation and dependency links. *Means-ends* links are used to describe how goals are in fact achieved. Each task connected to a goal by a means-ends link is an alternative way to achieve the goal. *Decomposition* links define the sub-components of a task. A *Contribution* link describe the impact that one element has on another. A contribution can be negative or positive. The extent of the contribution can be partial or sufficient based on Simon's concept of satisficing [12]. *Correlation* links describe the side effects of the existence of one element to others. *Dependency* links describe the inter-agent dependent relationships. Following are the graphical representations for links.

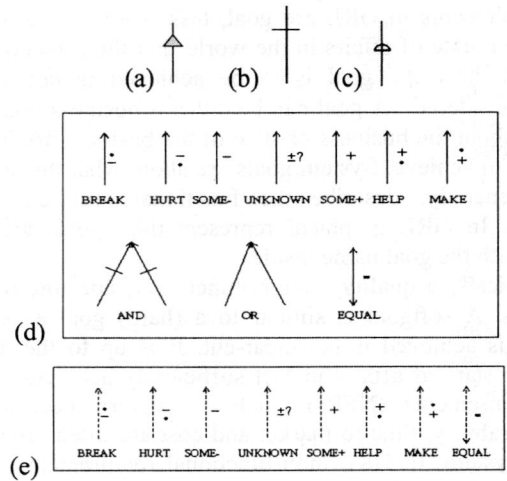

Fig. 1 (a) Means-Ends; (b) Decomposition; (c) Dependency; (d) Contribution; (e) Correlation

An *actor* is an active entity that carries out actions to achieve its goals by exercising know-how. It is an encapsulation of intentionally, rationality and autonomy [16]. Graphically, an actor may optionally have a boundary, with intentional elements inside. To model complex relationships among social actors, we further define the concepts of agents, roles, and positions, each of which is an actor in a more specialized sense.

An *agent* is an actor with concrete, physical manifestations, such as a human individual. A *role* is an abstract characterization of the behavior of a social actor within some specialized context or domain of endeavor. A *position* is intermediate in abstraction between a role and an agent. It is a set of roles typically played by one agent. Positions can *cover* roles, agents can *occupy* positions, and agents can also *play* roles directly. The „*INS*" construct represents the instance-and-class relation. The „*ISA*" construct expresses conceptual generalization/ specialization.

2.2 UCM

Use Case Maps (UCM)[1] provide a visual notation for scenarios, which is proposed for describing and reasoning about large-grained behavior patterns in systems, as well as the coupling of these patterns. The UCM notation employs scenario paths to illustrate causal relationships among responsibilities. It provides an integrated view of behavior and structure by allowing the superimposition of scenario paths on a structure of abstract components. Scenarios in UCM can be structured and integrated incrementally. This enables reasoning about and detection of potentially undesirable interactions between scenarios and components.

Basic elements of UCMs are start points, responsibilities, end points and components. *Start points* are filled circles representing pre-conditions or triggering causes. *End points* are bars representing post-conditions or resulting effects. *Responsibilities* are crosses representing actions, tasks or functions to be performed. *Components* are boxes representing entities or objects composing the system. *Use case Paths* are wiggle lines that connect start points, responsibilities and end points. A responsibility is said to be bound to a component when the cross is inside the component. In this case, the component is responsible for performing the action, task, or function represented by the responsibility.

When maps become too complex to be represented as a single UCM, a mechanism for defining and structuring sub-maps becomes necessary. A top level UCM, referred to as a root map, can include containers (called stubs) for sub-maps (called plug-ins). Stubs are represented as diamonds. Stubs and plug-ins are used to solve the problems of layering and scaling or the dynamic selection and switching of implementation details.

Other notational elements include OR-join, OR-fork, AND-join, AND-fork, timer, abort, failure point, and shared responsibilities. A detailed introduction to and examples of these concepts can be found in [1].

Although UCM can represent system designs in a high-level way, the tradeoffs between alternatives, and the intentional reasoning behind design decisions cannot be explicitly shown.

In our approach, we couple GRL with UCM to provide support for reasoning about scenarios by establishing correspondences between intentional GRL elements and functional components and responsibilities in the scenario models of UCM. The modelling of goals and scenarios is complementary and may aid in identifying further goals and additional scenarios (and scenario fragments) important to system design, thus contributing to the completeness and accuracy of requirements, as well as to the quality of system design.

3   A Design Methodology Based on Goal and Scenario Modelling

To support early requirements engineering and high-level system design, our goal and scenario modelling methodology aims to elicit, refine and operationalize customer-specific requirements incrementally based on domain experts' knowledge, until a satisfactory design is found. In this process, the objectives of a system have to be clarified, the concrete behaviors and constraints of the system-to-be need to be elaborated, and functions should be assigned to responsible units in that system.

The goal and agent oriented modelling in GRL focuses on answering the „why" questions of requirements (such as „why does the system need to be redesigned?" or „why is the interface designed as it is?"). The strength of GRL modelling is that it puts the design in a broader context, it considers from different stakeholders' viewpoint, and seeking for a balanced solution for all. Another advantage of GRL is that not only functional requirements but also non-functional requirements (in other words, the quality requirements) are dealt with. While goal-orientation can be highly useful for requirements engineering, goals are sometimes too abstract to capture all at once. Often they are discovered and become explicit only after a deeper understanding of the system has been achieved.

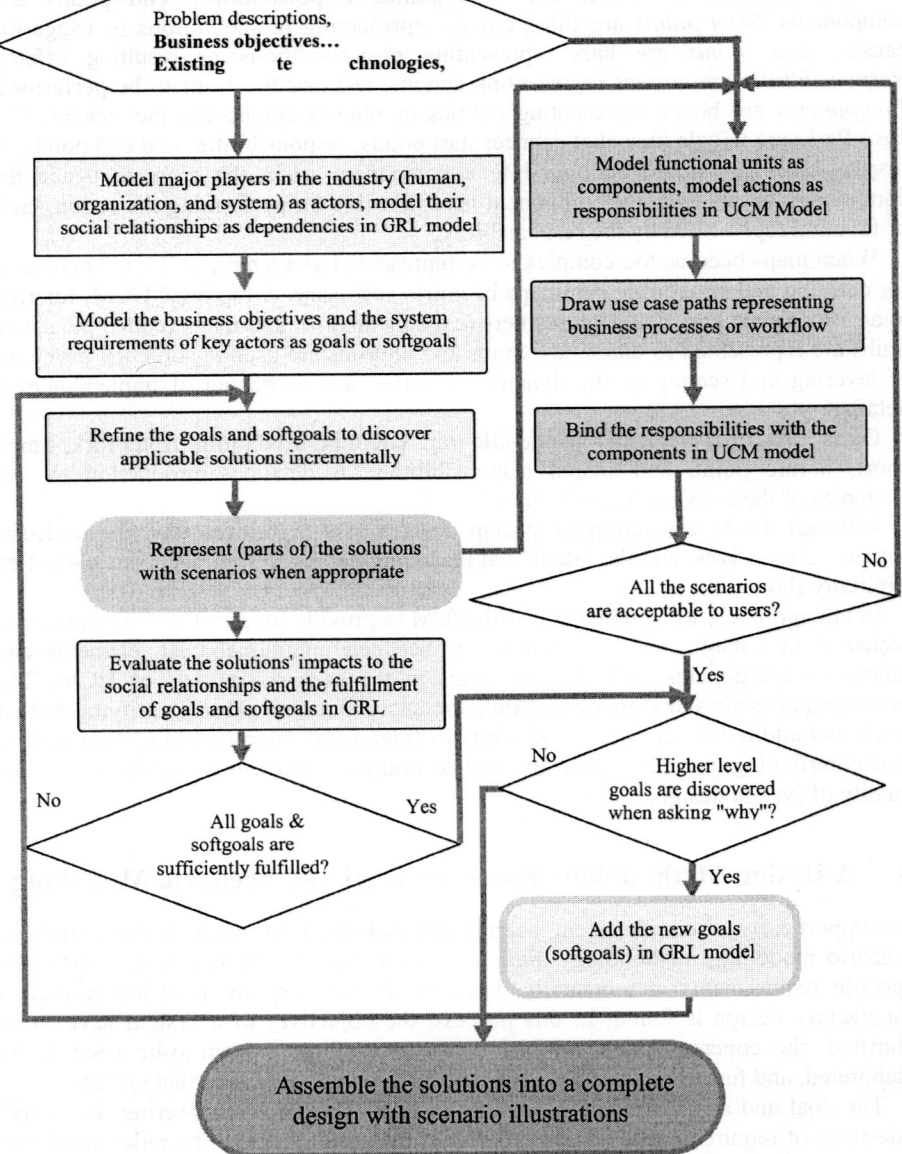

Fig. 2 Goal and scenario modelling based system design process

In comparison, it is often possible to create operational scenarios about using the hypothetical system relatively easily. In our approach, in parallel with goal-oriented modelling, UCM scenarios are used to describe the behavioral features and designs of the intended system in some restricted usage contexts. The scenarios basically answers the „what" questions such as „what should the system do to provide activity centered electronic lessons?" or „what is the process of giving learner customized tutorial?" Then, by raising „why" questions about these scenarios (e.g. „why let learners lead the class instead of instructor?") some implicit system goals are made explicit.

The general steps of the process are illustrated in Figure 2. From the flow chart, we can see that goal modelling and scenario modelling proceed in parallel, and they can interact at certain points in each round. In the goal-oriented modelling process, first actor dependency models are created, then the original business objectives and system requirements are identified and operationalized, until some concrete design options are obtained. These design options are explored UCM scenarios. On the UCM side, business process or workflow, as well as responsibility assignment are visualized and analyzed. On both sides, new requirements may become evident by asking why questions, and be entered into the GRL model. When all scenarios are acceptable, and all goals and softgoals are sufficiently fulfilled, the solution fragments for each independent goal can be assembled to form a complete design for the intended system. Scenarios illustrating the business processes or workflow are also obtained.

4   Case Study: Designing a Web-Based Training System

To illustrate the complementary application of GRL and UCM, we use the example of designing a Web-Based Training (WBT) System [6]. The approach is applicable to information systems in general, where there are conflicting goals and tradeoffs during design. A case study in telecommunication domain is discussed in [10], which focuses more on using goal and scenario together in software architectural design. Starting from the identification of the major stakeholders of the domain, we explain in sequence how to capture the original business objectives of the stakeholders, refine and operationalize these objectives into applicable design alternatives with GRL and how to visualize and concretize some solutions with UCM.

Step 1: Placing system design within its broader social context [15] (as in Figure 3), the proposed modelling approach can help to address the following questions systematically: Who are the major players in the business domain? What kinds of relationships exist among them? What are the business objectives and criteria of success for these players? In Figure 3, circles denote actors in the domain. If there is a line above the actor's name, the actor is an agent (or class of agent) with physical existence. Actors with a line under their name are abstract roles that can be played by agents.

The various dependency links in the model depict that in web-based training, the course provider is a key player, who provides web-based education service to learners. At the same time, he/she may depend on the support of web-technology expert, course content provider and web training consultant. Apart from the three instance level agents - "Mortgage Bankers Association of America", "Mortgage Banker Jim", and "William Horton Consulting", the model represents the common practices of e-training domain, and is a reusable domain knowledge model.

44 Lin Liu and Eric Yu

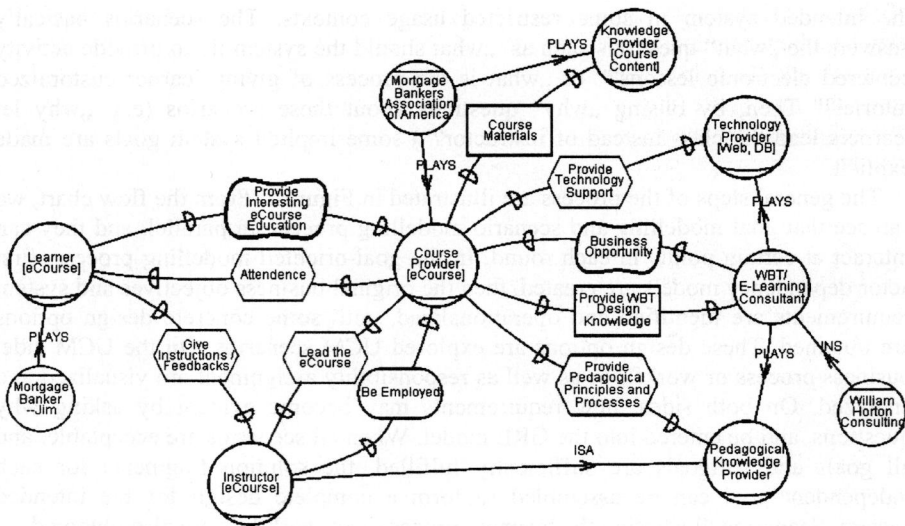

Fig. 3 Major players in E-Learning domain, agent dependency relationships, role-playing relationships and agent classification

Step 2: After the main vendors are identified, we ask them what are their business objectives, i.e., what they hope to accomplish for their organization, their sponsors, or their financial backers. Assume that, in our specific e-training system, the course provider is "Mortgage Bankers Association of America", who has two things in mind:

- Earn $200,000 by selling courses
- Reduce costs of training by 50% over the next year

They are represented as two softgoals in the initial GRL goal model in Figure 4.

Step 3: Explore the alternative business processes, methods or technologies used in this industry or business. Evaluate how are these alternatives serving the specific business objectives and the quality expectations of stakeholders.

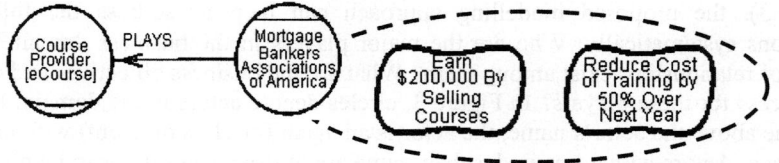

Fig. 4 Business objectives represented as softgoals in original goal model

In Figure 5, we see how the two solutions „Web-Based Training" and „Conventional Classroom Training" (represented as task nodes) contribute differently to the goals. By using contribution links labelled with numbers or different symbolic types, the model portrayed that WBT *makes* the goal of „Reduce Cost of Training by 50% Over Next Year" satisfiable, while conventional training method *hurts* the fulfillment of this goal. Furthermore, the fulfilling of this goal *helps* the achievement of „Earn $200,000 By Selling Courses". The result of this analysis suggests that WBT may be a better option for current stakeholder. The upper part of this model (the two softgoals and the help relationship between them) is only applicable to current system, while the lower part (the structure showing the different resource consumption of the two solutions) depicts generic domain knowledge reusable to all course providers of web-based training system.

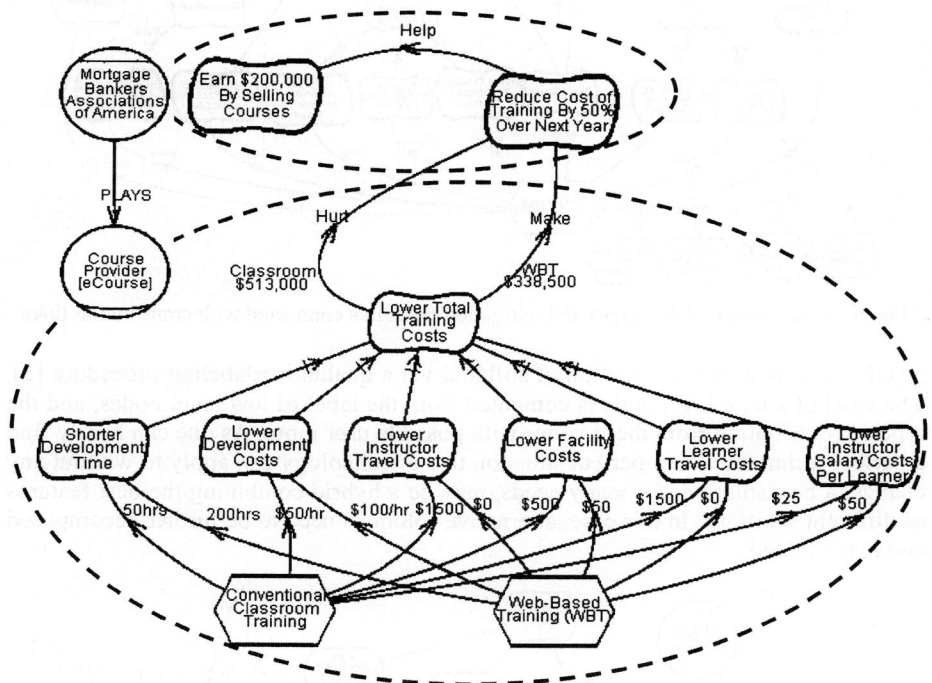

Fig. 5 Evaluate alternative technologies by comparison of resource consumption

Step 4: The advantages and disadvantages of the candidate solution are further investigated by evaluating its contributions to other concerned softgoals. For each disadvantage, mitigation plans are considered to complement the current solution.

The corresponding goal model (Figure 6) shows that the advantages of WBT include „Costs Saved", „Better Teaching Techniques Enabled", „Collaborative Learning Promoted", and „Effective Learning Technologies Used". Consequently, the overall „Quality of Learning Improved". It also contributions positively to „Globalization", „Flexibility", both of which contribute positively (helps) to the learner's satisfactory, as the right hand side of the model suggests. On the left side, disadvantages are considered, e.g., the inherent „High Dropout Rates" and „More Efforts" on „Conversion" and „Electronic Delivery" of WBT hurts the high level goals of the stakeholder. These disadvantages can be mitigated by countermeasures such as „Require Commitment", which are represented tasks connected with a negative correlation links (the dotted lines with arrows) to the unfavorable contributions links in the graph.

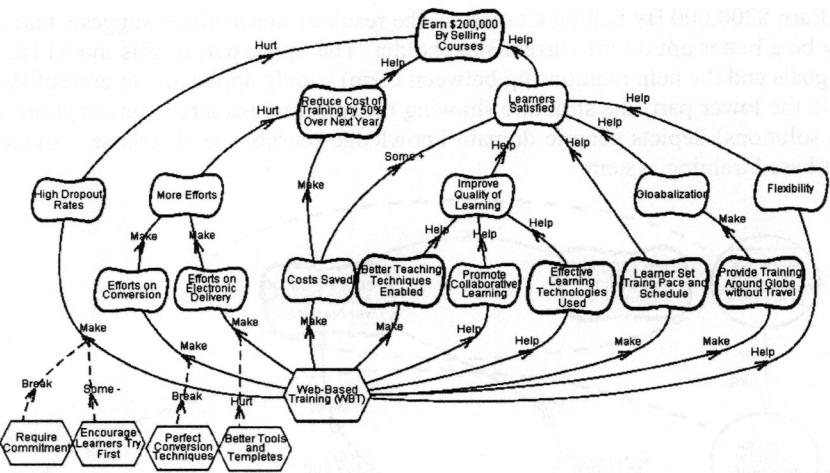

Fig. 6 Advantages, disadvantages and mitigation measures connected with contribution links

GRL evaluates the satisfaction of softgoal via a qualitative labeling procedure [3]. The label of a high level node is computed from the label of low level nodes, and the type of contribution from these nodes with possible user input. As one can hardly find a perfect technology, or a perfect situation that a technology can apply to without any change, a best solution, for many needs, may be a hybrid combining the best features of different solutions. In this case, alternative solutions need to be further decomposed and reassembled.

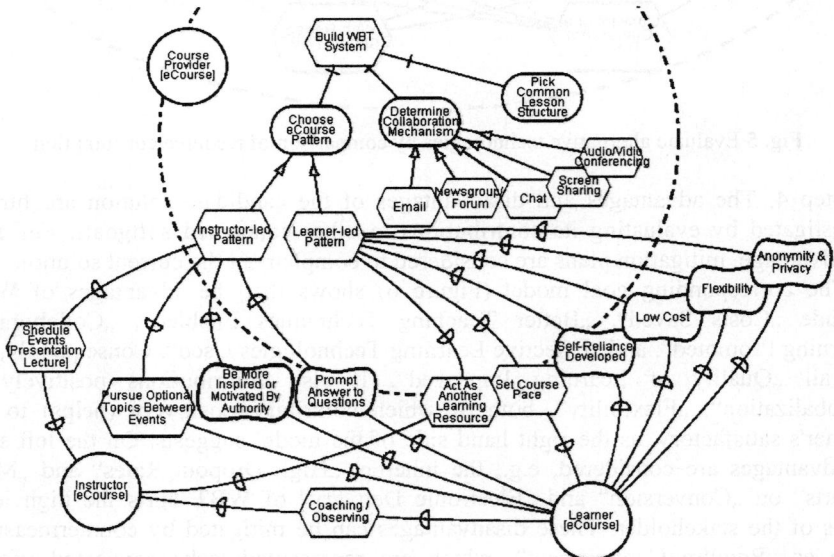

Fig. 7 Alternatives to implement essential sub-components and their impacts on actor dependencies

Step 5: Identify the alternative essential sub-processes/components to implement the candidate solution. The model in Figure 7 elaborates the generic knowledge about „Build a WBT System". First of all, an e-course provider needs to „Choose e-Course Pattern", decide whether to use „Collaboration Mechanisms" and what mechanism to use, and „Pick a Lesson Structure" for the course. As all of these sub-processes are necessary steps for the finishing of the root task, they are represented as subgoals connected to the root task with decomposition links.

Considering course patterns, the designers have two main options: instructor-led course and learner-led course. In Figure 7, the two task nodes are connected to parent goal with means-ends link. The dependency links pointing from these two tasks tell us that the two solutions lead to quite different role designations – the teacher is the driving force in instructor-led courses, but only acting as one of the optional learning resources in learner-led training. Conversely, the dependencies pointing to the two task nodes show that they have different capabilities and qualities to offer. Learner-led training has „Lower Costs". Learners are more „Flexible" on their schedule and learning content, and they also appreciate the „Anonymity and Privacy". In instructor-led training, instructors can „Answer questions and solve problems promptly" (as they arise), provide the authority needed by some learners for „Motivation", and urge and „Inspire" learners in a humanized way.

Similarly, existing collaboration mechanisms are connected to the goal „Determine Collaboration Mechanisms" with means-ends links. Their impacts to social dependencies and contributions to course provider's business objectives will be further explored. By making tradeoffs among the possible solutions, one can work out an acceptable design.

Step 6: As the goal-oriented design proceeds, finer-grained analysis needs to be conducted, hence the scenario-based notation comes into use. To elaborate the goal „Pick Lesson Structure" in Figure 7, alternative structures are denoted in the GRL model in Figure 8 as task nodes having different usage. For instance, „Classic Tutorials" are good to teach basic knowledge and skills, as they provide a „Safe", „Reliable" and „Simple" way.

On the right side of Figure 8, each of the first five class structures is described as a UCM scenario. WBT System and Learner, are represented as agent components (rectangles), holders of responsibilities (small crosses along on the wiggle lines). The first scenario means that, in a classic tutorial, after an introduction, learners read through a series of sessions, each teaching a more difficult concept or skill. At the end of the sequence (denoted with a use case path, the wiggle line with filled circle head, and small bar tail) is a summary and a test. Examples and practice are also provided in each session.

The second and fourth scenarios read similarly as the first one. In the third scenario, the use case path branches for different learners if they choose different subjects in the course. In the fifth scenario, the learner and the WBT system collaborates on searching on the web for materials the learner is interested in, so they are sharing responsibilities (denoted by adding a square „S" between the shared responsibilities).

The last scenario uses GRL and UCM modelling constructors jointly, as neither GRL nor UCM can describe this case on their own. In this scenario, both static and dynamic features needs to be considered. Tasks and decomposition links are used to describe the composition of the course materials, while the use case path is used to capture the dynamic generation of course structure at runtime. This model suggests that a close coupling of the two notations is needed for some applications.

In the case study above, the UCM model are rather simplistic because we have only tackled the highest level of process design, and the process in e-training is not very complicated. As we go down to a sufficiently detailed design, a UCM model may be fairly complex, and more modelling constructs need to be used. Having analyzed the benefits and tradeoffs of these structures, we can see that UCM is a useful counterpart to GRL in the process from requirements to high-level design, because it provides a concrete model of each design alternative. Based on the features in such a model, new non-functional requirements may be detected and added to the GRL model. At the same time, in the GRL model, new means to achieve the functional requirements can always be explored and concretized in a UCM model. Thus the above design process may iterate several rounds until an acceptable design is made.

5 Related Work

The work of this paper builds on an original submission to ITU-T Study Group 10 on the topic of User Requirements Notation (URN) [13]. The User Requirements Notation (URN) is intended to allow software engineers to specify, review for correctness, and possibly discover requirements for a proposed new system or for extensions to an existing system. This standard shall specify functional requirements in UCM and non-functional requirements in GRL as well as a set of relationships between the GRL and UCM. The methodology introduced in this paper is a follow-up step in relating the two modelling notations.

The combined use of goals and scenarios has been explored within requirements engineering, primarily for eliciting, validating and documenting software requirements. Van Lamsweerde and Willement studied the use of scenarios for requirements elicitation and explored the process of inferring formal specifications of goals and requirements from scenario descriptions in [8]. Though they treat goal elaboration and scenario elaboration as intertwined processes, their work regarding scenarios in [8] mainly focuses on goal elicitation. Our emphasis is the other way around, i.e., how to use goal model (especially NFRs) to direct design based on scenarios. The fundamental point is that both the goal-oriented modelling in GRL and the scenario-based modelling in UCM run through requirements to design, and also their interactions.

In the CREWS project, Rolland et al. have proposed the coupling of goals and scenarios in requirements engineeing with CREWS-L'Ecritoire [11]. In CREWS-L'Ecritoire, scenarios are used as a means to elicit requirements/goals of the system-to-be. Both goals and scenarios are represented as structured text. The coupling of goal and scenario could be considered as a „tight" coupling, as goals and scenarios are structured into <Goal, Scenario> pairs, which are called „requirement chunks". Their work focuses mainly on the elicitation of functional requirements/goals. In GRL, both functional and non-functional requirements are considered, with special attention being paid to non-functional requirements. The modelling process involves both requirements engineering activities and high-level architectural and process design.

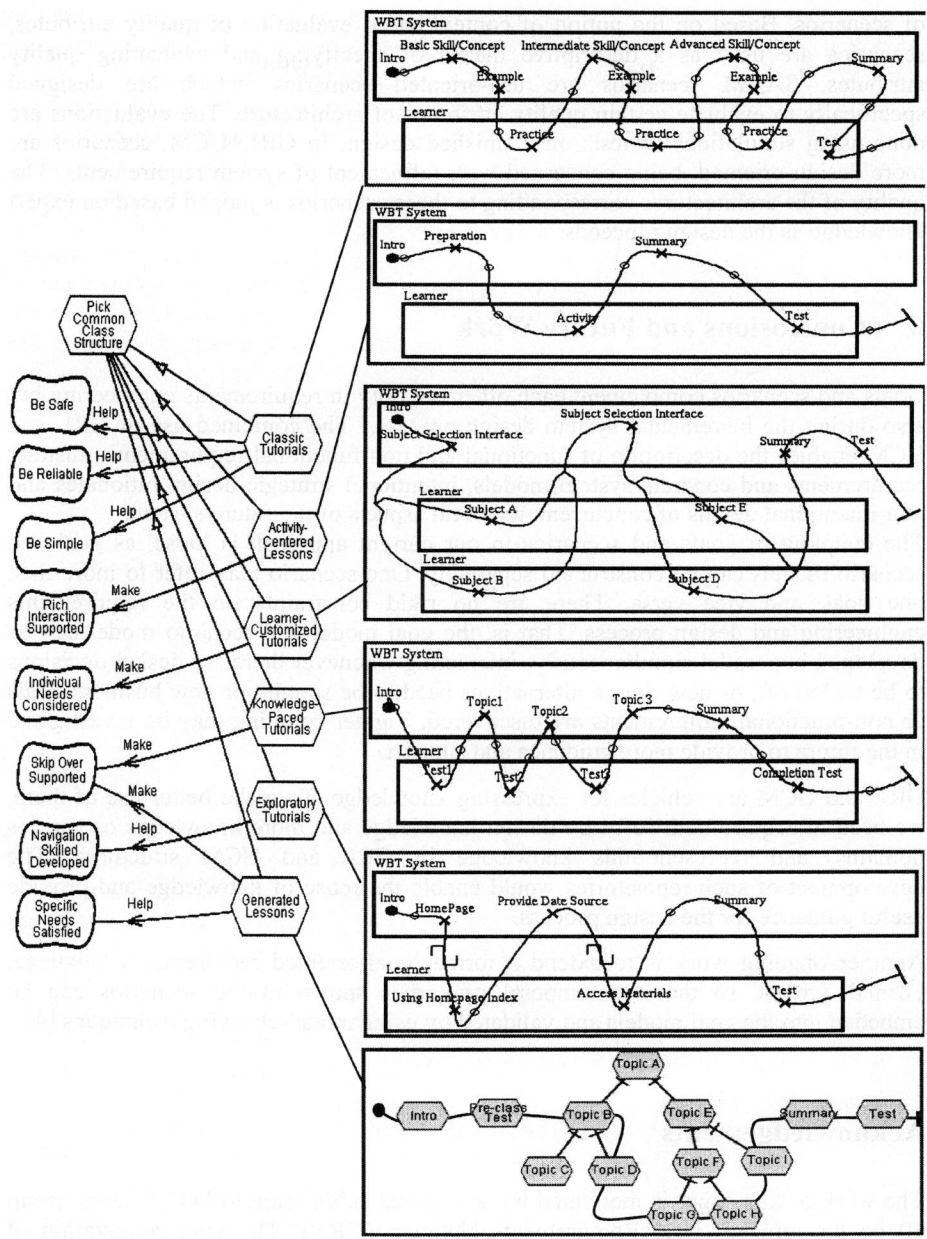

Fig. 8 Design alternatives represented as tasks, and their corresponding scenarios

The Software Architecture Analysis Method (SAAM) [7] is a scenario-based method for evaluating architectures. It provides a means to characterize how well a particular architectural design responds to the demands placed on it by a particular set of scenarios. Based on the notion of context-based evaluation of quality attributes, scenarios are used as a descriptive means of specifying and evaluating quality attributes. SAAM scenarios are use-oriented scenarios, which are designed specifically to evaluate certain quality attributes of architecture. The evaluations are done using simulations or tests on a finished design. In GRL+UCM, scenarios are more design-oriented, being concerned with refinement of system requirements. The quality of the architectures corresponding to these scenarios is judged based on expert knowledge as the design proceeds.

6 Conclusions and Future Work

Goals and scenarios complement each other not only in requirements engineering but also during the incremental system design process. The combined use of GRL and UCM enables the description of functional and non-functional requirements, abstract requirements and concrete system models, intentional strategic design rationales and non-intentional details of concurrent, temporal aspects of the future system.

The coupling of goals and scenarios in our current approach is loose, as goal and scenario models can be constructed separately. One scenario may refer to more than one goal, and vice versa. There are no rigid constraints on the requirements engineering and design process. That is, the goal model and scenario model can be developed in parallel simultaneously, interacting whenever there are design decisions to be traded off, or new design alternatives need to be sought, or new business goals or non-functional requirements are discovered. Tighter coupling may be investigated in the future to provide more guidance and support.

GRL and UCM are vehicles for expressing knowledge. To make better use of them, we need to acquire both software design knowledge and more knowledge of various domains, and represent this knowledge in GRL and UCM structures. The development of such repositories would enable the reuse of knowledge and provide useful guidance for the design process.

Another ongoing work is to extend a formal goal-oriented requirements language, Formal Tropos, so that the temporal properties shown in the scenarios can be embed into the goal models and validated by using model-checking techniques [4].

Acknowledgements

The work of this paper is motivated by an original submission to ITU-T study group 10 on the topic of User Requirements Notation (URN). The kind cooperation of people from Mitel Networks, Nortel Networks and other institutions is gratefully acknowledged. This work received financial support from NSERC, CITO, and Mitel Networks.

References

1. Buhr, R. J. A. Use Case Maps as Architectural Entities for Complex Systems. In: Transactions on Software Engineering, IEEE, Vol. 24, No. 12, December 1998, pp. 1131-1155.
2. Carroll, J. M. Introduction: The Scenario Perspective on System Development. In Scenario-Based Design: Envisioning Work and Technology in System Development, Ed Caroll, J. M. 1995. pp. 1-17.
3. Chung, L., Nixon, B. A., Yu, E.and Mylopoulos, J. Non-Functional Requirements in Software Engineering. Kluwer Academic Publishers, 2000.
4. Fuxman, A., Pistore, M., Mylopoulos, J., and Traverso, P. Model Checking Early Requirements Specifications in Tropos. In Proceedings of the 5th IEEE International Symposium on Requirements Engineering. August 2001. Toronto, Canada. 174-181.
5. GRL web site. http://www.cs.toronto.edu/km/GRL/.
6. Horton, W. Designing Web-Based Training, John Wiley & Sons, 2000.
7. Kazman, R., Bass, L., Abowd, G. and Webb, M. SAAM: A Method for Analyzing the Properties of Software Architectures. In *Proceedings of the 16th International Conference on Software Engineering*. May 1994. Sorrento, Italy. 81-90.
8. Lamsweerde, A. V., Willemet, L. Inferring Declarative Requirements Specifications from Operational Scenarios. *IEEE Transactions on Software Engineering*, Special Issue on Scenario Management, December 1998.
9. Lamsweerde, A. V. Requirements Engineering in the Year 00: A Research Perspective. In the *Proceedings of 22nd International Conference on Software Engineering*. Limerick, June 2000, ACM press.
10. Liu, L., Yu, E. From Requirements to Architectural Design - Using Goals and Scenarios. ICSE-2001 Workshop: From Software Requirements to Architectures (STRAW 2001) May 2001, Toronto, Canada. pp.22-30. Toronto, Canada, May 14, 2001. On-line at: http://www.cs.toronto.edu/~liu/.
11. Rolland, C., Grosz, G. and Kla, R. Experience With Goal-Scenario Coupling In Requirements Engineering. In *Proceedings of the IEEE International Symposium on Requirements Engineering* 1998. June 1999. Limerick, Ireland.
12. Simon, A. H. The Sciences of the Artificial, Second Edition. Cambridge, MA: The MIT Press, 1981.
13. URN web site. http://www.usecasemaps.org/urn/.
14. Yu, E. and Mylopoulos, J. Why Goal-Oriented Requirements Engineering. In *Proceedings of the 4th International Workshop on Requirements Engineering: Foundations of Software Quality*. June 1998, Pisa, Italy. E. Dubois, A.L. Opdahl, K. Pohl, eds. Presses Universitaires de Namur, 1998. pp. 15-22.
15. Yu, E. Agent-Oriented Modelling: Software Versus the World. In *the Proceedings Agent-Oriented Software Engineering AOSE-2001 Workshop*. LNCS 2222. On-line at: http://www.fis.utoronto.ca/faculty/yu.
16. Yu, E. Agent Orientation as a Modelling Paradigm. Wirtschaftsinformatik. 43(2) April 2001. pp. 123-132.

A State Machine Based Approach for a Process Driven Development of Web-Applications

Rakesh Mohan, Mitchell A. Cohen, and Josef Schiefer

IBM Watson Research Center
PO Box 704, Yorktown Heights, NY 10598
{rakeshm,macohen,josef.schiefer}@us.ibm.com

Abstract. Traditional workflow systems are not suited for highly interactive online systems. We present a state machine based workflow system, named FlexFlow, which formally describes Internet applications using statecharts. The FlexFlow engine uses these descriptions to directly control the execution of web applications. FlexFlow helps in generating controls for user interactions on web pages. Different versions of an application can be generated by visually editing its FlexFlow description, with minimal incremental effort in rewriting application code or related web pages. FlexFlow provides an efficient way to customize online systems and supports different versions of business processes in the same e-business system for different sets of industries, organizations, users, or devices. We demonstrate FlexFlow's use for rapid prototyping of business processes and describe how we have used FlexFlow in commercial platforms for B2B e-commerce.

1 Introduction

In business systems, abstraction of the process logic from the embedded task logic enables the business processes to be modified independent of application code. The implementation of an e-commerce platform at a company often requires a customization of processes, such as an order process or a Request for Quotes, to the existing environment of that company. Workflow technology is prevalent for the modeling, analysis and execution of business processes [4], [13].

Business process management is critical in a three- or multi-tier environment of e-business systems. Business rules and process information is extracted from the business logic tier and is presented in a workflow-based environment, which manages the execution of the business processes. Consequently, this approach greatly simplifies the application logic at each step. Business rules become explicit, visible, and rapidly changeable. System changes are stimulated and can be easily communicated between the development team and the business, and between the business and its partners, i.e., the customers and suppliers.

Business processes vary with a company's business model, and its industry sector. In e-commerce systems, trading mechanisms, such as auctions and negotiations are varied to suit particular business partners, product categories or market conditions. Business processes are customized to the role of the user and the terms and conditions of a contract with the user's organization. For example, the registration process for an administrator may be different from that of a buyer, and whether payment precedes or follows order confirmation may depend on the terms of a contract. E-commerce platforms thus need to provide both an easy way to modify business processes and to maintain variations of business processes. The separation of process and task logic allows both the easy customization of business process and reuse of the task logic in the variants of a business process.

In most current e-commerce systems, the steps of a business process, or the actions a system takes in response to user requests, are not made explicit, but are buried in software code for both the dynamic pages and the application server. This makes the modification of implemented business processes extremely difficult and fragile. For example, to change the ordering of the process steps requires substantial rewriting of the software for the application and the web pages for the user interface. For e-commerce platforms made to be used by different companies, this presents a big problem as most companies' business processes differ from those of other companies to a small or large extent. Thus, deployment of such e-commerce platforms incurs a large overhead in terms of time and money required to rewrite the business processes. Often, this overhead actually forces companies to adjust their business processes to conform to an e-commerce system instead of modifying the system to match their preferred processes.

In this paper, we present a state machine based approach for managing web-based business processes that is more suited for the interactive nature of online systems than traditional workflow systems. We introduce a system which facilitates communication about system change with a descriptive model in which "as-is" and "as-to-be" models represent business processes. Since the e-business environment is so dynamic, change often overtakes models before delivering any significant results. Business people, rather than information technology experts, must be able to develop and extend the business process model. Hence, tools are required that facilitate business experts in communicating their vision and insights via a descriptive model.

Additionally, we show how to employ the formal method of statecharts [6], [7] for the specification of processes for e-commerce platforms. By using statecharts as our specification method, we are able to model business processes which can be automatically executed by a workflow engine. Our contribution is the introduction of process state diagrams, which use the statechart notation for modeling business processes. Furthermore, we introduce the FlexFlow system, which supports the formal specification of process state diagrams, including the simulation and execution of processes modeled with these diagrams. FlexFlow is suited for interactive applications and is lightweight. It uses state machines to (a) describe the actions that can be taken by a particular user at particular points in a process based on the role of the user, (b) to enforce the validity of user requests, (c) to track the execution of actions within an instance of the business process, (d) to provide the user interface with a list of actions available to a user working on an instance of the business process, (e) to provide coordination between state machines, and (f) to allow different organizations to have varied business processes.

First, we discuss existing related work. Then, we give an overview of the FlexFlow system, introduce the FlexFlow process model, and explain how defining business processes with FlexFlow can drive e-commerce development. We wrap up with our real world experiences using FlexFlow and where we can go with it next.

2 Related Works

Business Process (Re-)Engineering [5] is an important driving force for workflow management. It aims to make business processes more efficient and quickly adjustable to the ever-changing needs of customers. In contrast to specifications of business processes, workflow specifications serve as a basis for the largely automated execution of processes. Workflow specifications are often derived from business process specifications by refining the business process specification into a more detailed and more concrete form. Automated and computer-assisted execution means that a workflow management system (WfMS) [4], [9], [12] controls the processing of activities, which have to be performed in the workflow. Some activities may have a manual or intellectual part, to be performed by a human. But the workflow management system is in charge of determining the (partial) invocation order of these activities. In contrast to business process specifications, this requires a formal specification of control flow and data flow.

Workflow specifications based on script languages contain control flow and data flow constructs which are specifically tailored to workflow applications. Such script languages are popular in current WfMS products. They provide a compact representation making them easy to use. A drawback of most script languages is their lack of a formal foundation. Their semantics is mostly 'defined' by the code of the script interpreter used.

Leymann argues in [11] that state transition nets are a good choice when a graphical visualization of workflow specifications has high priority. In state transition nets, activities are represented by nodes, and control flow is represented by edges. In fact, almost all WfMS products provide means for graphical specifications similar to state transition nets.

Considering only net-based methods with a formal foundation, we have to restrict ourselves more or less to statecharts [6] and Petri nets [3], [15]. Variants of Petri nets, especially predicate transition nets, are used in a number of research prototypes as well as in several WfMS products [2], [14]. Some workflow management systems use variants of Petri nets for the internal representation of the workflow engine, e.g., [16]. Statecharts [6], [7] have received little attention in workflow management, but they are well established in software engineering, especially for specifying reactive systems. In the MENTOR project [21], statecharts are used as a formal foundation for workflow specification.

Event-Condition-Action-Rules (ECA) rules are used in active database systems and have been adopted by a number of projects in the workflow area (e.g., [10]). ECA rules are used to specify the control flow between activities. Like for other methods that are not based on nets, the graphical visualization of sets of ECA rules is a non-trivial task. Large sets of ECA rules are hard to handle, and a step-wise refinement is not supported [17]. In terms of their formal foundation, ECA rules are typically mapped to other specification methods, especially variants of Petri nets or temporal logic.

The pattern of user interaction with e-commerce business processes is very different from that of traditional workflow systems. Online business systems are highly interactive. Internet applications follow the request-response model. In online business systems, a user takes an action, such as clicking a submit button on a web page. This results in the form data on that page being sent to the system and the system acting on it and presenting another page to the user. For example, a user goes to a shopping web site, fills out the login page and clicks the submit button. This results in her user name and password being sent to the system, which authenticates the user and returns the catalog page. Then the system waits until the user selects products to fill the shopping basket. This interactive, conversational pattern of the system acting based on a user request and then waiting for the user to initiate the next step is not well modeled by existing workflow systems. This modeling difficulty is a major reason why online e-business applications do not use workflow systems.

Another problem is the complexity, cost, and size of workflows systems cause a high cost of deployment and limit the responsiveness when servicing a large number of concurrent requests. Microflows [1] have been proposed to address this drawback of workflow systems. Microflows are small footprint workflow systems crafted for a particular class of applications. They provide minimal or no support for services provided by full workflow systems such as transaction management, guaranteed messaging and worklists. Microflows provide the benefits of abstracting process logic from task logic while at the same time improving the responsiveness and reducing the cost as compared to industrial strength workflow systems.

State machines are widely used for implementation of network protocols to describe the conversation between a sender and receiver. Business processes for e-commerce platforms also interact frequently with each other. Examples are negotiation scenarios between buyers and sellers, where the current state determines the next available actions to each. State machines have been also used to model negotiations [18]. They have been used for real-time systems; a system reacts or responds to events with a quick, nearly instantaneous response [19]. Thus, there is strong evidence to support that state machines would be useful for interactive, conversational and responsive online business systems.

3 Flexflow Overview

Fig. 1 shows the lifecycle of business processes in the FlexFlow system. A visual modeling tool is used to design business processes as process state diagrams. The visual modeling tool generates from the process state diagrams an XML representation, which is a full description of the business process. It contains all the information required by the FlexFlow engine to control the execution of the business process. This XML description is compiled and loaded into the FlexFlow system database tables. An additional table is used to store the current state of each instance of a business process running at a given time in the business system. The FlexFlow engine uses these tables to control the execution of business processes as well as the user interface.

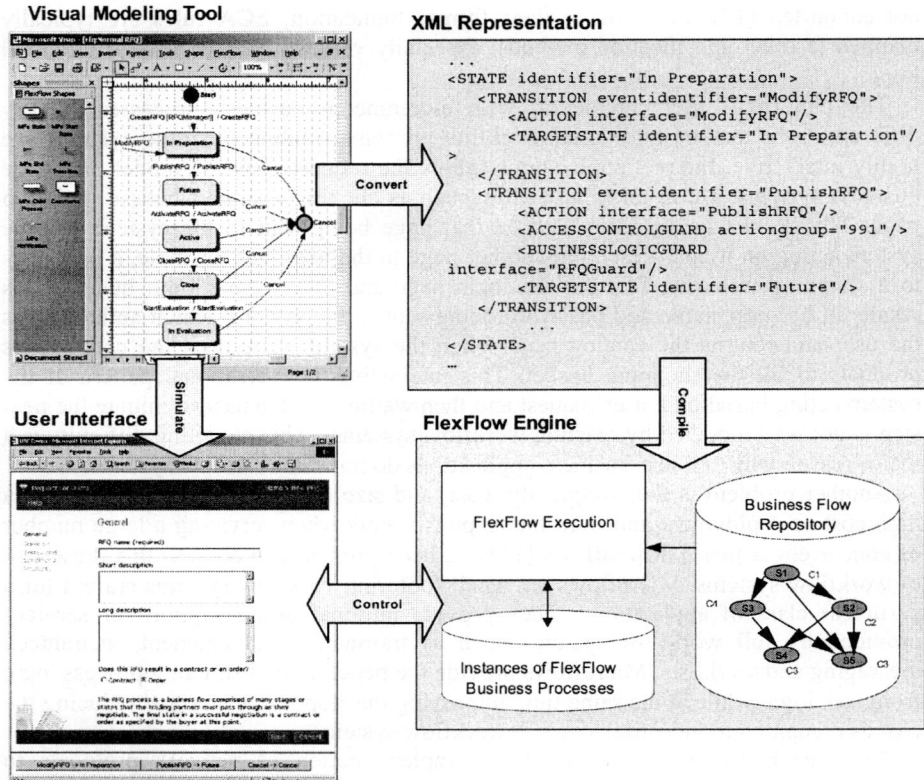

Fig. 1: FlexFlow - Lifecycle of a business process

The visual modeling tool is also used to modify definitions of business processes. Different versions of the business process are stored in the business flow storage. Business processes can be changed with limited or no change to the task logic or computer programs that are implementations of the business actions. Simply reconfiguring its corresponding state machine reconfigures a commerce function.

The FlexFlow system also includes a component for simulating business processes. Thereby, users and developers can explore process variations to reach a common vision of how the user might interact with the system to perform a task.

4 The Flexflow Process Model

FlexFlow models e-commerce business processes as Unified Modeling Language (UML) state diagrams [20], which are an adaptation of Harel's statecharts [6], [7]. UML uses state diagrams to describe the behavior of objects, whereas, FlexFlow uses statecharts to describe processes. We adopt the UML state diagram notation for the FlexFlow.

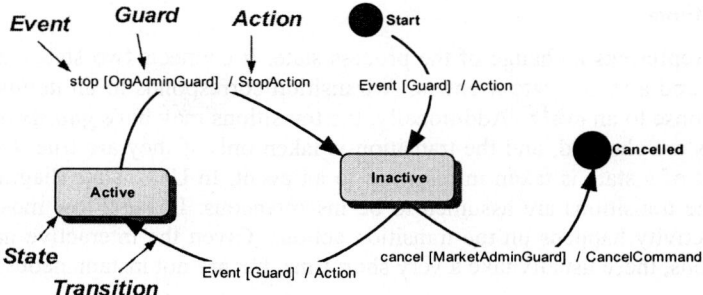

Fig. 2: FlexFlow state diagrams

UML state diagrams are directed graphs with nodes called *states* and the directed edges between them called *transitions* (see Fig. 2). FlexFlow models interactive online business processes with these state diagrams. However, unlike UML, where state diagrams describe the behavior of objects, FlexFlow state diagrams describe processes. In addition to the functionality of Harel statecharts and UML state diagrams, FlexFlow adds three key features: 1) the concept of roles, 2) the coordination of interactions of multiple parties, and 3) the ability to allow different organizations to use different versions of the business process. Business processes are versioned as different state diagrams. Versions can be selected based on membership at the organization level. Versions can also be selected based on other factors including the mode of interaction, such as device, browser, and messaging method. The UML notation used by FlexFlow consists of states, transitions, events, guards, and context.

4.1 Actions

Actions correspond to task logic being executed at the application server. For FlexFlow they are atomic units of business work. Actions can appear in states and transitions. An action can be used to interface to an external system, such as a workflow system handling its own set of functionality. An action can be a conglomeration, or sequence, of pre-defined internal commerce actions. All actions caused by the processing of an event are run within the same transaction.

4.2 States

States correspond to stages in a business process. A state identifies a precise point within the process. In a given business process at a given state, the actions that can be taken by various parties are completely defined by the set of outgoing transitions. A state may have an *entry action*, an action that is executed upon entering the state, and an *exit action*, an action that is executed upon leaving the state. In FlexFlow, *entry actions* are allowed to trigger new events, which in turn get processed by FlexFlow.

4.3 Transitions

A transition represents a change of the process state. It connects two states, a source state it exits and a target state it enters. A transition corresponds to an *action* that is taken in response to an *event*. Additionally, the transitions may have *guards* on them. These guards are checked, and the transition is taken only if they are true. Only one transition out of a state is taken in response to an event. In UML state diagrams, the actions on the transitions are assumed to be instantaneous. In FlexFlow most of the processing activity happens on the transition actions. Given the interactive nature of the applications, these usually take a very short time, but are not instantaneous.

4.4 Events

An event is a named message needing to get processed. In Internet applications, an event is usually an HTTP client request generated by a user pressing a hyperlink, button, etc. on a web page. It can also be an incoming Simple Object Access Protocol (SOAP) request or a Java Message Service (JMS) message. It can also be an event generated by another process such as a scheduler or another FlexFlow process. It can even be an event generated in the same FlexFlow process by a transition or a state entry action.

4.5 Guards

A guard is a set of conditions that need to be true before the action can be taken. Conditions are Boolean computations on the *context* of the business process and/or the parameters of the event. In general, the guards can be rules. In our implementation, an access control condition is always present in the guard. Thus, the action on a transition is taken only if access is allowed. If no access control policy is explicitly specified, the default access control mechanism is used.

4.6 Context

Context is data associated with a business process. It consists of

- The session information that includes information about the user including roles and permissions, and
- The data submitted by the user such as form entries and the data stored in the form such as the identification of the process and the business object. For example, if a user submits a bid for an auction, the context would contain the username and roles as well as the amount of the bid. The event would include an identifier for the auction on which the bid is made. Also included in the context is more general information about the process such as auction start and end time, number of bids, etc.

This context can be referenced in guards as well as read and updated in actions. Fig. 3 shows a FlexFlow model for a simple bilateral negotiation process between a buyer and a seller. The top right transition shows that on the event "Offer" the action "RecordOffer" is taken. The guard checks that the user making the offer is the

"Buyer". As the action for the other "Offer" transitions is also "RecordOffer" we do not show it here for simplicity. There is no action corresponding to the "Accept" or "Reject" events. On entry to the final state "Deal" a "RecordDeal" action is taken.

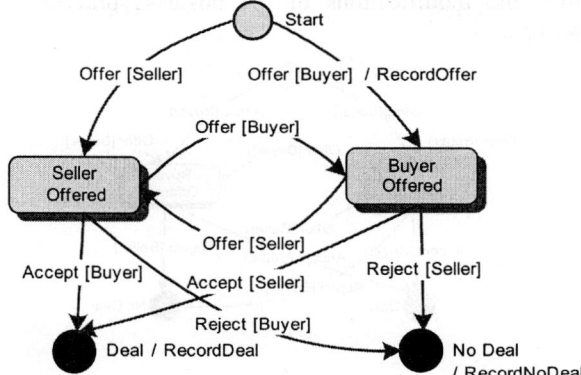

Fig. 3: A simple state diagram for bilateral negotiation

Fig. 4 shows two variations of the bilateral negotiation process shown in Fig 3. The process in Fig. 3 forces the buyer and seller to alternate their bids, i.e., once a participant makes an offer, she has to wait for the other party to make a counter offer. In Fig. 4 (a), the parties can improve their offers without waiting for a counter offer. In Fig. 4 (b), the parties can make a final offer which forces the other party to either accept of reject the offer but does not allow them to counter offer. As is obvious from the process diagrams, the three variants of the business process reuse the code for just three actions "RecordOffer", "RecordDeal" and "RecordNoDeal".

5 User Interaction with FlexFlow

We have observed that a common practice for designing web sites, such as e-commerce sites, is to first mock-up the flow of web pages for user interactions, and then to use this flow to drive the development of application logic. This practice works when the business process is simple and when only one party (the user) is interacting with the system. However, this design practice does not scale to complex business processes, especially where multiple parties are participating in the business process, such as two users in a bilateral negotiation or a buyer and multiple sellers in an RFQ, along with schedulers for timeouts etc. Another drawback of this design practice is that process logic gets embedded both in web pages and application code further complicating any modification of the business process.

5.1 Process Reflection

The FlexFlow process model has sufficient information for deriving user interactions from the state diagram. The process reflection mechanism of FlexFlow allows clients to discover or query process information at run time. This mechanism can be used to drive the user interface or the future user interaction. Thus, with FlexFlow, the design practice is to first design the process and then to automatically derive the flow of user interactions. As the user interaction information is added dynamically to the web pages at run time, the modifications of the business process get automatically reflected in the web pages.

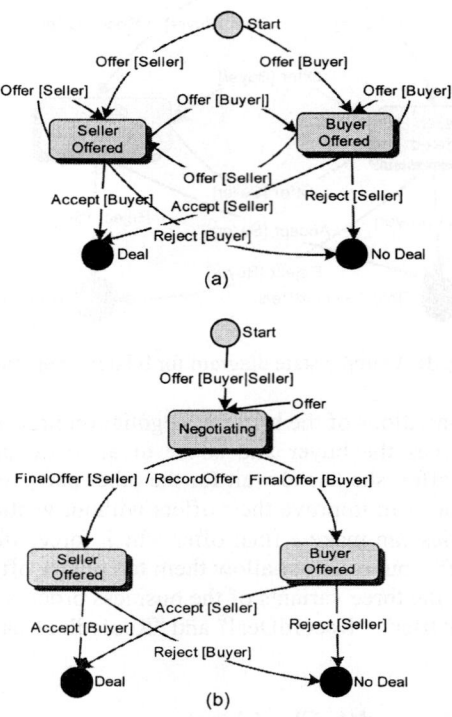

Fig. 4: Two variations of the bilateral negotiation process

Process reflection allows users to query a list of actions that are valid for a given user role at the current state of the business process. At each given state, the FlexFlow system knows the next possible set of actions a particular user can perform by using the guards on all the outgoing transitions. Thus, FlexFlow can provide relevant information for the rendering of the user output (i.e., FlexFlow can determine whether buttons should be enabled or disabled). If web designers use this reflection mechanism, web pages can be shared among different process versions. Using reflection also reduces the effort for modifying FlexFlow processes [8].

We illustrate this in Fig. 5 for a simple bilateral negotiation. There is web page for each state for each user where the user can take an action. The seller's pages are outlined in blue and the buyer's pages are outline in green. At the start state, either party can make an offer to start the negotiation so the both the buyer's and seller's page show a button (or other control) for making an offer. If the seller makes an offer, the process moves to the "Seller Offered" state and the page for the seller will show no buttons (corresponding to this instance of the bilateral negotiation) while the buyer's page will display the options to make a counter offer or to accept or reject the current offer. As the controls are generated dynamically via reflection on the process model, when the process is changed, for example as shown in Fig. 4, the controls on the web pages will show the correct set of actions without any rewriting.

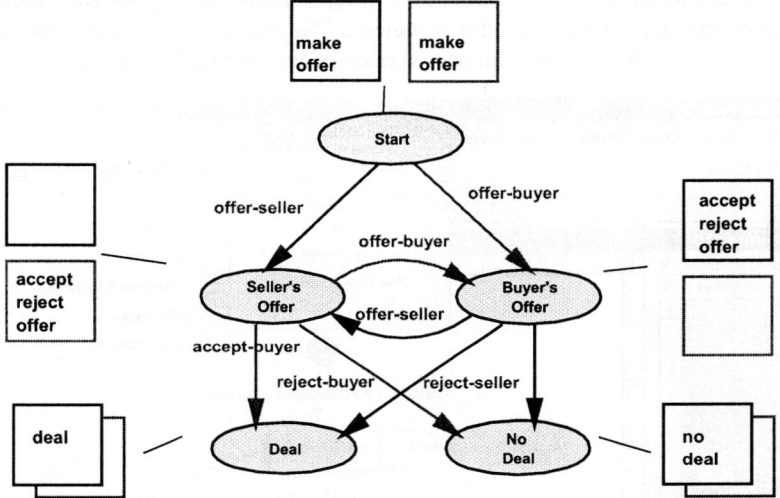

Fig. 5: Controls on web forms for user interactions are created using FlexFlow. The blue outlined page is for the seller, the green for the buyer. The text in black corresponds to buttons on the forms

6 Visual Modeling & Simulation

The FlexFlow engine uses an XML representation of the process definition. To allow business managers to easily create and change FlexFlow processes, we extended popular COTS (commercial off-the-shelf) modeling tools. Since statecharts are a part of the popular UML notation, a number of graphical tools are available. For managing FlexFlow processes, we have added extensions to both Microsoft Visio® and Rational Rose®. Therefore, business managers can use a familiar modeling environment, which provides the following key functionalities:

- Easy-to-use modeling interface for creating or modifying business processes by changing, adding, and/or removing states and transitions from the process state diagram.
- XML generation of the process definition based on the process state diagram.
- Import / Export of the XML process definition
- Management of different versions of process state machines.
- Simulation of the FlexFlow processes

The states and transitions of FlexFlow state diagrams have additional attributes like response views, additional guard properties and priorities. Business managers can import and export XML process definitions via a file or a web-service.

Different versions of a business process can be maintained based on membership at the organization level. Versions can also be selected based on the mode of interaction, such as device, browser, and messaging. Fig. 6 shows the default version of a RFQ process. By specifying new flows, the modeling tool allows administrators to manage several variations of a RFQ process. This way, business managers can model and maintain several RFQ processes (for instance a "Normal RFQ" process, and a "Fast RFQ" process, which is a more compact version of the normal RFQ process).

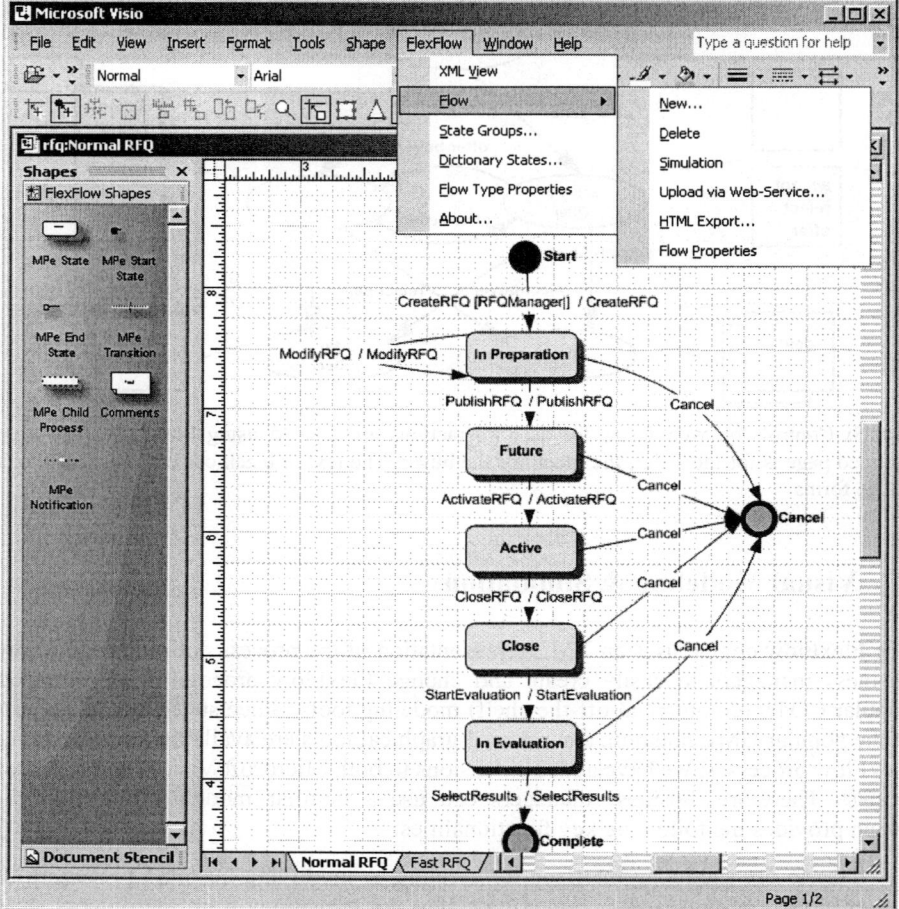

Fig. 6: Visio modeling tool for FlexFlow

6.1 Process Simulation

In a typical web application, users can navigate to a limited number of web pages based on the actions they take. The number of possible navigation paths can be very large in a complex graphical user interface, but the number is finite and the options usually are known. User interfaces also must stay in sync with the underlying business process. Therefore, process state diagrams reflect the navigation paths of the user at a high level of abstraction.

Process state diagrams can be used to explore hypothetical process models and user interface concepts based on the understanding of the requirements. Users and developers can study a process state diagram to reach a common vision of how the user might interact with the system to perform a task. The business process, business rules and the user experience can be incrementally and iteratively optimized by simulating the business process with user scenarios. These simulations can occur without implementing the business logic. This way, conflicts between the business process and the user interface can be easily discovered.

Process state diagrams capture the essence of the user-system interactions and task flow without getting one bogged down too soon in specifying the details of web pages or data elements. Users can trace through a process state diagram to find missing, incorrect, or superfluous transitions, and hence missing, incorrect, or superfluous requirements.

The FlexFlow modeling tool includes a simulation component that allows development of a horizontal prototype which displays the facades of user interface screens from the web application, possibly allowing some navigation between them. The tool does not show real data and contains little or no real functionality. The information that appears in response to a client's request is faked or static, and report contents are hard-coded. Nevertheless, the simulation component allows a process-oriented navigation through the web application. It allows users to change the status of the current process by selecting one of the available actions on the simulation panel. For the simulation, we can include web pages of existing web solutions or new web pages, which can be instantly created and modified. Fig. 7 shows the simulation of the RFQ process. The buttons in the simulation panel at the bottom of the screen show the available navigations paths based on the RFQ process state diagram.

Note, that not all page flows are represented by the control flows of a process. For instance, wizards, like in Fig., or other UI facilitators which have a predefined sequence of processing steps, are implemented solely in the presentation layer and have no impact the process itself. UI components of the presentation layer use the process reflection mechanism to determine functionality, which should be available to the user.

This type of simulation is often sufficient to give the users a feeling for the web application and lets them judge whether any functionality is missing, wrong, or unnecessary. The simulation prototypes represent the concepts to the developers of how the business process might be implemented. The user's evaluation of the prototype can point out alternative courses for a business process, new missing process steps, previously undetected exception conditions, or new ways to visualize information.

By modeling and executing business processes as state machines, FlexFlow enables its process to be modified with minimal changes to the underlying implementation of the business processes. A commerce process can be modified simply by reconfiguring its corresponding state diagram.

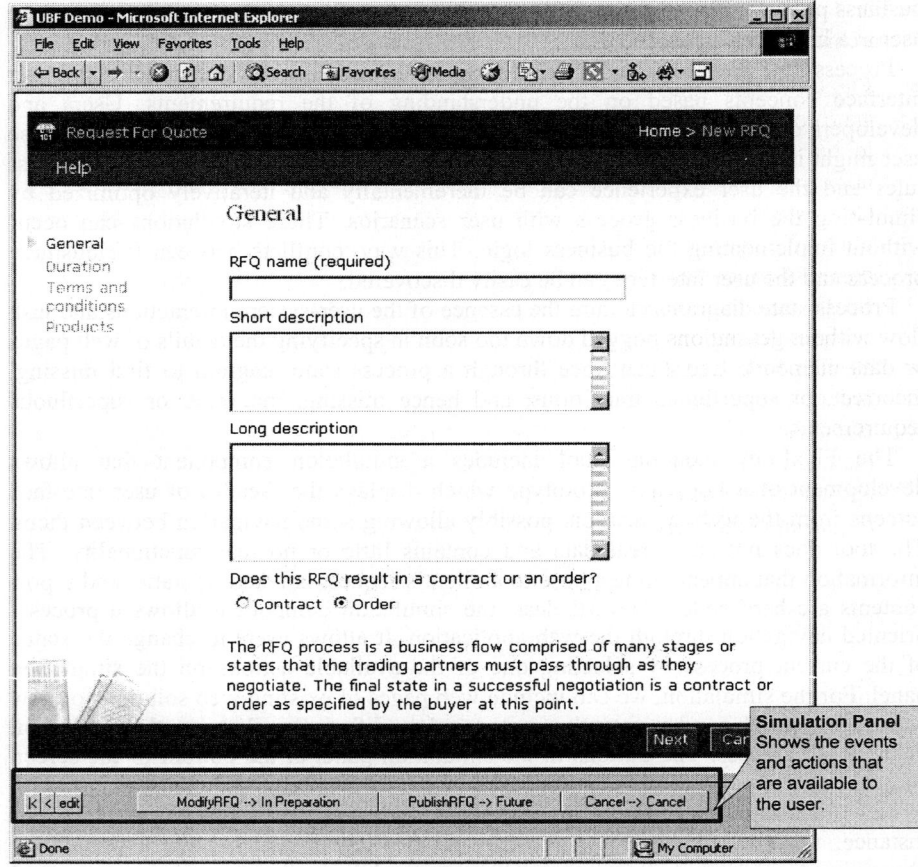

Fig. 7: Simulation of a RFQ process

7 Conclusion & Future Work

Web applications are difficult to build with traditional workflow management systems. In this paper, we presented an approach for managing web-based business processes and introduced a state machine based model for the specification of these business processes. Since e-commerce environments are highly dynamic, we argued that a descriptive model in which business processes are represented "as-is" and "as-to-be" models is advantageous compared to workflow management systems, where separate models are used.

We have shown the FlexFlow system, which supports the modeling, simulation and execution of process state machine. Using the FlexFlow system, developers start the development of a web application with a business process model and afterwards, they can incrementally and iteratively implement all functionalities for this process. Furthermore, web applications remain with FlexFlow customizable and extendible.

Further problems we want to consider in the future include the management of hierarchical states as well as the concurrent execution of FlexFlow processes:

- FlexFlow state machines can be denoted as super-states, whereby each super-state corresponds to a state machine. We want to extend our model to allow states to be nested an arbitrary number of times. Nested states would also allow a notional simplicity for handling duplicate transitions and interrupts.
- Concurrent process state machines sometimes need to be synchronized with each other. Web applications with many business processes demand the ability to start business processes together, run them independently until a certain state and finally re-synchronize them. Forks and joins will allow us to specify more complex transitions to allow this kind of synchronization.
- Besides forks and joins, we want to include a sync vertex in our process model in order to synchronize concurrent regions in a process state machine. A sync vertex is different from a state in the sense that it is not mapped to a Boolean value (active, not active), but an integer. It is used in conjunction with forks and joins to insure that one region of a state machine leaves particular states before another region can enter particular states.

References

1. Dragos A. Molescu, Ralph E. Johnson, A Micro Workflow Framework for Compositional Object Oriented Software Development, OOPSLA, 1999
2. Ellis, C. A., Nutt, G. J., Modeling and Enactment of Workflow Systems, 14th International Conference on Application and Theory of Petri Nets, 1993
3. Genrich, H. J., Predicate/Transition Nets. In: Advances in Petri Nets, 1986, Springer, LNCS 254
4. Georgakopolaus, Diimitiros and Hornik, Mark, An Overview of Workflow Management: From Process Modeling to Workflow Automation Infrastructure, Distributed and Parallel Databases, 3, 119-153, 1995
5. Hammer, M., Champy, J., Reengineering the Cooperation, A Manifesto for Business Revolution, New York, 1993
6. Harel D., Statecharts: A Visual Formalism for Complex Systems, Science of Computer Programming, Vol. 8, 1987
7. Harel, D., On Visual Formalisms, Communications of the ACM Vol.31 No.5, 1988
8. Ian Horrocks, Constructing the User Interface with Statecharts, Addison-Wesley, 1999
9. Jablonski, S., Bussler, C., Workflow-Management, Modelling Concepts, Architecture, and Implementation, International Thomson Computer Press, 1996
10. Kappel, G., Lang, P., Rausch-Schott, S., Retschitzegger, W.: Workflow Management Based on Objects, Rules, and Roles, IEEE Bulletin of the Technical Committee on Data Engineering, Vol. 18/1, March 1995, pp. 11-17
11. Leymann, F., Altenhuber, W., Managing Business Processes as an Information Resource, IBM Systems Journal Vol.33 No.2, 1994

12. Mohan, C.: State of the Art in Workflow Management Research and Products, SIGMOD, Montreal, Canada, 1996
13. Mohan, C., Recent Trends in Workflow Management Products, Standards and Research, NATO, 1997
14. Oberweis, A., Modeling and Execution of Workflows with Petri-nets, Teubner, 1996
15. Reisig, W., Petri Nets: An Introduction, Springer, 1985
16. Reuter, A., Schwenkreis, F., ConTracts - A Low-Level Mechanism for Building General-Purpose Workflow Management Systems, IEEE Computer Society, Bulletin of the Technical Committee on Data Engineering, 18(1):4-10, 1995
17. Simon, E., Kotz-Dittrich, A.: Promises and Realities of Active Database Systems, International Conference on Very Large Data Bases, Zurich, 1995
18. J. Sprinkle, C. P. van Buskirk and G. Karsai, Modeling Agent Negotiation, Proceedings of the IEEE Systems, Man, and Cybernetics Conference, October 2000
19. Tsai J. J. P., Yang, S., Bi, Y., Smith, R., Distirbuted Real-Time Systems, John Wiley and Sons Inc., 1996
20. Unified Modeling Language Specification, version 1.4, http://www.omg.org/technology/documents/formal/uml.htm, 2001
21. Weißenfels, J., Wodtke, D., Weikum, G., Kotz-Dittrich, A., The MENTOR Architecture for Enterprise-wide Workflow Management, Workflow and Process Automation in Information Systems, 1996

Supporting Dimension Updates in an OLAP Server

Alejandro A. Vaisman[1], Alberto O. Mendelzon[2],
Walter Ruaro[1], and Sergio G. Cymerman[1]

[1] Universidad de Buenos Aires
{avaisman,wruaro,scymer}@dc.uba.ar
[2] University of Toronto
mendel@db.toronto.edu

Abstract. Commercial OLAP systems usually treat OLAP dimensions as static entities. In practice, dimension updates are often needed to adapt the warehouse to changing requirements. In earlier work, we defined a taxonomy for these dimension updates and a minimal set of operators to perform them. In this paper we present *TSOLAP*, an OLAP server supporting fully dynamic dimensions. *TSOLAP* conforms to the *OLE DB for OLAP* norm, so it can be used by any client application based on this norm, and can use as backend any conformant relational server. We incorporate dimension update support to *MDX*, Microsoft's language for OLAP, and introduce *TSShow*, a visualization tool for dimensions and data cubes. Finally, we present the results of a real-life case study in the application of *TSOLAP* to a medium-sized medical center.

1 Introduction

The term OLAP (On Line Analytical Processing) refers to data analysis over large collections of historical data(*data warehouses*), supporting the decision-making process, allowing the analysis of factual data (*e.g.* daily sales in the different branches of a supermarket chain) according to dimensions of interest (*e.g.* regions, products, stores, etc.). Several formal models for OLAP applications have been proposed [4,2,1]. Most of these are based on the original idea of the "star schema" [8], in which data is stored in sets of *dimension* and *fact tables*. The usual assumption here is that data in the fact tables reflect the dynamic aspect of the data warehouse, whereas data in the dimension tables represent basically static information. In practice, however, the evolution of the information stored in the warehouse often requires updating some dimensions due to changing user requirements or changes in the data sources.

In this paper we present an OLAP server supporting dimension updates and view maintenance under these updates, built following the *OLE DB for OLAP* [10] proposal. We extend *MDX*, Microsoft's language for OLAP with a set of statements supporting dimension update operators. We also introduce a visualization tool for dimensions and data cubes. We present the results obtained in a real-life case study, a medical center in Argentina. These results suggest that execution times are compatible with real-life application requirements. Moreover, we show that our view maintenance algorithm largely outperforms the Summary-Delta algorithm for maintaining summary tables in a data warehouse [11].

The remainder of the paper is organized as follows: in Section 2 we review the multidimensional model and dimension updates; in Section 3 we describe our implementation in detail. Section 4 presents the case study and discusses the results. We conclude in Section 5.

2 Multidimensional Model and Dimension Updates

In previous work, Hurtado *et al.* [6,7] introduced a multidimensional model that includes a framework for dimension updates and a set of dimension update operators. Due to space limitations we will only give a quick overview of that model, and refer the reader to these works for details.

A *dimension schema* is a directed acyclic graph $G(L, \preceq)$ where each node represents a dimension level, and $\preceq$ is a relation between levels such that its transitive and reflexive closure, $\preceq^*$, is a partial order with a unique bottom level l_{inf}, and a unique top level *All*.

An *instance* of a dimension is an assignment of a set of *elements* to each dimension level. Moreover, between every pair of levels l_i and l_j such that $l_i \preceq l_j$ there is a function $\rho_{l_i}^{l_j}$ called *rollup*. A dimension instance must satisfy the *consistency condition*, meaning that for every pair of paths from l_i to l_j in $\preceq$, the composition of the rollup functions yields identical functions.

Example 1. Figure 1(a) shows dimension schema for a dimension *Geography,*, where for $L = \{city, province, country, All\}$. Relation $\preceq$ contains the following pairs: $city \preceq province, province \preceq country, country \preceq All$. Figure 2(a) shows an instance of the dimension.

Factual data is stored in *fact tables*. Given a set of dimensions D, a fact table has a column for each dimension in D and one or more columns for a distinguished type of dimension called *Measure*. A *base fact table* is a fact table such that its attributes are the bottom levels of each one of the dimensions in D. A *multidimensional database* is a set of dimensions and fact tables. A *cube view* is a view computed by aggregating data over the measure of a base fact table.

2.1 Dimension Updates and View Maintenance

We will now briefly review the set of operators that modify either the schema or an instance of a given dimension. There are two kinds of update operators: structural operators, that modify the schema, and instance operators, that modify an instance.

The *structural* operators are the following. *Generalize* adds a new level above a given one. *Relate* links two independent levels in a dimension. *Unrelate* deletes an edge between two levels. *DelLevel* deletes a level and its rollup functions. *Specialize* adds a new level to a dimension, below the bottom level l_{inf}. Although

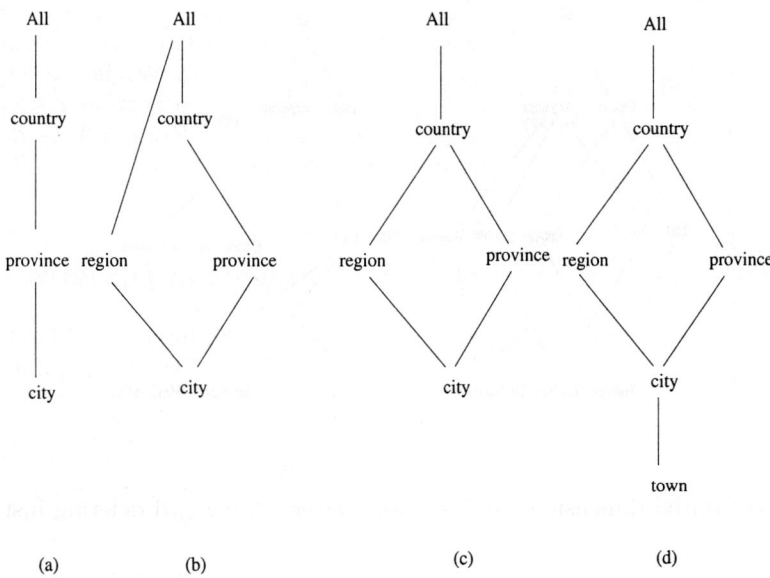

Fig. 1. Dimension *Geography*, and a series of updates

Specialize can be defined in terms of some of the operators above [13] this would lead to an inefficient implementation so we prefer to treat it as a separate operator. The *instance* operator *AddInstance* inserts a new element into a level, while *DelInstance*, deletes an element from a level.

Example 2. Figure 1 shows a sequence of structural dimension updates to the *Geography* dimension. Figure 1(b) depicts a generalization of level *city* to level *region*. Figure 1(c) shows the dimension schema after relating levels *region* and *country* (i.e. this defines that one region cannot belong to two different countries). Finally, Figure 1(d) shows a specialization of level *city* to a finer grain, represented by the level *town*. Deleting *town* would yield the dimension of Figure 1(c). Figure 2(b) depicts the dimension instance after having deleted the city *San Juan City,* and added *Mendoza City,* to the instance of Figure 2(a).

Many common updates to dimensions would result in long sequences of primitive instance updates. Thus, the works cited above define *complex instance update operators*, capturing such common sequences and encapsulating them in a single operation [6,7].

When an update to a dimension occurs, any cube views that have been materialized in the data warehouse must be updated accordingly. Previous works [6,13] present algorithms that outperform traditional incremental maintenance algorithms for materialized views with aggregates [11] by exploiting the special structure of dimension updates. In Section 4 we compare the performance of these algorithms for the *DelInstance* operation and the *SUM* aggregate function, against a summary-delta algorithm developed by Mumick et al [11].

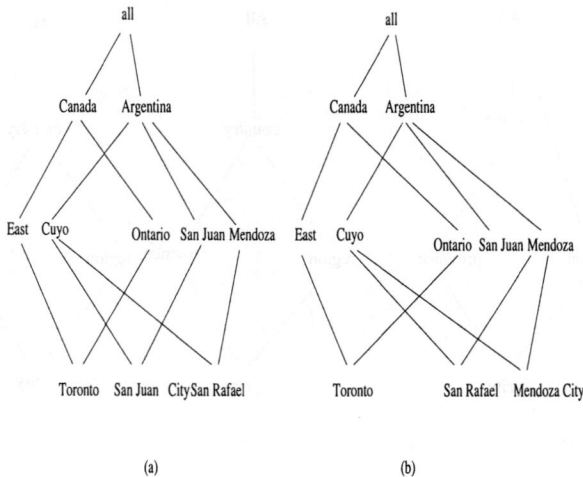

Fig. 2. (a) Initial dimension (b) Dimension after adding and deleting instances

2.2 Mapping Dimensions to Relations

In previous work [7] Hurtado and some of the authors discussed different ways in which dimensions can be represented in the relational model. The relational representation of a dimension schema that we adopted in the implementation discussed in Section 3 is a relation containing one attribute for each dimension level; each dimension instance contains a tuple for each element to which no other element in the dimension instance rolls up.

Formally, let us denote the relational representation of a dimension d as a pair $R_d = (S_d, T_d)$, where $S_d = (rname, A, \mathcal{F})$ is the schema of the relation; $rname$ is the name of the dimension, and also the name of the relational schema, A is the set of attributes of the relational schema, and $\mathcal{F}$ is a set of functional dependencies such that $dom(\mathcal{F}) \cup ran(\mathcal{F}) \subseteq A$. T_d is the set of tuples in the relation representing d. A tuple $R_d = (S_d, T_d)$ represents the dimension, where: (a) $S_d = (rname, A, \mathcal{F})$ is the dimension schema, such that: $rname$ is the name of the dimension; A contains an attribute l for each level $l \in L$; $\mathcal{F}$ contains a functional dependency $l_a \rightarrow l_b$ for each pair of levels $l_a, l_b \in L$ such that $l_a \preceq l_b$; (b) T_d, is the set of tuples in the relation. Let us define the leaves of a level $l \in L$, $Leaves(l)$, as the set of elements in a dimension level not reached by any other element below them in the dimension instance. For every level l, and for every element $e \in Leaves(l)$, there is a tuple t in T_d such that $t(l_i) = \rho *_l^{l_i}(e)$, if $l \preceq^* l_i$, or $t(l_i) = null$ otherwise, where ρ^* is the transitive and reflexive closure of ρ.

We assume that the functional dependencies are only applied over non-null values, i.e., a null in a level l_a can be related to two different elements in l_b even if we have $l_a \rightarrow l_b$ in $\mathcal{F}$.

Example 3. The denormalized representation of the dimension depicted in Figure 2(a) is the following:

city	province	region	country
$Toronto$	$Ontario$	$Cuyo$	$Canada$
$SanJuanCity$	$SanJuan$	$Cuyo$	$Argentina$
$SanRafael$	$Mendoza$	$Cuyo$	$Argentina$

3 Implementation of Dimension Updates

In this section we present a relational implementation of the model introduced in Section 2. We decided to build an implementation that could be accessed by multiple clients and served by multiple back-ends using reasonably standard interfaces. We chose for this purpose Microsoft's *OLEDB for OLAP* set of interfaces. To express dimension updates, we extended the *MDX* language, the language proposed by Microsoft as a standard for multidimensional database access [10]. The reason for this choice was the wide set of OLAP vendors supporting OLEDB for OLAP, including companies such as Business Objects, SAS Institute, Cognos, and Hyperion, among others. A commitment to this standard was subscribed in the Data Warehouse Alliance [9]. Further, the recently released *XML for Analysis* protocol extends OLE DB for OLAP and OLE DB for DM, allowing standard data access between a client and a provider over the web. However, an implementation could also be built on alternative proposals such as JOLAP [12], a Java-based OLAP API initiative led by ORACLE and IBM.

Roughly speaking, *OLE DB* is a set of low level interfaces for access and manipulation of different data types using the OLE Component Object Model (COM). Thus, OLE DB is more powerful that the well-known ODBC because it is not restricted to relational data. In an OLE DB architecture, a *consumer* is any object consuming an OLE DB interface, while a *provider* is a software component which offers OLE DB interfaces. *OLE DB for OLAP* is an OLE DB extension allowing access and manipulation of multidimensional data like cubes, dimensions, levels and measures, no matter how these data are physically stored. For querying multidimensional data, OLE DB for OLAP employs *multidimensional expressions* written in the *MDX* query language.

Data Cubes are created in MDX using the DDL(Data Definition Language) statement **CREATE CUBE**. However, MDX does not provide update statements for dimensions. Once dimensions and data cubes are created, they remain unchanged "forever." If a situation requiring a dimension update arises, the dimension must be rebuilt from scratch, along with the data cube. We would like to be able to update dimensions and data cubes as soon as it is required, without discarding any current data. Moreover, MDX does not support multiple-path hierarchies (i.e., hierarchies where there are at least two paths between some pair of levels). Instead, we are forced to treat such hierarchies as as a set of single-path hierarchies, which seems rather unnatural. We believe that from the analyst's point of view, it is important to address multiple hierarchies in a more natural way, providing a higher level of abstraction.

In order to give a solution to these drawbacks, we developed an OLE DB for OLAP data provider called *TSOLAP* that supports dimension updates and performs incremental view maintenance under these updates, together with an MDX extension denoted *MDDLX*.

3.1 TSOLAP Architecture

We considered four possible architectures for bringing dimension updates into OLAP: (a) building an application implementing dimension updates over a relational database; (b) modifying an existing OLAP server; (c) developing a hybrid architecture by storing the data cube in a commercial OLAP server, and a catalog in a relational database; (d) implementing a ROLAP server.

We discarded alternative (a) because it meant dimension updates could only be performed by the application program. Alternative (b) was not practical given that we had no access to the internals of an OLAP server. Alternative (c) would not allow maintenance of materialized cube views, as the data cube would be stored in the OLAP server. We chose alternative (d), with the architecture shown in Figure 3.

The ROLAP repository is built on top of a Relational Database. We extended OLE DB for OLAP with a Data Definition Language(MDDLX), and introduced a layer between OLE DB for OLAP and the data source for implementing dimension updates and view maintenance. The data sources can be accessed either through OLE DB or via ODBC (using MSDASQL, an OLE DB provider for ODBC). Configuring the ROLAP server for ODBC allows accessing a wide set of databases. Figure 3 shows that an application could also connect to an OLE DB for OLAP provider via ADO, a set of components and objects allowing data access using a high level programming language. This would require implementing the corresponding ADO interfaces.

3.2 Adding Dimension Update Support to MDX

With the support of the architecture described in the previous subsections, we developed a *Multidimensional Data Definition Language* which we called *MDDLX,* an extension to MDX supporting the model of Section 2. We provide statements for the primitive structural and instance update operators, as well as for the complex operators, remaining as faithful as possible to the formal definition of these operators. We also provide a limited **SELECT** statement for displaying the results, although this was not the focus of our work. The **CREATE CUBE** clause creates a data cube. The following statement creates a data cube *Services* for the case study we will present in Section 4.

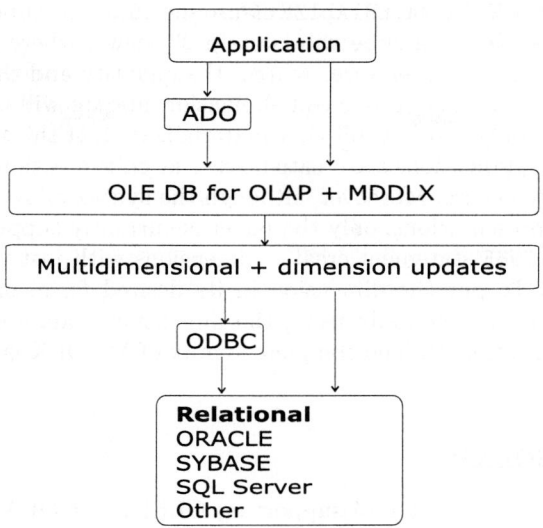

Fig. 3. TSOLAP architecture

```
CREATE CUBE Services (
   DIMENSION Doctor BOTTOM LEVEL doctorId TYPE CHAR(6),
   DIMENSION Procedure BOTTOM LEVEL procedureId TYPE CHAR(6),
   DIMENSION Patient BOTTOM LEVEL patientId TYPE CHAR(6),
   TIME DIMENSION Time GRANULARITY DATETIME FROM 01/01/2000 00:00:00
      TO 30/06/2000 23:00:00,
   MEASURE qty TYPE NUMERIC(5,0) FUNCTION SUM,
   MEASURE value TYPE NUMERIC(10,2) FUNCTION SUM)
FROM TABLE data_clinic
WITH MATERIALIZE
```

Here, *data_clinic* is the table from which data is downloaded, with schema (Doctor, Procedure, Patient, Date, qty, value). Attributes corresponding to dimensions must have the same name as the dimension they represent. It is assumed that *data_clinic* has gone through the data extraction and cleaning processes. This table may also include columns that will not be loaded into the cube. The base fact table for the cube will be generated at cube creation time as a materialized view with the least level of aggregation. A new dimension is created for each DIMENSION statement, such that a value in the corresponding column of *data_clinic* becomes a value in the bottom level of the dimension. In summary, after the CREATE CUBE Services is executed we will have four one-level (plus the distinguished level *All*) dimensions, *Doctor, Procedure, Patient* and *Time*. The TIME dimension is generated on-the-fly, taking into account the time column in the table *data_clinic*, which is mandatory. Then, the base fact table will be populated with data facts in the interval defined in the the FROM clause. Further, the `WITH MATERIALIZE` clause specifies that cube materialization is required. Thus, the data cube will contain 2^n views, where n is the number of dimensions. Two measures were created, the quantity and the dollar value of the service delivered. Any subsequent dimension update will also require view maintenance. We only support full view materialization at this time. This means that all possible aggregations are created either at cube creation time, or when a dimension update occurs. Moreover, although the syntax allows normalized and denormalized representations, only the latter is currently supported.

The `CREATE CUBE` statement creates dimensions with just two levels, one of them being *All*. To put the dimension in its desired form, once it is created it must be grown incrementally using the dimension update statement `ALTER DIMENSION` (see Section 4). The complete syntax of MDDLX is described in the full paper [14].

3.3 Using TSOLAP

We claimed that any client tool supporting OLEDB for OLAP could be used to display multidimensional data stored in TSOLAP. To show this, we execute our statements using a preexisting client tool, an OLEDB for OLAP consumer called *DataSetViewer*, provided by Microsoft as part of *MDAC2.0* (Microsoft Data Access Components). The *DataSetViewer* allows editing a *MDDLX* query and displaying query results.

An important objective of our work is enhancing the user's capabilities for data analysis. Along these lines, we built a client tool called TSShow for visualizing the structure and instances of the dimensions of every cube in the system. TSShow accesses the catalog tables to display the system's metadata, like cubes, hierarchies, levels and so on. Information about the dimension instances is retrieved from the dimension tables themselves. This tool becomes important in an environment supporting schema and instance updates. Although most of the commercial OLAP systems provide a visualization tool, TSShow not only displays the dimension's structure and instances, but also the rollup functions which hold between elements in the dimension's levels. Figure 4 presents a TSShow screen displaying the cubes and the dimensions in the system. We can see that two cubes were created, *Salescube* and *Services* (see Section 4). The hierarchies of the dimensions are also displayed.

4 A Case Study: A Medical Data Warehouse

In Section 3 we presented our implementation of the multidimensional model introduced in Section 2, called TSOLAP. In this section, we apply TSOLAP to a real life case study, a medical center in Argentina. We introduce the problem and describe how the cube and dimensions were built. After this, we discuss different ways in which TSOLAP could be applied to the case study, establish the goals of our experiments, and the hardware we used for the tests. Finally, we present our experimental results.

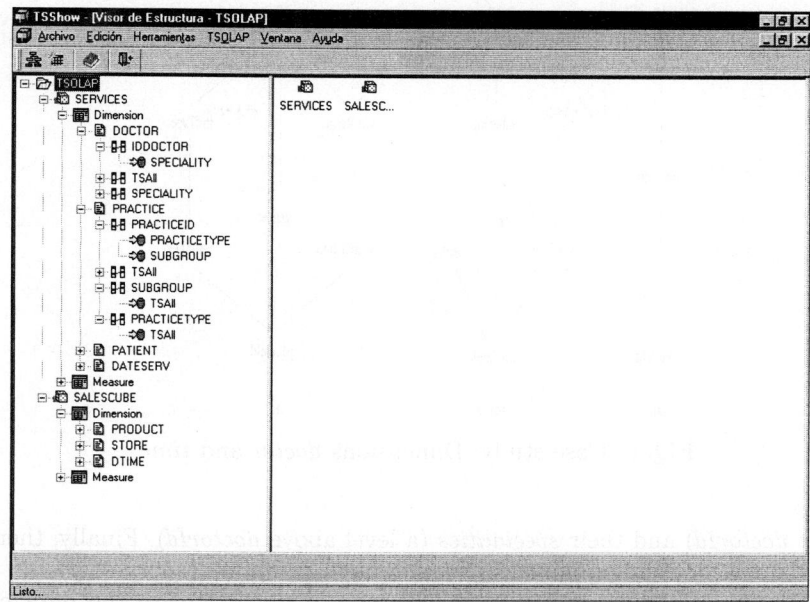

Fig. 4. Cube and dimension information with *TSShow*

4.1 The Problem

We tested the model and its implementation on a real case, a medical center in Buenos Aires, using six months of data about medical procedures performed on patients. Each patient receives different services, including radiographies, electrocardiograms, and so on. These services are called "Procedures," and are grouped into a classification hierarchy. For instance, a procedure like "Special Radiography" belongs to the subgroup "Radiography" and is further classified into the group denoted "Radiology". Medications given to a patient and disposable supplies are also considered "Procedures." The data were extracted from several tables in the operational database. Taking into account the available data, we designed the data warehouse as follows (see Figures 5 and 6).

A dimension *Procedure,* with bottom level *procedureId,* and levels *procedureType, subgroup* and *group,* gives information about the different procedures available to patients. *Patient,* with bottom level *patientId,* represents information about the person under treatment. As data about the age and gender of the patient are available, we also defined the dimension levels *yearOfBirth* and *gender.* Moreover, we found it interesting to analyze data according to age intervals, represented by a dimension level called *yearRange.* Patients are also grouped according to institutional affiliation. This information could be useful e.g. to categorize patients delivered by various health insurance institutions. Moreover, these institutions are grouped into types such as private companies, unions, and so on. Dimension *Doctor* gives information about the available doctors (identi-

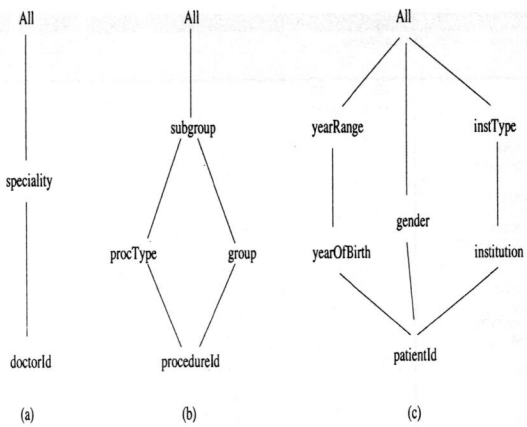

Fig. 5. Case study: Dimensions *doctor* and *time*

fied by *doctorId*) and their *specialities* (a level above *doctorId*). Finally, there is a *Time* dimension, as explained in Section *addingdimup*.

When the design was completed, we were ready to create the data cube using MDDLX statements. The **CREATE CUBE** statement in Section 3.2 creates the cube from a table *data_clinic*, with data from the first six months of the year 2000 (631,000 records). Each record in this table contains information about a *procedure* conducted on a certain *patient* by a given *doctor* on a given *date*.

It is now possible to update these dimensions using MDDLX statements, in order to obtain the dimensions depicted in Figures 5 and 6. For example, the following statement generalizes level *patientId* to level *gender*, which is of type CHAR(1) ('M' or 'F'), using the rollup function specified by the table data3gidintengender. This table has two columns, one named *patientId* and the other named *gender*, with *patientId* being the key, so each tuple stores the gender of a patient. The complete sequence of statements used to set up the dimensions can be found in the full paper [14].

```
ALTER DIMENSION Services.Patient
GENERALIZE LEVEL patientId
    TO LEVEL gender TYPE CHAR(1)
    USING ROLLUP FUNCTION data3gidintengender
```

4.2 What Can We Do with Dimension Updates?

We argue that building dimensions using our approach is, most of the time, more efficient and flexible than building a dimension from scratch every time an update occurs. Moreover, it is possible to add or remove elements from dimensions, or change classification levels in order to query hypothetical database states. Some

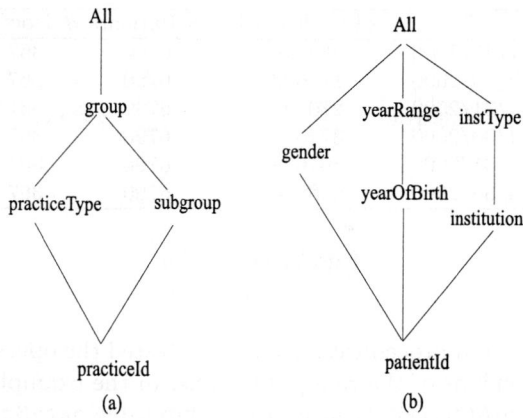

Fig. 6. Case study: Dimensions *procedure* and *patient*

examples of these kinds of situations are: (a) in a clinic like the one described in this study, dimension instances are updated all the time. For example, new doctors are hired or leave frequently and new patients are serviced every day. On the other hand, instance updates to the *Procedure* dimension are less frequent; (b) modifying the "yearRange" field in the *Patient* dimension allows finding out which age range is getting more services. This can be done by deleting the *yearRange* level, and then generalizing it again using a different (prepared off-line) rollup function. In a state-of-the-art OLAP system, this would require rebuilding the data cube once for each range test; (c) generalizing the *doctorId* level in dimension *Doctor* to level *doctorAgeRange* is useful to analyze the number of patients served depending on the doctors' age; (d) the model allows inserting, in an on-line fashion, new patients, institutions, institution types, and so on; (e) simulation data could be inserted on-line in order to query different hypothetical database states. Hypothetical situations could be easily modeled by replacing the actual rollup functions with the ones we wish to test. For instance, we could delete the level *yearOfBirth* and generalize level *patientId* again, with data such that seventy percent of the patients are more than sixty years old.

4.3 Objectives and Description of the Experiments

From the discussion in Subsection 4.2 it follows that TSOLAP is a very useful tool for data analysis. However, we must show that our approach can reach a performance that can cope with the requirements of everyday applications. Thus, getting a set of data large enough to allow representative results was a requirement. We used six months of data, involving almost 631,000 records; we partitioned this set into the six subsets shown in the table of Figure 7 in order to run the tests over each one of them, to test the performance of the system as the size of the data cube changed. Note that the six subsets contain the same number

Case #	From	To	# of tuples in FT	# Patients	# Doctors	# Procedures
1	1/1/2000	1/31/2000	90825	6790	367	3750
2	1/1/2000	2/29/2000	178698	6790	367	3750
3	1/1/2000	3/31/2000	270127	6790	367	3750
4	1/1/2000	4/30/2000	374674	6790	367	3750
5	1/1/2000	5/31/2000	501628	6790	367	3750
6	1/1/2000	6/30/2000	630844	6790	367	3750

Fig. 7. Data sets

of patients, doctors and procedures, because we tested the operators using all the elements in the domains of the rollup functions. In the example above (generalization from *patientId* to *gender* using the rollup table data3gidintengender), although the table holds the gender of all the patients, only doctors who actually delivered services before January 31st will be generalized.

In order to test the performance of dimension updates, we executed a set of MDDLX commands over the data cube described in Section 4.1. Our intuition was that performance could be strongly influenced by the order in which operations are performed. Thus, we decided to perform the dimension updates in two different sequences: in the first one, we updated the dimensions in the following order: *Patient, Doctor, Time* and *Procedure*; in the second sequence, we first performed all the updates over the *Time* dimension, then the ones over *Doctor, Procedure* and *Patient*, in that order. Thus, for instance, when performing a generalization over *Procedure*, more materialized views must be updated in the first sequence than in the second one. Both sequences can be found in the full paper.

Our second goal was testing the influence of view maintenance overhead on dimension update performance. To meet this goal, we created the same cube described above, but with the NO MATERIALIZE option, and executed the first sequence of updates. Of course, there is no reason for executing both sequences, because no view must be updated in this case.

The third goal was studying query performance when no view materialization is done. To this effect we ran the query " *list the total number of procedures by doctor, subgroup and institution type*" under full materialization, and computing the aggregation on-the-fly. This query involves taking the join of three dimensions of the cube.

Finally, we were interested in comparing the performance of the maintenance algorithm introduced in previous work [6], against a non-optimized algorithm like the standard Summary-Delta method [11]. We performed the tests for a DELETE INSTANCE update. We used only three months of data(270,000 tuples in the base fact table), since we expected a non-optimized algorithm on the fully materialized data cube to be too inefficient to run over the full data set. We created two data cubes, one with aggregate function SUM, and one with MAX. The latter allows no optimization because base data must always be accessed (recall that

MAX is not self-maintainable with respect to deletions [3]). Thus, view maintenance techniques cannot avoid the joins. We then applied the following updates: generalize level *datetime* to *date,* generalize *procedureId* to *procedureType,* and generalize *procedureId* to *subgroup,* in this order. The tests were carried out by deleting an element in level *procedureId* over each data cube.

Hardware. The tests were run on a PC with an Intel Pentium III 600Mhz processor, with 128 Mb of RAM memory and a 9Gb SCSI Hard Disk. The Database Management System was SQL Server 7.0 database running on top of a Windows NT 4 (Service Pack 5) Operating System, We also ran our tests on an ORACLE 8.04 DBMS, but do not report these results because further experimentation seems neeeded.

4.4 Experimental Results

In this section we describe the results of our experiments, following the order in which we stated our objectives in Subsection 4.3.

The creation times for fully materialized data cubes ranges from 60 to 470 seconds, while not materialized data cubes are created in less than 4 seconds for the full set of data (600.000 tuples). Figures 8 and 9 depict generalization time, comparing generalizations of fully materialized data cubes at different aggregation levels, for the two sequences described above. Notice that, even when the generalization from level *yearOfBirth* to level *yearRange* is performed *after* the generalization from *patientId* to level *institution* (sequence 2), the former takes less time to perform, because it affects levels located higher in the dimension's hierarchy. The charts show that the behavior of the operators and view updates is close to linear with respect to the number of tuples in the base fact table. Also notice that in Figure 8 the curve corresponding to the generalization over *Patient* is below the two other ones, while in Figure 9 it is above them, reflecting the influence of the number of updated views. The interested reader can find a more comprehensive description of the results in the full paper.

Updates to instances of dimensions are applied once all the views have been materialized(the same occurs in the case of *DelLevel*). Thus, the sequence of operations in these cases is irrelevant. Figure 10 shows the performance of the *DelInstance* operator.

Our second goal was measuring the time consumed by the operators themselves. Thus, as we explained in Section 4.3, we executed the updates over the cube created with the NO MATERIALIZE option. The results we obtained had shown that GENERALIZE statements were executed in less than fifteen seconds, for the full data set(*i.e.* 6300.000 tuples).

The results presented above show that execution times are compatible with application requirements. However, the tests over the non-materialized cube demonstrate that almost all the processing time is consumed by the view maintenance operations, suggesting that a partially materialized strategy (i.e. an approach like the one proposed by Harinarayan et al [5]) would be the best option when an evolving scenario like the one proposed here is implemented. As this

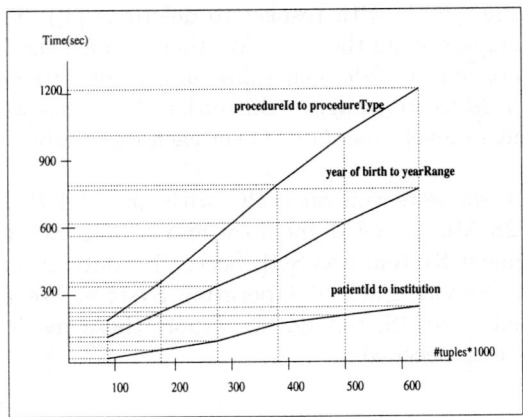

Fig. 8. Performance results for *generalize*(sequence 1)

alternative is dependent on query performance, our third experiment focused on studying how an MDDLX query could perform when no view is materialized. We executed the query " *total number of procedures by doctor, subgroup and institution type*" over both cubes under test. For the complete set of data, and no view materialization, the execution time takes two minutes, which seems to be an acceptable result. Of course, queries perform faster under the full materialization strategy, because performing a query under this strategy implies just a sequential scan of the desired view.

Figure 11 gives a summary of the disk space consumed by the database for the six different sets of data, comparing data and index spaces(the data cube contained 630 materialized views after all updates were performed). Notice that the relation between data and index spaces decreases as the data space increases.

Finally, we compared our maintenance algorithm against a non-optimized algorithm for the *DelInstance* operator with different numbers of materialized views. Avoiding unnecessary joins dramatically improves performance, reducing update times by a factor between five and eight.

5 Discussion and Summary

We have presented TSOLAP, an implementation of the multidimensional model introduced in previous works by Hurtado and some of the authors [6], and an extension to MDX supporting dimension updates. We also introduced TSShow, a visualization tool for dimensions and data cubes.

We used TSOLAP in a real-life case study. The results showed that our model can be useful not only for database administrators who could avoid rebuilding the multidimensional database each time a dimension is updated, but also for analysts who could benefit from the chance of easily posing hypothetical queries to the system.

Supporting Dimension Updates in an OLAP Server

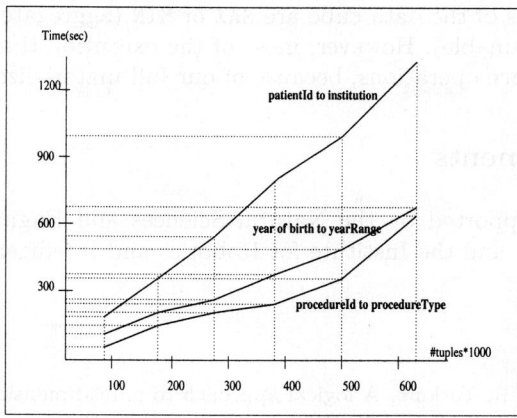

Fig. 9. Performance results for *generalize*(sequence 2)

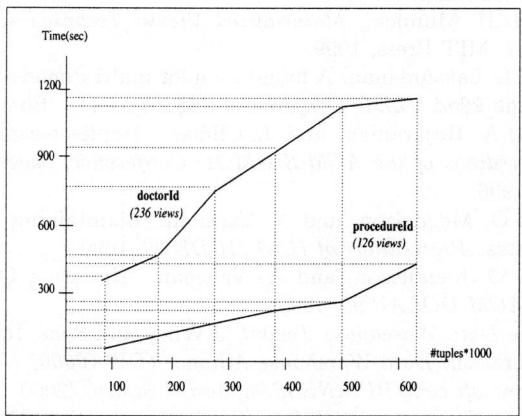

Fig. 10. Performance results for *DelInstance*

Case #	Data space(Mb)	Index space(Mb)	rate
1	324	634	1.98
2	568	1025	1.80
3	825	1423	1.72
4	1108	1854	1.67
5	1423	2333	1.63
6	1734	2816	1.62

Fig. 11. Data and index disk space

The DELETE INSTANCE statement is the most expensive, especially when the aggregate functions of the data cube are MAX or MIN (aggregate functions which are not self-maintainable). However, most of the execution time was consumed by view maintenance operations, because of our full materialization strategy.

Acknowledgements

This work was supported by the Natural Sciences and Engineering Research Council of Canada and the Institute for Robotics and Intelligent Systems.

References

1. L. Cabibbo and R. Torlone. A logical approach to multidimensional databases. In *EDBT'98: 6th International Conference on Extending Database Technology*, pages 253–269, Valencia, Spain, 1998.
2. A. Golfarelli, D. Maio, and S. Rizzi. Conceptual design of data warehouses from E/R schemes. In *Proceedings of the Hawaii International Conference on System Sciences*, Kona, Hawai, 1998.
3. A. Gupta and I. H. Mumick. *Materialized Views: Techniques, Implementations and Applications*. MIT Press, 1999.
4. M. Gyssens and L. Lakshmanan. A foundation for multi-dimensional databases. In *Proceedings of the 22nd VLDB Conference*, pages 106–115, Bombay, India, 1996.
5. V. Harinarayan, A. Rajaraman, and J. Ullman. Implementing data cubes efficiently. In *Proceedings of the ACM-SIGMOD Conference*, pages 205 – 216, Montreal, Canada, 1996.
6. C. Hurtado, A. O. Mendelzon, and A. Vaisman. Maintaining data cubes under dimension updates. *Proceedings of IEEE/ICDE'99*, 1999.
7. C. Hurtado, A. O. Mendelzon, and A. Vaisman. Updating OLAP dimensions. *Proceedings of ACM DOLAP'99*, 1999.
8. R. Kimball. *The Data Warehouse Toolkit*. J.Wiley and Sons, Inc, 1996.
9. Microsoft Corporation. *Data Warehouse Alliance (DWA2000) (Internet Document http://www.microsoft.com/BUSINESS/bi/dwa/dwa.asp)*, 2000.
10. Microsoft Corporation. *OLEDB for OLAP Specification (Internet Document http://www.microsoft.com/data/oledb/olap)*, 2000.
11. I. Mumick, D. Quass, and B. Mumick. Maintenance of data cubes and summary tables in a warehouse. In *Proceedings of the ACM - SIGMOD Conference*, Tucson, Arizona, 1997.
12. Sun Microsystems. *JOLAP: Java OLAP Interface (Internet Document http://jcp.org/jsr/detail/069.jsp)*, 2001.
13. A. Vaisman. Updates, view maintenance and time management in multidimensional databases. *Phd Thesis, http://www.cs.toronto.edu/ avaisman/publications*, 2001.
14. A. Vaisman, A. O. Mendelzon, W. Ruaro, and S. Cymerman. Supporting dimension updates in a ROLAP server(full paper). In *Internet Document http://www.cs.toronto.edu/ avaisman/publications*, 2002.

The COMET Metamodel for Temporal Data Warehouses

Johann Eder[1], Christian Koncilia[1], and Tadeusz Morzy[2]

[1] Dep. of Informatics-Systems, University of Klagenfurt
{eder,koncilia}@isys.uni-klu.ac.at
[2] Institute of Computing Science, Poznan University of Technology
morzy@put.poznan.pl

Abstract. "The Times They Are A-Changing" (B. Dylan), and with them the structures, schemas, master data, etc. of data warehouses. For the correct treatment of such changes in OLAP queries the orthogonality assumption of star schemas has to be abandoned. We propose the COMET model which allows to represent not only changes of transaction data, as usual in data warehouses, but also of schema, and structure data. The COMET model can then be used as basis of OLAP tools which are aware of structural changes and permit correct query results spanning multiple periods and thus different versions of dimension data. In this paper we present the COMET metamodel in detail with all necessary integrity constraints and show how the intervals of structural stabilities can be computed for all components of a data warehouse.

1 Introduction and Motivation

A data warehouse is an integrated, materialized view over several data sources which can be conventionally structured or semi-structured data. Data Warehouses are building blocks for many information systems, in particular systems supporting decision making, controlling, revision, customer relationship management (CRM), etc.[HLV00]

Data warehouses are used for analyzing data by means of OLAP (On-Line Analytical Processing) tools which provide sophisticated features for aggregating, analyzing, and comparing data and for discovering irregularities. Data warehouses differ from traditional databases in the following aspects: They are designed and tuned for answering complex queries rather than for high throughput of a mix of updating transactions, and they typically have a longer memory, i.e., they do not only contain the actual values (snapshot data) but also historical data needed for the purposes outlined above. Historical data can be stored either directly as in temporal databases or - more frequently - as already aggregated and abstracted data.

The most popular architecture for data warehouses are multidimensional data cubes, where transaction data (called cells, fact data or measures) are described in terms of master data (also called dimension members) hierarchically organized in dimensions, where the facts of the upper levels are computed from the facts of the lower levels by some consolidation functions.

This multi-dimensional view provides long term data that can be analyzed along the time axis, whereas most OLTP (On-Line Transaction Processing) systems only supply snapshots of data at one point of time. Available OLAP systems are therefore prepared to deal with changing measures, e. g., changing profit or turnover. Surprisingly, they are not able to deal with modifications in dimensions, e. g., if a new branch or division is established, although time is usually explicitly represented as a dimension in data warehouses.

Consider the following example: Diagnoses for patients were represented in a data warehouse using the "International Statistical Classification of Diseases and Related Health Problems" (ICD) code. However, codes for diagnoses changed from ICD Version 9 to ICD Version 10. For instance the code for "malignant neoplasm of stomach" has changed from 151 in ICD-9 to $C16$ in ICD-10. Other diagnoses were regrouped, e.g. "transient cerebral ischaemic attacks" has moved from "Diseases of the circulatory system" to "Diseases of the nervous system". Even worse, the same code described different diagnoses in ICD-9 and ICD-10. Other ICD-9 codes are a subset of ICD-10 codes, i.e. the granularity of codes changed (in fact ICD-10 comprises about 8,000 unique codes, over 3,000 more than ICD-9). The question is now: how can we get correct results for queries like "did liver cancer increase over the last 5 years". Without knowing the above changes we will end up with incorrect results.

The reason for this disturbing property of current data warehouse technology is the implicitly underlying assumption paradigmatically visible in the Star-Schema for data warehouses that the dimensions are orthogonal. Orthogonality with respect to the dimension time means the other dimensions ought to be time-invariant. This silent assumption inhibits the proper treatment of changes in dimension data. We have to be aware that the dimensions data, i.e. the structure, the schema and the instances of the dimensions of a data warehouse may change over time.

We propose an architecture for representing the changes of a data warehouse schema and of the dimension data in a way that correct analysis of data is made possible. Since it means recognizing that the shape and content of a star (-schema) may change over time we call this a *COMET* Schema. In particular, we propose a temporal data warehouse architecture which extends multidimensional data warehouses to achieve the following features:

1. Representation of changes in master data, units and schema of data warehouses.
2. Identification of structure versions as changeless periods.
3. Provision of mappings of transaction data between structure versions.
4. Supporting queries which touch data spanning several structural versions.
5. Analysis of data according to new and old versions of the structure

In this paper we focus on the first two aspects. We propose a metamodel for data warehouses which is a temporal database of all components of a data warehouse: schema, master date (also called dimension members), hierarchical relationships etc. The data of this model is the necessary basis for achieving the other goals.

Related Work. Our concept builds on the techniques developed in temporal databases [JD98], schema evolution and schema versioning of databases [FGM00]. However, all these approaches are not designed for analytical queries like data warehouses. Therefore, extensions and adaptions for the particularities of data warehouses are necessary.

We first presented the problem and a concept for solution for simple data warehouses by transformation functions in [EK01]. The work presented here extends this approach for fact constellation schemas and provides a metamodel together with integrity constraints which covers changes in a much more detailed way, i.e., on both the schema and the instance level.

Other approaches for temporal data warehouses are [Yan01, BSH99, Vai01, CS99]. They are more (e.g, [Yan01]) or less (e.g., [CS99]) formal. To our best knowledge, only [Vai01] deals with both schema and instance modifications. However, the approach proposed in [Vai01] supports only schema/instance evolution and no versioning. Furthermore, none of the mentioned papers supports a mechanism to introduce relationships between instances in different structural versions, i.e., transformation functions for instances between different versions of structure. Hence, none of these approaches supports correct results for queries spanning multiple versions of structure.

Outline. The rest of the paper is organized as follows: In section 2 we present the concept of our temporal data warehouse approach. In section 3 we present our COMET model for temporal data warehouses. In section 4 we show how we can compute the changeless time intervals for a given dimension member. A prototype implementation of this model is sketched in section 5. Finally we draw some conclusions.

2 Temporal Multidimensional Systems

Our concept extends the well known data warehouse approach with aspects of temporal databases and schema versioning. The changes we have to cope with are not only schema changes, but also changes in the dimension data (also called master data). The dimension *Time* ensures to keep track of the history of transaction data, i.e., measures. Nevertheless, for correct query results after modifications of dimension data we have to track modifications of these data [EK01].

Therefore, we extended the well known data warehouse approach with the following aspects [EK01]:

- **Temporal extension**: dimension data has to be time stamped in order to represent their *valid time*. The *valid time* represents the time when a "fact is true in the modeled reality" [JD98].

- **Structure versions**: by providing time stamps for dimension data the need arises that our system is able to cope with different versions of structure.
- **Transformation functions**: Our system has to support functions to transform data from one structure or schema version into another.

All dimension members and all hierarchical links between these dimension members have to be time stamped with a time interval $[T_s, T_e]$ representing the valid time where T_s is the beginning of the valid time, T_e is the end of the valid time and $T_e \geq T_s$. Furthermore, we timestamp all schema definitions, i.e. dimensions, categories and their hierarchical relations, in order to keep track of all modifications of the data warehouse schema [EKM01].

If we represent all time stamps of all modifications within our data warehouse on a linear time axis the interval between two succeeding time stamps on this axis represents a structure version. This means that a structure version is a view on a temporal data warehouse valid for a given time period $[T_s, T_e]$. Therefore, within a structure version the structure of dimension data on both the schema level and on the instance level is stable. Information about structure versions can be gained from our temporal data warehouse using temporal projection and temporal selection [JD98].

The data returned by a query may originate in several (different) structure versions. Hence, it is necessary to check whether the data needed for answering the query (the relevant sub-cube) was affected by structural changes. This is important since not all structural changes affect all data. If data was affected by structural changes, it is necessary to provide transformation functions mapping data from one structure version to a different structure version.

Using transformation functions enables us to assure that a successful analysis can be made even though there might be changes in the dimension data and dimension structure. The combination of structure versions and transformation functions enables the user to analyze data with dimension data and dimension structures "backward" or "forward" in the time axis.

3 The COMET Model

In this section we will specify our generic temporal data warehouse model COMET. The COMET model allows to register all changes of schema and structure of data warehouses.

3.1 Goals and Features

In contrast to the well known modelling techniques for data warehouses, e.g. the Star Schema modelling technique, our COMET Model allows to model data warehouses that do evolve over time.

The COMET model offers the following features for the definition of data warehouses:

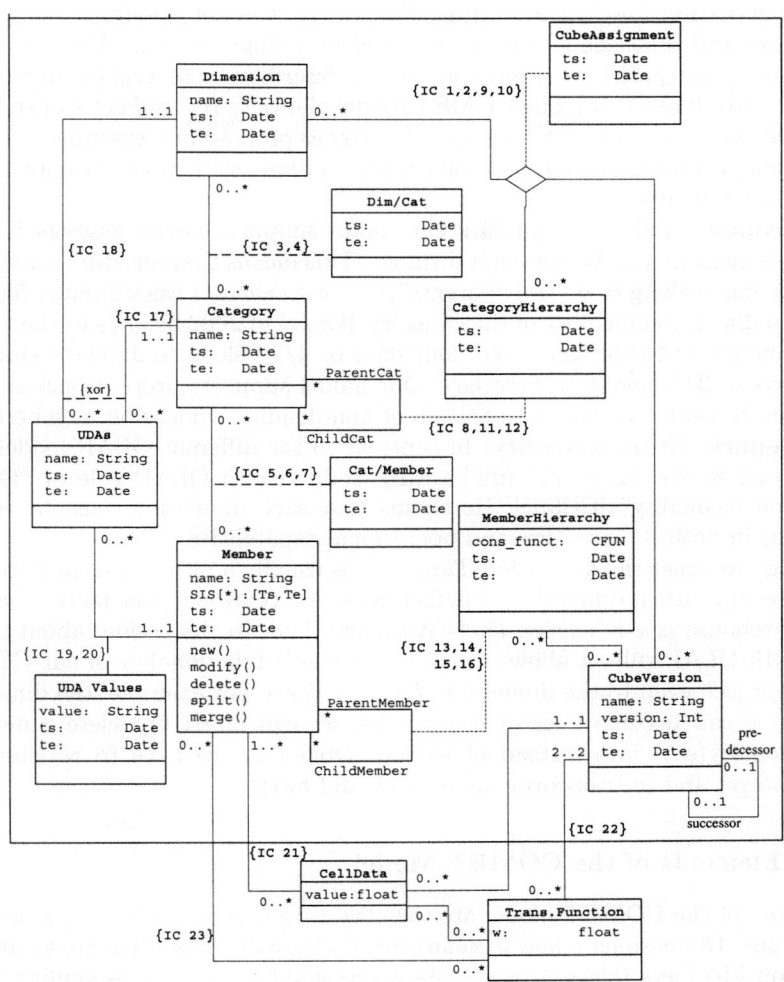

Fig. 1. The COMET Model (using UML notation)

- **Temporal Data Warehousing**: The COMET model enables us to keep track of modifications on both the instance level and the schema level.
  - Instance Level: Instances, i.e. dimension members may change over time. For example new products may become a part of the product port-folio of the company, divisions may split up into several subdivisions or the way how to compute facts may change over time.
  - Schema Level: The schema of the defined data warehouse may change over time. For example dimensions may be deleted or categories may be inserted.

- **Fact-Constellation Schemas**: Frequently it is not possible that all measures and dimensions can be captured in a single schema. Usually, a data warehouse consists of several fact tables described by several (shared or non-shared) dimensions. The COMET model allows to set up Fact-Constellation Schemas (also known as Galaxy Schemas) as proposed for example in [AV98]. Thus, it allows shared dimensions, e.g., a dimension *Products* may be part of several cubes.
- **Proportional Aggregation**: Our model supports correct aggregation even if dimension members are not disjunct. This means that one dimension member may belong to several "parents", e.g., the calendar week number 5 (which is a dimension member of the category *Weeks*) of 2002 belongs to the months January and February where four days or 4/7 belong to January and three days or 3/7 belong to February. Our model supports proportional aggregation to enable correct aggregation of non-disjunct dimension members.
- **Generic Dimensionality**: In contrast to the different OLAP models proposed so far our model fulfills E.F. Codd's sixth OLAP rule of "Generic Dimensionality" [CCS93]. He claims that each dimension must be equivalent in both its structure and operational capabilities.

  E.g., we treat the dimension *Time* that is usually a part of a data warehouse like any other dimension. Furthermore, we represent the facts of a data warehouse as a dimension *Facts*. Although there are discussions about Codd's sixth OLAP rule, it allows to apply the whole functionality of our COMET approach even to the dimension *Time* or *Facts*. For example, the dimension Time can become finer or coarser, i.e. we can insert or delete a new leaf category(say days instead of weeks). Obviously we have to register such changes and to transform values back and forth.

3.2 Elements of the COMET Model

The core of the COMET model are the classes to represent Cubes (class `CubeVersion`), Dimensions (class `Dimension`), Categories (class `Category`) and Dimension Members (class `Member`). As represented by the corresponding multiplicities in Fig. 1, a cube consists of several dimensions and each dimension consists of several categories.

Categories are represented in the class `Category` and are in a hierarchical order. E.g., the categories "Country", "State", "Region" and "City" are in the following order $Country \leftarrow State$, $Country \leftarrow Region$, $State \leftarrow City$ and $Region \leftarrow City$ were $X \leftarrow Y$ means Y rolls-up to X. This is represented by the recursive association of the class `Category`.

The same applies for dimension members which are also in a hierarchial order represented by the recursive association of the class `Member`. For example the dimension members "USA", "Texas", "South" and "Dallas" are in the order $USA \leftarrow Texas$, $USA \leftarrow South$, $Texas \leftarrow Dallas$ and $South \leftarrow Texas$.

As both hierarchical relations between categories and between dimension members may change over time we have to represent the valid time of these relations with timestamp represented in the classes `CategoryHierarchy` and `MemberHierarchy`.

Furthermore, we have to represent how data may be aggregated. We represent this with the attribute `cons_func` in the class `MemberHierarchy`. Moreover, this attributes allows the representation of proportional aggregation functions for non-disjunct members. For example, an salesman may be assigned to two divisions $Div1$ and $Div2$. The amount of sales attained by this salesman may be assigned with the factors 40% and 60% to the divisions $Div1$ and $Div2$.

Another important aspect that the COMET model has to fulfill is that the relation between dimensions and categories may change over time. The same applies for the relation between categories and dimension members. This is represented with the time stamps (attributes t_s and t_e) in the association classes `Dim/Cat` and `Cat/Member`.

We have to deal with different versions of a cube due to the fact that the schema and/or instances of a cube may change over time and the fact that the COMET model supports not only schema evolution but schema versioning. Each version of a cube may have a preceding and a succeeding version and each version is valid for a given valid time. We represent this with the the class `CubeVersion` and the recursive relation for this class.

The COMET model supports transformation of data from one structure and/or schema version into the (immediate) succeeding or preceding version. We represent these transformation functions within the class `Trans.Function`. Each transformation function transforms several cell data entries from exactly one version into its preceding or succeeding version. Moreover, several transformation functions may be defined to transform a cell value from one version into its preceding and succeeding version.

Transformation functions are only allowed between contiguous cube version (two versions V_i and V_k are contiguous if $T_{s,i} = T_{e,k} + Q$ or if $T_{s,k} = T_{e,i} + Q$ where Q is the defined chronon of the data warehouse). As described in section 2 we can represent these transformation functions as matrices. In order to increase query performance, we are able to automatically compute transformation matrices between two non-contiguous version by multiplying all corresponding transformation matrices. Consider for example two transformation matrices $M_{1\to 2}$ to transform data from version V_1 into version V_2 and $M_{2\to 3}$ to transform data from version V_2 into version V_3. By multiplying these transformation matrices we can compute a transformation function $M_{1\to 3}$ to transform data directly from version V_1 into V_3.

As described above the COMET model allows us to assign different dimensions to a cube. On the other hand each dimension may be assigned to several cubes in order to allow fact-constellation schemas. Furthermore, if a dimension is assigned to more then one cube it may consist of a different structure, i.e. a different set of categories and their hierarchical assignments, in each of these cubes. This is represented by the tertiary association between the classes `CubeVersion`, `Dimension` and `CategoryHierarchy`.

Furthermore, each dimension member may have different *User Defined Attributes* (UDA), e.g. the products stored in the data warehouse may have a "Color" and a "Weight". Hence, UDAs are attributes describing a dimension member. In contrast to dimensions UDAs do not allow the appliance of OLAP functionality, e.g. Drill-Down, Roll-Up, Slice, etc.

COMET allows the definition of UDAs for each defined Dimension or Category. The UDAs defined for a certain dimension define the UDAs applicable for all dimension members assigned to this dimension (all dimension members that are assigned to a category which is assigned to the specific dimension). The UDAs defined for a certain category define the UDAs applicable for all dimension members assigned to this category. E.g., one may want to assign a "Color" to each product and hence define this UDA through the dimension *Products*, but only products that do belong to the category "Video Cassette Recorder" have a UDA "Number of Heads". The attributes t_s and t_e in the class UDAs represent the valid time of a UDA.

The association class UDAValues specifies the value of a specific UDA for a specific dimension member. The attributes t_s and t_e in the class UDA Values represent the valid time of a value defined for a specific UDA and a specific dimension member.

The measures of the defined data warehouse are stored in the class CellData. A measure, i.e., a cell in a n-dimensional data cube contains a value and is referenced by a vector $\nu = (DM_{D_1}, ..., DM_{D_N})$ where DM_{D_i} is a dimension member DM that is assigned to a dimension D_i [Kur99].

Due to the temporal extensions that are a part of the COMET model a lot of integrity constraints have to be taken into consideration. In the next section, we will discuss these constraints in detail.

3.3 Integrity Constraints

We will now discuss the constraints that have to be fulfilled in order to guaranty the integrity of our temporal data warehouse model.

A basic constraint is that for all time stamps $[T_s, T_e]$ in the COMET model $T_s \leq T_e$ has to be true, i.e., a *temporal component* may not end before it starts. A *temporal component* is an object of any class that has attributes to represent the valid time (attributes t_s and t_e), e.g., a dimension, a category, a dimension-member and so on.

In order to give a formal description of the integrity constraints we introduce the predicates *overlaps* and *exists_in* as follows:

- $overlaps(C_i, C_j)$: describes that the valid time of temporal component C_i overlaps the valid time of temporal component C_j and vice-versa.
  $overlaps(C_i, C_j)$ is true if $\exists t \bullet (T_s^{C_i} \leq t \leq T_e^{C_i}) \wedge (T_s^{C_j} \leq t \leq T_e^{C_j})$, i.e. it is fulfilled, if there exists at least one point in time where both temporal components are valid.

- $exists\_in(C_i, C_j)$: describes that the time interval representing the valid time of temporal component C_i is a subset of the time interval representing the valid time of temporal component C_j.
  $exists\_in(C_i, C_j)$ is true if $\forall t \in [T_s^{C_i}, T_e^{C_i}] \bullet t \in [T_s^{C_j}, T_e^{C_j}]$.

Furthermore, we will use the notation $A.X$ as a reference to the component X of the assignment A. An assignment may be an object of the classes Dim/Cat, Cat/Member, CubeAssignment, CategoryHierarchy or MemberHierarchy.

- **IC 1:** A dimension D can be assigned to a Cube C if the valid time intervals of both components are overlapping. Furthermore, both components have to be valid within each timepoint of the valid time of the assignment:

$$\forall A \in \text{CubeAssignment} : exists\_in(A, D) \wedge exists\_in(A, C) \qquad (1)$$

- **IC 2:** Within the valid time interval of an assignment $A^C.D$ between a dimension D and a cube C the dimension D must not be assigned more than once to this cube:

$$\forall D_x, D_y \in \{A^C.D_1, ...A^C.D_N\} : D_x = D_y \rightarrow \neg overlaps(A^C.D_x, A^C.D_y) \qquad (2)$$

- **IC 3:** A category G can be assigned to a dimension D if the valid time intervals of both components are overlapping. Furthermore, both components have to be valid within each timepoint of the valid time of the assignment:

$$\forall A \in \text{Dim/Cat} : exists\_in(A, G) \wedge exists\_in(A, D) \qquad (3)$$

- **IC 4:** Within the valid time interval of an assignment $A^D.G$ between a category G and a dimension D the category G must not be assigned more than once to this dimension:

$$\forall G_x, G_y \in \{A^D.G_1, ...A^D.G_N\} : G_x = G_y \rightarrow \neg overlaps(A^D.G_x, A^D.G_y) \qquad (4)$$

- **IC 5:** A dimension member M can be assigned to a category G if the valid time intervals of both components are overlapping. Furthermore, both components have to be valid within each timepoint of the valid time of the assignment:

$$\forall A \in \text{Cat/Member} : exists\_in(A, M) \wedge exists\_in(A, G) \qquad (5)$$

- **IC 6:** Within the valid time interval of an assignment $A^G.M$ between a dimension member M and a category G the dimension member M must not be assigned more than once to this category:

$$\forall M_x, M_y \in \{A^G.M_1, ...A^G.M_N\} : \qquad (6)$$
$$M_x = M_y \rightarrow \neg overlaps(A^G.M_x, A^G.M_y)$$

- **IC 7:** Furthermore, within the valid time interval of an assignment A between a dimension member M and a category G - were G is again assigned to a dimension D_1 - the dimension member M must not be assigned to another category assigned to a different dimension D_2 were D_1 and D_2 are assigned to the same cube C:

$$\forall (M, G_i), (M, G_j) \in \text{Cat/Member} \qquad (7)$$
$$\forall t : T_s^{(M,G_i)} \leq t \leq T_e^{(M,G_i)} \wedge T_s^{(M,G_j)} \leq t \leq T_e^{(M,G_j)} \bullet$$
$$G_i \neq G_j \wedge$$
$$(((G_j, D) \in \text{Dim/Cat} \wedge (G_i, D) \in \text{Dim/Cat}) \vee$$
$$((G_j, D_1) \in \text{Dim/Cat} \wedge (G_i, D_2) \in \text{Dim/Cat} \wedge$$
$$(D_1, C_1) \in \text{CubeAssignment} \wedge (D_2, C_2) \in \text{CubeAssignment} \wedge$$
$$C_1 \neq C_2))$$

Please note that this constraint does allow a dimension member to be assigned to different categories of the same dimension, e.g. "Diet-Cola" may be part of "Diet-Drinks" and "Soft-Drinks" where both "Diet-Drinks" and "Soft-Drinks" are part of dimension "Products".

- **IC 8:** The assignment between two categories G_1 and G_2 as *ChildCat* and *ParentCat* within the class `CategoryHierarchy` is allowed if the valid time intervals of both categories are overlapping. Furthermore, both categories have to be valid within each timepoint of the valid time of the assignment:

$$\forall A \in \text{CategoryHierarchy} : exists\_in(A, G_1) \wedge exists\_in(A, G_2) \qquad (8)$$

- **IC 9:** An assignment between a dimension D and two categories G_1 and G_2 (`CategoryHierarchy`) may be a part of the relation `CubeAssignment` if both categories are assigned to the dimension D:

$$\forall A \in \text{CubeAssignment} : \exists y_1, y_2 \in \text{Dim/Cat} \bullet \qquad (9)$$
$$y_1.D = A.D \wedge y_2.D = A.D \wedge$$
$$(y_1.G, y_2.G) = A.(G_1, G_2)$$

- **IC 10:** Furthermore, all components (a dimension D, an assignment AG between two categories and a `CubeVersion` C) that are a part of a relation `CubeAssignment` have to exist during the valid time of the relation:

$$\forall A \in \text{CubeAssignment} : exists\_in(A.D, A) \wedge exists\_in(A.AG, A) \wedge \qquad (10)$$
$$exists\_in(A.C, A)$$

- **IC 11:** The assignment A between two categories as *ChildCat* and *ParentCat* is allowed if there does not already exist an assignment for the time interval of the assignment A:

$$\forall A_i, A_j \in \text{CategoryHierarchy} : (A_i.G, D) = (A_j.G, D) \rightarrow A_i = A_j \qquad (11)$$

- **IC 12:** There must not be any cycles within the assignments in the class `CategoryHierarchy`:

$$childsC(P) = \{x \in \text{Category} : \exists A \in \text{CategoryHierarchy} \bullet A = (P, x) \cup \quad (12)$$
$$childsC(x)\}$$

$$\nexists A \in \text{CategoryHierarchy} : (A.P, A.x) \wedge P \in childsC(P) \quad (13)$$

- **IC 13:** The assignment between two dimension members as *ChildMember* and *ParentMember* within the class `MemberHierarchy` is allowed if both members M_x and M_y are assigned to the same category G for each timepoint t within the time interval representing the valid time of the assignment. Furthermore, both components (*ChildMember* and *ParentMember*) have to be valid within the time interval of the assignment:

$$\forall\, A \in \text{MemberHierarchy} : (A.M_x, G) \in \text{Cat/Member} \wedge \quad (14)$$
$$G \in \text{Category} \wedge$$
$$(A.M_y, G) \in \text{Cat/Member} \wedge$$
$$exists\_in(A, (A.M_x, G)) \wedge$$
$$exists\_in(A, (A.M_y, G))$$

- **IC 14:** The assignment A between two dimension members as *ChildMember* and *ParentMember* is allowed if there does not already exist an assignment for the time interval of the assignment A:

$$\forall A_i, A_j \in \text{MemberHierarchy} : (A_i.M, G) = (A_j.M, G) \rightarrow A_i = A_j \quad (15)$$

- **IC 15:** An assignment A between two dimension members M_1 and M_2 as `MemberHierarchy` is allowed if there exists an assignment between two categories G_1 and G_2 as `CategoryHierarchy` and if both components of the MemberHierarchy M_1 and M_2 are assigned to both components of the CategoryHierarchy G_1 and G_2 such that M_1 is assigned to G_1 and M_2 is assigned to G_2:

$$\forall\, A \in \text{MemberHierarchy} : \quad (16)$$
$$\exists A_{CH} \in \text{CategoryHierarchy} \wedge \exists B_1, B_2 \in \text{Cat/Member} \bullet$$
$$A.M_1 = B_1.M \wedge A.M_2 = B_2.M \wedge$$
$$A_{CH}.G_1 = B_1.G \wedge A_{CH}.G_2 = B_2.G$$

- **IC 16:** There must not be any cycles within the assignments in the class `MemberHierarchy`:

$$childsM(P) = \{x \in \text{Member} : \exists A \in \text{MemberHierarchy} \bullet A = (P, x) \cup \quad (17)$$
$$childsM(x)\}$$

$$\nexists A \in \text{MemberHierarchy} : (A.P, A.x) \wedge P \in childsM(P) \quad (18)$$

- **IC 17:** An assignment between an UDA U and a category G is allowed, if the valid time of the UDA is within the valid time of the category:

$$\forall G \in \text{Category} : \mathit{exists\_in}(G.UDA, G) \tag{19}$$

- **IC 18:** An assignment between an UDA U and a dimension D is allowed, if the valid time of the UDA is within the valid time of the dimension:

$$\forall D \in \text{Dimension} : \mathit{exists\_in}(D.UDA, D) \tag{20}$$

- **IC 19:** An assignment between an UDA U and a dimension member M within UDA Values is allowed, if the valid time of the UDA value is within the valid time of both components:

$$\forall A \in \text{UDAValues} : \mathit{exists\_in}(A, M) \land \mathit{exists\_in}(A, U) \tag{21}$$

- **IC 20:** Furthermore, as assignment between an UDA U and a dimension member M within UDA Values is allowed, if the UDA is assigned to a category G and the dimension member is assigned to this category, or if the UDA is assigned to a dimension D and the dimension member is assigned to this dimension:

$$\forall x \in \text{UDAValues} : \tag{22}$$
$$(\exists y \in \text{Cat/Member} \bullet$$
$$y.M = x.M \land y.G = x.U.G) \lor$$
$$(\exists y \in \text{Dim/Cat} \bullet$$
$$\exists z \in \text{Cat/Member} \bullet$$
$$z.G = y.G \land z.M = x.M \land y.D = x.U.D)$$

- **IC 21:** The number of dimension members used to reference a CellData must be equal to the number of dimensions assigned to the cube: Let $\mathbb{M} = \{M_1, ..., M_n\}$ be the set of dimension members used to reference a cell V and let $\mathbb{D} = \{D_1, ..., D_m\}$ be the set of dimensions assigned to a cube C. V may be assigned to C if $n = m$.

- **IC 22:** A transformation function Trans.Function may be used to transform cell values between two contiguous versions of a cube CV_1 and CV_2 (Q is the defined chronon of the data warehouse):

$$\forall x \in \text{Trans.Function} \bullet (x.CV_1.T_e + Q = x.CV_2.T_s) \lor \tag{23}$$
$$(x.CV_1.T_s - Q = x.CV_2.T_e)$$

Transformation functions between non-contiguous version can be automatically computed by multiplying the given transformation matrices as proposed in [EK01].

- **IC 23:** A transformation function Trans.Function may be applied to lower-level dimension members only (dimension members without successors):

$$\forall x \in \text{Trans.Function} : \tag{24}$$
$$\nexists A \in \text{MemberHierarchy} \bullet A(x.Member, \_)$$

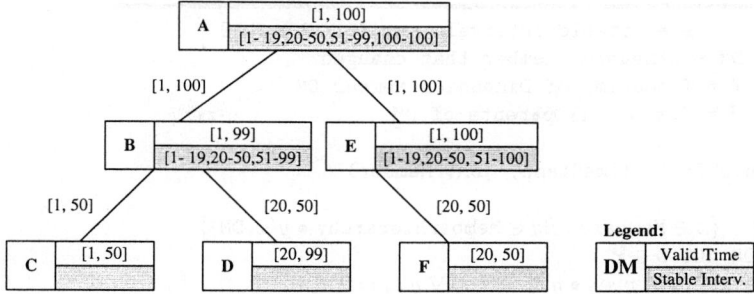

Fig. 2. Stable intervals sets

4 Stable Intervals

In this section, we will discuss an important aspect of our COMET approach – called *Stable Intervals Sets* – that enables us to increase query performance of queries spanning multiple structure versions.

The basic idea is that we want to compute the largest stable interval for upper-level dimension members (a dimension member with at least one successor). A stable interval of an upper-level dimension member DM is an interval in which no modification to another component does affect query results for DM.

As described in section 2 each dimension member and each hierarchical relation between dimension members has a timestamp that represents the valid time of the corresponding object. Nevertheless, this does not mean that changes "beneath" an upper-level dimension member do not affect the data computed for this dimension member during the given time interval of the valid time.

Consider for example a temporal data warehouse that stores information about a faculty. The faculty did not change but the departments within the faculty, the staff, etc. might have changed. Hence, if a query retrieves data for the faculty within the valid time interval of the faculty it still might be affected by wrong computations due to structural evolution of departments, etc. On the other hand, we do not want to perform transformations for all queries, with several structure versions within the relevant time interval of the query, if these structure versions stem from changes in parts from the data warehouse which are not relevant for the given query.

The stable intervals set of a dimension member is now a set of time intervals where for each interval the structures influencing (derived) cell-data for this dimension member did not change. So if a query stays with a stable interval, there is no need to transform data.

More formal we can define the following: let $G_{DM} = (\mathcal{N}, \mathcal{E})$ be a directed graph that represents all dimension members their hierarchical relations between dimension members consolidating in a dimension member DM where $\mathcal{N}$ is the set of all dimension members (=nodes) and $\mathcal{E}$ is the set of all hierarchial relations

```
REM: O.sis = stable intervals set for object O
REM: DM = Dimension Member that changed
REM: T  = Timestamp of Dimension Member DM
REM: ℙ  = Set of all parents of DM

ComputeSIS(↓T:TimeStamp, ↓DM: Member)
{
    ℙ = {x ∈ Members : ∃y ∈ MemberHierarchy • y(x, DM)}
    FOR ALL p ∈ ℙ :
        IF ∄y ∈ p.sis • y.t_s = T.t_s ∨ y.t_e = T.t_s
            I = y ∈ p.sis • y.t_s < T.t_s ∧ y.t_e > T.t_s
            p.sis = p.sis ∪ [T.t_s, I.t_e]
            I.t_e = T.t_s − 1
        ENDIF
        IF ∄y ∈ p.sis • y.t_s = T.t_e ∨ y.t_e = T.t_e
            I = y ∈ p.sis • y.t_s < T.t_e ∧ y.t_e > T.t_e
            p.sis = p.sis ∪ [T.t_e, I.t_e]
            I.t_e = T.t_e − 1
        ENDIF
        ComputeSIS(T, p)
    ENDFOR
}
```

Fig. 3. The ComputeSIS algorithm

between those dimension members (=edges). Both $\mathcal{N}$ and $\mathcal{E}$ are defined through the class MemberHierarchy of our COMET model.

The Stable Intervals Set for leaf dimension members (a dimension member without successors) is equivalent to the valid time defined for this member. The Stable Intervals Set of a non-leaf dimension member DM changes with each modification within the graph G_{DM} as defined below. In the COMET model the Stable Intervals Set is represented with the attribute SIS of the class Member.

Figure 2 shows how we represent the set of stable intervals within dimension members. For instance, the set of stable intervals of the dimension member B is derived from the valid time of all succeeding dimension members (C and D) and hierarchical relations ($B \leftarrow C$ and $B \leftarrow D$).

Figure 3 sketches the algorithm to propagate changes of dimension members that affect the Stable Intervals Set. The algorithm to propagate changes of hierarchical relations ($Parent \leftarrow Child$) is similar to the proposed algorithm except that it first computes the Stable Intervals Set for the $Parent$ and then calls ComputeSIS(T, P) where T is the timestamp of the hierarchical relation and P is the $Parent$.

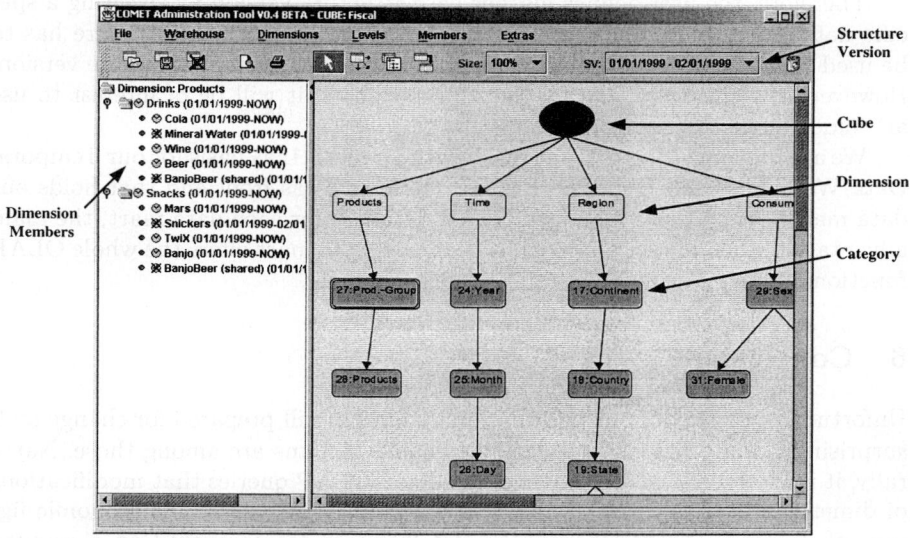

Fig. 4. The COMET administration tool

5 Implementation

In [EKM01] we discussed different implementation architectures. We are currently prototypically implementing a temporal data warehouse based on our COMET model with the *indirect approach* [EKM01].

The COMET prototype consists of three parts: the Temporal Data Warehouse (holds the required information about structure versions, cell data and transformation functions) implemented in Oracle 8.1, the Transformer (maps all required cell values from all required structure versions into the chosen base structure version by using the defined transformation functions) and the Administration Tool (allows to define the schema and structure of a temporal data warehouse, to modify schema and structure and to import cell data into the temporal data warehouse).

In Fig. 4 we show a screen shot of the main window of the Administration Tool. This window shows a cube and all assigned components (dimensions, categories and dimension members). The administrator may select a specific version of this cube by selecting the corresponding structure version in the selection list *SV* (top right).

The main idea of the indirect approach is that the Transformer generates a data mart for each structure version needed by the user. In most cases, this will only be the actual structure version. Each data mart consists of all fact data that are valid for the same time interval as the corresponding structure version plus it consists of all fact data that could be transformed by the defined transformation functions from all other structure versions.

Therefore, the user defines his/her base structure version by selecting a specific data mart. This base structure version determines which structure has to be used for the analysis. In most cases this will be the current structure version. However, in some cases, e.g. for auditing purposes, it will be of interest to use an "older" structure version.

We are implementing this approach with Oracle 8.1i as basis for our Temporal Data Warehouse and Hyperion Essbase (Release 6) as front end that holds our data marts. As we use a standard OLAP database for each data mart, the main advantage of the indirect approach is that each data mart offers the whole OLAP functionality, e.g., drill-down, roll-up, slice, dice, etc.

6 Conclusions

Unfortunately, many of our information systems are ill prepared for change and, surprisingly, multidimensional data warehouse systems are among those. Naturally, it is vital for the correctness of results of OLAP queries that modifications of dimension data is correctly taken into account. E.g., when the economic figures of European countries over the last 20 years are compared on a country level, it is essential to be aware of the re-unification of Germany, the separation of Czechoslovakia, etc.

Business structures and even structures in public administration are nowadays subject to highly direct changes. Comparisons of data over several periods, computation of trends, computation of benchmark values from data of previous periods have the necessity to correctly and adequately treat changes in dimension data. Otherwise we face meaningless figures and wrong conclusions triggering bad decisions. From our experience we could cite too many such cases.

The COMET model we propose in this paper allows to register all changes of schema and structure of data warehouses. The innovation lies in the complete registration and temporal attribution of *all* elements of a data warehouse. This is then the basis for OLAP tools, transformation operations, the derivation of (correctly) star shaped data marts etc. with the goal to reduce incorrect OLAP results.

References

[AV98] C. Adamson and M. Venerable. *Data Warehousing Design Solutions*. Wiley, New York, 1 edition, 1998.

[BSH99] M. Blaschka, C. Sapia, and G. Höfling. On Schema Evolution in Multidimensional Databases. In *Proc. of the DaWak'99 Conference*, 1999.

[CCS93] E. Codd, S. Codd, and C. Smalley. *Providing OLAP to User-Analysts: An IT Mandate*. Hyperion Solutions Corporation, California, 1993.

[CS99] P. Chamoni and S. Stock. Temporal Structures in Data Warehousing. In *Data Warehousing and Knowledge Discovery (DaWaK) 1999*, pages 353–358, Italy, 1999.

[EJS98] O. Etzion, S. Jajodia, and S. Sripada, editors. *Temporal Databases: Research and Practise*. Number LNCS 1399. Springer-Verlag, 1998.

[EK01]   J. Eder and C. Koncilia. Changes of Dimension Data in Temporal Data Warehouses. In *Proc. of the DaWak 2001 Conference*, 2001.
[EKM01]   J. Eder, C. Koncilia, and T. Morzy. A Model for a Temporal Data Warehouse. In *Proc. of the Int. OESSEO 2001 Conference*, Rome, Italy, 2001.
[FGM00]   E. Franconi, F. Grandi, and F. Mandreoli. Schema Evolution and Versioning: a Logical and Computational Characterisation. In *Workshop on Foundations of Models and Languages for Data and Objects*, 2000.
[HLV00]   B. Hüsemann, J. Lechtenbörger, and G. Vossen. Conceptual Data Warehouse Design. In *Proc. of the International Workshop on Design and Management of Data Warehouses (DMDW 2000)*, Stockholm, 2000.
[JD98]   C. S. Jensen and C. E. Dyreson, editors. *A consensus Glossary of Temporal Database Concepts - Feb. 1998 Version*, pages 367–405. Springer-Verlag, 1998. in [EJS98].
[Kur99]   A. Kurz. *Data Warehousing - Enabling Technology*. MITP-Verlag, 1999.
[Vai01]   A. Vaisman. *Updates, View Maintenance and Time Management in Multidimensional Databases*. Universidad de Buenos Aires, 2001. Ph.D. Thesis.
[Yan01]   J. Yang. *Temporal Data Warehousing*. Stanford University, 2001. Ph.D. Thesis.

Exploring RDF for Expertise Matching within an Organizational Memory

Ping Liu, Jayne Curson, and Peter Dew

Informatics Research Institute, School of Computing, University of Leeds
Leeds, LS2 9JT, United Kingdom
{pliu,dew}@comp.leeds.ac.uk
j.m.curson@leeds.ac.uk

Abstract. Organizations have realized that effective development and management of their organizational knowledge base is very important for their survival in todays competitive business environment. People, as a special knowledge asset, also attract the interest of many researchers because, only through people communicating with one another, can they really share their tacit knowledge and skills that can be more valuable than explicit documentation. The need to be able to quickly locate experts among the heterogeneous data sources stored in the organizational memory has been recognized by many researchers. This paper examines the advantages of using RDF (Resource Description Framework) for Expertise Matching. The major challenge is to semantically integrate heterogeneous data sources stored in the organizational memory and facilitate users to locate the right people. We present a practical application of this using a case study where PhD applicants can locate potential supervisors before they formally apply to a university.

1 Introduction

In the current economic environment, organizations have realized that effective development and management of an enterprise's organizational knowledge base will be a crucial success factor in the knowledge-intensive markets of the current century [1]. An Organizational Memory[1] is designed to store what employees have learned from the past in order for it to be reused by current employees in solving problems more effectively and efficiently. There are two kinds of retrieval in the organizational memory. One is *"information retrieval"* which aims to provide the knowledge required by the task at hand. However, access to information only is not sufficient, people often need to communicate with each other in order to find more important information which cannot be obtained from explicit documentation. That is

---

[1] In this paper, Organizational Memory is synonymous to Organizational Memory Information System because we focus on the technical aspects of OM. See [1] for a definition of OMIS.

why we need another kind of retrieval – "*people retrieval*". The process of finding relevant people who have similar interests is also called Expertise Matching. As noted by many researchers [2,4,6,9,15,25,36,39,40], employees learn more effectively by interacting with other employees because the tacit knowledge and expertise people possess are difficult to codify and store in a knowledge management system. There is widespread agreement that the highest-value knowledge is the tacit knowledge stored in peoples heads [27]. Consequently, we put our research emphasis on how to support "people retrieval" rather than "information retrieval".

If users wish to search information in web pages they can use search engines. However, if they want to locate somebody with the required expertise, there is no existing system which provides a satisfactory result. Users have to manually check different data sources stored in the organizational memory in order to find pieces of information relevant to an expert and then combine them manually. Considering the huge amount of information that the organizational memory stores, it is no surprise that searching for people with specific expertise is a common problem in nearly every company [31]. The main challenge addressed in our work is that of how "people retrieval" can be improved by extracting relevant information associated with an expert from different data sources and semantically integrating them.

This paper is organized as follows: It begins with an analysis of the Expertise Matching problem in Section 2. Section 3 describes the possible approaches and justifies the use of RDF in our solution of the Expertise Matching problem. Section 4 demonstrates our solution of Expertise Matching in a Brokering System which is currently being developed at the University of Leeds to help PhD applicants locate potential supervisor(s). It also describes the rationale for the system and presents the architecture. The use of the system is illustrated in Section 5 along with the key results. Finally, Section 6 compares our work with other related research and indicates areas that require further investigation.

2   Analysis of the Problem

There are many definitions of expertise. One definition from Webster's dictionary is "processing special skill or knowledge; trained by practice; skillful or skilled" [23]. Bedard gave a similar definition, "a combination of knowledge and ability, and the capability to achieve results with this knowledge" [5]. It is also defined as "a process by which individuals develop the ability to achieve task-specific superior performance" [32] and "the ability, acquired by practice, to perform qualitatively well in a particular domain" [22]. However, the substance of skills, knowledge and ability is a hidden variable and difficult to codify. This is why databases such as COS[2], VTED[3], BATH[4], New England[5] express expertise in terms of several keywords. REPIS[6] is distinct from these and a brief description of the system is given here. The

---

[2] COS Expertise http://expertise.cos.com/dics/expfields.shtml
[3] The Virginia Tech Expertise Database http://www.rgs.vt.edu/vted/
[4] University of BATH Directory of Expertise http://www.bath.ac.uk/expertise
[5] University of New England Expertise Search http://research.une.edu.au/
[6] University of Leeds Research Expertise and Publication Information System http://repis.leeds.ac.uk

University of Leeds Research Expertise and Publications Information System (REPIS) is a web-based information management system. It stores information about publications and research projects acquired from a variety of different sources. The principal objectives of REPIS are to provide a directory of research expertise across the University and to provide an introduction to the University's research activities for potential collaborators in academia, industry, government and charities. The REPIS Expertise Matcher acts as a *knowledge broker* connecting knowledge seekers and knowledge providers as shown in Figure 1. The difference between REPIS and other systems is that expertise is not input by the individual academics themselves but derived from their associated work outputs, in other words, their publications and projects. The current REPIS system uses search methods employed by SQL Server 2000 to search publication and project databases in order to locate the most appropriate expert(s).

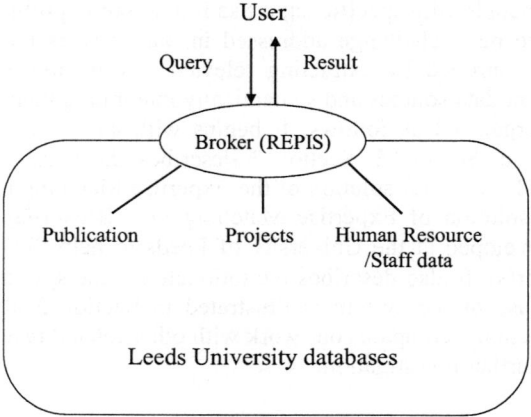

Fig. 1. Expertise matcher as a knowledge broker linking users and experts

There are limitations associated with DBMS techniques. Firstly, users looking for experts in a particular field need a lot of information in order to assess if this is the right person to contact. For example, users need to know the experts' position(s), their research interests, the project(s) they are working on or have worked on in the past, records of activities, and they may even want to read research papers they have produced. Manually creating a database to store all this information is very difficult and expensive. Secondly, there is the critical problem of maintaining up-to-date information. A person's expertise changes over time and it is not feasible to rely on the individual to report developments to their expertise profile and even so, the database maintenance task would be significant if many individuals were involved, for example, there are nearly 4000 academic related staff at the University of Leeds.

One important question is: "The information required is stored in the organizational memory, is it possible to automatically extract the relevant information from disparate data sources and integrate them?". To answer this question, it is necessary to examine closely what type of information is often stored in the organizational memory. There are a number of different data sources varying from structured data (such as databases), semi-structured data (such as web pages), to unstructured data (such as text files). This heterogeneity brings many difficulties in knowledge sharing. Busse [12], Seligman [34] and Sheth [35] present different classifications of heterogeneity, which can be summarized into 5 types, (1) *Heterogeneous interfaces;* (2) *Heterogeneous attribute representations;* (3) *Heterogeneous schemas;* (4) *Heterogeneous semantics;* (5) *Object identification.*

3 Approaches to Solving the Heterogeneous Problems

The problems of heterogeneity have been addressed in various projects and corresponding techniques have been proposed. Traditional approaches, which include standards like ODBC, middleware, federated database system (FDBS), and mediator-based information system, all suffer certain limitations. For example, middleware may be *costly* and may be *inefficient* compared to using native interfaces [34]. FDBS is only *applicable* to databases whilst mediator-based information systems require the software developers to have a clear understanding of a variety of metadata, as well as a comprehensive understanding of schematic heterogeneity [35]. In rule-based mediators, rules are mainly designed in order to reconcile structural heterogeneity [24], whilst for the reconciliation of the semantic heterogeneity problems, the semantic level also has to be considered [37]. The literature on integration is more concentrated on syntax and structure with few people focusing on semantic interoperability (see for example [21], [37]).

Extensible Markup Language (XML) [10] is accepted as the emerging standard for data interchange on the web. XML has defined a neutral syntax that can transform diverse data structures into graph-structured data as nested tagged elements [34]. In this way, heterogeneous data structures can be represented in a uniform syntax – XML. Using XML, three problems listed above can be alleviated, i.e. heterogeneous DBMSs, heterogeneous attribute representations, and heterogeneous schemas. However, XML cannot support integration at the semantic level. For example, there are two expressions: <Surname> Black </Surname> and <Lastname> Black </Lastname>, which seem to carry some semantics. However, the system does not understand that Surname and Lastname mean the same thing and that they are related to another concept, for example, "Person". XML Schema provides support for explicit structural cardinality and data typing constraints, but does not provide much support for the semantic knowledge necessary to integrate information [28]. Again, XML does not play a very significant role in object identification.

RDF (Resource Description Framework) [30] and RDFS (the Schema Language for RDF) [11] are W3C recommendations for describing metadata on the web. They can be used to solve the semantic heterogeneous problem. RDF provides a standard representation language for web metadata based on directed labelled graphs [29]. It consists of three object types: Resource, Property and Statement. Every resource has a Uniform Resource Identifier (URI). The use of URIs to unambiguously denote objects, and of properties to describe relationships between objects, distinguish it fundamentally from XML's tree-based data model [19]. The same RDF tree can be expressed differently in many XML trees because the order of elements in an XML document is very meaningful. So RDF successfully avoids the problem of querying XML trees which attempts to convert the set of all possible representations of a fact into one statement [7].

In order to solve the heterogeneous semantics problem, a shared set of terms describing the application domain with a common understanding is needed. Such a set of terms is called an ontology or a conceptual model[7], which includes not only the definition of the terms, but also the relationships between these terms. The most important role for RDFS is to define the ontology [28]. RDFS enables the interpretation of RDF descriptions. Through using ontologies to make the implicit meaning of their different terminologies explicit, it is then possible to dynamically locate relevant data sources based on their content and to integrate them as the need arises [16].

Having justified the importance of RDF/RDFS for semantic information integration, the use of RDF/RDFS in an organizational memory is now being explored. The aim is to provide a coherent and meaningful view of the integrated heterogeneous information sources associated with each particular expert. In the next section, this is illustrated through a practical application, namely a brokering system, which matches PhD applicants with potential supervisors in the School of Computing at the University of Leeds.

4 Experiment and Rationale

The School of Computing in the University of Leeds is a large department which each year attracts approximately 50 applications from potential research students. Potential research students can either trawl through web pages and search databases to try and locate information about potential suitable supervisors or they may simply ask the School's PhD Admissions Tutor to select a suitable supervisor for them based on their proposed research topic. The problems are (1) It is still very difficult for the PhD Admissions Tutor to recall up-to-date details of all the expertise and research interests for each academic as individual expertise and research interests may continually change and develop. (2) The PhD Admissions Tutor may not fully understand the applicants' intents because some applicants use quite specific technical terminology. As a result, the supervisor that the PhD Admissions Tutor recommends may not be the most suitable, and there exists a real possibility that some appropriate applicants are rejected because their needs cannot be appropriately matched in this way.

The design of our Brokering System aims to improve the process of matching supervisors and potential research students by enabling the potential applicant to make more informed choices about their supervisor before they formally apply to the University and benefiting both the School and the applicant in the long-run.

---

[7] The difference between Ontology and Conceptual Model is that "Ontology is external to information systems and is a specification of possible worlds in some particular domain that covers multiple and often a priori unknown information systems while a conceptual model is internal to information systems and is a specification of one possible world of that domain" [8].

4.1 User Study

To identify the support tasks needed in this Brokering System, let us consider the following scenario, which represents a typical case of the problem described above:

Mary is a Masters student at the University of Manchester and plans to study for a PhD. She searches the web pages of several universities, including the University of Leeds; her preferred research interest is "heterogeneous database systems". Mary first navigates the School of Computing website at the University of Leeds and browses the homepage of each member of staff. She quickly finds that there are a large number of staff in the School and many of whom are not active researchers. Then she decides to browse the research groups in order to quickly locate a potential supervisor. She finds these websites are not well organized. Although she searches very carefully, she still does not find an academic who can match her requirements. She thinks that maybe there are no academics conducting research in this area and she should give up applying to Leeds University.

This is not the desired outcome as there are people who could supervise her at Leeds. The scenario draws attention to the following problems involved in identifying the potential supervisor(s):

- *Low recall*: This means that some relevant people are missed. This is mainly due to: (1) There is a large number of staff in the School and it is a very time consuming task for the user to access each person's homepage; (2) The web page of each research group does not give detailed information on the individuals in the group. As a consequence, the user may not find the relevant person even when searching carefully.
- *Low precision*: This means that some of the people found are not experts in the preferred research area. It is not always the case that researchers working in the same research group have very similar research interests or expertise. Users still need to conduct further assessment by looking carefully at the detail of each researcher in order to determine if that individual is a suitable supervisor. Therefore, the number of real experts is very small compared to the total number of people retrieved.

The following is the ideal situation that Mary wants the system to provide:

When Mary conducts a search by entering her research interests, several relevant research areas are returned. Mary chooses "Information Integration and Databases" as her preferred research area, and two researchers are displayed. Each researcher has his/her own detailed information including research interests, the projects they are working on or have worked on, the papers they have published, and the technical reports which can be downloaded. Mary compares these two researchers and reads abstracts of 2 papers, she then chooses one of the two to be her preferred supervisor and starts completing the application form.

From the ideal situation above we can identify the most significant support tasks required of the Brokering System:

- Understanding user needs/identification of expertise requirements;
- Understanding the domain knowledge in order to provide translation between researchers' expertise and user interests;
- Providing an integrated view to the user from the different/diverse information sources;
- Capturing changes to the expertise profile of researchers.

4.2 The Proposed Architecture of Our Brokering System

The architecture for a typical Brokering System is described in [38]. This architecture has been adopted here and can be divided into five separate layers as shown in Figure 2 below. Figure 2 also illustrates the different data sources used in our case study.

- *Source Layer*: Contains data sources that are relevant to identifying the expertise of each potential supervisor such as personal homepages which includes personal contact information, research interests, associated research group(s), and recent publications; the REPIS database which stores information about publications and projects across the University; and technical reports which are online documents stored in the School of Computing database. These data sources are built by different people for different objectives or different users, some of the data across these three data sources is duplicated. For example, information on a particular publication authored by a member of staff may be stored in all these data sources.
- *XML Instance Layer*: Presents the serialized XML data transferred from the original data sources. This is through DB-XML wrappers or HTML-XML wrappers. For these unstructured data, some manual processes are needed such as adding metadata in XML according to the vocabularies stored in the Conceptual Model.
- *XML2RDF Layer*: Identifies the relevant concepts in the XML sources and replaces them with the concepts in the Conceptual Model; the mapping rules are specified in XSLT [13]. These mapping rules are defined by the application designer and can be modified if the concepts of the source change. However, the underlying Conceptual Model should be stable as it is the basis for the semantic integration; if it has to be changed, then the RDF model and the mapping rules should be modified accordingly. This layer also creates the RDF data from the XML instance in order to provide the actual response to a mediator's query.
- *Mediator Layer*: Maintains the Conceptual Model (shown in Figure 3). This layer identifies which data sources are relevant to the query, transfers the query to subqueries, and gets subresults from brokers. These subresults are input into RDFDB[8], and through searching RDFDB, the final results arrive at the application layer.
- *Application Layer*: Receives the query from the user and produces a result to the user.

---

[8] An RDF database http://web1.guha.com/rdfdb/

Exploring RDF for Expertise Matching within an Organizational Memory   107

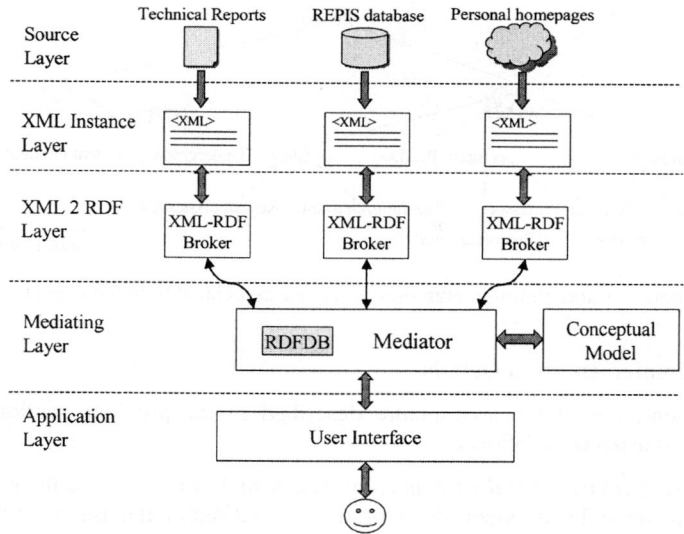

Fig. 2. Architecture of integration of heterogeneous information sources

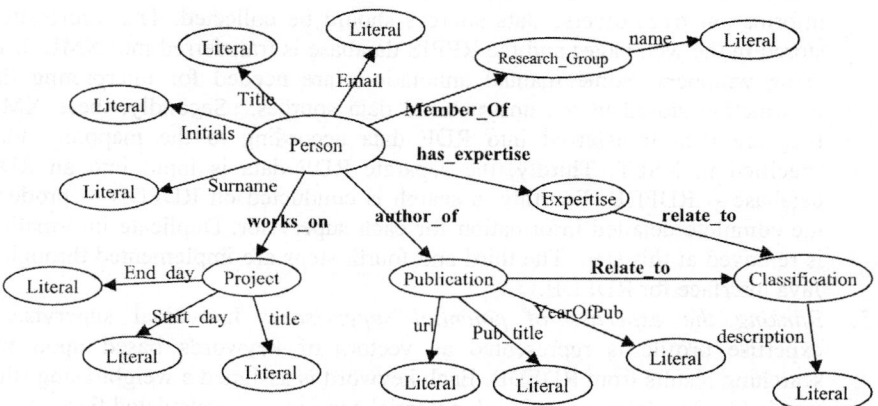

Fig. 3. Sample conceptual model used in the brokering system

Note: This is a simplified diagram and hierarchical relationships have not been included due to the space constraints. An example of the underlying hierarchical structure associated to concept "Person" is given in Figure 4. The major concept in Figure 3 is "Person"; the others are "Publication", "Expertise", "Project", "Research_Group" and "Classification". The relationships between the concepts and the attributes related to each concept are also specified in the conceptual model. For example, a resource of type "Person" may have a property "author_of" whose value is a resource of type "Publication". In the meantime, it can have another property "email" with value "Literal". "author_of" represents the relation between concepts "Person" and "Publication" while "email" represents the attribute related to concept "Person".

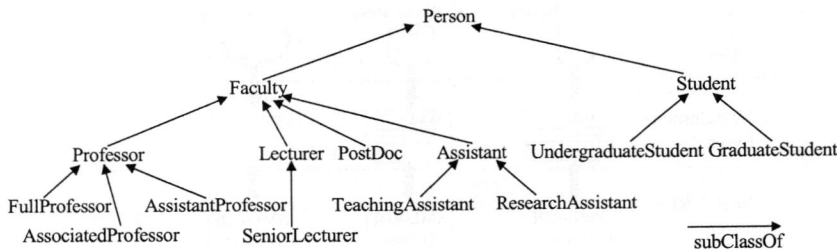

Fig. 4. Example of underlining hierarchical structure associated with the concept "Person"

4.3 Brief Implementation Details

The implementation of the architecture described in the previous section includes several crucial aspects as follows:

1. *Indexing and retrieval of concepts:* The actual concepts and their associated keywords and supervisors are stored in a relational database. This database is connected to the Java system code via JDBC. The possible relevant concepts are retrieved based upon the research interests that the user inputs.
2. *Constructing the detailed information for supervisors:* Firstly, relevant information from diverse data sources should be collected. The information stored in the web pages and the REPIS database is transferred into XML form using wrappers. Some manual annotations are needed for interpreting the information stored in the unstructured data sources. Secondly, these XML files are then transferred into RDF data according to the mapping rules specified in XSLT. Thirdly, the separate RDF data is input into an RDF database -- RDFDB. Fourthly, a search is conducted on RDFDB to produce the complete detailed information for each supervisor. Duplicate information is removed at this step. The third and fourth steps are implemented through a Java interface for RDFDB.
3. *Ranking the expertise of potential supervisors:* Individual supervisor's expertise profile is represented as vectors of keywords based upon the searching results from RDFDB. Each keyword is assigned a weight using tfidf metric [3]. The relevance of each potential supervisor is calculated through the similarity between the profile of each potential supervisor and the set of keywords used to describe the main concepts. The weight attributed to each potential supervisor is then converted into a percentage value by dividing the weight attributed to the individual by the sum of the weights of all the potential supervisors.
4. *Displaying the semantically integrated information of potential supervisors:* This is also implemented using Java programming. The search results from RDFDB are firstly constructed to a XML file, and then into an HTML file which is presented to users through XSLT.

4.4 Data Validation

In order to provide high quality information about each expert, it is unavoidable to rely on accurate information being available. For example, personal homepages and technical reports should be updated annually. In our case, the REPIS database, as a core data source, is heavily relied upon. This is because the data stored in REPIS on individual academics has been validated by the administrator of each department. There are also a number of automated validation processes built into REPIS. For example, one data source held in REPIS is ULRICHs[9] the authorative serials bibliographic database providing details of title and the International Standard Serial Number (ISSN) for journals published throughout the world. If an administrator tries to input details for a publication type of 'academic journal paper' and indicates an incorrect journal and/or ISSN then they will be automatically informed of this and provided with the correct title and/or ISSN details. The other data sources (such as personal homepage and technical reports) are complementary to REPIS in order to provide a richer description of each expert.

5 System Walk through and Key Results

A prototype brokering system, using the architecture described above, has been built and used to match PhD applicants with potential supervisors. The search for potential supervisor(s) follows 3 steps which are described below:

1. The user inputs a description of preferred research interest(s) and selects individual research areas which are the most relevant.
2. The user views the name of each academic working in the relevant research area.
3. The user views the detail of the preferred supervisor.

Step1: Initially the user inputs a brief description of their general research interests. This description is formulated in natural language. A list of relevant research areas will then be displayed (Figure 5). The selection of the relevant research areas is on the domain ontology which is a combination of ACM Computing Classification[10] and the computing dictionary[11]. The relevant research areas are ranked according to the number of keywords contained in the resarch interest field entered by the user which are relevant to each research area. Each result consists of three parts. First, the value which indicates the number of keywords that the user inputs which are relevant to the research area; second, the research area which is displayed in upper case; third, a list of the relevant keyword stems which are used to search all variants of the same keyword. The user can view the detailed information of each research area by clicking on "Show me the detail" or they can "Accept" the research area if they feel this is an area in which they would like to conduct research. They may accept as many research areas as they wish.

---

[9] ULRICHs http://www.ulrichsweb.com/
[10] ACM Computing Classification http://www.acm.org/class/1998
[11] Online computing dictionary http://foldoc.doc.ic.ac.uk/foldoc/index.html

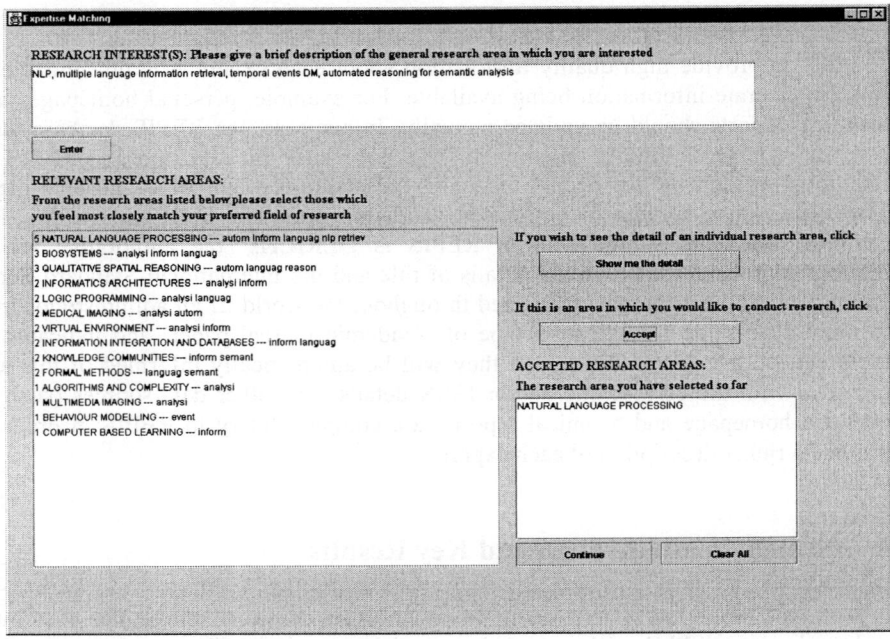

Fig. 5. Step 1 user interface for inputting research interests

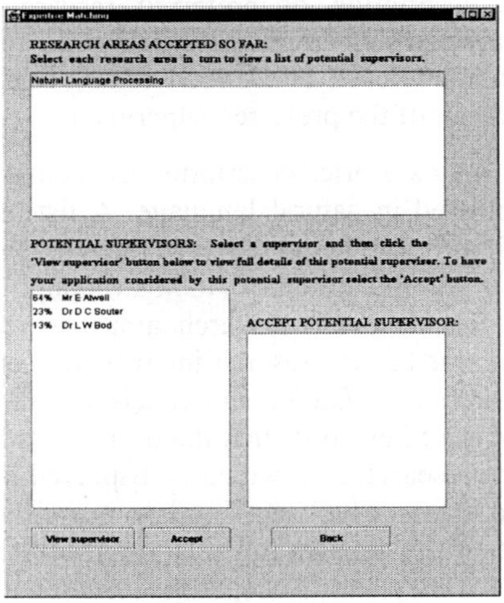

Fig. 6. Step 2 display the potential supervisor(s) for each preferred research area selected

Step2: The user can select any relevant reseach area in order to view a list of potential supervisors working in that research area (as shown in Figure 6). The potential supervisors are ranked according to how likely it is that this person will be selected as the potential supervisor. The example shown in Figure 6 indicates that there is a 64%

chance of choosing Mr E Atwell as the potential supervisor, a 23% chance for Dr. D. C. Souter and a 13% chance for Dr. L. W. Bod. The technique used to calculate the possibility for each potential supervisor being chosen is based on the Vector Model of information retrieval [3]. The detailed process of calculating this is outside the scope of this paper; a similar algorithm has been developed by [18].

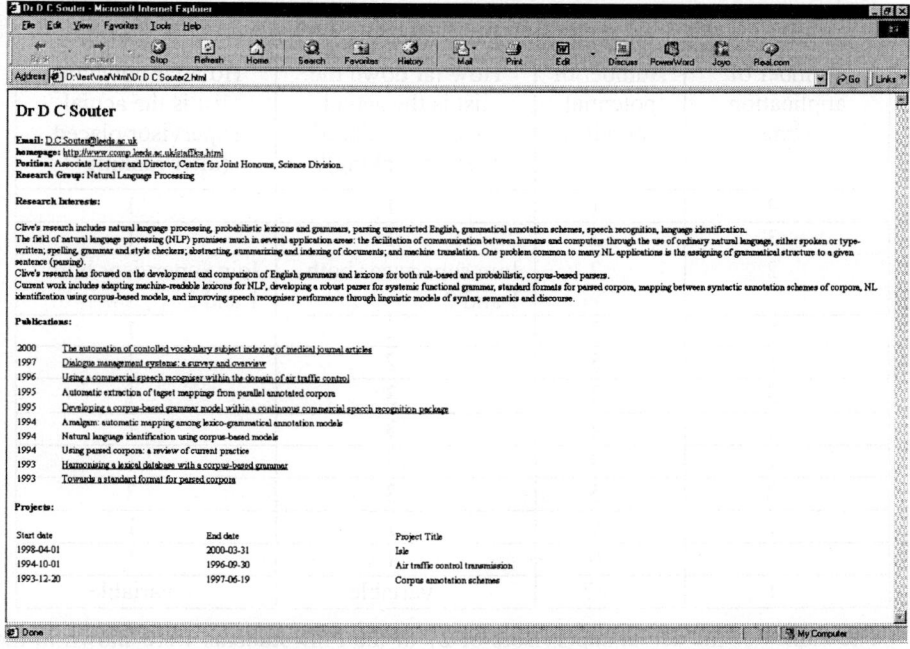

Fig. 7. Step 3 detailed information on the selected potential supervisor

Step 3: The complete personal profile of the particular potential supervisor (as shown in Figure 7) will be displayed if the user clicks on "View supervisor". The full detail page of Dr. D. C. Souter appears like a standard personal homepage currently existing in the School of Computing, but when we take a closer look at it, we find that it includes information taken from different data sources. As shown in Figure 7, the data is retrieved as follows: (1) The personal contact information and research interests are retrieved from the personal homepage; (2) The publication section is a combination of information from the personal homepage, from a series of technical reports which can be downloaded from the REPIS database. The duplicate information is deleted and the final results are reorganized so that the user is not aware where this information comes from; (3) The project information is also retrieved from the REPIS database.

The prototype system has been tested using the application forms of 28 current PhD students. For each applicant, the research interests from each application form were input into the research interests field of our Brokering System. The relevant research areas were then selected and the potential supervisors selected by through checking the detail of the individuals who were working in these areas. The initial results were then checked to determine whether the names of their actual supervisors were in the final lists of accepted potential supervisors. In order to find out if there is a benefit when the potential supervisors are ranked according to how likely it is that each potential supervisor will be selected, the prototype system was tested again using the same application forms after the ranking function had been added. The initial testing results are shown in Table 1; in particular, we can highlight the following:

Table 1 Initial results of searching for a potential supervisor

Number of application forms	Number of potential supervisors	How far down the list is the actual supervisor placed (before ranking)?	How far down the list is the actual supervisor placed (after ranking)?
4	1	1	1
3	2	1	1
2	2	Join supervisor both 1 and 2	Join supervisor both 1 and 2
5	2	2	1
1	3	2	1
5	3	3	1
2	4	3	1
1	4	4	1
2	5	3	3
1	5	1	1
1	6	1	1
1	>7	variable	variable

The names of the actual supervisors of 27 of the PhD students were shown in the final lists of the accepted potential supervisors. Only in one case was it difficult to ascertain if the actual supervisor was in the final list. This is because the applicant indicated many research interests on his application form, and as a result, lots of researchers could potentially serve as his potential supervisor which makes the selection more difficult.

It is noted that after the ranking function has been added, the names of the 14 PhD students' supervisors were listed higher than before. Although we cannot say for certain that the actual supervisor of each student is the most appropriate supervisor, it should be noted that the supervisor of each student is selected manually and methodically by the students themselves or by the PhD Admissions Tutor. This means that if the names of the actual supervisors are placed at the top of the results list most of time then the system is considered to be successful.

6   Conclusion and Directions of Future Work

The strengths and weaknesses of the work reported here is compared with several related projects concerned with searching web documents, searching XML-based documents in an organizational memory, and searching for people in organizations.

1. Searching web documents: SHOE (Simple HTML Ontology Extensions language) project [26] is one of the earliest trials on adding semantic information to web pages according to predefined vocabularies or ontology. On2broker [21] also provides languages to allow web page authors to annotate their web documents with ontological information. It allows users to access information and knowledge from the web and infer new knowledge with an inference engine.
2. Searching XML-based documents in an organizational memory: Osirix [33] tries to solve the heterogeneous data source problem in organizational memory using XML technology. Annotated XML documents are created and then searches are conducted on these XML documents.
3. Searching for people in organizations: CKBS [31] system, as part of organizational memory, builds upon an ontology-based model of competence fields. Expert Locator [14] uses concepts, a large pre-built, technical thesaurus as the initial ontology and enhances it using simple AI techniques. This results in a reduction of the ambiguity of the single keyword problem and also exploits domain knowledge for the search. Knowledge maps [20] make expertise accessible through visual interface based on a common framework or context to which the employees of a company can relate.

The major challenge of our system is that the different technologies from different research areas have been integrated and applied to the Expertise Matching problem. Firstly, our Brokering System does not restrict the data source to webpages in the case of SHOE and On2broker. Secondly, it also provides the semantic interoperability which is not addressed in Osirix system. Thirdly, it makes full use of all the information stored in the organizational memory and provides dynamically updated information about each person, which is richer than CKBS and Expert Locator. Fourthly, it can be used by both internal and external users rather than the employees of a company as in the case of Knowledge maps. The major advantages of using RDF for Expertise Matching are its abilities to: (1) integrate the pieces of information from the organizational memory to form a new up-to-date profile of each expert; and (2) improve the quality of the information through removal of duplicate data.

In this paper, we explore the use of RDF in matching PhD students and their potential supervisors. The same technology will be used in the KiMERA[12] project which aims to help people from industry to locate relevant experts in academia and facilitate collaboration. The internal users, who are employees of the University of Leeds, can also benefit from finding people who are doing similar things and exchange tacit knowledge. To date our prototype system has been tested using 28 PhD application forms. The initial results are very promising. Further user experiments will be conducted in the near future in order to evaluate our system against two main criteria: (1) How accurate the results are in terms of finding the right experts; (2) Whether there is any benefit to using semantic web technology (such as RDF) in terms of improving Expertise Matching performance.

---

[12] The Knowledge Management for Enterprise and Reachout Activity http://kimera.leeds.ac.uk

Acknowledgements

We wish to thank Dr Richard Drew from Symularity Ltd for helpful advice on the Brokering System and for his work contributing to the REPIS database. We also thank Dr Vania Dimitrova for helpful comments on the text.

References

1. Abecker, A. and Decker, S. Organizational Memory: Knowledge Acquisition, Integration, and Retrieval Issues in Knowledge-Based Systems, Lecture Notes in Artificial Intelligence, Vol. 1570, Springer-Verlag, Verlin, Heidelberg, pages 113-124, (1999)
2. Ackerman, M. S. and Halverson, C., Considering an Organization's Memory, in Conference on CSCW'98 pages 39-48, ACM Press, Seattle, WA, (1998)
3. Baeze-Yates, R. and Ribeiro-Neto, B., Modern information retrieval Imprint Addison-Wesley Longman (1999)
4. Bannon, L. and Kuuti, K. Shifting Perspective on Organizational Memory From Storage to Active Remembering in Proceeding of the HICSS'96, IEEE Computer Press, (1996), 156-167
5. Bedard, J. Expertise and its Relation to Audit Decision Quality, Contemporary Accounting Research, Fall, pp.198-222 (1991)
6. Bennis, W., Organizing genius: the secrets of creative collaboration Addison-Wesley: Reading, Mass. (1997)
7. Berners-Lee, T., Why RDF model is different form the XML model (1998) available online: http://www.w3.org/DesignIssues/RDF-XML.html
8. Bishr, Y., Kuhn, W. Ontology-Based Modelling of Geospatial Information 3rd AGILE Conference on Geographic Information Science, Finland, May 25th-2th, (2000)
9. Bishop, K., Heads or Tales: Can Tacit Knowledge Really be Managed Proceeding of ALIA (2000) Biennial Conference, 23-26 October, Canberra, available online at http://www.alia.org.au/conferences/alia2000/proceedings/karen.bishop.html
10. Bray, T., Paoli, J., Sperberg-McQueen, C., and Maler, E., Extensible Markup Language (XML) 1.0. W3C Recommendation, 6-October-2000. http://www.w3.org/TR/REC-xml
11. Brickley, D. and Guha, R.V., Resource Description Framework (RDF) Schema Specification 1.0, W3C Candidate Recommendation, World Wide Web Consortium, (2000), http://www.w3.org/TR/rdf-schema
12. Busse, S., Kutsche, R., Leser, U., and Weber, H. Federated Information Systems: Concepts, Terminology and Architectures Forschungsberichte des Fachbereichs Informatik 99-9, (1999) available online at http://citeseer.nj.nec.com/busse99federated.html
13. Clark, J. XSL Transformations (XSLT) Version 1.0 W3C Recommendation 16 November 1999, http://www.w3.org/TR/xslt.html

14. Clark, P., Thompson, J., Holmback, H., and Duncan, L. Exploiting a Thesaurus-Based Semantic Net for Knowledge-Based Search In Proceeding 12th Conference on Innovative Applications of AI (AAAI/IAAI'00), (2000), 988-995
15. Cross, R. and Baird, L., Technology Is Not Enough: Improving Performance by Building Organizational Memory MIT Sloan Management Review Spring (2000) Vol. 41, No.3 page 69-78
16. Cui, Z., Tamma, V., and Bellifemine, F. Ontology management in enterprises BT Technology Journal Vol. 17 No 4 October (1999)
17. Davenport, T. H. and Prusak, L. Working Knowledge: how organizations manage what they know Boston, Mass, Harvard Business School Press, (1998)
18. Davies, N. J., Stewart, S. and Weeks, R, Knowledge Sharing Agents over the World Wide Web, WebNet '98, Florida, USA, November (1998)
19. Decker, S., Mitra, P., and Melnik, S., Framework for the Semantic Web: an RDF tutorial. IEEE Internet Computing, 4 (6), November/December, (2000), 68-73
20. Eppler, M.J. Making Knowledge Visible Through Intranet Knowledge Maps: Concepts, Elements, Cases System Sciences, Proceedings of the 34th Annual Hawaii International Conference, (2001), 1530 –1539
21. Fensel, D., Angele, J., Decker, S., Erdmann, M., Schnurr, H. P., Staab, S., Studer, R., and Witt, A., On2broker: Semantic-based access to information sources at the WWW in World Conference on the WWW and Internet (WebNet99), Honolulu, Hawaii, (1999)
22. Frensch, P. A. and Sternberg, R. J. Expertise and Intelligent Thinking: When is it Worse to Know Better, Sternberg, R. (ed.), Advances in the Psychology of Human Intelligence, pp.157-188 (1989)
23. Gaines, B. R. The Collective Stance in Modeling Expertise in Individuals and Organizations, available online at http://ksi.cpsc.ucalgary.ca/articles/Collective/Collective2.html
24. Garcia-Molina, H., Papakonstantinou, Y., Quass, D., Rajara-man, A., Sagiv, Y., Ullman, J., and Widom, J. The tsimmis approach to mediation: Data models and languages. In Next Generation Information Technologies and Systems (NGITS-95), Naharia, Israel, November 1995. Extended Abstract
25. Gibson, R. ed 1996 Rethinking the Future Nicholas Brealey Publishing:London
26. Heflin, J. and Hendler, J. Searching the Web with SHOE In Artificial Intelligence for Web Search. Papers from the AAAI Workshop. WS-00-01, pages 35-40. AAAI Press, (2000)
27. Horvath, J., Working with Tacit Knowledge available online at http://www-4.ibm.com/software/data/knowledge/media/tacit_knowledge.pdf
28. Hunter, J. and Lagoze, C., Combining RDF and XML Schemas to Enhance Interoperability Between Metadata Application Profiles Tenth International World Wide Web Conference, HongKong, May (2001)
29. Karvounarakis, G., Christophides, V., and Plexousakis, D., Querying Semistructured (Meta)Data and Schemas on the Web: The case of RDF & RDFS Technical Report 269, ICS-FORTH, (2000). available at http://www.ics.forth.gr/proj/isst/RDF/rdfquerying.pdf
30. Lassila, O. and Swick, R., Resource Description Framework (RDF) Model and Syntax Specification; World Wide Web Consortium Recommendation http://www.w3.org/TR/REC-rdf-syntax/

31. Liao, M., Hinkelmann, K., Abecker, A., and Sintek, M. A Competence Knowledge Base System as Part of the Organizational Memory In: Frank Puppe (ed.) XPS-99 / 5. Deutsche Tagung Wissensbasierte Systeme, Würzburg, Springer Verlag, LNAI 1570, March (1999)
32. Marchant, G. Analogical Reasoning and Hypothesis Generation in Auditing, The Accounting Review 64, July, pp.500-513, (1989)
33. Rabarijaona, A., Dieng, R., Corby, O., and Ouaddari, R. Building and Searching XML-based Corporate Memory IEEE Intelligent Systems and their Applications, Special Issue on Knowledge Management and the Internet, May/June (2000) 56-63
34. Seligman, L. and Rosenthal, A. The Impact of XML on Databases and Data Sharing, IEEE Computer (2001)
35. Sheth, A. Changing Focus on Interoperability in Information Systems: from System, Syntax, Structure to Semantics, in Interoperating Geographic Information Systems, M. F. Goodchild, M. J. Egenhofer, R. Fegeas, and C. A. Kottman (eds.), Kluwer, (1998)
36. Stewart, T. In interview Tom Stewart on Intellectual Capital Knowledge Inc., May (1997) available online at: http://webcom/quantera/llstewart.html
37. Stuckenschmidt, H., Using OIL for Intelligent Information Integration In Proceedings of the Workshop on Applications of Ontologies and Problem-Solving Methods at ECAI (2000)
38. Vdovjak, R., and Houben, G. RDF Based Architecture for Semantic Integration of Heterogeneous Information Sources Workshop on Information Integration on the Web (2001) 51-57
39. Wellins, R. S., Byham, W. C., and Wilson, J. M. Empowered Teams: creating self-directed work groups that improve quality, productivity, and participation Jossey-Bass: San Francisco (1993)
40. Yimam, D. Expert Finding Systems for Organizations: Domain Analysis and the DEMOIR approach ECSCW 99 Beyond Knowledge Management: Management Expertise Workshop, (1999)

Describing and Communicating Software Architecture in Practice: Observations on Stakeholders and Rationale

Kari Smolander[1] and Tero Päivärinta[2]

[1] Lappeenranta University of Technology, Telecom Business Research Center
P.O. Box 20, 53851 Lappeenranta, Finland
kari.smolander@lut.fi
[2] Agder University College, Dept. of Information Systems
Serviceboks 422,4604 Kristiansand, Norway
tero.paivarinta@hia.no

Abstract. Despite considerable attention paid on software architecture, the organizational aspects of architecture design remain largely unexplored. This study analyses the stakeholders participating in architecture design in three software companies, their problems in relation to architecture, and the rationale for architecture description they emphasize. This qualitative, grounded-theory-based, study shows how the stakeholders' rationales for describing architecture exceed the plain programming-in-the-large metaphor, emphasizing such issues as organizational communication, and knowledge creation and management. Whereas designers alone highlighted architecture as the basis for further design and implementation, the other stakeholders emphasized architecture mostly as a means for communication, interpretation, and decision-making. The results suggest a need for further research on practices and tools for effective communication and collaboration among the varying stakeholders of the architecture design process.

1 Introduction

Software technologies have been under enormous change. The complexity of software and information systems has exploded in several domains. The trends include the diversification of user interfaces, the distribution of processing and data, and the utilization of mobile and Internet technologies; emphasizing the issue of architecture in the software engineering research as well as in practice.

Constructive and theoretical research approaches have dominated the software architecture research. The constructions of numerous architecture description languages (ADLs [1]) represent an example of this. The ADL school pursues "right" and "exact" high-level structures of software architecture, which are inspected and evaluated according to the requirements and then, ideally, generated to executable artifacts [e.g. 2, 3]. Architecture is thus regarded mainly, often plainly, as a means for further design and implementation, "programming-in-the-large" [4], from the viewpoint of the "system designer" [5-8].

Other possible rationale for architecture, such as organizational knowledge creation or achievement of mutual understanding among diverse stakeholders of software development, are rarely discussed in the research reports or it is just assumed that these are in-line with the programming-in-the-large, which represents the primary challenge. Among the rare reports discussing some organizational aspects related to architecture, Kazman et al. [9, 10] have implicitly recognized the existence of different stakeholders in actual software-producing organizations. However, they regard other stakeholders than software architects only as informants for the generic architecture design process instead of active stakeholders with the needs and purposes for architecture of their own. Bosch [11] presents a case study on the possibilities for organizing software product lines. Still, he discusses little about the rationale and needs of different stakeholders in architecture design and description. Robbins and Redmiles [12] consider the idea of diverse knowledge and the theory of reflection-in-action [13], but focus on the design work of a single architect leaving other possible stakeholders and their interests untouched. Grinter's [14] qualitative study covering 17 architects in a telecom corporation highlights the communicational and political skills required from architects, as they must communicate with (and influence to) other stakeholders in numerous situations. Still, the role of the other stakeholders remains vaguely discussed.

Our paper attempts to delve into the rationale of architecture design and description in practice, taking the roles of diverging stakeholders into account. Given that the structures of software-producing organizations vary, software products vary, and business strategies and practices vary, does the rationale for designing and describing architectures vary? Which purposes of architecture design and description emerge in practice? Is practical architecture design and description guided only by the needs for technical design and implementation from the viewpoint of the architects and designers? The state-of-the-art reports discuss little about these questions [15], and the other than the technical purposes of architecture are often referred to with ad-hoc lists [16-18] without explicit empirical grounding or verification of their importance.

In three software-producing organizations, we examined the participating stakeholders, the problems they face in relation to architecture, the rationale for architecture description they emphasize, and the architectural viewpoints they use when dealing with architecture. We hypothesized that the rationale for describing architecture exceeds the plain programming-in-the-large metaphor, covering also such issues as organizational and inter-organizational communication, and knowledge creation and management. Especially, we wished to focus on the combinations and relationships between the rationale, stakeholders, and viewpoints used in the architecture design and description process.

Architecture descriptions cover the documents, presentations, plans, sketches, and other genres of communication that are used in the architecture design and utilization. This represents an idea somewhat broader from that of the IEEE 1471 recommended practice, which emphasizes the architecture's documentation [16]. A stakeholder is a person or a group of people involved in creating or using architecture descriptions in a way or another: e.g. designer, project manager, architect, general management, customer. The repertoire of stakeholders varies between individual organizations.

A rationale is an underlying reason for creating architecture descriptions. In the IEEE recommended practice [16], a viewpoint is a specification from which individual views are developed by establishing the purposes and audience for the views and the techniques for their creation and analysis. Instead of necessitating any existing specification to identify a viewpoint in our analysis as such, a view and its specifying viewpoint were not explicitly defined beforehand, as we hypothesized that the organizations likely had shortcomings in such definitions, and our prejudice on the viewpoint definition might have constrained the data collection and analysis.

The paper is structured as follows. Section 2 explains the qualitative research process that took place in three software-producing organizations. Section 3 describes the key stakeholders of architecture design in the target organizations accompanied with their emerging problems and emphasized rationale, and a comparison of the differences and similarities identified among the organizations. Section 4 discusses implications for practice and research. Finally, Section 5 ends the paper with conclusions.

2 Research Process

We had access to three software-producing companies, hereinafter referred to as Alfa, Beta, and Gamma (Table 1), which had recognized the importance of architectural design for several years. Their parallel analysis and comparison was particularly interesting for our research purpose, as the nature of the organizations' products and customer relationships varied.

The research followed the grounded theory method, a research approach for creating and elaborating new theory from qualitative data to be collected within the research theme in question [19]. Qualitative approaches have been regarded as useful starting points in those fields whose literature base is in its infancy [20] – as is the case of research on software architecture design in real-life organizations. The grounded theory approach can also provide new insight into the already accepted theories, even "paradigms", of the research field in question [19] – as is the case concerning the programming-in-the-large metaphor in the software architecture research.

Table 1. Three target organizations

	Alfa	Beta	Gamma
Size (people in sw process)	200	200	400 + 600 (in two divisions)
Typical products	Embedded software products (within a certain technology) for mobile terminals	Software-based telecom-services and service platforms (running on servers)	Tailored information systems (also mobile and web-based) and services
Typical customers	Manufacturers of mobile hardware	In-house customers (providers of commercial telecom services) within the corporation	Project-by-project varying customers (telecom operators, public administration…)
Interviewed stakeholders	1 architect, 1 designer, 4 managers (1 project manager)	2 architects, 2 designers, 2 managers, 1 manager of an in-house customer	3 architects, 1 designer, 2 managers

Two researchers designed the data collection and analysis process collaboratively. The first author had conducted preliminary discussions with the intermediaries of each target organization in spring 2001. Those discussions had revealed the fuzziness of the concept of software architecture in each of those organizations, making them eager to participate in this research so that the situation would be clarified also for their development efforts, in addition to our "pure" research goals. The first author conducted altogether 19 interviews of the key stakeholders named by the organizations' intermediaries (Table 1) during August and September 2001. The semi-structured interviews covered the themes and sub-themes listed in Table 2. In addition, the intermediaries and interviewees provided documents about the organizations' existing software process specifications and examples of actual architectural descriptions. The role of the second author, an outsider from practical data collection, aimed at more "distance" compared to the first author, to facilitate data analysis [21].

Table 2. Interview themes and sub-themes

Theme	Subquestions
Role and tasks	Your role in relation to software development? What kind of products are you developing? How is their architecture described?
Need of architecture descriptions	Do you need architecture descriptions in your work? What kind? Why and for what purpose? Do you produce architecture descriptions in your work? What kind? Why and for what purpose?
Role of other stakeholders	What other parties or stakeholders need and produce descriptions? For what purpose? Explain the role of each stakeholder in detail.
History and experiences	How long has architecture been described like this? Do you remember any changes in the way of doing? Why there have been changes?
Change management	Will there be changes to architectural descriptions during the system's lifecycle? Who will update the descriptions?
Description practices	What is missing from the current architectural descriptions and what would you need more? Do you think that architectural descriptions should be improved? Why? Do you have any ideas about that?
Tools and languages	What kinds of tools for architecture design are available in your organization? What kinds of deficiencies do they have? What kinds of tools would you need in addition to the present tools when describing architecture? Why? How would you improve the situation? What kinds of description languages are needed for architecture description? What do you need to describe with these languages? Why?

The basic idea of the grounded-theory-based data analysis resides in finding conceptual categories and abstractions related to the research goal from a rich set of interviewees' mentions and other data, and in combining these categories meaningfully to provide theoretical insight into the phenomenon in question [22]. For the analysis, the interviews were tape-recorded and transcribed, resulting in c. 400 pages of text. A software tool designed for grounded-theory-based data analysis (ATLAS.ti™) was used for managing and analyzing the data, including also the documents about software processes and the examples of architecture descriptions. We started the analysis simply by searching for mentions about different stakeholders related to the architecture description process – we also had decided beforehand to focus on the mentions about the rationale of those stakeholders for producing or using architecture descriptions. The conceptual categories of 'stakeholder' and 'rationale' can thus be regarded as the high-level "seed categories" [23] of the data analysis. This "open coding" phase proceeded iteratively in parallel with the "axial coding" phase, in which relationships between the identified categories were built [19]. The first author conducted the initial coding iterations, after which the categorizations and interpretations were discussed and re-checked against the data collaboratively between the both authors.

Table 3. Identified stakeholder roles

Customer	System analyst	Testing & quality assurance
Business responsible	Product engineer	Tester
Technology responsible	Data administration	Quality manager
Designer	Internal data	UI Designer
Chief designer	administration	Technical designer
Project manager	Customer's data	User experience team
Technical project	administration	Production organization
manager	Product management	At customer's site
Architect	Other projects &	At vendor's site
Chief architect	organization	3rd party service
Project architect	Other suppliers	Support
Customer management &	Subcontractors	Technology management
marketing	Suppliers of connecting	Authorities
Account manager	systems	Process development
Salesman	Hardware vendors	Hardware integrator
General management	User	Documentation specialist
Project steering group	Known users	Consultant
Department manager	Anonymous users	
Team leader		

3 Stakeholders of Architecture Design and Description

3.1 Stakeholder Roles in Three Organizations

More than 20 stakeholder roles altogether (Table 3) were mentioned in the data. Each of them participated in the architecture design and description process, either by designing or describing architecture or by using the descriptions. The general-level stakeholders that carried similar connotations of their roles in the target organizations according to our interpretation are shown at the first level of indentation. The second level of indentation contains some variance inside the conceptualized stakeholder role in question (is-a relationship). In practice, an individual can play several roles. For example, a person affiliated as a 'designer' may operate also in the product support, as an architect in small projects, or even as a project manager. People assigned to the general management can be (and usually are) strongly involved in the customer management and marketing alike.

In the following, we describe the stakeholder roles in each target organization. Those roles that were mentioned more than once in the data were included in our maps describing the occurrences of the stakeholders in individual organizations.

3.1.1 Alfa

Figure 1 depicts the identified stakeholder roles in Alfa. The boxes represent a stakeholder role or a wider organizational entity that includes roles. A stakeholder role located inside a box operates within that organizational entity: for example, a project manager typically operates within a project and the project within a development organization. In Alfa (as well as in Beta and Gamma), a project designs and produces the software, including its architecture. A set of designers implements the software, and a project manager coordinates the project. Hardware integrators integrate the software to the constraining hardware. Three roles overlap the project border. The user experience team and quality management operate, in part, independently from the projects. The role of an architect was evolving at the time of the interviews. The number and resources of dedicated architects appeared to be very limited, and due to that fact, the architects operated rather independently from the projects and vice versa.

Alfa's management had a strong technology orientation. Four management roles and the role of process development were identified in the context of architecture design and description (Figure 1). Rapidly evolving mobile technologies and Alfa's strategic commitment to a certain technology necessitated that the general management took a number of conscious and serious risks related to the product's architecture. Moreover, as Alfa's business was rather product-based, the product management guided the architecture design and description process as well.

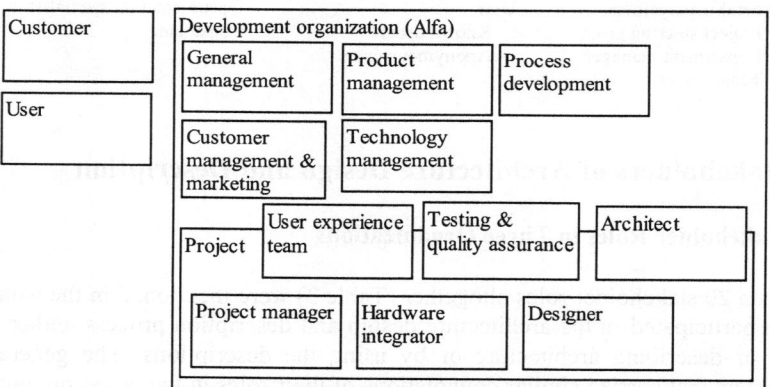

Fig. 1. Map of identified stakeholder roles in Alfa

The external stakeholders played less important roles compared to Beta and Gamma. The customer was definitely a key stakeholder of architecture design, although their relationship to projects, including designers, project managers, and architects, was rather distant. One explanation resides in the fact that Alfa operated as a subcontractor delivering specified product components based on formal documents provided by the customer, and Alfa's customers did not always want to share their technical knowledge with Alfa for competitive reasons, therefore limiting their interaction. Alfa thus developed its products and components quite independently from its customers. The actual software users were mostly anonymous from the viewpoint of Alfa's internal stakeholders.

3.1.2 Beta

In Beta's project-centric development organization (Figure 2), a project includes a manager, a product engineer, or a system analyst specifying requirements, designers, and a user interface (UI) designer and a documentation specialist in lesser roles. A project can include also a so-called project architect working at a level more detailed than the chief architect, who carries the responsibility for general-level solutions and policies. The product support and quality management are partly organized according to projects. No formal, fully project-independent support organization existed, as the customer operated within the borderlines of the same corporation, and the customer organized the support. The general management of Beta was somewhat technically oriented, being involved in architecture design and description. The management had initiated several development programs for enhancing design practices.

Beta, as an in-house developer, interacts intensively with the customers, who define the business, coordinating the relationships to external stakeholders, such as telecom service users, external customers, and telecom authorities. The subcontractor plays another role of external stakeholder. Based on the process documents, Beta was supposed to interact directly with subcontractors. In the interviews, however, no subcontractors were mentioned. Customers own the software products developed by Beta. The software development projects thus took place typically in parallel with the customer's product development initiatives, including business and concept development for telecom services. In addition to product development, customers run the software (production organization) and interfaces to the billing systems and other operative information systems (data administration). (Figure 2)

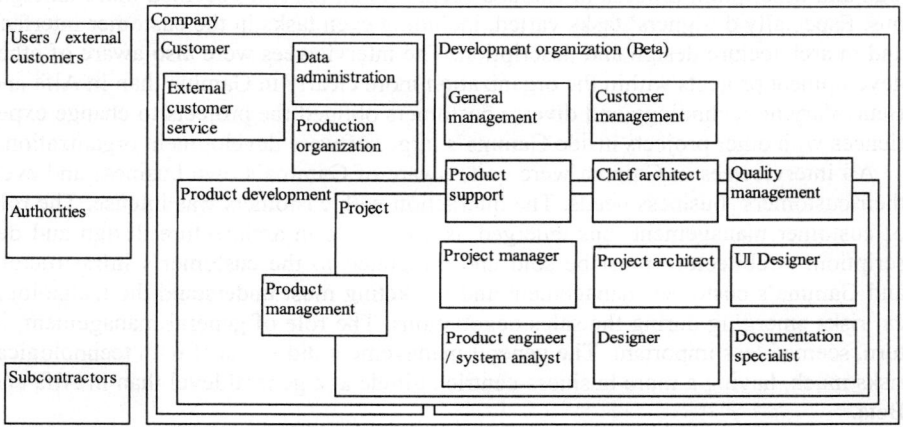

Fig. 2. Map of identified stakeholder roles in Beta

3.1.3 Gamma

The number of Gamma's stakeholder roles (Figure 3) appeared rather low compared to Alfa and Beta. However, after a second glance, the situation gets more complicated. The external stakeholders evidently play the most significant role in Gamma. Customers interact tightly with the development organization and the variation within the set of customers and inside their organizations is evident. Gamma co-operates with customers' data administration organizations, future users, and business representatives who own the delivered systems. In the systems delivery process, Gamma negotiates intensively also with diverging kinds of suppliers: such as other system development organizations interfacing the systems under development, software producers and importers, and hardware vendors.

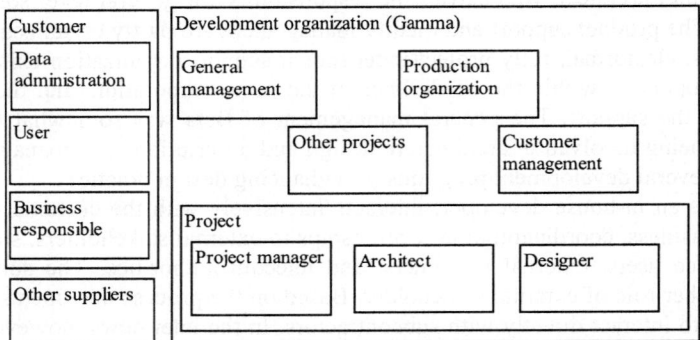

Fig. 3. Map of identified stakeholder roles in Gamma

Gamma's projects seem to be organized quite uncomplicatedly (Figure 3) compared to Alfa and Beta. This indicates fuzzier role clarity [cf. 24] within projects than in the other two organizations. While the number of explicit roles in architecture design and description process in Gamma seems small, the roles seemed more ambiguous. Especially designers' tasks varied, including even tasks in the customer interface and in architecture design and description. The interviewees were also aware of other development projects within the organization more clearly in Gamma than in Alfa and Beta. Varying technology and diverse customers obliged the projects to change experiences with other projects inside Gamma's large software development organization.

All interviewees in Gamma were quite aware of Gamma's own business and even their customers' business needs. The interaction with customers was intense. The role of customer management thus emerged as a key role in architecture design and description. Architecture must be sold and integrated to the customer's infrastructure and Gamma's customer management and marketing must understand the technological risks emerging during the sales negotiations. The role of general management, in turn, seemed less important. The general management did not deal with technological risks much, having a more business-centric attitude at a general level than in Alfa and Beta.

3.2 Key Stakeholder Roles and Their Rationale for Architecture Description

As it is rather unfeasible to give detailed descriptions of all the stakeholder roles we found (Figure 3), we focused on identifying and discussing key stakeholder roles and their characteristics in the architecture design and description process. Six roles occurred in all three organizations: 'customer', 'designer', 'project manager', 'architect', 'customer management and marketing', and 'general management'. Hence, we regarded these as the key stakeholders. They were also most frequently mentioned in the data. The role of 'system analyst' was important in Beta as the requirements gatherer. In Alfa, it did not occur at all, and in Gamma it was mixed with the roles of project manager and designer – no separate mentions of 'system analyst' existed in Gamma. Hence, we excluded it from the further analysis. Table 4 lists the key stakeholder roles with their typical tasks and the observed variation within each role. Each stakeholder has a typical relationship and perspective to architecture, which cause certain pertinent problems and challenges. A stakeholder's relationship to architecture and the emerging problems then emphasize certain rationale for each of them (Table 5).

Table 4. The key stakeholder roles in architecture design and description

Stakeholder/role	Typical tasks	Observed variation
Customer	Buying the system Setting requirements Utilizing the system Running the system	Includes both business and technology oriented people at customer side
Designer	Detailed design Programming	Tasks vary according to skills and experience
Project manager	Project management	Some projects include separate technical and business project managers
Architect	Evaluation of high level solutions Deciding about technology High-level design	Occurrences of more experienced 'chief architects' and less experienced or skilled 'project architects'
Customer management & marketing	Selling Negotiation	Account managers, salesmen
General management	Resource management Deciding strategies	Project steering groups, department managers, team leaders

A customer must comprehend a software system also at a technical and architectural level. The customer builds and operates the technical infrastructure (e.g., data communications and processing services) for the system or purchases it as a service. All this requires communication at an architectural level possibly leading to the problems in technical maturity (e.g. lacking technical skills and knowledge) and in the interpretation of meanings of the technical descriptions. According to numerous mentions in the data, the architecture descriptions were often considered too "technical" for the customer. As well, the problems of trust and security between the customer and the development organization were frequently mentioned. Due to the relationship to architecture and the related problems, communication and understanding were emphasized as the major rationale when customers were mentioned. Naturally, a customer must evaluate the technology and make decisions about it as well as the development organization.

All the organizations used explicitly the term 'designer' instead of 'software engineer', which could also appropriately label this role. Designers create detailed designs and system implementations according to architecture descriptions. Designers' detailed interest in the parts of the system tends to be somewhat isolated from the whole. This was mentioned as a problem in several occasions. The rationale emphasized in relation to the designer can most clearly be associated with the programming-in-the-large conception. Designers need architecture descriptions for design and implementation, for enabling reuse, and for documentation purposes. It was, however, realized that designers must first be able to understand and interpret the descriptions. Current state-of-the-art in the target organizations showed many imperfections in their description practices thus hindering the interpretation also among the designers.

Project manager was also considered a key stakeholder role in the architecture design and description. Architecture was often mentioned as one of the important sources of information for dividing a project into detailed work assignments. Resource or schedule constraints, such as unrealistic schedules or too little financing, were mentioned as possible causes leading to dubious compromises in architecture. A project manager must use architectural information and decide the critical path and the usage of resources in the subsequent development project. The project manager also discusses and negotiates about the architecture with the other stakeholders.

Table 5. Problems and rationale of the key stakeholder roles

Stakeholder role	Relationship to architecture	Emerging and emphasized problems	Emphasized rationale for architecture description/design
Customer	Varies. Must be able to rationalize the solutions, build and operate the technology infrastructure	Technical maturity Communication and interpretation of meanings and descriptions Security constraints	Communication Understanding Evaluation and deciding
Designer	Implements the software according to architecture	Isolated views Interpretation of descriptions	Understanding Design & implement Reuse Documentation
Project manager	Uses architecture for creating project breakdown structures.	Resource or schedule constraints	Project planning Communication Understanding Evaluation & deciding
Architect	The main creator of architecture	Skills and experience of other stakeholders Lack of resources	Communication Evaluation & deciding Documentation
Customer management & marketing	Uses architecture as a selling argument Demonstrates technical competency and compatibility with architecture	Understanding the descriptions Skills and experience Making resource estimates Isolated views	Communication Understanding Licensing and pricing Resource planning Selling
General management	Must have some understanding and analysis capability concerning technology	Knowledge management Interpretation of descriptions Organizational obstacles	Understanding Communicating Resource planning Quality management

The role called architect was identified as the main creator of architecture in all the three organizations. Architects are invariably technically skilled, being selected among the most technically advanced personnel with a broad view on technology. This causes also problems. No matter how skilled the architects are they must communicate with other stakeholders, who often lack the technological skills and insight, to get their message clear. An architect must be able to communicate with various stakeholders at several levels of abstraction and difficulty with different kinds of descriptions. The evaluation and decision-making on alternative solutions represents another rationale for architecture descriptions by the architects. The observed role of architects corresponded rather directly to Grinter's [14] in-depth observations. In addition, due to the continuous lack of skilled architects, architecture should also be well documented so that the needs for personal presence of the architects the numerous meetings and negotiations of the development process could be minimized.

Customer management and marketing utilizes architecture descriptions in sales negotiations. They must also demonstrate the vendor's technical competency and compatibility to a customer's environment. The employees involved in customer management and marketing may lack technological insight. Hence, the understanding of architecture descriptions may become a problem. Without a realistic picture of architecture, usable resource estimates in customer-vendor negotiations can be hard to reach. The data showed a tendency of cultural and operational isolation between the customer-oriented and technically oriented people. The rationale for architecture design and description among customer management and marketing thus resided in the understanding of architecture at some level, in communicating with the descriptions, in rationalizing the licensing and pricing requirements, in initial planning for development resources, and in "selling" the architecture to customers (in which even the visual attractiveness of the architecture descriptions counts as a factor to be considered).

The general management wanted as well to understand and analyze the technological and architectural issues. The general management had an urge to locate the necessary information concerning the ongoing and planned projects, to encourage the creation of architectural knowledge, and to disperse that knowledge in the organization. The data hinted about possible organizational obstacles, such as barriers between organizational units or different professional backgrounds of the stakeholders that might impede efficient architectural design and description processes. Quality management was considered especially as the rationale held by the general management. The other rationale held by general-level managers corresponded rather closely to those of customer management's.

3.3 Similarities and Differences among the Role Occurrences

Within the three target organizations, the roles of customer management and marketing, designer, and project manager appeared quite similar when observing the rationale for architecture descriptions. Their roles were rather uniformly defined and the emphasized rationale for architecture were well understood among the stakeholders.

More variation in the emphasized rationale for architecture descriptions emerged among architects and customers. An architect's role varied according to questions such as to what extent project management responsibilities were assigned to architects, or how much an architect was expected to control the conformance to the technological strategies and architectural policies of the organization. In addition, the role of customer included some variation in the rationale. The questions that affected to the variation were, for example: how much architectural descriptions were used during the process of purchasing negotiations, how much the customer's data administration was involved in architecture design, and what was the role of the customer's legacy interfaces and the run-time environment.

The role of general management varied most clearly among the target organizations. In Gamma, general management had only a minor role related to architecture, whereas in Alfa, general management was considered as a key stakeholder related to architecture. An explanation lies in the degree of how much general management was involved in the management and evaluation of technological risks when designing architecture. When the technological and operational risks were decentralized to individual projects (e.g., in Gamma), general management's role related to architecture decreases. On the other hand, when the risks were included in business and technology strategies created by the general management (in Alfa), general management must certainly be regarded as a key stakeholder.

Other stakeholder roles that included considerably variance or that were unique among the organizations were, for example, the roles of data administration or production organization (the importance of run-time architecture), maintenance and support (the role of documentation), other projects (reuse and knowledge management across projects), and other suppliers (communication between vendors, subcontractors, and authorities). The list of observed stakeholders is by far not complete. By extending the sample to additional target organizations, we could evidently find also other unique or varying stakeholder roles not included here.

Table 6. Common rationale for architecture description

Stakeholder role	Common rationale for architecture description
Architect	Must communicate about architecture with other stakeholders
Customer	Must communicate about architecture with other stakeholders Must evaluate the architecture and make decisions about it Must use 3rd party products and services associated with architecture
Customer mgmt and marketing	Must communicate about architecture with other stakeholders Must understand the architecture at some level
Designer	Must design and implement the system according to architecture Must understand the architecture
Project manager	Must communicate about architecture with other stakeholders Must plan the project and its resources against architecture

Table 6 lists those rationales that occurred uniformly in the three organizations in relation to a particular stakeholder role. The rationales are quite obviously evidenced by common sense. Nevertheless, they show the importance of communication and the richness of architecture as a concept.

3.4 Implicit Relationships of Architecture, Viewpoints, Stakeholders, and Rationale

Our original objective was to find out the combinations and relationships between rationale, stakeholders, and used viewpoints in the architecture design and description process. We did not define beforehand what we meant by 'architecture'. Based on the initial discussions, we already knew that the concept would carry ambiguous connotations in the organizations and therefore we did not want to constrain the data by artificial definitions. Instead, we let the interviewees to define their own points-of-view to architecture and analyzed the meaning from the transcripts. The concept of architecture carried varying connotations, indeed. To some, it included only the structure of software components, and to some, it included system's stakeholders and their required functionality, packages of business operations, network topologies, among many other features of the system.

With regard to the issue of viewpoints, the interviewees were not explicitly aware of such specific viewpoints recommended or defined in the literature [e.g. 5]. The concept of a viewpoint was not explicitly present in the target organizations' process documents or architecture descriptions, nor recalled in the interviews. On the other hand, so-called "rich descriptions", informally constructed and communicated among the key stakeholders, were used in all kinds of situations; obeying no explicit viewpoint definition [as defined in 16]. These "rich descriptions" were used in negotiations with customers as well as in internal meetings and communication among the stakeholders. Typically, they included PowerPoint™ presentations and extensive textual documents comprising often tens of pages of text and pictures; e.g., imported UML-based models created with design tools such as Rational Rose™, which was used as well for architecture descriptions in all target organizations. Those textual documents were often regarded as "too specific" for other stakeholders than designers.

Furthermore, several interviewees were also rather unaware of the rationales behind the descriptions. Some created architecture descriptions simply because it was defined obligatory in the process model and some were aware only of a proportion of the uses of their descriptions. These reasons led us to abandon the original idea of trying to relate viewpoints explicitly to particular rationale and stakeholders (at least based on our contemporary amount of data).

4 Implications

The observed multitude of stakeholder roles, with their problems and rationale related to software architecture raised a number of implications for practice and research, to be discussed as follows.

4.1 Implications for Practice

The repertoires of stakeholder roles clearly varied in the target organizations. More variation could be probably found by extending the sample. Certain key roles (customer, general management, architect) included more variation in relation to architecture than others (project manager, designer). Any generic methodology or process model for architecture design thus seems unlikely usable straightforwardly as such in practice. Our findings suggest that organization-specific aspects should be carefully considered in connection to the development of architecture design methods and processes. The process, methods, and tools for architecture design and description should be adapted to the needs of the stakeholders in a particular context. This adaptation could start with an explicit definition for the stakeholders in the organization in question, their architectural tasks, and the rationale they have for architecture design and description. The role of customers and other external stakeholders was highlighted. In our sample, the role of customer affected architecture design and description. The more customer-orientation was observed in architecture design and description, the more emphasis in architecture descriptions was put on communicational aspects and interpretation, instead of the detailed design and implementation.

Architecture design and description should not be approached separately from the other processes of software engineering, representing the core of work for a part of the key stakeholders. These processes include at least requirements management, project management, customer management, and technology management. In the target organizations, architecture emerged as a rich concept with a multitude of meanings for diverging stakeholders, and its design and description was intertwined with all these other processes, which provided additional and necessary knowledge and understanding for architecture design, and vice versa. The plain viewpoint of the 'architect' thus cannot explain the architecture design process in itself.

We noticed that designers, together with plainly technologically oriented architects, could be satisfied with current architecture description practices, although the descriptions were varying and their contents were all but formalized or standardized. Other stakeholders, such as management, were more concerned with standardized practices. The management worried clearly more about the reuse and the aspects of knowledge creation and management, whereas the technical people were relatively happy with the current situation, project-by-project. There are several possible explanations to this phenomenon. Managers have a wider view to architecture, including also the business and resource management aspects, being unable to locate that information in relation to the contemporary descriptions. They also needed to coordinate a number of projects. Moreover, architecture descriptions were traditionally designed to serve designers, rather than managers. The detailed architecture descriptions for the implementation purposes were too specific for managers, hindering quick overviews of the general situation across projects. The information needed from the architecture descriptions thus greatly varied depending on the diverging use situations, e.g., if the aim is to communicate and make business decisions versus the information needed for designing and implementing the system (i.e., programming-in-the-large). The stakeholders of the architecture design and description process must be aware of these differences between the needs and conceptions of the stakeholders in order to achieve common understanding of the varying rationale for architecture design and description.

4.2 Implications for Research

Our study suggests that further research on the software architecture design and description should consider a wider scale of issues than the programming-in-the-large rationale or the plain viewpoint of the software architect. Current conceptions on architecture design and description, including the proliferation of the formal languages and models that currently dominates the research on software architecture are somewhat based on such presuppositions about the rationale for architectural design that do not correspond with practice.

The rationales most emphasized among the key stakeholders were related to the issues of communicating and understanding the architecture, and making evaluations and decisions about it. The practical problems mentioned were rather unassociated with achieving the "right" or "most efficient" solution. Instead, they were mostly associated with communication, interpretation of the descriptions, skills and experience, and other "soft" aspects of software engineering. The aim to design and implement the system according to an architecture description appeared to be central only to designers. An architecture description was primarily considered a means for creating common understanding about the technological solutions and about the way of structuring associated with the system. The multiple stakeholders with multiple rationales identified in the target organizations call for empirical research on communication in architecture design and how it could be enhanced. The research should cover the evaluation of the role of formal and informal models and descriptions in architecture design – to what extent knowledge is created and transferred through formal models and to what extent through informal pictures, textual descriptions, and other social interaction. After that, we can determine effective means and tools to develop the architecture design and description process. These means might slightly differ from the current focus on formal issues of architecture design.

Our study thus sets modest challenges to the contemporary work around ADLs. If the emergence of informal "rich descriptions" of architecture aiming mostly at facilitating communication between diverse stakeholders increases among the software-producing organizations, the ADL developers might want to elaborate visual, flexible, communicative, and collaborative tools that could support all stakeholders (alongside architects and designers), still trying to retain the advantages of the programming-in-the-large metaphor and formality that have been already reached. On the other hand, UML was used extensively in all the three organizations, and designers and some of the architects seemed quite content with UML's ability to model architecture. This raises a paradox: if designers and architects remain unaware of the advantages of specific formal ADLs, then who would or should be aware of them, and what would be the practical rationale for those in the first place? As long as the lack of reported experiences from applying ADLs in real-life software producing companies continues, their contribution remains at a somewhat theoretical level. Practice-oriented research strategies, e.g. that of action research [see e.g. 25], might fruitfully shed additional light on this issue.

5 Conclusions

Different stakeholders have different purposes for architecture and they emphasize different rationales for architecture description. Whereas only designers emphasized architecture as a basis for further design and implementation, the other stakeholders emphasized it rather as a means for communication, interpretation, and decision-making. This observation challenges the common conception of architecture design as programming-in-the-large. Instead, architecture design and description can be regarded primarily as a means for coping with complex solutions and technology, reached through communication between diverse stakeholders with varying skills and experience. The primary focus of the software architecture research should be shifted onto the non-technical rationale and common understanding of technical complexity of software in relation to the relevant organizational and business environments.

References

1. Medvidovic, N. and Taylor, R. N., "A Classification and Comparison Framework for Software Architecture Description Languages," *IEEE Transactions on Software Engineering*, vol. 26, no. 1, 2000, pp. 70-93.
2. Luckham, D. C. and Vera, J., "An Event-Based Architecture Definition Language," *IEEE Transactions on Software Engineering*, vol. 21, no. 9, 1995, pp. 717-734.
3. Allen, R. and Garlan, D., "A formal basis for architectural connection," *ACM Transactions on Software Engineering and Methodology*, vol. 6, no. 3, 1997, pp. 213-49.
4. DeRemer, F. and Kron, H. H., "Programming-in-the-Large Versus Programming-in-the-Small," *IEEE Transactions on Software Engineering*, vol. SE-2, no. 2, 1976, pp. 80-86.
5. Kruchten, P. B., "The 4+1 View Model of Architecture," *IEEE Software*, vol. 12, no. 6, 1995, pp. 42-50.
6. Monroe, R. T., Kompanek, A., Melton, R., and Garlan, D., "Architectural styles, design patterns, and objects," *IEEE Software*, vol. 14, no. 1, 1997, pp. 43-52.
7. Hofmeister, C., Nord, R., and Soni, D., *Applied Software Architecture*. Reading, MA: Addison-Wesley, 1999.
8. Gomaa, H., Menascé, D. A., and Shin, M. E., "Reusable Component Interconnection Patterns for Distributed Software Architectures," *ACM SIGSOFT Software Engineering Notes*, vol. 26, no. 3, 2001, pp. 69-77.
9. Kazman, R., Abowd, G., Bass, L., and Clements, P., "Scenario-Based Analysis of Software Architecture," *IEEE Software*, vol. 13, no. 6, 1996, pp. 47-55.
10. Kazman, R., Barbacci, M., Klein, M., Carrière, S. J., and Woods, S. G., "Experience with Performing Architecture Tradeoff Analysis," Proceedings of the 1999 International Conference on Software Engineering, 1999, pp. 54-63.
11. Bosch, J., Design and Use of Software Architectures: Adopting and Evolving a Product-Line Approach: Addison-Wesley, 2000.

12. Robbins, J. E. and Redmiles, D. F., "Software Architecture Critics in the Argo Design Environment," *Knowledge-Based Systems*, vol. 11, no. 1, 1998, pp. 47-60.
13. Schön, D., The Reflective Practitioner: How Professionals Think in Action. New York: Basic Books, 1983.
14. Grinter, R. E., "Systems Architecture: Product Designing and Social Engineering," *ACM SIGSOFT Software Engineering Notes*, vol. 24, no. 2, 1999, pp. 11-18.
15. Shaw, M., "The Coming-of-Age of Software Architecture Research," Proceedings of the 23rd International Conference on Software Engineering (ICSE 2001), 2001, pp. 657-664a.
16. IEEE, "IEEE Recommended Practice for Architectural Description of Software-Intensive Systems," IEEE, IEEE Std 1471-2000, 2000.
17. Garlan, D., "Software Architecture: a Roadmap," in *The Future of Software Engineering*, A. Finkelstein, Ed.: ACM Press, 2000.
18. Bass, L., Clements, P., and Kazman, R., *Software Architecture in Practice*: Addison-Wesley, 1998.
19. Strauss, A. L. and Corbin, J., *Basics of Qualitative Research: Grounded Theory Procedures and Applications*. Newbury Park, CA: Sage Publications, 1990.
20. Galliers, R., "Information Systems Research: Issues, Methods and Practical Guidelines." Oxford: Blackwell, 1992.
21. Nandhakumar, J. and Jones, M., "Too Close for Comfort? Distance and Engagement in Interpretive Information Systems Research," *Information Systems Journal*, vol. 7, no., 1997, pp. 109-131.
22. Glaser, B. and Strauss, A. L., The Discovery of Grounded Theory: Strategies for Qualitative Research. Chigago: Aldine, 1967.
23. Miles, M. B. and Huberman, A. M., *Qualitative Data Analysis: A Sourcebook of New Methods*. Beverly Hills: Sage, 1984.
24. Goodman, R. A. and Goodman, L. P., "Some Management Issues in Temporary Systems: A Study of Professional Development and Manpower - The Theater Case," *Administrative Science Quarterly*, vol. 21, no. Sep 1976, 1976, pp. 494-501.
25. Avison, D., Lau, F., Myers, M. D., and Nielsen, P. A., "Action Research," *Communications of the ACM*, vol. 42, no. 1, 1999, pp. 94-97.

The Individual Deployment of Systems Development Methodologies

Magda Huisman [1] and Juhani Iivari [2]

[1] Department of Computer Science and Information Systems, Potchefstroom
University for CHE,
Private Bag X6001, Potchefstroom, 2531, South Africa
rkwhmh@puknet.puk.ac.za
[2] Department of Information Processing Science, University of Oulu
P.O.Box 3000, 90014 Oulun yliopisto, Finland
juhani.iivari@oulu.fi

Abstract. This paper reports results of a survey that investigated factors affecting the deployment of systems development methodologies by individual systems developers. The results show that relative advantage, compatibility and trialability of a systems development methodology, an individual's experience in systems development and his/her experience in systems development methodologies, management support and peer developer support, and uncertainty about the continued existence of the IS department significantly influence the deployment of systems development methodologies.

1 Introduction

There exists a widespread belief that adherence to systems development methodologies (SDM) is beneficial to an organization ([7],[13]). This belief is manifested in the pressure that practitioners face today to use SDM [7]. Despite the high investment in the development of SDM and the pressure to use it, their practical usefulness is still a controversial issue ([7],[20],[28]). Recent surveys on their use also indicate quite consistently that many organizations claim that they do not use any methodologies ([13],[2],[8]). Apart from this, we do not know why SDM are used or not used, and what factors influence its use and effectiveness.

In this paper we investigate the deployment of SDM among individual systems developers. A decision by IS management to adopt SDM in an IS department does not guarantee that all developers will use the methodology, or that they will use it to its full potential. The purpose of this paper is to determine which factors influence the individual deployment of SDM.

2 Conceptual Research Model and Research Hypotheses

2.1 Theoretical Background

Most of the previous research into SDM did not have any theoretical orientation but the idea had been just to report the state of use of SDM and techniques in purely descriptive terms, e.g. [13] and [2]. In general terms the present work is influenced by the diffusion of innovations (DOI) theory [35], which is becoming an increasingly popular reference theory for empirical studies of information technologies ([5],[31]).

More specifically, our work is based on the IS implementation model suggested by Kwon and Zmud [23]. They combined IS implementation research and the DOI theory. This resulted in an enlarged model that identifies five categories of factors affecting IS implementation: individual factors, structural (organisational) factors, technological factors (innovation characteristics), task-related factors, and environmental factors. This categorisation provides the overall conceptual framework for our work (Figure 1). However, our selection of individual factors does not follow the model of [23] precisely for two reasons. Firstly, their list of 23 factors is quite comprehensive to be tested in one study. Secondly, we wished to identify factors that are more specific to SDM than many of the factors they identified.

According to the tri-core model presented by [36], SDM are IS technological process innovations of Type 1b, which focus on the technical core of the IS department, and change the nature of IS work. The social system that we study is an organisation. In terms of [35], SDM are contingent innovations with organisations as primary adopting units and individuals as secondary adopting units. [4] stresses that a distinction should be made between the adoption and acquisition of technology at the organisational level and its adoption and implementation at the individual level. In this study we will focus on the individual systems developer as the adopting unit. The adoption and implementation at the organisational level are reported in another study.

The DOI theory has also been criticised. [5] points out that it has mainly addressed individual adoption of relatively simple innovations. Despite of our recognition that SDMs are contingent innovations [35], our focus in this paper lies on individual adoption of SDM. It is also obvious that SDM are fairly complex innovations. They are technologies of Type 2 [5], which are characterised by a high knowledge burden or high user interdependencies. This means that our study tests the validity of DOI theory partly outside its major focus area. Therefore the detailed hypotheses concerning the deployment of SDM, derived from the classical DOI theory, are quite tentative.

As pointed above there is not much theoretically oriented empirical research into the adoption of SDM, on which we can draw in our discussion of detailed hypotheses. To compensate this we mainly use existing empirical research on the adoption of CASE technology. There are two reasons for this. Firstly, CASE tools represent relatively complex technologies which are contingent innovations just as SDM. Secondly, the methodology companionship of CASE tools [38] implies that their adoption includes a significant aspect of SDM.

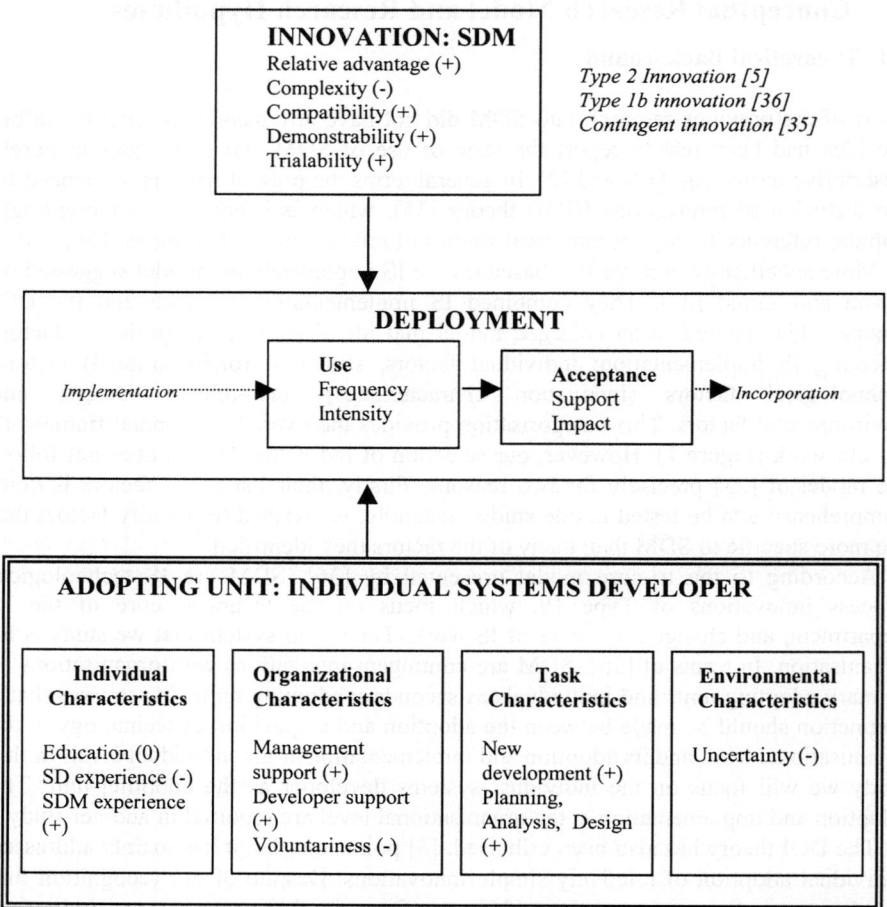

Fig. 1 Conceptual research model for the individual deployment of SDM

2.2 The Innovation: SDM

Trying to define SDM is no easy task. There is no universally accepted, rigorous and concise definition of SDM ([1],[39],[18]). [1] argues that the term methodology is a wider concept than the term method, as it has certain characteristics that are not implied by method, i.e. the inclusion of a philosophical view. We use the term „methodology" to cover the totality of systems development approaches (e.g. structured approach, object-oriented approach), process models (e.g. linear life-cycle, spiral models), specific methods (e.g. IE, OMT, UML) and specific techniques.

Individuals' responses to an innovation are primarily influenced by attributes of the innovation and the implementation process [25]. The characteristics of SDM that we will study was suggested by [35], namely perceived relative advantage, compatibility, complexity, trialability and observability.

Relative advantage

Relative advantage is the degree to which an innovation is perceived as being better than the idea it supersedes [35]. After a decade's intensive research on TAM [3] in particular, there is significant empirical evidence that relative advantage or perceived usefulness [27] is positively related to innovation use, even though [17] discovered it to have a significant relationship with CASE usage only at the organizational level but not at the individual level. This overwhelming evidence leads us to the following hypothesis:

- H1: There is a positive relationship between relative advantage and the individual deployment of SDM.

Complexity

Complexity is the degree to which an innovation is perceived as difficult to understand and use [35]. It is generally believed that the more complex an individual perceives an innovation to be before using it, the less likely it is that the innovation will be adopted and implemented. Although perceived complexity has generally been assumed to be negatively related to the adoption of innovations ([3],[27],[35]), the empirical results regarding the relationship between perceived complexity (or perceived ease of use when inversed [27]) and use has been inconclusive [9]. This is also the case in the adoption of CASE tools ([26],[17]). Despite the inconclusive empirical evidence, we postulate in accordance with the DOI theory [35] and TAM [3] the following:

- H2: There is a negative relationship between complexity and the individual deployment of SDM.

Compatibility

Compatibility is the degree to which an innovation is perceived as being consistent with the existing values, past experiences and needs of potential adopters, and it is positively related to innovation use [35]. Compatibility is sometimes described as the „fit" between an innovation and a particular context, which implies that an innovation must match its context in order to be effective. [26] remarks that a detailed assessment should be made of the „fit" between CASE methodology and the systems development tasks it is designed to support, when studying the acceptance of CASE methodology. [17] also found some evidence for the significance of compatibility for CASE usage. Following the DOI theory, we postulate the next hypothesis as follows:

- H3: There is a positive relationship between compatibility and the individual deployment of SDM.

Demonstrability

[35] uses the term „observability" and defines it as the degree to which the results of an innovation are visible to others. He argues that the easier it is for individuals to see the results of an innovation, the more likely they are to adopt it. [27] found that „observability" as originally defined by Rogers consist of two constructs, namely result demonstrability and visibility. Software-dominant innovations are less visible than hardware-dominant innovations ([27],[35]). Therefore we used the construct for result demonstrability and we postulate the following hypothesis:

- H4: There is a positive relationship between demonstrability and the individual deployment of SDM.

Trialability

[35] defines trialability as the degree to which an innovation may be experimented with on a limited basis. He argues that innovations, which are trialable, will be adopted more quickly, because it represents less uncertainty to the individual. We formulate the fifth hypothesis:
- H5: There is a positive relationship between trialability and the individual deployment of SDM.

2.3 Innovation Diffusion Process

Our main focus is on the deployment of SDM, which is related to the implementation and confirmation stages of the innovation-decision process as described by [35]. Since deployment is part of the post-implementation stage, we use the description of [26] in our conceptual research model. After implementation, deployment will follow, which in turn is followed by incorporation. We visualise deployment as two stages, namely use followed by acceptance.

Use will be studied along two dimensions, namely frequency of use and intensity of use. The acceptance of SDM will be studied from two perspectives, namely their impact on systems development and the perceived support it provides [26]. When studying the impact of SDM, we will focus on their impact on both the developed system and the development process ([14],[39]). The support that SDM provide will be studied along three dimensions, namely the perceived support as production technology, control technology, and cognitive/co-operative technology [15]. In Table 1 we summarise the different perspectives that we use to study deployment.

Table 1. Perspectives used to study deployment of SDM

Use	Acceptance	
	Support provided	Impact
Frequency of use	Production technology	Quality of developed system
Intensity of use	Control technology	Quality and productivity of development process
	Cognitive/co-operative technology	

2.4 Individual Characteristics

Education

Empirical results regarding the influence of education on the innovation process have been inconclusive. [23] states that negative associations have been found between education and innovation usage, mixed results have been reported for performance,

and negative associations have been found between education and satisfaction with the innovation. This leads to the next hypothesis in its null form:
- H6: There is no relationship between education and the individual deployment of SDM.

Experience in systems development

Research suggests that the experience profile of an individual is an important factor in the acceptance and use of SDM. The findings suggest that inexperienced developers are more likely to use SDM and CASE tools ([24],[29]), while experienced developers may resist using them [37]. We formulate the following hypothesis:
- H7: There is a negative relationship between an individual's experience in systems development and the individual deployment of SDM.

Experience in SDM

Contrary to Hypotheses H7 [25] argues that experienced developers are more likely to use SDM as they would be more aware of the benefits. Assuming that SDM have benefits, one can assume experienced developers who have experience of using a particular SDM to be more likely to use SDM. Therefore, we postulate the following hypothesis:
- H8: There is a positive relationship between an individual's experience with SDM and the individual deployment of SDM.

2.5 Task Characteristics

SDM are primarily used in the development of new systems, and are often not as helpful in the enhancement of operational systems [30]. Furthermore, SDM are most effective for analysing the functionality of a newly developed system [21]. We formulate the next hypotheses as follows:

H9: There is a positive relationship between the time an individual spends on the development of new systems and the individual deployment of SDM.

H10: There is a positive relationship between the time an individual spends on the planning, analysis and design of a new system and the individual deployment of SDM.

2.6 Organisational Characteristics

Individual systems developers do not work and deploy SDM in vacuum but under various social influences. The Theory of Reasoned Action [6] posits that an individual's behavior is influenced by his/her perception of the social pressure (subjective norm) to perform or not to perform the behavior. Subjective norm is defined as a multiplicative function of his/her normative beliefs (i.e. perceived expectations of specific referent individual and groups) and his/her motivation to comply with these expectations. The relevant referent groups may be top managers, supervisors, peers and friends. [22] tested the influence of a number of referent groups on the subjective norms of potential *adopters* and *users* of Microsoft Windows 3.1 software. They found that top management, supervisors and peers significantly underlie subjective norms for both groups, and additionally local computer specialists for users. On the other hand, they discovered subjective norms to have a significant influence on behavioral intention to adopt but not on behavioral intention to continue using. In line with [22] we will focus on manager influence, including both top management and IT managers, and peer developer influence. We do not make a distinction between potential adopters and users since SDM deployment concerns continued use, rather than potential adoption. Partly contrary to [22] findings we assume management and peer support to influence positively continued use of SDM, as explained below.

Management Support

Management support is consistently reported to facilitate IS implementation [10]. When we consider SDM, [21], [33], and [34] list a lack of management commitment as one of the biggest obstacles to implementing SDM. [17] also reports management support to have significant effects on CASE usage both at the individual and organizational level. This leads to our next hypothesis:
- H11: There is a positive relationship between management support and the individual deployment of SDM.

Developer support

To our knowledge there is not much previous research on peer influence on the use and acceptance of innovations in general, IT innovations more specifically, and SDM innovations in particular. Despite that we propose the following hypothesis:
- H12: There is a positive relationship between developer support for the systems development methodology and the individual deployment of SDM.

Voluntariness

Voluntariness is the degree to which an innovation is perceived as being voluntary or of free will [27]. When we consider contingent innovations, the secondary adopters rarely have complete autonomy regarding their adoption and use in the workplace. Furthermore, SDM are complex innovations, and unless management declares their use mandatory, systems developers will have difficulty to fit them into their tight schedule. [17] found strong support for the negative influence of voluntariness on CASE usage and [11] reports a strong negative influence of voluntariness on the use of the Personel Software Process innovation. This leads to our next hypothesis:

H13: There is a negative relationship between voluntariness and the individual deployment of SDM.

2.7 Environmental Characteristics

Uncertainty

The deployment of SDM can be justified as an investment in the maintainability of systems, supported by proper documentation and proper modular structuring. Therefore, if the future of the IS department is uncertain or under threat, it may decrease the motivation to deploy the SDM. Unfortunately, to our knowledge there is no previous work on this relationship. [32] concluded that users may be unwilling to

support new initiatives in an IS department in which they have limited confidence. On the other hand, uncertainty is believed to stimulate innovation through an organisation's effort to survive and grow [23]. On the whole, we formulate our next hypothesis as follows:
- H14: There is a negative relationship between the uncertainty about the continued existence of an IS department and the individual deployment of SDM.

3 Research Design

3.1 The Survey

This study is part of a larger survey on the deployment of SDM in South Africa, which was conducted between July and October 1999. The 1999 IT Users Handbook (the most comprehensive reference guide to the IT industry in South Africa) was used and the 443 listed organizations were contacted via telephone to determine if they were willing to participate in the study. 213 organizations agreed to take part. A package of questionnaires was sent to a contact person in each organization who distributed it. This package consisted of one questionnaire to be answered by the IT manager, and a number of questionnaires to be answered by individual systems developers in the organization. The response rate of the survey was as follows: 83 organizations (39%), 234 developers (26%) and 73 managers (34%) responded. The responses came from organisations representing a variety of business areas, manufacturing (33%) and finance/banking/insurance (15%) as the major ones. At the individual level the respondents reported considerable experience in SD, 22% between 3 and 5 years, 23% between 5-19 years and 38% more than 10 years.

3.2 Measurement

3.2.1 Measurement of Dependent Variable: Deployment

In Table 2 we summarise the measurement of the different aspects that we used to study deployment. Frequency of use was measured using a question of how frequently the respondent needed or applied SDM knowledge (never; once a month or less: a few times in a month; several times in a week; every working day). Intensity of use was measured as the maximum of the individual usage of 29 listed methods, possible other commercial methods and possible in-house developed methods.

One might also ask what independent variables explain deployment in total. To answer this question, factor analysis on the seven aspects of deployment was performed, and this resulted in one factor with a reliability of 0.82. To measure total individual deployment we used the factor scores resulting from the factor analysis.

Table 2. Measurement of deployment

Deployment aspects	Perspectives	Measurement	Reliability
Use	Frequency of use	2 items	0.84
	Intensity of use		
Support	Production technology	11 items (see [19])	0.94
	Control technology	9 items (see [19])	0.94
	Cognitive/co-operation technology	11 items (see [19])	0.91
Impact	Quality of developed systems	8 items (see [19])	0.95
	Quality and productivity of development process	10 items (see [19])	0.94

3.2.2 Measurement of Independent Variables

The measurement of the independent variables is summarised in Table 3. As Table 3 shows most measures were adopted from earlier research, and they have high reliability. The two items of uncertainty concerned the threat that the IS department is disbanded and the uncertainty of the future of the IS department in the organization.

3.3 Data Analysis

Data analysis was performed on the developer responses using Statistica (version 5) software. In the first analysis the seven different aspects of deployment was treated separately as the dependent variables. To identify the most important independent variables that explain the dependent variables, best subset multiple regression analysis was performed. In a second analysis, total deployment was treated as the dependent variable, and best subset multiple regression was performed.

Multiple regression analysis assumes interval or ratio scale measurement, linearity, homoscedasticity, i.e. the constancy of the residual terms across the values of the predictor variables, independence of residuals, normality of residuals, and no multicollinearity [12]. These assumptions were tested and no violations were detected.

4 Results

The results of the best subset multiple regression analysis with the seven different aspects of deployment of SDM as the dependent variables are presented in Table 4 and Table 5.

The last column of Table 5 contains the results of the regression analysis where total deployment was the dependent variable. To confirm the results of the regression analysis with total deployment as the dependent variable, we performed canonical analysis. Canonical analysis is used to determine the relationship between two sets of variables. The seven different aspects of deployment formed the first set, and the fourteen independent variables the second set. The resulting Canonical R was 0.90 at the level of p ≤ 0,001, and the eigenvalue of the first root was 0.81. The factor structures of the two sets confirmed the results of the factor analysis and the regression analysis.

Table 3. Measurement of independent variables

Type	Characteristic	Measurement	Reliability
Innovation Characteristics	Relative advantage	5 items (adapted from [27])	0.94
	Complexity	3 items (adapted from [27])	0.88
	Compatibility	3 items (adapted from [27])	0.91
	Demonstrability	3 items (adapted from [27])	0.85
	Trialability	2 items (adapted from [27])	0.70
Individual Characteristics	Education	Highest qualification obtained	-
	Experience in systems development	Number of years	-
	Experience in the use of SDM	Number of years	-
Task Characteristics	Time spent on the development of new applications	%	-
	Time spent on planning, analysis, and design activities	%	-
Organisational Characteristics	Management support	2 items (adapted from [17])	0.86
	Developer support	1 item	-
	Voluntariness	2 items (adapted from [27])	0.82
Environmental Characteristic	Uncertainty	2 items	0.90

5 Discussion and Final Comments

In this paper our purpose was to study factors that influence the individual deployment of SDM. We identified fourteen possible factors, postulating fourteen hypotheses about their relationship with the individual deployment of SDM. These are summarised in Table 6.

Table 4 Results of the regression analysis

N=173	Frequency of use	Intensity of use	Support: Production technology	Support: Control technology	Support: Cognitive/co-operation technology
Relative advantage	0.34**	0.24'	0.25**	0.45***	0.49***
Complexity			0.09		
Compatibility	-0.15	-0.20	0.20*	0.11	
Demonstrability		0.15'			
Trialability	0.08	0.11	0.08	0.10'	0.12*
Education			0.06		
SD experience	-0.17*		-0.12*		
SDM experience	0.45***	0.21**	0.10		0.07
Time: Develop new applications					0.10'
Time: Planning, Analysis, Design	0.23***				
Manager support	-0.16*		0.29***	0.25***	0.10
Developer support	0.10		0.11'		0.20**
Uncertainty	-0.08		-0.13**	-0.15**	
Voluntariness	-0.13'		0.07		
R	0.71	0.40	0.82	0.75	0.77
R²	0.51	0.16	0.68	0.57	0.60
Adjusted R²	0.48	0.13	0.66	0.56	0.58
F	17.65***	6.60***	32.11***	45.28***	41.88***

' $p \leq 0,10$ * $p \leq 0,05$ ** $p \leq 0,01$ *** $p \leq 0,001$

5.1 Implications for Theory

The above results shed new light into the factors affecting the deployment of SDM. Overall, they show that the classical DOI theory [35] is relevant and useful in the case of individual deployment of complex innovations such as SDM (see [5]). The results indicate that especially relative advantage, compatibility less systematically and trialability more weakly have significant positive relationships with the individual deployment of SDM. Relative advantage is positively related to all seven different aspects of individual deployment. This suggests that individual systems developers' decisions to deploy SDM mainly takes place on rational grounds. If a systems developer sees SDM to provide relative advantage he or she is prepared to use it and to derive the benefits of using it. While compatibilty is strongly related to the perceived impact of SDM on the developed system and the development process, it is perplexing that it has negative, although not significant, beta coefficients with the methodology use. One explanation may be that when a SDM is highly compatible with a developer's way of working, its use may be quite routine and even tacit. It may be that our items measuring methodology use were not fully able to capture this routine or tacit nature of SDM use. On the other hand, when a methodology is perceived to be compatible with one's way of working, its benefits are perceived to be higher in terms of its impact on the quality of the system to be developed and the development process. Although trialability is not significantly related to the many aspects of deployment, it is related to deployment in total. On the other hand, contrary to the predictions of the DOI theory, complexity and demonstrability were not significantly related to the individual deployment of SDM.

Table 5. Results of the regression analysis

N=173	Impact: System	Impact: Process	Total deployment
Relative advantage	0.17'	0.39***	0.39***
Complexity			
Compatibility	0.44***	0.27**	0.17*
Demonstrability	0.10'		0.06
Trialability		0.08	0.10*
Education		0.06	
SD experience	-0.12*	-0.09'	-0.11*
SDM experience			0.14**
Time: Develop new applications		0.08	0.05
Time: Planning, Analysis, Design			
Manager support	0.10	0.18**	0.16**
Developer support	0.08		0.11'
Uncertainty	-0.07	-0.10'	-0.09*
Voluntariness		0.07	
R	0.76	0.78	0.86
R²	0.58	0.60	0.74
Adjusted R²	0.56	0.58	0.73
F	33.39***	27.94***	46.43***

' $p \leq 0,10$ * $p \leq 0,05$ ** $p \leq 0,01$ *** $p \leq 0,001$

Systems development experience was negatively related to the individual deployment of SDM. This is in accordance with earlier findings that methodologies are used more by beginners than experienced developers ([24],[29]). However, to complicate the situation, experience with SDM was positively related to the individual deployment of SDM. More experienced systems developers had more experience with SDM as indicated by the correlation coefficient (r = 0,47, p ≤ 0,001). So, as individuals they comprise two characteristics that are opposite to each other with regard to the deployment of SDM: experience with SDM being positively associated with the deployment and SD experience being negatively associated with the deployment. When we consider the different aspects of deployment the picture becomes a bit clearer. SD experience is mainly negatively related to the perceived impact of SDM on the developed system and the development process, and SDM experience is strongly positively related to the use of SDM.

Table 6. Summary of results

H1	There is a positive relationship between relative advantage and the individual deployment of SDM	Strongly supported
H2	There is a negative relationship between complexity and the individual deployment of SDM	Not supported
H3	There is a positive relationship between compatibility and the individual deployment of SDM	Partially supported
H4	There is a positive relationship between demonstrability and the individual deployment of SDM	Not supported
H5	There is a positive relationship between trialability and the individual deployment of SDM	Weakly supported
H6	There is no relationship between education and the individual deployment of SDM	Supported
H7	There is a negative relationship between an individual's experience in systems development and the individual deployment of SDM	Partially supported
H8	There is a positive relationship between an individual's experience with SDM and the individual deployment of SDM	Partially supported
H9	There is a positive relationship between the time an individual spends on the development of new systems and the individual deployment of SDM	Not supported
H10	There is a positive relationship between the time an individual spends on the planning, analysis and design of a new system and the individual deployment of SDM	Not supported
H11	There is a positive relationship between management support and the individual deployment of SDM	Supported
H12	There is a positive relationship between developer support for the systems development methodology and the individual deployment of SDM	Weakly supported
H13	There is a negative relationship between voluntariness and the individual deployment of SDM	Not supported
H14	There is a negative relationship between the uncertainty about the continued existence of an IS department and the individual deployment of SDM	Weakly supported

The results also lend support for the significance of social influences on the individual deployment of SDM. A significant positive relationship was found between management support and the individual deployment of SDM. Furthermore, an almost significant positive relationship was found between developer support and the individual deployment of SDM. These results are in line with previous research on the adoption of complex innovations [5] and confirm earlier findings on the significance of management support in the case of software process improvement initiatives [16].

5.2 Practical Implications

The above results have clear practical implications. Assuming that deployment of SDM is desirable, one should attempt to ensure that the individual systems developers perceive the methodologies to have relative advantage and compatibility with their work. The potential benefits of a methodology and reasons for its introduction should be made clear and communicated to the systems developers. However, we do not believe that these perceptions can be changed using unilateral communication, but the benefits and compatibility should be discussed openly with systems developers. The significance of compatibility suggests that one should also be prepared to adapt and customise a methodology to fit the organization and the project as far as it does not threat the central reasons of introducing a methodology.

The trialability of SDM was also found significant. This would suggest that one should pay attention to the way of introducing a methodology. It can take place in pilot projects or applying only part of a methodology (e.g. starting from requirements engineering). As always in pilot projects one should pay attention to their selection as well to the selection of the participants. The participants should be motivated. Although it is not tested in this study, it would also be useful if they could serve as opinion leaders later, if the methodology is to be diffused more widely in the organisation. Referring to the significance of experience, it is important to ensure that the pilot project is as pleasant an experience as possible. The pilot project may be introduced as an opportunity to learn a new methodology that enhances and possibly updates the expertise of the participants (as could be the case when introducing some OO methodology).

It is also significant that management communicates its support for the SDM introduction and deployment. The results also suggest that uncertainty concerning the future of the IS department is detrimental to methodology deployment. Therefore, if the IS department is not under real threat, one should attempt to decrease such uncertainty.

References

1. Avison, D. E., Fitzgerald, G. (1995) *Information Systems Development: Methodologies, Techniques and Tools*, McGraw-Hill, Berkshire, England
2. Chatzoglou, P. D., Macaullay, L. A. (1996) Requirements capture and IS methodologies, *Information Systems Journal*, Vol. 6, pp. 209-225

3. Davis, F. D., Bagozzi, R. P., Warshaw, P. R. (1989) User acceptance of computer technology: A comparison of two theoretical models, *Management Science*, Vol. 35, No. 8, pp. 982-1003
4. Dietrich, G. B., Walz, D. B., Wynekoop, J. L. (1997) The failure of SDT Diffusion: A Case for Mass Customization, *IEEE Transactions on Engineering Management*, Vol. 44, No. 4, pp. 390-398
5. Fichman, R. G. (1992) Information Technology Diffusion: A review of empirical research, in DeGross, J. I., Becker, J. D., Elam, J. J. (eds.) *Proceedings of the Thirteenth International Conference on Information Systems*, Dallas, TX, pp. 195-206
6. Fishbein, M., Ajzen, I. (1975) Belief, Attitude, Intention and Behavior: An Introduction to Theory and Research, Addison-Wesley, Reading, MA
7. Fitzgerald, B. (1996) Formalized SDM: a critical perspective, *Information Systems Journal*, Vol. 6, pp. 3-23
8. Fitzgerald, B. (1998) An empirical investigation into the adoption of SDM, *Information & Management*, Vol. 34, pp. 317-328
9. Gefen, D., Straub, D. W. (2000) The relative importance of perceived ease of use in IS adoption: A study of e-commerce adoption, *Journal of the Association for Information Systems*, Vol. 1, 2000
10. Ginzberg, M. J. (1981) Key recurrent issues in the MIS implementation process, *MIS Quarterly*, Vol. 5, pp. 47-59
11. Green, G. C. and Hevner, A. R., Perceived Control of Software Developers and its Impact on the Successful Diffusion of Information Technology, CMU/SEI-98-SR-013, Carnegie Mellon, Software Engineering Institute, Pittsburgh, PA, 1999, http://www.sei.cmu.edu/pub/documents/98.reports/pdf/98sr013.pdf
12. Hair, J. F., Anderson, R. E., Tatham, R. L., Black, W. C. (1992), *Multivariate Data Analysis with Readings*, Macmillan, New York
13. Hardy, C. J., Thompson J. B., Edwards H. M. (1995) The use, limitations and customization of structured systems development methods in the United Kingdom, *Information and Software Technology*, Vol. 37, No. 9, pp. 467-477
14. Heineman, G. T., Botsford, J. E., Caldiera, G., Kaiser, G. E., Kellner, M. I., Madhavji, N. H. (1994) Emerging technologies that support a software process life cycle, *IBM Systems Journal*, Vol. 33, No. 3, pp. 501-529
15. Henderson, J. C., Cooprider, J. G. (1990) Dimensions of I/S planning and design aids: A functional model of CASE technology, *Information Systems Research*, Vol. 1, No. 3, pp. 227-254
16. Herbsleb, J., Zubrow, D., Goldenson, D., Hayes, W., Paulk, M. (1997) Software quality and the Capability Maturity Model, *Communications of the ACM*, Vol. 40, No. 6, pp. 30-40
17. Iivari J. (1996) Why are CASE Tools not used?, *Communications of the ACM*, Vol.39, No.10, pp. 94-103
18. Iivari, J., Hirscheim, R., Klein, H. K. (1999) Beyond Methodologies: Keeping up with Information Systems Development Approaches through Dynamic Classification, *Proceedings of the 32nd, Hawaian International Conference on Systems Sciences*, pp.1-10

19. Iivari, J. and Huisman, M. (2001) The relationship between organisational culture and the deployment of systems development methodologies, in Dittrich, K., Geppert, A. and Norrie, M. C., *Advanced Information Systems Engineering*, Springer-Verlag, Berlin, 2001, pp. 234-250
20. Introna, L. D., Whitley, E. A. (1997) Against methodism, Exploring the limits of methods, *Information Technology & People*, Vol.10, No. 1, pp. 31-45
21. Isoda, S., Yamamoto, S., Kuroki, H., Oka, A. (1995) Evaluation and Introduction of the Structured Methodology and a CASE Tool, *Journal of Systems Software*, Vol.28, No.1, pp. 49-58
22. Karahanna, E., Straub, D. W., Chervany, N. L. (1999) Information technology adoption across time: A cross-sectional comparison of pre-adoption and post-adoption beliefs, *MIS Quarterly*, Vol. 23, No. 2, pp. 183-213
23. Kwon, T. H., Zmud, R. W. (1987) Unifying the Fragmented Models of Information Systems Implementation, in Boland, R. J., Hirschheim, R. A. (eds.) *Critical Issues in Information Systems Research*, John Wiley & Sons, New York, pp. 227-251
24. Lee, J., Kim, S. (1992) The relationship between procedural formalization and MIS success, *Information and Management*, Vol.22, pp. 89-111
25. Leonard-Barton, D. (1987) Implementing structured software methodologies: a case of innovation in process technology, *Interfaces*, Vol. 17, No. 3, pp. 6-17
26. McChesney, I. R., Glass, D. (1993) Post-implementation management of CASE methodology, *European Journal of Information Systems*, Vol. 2, No. 3, pp. 201-209
27. Moore, G. C., Benbasat, I. (1991) Development of an instrument to measure the perceptions of adopting an Information Technology innovation, *Information Systems Research*, Vol. 2, No. 3, pp. 192-222
28. Nandhakumar, J., Avison, D. E. (1999) The fiction of methodological development: A field study of information systems development, *Information Technology & People*, Vol. 12, No. 2, pp. 176-191
29. Orlikowski, W. J. (1993) CASE Tools as Organizational change: Investigating Incremental and Radical changes in Systems Development, *MIS Quarterly*, Vol. 17, No. 3, pp. 309-340
30. Peacham, D. (1985) Structured methods – ten questions you should ask, *Data Processing*, Vol. 27, No. 9, pp. 28-30
31. Prescott, M. B., Conger, S. A. (1995) Information Technology Innovations: A Classification by IT Locus of Impact and Research Approach, *The DATABASE for Advances in Information Systems*, Vol. 26, No. 2/3, pp. 20- 42
32. Rai, A., Howard, G. S. (1994) Propagating CASE usage for Software Development: An Empirical Investigation of Key Organizational Correlates, *OMEGA*, Vol. 22, No. 2, pp. 133-147
33. Roberts, T. L., Hughes, C. T. (1996) Obstacles to implementing a systems development methodology, *Journal of Systems Management*, Vol. 47, pp. 36-40
34. Roberts, T. L., Gibson, M. L., Fields, K. T., Rainer, R. K. (1998) Factors that impact implementing a SDM, *IEEE Transactions on Software Engineering*, Vol. 24, No.8, pp. 640-649
35. Rogers, E. M. (1995) *Diffusion of Innovations*, The Free Press, New York

36. Swanson, E. B. (1994) Information Systems Innovation Among Organizations, *Management Science*, Vol. 40, No. 9, pp. 1069-1092
37. Tesch, D. B., Klein, G., Sobol, M. G. (1995) Information System Professionals' Attitudes: Development Tools and Concepts, *Journal of Systems Software*, Vol. 28, No.1, pp. 39-47
38. Vessey, I., Jarvenpaa, S. L., Tractinsky, N. (1992) Evaluation of vendor products: CASE tools and methodology companions, Communications of the ACM, Vol. 35, No. 4, pp. 90-105
39. Wynekoop J.L., Russo N.L. (1997) Studying SDM: an examination of research methods, Information Systems Journal, Vol. 7, pp. 47-65

Supporting the Deployment
of Object-Oriented Frameworks

Daqing Hou, H. James Hoover, and Eleni Stroulia

Department of Computing Science, University of Alberta
Edmonton, Alberta Canada T6G 2E8
{daqing,hoover,stroulia}@cs.ualberta.ca

Abstract. Although they are intended to support and encourage reuse, Object-Oriented application frameworks are difficult to use. The architecture and implementation details of frameworks, because of their size and complexity, are rarely fully understood by the developers that use them. Instead, developers must somehow learn just enough about the parts of the framework required for their task. Faced with a framework problem, the developer will ask for assistance or muddle through using a trial-and-error approach. In many cases, they will not learn what the framework designer had in mind as the proper solution to their problem, and thus misuse the framework.

This paper is a preliminary look at the kinds of problems faced by framework users, and how the framework developer can assist in mitigating these problems. Our goal is to develop mechanisms for detecting when the framework user has violated the conditions of use intended by the framework developer, using static analysis of structure, and dynamic analysis of behavior.

Keywords Object-Oriented frameworks, framework deployment, static analysis, model checking

1 Introduction

Object-Oriented frameworks are composed of collaborating classes that provide standard solutions to a family of problems commonly encountered among applications in some domain. Framework builders provide mechanisms, the variation points, that enable developers to use the framework to construct their specific application.

While a deep understanding of general framework based development [4] remains a research problem, there are many frameworks used for production development. Having chosen a framework, how does the development team address the problem of correct usage of the chosen framework?

The size and complexity of frameworks, and their notorious lack of design and intended-usage documentation make framework-based development a learning-intensive and error-prone process. It is quite common for framework users to misunderstand the relation between their application and how the framework designer intended the framework to be used, resulting in overly complex solutions, or subtle bugs.

Experience with using industrial strength frameworks has shown that in order for frameworks users to understand and properly use a framework, precise, concise, and complete documentation is needed. However, textual and diagrammatic documents are informal and in general, we do not know yet how to judge whether a programmer has understood a document [7]. Other conventional approaches such as framework design review, manual code inspection, and testing can also be helpful.

Frameworks are supposed to capture commonality in a way that makes reuse easier. But applying most current frameworks requires a nontrivial body of knowledge about the framework on the part of users. Lack of understanding makes debugging difficult because it can be hard to follow a thread of execution that is mostly buried in the framework code. Testing is similarly difficult, since it often requires a fundamental understanding of the architecture of the framework.

For the framework user with shallow knowledge, something more akin to type-checking is desirable. That is, the framework developer takes on the burden of describing how to properly use the framework, and then compliance by the framework user is checked mechanically. Although correct type matching is no guarantee that one has called a function properly, it does catch many common mistakes. We would like something similar to hold for framework use.

We use the term *framework constraint* to denote the knowledge that a user needs to know in order to use a framework properly. The idea is to formalize the framework constraints on hot spots and check whether a framework instantiation satisfies these constraints. Our goals are to create specification languages and tools that enable framework builders to encode their knowledge about the framework and use the knowledge to check user applications.

We investigate the feasibility of two technologies, namely, static analysis and model checking, to the problem. Along that line, framework constraints can be categorized into *structural constraints* and *behavioral constraints*. Structural constraints can be evaluated by parsing and analyzing source code while behavioral constraints could be dealt with by model checking.

The rest of section 1 formulates some related framework concepts. After that, section 2 analyzes the framework use problems and causes. The bulk of the paper, from section 3 to 5 describes our proposed solution and experience: Section 3 describes a preliminary version of our specification language FCL for structural constraints. Section 4 gives a specific example for FCL. Section 5 describes our experience with using SPIN/Promela to model check frameworks. Finally, section 6 concludes the paper, summarizing the identified problems and some future work.

1.1 Related Concepts of OO Frameworks

For the clarity of presentation, this subsection defines the following terms: *framework builder, framework user, framework architecture, framework classes, inter-*

nal classes, framework derived classes, framework parts, application classes, hot spots, framework instantiation, framework instance/application, and *framework constraints.*

People who build the framework are referred to as *framework builders* and people who use the framework are called *framework users*. When no confusion occurs, we may also use *builders* and *users* instead. The process of building applications based on frameworks is called *framework instantiation* and the generated application is referred to as *framework instance* or simply *application* when appropriate.

Framework architecture (or *architecture*) defines the typical software architecture for problems in the domain. It comprises both abstract and concrete classes, which can be collectively referred as *framework classes*. Some framework classes are *internal classes* and are not intended to be visible to framework users. Only concrete framework classes can be internal. In most cases, framework users create additional classes by subclassing abstract classes. We call these additional classes *framework derived classes* and the abstract classes *hot spots* [14] or *variation points*. Sometimes, framework builders can predict potential subclasses and provide them as accompanying parts of the framework. For example, in MFC [15] (Microsoft Foundation Classes), class `CCtrlView` has the predefined concrete subclasses `CEditView`, `CListView`, `CRichEditView`, and `CTreeView` [17]. These additional classes capture common implementations of the framework architecture and are referred to as *framework parts*. For those parts of the application design not covered by frameworks, new classes need to be developed to fulfill the actual applications requirements. We refer to these new classes as *application classes*. Collectively, framework derived classes and application classes are sometimes called a *framework extension*.

Thus, in the context of frameworks, an application can be composed of one or more framework architectures, framework parts of each framework (if any), framework derived classes, and application classes.

Framework constraints (see section 3) are rules and conventions for a framework to which any framework extension has to conform. Quite often, these rules and constraints are either implicit in or missing from existing documentation. Making them explicit and checkable should help framework users verify that they have used the framework as intended.

2 Problems Faced by Framework Users

Any tools that purport to support framework use should initially focus on the most common problems. What kinds of problems do framework users face in practice, and is it possible to mitigate them? Although frameworks vary in size and complexity, users face the same kinds of problems. We began by examining two frameworks, Microsoft's MFC and our own CSF (Client/Server Framework). MFC is probably the most successful industrial foundation framework. CSF was developed to as part of our research on frameworks at the University of Alberta and has been used in an undergraduate project course for several terms.

2.1 Common Types of Questions on Frameworks

We did a short investigation of MFC's architecture and implementation, collecting and analyzing questions which users posted to two MFC news groups, comp.os.mswindows.programmer.tools.mfc and microsoft.public.vc.mfc. We then developed a preliminary classification taxonomy for these questions, consisting of the following five areas.

- "Where" Questions
  Developers often need to introduce application-specific behavior to override or specialize the default behavior of the framework, but do not know where to start. Due to the difficulty of understanding framework code and improper documentation, frequently framework users are unclear or even unaware about the "template methods" they should reuse and the nature of the "hook" methods they should develop [16,8].
- "How to" Questions
  Many questions asked about MFC are of the "how to" type. Examples of this category are "how to translate an Enter key into Tab key so that you can use the Enter key to traverse widgets in a way similar to using the Tab key", or "how to change an Edit's background at run time". To answer this type of questions, the application developer needs to understand the architecture of the underlying framework, specifically, the message and command routing logic [5].
- "Why" Questions
  Quite often, errors in the developers' assumptions about the framework architecture lead to improper extensions that exhibit bizarre behavior. The precise error is difficult to localize, since it is not necessarily in the application code itself and debugging requires a deeper understanding of the framework architecture and possibly its code structure.
- "Does it support" Questions
  Quite often, ambiguities in the framework documentation result in the developer wondering whether or not a particular feature required of the application is possible to implement within the framework. These issues are especially critical, because application development cannot even start without having a resolution for them.
- "What If Not Supported" Questions
  Finally, a large number of questions deal with deficiencies of the framework. Sometimes, a poor choice of framework leads to architectural conflicts or mismatch [9] between the desired application and the framework, in which case little can be done. Often there are simply gaps in the framework where it was never designed to accommodate the users' desired extensions. In this case, it may be possible to evolve the framework to fill these gaps in a manner consistent with the original framework designers intent.

Our study of the use of the CSF framework and the questions asked by the undergraduates students who used it in their course projects revealed, not surprisingly, the same types of questions.

2.2 Underlying Causes

It is difficult to communicate the intended use of a framework to the users who need to develop applications. Sheer size can be one factor: a framework with hundreds of classes, like MFC, is quite daunting to learn even for an expert. Often domain-specific knowledge must first be acquired in order to appreciate how to use the framework [3]. Even small frameworks can have complex behavior that is not obvious from reading static artifacts like code. Here is a brief list of common hurdles in understanding a framework.

Environmental Dependency Frameworks are usually built on top of a certain platform, depend on some supporting techniques, and serve a specific domain. For example, several key design decisions of MFC are based on the Microsoft implementation of the concepts of message queues, event looping and dispatching, window structure, window class, window procedure, and window subclassing. As a result, to understand and use MFC, a programmer must first get familiar with the Windows operating system.

Structural Coupling One problem in using and understanding frameworks is the numerous and varied dependencies between their classes. These structural dependencies comprise an important part of the complexity of frameworks. There are several ways for two classes to work together. Suppose that we have two objects, X and Y, and X needs a reference, *ref*, to Y. Four techniques are commonly used to retrieve the reference:

- X creates and uses Y and then discards it. *ref* is a local variable of some method of X's class; the type of *ref* (i.e. a class) is statically compiled into X's class;
- *ref* is an instance variable of X and references Y. This is a more flexible approach because *ref* can be changed at run-time;
- Y is passed to X as a parameter of some method. This is even more flexible because the responsibility of obtaining a reference no longer lies in X's class;
- Y is retrieved from another object. This object can, for instance, be a factory or a collection.

For example, the Observer pattern [8], used in this paper to illustrate our method, uses techniques 3 and 4. Firstly, the *observer* is registered as being interested in certain event originating from the *subject*. This is done using technique 3: *observer* is passed to the *subject* as a parameter of its **attach** method and the *subject* stores the reference to the *observer* in its collection (usually a list). Later, whenever the event occurs, the *subject* retrieves the previously stored reference from its collection property and calls the *observer*'s **update** method.

Behavioral Coupling O-O systems have complex message dispatch mechanisms that make behavior difficult to comprehend. One example of behavioral coupling is the interaction and dependency between the so-called template [16,8] and hook methods. Template methods define the generic flow of control and interaction between objects; hook methods enable the customization of the behavior of a template method, through interface implementation, or class extension and method overriding [14,10]. Although in theory we have accumulated a body of knowledge on the forms of method interaction, in practice it is not easy for users to recognize the nature of the interaction from the code. A message from the MFC newsgroup amply demonstrates this:

> "This (*when or if you should call the base class version (of functions) from within your overridden version? ... And if you do call the base class version, should you call the base class version before the code in your version or after*) is (*what*) I think one of the most confusing things about MFC... I really think the documentation for all these CWnd virtual functions and message handlers should spell this out clearly, case by case. As it is, the only way is to look at the source code for the base class, but since these functions may or may not be implemented at each level of the class hierarchy it is not that easy."

3 The Framework Constraints Language – FCL

In our study of frameworks, we have encountered recurrent types of rules and conventions regulating how to correctly use a framework; we call these rules *structural constraints*. Simple examples of structural constraints can be the cardinality of certain objects, their creation and deletion, and method invocation etc. To formally specify structural constraints we are in the process of developing a language called FCL (Framework Constraints Language). The language is still very preliminary and evolving rapidly as we use it.

This section introduces the main types of constraints that have been identified to date. To help understand the grammar (the appendix to this paper), the corresponding non-terminal symbols are also provided for the description of each construct. A concrete example of the FCL specification for the Observer pattern is given in the next subsection.

An FCL specification starts with a class list section. The section can be used to organize classes into groups such as framework classes, abstract classes, and concrete classes (*ClassListSection*) etc. The class list section is followed by one or more units (*Unit*). Each unit consists of a scope (*Scope*) and a list of constraints. A scope can specify a group of classes either explicitly through class names or through pattern matching. The scope is then followed by the list of constraints (*Constraints*). All classes in the scope must conform to the constraints.

Constraints are further decomposed into primitive and compound ones. Primitive constraints for classes can be either about variables (*OnVar*) or about methods (*OnMethod*). Constraints on the definition of variables (*OnVar*) include their types, cardinality, visibilities, and access scope (i.e., *iVar* for instance variable, *gVar* for global variable, and *lVar* for local variable).

A method constraint has two parts: a method signature and a body (*OnMethod*). The signature identifies the method that will be restricted. The body contains constraints that the method has to satisfy. The constraints on methods (*MethodConstraint*) can be method invocation (*MethodCall*) and sequence (*Sequential*). They can be used to specify causal and temporal relations among methods, i.e., m1 calls m2 and m1; m2, respectively. There are also two predefined predicates on variables, *use* and *change*, which allow one to specify constraints on the usage and modification of variables.

A constraint may depend on other constraints. For instance, *"if you subclass X then you must also subclass Y"*. Compound constraints are formed by connecting constraints with the usual logic connectives, implication, negation, conjunction, and disjunction (*Constraint*).

Some example constraints are as follows:

- For a framework class X, one constraint can be *"framework users must/must not subclass X"* (*Subclass*). In order to specify limits on the number of subclasses, the integral range is introduced. It includes greater than, less than or equal, and their combination (*Dim*). Integral ranges can also be used to restrict the number of variables and methods.
- Although the advocated mechanism for using a whitebox framework is inheritance, framework builders may also permit users to augment class X directly. Correspondingly, other constraints on X can be *"must/mustn't add certain instance variables"*, *"cardinality and/or type of instance variables Y must/mustn't satisfy certain condition"* (*OnVar*), *"must/mustn't add/call certain methods"* (*OnMethod*). These can also be applied to framework derived classes.
- For a framework derived class X, constraints may be *"class X must/mustn't override a certain method"* (*MethodHead*), *"must/ mustn't add certain instance variables"*, *"cardinality and/or type of instance variables Y must/mustn't satisfy certain condition"* (*OnVar*), *"must/mustn't add a certain method"* (*OnMethod*).
- Constraints on a hook method can be: *"must/mustn't delete/change/use parameter variable"* (*Predicate*), *"must/mustn't define variables"* (*OnVar*), *"must call methods before/after some point"* (*MethodCall* and *Sequential*), etc. (*MethodConstraint*)

4 An Example: Structural Constraints for the Observer Pattern

Design patterns can be seen as small frameworks made of a few classes. Although we could have given other examples, for the purpose of presentation, we choose to use the Observer pattern to discuss some of the constraints on the pattern and how to specify them in FCL.

As shown in figure 1, Subject and Observer are the framework classes of the Observer pattern. A Subject may have one or more Observers associated with it. All observers are notified whenever the Subject changes its state. In response, each Observer will query the Subject to synchronize its state with the Subject.

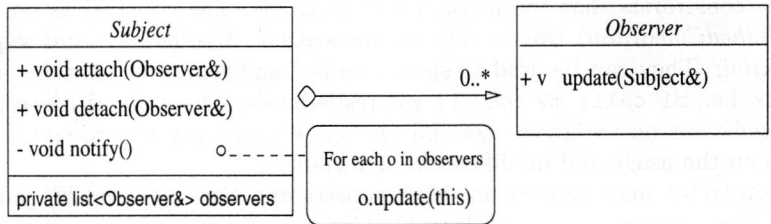

Fig. 1. Class diagram for the observer pattern

```
//Abstract classes
abstractclass = [Subject, Observer]
frameworkclass = [abstractclass, model, view]
```

These two statements define two class lists, one for the abstract classes, Subject and Observer, the other for Subject, Observer, and their subclasses, model and view.

```
subclass model of Subject conforms to
{
        iVar vars (>0)
        private(vars)
        method methods (>1)
        exists m: methods, v: vars
        { change(v); notify()
        }
}
```

This constraint requires that, in the framework extension, there must be exactly one subclass of class Subject, which is referred to as model (here model is only a place holder, the actual subclass can use any name, say clock).

The statements in the curly brackets are constraints on the class model. The first statement, iVar vars (>0), says that class model must define at least one extra instance variable. However, we can predict nothing more about their types and cardinalities. The second statement requires these variables to be private. Similarly class model also must define at least two methods (see the third statement) because at least one method is needed to change state and the other to query the state (note that method is a keyword of FCL whereas methods is only an FCL variable that represents the set of methods of model). The last statement says that there must be at least one method, say m, in class model, which satisfies the following requirements:

- firstly, m changes some variable v in set vars;
- secondly, m must call the inherited notify method;
- and thirdly, the change must happen before the notify method is called.

```
subclass view (>=1) of Observer conforms to
{
        override update(Subject s)
        {
                s.methods
                !s.m
                !delete(s)
                !change(s)
        }
}
```

This constraint requires that in the framework extension, there must be at least one subclass of class Observer. These subclasses are collectively referred to as `view`. All classes in `view` must override the `update` method. Furthermore, this `update` method is required to call some methods of the actual parameter `s`, but not `m` (recall that `m` is defined in Subject and calls `notify` and `notify` invokes `update` in turn). The method `update` is also not permitted to delete or change `s`.

```
oneclass in !frameworkclass conforms to
{
        model o
        view v (>0)
        o.attach(v)
        o.m
        o.detach(v)
}
```

This statement requires that there must exist exactly one application class, which is referred to as `oneclass`, satisfying the followinf constraint: inside class `oneclass`, there is exactly one object of `model` created (`model o`) and at least one object of class `view` created (`view v(>0)`); there must be the invocations of methods `attach`, `m`, and `detach` of the object `o`.

```
!frameworkclass conforms to
{
        !model::notify()
        !view::update(*)
}
```

This statement says that in all classes except those in `frameworkclass`, there must not be the direct invocations of the methods `model::notify` and `view::update`.

5 Behavioral Constraints

Informally, behavioral constraints are the requirements that are put on applications by the framework but cannot be checked by static program analysis.

Typically such constraints specify a pattern of (two and more) states and/or events that characterizes applications' behavior. Examples of behavioral constraints are as follows:

1. Object interface protocols which are the FSM (finite state machine) specification of the method invocation order of objects. One formal treatment of object protocols appears in [13];
2. Control reachability, e.g., all hook methods must eventually be called, or, in MFC, all user defined message handlers must eventually be called;
3. Livelock-freedom, e.g., no livelocks are permitted in GUI programming.
4. Target existence, e.g., an object must exist when others send message to it.

A variety of temporal logics might be used for encoding behavioral constraints. We experimented with linear temporal logic (LTL) in our work, which is supported by a mature model checker, SPIN [11]. LTL is a propositional logic with the standard connectives &&, ||, ->, and !. It includes three temporal operators: <>p says that p holds at some point in the future, []p says that p holds at all points in the future, and the binary p U q operator says that p holds at all points up to the first point where q holds. An example LTL specification for the response property "all requests for a resource are followed by granting of the resource" is [](request -> <>granted).

Many efforts have been made to apply model checking to software artifacts including requirements specifications [1,2], architectures [12], and implementations [6]. When model checking software, one describes the software as a finite state-transition system, specifies system properties with a temporal logic formula, and checks, exhaustively, that all sequences of states satisfy the formula. Specifically, in the case of the model checker SPIN, its finite state model is written in the Promela language and its correctness properties in LTL. Users specify a collection of interacting processes whose interleaved execution defines the finite state model of system behavior. SPIN performs an efficient nonempty language intersection test to determine if any state sequences in the model conform to the negation of the property specification. If there are no such sequences then the property holds, otherwise the sequences are presented to the user as exhibits of erroneous system behavior.

In this approach, framework builders are responsible for constructing the validation model of the framework and defining its properties. Together with the framework, the validation model and the properties will be delivered to framework users to model-check the application. Since frameworks are meant for massive reuse, we argue that the framework builders' investment in constructing the validation model and defining the properties will be quickly amortized.

One of the major problems in model checking software is model construction: given real world software components built with sophisticated programming constructs which give rise to gigantic state spaces, generate correct compact representations for tractable model checking. In the next subsection, we describe our experience with using Promela to manually construct finite state models.

5.1 Using Promela to Model The Observer Pattern

We used the following strategy to model the behavior of the observer pattern. Classes are modeled as processes. These processes are embedded in an *atomic* statement to eliminate unnecessary interleaving execution.

Given a class P, to create an object for it, we use `run P(parameter list)`. Each object has a unique id, which is modeled by process id. Therefore, to create an object and get a reference to it, use `byte id; id = run P(parameter list)`. Note that we have defined `id` as type of byte, this is because currently SPIN supports at most 256 processes (that is, 256 objects in our case) simultaneously. Once created, the object keeps observing a rendezvous channel for messages intended for it.

In a sequential program, at any time, there is only one active method. Therefore, we define one single global rendezvous channel to synchronize method invocation among all objects. All objects keep polling the channel to look for messages directed to them. For an object, if there is no message or the message is not for it, it's blocked (this is implemented with the *eval* and *_pid* feature of Promela). The rendezvous channel is defined as follows:

```
chan Rendezvous = [0] of {
object,returnChannel,message,p1,p2, ...,pn}
```

This statement defines the variable `Rendezvous` as a rendezvous channel (as indicated by the dimension of 0) and the message format for the channel. A message consists of following elements:

- `object`: specifies the message reception object;
- `returnChannel`: is used to synchronize caller and callee;
- Method name (`message`): is type of `mtype`, which is the default enumeration type of SPIN; Currently, we assume no method name conflict among all classes and treat all method names as enumeration members of this type; If there are more than 256 messages, we could also model them as integer constants.
- n: is the largest number of parameters of all the methods.

In general, methods can also be modeled as processes. However, because of the potential state space explosion problem, we recommend inlining them into class processes whenever possible. Instance variables are modeled as local variables of processes.

Method invocation is synchronized using rendezvous. For each invocation, the caller site provides: object id (`object`), a rendezvous channel (`returnChannel`), method name (`message`), and a list of parameters (p1, p2, ..., pn).

The following two code segments illustrate how method calls are modeled. The caller site uses the following pattern:

```
...
//Each caller must define one local rendez-vous
chan returnChannel = [0] of {int};
...
```

```
Rendezvous!object,returnChannel,message,p1,p2,..., pn
returnChannel? returnValue;
// vp: Variable Parameters
returnChannel? vp1;
...
returnChannel? vpm;
```

The callee site uses the following pattern:

```
do
::Rendezvous?this,returnChannel,msg,p1,...,pn
      if
      ...
      ::msg == message -> do something;
            returnChannel!returnValue;
            returnChannel!vp1;
            ...
            returnChannel!vpm;
      ...
      :: msg == delete -> break;
            returnChannel!NULL
      fi
od
```

In the code, `this` represents the callee's pid. `returnChannel`, `msg`, and `p1` to `pn` are local variables of the callee process.

The purpose of `returnChannel` is to prevent the caller from proceeding unless the callee returns. When the callee finishes, it first sends the caller its return value, then the value of each variable parameter, if any.

Inheritance is also modeled. Each object of a concrete subclass automatically creates one internal object for each of its superclasses. All messages that are not recognized by one object are dispatched to its superclass objects.

For the Observer pattern, a small model was manually constructed. To test it, several artificial bugs were seeded into the model.

– The first bug is that the user code calls `update` directly;
– The second is sending a message to an already-deleted observer object;
– The third is terminating the program without freeing an object.

The frameworks constraints specifying the permitted patterns on method calls should ideally be expressed as trace clauses over the traces of the system. However, as discussed below, SPIN is limited in its capability for specifying event patterns. Instead, the constraints were specified using assertions.

The result is somewhat dissatisfying: model checking quickly found all the bugs, but it is not clear how well this technique generalizes and extends.

LTL supports only the specification of properties of state sequence instead of action/event sequence. But sometimes we need to write properties directly in terms of events, such as method invocation and return. On the surface, it seems that SPIN/Promela's trace assertion can be used for this purpose. But our initial experiment revealed several problems:

- SPIN can only trace events on a global channel;
- It does not support non-determinism;
- When specifying properties for sequential programs, constructs that can distinguish between causal relation and temporal relation between events are needed.

Specially, SPIN seems not to be designed to support the last point above. Actually, during our exploration of SPIN, we have found one bug in SPIN's implementation of trace assertion. This shows that probably the trace mechanism has not been extensively used [Gerard Holzmann, Personal Communication] in practice. Although we could work around by defining extra boolean variables to mark the invocation and return of method, thus express properties on events by state based LTL formula, this method is neither efficient nor straightforward.

Due to space limitation, readers are referred to [18] for further details.

6 Conclusions and Further Work

Many structural constraints are feasible to check. Checking these could achieve benefits similar to what compilers have done with static type checking.

A checker program is envisaged that understands the FCL specification, parses the application, and performs the conformance checking. In addition, our FCL definition is still in the demonstration stage, thus needs revision to add new types of constraints. One of our ongoing tasks is to formalize the core architecture of MFC and identify checkable structural constraints.

Checking behavioral constraints is more problematic. Since we use processes to model objects, one problem is how to model the visibility of objects. In addition, languages such as C++ and Java permit direct reference to the public variables of objects, thus the capability of modeling visibility would also be needed. Earlier versions of SPIN did support remote referencing, which could be used to achieve this. Unfortunately, to support partial order reduction of the state space, this feature has been removed from the newer versions. Although SPIN is not suited, other formalisms such as CTL (Computation Tree Logic) are worth investigating.

By the very nature of frameworks, the validation model must be incomplete. Therefore, there are two other important problems left:

- how to extract the other part of the validation model from application classes, and
- how to combine the two models to get a complete validation model of the application so that we can run model checking on it.

Further investigation to these problems is also needed.

Finally, section 2 only briefly summarizes the types of questions that framework users may have: they are by no means either the best classification or complete. Further empirical study is needed to provide more fine-grained knowledge.

Acknowledgements

The authors thank Marsha Chechik, Jim Cordy, Garry Froehlich, Amr Kamel, Rudolf Keller, Andrew Malton, and Keny Wong for their discussion and assistance during various stages of the project. We also want to thank the three anonymous reviewers for their very insightful comments on the paper.

This work was supported by the Natural Sciences and Engineering Research Council of Canada, and the Alberta Science Research Authority.

References

1. R. Anderson, P. Beame, S. Burns, W. Chan, F. Modugno, D. Notkin, and J. Reese. Model Checking Large Software Specifications, Software Engineering Notes, 21(6):156–166, November 1996.
2. J. Atlee, J. Gannon. State-based Model Checking of Event-driven System Requirements, IEEE Transactions on Software Engineering, 19(1):24–40, June 1993.
3. A. Birrer, T. Eggenschwiler. Frameworks in the Financial Engineering Domain: An Experience Report, Proceedings of ECOOP 93, 1993.
4. J. Bosch, P. Molin, M. Mattsson and P. Bengtsson. Obstacles in Object-Oriented Framework-based Software Development, ACM Computing Surveys Symposia on Object-Oriented Application Frameworks, 1998.
5. P. DiLascia. Meandering Through the Maze of MFC Message and Command Routing, Microsoft System Journal, July 1995. Available at <http://www.microsoft.com/msj/0795/dilascia/dilascia.htm>
6. M. Dwyer, V. Carr, and L. Hines. Model Checking Graphical User Interfaces Using Abstractions, In LNCS 1301, pages 244–261. Proceedings of the 6th European Software Engineering Conference held jointly with the 5th ACM SIGSOFT Symposium on the Foundations of Software Engineering, September 1997.
7. G. Froehlich, H. J. Hoover, L. Liu, P. G. Sorenson. Hooking into Object-Oriented Application Frameworks, Proceedings of the 1997 International Conference on Software Engineering, Boston, Mass., May 17-23, 1997.
8. E. Gamma, R. Helm, R. E. Johnson, J. O. Vlissides. Design Patterns–Elements of Reusable Object-Oriented Software, Addison Wesley, 1994.
9. D. Garlan, R. Allen, J. Ockerbloom. Architectural Mismatch or Why it is so hard to build systems out of existing parts, Proceedings of the 17th International Conference on Software Engineering, April 1995.
10. R. Helm, I. M. Holland, D. Gangopadhyay. Contracts: Specifying behavioral Compositions in Object-Oriented Systems, Proceedings of ECOOP/OOPSLA 90, Ottawa, Canada, 1990.
11. G. Holzmann. Design and Validation of Computer Protocols, Prentice Hall, Englewood Cliffs, NJ, 1991.
12. G. Naumovich, G. Avrunin, L. Clarke, and L. Osterweil. Applying Static Analysis to Software Architectures. In LNCS 1301. The 6th European Software Engineering Conference held jointly with the 5th ACM SIGSOFT Symposium on the Foundations of Software Engineering, September 1997.
13. O. Nierstrasz. Regular Types for Active Objects, Object-Oriented Software Composition, O.Nierstrasz and D.Tsichritzis eds, Prentice Hall, 1995, pp.99–121.
14. W. Pree. Design Patterns for Object-Oriented Software Development, Addison Wesley, 1995.

15. G. Shepherd, S. Wingo. MFC Internals: Inside the Microsoft Foundation Class Architecture, Addison Wesley, 1996.
16. R. J. Wirfs-Brock, B. Wilkerson, and L. Wiener. Designing Object-Oriented Software, Prentice Hall, Englewood Cliffs, NJ, 1990.
17. Microsoft Developer Network. Available at <http://www.msdn.microsoft.com>
18. Promela Model for the Observer Pattern. Available at <http://www.cs.ualberta.ca/~daqing/frameworks/so>
19. The Client Server Framework Web Site. Available at <http://www.cs.ualberta.ca/~garry/framework>

A Appendix: FCL Grammar

```
Legend note: all symbols starting with capital letters are nontermi-
nal. ::=, [], {}+, | and empty are preserved as meta-symbols. All
others are terminal symbols.
LType and LMethodProt are programming language specific definition
of type and method signature, which are omitted.

FrameworkConstraint ::= ClassListSection Toplevel

    ClassListSection ::= ClassList | ClassList ClassListSection
        ClassList::= ListName = "[" List "]"
        List       ::= Class | Class , List
        Class      ::= Id | ListName
        ListName ::= Id

    Toplevel ::= Unit | Unit Toplevel
        Unit ::= Scope [conform|conforms] to { Constraints }
                 | Unit->Unit
    Scope ::= ListName | SubClass | !Scope
              | NameDecl in Scope
        SubClass ::= subClass NameDecl of Class
        NameDecl ::= Id [(Dim)]
        Dim       ::= BasicDim | BasicDim, BasicDim
        BasicDim ::= Constant | > Constant | <= Constant

    Constraints ::= Constraint | Constraint Constraints

    Constraint  ::= OnVar | OnMethod |
        Constraint -> Constraint | !Constraint |
        {Constraints} | Constraint "||" Constraint
        OnVar ::= Type NameDecl | Predicate ( Ids )
            Type ::= LType | iVar [LType] | lVar [LType]
                   | gVar [LType]
            OnMethod   ::= MethodHead { MethodConstraints }
                         | MethodConstraint
            MethodHead ::= [override] LMethodProt | Qualified
                         | method NameDecl
                Qualified  ::= [exists] {Id: Id [,]}+
```

```
                              | forall {Id: Id[,]}+
            MethodConstraints ::= MethodConstraint
                              | MethodConstraint MethodConstraints
            MethodConstraint  ::= OnVar | Predicate ( Ids )
                              | MethodCall [(Ids)] | Sequential
                              | MethodConstraint->MethodConstraint
                              | !MethodConstraint
                              | { MethodConstraints }
                              | MethodConstraint "||" MethodConstraint
                  MethodCall  ::= [Class::] Id | Id.Id
                  Predicate   ::= use | change | delete
                              | public | protected | private
                  Sequential  ::= MethodConstraint ; Sequential
                              | MethodConstraint ; MethodConstraint
/*
*Simple non terminal symbols
*/
Constant ::= integer constant
Id       ::= Identifier
Ids      ::= empty | Id | Id, Ids | *
```

A Conceptual Modeling Approach to Semantic Document Retrieval

Terje Brasethvik [1] and Jon Atle Gulla [2]

[1] Norwegian University of Science and Technology, Trondheim
brase@idi.ntnu.no
[2] Elexir Sprach- und Informationstechnologie, Munich*
jag@elexir.de

Abstract. This paper describes an approach to semantic document retrieval geared towards cooperative document management. In our conceptual modeling approach, a semantic modeling language is used to construct a domain model of the subject domain referred to by the document collection. This domain model is actively used for the tasks of document classification and search. Moreover, linguistic techniques are used to facilitate both the construction of the model and its use. This paper presents our prototype model-based classification and search tool and how it is applied on a document collection from a Norwegian company.

1 Introduction

Conceptual modeling languages, techniques and tools serve different purposes with respect to Information Systems. In particular conceptual models serve as a vehicle of communication between various stakeholders, they facilitate information exchange and they provide (a formalized) documentation of several perspectives of the system as well as the Universe of Discourse. In areas like information and knowledge management and ERP systems, models are not only used during system development, but may also be used actively as access points to information during the whole system lifecycle [1]

Several approaches to using conceptual models in the design of web-based information systems have been proposed (see e.g. [2][3]). However, there are relatively few approaches that use conceptual modeling techniques as access points to information on the Web. This is rather surprising, as the ability to describe information precisely is central in much current research and standardization efforts, such as the Semantic Web [4] and the OntoWeb [5] initiatives. Of particular importance here is the construction of ontologies to facilitate information exchange. So far, efforts in these areas have come from Artificial Intelligence and Library Science, rather than from the modeling communities. One possible reason for this is that conceptual modeling techniques can be too labor intensive for the magnitude of the world wide web in general.

---

* Elexir is a subsidiary of Fast Search & Transfer, http://www.fast.no.

It is our claim that conceptual modeling languages are useful in information retrieval and information management on the web. In smaller and more restricted settings than the whole web, such as Intranets, Special Interest Groups and Project web sites, these techniques may be made to scale. Also, in these settings web tools will have to be more situation-specific and are often designed to support the activities of the users, particularly with respect to document classification and retrieval.

This paper describes an approach to semantic document retrieval geared towards cooperative document management. A semantic modeling language is used to construct a domain model of the subject domain referred to by the document collection. Whereas this domain model is central in document classification and search, linguistic techniques are used to facilitate both the construction of the model and its use. The techniques represent an interface between the textual documents and the formal concepts represented in the model and partly automate the user tasks.

We start in Section 2 by describing the notion of cooperative document management and the problems related to semantic document retrieval. Section 3 describes our approach in detail, while Section 4 presents our prototype applied on a small example from a Norwegian company, while section 5 gives a presentation of related work.

2 Cooperative Document Management

Work in organizations today is document intensive. A substantial amount of information in an organization is resident in documents. The ability to retrieve and extract information from these documents is becoming increasingly important [6][7] and is a natural part of such efforts as knowledge management and organizational memories: *"Insights drawn from the documents are seldom made explicit, although persons who work in teams, form a group or belong to a community would greatly profit from sharing their knowledge." [6]*.

In semantic document retrieval, the challenge is to express document semantics in a formalism that enables efficient document retrieval and increases reuse of documents and their enclosed knowledge. This is a distinguishable part of document management and is something we will refer to as *cooperative document management* for the rest of this paper.

As long as documents are in their production phase, they are often subject to *local management*, i.e. they are guarded by their authors and distributed to a limited audience like the project group. The problem of document management arises when these documents are to be made available outside their local production context, i.e. when they are to be used and reused by other actors, possibly in different settings and locations. Web technology in various flavors is used to make documents available, as in Intranets and community web sites. However, there are no explicit mechanisms available to describe the semantics of these documents and to classify and organize them for the benefit of later retrieval and use. For these purposes, one turns to document descriptive meta-data [8][9]. The need for meta-data is situation specific. Various schemes for describing document semantics for example use of selected keywords, written abstracts, text-indices or auto-summaries and even collectively created free-text descriptions. Our approach draws on the use of keywords from controlled vocabularies.

2.1 The Use of Conceptual Modeling

With controlled vocabularies, most of the work is put into the definition of the concepts in the vocabulary. A well-defined vocabulary becomes a tangible representation of the subject domain of the documents that can be applied directly in semantic description and retrieval of documents. Vocabularies are often created and expressed in their own "subject languages" and are useful in their own right: *"Using these to retrieve information provides a value added quality, can transform information into knowledge. When this happens, the subject language becomes an analogy for knowledge itself."* [10, p 127]

Fundamental to our approach is the idea that both document descriptions and query expressions can be created using concepts from the vocabulary. The "language problem" in retrieval systems arises when the descriptions and queries do not match.

With controlled vocabularies, the language problem is approached by the proper definition of the vocabulary and by the way this vocabulary is put to use in the actual semantic description and retrieval system. In our approach, concepts in the vocabulary must be given a domain specific definition and users must be able to interpret these concepts in order to create document descriptions and query expressions.

Models are constructed whenever knowledge should be communicated to others and examined independently of the knowledge originator [11]. Modeling languages provide the necessary mechanisms for converting personal knowledge into publicly available representations. Given appropriate tool support, modeling languages are in their very nature intended to support the shared construction of domain semantics, a process quite similar to the construction of domain vocabularies for document management. Conceptual modeling languages allow us to define concepts, their properties and interrelations, and to communicate this information to the stakeholders.

In an approach to document retrieval, the definition of concepts in the model must be textually grounded, i.e. the definition of a concept must be related to its appearances in the document text. We use linguistic analysis to create a *domain model lexicon* containing text level terms and word forms, thus representing the interface between the conceptual model and the document text.

2.2 The Example of Company N

Throughout this paper, we will illustrate our approach with an example from a large-scale Norwegian company, *Company N*. When projects are carried out, all documentation is stored in separate project databases in Lotus Notes, where documents are organized according to the appropriate project activity (or sub activity and task). Documents in this sense can mean anything from small half-a-page notes, written directly in the Notes text editor, to special documents like requirements specifications, that may be several hundred pages long and are added to the database as attachments. For documents written in Notes, the system offers a free-text search facility. The database naturally structures information according to properties relevant for projects, such as activity names, titles, descriptions, responsible, deadlines and so on. These are the contextual meta-data attributes that facilitate browsing and retrieval from the database.

Even if Lotus Notes provides advanced search facilities, these are hampered by several factors; Notes search is not efficient in cases where the volume of documents increase, there are large variances in document types, and of course when the document text is not available in Notes, but only as a "binary" attachment. Consequences of this is that users feel they have to really know which database to search, and even sometimes be familiar with the structure of the database in order to successfully find documents. Company N also uses a web-based Intranet built on top of Lotus Notes. In order to improve distribution of documents and information, selected documents are extracted from the Lotus Notes database and published on the fixed intranet.

3 The Approach

Our approach to semantic document retrieval is based on two fundamental assumptions: First, we believe that it is possible to create a domain model that defines the semantics of the subject domain and that both semantic document descriptions and query expressions can be created as selections – or fragments - of this domain model. Second, we believe that the users may use this domain model interactively in order to classify and retrieve documents semantically.

3.1 Overall Description

The functionality of the document system includes three fundamental processes:

> The construction of the domain model. This is mainly a manual process, though the model must reflect the subject domain of the documents. To speed up the modeling, we run several linguistic techniques on representative sets of documents from the domain.
>
> The classification of documents is done by selecting the appropriate domain model fragments and providing some meta data. Classifications may be made more precise by labeling relationships between the concepts. The process involves the automatic matching of document text against domain model concepts and leads to a proposal that shows the users which concepts were found in the model.
>
> The retrieval of documents is normally done by entering text queries that are matched against the model before they are sent to the retrieval system. However, the domain model may also be used interactively both for creating the search expression and for subsequent query refinement.

Figure 1 illustrates the construction of the domain model. In addition to the manual modeling and definition effort, we include two additional steps. We start out by analyzing a set of representative documents from the domain. The text of the documents is prepared by some linguistic techniques (described in section 3.3) before being compared with a reference document corpus. The result is a list of high-frequented terms from the document domain, as well as a correlation analysis that indicates some possible relations between these terms. This list is then taken as input to the cooperative and manual modeling process.

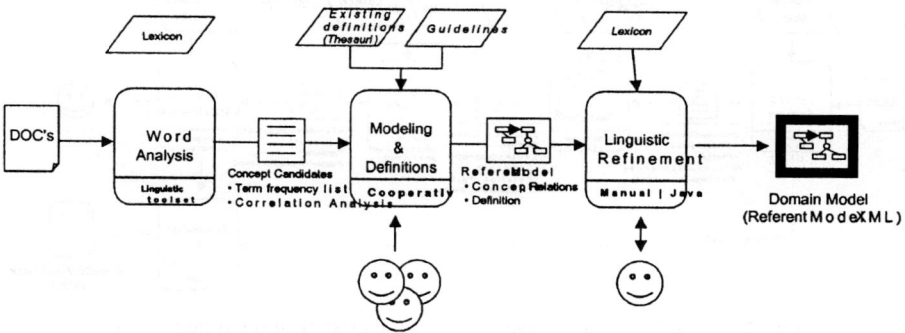

Fig. 1. Constructing the domain model

In our system we use the Referent Model Language [12] and the corresponding "Refedit" [13] modeling editor to define concepts and their properties. In order to prepare the models for automated matching against document text, we perform what we call a linguistic refinement of the model. For each concept in the model we add textual definitions of the concept, as well as what we call a term list, i.e. the list of terms/words that we will look for in a text as designators for concepts. Today this list is created manually, but this could be partly automated with the use of a synonym dictionary or some linguistic domain analyses to be described later. Furthermore, we add all conjugated word forms for the terms in the list. For Norwegian, these word forms are extracted from a full-form dictionary.

The process of classifying documents is described in figure 2. Again, this could be performed as a completely manual process, having the user interact with the model in order to select and refine the model fragment that best describes the semantics of the document at hand and to enter the meta-data attributes appropriate for this domain. However, if the model is prepared with the linguistic enhancements, we may perform an automated matching of the document text to give the users an indication as to which concepts could be relevant for a document. The user may also work simultaneously on a group of documents. For a group of documents, the matching provides an overview of how the text in the documents is reflected by the domain model concepts.

To utilize the relations between concepts, there are several possibilities. The correlation analysis from the initial document analysis step provides a statistical measure that indicates the strength of a relationship. These strengths or weights can be used to suggest expansions to either the document classification or the later queries. Simpler weighting algorithms such as counting the times a relation is used, is found in indexing approaches [14]. Our approach has so far been to go with the traditional modeling way, i.e. to provide meaningful names for a relation. For the task of classifying documents, these names can be entered at classification time for each document. Provided relation names are stored with the model as synonyms for the relation and then provided as "synonyms" for the relations in subsequent classification tasks.

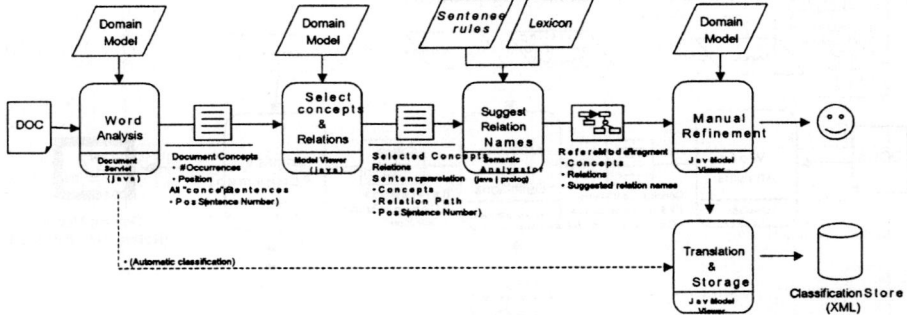

Fig. 2. Using the domain model for semantic classification of documents

In the end, the completed document description is converted to an appropriate storage format and installed in a classification store. The intention is to apply a standard meta-data representation format (such as the Dublin Core, RDF-XML serialization syntax) or to be able to use whatever indexing and retrieval machinery is available in the intranet setting. Today, we create our own DC-like description file in XML format.

Documents are retrieved by selecting model fragments that reflect the information need of the user. Even if the queries have to be created in terms of model concepts, the user may start with a text only query that is matched against the model in a similar way as for classification. However, in order to exploit the fact that the domain model represents "a map of available" information, our system supports a model-based interface to document retrieval that allows the users to interactively create and refine query expressions and visualizes how the result set is distributed in terms of model concepts.

3.2 System Architecture

An overview of the system architecture is presented in. The client, denoted CnS client (classification and search), is implemented as a standalone Java application. The CnS client has two modes, as indicated by the name. For classification, the client supports working simultaneously on a set of documents that are locally managed in a user profile. Also the linguistic enhancement of the model is performed using this client. In the search mode, the client communicates with a standard Web-browser for listing and viewing documents.

The server side components are implemented as a variety of add-ons to a standard Web server; mainly cgi-scripts and servlets. The client communicates with the server by executing http get/post commands and receiving XML encoded replies. As it is our goal to interface our system with existing retrieval machinery or document storage systems, we have not developed any extensive solutions to these functions, they are best considered working prototypes that are applicable in stand-alone settings.

A Conceptual Modeling Approach to Semantic Document Retrieval

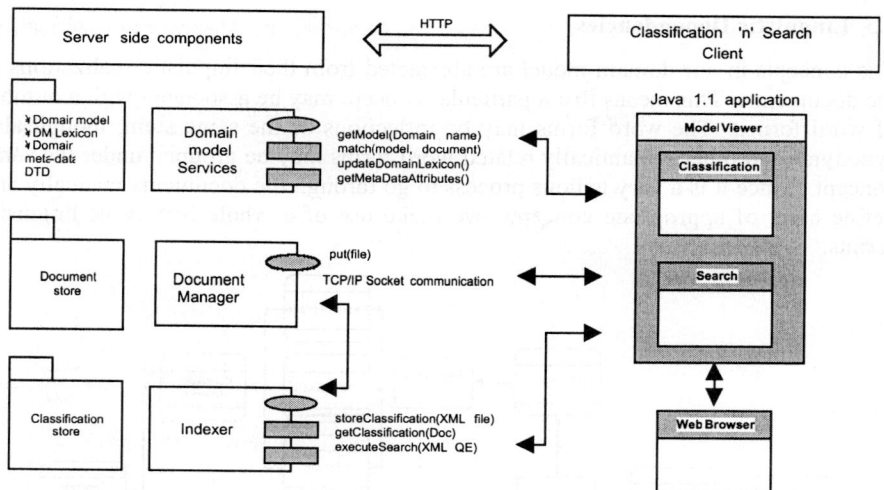

Fig. 3. Overview of system architecture

Currently all server-side storage of information is done using XML files. The main components on the server-side are:

- Domain services: these are cgi-scripts written in Perl that "deliver" the domain model and its additional files upon request. Models are stored as XML files. The linguistic enhancements, which we may denote the *domain model lexicon,* are stored in a separate XML file that refers to the concepts and relations in the model file. This lexicon is updated from the client.
- The domain services also include the document-model matcher that is used to match the text of a document against the concepts in the model by using the corresponding domain model lexicon. The matcher returns match-sets, describing for each matched concept, the match count as well as the list of sentences that included a reference to this concepts. The sentences are used to provide examples of concept occurrences and to provide input to the naming of relations. Currently the matcher only accepts pure text and HTML documents.
- The document manager is a simple Java servlet that accepts documents and stores these in a document directory, providing a unique URL for these. This component is only used when necessary in order to ensure that all documents can be accessed through a URL, the preferred point of access to documents from the other components.
- The indexer is a cgi-script written in Scheme. The name is somewhat misplaced, as no actual indexing takes place in our prototype, the script just accepts the final document description XML files created by the client and stores and manages these. The name indicates however, that in a real setting, this module will be replaced by an interface to existing indexing and retrieval machinery. The indexer also accepts query expressions in XML format, evaluates these against the stored description files and formulates the XML containing the query results returned to the client.

3.3 Linguistic Dependencies

The concepts in our domain model are abstracted from their linguistic realizations in the documents. This means that a particular concept may be associated with a number of word forms. The word forms may be inflections of the same stem, though also synonyms and other semantically related word forms may be grouped under the same concept. Since it is a very tedious process to go through the documents manually and define a set of appropriate concepts, we make use of a whole battery of linguistic scripts.

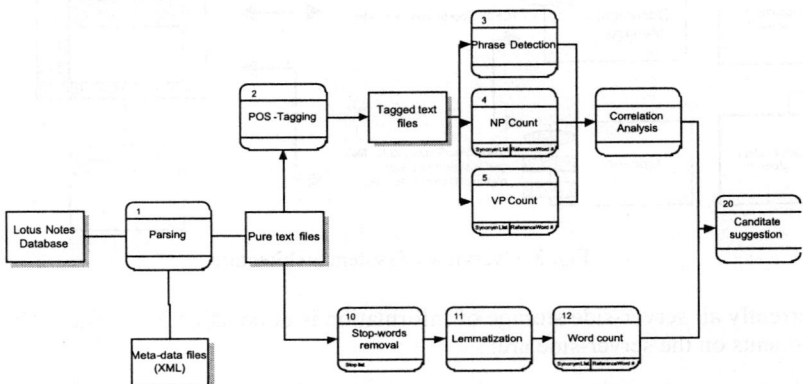

Fig. 4. Performing a linguistic analysis of documents in order to suggest concept candidates

Consider the document flow in figure 4, which shows how candidate concepts are generated from a set of Notes documents in Company N. After stripping off Notes-specific tags and other structural information in the documents, we use the resulting text files for two kinds of analyses:

- Detection of prominent phrases: Noun phrases (NPs) and verb phrases (VPs) may be good indications of concepts to be included in the domain model. To analyze grammatical phrases, we first tag the text with a simple part-of-speech tagger. Highly frequent phrases are detected, counted and inserted into our list of candidate concepts. For the relationships between concepts, we also need to expose the verbs commonly used in connection with these prominent nouns and noun phrases.
- Detection of prominent stems: After removing stop words from the document, we replace the word forms with the corresponding stems (lemmatization). We then count the number of occurrences of each stem and enter the most frequent stems into the list of candidate concepts.

With this approach, we help the domain experts in defining the concepts to be included in the domain model. A list of candidate multi-term concepts and a list of single-term concepts are presented to the user. However, we are only able to generate concept candidates, and a manual verification and refinement of this candidate set is necessary before creating the actual model.

4 System Walkthrough

In this section we go through a case study, in which our system was used to classify project documents for Company N. Our example is selected from an actual project database in Lotus Notes. For the subject domain "collaboration technologies" - a high level terminology document with definitions of central terms from the domain has formed the basis for our domain model. These terminology definitions are part of an initial "mission statement" for the project. However, the abstract terms found here are rarely found in the text of the actual project documents. Thus, in order to bridge the gap between the texts and the high-level terminology document, we have to add more detailed concepts to the model. In particular, we use the general abstraction mechanisms of our modeling language to specialize the original abstract concepts. Furthermore, we run the texts through the linguistic analysis in order to extract terms that can be associated with the concepts in the model. It is interesting to note that in the Company N example, the linguistic analysis discovers exactly the same terms in both Norwegian and English. Most of the documents are written in both languages. Since classification and retrieval is performed by concepts and we can attach terms in both languages to these concepts, our approach can just as easily classify documents in both languages.

4.1 Classification

Figure 5 shows our CnSClient in classification mode with a fragment of the particular domain model and a small set of corresponding documents. The domain model fragment shows the hierarchy of collaborative processes, which in the terminology definitions from Company N is defined as an aggregation of coordination, production and other activities. The fragment also shows the specialization of the concepts representing *coordination* and *production* activities.

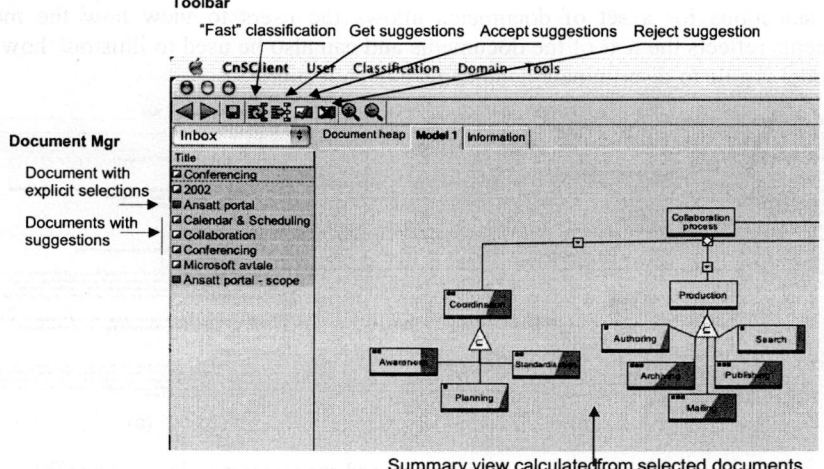

Fig. 5. The CnS tool: Classification modus - a working set of documents classified by way of the domain model

The classification of a document according to the domain model amounts to selecting the model concepts considered relevant for this document. In the classification mode, the toolbar provides the user with the options of getting suggestions from the server-side model-matcher as well as quick-keys for accepting or rejecting these suggestions. The "Fast" classification button lets the user accept whatever suggestions the server provides without further examination – our alternative to automatic classification. The document management function allows the user to manage a local set of documents that are under classification, these may be divided in folders. As is illustrated in the figure, the user may work with both one document at a time or a selection of documents simultaneously. The figure shows a summary view of all the selected documents. In this view the user has first received suggestions from the model-matcher and is now manually refining these suggestions. Suggestions are marked with a green triangle. In the document list, documents with unprocessed suggestions are marked with a small green triangle, while documents where the user has made actual selections (or accepted the suggestions) is marked with a filled rectangle.

The model-view shows a summary of how all the selected documents match the model. Green triangles illustrate concepts that have suggestions, the size of the triangle (along the bottom line) illustrates the percentage of documents in which this concept is suggested. The more suggestions, the more the triangle grows from right to left. Similarly, if a suggestion is accepted or a concept is manually selected, the triangle becomes a rectangle. As with suggestions, in the summary view the top of the rectangle grows from right to left according to the relative amount of documents in which this concept is selected. For example the concept of *archiving* is suggested in a little more than half of the documents, while it is actually selected in roughly one third. The concept of *authoring* however has only a small amount of suggestions and no actual selections. The blue dots in the upper left corner of the concepts is a proportional measure on how many hits this concept had in the last matching, and this number is unaltered by the actual selections. The way of summarizing the matches and selections for a set of documents allows the users to view how the model-concepts reflects the text of the documents and can also be used to illustrate how well a model is able to discriminate documents in a collection.

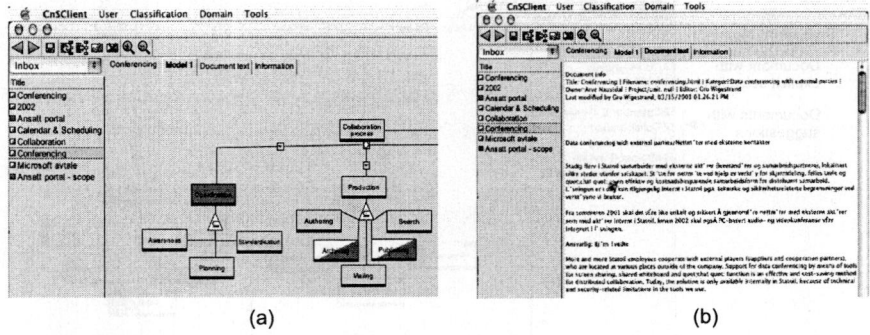

Fig. 6. Classfication of one document (a) and examining one documet text (b)

Figure 6a shows a user working on one single document. The coloring of the concepts follows the same rules as in the summary view, but with a single document, the suggestions are shown as a full triangle (archiving and publishing) and actual selections become a fully colored green rectangle (coordination). Users may accept and reject a single suggestion by clicking either on the green or white part of the concept respectively, or all suggestions at once by using the toolbar buttons. When examining classifications for one document, the user can examine the full text of the document by clicking on the document tab figure 6b.

Before saving the finished classifications, also the selected contextual meta-data attributes for the documents must be entered. Before storing the final classifications, the client performs a check of the selected document's classifications and provides warnings to the user according to some predefined rules. Currently the system will also signal if documents are classified according to only one concept or if a whole set of documents are all classified according to the exact same concepts.

4.2 Retrieval

In the retrieval mode, the user may start with a string representation of the query and then refine the query by interacting with the model. Search results are computed continuously during model interaction. Figure 7 illustrates the mapping of a search string to a model concept (collaboration process). By default, query expressions are expanded along the hierarchical abstraction mechanisms of the model (here aggregation and generalization) illustrated by a lighter shade of green the default expansion may be overridden simply by clicking on the abstraction symbol. Also in search mode, the blue dots are used to indicate the number of hits for a concept. They are shown also for concepts not included in the selection, in order to illustrate which concepts will return more documents in a subsequent refined search.

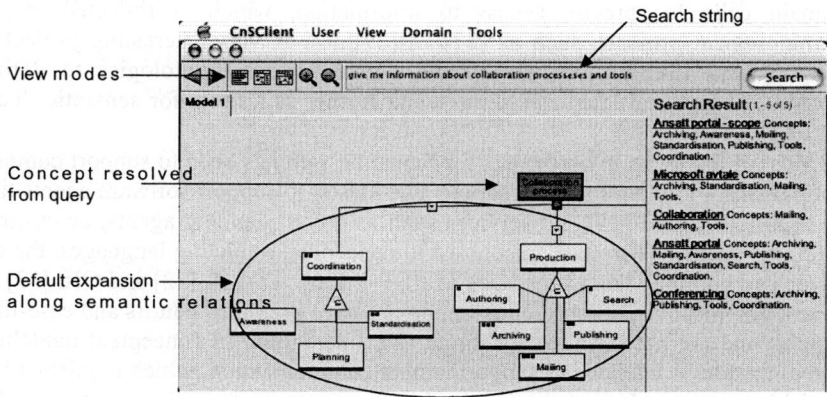

Fig. 7. Retrieval: Interacting with the model to create a search expression

5 Related Work

We define our approach as a cooperative document management system. Shared or common information space systems in the area of CSCW, like BSCW [15], ICE [16] or FirstClass [17] mostly use (small) static contextual meta-data schemes, connecting documents to for example people, tasks or projects. In general these systems rely on free-hand descriptions of the semantics of documents. An interesting approach to semantic classification of text in a cooperative system is found in the ConceptIndex system [6], where concepts are defined by attaching them to phrases – or text fragments – from the documents. Concepts are only defined by their occurrences and the actual domain vocabulary is not visible in the approach. This is contrary to our use of conceptual modeling, which provides mechanisms for explicit definition of the domain model.

The idea that users putting information on the web should also describe the semantics of this information, is at the very heart of the Semantic web initiative [18][4]. Semantic web relies on the Resource Description Framework [19] a semantic network inspired language for constructing meta-data statements. Pure RDF does however not include a facility for specifying the vocabulary used in the meta-data statements. This is however under development through what is denoted RDF-Schemas [20] and there are interesting work on document query-facilities that exploits the information in the RDF-schema when querying for documents [21]. Also, pure RDF does not include mechanisms to ensure shared semantics of information. For this, RDF statements should be connected to Ontologies. Ontologies [22][23] are nowadays being collaboratively created [24] across the Web, and applied to search and classification of documents. Ontobroker [25] and Ontosaurus [26] allow users to search and also annotate HTML documents with "ontological information". Domain specific ontologies or thesauri are used to improve search-expressions. The medical domain calls for precise access to information, which is reflected in several terminological projects, such as [27][28][29][30]. A very interesting project is the "OntoQuery" [31] project which uses domain specific ontologies to define the semantics of natural language phrases and further as a basis for semantic document retrieval.

Most of the focus in ontologies for Semantic web has been to support computers – not humans – looking for information. The idea is to support software agents that can be used to enable intelligent services such as travel planning agents, or eCommerce shopping agents. Therefore, in contrast to conceptual modeling languages, the current advocated ontology languages, such as RDF-S [20], DAML [32] and OIL [33] do not have a graphical visual representation, do not have graphical editors and case-like tool support and are not intended for direct user interaction. In conceptual modeling, the domain model is intended to support human communication, which requires a human-readable notation. In our approach, this is necessary to make the model directly applicable in the classification and search interface. Web search engines today increasingly use language technology to improve their search. Natural Language Analysis enables the use of phrases or semantic units, rather than "simple" words in retrieval. Phrase extraction from text has led to advances in IR and has been the basis for Linguistically Motivated Indexing - LMI – [34][35][36]. [37] provide a survey of NLP techniques and methods such as stemming, query expansion and word sense disambiguation to deal with morphological, lexical, syntactic and semantic variation when indexing text. An increasing number of search tools offer categorization as part of the search functionality. Posting a query, the user may also select one or more categories for the search. Each category is defined internally by means of a domain dictionary that contains the characteristic words and phrases in the category. The document category is included in the index, making it possible to restrict the search to one or more categories. The scientific search tool from Elsevier Science, Scirus [38] is a good example of this approach. The Northern Lighthouse web search engine applies automated generation of categories to let users refine their search expressions.

Like our model-based search approach, category-based search establishes links between documents and abstract semantic units. A category is an abstraction of related concepts, forms a semantically meaningful unit, and can be both part of a super-category and decomposed into sub-categories. Compared to our model approach, the categories tend to be at a higher level of abstraction. Even though you may specify a model describing a vast area like "scientific publications," you would usually use the model approach on fairly small, but well-defined domains. Category-based search and model-based search are in fact compatible, in the sense that domain models may be employed to describe the actual concepts defining the lowest-level categories. This exposes the concepts underlying the category to the user and allows the user to explore the whole category in a systematic way. Work on the connection between Natural language statements and formal statements of some kind in a CASE tool have been a challenge for many years [39]. Constructing models from a larger set of documents, however, the system needs more sophisticated techniques for handling linguistic variation when proposing model elements. [40][41] give examples of CASE tools that have integrated advanced parsing and understanding [39].

6 Concluding Remarks

This paper presented an information retrieval system that concentrates on concepts rather than on key words. Whereas traditional systems depend on syntactic matching of query terms with document key words, our system abstracts concepts from the documents and matches these against query concepts. Problems linked to word inflections, synonyms, phrasing and spell-checking are easier to handle in this framework. An additional feature of concept-based retrieval is that we do not see the words in isolation, but also take into account how words or concepts are semantically related to each other.

Also, the retrieval system represents a shift from traditional text-based retrieval interfaces to graphical model-based ones. Whereas text-based retrieval is fast for small, independent queries, the model-based approach allows the user to explore the structure of the domain while formulating his query. A more explorative retrieval method is made available, where the user is given feedback even before any documents are retrieved. In this way, the user learns more about the domain as a whole and can take the distribution of documents into account before posting his query.

It should be noted that we do not consider our retrieval system a replacement of traditional search engines The system presented here is not intended as a general-purpose search engine. Domain models assume that the document collections address structured, well understood domains. For unstructured domains, the models would be too fragmented or unreliable to be of any help. Also, in spite of the abstraction mechanisms in modeling languages, domain models seem more effective in small domains than in large ones. For large, complex domains, the challenge is to come up with domain models that are small and easy to use for the end-users. We must be able to handle several views of a model, or even several models. In addition, it should be possible to focus the models into an area of interest (other than just zooming). This is most notable during search, when users want to specialize their search expressions by narrowing in on the interesting concepts. Our blue-dot symbols for concepts with hits, illustrates the concepts that may be used to narrow a search expression. We are currently experimenting with allowing the users to "dim away" concepts without hits and then to compress the remaining concepts by squeezing them closer together.

Acknowledgements

This work is performed at the Information Systems group at IDI, NTNU, directed by Professor Arne Sølvberg. The CnSClient application is implemented by Audun Steinholm, while most of the server side scripts is written by Arne Dag Fidjestøl.

References

1. Gulla, J. A. and T. Brasethvik (2001). A model driven ERP Environment with search facilities. Applications of Natural Language to Information Systems NLDB, 2001.
2. Poncia, G. and B. Pernici (1997). A methodology for the design of distributed web systems. CAISE*97, Barcelona, Spain, Springer Verlag, 1997.
3. German, D. M. and D. D. Cowan (1999). Formalizing the specification of Web applications. Advances in conceptual modeling (Workshop of ER'99), Paris, Springer Verlag, 1999.
4. W3CSW (2001). Semantic Web Initiavive, http://www.w3c.org/2001/sw/, Accessed:December 2001.
5. Fensel, D. (2001). The Ontoweb Project, http://www.ontoweb.org: http://www.ontoweb.org, Accessed:July 2001
6. Voss, A., K. Nakata, et al. (1999). Collaborative information management using concepts. 2nd International Workshop IIIS-99, Copenhague, DK, Postproceedings published by IGP, 1999.
7. Sulllivan, D. (2001). Document Warehousing and Text Mining, Wiley Computer Publishing.
8. Weibel, S. (1995). "Metadata - The foundations for resource descriptions." D-LIB Magazine(July 1995).
9. Miller (2001). Semantic web and digital libraries. European Conference on Research and Advanced Technology for Digital Libraries, Germany, 2001.

10. Svenonius, E. (2000). The intellectual foundation for organising information. Cambridge, MIT Press.
11. Bunge, M. (1998). The Philosophy of science - from problem to theory, revised edition, Transaction Publishers.
12. Sølvberg, A. (1998). Data and what they refer to. Conceptual modeling: Historical perspectives and future trends, In conjunction with 16th Int. Conf. on Conceptual modeling, Los Angeles, CA, USA, 1998.
13. Refedit (2000), "The referent model editor homepage", http://www.idi.ntnu.no/~ppp/referent/, Accessed: February 2002.
14. Pubgene (2001). The Pubgene database and tools, http://www.pubgene.org, Accessed:December 2001.
15. BSCW (1999). Basic Support for Cooperative Work on the WWW, http://bscw.gmd.de, Accessed:May 1999.
16. Farshchian, B. A. (1998). ICE: An object-oriented toolkit for tailoring collaborative Web-applications. IFIP WG8.1 Conference on Information Systems in the WWW Environment, Beijing, China., 1998.
17. FirstClass (1999). FirstClass Collaborative Classroom, http://www.schools.softarc.com/, Accessed: May, 1999
18. Berners-Lee, T., J. Hendler, et al. (2001). "The Semantic Web." Scientific Amerian(5).
19. W3CRDF (1998). Resource Description Framework - Working Draft, http://www.w3.org/Metadata/RDF/, Accessed:March 2000
20. W3CRDFS (2000). The RDF Schema Specification, http://www.w3.org/TR/2000/CR-rdf-schema-20000327/.
21. Karvounarakis, G., V. Christophides, et al. (2000). Querying semistructured (meta)data and schemas on the web: The case of RDF and RDFS, http://www.ics.forth.gr/proj/isst/RDF/rdfquerying.pdf, September 2000.
22. Gruber, T. (1995). "Towards Priciples for the Design of Ontologies used for Knowledge Sharing." Human and Computer Studies 43(5/6): 907-928.
23. Uschold, M. (1996). Building Ontologies: Towards a unified methodology. The 16th annual conference of the British Computer Society Specialist Group on Expert Systems, Cambridge (UK), 1996.
24. Domingue, J. (1998). Tadzebao and WebOnto: Discussing, Browsing, and Editing Ontologies on the Web. 11th Banff Knowledge Aquisition for Knowledge-based systems Workshop, Banff, Canada, 1998.
25. Fensel, D., J. Angele, et al. (1999). On2Broker: Improving access to information sources at the WWW: http://www.aifb.uni-karlsruhe.de/WBS/www-broker/o2/o2.pdf, Accessed: May, 1999.
26. Swartout, B., R. Patil, et al. (1996). Ontosaurus: A tool for browsing and editing ontologies. 9th Banff Knowledge Aquisition for KNowledge-based systems Workshop, Banff, Canada, 1996.
27. Galen (1999). Why Galen - The need for Integrated medical systems, http://www.galen-organisation.com/approach.html, Accessed:March 2000.
28. OMNI (1999). OMNI: Organizing Medical Networked Information, http://www.omni.ac.uk/, Accessed: May, 1999.

29. Soamares de Lima, L., A. H. F. Laender, et al. (1998). A Hierarchical Approach to the Automatic Categorization of Medical Documents. CIKM*98, Bethesda, USA, ACM, 1998.
30. Spriterm (1999). Spriterm - hälso och sjukvårdens gemensamma fakta och termdatabas, http://www.spri.se/i/Spriterm/i-prg2.htm, Accessed:March 2000.
31. Ontoquery (2001). The Ontoquery project - description, http://www.ontoquery.dk, Accessed:December 2001.
32. DAML, P. (2000). The DARPA Agent Markup Language Homepage, http://www.daml.org, Accessed:December 2001.
33. OIL (2001). Ontology Interface Layer, http://www.ontoknowledge.org/oil/, Accessed: December 2001.
34. Schneiderman, B., D. Byrd, et al. (1997). "Clarifying Search: A User-Interface Framework for Text Searches." D-Lib Magazine(January 1997).
35. Strzalkowski, T. (1999). Natural Language Information Retrieval, Kluwer Academic Publishers.
36. Strzalkowski, T., G. Stein, et al. (1998). Natural Language Information Retrieval - TREC-7 report. TREC-7, 1998.
37. Arampatzis, A. T., T. P. van der Weide, et al. (1999). Linguistically Motivated Information Retrieval, University of Nijmegen.
38. Scirus (2001). SCIRUS for scientific information only, http://www.scirus.com, Accessed:December 2001.
39. Métais, E. (1999). The role of knowledge and reasoning i CASE Tools, University of Versailles.
40. Fliedl, G., C. Kop, et al. (1997). NTS-based derivation of KCPM Perspective Determiners. 3rd Int. workshop on Applications of Natural Language to Information Systems (NLDB'97), Vancouver, Ca, 1997.
41. Tjoa, A. M. and L. Berger (1993). Transformation of Requirement Specifications Expressed in Natural Language into EER Model. 12th Int. conceference on Entity-Relation approach, 1993.

Multidimensional Semistructured Data: Representing Context-Dependent Information on the Web

Yannis Stavrakas[1,2] and Manolis Gergatsoulis[2]

[1] Knowledge & Database Systems Laboratory, National Technical University of Athens (NTUA)
157 73, Athens, Greece
[2] Institute of Informatics & Telecommunications, National Centre for Scientific Research (N.C.S.R.) 'Demokritos'
153 10 Aghia Paraskevi Attikis, Greece
{ystavr,manolis}@iit.demokritos.gr

Abstract. In this paper, we address a problem common in the frame of WWW, namely, representing information that assumes different facets under different *contexts* (sets of *worlds*). For expressing context-dependent (or *multidimensional*) data, we introduce *Multidimensional Semistructured Data*, where context is defined through (*dimension, value*) pairs. An extension of OEM called *Multidimensional Object Exchange Model (MOEM)* is introduced, for representing multidimensional data. We discuss the properties of MOEM and define a transformation that, for any given world, reduces MOEM to a conventional OEM holding under that world. As a case study, we show how MOEM can be used to represent changes over time in an OEM database.

1 Introduction and Motivation

The nature of the Web poses a number of new problems [4]. While in traditional databases and information systems the number of users is more or less known and their background is to a great extent homogeneous, Web users do not share the same background and do not apply the same conventions when interpreting data. Such users can have different perspectives of the same entities, a situation that should be taken into account by Web data models. Similar problems appear when integrating information from various sources [10], where the same conceptual entity may exhibit different structure, or contain conflicting data.

Those problems call for a way to represent information entities that manifest different facets, whose contents can vary in structure and value. As a simple example imagine a report that must be represented at various degrees of detail and in various languages. A solution would be to create a different report for every possible combination of variations. Such an approach is certainly not practical, since it involves excessive duplication of information. What is more, different variants are not associated as being parts of the same entity. Although existing web data models, such as OEM [7], are in principle capable to represent such multi-facet entities, they fall short for a number of reasons, namely (a) hidden semantics: by not addressing directly the issue of multiple facets, it is the responsibility of an application to assign semantics in an ad-hoc manner, (b) cumbersome notation: representing multiple facets of an entity cannot be done in an elegant way, and (c) duplication of information: information that is common can be duplicated, which is undesirable.

In this paper we introduce *multidimensional semistructured data* and an extension of OEM called *multidimensional OEM*, that incorporate ideas from multidimensional programming languages [3] and associate data with *dimensions*, in order to tackle the aforementioned problems. We show how multidimensional OEM can be reduced to OEM under a specific *world*. As an example application of multidimensional OEM, we consider the problem of representing histories of changes in an OEM database. This problem has been also investigated in [8], where the need for an OEM extension has been recognized. In Section 5 we discuss [8] further. A model for semistructured data that deviates from OEM has been proposed in [6], where edge labels are themselves pieces of semistructured data. The model we propose views labels as containing metadata rather than data. In [9], an extensible semistructured data model has been proposed that uses sets of properties of the form "property_name: property_value" as edge labels. By attaching properties at will, the graph becomes rich in metadata. Different properties may have different semantics, which results in a model of increased generality, but on the other hand makes the formulation of queries more complicated. The goal of our approach is to represent information that presents different facets. This leads to common semantics for the metadata, which is used solely to embody *context* information. In addition, our model retains OEM labeled edges and attaches context metadata to a new type of edges; graph models such as OEM become special cases of the model we propose.

Our work was influenced by *Intensional HTML* [16], a Web authoring language that incorporates ideas presented in [13] and allows a single Web page to have different variants and to dynamically adapt itself to a user-defined context. Our previous work on *Multidimensional XML* (MXML) [14,11,12] has also played a major role in shaping the data model we describe in this paper. MXML is an extension of XML that treats context as first class citizen. In MXML, elements and attributes can assume different values or structure, depending on the context. A multidimensional DTD (MDTD) has also been proposed for defining constraints on MXML documents.

In this paper, we address the representation of context-dependent semistructured data in general. We define an extended formalism for contexts, and investigate various aspects of a multidimensional model for semistructured data. The structure of the paper is as follows. In Section 2 we give a formalism for contexts. In Section 3 we introduce a graph data model and syntax for multidimensional semistructured data, we discuss validity issues of the proposed model, and define a process for obtaining conventional graphs from a multidimensional graph. Querying multidimensional semistructured data is briefly discussed in Section 4.

In Section 5, a way to model OEM histories using multidimensional OEM is presented. Finally, Section 6 concludes the paper.

2 A Formalism for Contexts

Multidimensional semistructured data (*MSSD* in short) are semistructured data (*SSD* in short) [15] which present different facets under different worlds. The notion of *world* is fundamental in our approach. A world represents an environment under which data obtain a substance. In the following definition, we specify the notion of world using a set of parameters called *dimensions*.

Definition 1. *Let $\mathcal{D}$ be a nonempty set of dimension names and for each $d \in \mathcal{D}$, let $\mathcal{V}_d$ be the domain of d, with $\mathcal{V}_d \neq \emptyset$. A world w with respect to $\mathcal{D}$ is a set whose elements are pairs (d, v), where $d \in \mathcal{D}$ and $v \in \mathcal{V}_d$, such that for every dimension name in $\mathcal{D}$ there is exactly one element in w.*

The main difference between conventional semistructured data and multidimensional semistructured data is the introduction of *context specifiers*, that are used to qualify semistructured data expressions (*ssd-expressions*) [1] with contexts. The context of an ssd-expression can be seen as a set of worlds under which that ssd-expression holds; it becomes therefore possible to have at the same time variants of the same information entity, each holding under a different set of worlds. An information entity that encompasses a number of variants (also called *facets*) is called *multidimensional entity*. If the facets $e_1, e_2, \ldots, e_n$ of a multidimensional entity e hold under a world w (or, under every world defined by a context specifier c), then we say that e evaluates to $e_1, e_2, \ldots, e_n$ under w (under c, respectively).

In order to define context specifiers and explain their relation to worlds, we first discuss *context specifier clauses*.

Definition 2. *Let $\mathcal{D}$ be a set of dimension names and for each $d \in \mathcal{D}$, let $\mathcal{V}_d$ be the domain of d, with $\mathcal{V}_d \neq \emptyset$. Then a dimension specifier s of a dimension d is a pair (d, V) where $d \in \mathcal{D}$ and $V \in 2^{\mathcal{V}_d}$. A context specifier clause cc is a set of dimension specifiers, such that for any dimension $d \in \mathcal{D}$ there exists at most one dimension specifier (d, V) in cc.*

A context specifier clause cc is called *empty* and is denoted by $\emptyset_{cc}$, if for some dimension d, $(d, \emptyset) \in cc$. The empty context specifier clause $\emptyset_{cc}$ represents the empty set of worlds $\mathcal{E}_c$ (empty context). If $cc = \emptyset$, then cc is called *universal* context specifier clause, and represents the set of all possible worlds $\mathcal{U}_c$ (universal context). Any number of dimensions can be combined to form a context specifier clause, in other words, it is not necessary for a context specifier clause to contain an element (dimension specifier) for every possible dimension. The meaning of omitting dimensions becomes evident in what follows, where we explain how a context specifier clause is interpreted as a set of worlds.

Definition 3. *The* extension $\otimes cc$ *of a context specifier clause cc is defined as follows: if* $cc=\emptyset$, *then* $\otimes cc = \mathcal{U}_c$; *if* $cc=\emptyset_{cc}$, *then* $\otimes cc = \mathcal{E}_c$; *else if* $cc=\{(d_1,V_1), (d_2,V_2), \ldots, (d_n,V_n)\}$, *then* $\otimes cc = \{ \{(d_1,v_1),(d_2,v_2),\ldots,(d_n,v_n)\} \mid v_i \in V_i$ *with* $1 \leq i \leq n\}$.

The extension of a context specifier clause gives a set of sets of *(dimension, value)* pairs. To determine whether each set of pairs represents a world or not, the set $\mathcal{D}$ of all the dimensions must be taken into account. For a dimension in $\mathcal{D}$ that does not exist in a context specifier clause, the inclusion of all values in its domain is implied. The following defines an expansion of context specifier clauses in order to take into account the set of dimensions $\mathcal{D}$.

Definition 4. *Let $\mathcal{D}$ be a set of dimensions and for each $d \in \mathcal{D}$, let $\mathcal{V}_d$ be the domain of d, with $\mathcal{V}_d \neq \emptyset$. Let cc be a context specifier clause. Then the* expansion *of cc with respect to $\mathcal{D}$ is a context specifier clause, denoted by $exp(cc)$, that contains the following elements: (a) if $(d,V) \in cc$, then $(d,V) \in exp(cc)$; (b) if $d \in \mathcal{D}$ and $(d,V) \notin cc$ for any V, then $(d,\mathcal{V}_d) \in exp(cc)$.*

Assuming a set of dimensions $\mathcal{D}$, the worlds specified by cc with respect to $\mathcal{D}$ are given by the extension of the expansion of cc, $W_{\mathcal{D}}^{cc}(cc) = \otimes(exp(cc))$. Consequently, (a) what represents a world with respect to a set of dimensions D, represents a set of worlds with respect to every $D' \supset D$, and (b) what represents a world with respect to a set of dimensions D, also represents a world with respect to every $D' \subset D$.

The intersection of two context specifier clauses cc_1 and cc_2, is a context specifier clause that represents the worlds specified by both cc_1 and cc_2.

Definition 5. *Let cc_1, cc_2 be two context specifier clauses. The* context specifier clause intersection $cc_1 \cap_{cc} cc_2$, *is a context specifier clause cc_3 such that:*
$cc_3 = \{(d,V) \mid (d,V) \in cc_1$ *and there is no element* (d,V') *in* $cc_2\} \cup \{(d,V) \mid (d,V) \in cc_2$ *and there is no element* (d,V') *in* $cc_1\} \cup \{(d,V) \mid (d,V_1) \in cc_1$ *and* $(d,V_2) \in cc_2$ *and* $V = V_1 \cap V_2\}$

Note that $cc \cap_{cc} \emptyset_{cc} = \emptyset_{cc}$, and $cc \cap_{cc} \emptyset = cc$.

Consider the dimension *language* ranging over *English, French, Greek*, the dimension *detail* ranging over *low, medium, high*, and the dimension *format* ranging over *ps, pdf*. Consider also the context specifier clauses $cc_1 = \{(lang, \{en, gr\}), (detail, \{medium, high\})\}$ and $cc_2 = \{(lang, \{gr, fr\})\}$. Then, $cc_1 \cap_{cc} cc_2 = \{(lang, \{gr\}), (detail, \{medium, high\})\}$, and represents the worlds: $\{(lang, gr), (detail, medium), (format, ps)\}$, $\{(lang, gr), (detail, medium), (format, pdf)\}$, $\{(lang, gr), (detail, high), (format, ps)\}$, $\{(lang, gr), (detail, high), (format, pdf)\}$.

Definition 6. *A* context specifier *c is a nonempty set of context specifier clauses.*

A context specifier $c = \{cc_1, cc_2, \ldots, cc_n\}$, $n \geq 1$, represents the set of worlds $W_{\mathcal{D}}^c(c) = W_{\mathcal{D}}^{cc}(cc_1) \cup W_{\mathcal{D}}^{cc}(cc_2) \cup \ldots \cup W_{\mathcal{D}}^{cc}(cc_n)$. In analogy to context specifier clauses, the *empty context specifier* $\emptyset_c$ is a context specifier that contains only empty clauses $cc_1 = cc_2 = \ldots = cc_n = \emptyset_{cc}$, and does not represent any world. A context specifier that contains at least one universal clause represents the set of all possible worlds, is called *universal context specifier*, and is denoted by $\{\emptyset\}$.

We now define how the intersection and union of worlds is performed at the level of context specifiers. The intersection of context specifiers $\cap_c$ is based on the intersection of clauses $\cap_{cc}$, while the union of context specifiers $\cup_c$ is not different from conventional set union, and is introduced for uniformity of notation.

Definition 7. *Let c_1, c_2 be two context specifiers. Then the context specifier intersection $c_1 \cap_c c_2$, is a context specifier c_3 such that: $c_3 = \{cc_i \cap_{cc} cc_j \mid cc_i \in c_1, cc_j \in c_2\}$. The context specifier union $c_1 \cup_c c_2$, is a context specifier c_4 such that: $c_4 = c_1 \cup c_2$.*

Consider the context specifiers $c_1 = \{\{(lang, \{en, gr\}), (detail, \{high\})\}\}$ and $c_2 = \{\{(lang, \{en\}), (detail, \{low\})\}, \{(lang, \{gr\})\}\}$. Then $c_1 \cap_c c_2 = \{\emptyset_{cc}, \{(lang, \{gr\}), (detail, \{high\})\}\} = \{\{(lang, \{gr\}), (detail, \{high\})\}\}$, and $c_1 \cup_c c_2 = \{\{(lang, \{en, gr\}), (detail, \{high\})\}, \{(lang, \{en\}), (detail, \{low\})\}, \{(lang, \{gr\})\}\}$.

It is easy to show that the context specifier intersection and union are equivalent to the intersection and union of the corresponding sets of worlds. More formally, if c_1 and c_2 are context specifiers, then:

$W_\mathcal{D}^c(c_1) \cap W_\mathcal{D}^c(c_2) = W_\mathcal{D}^c(c_1 \cap_c c_2)$
$W_\mathcal{D}^c(c_1) \cup W_\mathcal{D}^c(c_2) = W_\mathcal{D}^c(c_1 \cup_c c_2)$

A context specifier may contain clauses that define overlapping sets of worlds. In the example above, the worlds matching $\{(lang, gr), (detail, high), \ldots\}$ are covered by the first and the third context specifier clause of c_4. The context specifier c_4 can be simplified as follows: $c_4 = \{\{(lang, \{en\}), (detail, \{high\})\}, \{(lang, \{gr\}), (detail, \{high\})\}, \{(lang, \{en\}), (detail, \{low\})\}, \{(lang, \{gr\})\}\} = \{\{(lang, \{en\}), (detail, \{high\})\}, \{(lang, \{en\}), (detail, \{low\})\}, \{(lang, \{gr\})\}\} = \{\{(lang, \{en\}), (detail, \{low, high\})\}, \{(lang, \{gr\})\}\}$.

Definition 8. *Two context specifier clauses cc_1, cc_2 are said to be* mutually exclusive *iff $cc_1 \cap_{cc} cc_2 = \emptyset_{cc}$. Two context specifiers c_1, c_2 are said to be* mutually exclusive *iff $c_1 \cap_c c_2 = \emptyset_c$.*

Mutually exclusive context specifier clauses and context specifiers define disjoint sets of worlds. The context specifier clauses $cc_1 = \{(lang, \{en\})\}$ and $cc_2 = \{(detail, \{low\})\}$ are not mutually exclusive, since the worlds matching $\{(lang, en), (detail, low), \ldots\}$ are covered by both cc_1 and cc_2. In contrast, the context specifier clause $cc_3 = \{(lang, \{gr, fr\}), (detail, \{high\})\}$ is mutually exclusive with both cc_1 and cc_2.

Section 3.2 defines a syntax for context specifiers in ssd-expressions, which will be used throughout the paper. As an example, consider the expressions:

```
[time=07:45]
[language=greek, detail in {low,medium}]
[season in {fall,spring}, daytime=noon | season=summer]
```

The last context specifier contains two clauses, and represents the worlds where it is either summer or fall/spring noons. The universal context specifier is denoted by [] while the empty context specifier is denoted by [-].

3 Supporting Contexts in SSD

In this section we propose a graph model for representing MSSD, specify a syntax for expressing multidimensional semistructured data, and discuss some properties of multidimensional data graphs.

3.1 Multidimensional OEM

A predominant graph model for SSD is *Object Exchange Model* (OEM) [2], that was originally designed in Stanford as part of the TSIMMIS project [7]. OEM is a rooted directed labeled multigraph, flexible enough to tolerate the irregularities of SSD. We retain that flexibility, and extend OEM with two new basic elements:

- *Multidimensional nodes*: a multidimensional node represents a multidimensional entity, and is used to group together nodes that constitute facets of that entity. Facets of entities can use multidimensional nodes to connect to each other, as a multidimensional node plays the role of a surrogate for its facets. In our graph model, multidimensional nodes have a rectangular shape to distinguish them from conventional circular nodes.
- *Context edges*: context edges are directed labeled edges that connect a multidimensional node to its variants. The label of a context edge pointing to a variant p, is a context specifier that defines the set of worlds under which p holds. Context edges are drawn as thick or double lines, to distinguish them from conventional edges.

We call the new model *Multidimensional Object Exchange Model* (*MOEM* in short). In MOEM the conventional circular nodes of OEM are called *context nodes* and represent variants associated with some context. Conventional (thin) OEM edges are called *entity edges* and define relationships between objects.

As in OEM, all MOEM nodes are considered objects, and have a unique *object identifier* (oid). In what follows, the terms *node* and *object* will be used interchangeably in the frame of MOEM. Context objects are divided into *complex objects* and *atomic objects*. Atomic objects have a value from one of the basic types, e.g. integer, real, strings, etc. The value of a complex object is a set of *object references*, represented by entity edges. The value of a multidimensional object is also a set of object references, represented by context edges.

The MOEM in Figure 1 is an example of a context-dependent recreation guide. For simplicity, the graph is not fully developed and some of the atomic objects do not have values attached. The dimensions and their respective domains in Figure 1 are as follows: season ranging over {summer, fall, winter, spring}, daytime ranging over {noon, evening}, detail ranging over {high,

Multidimensional Semistructured Data   189

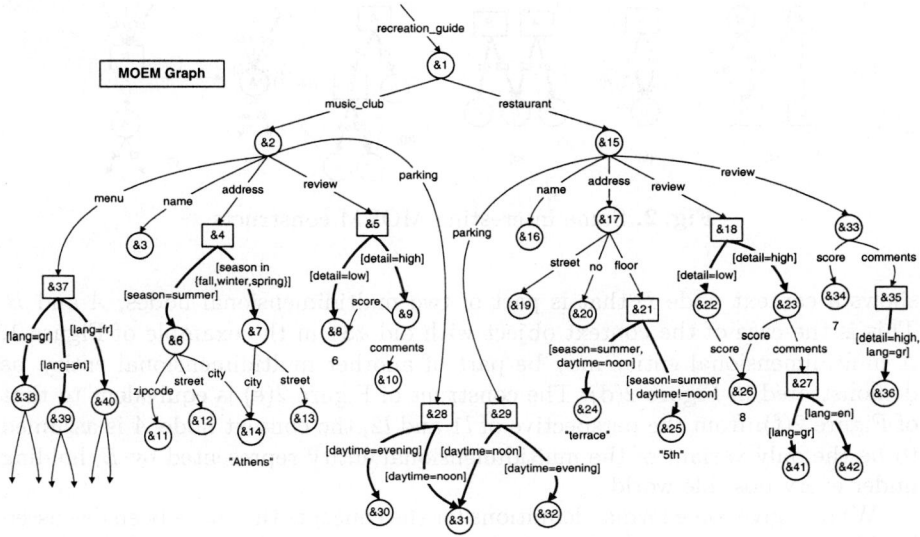

Fig. 1. A multidimensional recreation guide

low}, and `lang` ranging over {`en, fr, gr`}. The `restaurant` with oid &15 normally operates on the fifth floor, but at summer noons it operates on the terrace. Therefore, `floor` with oid &21 is a multidimensional object whose (atomic) value depends on dimensions `season` and `daytime`. Except from having a different value, context objects can have a different structure, as is the case of &6 and &7 which are variants of the multidimensional object `address` with oid &4. In this case, the `music_club` with oid &2 operates on a different address during the summer than the rest of the year (in Athens it is not unusual for clubs to move south close to the sea in the summer period, and north towards the city center during the rest of the year). The `menu` of the club is available in three languages, namely English, French and Greek. The restaurant and the club have a number of `reviews` that can be detailed or brief, depending on the dimension `detail`. In addition, each has a couple of alternative `parking` places, depending on the time of day as expressed by the dimension `daytime`.

The existence of two kinds of nodes and two kinds of edges raises the question of which node - edge combinations are meaningful. Starting with what is not legal, a context edge cannot start from a context node, and an entity edge cannot start from a multidimensional node. Those two are the only constraints on the morphology of an MOEM graph.

Figure 2 depicts some legal non-trivial MOEM constructs. In Figure 2(b) more than one context edges connect a multidimensional node with the same context node. The multidimensional node A evaluates to B under the union of the worlds specified by $c1$ and $c2$. The two context edges can, therefore, be replaced by a single one with context specifier $c3 = c1 \cup_c c2$. Figure 2(c)

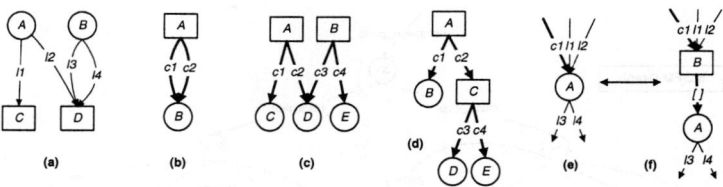

Fig. 2. Some interesting MOEM constructs

shows a context node D that is part of two multidimensional nodes, A and B. This is the case of the context object with oid &31 in the example of Figure 1. A multidimensional entity may be part of another multidimensional entity, as demonstrated in Figure 2(d). The construct of Figure 2(e) is equivalent to that of Figure 2(f): from the perspective of $l1$ and $l2$, the context node A is assumed to be the only variant of the multidimensional entity represented by B, holding under every possible world.

We now give some formal definitions for the concepts that have been discussed in this section. We start by introducing *multidimensional data graphs*.

Definition 9. *Let C be a set of context specifiers, $\mathcal{L}$ be a set of labels, and $\mathcal{A}$ be a set of atomic values. A* multidimensional data graph *is a finite directed edge-labeled multigraph $G = (V, E, r, C, \mathcal{L}, \mathcal{A}, v)$, where:*

1. *The set of nodes V is partitioned into* multidimensional nodes *and* context nodes *$V = V_{mld} \cup V_{cxt}$. Context nodes are further divided into* complex nodes *and* atomic nodes *$V_{cxt} = V_c \cup V_a$.*
2. *The set of edges E is partitioned into* context edges *and* entity edges *$E = E_{cxt} \cup E_{ett}$, such that $E_{cxt} \subseteq V_{mld} \times C \times V$ and $E_{ett} \subseteq V_c \times \mathcal{L} \times V$.*
3. *$r \in V$ is the* root, *with the property that there exists a path from r to every other node in V.*
4. *v is a function that assigns values to nodes, such that: $v(x) = M$ if $x \in V_{mld}$, $v(x) = C$ if $x \in V_c$, and $v(x) = v'(x)$ if $x \in V_a$, where M and C are reserved values, and v' is a value function $v' : V_a \to \mathcal{A}$ which assigns values to atomic nodes.*

It is easy to recognize that OEM is a special case of multidimensional data graph, where there are no multidimensional nodes and context edges.

An important issue is whether or not, given a specific world, it is always possible to reduce a multidimensional data graph to a conventional graph holding under that world. To be able to safely "disassemble" a multidimensional data graph, each multidimensional entity in the graph must evaluate to at most one variant under any world. This leads to the definition of *context deterministic* multidimensional data graphs, where the context specifiers of each multidimensional entity are mutually exclusive.

Definition 10. *A multidimensional data graph $G = (V, E, r, C, \mathcal{L}, \mathcal{A}, v)$ is* context-deterministic *iff for every (p, c_1, q_1), (p, c_2, q_2) in E_{cxt}, with $q_1 \neq q_2$, $c_1 \cap_c$*

$c_2 = \emptyset_c$. An MOEM graph *is a context-deterministic multidimensional data graph.*

Note that, in any case, a multidimensional entity may evaluate to no variant under some world(s). A context-deterministic graph merely assures that an entity cannot evaluate to more than one variants under any specific world.

For the rest of this paper we assume context-deterministic graphs. This does not imply that context-nondeterministic graphs are of no interest; however, the investigation of context-nondeterministic graphs is out of the scope of this paper.

3.2 MSSD-Expressions

As pointed out in [1], the cornerstone of SSD syntax is *ssd-expression*. We define *mssd-expression* by extending SSD syntax to incorporate context specifiers. The grammar of mssd-expression is given below in Extended Backus-Naur Form (EBNF), where symbols that can be defined by a regular expression start with a capital letter.

```
mssd-expr    ::= value | Oid value | Oid
value        ::= Atomicvalue | "{" complexvalue "}" | "(" multidimvalue ")"
complexvalue ::= Label ":" mssd-expr ("," complexvalue)?
multidimvalue ::= contspec ":" mssd-expr ("," multidimvalue)?
```

It is evident that `multidimvalue` corresponds to the multidimensional node of MOEM, while `atomicvalue` and `complexvalue` correspond to context nodes. Note that `multidimvalues` can have object identifiers, just like complex and atomic values. The conventions concerning the syntax of labels, atomic values, and object identifiers, as well as the requirements for the consistency of ssd-expressions [1] also hold for mssd-expressions.

A context specifier is of the form:

```
contspec     ::= "[" contspecclause ("|" contspecclause)* "]"
contspecclause ::= "" | "-" | dimlist
dimlist      ::= dimspec ("," dimspec)*
dimspec      ::= dimname (atomicop Dimvalue | setop "{" setdimvalue "}")
atomicop     ::= "=" | "!="
setop        ::= "in" | "not in"
setdimvalue  ::= Dimvalue ("," Dimvalue)*
```

As an example, consider the following mssd-expression that describes the music_club object with oid &2 in Figure 1:

```
&2 {menu: &37 ([lang=gr]: &38 {...},
               [lang=en]: &39 {...},
               [lang=fr]: &40 {...}),
    name: &3,
    address: &4 ([season=summer]:
                 &6 {zipcode: &11, street: &12, city: &14 "Athens"},
```

```
                 [season in {fall,winter,spring}]:
                     &7 {city: &14, street: &13}),
    review: &5 ([detail=low]: &8 6,
                [detail=high]:
                     &9 {score: &8, comments: &10}),
    parking: &28 ([daytime=evening]: &30,
                  [daytime=noon]: &31)
  }
```

In this paper we assume finite dimension domains, which the proposed syntax describes by enumerating their elements. Other ways of representation as well as infinite domains may be useful and are not excluded, they are, however, out of the scope of this paper. In Section 5.2 we introduce a shorthand for representing intervals over a bounded, discrete, and totally ordered time domain.

3.3 Properties of Multidimensional Data Graphs

Multidimensional data graphs present interesting properties, a discussion of which cannot be exhausted in the present section. In what follows, we introduce some basic concepts starting with the definitions of *explicit context* and *inherited context*.

Definition 11. *Let $G = (V, E, r, \mathcal{C}, \mathcal{L}, \mathcal{A}, v)$ be a multidimensional data graph. The* explicit context *of an edge $h = (p, k, q) \in E$ is given by the context specifier ec, defined as follows: if $h \in E_{cxt}$ then $ec = k$; otherwise, $ec = \{\emptyset\}$.*

The explicit context can be considered as the "true" context only within the boundaries of a single multidimensional entity. When entities are connected together in a multidimensional graph, the explicit context of an edge is not the "true" context, in the sense that it does not alone determine the worlds under which the destination node holds. The reason for this is that, when an entity e_2 is part of (pointed to through an edge) another entity e_1, then e_2 can have substance only under the worlds that e_1 has substance. This can be conceived as if the context under which e_1 holds is inherited to e_2. The context propagated in that way is combined with (constrained by) the explicit context of each edge to give the *inherited context* for that edge. In contrast to edges, nodes do not have an explicit context; like edges, however, they do have an inherited context. The inherited context of a node or edge is the set of worlds under which the node or edge is taken into account, when reducing the multidimensional graph to a conventional graph (as explained later in this section).

Definition 12. *Let $G = (V, E, r, \mathcal{C}, \mathcal{L}, \mathcal{A}, v)$ be a multidimensional data graph, ic_r be a context specifier giving the inherited context of the root r, and p, q be nodes in V with $p \neq r$. The inherited context of node p is given by the context specifier $ic_p = ic_1 \cup_c ic_2 \ldots \cup_c ic_n$, with $n \geq 1$, where $ic_1, ic_2, \ldots, ic_n$ give the inherited contexts of the edges in E that lead to p. Let ic_q be a context specifier giving the inherited context of node q, h be an edge in E that departs from q, and*

ec_h be a context specifier giving the explicit context of h. The inherited context of edge h is the least set of worlds given by a context specifier ic_h, such that $ic_h = ic_q \cap_c ec_h$.

If the root r of an MOEM graph G is assumed to hold under every possible world, the inherited context of the root becomes the universal context. A point that requires attention, is that the inherited context of an edge which constitutes part of a cycle is eventually defined in terms of itself. It is easy, however, to show that in such cases there exists a least fixed point, which gives the inherited context of the edge.

Multidimensional entities are not obliged to have a facet under every possible world. However, they must provide enough coverage to give substance to each incoming edge under at least one world. The validity of a multidimensional data graph ensures that edges pointing to multidimensional nodes do not exist in vain. As an example, consider the MOEM in Figure 3(a), which is a variant of a part of the MOEM in Figure 1 where the context specifier c of the context edge (&18, c, &23) has been changed to [detail=high,lang=fr]. Now, the entity edge (&23, "comments", &27) does not hold under any world and is *invalid*, since there does not exist any world under which &23 holds together with one of &41, &42. If node &27 pointed also to a third context node through a context edge with explicit context [lang=fr], the entity edge in question would be valid.

Definition 13. *Let $G = (V, E, r, \mathcal{C}, \mathcal{L}, \mathcal{A}, v)$ be a multidimensional data graph. Let $h = (p, k, q)$ be an edge in E that leads to a node q in V, let ic_h give the inherited context of h, and let $ec_1, \ldots, ec_n$, with $n \geq 1$, give the explicit contexts of the edges in E that depart from q. Then, the edge h is invalid iff $ic_h \neq \emptyset_c$ and $ic_h \cap_c (ec_1 \cup_c \ldots \cup_c ec_n) = \emptyset_c$. The multidimensional data graph G is valid iff none of its edges is invalid.*

Each MOEM comprises a number of conventional OEM graphs. The facet of an MOEM graph G under a world w, is an OEM graph G_w that holds under w. Given a world w expressed as a context specifier c_w, the graph G_w can be obtained from G through the following process:

Procedure reduce_to_OEM (G, c_w, G_w) is Initialize G_w to G. With G_w do the following.

Step 1: Remove every node in V and edge in E with $c_w \cap_c ic = \emptyset_c$, where ic gives the inherited context of the node or edge respectively.

Step 2: For every edge $(p, l, m_1) \in E_{ett}$ with $m_1 \in V_{mld}$, follow the path of consecutive context edges $(m_1, c_1, m_2), \ldots, (m_n, c_n, q)$, $n \geq 1$, until no more context edges can be followed. Then, if $q \in V_{cxt}$ add a new entity edge (p, l, q) in E_{ett}.

Step 3: Remove all multidimensional nodes in V_{mld}. Remove all edges in E departing from or leading to the removed nodes. □

Intuitively, explicit contexts can be seen as defining constraints that are accumulated from the root to the leaves to form inherited contexts. Inherited contexts

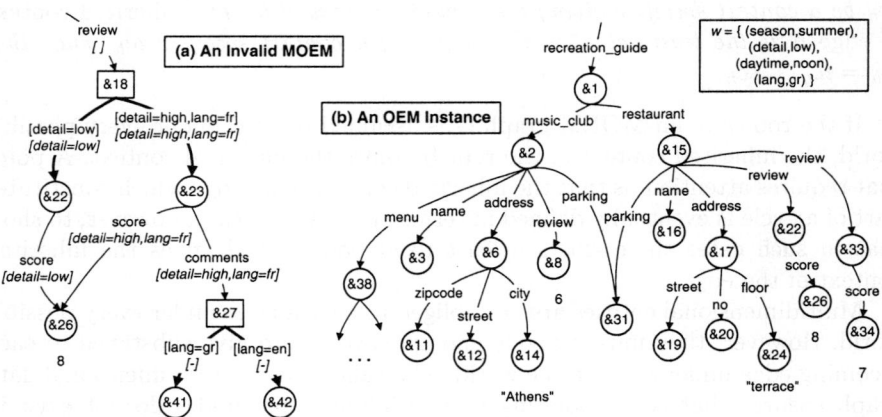

Fig. 3. Figure 3(a) depicts an invalid MOEM, annotated with the inherited contexts of edges (second line of labels), and Figure 3(b) the OEM instance, holding under the world w, of the MOEM in Figure 1

are used to identify parts of the graph that are unreachable under some context, and that can be removed in order to obtain the facet corresponding to a specific world. As an example, consider the MOEM in Figure 1. By applying the above steps on the MOEM for the world $w = \{(season, summer), (detail, low), (daytime, noon), (lang, gr)\}$, we get the OEM in Figure 3(b). Notice how the two parking multidimensional entities with oids &28 and &29 are represented by the object with oid &31. Also, notice how the comment object with oid &35 is excluded from the resulting OEM.

4 Querying Multidimensional Data Graphs

An issue that arises is how to query [5,2] multidimensional semistructured data. In this section, we discuss briefly what a "multidimensional" query is, mention the directions of our ongoing work, and argue that an MOEM graph is something more than the sum of the OEMs it can be "decomposed" to.

Similarly to an OEM database, we define an *MOEM database* as a database whose model is an MOEM graph. Suppose that an MOEM database M is reduced to an OEM database O_w under the world w. Then, a "multidimensional" query $q = (q_w, w)$ on M can be expressed as a query q_w on O_w. For example, consider the query q *"give me the addresses of restaurants at summer noons in low detail in Greek"* on the MOEM database M of Figure 1. Then q is equivalent to q_w *"give me the addresses of restaurants"* on the OEM facet O_w of M for $w = \{(season, summer), (detail, low), (daytime, noon), (lang, gr)\}$.

However, reducing M to O_w is not a necessary step for evaluating q; the processing of q can take place directly on M. Intuitively, q_w can be used for navigating through MOEM entity edges, while w can guide the navigation through MOEM context edges.

In addition, the fact that multidimensional data graphs group variants of entities together, allows a "cross-world" type of queries. As an example, consider the music_club in Figure 1, and the query: *"give me the name and the address in winter of a club whose summer address is given"*. We believe that such queries show the potential of multidimensional data graphs, and that query processing for multidimensional data graphs is an interesting research direction.

5 Using MOEM to Represent Changes

In this section, we will give an example of how MSSD can be applied to a tangible problem: we will use MOEM to represent changes in an OEM database. In short, the problem can be stated as follows: given a static OEM graph that comprises the database, we would like a way to represent dynamically changes in the database as they occur, keeping a history of transitions, so that we are able to subsequently query those changes.

The problem of representing and querying changes in SSD has been studied in [8] where *Delta OEM*, which extends OEM with annotations, is proposed. Our approach, although quite different, is based on the same framework, which we outline in Section 5.1. The approach that we propose will be developed in Section 5.2. An important advantage of MOEM is that a single model can be applied to a variety of problems from different fields; representing valid time is a problem that we discuss here as a case study.

5.1 Basic Concepts

In order to modify an OEM database O, four basic change operations were identified in [8]:

creNode(*nid, val*): creates a new node, where *nid* is a new node oid ($nid \notin V$), and *val* is an atomic value or the reserved value C.

updNode(*nid, val*): changes the value of an existing object *nid* to a new value *val*. The node *nid* must not have any outgoing arcs (in case its old value is C, the arcs should have been removed prior to updating the value).

addArc(*p, l, q*): adds a new arc labeled l from object p to object q. Both nodes p and q must already exist in V, and (p, l, q) must not exist in E.

remArc(*p, l, q*): removes the existing arc (p, l, q). Both nodes p and q must exist in V.

Arc removals can be used for deleting objects, as in OEM the persistence of an object is determined by whether or not the object is reachable from the root. Sometimes the result of a single basic operation u leads to an inconsistent state: for instance, when a new object is created, it is temporarily unreachable from the root. In practice however, it is typical to have a sequence $L = u_1, u_2, \ldots, u_n$ of basic operations u_i, which corresponds to a higher level modification to the database. By associating such higher level modifications with a timestamp, an OEM history H is defined as a sequence of pairs (t, U), where U denotes a set of basic change operations that corresponds to L as defined in [8], and t is the associated timestamp. Note that within a single sequence L, a newly created node may be unreachable from the root and still not be considered deleted. At the end of each sequence, however, unreachable nodes are considered deleted and cannot be referenced by subsequent operations.

5.2 Modeling OEM Histories with MOEM

Given an MOEM database M, the following MOEM basic operations are introduced: **createCNode** for creating a new context node, **updateCNode** for changing the value of an atomic context node, **createMNode** for creating a new multidimensional node, **addEEdge** for creating a new entity edge, **remEEdge** for removing an entity edge, **addCEdge** for creating a new context edge, and **remCEdge** for removing a context edge.

We will now use the framework outlined in the previous section and the MOEM operations introduced above to represent changes in an OEM database using MOEM. Our approach is to map the four OEM basic change operations to MOEM basic operations, in such a way, that new variants of an object are created whenever changes occur in that object. In this manner, the initial OEM database O is transformed into an MOEM graph, that uses a dimension d whose domain is time to represent an OEM history H valid [8] for O. We assume that our time domain T is linear and discrete; we also assume: (1) a reserved value *now*, such that $t < now$ for every $t \in T$, (2) a reserved value *start*, representing the start of time, and (3) a syntactic shorthand $v_1..v_n$ for discrete and totally ordered domains, meaning all values v_i such that $v_1 \leq v_i \leq v_n$. The dimension d denotes, for each context node it qualifies, the time period during which this context node is the holding node of the corresponding multidimensional entity.

Figure 4 gives an intuition about the correspondence between OEM and MOEM operations. Consider the sets U_1 and U_2 of basic change operations, with timestamps t_1 and t_2 respectively. Figure 4(a) shows the MOEM representation of an atomic object, whose value "A" is changed to "B" through a call to the basic change operation *updNode* of U_1. Figure 4(b) shows the result of *addArc* operation of U_1, while Figure 4(c) shows the result of *remArc* operation of U_2, on the same multidimensional entity. It is interesting to notice that three of the four OEM basic change operations are similar, in that they update an object be it atomic (*updNode*) or complex (*addArc*, *remArc*), and all three are mapped to MOEM operations that actually update a new facet of the original object. Creating a new node with *creNode* does not result in any additional MOEM operations; the new node will subsequently be linked with the rest of the graph (within the same set U) through *addArc* operation(s), which will cause new object variant(s) to be created. It is worth noting that the changes induced by the OEM basic change operations affect only localized parts of the MOEM graph, and do not propagate throughout the graph.

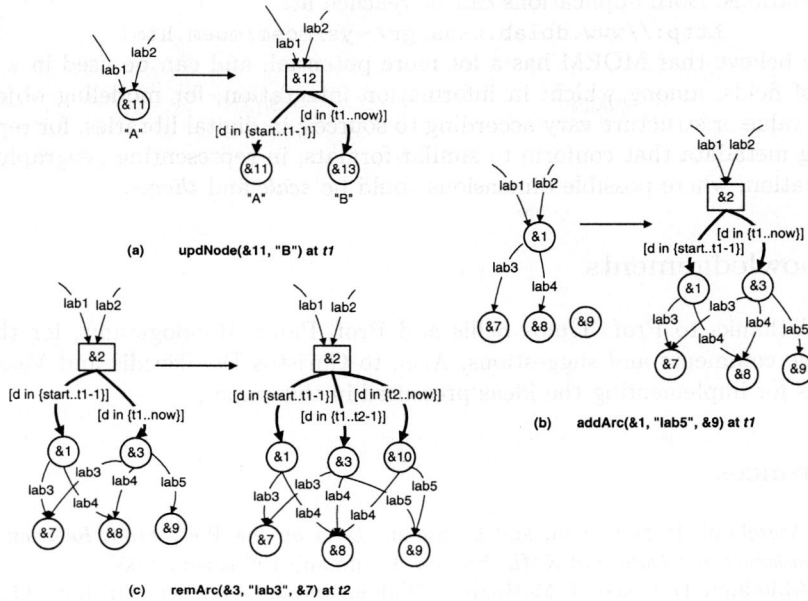

Fig. 4. Modeling OEM basic change operations with MOEM

Based on the above, each OEM basic change operation can be mapped to a procedure implemented through calls to MOEM basic operations, thus defining a process for encompassing an OEM History into an MOEM database. Given an MOEM database M created through such a process, it is possible to specify a time instant and get an OEM database O which is a temporal instantiation of M. In other words, a time instant t is a world for M and we can apply the process described in Section 3.3 to reduce M to an OEM holding under t.

6 Conclusions

In this paper, we presented a formalism for *contexts*, we introduced *multidimensional semistructured data*, specified their syntax, and proposed a new data model called *multidimensional OEM*, which is a graph model that extends OEM by incorporating *dimensions*. We defined the concept of a *multidimensional data graph*, gave a validity criterion for that graph, and specified a process for reducing multidimensional OEM to a conventional OEM under a specific *world*. As a case study of multidimensional OEM, we showed how it can be used to represent the history of an OEM database.

The implementation of the above comprises two applications: "MSSDesigner" that allows to design, validate and reduce MOEM graphs, and "OEM History" that models the history of an OEM database and allows to get OEM temporal

instantiations. Both applications can be reached at:
http://www.dblab.ntua.gr/~ys/moem/moem.html
We believe that MOEM has a lot more potential, and can be used in a variety of fields, among which: in information integration, for modeling objects whose value or structure vary according to sources; in digital libraries, for representing metadata that conform to similar formats; in representing geographical information, where possible dimensions could be *scale* and *theme*.

Acknowledgements

Special thanks to Prof. Timos Sellis and Prof. Panos Rondogiannis, for their valuable comments and suggestions. Also, to Christos Doulkeridis and Vassilis Zafeiris for implementing the ideas presented in this paper.

References

1. S. Abiteboul, P. Buneman, and D. Suciu. *Data on the Web: From Relations to Semistructured Data and XML*. Morgan Kaufmann Publishers, 2000.
2. S. Abiteboul, D. Quass, J. McHugh, J. Widom, and J. L. Wiener. The Lorel Query Language for Semistructured Data. *International Journal on Digital Libraries*, 1(1):68–88, 1997.
3. E. A. Ashcroft, A. A. Faustini, R. Jagannathan, and W. W. Wadge. *Multidimensional Programming*. Oxford University Press, 1995.
4. Ph. A. Bernstein, M. L. Brodie, S. Ceri, D. J. DeWitt, M. J. Franklin, H. Garcia-Molina, J. Gray, G. Held, J. M. Hellerstein, H. V. Jagadish, M. Lesk, D. Maier, J. F. Naughton, H. Pirahesh, M. Stonebraker, and J. D. Ullman. The Asilomar Report on Database Research. *SIGMOD Record*, 27(4):74–80, 1998.
5. P. Buneman, M. Fernandez, and D. Suciu. UnQL: A Query Language and Algebra for Semistructured Data Based on Structural Recursion. *The VLDB Journal*, 9(1):76–110, 2000.
6. Peter Buneman, Alin Deutsch, and Wang-Chiew Tan. A Deterministic Model for Semistructured Data. In *Workshop on Query Processing for Semistructured Data and Non-Standard Data Formats*, 1998.
7. S. Chawathe, H. Garcia-Molina, J. Hammer, K. Ireland, Y. Papakonstantinou, J. Ullman, and J. Widom. The TSIMMIS project: Integration of Heterogeneous Information Sources. In *Proceedings of IPSJ Conference, Tokyo, Japan*, pages 7–18, October 1994.
8. S. S. Chawathe, S. Abiteboul, and J. Widom. Managing Historical Semistructured Data. *Theory and Practice of Object Systems*, 24(4):1–20, 1999.
9. C. E. Dyreson, M. H. Böhlen, and C. S. Jensen. Capturing and Quering Multiple Aspects of Semistructured Data. In *Proceedings of the 25th International Conference on Very Large Data Bases (VLDB'99)*, pages 290–301, 1999.
10. H. Garcia-Molina, Y. Papakonstantinou, D. Quass, A. Rajaraman, Y. Sagiv, J. Ullman, V. Vassalos, and J. Widom. The TSIMMIS Approach to Mediation: Data Models and Languages. *Journal of Intelligent Information Systems*, 8(2):117–132, 1997.

11. M. Gergatsoulis, Y. Stavrakas, and D. Karteris. Incorporating Dimensions to XML and DTD. In *Database and Expert Systems Applications (DEXA' 01)*, Munich, Germany, September 2001, LNCS Vol. 2113, pages 646–656.
12. M. Gergatsoulis, Y. Stavrakas, D. Karteris, A. Mouzaki, and D. Sterpis. A Web-based System for Handling Multidimensional Information through MXML. In *Advances in Databases and Information Systems (ADBIS' 01)*, September 2001, LNCS Vol. 2151, pages 352–365.
13. J. Plaice and W. W. Wadge. A New Approach to Version Control. *IEEE Transactions on Software Engineering*, 19(3):268–276, 1993.
14. Y. Stavrakas, M. Gergatsoulis, and T. Mitakos. Representing Context-Dependent Information Using Multidimensional XML. In *Research and Advanced Technology for Digital Libraries, 4th European Conference ECDL'2000*, LNCS 1923, pages 368–371, 2000.
15. D. Suciu. An Overview of Semistructured Data. *SIGACT News*, 29(4):28–38, December 1998.
16. W. W. Wadge, G. D. Brown, M. C. Schraefel, and T. Yildirim. Intensional HTML. In *Proceedings of the Fourth International Workshop on Principles of Digital Document Processing (PODDP '98)*, March 1998, LNCS 1481, pages 128–139.

The Role of Semantic Relevance in Dynamic User Community Management and the Formulation of Recommendations[*]

Nick Papadopoulos[1] and Dimitris Plexousakis[1,2]

[1] Institute of Computer Science, Foundation for Research and Technology - Hellas
P.O. Box 1385, GR-71110, Heraklion, Greece
{npap,dp}@ics.forth.gr
[2] Department of Computer Science, University of Crete
P.O. Box 2208, GR-71409, Heraklion, Greece

Abstract. In recent years, an increasing interest in recommendation systems has emerged both from the research and the application point of view and in both academic and commercial domains. The majority of comparison techniques used for formulating recommendations are based on set-operations over user-supplied terms or internal product computations on vectors encoding user preferences. In both cases however, the "identical-ness" of terms is examined rather than their actual semantic relevance. This paper proposes a recommendation algorithm that is based on the maintenance of user profiles and their dynamic adjustment according to the users' behavior. Moreover, this algorithm relies on the dynamic management of communities, which contain "similar" and "relevant" users and which are created according to a classification algorithm. The algorithm is implemented on top of a community management mechanism. The comparison mechanism used in the context of this work is based on semantic relevance between terms, which is evaluated with the use of a glossary of terms.

1 Introduction

In recent years, an increasing interest in recommendation systems has emerged both from the research and the application points of view, and in both academic and commercial domains. Many online "e-shops" have adopted recommendation techniques to recommend new items to their customers based on a logged history of previous purchases or transactions. The majority of existing recommendation systems does not adequately address the information filtering needs of their users. A principal requirement main reason for such systems is the employment of a mechanism for filtering

---

[*] This research has been supported by project CYCLADES (IST-2000-25456): An Open Collaborative Virtual Archive Environment.

information that is available through the Web, and dynamically adjust it to the user's needs and interests [1]. Information filtering and its subsequent tailoring to the user's interests constitute the ultimate goals of recommendation systems. Modern recommendation systems mainly base their functionality on one of two approaches, in order to recommend a document or product to a user. These two approaches are *content-based filtering* and *collaborative-filtering* [2,3,6,7] respectively. The adoption of the former or the latter depends on the type of information that a system aims to provide to its users.

In the *content-based* approach, the system filters information (typically a document) and aims to provide recommendations based on the contents of this document. Hence, given their preferences, recommendations for documents that are relevant to their interests are forwarded to the users [2,3]. Such an approach has been mainly adopted by information retrieval [7,8] and machine learning systems [9,10,11]. For instance, in the case of text documents, recommendations are provided based on the degree of matching between the content of a document and a user's profile. The user's profile is built and maintained according to an analysis that is applied to the contents of the documents that the user has previously rated [11,12]. The user's ratings in combination with a mechanism for obtaining the feature terms of a document [2,3,4,5] are the only requirement of these systems.

On the other hand, systems adopting the *collaborative-filtering* approach, aim to identify users that have relevant interests and preferences with a particular user. Thereafter, the documents that these users prefer are recommended to that particular user. The idea behind this approach is that, it may be of benefit to one's search for information to consult the behavior of other users who share the same or relevant interests and whose opinion can be trusted [4]. Such systems take advantage of the documents that other users have already "discovered" and rated. In order for these systems to be able to "detect" the relevance between users, there must be a comparison mechanism, which in this case too, is the usage of user profile information [11,12]. The requirement imposed by such systems is that new users have to rate some documents, so that profiles can be built for them [2,3,4,5].

If these two approaches are applied separately, they present crucial disadvantages and suffer from specific problems. In order for these problems to be dealt with, hybrid approaches need to be devised. Motivated by these issues, this paper presents such a hybrid approach in which the semantic (and not solely lexical) relevance of terms in dynamically maintained user profiles is exploited for the formulation of recommendations.

The rest of the paper is organized as follows. Section 2 presents a comparison between content-based filtering and collaborative filtering as well as the benefits of hybrid approaches. Section 3 describes the proposed algorithm for formulating recommendations. Section 4 presents preliminary experimental results. Section 5 summarizes our contribution and draws directions for further research.

2 Comparing Content-Based and Collaborative Filtering

A representation of the data available in a recommendation system is depicted in Figure 1. Data are represented by means of a matrix whose rows correspond to users and columns correspond to items. Each item is associated with a feature vector. A feature vector can represent an item in different ways. For example we can consider the case of text documents where the (binary) feature vector denotes whether a term is presented or not in a certain document. This means that '1' would denote the appearance of a certain term in the document while '0' would denote the opposite. The elements of this matrix are binary, indicating whether a user has rated an item.

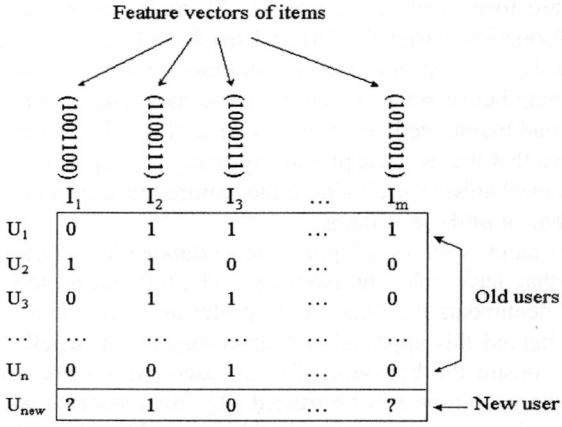

Fig. 1. Representation of data in recommendation systems

The main difference between content-based and collaborative-filtering systems is found in the way they use the available data. Content-based system use only the feature vector of the item that a user has rated (columns with '1') and ignore the items that other users have rated. Therefore, they utilize only the last row of the matrix and the feature vector of the items, ignoring the data in the first n rows [4,5].

Systems adopting collaborative filtering on the other hand, formulate their recommendations based solely on the ratings of other users that are considered relevant to a given user. Thus, in this case, only the data within the matrix and not the feature vectors are used. These systems identify the users, which are interested in the items that a given user is also interested in, by checking the columns with '1' in the last row and the preceding n rows with '1' in the same columns [2,4].

Both approaches have certain shortcomings. One problem with content-based systems is that, in some applications, it is often difficult, and in others even infeasible, to describe the items as vectors or as some other form (such items for example are images, movies and general multimedia items). As a result, we are not able to compare the relevance of such items; we can only check their identity. A second problem is over-specialization, meaning that recommendations can only be made for items that are similar to what a user has already rated [2,3,4,5]. Finally, a less severe problem[1] is that each new user starts with an empty profile. In order for the recommendation system to achieve a high degree of accuracy, the user must rate a number of items. The users' ratings constitute the only factor that influences the subsequent performance of the system [2,4].

Collaborative filtering systems avoid the aforementioned problems of content-based systems but suffer from others. Specifically, an item can be recommended to a user, even if it is not so similar to those the user has already rated. Recommendations for this particular item are based on the preferences of other "relevant" users. In these systems, rather than computing the similarity of items, the similarity of users is computed [2]. However, if a new item appears in the system's database, the system cannot consider it and thus it will not be able to provide recommendations for that until another user rates it. Furthermore, for a user whose preferences and, thus, profile, are "unusual" compared to the rest of the users, there will probably not be any good recommendations, since there will not be any other relevant users [2,4,5].

It is becoming obvious that techniques that base their functionality on either of these approaches or both but apply them separately present crucial disadvantages. In order for these problems to be dealt with, hybrid approaches combining techniques from both types of systems are adopted. Hence, content-based techniques are usually used in order to build and maintain users' profiles. Then, collaborative filtering techniques are applied on these profiles, so that the relevant users can be identified and can thereafter form a community. Furthermore, collaborative filtering techniques are applied on these communities in order for recommendations to be provided. Each such community can also be considered as a single user and it is feasible thereafter recommendations to be provided to an entire community.

3   User Classification and Recommendations

In this section, a general recommendation algorithm that adopts a hybrid approach is presented. This algorithm is based on the maintenance of a user-profile for each user and on the dynamic adjustment of this profile to the user's behavior. Moreover, the algorithm is based on the dynamic management of communities that encompass "relevant" users [12,13]. The classification of users into communities and the identification of "relevant" users are based on the examination of users' profiles.

The goal is to devise techniques that are applicable for both content-based and collaborative filtering. The maintenance of the profiles is performed according to a user's behavior, always taking into account the user's ratings on documents [1,13,14]. Hence, techniques from content-based systems are used in order for the documents to be analyzed and the user profiles to be properly updated. Thereafter, the algorithm for user classification into communities is activated with the result of classifying relevant users into the same community. Subsequently, techniques from collaborative filtering are applied on the derived communities, in order for recommendations to be provided to their members.

---

[1] Many do not consider this as a problem at all.

We believe that the suggested method deals well with the problems of the recommendations systems. The only requirement imposed to users is that they must rate some documents, so that a profile can be build for them. The larger the number of documents a user rates, the better and more adequate are the recommendations that this user will receive. We also claim that, regardless of a user's distinctiveness, the classification algorithm will classify that user into the appropriate communities. A user must have a quite idiomorphic profile, so as to be left out of all the communities.

The above claim is founded on the fact that the comparison mechanism of the algorithm bases its functionality not on "identicalness" of the users but on *semantic relevance* of them. To be more specific, users' semantic relevance implies terms' semantic relevance and terms' semantic relevance is evaluated according to various criteria (e.g., synonymity, subsumption) of semantic relevance. Such criteria for evaluation can be provided by dictionary of terms such as WordNet [26]).

3.1 Characterizing User Interests: User Profiles

The interests and the preferences of each user are expressed through terms that participate into the user's profile that is built and dynamically maintained. The next paragraphs describe user profiles and the way the profiles are maintained.

Each term in a user profile expresses, in a certain degree, the likes of a particular user. A weight is associated to each term for denoting this degree. This weight indicates the importance of the term in the user's interests [1,15]. The weights dynamically change as a result of the user's behavior, and so the importance of that term in the user's interests changes as well [1,15,16,17,18,19,20,21,22]. Moreover, if the weight of a term becomes zero, that term is removed from the profile.

According to their associated weights, all terms in a profile are classified into two groups: one that contains "heavier" terms (called "LONG-TERMS"), and one containing the "lighter" ones (called "SHORT-TERMS"). This classification / characterization denotes whether a term expresses the user's interests at a high or low degree respectively [1,21,23]. As an example, Figure 2 depicts the weights and respective characterizations of terms relevant to Computer Science bibliography for a weight threshold of 20. This characterization is closely related to the weights, meaning that whenever the weight changes, according to the user's behavior, this characterization may also change accordingly. If the weight of a term exceeds a certain threshold then the characterization will automatically change to "LONG-TERM" and if it falls below that threshold it will change to "SHORT-TERM". The usage of that characterization is mainly adopted for practical reasons and is particularly helpful in order for the terms to be visibly distinguishable.

Every time a user rates a document, the user profile is properly adjusted according to the relevance the document has with her interests. This means that, depending on whether the rating is positive or negative, the weight of some terms (and consequently the characterization) will change and either increase or decrease accordingly. Moreover, if the rating is positive then some new terms might be inserted into profile.

For example, if the user rates positively a document, which contains the term 'Artificial Intelligence', then that term's weight will increase. If this happens again and again then the weight will exceed the threshold and thus the term will be considered as a "LONG-TERM". More details are presented in the following subsections.

Term	Weight	Characterization
Software Engineering	32	LONG-TERM
Computer	40	LONG-TERM
Data processing	6	SHORT-TERM
Applications	28	LONG-TERM
Electronic Circuit	15	SHORT-TERM
Artificial intelligence	18	SHORT-TERM
⋮	⋮	⋮

Fig. 2. A user profile (with threshold of change equal to 20)

3.1.1 Automatic Profile Maintenance

The maintenance of profiles is carried out by applying a gradual decrement of all term weights in a profile. This decrement is performed without being noticed by the user and it is applied periodically at appropriate times. The exact time intervals between successive applications of weight modification may depend on the application in question. It is obvious that automatic profile maintenance cannot be applied, say every day, because a user may not carry out any action for the time span of a day and so it would be unwarranted to change the profile in any way. Thereafter, it is important to define precisely the appropriate time points, which in our case are considered to be the time points at which a user acts and which are expressed by the ratings of the documents.

In the previous subsection, we mentioned that whenever the user rates some documents, an adjustment of the profile is performed and either new terms are inserted into profile or the weights of some terms are appropriate updated. The terms inserted into the profile, are the "characteristic terms" of the rated documents. "Characteristic terms" are meant to be those terms of the documents, which are produced by a textual analysis that is performed so that the "stop words" (terms which do not have any special meaning for the document) are discarded [24,25].

In addition to the above procedure, which is directly related to the documents that a user has rated, a further adjustment of the profile is deemed necessary. This adjustment is based on continuous and gradual decrement of the weight of each term, independently of the rated documents. In this manner, all terms automatically lose some degree of importance as far as user interests are concerned. The main goal of this procedure is to achieve better and more "fair" distinction of the terms in the "LONG-TERM" and "SHORT-TERM" lists. Hence, as long as a term is not affected by the user's ratings, its weight decreases and so this term will soon be considered as a "SHORT-TERM", meaning that it loses some of the importance it has among the rest of the user's interests.

On the other hand, a term that is usually affected positively by the user's ratings has a high weight value and thus, if the weight has exceeded a certain value, it is considered "LONG-TERM". This means that user's likes are well expressed by that term and due to its high weight it will not be affected immediately by the automatic profile maintenance. Consequently, the more important a term is the more it will take for it to lose that importance. Conversely, the less important a term is the less it will take for it to lose that importance.

By applying this procedure for automatic profile maintenance, an additional goal is achieved. The weights of terms which are not affected by the user's ratings, meaning that they probably do not have any importance in her interests, gradually decrease until they become zero and are removed from the profile. Hence, by applying automatic profile maintenance, terms which no longer express the likes of a user, are automatically and without that user's interference removed from her profile.

3.2 Description of the Algorithm

The algorithm, which is proposed in this paper, forms the basis for a dynamically adjustable to a user's behavior recommendation algorithm. The goal of this algorithm is the users' classification into communities according to their relevant interests.

3.2.1 Algorithm's Requirements

The algorithm bases its functionality on user profiles. It expects that the terms in those profiles are associated with a weight, which denotes the importance of that term. Also, it expects that the terms in a profile can be distinguished into two groups, "LONG-TERMS" and "SHORT-TERMS", as described in section 3.1 above.

3.2.2 Algorithm's Operational Procedure

Given the fact that each user can be described by a set of terms, checking users' relevance is reduced to checking the relevance of their associated sets of terms. Hence, the algorithm must consider the creation of such a set per user. In order for these sets to be created, all the "LONG-TERMS" are selected at first and are inserted into that set. All "LONG-TERMS" are selected, without any discrimination, because they express the user's likes at a high degree and it is considered fair to select them all. In addition to this selection, a portion of the rest of terms, which are characterized as "SHORT-TERMS", is selected. This is a percentage value specified as a parameter for the algorithm *(selection percentage)* and thus it can vary. The portion of the "SHORT-TERMS" selected comprises the most important terms according to the weights. Eventually, a set of terms, which contains all the "LONG-TERMS" of the profile and a portion of the "SHORT-TERMS", is created for each user.

For instance, consider the user profile shown in the left part of Figure 3 where the terms that are eventually going to be selected have been emphasized. The right part of Figure 3 shows the set of terms that will be created by the algorithm. In this example the selection percentage equals 20% and one term is finally selected, since there are only 3 "SHORT-TERMS". The "SHORT-TERM" which is selected is the one with the greatest weight (in our example it is 'Artificial Intelligence' with weight 18).

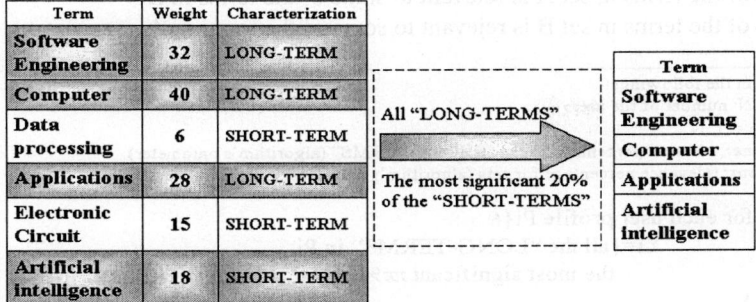

Fig. 3. Selection of terms from a user profile with 20% selection percentage

The above procedure for term selection is defined so that the terms, which more accurately express the likes and the interests of each user be selected. Since the "LONG-TERMS" express the user's likes at a high degree, they are all selected without any distinction. Moreover, a portion of the most significant "SHORT-TERMS" is also selected. This is mainly done so that users with no "LONG-TERMS" in their profile can be taken into account as well.

Concerning the selection percentage, this is adopted so that the algorithm acts in a fair manner for all users, independently of the terms in each profile. That means that the more "SHORT-TERMS" are contained in a user profile, the more terms will be selected for the set, which will be created for that user by the algorithm. So, for the users who have a huge profile, which statistically implies many "SHORT-TERMS" in it as well, a lot of terms will finally be selected in addition to the "LONG-TERMS", which are selected in their totality in any case.

The previous distinction implies that users with big profiles are described in a more "detailed" manner as compared to users with small ones. Besides, big profiles usually reveal users with high activity and behavior, as accrued by their ratings. Hence, it would be fair for them to participate in the algorithm's operational procedure with more terms. On the other hand, in order for a user with a small profile, and thus low activity, not to be excluded at all, they can participate too but with fewer terms.

Obviously, the set of terms created for each user is a subset of that user's profile. Thereafter, these sets are examined and compared so that the ones with relevant terms can be identified. If two or more such sets are found, then the respective users are considered relevant and they are grouped together in the same community.

The following figures depict the algorithm in pseudocode (fig. 4) and a graphical representation of the algorithm's operational procedure (fig. 5).

3.2.3 User Comparison and Relevance

The comparison of users is performed according to the sets of terms created by the algorithm. Again, a percentage is used as a parameter of the algorithm *(relevance percentage)* to denote how similar two sets must be so as to be considered relevant. Specifically, given two sets, say A and B, and a relevance percentage, say π, A and B are considered relevant if one of the following two conditions hold:

- $\pi\%$ of the terms in set A is relevant to some of the terms in B
- $\pi\%$ of the terms in set B is relevant to some of the terms in A

```
In the followings:
N: number of the users
i = 1..N
πs: selection percentage of the "SHORT-TERMS" (algorithm's parameter)
πσ: relevance percentage for sets (algorithm's parameter)

for each user profile Pi{
        Σi={all the "LONG-TERMS" in Pi,
             the most significant πs% of the "SHORT-TERMS" in Pi}
}

for each Σi {
        for the rest Σj {           // j = (i+1)..N
                Compare Σi to Σj;
                if (Σi relevant to Σj by πσ%){
                        Classify user j into community i;
                }
        }
}
```

Fig. 4. Algorithm in pseudocode

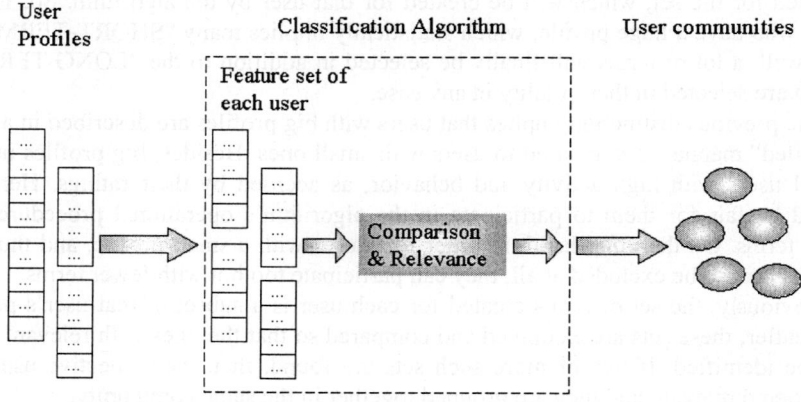

Fig. 5. Graphical representation of the algorithm's operational procedure

Consequently, in order for two sets to be considered relevant, it suffices for these sets to be relevant upon a percentage of their terms. In order for these conditions to be evaluated, each term in one set must be compared to each term of the other. Of course this induces a latency, which is partly avoided if set operations are used for checking the similarity of two sets. However, we believe that the degree of relevance that is finally achieved among sets, and thereafter among users, results in high-quality recommendations to the users. This quality of recommendations balances the drawback of the high cost of term comparisons. Furthermore, one can select the invocation times of the algorithm so that it does not become a burden on system performance. For example, it could be activated during certain periods of time (low user 'traffic-jam') and possibly on a snapshot of the system's data.

As it has become apparent from the preceding discussion, it is of great importance to be able to decide when two terms might be considered relevant and how someone could come to that conclusion. It is mentioned that the algorithm uses semantic relevance and in order for this semantic relevance to be examined, a hierarchical semantic relevance model is adopted. That means that, whenever a term is included in another term's thematic domain or it expresses a notion which is "equal to " or "subsumed by" the notion that the other term expresses, then these two terms may be considered relevant. The concept of "equality" can be defined in terms of the synonymity of terms or in terms of the same thematic domain, whereas the notion of "subsumption" can de defined in terms of the hyponyms of a term.[2] Such a hierarchical semantic model can be provided by thesauri or dictionaries of terms, such as WordNet [26]. It should be mentioned here that it is possible to specify whether or not semantic relevance will be applied by the algorithm; it is the third parameter of the algorithm. So the algorithm is capable of functioning in two ways, one that employs semantic relevance is applied and another that doesn't.

Let now examine these two functional ways by means of a simple example. Consider the "representative" sets for two users, which are the ones that were created during the algorithm's operational procedure and will form the base for user comparison and relevance. These sets are depicted in Figure 6 in which the bold line separates "LONG-TERMS" from "SHORT-TERMS" and the common terms are emphasized. If the relevance of these sets is examined by applying set intersection, then it is obvious that these sets are not highly relevant since the common terms are really few. Specifically, since there are only three common terms to these sets, this means that user 1 is relevant to user 2 by 3/18 = 16,67% and user 2 is relevant to user 1 by 3/12 = 25%. Alternatively, if semantic relevance is applied, then almost all the terms in the second user's set are related to some terms in first user's set (fig. 7). Now user 2 is relevant to user 1 by 10/12 = 83,33% (25% previously) and user 1 is relevant to user 2 by 9/18 = 50% (16,67% previously).

3.2.4 Algorithm's Complexity

In this section, we assess the complexity of the proposed algorithm. Assume that each profile contains l "LONG-TERMS" and s "SHORT-TERMS", hence it contains $l+s$ terms in total. Also assume that the total number of users is n.

It has already been mentioned that during the algorithm's operation some terms are selected from each user profile and a set of terms is created for each user. This set of terms represents the user in the rest of the procedure. These sets are created by including the l "LONG-TERMS", and a percentage, π, of the s "SHORT-TERMS". Eventually, each set contains $l+s*\pi$ terms. Hence, the term selection requires $n*(l+s*\pi)$ operations.

---

[2] A hyponym of a term is defined to be a term that expresses a more specific concept.

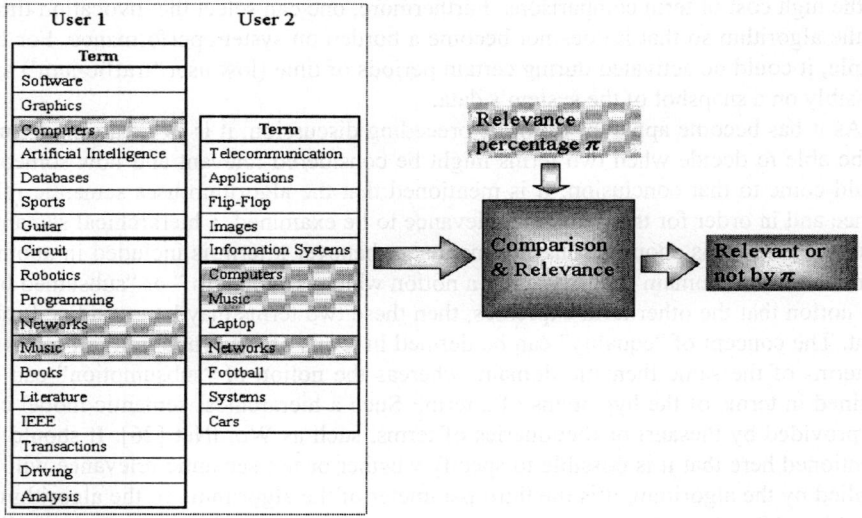

Fig. 6. Comparing two users

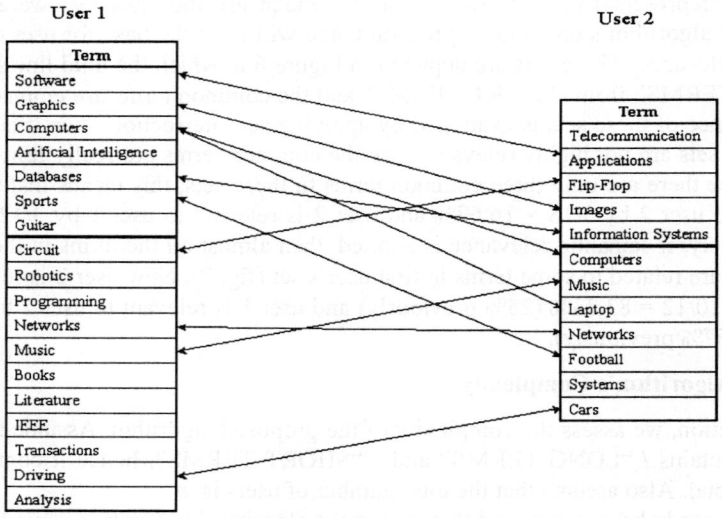

Fig. 7. Term relevance of two sets by applying semantic relevance

The algorithm examines all those sets, which on average contain $t=l+s*\pi$ terms. Specifically, all the terms of each set are compared to all the terms of the rest of the sets, where the total number of such sets is n. Each term in the first set is compared to all the terms in the second, requiring $t*t=t^2$ operations. After that, the first set is compared to the third, so an overall number of $t^2*t=t^3$ operations is required. The same procedure is performed for all n sets. As a result, in order for the first set to be examined, an overall number of t^n operations is required.

Similarly, the second set will be compared to all the remaining sets, but now the number of sets for comparison is $n-1$, since the first set has already been examined. Hence, a total number of t^{n-1} operations is required. For the third set, an overall number of t^{n-2} operations is required and so on. In total, the number of operations that are required equals: $t^n+t^{n-1}+...+t^2$ or $t^2+t^3+...+t^n$. This can be represented by the sum of a geometric sequence: $\Sigma=a_1*(L^n-1)/(L-1)$, where $a_1=t^2$ and $L=t$. Hence, the total number of operations that are required equals $\Sigma=t^2*(t^n-1)/(t-1)$.

Hence, that algorithm's complexity is $\mathbf{O}(t^n)$. This is of course quite a large figure for a large number of users. This is due to the exhaustive comparison that is being performed, in order to make sure that all the terms in all sets are examined. All the users must be exhaustively examined and compared to one another, in order for the relevant ones to be found and grouped together in communities. The following section presents preliminary performance results on the algorithm's implementation.

4 Experimental Results

We have performed some preliminary experiments so as to get a notion of the algorithm's performance. In all executions the parameters of the algorithm are the same, while the number of users increases. Particularly, the selection percentage is set to 20%, the relevance percentage to 30% and the function mode is set so as semantic relevance is applied.[3] The larger a profile is, the higher the relevance percentage should be, ranging between 20%-40% or maybe slightly more at times. Each set created by the algorithm contains about 60 terms.

As mentioned before, the algorithm's complexity is $\mathbf{O}(t^n)$, which means that adding a new user causes the execution time to rise geometrically. Figure 8 depicts a graph that shows the execution time required in respect of the users. As the number of users increases the execution time of the algorithm rises.

Remarkably, we notice that in a particular execution (for nine users) the execution time instead of rising, it falls off. This is quite noteworthy and it is worth explaining.

We have seen that the algorithm exhaustively compares all the users. Thus, the first user is compared to all the others, the second to the rest of them, and so on. If two or more users are considered to be relevant then they are grouped together into the same community. But, in that way, if the first user has many and various likes and interests, then there is a high possibility for her to be considered relevant to many other users. Therefore, all these users will be grouped together, and thus they will be excluded from the rest of the procedure. That leads to considerable reduction of the users, which must be furthermore compared by the algorithm.

The above analysis reveals a methodology, which could be followed in order for the execution time to be reduced. If the profiles were sorted in ascending order according to their size prior to the execution of the algorithm, this would result in the aforementioned situation where users with large profiles will be examined first.

---

[3] The selection of these values was based on experiments as well.

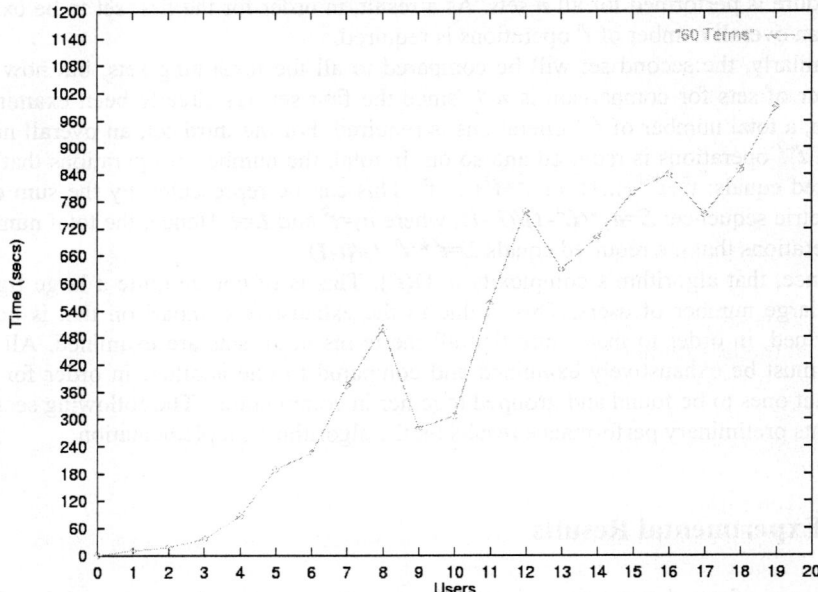

Fig. 8. Execution time for profiles with 60 terms

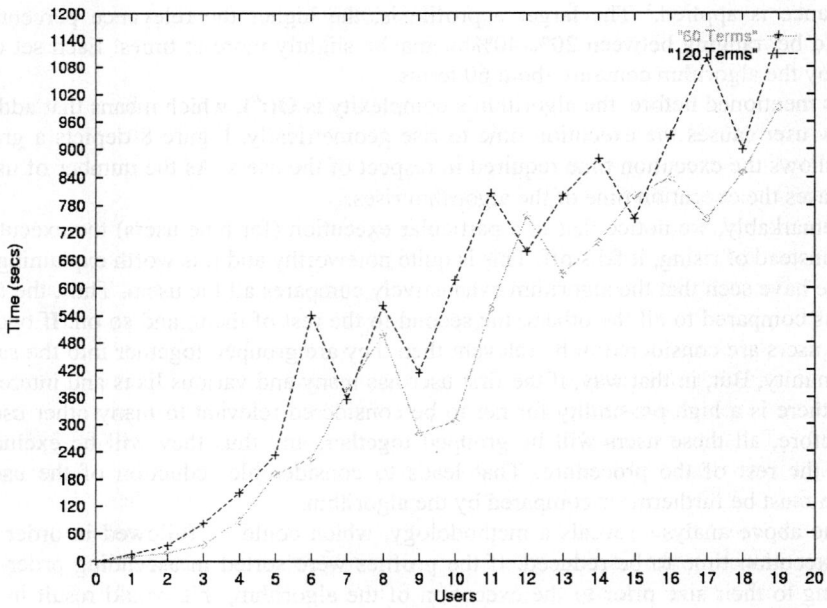

Fig. 9. Execution time for profiles with 60 and 120 terms

Figure 9 depicts the previous graph in comparison to a new one, which shows the execution time of the algorithm under the same circumstances as previously, but with twice the number of terms in the sets. Execution times are higher this time, but it is remarkable that the phenomenon, which was described above, is occurring more often. That is expected since user profiles are almost doubled and thus users have more and different likes.

5 Conclusions and Further Research

This paper proposes an algorithm that examines and compares all user profiles with the goal of classifying them into communities. In order for this to be achieved, all the sets that are created for each user are examined. The operation of the algorithm ensures that a user may participate in more than one community, which is really desirable especially for users with a great variety of interests and thus big profiles. Additionally, a user might not participate to any community, as is the case for new users, who haven't provided enough ratings so that a profile can be built for them, and for users with idiomorphic likes and interests, who are not relevant to any other user. In a nutshell, after the algorithm terminates, a user might belong to none, one or more communities.

It is also possible that two or more users participate in the same communities. But they are included in each one of the communities because different interests were considered for each of the users, or because of their relevance to different users. This is more probable to happen in the case of numerous users with big profiles and thus many terms in them. Since the algorithm is based on the selection of a percentage of terms, the larger the number of terms in the term sets, the higher is the possibility for these sets to be considered relevant concerning various thematic domains and, thus, more communities are likely to be created. Hence, the respective users will all be classified in these communities, which is of course desirable so that the users are able to receive recommendations from all of them.

The algorithm adequately addresses the case of idiomorphic users that may exist and classifies them in the appropriate communities. If there is a possibility for two users to be considered relevant, then this will be done so by the application of the algorithm, since user relevance is based on set relevance. Set relevance is in turn based on the semantic relevance of their terms. So, even though two particular terms have no apparent (i.e., lexical) similarity, these terms may be closely related and may sometimes express the same notion. For example, consider the terms 'car' and 'motor vehicle'. These terms semantically express the same concept since the term 'car' belongs to hyponyms of the term 'motor vehicle'.

As far as the complexity of the algorithm is concerned, we argue that it is balanced by the expected high quality and accuracy of the recommendations that are provided and are based on the user classification into communities. Our preliminary experimental results show that as new users are added the execution time of the algorithm rises, but also reveal a methodology, which could be followed in order for these execution times to be reduced.

We are currently investigating aspects of reducing even more the execution time both "directly", by means of implementation, and "indirectly". The algorithm creates the user communities from scratch and whenever it is applied the old communities are destroyed. This wouldn't be desirable, especially if new users could be accommodated to the existing communities. Therefore, a "differential" classification algorithm could be applied only on new users, in order for them to be grouped to existing communities. This may be performed by comparing new users to existing communities and is feasible due to the fact that each community has its own profile, which is produced as the union of the profiles of all users in community. So each community could be treated as a single user and thus compared to other users. Such an algorithm is expected to have shorter execution time and could be executed more often than the algorithm presented in this paper, which could be executed rarely, so as to cover the cases in which the likes of some users already in a community have changed and are no longer relevant to those of other users in the community.

Finally, one could investigate the case where users with huge profiles (and thus with various and different likes) would act as anchors and organize communities around them. That would result in having incoherent sub-communities inside a community. To deal with these cases a pre-processing of all profiles would be performed so as to distinguish between the various sub-profiles of a user. The algorithm then could be applied on these sub-profiles.

References

1. D. H. Widyantoro, T. R. Ioerger, and J. Yen. "Learning User Interest Dynamics with, Three-Descriptor Representation". *Journal of the American Society for Information Science (JASIS)*, 2000.
2. M. Balabanovic and Y. Sholam. "Combining Content-Based and Collaborative Recommendation". *Communications of the ACM*, 1997.
3. G. Karypis. "Evaluation of Item-Based Top-N Recommendation Algorithms", 2000. In *Proceedings of CIKM*, 2001, pp. 247-254, 2001.
4. M. Keim Condliff, D. D. Lewis, D. Madigan, and C. Posse. "Baeysian Mixed-Effects Models for Recommendation Systems". In *Proceedings of ACM SIGIR Workshop on Recommendation Systems*, 1999.
5. M. Newman, and D. Fisher. "A News Article Recommendation System for Informavores", http://www.cs.berkeley.edu/~danyelf/inf/.
6. J. Konstant, B. Miller, B. Maltz, J. Herlocker, L. Gordon, and J. Riedl. "Grouplens: applying collaborative filtering to Usenet news". *Communications of the ACM*, 40(3):77-87, 1997.
7. P. Resnick, N. Iacovou, M. Suchak, P. Bergston, and J. Riedl. "Grouplens: An open architecture for collaborative filtering of netnews". In *Proceedings of CSCW*, 1994.
8. R. Baeza-Yates, B. Ribeiro-Neto. *"Modern Information Retrieval"*. Addison Wesley, 1999.
9. T. Mitchell *"Machine Learning"*. NY:McGraw-Hill, 1997.

10. G. Widmer, and M. Kubat "Learning in the Presence of Concept Drift and Hidden Contexts". *Machine Learning Journal, 1*, 69-101, 1996.
11. M. Pazzani and D. Billsus. "Learning and revising user profiles: The identification of interesting web sites". *Machine Learning*, 27:313-331, 1997.
12. D.H. Widyantoro *"Learning User Profile in Personalized News Agent"*. Master's thesis, Department of Computer Science, Texas A&M University, 1999.
13. B. Mobasher, H. Dai, T. Luo, M. Nakagawa, and J. Witshire. "Discovery of aggregate usage profiles for web personalization". In *Proceedings of the WebKDD Workshop*, 2000.
14. P. Chan. "A non-invasive learning approach to building web user profiles". In *Proceedings of ACM SIGKDD International Conference*, 1999.
15. C. Buckley and G. Salton. "Optimization of Relevance Feedback Weights". In *Proceedings of the 18th Annual Intl ACM SIGIR Conference, Seattle*, 1995.
16. M.Balabanovic. "An Adaptive Web Page Recommendation Service". In *Proceedings of First International Conference on Autonomous Agents*, pp. 378-385, 1997
17. G. Salton, and M.J. McGill. *"Introduction to Modern Information Retrieval"*.McGraw-Hill, 1983.
18. J. Allan. "Incremental Relevance Feedback for Information Filtering". In Proceedings of the Nineteenth Annual International ACM SIGIR Conference on Research and Development in Information Retrieval, pp. 270-278, ACM, 1996.
19. J. J. Rocchio, "Relevance feedback in information retrieval". In G. Salton, The SMART Retrieval System: Experiments in Automatic Document Processing, pp. 313-323, Englewood Cliffs, NJ, 1971. Prentice Hall, Inc.
20. M. Balabanovic. *"Learning to Surf: Multi-agent Systems for Adaptive Web Page Recommendation"*. PhD thesis, Department of Computer Science, Stanford University, 1998.
21. D. Billsus and M. Pazzani. "A personal news agent that talks, learns and explains". In *Proceedings of the third International Conference on Autonomous Agents (Agents '99)*, pages 268--275, Seattle, WA, 1999
22. B.D. Sheth, *"A Learning Approach to Personalized Information Filtering"*. Master's Thesis, Department of Electrical Engineering and Computer Science, MIT, 1994.
23. D.H.Widyantoro, T.R. Ioerger, and J. Yen. "An Adaptive Algorithm for Learning Changes in User Interests". In *Proceedings of the Eight International Conference on Information and Knowledge Management*, pp. 405-412, 1999.
24. C. Fox, *"Lexical Analysis and Stoplists"*, in *Information Retrieval: Data structures and Algorithms*, edited by W. B. Frakes and R. Baeza-Yates, 1992, Prentice-Hall, pp. 102-130.
25. E. Riloff, "Little words can make a big difference for text classification". In Proceedings, 18th Annual International ACM SIGIR Conference on Research and Development in Information Retrieval (SIGIR'95), pp. 130-136, Seattle, 1995.
26. WordNet, a lexical database for the English language, http://www.cogsci.princeton.edu/~wn/.

Can We Ever Build Survivable Systems from COTS Components?

Howard F. Lipson, Nancy R. Mead, and Andrew P. Moore

CERT® Coordination Center, Software Engineering Institute
Pittsburgh, PA 15213 USA
{hfl,nrm,apm}@sei.cmu.edu
http://www.cert.org/research/

Abstract. Using commercial off-the-shelf (COTS) components to build large, complex systems has become the standard way that systems are designed and implemented by government and industry. Much of the literature on COTS-based systems concedes that such systems are not suitable for mission-critical applications. However, there is considerable evidence that COTS-based systems are being used in domains where significant economic damage and even loss-of-life are possible in the event of a major system failure or compromise. Can we ever build such systems so that the risks are commensurate with those typically taken in other areas of life and commerce?

This paper describes a risk-mitigation framework for deciding when and how COTS components can be used to build survivable systems. Successful application of the framework will require working with vendors to reduce the risks associated with using the vendors' products, and improving and making the best use of your own organization's risk-management skills.

1 Introduction

Lower upfront costs, and a belief that the cost savings extend throughout the system's lifecycle, are primary motivators in the shift from custom-designed to COTS-based systems. The disadvantages associated with COTS-based design include the absence of source code and lack of access to the artifacts of the software engineering process used to design the COTS components.

Whether you've built your system using COTS components from many vendors, or a single vendor has provided you with an integrated solution, many of the risks associated with system management and operation are not in your direct control [2], [3], [8], [10]. Each vendor that plays a role in the design, development, acquisition, integration, deployment, maintenance, operation, or evolution of part (or all) of your system affects the risks you face in your attempt to survive cyber-attacks, accidents, and subsystem failures. We propose

---

® "CERT" and "CERT Coordination Center" are registered in the U.S. Patent and Trademark Office.

continual vendor-based risk evaluations as a critical part of the system lifecycle for mission-critical systems that use COTS components.

Survivable systems are those that continue to fulfill their missions (perhaps at a reduced level of service), despite having components or subsystems that are damaged or compromised by attack, accident, or failure. SEI research into the design and analysis of survivable systems [9], [6] has shown that system survivability is dependent upon well-reasoned tradeoffs among the various quality attributes of a system's architecture and implementation. The design rationale and quality attribute tradeoffs are among the many engineering artifacts that are not available to the consumers of COTS components. Is it then impossible to build survivable systems out of COTS components?

Risk management is central to the achievement of survivability [11]. Those who acquire, design, implement, operate, maintain, and evolve systems that use COTS components can significantly enhance the survivability of such systems by working with vendors to reduce the risks inherent in the vendors' products and processes, and by improving and making the best use of their own organization's risk management skills. This paper suggests approaches that point the way towards future COTS components and vendor processes that provide sufficient visibility into a product's internals to give ample evidence that the use of these components can contribute to the assurance of overall system survivability.

2 Survivability and COTS Components

Survivability cannot be achieved without a clear understanding of the context in which modern systems typically operate – unbounded domains. Unbounded domains, such as the Internet, are characterized by a lack of central control, and a lack of complete, timely, or precise information. Moreover, a typical contemporary system constitutes an unbounded domain. In the absence of full control and full visibility into a system and its environment, achieving survivability (i.e., fulfilling the mission of a system) is an exercise in risk-management and risk tolerance. If your system is primarily composed of COTS components, then you have a rather extreme case of lack of control and lack of visibility regarding the ultimate behavior of your system under a variety of circumstances that could threaten its survival [12].

System vulnerabilities that are extremely unlikely to cause mission failure due to the actions of a normal user may very likely be exploited by an intelligent adversary, e.g., by taking advantage of buffer overflow vulnerabilities [5], particularly when scripts are developed that encode the often intricate and detailed steps needed for successful exploitation. Survivability, therefore, demands high assurance that (1) such vulnerabilities do not exist or cannot be exploited, or (2) that their exploitation does not compromise the mission or can be recognized and recovered from to continue the mission [6]. This need for high assurance is what makes the use of COTS components in mission-critical systems so difficult.

Of course, COTS components can always be used to implement non-critical system functions, that is, functions whose properties do not impact system survivability. Some architectures have demonstrated how to structure a system so that the critical function is isolated to small, high assurance components, thus allowing COTS components to be used anywhere else [7]. Unfortunately, such approaches are currently limited to fairly narrow properties, such as military confidentiality.

Where such approaches are not available, the question is whether COTS components can be used to implement critical system functions. Survivability techniques often rely on redundancy to tolerate compromises of individual components. Layered defenses (e.g., using intrusion detection and recovery to complement resistance measures) also help to tolerate failures in critical function implementations. As a result of a design team's judicious use of replication, redundancy, and diversity, the property of system survivability can emerge from the interactions among the individual components of a system even when the components themselves are not survivable. But what assurances are required of COTS components that implement critical system functions?

The criticality of a system influences the assurance requirements for COTS components that implement essential services. A system has high criticality if the consequences of system failure are severe. A system has low criticality if the consequences of system failure are negligible. Fig. 1 maps the COTS component assurance required as a function of system criticality. There are many factors that influence COTS component assurance, which will be elaborated later in the paper. However, for the purposes of discussing the figure, we treat COTS component assurance abstractly, assuming only that assurance can vary greatly.

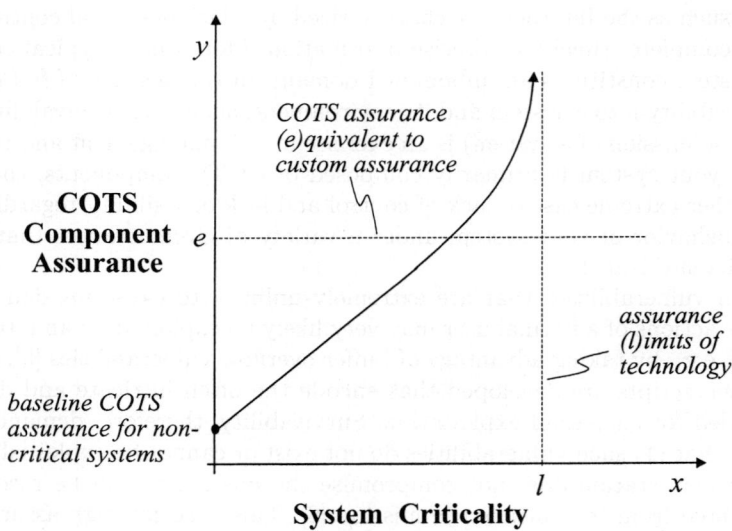

Fig. 1. COTS Component Assurance Required as Function of System Criticality

We assume in Fig. 1 that there is some baseline COTS component assurance required even for non-critical systems. Suppose (c, a) is a particular point along the curve, where $c < l$ is the criticality of the system being built. Then a represents the minimal assurance permitted of any COTS component used to implement the system's essential services. The area above the curve represents acceptable use of COTS components, while the area below the curve represents unacceptable use. We assume that the proposed system relies on the use of COTS for the survival of the system's mission. We also assume that there is a point at which the potential impact is so severe that computing/network technology should not be used regardless of the assurances that the technology affords. This limit is shown as the dashed line l in Fig. 1. The asymptotic nature of the curve to the limit l reflects the need for "infinite" COTS component assurance to implement such high consequence systems.

The dashed line labeled e in Fig. 1 represents COTS component assurance that is as convincing as the custom development assurance. While this varies with the custom development process used, postulating such a point reflects the real possibility that COTS assurance can exceed that of custom development. Some may argue that COTS components with such high assurance do not currently exist and, even if they did, they could not be considered to actually be COTS at that point. We do believe, however, that within our characterization of COTS, COTS components may have certain assurance benefits over custom development – for example, vendor expertise, history of use, and ensured evolution. Given this, the part of the curve above the dashed line e represents systems that are so critical that they actually require the use of very high-assurance COTS components instead of custom development.

3 COTS vs. Custom Design — A Binary Choice, or a Spectrum of Choices?

The term COTS, as it is generally understood, refers to widely-available commercially produced software supplied as object code, for which the only information you might have about the product is the purchase price, a list of features, a user's manual, some vendor claims about the product, a license agreement, an application programming interface (API) specification, and your own experience with the product or trial version (or some third-party experience or test results of which you are aware). Hence, your visibility into the product and the process used to construct it is limited in the extreme. The only control you have over the product is whether to buy it and how many copies you'll purchase.

At the other extreme of the software development world is custom-designed software and systems. However, software design and development always involves risk management, since the processes for even well-engineered custom-designed software involve a lack of full control and a lack of full visibility. The iterative analysis and design methodologies that help to determine the ultimate functional and non-functional attributes of a system, and the tradeoffs among the software quality attributes, functionality, and cost, are suspended when you feel comfortable that the risks associated with the design, implementation, deployment, and use of the system are below your risk-tolerance threshold [9]. Moreover, your compiler and other programming tools are likely to be COTS products, as are your development and target platforms. You can never be completely aware of the backgrounds and skills of the personnel building your system, though the efforts you make in terms of background and reference checks help to reduce your risk, in exchange for some additional time and expense.

Therefore, we wish to dispel the notion that organizations seeking to build survivable systems have only a binary choice, COTS or custom, where COTS-based systems lack almost all control and visibility, but are relatively inexpensive, and custom-built systems give you full control and visibility, albeit at much greater up-front cost. We believe there is a middle spectrum of design choices, ranging from 100% black-box COTS component integration to 100% custom-design, that allows a much more flexible, cost-effective, and risk-mitigating approach to the design of survivable systems. The *V-RATE* method, described in the next section, outlines a set of enabling strategies for mitigating the risks associated with using COTS products. Some of the strategies enable risk reduction by providing more control and more visibility into the internals of a product and the processes used to construct it. However, V-RATE includes other alternatives for mitigating risk that don't involve increasing control and visibility.

4 The V-RATE (Vendor Risk Assessment & Threat Evaluation) Method

Building survivable systems using COTS components is a daunting task because the developer has little or no access to the artifacts of the software engineering process used to create the components. These artifacts are the primary sources from which assurance evidence for a composite system is derived. One way to partially compensate is to use vendor risk assessments as a tool to help you build, maintain, and evolve survivable systems. Such an assessment can be used as a new source of assurance evidence of a system's survivability.

Our proposed vendor risk assessments are based on a *V-RATE (vendor risk assessment and threat evaluation) taxonomy* described below. Two broad categories are at the highest level of our taxonomy: (1) vendor-inherent risk elements and (2) vendor risk elements associated with your own risk management skills. The output of an assessment based on the V-RATE taxonomy is a *vendor-risk profile* for the system being evaluated. We envision a large and growing collection of vendor-risk profiles tied to real-world performance histories, providing empirical data against which a newly generated risk profile can be compared. A vendor-risk profile can be used to assess the risk associated with the use of a product in a particular threat environment, and to identify areas for additional risk-mitigation activities. Because a single numerical rating would not provide sufficient guidance for these risk-mitigation activities, the vendor-risk profile helps you to identify your risks in each of the V-RATE taxonomy areas, and allows you to consider your risk tolerance with respect to each element of the taxonomy.

4.1 The V-RATE Taxonomy

Elements of the V-RATE taxonomy include:

1. **Vendor's Inherent Risk Elements**
    1.1 *Visibility of Product Attributes*
        1.1.1 Openness – Degree of visibility into design and engineering processes
        1.1.2 Independent testing organizations
    1.2 *Technical Competence*
        1.2.1 Survivability capability maturity
        1.2.2 Existence of vendor ratings/certifications
        1.2.3 Evidence of adherence to applicable industry standards and government regulations
        1.2.4 Demonstrated diversity and redundancy in a vendor's products and services
        1.2.5 Existence of a vendor team that deals effectively with security/survivability issues
    1.3 *Performance History*
    1.4 *Compliance*
        1.4.1 Responsiveness to security/survivability issues (which can include related quality issues such as reliability, performance, safety, and usability)
        1.4.2 Responsiveness to requests for new features and improvements
        1.4.3 Willingness to cooperate with third-party testers and certifiers
    1.5 *Trustworthiness*
        1.5.1 Track record / Word-of-mouth
        1.5.2 Evidence of skill at evaluating trustworthiness of personnel
    1.6 *Business Management Competence*
        1.6.1 Economic viability
        1.6.2 Vendor's risk-management skills in dealing with subcontractors
    1.7 *Controlled Evolution*
        1.7.1 Clearly specified (or discernible) evolutionary path
        1.7.2 Product integration stability
        1.7.3 Product evolution supports continual survivability improvement
2. **Vendor Risk Elements Associated with Your Risk Management Skills in Dealing with Vendors**
    2.1 *Technical Risk-Mitigating Factors*
        2.1.1 Your skill at evaluating a product's quality attributes (in particular, those quality attributes that can contribute to system survivability, such as security, reliability, performance, safety, and usability)
        2.1.2 Your skill at evaluating vendor technical competence
        2.1.3 Awareness of existing vendor ratings and certifications

2.1.4 Demonstrated diversity and redundancy in the integration of vendor products and services
2.1.5 Use of architectural tools and techniques (e.g., wrappers) to limit risks associated with a vendor product
2.1.6 Your association with expert security/survivability organizations, and the existence of a dedicated security/survivability group within your own organization

2.2 *Non-Technical Mitigation of Risk*
2.2.1 Legal
2.2.2 Economic
2.2.3 Political and social

2.3 *Independence / Interdependence*
2.4 *Your Exposure*
2.5 *Mission Alignment / Vendor Compatibility*
2.6 *Your Negotiating Skill / Bargaining Power*

4.2 Specific Vendor Risk Reduction Techniques

The V-RATE method provides a framework for assessing survivability risks associated with COTS products. Although there are many risks and much work to be done, there are specific ways that risk can be reduced. In the long term, we would like to see a full list of vendor risk reduction techniques. Each technique could be assigned a value that could be used in the V-RATE calculation to show reduction of overall survivability risk associated with specific COTS products.

For each element of the V-RATE method, specific strategies should be developed to reduce risk. In Table 1 we provide some brief examples of ways in which risk can be reduced. We align these examples with the V-RATE taxonomy.

The following are expanded examples for two of the items in the table. This expansion could be done for the entire table to form a comprehensive set of examples/strategies.

Example of V-RATE Taxonomy Section 1.4, Compliance. The vendor shows a willingness to respond to security and survivability concerns by:

- making security patches available quickly.
- allowing the client to *turn off* unneeded features and thus reduce the risks associated with those features. In this way the client can select a *core* set of needed services, rather than be forced to live with the consequences of "one size fits all."
- building recovery mechanisms into the software. Examples of such mechanisms are automated back up of data and retention of state data.
- building security (resistance) mechanisms into the software. Examples are encryption, password protection, and diversity.
- putting specific software engineering practices in place to improve security, such as inspections, testing, the use of strongly typed languages, and processes that support good programming practices. Another positive response to customer concerns would be to initiate or increase education and training in security and software engineering for the vendor's technical staff

Table 1. V-RATE Risk Reduction Examples

V-RATE Element	Example
1.1 Visibility of Product Attributes	The vendor is willing to allow client to see source code corresponding to installed binaries.
1.2 Technical Competence	The vendor has demonstrated (rated) competence in key survivability activity/practice areas (using a survivability capability maturity model).
1.3 Performance History	The vendor has a track record – experience, statistics, testimonials, and word-of-mouth.
1.4 Compliance	The vendor makes security patches available quickly.
1.5 Trustworthiness	The vendor consistently checks character references of new hires and periodically re-checks all personnel.
1.6 Business Management Competence	The vendor's prospects for long-term economic health are good.
1.7 Controlled Evolution	The vendor shares plans and procedures that indicate controlled product evolution.
2.1 Technical Risk-Mitigating Factors	You have the skills needed for direct technical risk evaluation (including, but not limited to Survivable Systems Analysis).
2.2 Non-Technical Mitigation of Risk	You have access to legal or economic protection, such as insurance, warranty and license agreements, performance clauses and penalties, regulatory protection, and performance bonds.
2.3 Independence / Interdependence	You examine the vendor products and services associated with your system and look for interdependencies that could threaten survivability.
2.4 Your Exposure	You determine what elements of the system are dependent upon the competence, trustworthiness, and thoroughness of the vendor.
2.5 Mission Alignment / Vendor Compatibility	You evaluate alignment of your mission and required software quality attributes (SQA's) with vendor mission and SQA's.
2.6 Your Negotiating Skill / Bargaining Power	You partner with vendor to obtain early notification of potential security/survivability problems.

Example of V-RATE Taxonomy Section 1.7, Controlled Evolution.
The vendor's plans and procedures indicate controlled product evolution as follows:

- Vendor upgrades do not require massive re-integration (such as major rewrites of API glue code).
- Applying security patches should not be delayed by the ripple effects of changes in the vendor product.
- There is a low degree of feature coupling.
- Changes in a few features do not cause massive maintenance headaches.

– The vendor is willing to provide insight into business plans for the product, so that the client has some idea of the stability of the product.
– The vendor agrees to support the product, particularly from a security and survivability perspective, over the long term.

5 A V-RATE Example

Although the V-RATE framework is at a very early stage of development, it is crucial to understand from the outset that it is not the goal of this research to assign a single or small number of composite numerical ratings to vendor product and processes for purposes of direct comparison. We instead envision that the output of the application of the V-RATE method will be a vendor-risk profile that is personalized to the specific organization that is interacting with a vendor or group of vendors for the purpose of acquiring, developing, operating, or maintaining a mission-critical COTS-based system. Each element of the V-RATE taxonomy represents an area of added risk that is not present in custom-designed systems. A heightened awareness of these risks (which enables you to take steps to reduce them) is the main benefit to be achieved by mapping the V-RATE taxonomy onto an existing or proposed design that includes COTS components.

Let's consider an e-commerce system that is used for Internet purchases as exemplified in Fig. 2, incorporating a number of COTS products, such as a Web server, a firewall, and a database application. The V-RATE taxonomy can serve

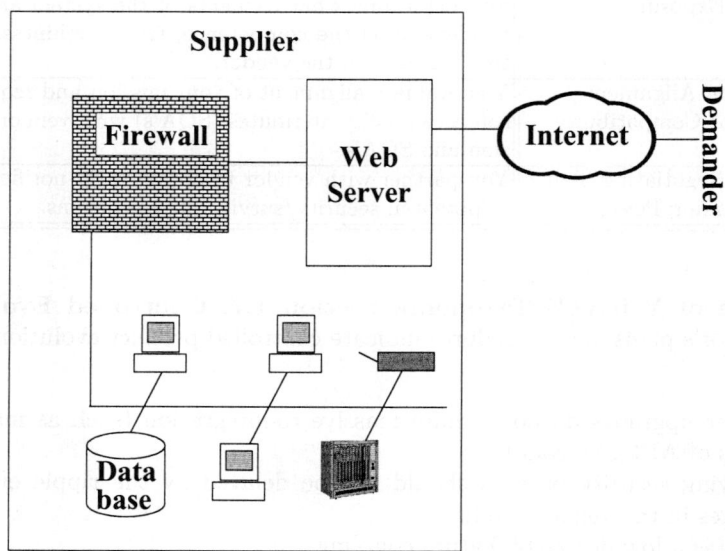

Fig. 2. Example E-Commerce System Architecture

as a road map to examine each of the COTS products used to implement the architecture and can be used in conjunction with architectural modifications, based on architectural-level survivability strategies, to enhance the survivability of the system. This process is inherently iterative and risk-driven.

Once mission requirements are defined, the design team should examine the existing (or proposed) e-commerce system architecture and modify it to support high-level survivability strategies, in the context of scenarios that threaten the business mission. Based on this scenario-driven examination of the architecture, the designers may decide, for example, to

- Add a second firewall (i.e., a DMZ) for defense-in-depth against cyber-attack, and a backup Web server in the event of accident or attack.
- Deploy redundant (and diverse) databases to recover from data loss or corruption.
- Contract with redundant (and diverse) service providers for more survivable Internet connectivity.

Once the architectural-level survivability strategies are in place, the design team must ensure that the components used to implement the architecture are technically sound. The V-RATE taxonomy can be used to gather evidence of assurance. The first step is to annotate a representation of the architecture with vendor names, and other vendor attributes, to identify areas of exposure. For example, it is well known that apparently independent telecommunications service providers offer connectivity solutions that share the same physical fiber. Designers should ask the right questions of their service providers (or use other means) to ensure diversity.

Next, proceed down the taxonomy to gather evidence of assurance. First, consider the openness of a vendor's component. Can you negotiate full access to the source, and other engineering and design artifacts (perhaps under a confidentiality agreement)? If you can, does your staff have the expertise to do the analysis and testing necessary to provide the required assurance? If not, perhaps third-party testing and analysis will provide the expertise and assurance you need, and might actually be superior to giving your own staff access to the source code. This might be an example of a situation where COTS can be superior to custom-built, for instance, if a vendor with a high degree of expertise and experience in a given industry problem domain is willing to make the results of their testing and analyses available. COTS-related risks would be further reduced by verifying the vendor's detailed technical claims through competent third-party testing and analysis.

Continue, in this manner, step-by-step down the V-RATE taxonomy. In particular, carefully consider the value of non-technical approaches to mitigate risk, such as performance bonds, legal disclaimers, and insurance. The process of survivable architecture refinement and COTS-product risk assessment proceeds iteratively as required by mission demands and business constraints.

Use the V-RATE taxonomy to gather evidence of assurance for the set of COTS products under consideration. This collection of evidence will then allow you to compare the products. Numerical ratings within each category (indicating both strength of assurance and importance of this evidence to the system owner) and composite ratings that represent accumulated evidence across categories, allow for relative rankings of concerns, with the caveat that composite rankings derived from such numbers may only be used with extreme caution. Composite ratings suffer from the danger that ratings for taxonomy elements important to your organization will be cancelled out by ratings associated with elements that are not of concern to you.

On the other hand, a detailed vendor-risk profile would provide ratings across a number of risk-relevant elements that are keyed to emphasize what a specific organization deems important. We envision tools that provide

- multiple views or perspectives of a vendor-risk profile
- the ability to group or ungroup related taxonomy elements to yield a wide range of composite representations
- views that are suitable for "what-if" analyses and comparison of design or acquisition alternatives.

However, the specific numerical ratings and vendor-risk profiles that result from the V-RATE process are not as important as what can be learned by going through the process itself. We believe that risk will be significantly reduced if the system owner goes through the exercise of assigning importance to each V-RATE category and assessing the risks associated with the vendor's products and processes, as well as the system owner's management processes. Further gains can be achieved by obtaining the support of the vendor in this exercise.

6 How V-RATE Relates to the Common Criteria

The Common Criteria (CC), ISO International Standard 15408, represents an attempt to provide a structured, yet flexible approach to help consumers and vendors of security-relevant COTS products agree on and evaluate required product function and product/process assurance [4]. The CC promotes creating two documents called the Protection Profile and the Security Target. Consumers develop a Protection Profile for a class of security-relevant products of interest, such as firewalls, operating systems, and smart cards. The Protection Profile specifies the function and assurances required by a broad consumer base for the class of product independent of any particular implementation. A vendor develops a Security Target to describe their implementation of a product intended to conform to a particular Protection Profile. The Security Target specifies the security functions supported, the development process used, and an argument for why the functions and processes conform to the Protection Profile targeted. The CC sets forth guidelines for the production and independent evaluation of a vendor's Security Target in response to a consumer Protection Profile.

While originally intended as a vehicle for internationally-accepted IT security evaluation, the CC may provide a model for using V-RATE to promote increased trustworthiness of COTS products. V-RATE provides criteria for the vendor's product and process that aid the evaluation of COTS technology for use in achieving a particular mission. V-RATE's criteria are technology-independent and thus, more abstract than the CC. V-RATE also includes criteria for assessing the consumer's own ability to deal with COTS vendors and the inherent risks associated with COTS technology. One of the criticisms of the CC is the large amount of overhead needed to produce and evaluate products within its framework. V-RATE may provide a middle ground between the black-box acceptance of COTS and a CC-evaluated product.

A significant difference between the Common Criteria and V-RATE is that V-RATE is conducted by, or on behalf of, the party whose security and survivability is at risk (and from that party's perspective), whereas a Common Criteria evaluation is typically paid for by the vendor, and is conducted on the vendor's behalf [1].

7 Summary and Future Work

Too many organizations take an all-or-nothing view with regard to the use of COTS in mission-critical systems (e.g., either COTS components are never safe to use, or COTS use should be maximized). This paper describes V-RATE criteria to help decide when and how COTS products can be used to build survivable systems. Factors that influence this decision include not only attributes of the COTS products themselves, but also attributes of the system's mission, the vendor, the vendor's development lifecycle process, and your own organization's risk management skills.

Increased vendor cooperation will improve the V-RATE method's effectiveness. Organizations often expect too little of their vendors, in terms of visibility into the internals of vendor products and processes, or meaningful guarantees of quality. Expectations need to be raised so that vendors more directly support the risk assessment and risk reduction efforts of their customers. Moreover, appropriate economic incentives to encourage vendor cooperation need to be explored.

Future work will investigate how to put the V-RATE method on a more scientific basis. Ongoing development of V-RATE may provide input into a model similar to the Capability Maturity Model® that would help acquirers to more systematically assess a developer's maturity for producing COTS components for survivable systems. More rigorous foundations will require quantitative measures of a system's capability to survive malicious attacks, and ways to measure the contribution of a given COTS product (or set of COTS products) to promoting or obstructing that capability. This must include the ability to measure the impact on system survivability of interactions among multiple COTS components.

We also plan to incorporate the V-RATE criteria into suitable system development lifecycle models, such as the Spiral Model. The process of refining a survivable architecture using COTS products is inherently iterative. Unacceptable product or vendor risks found during one iteration may require backtracking

---

® Capability Maturity Model is a registered trademark of Carnegie Mellon University.

to a previous iteration to incorporate different vendor or custom products within the architecture. The iterative, risk-driven nature of the Spiral Model makes it particularly appropriate for incorporating the V-RATE method.

Our plan to incorporate the V-RATE criteria into software development lifecycle models will require us to take a close look at the concept of *open-source software*, which has been gaining increasing acceptance over the past few years. Open-source software provides access to the source code of a product for little or no cost, thereby encouraging the programming community to read, modify, and redistribute the source code, potentially leading to rapid evolution and improvement. We will investigate the suitability of open-source components for the design, development, maintenance, and evolution of survivable systems, in the context of the V-RATE criteria and integration with more traditional COTS components.

Finally, we plan to apply V-RATE to real-world, mission-critical systems. Such case studies will help us to fine-tune and validate the method, and demonstrate its use within a realistic lifecycle process. These studies will also help us to understand the risks associated with using COTS components for specific system missions. The details of the application of V-RATE (such as the specific evidence that needs to be gathered) may differ for different domains (e.g., military mission-critical systems, e-commerce systems, and financial systems). Since survivability is heavily dependent upon the context of the mission, understanding these differences is critical to V-RATE's successful application.

We intend to focus our research activities in these areas and encourage others to do the same. Only then will we be able to determine with assurance when and how we can use COTS components to build survivable systems.

Acknowledgment

We would like to express our gratitude to Dr. Carol A. Sledge, a colleague at the Software Engineering Institute, for her valuable comments and suggestions based on her review of an earlier draft of this paper.

References

1. R. Anderson. *Security Engineering: A Guide to Building Dependable Distributed Systems*, pages 527–529. John Wiley & Sons, 2001.
2. V. R. Basili and B. Boehm. COTS-based systems top 10 list. *IEEE Software*, 34(5):91–93, May 2001.
3. L. Brownsword, P. Oberndorf, and C. Sledge. An activity framework for COTS-based systems. *Crosstalk: The Journal of Defense Software Engineering*, 13(9), September 2000.
4. Common Criteria Implementation Board. *Common Criteria for Information Technology Security Evaluation, Version 2.1.* Number CCIMB-99-031. August 1999. See: http://csrc.ncsl.nist.gov/cc/.

5. C. Cowan, P. Wagle, C. Pu, S. Beattie, and J. Walpole. Buffer overflows: Attacks and defenses for the vulnerability of the decade. In *DARPA Information Survivability Conference and Expo (DISCEX)*, Hilton Head, SC, January 2000. IEEE Computer Society.
6. R. J. Ellison, D. A. Fisher, R. C. Linger, H. F. Lipson, T. A. Longstaff, and N. R. Mead. Survivable systems: An emerging discipline. In *Proceedings of the 11th Canadian Information Technology Security Symposium (CITSS'99)*, Ottawa, Ontario, May 1999. Communications Security Establishment, Government of Canada. See: http://www.cert.org/research/ for additional papers on this topic.
7. J. Froscher and M. Kang. A client-server architecture supporting MLS interoperability with COTS components. In *Proc. MILCOM 97*, Monterey, CA, November 1997.
8. S. A. Hissam, D. Carney, and D. Plakosh. *DoD Security Needs and COTS-Based Systems*. SEI Monographs on the Use of Commercial Software in Government Systems. Software Engineering Institute, Carnegie Mellon University, Pittsburgh, PA, September 1998. See: http://www.sei.cmu.edu/cbs/papers/monographs/dod-security-needs.htm.
9. R. Kazman, M. Klein, M. Barbacci, T. Longstaff, H. F. Lipson, and S. J. Carriere. The architecture tradeoff analysis method. In *Proceedings of the IEEE International Conference on Engineering of Complex Computer Systems*, Monterey, CA, August 1998. IEEE Computer Society. See: http://www.sei.cmu.edu/ata/ for additional papers on this topic.
10. U. Lindqvist and E. Johnson. A map of security risks associated with using COTS. *IEEE Computer*, pages 60–66, June 1998.
11. H. Lipson and D. Fisher. Survivability – A new technical and business perspective on security. In *Proceedings of the New Security Paradigms Workshop*. ACM, September 1999.
12. N. R. Mead, H. F. Lipson, and C. A. Sledge. Towards survivable COTS-based systems. *Cutter IT Journal*, 14(2):4–11, February 2001.

Towards a Data Model for Quality Management Web Services: An Ontology of Measurement for Enterprise Modeling

Henry M. Kim[1] and Mark S. Fox[2]

[1] Schulich School of Business, York University
Toronto, Ontario M3J 1P3
hkim@schulich.yorku.ca

[2] Department of Mechanical and Industrial Engineering, University of Toronto
Toronto, Ontario M5S 3G9
msf@mie.utoronto.ca

Abstract. Though the WWW is used for business process automation to lower costs and shorten leadtimes, arguably its use has been limited for another metric of business success: Improving quality. A promising advancement to the WWW is the development of the Semantic Web, which relies upon using machine process-able domain knowledge represented in ontologies. Therefore, one promising area of research and application is the development of ontologies used as data models to provide quality management services on the Semantic Web. In this paper, the TOVE Measurement Ontology is presented as a formal model of a fundamental domain, which needs to be represented to provide these services. Measurement is fundamental for representing quality because before quality is evaluated and managed, it must first be measured. An assessment system for measuring attributes of an entity, activities for measurement, and quality as conformance to requirements are the core concepts represented in the ontology. The formal representation of measurement is emphasized over detailing context of ontology use, since this is an issue not heavily examined by the ontology community and one that needs to be detailed in order develop data models to provide Semantic Web based quality management services.

1 Introduction

Using Internet technologies to enable novel business processes and link globally disparate entities has led to benefits such as lowered transaction costs and leadtimes. However, what about quality? Though technologies can be used to automate rote operational business processes, quality management processes are often knowledge intensive. It is difficult then to abstract processes' steps, and automate them to computer readable instructions. A (computational) enterprise model[1], "a computational representation of the structure, activities, processes, information, resources, people, behavior, goals, and constraints of a business, government, or other enterprise" [1], can be used to encode organizational knowledge. An expressive model represents rich knowledge required for some quality management business processes. A precise model represents this knowledge such that computers can interpret instructions and data as intended by the encoders.

Ontology-based enterprise models are expressive and precise (minimize ambiguity in interpretation). An ontology is a data model that "consists of a representational vocabulary with precise definitions of the meanings of the terms of this vocabulary plus a set of formal axioms that constrain interpretation and well-formed use of these terms" [2]. An ontology can also be considered an explicit representation of shared understanding [3]: Since precise definitions and axioms exist, proper interpretations by and sharing with a computer or a decision maker that did not develop the definitions and axioms are possible.

Yahoo! [4] and *VerticalNet* [5] use ontologies commercially. In Tim Berners-Lee's vision of the Semantic Web [6], computers on the web will automatically find and interpret semantics of key terms and rules, represented in ontologies, necessary for providing web services. If this vision is realized, there are huge implications for businesses. IBM states the provision and use of web services as part of "dynamic e-business, the evolution of our e-business strategy" [7]. Potentially, some quality management functions can be performed as web services, and these in turn can be enabled using quality management ontologies.

Though not explicitly designed for use on the Semantic Web, Kim [8] identifies measurement, traceability, and quality management system as domains fundamental to represent to describe quality. In particular, according to the definition of quality as "conformance to requirements" [9], a more definitive statement about the quality of an entity is possible after measurements are taken and conformance to requirements, evaluated. For instance, Federal Express' quality motto was "measure, measure, measure" [10].

In this paper then, an ontology of measurement is detailed to provide evidence that enterprise models constructed using the ontology can someday enable and automate business processes for provision of quality management web services. In particular, the representations themselves are detailed rather than the context of their uses. This paper is organized as follows. In §2, the ontological engineering methodology used is introduced. In §3, development of ontology representations according to the steps of the methodology is presented. Finally in §4, concluding remarks are made, along with statements about how this work can be extended to provide quality management services via the Semantic Web.

2 Methodology

Shown below is an overview of the methodology [11] used to engineer the TOVE Measurement Ontology.

---

[1] Hereto forth, 'enterprise model' refers to computational enterprise model.

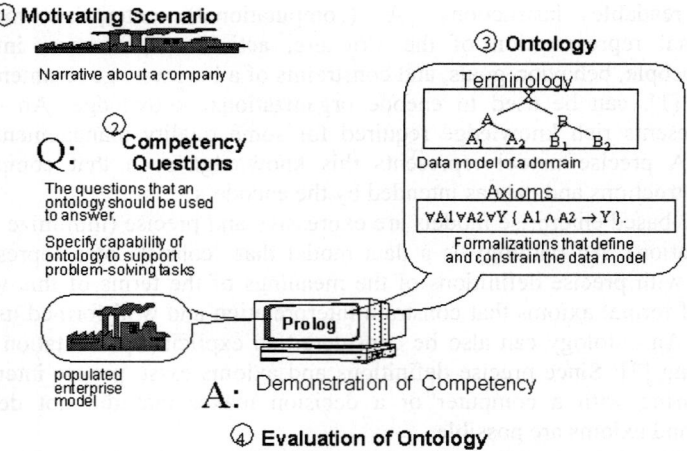

Fig. 1. TOVE Ontological Engineering Methodology

A *Motivating Scenario* is a detailed narrative about a specific enterprise, where emphasis is placed on problems or tasks it faces. When the Motivating Scenario is analyzed, enterprise-independent, generic concepts are abstracted and serve to characterize *Informal Competency Questions* in natural language. Terms with which such queries can be composed comprise the *Terminology*, or data model, of the ontology. Queries re-stated using the terminology are called *Formal Competency Questions*. Answers to these questions can be automatically deduced if *Axioms* that define and constrain the terminology are developed in a formal language with restrictive syntax and semantics, such as First-Order Logic. In this methodology, ontologies are defined using building block ontologies that formalize core enterprise concepts. So, axioms of the measurement ontology are defined using its own terms and/or those from the TOVE Core Ontologies —a collective term for ontologies of activity-state, causality, time, resource, and organizational structure. Deductions using the axioms constitute a *Demonstration of Competency*, which can be implemented in a declarative language like Prolog. If this ontology is used as a schema to construct a populated enterprise model for the specific enterprise analyzed in the Motivating Scenario, the demonstration of competency serves as query-based analysis to solve the enterprise's problems.

3 Measurement Ontology

3.1 Motivating Scenario

BHP Steel is an industrial collaborator for the TOVE Measurement Ontology development. The following excerpt describes its losses with respect to cost, time, and revenue when products of unacceptable quality (called non-prime products) are produced. The key concept abstracted from this excerpt is the following: *There must be a systematic way of describing how a particular physical characteristic is to be measured and this description must be used to meet the customer expectations of quality* (**C1**)[2].

- As raw materials are transformed by the different production units of BHP Steel's supply chain, non-prime products may be produced. These are the products whose physical properties do not satisfy necessary tolerance specifications. Non-prime products lead to lost revenue due to re-grading and scrapping, increased costs due to additional rework, carrying of excess inventory to meet delivery promises, and increased variability of leadtime performance.

The next excerpt describes BHP Steel's need to understand and improve its inspection system, the collection of activities that assesses whether a product is non-prime. The key concept is the following: *Quality assessment is made through a system of activities that perform measurement; this is a view of measurement as an activity* (**C2**).

- If products are consistently found to be non-prime, this is an indication that there is something faulty in the production unit. A cause for this occurrence is suspected to be an inadequate inspection processes.

The following excerpt specifies what is entailed in determining a product as non-prime. The key concept is the following: *Every quality assessment is a decision that begins with a value of measurement at a given point in time* (**C3**).

- Especially when the product is shipped to the customer, it is essential that the product satisfy the tolerance specifications of the customer. Therefore, the product's physical characteristics are measured, compared against tolerance specifications, and a decision about whether the product is non-prime is made.

3.2 Informal Competency Questions

Measurement Description System. In order to elaborate (C1), the transformation of the relationship between an entity and its attributes into the more tractable domain of terms, numbers and operators must be modeled. Relationships that describe quality can be represented as requirements on an entity, expressed as a series of equations, $A \otimes B$, where A and B denote qualitative or quantitative measurements upon attributes, and $\otimes$ denotes a comparison operator. The following then are informal competency questions (ICQ's) about requirements:

- Is this a quality requirement? (**ICQ-1**)
- What are the physical characteristics that are measured? (**ICQ-2**)

In measuring physical characteristics, one important aspect is sampling, which occurs when a subset of a population of an evaluated entity is measured, rather than the whole population [12]. The following are some questions for representing sampling:

- Is every entity that is produced measured? (**ICQ-3**)

---

[2] stands for Concept #1

- If the product is a batch, is a sample taken from that batch and measured? **(ICQ-4)**
- If a sample is taken and measured, is the value for the measurement some aggregate (e.g. average) of the measurement upon individual units of that sample? **(ICQ-5)**
- Or, is the value of the measurement a measure of whether or not individual units of the sample passed or failed a certain threshold (e.g. % of widgets of the sample which are <10cm)? **(ICQ-6)**

In order to measure, there must be a way to systematically describe a measurement. This description system must minimally include the appropriate attributes of an entity to measure, as well as each of the attributes' mean (μ), distribution (connoted by its standard deviation, σ), and comparison operator ($\otimes$) for comparing measured values against μ and σ. Hopefully, the value of a measurement for a physical characteristic falls within certain tolerance specifications, which can be described with μ, σ and $\otimes$. So, the following can be asked:

- What ought to be the measured value; that is, what is the expected value for that physical characteristic? **(ICQ-7)**
- What are the tolerance specifications for a physical characteristic that is measured? **(ICQ-8)**

Measurements are ambiguous without their relevant units of measurements. So, the following can be asked:

- What is the unit of measurement for a physical characteristic of an entity? **(ICQ-9)**

Measurement Activities. In order to elaborate (C2), the following questions about measurement and inspection can be asked.

- Is this an activity that performs measurement? **(ICQ-10)**
- Is this an inspection activity? **(ICQ-11)**

Measurement Points. In order to elaborate (C3), the elemental piece of information needed to make a quality assessment decision can be represented as the value of a measurement taken at a point in time. Following are questions about quality that build on this.

- What is the measured value for a physical characteristic at a given point in time? **(ICQ-12)**
- What are the measured values for a physical characteristic during a given period of time? **(ICQ-13)**
- Is an entity of "good" quality at a given point in time? **(ICQ-14)**
- Is an entity of "bad" quality at a given point in time? **(ICQ-15)**
- Is an entity of conforming quality over a given period of time? **(ICQ-16)**

These questions need to be expressed more formally using terms from the TOVE Measurement Ontology, which are shown next.

3.3 Terminology & Formal Competency Questions

Measurement Description System. To formally express (ICQ-1) and (ICQ-2), the following terms are included in the TOVE Measurement Ontology:

quality_requirement(Qr) **(Term-1)**
   <Qr> A quality related organizational constraint
measured_attribute(At) **(Term-2)**
   <At>[3] A physical characteristic for an entity that has a bearing on the quality of the entity

To formally express (ICQ-3) to (ICQ-6), the relationship between an attribute <Atr> of a *resource*—e.g. 'arm length' of an 'arm assembly'—and a measured attribute <At> of a set or batch (also called a *traceable resource unit* or *tru*) of that resource—e.g. 'average arm length' of the measured sample from a 'lot of arm assemblies'—is represented. tru and resource are terms from the TOVE Core Ontologies.

- samples_attribute(Atr,At) **(Term-3)**

There are two additional issues regarding sampling.

- *sample size*: How many individuals in a set are measured in order to model the characteristics of the set? Sample size type <Sz> can be classified as one of:
  - *sample*: set size > sample size > 1
  - *unit sample*: set size > sample size = 1
  - *unit population*: set size = sample size = 1
  - *population*: set size = sample size > 1
- *sampling plan*: When determining an aggregate value from the sample, does it refer directly to the actual attribute that is physically measured—e.g. 'average arm length'—or is the reference indirect—e.g. '# nonconforming of a sample'? In statistics, the former sampling plan type <Sp> is called *variable sampling*, the latter, *attribute sampling*.

So the following are represented:
- has_sample_sizing(At,Sz) **(Term-4)**
- has_sampling_plan(At,Sp) **(Term-5)**

To formally express (ICQ-7) to (ICQ-8), a standard mean value μ <Mu> for what the value of a measured attribute <At> must be is represented as well as a function of μ and σ^2 ($f(\mu,\sigma^2)$) and an operator ($\otimes$). Then, the value of each measurement can be compared to this function, so that some evaluation of "acceptability" of the entity measured can be made. The challenge for representation is the following: How can $f(\mu,\sigma^2)$ and $\otimes$ be represented when measured values are not of ratio scale? Although σ^2 cannot be represented non-numerically, $f(\mu,\sigma^2)$ can, if it is assumed that $f(\mu,\sigma^2)$ is a subset of the range of all possible measured values. For a measured attribute <At>, this subset is given a generic term called a *specification set* <SL>, where elements of this subset denote "acceptable" measurement values:

---

[3] A variable or parameter of a term is denoted within <> brackets when the term is defined. <At> denotes that 'At' is one of the variables of the term *measured attribute*, e.g. if At='average widget length' for the expression measured_attribute(At) then this is read as "average widget length is a measured attribute."

- has_standard_value(At,Mu) (**Term-6**)
- has_specification_set(At,SL) (**Term-7**)

To formally express (ICQ-9), a description system for a measured attribute <At> that describes a unit of measurement <U> is represented:

- has_unit_of_measurement(At,U) (**Term-8**)

Below is a data model of the Measurement Description System represented in the TOVE Measurement Ontology.

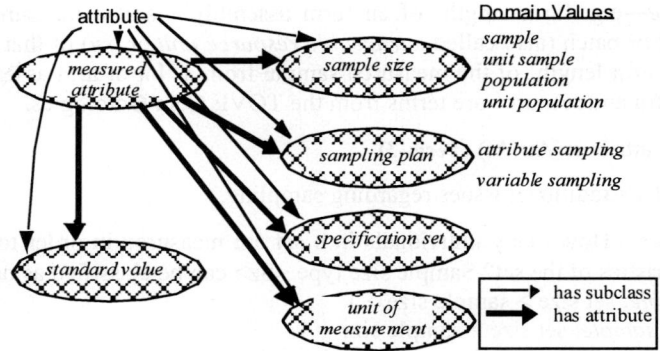

Fig. 2. Measurement Description System Data Model

Measurement Activities. The simplest measurement action is the measurement of one measured attribute of one tru at one point in time. When this measurement is performed using a special resource <R> called a *measuring resource*, this activity <A> is a *primitive measure* activity. A primitive measure activity or an aggregation of primitive measure activities is a *measure* activity. An *inspection and test* activity is a form of a measure activity. The following terms then are used to formally express (ICQ-9) and (ICQ-10).

- measuring_resource(R) (**Term-9**)
- primitive_measure(A) (**Term-10**)
- measure(A) (**Term-11**)
- inspect_and_test(A) (**Term-12**)

Measurement Point. To formally express (ICQ-12) and (ICQ-13), the result of a measurement activity is represented using a *measurement point* <Mp>, which relates the value of the measurement, and concomitantly the measured attribute <At>, the time of measurement <Tp>, and tru measured <Rt>.

- measurement_pt(Rt,At,Mp,Tp) (**Term-13**)

If a measurement point is assessed to be "acceptable"—i.e. the point is an element within the specification set—then a *conformance point* <Q> is represented along with the related tru <Rt>, measured attribute <At>, and time of measurement <Tp>. If it is not "acceptable" then a *nonconformance point* with the same related variables is represented.

- conformance_pt(Q,Rt,At,Tp) **(Term-14)**
- nonconformance_pt(Q,Rt,At,Tp) **(Term-15)**

A given quality requirement <Qr> on an entity <X> can then be written as a composition of conformance points—e.g. "X meets its quality requirements if all measurement points for a measured attribute of various trus whose measurements related to X's quality during a given time period are conformance points." The following term then represents the concept that "quality is conformance to requirements."

- conforming_quality(X,Qr) **(Term-16)**

With these terms that describe measurement points, (ICQ-14) to (ICQ-16) can be formally expressed. Informal competency questions can now be stated formally since the terminology with which the questions can be re-posed are developed.

3.4 Formal Competency Questions

For brevity, only some of the competency questions are presented, and in the following manner:

- The informal competency question is stated.
- The informal competency question is re-stated in English with the terminology developed from the ontology
- The competency question is stated formally in First-Order Logic.

For consistency with other TOVE ontologies, the situation calculus [13] is used to represent measurement ontology expressions. In situation calculus, each perturbation to the modeled world changes the world from one *situation* <s> to another. If the truth value of a term that describes an entity in this world or a relationship between entities varies from situation to situation, then the term is a *fluent* <f>. A fluent *holds* in a given situation if the term is true in that given situation. So, ontology expressions are of the form *holds(f,s)*.

Measurement Description System.

- Is this a quality requirement? Does there exist a quality requirement '$\theta\rho$'[4] in a situation 'σ'?

$$holds(quality\_requirement(\theta\rho),\sigma). \hspace{2cm} \textbf{(CQ-1)}[5]$$

- What are the physical characteristics that are measured? Does there exist a measured attribute <At> for a tru 'κ' in a situation 'σ'?

$$\exists At\ [holds(tru(\kappa),\sigma) \land holds(has\_attribute(\kappa,At),\sigma) \land \\ holds(measured\_attribute(At),\sigma)]. \hspace{1cm} \textbf{(CQ-2)}$$

---

[4] Facts or constants (as opposed to variables) expressed in competency questions are denoted within single quotes. For example, 'σ' and 'sample_population' are constants that are bound to variables.

[5] Stands for Competency Question #1, which is the formal representation of Informal Competency Question #1

has_attribute(X,At) is from Core Ontologies: an object <X> has an attribute named <At>.

- If the product is a batch, is a sample taken from that batch and measured? That is, for a measured attribute 'α' of a tru 'κ' in a given situation 'σ', does it have a 'unit sample' or 'sample' sample sizing plan?

$$holds(tru(\kappa),\sigma) \wedge holds(has\_attribute(\kappa,\alpha),\sigma) \wedge \\ holds(measured\_attribute(\alpha),\sigma) \wedge$$

$$(holds(has\_sample\_sizing(\alpha,unit\_sample),\sigma) \vee \\ holds(has\_sample\_sizing(\alpha,sample),\sigma)).$$

(CQ-4)

- What are the tolerance specifications for a physical characteristic that is measured? For a measured attribute 'α' in a given situation 'σ', does there exist a specification set (expressed as an interval [<T_1>,<T_2>] or a list {<W_i>}?

$$\exists T_1 \exists T_2 \exists \{W_i\} \; [holds(measured\_attribute(\alpha),\sigma) \wedge$$

$$(holds(has\_specification\_set(\alpha,[T_1,T_2]),\sigma) \vee \\ holds(has\_specification\_set(\alpha,\{W_i\}),\sigma))].$$

(CQ-8)

Measurement Activities.

Is this an activity that performs measurement? Is 'α' a measure activity in a situation 'σ'?

$$holds(measure(\alpha),\sigma).$$

(CQ-10)

Measurement Points.

What are the measured values for a physical characteristic during a given period of time? What are the measurement points <Mp> for a measured attribute 'κ' of an entity 'ξ' for time points <Tp> within the duration ['τ_1',τ_2'] for a given situation 'σ'?

$$holds(measurement\_pt(\xi,\kappa,Mp,Tp),s) \wedge Tp \geq \tau_1 \wedge Tp \leq \tau_2 \rightarrow f(Tp,Mp).$$
Where $f(Tp,Mp)$ is just a graphing function that plots Tp vs. Mp.

(CQ-13)

Is an entity of conforming quality over a given period of time? For all time points <Tp> within a given time duration ['τ_1',τ_2'] for a given situation 'σ', does there always exist a conformance point <Q> for different trus <Rt> comprised of resource 'ξ', for the attribute 'κ'?

$$\forall Rt \forall Tp \; [Tp \geq \tau_1 \wedge Tp \leq \tau_2 \wedge \tau_1 < \tau_2 \wedge holds(has\_tru(\xi,Rt),s) \rightarrow \\ \exists Q \; holds(conformance\_pt(Q,Rt,\kappa,Tp),\sigma)].$$

(CQ-16)

Next, some of the axioms required to deduce answers to these questions are stated.

3.5 Axioms

Measurement Description System. A *quality requirement* is stated as a *primitive term*—a term that is instantiated and stated as a fact in the populated enterprise model. All *definition* axioms of an ontology are ultimately formally defined in terms of primitive terms. By applying *constraint* axioms, proper use of primitive terms is enforced. Primitive terms are populated (instantiated) as *ground terms*; e.g. a fact that 'widget119' is a resource is represented as a ground term, resource(widget119), which is an instance of the primitive term, resource(R). The term, *measured attribute*, is also a primitive term. In the TOVE Measurement Ontology, the quality of an activity is evaluated by the quality of resources associated with that activity; and the quality of a resource (prototypical product) is gauged by the quality of trus comprised of individual units of that resource. The following axioms express this:

A measured attribute must be an attribute of a tru. **(Cons-1)**[6]
A measured attribute must be sampled from an attribute of a resource.

$$\forall At \forall s \ [\ holds(\text{measured\_attribute}(At),s) \rightarrow \\ \exists Atr \exists R \ (\ holds(\text{samples\_attribute}(Atr,At),s) \land \\ holds(\text{has\_attribute}(R,Atr),s) \land holds(\text{resource}(R),s) \ ) \ ].$$

<At> measured attribute (Cons-2)
<Atr> attribute sampled for At
<Rt> tru for which At is an attribute
<R> resource for which Atr is an attribute
<s> an extant or hypothetical situation

In order to express the above constraint, the term, *samples attribute*, is also represented as a primitive term. These axioms ensure valid answers for (CQ-1) and (CQ-2). Additional such constraints constrain the use of the primitive terms, *has sample sizing, has sampling plan, has standard value, has specification set,* and *has unit of measurement.* The following axiom ensures valid answers for (CQ-8).

All measured attributes must have a specification set, and the standard value for that measured attribute must be an element of the specification set.

$$\forall At \forall Mu \forall s \ [holds(\text{has\_standard\_value}(At,Mu),s) \rightarrow \\ \exists T_1 \exists T_2(holds(\text{has\_specification\_set}(At,[T_1,T_2]),s) \land T_1 \leq Mu \leq T_2) \lor \\ \exists \{W_i\} \ (holds(\text{has\_specification\_set}(At,\{W_i\}),s) \land Mu \in \{W_i\}) \ ]$$

<At> a measured attribute (Cons-3)
[<T_1>,<T_2>] upper and lower bounds of a specification set for a measured attribute of ratio scale
{W_i} a set of "acceptable" values for the measured attribute
<Mu> the standard value for At
<s> an extant or hypothetical situation

Measurement Activities. A *primitive measure* activity is a *primitive activity* (an activity without any sub-activities) that *uses* a *measuring resource* (a primitive term) to measure the measured attribute of a *consumed* tru.

---

[6] Stands for Constraint #1

∀A ∀s ∃R ∃At ∃Rt [holds*(primitive_activity(A),s)* ∧
holds*(use_res_tru(A,R),s)* ∧
holds*(measuring_resource(R),s)* ∧
holds*(consume_res_tru(A,Rt),s)* ∧
holds*(has_attribute(Rt,At),s)* ∧ holds*(tru(Rt),s)* ∧
holds*(measured_attribute(At),s)*)
→ holds*(primitive_measure(A),s)]*.

        \<At\> measured attribute
        \<A\> primitive measure activity
        \<Atr\> attribute sampled for At   **(Defn-1)**[7]
        \<Rt\> tru for which At is an attribute
        \<R\> resource for which Atr is an attribute
        \<s\> an extant or hypothetical situation
        - primitive_activity(A) is from Core Ontologies
        - use_res_tru(Ax,Rx) and consume_res_tru(Ax,Rx) are from Core Ontologies. If an activity \<Ax\> uses a resource or tru \<Rx\>, then it does not materially change Rx; if \<Ax\> consumes \<Rx\>, then it changes a fundamental property of \<Rx\>. Note \<A\> ⊆ \<Ax\>, \<R\> ⊆ \<Rx\>, and \<Rt\> ⊆ \<Rx\>.

Then, any *measure* activity can be composed from primitive measure activities; i.e. it is a primitive measure activity or an aggregation of measure activities (**Defn-2**). This definition ensures an answer for (CQ-10).

Measurement Points. A *measurement point* is defined to be the *value* for the measured attribute of a tru that is measured by a primitive measure activity at a *time point* included in the *activity duration* for that primitive measure activity. Using the axiom below, (CQ-13) can be answered.

∀Rt ∀At ∀Mp ∀s ∃T ∃Tp [holds*(measured_attribute(At),s)* ∧
holds*(has_attribute(Rt,At),s)* ∧
holds*(has_attribute_value(Rt,At,Mp),s)* ∧
∃A (holds*(tru(Rt),s)* ∧ holds*(consume_res_tru(A,Rt),s)* ∧
    holds*(primitive_measure(A),s)* ∧
    activity_duration(A,T) ∧ *has_point(T,Tp)*) →
    holds*(measurement_pt(Rt,At,Mp,Tp),s)]*.   **(Defn-3)**

    \<Rt\>   a tru for which there exists a measurement point
    \<At\>   a measured attribute of Rt
    \<Tp\>   time point for which Mp is the measurement point for Rt
    \<Mp\> value of that measurement point
    \<T\>   time period in which the measurement takes place
    \<A\>   the primitive measure activity that ascertains the measurement point

---

[7] Stands for Definition #1

<s> an extant or hypothetical situation
has_attribute_value(X,Atx,V) is from the Core Ontologies: An object <X> has a value <V> for its attribute <Atx>. Note <Rt> $\subseteq$ <X>, <At> $\subseteq$ <Atx>, and <Mp> $\subseteq$ <V>.
activity_duration(Ax,Tx) is from the Core Ontologies: Any activity <Ax> is performed during a time period <Tx>. Note <A> $\subseteq$ <Ax> and <T> $\subseteq$ <Tx>.
has_point(Tx,Tpx) is from the Core Ontologies: Time points <Tpx> are within the time period <Tx>. Note <T> $\subseteq$ <Tx> and <Tp> $\subseteq$ <Tpx>.

A *conformance point* is defined as a measurement point of a tru that lies within the specification set (**Defn-4**). Otherwise, that measurement point is a *nonconformance point* (**Defn-5**).

Then, conformance points of other entities like resources, activities, or even organization agents can be defined in terms of conformance points of trus. For example, conformance points of an activity can be defined in terms of conformance points of trus produced by the activity, and conformance points of an organization agent can be defined in terms of conformance points of trus produced by activities performed by that agent.

3.6 Quality Management Analysis

In the TOVE Core Ontologies, an *agent constraint* is a special fluent that represents a constraint upon an *organization agent,* which must be satisfied in order for that agent to achieve some goal. For instance, ISO 9000 compliance can be represented as goal that is achieved if a set of quality-related agent constraints upon an enterprise is satisfied. The following is the formal representation:

Holds*(agent_constraint(Oa,c($\underline{X}$)),s)* $\leftrightarrow$ $\Phi(Oa,\underline{X},s)$.

<s> a given situation
<Oa> an organization agent which seeks to achieve a goal in situation s
<$\underline{X}$> entities that must be represented in order to represent the (**Defn-6**) constraints on Oa; $\underline{X}$ is a vector with none, one, or more entities
<c($\underline{X}$)> predicate name for the agent constraint
<Φ(A,$\underline{X}$,s)> a first-order logic expression for the constraint described as c($\underline{X}$)

Since a key concept set before developing the Measurement Ontology is that *every quality assessment is a decision that begins with a value of measurement at a given point in time,* it follows that a quality requirement should be expressed as a composition of conformance and nonconformance points. Regardless of how it is expressed, if an agent constraint that constrains an entity <X>, is satisfied in situation <s> and is a quality requirement <Qr>, then the entity is evaluated as *of conforming quality* with respect to that quality requirement.

$\forall X \, \forall Qr \, \forall s \, [\text{holds}(conforming\_quality(X,Qr),s) \leftrightarrow$
  $\text{holds}(agent\_constraint(X,Qr),s) \wedge$ **(Defn-7)**
  $\text{holds}(quality\_requirement(Qr),s) \,].$

With these axioms, (CQ-16) can be answered. In fact, it looks like a prototypical quality requirement: Within time interval ['τ_1','τ_2'], all measurements for the attribute 'κ' of batches (or lots) of the resource 'ξ' must be within specs.

Then quality analysis using the TOVE Measurement Ontology can follow the same steps used to construct the ontology:

1. *Motivating Scenario*: Write a narrative about a specific quality issues related to an entity.
2. *Informal Competency Questions*. Write out the quality requirements for the entity informally in natural language.
3. *Terminology*: Organize useful terminology from existing ontologies.
4. *Formal Competency Questions*: State informally stated quality requirements as a First-Order Logic expression using ontology terminology, especially conformance and nonconformance points.
5. *Axioms*: Organize the axioms that constrains or defines the relevant terminology.
6. *Answer Competency Questions*: If the facts about an entity are represented as ground terms—e.g. *holds*(measured_attribute(average_length),s10) and *holds*(measurement_pt (tru123,average_length,2, 10),s10)—axioms are applied to ground terms to deduce whether a quality requirement is satisfied.

For brevity, the demonstration of competency is not shown. It can be found in [8].

4 Conclusion

First, though the WWW is used for business process automation to lower costs and shorten leadtimes, its use is limited for another metric of business success: Improving quality. Second, a promising advancement to the WWW is the development of the Semantic Web, which relies upon using machine process-able domain knowledge represented in ontologies. Therefore, one promising area of research and application is the development of ontologies as data models to provide quality management services on the Semantic Web. In this paper, the TOVE Measurement Ontology is presented as a formalization of a fundamental domain, which needs to be represented to provide these services. The following summarizes the generic concepts represented:

- A system for assessing measurements includes the appropriate *measured attribute*, as well as its *standard value* (μ), *sampling plan* and *size*, *specification set* of "acceptable values" of $f(\mu,\sigma^2)$, and *unit of measurement*. Measurement of attributes are recorded as *measurement points* in time that are assigned a value as a result of some *measure* activity. These representations are the basic ones necessary to model any form of measurement.
- Quality can be represented as some composition of *conformance points*, which are "conforming" *measurement points* with respect to some *quality requirement*.

Representing quality requirements, measurement points, and conformance points makes it possible to model and assess any entity within an enterprise as of *conforming quality*.

These concepts are formally represented by: Posing competency questions, analyzing the domain of measurement, stating assumptions, and developing terminology and axioms.

The main contribution of this paper is that representations themselves and the methodology used to develop them are detailed. These have been emphasized over discussions of other important issues such as related works in measurement modeling [14], mechanics of providing web services (e.g. use of software agents [15]), and whether ontologies and the Semantic Web will even be commercially adopted [16][17] In this paper, the content of quality management ontologies are disseminated over the context of their uses.

The "content vs. context" dichotomy serves as a framework for future work. For content, formally representing other domains fundamental to quality management such as traceability and the quality management system is planned, as is applying these ontologies for providing a quality management service—automatic ISO 9000 compliance evaluation. For context, an interesting research area is in ontological engineering methodologies for the Semantic Web. The ontological engineering community has known that in order for ontologies to be adopted, they must be competent for "local," known applications yet re-usable for "foreign," unknown applications in order to justify the substantial effort in knowledge representation. However, possible emergence of the Semantic Web as a readily accessible infrastructure means that assumptions about "foreign" applications inherent in many existing methodologies —e.g. that those using others' ontologies are ontological engineers, who have reasonable knowledge of the domain represented in shared ontologies—may not necessarily hold, inasmuch as the accessibility of the WWW enabled access to documents by those whom the documents' authors could not have anticipated as readers. The opportunity then is in researching development of adaptive and flexible ontologies.

References

1. Fox, Mark S. and Grüninger, Michael. "Enterprise Modeling", *AI Magazine*, AAAI Press, Fall (1998), 109-21.
2. Campbell, A. E. and Shapiro, S. C. "Ontological Mediation: An Overview", *IJCAI Workshop on Basic Ontological Issues in Knowledge Sharing*, AAAI Press: Menlo Park, (1995).
3. Gruber, Thomas R. "Towards Principles for the Design of Ontologies Used for Knowledge Sharing", In *International Workshop on Formal Ontology, Guarino, N. & Poli, R. (Eds.)*, Padova, Italy (1993).
4. Labrou, Y. and Finin, T. "Yahoo! as an Ontology - Using Yahoo! Categories to Describe Documents", In: *8th CIKM*, Kansas City, MO, November (1999), 180-7.

5. Das, Aseem, Wu, Wei, and McGuinness, Deborah L. "Industrial Strength Ontology Management", In *Proceedings of the International Semantic Web Working Symposium*. Stanford, CA, July (2001).
6. Berners-Lee, Tim, Hendler, James, and Lassila, Ora, "The Semantic Web", *Scientific American*, May (2001).
7. IBM Software Solutions, "Web services by IBM: Overview", (2001, November - last update). Available - *http://www-4.ibm.com/software/solutions/webservices/overview.html*, (Accessed: November 9, 2001).
8. Kim, Henry M., "Representing and Reasoning about Quality using Enterprise Models", *Ph.D. Thesis*, Department of Mechanical and Industrial Engineering, University of Toronto, Toronto, Ontario Canada M5S 3G9 (1999).
9. Crosby, P. B., *Quality is Free: The Art of Making Quality Certain*, McGraw-Hill: New York, NY (2001).
10. American Management Association, *Blueprints for Service Quality: The Federal Express Approach*, AMA Publications: NY, (1992).
11. Grüninger, M., and Fox, M.S. "Methodology for the Design and Evaluation of Ontologies", *Workshop on Basic Ontological Issues in Knowledge Sharing, IJCAI-95*, Montreal (1995).
12. Scheaffer, Richard L. and McClave, James T. *Statistics for Engineers*, PWS Publishers: Boston, MA: (1982).
13. McCarthy, J., and Hayes, P. J., "Some Philosophical Problems from the Standpoint of AI", in *Machine Intelligence 4*, Meltzer B. and Michie D. (eds.), Edinburgh, UK: Edinburgh University Press (1969), 463-501.
14. Kim, Henry M., "Enterprise Models of Measurement: A Comparison of Existing Models Used for Quality Management and E-Business", *Work Report*, Schulich School of Business, York University, Toronto, Ontario, Also: (2000, August 2000 - last update), Available - http://www.yorku.ca/hmkim/files/wits%20paper%202000.PDF, (Accessed: November 21, 2001).
15. Jennings, N., Sycara, K., and Woolridge, M., "A roadmap of agent research and development", *Journal of Autonomous Agents and Multi-Agent Systems*, Vol. 1 (1998), 275-306.
16. Uschold, Mike, "Where Are the Killer Apps?", In: Proceedings of ECAI-98 Workshop on Applications of Ontologies and Problem-Solving Methods (1998).
17. Kim, Henry M., "Predicting how the Semantic Web Will Evolve", *Communications of the ACM*, February, Vol. 45, No. 2, 48-54 (2002).

A Modelling Approach to the Realisation of Modular Information Spaces

Moira C. Norrie and Alexios Palinginis

Department of Computer Science
ETH Zurich, CH-8092 Zurich, Switzerland
{norrie,palinginis}@inf.ethz.ch

Abstract. We present a metamodel which forms the basis for the design and implementation of modular information systems supporting a cooperative working environment. The model consists of four separate, but interconnected, sub-models dealing with all aspects of modular systems from the database *meta and object model* down to a possible *storage model*. The database *connectivity metamodel* is crucial in supporting the implementation of the database and connectivity models which enable users to dynamically dock on a foreign database module. At the centre is the *user model* which serves to tie the other sub-models together and this reflects our human-centric approach to cooperative environments. Consistency of each database module is maintained through our model of personal and shared workspaces. The global consistency of interconnected database modules can be achieved through synchronisation and cooperation of the conflicting parties over personal and history data.

1 Introduction

When designing a complete information system, many invariants such as a clear information model, data consistency, efficient query and recovery operations, must be ensured in the lifetime of the application. On the other hand, free collaboration between multiple users, physical storage distribution, replication and interchange mechanisms must be enabled, which may often introduce undesirable side-effects to the information system invariants.

With the goal of solving the problem of legacy database integration, we have seen major efforts within the information system community in the areas of schema integration, data heterogeneity and federated databases [HM85, SL90, Bro92]. In the mean time, modularity has become a standard tool for software engineering and componentware is gaining broad acceptance in the object-oriented programming world. Nevertheless, every day new database applications are created still based on old information and distribution models. This results in a large impedance mismatch between data and application modelling and design techniques, thereby preventing the full exploitation of new technological advances, while retaining many of the old pitfalls. We notice that the current middleware emphasis is justified by its success to close the gap between such technological mismatches. However, we still believe that, for new applications built from scratch, new models and techniques must be used, not only at the application level, but also at that of the information itself.

The overall complexity of distribution in an information system is a major drawback in terms of, not only its design, but also its implementation and efficiency. In the past years, many communication and synchronisation protocols [Gri98] that support distribution have been studied and proposed. Nevertheless most of them are at a very low level: They support object-orientation only at the level of programming languages and processes and not in terms of information abstractions and cooperative work activities. Thus, while they are useful to solve the problems of communication between distributed objects, a lot more is required to achieve the goal of modular information systems. The effort involved in designing and implementing a complete information system application is still a very time-consuming and difficult task.

We are therefore seeking both a methodology and a model to support the design and implementation of an information system in terms of modular components. To achieve this goal, the approach taken must be total and at a higher level of abstraction than just that of a communication protocol: It must aim to solve the problem of the distribution of information, rather than the problems of the communication and synchronisation of data arising from it. Existing distributed protocols can be integrated into the methodology and model by defining the operational specifications of the special partial problems that they address.

Our system focuses on the extensibility and reusability of databases in a user-centric approach, rather than purely on the underlying data. Information is indeed formed out of data and their consistency is crucial. Still, the perception of information is user and situation dependent. Each user must have a consistent information space, but it is not guaranteed that this will be part of a consistent extended space when participating in a community. Nevertheless, it is desirable for a user to dynamically participate in other communities. An information system must then be able to dynamically dock on other systems and resolve possible conflicts through cooperation and contract definitions.

Thus we are working on a logical rather than physical distribution schema. Contrary to a transparent distribution environment, the users view the entire information space in terms of logical, user-aware sub-spaces. As stated above, physical distribution techniques can still be used and applied to each logical application entity, but, by defining logical application modules and their interaction and evolution, we achieve a system suited to cooperative working environments.

We identify the following four major conceptual areas, with their respective models, that influence the design and implementation of such a system:

- A rich information model.
- Database modules and their interconnection model.
- A flexible storage model that supports cooperative working environments.
- A user model for our human centric approach and security aspects.

In the following sections, we will describe each of these models in turn and investigate the dependencies between them. We begin with a discussion of the general requirements in Section 2. In Sections 3 to 5, we describe each of the submodels, focusing on the features that enable better understanding and control of the distribution aspects of a modular information space. In Section 6, we examine how these models are combined. We give concluding remarks in Section 7.

2 Requirements

In this section, we briefly introduce the four sub-models proposed by examining the general requirements. An overview of the four components is given in Figure 1.

First of all, the information system must be defined clearly, completely and orthogonally in terms of an *information model* and its corresponding metamodel. This model must be kept as *simple* as possible to avoid unnecessary complications when distribution comes into play. "Simple" refers to the concepts used and the operations applied to the abstractions offered by the model. The model should be complete and orthogonal with respect to operations and constructs, thus ensuring the robustness of the system in delicate situations that may be introduced by distributed operation (disconnected operation, replication, partitioning etc.). The entities of the system must be uniquely identified, not only in the scope of the database module in which they reside, but also in the entire potential cooperation universe in which they might participate now or in the future.

We see a great significance in the existence of a *database connectivity model*, which models how the different peers should be connected and what kind of entities are represented alone or in conjunction with each other. We handle a database (or a piece of it) as an object itself which can have attributes, operations and can reference other databases, thereby building up hierarchies on which inheritance and encapsulation can be applied.

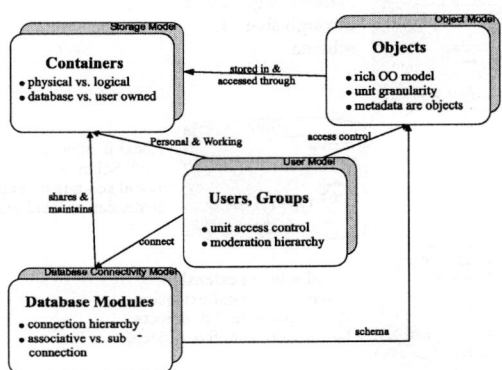

Fig. 1. Metamodel components

The distribution aspect is indeed tightly coupled with the storage of the information, making the introduction of a general object *storage model* inevitable. We use a model based on storage containers, which represent units of storage at a logical or physical abstraction level. A user view is an information space which is constructed dynamically from a set of storage containers in terms of set operators over these containers.

Last, but not least, a *user model* is required. As a result of our aim to support cooperative human environments, the user model is actually the interface and interconnection between all of the sub-models mentioned above. The user is aware of the high-level logical distribution and database connection models. Behind the scenes, the user model drives part of the storage model and gives admission to the visibility of the object model.

Before discussing each model in detail, we present an example to illustrate our vision of a modular information space. Assume we want to model a population database for Switzerland which tracks all inhabitants in databases distributed across the country and maintained by the cantons (autonomous regions of the Swiss confederation). The canton of Zurich may have a database where information on all inhabitants of Zurich are stored under the guidance provided by the federal inhabitants schema, located in the Swiss capital, Bern. Due to its autonomy, Zurich could enrich the basic inhabitants data, based on the schema from Bern, with other information and operations, such as information on local taxes/statistics and/or some local rules or restrictions. This schema extension would involve the creation of one or more local subtypes, e.g. ZH_person as a subtype of person as shown in Figure 2.

ETH Zurich, one of the two Swiss federal universities, is located in Zurich. Assume a restriction that employees of ETH Zurich must live in the local canton. ETH has access to the information about its employees from the local canton

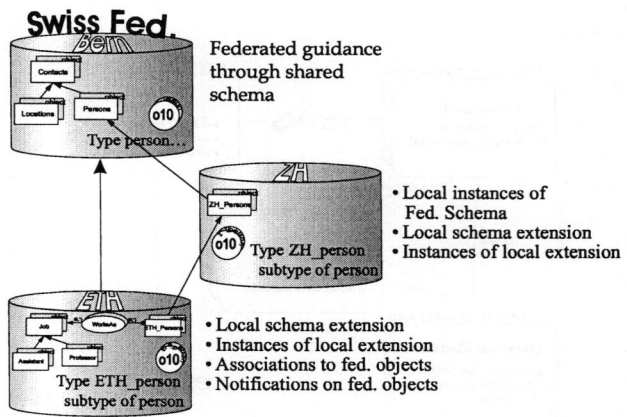

Fig. 2. Inhabitants DB Example

inhabitants database and, again, it is free to extend it through additional subtypes as required, e.g. ETH_person as a subtype of ZH_person. However, in this case, control of the inhabitant objects remains with the canton and ETH stores only the information units corresponding to its local extension in its database and not the whole object. Thus, only the methods and attributes defined for type ETH_person and not the inherited properties are stored at ETH.

We clearly see that the physical distribution is based on and driven by the logical application model. Such a structure could be further extended to deal with, for example, ETH internal organisations which may have requirements to share both schema and data, with or without taking control over the management of the relevant objects. At each level of sharing, it is, of course, necessary to specify which information is accessible to other systems. Thus both data and metadata are subject to access controls.

In addition, the situation may arise where a user wants to update data that is not within their control. For example, assume that ETH wants to change the employment conditions of one of its employees. ETH may update this information in the local database, but it ultimately requires the approval of the canton of Zurich, which issues work permits and processes tax information. In such a case, ETH may either be given full privileges to alter the information on the database of Zurich, or, it may apply for an update through a "change request" submission. Thus, the process is not simply one of update synchronisation, but rather of cooperation between the users of data.

3 Information Model and Metamodel

An information system is defined through its schema and the corresponding metadata defines the general concepts of the application. The metadata provides the system with crucial information, even at run-time, about the structure and status of the application data. This information can also be used to support the distribution strategy. Our aim is to give a user the ability to dynamically dock on a foreign database, use it and even extend it, without any administrator or designer intervention. It is therefore of crucial importance that the metadata are also represented and handled as normal objects.

Object-oriented metamodels [ABD+89] are powerful due to the fact that the notion of an object is a simple orthogonal abstraction, based on which, all of the concepts of an application can be modelled. Providing distribution of the object abstraction, in the form of types, entities or operations, will yield some kind of application distribution. The same applies to relational metamodels which have also been used successfully as a basis for distribution. However, as stated in the introduction, our overall aim is to obtain a methodology and a model to support overall information system application design. Therefore, the existence and completeness of an information model alone is not sufficient.

In our aim to support extensibility and reusability, concepts such as finegrained object decomposition, collections of relevant objects and object relationships through references are important characteristics. We therefore need an information model that incorporates such constructs. Through a rich object-oriented model that encapsulates many application concepts, the implementation of a distributed information system is greatly simplified. Although the addition of certain semantic constructs to the core of the system may initially appear to introduce unnecessary complexity, it in fact pays off in terms of simplifying application development.

We have based our prototype on the OMS Pro data management system [Wue00, KNW98]. It, in turn, is based on OM, an object-oriented model with support for object collections and associations, a rich collection algebra and object evolution [Nor93]. OMS Pro handles all information, metadata and data with the same object concept. In fact, when it comes to the implementation, metadata is handled slightly differently in order to achieve efficiency, but the logical behaviour is common to all database objects. As a result, when a client database connects to a server database, the client can have full access (subject to access controls) to the metadata enabling the remote data to have known type and structure. Moreover, the choice of a model which clearly separates notions of entity representation and classification within its type and value system [Nor95] allows us to even work with parts of an object or even to reference objects that are private. The system and model were both developed within our research group which gave us the freedom and resources to introduce distribution concepts into the core of the system. Due to the fact that OM is orthogonal with respect to operations and constructs, it demonstrates the benefits of making as many information systems concepts distribution-aware as possible.

Returning to our Swiss inhabitants example, the shared schema would be stored in a shared database in Bern. A canton could create **person** objects locally according to this shared schema. No special handling of this metadata must be undertaken due to the fact that distribution, partitioning, replication and synchronisation of metadata are treated as normal objects. The canton of Zurich can then extend the remote shared schema by creating locally additional metadata. For example, since local cantons manage taxes autonomously, the canton of Zurich could create a local subtype of the shared schema's **person** type with the relevant tax-related attributes and methods.

In Figure 3, we present the object and metamodel of the OMS database in the OM notation. Rectangles represent collections of objects and ovals represent associations between collections, i.e. a collection of reference pairs. Classification hierarchies are formed through subcollection relationships between collections as specified by `cisa` objects, indicated graphically through directed edges between collections.

In the shaded part of collection rectangles, the type of the member objects is indicated. Type hierarchies are built from subtype relationships represented as `tisa` objects. Active objects represent the operational part of the database through methods, triggers and macros (database operations).

One can see that metadata are also normal objects with an appropriate type and possibly methods. Of course, in the definition of the basic persistent type

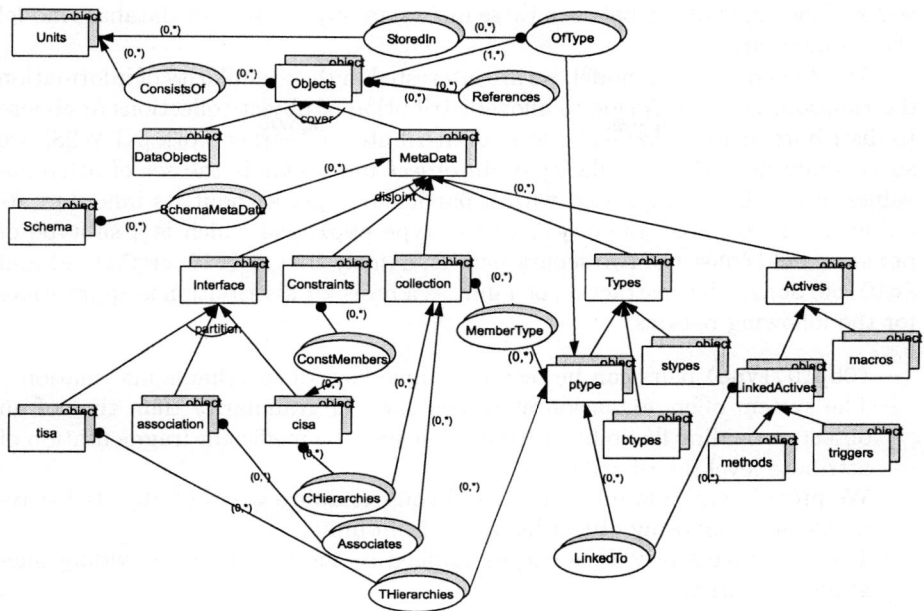

Fig. 3. Information Model and Metamodel

and object (`ptype` and `object`), we arrive at a classic fix-point situation where those objects must be defined using themselves.

Although we cannot provide details of the OM model and its metamodel here, the main constructs of the model can be summarised as:

- Unique objects which may be instances of arbitrary types with attributes of base/structured or reference type.
- Types and subtype (tisa) relationships.
- Methods, triggers and macros.
- Collections with subcollection (cisa) relationships and constraints such as disjoint and partition over them.
- Associations between objects participating in collections.

These are the logical constructs that actually influence database consistency and, as seen later, form one dimension that influences the distribution strategy. Although the presence of collections, associations and their constraints increases the complexity of the core system in comparison to a simple object-type model, we prefer to deal with these concepts once in the core of the system rather than having to provide ad-hoc distribution of rich constraints within the application.

The various forms of relationship metadata objects — `association`, `cisa` and `tisa` — are treated as special cases in our model. They represent the linking between objects used as the basis for connection and extension when interconnecting databases. After explaining the database connectivity model in the next section, the dependency between these metadata objects and the database model should be clear.

Apart from the metamodel, we are interested in the granularity of information distribution. One can decide to allow distribution of object collections or choose to distribute at the granularity level of attributes. In earlier work [NPW98], we successfully used the granularity of an object unit. This is the set of attribute values of an object associated with a particular type, without its inherited attributes. For example, the object o10 of type employee which is a subtype of person would consist of two separate units, namely that of (o10,employee) and (o10,person). The abstraction of a unit as a basis for distribution is appropriate for the following reasons:

- (ObjID,Type) pairs can be seen as unique keys of searchable information.
- The system offers extension at a finer level of granularity than that of an object, providing flexibility without reaching the inefficient fragmentation of attribute level distribution.
- We provide multiple inheritance and context-aware views of objects by dynamically composing object instances from units.
- The user access privileges can be applied to the unit level, providing fine-grained security.

Last but not least, dealing with units at the physical level of the system, enables us to provide rich functionality and flexibility to the upper logical abstraction levels, while keeping the underlying implementation simple and efficient.

4 Database Connectivity

We now discuss some database connectivity issues and the corresponding part of the metamodel. As stated previously, we want to create a dynamic, shareable, distributed information system. The usual client/server architecture would be very limited for this purpose, as it should be possible that a database shares its data and schema and, at the same time, acts as a client on other databases. A database module should be autonomous, allow other modules to extend it and be able to be an extension from other modules. However, allowing such flexibility could introduce some problems. What if, for instance, a cycle of interconnected databases occurs? Where must the data, and above all the metadata, be stored? How can we control propagations among database modules?

To give solutions to such problems, one must define what a database module is and how it relates to the information model. As seen in the previous section, a database is defined by its schema. The question that arises in a distributed interconnected environment of database modules, is how can we decide which part of the schema belongs to which module and, further, when can we say that a database module is consistent?

The straightforward answer used in many object-oriented systems is to use the transitive closure of objects, defined as the information of an object plus the information of all objects that are linked or referenced from it. If we have all this information and it is consistent, then the module itself is in a consistent state. Recall now from our requirements that a user of a database module should be able to dynamically attach to and extend a foreign module. If we base our model on the transitive closure concept, such interconnected and linked modules could never be disconnected again! We therefore looked for another approach.

We distinguish two kinds of module connections:

- Applications that are logically autonomous and one can shift the focus to another logical application through linked information.
- Applications that are more tightly linked together and build a hierarchy.

It is clear that, in the first case, the consistency of the application is separate from the consistency of the linked information. The user is focused on the application domain of the module but has the opportunity to attach dynamically to further information and use another application. The user can later detach from the other module without influencing its consistency. If desired, the first working scenario can migrate to the second, more strict scenario, where the two parties are willing to cooperate and build a community that must also be consistent due to some kind of contract (new extended consistency).

We therefore see a database module as a logical application abstraction. When modelling large applications, one can easily come up with sub-schemas interconnected with each other via association, subtype or subcollection relationships, representing logical domains of the whole application. Even graphically, we tend to draw partial application spaces adjacent to each other. Based on these considerations, we introduce the following definition:

"A consistent database module schema consists of all metadata objects of a logical application domain and all further objects that build up their transitive *application consistent* closure."

Notice that the transitive *application consistent* closure is a subset of the absolute transitive closure. Taking advantage of the reference semantics of an association and, using the unit model described in the previous section, we are able to define the application borders through those constructs.

In OM, associations are the connection points between objects. If we were to ignore them, we would reduce the logical application, but could then easily ensure the consistency of the remaining parts of the application domain. From a particular part of a schema, we can regard associations as the bridges to the neighbouring database modules. If we close these bridges, we can still remain and work effectively within our own information island, as long as that island is itself a meaningful sub-space of the overall application information space.

Some contexts in which an application object resides can also be set apart if desired. As mentioned before, OM models object roles that can define context-sensitive properties and behaviour. For example, a person can have both a student and a private context for two different application sub-spaces. If it makes logical sense, a context can be omitted. Thus, the specialisation relationships declared through subtype (tisa) and subcollection (cisa) relationships can also be seen as bridges to neighbouring contexts. Because the object model is physically structured in terms of units, the partitioning of objects over contexts is straightforward. For this reason, we see in Figure 3 that associations, tisas and cisas are all regarded as special forms of interface metadata.

In summary, a database module represents a logical information space, defined by a consistent schema and composed of objects according to that schema. Through connectivity with other database modules, the information space can be extended through associations and/or contexts defined by interface metadata. The database modules can then build-up a hierarchy. A module can view only the immediate connected modules, thereby avoiding major propagation and security issues. If a module A wishes to use a module B that extends another module C, then the module A must connect explicitly to module C. The system supports this by providing the dependencies of a module to the connected clients.

The resulting connectivity model is shown in Figure 4. We further distinguish connections (Connection), based on the kind of interface metadata used to connect the databases, into Associative (AssocDB) and Submodule (SubDB) connections. This is mainly due to the fact that the connection through an associative bridge, represents a more loosely-coupled connection than that of a submodule connection. Making this distinction enables us to optimise aspects of performance in the implementation.

In our inhabitants example, every canton would have at least one database module. A shared database module, namely that of the federation, is maintained in Bern. The federation would have many such modules for further applications, such as federation laws and foreign policy. Associations across these logically separated application modules enables them to be connected to each other. Suppose the traffic department of the canton of Zurich now wants to work on traffic data that they created locally and associated to the inhabitant data based on the shared schema. They can perform this operation by simply using their traffic database module and connecting to the inhabitant module of Bern. There is no need to connect to the federation foreign policy module, even if this is interconnected to the inhabitants module. An associative connection between the database modules is created automatically.

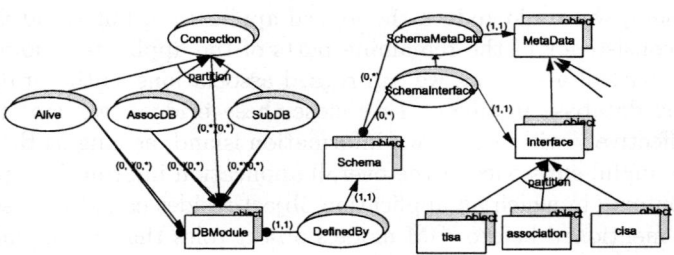

Fig. 4. Connectivity Model

On the other hand, ETH also uses the inhabitants module, this time of the canton of Zurich, and can extend the schema by introducing new subtypes locally, such as ETH_person, student and professor with new attributes and methods. The information units of each student or professor object will be stored locally, while the person units will still be maintained in the canton of Zurich database. Once ETH has established such a connection, it has a database module that is strongly connected to the inhabitant database of canton of Zurich. In effect, they are building a submodule hierarchy. The information units of each student and professor must be available to ETH from the different cantons. Moreover, due to the fact that we actually distribute objects based on logical criteria, the system can automate the replication process using the metadata [Pit96] and copy the student/professor inhabitant units locally to ETH, increasing not only the response time, but also the ability to work further in a case of a connection failure.

Having this connectivity model, we still have not answered the question as to where the objects are stored and how the users are involved. To answer this, we first need to present a storage model appropriate for a distributed, cooperative working environment.

5 Storage Model

A major property of information systems is to guarantee consistency of the stored data. Most of the proposed approaches are based on a short transaction scheme. An update, typically carried out from a task or a batch command, locks a resource, applies the update and frees the resource again. In our system which focuses on cooperative working environments, we take another approach.

An OMS transaction represents a particular logical work activity on the database which may even span several OMS user sessions. The length of such a transaction will definitely be too large to apply traditional locking techniques. Apart from the logical consistency of the system, we must ensure further physical consistency. All user interactions must be made persistent automatically and recovery must be ensured in the case of failure. OMS Pro was originally designed as a rapid prototyping tool, and, in such a development environment, physical consistency is crucial since "mistakes" are not excluded. Further, a human cooperation environment could lead to inconsistencies due to the different perspectives of each user.

We therefore built a system that gives each individual the flexibility to always secure his/her work and to support the resolution of logical conflicts by either providing synchronisation tools or a personal view over the information. The decision to use information units as our level of granularity, as discussed in Section 3, supports such a strategy by providing quite small granularity and thereby restricting the level of conflicting information. In this section, we focus therefore on information units as the physical level of information storage, rather than whole objects.

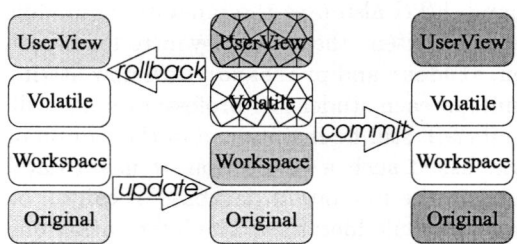

Fig. 5. Information Spaces

The information units are stored in what we call "information storage containers". These containers may be either physically stored or virtual containers derived from other containers (for example, views defined in terms of set operators). This means that to retrieve a unit given its key (recall from section 3 that the pair (ObjID,type) is the unique key of a unit) from a virtual container V, the request sent to V will be propagated to the containers in terms of which V is defined. This may seem complicated initially, but it allows us to be very flexible and enables us to model many distribution scenarios. With special storage structures, we are even able to reduce the overheads introduced.

To give a better understanding of how we work with information containers, let us study the use of such containers to implement the single user storage solution of Figure 5. It comprises one logical and three physical containers. *Original* is a physical container holding the database consistent state. This container is implemented in a similar manner to a conventional object repository, providing indexing, recovery etc. Each user has his own *Workspace* container where all the changes are immediately made persistent. A workspace is also a physical container but, because it holds a small number of units, indexing may not be so crucial. Temporary objects are stored in the *Volatile* container which, although it is a physical container, is implemented in memory. The *UserView* container is then a virtual space that is defined as follows:

$$UserView = \{x|\ (x \in Original \wedge x \notin Workspace)\ \vee$$
$$x \in Workspace \vee x \in Volatile\}, \quad \text{where x is a unit}$$

The user always views the UserView container, while the system writes updates only to the Workspace or Volatile container, thereby avoiding fragmentation of the Original container and decreasing the possibility of loss of information due to failures in the Original container. On commit, the UserView is checked for consistency and, if the check succeeds, the changes in Workspace are "melted" into the Original; the Workspace and Volatile containers are emptied for the next session. To support some functionality required for logging, versioning and rollback through the different logical commit stages, the Workspace is actually copied to a history container. Any snapshot of the Original container over time can consequently be reconstructed from the subsequent union of its History containers.

The abstraction of information containers, combined with the concepts of information unit uniqueness and small granularity, gives us the flexibility to, not only easily introduce new virtual storage containers by just defining a name and the corresponding dependencies between others, but also to optimise the implementation of physical containers or even re-distribute the units of one physical container into many other containers. For example, the Original container in OMS is actually partitioned into three physical containers according to the category of units in terms of whether they are meta-, user- or classification-data.

To extend the single user case just discussed into a multi-user cooperative environment, we next present the user model.

6 User Model and the Model in its Entirety

The user has an important role in our system in actually binding together the models discussed so far and their properties (see Figure 1 or Figure 6 for a more detailed view). Therefore, while presenting the user model, we will also explain the model in its entirety.

One can notice that the user model authenticates access to objects and forms connections between database modules. Although, at this stage of our project, security is not a major focus, we model and implement access privileges through user groups. We perform security checking on the physical information level, i.e. that of the information unit. Introducing security at such a fine-grained level causes some additional loss of efficiency of the system. For the moment, we have a naive and rather slow implementation that we aim to improve in the future.

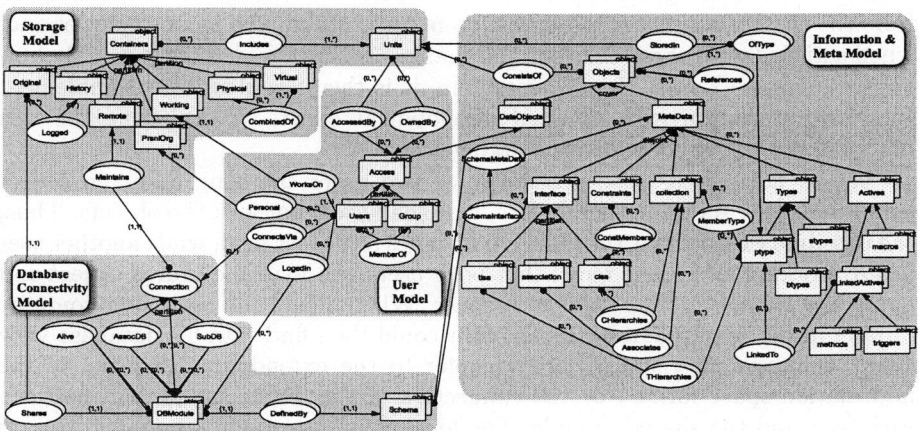

Fig. 6. The total detailed Model

It is worth noting that the User notion is also an object of our information model, but it has to be treated specially at the physical storage level to increase performance.

Having introduced information containers as storage abstractions and explaining the single user solution, let us now extend the abstraction in the context of cooperative working environments. Every database module has a single Original space where it stores consistent units defined by the database schema as mentioned in the previous section. When a user logs into the database and at the same time connects to a remote database module, they will view a union of both modules (subject to access controls). The uniqueness of the objects in the new environment is guaranteed by a hierarchical registration process which was presented in a previous publication [NPW98]. The user can then decide to use the connected database either by extending it through the creation of tisa relationships, or by designing affinities through the creation of associations. As mentioned before, all changes will immediately become persistent in the user's working containers (*Workspace* and *Volatile*).

For every connection, the system maintains a virtual container *Remote* (see upper-left corner of Figure 6). It comprises all objects made accessible through the connection. The user can further extend its functionality by introducing a physical sub-container of *Remote* that acts as network cache. The system can be directed to keep in the network cache all referenced objects that are requested together with their consistent transient closures. For large amounts of data, this could be time consuming, but it enables additional important features such as disconnected operation.

When the user decides that they have reached a logical working milestone, they would check the new state and, if consistent, the system will "melt" the changes into the shared Original container. This working scheme can be observed frequently in development processes such as web site development and Software Configuration Management [Est01]. Developers will change some information from the current consistent state, test them for mistakes and inconsistencies and, when satisfied with these changes, the changes are deployed. This is exactly how our system core works. Using our system, it is therefore possible to implement such an application with minimal development effort, by exploiting the rich functionality of the cooperative working schema.

Let us now discuss the possibility of two users changing a shared object simultaneously. As mentioned before, we usually will not lock the objects. Thus, the possibility exists that the first user changes an object field, while another user is also working on it. But recall that both users will read the shared object and apply any change to their own Workspace. When one of the users first commits objects in the shared database, the other could then find that his database view is in an inconsistent state. Here we refer to the extended consistency of the information space formed by the connection of the database modules between each user and the shared module. The local consistency will stay intact due to the absence of the bridge objects that extend the information space, as explained in section 4. But what motivates us to allow such a possibility?

In a cooperative working environment, and most of all when the parties are loosely connected, an information unit can evolve in an application domain without the awareness of foreign application domains. In such cases, we arrive at a conflict situation. The involved parties can view the different versions and cooperate to resolve the conflict. In our system we support two different scenarios. On one hand, the cooperative environment may have some kind of hierarchical structure, whether it is an organisational, operational or even task-oriented hierarchy. Thus giving priority to the changes introduced by the party higher in the hierarchy. On the other hand, an application could support a more liberal, democratic way where multiple perceptions can be accepted. We therefore model this fact by associating the user model with the storage model as shown in Figure 6.

In both cases, the server database should only be updated if the docked user has update privileges. If not, the user will get a personal view of the remote database for any changes that will be made: The changes will be melted into the user's *Personal* container ensuring the consistency of the user information space and avoiding the introduction of further conflicts with other users of the shared module, thereby giving a solution to the democratic view-point with personal versions.

To support the hierarchical working model, the users of a particular database are building up a priority hierarchy. This may enable more users to access and even update data, while giving moderation privileges over the data and its synchronisation in conflict situations. This scheme is ideal for multi-user applications working in a workflow manner commonly used in all hierarchical organisational working models. In the case that the working model changes over time, it is always possible to again publish your personal view of the information or vice-versa.

Imagine in our ETH example that a teaching assistant wants to reduce their working time by half. The personnel department makes the appropriate ETH internal changes to the database. Recall that the canton of Zurich tracks all working profiles to adapt the taxes or work permits of its inhabitants. Consequently, the occupation information must also be altered in the database of Zurich. Because ETH has no direct write access to the data, the changes are stored at the ETH personnel container and a notification of the situation is sent to the canton of Zurich database. The responsible person in the employment centre of Zurich, the *moderator* that handles ETH cases, is informed from the system about the request for occupation change. He can either accept the change by adopting the ETH personnel copy of the employment object or resolve the inconsistency due to this change in cooperation with the ETH personnel department. In this way, the central office retains control of the data, but clients of that data may notify them of changes.

7 Conclusions

We have identified four major concept areas that must be investigated when building a distributed information system for a cooperative working environment. The model presented defines the concepts of each area and interconnects them to support both data and schema sharing in modular information spaces.

The process of modelling our system in this way, led to a better understanding of the existing concepts that influence overall system design and the interoperability between them. This, in turn, led to improved functionality and efficiency of the current platform over an initial prototype.

To perform such metamodelling, it is important to use a rich and expressive data model that increases the semantic information about the data, which can, in turn, be used to drive the distribution. Moreover the overall implementation of the application will be easier by using distribution, replication and synchronisation concepts already introduced in the core of the system with a clear logical model. A flexible object storage model must exist to support distribution and interoperability between users. The granularity of information is crucial, not only for reasons of efficiency, but also flexibility. Finally, the user plays a central role in the system, controlling the connectivity within his environment. Two working strategies are supported by the system: A user privilege schema organised hierarchically, that supports user cooperation and a more autonomous solution based on versioning.

References

[ABD+89] M. Atkinson, F. Bancilhon, D. DeWitt, K. Dittrich, D. Meier, and S. Zdonik. The Object-Oriented Database System Manifesto. In *Proc. 1st Int. Conference on Deductive and Obect-Oriented Databases (DOOD)*, Japan, 1989.

[Bro92] M. L. Brodie. The Promise of Distributed Computing and Challenges of Legacy Information Systems. In D. K. Hsiao, E. J. Neuhold, and R. Sacks-Davis, editors, *Proceedings of IFIP DS-5 Semantics of Interoperable Database Systems*, volume 1, pages 1–30, Lorne, Victoria, Australia, November 1992.

[Est01] J. Estublier. Objects Control for Software Configuration Management. In *Proc. of 13th Conference on Advanced Information Systems Engineering (CAiSE'01)*, jun 2001.

[Gri98] Rebecca E. Grinter. Recomposition: Putting it all back together again. In *Computer Supported Cooperative Work*, pages 393–402, 1998.

[HM85] D. Heimbigner and D. McLeod. A Federated Architecture for Information Management. *ACM Transactions on Office Information Systems*, 3(3):253–278, 1985.

[KNW98] A. Kobler, M. C. Norrie, and A. Würgler. OMS Approach to Database Development through Rapid Prototyping. In *Proc. 8th Workshop on Information Technologies and Systems (WITS'98)*, Helsinki, Finland, December 1998.

[Nor93] M. C. Norrie. An Extended Entity-Relationship Approach to Data Management in Object-Oriented Systems. In *12th Intl. Conf. on Entity-Relationship Approach*, pages 390–401, Dallas, Texas, December 1993. Springer-Verlag, LNCS 823.

[Nor95] M. C. Norrie. Distinguishing Typing and Classification in Object Data Models. In *Information Modelling and Knowledge Bases*, volume VI, chapter 25. IOS, 1995. (originally appeared in Proc. European-Japanese Seminar on Information and Knowledge Modelling, Stockholm, Sweden, June 1994).

[NPW98] M. C. Norrie, A. Palinginis, and A. Würgler. OMS Connect: Supporting Multidatabase and Mobile Working through Database Connectivity. In *Proc. Conference on Cooperative Information Systems*, New York, USA, August 1998.

[Pit96] E. Pitoura. A Replication Schema to Support Weak Connectivity in Mobile Information Systems. In *Proc. of 7th Intl. Conf. on Database and Expert System Applications (DEXA)*, sep 1996.

[SL90] A. Sheth and J. Larson. Federated Database Systems for Managing Distributed, Heterogeneous, and Autonomous Databases. *ACM Computing Surveys*, 22(3):183–236, September 1990.

[Wue00] A. Wuergler. *OMS Development Framework: Rapid Prototyping for Object-Oriented Databases*. PhD Thesis, Department of Computer Science, ETH, CH-8092 Zurich, Switzerland, 2000.

Data Integration under Integrity Constraints

Andrea Calì, Diego Calvanese, Giuseppe De Giacomo, and Maurizio Lenzerini

Dipartimento di Informatica e Sistemistica, Università di Roma "La Sapienza"
Via Salaria 113, I-00198 Roma, Italy
lastname@dis.uniroma1.it,
http://www.dis.uniroma1.it/~*lastname*

Abstract. Data integration systems provide access to a set of heterogeneous, autonomous data sources through a so-called global schema. There are basically two approaches for designing a data integration system. In the global-centric approach, one defines the elements of the global schema as views over the sources, whereas in the local-centric approach, one characterizes the sources as views over the global schema. It is well known that processing queries in the latter approach is similar to query answering with incomplete information, and, therefore, is a complex task. On the other hand, it is a common opinion that query processing is much easier in the former approach. In this paper we show the surprising result that, when the global schema is expressed in the relational model with integrity constraints, even of simple types, the problem of incomplete information implicitly arises, making query processing difficult in the global-centric approach as well. We then focus on global schemas with key and foreign key constraints, which represents a situation which is very common in practice, and we illustrate techniques for effectively answering queries posed to the data integration system in this case.

1 Introduction

Integrating heterogeneous data sources is a fundamental problem in databases, which has been studied extensively in the last two decades both from a formal and from a practical point of view [1,2,3,4,5,6]. Recently, mostly driven by the need to integrate data sources on the Web, much of the research on integration has focussed on so called *data integration* [7,8,6]. Data integration is the problem of combining the data residing at different sources, and providing the user with a unified view of these data. Such a unified view is structured according to a so-called global schema, which represents the intensional level of the integrated and reconciled data, and provides the elements for expressing the queries over the data integration system. It follows that, in formulating the queries, the user is freed from the knowledge on where data are, how data are structured at the sources, and how data are to be merged and reconciled to fit into the global schema.

The interest in this kind of systems has been continuously growing in the last years. Many organizations face the problem of integrating data residing in several sources. Companies that build a Data Warehouse, a Data Mining, or an Enterprise Resource Planning system must address this problem. Also, integrating data in the World Wide Web is the subject of several investigations and projects nowadays. Finally, applications requiring accessing or re-engineering legacy systems must deal somehow with data integration.

The design of a data integration system is a very complex task, which requires addressing several different issues. Here, we concentrate on two basic issues:

1. specifying the mapping between the global schema and the sources,
2. processing queries expressed on the global schema.

With regard to issue (1), two basic approaches have been used to specify the mapping between the sources and the global schema [7,7,9]. The first approach, called *global-centric* [10,11,12], requires that the global schema is expressed in terms of the data sources. More precisely, to every element of the global schema, a view over the data sources is associated, so that its meaning is specified in terms of the data residing at the sources. In general, the views associated to the elements of the global schema are considered *sound*, i.e., all the data provided by a view satisfies the corresponding element of the global schema, but there may be additional data satisfying the element not provided by the view. The second approach, called *source-centric* [13,14,15], requires the global schema to be specified independently from the sources. In turn, the sources are defined as views over the global schema. Comparisons of the two approaches are reported in [8,16]. In this paper, we study global-centric data integration systems, and, according to the usual approach, we assume that the views associated to the elements of the global schema are sound.

Issue (2) is concerned with one of the most important problems in the design of a data integration system, namely, the choice of the method for computing the answer to queries posed in terms of the global schema. For this purpose, the system should be able to reformulate the query in terms of a suitable set of queries posed to the sources. These queries are then shipped to the sources, and the results are assembled into the final answer. It is well known that processing queries in the source-centric approach is a difficult task [8,17,14,18,19]. Indeed, in this approach the only knowledge we have about the data in the global schema is through the views representing the sources, and such views provide only partial information about the data. Therefore, extracting information from the data integration system is similar to query answering with incomplete information, which is a complex task [20]. On the other hand, query processing is considered much easier in the global-centric approach, where in general it is assumed that answering a query basically means unfolding its atoms according to their definitions in terms of the sources [7]. The reason why unfolding does the job is that the global-centric mapping essentially specifies a single database satisfying the global schema, and evaluating the query over this unique database is equivalent to evaluating its unfolding over the sources.

While this is a common opinion in the literature, we show in this paper that the presence of integrity constraints in the global schema poses new challenges, specially related to the need of taking the semantics of constraints into account during query processing. The importance of allowing integrity constraints in the global schema has been stressed in several work on data integration [15,21,22]. Since the global schema acts as the interface to the user for query formulation, it should mediate among different representations of overlapping worlds, and therefore the schema definition language should incorporate flexible and powerful representation mechanisms, such as the ones based on semantic integrity constraints.

The first contribution in this paper is to show that, when the global schema contains integrity constraints, even of simple forms, the semantics of the data integration system is best described in terms of a set of databases, rather than a single one, and this implies that, even in the global-centric approach, query processing is intimately connected to the notion of querying *incomplete databases*. The fact that the problem of incomplete information is overlooked in current approaches can be explained by observing that traditional data integration systems follow one of the following strategies: they either express the global schema as a set of plain relations without integrity constraints, or consider the sources as exact (see, e.g., [23,24]), as opposed to sound. On the contrary, the goal of our work is to study the more general setting where the global schema contains integrity constraints, and sources are considered sound (but not necessarily complete). The above result demonstrates that, in this case, we have to account for multiple global databases.

The second contribution of the paper is to study the case of global schemas expressed in the relational model with key and foreign key constraints, which represents a situation very common in practice. Although the problem of multiple global databases arises in this case, we have devised techniques for effectively answering queries posed to the data integration system. The resulting algorithm runs in polynomial time with respect to data complexity, i.e., with respect to the size of data at the sources.

The paper is organized as follows. In Section 2 we describe a formal framework for data integration. In Section 3 we show that the presence of integrity constraints in the global schema complicates the task of query processing. In Sections 4 and 5 we present our query processing algorithm for the case of global relational schema with key and foreign key constraints. Section 6 concludes the paper.

2 Framework for Data Integration

In this section we illustrate our formalization of a data integration system, which is based on the relational model with integrity constraints.

In the relational model, predicate symbols are used to denote the relations in the database, whereas constant symbols denote the objects and the values stored in relations. We assume to have a fixed (infinite) alphabet Γ of constants, and, if not specified otherwise, we will consider only databases over such alphabet. We adopt the so-called *unique name assumption*, i.e., we assume that different constants denote different objects. A *relational schema* $\mathcal{C}$ is constituted by:

- An *alphabet* $\mathcal{A}$ of predicate (or relation) symbols, each one with the associated arity, i.e., the number of arguments of the predicate (or, attributes of the relation). We do not use names for referring to attributes, rather, we simply use the numbers corresponding to their positions.
- A set of *integrity constraints*, i.e., assertions on the symbols of the alphabet $\mathcal{A}$ that express conditions that are intended to be satisfied in every database coherent with the schema.

A relational database (or simply, database) $\mathcal{DB}$ for a schema $\mathcal{C}$ is a set of relations with constants as atomic values, and with one relation $r^{\mathcal{DB}}$ of arity n for each predicate symbol r of arity n in the alphabet $\mathcal{A}$. It is well known that a database can be seen as a first-order interpretation for the relation symbols in the schema: the relation $r^{\mathcal{DB}}$ is the interpretation of the predicate symbol r in $\mathcal{DB}$, in the sense that it contains the set of tuples that satisfy the predicate r in $\mathcal{DB}$. A database $\mathcal{DB}$ for a schema $\mathcal{C}$ is said to be *legal* if every constraints of $\mathcal{C}$ is satisfied by $\mathcal{DB}$. The notion of satisfaction depends on the type of constraints.

In our framework we consider the relational model with two kinds of constraints:

- *Key constraints*: given a relation r in the schema, a key constraint over r is expressed in the form $key(r) = \mathbf{A}$, where $\mathbf{A}$ is a set of attributes of r. Such a constraint is satisfied in a database $\mathcal{DB}$ if for each $t_1, t_2 \in r^{\mathcal{DB}}$ we have $t_1[\mathbf{A}] \neq t_2[\mathbf{A}]$, where $t[\mathbf{A}]$ is the projection of the tuple t over $\mathbf{A}$.
- *Foreign key constraints*: a foreign key constraint is a statement of the form $r_1[\mathbf{A}] \subseteq r_2[\mathbf{B}]$, where r_1, r_2 are relations, $\mathbf{A}$ is a sequence of distinct attributes of r_1, and $\mathbf{B}$ is a sequence formed by the distinct attributes forming the key of r_2. Such a constraint is satisfied in a database $\mathcal{DB}$ if for each tuple t_1 in $r_1^{\mathcal{DB}}$ there exists a tuple t_2 in $r_2^{\mathcal{DB}}$ such that $t_1[\mathbf{A}] = t_2[\mathbf{B}]$.

A *relational query* is a formula that specifies a set of tuples to be retrieved from a database. In this work, we restrict our analysis to the class of conjunctive queries. Formally, a *conjunctive query* (CQ) q of *arity* n is written in the form

$$q(x_1, \ldots, x_n) \leftarrow conj(x_1, \ldots, x_n, y_1, \ldots, y_m)$$

where: q belongs to a new alphabet $\mathcal{Q}$ (the alphabet of queries, that is disjoint from both Γ and $\mathcal{A}$); $conj(x_1, \ldots, x_n, y_1, \ldots, y_m)$ is a conjunction of atoms involving the variables $x_1, \ldots, x_n, y_1, \ldots, y_m$, and a set of constants from Γ; and the predicate symbols of the atoms are in $\mathcal{C}$.

The answer to a query q of arity n over a database $\mathcal{DB}$ for $\mathcal{G}$, denoted $q^{\mathcal{DB}}$, is the set of n-tuples of constants $(c_1, \ldots, c_n)$, such that, when substituting each c_i for x_i, the formula $\exists (y_1, \ldots, y_n).conj(x_1, \ldots, x_n, y_1, \ldots, y_m)$ evaluates to true in $\mathcal{DB}$. Note that the answer to q over $\mathcal{DB}$ is a relation whose arity is equal to the arity of the query q.

We now turn our attention to the notion of data integration system.

Definition 1. *A data integration system $\mathcal{I}$ is a triple $\mathcal{I} = \langle \mathcal{G}, \mathcal{S}, \mathcal{M}_{\mathcal{G},\mathcal{S}} \rangle$, where $\mathcal{G}$ is the* global schema, *$\mathcal{S}$ is the* source schema, *and $\mathcal{M}_{\mathcal{G},\mathcal{S}}$ is the* mapping *between $\mathcal{G}$ and $\mathcal{S}$.*

Now we describe the characteristics of the components of a data integration system in our approach. In particular, we specialize the general framework as follows:

- The *global schema* is expressed in the relational model with both key and foreign key constraints. We assume that in the global schema there is exactly one key constraint for each relation.
- The *source schema* is expressed in the relational model without integrity constraints. In other words, we conceive each source as a relation, and we consider the set of all relations as a unique schema, called source schema.
- The *mapping* $\mathcal{M}_{\mathcal{G},\mathcal{S}}$ is defined in the global-centric approach: to each relation r of $\mathcal{G}$ we associate a query $\rho(r)$ over the source schema. No limitation is posed on the language used to express queries in the mapping $\mathcal{M}_{\mathcal{G},\mathcal{S}}$.
- Queries over the global schema are *conjunctive queries*.

Example 1. An example of data integration system is $\mathcal{I}^1 = \langle \mathcal{G}^1, \mathcal{S}^1, \mathcal{M}^1_{\mathcal{G},\mathcal{S}} \rangle$ where $\mathcal{G}^1$ is constituted by the relation symbols student($Scode, Sname, Scity$), university($Ucode, Uname$), and enrolled($Scode, Ucode$) and the constraints

$$key(\text{student}) = \{Scode\}$$
$$key(\text{university}) = \{Ucode\}$$
$$key(\text{enrolled}) = \{Scode, Ucode\}$$

enrolled$[Scode] \subseteq$ student$[Scode]$
enrolled$[Ucode] \subseteq$ university$[Ucode]$

$\mathcal{S}^1$ consists of three sources. Source s_1, of arity 4, contains information about students with their code, name, city, and date of birth. Source s_2, of arity 2, contains codes and names of universities. Finally, Source s_3, of arity 2, contains information about enrollment of students in universities. The mapping $\mathcal{M}^1_{\mathcal{G},\mathcal{S}}$ is defined by

$$\rho(\text{student}) = \text{st}(X,Y,Z) \leftarrow \text{s}_1(X,Y,Z,W)$$
$$\rho(\text{university}) = \text{un}(X,Y) \leftarrow \text{s}_2(X,Y)$$
$$\rho(\text{enrolled}) = \text{en}(X,W) \leftarrow \text{s}_3(X,W)$$

In order to define the semantics of a data integration system $\mathcal{I} = \langle \mathcal{G}, \mathcal{S}, \mathcal{M}_{\mathcal{G},\mathcal{S}} \rangle$, we start from the data at the sources, and specify which are the data that satisfy the global schema. A *source database* $\mathcal{D}$ for $\mathcal{I}$ is constituted by one relation $r^\mathcal{D}$ for each source r in $\mathcal{S}$. We call *global database* for $\mathcal{I}$, or simply *database* for $\mathcal{I}$, any database for $\mathcal{G}$. A database $\mathcal{B}$ for $\mathcal{I}$ is said to be *legal* with respect to $\mathcal{D}$ if:

- $\mathcal{B}$ satisfies the integrity constraints of $\mathcal{G}$.
- $\mathcal{B}$ satisfies $\mathcal{M}_{\mathcal{G},\mathcal{S}}$ with respect to $\mathcal{D}$, i.e., for each relation r in $\mathcal{G}$, the set of tuples $r^\mathcal{B}$ that $\mathcal{B}$ assigns to r is a subset of the set of tuples $\rho(r)^\mathcal{D}$ computed by the associated query $\rho(r)$ over $\mathcal{D}$, i.e., $\rho(r)^\mathcal{D} \subseteq r^\mathcal{B}$.

Note that the above definition amounts to consider any view $\rho(r)$ as *sound*, which means that the data provided by the sources are not necessarily complete. Other assumptions on views are possible (see [14,18]). In particular, views may be *complete*, i.e., for each r in $\mathcal{G}$, we have $\rho(r)^\mathcal{D} \supseteq r^\mathcal{B}$, or *exact*, i.e., for each r in $\mathcal{G}$, we have $\rho(r)^\mathcal{D} = r^\mathcal{B}$. In this paper, we restrict our attention to sound views only, which are typically considered the most natural in a data integration setting.

At this point, we are able to give the semantics of a data integration system, which is formally defined as follows.

Definition 2. *If* $\mathcal{I} = \langle \mathcal{G}, \mathcal{S}, \mathcal{M}_{\mathcal{G},\mathcal{S}} \rangle$, *and* $\mathcal{D}$ *is a source database for* $\mathcal{I}$, *the semantics of* $\mathcal{I}$ *w.r.t.* $\mathcal{D}$, *denoted* $sem^{\mathcal{D}}(\mathcal{I})$, *is the set of databases for* $\mathcal{I}$ *that are legal w.r.t.* $\mathcal{D}$, *i.e., that satisfy both the constraints of* $\mathcal{G}$, *and the mapping* $\mathcal{M}_{\mathcal{G},\mathcal{S}}$ *with respect to* $\mathcal{D}$. *If* $sem^{\mathcal{D}}(\mathcal{I}) \neq \emptyset$, *then* $\mathcal{I}$ *said to be* consistent *w.r.t.* $\mathcal{D}$.

By the above definition, it is clear that the semantics of a data integration systems is formulated in terms of a *set* of databases, rather than a single one. Indeed, as we will show in the sequel, the cardinality of $sem^{\mathcal{D}}(\mathcal{I})$ is in general greater than one. The impact of this property on query answering will be studied in the next section.

3 Query Answering in the Presence of Constraints

The ultimate goal of a data integration system is to answer queries posed by the user in terms of the global schema. Answering a query posed to a system representing a set of databases, is a complex task, as shown by the following example.

Example 2. Referring to Example 1, suppose to have the following source database $\mathcal{D}^1$:

$s_1^{\mathcal{D}^1}$:
12	anne	florence	21
15	bill	oslo	24

$s_2^{\mathcal{D}^1}$:
AF	bocconi
BN	ucla

$s_3^{\mathcal{D}^1}$:
12	AF
16	BN

Now, due to the integrity constraints in $\mathcal{G}_1$, 16 is the code of some student. Observe, however, that nothing is said by $\mathcal{D}^1$ about the name and the city of such student. Therefore, we must accept as legal all databases that differ in such attributes of the student with code 16. Note that this is a consequence of the assumption of having sound views. If we had exact or complete views, this situation would have lead to an inconsistency of the data integration system. Instead, when dealing with sound views, we can think of extending the data contained in the sources in order to satisfy the integrity constraint over the global schema. The fact that, in general, there are several possible ways to carry out such extension implies that there are several legal databases for the data integration systems.

Let us now turn our attention to the notion of answer to a query posed to the data integration system. In our setting, a query q to a data integration system $\mathcal{I} = \langle \mathcal{G}, \mathcal{S}, \mathcal{M}_{\mathcal{G},\mathcal{S}} \rangle$ is a conjunctive query, whose atoms have symbols in $\mathcal{G}$ as predicates. Our goal is to specify which are the tuples that form the answer to a certain query posed to $\mathcal{I}$. The task is complicated by the existence of several global databases which are legal for $\mathcal{I}$ with respect to a source database $\mathcal{D}$. In order to address this problem, we adopt the following approach: a tuple $(c_1, \ldots, c_n)$ is considered an answer to the query only if it is a *certain* answer, i.e., it satisfies the query in *every* database that belongs to the semantics of the data integration system.

Definition 3. Let $\mathcal{I} = \langle \mathcal{G}, \mathcal{S}, \mathcal{M}_{\mathcal{G},\mathcal{S}} \rangle$ be a data integration system, let $\mathcal{D}$ be a source database for $\mathcal{I}$, and let q be a query of arity n to $\mathcal{I}$. The set of certain answers $q^{\mathcal{I},\mathcal{D}}$ to q with respect to $\mathcal{I}$ and $\mathcal{D}$ is the set of tuples $(c_1, \ldots, c_n)$ such that $(c_1, \ldots, c_n) \in q^{\mathcal{B}}$, for each $\mathcal{B} \in sem^{\mathcal{D}}(\mathcal{I})$.

As mentioned, it is generally assumed that query answering is an easy task in the global-centric approach. Indeed, the most common technique for query answering in this approach is based on *unfolding*, i.e. substituting to each relation symbol r in the query its definition $\rho(r)$ in terms of the sources. We now show a simple unfolding strategy is not sufficient for providing all correct answers in the presence of integrity constraints.

Example 3. Referring again to Example 1, consider the query

$$q(X) \leftarrow \mathsf{student}(X, Y, Z) \wedge \mathsf{enrolled}(X, W)$$

The correct answer to the query is $\{12, 16\}$, because, due to the integrity constraints in $\mathcal{G}_1$, we know that 16 appears in the first attribute of student in all the databases for $\mathcal{I}$ that are legal w.r.t. $\mathcal{D}_1$. However, we do not get this information from $\mathsf{s}_1^{\mathcal{D}_1}$, and, therefore, a simple unfolding strategy retrieves only the answer $\{12\}$ from $\mathcal{D}^1$, thus proving insufficient for query answering in this framework. Notice that, if the query asked for the student name instead of the student code (i.e., the head is $q(Y)$ instead of $q(X)$), then one could *not* make use of the dependencies to infer additional answers.

The above example shows that, in the presence of integrity constraints, even in the global-centric approach we have to deal with incomplete information during query processing.

4 General Description of the Approach

We present the general ideas that are at the basis of our method for query answering in data integration systems.

Let $\mathcal{I} = \langle \mathcal{G}, \mathcal{S}, \mathcal{M}_{\mathcal{G},\mathcal{S}} \rangle$ be a data integration system. In this paper we assume that, for each relation r of the global schema, the query $\rho(r)$ over the source schema that the mapping $\mathcal{M}_{\mathcal{G},\mathcal{S}}$ associates to r preserves the key constraint of r. This may require that $\rho(r)$ implements a suitable duplicate record elimination strategy that ensures that, for every source database $\mathcal{D}$ no pairs of tuples are extracted from $\mathcal{D}$ by $\rho(r)$ with the same value for the key of r. The problem of duplicate record elimination, and, more generally, of data cleaning, is a critical issues in data integration systems, however it is orthogonal to the problem addressed here. We refer to [25,26] for more details.

Let q be a query posed to $\mathcal{I}$, and $\mathcal{D}$ a source database for $\mathcal{I}$. We illustrate a naive method for computing the answer $q^{\mathcal{I},\mathcal{D}}$ to q w.r.t. $\mathcal{I}$ and $\mathcal{D}$. The naive computation of $q^{\mathcal{I},\mathcal{D}}$ proceeds as follows.

1. For each relation r of the global schema, we compute the relation $r^{\mathcal{D}}$ by evaluating the query $\rho(r)$ over the source database $\mathcal{D}$. The various relations so obtained form what we call the *retrieved global database* $ret(\mathcal{I}, \mathcal{D})$. Note

that, since we assume that $\rho(r)$ does not violate the key constraints, it follows that the retrieved global database satisfies all key constraints in $\mathcal{G}$.

2. If, additionally, the retrieved global database satisfies all foreign key constraints in $\mathcal{G}$, then we are basically done: we simply evaluate q over $ret(\mathcal{I}, \mathcal{D})$, and we obtain the answer to the query.

   Otherwise, based on the retrieved global database, we can build a database for $\mathcal{I}$ still satisfying the key constraints by suitably adding tuples to the relations of the global schema in such a way that also the foreign key constraints are satisfied.[1] Obviously, there are several possible ways to add tuples to the global relations.

   We may try to infer all the legal databases for $\mathcal{I}$ that are coherent with the retrieved global database, and we compute the tuples that satisfy the query q in all such legal databases. However, such a solution is not easy to pursue. Indeed, the direct way to implement it, i.e., building all the legal databases for $\mathcal{I}$ that are coherent with the retrieved global database, is not feasible: in general, there is an infinite number of legal databases that are coherent with the retrieved global database. Fortunately, starting from the retrieved global database, we can build another database, that we call *canonical*, that has the interesting property of faithfully representing all legal databases that are coherent with the retrieved global database.

Let us start by showing how to build the canonical database. First of all, we define the domain of such database, which we denote $HD(\mathcal{D})$, as follows. Based on the global schema $\mathcal{G}$ of $\mathcal{I}$, we introduce the following set of function symbols:

$$HT(\mathcal{G}) = \{f_{r,i} \mid r \in \mathcal{G} \text{ and } i \leq arity(r) \text{ and } i \notin key(r)\}$$

Thus, each $f_{r,i}$ is a function symbol, and such a function symbol has the same arity as the number of attributes of $key(r)$, i.e., $arity(f_{r,i}) = arity(key(r))$. From $\mathcal{D}$, we now define the domain $HD(\mathcal{D})$ as the smallest set satisfying the following conditions:

- $\Gamma \subseteq HD(\mathcal{D})$,
- if $\alpha_1, \ldots, \alpha_k \in HD(\mathcal{D})$, and $f_{R,i} \in HT(\mathcal{G})$, with $arity(f_{R,i}) = k$, then $f_{R,i}(\alpha_1, \ldots, \alpha_k) \in HD(\mathcal{D})$.

Now, given the retrieved global database $ret(\mathcal{I}, \mathcal{D})$, we obtain the canonical database $can(\mathcal{I}, \mathcal{D})$ over the domain $HD(\mathcal{D})$ by repeatedly applying the following rule:

if $(x_1, \ldots, x_h) \in r[\mathbf{A}]$, and the foreign key constraint $r_1[\mathbf{A}] \subseteq r_2[\mathbf{B}]$ is in $\mathcal{G}$,
then insert the tuple t in r_2 such that

---

[1] Note that, since views are sound, i.e., they return a *subset* of the tuples in a global relation, we cannot conclude that the data integration system violates the foreign key constraints of $\mathcal{G}$. Indeed, it may be the case that the tuples needed to satisfy such constraints are not part of the retrieved subsets.

- $t[\mathbf{B}] = (x_1, \ldots, x_h)$, and
- for each $i \leq \mathit{arity}(r_2)$ not in $\mathbf{B}$, $t[i] = f_{r_2,i}(x_1, \ldots, x_h)$.

Observe that $\mathit{can}(\mathcal{I}, \mathcal{D})$ is indeed a database over the domain $HD(\mathcal{D})$, and that, in general, $\mathit{can}(\mathcal{I}, \mathcal{D})$ is infinite. However, it enjoys important properties, as shown below. The first property is related to the satisfaction of the constraints of $\mathcal{G}$.

Theorem 1. *If $\mathcal{I} = \langle \mathcal{G}, \mathcal{S}, \mathcal{M}_{\mathcal{G},\mathcal{S}} \rangle$, and $\mathcal{D}$ is a source database for $\mathcal{I}$, then $\mathit{can}(\mathcal{I}, \mathcal{D})$ does not violate any foreign key constraint in $\mathcal{G}$.*

Proof. Suppose by contradiction that the foreign key constraint $r_1[\mathbf{A}] \subseteq r_2[\mathbf{B}]$ is violated in $\mathit{can}(\mathcal{I}, \mathcal{D})$. This implies that there is a tuple t in r_1 such that for no tuple t' in r_2 $t'[\mathbf{B}] = t[\mathbf{A}]$. But this would imply that we can apply the rule and insert a new tuple t'' in r_2 such that $t''[\mathbf{B}] = t[\mathbf{A}]$, and for each $i \leq \mathit{arity}(r_2)$ not in $\mathbf{B}$, $t'[i] = f_{r_2,i}(t[\mathbf{A}])$. But this contradicts the assumption.

We now show that there exists a legal database for $\mathcal{I}$ w.r.t. $\mathcal{D}$ (called $\mathit{can}^-(\mathcal{I}, \mathcal{D})$), which implies that $\mathcal{I}$ is consistent w.r.t. $\mathcal{D}$, if and only if $\mathit{ret}(\mathcal{I}, \mathcal{D})$ does not violate any key constraint in $\mathcal{G}$.

Theorem 2. *If $\mathcal{I} = \langle \mathcal{G}, \mathcal{S}, \mathcal{M}_{\mathcal{G},\mathcal{S}} \rangle$, and $\mathcal{D}$ is a source database for $\mathcal{I}$, then there exists a legal database for $\mathcal{I}$ w.r.t. $\mathcal{D}$ if and only if $\mathit{ret}(\mathcal{I}, \mathcal{D})$ does not violate any key constraint in $\mathcal{G}$.*

Proof. It is immediate to see that if $\mathit{ret}(\mathcal{I}, \mathcal{D})$ violates some key constraint in $\mathcal{G}$, then no legal database exists for $\mathcal{I}$ w.r.t. $\mathcal{D}$.

It remains to show that, if $\mathit{ret}(\mathcal{I}, \mathcal{D})$ does not violate any key constraint in $\mathcal{G}$, then there exists a legal database $\mathit{can}^-(\mathcal{I}, \mathcal{D})$ for $\mathcal{I}$ w.r.t. $\mathcal{D}$, which implies that $\mathcal{I}$ is consistent w.r.t. $\mathcal{D}$. We construct $\mathit{can}^-(\mathcal{I}, \mathcal{D})$ from $\mathcal{G}$ and $\mathcal{D}$ similarly to $\mathit{can}(\mathcal{I}, \mathcal{D})$, with the only difference that we use the rule:

If $(x_1, \ldots, x_h) \in r_1[\mathbf{A}]$, $(x_1, \ldots, x_h) \notin r_2[\mathbf{B}]$, and the foreign key constraint $r_1[\mathbf{A}] \subseteq r_2[\mathbf{B}]$ is in $\mathcal{G}$,
then insert the tuple t in r_2 such that
- $t[\mathbf{B}] = (x_1, \ldots, x_h)$, and
- for each $i \leq \mathit{arity}(r_2)$ different from $\mathbf{B}$, $t[i] = f_{r_2,i}(x)$.

It is easy to see that $\mathit{can}^-(\mathcal{I}, \mathcal{D}) \subseteq \mathit{can}(\mathcal{I}, \mathcal{D})$. To show that $\mathit{can}^-(\mathcal{I}, \mathcal{D})$ is indeed a legal database for $\mathcal{I}$ w.r.t. $\mathcal{D}$, we consider key and foreign key constraints separately. As for key constraints, it is easy to see that the tuples inserted during the process of computing $\mathit{can}^-(\mathcal{I}, \mathcal{D})$ cannot violate any key constraints of $\mathcal{G}$. Indeed, in computing $\mathit{can}^-(\mathcal{I}, \mathcal{D})$, we insert a tuple into a relation r only when the key component of that tuple is not already present in r. Since $\mathit{ret}(\mathcal{I}, \mathcal{D})$ does not violate any key constraint in $\mathcal{G}$, it follows that no key constraint of $\mathcal{G}$ is violated in $\mathit{can}^-(\mathcal{I}, \mathcal{D})$. As for foreign key constraints, suppose by contradiction that the foreign key constraint $r_1[\mathbf{A}] \subseteq r_2[\mathbf{B}]$ is violated in $\mathit{can}^-(\mathcal{I}, \mathcal{D})$. This implies that there is a tuple t in r_1 such that for no tuple t' in r_2 $t'[\mathbf{B}] = t[\mathbf{A}]$. But this would imply that we can apply the above rule and insert a new tuple t'' in r_2 such that $t''[\mathbf{B}] = t[\mathbf{A}]$, and for each $i \leq \mathit{arity}(r_2)$ not in $\mathbf{B}$, $t'[i] = f_{r_2,i}(t[\mathbf{A}])$. But this contradicts the assumption.

The canonical database $can(\mathcal{I}, \mathcal{D})$ has the interesting property of faithfully representing all legal databases that are coherent with the retrieved global database $ret(\mathcal{I}, \mathcal{D})$.

Theorem 3. *Let $\mathcal{I} = \langle \mathcal{G}, \mathcal{S}, \mathcal{M}_{\mathcal{G},\mathcal{S}} \rangle$, let $\mathcal{D}$ be a source database for $\mathcal{I}$, and let $\mathcal{B}$ be a legal database for $\mathcal{I}$ w.r.t. $\mathcal{D}$. There is a total function ψ from $HD(\mathcal{D})$ to Γ such that, for each relation r of arity n in $\mathcal{G}$, and each tuple $(c_1, \ldots, c_n)$ constituted by elements in $HD(\mathcal{D})$, if $(c_1, \ldots, c_n) \in r^{can(\mathcal{I},\mathcal{D})}$, then $(\psi(c_1), \ldots, \psi(c_n)) \in r^{\mathcal{B}}$.*

Proof. We define the function ψ from $HD(\mathcal{D})$ to Γ inductively, and we simultaneously show that for each relation r of arity n in $\mathcal{G}$, and each tuple $(c_1, \ldots, c_n)$ constituted by elements in $HD(\mathcal{D})$, if $(c_1, \ldots, c_n) \in r^{can(\mathcal{I},\mathcal{D})}$, then $(\psi(c_1), \ldots, \psi(c_n)) \in r^{\mathcal{B}}$.

We proceed by induction on the application of the rule used during the construction of $can(\mathcal{I}, \mathcal{D})$. As a base step, the function ψ maps each constant in $ret(\mathcal{I}, \mathcal{D})$ into itself. It follows that, for each r, if $c_1, \ldots, c_n$ are constants, and $(c_1, \ldots, c_n) \in r^{ret(\mathcal{I},\mathcal{D})}$, then it is obvious that both $(c_1, \ldots, c_n) \in r^{can(\mathcal{I},\mathcal{D})}$, and $(\psi(c_1), \ldots, \psi(c_n)) \in r^{\mathcal{B}}$.

Inductive step. Suppose, without loss of generality, that in the application of the rule, we are inserting the tuple $(\alpha, f_{r,i_1}(\alpha), f_{r,i_2}(\alpha))$ in $r^{can(\mathcal{I},\mathcal{D})}$ where r has arity 3, $key(r) = \{1\}$, and the tuple is inserted in $r^{can(\mathcal{I},\mathcal{D})}$ because of the foreign key constraint $w[j] \subseteq r[1]$. Since we are applying the rule because of the constraint $w[j] \subseteq r[1]$, we have that there is a tuple t in $w^{can(\mathcal{I},\mathcal{D})}$ such that $t[j] = \alpha$. For the induction hypothesis, there is a β in Γ such that $\psi(\alpha) = \beta$, and there is a tuple $t' \in w^{\mathcal{B}}$ such that for each i, $t'[i] = \psi(t[i])$, and $t'[j] = \psi(\alpha) = \beta$. Because of the constraint $w[j] \subseteq r[1]$, and because $\mathcal{B}$ is legal, there is one and only one tuple (β, γ, δ) in $r^{\mathcal{B}}$ (since 1 is a key of r, β appears once in $r^{\mathcal{B}}[1]$). Then, we set $\psi(f_{r,i_1}(\alpha)) = \gamma$, $\psi(f_{r,i_2}(\alpha)) = \delta$, and we can conclude that $(\psi(\alpha), \psi(f_{r,i_1}(\alpha)), \psi(f_{r,i_2}(\alpha))) \in r^{\mathcal{B}}$.

Finally, we show that, if $\mathcal{I}$ is consistent w.r.t. $\mathcal{D}$, then a tuple t of constants is in $q^{\mathcal{I},\mathcal{D}}$ if and only if t is in the answer to q over the database $can(\mathcal{I}, \mathcal{D})$.

Theorem 4. *Let $\mathcal{I} = \langle \mathcal{G}, \mathcal{S}, \mathcal{M}_{\mathcal{G},\mathcal{S}} \rangle$, let q be a query posed to $\mathcal{I}$, $\mathcal{D}$ a source database for $\mathcal{I}$, and t a tuple of constants of the same arity as q. If $\mathcal{I}$ is consistent w.r.t. $\mathcal{D}$, then $t \in q^{\mathcal{I},\mathcal{D}}$ if and only if t is in the answer to q over $can(\mathcal{I}, \mathcal{D})$.*

Proof. For the "if" direction, we show that if t is in the answer to q over $can(\mathcal{I}, \mathcal{D})$, then $t \in q^{\mathcal{I},\mathcal{D}}$. Indeed, consider any $\mathcal{B}$ that is a legal database for $\mathcal{I}$ w.r.t. $\mathcal{D}$. By theorem 3, there is a total function ψ from $HD(\mathcal{D})$ to Γ such that, for each relation r of arity n in $\mathcal{G}$, and each tuple $(c_1, \ldots, c_n)$ constituted by elements in $HD(\mathcal{D})$, if $(c_1, \ldots, c_n) \in r^{can(\mathcal{I},\mathcal{D})}$, then $(\psi(c_1), \ldots, \psi(c_n)) \in r^{\mathcal{B}}$. The fact that t is in the answer to q over $can(\mathcal{I}, \mathcal{D})$ means that there is an assignment α from the variables of q to objects in $HD(\mathcal{D})$ such that all atoms of q are true with respect to the assignment. It is easy to see that the assignment $\alpha \cdot \psi$ can be used to show that t is in the answer to q over $\mathcal{B}$.

As for the "only-if" direction, first note that, by hypothesis $\mathcal{I}$ is consistent w.r.t. $\mathcal{D}$, and, therefore, by theorem 2, $ret(\mathcal{I},\mathcal{D})$ does not violate any key constraint in $\mathcal{G}$, which implies that $can^-(\mathcal{I},\mathcal{D})$ is a legal database for $\mathcal{I}$ w.r.t. $\mathcal{D}$. Now, since $can^-(\mathcal{I},\mathcal{D}) \subseteq can(\mathcal{I},\mathcal{D})$, and since q is a conjunctive query, the fact that t is not in the answer to q over $can(\mathcal{I},\mathcal{D})$ implies that t is not in the answer of q over $can^-(\mathcal{I},\mathcal{D})$. Therefore, we can conclude that $t \notin q^{\mathcal{I},\mathcal{D}}$.

Based on the above results, we can conclude that $can(\mathcal{I},\mathcal{D})$ is the right abstraction for answering queries posed to the data integration system. In the next section we show that, in processing a query q posed to the data integration system, we can find the answers to q over $can(\mathcal{I},\mathcal{D})$ without actually building $can(\mathcal{I},\mathcal{D})$.

5 Query Reformulation

The naive computation described in the previous section is impractical, because it requires to build the canonical database, which is in general infinite. In order to overcome the problem, we have devised an algorithm, whose main ideas are as follows.

1. First, as we said in the previous section, we assume that, for each relation r of the global schema, the query $\rho(r)$ over the source schema that the mapping $\mathcal{M}_{\mathcal{G},\mathcal{S}}$ associates to r preserve the key constraint of r.
2. Instead of referring explicitly to the canonical database for query answering, we transform the original query q into a new query $exp_{\mathcal{G}}(q)$ over the global schema, called the *expansion of q w.r.t. $\mathcal{G}$*, such that the answer to $exp_{\mathcal{G}}(q)$ over the retrieved global database is equal to the answer to q over the canonical database.
3. In order to avoid building the retrieved global database, we do not evaluate $exp_{\mathcal{G}}(q)$ on the retrieved global database. Instead, we unfold $exp_{\mathcal{G}}(q)$ to a new query, called $unf_{\mathcal{M}_{\mathcal{G},\mathcal{S}}}(exp_{\mathcal{G}}(q))$, over the source relations on the basis of $\mathcal{M}_{\mathcal{G},\mathcal{S}}$, and we use the unfolded query $unf_{\mathcal{M}_{\mathcal{G},\mathcal{S}}}(exp_{\mathcal{G}}(q))$ to access the sources.

We refer to steps 1 and 2 as the "query reformulation" step. Step 3 is called the "source access". In the rest of the section we discuss the first two steps.

Let $\mathcal{I} = \langle \mathcal{G}, \mathcal{S}, \mathcal{M}_{\mathcal{G},\mathcal{S}} \rangle$ be a data integration system, let $\mathcal{D}$ be a source database, and let q be a query over the global schema $\mathcal{G}$. We show how to reformulate the original query q into a new query $exp_{\mathcal{G}}(q)$ over the global schema, called the expansion of q w.r.t. $\mathcal{G}$, such that the answer to $exp_{\mathcal{G}}(q)$ over the (virtual) retrieved global database is equal to the answer to q over the canonical database.

The basic idea to do so is that the constraints in $\mathcal{G}$ can be captured by a suitable *logic program* $\mathcal{P}_{\mathcal{G}}$. To build $\mathcal{P}_{\mathcal{G}}$, we introduce a new relation p' (called primed relation) for each relation p in $\mathcal{G}$. Then, from the semantics of $\mathcal{G}$ we devise the following rules for $\mathcal{P}_{\mathcal{G}}$ (expressed in Logic Programming notation [27]):

- for each relation r, we have:

$$r'(X_1,\ldots,X_n) \leftarrow r(X_1,\ldots,X_n)$$

- for each foreign key constraint $r_1[\mathbf{A}] \subseteq r_2[\mathbf{B}]$ in $\mathcal{G}$, where $\mathbf{A}$ and $\mathbf{B}$ are sets of attributes and $\mathbf{B}$ is a key for r_2 (assuming for simplicity that the attributes involved in the foreign key are the first h):

$$r'_2(X_1,\ldots,X_h, f_{h+1}(X_1,\ldots,X_h),\ldots, f_n(X_1,\ldots,X_h))$$
$$\leftarrow r'_1(X_1,\ldots,X_h,\ldots,X_m)$$

where f_i are fresh function symbols, called Skolem functions.

We can use the logic program $\mathcal{P}_\mathcal{G}$ to generate the query $exp_\mathcal{G}(q)$ associated to the original query q. This is done as follows.

1. First, we rewrite q by substituting each relation symbol r in the body $body(q)$ of q with a new symbol r'. We denote by q' the resulting query. In the following we call "primed atom" every atom whose relation symbol is primed, i.e., it has the form r' for some r.
2. Then we build a *partial evaluation tree* for q', i.e., a tree having each node labeled by a conjunctive query g, with one of the atoms in $body(g)$ marked as "*selected*", obtained as follows.
   (a) The root is labeled by q', and has one (primed) atom (for example the first in left-to-right order) marked as selected.
   (b) Except if condition (2c) below is satisfied, a node, labeled by a query g having a "selected" atom α, has one child for each rule ϕ in $\mathcal{P}_\mathcal{G}$ such that there exists a most general unifier[2] $mgu(\alpha, head(\phi))$ between the atom α and the head $head(\phi)$ of the rule ϕ, such that the distinguished variables are not assigned to terms involving Skolem functions. Each of such children has the following properties:
      - it is labeled by the query obtained from g by replacing the atom α with $body(\phi)$ and by substituting the variables with $mgu(\alpha, head(\phi))$;
      - it has as marked "selected" one of the primed atoms (for example the first in left-to-right order).
   (c) If a node d is labeled by a query g, and there exist a predecessor d' of d labeled by a query g' and a substitution θ of the variables of g' that makes g' equal to g, then d has a single child, which is labeled by the empty query (a query whose body is false).
3. Finally we return as result the query $exp_\mathcal{G}(q)$ formed as the union of all non-empty queries in the leaves of the partial evaluation tree.

Theorem 5 (Termination). *The algorithm above always terminates.*

---
[2] We recall that given two atoms α and β the most general unifier $mgu(\alpha, \beta)$ is a most general substitution for the variables in α and β that makes α and β equal [27].

Proof. The termination of the algorithm follows directly from the following observations:

- The queries in all nodes on the tree have exactly the same number of atoms as the original query q. This is an immediate consequence of the fact that for rule ϕ in $\mathcal{P}_\mathcal{G}$, $body(\phi)$ is formed by exactly one atom.
- Condition (2c) guarantees a finite bound on the nesting of Skolem functions in the queries in the nodes.

As a consequence, the number of queries along each branch of the partial evaluation tree must be finite, hence the thesis holds.

Our goal now is to show that if $\mathcal{I}$ is consistent w.r.t. $\mathcal{D}$, then $t \in q^{\mathcal{I},\mathcal{D}}$ if and only if t is in the answer to $unf_{\mathcal{M}_{\mathcal{G},\mathcal{S}}}(exp_\mathcal{G}(q))$ over $\mathcal{D}$. We will prove such result by applying results from the logic programming theory [27] and, in particular, results on the partial evaluation of logic programs [28]. We first observe that $ret(\mathcal{I},\mathcal{D})$ can be seen as a (finite) set of ground facts in logic programming terms. We proceed by proving a series of lemmas, each dealing with a particular aspect of the proof. The relationship between the *logic program* $\mathcal{P}_\mathcal{G}$ and the canonical database of the data integration system $\mathcal{I}$ is characterized by the following lemma.

Lemma 1. *Up to the renaming of each relation symbol r by the corresponding primed symbol r', $can(\mathcal{I},\mathcal{D})$ coincides with the minimal model of $\mathcal{P}_\mathcal{G} \cup ret(\mathcal{I},\mathcal{D})$.*

Proof. The thesis is an immediate consequence of the semantics of $can(\mathcal{I},\mathcal{D})$ and $\mathcal{P}_\mathcal{G} \cup ret(\mathcal{I},\mathcal{D})$ [27].

Next we focus on SLD-refutation. We observe that, since the query q is a conjunctive query, the query q' is a union of conjunctive queries:

$$q'(X_1,\ldots,X_n) \leftarrow disj_1 \vee \cdots \vee disj_k$$

An SLD-refutation for $\mathcal{P}_\mathcal{G} \cup ret(\mathcal{I},\mathcal{D}) \cup \neg q'(t)$ is defined as an SLD-refutation for $\mathcal{P}_\mathcal{G} \cup \mathcal{P}'_q \cup ret(\mathcal{I},\mathcal{D}) \cup \neg q'(t)$, where $\mathcal{P}'_q$ is constituted by the rules:

$$q(X_1,\ldots,X_n) \leftarrow disj_1$$
$$\cdots$$
$$q(X_1,\ldots,X_n) \leftarrow disj_k$$

one for each disjunct $disj_i$ of the query q' (see [27]).

Lemma 2. $q'(t)$ *is true in the minimal model of $\mathcal{P}_\mathcal{G} \cup ret(\mathcal{I},\mathcal{D})$ iff there is an SLD-refutation for $\mathcal{P}_\mathcal{G} \cup ret(\mathcal{I},\mathcal{D}) \cup \{\neg q'(t)\}$.*

Proof. The thesis follows directly from the soundness and completeness of SLD-resolution for definite logic programs, see e.g., [27].

Next, let us consider a slight modification of the algorithm above where Condition (2c) is replaced by the following one:

If a node d that is labeled by a query g and there exists a predecessor d' of d labeled by a query g' and a substitution θ of the variables of g' that makes g' equal to g, then d has a single child, which is labeled by g itself but without any atom marked as selected.

Let us call $exp_{\mathcal{G}}^-(q)$ the query obtained from such a modified algorithm. For $exp_{\mathcal{G}}^-(q)$, we have the following result.

Lemma 3. $\mathcal{P}_{\mathcal{G}} \cup ret(\mathcal{I}, \mathcal{D}) \cup \{\neg q'(t)\}$ has an SLD-refutation iff $ret(\mathcal{I}, \mathcal{D}) \cup \{\neg exp_{\mathcal{G}}^-(q)(t)\}$ has an SLD-refutation.

Proof. It is easy to see that the modified algorithm generates a so-called partial evaluation [28] of the program $\mathcal{P}_{\mathcal{G}}$ w.r.t. the query q'. From the results in [28] on soundness and completeness of partial evaluation of logic programs, the thesis follows.

Lemma 4. $\mathcal{P}_{\mathcal{G}} \cup ret(\mathcal{I}, \mathcal{D}) \cup \{\neg q'(t)\}$ has an SLD-refutation iff $ret(\mathcal{I}, \mathcal{D}) \cup \{\neg exp_{\mathcal{G}}(q)(t)\}$ has an SLD-refutation.

Proof. The difference between $exp_{\mathcal{G}}^-(q)$ and $exp_{\mathcal{G}}(q)$ is that in $exp_{\mathcal{G}}(q)$ we drop the disjuncts coming from those nodes labeled by a query g such that there exists a query g' and a substitution θ of the variables of g' that makes g' equal to g. Next we show that, in doing this we do not loose any potential SLD-refutation of $\mathcal{P}_{\mathcal{G}} \cup ret(\mathcal{I}, \mathcal{D}) \cup \{\neg q'(t)\}$.

Suppose that the shortest (possibly the only one) SLD-refutation for $\mathcal{P}_{\mathcal{G}} \cup ret(\mathcal{I}, \mathcal{D}) \cup \{\neg q'(t)\}$ goes through a node labeled by one such g. Let us say the length of the SLD-refutation is n, and that node labeled by g is the k-th node along the SLD-refutation. From such SLD-refutation we get an SLD-refutation for $\mathcal{P}_{\mathcal{G}} \cup ret(\mathcal{I}, \mathcal{D}) \cup \{\neg g(t)\}$ of length $n - k$. Observe that, by the so called Lifting Lemma [27], such an SLD-refutation is also an SLD-refutation for $\mathcal{P}_{\mathcal{G}} \cup ret(\mathcal{I}, \mathcal{D}) \cup \{\neg g'(t)\}$. Hence there exists an SLD-refutation for which occurs in a node of the SLD-refutation for $\mathcal{P}_{\mathcal{G}} \cup ret(\mathcal{I}, \mathcal{D}) \cup \{\neg q(t)\}$ that is shorter than n, which leads to contradiction. It follows that for each SLD-refutation for $\mathcal{P}_{\mathcal{G}} \cup ret(\mathcal{I}, \mathcal{D}) \cup \{\neg q'(t)\}$ going through a node satisfying Condition (2c) there is also another (a shorter one in fact) that does not go through that node. Hence we may drop from the partial evaluation $exp_{\mathcal{G}}^-(q)$ all the conjuncts involving such nodes, thus getting $exp_{\mathcal{G}}(q)$ without loosing any SLD-refutation for the original query.

Finally, we observe that, since $exp_{\mathcal{G}}(q)$ does not involve any prime atom, the rules in $\mathcal{P}_{\mathcal{G}}$ cannot be applied along an SLD-refutation for $\mathcal{P}_{\mathcal{G}} \cup ret(\mathcal{I}, \mathcal{D}) \cup \{\neg exp_{\mathcal{G}}(q)(t)\}$. Hence every SLD-refutation for $\mathcal{P}_{\mathcal{G}} \cup ret(\mathcal{I}, \mathcal{D}) \cup \{\neg exp_{\mathcal{G}}(q)(t)\}$ is also an SLD-refutation for $\mathcal{P}_{\mathcal{G}} \cup ret(\mathcal{I}, \mathcal{D}) \cup \{\neg exp_{\mathcal{G}}(q)(t)\}$.

With this lemma in place we can finally present our main theorem.

Theorem 6 (Soundness and Completeness). *Let* $\mathcal{I} = \langle \mathcal{G}, \mathcal{S}, \mathcal{M}_{\mathcal{G},\mathcal{S}} \rangle$, *let* q *be a query posed to* $\mathcal{I}$, $\mathcal{D}$ *a source database for* $\mathcal{I}$, *and* t *a tuple of constants of the same arity as* q. *If* $\mathcal{I}$ *is consistent w.r.t.* $\mathcal{D}$, *then* $t \in q^{\mathcal{I},\mathcal{D}}$ *if and only if* t *is in the answer to* $unf_{\mathcal{M}_{\mathcal{G},\mathcal{S}}}(exp_{\mathcal{G}}(q))$ *over* $\mathcal{D}$.

Proof. By Lemma 1, Lemma 2, Lemma 4, we have that $q(t)$ is true in $can(\mathcal{I},\mathcal{D})$ iff $ret(\mathcal{I},\mathcal{D}) \cup \{\neg exp_\mathcal{G}(q)(t)\}$ has an SLD-refutation. That is by, again applying Lemma 2, $q(t)$ is true in $can(\mathcal{I},\mathcal{D})$ iff t is in the answer to $exp_\mathcal{G}(q)$ over $ret(\mathcal{I},\mathcal{D})$, i.e., by the semantics of $ret(\mathcal{I},\mathcal{D})$, iff t is in the answer to $unf_{\mathcal{M}_{\mathcal{G},\mathcal{S}}}(exp_\mathcal{G}(q))$ over $\mathcal{D}$.

With regard to the characterization of the computational complexity of the algorithm, we observe that the number of disjuncts in $exp_\mathcal{G}(q)$ can be exponential in the number of rules in the logic program $\mathcal{P}_\mathcal{G}$ (and therefore in the size of the global schema $\mathcal{G}$), and in the number of variables in the original query q. Note, however, that this bound is independent of the size of $\mathcal{D}$, i.e., the size of data at the sources. We remind the reader that the evaluation of a union of conjunctive queries can be done in time polynomial with respect to the size of the data. Since $exp_\mathcal{G}(q)$ is a union of conjunctive queries, as the queries associated by $\mathcal{M}_{\mathcal{G},\mathcal{S}}$ to the elements of $\mathcal{G}$ are, then evaluating $unf_{\mathcal{M}_{\mathcal{G},\mathcal{S}}}(exp_\mathcal{G}(q))$ over $\mathcal{D}$ is also polynomial in the size of the data at the sources. It follows that our query answering algorithm is polynomial with respect to data complexity.

The following example illustrates the application of the expansion algorithm in a simple case.

Example 4. Suppose we have the following relations in the global schema $\mathcal{G}$ of a data integration system:

person($Pcode, Age, CityOfBirth$)
student($Scode, University$)
city($Name, Major$)

with the following integrity constraints:

key(person) = $\{Pcode\}$ person[$CityOfBirth$] $\subseteq$ city[$Name$]
key(student) = $\{Scode\}$ city[$Major$] $\subseteq$ person[$PCode$]
key(city) = $\{Name\}$ student[$SCode$] $\subseteq$ person[$PCode$]

The logic program $\mathcal{P}_\mathcal{G}$ makes use of the predicates person$'$/3, student$'$/1, city$'$/2 and constitutes of the following rules:

person$'(X,Y,Z)$ ← person(X,Y,Z) city$'(X, f_1(X))$ ← person$'(Y,Z,X)$
student$'(X,Y)$ ← student(X,Y) person$'(Y, f_2(Y), f_3(Y))$ ← city$'(X,Y)$
city$'(X,Y)$ ← city(X,Y) person$'(X, f_4(X), f_5(X))$ ← student$'(X,Y)$

Suppose the user query is q(X) ← person(X,Y,Z).

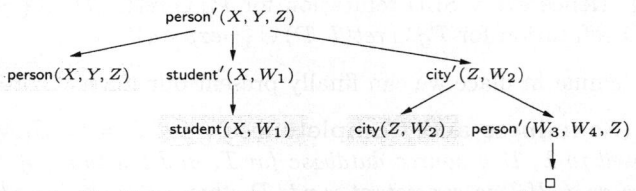

Fig. 1. Partial evaluation tree for the query of Example 4

The partial evaluation tree of q is shown in Figure 1. Note that in the rightmost branch, Condition (2c) is verified and hence the evaluation stops, producing the empty clause $\square$. This prevents the evaluation process to get into an infinite branch. The new variables W_1, W_2, and W_3 are introduced in order to avoid variable clashes when performing unification. The non-empty leaves, shaded in the figure, provide the following expansion $q' = exp_{\mathcal{G}}(q)$ of the query q:

$$q'(X) \leftarrow \mathsf{person}(X, Y, Z)$$
$$q'(X) \leftarrow \mathsf{student}(X, W_1)$$
$$q'(W_2) \leftarrow \mathsf{city}(Z, W_2)$$

Intuitively, we see that the expanded query searches for codes of persons not only in the relation **person**, but also in **student** and **city**, where, due to the integrity constraints, it is known that codes of persons are stored.

6 Conclusions

While it is a common opinion that query processing is an easy task in the global-centric approach to data integration, we have shown the surprising result that, when the global schema contains integrity constraints, even of simple forms, query processing becomes more difficult. The difficulties basically arise because of the need of dealing with incomplete information, similarly to the case of the source-centric approach to data integration. We have studied the case of global schemas expressed in the relational model with key and foreign key constraints, and we have presented techniques for effectively answering queries posed to the data integration system in this case.

As future work, we aim at considering more forms of integrity constraints in the global schema, with the goal of modifying the algorithm described in this paper in order to take into account the new classes of constraints during query processing.

References

1. Batini, C., Lenzerini, M., Navathe, S. B.: A comparative analysis of methodologies for database schema integration. ACM Computing Surveys **18** (1986) 323–364
2. Sheth, A. P., Larson, J. A.: Federated database systems for managing distributed, heterogeneous, and autonomous databases. ACM Computing Surveys **22** (1990) 183–236
3. Thomas, G., Thompson, G. R., Chung, C. W., Barkmeyer, E., Carter, F., Templeton, M., Fox, S., Hartman, B.: Heterogeneous distributed database systems for production use. ACM Computing Surveys **22** (1990) 237–266
4. Litwin, W., Mark, L., Roussopoulos, N.: Interoperability of multiple autonomous databases. ACM Computing Surveys **22** (1990) 267–293
5. Catarci, T., Lenzerini, M.: Representing and using interschema knowledge in cooperative information systems. J. of Intelligent and Cooperative Information Systems **2** (1993) 375–398
6. Hull, R.: Managing semantic heterogeneity in databases: A theoretical perspective. In: Proc. of PODS'97. (1997)

7. Halevy, A. Y.: Answering queries using views: A survey. VLDB Journal **10** (2001) 270–294
8. Ullman, J. D.: Information integration using logical views. In: Proc. of ICDT'97. Volume 1186 of LNCS., Springer (1997) 19–40
9. Li, C., Chang, E.: Query planning with limited source capabilities. In: Proc. of ICDE 2000. (2000) 401–412
10. Garcia-Molina, H., Papakonstantinou, Y., Quass, D., Rajaraman, A., Sagiv, Y., Ullman, J. D., Vassalos, V., Widom, J.: The TSIMMIS approach to mediation: Data models and languages. J. of Intelligent Information Systems **8** (1997) 117–132
11. Anthony Tomasic, Louiqa Raschid, P. V.: Scaling access to heterogeneous data sources with DISCO. IEEE Trans. on Knowledge and Data Engineering **10** (1998) 808–823
12. Goh, C. H., Bressan, S., Madnick, S. E., Siegel, M. D.: Context interchange: New features and formalisms for the intelligent integration of information. ACM Trans. on Information Systems **17** (1999) 270–293
13. Kirk, T., Levy, A. Y., Sagiv, Y., Srivastava, D.: The Information Manifold. In: Proceedings of the AAAI 1995 Spring Symp. on Information Gathering from Heterogeneous, Distributed Enviroments. (1995) 85–91
14. Abiteboul, S., Duschka, O.: Complexity of answering queries using materialized views. In: Proc. of PODS'98. (1998) 254–265
15. Calvanese, D., De Giacomo, G., Lenzerini, M., Nardi, D., Rosati, R.: Data integration in data warehousing. Int. J. of Cooperative Information Systems **10** (2001) 237–271
16. Calì, A., De Giacomo, G., Lenzerini, M.: Models for information integration: Turning local-as-view into global-as-view. In: Proc. of Int. Workshop on Foundations of Models for Information Integration (10th Workshop in the series Foundations of Models and Languages for Data and Objects). (2001)
17. Gryz, J.: Query folding with inclusion dependencies. In: Proc. of ICDE'98. (1998) 126–133
18. Grahne, G., Mendelzon, A. O.: Tableau techniques for querying information sources through global schemas. In: Proc. of ICDT'99. Volume 1540 of LNCS., Springer (1999) 332–347
19. Calvanese, D., De Giacomo, G., Lenzerini, M., Vardi, M. Y.: Query processing using views for regular path queries with inverse. In: Proc. of PODS 2000. (2000) 58–66
20. van der Meyden, R.: Logical approaches to incomplete information. In Chomicki, J., Saake, G., eds.: Logics for Databases and Information Systems. Kluwer Academic Publisher (1998) 307–356
21. Fernandez, M. F., Florescu, D., Levy, A., Suciu, D.: Verifying integrity constraints on web-sites. In: Proc. of IJCAI'99. (1999) 614–619
22. Fernandez, M. F., Florescu, D., Kang, J., Levy, A. Y., Suciu, D.: Catching the boat with strudel: Experiences with a web-site management system. In: Proc. of ACM SIGMOD. (1998) 414–425
23. Carey, M. J., Haas, L. M., Schwarz, P. M., Arya, M., Cody, W. F., Fagin, R., Flickner, M., Luniewski, A., Niblack, W., Petkovic, D., Thomas, J., Williams, J. H., Wimmers, E. L.: Towards heterogeneous multimedia information systems: The Garlic approach. In: Proc. of the 5th Int. Workshop on Research Issues in Data Engineering – Distributed Object Management (RIDE-DOM'95), IEEE CS Press (1995) 124–131

24. Li, C., Yerneni, R., Vassalos, V., Garcia-Molina, H., Papakonstantinou, Y., Ullman, J. D., Valiveti, M.: Capability based mediation in TSIMMIS. In: Proc. of ACM SIGMOD. (1998) 564–566
25. Galhardas, H., Florescu, D., Shasha, D., Simon, E.: An extensible framework for data cleaning. Technical Report 3742, INRIA, Rocquencourt (1999)
26. Bouzeghoub, M., Lenzerini, M.: Introduction to the special issue on data extraction, cleaning, and reconciliation. Information Systems **26** (2001) 535–536
27. Lloyd, J. W.: Foundations of Logic Programming (Second, Extended Edition). Springer, Berlin, Heidelberg (1987)
28. Lloyd, J. W., Shepherdson, J. C.: Partial evaluation in logic programming. J. of Logic Programming **11** (1991) 217–242

Babel: An XML-Based Application Integration Framework

Huaxin Zhang and Eleni Stroulia

Computing Science Department,
University of Alberta,
Edmonton, AB, T6G 2E8, Canada
{hxzhang,stroulia}@cs.ualberta.ca

Abstract. One of the major problems in integrating independently developed applications is the divergence between the data and control-of-processing models assumed by these applications. Research on database integration has focused on establishing and maintaining a canonical schema on top of the schemas of the underlying databases. At the same time, web-accessible software systems have been adopting a multi-layer architecture style, with databases in the lowest tier, business logic in the middle tier and user interfaces in the top-most tier. However, as the time-to-market window shrinks, new software is presented with the challenge of reusing and integrating the functionalities of existing whole applications, instead of simply their database back-ends. The Babel framework provides support for specifying existing applications in terms of the functionalities they deliver and the data they manipulate. In addition, it supports the specification of the "logic" defining how these functionalities should be integrated. Based on these specifications, Babel produces a run-time mediator that monitors the behavior of the underlying applications, evaluates the defined logic on the global state of the integrated system, and generates triggers for new functionalities to be accomplished according to these rules.

1 Motivation and Background

As the number of alternative technologies underlying software development increases, the need to develop methods and tools to support the integration of heterogeneous software assets becomes more pressing.

Research efforts to that end aimed originally at integrating heterogeneous databases. As the object-oriented paradigm usurped the more traditional procedural approach to software design and development, object-oriented databases were proposed as an alternative to relational databases. As a result, a new area of research was born, focusing on methods for developing object-oriented views of relational data [20]. However, even when developed with the same design paradigm for the same application domain, different databases differ in terms of the syntax they adopt for the representation of (potentially the same) data and the semantic [7] interpretation of the data by the applications supported by these databases. Thus, a substantial research effort has been invested in integrating the schemas of heterogeneous databases or constructing unified views of their data [2,3,4] and creating new query languages to query distributed heterogeneous databases [10].

More recently, the advent of XML has inspired a whole new area of database research aiming at developing database support for managing XML data [6] and integrating XML-based databases [11]. At the same time, XML provides a flexible syntax for representing semi-structured data and can be used as the medium to represent information extracted from all types of different sources, such as HTML documents [24], and textual information repositories [25]. The scope of the integration problem has thus expanded from database to information integration [13].

The next logical step in this evolution of the integration research agenda is application integration; not only should data, structured in databases or unstructured in informal repositories, be integrated, but also complete applications. The problem of application integration however raises a new important question: how to coordinate the behavior of independent applications that have been designed with different assumptions regarding their context of operation and different expectations on how they may be called from their environment [22,23].

Several approaches have been developed to address this problem, making strong assumptions regarding the underlying integration infrastructure as well as the re-engineering of the applications to be integrated. Object-oriented integration frameworks, such as CORBA for example, require that the applications to be integrated are developed in the object-oriented style and that the interfaces of their classes be represented in a proprietary specification language in order to be advertised and brokered by the central mediator (Object Request Broker). Such approaches are therefore applicable to a specific type of applications and require specialized technical skills and substantial development effort.

This is exactly the motivation behind more lightweight, event-driven approaches, such as XWrap/CQ [26] and CoopWare [5,12]. CQ aims at developing a framework for integrating applications, by monitoring the updates to the information they contain in distributed open environments such as the web for example. Furthermore it combines traditional database-style pull-based query-answering services with push-enabled event-driven update monitoring services. CoopWare is an event-based integration architecture based on active-database technology; update events in the underlying databases trigger rules in a central coordinator module that can, in turn, invoke SQL-like transactions in the underlying databases.

In our work, we have also been investigating methods for lightweight integration of distributed, heterogeneous, independently developed applications. Babel [21], like CQ, assumes XML as the syntax for representing the data extracted from the underlying applications. Like CQ and CoopWare, it assumes that the coordination behavior of the mediator is triggered by events generated by the underlying resources. Unlike CQ and CoopWare, Babel does not assume SQL-like queries integrating the underlying resources; instead, it assumes that the underlying applications are wrapped with a particular style of adapter wrappers that expose a task-based interface of the applications' behaviors of interest. In the context of the CelLEST project [17], we have also developed Mathaino [9], a tool that implements a semi-automated method for construction of such wrappers for legacy systems running on ASCII-based protocols such as tn3270. Furthermore, Babel pr ovides a design-time environment, with an easy-to-use interface, for specifying the logic of the coordination among the wrapped applications being integrated.

The rest of the paper is organized as follows. Section 2 discusses the overall Babel architecture, its components and its approach to data modeling and coordination control. Section 3 briefly describes the design-time environment of Babel that can be used to support the specification of the coordination logic. Section 4 discusses the run-time behavior of Babel. Section 5 describes Babel's implementation and our experiments with it evaluating its performance, scalability and robustness. Finally, Section 6 summarizes the approach and concludes by identifying its novel contributions to the area.

2 The Babel Architecture

Figure 1 diagrammatically depicts the overall architecture of the Babel framework. It consists of two loosely coupled environments: a design-time environment called Visual X-logic Generator (VXG), which supports the "visual programming" of the mediation logic, and a run-time environment, which monitors the execution of the underlying wrapped applications and executing the mediation logic.

The run-time mediator of Babel enables the reactive integration of heterogeneous applications, wrapped within a particular type of adapter wrappers. These wrappers "translate" the original application interface into an event-based interface; they execute specific tasks on the original applications in response to input events, and they produce output events in response to the completion of these tasks. These events are monitored by the Babel mediator and recorded in the mediator's repository. In addition to maintaining the task history, the Babel mediator also maintains a registry of Event-Condition-Action (ECA) rules and workflow-session definitions, which specify the "logic" of the mediation. Upon receiving a task event form one of the wrapped applications, the mediator identifies the relevant rules and sessions. The events resulting from the rule execution are forwarded to the appropriate wrappers that proceed to exec

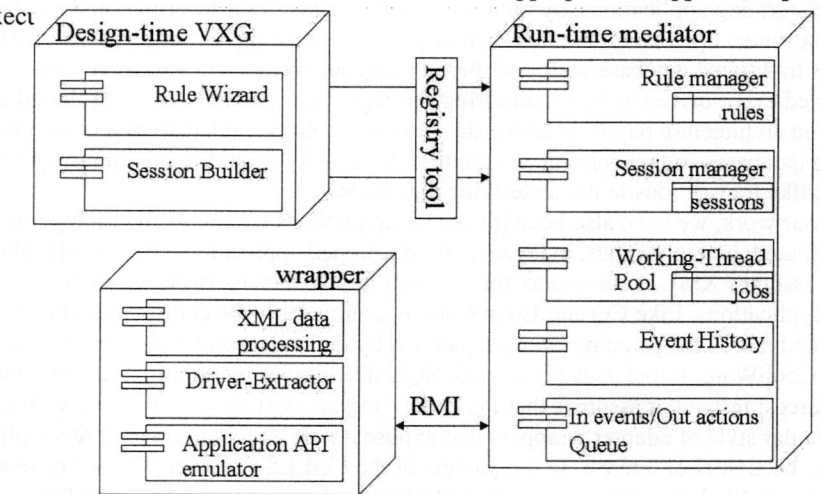

Figure 1: The overall Babel Architecture

VXG helps to alleviate the problem of "programming" the mediation logic. It consists of a "Rule Wizard", which guides the user to define the mediation application's ECA rules. VXG also provides a "Session Builder", i.e., a lightweight workflow-process definition tool, to define higher-level coordination logic based on these ECA rules. Upon the completion of the visual programming, VXG "compiles" XSLT programs, implementing the defined rules and sessions, which are then registered with the run-time Babel mediator.

2.1 Application Wrapping

As is the case with all environments aiming at the integration applications of developed independently, Babel requires that all applications at the bottom tier of the runtime architecture be wrapped, in order to expose a canonical behavior to the mediator and thus hide their heterogeneity. There are two dimensions of heterogeneity that the Babel wrappers are designed to abstract away: the *data model* underlying the individual integrated applications and their *protocol of interaction* with their external environment.

Domain-specific data consumed as input (and produced as output) by the underlying applications are transformed from (and into) a canonical data model; this data model is the "lingua franca" of the overall mediation application [1]: all data exchanged at runtime between the wrappers and the mediator, as well as the coordination logic of the mediation application, are represented in terms of this model. It is therefore imperative that the syntax of the data-modeling language is expressive enough to succinctly model the data of realistically complex applications, so as not to complicate coordination logic that is based on top of it. Babel adopts XML as the syntax in which to specify the canonical data model of the mediation application. XML enables data modeling in terms of a "flexible" object-oriented syntax (XML schemas include support for inheritance and aggregation and allow for missing attributes). Furthermore, XML documents are self-documenting, since they include their underlying domain model in the tags surrounding their data, and can therefore be exchanged among applications, as long as these applications "agree" on the semantics underlying the domain model.

Different applications provide different modes of interaction with their environment. Legacy applications, running on mainframe hosts, are designed to have their services invoked from a ASCII terminal, implementing a protocol such as tn3270 or vt100. Others, designed in the client-server style, make their services accessible through HTTP requests issued by browsers. The Babel application wrappers abstract away these differences by viewing the applications as performing *tasks*. Tasks are abstractions of the interesting capabilities of the underlying applications [16], and are defined in terms of their type and their input and output information. Wrappers expose two types of events for each distinct task of their underlying application: a *task-initiation* event and *task-execution* event. Task-execution events flow from the wrappers to the mediator. Each such event constitutes, in effect, a record of a single execution of the task in question by the underlying application. The generation of task-execution events by the wrappers enables the mediator to monitor the behaviors of interest of the wrapped applications. The mediator generates task-initiation events, based on the task-execution events it has received and the coordination logic it enacts. Each such event

---

[1] We use the term "application mediation" to denote a specific instantiation of the Babel runtime environment, including the wrapped original applications, the domain model of the data exchanged among the wrappers and the Babel mediator, and the specific coordination rules and workflow sessions.

provides the necessary data for the application wrapper to execute the corresponding task of the underlying application. In this model, the integrated applications are viewed as components that accomplish a set of tasks by receiving events containing the required input for these tasks and by responding with events recording the task execution.

The domain-specific information contained in task-initiation and task-execution events is represented in terms of the canonical domain model of the mediation application. Each individual application wrapper is responsible for parsing the information contained in task-initiation events and using it to "drive" the underlying application so as to accomplish the desired task. Similarly, the wrapper is responsible for translating the data produced by the task execution into the canonical domain model to generate the corresponding task-execution event to the mediator.

Consider for example a digital library application that can be queried with a particular keyword, in response to which, it returns a set of three books with titles matching the keyword. An instance of this task, as represented in Babel, is shown in Figure 2.

```
<task>
    <t_type>Library1BookSearch</t_type>
    <t_id>1</t_id>
    <input>
        <information> type=book
            id=1
            keyword="databases"
        </information>
    </input>
    <output>
        <information> type=book
            id=1
            keyword="databases"
            title="Principles of Distributed Database Systems"
            author[1].last="Ozsu"
        </information>
        <information>
            ...
        </information>
        <information>
            ...
        </information>
    </output>
</task>
```

Figure 2: Representing the Library "BookQuery" task in Babel.

This task takes as input the "keyword" of a "book" and returns as output three book instances, each of which has four attributes, "author's last name", "keyword", "title", and "subject". In order to treat input and output objects uniformly, the task data model uses the "information"-structured data as input or output. The various types of "information" manipulated by the applications tasks constitute the overall domain of the mediation application. Information objects in Babel are represented in terms of the object type, object Id, and for each one of interesting attributes, an XPath-like expression characterizing the attribute in the context of the object and the attribute value. Finally, each task is characterized in terms of its "type", which uniquely identifies the wrapper consuming initiation events and produces execution events for this task, and its "Id", uniquely identifying each distinct execution of this task type on the underlying application. Note that task-initiation events forwarded by the mediator to the wrappers do not have values for the expected output information objects; task-execution events, on the other hand, have values for all pieces of information included in the task input and output.

2.2 Coordination Logic

After wrapping the applications of interest, the next step towards developing a mediation application with Babel is to define the "logic" of how these applications will be coordinated at run time. The Babel framework supports two types of coordination logic: Event-Condition-Action rules and lightweight workflow sessions.

2.2.1. Even-Condition-Action Rules: The Event-Condition-Action (ECA) rule paradigm was developed in the context of active-databases research and was originally intended to support daemons monitoring transactions of interest and triggering further transactions in response [27]. The underlying intent of this paradigm is to enable the specification of high-level consistency constraints and to provide a mechanism for their maintenance. Often, application integration is motivated by similar needs, i.e., to maintain a high-level of consistency over the loosely integrated applications. For example, it is often desired to propagate data-entry transactions form one application to another and to trigger desired global side-effects of a transaction in one application to related ones. This is why we adopted ECA rule-based integration as the basic level of coordination logic supported by Babel.

A Babel *rule* is an *event-condition-action* triple that specifies what task-initiation event should be invoked as the *action* generated in response to a task-execution *event* received, in the context of a particular *condition*. Babel rules are also specified in XML, in terms of a high-level, natural-language description of the rule, a type, and a unique id. Both the condition and the action elements of a rule are optional. Rules with no conditions are always applicable, upon receipt of their triggering event. Rules with no actions are only used to advance the state of the workflow sessions.

The conditions of Babel's rules are logical compositions of simple *constraints*. An individual constraint is a predicate that must hold true between the input information provided by the task-execution event triggering the rule and the information contained in the task (–initiation and –execution) events recorded in the mediator's history. In addition to defining the rules' conditions, constraints are also used to define how the information provided as input to the generated task-initiation event, i.e., the action of the rule, should be constructed. The action data could may be constructed based on rule parameters input by the mediation designer, the generating-event data as well as data of the tasks contained in the mediator's history.

Consider, for example, a help-desk mediation application that integrates multiple libraries and bookstores. One service that this mediation application provides is to receive through email keywords from its customers and, in response, search for relevant books in all the partner libraries. To support this service, the two rules, shown in Figure 3(a), have to be defined.

The first rule of Figure 3(a) specifies, that when the mediator receives a task-execution event from its EmailReceipt wrapper, it should check whether the subject of the received email is " BookQuery". If it is, then the mediator should generate a task-initiation event for its "Library1BookSearch" wrapper. The input information for this task-initiation event should be "keyword" whose value should be whatever is in the

"Content" of the received email. The second rule defines the reaction of the mediator, when it receives a task-execution event from its "Library1BookSearch" wrapper. Upon receipt of such an event, the mediator should look in its history of task events to identify all the past receipts of " BookQueries" for the same keyword as the keyword appearing in the input of the current task-execution event. For all such tasks in its history, the mediator should generate a task-initiation event of type " EmailSend" and it should forward the current task's output book to the senders of the corresponding "BookQueries", found in the history. Note that the representations of rules shown in Figure 3(a) are simplified demonstrations; rules are actually represented as XSLT programs.

- Rule1:
  - Event:
    - Task.Type="EmailReceipt"
  - Condition:
    - Task.Input.Subject="BookQuery"
  - Action:
    - Task.Type="Library1BookSearch"
    - Task.Input.Book.Keyword=Event.Task.Input.Content
- Rule2
  - Event:
    - Task.Type="Library1BookSearch"
  - Condition:
    - Exists a task, tsk, in history such that
      History.Task.Type="EmailReceipt" ^
      History.Task.Input.Subject="BookQuery" ^
      History.Task.Input.Content=Event.Task.Input.Keyword
  - Action:
    - Task.Type="EmailSend"
    - Task.Input.Book.Content=Event.Task.Output.Book
    - Task.Input.Receipient=tsk.Input.Sender

(a) (b)

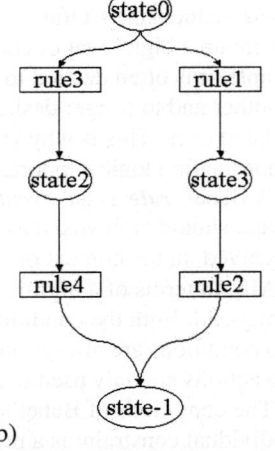

Figure 3: Two rules (a) and a session (b) for the Book Help Desk.

2.2.2 Workflow Sessions: Coordination based solely on ECA rules is not sufficient. Although, side effects can be effectively specified and maintained using such rules, more complex, multi-step processes are often desired. Workflow management systems provide the automated coordination, control and communication of work needed for multiple task execution [15], but to the best of our knowledge , no existing workflow model applies a similar event-based mediation approach yet.

In order to incorporate a lightweight workflow processing capability in the Babel mediator, we have extended the coordination language of Babel with the concept of a *session*. A session is a lightweight process that coordinates multiple tasks by combining multiple rules. Rule composition is based on sequencing, branching and looping operations. WFMC specifies nine valid run-time states for a workflow process instance [18]. The more limited Babel session incorporates the following states for its session instances:
- *Not Started:* the initial state of every session; a session requires the occurrence of a particular task-execution event to start;

- *Running:* after a session has started (the initiating task-execution event has occurred) and one of the rules applicable to this event has been successfully applied;
- *NotRunning:* after a session has transitioned to its new state and no incoming event has triggered any of the rules enabling a new transition from this state; and
- *Terminated:* after the session has completed, i.e., it has reached a state where no further rules are relevant.

The expressiveness of a workflow depends heavily on its flexibility. Several flow control formalisms being applied in workflow management systems (WFMS), such as Petri nets [1] and statecharts [19]. Babel is an event-based mediator and its control flow relies on (task-execution) events as triggers. Babel internally represents the defined workflow sessions as *Transition Vectors*. A *Transition Vector* holds all transitions involved in a workflow session definition. Each transition is defined in terms of a (from-state, rule, to-state[2]) triple. A session consists of a number of transitions, one or more of which may be *source* transitions. Source transitions have the 0th state as their "from-state", and they specify when a new session instance should be initialized. When the mediator receives a new task-execution event, it checks the received event against all the start-up transitions of the registered workflow sessions. If one of the rule conditions in these transitions is met, a new instance of this session is spawned and its state advances from the 0th state to the to-state specified by the transition. If the rule conditions of multiple start-up transitions are successful, the one with the lowest order in the transition vector will be followed. After a session instance is created, it switches to a "not-running" process state until another task-execution event is received. If any of the rules applicable to a received task-execution event is associated with a transition possible in the current state of the session instance, this session instance switches to the "running" process state and the rules' conditions are evaluated; if successful, the session instance advances to the to-state of the successful transition. If the all transitions at the current state of the session instance fail (the rules of the transitions fail), the session remains at its original state. Transitions with "to-state" as "-1" are *sink* transitions. Once a session instance passes one of its sink transitions, it expires, i.e., it switches to the "terminated" process state.

In order to prevent ambiguities, no two transitions with the same "from-state" and the same "rule" are allowed in the transition vector of a session. Moreover, each transition vector must have at least one start-up transition and one terminating transition.

Consider for example, the BookServices application introduced above. An additional service could be to search from for a book-price quote, if the same user searches for the same book title three times. This new service and the one we described in the section above are not independent; they are in fact two mutually exclusive alternatives, and it would be more efficient if this fact were represented with a workflow session. Figure 3(b) diagrammatically depicts the transition vector of such a session. Here rule3 is similar in content to rule1, with two exceptions: it is conditioned upon finding at least three similar "BookQuery" task-execution events in the history, and instead of generating a LibrarySearch task-initiation action, it generates a " BookstoreSearch"

---

[2] We use the term "state" to denote (a) the state of the process executing a session instance and (b) the logical states comprising a workflow session definition. Wherever ambiguous, we use the term "process state" to denote the former.

action. Rule 4 is similar with rule 2, in that it sends query result of the book from a book dealer (www.amazon.com) instead of from a library. This session will be activated when a task-execution event of the type " BookQuery" is received, in which case, either rule3 or rule1 will be successful. If rule3 succeeds, the first transition will lead the session instance to state2, and rule1 will not be evaluated. If rule3 fails, i.e., the first two times that the user requests information about the same book, rule1 will succeed and the session instance will move to state3. From state2 and state3, the session instance will move to state-1, i.e., it will expire, when it receives a "LibraryBookSearch" or a "BookstoreSearch" task-execution event when rule4 or rule2 will be applied correspondingly. The reason that rule 3 is always checked before rule 1 is that rule 3 is inside a transition with a lower order than rule 1.

3 VXG: The Babel Design-Time Environment

VXG, the Babel design-time environment supports the specification of ECA rules and workflow sessions through two visual-programming components, the *Rule Wizard* and the *Session Builder*. The Babel user can use VXG to define rules and sessions with simple dialog operations and drag-and-drop actions in response to the wizard prompts. The storyboard of Figure 4 below illustrates the rule- and session- definition process with Babel's VXG.

The interface supports the specification of rules (steps a – h) and sessions (steps i – l). To define a rule, the user has first, to give a short description (in English) of the logic that the rule is intended to implement (step a). Next, the user has to choose the type of events that can potentially activate the rule and the type of events that must have already occurred in the past on which the rule's activation may be conditioned (step b). The interface enables the user to select both these event types from a dropdown menu that is configured to include as choices all wrappers known to the system. These event types appear as components in the main panel of the interface. Then (steps c,d) the user can define functions on the various types of information associated with the chosen event types by dragging and dropping the corresponding ports of the selected components. Next (step e) the user selects the type of action that will result from the rule's invocation and defines the action's input in terms of information contained in the triggering and condition events (step f). Finally, the user may inspect and edit the XSLT program implementing the defined rule (step g), and, if it is correct, the rule is saved in the system's repository under a user-provided file name (step h).

To define a session, the user has, first, to import the relevant rules by selecting their specifications from the system (step i). The description of the imported rules is shown as a tool tip, when the user moves the mouse over the icon corresponding to the rule (step j). Then, in the main panel of the interface, she can select design a state-transition network, by defining new states and by using the imported rules to define the transition between them (steps k,l). The sessions defined in this manner are also "translated" by VXG into XSLT programs that are saved in Babel's environment.

Babel: An XML-Based Application Integration Framework 289

Figure 4: Defining ECA Rules and Workflow Sessions with Babel's VXG.

At the end of the process, VXG produces the XSLT programs corresponding to the defined rules and sessions. No XSLT knowledge is required to perform the tasks by using the Babel design-time to write the complex coordination logic.

4. The Babel Run-Time Environment

At run time, ECA rules and workflow sessions are dynamically registered with the Babel mediator. At the same time, the mediator receives task-execution events from the wrappers of the underlying applications. Whenever a data stream comes to the mediator, the mediator parses it, infers its content type, i.e., whether it is a rule or a session or a task event, and validates it according to the appropriate schema. If the input is a rule definition, the Babel mediator stores it in its *rule repository*. From this point onward, task-execution events of the type specified in the event field of the registered rule will activate this rule. If the input is a session definition, the Babel mediator registers this session with its *session manager*. If the input is a task-execution event, the Babel mediator places it into its *event queue* and gets ready for receiving the next input.

4.1 Processing Task-Execution Events

An independent thread, inside the Babel mediator, processes the event queue, according to First-In-First-Out policy. Given the type of the task-execution event being processed, the session manager, first, evaluates whether a new session instance should be initialized. If any of the start-up transitions of the registered sessions are conditioned upon a rule applicable to this task type and the rule is successful, a new instance is created (as discussed in Section 2.2 above). Second, all the currently active session instances are examined to evaluate whether they can advance to a subsequent state; these which are at a state waiting for the application of a rule conditioned upon an event of the current type are added to the *job pool*. Finally, for each of the registered rules applicable to the type of the task-execution event at hand, a corresponding "task-rule" *job* is added to the *job pool*.

Babel's *job pool* is a data structure that maintains a bag of jobs, i.e., pairs of task-execution events and the applicable rules. The Babel mediator processes these jobs in parallel -- each rule or session is applied on the task event by an independent thread. Babel adopts a *Working-Thread Pool* model for its parallel. When the Babel mediator is initialized, a fixed amount of threads are created and organized in a working thread pool. Working threads continuously look for pending jobs in the Job Pool. A thread either starts working on the selected job on successful job retrieval, or suspends itself until new jobs become available.

This Working Threads Pool (WTP) paradigm shortens processing latency because creating a thread is an expensive operation to be avoided during mediation runtime. Meanwhile, keeping a fixed number of threads ensures the stability of the system because threads will not grow indefinitely to exhaust system resources. Furthermore, since the jobs are dynamically assigned to the worker threads, workload is balanced among the threads. When all the worker threads have completed their processing, Babel dispatches all the task-initiation events generated to the corresponding wrappers, and updates its information repository to record these new events.

4.2 Application-Wrapper Processing

When the Babel mediator generates a task-initiation event for an application wrapper, the wrapper starts "driving" the underlying application in order to execute the task corresponding to the event it received.

A wrapper consists of three layers: the XML data interface layer, the driver and extractor layer, and the API to the underlying applications layer. The XML data interface layer retrieves from the mediator task-initiation events and parses them to extract the input required by the underlying application to execute the task. This layer also compiles the data output by the underlying application, after it has completed the task in question, into task-execution events and sends them back to the mediator. This layer is quite general and is shared by all application wrappers. The driver-and-extractor layer consists of wrapper-specific modules. The driver takes as input information provided from the Babel mediator to drive the underlying application. For instance, the email wrapper gets task data from mediator, extracts the email address and user name meta-data, and makes the system call to send the email. On the other end, information feedback from the applications is detected and sent to the Babel mediator by the extractor module. These two modules operate on top of the API layer, which consists of the APIs specific to the underlying applications.

The wrappers in the Babel environment can be constructed using the Mathaino tool of the CelLEST environment [9]. Mathaino (semi-)automatically constructs front-end interfaces for legacy user interfaces, based on traces of the legacy system-user interaction. Other types of applications, such as web-based applications accessible through browser thin-clients, are wrapped manually.

The Babel wrappers are heavy-weighted components that monitor and drive the underlying application. The Babel mediator communicates with the wrappers by sending and receiving data asynchronously. The Babel architecture also allows the wrappers to be built as light-weighted components, extensions of the mediator itself. The communication of the mediator with these extensions is synchronous. The Babel architecture provides a framework for building such extension services as hooks to this framework.

5 Implementation Overview and Performance Evaluation

Both the design-time and the run-time environments of the Babel framework are implemented using JDK1.3. The XML parser is provided by JAXP 1.1 [8] and the XSLT processing engine for the run-time rule and session enactment is based on SAXON 6.2.2 [14]. The mediator run-time includes an information repository module, currently implemented with flat XML files. At run time, the task-execution (-initiation) events from (to) the wrappers to (from) the mediator are XML data exchanged over RMI.

We evaluated the performance of the run-time Babel mediator in terms of efficiency, scalability and robustness with simulations performed on sun4u SPARC-SUNW, Ultra-30, under SunOS 5.6. Our experiments were designed to evaluate the performance of the Babel mediator, independent of the network latency in delivering events from (to) the wrappers and the wrapper processing itself.

A wrapper sends events to the mediator periodically, with constant time t_p between subsequent events. Timing starts when the mediator receives the event. The mediator de-serializes the object received from the RMI interface, reorganizes the data into a "raw" XML document, parses and validates it, and saves it in the event queue. Eventually, this event is retrieved from the queue and processed by the Rule Manager and the Session Manager. Then it is saved in the mediator's history. All these activities are recorded for mediator performance profiling. In the following simulation, costs in various aspects will be estimated.

5.1 Efficiency

For each experiment run, the time between every two events, sent to the mediator, is constant t_p. Suppose an event-message is received at t_r and that this message is processed and the resulting messages (if there are any) are placed in the message dispatching queues of each wrapper at t_f. Then the mediation processing time is $t_s = t_f - t_r$. The time elapsed between t_s and t_p measures the mediation efficiency, independent of the wrapper performance and communication issues. Different values of t_p were chosen as multiples of 200 milliseconds to evaluate the mediation performance.

Figure 5 shows a negligible service time for pure event processing with no rules triggered, which means that the message queuing, parsing, validating and information repository updating costs are trivial. The other three lines depict the average processing time when 1 rule, 2 rules, or 3 rules are triggered by the incoming task-execution event, correspondingly. In addition to the number of rules triggered, the complexity of the actual rules triggered may also have an effect to the processing times; the reported simulation results are averaged using different rules. We based our simulation result on 100 test runs, and the standard deviation ranges from *2.1—3.7*. This simulation shows that the average processing time decreases as the time gap increases, and at certain time gap, the average processing time becomes constant. A similar number reported in [5,12] is higher.

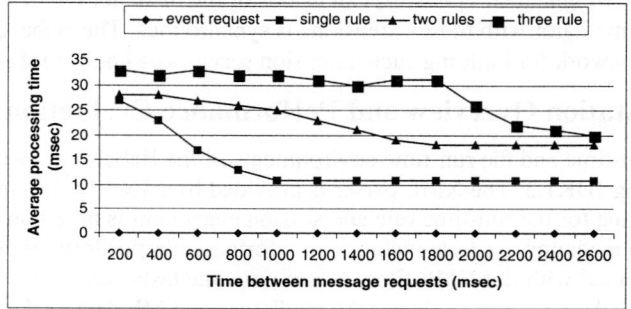

Figure 5: Average processing time (ts) vs. time between message requests.

5.2 Scalability

To evaluate the mediator's scalability, we defined several rules to be triggered by events of the same task type. After the mediator receives an event of this type, the Rule Manager retrieves a number of rules r_n already registered for this event and starts processing those rules against the current task event in parallel. In this simulation, 1 to 10 rules were registered to Babel and the corresponding average mediator processing time T_s (measured in the same way as first simulation) was recorded. Standard deviation ranges from *3.2–5.8*.

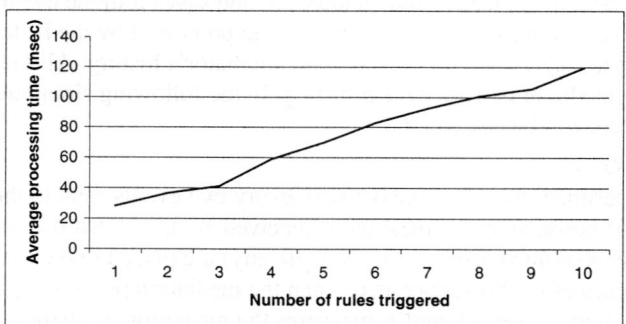

Figure 6: Average processing time (t_s) vs. Number of rules r_n.

As can be seen from Figure 6, the mediator shows very moderate increase in T_s with the increase of the number of triggered rules. Processing of 10 rules takes 119.6 milliseconds, while one rule takes 28.4 milliseconds. We can therefore infer that the parallel rule-processing model scales well with large number of concurrently triggered rules.

5.3 Robustness

Finally, another important metric to evaluate is the mediator's capability of handling message flooding, i.e., a large amount of events simultaneously sent to the mediator. In order to test this capability, we started a lot of wrapper instances on the machine on which the mediator runs, and bombarded the mediator with simultaneous messages. The time t_r, as needed for the mediator to process various number n_r of simultaneous messages, is recorded.

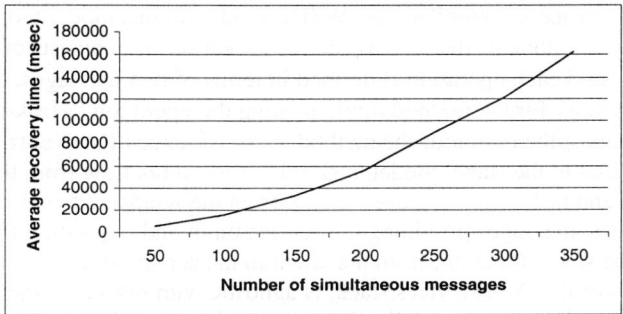

Figure 7: Average recovery time vs. Number of simultaneous messages.

As shown in Figure 7, the mediator is able to recover within a very short period of time (5.317 sec) for n_r =50 (standard deviation ranges from 0.49—0.83 sec). The mediation slows down as the number of messages increases and reaches 161.909 sec at 350 simultaneous messages, and does not crash under a very heavy load. However, this performance impact is attributed to the constant information repository updating. When the information repository increases, it takes much longer to update the flat XML file-based database.

6 Conclusions and Further Work

In this paper, we discussed Babel, an application-integration framework. Babel is certainly not unique in providing an infrastructure for rule-based mediation over independent applications. CoopWare [5,12] is a similar framework, on which in fact we based our evaluation of Babel. However, Babel's approach to application integration is novel in the following respects.

First, it enables both rule- and session-based integration of the underlying applications. Reactive rule-based integration is sufficient for establishing consistency rules between pairs of tasks across applications. However, as the execution of rules produces new events that may cause new rules to apply, tracing the overall consequences of the rules becomes difficult. If the rules are fairly independent, i.e., not many task-initiation *actions* and task-execution *events* refer to the same task types, then there are few secondary effects of the rule execution, and therefore few long-term consequences. If however this is not the case, and tightly controlling the overall integration behavior is important, then more complex process descriptions are required, and this type of integration is also supported by Babel, with workflow sessions.

Second, the coordination logic of a mediation application developed with Babel, i.e., the event-condition-action rules and the workflow sessions, are declaratively specified in XML. They are therefore easy to inspect and modify. Even more importantly, the VXG interface supports the specification of the coordination logic and thus alleviates the burden of the programmer. At the same time, by virtue of the fact that the logic is compiled into XSLT programs that are executable by the run-time Babel mediator, the mediation applications are easily extensible. If the programmer has a strong XSLT background, he/she can bypass VXG and manually program more complex rules to be executed by the mediator.

Finally, the event-based description of the underlying application services is similar to the recently proposed WebServices WSDL model. In this model too, applications are viewed as components that export services; each service consists of a set of operations (≈tasks) and each operation is defined in terms of two messages, one to provide the input necessary for the method implementing the operation (≈task-initiation event) and one to request the output of the method (≈task-execution event). An interesting difference is that in the Babel model, task-initiation events flow from the mediator to the wrappers and task-execution events flow from the wrappers to the mediator, where in WebServices, messages providing the service input and requesting the service output flow in the same direction, from the client to the server. WSFL, the workflow-level standard of the WebServices stack, is agnostic with respect to the integration style of the underlying server applications. In our future work, we plan to investigate whether or not (and how exactly) the Babel coordination logic can be translated in WSFL.

References

1. W.M.P. van der Aalst, "Petri-net-based Workflow Management Software", Proceedings of the NFS Workshop on Workflow and Process Automation in Information Systems, Athens, Georgia, May 1996, pp. 114-118.
2. Batini, C., Lenzerini, M. and Navathe, S.B., "A comparative analysis of methodologies for database schema integration", ACM Computing Surveys, Vol. 18, No. 4, Dec. 1986, pp. 323-364.
3. E. Bertino, "Integration of heterogeneous database applications though object-oriented interface", Information systems, 1989, pp. 407-420.
4. Y. Breitbart, P. Olson, and G. Thompson, "Database integration in a distributed heterogeneous database system", Proceedings of the 2nd International Conference on Data Engineering, Los Angeles, CA, February 1986, pp. 301-310.
5. A. Gal, J. Mylopoulos, "Supporting Distributed Autonomous Integration Services Using Coordination", International Journal of Cooperative Information Systems, vol.9, no.3 pp. 255-282, 2001.
6. R. Goldman, J. McHugh, and J. Widom. "From Semistructured Data to XML: Migrating the Lore Data Model and Query Language", Proceedings of the 2nd International Workshop on the Web and Databases (WebDB '99), pp. 25-30, 1999.
7. S. Heiler, "Semantic Interoperability", ACM Computing Surveys, 27(2):271-273, June 1995.
8. JavaTM APIs for XML Processing (JAXP), http://java.sun.com/xml/xml_jaxp.html

9. R. Kapoor, " Mathaino: Device Retargetable User Interface Migration UsingXML", University of Alberta, TR-01-112001.
10. A.Levy, A. Rajaraman, and J.Ordile, "Querying heterogeneous information sources using source description", Proceedings of the International Conference on VLDB, Bombay, India, 1996, pp. 251-262.
11. C. Baru, A. Gupta, B. Ludascher, R. Marciano, Y. Papakonstantinou, P. Velikhov, V. Chu, "XML-based information mediation with MIX", ACM SIGMOD, pp. 597-599, 1999.
12. J. Mylopoulos, A. Gal, K. Kontogiannis, M. Stanley, "A Generic Integration Architecture for Cooperative Information Systems", Proceedings of the 1st IFCIS Intl. Conference on Cooperative Information Systems, Brussels, Belgium, pp. 208-217, June 1996.
13. Y. Papakonstantinou, H. Garcia-Molina, J. Widom, "Object Exchange Across Heterogeneous Information Sources", In Proceedings of Eleventh International Conference on Data Engineering, Taipei, Taiwan, 251-260, 1995.
14. XSLT processor implementation, http://users.iclway.co.uk/mhkay/saxon/
15. A. Sheth, D. Georgakopoulos, S.M.M. Joosten, M. Rusinkiewicz, W. Scacchi, J. Wileden, A. Wolf, "Reports from the NSF Workflow and Process Automation in Information Systems", ACM SIGMOD Record, Volume 25 Number 4 December 1996.
16. Q. Situ and E. Stroulia, " Task-structure Based Mediation: The Travel-Planning Assistant Example", Proceedings of the 13 [th] Canadian Conference on Artificial Intelligence (AI'2000), 14-17 May, 2000, pp. 400-410, Montreal, Quebec, Canada.
17. E. Stroulia, M. El-Ramly, P. Sorenson, R. Penner, "Legacy Systems Migration in Cel L-EST", Proceedings of the 22nd International Conference on Software Engineering, Limerick, Ireland (June 4-11, 2000), pp. 790. IEEE Computer Society Press.
18. "The Workflow Reference Model", Workflow Management Coalition, Document Number TC00-1003, http://www.wfmc.org/standards/docs/tc003v11.pdf.
19. D. Wodtke and G. Weikum, "A formal foundation for distributed workflow execution based on statecharts", 6th International Conference on Database Theory (ICDT 97), pp. 230-246, 1997.
20. G. Wiederhold: Mediation and Software Maintenance; Technical Note STAN-CS-TN-95-26.
21. H. Zhang, and E. Stroulia, "Babel: Application Integration through XML specification of Rules", 23rd International Conference on Software Engineering (ICSE 2001), 12-19 May 2001, Toronto, Canada. 831-832. IEEE Computer Society Press.
22. D. Garlan, R. Allen, and J. Ockerbloom. Architectural Mismatch, or Why it is hard to build systems out of existing parts. In Proceedings 17th International Conference on Software Engineering, pp. 179-185, Seattle, Washington, April 1995. ACM SIGSOFT.
23. K. J. Sullivan and J. C. Knight. Experience Assessing an Architectural Approach to Large-Scale Systematic Reuse. Proceedings of 18th International Conference on Software Engineering, pp. 220-229, IEEE Computer Society Press.
24. A. Sahuguet and F. Azavant. "Looking at the Web through XML Glasses", Conference on Cooperative Information Systems, pp. 148-159, 1999.
25. B. Adelberg. NoDoSE: A tool for semi-automatically extracting semi-structured data from text documents. In Proc. Intl. Conference on Management of Data, pp. 283-294, 1998.
26. L. Liu and C. Pu. CQ: A personalized update monitoring toolkit. In Proc. of the ACM SIGMOD Conf., pp. 547--549, Seattle, 1998.
27. U. Dayal, E.N. Hanson, and J. Widom. Active database systems. In W. Kim, editor, Modern Database Systems: The Object Model, Interoperability, and Beyond. ACM Press, New York, 1994.

Integrating and Rapid-Prototyping UML Structural and Behavioural Diagrams Using Rewriting Logic

Nasreddine Aoumeur and Gunter Saake

Institut für Technische und Betriebliche Informationssystem
Otto-von-Guericke-Universität Magdeburg
Postfach 4120, D–39016 Magdeburg
{aoumeur,saake}@iti.cs.uni-magdeburg.de

Abstract. Although the diversity of UML diagrams provides users with different views of any complex software under development, in most cases system designers face challenging problems to keeping such diagrams coherently related. In this paper we propose to contribute to the tremendous efforts being undertaken towards rigorous and coherent views of UML-based modelling techniques. In this sense, we propose to integrate most of UML diagrams in a very smooth yet sound way. Moreover, by equipping such integration with an intrinsically concurrent and operational semantics, namely rewriting logic, we also provide validation by rapid-prototyping using MAUDE implementations.
More precisely, the diagrams we propose to smoothly integrate include: object- and class-diagrams with their related object constraints (using OCL), statecharts and life-cycle diagrams. The integration of such diagrams is based on very appealing Petri-net-like semi-graphical notations. As further advantages of the proposed integration we cite: (1) an explicit distinction between local features and observed ones in (the enriched) class-diagrams which offers a clean separation between intra- and inter-class-diagram reasoning; and (2) a full exploitation of rewriting logic reflection capabilities for expressing different object-life cycles in a runtime way.

1 Introduction

Standardized by the Object Management Group (OMG) in 1997, the Unified Modeling Language (UML) [BJR98, BJR97] methodology has been rapidly accepted and emerged as a suitable framework for modeling (and implementing) complex software-intensive systems. By providing numerous forms of very appealing semi-graphical diagrams with associated texts (i.e. using the object constraint language OCL), UML has been largely experienced in different categories of software-intensive systems. However, as designers attempt to go beyond the syntactical constructions of such diagrams—including object-, class-, sequence-, state-chart-, collaboration-, and component-diagrams with associated text descriptions—they face challenging problems in keeping such diagrams coherent and intrinsically related. Such coherence is a crucial requirements for ensuring consistency and completeness (using different verification/validation formal techniques) of the whole system before its implementation.

As a result of this unsatisfactory state of affair, several proposals have been forwarded recently aiming at bringing more rigor and coherence to these often redundant and incoherent views. Among these proposals we specifically cite the development of an adequate integration, denoted by `Casl-Ltl` [RCA01, ACR00], of the recently developed algebraic specification language `Casl` [Mos97] and a suitable form of labelled transition systems [Ast99]. Using this integration the authors show how almost all UML diagrams can find a rigorous formalization. Other approaches concentrating on the formalization and integration of some UML diagrams have been also put forward like the formalization using Object-Z, Graph-theory, Petri nets, etc (see the proceedings deserved to this methodology [FR99, EK00]).

The purpose of this paper fits within the direction of these research directions, and introduces a more coupled integration of most UML diagrams having in mind complex distributed information systems as a main application domain. That is, following our experiences in this field [AS99c, Aou00, JSHS96, CRSS98], we are concentrating more on object-, class- (with related text descriptions using OCL), transition- and statecharts' diagrams, that are in our view largely sufficient for covering most of structural as well as behavioural aspects in complex information systems. However, instead of describing (or after describing[1]) them separately when conceiving a complex information system, we rather propose to soundly integrate them in a smooth way keeping all their expressive advantages while overcoming most of their shortcomings. More precisely, the shortcomings we are tackling with—as triggers towards the proposed integration—include the following:

- By independently conceiving object constraints—particularly pre-, post-conditions and conditions to be associated with methods or operations in the class-diagrams—, in our view this does not only violate the *intrinsic dependency* of these constraints to associated operations and objects but also increases the degree of incoherence between the two parts, which in fact concern the same world entities. So, our contribution aims at intrinsically incorporating these constraints in the corresponding class- and/or object-diagrams.
- UML diagrams promote just a community-based perception of the system, whereas to cope with the ever-increasing complexity in real-life information systems rather a *component*-based perception is overwhelmingly needed. In this sense, an explicit distinction between local attributes / operations and observed ones, would allow each (hierarchy) of class-diagram—capturing an independent part of whole system— to be autonomously conceived as a

---

[1] We should point out here that the present proposal should be regarded just as complement artifacts helping the UML-based designers for more reliability rather than as a new alternative.

component. On the basis of observed features, such components may be then interconnected by hiding all their internal features.
- Although the object-orientation with its message-passing concept promotes true-concurrency and distribution, the UML (behavioural) diagrams offer only a very restricted form of interleaving (see [WMB99] for recent attempts to deal with concurrency in UML state-charts). That is, a true concurrent semantics would very be helpful for capturing the distributed nature of complex information systems.
- In the same spirit as for OCL descriptions against object and class-diagrams, we also argue that the modelling of life-cycle- and sequence-diagrams independently of class- and object-diagrams makes very hard the understanding and the coherence of whole specification as well as any further refinement steps towards efficient implementations.

In some detail, with the aim to overcome the above UML shortcomings the integration we are proposing may be sketched as follows. But before we should once again clearly point out that our integration is to be regarded as an *intermediate* phase between the UML modelling and implementation phases. The purpose of this intermediate phase, that could be generated (semi-)automatically from the original UML diagrams, is to bring more coherence, concurrency, more componentization and validation to the modelled system.

- First as we just mentioned, in any class-diagram we make an explicit distinction between local attributes / operations[2] and observed ones. Of course such distinction is intrinsically depending on the application at hand. Second, besides the attribute identifiers and their sorts (and eventually initial values), we propose to endow each attribute with a *variable*(s), which will play the role of a *current value* when we proceed to its interpretation using rewrite logic. In the same way, we equip each message argument with a corresponding variable.
- The second important step consists in constructing the dynamic of each message or method-invocation. To this aim we propose to construct for each local message a Petri-net-like 'transition', where the condition and post-operation or the resulting change have to be adapted from the corresponding OCL description when it exists; otherwise they have to be constructed from the intuitive meaning of such a message. A general pattern of such a dynamics is proposed. We will refer to such 'enriched by dynamics' class-diagrams as enriched class-diagrams or simply as components.
- With respect to such a general pattern, we propose to interpret the operations dynamics in terms of rewrite logic. That is, each operation or message dynamics is captured by a corresponding rewrite rule. By allowing objects to be created and deleted, using these rules we show how a true concurrent reasoning is possible with a full exhibition of intra- and inter-object concurrency using an adequate extension of MAUDE language that we have proposed in [AS99a].

---
[2] In order to emphasize the concurrent character of our integration, we will use later messages instead of operations or method-invocations.

- After associating with each class-diagram its corresponding local behaviour, the next step is to deal with the interconnection of different independent (i.e. related only through relationships) class-diagrams composing the system. We follow the same reasoning as for the internal behaviour. That is, for each message declared as observed in each class-diagram as well as for each (dynamical) relationship, we construct the corresponding dynamics using the same Petri-like notation, but at this level only observed features of interacting class-diagrams are to be selected. That is, from a methodological point we are proposing a two-level based perception: first, each independent component is constructed and rapid-prototyped and then the interaction is dealt with by hiding all local features.
- Using the reflection capabilities of rewrite logic, we directly provide how message rewrite rules are to be performed, where carefully chosen strategies will correspond to life-cycle diagrams. To capture sequence diagrams, we have to add to the list of attributes in each class-diagram a particular attribute we called state and construct an appropriate strategy reflecting its change.

The rest of this paper is organized as follows. Using a very simplified example, in the next section we present an overview of different UML diagrams we will be focusing on. In the third section, we concentrate on the syntactical integration of OCL descriptions into class-diagrams. In the four section we propose an adequate interpretation of this integration in terms of the extended MAUDE language. The last section recapitulates the achieved work and discusses some future improvements. Unfortunately, due to space limitation we could not presents the semantical part, that is the rewrite theory, of the MAUDE extension and the meta-level for capturing state-chart diagrams semantics; however, the extended version of this paper adressing these two issues is appearing as a technical report [AS02].

2 UML Diagrams through a Simplified Example

In this section we present a simplified illustration of different UML diagrams we are concerning with, namely class-, object-, and associated OCL descriptions. From a methodological point of view, the construction of such diagrams has to be seen as a first phase towards the modelling / validation of any system. In this simplified banking system we assume having two 'independent' (i.e. related only through relationships) class-diagrams, namely the account and the account owners diagrams. Before giving the detail of each diagram, the left-hand side of Figure 1 sketches the 'generic' form of class diagrams—where classes are composed as usual of a set of attributes and operations and may be related to each other through inheritance, role and associations.

Using this general form, the right-hand side of Figure 1 depicts the class-diagram of an account class hierarchy. In this hierarchy we have as a super-class current accounts. Attributes of this class are the balance, the account owner's identity and a constant, denoted by Limit, as a minimal value of the balance. As methods of this class we consider : the opening and deletion of any

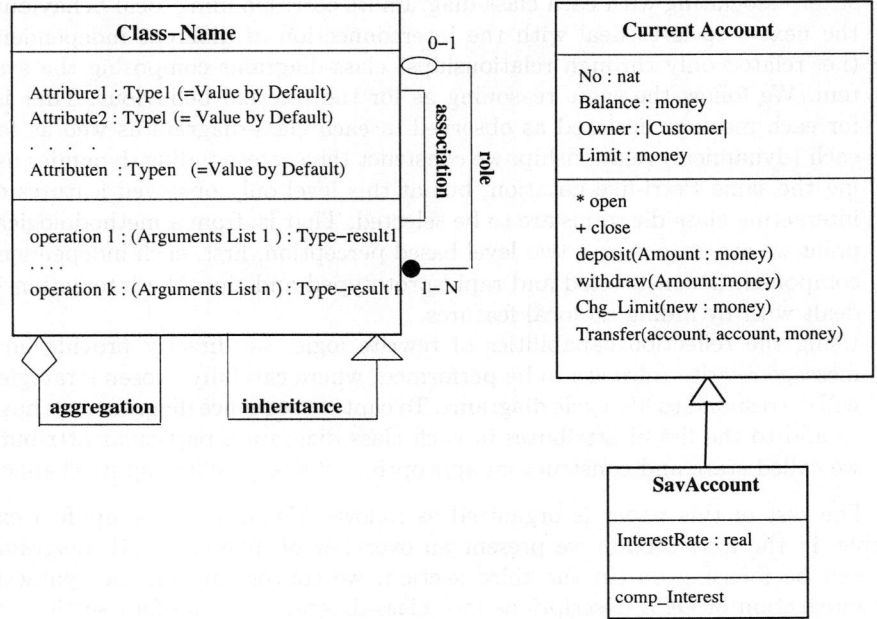

Fig. 1. The Generic form of UML class diagrams with the accounts example

account, the deposit of a given amount, the withdraw of a given amount, and the transfer of funds from an account to another. As a subclass we consider the class Sav-Account which is characterized by the interest percent. The interest percent of the balance is added up (at the end of each year for instance) to the current balance through the method comp_interest.

As a sketch of the OCL description part which will be the interest of our focus, we present in what follows the corresponding description to be associated, for instance, with the transfer method. This description is depicted in Table 1, where besides the signature of the method and its informal meaning, relevant is the condition Pre to be true to perform such a transfer, namely the account source balance has to the greater than the intended amount to be transferred. Relevant is also, the result of any operation, denoted by Post.

3 Integration of OCL Descriptions into Class-Diagrams

As we pointed out above, modelling separately OCL descriptions, and specifically different details about methods, does not only prevent a full respect of the object-oriented philosophy—that is, an *intrinsic* description of structural and behavioural aspects— but also prohibits any form of validation by rapid-prototyping. Indeed, it is very desirable that such a validation is performed at the specification level without requiring further refinements or implementations.

Table 1. A simplified illustration of OCL description using the transfer method

keywords	corresponding instantiation
Operation	Account :: transfer (src:Account, dest:Account, amount : Money)
Description	The system takes amount from the source, if there is, and places it on the destination
Pre:	src.balance $\geq$ amount
Post:	src.balance$-$ = amount $\wedge$ dest.balance$+$ = amount

However, we should be aware that although several OO existing modelling frameworks do achieve such intrinsic integration, only a few of them offer an appealing and high-comprehension level provided by UML diagrams. In other words, our objective is to *maintain* all the strengths of UML diagrams and just *enriching* them in such a way that OCL descriptions concerning operations could be smoothly *merged* in the class-diagrams. In the following we present step by step this enrichment of class-diagrams with related OCL descriptions.

3.1 Enrichment of Class-Diagrams by Variables and Scopes

The first step towards integrating behavioural aspects in UML class-diagrams consists in the following. In order to allow controlling the change of attribute values as well as the invoked objects and values of message parameters, we propose to endow each attribute (resp. operation parameter) with at least one variable which has to be of the same sort. Besides argument variables, we also make explicit the objects (identities) invoked in a given message. On the other hand, as we mentioned we want rather a component-oriented perception. To this aim, we associate with each attribute (resp. operation) a scope which may be *local* or *observed*—shortly l or o. Finally, in order to distinguish between invoked objects in a given operation (as in the transfer operation for instance), we also propose to include in the attribute box a list of (current) identifier variables preceeded by the (key)word Identity.

These enrichment are depicted in Figure 2, where with respect to the generic general form of class-diagrams we already introduced in Figure 1 we have added variables and scopes with each attribute and operations. In this enriched general form we have also separated (by using two boxes) between messages considered as local and those considered as observed ones.

Example 1. By restricting the account class-diagram to just the current accounts class, in the left-hand side of Figure 3 we have enriched this class by different variables for attributes as well as for message arguments. Also, we have distinguished between local and observed attributes and messages. However, the user may always change the scope of such attributes and messages at a need; for instance we have decided that the transfer operation be an observed one just for illustration purpose as will be subsequently made clear. In the right hand side, we have introduced a new 'enriched' class-diagram, namely the account owners' (or customer) class.

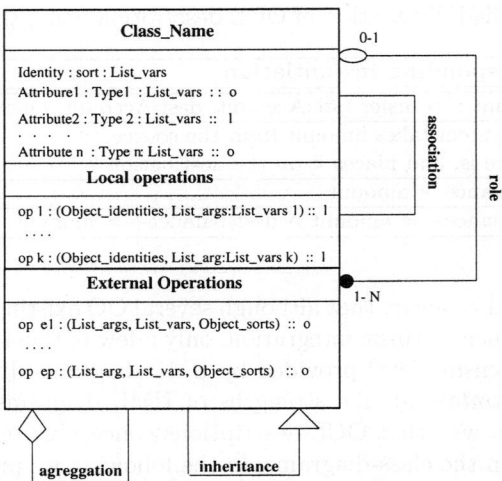

Fig. 2. The generic UML class-diagrams enriched by variables and scopes

3.2 Introducing New Notations for Behavioural Aspects

After enriching class-diagrams with the notions of variables and scopes, the next step consists in intrinsically incorporating in these diagrams the dynamics of each operation instead of (or after) describing them separately using OCL descriptions. In the endeavor to achieve this crucial step, we propose to add new semi-graphical notations we borrow from Petri-nets ones [Rei85]. More precisely, with respect to our objective of enhancing scalability and component-orientation, first, we present how class-diagrams' behaviour is conceptualized, and then we deal with the behaviour gouverning the interaction between 'independent' class-diagrams composing the whole system.

Internal behaviour within class-diagrams. As described in Figure 4, the incorporation of the dynamics associated with each local message—all observed messages are ignored at this level—consists in constructing a Petri-net like transition, with the following characteristics.

- The transition form we associate with each operation is represented as a rounded box. Within each rounded box we associate a condition (i.e. a boolean expression), we denote by Mes_cond, which has to be built on the invoked attributes and message argument variables using different comparison operators (e.g $=, >, <, \neq, \leq, \geq$) and / or boolean operators (e.g **and**, **or**).
- The (input) arrows or arcs going from the class to each rounded box are labelled by two information. On the one hand, the first inscription denoted by Invoked_Mes is to be always a local message of the form op_i(Id1, .., var1,..,vark); where op_i is any operation or message declared as local one in the corresponding class-diagram, and the parameters Id1, ...

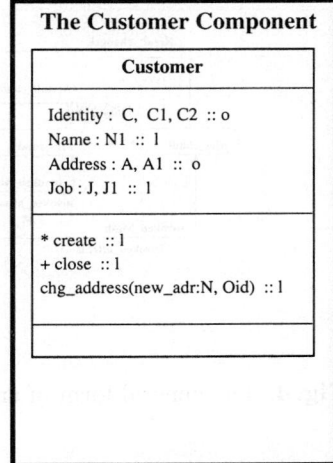

Fig. 3. The accounts and customers class-diagrams with variables and scopes

var1,..,vark have to reflect the object identifiers and other invoked parameters. The second inscription we denote by **Invoked attributes** has to be of the form:

$$Id_1.atr_1:Var_1,\ldots,Id_k.atr_k:Var_k$$

Intuitively each pair $Id_i.atr_i:Var_i$ corresponds to an invoked attribute belonging to an object Id_i with Var_i to be understood as a current value. The selected pairs should correspond to objects (identifiers) invoked in the corresponding message. In other words, they have to be involved either for changing these current values or participating in the condition. This will play an important role towards exhibiting intra-object concurrency as we show later.

– Finally, the inscription associated with the output arrow, we denoted by **Result_change**, has to be of the form.

$$Id_1.atr_1:Exp_1,\ldots,Id_k.atr_k:Exp_k.$$

Each expression Exp_i has to reflect the intended change of the corresponding value of the invoked attributes.

Example 2. Following this general form in integrating message dynamics into class-diagrams, Figure 5 illustrates the incorporation of different behaviour associated with local operations in both **Account** and **Account Owners** classes. For instance, to reflect the withdraw behaviour, first, we have to select an account and a corresponding amount: this fact is illustrated by the inscription withdraw(I,M), with I as account identifier and M the associated amount to

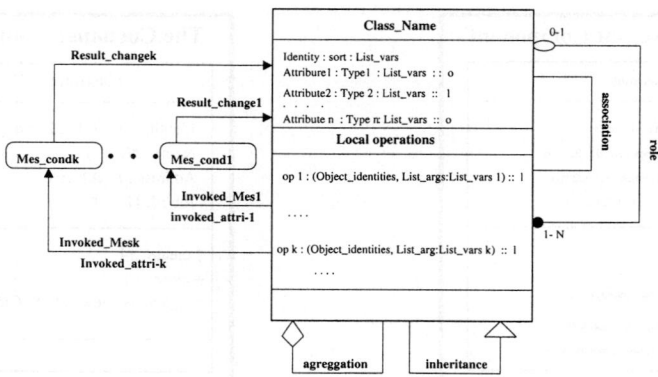

Fig. 4. The general form of enriching class-diagram by operations dynamic

be withdrawn. The second inscription, labelling the corresponding input arc of this method, namely I.balance:B, I.limit:L, involves the attributes of the invoked object (i.e. I) which are needed to express the corresponding state's change and conditions. As a condition of this method we require that the current value of the balance should by greater that M and the difference B-M be greater than L. Finally the resulting state's change has to be I.balance:B-M, I.limit:L which corresponds to the output arc inscription.

On the light of this explanation, all other operation dynamics are constructed following the same reasoning. It is worth-noting that all observed messages are simply omitted at this level.

Interaction between independent class-diagrams. As we pointed out in the introduction, we are proposing a two-level based methodology for integrating different UML diagrams. That is, after enriching each independent class-diagram with the appropriate behaviour as a first level, the next step is to deal with the interaction between different class-diagrams composing the whole system. To this purpose, we introduce very similar constructions with the following specificities. First as depicted in Figure 6, at this level in each class-diagram we have to deal only with those attributes and operations chosen to be observed. That is, the already constructed internal behaviour as well as all local attributes and messages have to be hidden at this inter-class diagrams' interaction level. Second, besides observed messages also relationships relating different class-diagrams may have corresponding behaviours. Third, technically the construction of such behaviour is exactly as for local messages except that now more than one class-digram is needed.

Example 3. In Figure 7 we have constructed the corresponding behaviour of the *transfer* message. In this construction we require for instance that for performing any money transfer between two accounts their corresponding owners should

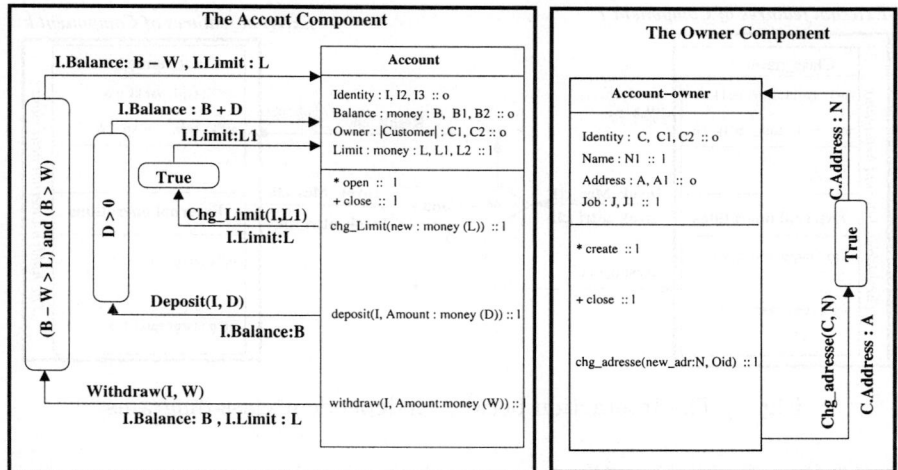

Fig. 5. The Account and Owner class-diagrams extended by messages behaviour

have the *same* address (the same city). With such a constraint we should now also involve the owner class-diagram.

4 Interpretation of the Proposed Integration in the Extended MAUDE

First as we pointed out in the introduction, due to space limitation we assume the reader fimiliar we the MAUDE language and the extension for intra-object concurrency and componentization we proposed in [AS99a]. This section is devoted to the theoretical underpinning of the proposed syntactical modelling artifacts. Our objective is to propose a semantical framework that allows fulfilling all the mentioned features, namely : (1) an indivisible integration of structural and behavioural aspects of objects within classes ; (2) a full exhibition of intra- and inter-object concurrency; (3) a satisfactory interpretation of all structuring abstractions within the enriched class-diagrams; (4) a clean separation between the internal description and reasoning within any class-diagram and the description and reasoning about the interaction between such class-diagrams. By reasoning we mainly understand the rapid-prototyping using the deduction rules of such an adequate semantical framework.

The semantical framework we are proposing is based on rewrite logic [Mes92], which has been proved very appropriate for dealing with concurrent OO systems in the recent years [Mes98]. Another advantage that makes this logic very practical is the current implementation of the MAUDE language [CDE+99], those programs are just theories in this logic.

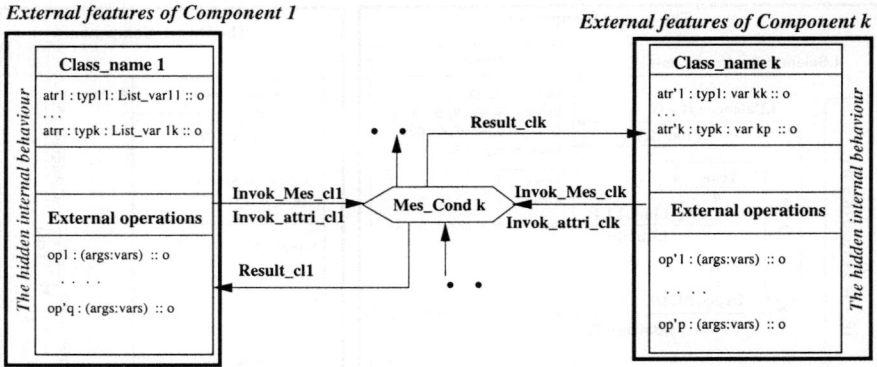

Fig. 6. The Interaction between independent class-diagrams

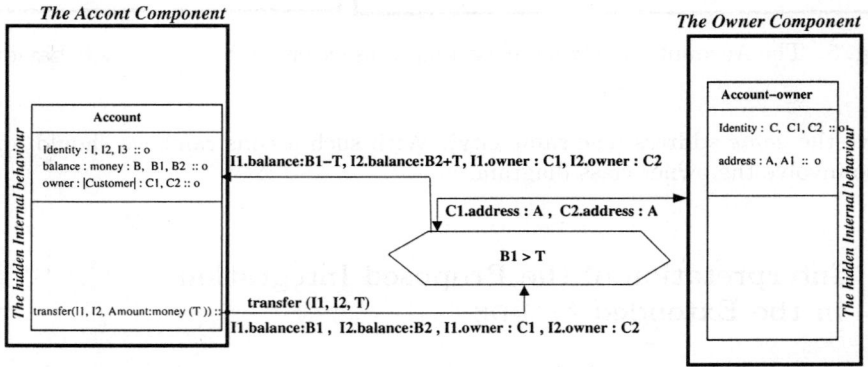

Fig. 7. The interaction between the account and the customer class-diagrams

More precisely, in the next subsection we will focus more on the way of translating the proposed integration to the extension of MAUDE we proposed in [AS99a, AS99b], which allows fulfilling all the mentioned (four) objectives.

4.1 Translating Extended Class-Diagrams into MAUDE

This subsection is devoted to the translation of our proposed variant of class-diagrams into the MAUDE language. To this aim, following the two-level suggested methodology, first, we have to deal with the translation of each independent class-diagram separately. Then, we should complete this translation by coping with the interaction between such independent class-diagrams composing the whole system.

Translating class-diagrams. By examining the general form of class-diagrams we proposed in Figure 4 and the MAUDE description it follows that such a translation is very straightforward. More precisely, the steps to be performed are the following.

1. The translation of structural aspects of any class-diagram is directly captured as a MAUDE module, where attributes are to be declared with their corresponding sorts and operations are conceived as messages. Besides that, in order to distinguish local attributes / messages and observed ones, instead of the OO MAUDE modules' keywords *class* and Msgs we will rather use class-loc and class-obs as well as Msg-loc and Msg-obs.
2. The translation of the behaviour we associated with each operation can also be intuitively expressed as a rewrite rule. More precisely, we have to perform the two follwoing two steps:
   - first, we have to reorganize input (resp. ouput) inscriptions from the form
   $$Id_1.atri_1 : val_1, \ldots, Id_k.atri_k : val_k$$
   (resp. $Id_1.atri_1$: exp_1, ... , $Id_l.atri_l$:exp_l) to the MAUDE form one, namely:
   $$\langle Id_1 | atri_1 : val_1 \rangle, \ldots, \langle Id_k | atri_k : val_k \rangle$$
   (resp. $\langle Id_1|atri_1 : exp_1\rangle, \ldots, \langle Id_l|atri_l : exp_l\rangle$);
   - each Petri-net like transition is then to be expressed as a rewrite rule of the form:
   $$\text{Invoked\_Mes}_i \quad \text{Invoked\_Attri}_i \Rightarrow \text{Result\_change}_i \quad \text{if}$$
   $$\text{Condition}$$

Example 4. With respect to these straightforward ideas, the corresponding structural MAUDE part of the account class, for instance, takes the following form:

```
omod Account is
  protecting Money .
  class-loc Account | Limit : Money .
  class-obs Account | Balance : Money, Owner : OId .
  msg-loc Chg_Limit : OId Money → Msg .
  msg-loc Deposit : OId Money → Msg .
  msg-loc Withdraw : OId Money → Msg .

  vars I, I2, I3 : OId .
  vars C, C1, C2 : OId .
  Vars B, B1, B2, L, L1, L2 : Money .
  vars W, D : Money .
```

On the other hand, following these very simple translating ideas, the corresponding rewrite rules of the messages in the account class-diagram, for instance, are as follows. In these rules we have considered the corresponding message names as rule labels.

Chg_Limit : $Chg\_Limit(I, L1) \; \langle I|Limit : L\rangle \Rightarrow \langle I|Limit : L1\rangle$
Deposit : $Deposit(I, D) \; \langle I|Balance : B\rangle \Rightarrow \langle I|Balance : B + D\rangle$ if $(D > 0)$
Withdraw : $Withdraw(I, W) \; \langle I|Balance : B, Limit : L\rangle \Rightarrow \langle I|Balance : B - W, Limit : L\rangle$ if $(B - W > L) \wedge (B > W)$

Translating inter-class interactions. The translation into extended MAUDE of the inter-class interactions is like the translation of intra-class structure and behaviour except that here we deal only with observed features in each class. Besides that, in order to separate the invoked messages and objects in each class, we adopt the notation

(Class_name$_1$, configuration$_1$) ⊗ ... ⊗ (Class_name$_k$, configuration$_k$)

Following that, the general form of rewrite rules to associate with the interaction pattern depicted in Figure 6 takes the following configuration:

(Class_name$_1$, Invok_Mes_cl1 Invok_attri_cl1) ⊗ ... ⊗ (Class_name$_k$, Invok_Mes_clk Invok_attri_clk) ⇒ (Class_name$_1$, Result_cl1) ⊗ ... ⊗ (Class_name$_k$, Result_clk)   if Mes_Condk

Example 5. Using the above general of rewrite rule, the rule corresponding to the observed message `transfer` in Figure 7 takes the form:

Transfer: $(Account, transfer(I1, I2, T)\langle I1|balance : B1, Owner : C1\rangle\langle I2|balance : B2, Owner : C2\rangle) \otimes (Accout - owner, \langle C1|address : A\rangle\langle C2|address : A\rangle) \Rightarrow (Account, \langle I1|balance : B1 - T, Owner : C1\rangle\langle I2|balance : B2_T, Owner : C2\rangle) \otimes (Accout - owner, \langle C1|address : A\rangle\langle C2|address : A\rangle)$ **if** $(B1 > T)$

5 Conclusions

In this paper, we have proposed a sound and intuitive integration of all relevant UML-diagrams for dealing complex distributed information systems. More specifically in our integration we have concentrated on object- and class-diagrams and OCL descriptions in particular pre- and post-conditions. Beside being syntactically and semantically well-founded, the proposed integration enhances concurrency with a full exhibition of intra- as well as inter-object concurrency, componentization as we explicitly separate between internal and object features in any enriched class-diagram, and rapid-prototyping of this coherent view of different system diagrams using rewriting techniques.

Methodologically, this proposed sound integration has to be regarded more as an intermediate phase between the UML modelling and implementation phases. That is, after specifying any complex information systems using UML diagrams, a semi-automatic translation or integration of these diagrams following the explained steps allows achieving at least the three above mentioned objectives. We argue that fulfilling such goals promotes more reliability, reusability and eliminate different errors and misunderstanding at an early stage.

As a future perspectives, first we are conscious that this proposal is just a first stone in bringing more coherence and reliability to the UML methodology, and it has to be improved, extended and be supported by appropriate software tools. In this sense, firstly we are currently working on more complex non-trivial studies to assess and enhance the practicability of this proposal. Such case studies have also to be validated using the current implementation of the MAUDE language. As a very promising extension we are working on dealing with dynamic evolution of such integration using the rewriting logic meta-level. This will offer in particular to change in a runtime way the scope, the internal behaviour as well as the interaction between different components.

References

[ACR00] E. Astesiano, M. Cerioli, and G. Reggio. Plugging data constructs into paradigm-specific languages: Towards an application to UML. In T. Rus, editor, *Proceedings Algebraic Methodology and Software Technology, 8th International Conference, AMAST 2000, Iowa City, Iowa, USA, May 2000*, volume 1816 of *LNCS*, pages 273-292. Springer, 2000.

[Aou00] N. Aoumeur. Specifying Distributed and Dynamically Evolving Information Systems Using an Extended Co-NETs Approach. In G. Saake, K. Schwarz, and C Tärker, editors, *Transactions and Database Dynamics*, volume 1773 of *Lecture Notes in Computer Science, Berlin*, pages 91-111. Springer-Verlag, 2000. *Selected papers from the 8th International Workshop an Foundations of Models and Languages for Data and Objects, Sep. 1999, Germany.*

[AS99a] N. Aoumeur and G. Saake. On the Specification and Validation of Cooperative Information Systems Using an Extended MAUDE. In K. Futatsugi, J. Goguen, and J. Meseguer, editors, *Proc. of 1 st Int. OBJ/CafeOBJ/Maude Workshop, at FM'99 Conference, Toulouse, France*, pages 197-211. The Theta Foundation Bucharest, Romania, 1999.

[AS99b] N. Aoumeur and G. Saake. Operational Interpretation of the Requirements Specification Language ALBERT Using Timed Rewriting Logic. In *Proc. of 5th Int. Workshop an Requirements Engineering: Foundation for Software Quality (REFSQ'99), Heidelberg, Germany*. Presses Universitaires de Namur, 1999.

[AS99c] N. Aoumeur and G. Saake. Towards an Object Petri Nets Model for Specifying and Validating Distributed Information Systems. In M. Jarke and A. Oberweis, editors, *Proc. of the 11th Int. Conf. an Advanced Information Systems Engineering, CAiSE'99*, volume 1626 of *Lecture Notes in Computer Science*, pages 381-395. Springer-Verlag, 1999.

[AS02] N. Aoumeur and G. Saake. Integrating and Rapid-prototyping UML Structural and Behavioural Diagrams Using Rewriting Logic. Preprint, Fakultät für Informatik, Universität Magdeburg, March 2002.

[Ast99] E. Astesiano. Algebraic Specification of Concurrent Systems. In E. Astesiano, 11.4. Kreowski, and B. Krieg-Brückner, editors, *IFIP 14.3 Volume an Foundations of System Specification, Chapter 1. To appear in Springer LNCS*, 1999.

[BJR98] G. Booch, I. Jacobson, and J. Rumbaugh, editors. *The Unified Modeling Language Reference Manual*. Addison-Wesley, 1997.

[BJR97] G. Booch, I. Jacobson, and J. Rumbaugh, editors. *Unified Modeling Language, Notation Guide, Version* 1.0. Addison-Wesley, 1998.

[CDE+99] M. Clavel, F. Duran, S. Eker, J. Meseguer, and M. Stehr. Maude. Specification and Programming in Rewriting Logic. Technical report, SRI, Computer Science Laboratory, March 1999. URL: http://maude.esl.sri.com.

[CRSS98] S. Conrad, J. Ramos, G. Saake, and C. Sernadas. Evolving Logical Specification in Information Systems. In J. Chomicki and G. Saake, editors, *Logics for Databases and Information Systems*, chapter 7, pages 199-228. Kluwer Academic Publishers, Boston, 1998.

[EK00] A. Evans and S. Kent. Proc. *3rd Int. Conf. Unified Modeling Language (UML'2000)*. LNCS. Springer, 2000.

[FR99] R. France and B. Rumpe. Modeling dynamic software components with UML. In *UML'99 - The Unified Modeling Language. Beyond the Standard. Second International Conference, Fort Collins, CO, USA, October 28-30. 1999, Proceedings*, volume 1723 of *LNCS*. Springer, 1999.

[JSHS96] R. Jungclaus, G. Saake, T. Hartmann, and C. Sernadas. TROLL - A Language for Object-Oriented Specification of Information Systems. *ACM Transactions an Information Systems*, 14(2):175-211, April 1996.

[Mes92] J. Meseguer. Conditional rewriting logic as a unified model for concurrency. *Theoretical Computer Science*, 96:73-155, 1992.

[Mes98] J. Meseguer. Research Directions in Rewriting Logic. In U. Berger and H. Schwichtenberg, editors, *Computational Logic, NATO Advanced Study Institute, Marktoberdorf, Germany*. Springer-Verlag, 1998.

[Mos97] P. Mosses. Cofi: The common framework initiative for algebraic Specification and development. In Proc. Intl. Symp. an *Theory and Practice of Software Development (TAPSOFT)*, volume 1214 of *LNCS*, pages 115-137. Springer, 1997. **COFi Homepage: http://www.brics.dk/Projects/CoFI**.

[RCA01] G. Reggio, M. Cerioli, and E. Astesiano. Towards a rigorous semantics of UML supporting its multiview approach. In H. Hussmann, editor, *Fundamental Approaches to Software Engineering. 4th International Conference, FASE 2001 Held as Part of the Joint European Conferences an Theory and Practice of Software, ETAPS 2001 Genova, Italy, April 2-6. 2001 Proceedings*, volume 2029 of *LNCS*, pages 171-186. Springer, 2001.

[Rei85] W. Reisig. Petri Nets. *EATCS Monographs an Theoretical Computer Science*, 4, 1985.

[WMB99] A. Wienberg, F. Matthes, and M. Boger. Modeling dynaanic software components with uml. In Robert France and Bernhard Rumpe, editors, *UML'99 - The Unified Modeling Language. Beyond the Standard. Second International Conference, Fort Collins, CO, USA, October 28-30. 1999, Proceedings*, volume 1723 of *LNCS*, pages 204-219. Springer, 1999.

Verification of Payment Protocols via MultiAgent Model Checking

M. Benerecetti[1], M. Panti[2], L. Spalazzi[2], and S. Tacconi[2]

[1] Dept. of Physics, University of Naples "Federico II"
Napoli, Italy
bene@na.infn.it
[2] Istituto di Informatica, University of Ancona
Ancona, Italy
{panti,spalazzi,tacconi}@inform.unian.it

Abstract. The paper presents a logic of belief and time (called MATL) that can be used to verify electronic payment protocols. This logic encompasses its predecessors in the family of logics of authentication. According to our approach, the verification is performed by means of MultiAgent Model Checking Checking, an extension of traditional model checking to cope with time and beliefs. In this framework, principals are modeled as concurrent processes able to have beliefs about other principals. The approach is applied to the verification of the Lu and Smolka protocol, a variant of SET. The results of our analysis show that the protocol does not satisfy some important security requirements, which make it subject to attacks.

1 Introduction

In this paper we show how *MultiAgent Model Checking* [6] (an extension of traditional model checking, see e.g. [10]) can be used for the verification of electronic payment protocols using a *logic of belief and time*. This work extends to payment protocols our previous work on authentication protocols [4,5].

The application of model checking to payment protocol verification is not new (e.g., see [13,15,17]). However, in the previous work, payment protocols are verified by introducing the notion of intruder and, then, by verifying whether the intruder can attack a given protocol. This approach makes it possible to directly find a trace of a possible attack, but it may not be clear what the protocol flaw really is. This work usually employs temporal logics or process algebras.

A different approach makes use of logics of belief or knowledge to specify and verifying both authentication protocols (see, e.g. [8,1]) and payment protocols (e.g., see [7,11,14]). The use of such logics requires no models of intruder, and allows one to find what the protocol flaw is, allowing to specify (and check) security properties in a more natural way. However, in this approach, usually verification is performed proof-theoretically.

Our approach can be seen as a combination of the above two: we employ a logic called MATL (MultiAgent Temporal Logic) which is able to represent both time and belief (thus it follows the line of the work based on logics of belief or knowledge and does not use any model of the intruder); but verification is performed by means of a symbolic model checker (called NuMAS [3], a model checker based on NuSMV [9]). NuMAS is built on the work described in [6], where model checking is applied to BDI attitudes (i.e., Belief, Desire, and Intention) of agents.

Our work aims at the use of MATL for modeling payment protocols and uses NuMAS for their verification. This goal is fulfilled in three steps. First, we capture traditional logics of authentication (e.g., as [1,8,18]) in MATL. Second, we extend the above work in order to capture typical issues of electronic payment protocols. MATL is expressive enough to fulfill both the previous steps. Third, we model *principals* participating to a payment protocol session as (concurrent finite state) processes able to have beliefs within the NuMAS system.

The specification of a principal has two orthogonal aspects: a temporal aspect, and a belief aspect. When we consider the temporal evolution of a principal we treat belief atoms (namely, atomic formulae expressing belief) as atomic propositions. The fact that these formulae talk about beliefs is not taken into consideration. When we deal with the beliefs of a principal P, we model its beliefs about another principal Q as the fact that P has access to a representation of Q as a process. Then, any time it needs to check the truth value of some belief formula about Q, e.g., $B_Q \phi$, P simply tests whether ϕ holds in its (appropriate) representation of Q. Beliefs are essentially used to control the "jumping" among processes. This operation is iterated in the obvious way in case of nested beliefs.

The paper is structured as follows. In Section 2 we briefly introduce the Lu and Smolka Protocol (a variant of the well-known Secure Electronic Transaction (SET) Protocol), as a running example. Section 3 describes MATL and its use as a logic of authentication. The use of MATL as a logic for payment protocols is described in Section 4. Section 5 describes the formal specifications for the usual security requirements of payment protocols. The results of the verification of the Lu and Smolka protocol are reported in Section 6. Finally, some conclusions are drawn in Section 7.

2 The Lu-Smolka Variant of the SET Protocol

The Secure Electronic Transaction (SET [16]) is an electronic commerce protocol jointly developed by Visa and Mastercard in order to guarantee secure transactions over open networks. SET is not a monolithic protocol, but a suite comprising seventeen subprotocols, each devoted to make secure a specific phase of a commercial transaction. The Lu-Smolka variant of this protocol [15], reported in Figure 1, is a simplified version of the subprotocol involved in the payment phase only. This subprotocol is supposed to be invoked during a web-based commercial transaction. In other words, a client (the cardholder) after selecting the goods/services that it wishes to purchase/request, the shipping address, and the billing address (if any), uses the protocol to perform the on-line payment. In Figure 1, C denotes the cardholder, M the merchant, and P the payment

(1) $C \to M\ : TIDR$ *Initiate Request*
(2) $M \to C\ : S_{K_M^{-1}}\{TID\}$ *Initiate Response*
(3) $C \to M\ : S_{K_C^{-1}}\{TID\}, \{TID, PA\}_{K_m}, S_{K_C^{-1}}\{\{TID, PY, CA\}_{K_p}\}$
     Purchase Request
(4) $M \to P\ : S_{K_C^{-1}}\{\{TID, PY, CA\}_{K_p}\}, S_{K_M^{-1}}\{TID\}, \{TID, AA, MA\}_{K_p}$
     Authorization & Capture Request
(5) $P \to M\ : S_{K_P^{-1}}\{TID, Tr\}$ *Authorization & Capture Response*
(6) $M \to C\ : S_{K_P^{-1}}\{TID, Tr\}$ *Purchase Response*

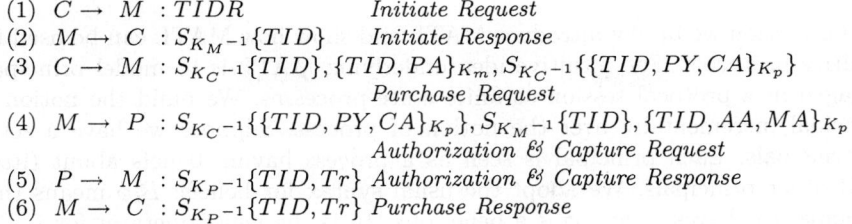

Fig. 1. The Lu-Smolka variant of SET

gateway. The notation $\{m\}_{K_x}$ denotes a message m encrypted with the public key of X, whereas $S_{K_x^{-1}}\{m\}$ denotes a message m signed by X with its private key. $TIDR$ represents a record containing initialization data for the protocol. TID represents the unique identifier of the transaction, it can be considered as a nonce. PA is the amount that the cardholder is supposed to pay, PY is the amount that the cardholder is willing to pay, and AA is the amount of charge that the merchant requests for authorization. CA and MA are the identifiers of the cardholder's account and of the merchant's account, respectively. Finally, Tr denotes the answer of the gateway that can be either an authorization or a negation of authorization.

Intuitively, the protocol works as follows. In step (1), C sends the request for a unique transaction identifier to M. M assigns the TID to the transaction, signs it, and returns it to C in step (2). At this point, in step (3), C sends the Ordering Information (OI, i.e., TID and PA) to M, together with the Payment Instruction (PI, i.e., TID,PY,CA). PY may be lower than PA, in case the cardholder is trying to deceive the merchant. Moreover, the PI is for the payment gateway, while OI is for the merchant. In step (4), M decrypts OI, checks if it is correct, then encrypts a new OI (OI' composed by TID,AA,MA) with the payment gateway's public key. Finally, M sends, in a single message, an authorization and capture request to P. Notice that AA may be higher than PY. In step (5), P authorizes C's payment card, checks for consistency between OI' and PI, performs appropriate account operations, and returns the transaction result Tr to M. In step (6), M reads the response, and forwards the message to C.

3 MATL as a Logic of Authentication

In this section we briefly introduce MATL and show how MATL can be used for security protocols. The intuitive idea underlying MATL is to model principals engaged in a protocol session as finite state processes. We build the notion of principal incrementally over the notion of process. Suppose we have a set I of principals. Each principal is seen as a process having beliefs about (itself and) other principals. We adopt the usual syntax for beliefs: $B_i \phi$ means that principal i believes ϕ, and ϕ is a belief of i. B_i is the belief operator for i. The idea is then to associate to each (level of) nesting of belief operators a *process evolving over time*, each of which intuitively correspond to a "view" about that process.

View Structure. Let $B = \{B_1, ..., B_n\}$, where each index $1, ..., n \in I$ corresponds to a principal. Let B^* denote the set of finite strings of the form $B_1, ..., B_n$ with $B_i \in B$. We call any $\alpha \in B^*$, a *view*. Each view in B^* corresponds to a possible nesting of belief operators. We also allow for the empty string, ϵ. The intuition is that ϵ represents the view of an external observer (e.g., the designer) which, from the outside, "sees" the behavior of the overall protocol.

Example 1. Figure 2 depicts the structure of views for the Lu and Smolka protocol. The beliefs of principal C correspond to the view B_C and are modeled by a process playing the cardholder's role in the protocol. The beliefs of principals M (the view B_M) and P (the view B_P) are modeled similarly. The beliefs that C has about (the behavior of) principal M correspond to the view $B_C B_M$ and are modeled by a process playing M's role in the protocol. Things work in the same way for any arbitrary nesting of belief operators.

Language. We associate a language $\mathcal{L}_\alpha$ to each view $\alpha \in B^*$. Intuitively, each $\mathcal{L}_\alpha$ is the language used to express what is true (and false) about the process of view α. We employ the Computational Tree Logic (CTL) [12], a well known propositional branching-time temporal logic widely used in formal verification. For each α, let P_α be a set of propositional atoms. Each P_α allows for the definition of a different language, called a MATL language (on P_α). A MATL language $\mathcal{L}_\alpha$ on P_α is the smallest CTL language containing the set of propositional atoms P_α and the belief atoms $B_i \phi$, for any formula ϕ of $\mathcal{L}_{\alpha B_i}$. In particular, $\mathcal{L}_\epsilon$ is used to speak about the whole protocol. The language $\mathcal{L}_{B_i}$ ($\mathcal{L}_{B_j}$) is the language adopted to represent i's (j's) beliefs. i's beliefs about j's beliefs are specified by the language of the view $B_i B_j$. Given a family $\{P_\alpha\}$ of sets of propositional atoms, the family of MATL languages on $\{P_\alpha\}$ is the family of CTL languages $\{\mathcal{L}_\alpha\}$. We write $\alpha : \phi$ (called labeled formula) to mean that ϕ is a formula of $\mathcal{L}_\alpha$. For instance, the formula $\mathsf{AG}\,(p \to B_i \neg q) \in \mathcal{L}_\epsilon$, (denoted by $\epsilon : \mathsf{AG}\,(p \to B_i \neg q)$), intuitively means that in every future state (the CTL operator AG), if p is true then principal i believes q is false.

The next step is the definition of an appropriate $\{P_\alpha\}$ in order to represent the usual propositions of a logic of authentication as in [1,8,18]. First of all, a logic of authentication is a logic of belief, i.e. it has formulae as P believes ϕ. Such formulae have a one-to-one mapping with MATL formulae as $B_P \phi$ (see

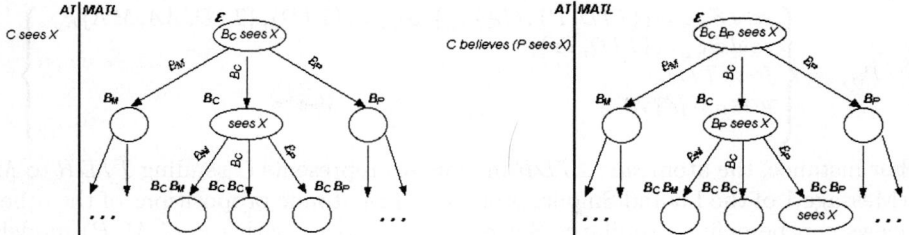

Fig. 2. The structure of views for the Lu and Smolka protocol and the proposition C sees X in MATL

Fig. 3. The structure of views for the Lu and Smolka protocol and the proposition C believes P sees X in MATL

Figure 3). Furthermore, a logic of authentication has propositions about which (fragments of) messages a principal (say P) sends or receives. For instance, in [1] they are expressed by propositions as P said X and P sees X (where X is a fragment of message). In MATL, such notions can be easily expressed by formulae as $B_P said\ X$ and $B_P sees\ X$ (see Figure 2). This means that we need to introduce the propositional atoms $said\ X$ and $sees\ X$ in P_{B_P}. A logic of authentication also has propositions as $fresh(X)$ that expresses the freshness of (fragments of) messages. Intuitive meaning is that X has been generated during the current protocol session. In MATL, we introduce the propositional atom $fresh(X)$. Usually, a logic of authentication also has propositions such as P says X to express that principal P has sent X recently. This can be expressed in MATL by the formula $B_P says\ X$. Propositions of the form $pubk_P\ K$ and $prik_{P,Q}\ K^{-1}$ mean that K is the public key of P and K^{-1} the corresponding secret key. They can be directly added as propositional atoms to the languages of MATL.

Example 2. We can set the atoms P_α for the views B_C, B_M and B_P as follows:

$$P_{B_C} = \begin{cases} said\ TIDR, \\ sees\ S_{K_M^{-1}}\{TID\}, \\ said\ S_{K_C^{-1}}\{TID\}, \{TID, PA\}_{K_m}, S_{K_C^{-1}}\{\{TID, PY, CA\}_{K_p}\}, \\ fresh\ S_{K_C^{-1}}\{TID\}, \{TID, PA\}_{K_m}, S_{K_C^{-1}}\{\{TID, PY, CA\}_{K_p}\}, \\ fresh\ TID, \\ pubk_M\ K_m, \\ ... \end{cases}$$

$$P_{B_M} = \begin{cases} sees\ TIDR, \\ said\ S_{K_M^{-1}}\{TID\}, \\ sees\ S_{K_C^{-1}}\{TID\}, \{TID, PA\}_{K_m}, S_{K_C^{-1}}\{\{TID, PY, CA\}_{K_p}\}, \\ fresh\ S_{K_C^{-1}}\{TID\}, \{TID, PA\}_{K_m}, S_{K_C^{-1}}\{\{TID, PY, CA\}_{K_p}\}, \\ pubk_P\ K_p, \\ ... \end{cases}$$

$$P_{B_P} = \left\{ \begin{array}{l} sees\ S_{K_C-1}\{\{TID, PY, CA\}_{K_P}\}, S_{K_M-1}\{TID\}, \{TID, AA, MA\}_{K_P}, \\ said\ S_{K_P-1}\{TID, Tr\}, \\ fresh\ TID, \\ prik_P\ K_P^{-1}, \\ ... \end{array} \right\}$$

For instance, the atom *said TIDR* in view B_C represents C sending $TIDR$ to M (Message 1 of the Lu and Smolka protocol). The atomic propositions of the other views can be defined similarly. Since each view αB_i (with $i = C, M, P$) models the (beliefs about the) behavior of principal i, the set of atomic propositions will be that of view B_i (see [5]).

Semantics. To understand the semantics of the family of languages $\{\mathcal{L}_\alpha\}_{\alpha \in B^*}$ (hereafter we drop the subscript), we need to understand two key facts. On the one hand the semantics of formulae depend on the view. For instance, the formula p in the view B_i expresses the fact that i believes that p is true. The same formula in the view B_j expresses the fact that j believes that p is true. As a consequence, the semantics associates *locally* to each view α a set of pairs $\langle m, s \rangle$, where: $m = \langle S, J, R, L \rangle$ is a CTL structure, with S a set of states, $J \subseteq S$ the set of *initial states*, R the transition relation, and $L : S \to \mathcal{P}(P)$ the *labeling function*; and s is a *reachable state* of m (a state s of a CTL structure is said to be reachable if there is a path leading from an initial state of the CTL structure to state s). On the other hand there are formulae in different views which have the same intended meaning. For instance $B_j p$ in view B_i, and p in view $B_i B_j$ both mean that i believes that j believes that p is true. This implies that only certain interpretations of different views are *compatible* with each other, and these are those which agree on the truth values of the formulae with the same intended meaning. To capture this notion of compatibility we introduce the notion of chain.

Definition 1 (Chain). *Let α be any view, a α-chain c is a finite sequence $\langle c_\epsilon, ..., c_\beta, ..., c_\alpha \rangle$, where $c_\beta = \langle m, s \rangle$ is an interpretation for $\mathcal{L}_\beta$ and β is a prefix of α (i.e., $\alpha = \beta\gamma$ for some index $\gamma \in B^*$). A compatibility relation C on $\{\mathcal{L}_\alpha\}$ is a set of α-chains, for every α.*

Intuitively, C will contain all those c's whose elements c_α, c_β (where α, β are two views in B^*) assign the same truth values to the formulae with the same intended meaning.

Example 3. Figure 4 shows some possible chains of the MATL structure for the Lu and Smolka protocol. The boxes in each view represent interpretations of the language associated with the corresponding view. The figure shows an interpretation for view ϵ, two interpretations for view B_M and two interpretations for view $B_M B_P$. Links connecting boxes in different views represent $B_M B_P$-chains. Figure 4 shows three $B_M B_P$-chains, $c = \langle c_\epsilon, c_{B_M}, c_{B_M B_P} \rangle$, $c' = \langle c'_\epsilon, c'_{B_M}, c'_{B_M B_P} \rangle$ and $c'' = \langle c''_\epsilon, c''_{B_M}, c''_{B_M B_P} \rangle$, where $c_\epsilon = c'_\epsilon = c''_\epsilon$, $c'_{B_M} = c''_{B_M}$ and $c_{B_M B_P} = c'_{B_M B_P}$. Let us assume that each interpretation satisfies the formula written close to it in figure. Therefore, the interpretation labeled c_{B_M} satisfies the formula $B_P said\ X$. The intended meaning of this formula in view B_M is that M

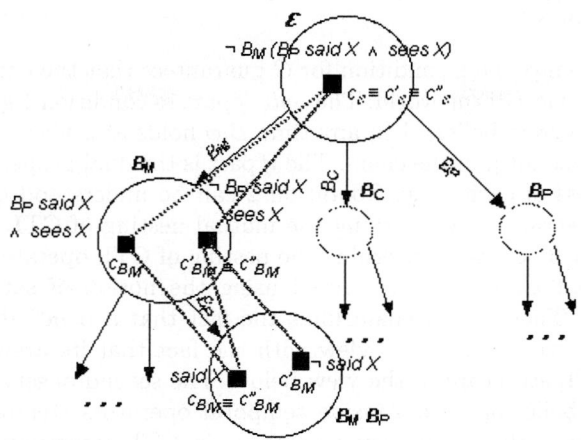

Fig. 4. Some chains of the Lu and Smolka protocol

believes that P believes it has sent message X to M. The formula *said* X in view $B_M B_P$ has the same intended meaning, as $B_M B_P$ models the beliefs of P seen from (the beliefs of) M. Therefore any $B_M B_P$–chain passing through the interpretation c'_{B_M} must reach an interpretation in $B_M B_P$ which satisfies the argument *said* X, as shown in the figure.

Let us now define the notion of satisfiability. We start with satisfiability local to views (first step) and suppose that for each view α there is a satisfiability relation between CTL structures and formulae of $\mathcal{L}_\alpha$. With an abuse of notation, we denote all these satisfiability relations with the same symbol $\models$. The context always makes clear which relation we mean. The second step is to define (global) satisfiability taking into account chains. To do this we need some further notation. Let $\models$ denote satisfiability also on chains. For any α–chain c and for any formula in $\mathcal{L}_\beta$, satisfiability relation $\models$ is defined only when either α is a prefix of β or β is a prefix of α. (i.e., when either $\alpha = \beta\gamma$ or $\beta = \alpha\gamma$). If $\alpha = \beta\gamma$ then $c_\beta \models \phi$ iff ϕ is true in c_β. If $\beta = \alpha\gamma$ then $c_\beta \models \phi$ for any ϕ. In other words, if a chain stops at a given level (e.g. α), then it satisfies every formula of the views (e.g., $\alpha\gamma$) which are below that level in the tree. Let us extend the satisfiability relation to sets of formulae: $x \models Y$ if and only if for any $y \in Y$, $x \models y$.

We are now ready to define the notion of model for MATL (called MATL structure), and then that of satisfiability between MATL structures and formulae of a view.

Definition 2 (MATL structure). *A nonempty compatibility relation C for a family of MATL languages on $\{P_\alpha\}$ is a MATL structure on $\{P_\alpha\}$ if for any $\alpha\beta$–chain $c \in C$,*

1. $c_\alpha \models B_i\phi$ *iff for every $\alpha\gamma$–chain $c' \in C$, $c'_\alpha = c_\alpha$ implies $c'_{\alpha B_i} \models \phi$;*

2. if $c_\alpha = \langle m, s \rangle$, then for any state s' of m, there is a $\alpha\beta$-chain $c' \in C$ such that $c'_\alpha = \langle m, s' \rangle$.

Briefly: the nonemptyness condition for C guarantees that the external observer has a consistent view of the world. The *only if* part in condition 1 guarantees that each view has correct beliefs, i.e., any time $B_i\phi$ holds at a view then ϕ holds in the view one level down in the chain. The *if* part is the dual property and ensures the completeness of each view. Condition 2 can be understood on the basis of two crucial observations, concerning the mutual nesting of CTL operators and belief operators. The first, concerning the nesting of CTL operators inside belief operators is that $c_\alpha \models \phi$ is computed using the notion of satisfiability in a CTL structure. Therefore, a chain links the fact that a belief atom holds in a state of a CTL structure in one view with the fact that its argument holds in a state of a CTL structure in the view below. The second observation concerns the nesting of belief operators inside temporal operators (temporal operators which involve no belief atoms are treated as in CTL structures, i.e., without jumping among views). Consider for instance the formula $\text{EX } B_i p$. To assess the truth of $\text{EX } B_i p$ we need to be able to assess the truth of $B_i p$ in some (reachable) next state s' (the CTL operator EX) of the CTL structure we are considering, e.g., $\langle\langle S, J, R, L\rangle, s\rangle$. The only way to establish this is to request that in s' we have a chain c' which gives access to a CTL structure in the view below. Given the fact that chains connect CTL structures only for what holds in their (reachable) states, the only solution is to request that s' is the state component of the structure $c'_\epsilon = \langle\langle S, J, R, L\rangle, s'\rangle$ with $c' \in C$. Given the fact that temporal operators allow us to state facts about all the states in a CTL structure, this operation must be repeated for each state $s \in S$. But this is exactly what Item 2 of Definition 2 says.

Example 4. Consider again Figure 4. The formula $\neg B_M (B_P \text{said } X \wedge \text{sees } X)$ is satisfied by the interpretation in view ϵ. By Item 1 of Definition 2 (only if direction), there must be a chain starting from the interpretation in view ϵ whose component for view B_M does not satisfy the argument of the belief, i.e., $B_P \text{said } X \wedge \text{sees } X$. This is indeed the case for both c' and c'', as $c'_{B_M} = c''_{B_M}$ and both of them do not satisfy $B_P \text{said } X$. This is due to the fact that there exists a chain whose component for view $B_M B_P$ does not satisfy the argument of the belief, i.e., $\text{said } X$. This is indeed the case for c' as $c'_{B_M B_P}$ does not satisfy $\text{said } X$. Assume now that c is the only chain passing through interpretation c_{B_M}. The component for view $B_M B_P$ of chain c passing through that interpretation, i.e., $c_{B_M B_P}$, satisfies the argument $\text{said } X$. Thus, by Item 1 of Definition 2 (if direction), c_{B_M} must satisfy $B_P \text{said } X$, as shown in Figure 4.

Given a MATL structure C, a formula ϕ and a view α, $C \models \alpha : \phi$ is read as ϕ is true in C (or equivalently, ϕ holds in C, or ϕ is satisfied by C) at view α, and it is defined as follows:

$$C \models \alpha : \phi \text{ iff for all } c \in C \text{ s.t. } c_\alpha = \langle\langle S, J, R, L\rangle, s\rangle \text{ and } s \in J, \; c_\alpha \models \phi \quad (1)$$

The intuition is that in order to check the satisfiability of ϕ at the view α we need to check all the interpretations of $\mathcal{L}_\alpha$ allowed by the compatibility imposed by the chains we are considering.

For any set of labeled formulae Γ, let Γ_α denote the set $\{\phi \mid \alpha : \phi \in \Gamma\}$.

Definition 3 (MATL Logical consequence). *A set of labeled formulae Γ logically entails $\alpha : \phi$, in symbols $\Gamma \models \alpha : \phi$, if for every MATL structure C and every $\alpha\beta$–chain $c \in C$, if for every γ prefix of α, $c_\gamma \models \Gamma_\gamma$ then $c_\alpha \models \phi$. A labeled formula is valid if it is a logical consequence of the empty set.*

Notice that MATL structures define a logic where each B_i has the same strength as a modal operator in the multimodal logic $K(m)$, where m is the number of principals.

Axioms. MATL is expressive enough to be used as a logic of authentication. Furthermore, it has a temporal component that usually is not present in the other logics of authentication (e.g., see [1,8,18]). In order to show how the properties of security protocols can be expressed within MATL, we shall now impose some constraints to the models in order to capture the intended behavior of a protocol. These constraints can be formalized with a set of sound axioms. This is similar to what happens with several logics of authentications (see for example [1,18]). Indeed MATL encompasses such logics. Here, for the sake of readability, we show how it is possible to translate in MATL some of the most significant axioms that has been proposed in most logics of authentication.

As a first example, let us consider the *message meaning* axioms. Usually, such axioms correspond to the following schema:

$$shk_{P,Q}K \land P\ sees\{X\}_K \to Q\ said\ X$$

Intuitively, it means that when a principal P receives a (fragment of) message encrypted with K, and K is a key shared by P and Q, then it is possible to conclude that the message comes from Q. The above axiom schema can be formulated in MATL as follows:

$$P : shk_{P,Q}K \land sees\{X\}_K \to B_Q said X \tag{2}$$

where with $P : Ax$ we also emphasize which view (P) the axiom Ax belongs to. Message meaning is often used with the *nonce verification*, that has the following schema:

$$Q\ said\ X \land fresh(X) \to Q\ says\ X$$

This schema expresses that when a principal Q has sent X (i.e., $Q\ said\ X$) recently (i.e., $fresh(X)$), then we can assert that $Q\ says\ X$. In MATL, this becomes

$$P : B_Q said X \land fresh(X) \to B_Q says X \tag{3}$$

As a consequence, it is important to establish whether a fragment of message is fresh. The following axioms help on this task:

$$fresh(X_i) \to fresh(X_1, \ldots, X_n)$$
$$fresh(X) \to fresh(\{X\}_K)$$

Intuitively, they mean that when a fragment is fresh, then the message that contains such a fragment (the encryption of the fragment) is fresh as well. In MATL, they can be inserted in the appropriate views without modification. Another important set of axioms establishes how a message can be decomposed. For instance, in [1] we have the following schemata:

$$P\ sees(X_1 \ldots X_n) \rightarrow P\ sees\ X_i$$
$$P\ sees\ \{X\}_K \wedge P\ has\ K \rightarrow P\ sees\ X$$

For instance, the intuitive meaning of the second schema is that a principal can decrypt a message encrypted with a given key when it knows such a key. Once again, in MATL the above axiom schemata can be inserted in a view without modification.

4 MATL as a Logic for Payment Protocols

In this section we discuss the main differences between our logic and previous logics of authentication. We especially take into account those differences which arise when the focus is on payment protocols. For what concerns atomic propositions, we introduce atoms of the form $rec\ X$ and $send_P\ X$ (where X can be a full message of a given protocol but not a fragment of message) that represent the communicative act of receiving X and sending X to P, respectively. This allows us to take into account the temporal aspects of a protocol. Indeed, such propositions represent when a principal actually receives or sends a message during a session. Therefore, we are able to recognize when such events occur by looking at the sequence of states. This is different from the notion of what are the fragments of messages that a principal has (atom *sees*) or uses when composing its messages (atom *said*). Furthermore, the atom *sees* represents both the notion of *possessing* (what a principal has because it is initially available or newly generated) and *seeing* (what has been obtained from a message sent by another principal). Notice that, for instance, Abadi and Tuttle [1] make for keys a different choice. Indeed, when they have a key K, they distinguish the proposition $P\ sees\ K$ by $P\ has\ K$. In our opinion this difference does not make much sense, as in their logic a principal happens to have all the keys it sees (e.g., see [18] where the authors introduce the axiom schema: $P\ sees\ K \leftrightarrow P\ has\ K$). The above facts have the following consequences in the corresponding axiom system. The following axiom schemata relate sent (received) messages to what a principal says (sees).

$$P : send_Q X \rightarrow said\ X \qquad (4)$$
$$P : rec\ X \rightarrow sees\ X \qquad (5)$$

The next axiom schemata capture the idea that a principal sees what it previously said or what it says.

$$P : said\ X \rightarrow sees\ X \qquad (6)$$
$$P : says\ X \rightarrow sees\ X \qquad (7)$$

The following schema represents the fact that a principal can compose a new message starting from the (fragment of) messages it already sees.

$$P : sees\ X_1 \land \ldots \land sees\ X_n \rightarrow sees(X_1 \ldots X_n) \tag{8}$$

For what concerns payment protocols, we have to take into account hash functions and signatures, as well. First of all, we assume a signature as a reliable schema without considering how such a schema is[1]. This allows us to focus on whether the protocol is trustworthy. This is similar to what is usually assumed for encryption algorithms in such a kind of verification. The corresponding axiom schemata are the following:

$$P : fresh(X) \rightarrow fresh(H(X)) \tag{9}$$
$$P : fresh(X) \rightarrow fresh(S_{K_Q^{-1}}\{X\}) \tag{10}$$
$$P : sees\ X \rightarrow sees\ H(X) \tag{11}$$
$$P : sees\ X \land sees\ K_P^{-1} \land prik_P\ K_P^{-1} \rightarrow sees\ S_{K_P^{-1}}\{X\} \tag{12}$$
$$P : sees\ X \land sees\ K_Q \land pubk_Q\ K_Q \rightarrow sees\ \{X\}_{K_Q} \tag{13}$$

where Q and P can be both substituted with the same principal or with different ones. The above schemata are the obvious extension to hash functions and signatures of the axioms about the freshness and the capability of composing messages.

The following axiom schema represents the capability of extracting the original message from its signed version when the principal has the corresponding public key.

$$P : sees\ S_{K_Q^{-1}}\{X\} \land sees\ K_Q \rightarrow sees\ X \tag{14}$$

The next schema corresponds to the *message meaning* axiom schema for signed messages.

$$P : sees\ S_{K_Q^{-1}}\{X\} \land pubk_Q\ K_Q \rightarrow B_Q saidX \tag{15}$$

Intuitively, it means that when a principal sees a message signed with the key of Q, then it believes that Q said such a message.

5 Specifications for Payment Protocol

Payment protocols are intended to protect business transactions, therefore they must achieve various security requirements. In literature, there's no common agreement about this issue. There are indeed different definitions of security requirements for payment protocols. In this work, we follow the taxonomy introduced in [2], where requirements are classified with respect to the security needs of each actor involved in an electronic payment. Indeed, [2] proposes a number of requirements expected by the customer, by the merchant, and by the payment gateway. When we formalize security requirements with MATL, it is

---
[1] The most common schema is the following: $S_{K_Q^{-1}}\{X\} = (X, H(X)_{K_Q^{-1}})$

indeed quite natural to state a specification for a principal as a formula in the view of the principal itself.

CUSTOMER REQUIREMENTS
Proof of Transaction Authorization by Payment Gateway. The customer must have a proof that the payment gateway authorized the transaction.

Example 5. In the case of the Lu and Smolka protocol, the above requirement can be written as follows:

$$C : \mathsf{AG}\,(\mathit{sees}\ \mathit{Tr} \to B_P \mathit{says}\ \mathit{Tr}) \tag{16}$$

Intuitively, it asserts that in the view of the customer C, in every future state, if C receives Tr, then C must believe that P has recently sent this information.

Receipt from Merchant. The customer must have a proof that the merchant who has made the offer has received payment and promised to deliver the good/service.

Example 6. For the Lu and Smolka protocol, such a requirement becomes:

$$C : \mathsf{AG}\,(\mathit{sees}\ \mathit{Tr} \to B_M \mathit{says}\ \mathit{Tr}) \tag{17}$$

This means that, in the view of C, in every future state, if C receives the gateway answer Tr, then it must believe that the merchant M has recently sent it (remember that in the Lu-Smolka protocol the answer is forwarded to the customer by the merchant).

MERCHANT REQUIREMENTS
Proof of Transaction Authorization by Payment Gateway. The merchant needs an unforgeable proof that the payment gateway has authorized the payment.

Example 7. For the Lu and Smolka protocol, we have

$$M : \mathsf{AG}\,(\mathit{sees}\ S_{K_P^{-1}}\{TID, Tr\} \to B_P \mathit{says}\ Tr) \tag{18}$$

Intuitively, this formula means that in the view of M, in every future state, if the merchant M receives $S_{K_P^{-1}}\{TID, Tr\}$, then it must believe that the gateway P has recently sent Tr.

Proof of Transaction Authorization by Customer. The merchant needs an unforgeable proof that the customer has authorized the payment before that the merchant receives the transaction authorization from the payment gateway.

Example 8. For the Lu and Smolka protocol, such a requirement becomes:

$$M : \mathsf{A}\,((B_C \mathit{says}\ PA)\ \mathcal{B} \tag{19}$$
$$(\mathit{send}_P\ S_{K_C^{-1}}\{\{TID, PY, CA\}_{K_p}\}, S_{K_M^{-1}}\{TID\}, \{TID, AA, MA\}_{K_p}))$$

Intuitively[2], the specification above asserts that the merchant M must believe that, in every future path, the customer C will have recently sent PA before the merchant M sends the *Authorization & Capture Request* message (message 3 of the protocol).

---
[2] $\mathsf{A}\,(p\ \mathcal{B}\ q)$ means that in every future path, p will be true before q holds.

Confidentiality of Customer Sensitive Information. The customer desires privacy of information related to its account.

Example 9. In order to formalize the fact that the merchant must not know the Customer Account (in particular its Credit Card Number) in the Lu and Smolka protocol, we write:
$$M : \mathsf{AG}\,(\neg sees\ CA) \qquad (20)$$

The above formula states that in the view of the merchant M, in every future state, M never sees the *Customer Account*.

PAYMENT GATEWAY REQUIREMENTS

Proof of Transaction Authorization by Customer. When the payment gateway debits a certain amount to the customer, the payment gateway must have an unforgeable proof that the customer has authorized this payment.

Example 10. For the Lu-Smolka protocol, such a requirement becomes:
$$P : \mathsf{AG}\,(sees\ S_{K_P^{-1}}\{TID, Tr\} \rightarrow B_C says\ PY) \qquad (21)$$

This formula asserts that in the view of the gateway P, in every future state, if P receives $S_{K_P^{-1}}\{TID, Tr\}$ then it must believe that the customer C has recently sent PY.

Proof of Transaction Authorization by Merchant. When the payment gateway authorizes a payment to a certain merchant, the payment gateway must have an unforgeable proof that this merchant has required that this payment must be made to him.

Example 11. For the Lu-Smolka protocol, we have:
$$P : \mathsf{AG}\,(sees\ S_{K_P^{-1}}\{TID, Tr\} \rightarrow B_M says\ AA) \qquad (22)$$

This formula asserts that in the view of the gateway P, in every future state, if P receives $S_{K_P^{-1}}\{TID, Tr\}$ then it must believe that the merchant M has recently sent AA.

6 Verification of the Lu and Smolka Protocol

The verification of the Lu and Smolka protocol with NuMAS requires to model each view as a finite state machine, to specify the security requirements in the appropriate views (see Section 5), and to check the specifications by means of the model checker. Modeling a view amounts at establishing what are the propositional atoms and the beliefs of the a view, and how they vary over time. The temporal evolution of the propositional atoms $send_P\ X$ and $rec\ X$ can be derived directly from the protocol description. The behavior of the other atoms derives from the axioms described in Section 3. The reader can refer to [4,5] for a description of how the views can be modeled in NuMAS and to [3] for a description of the symbolic model checking algorithm for MATL. Here we report

Table 1. The verification of the Lu and Smolka protocol

View	Specification	Result
C	(16)	False
C	(17)	True
M	(18)	False
M	(19)	True
M	(20)	True
P	(21)	False
P	(22)	False

the results of the verification (that required 0.3 sec. on a PC equipped with a Pentium III and 512 MB RAM). The results are summarized in Table 1. Notice that some expected security requirements concerning *transaction authorizations* are not satisfied. This means that the protocol suffers from weaknesses which make it vulnerable to attacks by dishonest entities. Indeed, following we describe a possible attack reported in [17] (see Figure 5). We write $X \to I(Y) : m$ when the dishonest entity intercepts a message m in transit from X to Y, preventing it from being received; we write $I(X) \to Y : m$ when the dishonest entity sends a message m to Y, impersonating X. The attack proceeds as follows. A

(α.1) $C \to I : TIDR$
 (β.1) $I(C) \to M : TIDR$
 (β.2) $M \to I(C) : S_{K_M^{-1}}\{TID\}$
(α.2) $I \to C : S_{K_I^{-1}}\{TID\}$
(α.3) $C \to I : S_{K_C^{-1}}\{TID\}, \{TID, PA\}_{K_i}, S_{K_C^{-1}}\{\{TID, PY, CA\}_{K_p}\}$
 (β.3) $I(C) \to M : S_{K_C^{-1}}\{TID\}, \{TID, PA\}_{K_m}, S_{K_C^{-1}}\{\{TID, PY, CA\}_{K_p}\}$
 (β.4) $M \to P : S_{K_C^{-1}}\{\{TID, PY, CA\}_{K_p}\}, S_{K_M^{-1}}\{TID\}, \{TID, AA, MA\}_{K_p}$
 (β.5) $P \to M : S_{K_P^{-1}}\{TID, Tr\}$
 (β.6) $M \to I(C) : S_{K_P^{-1}}\{TID, Tr\}$

Fig. 5. An attack on the protocol Lu-Smolka protocol

dishonest merchant I waits for a buyer C to start a session α with it. At this point, I opens a parallel session β, impersonating the client C towards another merchant M. The TID provided by M in step (β.2) is sent by I to C as the transaction identifier of session α. In this way I obtains a message having the two components with the TID signed by C in step (α.3). By means of these signed fragments, I can send the message in step (β.3) to M, masquerading as C. After receiving the above message, in step (β.4), M requires the payment authorization to the gateway P. For this purpose, it sends a message with the same fake $S_{K_C^{-1}}\{\{TID, PY, CA\}_{K_p}\}$ it received in the previous step. Notice that M blindly forwards this fragment, since it is encrypted with P's public key.

The gateway is unable to detect the cheat and thus authorizes the payment in favor of M, sending the message in step (β.5). Finally, M forwards the received message to C, but I intercepts and removes it, so that C has no suspects of the fraud. In this way, the session β ends, allowing I to masquerade as C towards M. As a consequence of the above attack on a commercial transaction, a dishonest buyer I succeeds in debiting to another buyer C a purchase that C in fact has never performed. Moreover, if the good is delivered via Internet (e.g., the content of a web-page) or I has altered the shipping address in the (often insecure) phase before the invocation of the protocol, I is able to obtain that good without paying it. As a final remark, notice that when M receives the message in step (3), it is not able to deduce the identity of the intended receiver. This problem has implications on the non-repudiation requirement, and exists in the original version of SET as well [19]. However, in SET, the presence of the merchant identifier in message (4) allows the gateway P to deduce the real identity of the intended merchant and, thus, to avoid the above fraud. This is however not true of the Lu and Smolka protocol, where Specification (21) is not satisfied and the attack in Figure 5 can occur.

7 Conclusions

In this paper we have described MATL, a logic of belief and time that can be used for the verification of payment protocols as well as other kinds of security protocols. The verification is fulfilled by means of NuMAS, a symbolic model checker based on MATL. This kind of verification has been applied to the Lu and Smolka protocol, a variant of SET. Even if this protocol was considered secure, we have discovered that the protocol does not satisfy some important requirements as the proof of transaction authorization. This kind of verification has been applied to SSL 3.0 and 3KP as well. For these protocols, all the security requirements are satisfied. Such verifications require few seconds with a normally equipped PC. For lack of space, in this paper we have described only the verification of the Lu and Smolka protocol.

Acknowledgments

We would like to thank Fausto Giunchiglia for his support to the present research. We also owe a lot to all the past and current members of the Information Systems Group at the Istituto di Informatica – University of Ancona. In particular, we would like to mention Johann Dimarti, Loïc Jay, and Luca Roganti who participated to the verification of the protocol described in this paper.

References

1. M. Abadi and M. Tuttle. A semantics for a logic of authentication. In *Proceedings of the 10th Annual ACM Symposium on Principles of Distributed Computing*, pages 201–216, 1991.

2. M. Bellare, J. A. Garay, R. Hauser, A. Herzberg, H. Krawczyk, M. Steiner, G. Tsudik, and M. Waidner. iKP-a family of secure electronic payment protocols. In *Proc. of the First USENIX Workshop of Electronic Commerce*, Berkeley, CA, USA, 1995. USENIX Assoc.
3. M. Benerecetti and A. Cimatti. Symbolic Model Checking for Multi–Agent Systems. In *CLIMA-2001, Workshop on Computational Logic in Multi-Agent Systems*, Paphos, Cyprus, December 1st 2001. Co-located with ICLP'01.
4. M. Benerecetti and F. Giunchiglia. Model checking security protocols using a logic of belief. In *Proc. of the 6th International Conference on Tools and Algorithms for the Construction and Analysis of Systems (TACAS 2000)*, Berlin, Germany, March 27th - April 1st 2000.
5. M. Benerecetti, F. Giunchiglia, M. Panti, and L. Spalazzi. A Logic of Belief and a Model Checking Algorithm for Security Protocols. In *Proc. of IFIP TC6/WG6.1 International Conference FORTE/ PSTV 2000*, Dordrecht, The Netherlands, 2000. Kluwer Academic Publisher.
6. M. Benerecetti, F. Giunchiglia, and L. Serafini. Model Checking Multiagent Systems. *Journal of Logic and Computation*, 8(3):401–423, June 1998.
7. D. Bolignano. Towards the Formal Verification of Electronic Commerce Protocols. In *Proceedings of 10th Computer Security Foundations Workshop*, pages 133–146, 1997.
8. Michael Burrows, Martin Abadi, and Roger Needham. A logic of authentication. *ACM Transactions on Computer Systems*, 8(1):18–36, February 1990.
9. A. Cimatti, E. Clarke, F. Giunchiglia, and M. Roveri. NuSMV: a new Symbolic Model Verifier. In *Proceedings of the International Conference on Computer-Aided Verification (CAV'99)*, Trento, Italy, July 1999.
10. E. Clarke, O. Grumberg, and D. Long. Model Checking. In *Proc. of the International Summer School on Deductive Program Design*, Marktoberdorf, Germany, 1994.
11. E. Clarke, S. Jha, and W. Marrero. A machine checkable logic of knowledge for specifying security properties of electronic commerce protocols. In *Proc. of the Workshop on Formal Methods and Security Protocols*, 1998.
12. E. A. Emerson. Temporal and Modal Logic. In J. van Leeuwen, editor, *Handbook of Theoretical Computer Science*, volume B, pages 996–1072, Amsterdam, The Netherland, 1990. Elsevier Science Publishers.
13. N. Heintze, J. D. Tygar, J. Wing, and H. C. Wong. Model Checking Electronic Commerce Protocols. In *Proc. of the 2nd USENIX Workshop on Electronic Commerce*, 1996.
14. R. W. Lichota, G. L. Hammonds, and S. H. Brackin. Verifying Cryptographic Protocols for Electronic Commerce. In *Proc. of the 2nd USENIX Workshop on Electronic Commerce*, pages 53–65, 1996.
15. S. Lu and S. A. Smolka. Model Checking the Secure Electronic Transaction (SET) Protocol. In *Proceedings of 7th International Symposium on Modeling, Analysis and Simulation of Computer and Telecommunication Systems*, pages 358–365. IEEE Computer Society, 1999.
16. Mastercard and Visa. *SET Secure Electronic Transaction Specification*. Mastercard & Visa, May 1997. Available at http://www.setco.org.
17. M. Panti, L. Spalazzi, and S. Tacconi. Verification of Security Properties in Electronic Payment Protocols. In *IFIP WG 1.7 Workshop on Issues in the Theory of Security (WITS '02)*, Portland, Oregon, January 2002. Co-located with POPL'02.

18. P. Syverson and P. C. van Oorschot. On Unifying Some Cryptographic Protocol Logics. In *Proceedings of the IEEE Symposium on Research in Security and Privacy*, pages 14–28, Oakland, CA, May 1994. IEEE Computer Society Press.
19. E. Van Herreweghen. Non-repudiation in SET: Open Issues. In *Proceedings of the 4th Conference on Financial Cryptography*, 2000.

SNet: A Modeling and Simulation Environment for Agent Networks Based on i* and ConGolog

Günter Gans[1], Gerhard Lakemeyer[1], Matthias Jarke[1,2], and Thomas Vits[1]

[1] RWTH Aachen, Informatik V
Ahornstr.55, 52056 Aachen, Germany
[2] Fraunhofer FIT
Schloss Birlinghoven, 53754 Sankt Augustin, Germany
{gans,lakemeyer,jarke}@cs.rwth-aachen.de

Abstract. SNet is a prototype environment supporting the representation and dynamic evaluation of designs for social networks comprising human, hardware, and software agents. The environment employs metadata management technology to integrate an extended version of the i* formalism for static network modeling with the ConGolog logic-based activity simulator. The paper defines the formal mappings necessary to achieve the integration and describes an operational prototype demonstration. SNet's intended application domain is requirements management and mediation support for inter-organizational and embedded process systems, as well as simulation support for inter-organizational studies e.g. in hightech entrepreneurship networks.

1 Introduction

The modeling of business processes has been an important aspect of information systems engineering for many years. In this research, a progress from pure drawing facilities towards a more formal semantics can be observed. This formal understanding enables consistency and completeness analysis of models as well as their semi-automatic transformation.

A further step in this progression is the modeling and simulation of dynamic business aspects. For many well-known business process formalisms, such as the event-process chains of the ARIS modeling formalism [Sch94], timed Petri nets ([OSS94], meanwhile commercialized by PROMATIS AG for the Oracle Designer environment), or simply automata-based mechanisms [PJ96], simulation environments have been developed from which the impact of different business strategies on operational efficiency and, in some cases, organizational memory and similar long-term factors can be assessed.

The modeling of dynamic inter-organizational relationships, especially for complex social networks involving many human, organizational, and possibly technological agents, is in a much less mature stage. While extensions of traditional business models do cover some important aspects of modern business concepts such as supply chain management, they often ignore the autonomy of the members within network settings, thus underestimating the independent evaluation of different agent goals, modulated by the strategic interdependences among them, and the resulting complex dynamics of negotiation and trust-based (or distrust based) activity. In this paper, we report on SNet, a modeling and simulation environment for agent networks that attempts to remedy some of these shortcomings.

The social networks we have in mind are in particular those created among independent organizations or individuals to pursue some shared strategic goals, but always at the risk of falling apart. To formalize such networks the agent-oriented requirements modeling language i* [Yu95] seems particularly suited since it explicitly allows one to capture the mutual dependencies among actors, which are key ingredients of such networks. However, representing the structural relationships among actors alone is not sufficient. As was argued in [GJK+01a], it is equally important to model the network dynamics because the interactions among the actors are to a large extent trust-based, and to understand the impact of trust one needs to consider interactions and their effects over time. To do so, the authors propose a multi-perspective modeling approach which includes an extension of i*, speech acts, and the action language ConGolog. While it was suggested already then to translate i* into executable ConGolog programs (see also [GJK+01b]), the mapping was preliminary and only partially developed. In this paper we consider a complete and automatic translation for a large fragment of extended i* models. Moreover, we report on a fully implemented prototype implementation. Having a system which takes as input graphical network representations based on (extended) i*, which can then be turned into executable programs, is valuable because it provides a tool for network participants to simulate various network scenarios whose outcome may give valuable information regarding the risks and benefits of taking certain actions.

The rest of the paper is organized as follows. In the next section we introduce i* and the extensions necessary to facilitate the translation into executable programs. In Section 3, we introduce ConGolog and present the translation from extended i* networks into ConGolog programs. In Section 4 we briefly go over the implemented system. Finally, we end with some conclusions and open issues.

2 Representing Social Networks in Extended i*

We begin this section by introducing the i* modeling language [Yu95], originally devised for early requirements engineering. i* is then extended to facilitate the automatic translation into executable programs. We also show that, by representing i* diagrams in the conceptual modeling language Telos [MBJK90], it becomes possible to perform a static analysis of a network or enforce integrity constraints with the help of the Telos query language.

2.1 The i* Modeling Language

i* is firmly based on the notions of *actor* and *goal* and assumes that social settings involve actors who depend on each other for goals to be achieved, tasks to be performed, and resources to be furnished. The framework includes the *strategic dependency (SD) model* for describing the network of relationships among actors, as well as the *strategic rationale (SR) model* for describing and supporting the reasoning that each actor performs concerning her relationships with other actors.

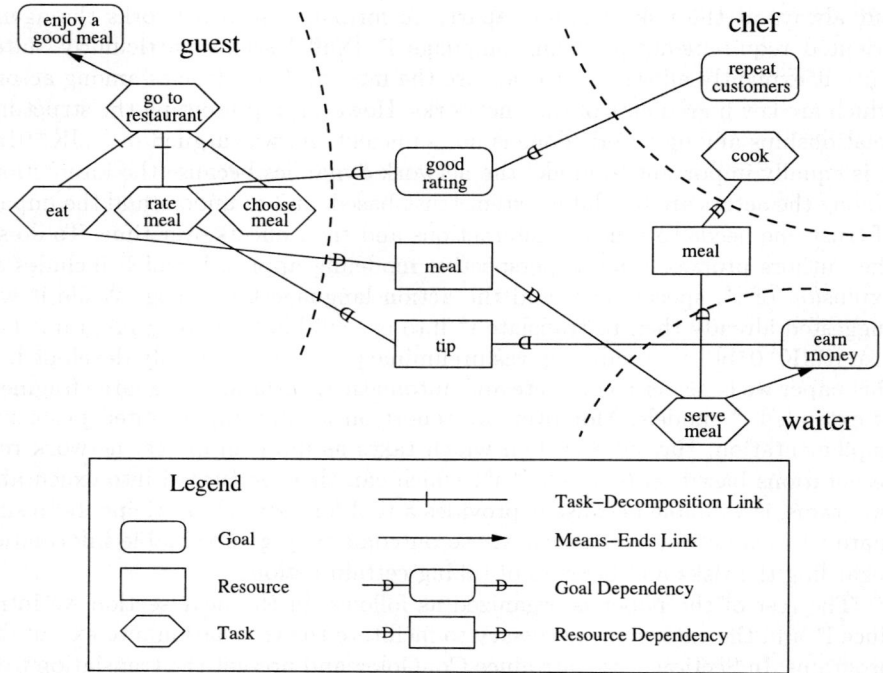

Fig. 1. Strategic rationale model of the "restaurant" example

We will not go over SD models here, but instead focus on SR models and illustrate some of their key features by way of a restaurant example shown in Figure 1 involving three actors: a *guest*, a *waiter*, and a *chef*.[1] The guest's main component is a *go_to_restaurant* task which serves to bring about the goal of enjoying a good meal and is decomposed into three subtasks. The guest depends on the waiter for the meal to be served. Conversely, to obtain a tip the waiter depends on the guest's favorable rating of the meal, which the chef also depends on in his goal to have repeat customers.

---

[1] While the example, which we use throughout the paper, is rather simple and the actors involved may not even share long-term strategic goals, it nevertheless serves to illustrate the main ingredients of our approach and has the advantage of being familiar to most readers.

2.2 Enriching Task Description

Our goal is to turn specifications of SR diagrams into agent programs ready for simulation. However, in their current form, i* models are not expressive enough for this purpose. For example, consider the decomposition of the *go_to_restaurant* task. Clearly, the subtasks need to be ordered, but the ordering is not determined by the model. In fact, in i* the semantics of this decomposition is left open. Here we interpret it as an *and-decomposition*, that is, all subtasks need to be performed, and we will give it a precise semantics in Section 3.2. Also, when tasks are decomposed, it is implicitly assumed that *all* subtasks are (eventually) performed. However, as we will see below in an example, there are cases where an or-decomposition is needed, that is, where only one of the subtasks should be performed. Finally, it is not clear at all when and how any of the tasks involved are actually activated.

To see how all this can be achieved, let us consider Figure 2, which enriches the task descriptions of Figure 1 in an appropriate way. From a syntactical point of view, the main new graphical feature are triangles. These are labeled with logical formulas whose predicates are so-called *fluents* whose truth value may vary during the execution of tasks. When a triangle points to a task like *trust_high_enough* pointing to *choose_meal*, then it serves as a *precondition*. When a task points to a triangle, then it denotes a *postcondition* or effect of that task, which in turn can be preconditions of other tasks.

Precondition triangles in bold face have a special meaning in that they serve as triggers or *interrupts* for the execution of the task they are pointing to. For example, *order_received* triggers the execution of *cook*. We require that only top-level tasks can have interrupts and that there can be at most one per task. Tasks without interrupts that trigger their execution are considered to be *exogenous*, like the *start* task in the example. Each graphical object has to be assigned to one actor. So, an exogenous task belongs to a special actor called *Exogenous*. Intuitively, these kinds of tasks are under external control and may be used, for example, to start a simulation run. Note that there may be more than one exogenous task present.

The decomposition of *rate_meal* is an example of an *or-decomposition*. In particular, we want to make sure that only one of *rate_good* or *rate_bad* is performed, not both. We will see in Section 3 that the semantics of or-decompositions is actually quite subtle.

Note that there are preconditions without any arrows directed to them. Where does, for example, the fluent *trust_high_enough* obtain its value from? The complete specification of this precondition refers to another fluent *confidence_guest* which, say, takes as value a positive real number and is initialized appropriately. It is then updated by the effects of *good_rating* and *bad_rating*, respectively. For example, when *good_rating* is activated, it raises the value of "guest-confidence" by some small amount.[2]

---

[2] We have not included these details in the diagram to avoid clutter. In the implementation discussed in Section 4, these details are usually also hidden, but can be made visible on demand (see Figure 3).

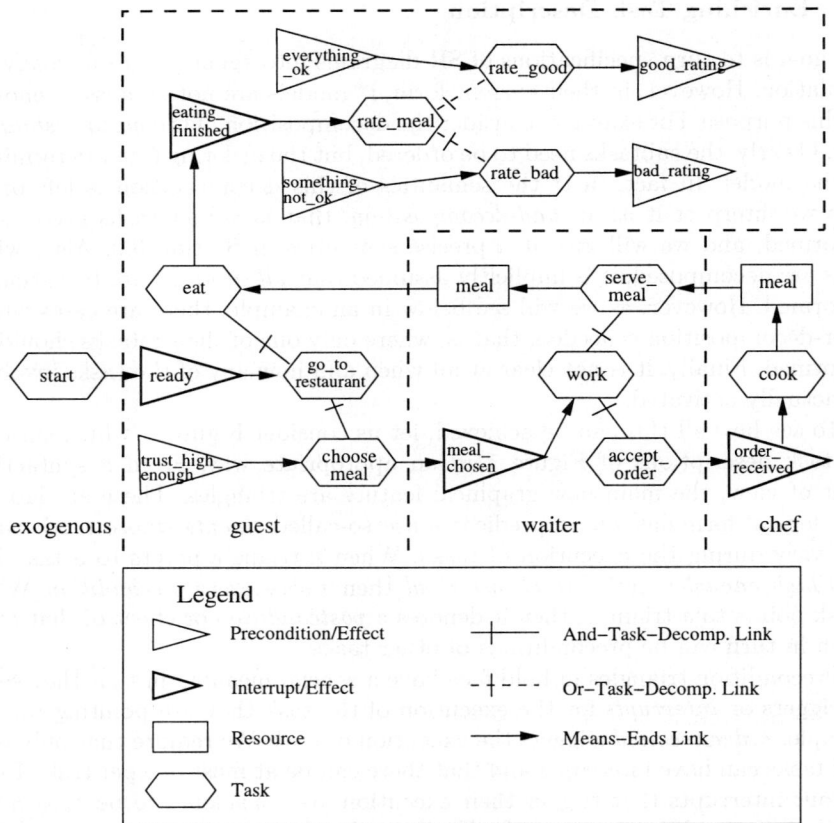

Fig. 2. Extended strategic rationale model of the "restaurant" example

Finally, note that the synchronization of tasks via pre- and postconditions gives rise to dependencies among actors in an implicit fashion. For example, the chef can only cook a meal after an order was accepted by the waiter, thus expressing a natural dependency between the waiter and the chef.

To summarize, the new features introduced into SR models are preconditions, postconditions, interrupts as a special kind of preconditions, and or-decompositions.

2.3 Static Analysis in ConceptBase

We use the *ConceptBase* metadata manager [JEG+95] based on the conceptual modeling language Telos [MBJK90] as the representation language of extended i* diagrams. This has the added benefit of providing us with a powerful query language which allows us to perform a static analysis of our networks. Syntactical checks are one application. For example it is useful to know whether there are network nodes with neither in- nor outgoing links, because isolated elements make no sense, which can be formulated as follows in the *ConceptBase Query Language*:

```
QueryClass elements_without_link isA SNetElement with
retrieved_attribute
   name: String
constraint
   rule: $not exists l/SNetLink (l from this) or (l to this)$
end
```

Another example describes that it is not allowed for subtasks to be a decomposition of more than one supertask. If there are tasks with more than one in-going task-decomposition-link (tdl) they will be found by the following query:

```
QueryClass subTask_with_n_tdls isA SNetTaskElement with
constraint
   rule: $exists tdl1,tdl2/SNetTaskDecompLink
          (tdl1 to this) and (tdl2 to this) and (not (tdl1==tdl2))$
end
```

As we will see in Section 3.2, queries to ConceptBase also play an important role to supply the relevant information for the translation from extended i* diagrams into ConGolog programs.

3 Simulation of Social Networks

3.1 ConGolog – A Short Introduction

In our methodology, plans are expressed in the logic-based language ConGolog. This section describes both ConGolog and its formal foundation, the situation calculus.

The *situation calculus* is an increasingly popular language for representing and reasoning about the preconditions and effects of actions [McC63]. It is a variant of first-order logic[3], enriched with special function and predicate symbols to describe and reason about dynamic domains. We will not go over the language in detail except to note the following features: all terms in the language are one of three sorts, ordinary objects, actions or situations; there is a special constant S_0 used to denote the *initial situation*, namely that situation in which no actions have yet occurred; there is a distinguished binary function symbol do where $do(a, s)$ denotes the successor situation to s resulting from performing the action a; relations whose truth values vary from situation to situation are called *relational fluents*, and are denoted by predicate symbols taking a situation term as their last argument; similarly, functions varying across situations are called *functional fluents* and are denoted analogously; finally, there is a special predicate $Poss(a, s)$ used to state that action a is executable in situation s.

---

[3] Strictly speaking, a small dose of second-order logic is required as well, an issue which should not concern us here.

Within this language, we can formulate theories which describe how the world changes as the result of the available actions. One possibility is a *basic action theory* of the following form [LPR98]:

- Axioms describing the initial situation, S_0.
- Action precondition axioms, one for each primitive action a, characterizing $Poss(a, s)$. For example, the fact that a robot can only pick up an object if it is next to the object and it is not holding anything can be formalized as follows: $Poss(pickup(r, x), s) \equiv NextTo(r, x, s) \wedge \forall y. \neg Holding(r, y, s)$.
  We use the convention that free variables are implicitly universally quantified.
- Successor state axioms, one for each fluent F, stating under what conditions $F(x, do(a, s))$ holds as a function of what holds in situation s. These take the place of the so-called effect axioms, but also provide a solution to the frame problem [Reiter 1991]. As an example, consider a simple model of time which progresses in a discrete fashion by 1 unit as a result of a special action *clocktick*. The time of a situation can then be specified with the help of a fluent $time(s)$ and the following successor state axiom:

$$time(do(a, s)) = t \equiv a = clocktick \wedge t = time(s) + 1$$
$$\vee a \neq clocktick \wedge t = time(s)$$

- Domain closure and unique-name axioms for actions.

ConGolog [dGLL00], an extension of Golog [LRL$^+$97], is a language for specifying complex actions (high-level plans). It comes equipped with an interpreter which maps these plans into sequences of atomic actions assuming a description of the initial state of the world, action precondition axioms and successor state axioms for each fluent. Complex actions are defined using control structures familiar from conventional programming languages such as sequence, while-loops, and recursive procedures, but also non-deterministic actions like choosing non-deterministically between two actions or performing an action an arbitrary number of times. In addition, parallel actions with or without priorities are possible as well.

α	primitive action
$\phi?$	test action
$[\sigma_1, \sigma_2]$	sequence
if ϕ then σ_1 else σ_2	conditional
while ϕ do σ	loop
$or(\sigma_1, \sigma_2)$	nondeterministic choice of actions
$pi(x, \sigma)$	nondeterministic choice of arguments
$star(\sigma)$	nondeterministic iteration
$conc(\sigma_1, \sigma_2)$	concurrent execution
$pconc(\sigma_1, \sigma_2)$	prioritized concurrent execution
$tryAll(\sigma_1, \sigma_2)$	concurrent execution until one terminates
$interrupt(\phi, \sigma)$	interrupts
$proc(\beta(\vec{x}), \sigma)$	procedure definition

When translating extended i* into ConGolog, the most important constructs are *conc*, *pconc*, *tryAll*, and *interrupt*. While the intuitive meaning of *conc* is the obvious, *pconc* says that σ_1 should be preferred over σ_2 whenever possible. *tryAll*[4] means that both programs σ_1 and σ_2 start executing concurrently, but the whole *tryAll*-construct terminates as soon as one of the two terminates. This is in contrast to *conc* and *pconc*, where both parts need to terminate. As we will see later, *tryAll* is needed to give semantics to the or-decomposition of subtasks in i*. Finally, $interrupt(\phi, \sigma)$ says that σ should be executed whenever the condition ϕ becomes true. In other words, interrupts serve as triggers to initiate actions.

We will not go over the formal semantics of ConGolog here except to note that it uses a conventional transition semantics defining single steps of computation and where concurrency is interpreted as an interleaving of primitive actions and test actions. For details see [dGLL00, GL00].

3.2 Transformation of Extended i* into Executable Programs

In this section we show how to automatically translate a large fragment of extended SR models, which includes all the new features added in Section 2.2, into executable ConGolog specifications. We will get back to the parts of SR models that are not dealt with at the end of this section.

The translation needs to specify two parts, the description of the application domain and the complex tasks operating on this domain. For the application domain we need to describe the fluents and primitive actions together with their preconditions and effects. Complex tasks correspond to ConGolog procedure definitions. Each fluent, primitive action, and procedure is also assigned a unique actor to which it belongs.

In what follows we use the Prolog syntax of the IndiGolog interpreter used for our implementation. IndiGolog [dGL99] is a variant of ConGolog developed for *on-line* execution, where the choice of the next primitive action alternates with its execution.[5]

Generating the Application Domain Description

To describe the application domain we use clauses (in the sense of Prolog) of the form prim_fluent(F), prim_action(a), and exog_action(e) for primitive fluents, primitive actions, and exogenous actions, respectively. The clauses initially(F,true) and poss(a,ϕ) are needed to initialize a fluent's value in situation S_0 resp. to define an action precondition axiom. A convenient feature of IndiGolog is that it suffices to declare the effects of actions, which are then

---

[4] We remark that the *tryAll*-construct was not present in the original ConGolog, but was later added in [GL00].
[5] IndiGolog can also be used in an off-line modus, where a whole action sequence is computed before execution. The on-line modus, however, seems more appropriate for simulation purposes.

automatically converted into successor state axioms introduced in Section 3.1. Effect axioms have the form `causes_val(a,F,newVal,cond)` with the reading that after performing an action `a`, the fluent `F` will obtain the new value `newVal`, if the condition `cond` holds.

Besides fluents which are explicitly specified in the extended SR model like *meal_chosen* or *confidence_guest*, interrupts and resources are also represented as relational fluents. The former are used to trigger the corresponding ConGolog interrupts inside procedures (see below). The latter are needed to describe the owner of a resource, who, unlike other components of the model, may change over time. In the restaurant example the *meal*'s owner initially obtains the default value "notexist." After the chef performs *cook* he owns the *meal*-resource. The waiter can only perform *serve_meal* if this resource is owned by the chef in that situation. Thus, in a sense, resources are formally treated like special task preconditions. There is one system-defined fluent *time* which keeps track of time and whose meaning is given by the successor state axiom in Section 3.1. Finally, initial values of fluents are generated from corresponding annotations in the SR model (see below for an example).

The primitive actions are generated by extracting the names of all tasks that are neither decomposed further nor an exogenous task. For example, *choose_meal* is considered a primitive action, while *go_to_restaurant* is not. There is one system-defined primitive action *clocktick* which advances time and which is executed with lowest priority.

A `poss(a,`ϕ`)`-clause for a primitive action `a` is generated by collecting the corresponding preconditions in the SR model and then computing the appropriate ϕ. For example, the task *rate_good* will not be performed unless the precondition *everything_ok* holds. Also, *everything_ok* held and *rate_good* has been performed, the *rate_bad* or-branch will be pruned, because or-decomposition applies the *tryAll*-construct (see above).

Exogenous actions are special primitive actions that are controlled by the user. In our model, an action is exogenous if it belongs to a special actor called "Exogenous." During a simulation, the user is able to invoke exogenous actions interactively. Because they are regarded as primitive, the corresponding task in the SR model may not be decomposed further. In our example, the task *start* is the only exogenous action and does the obvious. In general, exogenous tasks are not restricted to initiating simulation runs. For example, we could replace the *rate_meal* task by an exogenous *rate_meal_exog* task, which would give the user the chance to influence the meal-rating process from the outside.

How a fluent is affected by actions is determined in one of four ways: 1) it can be read off explicitly from the postconditions of tasks corresponding to primitive actions, as in *meal_chosen*, which is satisfied by the action *choose_meal*; 2) interrupt-fluents like *meal_chosen* are automatically reset at the end of the task they are pointing to; 3) resource-fluents are affected by changes in ownership; 4) the special fluent *time* is only affected by the action *clocktick*. In any case, appropriate `causes_val`-clauses are generated.

Here is an excerpt of the definitions generated for the restaurant example.

```
initially(confidence_guest, 0.5).
prim_action(choose_meal).
prim_fluent(meal_chosen).
prim_fluent(confidence_guest).
poss(choose_meal,confidence_guest > 0.45).
causes_val(rate_good,confidence_guest,X,X is confidence_guest+0.1).
causes_val(choose_meal , meal_chosen, true, true).
causes_val(work, meal_chosen, false, true).
```

Note that these clauses are generated completely automatically from the SR model. Since the SR model is stored in ConceptBase, we can easily collect the relevant information for clause generation by posing appropriate queries. For example, in order to define fluents for all interrupts in the model, we would use the following query:

```
QueryClass fluents isA SNetInterruptElement with
   retrieved_attribute
      name : String
end
```

Given the result of the query, it is then a simple matter to emit the right prim_fluent-definitions.

Generating Procedural Descriptions

For the generation of procedures from complex tasks, we only need a subset of the IndiGolog instructions, namely sequential and (prioritized) concurrent execution of actions ([A,B] resp. conc(A,B)) (pconc(A,B)), as well as control of actions by (prioritized) interrupts (interrupt(condition,body) resp. prioritized_interrupts(list_of_interr.)). The latter is an abbreviation of the prioritized concurrent execution of interrupts, where precedence in the list means higher priority.

For each actor in our model we need a procedure that describes its behavior. In particular, all interrupts and their following actions form the body of the procedures. Additionally, we need a start-procedure which both concurrently starts the procedures of all involved agents and provides other services for our simulation. (Again, the relevant information can be extracted automatically using ConceptBase queries.):

```
proc(agent_guest,
     conc(interrupt(eating_finished=true, decomp_rate_meal),
          interrupt(ready=true, decomp_go_to_restaurant))).
proc(agent_chef,
     interrupt(order_received=true, cook)).
proc(agent_waiter,
     interrupt(meal_chosen=true, decomp_work)).
proc(start_sim,
     prioritized_interrupts([interrupt(sim_running=true,
```

```
pconc(conc(conc(agent_guest,agent_chef),agent_waiter),
      interrupt(true,noOp))),
      interrupt(sim_running=false, noOp)])).
```

While primitive actions like *cook* are used directly, decomposed tasks like *go_to_restaurant* lead to auxiliary procedures which initiate the execution of the corresponding subtasks in a concurrent fashion. In other words, our interpretation of and-decomposition is that all subtasks are started concurrently and they all need to terminate successfully for the supertask to terminate. In the case of the and-decomposed task *work*, we obtain

```
proc(decomp_work,[conc(accept_order, serve_meal), work]).
```

Note that each procedure `decomp_[taskname]` ends with a primitive action `[taskname]`, which is used for things like switching off the interrupt or performing other direct effects of the task.

As for or-decompositions, recall that the intuition is that the termination of one of the subtasks should lead to the termination of the whole task. At first glance, one might be tempted to use the $or(\sigma_1,\sigma_2)$-construct provided by ConGolog, which nondeterministically chooses one of the σ_i for execution. However, this is problematic for on-line execution. After all, the interpreter needs to commit right away to one of the choices, but it may not have enough information to make the right choice. This is why we need the $tryAll(\sigma_1,\sigma_2)$-construct first proposed in [GL00], which starts executing both σ_1 and σ_2 concurrently and stops as soon as one of them reaches a final state. In the restaurant example, *rate_meal* is or-decomposed and the translation results in:

```
proc(decomp_rate_meal,[tryAll([rate_bad , rate_meal],
                              [rate_good, rate_meal])]).
```

This ends the description of the translation from extended SR diagrams into IndiGolog. Note that, since the mapping is completely automatic and since IndiGolog has a precise declarative semantics, we have also given extended SR models a precise meaning. The only caveat is that we have not yet considered all features of i*. *Goals* and *subgoals*, perhaps the most notable omissions, will be dealt with in the near future.[6] *Soft-goals* and *positive* resp. *negative contribution links* are more problematic because they are introduced as vague concepts, and it is not clear at all how to formally represent them.

4 SNet: A Software Environment for Modeling, Analysis, and Simulation of Social Networks

Extended i* diagrams are composed using a modification of the editor OME3 (Object Modeling Environment) [LY]. While OME3 was developed for the original i*, we extended it to cover the new features like preconditions and or-decompositions of tasks.

---

[6] If a task satisfies a goal, one idea would be to insert a test action corresponding to the goal as the final action of the procedure representing the task.

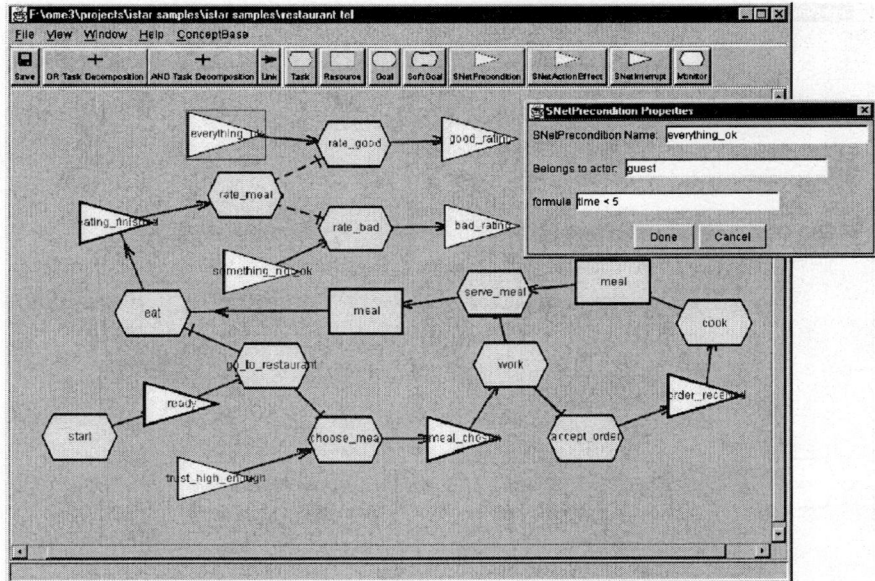

Fig. 3. OME(Object Modeling Environment)

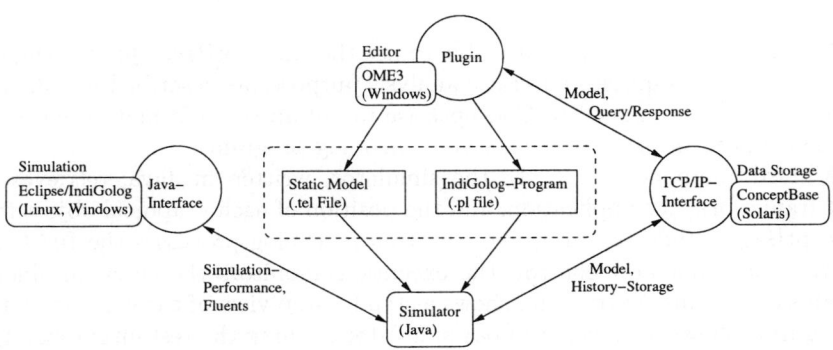

Fig. 4. SNet Software Architecture

In addition, we have attached Java plugins to OME3 to maintain a connection to a ConceptBase server (see below), initiate the static analysis of extended i* diagrams, and to perform the translation process to ConGolog programs. An OME-snapshot is shown in Figure 3.

In the context of static analysis in 2.3 we mentioned that we use *Concept-Base*, a deductive object manager for meta databases (for details see [JEG+95]). The role of ConceptBase will become clearer if we have a look at our implementation's architecture (Figure 4). By establishing a TCP/IP connection we are able to transfer the SNet framework as well as the current application model

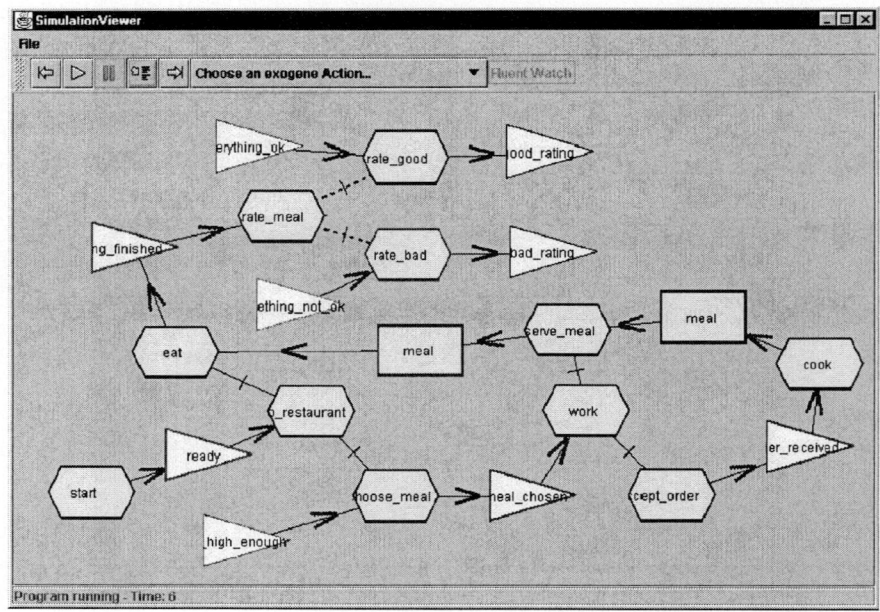

Fig. 5. SNet Simulator[7]

to ConceptBase. This way we are able to use the ConceptBase Query Language to perform certain queries for static analysis purposes as described in 2.3. Also, suitable queries are issued to ConceptBase to obtain the information necessary for the translation process to generate ConGolog programs.

A third component (Fig. 4), the simulator, written in Java, retrieves the SNet framework, the application, and the position of each graphical object from ConceptBase. While the interpreter written in Prolog processes the IndiGolog program, the simulator controls the execution, monitors the changing fluents, initiates exogenous actions, and shows a step by step view of the simulation run.

Figure 5 shows a snapshot of our simulator running the restaurant example. The user creates specific simulation runs by exogenous actions. Preconditions that hold are depicted with a green border, otherwise they have red borders. In the snapshot *something_not_ok* holds, which leads to the task *rate_bad* being performed. As a consequence the precondition *trust_high_enough* gets a red border. The red-bordered resource *meal* illustrates that the guest is it's owner.

5 Related Work

Lespérance et al. [LKMY99] are the first to demonstrate that ConGolog can be applied to model and simulate business processes. Similar in spirit to our work,

---

[7] For those labels in the screenshot which are not legible the reader is referred to Figure 2 instead, which shows the same network, only hand-drawn.

Wang and Lespérance [WL01] also propose to integrate i* and ConGolog, but in a way quite different from ours. Roughly, while we introduce a small number of new node and link types like task preconditions and or-decomposition into the graphical representation of SR models, they annotate the original SR diagrams with ConGolog constructs like while-loops, sequential task decompositions, and the like. While this allows very fine-grained control-flow specifications at the i*-level, it comes at the expense of burdening the user with choosing among the various control alternatives. Also, while we strive for automatic translations from extended i* into ConGolog, they still need considerable user interaction. Fuxman et al. [FPMT01] also start with i* and enrich it with constraints formalized in a linear time logic inspired by the KAOS language [DvLF93].

They then use model checking techniques [CCGRar] to verify the consistency of the specification. Models are presented by listing which fluents are true at certain time points and hence can be thought of as a form of simulation. However, the main motivation for model checking is finding counterexamples, that is, bugs in the specification. Our system, on the other hand, is mainly intended for the simulation of different scenarios for consistent specifications. Hence, the two approaches seem to complement each other well, an issue we want to explore further in the future.

6 Conclusions

In this paper we proposed a framework for modeling and simulating the complex interactions found in social networks. A graphical language based on Yu's i* is introduced for the specification of the network and the internal structure of the agents involved. The models are stored in the ConceptBase system, whose query language can be used for the static analysis of the models. These are then automatically translated into executable ConGolog programs and the prototype implementation provides a graphical interface to visualize simulation runs.

This work was originally motivated by our desire to understand and model the role of trust and distrust in social networks [GJK+01a]. Now that we have an implemented modeling and simulation environment, we are in a position to test existing theories about how trust and distrust evolve over time. Doing so will require collecting data from extensive simulation runs and storing the history of interactions in a suitable form. Storing the history in ConceptBase will have the advantage of making it accessible not only to the user for analysis but also to the agents in the network who can use it for further decision making.

Another important issue is to test our modeling and simulation environment on real data. One such application scenario is our ongoing case study in trans-Atlantic entrepreneurship networks. Using such a realistic application will likely lead to refinements and extensions of our methodology.

Acknowledgment

This work was supported in part by the Deutsche Forschungsgemeinschaft in its Focussed Research Programme on Socionics.

References

[CCGRar] A. Cimatti, E. Clarke, F. Giunchiglia, and M. Roveri. NuSMV: a new symbolic model checker. *Int. Journal on Software Tools for Technology Transfer (STTT)*, To appear.

[dGL99] G. de Giacomo and H. J. Levesque. An incremental interpreter for high-level programs with sensing. *Logical Foundations for Cognitive Agents*, pages 86–102, 1999.

[dGLL00] G. de Giacomo, Y. Lespérance, and H. J. Levesque. ConGolog, a concurrent programming language based on the situation calculus. *Artificial Intelligence*, 121(1-2):109–169, 2000.

[DvLF93] A. Dardenne, A. van Lamsweerde, and S. Fickas. Goal-directed requirements acquisition. *Science of Computer Programming*, 20(1-2):3–50, 1993.

[FPMT01] A. Fuxman, M. Pistore, J. Mylopoulos, and P. Traverso. Model checking early requirements specifications in tropos. In *Proceedings Fifth IEEE International Symposium on Requirements Engineering (RE01), Toronto, Canada*, August 27-31 2001.

[GJK+01a] G. Gans, M. Jarke, S. Kethers, G. Lakemeyer, L. Ellrich, C. Funken, and M. Meister. Requirements modeling for organization networks: A (dis)trust-based approach. In *Proceedings of the 5th IEEE International Symposium on Requirements Engineering (RE01)*, pages 154–163, Toronto, Canada, August 2001. Los Alamitos: IEEE Computer Society Press 2001, ISBN 0-7695-1125-2.

[GJK+01b] G. Gans, M. Jarke, S. Kethers, G. Lakemeyer, L. Ellrich, C. Funken, and M. Meister. Towards (dis)trust-based simulations of agent networks. In *Proceedings of the 4th Workshop on Deception, Fraud, and Trust in Agent Societies*, pages 49–60, Montreal, May 2001.

[GL00] H. Grosskreutz and G. Lakemeyer. Towards more realistic logic-based robot controllers. In *Proc. of AAAI-00*, 2000.

[JEG+95] Matthias Jarke, Stefan Eherer, Rainer Gallersdörfer, Manfred A. Jeusfeld, and Martin Staudt. ConceptBase - a deductive object base for meta data management. *Journal of Intelligent Information Systems, Special Issue on Advances in Deductive Object-Oriented Databases*, 4(2):167–192, 1995.

[LKMY99] Y. Lespérance, T. G. Kelley, J. Mylopoulos, and E. Yu. Modeling dynamic domains with congolog. In *Proceedings of CAiSE-99*, June 1999.

[LPR98] Hector Levesque, Fiora Pirri, and Ray Reiter. Foundations for the situation calculus. *Linköping Electronic Articles in Computer and Information Science*, 3(18), 1998.

[LRL+97] H. J. Levesque, R. Reiter, Y. Lespérance, F. Lin, and R. Scherl. Golog: A logic programming language for dynamic domains. *Journal of Logic Programming*, 31(1):59–84, 1997.

[LY] L. Liu and E. Yu. OME (Object Modeling Environment), http://www.cs.toronto.edu/km/ome/.

[MBJK90] J. Mylopoulos, A. Borgida, M. Jarke, and M. Koubarakis. Telos - representing knowledge about information systems. *ACM Transactions on Information Systems*, 8(4):325–362, October 1990.

[McC63] John McCarthy. Situations, actions and causal laws. Technical report, Stanford University, 1963. Reprinted 1968 in Minsky, M.(ed.): Semantic Information Processing, MIT Press.

[OSS94] A. Oberweis, G. Scherrer, and W. Stucky. INCOME/STAR: Methodology and tools for the development of distributed information systems. *Information Systems*, 19(8):643–660, 1994.

[PJ96] P. Peters and M. Jarke. Simulating the impact of information flows on networked organizations. In *Proceedings of the 17th International Conference on Information Systems, Cleveland, Ohio, USA*, pages 421–439, Dezember 1996.

[Sch94] A.-W. Scheer. *Business Process Engineering - Reference Models for Industrial Companies*. Springer Verlag, Berlin, 2 edition, 1994.

[WL01] Xiyun Wang and Yves Lespérance. Agent-oriented requirements engineering using ConGolog and i*. In *Working Notes of the Agent-Oriented Information Systems (AOIS-2001) Workshop, Montreal, QC*, May 2001.

[Yu95] E. Yu. *Modelling Strategic Relationships for Process Reengineering*. PhD thesis, University of Toronto, 1995.

Usage–Centric Adaptation of Dynamic E–Catalogs

Hye-young Paik, Boualem Benatallah, and Rachid Hamadi

School of Computer Science and Engineering, The University of New South Wales
Sydney, NSW, 2052, Australia
{hpaik,boualem,rhamadi}@cse.unsw.edu.au

Abstract. Although research into the integration of e-catalogs has gained considerable momentum over the years, the needs for building adaptive catalogs have been largely ignored. Catalogs are designed by system designers who have a priori expectations for how catalogs will be explored by users. It is necessary to consider how users are using catalogs since they may have different expectations. In this paper, we describe the design and the implementation of a system through which integrated product catalogs are continuously adapted and restructured within a dynamic environment. The adaptation of integrated catalogs is based on the observation of customers' interaction patterns.

1 Introduction

In recent years, integration of e–catalogs has gained considerable momentum because of the emergence of online shopping portals, increasing demand for information exchange between trading partners, prevalent mergers and acquisitions, etc [10]. In approaches that address the problem of e–catalogs organisation and integration, a product catalog is usually structured in a category–based hierarchy [10,7]. Catalogs are designed in a "one–view–fits–all" fashion, by a system designer who has a priori expectations for how catalogs will be "explored" by customers. However, the customers may have different expectations. Therefore, it is necessary to take into consideration how the customers are using the catalogs to continuously minimise the gap between expectations of the system designer and customers. For example, in a catalog for computer parts, assume that it is repeatedly observed that many users always use product category RAM right after using category CPU. If the administrator merges the two categories and creates a new category CPU&RAM, users now only need to visit this new category once for information of both products.

In this paper, we describe the design and the implementation of a system, called $WebCatalog^{Pers}$, through which existing online product catalogs can be integrated and the resulting integrated catalogs can be continuously adapted and restructured within a dynamic environment. The catalogs integration framework used in this paper originates from a previous project on integration of Web data, called $WebFINDIT$ [4]. Based on this framework, we propose a usage–centric technique for transforming catalogs organisation. It should be noted that the focus of this paper is not on catalogs integration. The objective is to *continuously* improve the organisation of catalogs by being responsive to the ways customers navigate them in searching for products. The proposed approach offers the following features: (i) *Catalog navigation and access model* – this model provides a set of actions, called catalog interaction actions, that users would perform while accessing catalogs, (ii) *Catalog transformation operations* – these operations are used to transform the structure and organisation of catalogs, and (iii) *Predefined sequences of catalog interaction actions* – these sequences represent pre–identified interaction patterns of users. They can be considered as heuristics for catalog transformations. Discovery of these patterns help administrators decide what kind of transformations would be desirable to improve the organisation of catalogs. Transformations of a catalog over time, result in offering improved alternative of its organisation based on user interaction patterns.

The remainder of this paper is organised as follows. Section 2 overviews the design of $WebCatalog^{Pers}$. Section 3 presents a formal model for integrated catalogs and user interaction actions. The catalog reorganisation operations, predefined interaction sequences (PISs), and the confidence of a PIS are introduced in Sect.4, Sect.5, and Sect.6 respectively. Section 7 presents the results of simulation studies. Finally, Sect. 8 discusses related work and concludes the paper.

2 $WebCatalog^{Pers}$: Design Overview

In this section, we give the intuition behind the main concepts that are used in $WebCatalog^{Pers}$, namely, catalog communities and eCatalogs–Net. The formalisation of these concepts will be presented in the next section.

2.1 Catalog Communities

A catalog community[1] is a container of catalogs which offer products of a common domain (e.g., community of Laptops). It provides a description of desired products without referring to actual sellers (e.g., a seller of IBM Laptops). We illustrate catalog communities with *computers and related services* domain (see Fig.1).

There are two types of relationships defined between catalog communities: *SubCommunity–Of* and *PeerCommunity–Of*. SubCommunity–Of relationships represent *specialisation* between domains of two catalog communities (e.g., Printer is a sub–community of Peripherals). We assume that, each catalog community has at most one super–community. PeerCommunity–Of relationships are viewed as a referral mechanism in that when the user can not find (or is not satisfied with) information from a catalog community, s/he can refer to other communities that the catalog community consider as its peers (e.g., community Display is a peer community of VideoCard). It should be noted that,

---
[1] We use the terms *catalog community* and *community* interchangeably.

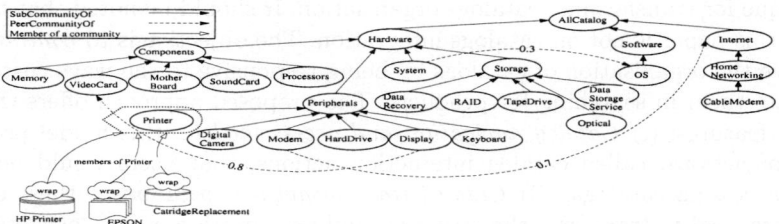

Fig. 1. eCatalogs–Net: Organising catalog communities

we do not assume that the opposite (i.e., `VideoCard` is a peer community of `Display`) systematically holds. A weight (a real value between 0 and 1) is attached to each PeerCommunity–Of relationship to represent the degree of relevancy as a peer. Note that communities can also forward queries to each other via PeerCommunity–Of relationship. We call this organisation of catalog communities *eCatalogs–Net*. Any catalog community that is not a sub–community of any other community is related to `AllCatalog` via SubCommunity–Of relationship.

Each catalog community has a set of attributes that can be used to query the underlying catalogs. We refer to the set of attributes as *community product attributes*. For example, catalog community that represents "CD-Readers and Writers" would have community product attributes such as `Maker`, `Read-WriteSpeed`, `Price`, etc.

2.2 Catalog Registration

In order to be accessible through a community, product sellers need to register their catalogs with the community. A catalog provider is known to a community by providing (i) a wrapper, (ii) an exported interface, and (iii) a mapping between exported interface and community product attributes. The wrapper translates $WebCatalog^{Pers}$ queries to local queries, and output of the local queries are translated back to the format used by $WebCatalog^{Pers}$. The exported interface defines the local product attributes for querying information at the local catalog. A local catalog supplier also should provide operations, such as ordering or payment for the products. However, the focus of this paper is not on specifying transactional operations. Detailed description on provisioning such operations in the context of Web services is presented in [1]. Users may use a community to express queries that require extracting and combining product attributes from multiple underlying product catalogs (e.g., price comparison). We refer to this type of queries as *global queries*. Global querying is achieved by using community product attributes which do not directly correspond to product attributes. Therefore, when a product catalog is registered with a community, the catalog provider should also define mapping between local product attributes and community attributes. We call this mapping *Source–Community mapping*. Note that a community can be registered with another community. By doing so, the members of the first community also become members of the second community.

2.3 Searching and Querying Product Information

Users in $WebCatalog^{Pers}$ will typically be engaged in two–step information–seeking activity: (i) navigating communities for product catalogs location and semantic exploration (e.g., get communities that are relevant to selling laptops) and (ii) querying selected communities or catalogs for products information (e.g., compare product prices). Users would have a specific task to achieve (e.g., product items they wish to purchase, a category of products they want to investigate) when using product catalogs. We assume that they use the following strategy[2]:

1. Start at the root (i.e., AllCatalog), or at a specific community (if they know the location of the catalog community).
2. While (current community C is not the target community T) do
   (a) If any of the SubCommunity–Of relationships of C seems likely to lead to T, follow the relationship that appears most likely to lead to T.
   (b) Else, if any of the PeerCommunity–Of relationships of C seems likely to lead to T, follow the relationship that appears most likely to lead to T.
   (c) Else, either backtrack and follow SuperCommunity–Of relationship of C, or give up.

Once the user has reached the target, s/he will submit a query to the target. If the user ends up in the same community again in step 2(a) or 2(b), s/he will follow a different relationship, since her/his reasoning of which relationship is likely to lead to the target has changed by then.

3 Modelling Catalog Communities and User Interaction

In this section, we present a model for formally representing communities, eCatalogs–Net, and consistency of eCatalogs–Net. The model also identifies a set of actions that users can perform when interacting with the eCatalogs–Net. The proposed model forms the basis for defining catalog restructuring operations and user interaction patterns (see Sect. 4 and Sect. 5).

3.1 eCatalogs–Net

We give the definition of a community first and then eCatalogs–Net.

Definition 1 (Catalog Community). *A catalog community C is a tuple* C = (NameC, GeneralInfo, CommunityProductAttr, Members) *where:*

– NameC *is the name of the community* C,

---
[2] [13] uses a similar strategy for browsing and searching Web documents.

- GeneralInfo *is a set of pairs* (p, v), *where* p *is a property of the community and* v *is a value of* p *(e.g., (Domain, "CD Writers"))*,
- CommunityProductAttr *is a set of attribute-type pairs* (att, type), *where* att *is a community product attribute (i.e., a global attribute) and* type *is the type of* att *(e.g., ("ModelNumer", Integer))*,
- Members *is a set of members. A member can be either a product catalog or another catalog community and is defined as a pair* (mid, map) *where* mid *represents the identifier of the member and* map *contains the Source–Community mapping.* □

Definition 2 (eCatalogs–Net). *An eCatalogs–Net is a labelled directed graph* $G = (N, E_1, E_2, W, \ell)$, *where:*

- N *is a finite set of nodes. A single node represents a catalog community,*
- $E_1 \subseteq N \times N$ *is a finite set of directed edges (representing SubCommunity-Of),*
- $E_2 \subseteq N \times N$ *is a finite set of directed edges (representing PeerCommunity-Of),*
- $W : E_2 \rightarrow [0, 1]$ *is a weighting function (initially each edge in* E_2 *receives a neutral weight of 0.5), and*
- $\ell : N \rightarrow C$ *is a naming function where* C *is a set of catalog community names.* □

To be *consistent*, an eCatalogs–Net must satisfy the conditions given in the definition below:

Definition 3 (Consistent eCatalogs–Net). *The eCatalogs–Net* $G = (N, E_1, E_2, W, \ell)$ *is consistent if and only if the following conditions are satisfied:*

1. *The naming function ℓ is injective (that is, there will not be two communities with the same name),*
2. *The graph* $G_1' = (N, E_1^{-1}, \ell)$ *(generated from the sub-graph* $G_1 = (N, E_1, \ell)$ *of* G *by inverting the edges) is a tree. The root of the tree is* AllCatalog,
3. $E_2 \cap (E_1 \cup E_1^{-1})^+ = \varnothing$ *(where* E^+ *denotes the transitive closure of* E, *i.e.,* $(i, j) \in E^+$ *iff there is a directed path from* i *to* j *in* E*).* □

3.2 Permissible User Actions

The permissible actions, noted $\mathcal{A}$, for exploring eCatalogs–Net are listed in Table 1. By modelling user interaction actions, the system can capture them for future use.

Every time a user invokes one of the permissible actions at a catalog community, $WebCatalog^{Pers}$ keeps that event in the system log file. The log file is, later, organised into *sessions* and for each SubmitQuery action in a session, all of the product attributes selected by the query are identified. A session in $WebCatalog^{Pers}$ is an ordered sequence of actions performed by a single user, where the time difference between any two consecutive actions in the sequence should be within a time threshold, $T_{threshold}$ defined by an administrator.

Table 1. Permissible User Actions $\mathcal{A}$ in eCatalogs–Net

Action Name	Description
NavigateToSub(Community c)	The user goes from the current catalog community to one of its sub–communities c.
NavigateToSuper()	The user goes from the current catalog community to its super–community.
NavigateToPeer(Community c)	The user goes from the current catalog community to one of its peer communities c.
LeaveCatalogCommunity()	The user leaves the current catalog community. The user is taken to AllCatalog.
ShowMembers(Constraint s)	The user requests to show members of the current catalog community satisfying the constraint s.
SubmitQuery(Query q)	The user submits the query q to the current catalog community. It could be a global query which uses the community product attributes, or a source query which concerns one member of the community.

4 Restructuring eCatalogs–Net

We now describe a set of restructuring operations on eCatalogs–Net. These operations are used, for example, to change the relationships between catalog communities, remove a catalog community, or merge catalog communities. They can be performed at an administrator's own discretion. In the next section, we will introduce predefined interaction sequences which provide means to observe the user's interaction patterns. The observation will help decide which operation to perform in order to improve the organisation of the eCatalogs–Net.

An operation is applied to a consistent eCatalogs–Net $G = (N, E_1, E_2, W, \ell)$ and produces a consistent eCatalogs–Net $G' = (N', E_1', E_2', W', \ell')$. For space reasons, we do not give detailed description of each operation. We only describe operations for merging and splitting catalog communities. It should be noted that each high level operation is defined as a sequence of primitive operations. The primitive and high level restructuring operations are summarised in Table 2.

Moving a Community. The operation moveCatComm() moves a community c from one place to another, by changing its super–community. This operation is used, e.g., when an administrator is convinced that the current super–community of c does not represent the domain of products in c properly. For example, in Fig.1, assume that the community HardDrive is sub–community of Peripherals and the user navigation behaviour shows that community Storage is more suitable super–community for HardDrive. This may suggest that it is beneficial to move HardDrive to Storage. When a community c is moved, all of its sub–communities are moved with it. Having this assumption creates less overhead,

Table 2. eCatalogs–Net Restructuring Operations

Primitive Operations
`setCatalogName(Community c, String n)` : Set the name of `c` to `n`.
`addPeer(Community` c_i`, Community` c_j`)`: Add PeerCommunity–Of from c_i to c_j.
`delPeer(Community` c_i`, Community` c_j`)`: Delete PeerCommunity–Of from c_i to c_j.
`updatePeer(Community` c_i`, Community` c_j`, Weight w)`: Update the weight of PeerCommunity–Of from c_i to c_j by `w`.
`addSub(Community` c_i`, Community` c_j`)`: Add SubCommunity–Of from c_i to c_j.
`delSub(Community` c_i`, Community` c_j`)`: Delete SubCommunity–Of from c_i to c_j.
`createCatComm(Name n, GeneralInfo gi, Members m, CommunityProductAttr gs)`: Create a new catalog community with the information given. `create-CatComm` must be followed by `addSub` operation.
`superCatComm(Community c)`: Return the super–catalog community of `c`.
`subCatComm(Community c)`: Return a set of catalog communities which directly have SubCommunity–Of relationship with `c` (direct sub–communities).
`indSubCatComm(Community c)`: Return a set of catalog communities which, directly or indirectly, have SubCommunity–Of with `c` (indirect subcommunities).
High Level Operations
`mergeCatComm(Community` c_i`, Community` c_j`, Name n)`: Merge two existing communities c_i and c_j and set the name of the new catalog community to `n`.
`splitCatComm(Community c, GeneralInfo gic, Name n, GeneralInfo gi, CommunityProductAttr cpa, Query q, setOfCommunities sub)`: Split catalog community `c` into two separate communities. `gic` contains new specification of `GeneralInfo` for `c`. `n`, `gi`, and `cpa` contain specification of the new community (`Name`, `GeneralInfo`, and `CommunityProductAttr` respectively). `q` is a query which will be used by the operation to select members to be moved from `c` to the new community. `sub` is a set of sub–communities to be moved to the new one.
`delCatComm(Community c)`: Remove the catalog community `c` from eCatalogs–Net. Used, for example, when a community becomes obsolete (e.g., has no useful existence inside the eCatalogs–Net).
`moveCatComm(Community` c_i`,Community` c_j`)`: Move c_i to new super–community c_j.

since sub–communities of c do not get affected by the change. The effects of this operation are described in Fig.2.

The community E is moved from its super–community B to the new super–community C. E's sub–communities, i.e., G and H remain as sub–communities of E. However, since a catalog community cannot be a peer of its super–community, the PeerCommunity–Of relationship from H to C has to be deleted.

Merging Communities. The operation `mergeCatComm()` merges two communities c and c' which have the same super–community[3]. It is used, e.g., when

---
[3] Note that, in this paper, we only consider merging of two communities, but the operation can be generalised to more than two communities.

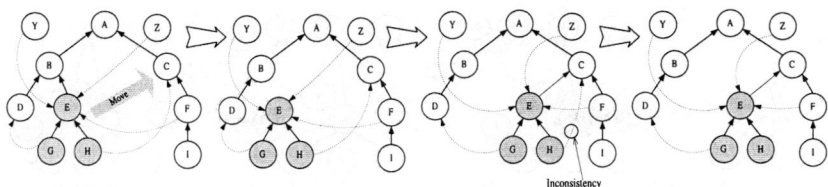

Fig. 2. Moving a catalog community

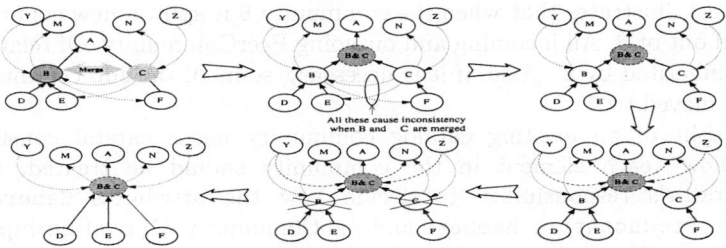

Fig. 3. Merging two catalog communities of the same super–community

it is observed that the two catalog communities c and c' are always accessed together. Hence, it is beneficial that these two catalog communities are merged, so that the majority of users do not have to visit two separate communities each time. Figure 3 illustrates the effects of mergeCatComm().

It shows that a new community is created from merging communities B and C. The super-community of the new community is the super-community of B and C (i.e., A). All sub–communities of B and C (i.e., D, F and G) are sub-communities of the new community. All PeerCommunity–Of relationships between B and C, as well as between B and all of C's sub–communities, C and B's sub-communities should be deleted to maintain the consistency of the eCatalogs–Net. Also, all PeerCommunity–Of relationships coming from other communities into B and C need to be updated, i.e, the PeerCommunity–Of relationships would refer to the name of the new community, instead of B and C.

Splitting a Community. The operation splitCatComm() splits an existing catalog community into two separate communities. This operation is used, e.g., when it is observed that the community represents a domain (described by community product attributes) which can be divided into smaller sub-domains. This situation is illustrated in Fig.4. Note that as a result of split, one new community is created out of an existing one. The definition of the existing community is updated to reflect this change (e.g., remove community product attributes, or members that have been moved to the new community).

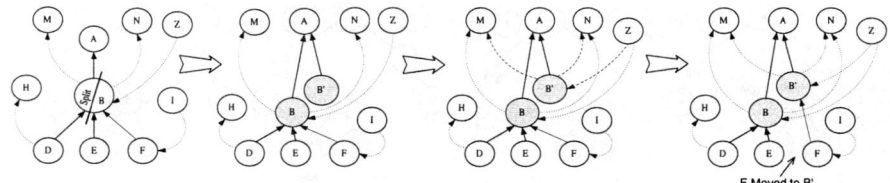

Fig. 4. Splitting a catalog community

Figure 4 illustrates that when the community B is split, a new community B' is created out of B. All incoming and outgoing PeerCommunity–Of relationships of B are inherited by B'. Also, if it is necessary, some of the sub communities of B can be moved to B'.

The split of an existing catalog community needs careful consideration about "how" each element in the community should be treated. It is an administrator's responsibility to decide how the attributes `GeneralInfo`, `CommunityProductAttr`, `Members` and SubCommunity–Of relationships should be initialised. This information is specified via the operation parameters (see Table 2).

5 Predefined Interaction Sequences

Predefined interaction sequences represent foreseeable user's interaction behaviour, therefore can be predefined. In our approach, we use these sequences of actions to help identify situations where the organisation of an eCatalogs–Net may be improved through restructuring operations. Any particular sequence of actions with prevalent occurrences should be recognised as a recurring user interaction pattern. Each interaction pattern identified suggests a restructuring operation. A *Predefined Interaction Sequence* (PIS) is formally defined as follows:

Definition 4 (Predefined Interaction Sequence (PIS)). *A predefined interaction sequence PIS of length n ($n > 0$) is a vector of ordered user actions* $PIS = \langle a_1, a_2, ..., a_n \rangle$ *where $a_i \in \mathcal{A}$ (see Table 1) ($i = 1, .., n$).* □

For a given PIS, there may exist a session s such that the exact order of actions in PIS can be found in s. A predefined interaction sequence is matched against each session in the processed log file to check whether the sequence exists in the session. We refer to the number of occurrences of a PIS in the log file as *Frequency* (see Sect. 6).

In the following subsections, we present a set of predefined interaction sequences. We describe some of the PISs in details. The rest are listed in Tables 3 and 4. We use the action `SubmitQuery` as the most appropriate action in indicating user's strong interests in a community. However, an administrator may decide to choose other actions (or define new ones, e.g., PurchaseItem) for the same purpose.

Table 3. Other Predefined Interaction Sequences

Predefined Interaction Sequences
Deleting a community : Identify a community from which users are constantly leaving without performing any further action. $PIS_{delComm} = \langle\, a(c_i, c_j), \texttt{LeaveCatalogCommunity}(c_j)\rangle$, where $c_i, c_j \in N$, $(c_i, c_j) \in E_1 \cup E_1^{-1}$, and $a \in \{\texttt{NavigateToSub}, \texttt{NavigateToSuper}\}$.
Merging communities (Case 1): Identify two sub–communities of the same super–community which are always accessed together (not via PeerCommunity–Of). $PIS_{merge1} = \langle\, \texttt{SubmitQuery}(c_i, q_1), \texttt{NavigateToSuper}(c_i, c_k), \texttt{NavigateToSub}(c_k, c_j),$ $\texttt{SubmitQuery}(c_j, q_2)\,\rangle$, where $c_i, c_j, c_k \in N$ and $(c_i, c_k), (c_j, c_k) \in E_1$.
Merging communities (Case 2): Identify a catalog community and its super community are always queried together. $PIS_{merge2} = \langle\, \texttt{SubmitQuery}(c_i, q_1), a(c_i, c_j), \texttt{SubmitQuery}(c_j, q_2)\,\rangle$, where $a \in \{\texttt{NavigateToSuper}, \texttt{NavigateToSub}\}$, $c_i, c_j \in N$, and $(c_i, c_j) \in E_1 \cup E_1^{-1}$.
Merging communities (Case 3): Same as PIS_{merge1}, but uses NavigateToPeer $PIS_{merge3} = \langle\, \texttt{SubmitQuery}(c_i, q_1), \texttt{NavigateToPeer}(c_i, c_j), \texttt{SubmitQuery}(c_j, q_2)\,\rangle$ where $c_i, c_j \in N$ and $(c_i, c_j) \in E_2$.

5.1 Merging Communities

Here, we introduce a generic sequence that describes situations where merging of communities may be beneficial. We identify some interesting sequences which represent special cases of the generic sequence[4].

Definition 5 ($PIS_{GenericMerge}$). $PIS_{GenericMerge}$ *which represents the situations where two communities are always queried together is:*

$$PIS_{GenericMerge} = \langle\, \texttt{SubmitQuery}(c_i, q_1), a_1, ..., a_n, \texttt{SubmitQuery}(c_j, q_2)\,\rangle$$

where $c_i, c_j \in N$, $a_k \in \{\texttt{NavigateToSub}, \texttt{NavigateToSuper}, \texttt{NavigateToPeer}\}$ ($k = 1, .., n$), *and* q_1, q_2 *are global query attributes (i.e., community product attributes).* □

$PIS_{GenericMerge}$ captures interaction sequences where users, within a catalog community c_i, first submit a query then perform several navigation actions to reach a community c_j from where they finally submit another query. Figure 5 presents three particular cases of $PIS_{GenericMerge}$.

5.2 Splitting a Community

A catalog community may be split if a subset of community product attributes are always queried together and the subset can represent a specific domain by

---

[4] Note that, even though actions in Table 1 do not include source catalog community parameters, we add them when defining PIS for clarity reasons.

Table 4. More PISs (on PeerCommunity–Of relationship)

Predefined Interaction Sequences
Upgrading the weight of a PeerCommunity-Of: Consolidates the relevancy of the relationship. Consider that many users navigate from community c_i, via PeerCommunity-Of relationship, to community c_j, and submit a query to c_j. This indicates that the PeerCommunity – Of relationship from c_i to c_j positively contributed in finding the target community. $PIS_{upgrade} = \langle\, \texttt{NavigateToPeer}(c_i, c_j), \texttt{SubmitQuery}(c_j, q)\, \rangle$, where $c_i, c_j \in N$, $(c_i, c_j) \in E_2$, and q is global query attributes.
Downgrading the weight of a PeerCommunity-Of: Consider that many users who followed a PeerCommunity-Of relationship and arrived at a community c_j, ultimately leave the community without performing any further action. This may indicate that c_j is not relevant to these users. To leave c_j, use LeaveCatalogCommunity or NavigateToPeer. $PIS_{downByLeave} = \langle\, \texttt{NavigateToPeer}(c_i, c_j), \texttt{LeaveCatalogCommunity}(c_j)\, \rangle$, where $c_i, c_j \in N$, and $(c_i, c_j) \in E_2$. $PIS_{downByPeer} = \langle\, \texttt{NavigateToPeer}(c_i, c_j), \texttt{NavigateToPeer}(c_j, c_i)\, \rangle$, where $c_i, c_j \in N$, and $(c_i, c_j), (c_j, c_i) \in E_2$.
Creating a new PeerCommunity--Of: Identify communities that are constantly used as stop-overs. It may be beneficial to create direct PeerCommunity–Of relationship so that users can by-pass them. $PIS_{createPeer}$ represents a situation where there are one or more navigational actions between NavigateToPeer and SubmitQuery. This suggests the creation of Peer-Community–Of between c_i and c_k. $PIS_{createPeer} = \langle\, \texttt{NavigateToPeer}(c_i, c_k), a_1, .., a_n, \texttt{SubmitQuery}(c_j, q)\, \rangle$, where $a_p \in \{\texttt{NavigateToSub}, \texttt{NavigateToSuper}, \texttt{NavigateToPeer}\}$ $(p = 1, .., n)$, $c_i, c_j, c_k \in N$, $(c_i, c_k) \in E_2$, and $(c_i, c_j) \notin E_1 \cup E_1^{-1} \cup E_2$.
Deleting a PeerCommunity-Of: No pattern specifically defined. We consider $PIS_{downByLeave}$, and $PIS_{downByPeer}$. When it is observed that the weight of a PeerCommunity–Of in a community reaches the lower threshold (given by an administrator), the relationship is considered to be irrelevant and can be removed.

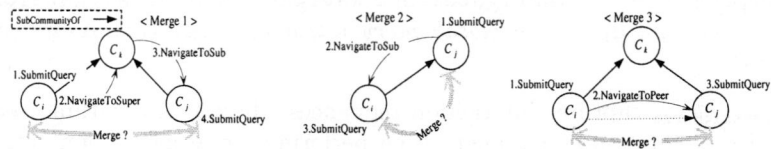

Fig. 5. Three particular cases of $PIS_{GenericMerge}$

itself. One way to detect this situation is to observe the way the community product attributes are queried. The following pattern is used to identify a subset of attributes that are always queried together. In this pattern, an administrator has a specific catalog community in mind (c_i) that s/he wants to examine for possibility of splitting and a set of attributes s/he predicts to be queried together.

Definition 6 (PIS_{split}). PIS$_{split}$ which represents the pattern for splitting a catalog community is: PIS$_{split}$ = ⟨ SubmitQuery(c$_i$, "attr$_1$,..,attr$_n$") ⟩, where c$_i$ ∈ N, and attr$_1$,..,attr$_n$ are community product attributes in c$_i$ that are likely to be queried together. □

6 Confidence of Patterns

In this section, we provide two definitions, namely *frequency* and *confidence* of a PIS. They are used to decide whether a PIS can be considered as a pattern for which a restructuring operation is suggested.

Definition 7 (Frequency). *A frequency of a PIS, denoted by* Frequency(PIS), *is number of occurrences of PIS in the processed log file.* □

The frequency of a predefined interaction sequence is used to decide whether the result of the match is significant enough to consider performing eCatalogs–Net restructuring operations. We discuss some of the issues that arise from using the patterns.

First, there is an issue of conflicting patterns where discovery of one pattern suggests a certain restructuring operation, whereas another pattern leads to a different operation on the same relationships or communities. For instance, it is possible that the pattern PIS$_{upgrade}$ shows that the weight of PeerCommunity–Of relationship between community A and B needs to be upgraded, but at the same time, the pattern PIS$_{downByPeer}$ may suggest that the same relationship should be downgraded.

On the other hand, there is an issue of knowing patterns that can consolidate each other. We refer to these patterns as consolidating patterns. These patterns, when used together, can reinforce each other's findings. For example, suppose that the pattern PIS$_{downByLeave}$ suggests that PeerCommunity–Of relationship between community A and B should be downgraded. When PIS$_{downByPeer}$ pattern also suggests downgrading of the same relationship, it helps choosing a restructuring operation with much more assurance. Table 5 lists the identified conflicting and consolidating patterns among the predefined interaction patterns presented in this paper.

Definition 8 (Confidence). *A confidence of a PIS denoted by Confidence(PIS) is defined as:*

$$\text{Confidence}(\text{PIS}) = \frac{\text{Frequency}(\text{PIS}) + A}{(\text{Frequency}(\text{PIS}) + A) + B} \quad \text{where}$$

A *is sum of frequency of all consolidating patterns of PIS and* B *is sum of frequency of all conflicting patterns of PIS.* □

For a PIS to be considered, (i) its frequency should be greater than a frequency threshold and (ii) its confidence should be greater than a confidence threshold. Those two thresholds can be defined by an administrator.

Table 5. Conflicting and Consolidating Patterns

Name of PISs	downBy Leave	downBy Peer	create Peer	del Comm	merge1	merge2	merge3	split
upgrade	−	−	+	n	n	n	+	n
downByLeave	.	+	−	+	n	n	−	n
downByPeer	.	.	−	+	n	n	−	n
createPeer	.	.	.	−	n	n	n	n
delComm	.	.	.	.	−	−	−	−
merge1	.	.	.	.	.	n	n	−
merge2	.	.	.	.	.	.	n	−
merge3	.	.	.	.	.	.	.	−
split	.	.	.	.	.	.	.	.

Legend: n=no conflict, −=conflict, +=consolidation

7 Evaluation

The eCatalogs–Net (see Fig.1) used in the experiments represents an integrated view of 27 catalog communities in *computers and related services* domain. Overall, all components in $WebCatalog^{Pers}$ have been implemented using Java, JSP/Servlets, and JDBC. For persistent storage (log data and metadata repository), an XML-supported repository (Oracle 8i database) is used. The metadata repository stores information about community attributes, relationships, members, etc. It should be noted that our initial studies were conducted under simulated scenarios, in which, we restricted the users' interactions in terms of number of moves (e.g., mouse clicks) they can make. We show any measurable improvement by comparing the number of users who find the target (what they were looking for) before restructuring and after restructuring. The primary goal of this simulation study is to demonstrate that given the same constraint (i.e., limited number of moves), more users find targets after restructuring.

7.1 Experiment Framework

We used *task agents* that played the role of customers who wanted to find out information about the products. A Java class called *AgentFactory* was used to create agents. More precisely, the class AgentFactory implements a software component made up of a container and a pool of objects which represent agents. The container is a process that, once created, runs *continuously*, listening to a socket, through which an instantiation message from a predefined script (used to create an agent) is received. An agent interacts with a module called *Community Manager* (implemented as JavaBean) which provides various methods for exploring the community relationships (e.g., getSubCommunityOf(), getPeerCommunityOf() etc.). The agent's search and query behaviour is based on the same search and query strategy which is presented in Sect. 2.3. The agents are equipped with two kinds of information for autonomous interaction with communities. First, the agents have access to the relationships (i.e., Sub, PeerCommunity–Of) between communities. The second information provided to the agents is called *Likelihood Table*. In the likelihood table, for a given a target community, every community in eCatalogs–Net is assigned a number value, which represents a degree of "closeness" (i.e., relevance) of the community to the target community. Hence, the higher the value, the *more likely* the community will lead the agent to the target. We will refer to this value as a *likelihood* and the list of likelihood values as a *likelihood table*.

Having the likelihood values fixed in the table makes the agents' interaction sequence to be always predictable. Agents should be able to make spontaneous and irregular decisions, resulting in unpredictable behaviour. We introduced a variant factor which would diverge a likelihood value. Each time, when an agent is given the likelihood values, the agent dynamically recalculates all likelihood values according to the factor before starting navigation.

The agent takes the following inputs to run; (1) name of the file that contains likelihood table, (2) name of the target community to find, (3) maximum number of moves an agent can make before giving up. For the purpose that stated earlier in Sect. 7, we limited the MaxMove to 14 for all experiments. The parameter VF (Variant Factor) represents the value of the variant factor for likelihood table. We asked four people who are familiar with the domain to produce the likelihood tables. The actual likelihood values used in the experiments took the average values of the four. The VF has three settings, 5%, 10% and 15%. Higher the VF, bigger the deviation from given likelihood values[5].

7.2 Experiments and Results

We now describe the results of experiments that investigated the effect of two restructuring operations (addPeer, moveCatComm) and the experiment parameter VF. The experiments carried out were based on two simulation scenarios. In the first scenario, we experimented on a PeerCommunity–Of relationship. For initial runs, 3000 agents were created and given the task of finding the community CableModem (see 'Before' in Fig.6). From the initial runs, observation showed that about 28% of the agents who found target followed the PeerCommunity–Of relationship from Modem to Internet, and Internet, HomeNetworking were used as stop-overs. We performed addPeer operation to create a new PeerCommunity–Of relationship from Modem to CableModem. Then we ran the 3000 agents again (see 'After' in Fig.6).

Varying VF: We measured the improvement made by the restructuring and study the effect of different values of the variant factor. We varied VF from 15% to 10%, and then to 5%. As shown in Fig.6, there were visible improvements in the number of agents found target. Irrespective of creation of the relationship,

---

[5] Note that other experimental parameters related to likelihood table have been defined, such as number of the tables participated in the experiment, range of likelihood values, etc. However, we only present the experiments with VF.

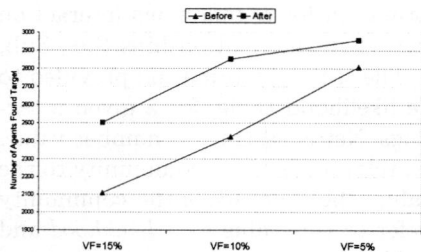
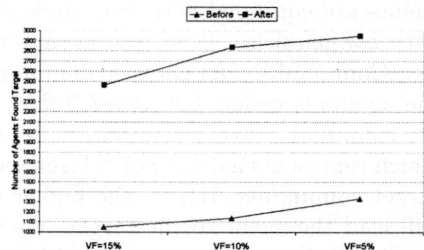

Fig. 6. Varying VF: First Scenario **Fig. 7.** Varying VF: Second Scenario

as VF decreases the more agents were able to find targets. VF randomises the likelihood values from a given table. This result demonstrates that agents are likely to find the target if their likelihood values are less deviated from the given likelihood values. Given the fact that the likelihood values used described the relationships of communities in relatively precise manner, this result can be interpreted that the user whose understanding does not deviate much from that of domain experts is more likely to find targets easily. Also, the biggest improvement was made when VF was 15 (i.e, having the highest deviation from given likelihood values). This indicates that the restructuring of eCatalogs–Net can benefit the most when the user's understanding deviates much from the expert.

In the second scenario, we experimented on moving a community to a new super–catalog community. In the initial structure of eCatalogs–Net (Fig.1), HardDrive is sub catalog community of Peripherals. The likelihood values used reflected the Storage as the expected location of the target. In the initial runs, 3000 agents were created and given the task of finding the community HardDrives. For the second runs, we performed moveCatComm() operation to move HardDrives from Peripherals to Storage and ran 3000 agents again. As shown in Fig.7, clear improvements were made after the restructuring.

Overall, we saw obvious improvements made after restructuring of eCatalog–Net across various experiment settings. This demonstrates that adaptive structuring of e–catalogs can help users have more streamlined and easier navigation/search experience. The experiments with VF parameter showed that for the users whose understanding deviates very much from the experts, can benefit the most from having communities restructured.

8 Related Work and Conclusions

We identify two major areas to discuss related work, namely building adaptive Web sites and navigation mining techniques in Web content personalisation. [11] automatically constructs index pages that supplement an existing organisation by looking at co–occurring pages, so that users can easily locate pages that are conceptually and strictly related to one topic. In [9], a technique that discovers the gap between Web site designer's expectation and user's behaviour is proposed. The technique uses inter page conceptual relevance vs. inter page access co-occurrence. [13] developed an algorithm to identify "expected locations" of a Web page and create a link from the expected location to the page. [14] extract related pages from a given page, then investigate the relationships between two Web pages based on how each page drives other pages as related page. It is worth noting that, while basic principles of this area are complementary to our work, most approaches only deal with Web pages, which is quite different from the concept of communities we proposed. In our work, communities are individual and autonomous entities (rather than network of Web pages) with which users and members of the community can have various interactions (submitting a query to, invoking operations from, register with, etc.).

In the area of mining access patterns, [6] uses Web usage mining concept to dynamically predict user's next behaviour and to make a recommendation. [3] uses Hypertext Probabilistic Grammar also to predict the user's navigation path. [5,8] discuss issues and processes involved in preparation/transformation of data from Web server logs to a format suited for purpose of mining. In typical sequence or Web usage mining, an access pattern is a sequence of visited Web documents which have a large occurrence frequency. It extracts frequently visited nodes, or nodes that are visited together, but these kind of access pattern does not reflect how users navigate the imposed structure. [12,2] proposed a Web Usage Mining (WUM) system to evaluate effectiveness of the Web site organisation. It uses a concept of g-sequence to model sequence of navigation of users. We use a similar concept to model sequence of user interaction actions.

Another work worth mentioning is [15], in which decision trees are used to automatically construct catalogs based on popularity of product items (i.e., frequency of visits) and weighted product attributes. The algorithm of construction is designed in a way that the depth of product hierarchy (which is a tree) is minimised, pushing the popular product items/attributes to upper levels so that customers can find them easily (with fewer clicks). However, it does not discuss the ongoing adaptivity of the catalogs. Also, *WebFINDIT* [4] considers addition and deletion of links between communities. However, the mechanism is based on link-monitoring agents, which is different from mining user access patterns.

In summary, in this paper, we presented a usage-centric approach for transforming and improving integrated catalogs structure and organisation. We proposed catalog restructuring operations as well as predefined interaction sequences that help decide which operation to perform. We also illustrated the viability of the proposed approach and demonstrated that restructuring increase the chances of the user finding his/her targets through simulated experiments. Ongoing work includes case studies to evaluate $WebCatalog^{Pers}$ in a distributed environment. We also plan to extend the proposed approach by grouping people with similar interaction patterns.

References

1. B. Benatallah, M. Dumas, Q.Z. Sheng, and A.H.H. Ngu. Declarative Composition and Peer-to-Peer Provisioning of Dynamic Web Services. In *Proc. of the International Conference on Data Engineering*, San Jose, California, February 2002.
2. B. Berendt and M. Spiliopoulou. Analysis of Navigation Behaviour in Web Sites Integrating Multiple Information Systems. *The VLDB Journal*, 9(1):56–75, 2000.
3. J. Borges and M. Levene. Data Mining of User Navigation Patterns. In *Proc. of the Workshop on Web Usage Analysis and User Profiling (WEBKDD'99)*, San Diego, CA, August 1999.
4. A. Bouguettaya, B. Benatallah, L. Hendra, M. Ouzzani, and J. Beard. Supporting Dynamic Interactions among Web-based Information Sources. *IEEE Transaction on Knowledge and Data Engineering*, 12(5):779–801, Sept/Oct 2000.
5. R. Cooley, B. Mobasher, and J. Srivastava. Data Preparation for Mining World Wide Web Browsing Patterns. *Journal of Knowledge and Information Systems*, 1(1), 1999.
6. A. Datta, K. Dutta, D. VanderMeer, K. Ramamritham, and S. B. Navathe. An Architecture to Support Scalable Online Personalization on the Web. In *Proc. of the 2nd ACM Conference on Electronic Commerce (EC'00)*, Minneapolis, Minnesota, October 2000.
7. J. Jung, D. Kim, S. Lee, C. Wu, and K. Kim. EE-Cat: Extended Electronic Catalog for Dynamic and Flexible Electronic Commerce. In *Proc. of the IRMA2000 International Conference*, Anchorage, Alaska, May 2000. IDEA Group Publishing.
8. B. Mobasher, R. Cooley, and J. Srivastava. Automatic Personalization Based on Web Usage Mining. *Communications of the ACM*, 43(8), August 2000.
9. T. Nakayma, H. Kato, and Y. Yamane. Discovering the Gap Between Web Site Designers' Expectations and User's Behaviour. In *Proc. Of 9th International World Wide Web Conference*, Amsterdam, May 2000.
10. S. Navathe, H. Thomas, M. Satits Amitpong, and A. Datta. A Model to Support E-Catalog Integration. In *Proc. of the IFIP Conference on Database Semantics*, Hong Kong, April 2001. Kluwer Academic Publisher.
11. M. Perkowitz and O. Etzioni. Adaptive Web Sites. *Communications of the ACM*, 43(8), August 2000.
12. M. Spilopoulou. Web Usage Mining for Web Site Evaluation. *Communications of the ACM*, 43(8), August 2000.
13. R. Srikant and Y. Yang. Mining Web Logs to Improve Website Organization. In *Proc. of 10th International World Wide Web Conference*, Hong Kong, May 2001.
14. M. Toyoda and M. Kitsuregawa. A Web Community Chart for Navigating Related Communitie. In *Proc. of 10th International WWW Conference*, Hong Kong, May 2001.
15. D. Yang, W. Sung, S. Yiu, D. Cheung, and W. Ho. Construction of Online Catalog Topologies Using Decision Trees. In *Proc. of Second International Workshop on Advance Issues of E-Commerce and Web-Based Information Systems (WECWIS 2000)*, Milpitas, California, June 2000.

Reengineering of Database Applications to EJB Based Architecture

Jianguo Lu

Department of Computer Science, University of Toronto
jglu@cs.toronto.edu

Abstract The advent and widespread use of Enterprise JavaBean (EJB) technology not only demands more reengineering support for legacy database applications, but also changes the reengineering practice. Initiated from our experience of reengineering database applications to EJB based architecture, this paper addresses two challenges in the mapping between database queries and EJBs. The first is to map a SQL to the equivalent EJB client code when the enterprise beans exist. The second is to generate enterprise beans from the set of legacy SQL expressions when the EJB architecture does not exist in the first place. We propose the EJB-SQL mediator to solve the first problem, and a view selection algorithm to solve the second one.

1 Introduction

There has been a great divide between the object world and the relational world. Both techniques are successful in the mainstream industrial practice, one for programming and the other for data management. In many cases these two worlds cohabitate peacefully, not interfering with each other. Unfortunately, many large applications, especially multi-tier e-commerce ones, need to use objects as the programming interface and use relations to manage the data. Current common practice in combining the two worlds is to imbed SQL expressions inside the classes. This close coupling of the object and relation runs against many software engineering principles, such as modularity, information encapsulation, usability, maintainability, etc.

One of the objectives of the Enterprise JavaBean (EJB) [34] technology is to address gracefully this object-relation interface. EJB can be seen as, among other things, the object view of the relational database system. With EJB, databases are transparent to application developers.

EJB based applications are seldom developed from scratch. In most cases they are reengineered from existing systems, especially the multi-tier applications that use relational databases as their back-ends. In particular, such legacy applications include large amount of SQL queries imbedded in various programming or scripting languages such as C++, or proprietary languages such as PL/SQL[18] and Net.Data [15]. While reengineering such systems to EJB-based architectures, there are three problems need to be addressed. First, how to map the relational schema to the object model in EJB. Second, how to translate the legacy queries to the EJB client code that access the enterprise beans. Third, when the enterprise beans do not exist, how to generate those beans and the behavior part of the EJB model from the set of queries of the legacy system.

The first problem can be viewed as the traditional object-relational mapping problem that has been thoroughly studied for a long time [22] [3] [4]. Those studies have proposed a variety of methods and tools to support such a mapping, ranging from design patterns [5] to tools that generate the EJB skeletons from database schemas [17].

This paper focuses on the second and the third problems, which can be viewed as the other half of the object-relational mapping, i.e., the mapping between the relational queries and the behaviors of the objects. This part of object relational mapping has been barely touched in literature.

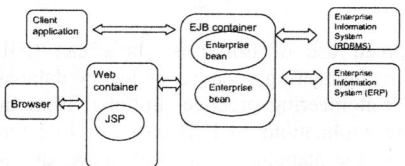

Fig 1. EJB architecture   Fig. 2. Varieties of enterprise beans

By viewing EJBs as wrappers that represent the object views for the underlying database systems, the translation of a query to the EJB client code can be formulated as the query rewriting problem, a problem that has been widely studied [26][25]. Likewise, the EJB generation from legacy queries can be formalized as the view selection problem in databases [27].

In this paper, we propose an SQL-EJB mediator in order to generate the EJB client code. The mediator accepts a legacy query and uses descriptions of the query answering capabilities of available enterprise beans in order to translate that query into the equivalent EJB client code. The paper also proposes an enterprise bean generator that accepts a set of legacy queries as input, and produces a set of enterprise beans that can accommodate these queries.

Mapping SQLs into EJB architecture is an important problem for many reasons. Firstly, there are many legacy systems are being reengineered into EJB based applications. Secondly, the design of the EJB architecture itself should rely not only on the relational schemas of the underlying databases, but also on SQL expressions in the legacy system. In current practice, the methods attached to enterprise beans depend largely on developer experience. Providing developers with comprehensive information on the legacy queries that the EJB architecture will have to accommodate can facilitate the bean design process and make it less ad hoc. Thirdly, our research has implications not only in the reengineering of database applications to EJB architecture, but also for the developing of application that have object-relational mappings.

This paper is organized as follows. Section 2 introduces the background knowledge of EJB, Object-relational mapping and query rewriting. Section 3 introduces the overall architecture of the EJB reengineering problem. Section 4 describes the transformation of SQL expressions to client code of EJBs, supposing the EJB architecture already exists. Section 5 discusses the generation of EJB architecture from the legacy SQL expressions. In section 6 we explain the experiments in the IBM Websphere Commerce Suite reengineering project. Section 7 discusses related and future work.

2 Background

2.1 EJB Architecture

EJB is a distributed component framework that provides services for transactions, security and persistence in the distributed multi-tier environment [34]. It separates the business logic from the low-level details so that developers can concentrate on the business solution. With the growing popularity of the EJB framework, more and more legacy systems and old web-based systems are being transitioned into EJB architecture. Typically, in the legacy systems there are large amount of SQL queries. On the other hand, in the EJB based applications, those SQL queries are not directly used. Instead, by adopting the popular model-view-control design pattern, queries are wrapped inside the EJBs. The web designers, like JSP writers, and other EJB clients access the data through EJBs instead of SQL statements. A typical EJB based application would look like *figure 1*.

In the center is the EJB container. It manages a set of enterprise beans. The beans connect with the backend systems, typically a relational database system. The web container typically uses JSP to access the EJB, and serve the JSP to the browser. Besides, EJB client applications other than JSP, such as Java applets or any other systems, can also access to the enterprise beans.

The enterprise beans in the middle tier function as wrappers over various systems, especially relational database systems. There are two kinds of enterprise beans, i.e., entity bean and session bean. Roughly speaking, session beans are the verbs and entity beans are the nouns of the application. An entity bean is a persistent object that represents an item in a storage system such as a database system. In a simple scenario, one bean could correspond to a row in the table. The selection of certain rows of the table corresponds to the selection of a group of beans satisfying certain condition. The selection of beans is accomplished by the finder method in the entity bean, which has SQL statement imbedded in the method. What we are interested in is the entity bean, especially the CMP entity bean. This is illustrated in *figure* 2.

By using EJB, web designers no longer need to learn the details of database structure. Also, any changes in the database are shielded off by the beans, thus making the maintenance of the JSP pages easier.

2.2 Object Relational Mapping in EJB

Object-relational mapping is the process of transforming between object and relational models and between the systems that are built on top of these models. While it has been extensively studied as for the mappings between relational and object models, the mappings between the SQL expressions and the behaviors of the objects are barely touched. With the introduction of Enterprise JavaBean (EJB), there are growing demands for supporting the transformation of SQLs in legacy systems to EJB.

A simple object–relational mapping can be illustrated in *figure* 3. In this mapping, the table Emp maps to the class EmployeeBean, the columns NAME and SAL corresponds to the attributes name and sal in the class, respectively. For the query in the relational database such as finding all the employees by name, there is a corresponding method called `findByName` in the entity bean that has a SQL expression embedded inside the method.

Object-relational mapping is often complicated in several ways. First, object and table may not be a simple 1-1 mapping. Instead, it may be a many-many mapping in many cases. The same applies to the attribute-column mapping. Second, there are relationships between objects, like association, aggregation, and inheritance. In the relational model there are also associations between tables realized by the foreign key. When mapping the relational model to the object model, we need to map those relationships as well. This can be illustrated in *figure* 4.

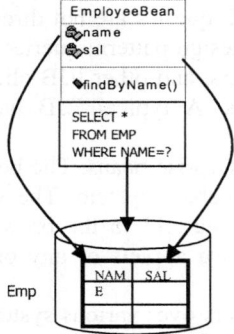

Fig. 3. Simple mapping

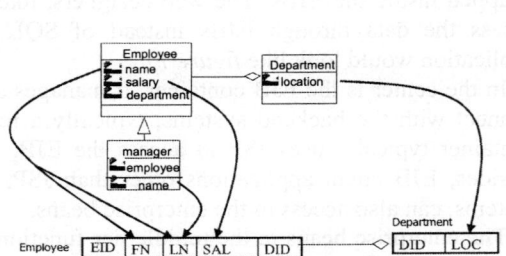

Fig. 4. Complex mapping

2.3 Query Rewriting

Query rewriting problem has been extensively studied in the areas of query optimization [10] and data integration [25]. Informally speaking, query rewriting problem can be formulated as follows. Given a query and a set of view definitions, how can we answer the query using the answers to the views? Following the common practice we use Datalog notation [35] in the following discussion.

Definition 2.1 (*Query containment and equivalence*) A query Q is contained in another query Q', denoted as Q⊆Q', if for any instance of the base relations, the set of tuples computed for Q is a subset of those computed for Q'. Two queries Q and Q' are equivalent (denoted as Q=Q') if Q⊆Q' and Q⊇Q'.

Definition 2.2 (*query rewriting*) Given a query Q and a set of views V, a *rewriting* of Q using V is a query Q' such that Q=Q', and Q' refers to one or more views in V.

3 EJB Reengineering Framework

Here we define a generic framework to reengineer database applications to EJB based architecture. When reengineering such applications, we face two challenges that are depicted in *figure* 5:

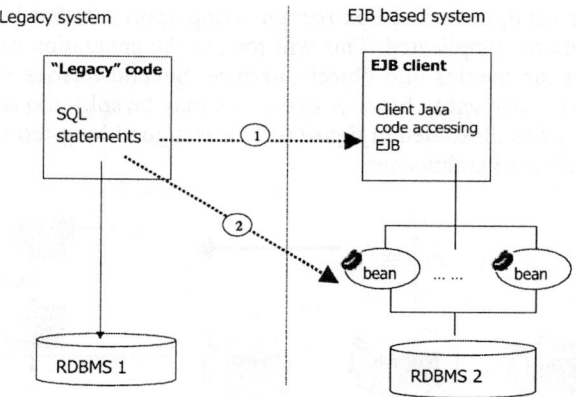

Fig. 5. Issues database application reengineering

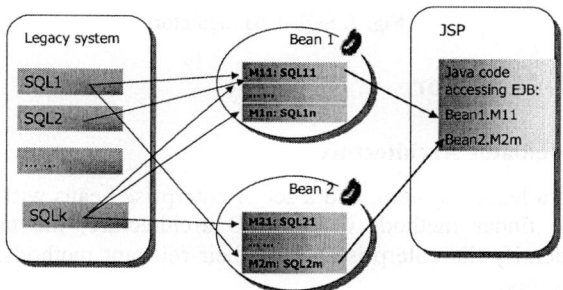

Fig. 6. White-box reengineering

1. When the enterprise beans are already provided, how to translate the queries embedded in the legacy code to the equivalent EJB client code?
2. When the enterprise beans are not provided, how to produce the beans, especially the finders and the queries inside finders according to the existing legacy queries?

In general these two tasks are not performed independently. The reengineering is an iterative process with intervention from EJB designers. In a typical scenario the EJB designer defines some entity beans first, then uses the SQL-EJB mediator to locate legacy SQL queries that can not be reproduced using the enterprise beans. Those queries are then used as the basis for EJB generation. By using the EJB generator, enterprise beans and the finder methods are recommended for the designer to choose. The selected beans are added into the existing system and we can iterate this process, run the SQL-EJB mediator once again.

As for the SQL to EJB reengineering, there are two approaches. One is the black-box reengineering. In this approach, the SQLs are not analyzed. Instead, they are directly copied into the methods of enterprise beans. This kind of reengineering requires generating some scaffolding code for the method so that it can access the database. In general, this approach will use session beans.

On the other hand, the white-box reengineering approach that is described in this paper is much more complicated. This will require the generation of entity beans and the rewriting of the queries into object interface. Several queries may be combined into one method in one entity bean, or one query may be split into several methods in different beans, or as illustrated in *figure* 6. This is a good long-term solution offering a clean object-oriented architecture.

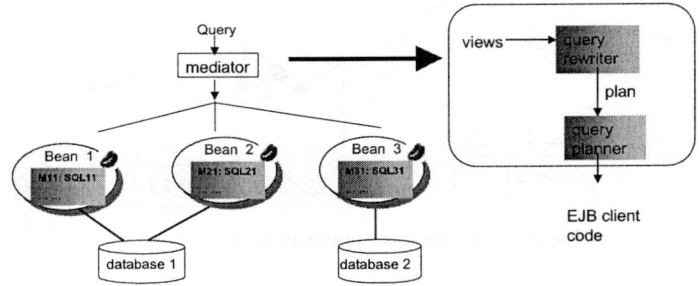

Fig. 7. SQL-EJB mediator

4 EJB-SQL Mediator

4.1 SQL-EJB Mediator Architecture

Given a query in a legacy system, and a set of enterprise beans with SQL statements imbedded in the finder methods in the EJB architecture, the task of SQL-EJB mediator is to identify the enterprise beans, their relevant methods, and the way to combine those methods.

Obviously, there are several questions need to be answered before we can automate the reengineering of the SQL queries to the client Java code in the EJB architecture:

1. For a query in the legacy system, is there a way to decide which finder method in EJB architecture is semantically equivalent to the query?
2. When there does not exist a single corresponding finder method, is there a way to find a bunch of finders that are semantically equivalent?
3. After we decompose the query into several sub-queries, how to combine them in the EJB client Java program?
4. When those sub-queries (finders) do not exist, what kind of finders we need to add? More specifically, what kind of finders we need to add so that it is guaranteed every query in the legacy system can be represented in the EJB?

If we regard the finders as the view definitions in database, we can see that the first question corresponds to query containment [8], the second corresponds to query rewriting using views [26], the third corresponds to query planning and the fourth the view selection [27][6].

The SQL-EJB mediator can be illustrated in *figure* 7, which resembles many of the information mediator systems [25]. The main difference is that we have enterprise beans instead of heterogeneous information sources, and we produce client Java code instead of actually running the queries. Like information sources, enterprise beans are wrappers of the one or more databases and have limited query answering capabilities.

4.2 Representing the Query Answering Capabilities of the Enterprise Bean

One factor that makes the query rewriting systems different is how the views are represented. Remember the views are the SQL queries in the finders in the entity beans. Due to the EJB specification, there are several format requirements for the view definition:

- The finder method always returns one entity bean or a collection of beans. That means the head of the view definition will always have attributes from one particular bean. It will never be able to contain attributes from different beans. Also, views always select all the attributes from a entity bean.
- The finders have arguments. That means the view definition would be parameterized.
- The entity bean will have getter for each attribute. That means by default there is a projection for every attribute in the base relation.

Using these observations, we extracted the view definitions from the EJB source code.

4.3 Maximal Query Rewriting in SQL-EJB Mediator

When designing a query rewriting system, there are two factors need to consider:

1. *What if there are multiple choices of the rewritings*. In the case of optimizing queries using rewriting [10], the best rewriting could be selected by comparing the cost of each candidate.
2. *What if there is no complete and equivalent rewriting of a query*. A complete rewriting is the one that contains view predicates only. In many cases, a complete and equivalent rewriting of a query using a set of views may not exist. When such a case occurs, there are two choices. One is to relax the completeness requirement and allow view predicates as well as base predicates occur in the rewriting. The other is to compromise the equivalent requirement and make the rewriting not equivalent but the maximally-contained rewriting.

When we design the rewriting system, we have the following considerations:

1. When there are multiple complete rewritings, we select the one that has fewer views. This is because each view will have separate database access. Less views means less database connections and travels. Also, there is less code at the client side to integrate the result
2. When there is not a complete rewriting, we sacrifice the completeness and minimize the number of base predicates. This is necessary since we want to have equivalent rewriting. Besides, the base predicates that can't be removed from the query will be suggested as new view definitions. Those new definitions will become the input of the EJB generator and finally will be added as some finders in some entity beans. We would like to see fewer views the better.

Given the above design desiderata, in the following we formalize those requirements and present the algorithm that satisfies those conditions.

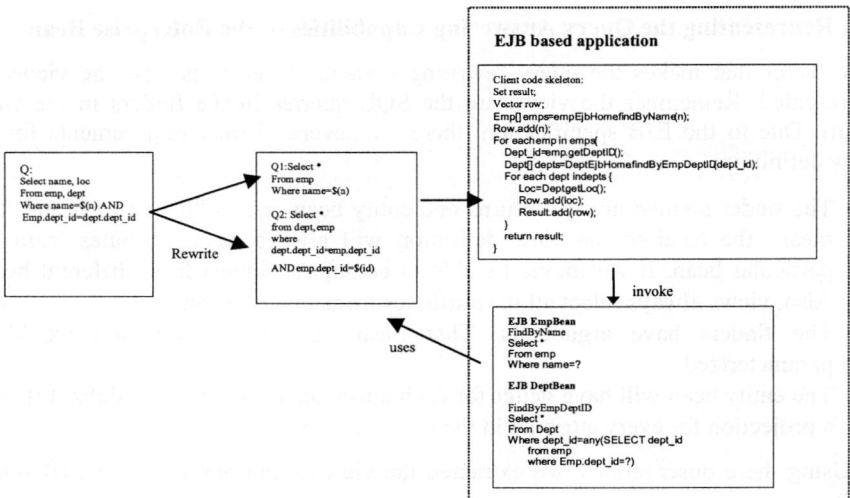

Fig. 8. Code generation

Definition 4.1 (*Partial and complete rewriting*) For a rewriting Q' of a query Q using a set of views V, when the body of Q' contains view predicates from V as well as base predicates, it is called *partial rewriting*. When the body of Q' contains view predicates only, it is called *complete rewriting*.

Definition 4.2. (*Maximal rewriting*) Given two partial rewritings Q' and Q'' of Q using views V. Q' is greater than Q'' if the number of base predicates in Q' is less than that of Q''. A partial rewriting Q' is *maximal* if there is no other partial rewriting Q'' of Q using V such that Q'' is greater than Q'.

Please note that the maximal rewriting is different from the maximally-contained rewriting[30].

4.4 Extended Bucket Algorithm

There are two classes of rewriting algorithms. One is used in query optimization that guarantees the efficiency and sacrifices the completeness, such as join enumeration [26]. The other is used in data integration that guarantees the completeness and sacrifices the equivalence, such as the Bucket algorithm [26] and Inverse-rule algorithm [26]. Our approach is to extend the Bucket algorithm so that equivalence and the maximalarity as defined in previous section are ensured. Besides, we have other requirements that are specific in our particular application area.

4.5 Generate the EJB Client Code

Once a rewriting is obtained, we need to generate a plan for the query so that client Java code could be generated to actually execute the query. A query plan is a sequence of accesses to the EJB methods interspersed with local processing operations. Given a query Q of the form:

$$Q(X):-V1(X1),\ldots,Vn(Xn).$$

A plan to answer it consists of a set of conjunctive plans. Conjunctive plans are like conjunctive queries except that each subgoal has input and output specification associated with it. For example, a plan for the above query could be

$$Q(X) :- V1(X_1)(In_1,Out_1), V2(X_2)(In_2, Out_2), \ldots \ldots Vn(Xn)(In_n, Out_n).$$

A plan is executable if the input of the i-th predicate appears in the output of the preceding predicates, i.e., $In_i \subseteq Out_1 \cup \ldots \cup Out_{i-1}$

Once we generated the execution plan, we can replace the view predicates with finder methods invocations, and provide the input parameters using input/output definitions.

Figure 8 explains a concrete example. The starting point is a SQL query like Q and a bunch of enterprise Java beans like `EmpBean` and `DeptBean`. In those entity beans there are some finder methods like `findByName` and `findByEmpDeptId`, which have their corresponding SQL queries. When page designers want to access database, they will use the beans instead the SQLs. In this case, we need to decompose query Q into Q1 and Q2, which corresponds to `findByName` and `findByEmpDeptID`, respectively. Then, according to the logic of the decomposition, we need to insert Java code to combine the results of the two finder methods.

5 EJB Architecture Generation

5.1 Rational for EJB Generation

The problem is given a set of legacy queries, how to produce the finder methods and SQLs inside the finder methods, so that all legacy queries have a rewriting using the finders?

Obviously, a naïve solution for this problem is to define a session bean for every legacy query. On the other end of extreme, for every base predicate we can define an entity that has finders for every attribute of the predicate. The former approach can be used in the black-box reengineering discussed in Section 3. The drawback is that we will have session beans only and henceforth, it loses the beauty of the entity bean and is not a really EJB system. Besides, queries in EJB have various format requirements. We need to transform the legacy queries anyway to fit in the EJB specification. Also, from the EJB design point of view, enterprise beans are meant for the programming interface for bean users. The interface should be kept simple and logically coherent. That entails the decomposition, classification, and the generation of a minimal set of finders.

The desiderata for the finder selection (or view selection) aiming at EJB architecture generation are as follows, in both semantic and syntactic aspects:

1. *Complete*: every query should have a rewriting using the finders.

2. *Minimal*: The set of queries that can be answered using the finders should not be much larger than the original query set. One of the purposes of adding the EJB layer on top of the database is to provide partial database query capabilities so that the modularity and security can be increased.
3. *Concise:* The number of views (i.e., the EJB finders) should not be very large. Remember that page designers use EJBs as an interface to access the data. The interface should be as succinct as possible. A direct consequence of this requirement is that the size of the views should not be very large. Smaller views can generate more queries.
4. *Efficient:* The views should do the time-consuming operations as much as possible. This is because the views (the finders) are supported by the underlying database, while composing the finders would be done outside of database which is not as efficient as the database.

In the following we formalize those requirements.

Balloon algorithm
Input: a set of queries Q, constants k_1 and k_2.
Output: A set of views V.
Steps:
1. Let V=Q.
2. For every V_i in V, suppose V_i is of the form:
    V_i:-P_{i1}, P_{i2}, ..., P_{im}.
   Let V_{i1} :- P_{i1}. , ..., V_{im} :- P_{im}.
   Add each V_{ij} to V.
3 For each combination of (P_{i1}, ..., P_{im}) in V_i with length less than k_1 do {
    Suppose the combination is P_{il}, ..., P_{in}.
    Let V_k=P_{il}, ..., P_{in}.
    Rewriting the queries in Q using V.
    Count the number of times that V_k is used in all the rewritings;
    If count > k_2 {
        For each view in {V_{il}, ..., V_{in}} {
            If every query in Q has a rewriting after removing the view
            Then remove the view.
        }
        Add V_k into V.
    }
}

Fig. 9 Balloon algorithm

5.2 The View Selection Problem

EJB architecture generation can be studied in the realm of view selection problem [27][14], which is a dual problem of query rewriting. Informally speaking, it can be formulated as: given a set of queries, how can we find a set of views so that all the queries have a rewriting using this set of views

Definition 5.1 *(covering view set)*: Let **Q**(V) denote the set of queries that have rewritings using V. Given a set of queries Q and a set of views V. V is a covering view set of Q if Q ⊆ **Q**(V), i.e., for every query q in Q there is a rewriting of q using V.

Note that in general Q ⊆ **Q**(Q).

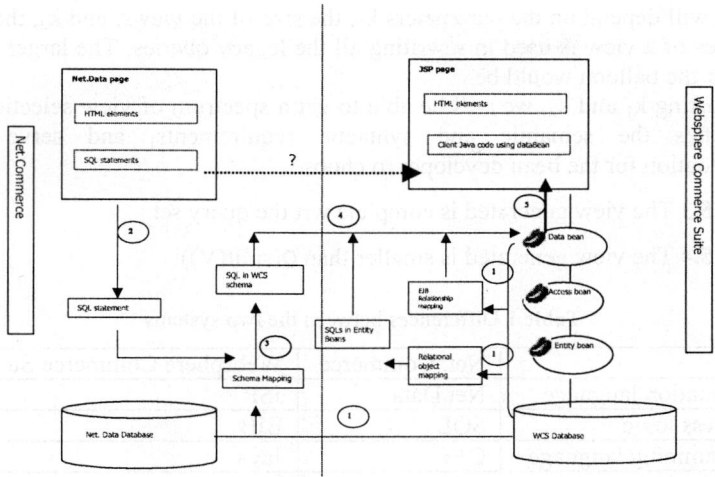

Fig. 10. Architecture of the Websphere reengineering tool

Definition 5.2 (*view set containment*) Given two view sets V1 and V2, V1 is contained in V2 (denoted as V1 ≤ V2) if $\mathbf{Q}$ (V1) ⊆ $\mathbf{Q}$ (V2), i.e., for every query Q, if Q is answerable using V1, then Q is also answerable using V2.

By the definition, it is straightforward that if V1 ⊆ V2, then V1 ≤ V2. But the vice versa does not hold.

The following property says that if we split a view in a view set, the view set becomes larger.

Property 5.1 For a view set V={V1,..., Vi, ..., Vn}. Let Vi:-P1,P2. Vi1:-P1. Vi2:-P2. V'={V1, ..., Vi1, Vi2, ..., Vn}. Then V ≤ V'.

Note that the view set containment is defined in terms of infinite number of queries. The following property ensures the containment is decidable.

Property 5.2 Given two view set V and V'. V ≤ V' if for every Vi in V, there is a rewriting of Vi using V'.

Using the view set containment relation, we can define the minimal covering view set.

Definition 5.3 (*minimal covering view set*) V is a minimal covering view set of Q, if V is a covering view set of Q and there is no other covering view set V' of Q such that V' ≤ V.

5.3 Balloon Algorithm

Based on the properties above, we present the balloon algorithm in *Figure 9*. The starting point is the set of queries Q. When we take the Q as the set of views, the queries that can be answered using Q is $\mathbf{Q}$ (Q), which is larger than Q. After that, we blow the balloon to its full extent, get the $\mathbf{Q}$ (split(V)). After that, we let some air out of the balloon $\mathbf{Q}$ (split(V)), but never let it smaller than $\mathbf{Q}$ (V). How large the solution balloon is will depend on the parameters k_1, the size of the views, and k_2, the number of the times of a view is used in rewriting all the legacy queries. The larger is the k_1, the smaller the balloon would be.

By adjusting k_1 and k_2, we will be able to get a spectrum of view selections, each one satisfies the semantic and syntactic requirements, and serve as the recommendation for the bean developer to choose.

Property 5.3 The view generated is complete wrt the query set.

Property 5.4 The view generated is smaller than $Q(split(V))$.

Table 1 Differences between the two systems

	Net. Commerce	Websphere Commerce Suite
Presentation language	Net.Data	JSP
Business logic	SQL	EJB
Programming language	C++	Java
Programming model	Ad hoc	MVC

6 A Case Study: Reengineering the IBM e-Commerce Framework

To validate the usability and feasibility of the approach discussed above, we have been carrying out an e-commerce reengineering project for IBM Toronto Lab. The project aims at the transition from the 5-year-old e-commerce framework Net.Commerce to the new architecture Websphere Commerce Suite that uses EJB technology.

Both Net.Commerce and Websphere Commerce Suite are frameworks for building e-commerce websites. They provide templates for realizing functionalities such as product catalog browsing, payment processing, product promotion, auction, and almost anything that can be carried out on the web. Both of them are multi-tier applications that use browsers at the client side, use web-servers in the middle, and use the RDBMS to manage the data.

Although there are many similarities, they are actually totally different systems. WCS is a successor of Net.Commerce. It is redesigned without the consideration for backward compatibility. Most notably, WCS uses EJB technology. Table 1 highlights the differences between the two systems. *Figure* 10 illustrates simplified architectural views of the two systems.

For the presentation language, Net.Commerce uses Net.Data, which is an IBM proprietary product for dynamic HTML, while WCS uses JSP (the Java Server Page) that is widely accepted for dynamic web pages. For the business logic, Net.Commerce uses SQL in many cases directly in C++ and Net.Data, while WCS uses EJB to access the database. For the programming language, Net.Commerce uses C++, while WCS uses Java. For the programming model, Net.Commerce is pretty ad hoc. Sometimes the separation of view, model, and control is not clear. WCS adopts a clean MVC (Model, View and Control) design pattern.

Given the huge size and complexity of the two frameworks, there are many reengineering tasks. Our focus is on the Net.Data to JSP reengineering, and especially, the SQL to EJB reengineering. *Figure* 10 shows the overall task and the steps we take. On the left side is the Net.Commerce architecture, right side is the WCS architecture. This picture is oversimplified to focus on the things we are interested in. Net.Commerce uses Net.Data to generate dynamic web pages. In Net.Data, there are SQL statements that can access databases. In WCS, JSP is used as the presentation language. In JSP there are Java code that accesses data beans. Data beans and access beans are IBM extensions to EJB framework to improve performance.

Our first step in the reengineering is to analyze the WCS source code to extricate several relationships. One is that between the data beans, access beans, and enterprise beans. The other is the relationship between the data beans such as inheritance and aggregation. The third is the relationship between the objects and relational database, such as the mappings between the objects and tables, between the attributes and columns, and between the methods and SQLS. In the meanwhile, we analyze the mapping between the two relational databases in the Net.Commerce and WCS.

The next step is to parse the Net.Data and the SQLs inside Net.Data. Using the mapping information extracted in the first step, the third step is to translate the SQL in the old schema to the equivalent one in the new schema. The fourth step is to compare the legacy SQL with the SQLs in the WCS and pick out the most relevant ones. Using the relationships between SQLs and objects and that of different objects, step 5 make the recommendations that the enterprise beans we should use in the JSP page.

We have implemented the system and have published it in IBM alpha works [24]. In addition to that carried out on the Websphere customer side, the tool has been tested on more than 500 Net.Data file, more than 600 SQLs. The largest Net.Data file is 152K. The WCS source code that we crawled through is 62MB. Altogether there are more than 200 tables and more than 200 entity bean. The view set collected from the WCS source code consists of about 600 of queries.

This e-commerce reengineering project shows that the white-box reengineering, especially the SQL-EJB mediator and the EJB architecture generator, is crucial for the success of EJB application development. Also, this project demonstrates the feasibility of our approach. Through this project, we also realized that EJB design should rely on not only the logics in queries, but also on the design strategies that have been evolved over time and experience, such as what granularity of the entity beans should have, when to use BMP or CMP entity bean, and when to use session bean. Those EJB design strategies need to be studied, formalized, and applied in the EJB generation.

7   Related Work and Conclusions

There are tools and methods to migrate EJB applications from one platform to another [1][20]. Our work differs from those approaches in that we are migrating the database applications to EJB architecture instead of moving EJB applications between different platforms. There are also tools for mapping database schemata or UML models to entity beans[18][17]. However, these do not address the SQL issues. Such tools are more relevant to the traditional object-relational mapping problem [2][12].

Database reverse engineering and schema mapping [21][36] are relevant to our work as well. Most database reverse engineering research attempts to map a relational schema to an object schema, or the transformation of relational queries to object-oriented queries [9][12]. In our case, we translate SQL expressions from database application to object wrappers of the relational database.

Compared with the work in query rewriting and view selection, we have several contributions as well. First, we proposed a new applications area for query rewriting and view selection which entails a different approach for query rewriting and view selection. For the query rewriting, we developed the notion of maximal rewriting and the extended bucket algorithm. The SQL-EJB mediator differs from other information mediators in several respects, such as the query capability representation in EJB and the query rewriting algorithm. More importantly, this is the largest query rewriting system ever used in real application. Up to now, the largest query rewriting system we know of is described in [30], which experimented with hundreds of views. However, the views and queries there are randomly generated. In our case, thousands of queries and hundreds of views come from real industry application. Thirdly, unlike other query rewriting system, we translate query plans to Java programs. For the view selection, we proposed the balloon algorithm in order to generate the EJB architecture.

The research on object-relational mapping has been largely on the schema level, i.e., between object and relational models. There has been few work on the study of the mappings between the systems that are built on top of these models, and in particular, the mapping and translation between the SQLs and the methods in the objects. In the settings of Enterprise JavaBean technology and software reengineering application area, this paper demonstrates the importance of such a mapping and presents the methods to do the translation. We should emphasize that our methods is applicable not only to the EJB reengineering problem, but also to other object persistent mechanism, such as JDO (Java Data Object).

From the reengineering point of view, we propose the reengineering of database applications using query rewriting and view selection techniques.

This is an on going project. There are several issues need to be investigated further.

Although a reengineering tool is constructed and commercialized, and the approach proposed in this paper is proved necessary and feasible in this reengineering environment, the implementation of the SQL-EJB mediator and EJB generator is still under way.

In this paper the EJB architecture is assumed to be a simple one that does not have inheritance and associations [17]. Also, we are only considering CMP entity beans. BMP entity beans and session beans are not considered.

When rewriting a query the cost model is not used for selecting a good rewriting over a bad one.

When selecting views from a set of queries, now each query is considered of equal importance. However, a more precise approach is to use the workload model, which is a set of queries and each query has a weight that reflects how often the query is used.

All our algorithms are assuming SPJ queries. How to deal with disjunctive queries, groupings etc needs to be investigated.

In the new version of EJB specification EJB 2.0, a vendor independent query language EJB-QL is defined. We need to expand our approach to cover the EJB-QL, instead of SQL.

Acknowledgements

The author would like to thank John Mylopoulos for the stimulating discussions of the problem and his valuable comments, modifications on this paper, also Kostas Kontogiannis, Terry Lau, Emily Xing and Erik Hedges for their input in the construction of the IBM E-commerce reengineering tool.

References

[1] Sanjay Agrawal, Surajit Chaudhuri, and Vivek Narasayya. Automated selection of materialized views and indexes in Microsoft SQL Server. VLDB 2000.
[2] R.S. Arnold, editor. *Software Reengineering*, Los Alamitos, CA, 1993. IEEE Computer Society Press.
[3] Andreas Behm and Andreas Geppert and Klaus R. Dittrich, *On the Migration of Relational Schemas and Data to Object-Oriented Database Systems*, in Proc. 5th International Conference on Re-Technologies for Information Systems, 13-33, 1997.
[4] S. Bergamaschi and A. Garuti and C. Sartori and A. Venuta, *The object wrapper: an object oriented interface for relational databases*, In Euromicro 1997.
[5] Kyle Brown, Handling N-ary relationships in VisualAge for Java, http://www.ibm.com/vadd, August 2000.
[6] Elliot Chikofsky and James Cross. *Reverse Engineering and Design Recovery: A Taxonomy*. IEEE Software, 7(1): 13-17, January 1990.
[7] Rada Chirkova, Alon Y. Halevy, Dan Suciu, A Formal Perspective on the View Selection Problem, VLDB 2001.
[8] A.K. Chandra, P.M. Merlin, *Optimal implementation of conjunctive queries in relational databases,* in Proceedings of the 9th Annual ACM Symposium on Theory of Computing, pages 77-90, 1977.
[9] Chang, Y., Raschid, L. and Dorr, B., *Transforming queries from a relational schema to an equivalent object schema: a prototype based on F-logic*, Proceedings of the International Symposium on Methodologies for Intelligent Systems, 1994.
[10] Surajit Chaudhuri, Ravi Krishnamurthy, Spyros Pptamianos, Kyuseok Shim, *Optimizing Queries with materialized views*, ICDE 1995.
[11] Cohen, Y.; Feldman, Y.A., *Automatic high-quality reengineering of database programs by temporal abstraction,* Proceedings of the 1997 International Conference on Automated Software Engineering (ASE '97) (formerly: KBSE)
[12] Fong, J., *Converting Relational to Object-Oriented Databases.* SIGMOD Record, Vol.26, No. 1, March 1997.
[13] H. Gupta, I. S. Mumick, *Selection of views to materialize under a maintenance cost constraint*, in Proceedings of ICDT, pages 453-470, 1999.

[14] H. Gupta, *Selection of views to materialize in a data warehouse*, in Proceedings of ICDT, pages 98-112, 1997.
[15] IBM, *IBM Net.Data Reference*, Version 7, http://www4.ibm.com/software/data/net.data/, June 2001 Edition.
[16] IBM, Websphere Commerce Suite Version 5.1: An introduction to the programming model, IBM white paper, Feb 2001.
[17] IBM, VisualAge for Java 3.5, IBM, 2001.
[18] In2j, Automated tool for migrating Oracle PL/SQL into Java, www.in2j.com, April, 2001.
[19] Ivar Jacobson , Fredrik Lindström, *Reengineering of old systems to an object-oriented architecture*, OOPSLA 1991, ACM SIGPLAN Notices, Volume 26 Issue 11.
[20] IPlanet, *Migration Guide, iPlanet Application Server*, Version 6.0, www.iplanet.com, May 2000.
[21] J. Jahnke and W. Schafer and A. Zundorf, A Design Environment for Migrating Relational to Object Oriented Database Systems, In Proceedings of the International Conference on Software Maintenance, IEEE Computer Society Press, 163--170, 1996.
[22] Yannis Kotidis, Nick Roussopoulos, DynaMat: A Dynamic View Management System for Data Warehouses, SIGMOD 99, June.
[23] Terry Lau, Jianguo Lu, Erik Hedges, Emily Xing, Migrating E-commerce Database Applications to an Enterprise Java Environment, CASCON'01.
[24] Terry Lau, Jianguo Lu, John Mylopoulos, Erik Hedges, Kostas Kontogiannis, Emily Xing, and Mark Crowley, *Net.Data to JSP Helper*, IBM alphaWorks, www.alphaworks.ibm.com/tech/netdatatojsp, 2001.
[25] Alon Levy, Anand Rajaraman, Joann J. Ordille, *Querying heterogeneous information sources using source descriptions*. In proceedings of the international conference on Very Large Data Bases, Bombay, India, 1996.
[26] Alon Levy, Answering queries using views: a survey, VLDB Journal 2001.
[27] Chen Li, Mayank Bawa, Jeffrey D. Ullman, Minimizing view sets without losing query-answering power, ICDT'01.
[28] R. J. Miller, L. M. Haas and M. Hernández. *Schema Mapping as Query Discovery*. VLDB 2000.
[29] Wie Ming Lim and John Harrison, *An Integrated Database Reengineering Architecture - A Generic Approach*, Proceedings of the 1996 Australian Software Engineering Conference (ASWEC '96).
[30] Rachel Pottinger, Alon Y. Levy, A Scalable Algorithm for Answering Queries Using Views, VLDB 2000.
[31] William J. Premerlani, Michael R. Blaha, An approach for reverse engineering of relational databases, CACM, 1994 Vol 37(5).
[32] Chandrashekar Ramanathan, *Providing Object-Oriented Access To Existing Relational Databases*, PhD dissertation, Mississippi State University, 1997.
[33] Sun, Enterprise JavaBeans 2.0 Specification, www.java.sun.com, 2001.
[34] Tech Metrix, *Moving from IBM Websphere 3 to BEA WebLogic Server 5.1*, White Paper, TechMetrix Research, September 2000.
[35] Jeffrey D. Ullman, *Principles of Database and Knowledge-base Systems*, Volumes I, II, Computer Science Press, Rockville MD, 1989.

Efficient Similarity Search for Time Series Data Based on the Minimum Distance*

Sangjun Lee, Dongseop Kwon, and Sukho Lee

School of Electrical Engineering and Computer Science, Seoul National University
Seoul 151-742, Korea
{freude,subby}@db.snu.ac.kr
shlee@cse.snu.ac.kr

Abstract. We address the problem of efficient similarity search based on the minimum distance in large time series databases. Most of previous work is focused on similarity matching and retrieval of time series based on the Euclidean distance. However, as we demonstrate in this paper, the Euclidean distance has limitations as a similarity measurement. It is sensitive to the absolute offsets of time sequences, so two time sequences that have similar shapes but with different vertical positions may be classified as dissimilar. The minimum distance is a more suitable similarity measurement than the Euclidean distance in many applications, where the shape of time series is a major consideration. To support minimum distance queries, most of previous work has the preprocessing step of vertical shifting that normalizes each time sequence by its mean before indexing. In this paper, we propose a novel and fast indexing scheme, called the segmented mean variation indexing(SMV-indexing). Our indexing scheme can match time series of similar shapes without vertical shifting and guarantees no false dismissals. Several experiments are performed on real data(stock price movement) to measure the performance of our indexing scheme. Experiments show that the SMV-indexing is more efficient than the sequential scanning in performance.

1 Introduction

Time sequences are of growing importance in many database applications, such as data mining and data warehousing[1,2]. A time sequence is a sequence of real numbers and each number represents a value at a time point. Typical examples include stock price movement, exchange rate, weather data, biomedical measurement, etc. Similarity search in time series databases is essential, because it helps predicting, hypothesis testing in data mining and knowledge discovery[1,2]. Many techniques have been proposed to support the fast retrieval of similar time sequences based on the Euclidean distance[5,6,17]. However, the Euclidean distance as a similarity measurement has the following problem: it is sensitive to the absolute offsets of time sequences, so two time sequences that have similar shapes but with different vertical positions may be classified as dissimilar.

---

* This work was supported by the Brain Korea 21 Project in 2001

Consider a query time sequence $Q = (4, 9, 4, 9, 4)$ and two data time sequences $A = (7, 5, 6, 7, 6)$ and $B = (14, 19, 14, 19, 14)$ in Figure 1. Note that shifting Q upward for 10 units generates B. Using the similarity definition of the Euclidean distance, A is a more similar to Q than B. However, B is more similar to Q in shape. From this example, the Euclidean distance is not a good measurement of similarity when we would like to retrieve the time sequences of similar shapes irrespective of their vertical positions in time series databases.

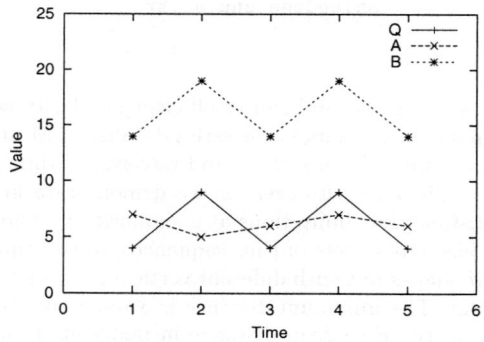

Fig. 1. Shortcoming of the Euclidean distance

In order to overcome the shortcoming of the Euclidean distance above mentioned, the minimum distance can be used for time sequence matching[18,19,22]. The minimum distance is the Euclidean distance between two time sequences, neglecting their offsets, that is, the minimum Euclidean distance over various shift factors. This can give a better estimation of similarity in shape between two time sequences irrespective of their vertical positions. To support minimum distance queries, most of previous work has to take the preprocessing step of vertical shifting which normalizes each time sequence by its mean before indexing[7,23,27]. This has the effect of shifting the time sequence in the value-axis such that its mean is zero, removing its offset. However, the vertical shifting has the additional overhead to get the mean of a time sequence and to subtract the mean from each element of the time sequence.

Time sequences are usually long, so the similarity calculation can be time consuming. As the size of time series databases increases, the sequential scanning scales poorly. To reduce the number of similarity calculations, an efficient indexing scheme is required. Indexing, however, on such multidimensional data doesn't seem to be easy because of dimensionality curse in making an index structure using a spatial access method such as R-tree[3] or R*-tree[4].

In this paper, we propose a novel and fast indexing scheme for time series, called the segmented mean variation indexing(SMV-indexing). This method is motivated by autocorrelation of time sequence, that is, the variation between two adjacent elements of time sequence is invariant under vertical shifting. This autocorrelation motivated the dimensionality reduction technique introduced in this paper. Our indexing scheme can match time series of similar shapes without vertical shifting and guarantees no false dismissals.

The remainder of this paper is organized as follows. Section 2 provides a survey of related work. We will give similarity measurements used in sequence matching in Section 3, and our proposed approach is described in Section 4. We will present the overall process of minimum distance queries in Section 5. Section 6 presents the experimental results. Finally, several concluding remarks are given in Section 7.

2 Related Work

Various methods have been proposed for fast matching and retrieval of time series. The main focus is to speed up the search process. The most popular methods perform feature extraction as dimensionality reduction of time series data, and then use a spatial access method such as R-tree to index the time series data in the feature space.

An indexing scheme called *F-index*[5] is proposed to handle sequences of the same length. The idea is to use Discrete Fourier Transform(DFT) to transform time sequence data from time domain to frequency domain, drop all but the first few frequencies, and then use the remaining ones to index the time sequence using a spatial access method such as R-tree. The results of [5] are extended in [6] and the *ST-index* is proposed for sequence matching of the different length. The methods proposed in [5,6] use the Euclidean distance as a similarity measurement without considering any transformation. As shown in Figure 1, it is better to consider the minimum distance as a similarity measurement in some applications.

In [7], the authors show that the similarity retrieval will be invariant to simple shifting and scaling if sequences are normalized before indexing. In [14,15], authors present an intuitive similarity measurement for time series data. They argue that the similarity model with scaling and shifting is better than the Euclidean distance. However, they do not present any indexing method. In [8], authors give a method to retrieve similar sequences in the presence of noise, scaling and transformation in time series databases. In [20], the authors propose a definition of similarity based on scaling and shifting transformations. In [9] authors present a hierarchical algorithm called *HierarchyScan*. The idea of this method is to perform correlation between the stored sequences and the template in the transformed domain hierarchically. In [18,19], authors propose the definition of similarity between sequences based on the slope of segments.

In [12], authors use vantage point trees for indexing and matching sequences of different lengths based on a modified version of the edit distance, considering two sequences similar if a majority of elements match. This technique is extended to matching of multidimensional data sequences such as sequences of images[13].

In [10], Singular Value Decomposition(SVD) is used for dimensionality reduction technique. SVD is a global transformation which maps the entire dataset into a much smaller one. SVD can be used to support ad hoc queries on large dataset of time sequences. The problem of SVD is the performance deterioration by update of an index structure. SVD has to examine the entire dataset again to update an index structure.

In [11], authors propose a set of linear transformations such as moving average, time warping, and reversing. These transformations can be used as the basis of similarity queries for time series data. The results of [11] are extended in [21] and authors propose the method for processing queries that express similarity in terms of multiple transformations instead of a single one. In [16,24], authors use time warping as distance function and present algorithms for retrieving similar time sequences under this function. However, a time warping distance does not satisfy triangular inequality and can cause false dismissals.

In [22], authors propose to use Discrete Wavelet Transform(DWT) for dimensionality reduction and compare this method to DFT. They argue that Haar wavelet transform performs better than DFT. However, the performance of DFT can be improved using the symmetry of Fourier Transforms and DWT has the limitation that it can only be defined for time sequences with a length of the power of two.

In [25], authors propose the *Landmark Model* for similarity-based pattern queries in time series databases. The *Landmark Model* integrates similarity measurement, data representation, and smoothing techniques in a single framework. The model is based on the fact that people recognize patterns by identifying important points.

In [23,27] the authors introduce new dimensionality reduction technique of time sequence by using segmented mean features. In this method, the time sequence is divided into non-overlapping segments. The feature of segment is represented by segment's mean value. Then, the time sequence is indexed in the feature space by a spatial access method. The same concept of independent research is proposed in [26]. They show that the segmented mean features can be used in arbitrary L_p norm. However, the segmented mean features cannot support minimum distance queries, vertical shifting is required in preprocessing raw data to support minimum distance queries.

3 Similarity Measurements for Sequence Matching

In this section, we will give two similarity measurements used in sequence matching. The first definition is based on the Euclidean distance between two time sequences.

Definition 1 (Euclidean Distance). *Given a threshold ϵ, two time sequences $A = \{a_1, a_2, \ldots, a_n\}$ and $B = \{b_1, b_2, \ldots, b_n\}$ of equal length n are said to be similar if*

$$L_2^{Euclidean}(A, B) = (\sum_{i=1}^{n} |a_i - b_i|^2)^{1/2} \leq \epsilon$$

A shortcoming of Definition 1 is demonstrated in Figure 1. Two time sequences B and Q are the same in shape, because B can be obtained by shifting Q upward 10 units. However, they can be classified as dissimilar by Definition 1. From this example, the Euclidean distance is not a suitable measurement of similarity when the shape is a major consideration.

Definition 2 (Minimum Distance). *Given a threshold ϵ, two time sequences $A = \{a_1, a_2, \ldots, a_n\}$ and $B = \{b_1, b_2, \ldots, b_n\}$ of equal length n are said to be similar in shape if*

$$L_2^{minimum}(A, B) = (\sum_{i=1}^{n} |a_i - b_i - m|^2)^{1/2} \leq \epsilon$$

$$\text{where} \quad m = \sum_{i=1}^{n}(a_i - b_i)/n$$

From Definition 2, two time sequences are said to be similar in shape if the minimum distance is less or equal to a threshold ϵ. This definition is a more flexible similarity measurement when we would like to retrieve time sequences of similar shapes from databases irrespective of their vertical positions.

4 Proposed Approach

The problem we focus on is the design of fast retrieval of similar time sequences in databases based on the minimum distance. To the best of our knowledge, this is the first work that examines indexing methods for minimum distance queries without vertical shifting for time series of an arbitrary length. We will now introduce the SMV-indexing and show that it guarantees no false dismissals.

4.1 Dimensionality Reduction

Our goal is to extract features that capture the information on the shape of a time sequence, and that will lead to the feature distance definition satisfying the lower bound condition of the minimum distance. Suppose that we have a set of time sequences of length n. The idea of our proposed feature extraction method consists of two steps. First, we divide each time sequence into m segments of equal length l. Note that the start point and end point of adjacent segments are the same, because the variation will be missed if the time sequence is divided disconnectedly. In case the length of time series is not $m(l-1)+1$, then we add the final element's values at the end of sequence. This has no effect on query results. Next, we extract a simple feature from each segment. We propose to use the mean variation as the feature of each segment. FA_j denotes the feature of the $j-th$ segment of the time sequence A. We define the feature vector of the time sequence A as follows.

Definition 3 (Segmented Mean Variation Feature). *Given a sequence $A = \{a_1, a_2, \ldots, a_n\}$ and the number of segments $m > 0$, define the feature vector $\overrightarrow{FA}$ of the time sequence A by*

$$\overrightarrow{FA} = (FA_1, FA_2, \ldots, FA_m)$$
$$= \frac{1}{l-1} \cdot \left(\sum_{i=1}^{l-1} |a_{i+1} - a_i|, \sum_{i=l}^{2(l-1)} |a_{i+1} - a_i|, \ldots, \sum_{i=(m-1)l+(2-m)}^{m(l-1)} |a_{i+1} - a_i| \right)$$

Figure 2 illustrates the dimensionality reduction technique used in this paper. A time sequence of length 11 is projected into two dimensions. The time sequence is divided into two segments and the mean variation of each segment is obtained.

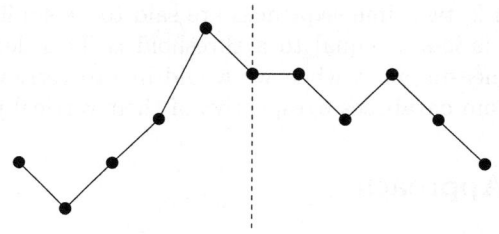

Sequence A=(5,4,5,6,8,7,7,6,7,6,5)

$$\overrightarrow{FA} = (MeanVariation(5,4,5,6,8,7), MeanVariation(7,7,6,7,6,5))$$
$$= (1.2, 0.8)$$

Fig. 2. Dimensionality Reduction Technique used in this paper

The algorithm to extract the feature vector is obviously simple. The mean variation of a segment is invariant under vertical shifting, so the segmented mean variation features can be indexed to support minimum distance queries. The proposed matching scheme is motivated by the following observation.

Observation 1 (Autocorrelation of Time Sequence) *The segmented mean variation is invariant under vertical shifting.*

Verifying its correctness is obvious. The following equality shows its correctness.

$$MeanVariation(A) = \frac{1}{(n-1)} \sum_{i=1}^{n-1} |a_{i+1} - a_i|$$

$$= \frac{1}{(n-1)} \sum_{i=1}^{n-1} |(a_{i+1} - m_a) - (a_i - m_a)|$$

$$\text{where} \quad m_a = \sum_{i=1}^{n} (a_i)/n$$

4.2 Lower Bounding of the Minimum Distance

In order to guarantee no false dismissals, we must show that the distance between feature vectors is the lower bound of the minimum distance between original sequences. Lower bounding the minimum distance with the feature distance is a condition that guarantees no false dismissals for similarity search in time series databases. It is not hard to show that the feature distance is the lower bound of the minimum distance.

$$L_2^{Euclidean}(\overrightarrow{FA}) \leq L_2^{minimum}(A)$$

In practice, however, the segmented mean variation feature vector $\overrightarrow{FA}$ is a poor approximation of the time sequence A, since it is essentially a down-sampling of time sequence. Much of the information will be lost, consequently, too many false alarms will occur. It is necessary to find a way to compensate the loss of information so that we could reduce the number of false alarms. More specifically, we find a factor $\alpha > 1$ such that,

$$\alpha \cdot L_2^{Euclidean}(\overrightarrow{FA}) \leq L_2^{minimum}(A)$$

Since $F(\cdot) = |\cdot|^2$ is a convex function on R, we can use the property of convex functions to find α. There is a well-known mathematical result on convex functions. We can use the following theorem from [26,28]

Theorem 1. *Suppose that $x_1, x_2, \ldots, x_n \in R$, and $\lambda_1, \lambda_2, \ldots, \lambda_n \in R$ such that $\lambda_i \geq 0$ and $(\sum_{i=1}^{n} \lambda_i) = 1$. If $F()$ is a convex function on R, then*

$$F(\lambda_1 x_1 + \lambda_2 x_2 + \ldots + \lambda_n x_n) \leq \lambda_1 F(x_1) + \lambda_2 F(x_2) + \ldots + \lambda_n F(x_n)$$

where R is the set of real numbers.

Proof. The proof is shown in [28]. □

Using the result of Theorem 1 by taking $\lambda_i = \frac{1}{n}$, we have the following corollary.

Corollary 1 *For any time sequence* $A = (a_1, a_2, \ldots, a_n)$, *the following holds.*

$$(n-1) \cdot |MeanVariation(A)|^2$$
$$\leq \sum_{i=1}^{n-1} |a_{i+1} - a_i|^2$$
$$\leq 2 \cdot (\sum_{i=1}^{n-1} |a_i - m_a|^2 + \sum_{i=2}^{n} |a_i - m_a|^2)$$
$$\leq 2^2 \cdot \sum_{i=1}^{n} |a_i - m_a|^2$$
$$where \quad m_a = \sum_{i=1}^{n} (a_i)/n$$

or, equivalently, for each segment S_j, $1 \leq j \leq m$, *we have*

$$(l-1) \cdot |MeanVariation(S_j)|^2$$
$$\leq \sum_{i=(j-1)l+(2-j)}^{j(l-1)} |a_{i+1} - a_i|^2$$
$$\leq 2 \cdot (\sum_{i=(j-1)l+(2-j)}^{j(l-1)} |a_i - m_a|^2 + \sum_{i=(j-1)l+(3-j)}^{j(l-1)+1} |a_i - m_a|^2)$$
$$where \quad m_a = \sum_{i=1}^{n} (a_i)/n$$

Now, we present our main theorem as follows.

Theorem 2. *For any time sequence* $A = (a_1, a_2, \ldots, a_n)$, *the following holds.*

$$\sqrt{l-1} \cdot L_2^{Euclidean}(\overrightarrow{FA}) \leq 2 \cdot (\sum_{i=1}^{n} |a_i - m_a|^2)^{1/2}$$
$$= 2 \cdot L_2^{minimum}(A)$$
$$where \quad m_a = \sum_{i=1}^{n} (a_i)/n$$

Proof. Based on the definitions of L_2 and $\overrightarrow{FA}$,

$$(l-1) \cdot L_2^{Euclidean}(\overrightarrow{FA})^2 = (l-1) \cdot \sum_{j=1}^{m} |MeanVariation(S_j)|^2$$

By Corollary 1, we can get the following inequality.

$$(l-1) \cdot \sum_{j=1}^{m} |MeanVariation(S_j)|^2$$

$$\leq 2 \cdot \{\sum_{i=1}^{l-1} |a_i - m_a|^2 + \sum_{i=2}^{l} |a_i - m_a|^2\}$$

$$+ 2 \cdot \{\sum_{i=l}^{2(l-1)} |a_i - m_a|^2 + \sum_{i=l+1}^{2(l-1)+1} |a_i - m_a|^2\}$$

$$+ \ldots$$

$$+ 2 \cdot \{\sum_{i=(j-1)l+(2-j)}^{j(l-1)} |a_i - m_a|^2 + \sum_{i=(j-1)l+(3-j)}^{j(l-1)+1} |a_i - m_a|^2\}$$

$$\leq 2^2 \cdot \sum_{i=1}^{n} |a_i - m_a|^2$$

$$= 2^2 \cdot L_2^{minimum}(A)^2$$

where $\quad m_a = \sum_{i=1}^{n} (a_i)/n$

By taking square root of both sides, we prove the theorem. □

Owing to Theorem 2, we can efficiently handle minimum distance queries with the segmented mean variation features. We know that $L_2^{minimum}(A, B) \leq \epsilon$ represents $L_2^{Euclidean}(\overrightarrow{FA}, \overrightarrow{FB}) \leq 2 \cdot \epsilon/\sqrt{l-1}$ by Theorem 2. Consequently, minimum distance queries can be correctly converted to simple Euclidean distance queries in the feature space without false dismissals. We can reduce the search space by a factor of $2/\sqrt{l-1}$.

5 Query Processing

In this section, we will first present the sequential scanning which is the simplest searching algorithm for time sequence matching. Then, we will present the overall process of the SMV-indexing scheme.

5.1 Sequential Scanning

The sequential scanning searches entire databases. It computes the minimum distance between query time sequence and all data time sequences in databases. If the minimum distance is within a given error bound, the data time sequence is classified as similar to the query time sequence. Otherwise, it is classified as dissimilar to the query time sequence and rejected. The sequential scanning processes above procedure to all data time sequences in databases. The sequential scanning guarantees that no qualified data time sequence is falsely rejected. However, the sequential scanning is slow because it has to access all data time sequences in databases. As the size of time series databases increases, the sequential scanning scales poorly. The implementation of the sequential scanning is described in Algorithm 1.

Algorithm 1: Sequential Scanning
---

begin
    Input: query time sequence Q, error bound ϵ
    Output: data time sequences within error bound ϵ

    Result $\leftarrow$ NULL;
    for all $D_i \in$ databases **do**
        if ComputeMinimumDistance(Q, D_i)$\leq \epsilon$ **then**
            Result $\leftarrow D_i \bigcup$ Result;
        else
            Reject D_i;
        end
    end
    return Result;
end

5.2 Segmented Mean Variation Indexing (SMV-Indexing)

We present the overall process of our time series indexing scheme. Before a query is performed, we shall do some preprocessing to extract feature vectors from time sequences, and then to build an index. After the index is built, the similarity search can be performed to select candidate sequences from databases.

Pre-processing

    •**Step 1. Feature Extraction** : Each time sequence is divided into m segments. Then, the feature vector is extracted from the time sequence using the dimensionality reduction technique mentioned in Section 4.1 for all time sequences in databases.
    •**Step 2. Index Construction** : We build a multidimensional index

structure such as R-tree using the feature vectors extracted from time sequences.

Index Searching After an index structure has been built, we can perform the similarity search against a given query time sequence. The searching algorithm consists of two main parts. The first is for candidate selection and the other is postprocessing to remove false alarms. Some non-qualifying time sequences may be included in the results of candidate selection because the feature distance is the lower bound of the minimum distance. The actual minimum distance between query time sequence and candidate sequences are computed and only those within the error bound are reported as the query results. The implementation of the SMV-indexing is described in Algorithm 2.

Algorithm 2: SMV-indexing

begin
    Input: query time sequence Q, error bound ϵ
    Output: data time sequences within error bound ϵ

    Result $\leftarrow$ NULL;
    Candidate $\leftarrow$ NULL;
    // project the query time sequence Q into the index space,
    $\overrightarrow{FQ} \leftarrow$ FeatureExtraction(Q);
    // candidate selection using a Spatial Access Method,
    Candidate $\leftarrow$ IndexSearching($\overrightarrow{FQ}$,SAM,$\frac{2 \cdot \epsilon}{\sqrt{l-1}}$);
    // postprocessing to remove false alarms,
    for all $C_i \in Candidate$ do
        if $ComputeMinimumDistance(Q,\ C_i) \leq \epsilon$ then
            Result $\leftarrow C_i \bigcup$ Result;
        else
            Reject C_i;
        end
    end
    return Result;
end

---

6 Performance Evaluation

We implemented both the SMV-indexing and the sequential scanning in C++ on a Linux machine (Redhat 7.1, Kernel version 2.4.2) with dual Pentium III 500MHz CPUs, 512MB of memory and 40GB HDD. The size of disk page is set to 4KB. For a spatial access method, we used the Katayama's R*-tree source codes[1].

The real time sequences were obtained from Seoul Stock Market, Korea[2]. The stock database consisted of 2000 stocks and for each stock its daily closing prices for 128 days. We have run 25 random queries over real dataset to find similar time sequences based on the minimum distance. The query time sequences were randomly selected from the stock database.

First, we compared the SMV-indexing with the sequential scanning in terms of the number of actual computations required by varying error bound. We evaluated the search space ratio to test the filtering power of removing irrelevant time sequences in the process of index searching. The search space ratio is defined as follows.

$$search\ space\ ratio = \frac{the\ number\ of\ candidate\ sequences}{the\ number\ of\ time\ sequences\ in\ databases}$$

Figure 3 shows the experimental result. Figure 3 shows that there is a significant gain in reducing search space by the SMV-indexing.

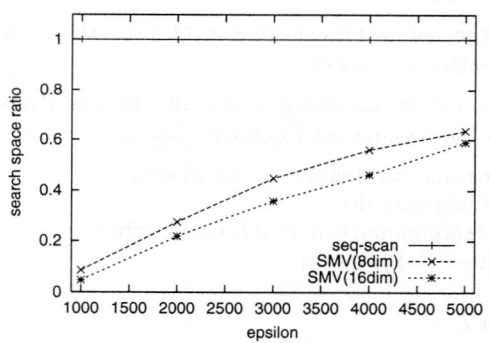

Fig. 3. Search Space Ratio: SMV-indexing vs. Sequential Scanning

Good filtering effect dose not always result in good performance since the spatial access method can be affected by the dimensionality of feature vectors. To verify the performance of the SMV-indexing, we compared the SMV-indexing with the sequential scanning with respect to the average execution time. Figure 4 shows the experimental result. The result shows that the SMV-indexing is more efficient than the sequential scanning in performance. However, as shown in

---
[1] The Katayama's R*-tree source codes can be retrieved from
 http://research.nii.ac.jp/~katayama/homepage/research/English.html
[2] This data can be retrieved from http://www.kse.or.kr/kor/stat/stat_data.htm

Figure 4, the average execution time increases as the given error bound increases, eventually, the performance of the SMV-indexing becomes worse than that of the sequential scanning. This is because the number of retrieved time sequences for a larger error bound increases more rapidly than the number of relevant time sequences. Consequently, the postprocessing time to remove false alarms increases with a larger error bound.

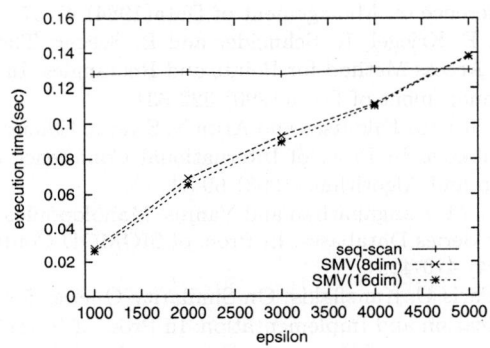

Fig. 4. Execution time: SMV-indexing vs. Sequential Scanning

7 Conclusion

We focused on fast similarity search in large time series databases, when the similarity measurement is the minimum distance. The Euclidean distance is the most popular similarity measurement for sequence matching. However, the Euclidean distance has the potential drawback that it cannot support the shape queries based on the minimum distance. To support minimum distance queries, most of previous work has to take the preprocessing step of vertical shifting that normalizes each time sequence by its mean before indexing. In this paper, we have proposed a novel time series indexing scheme that supports minimum distance queries without vertical shifting. Our indexing scheme is motivated by autocorrelation of time sequence, that is, the mean variation of time sequence is invariant under vertical shifting.

The major contributions of this work are: 1) introducing the similarity matching scheme that allows indexing of time series based on the minimum distance without vertical shifting, 2) introducing lower bound of the minimum distance to filter out dissimilar time sequences without false dismissals.

Our approach can be extended to the matching time series of similar shapes in arbitrary L_p norm. We are currently working in this direction for fast retrieving and matching time series of similar shapes in arbitrary L_p norm.

References

1. Rakesh Agrawal, Tomasz Imielinski and Arun N. Swami: Database Mining: A Performance Perspective. IEEE TKDE, Special issue on Learning and Discovery in Knowledge-Based Databases 5-6(1993) 914-925
2. Usama M. Fayyad, Gregory Piatetsky-Shapiroa and Padhraic Smyth: Knowledge Discovery and Data Mining: Towards a Unifying Framework. In Proc. of International Conference on Knowledge Discovery and Data Mining(1996) 82-88
3. A. Guttman : R-trees: A Dynamic Index Structure for Spatial Searching. In Proc. of SIGMOD Conference on Management of Data(1984) 47-57
4. N. Beckmann, H. P. Kriegel, R. Schneider and B. Seeger: The R*-tree: An Efficient and Robust Access Method for Points and Rectangles. In Proc. of SIGMOD Conference on Management of Data(1990) 322-331
5. Rakesh Agrawal, Christos Faloutsos and Arun N. Swami: Efficient Similarity Search In Sequence Databases. In Proc. of International Conference on Foundations of Data Organization and Algorithms(1993) 69-84
6. Christos Faloutsos, M. Ranganathan and Yannis. Manolopoulos: Fast Subsequence Matching in Time-Series Databases. In Proc. of SIGMOD Conference on Management of Data(1994) 419-429
7. Dina Q. Goldin, Paris C. Kanellakis: On Similarity Queries for Time-Series Data: Constraint Specification and Implementation. In Proc. of International Conference on Principles and Practice of Constraint Programming(1995) 137-153
8. Rakesh Agrawal, King-Ip Lin, Harpreet S. Sawhney and Kyuseok Shim: Fast Similarity Search in the Presence of Noise, Scaling, and Translation in Time-Series Databases. In Proc. of International Conference on Very Large Data Bases(1995) 490-501
9. Chung-Sheng Li, Philip S. Yu and Vittorio Castelli: HierarchyScan: A Hierarchical Similarity Search Algorithm for Databases of Long Sequences. In Proc. of International Conference on Data Engineering(1996) 546-553
10. Flip Korn, H. V. Jagadish and Christos Faloutsos: Efficiently Supporting Ad Hoc Queries in Large Datasets of Time Sequences. In Proc. of SIGMOD Conference on Management of Data(1997) 289-300
11. Davood Rafiei, Alberto O. Mendelzon: Similarity-Based Queries for Time Series Data. In Proc. of SIGMOD Conference on Management of Data(1997) 13-25
12. Tolga Bozkaya, Nasser Yazdani and Z. Meral Ozsoyoglu: Matching and Indexing Sequences of Different Lengths. In Proc. of International Conference on Information and Knowledge Management(1997) 128-135
13. Nasser Yazdani and Z. Meral Ozsoyoglu: Sequence Matching of Images. In Proc. of International Conference on Scientific and Statistical Database Management(1996) 53-62
14. Gautam Das, Dimitrios Gunopulos and Heikki Mannila: Finding Similar Time Series. In Proc. of European Conference on Principles of Data Mining and Knowledge Discovery(1997) 88-100
15. Bela Bollobas, Gautam Das, Dimitrios Gunopulos and Heikki Mannila: Time-Series Similarity Problems and Well-Separated Geometric Sets. In Proc. of Symposium on Computational Geometry(1997) 454-456
16. Byoung-Kee Yi, H. V. Jagadish and Christos Faloutsos: Efficient Retrieval of Similar Time Sequences Under Time Warping. In Proc. of International Conference on Data Engineering(1998) 201-208

17. Davood Rafiei and Alberto O. Mendelzon: Efficient Retrieval of Similar Time Sequences Using DFT. In Proc. of International Conference on Foundations of Data Organization and Algorithms(1998)
18. Sze Kin Lam, Man Hon Wong: A Fast Projection Algorithm for Sequence Data Searching. Data and Knowledge Engineering 28-3(1998) 321-339
19. Kelvin Kam Wing Chu, Sze Kin Lam and Man Hon Wong: An Efficient Hash-Based Algorithm for Sequence Data Searching. The Computer Journal 41-6(1998) 402-415
20. Kelvin Kam Wing Chu, Man Hon Wong: Fast Time-Series Searching with Scaling and Shifting. In Proc. of Symposium on Principles of Database Systems(1999) 237-248
21. Davood Rafiei: On Similarity-Based Queries for Time-Series Data. In Proc. of International Conference on Data Engineering(1999) 410-417
22. Kin-pong Chan, Ada Wai-chee Fu: Efficient Time Series Matching by Wavelets. In Proc. of International Conference on Data Engineering(1999) 126-133
23. Eamonn J. Keogh, Michael J. Pazzani: A Simple Dimensionality Reduction Technique for Fast Similarity Search in Large Time Series Databases. In Proc. of Pacific-Asia Conference on Knowledge Discovery and Data Mining(2000) 122-133
24. Sanghyun Park, Wesley W. Chu, Jeehee Yoon and Chihcheng Hsu: Efficient Searches for Similar Subsequences of Different Lengths in Sequence Databases. In Proc. of International Conference on Data Engineering(2000) 23-32
25. Chang-Shing Perng, Haixun Wang, Sylvia R. Zhang and D. Stott Parker: Landmarks: a New Model for Similarity-based Pattern Querying in Time Series Databases. In Proc. of International Conference on Data Engineering(2000) 33-42
26. Byoung-Kee Yi, Christos Faloutsos: Fast Time Sequence Indexing for Arbitrary Lp Norms. In Proc. of International Conference on Very Large Data Bases(2000) 385-394
27. Eamonn J. Keogh, Kaushik Chakrabarti, Sharad Mehrotra and Michael J. Pazzani: Locally Adaptive Dimensionality Reduction for Indexing Large Time Series Databases. In Proc. of SIGMOD Conference on Management of Data(2001) 151-162
28. M. H. Protter and C. B. Morrey: A First Course in Real Analysis. Springer-Verlag(1977)

A High-Performance Data Structure for Mobile Information Systems

John N. Wilson

Department of Computer and Information Sciences, University of Strathclyde
26, Richmond St, Glasgow, G1 1XH, UK
jnw@cis.strath.ac.uk

Abstract. Mobile information systems can now be provided on small form-factor computers. Dictionary-based data compression extends the capabilities of systems with limited processing and memory to enable data intensive applications to be supported in such environments. The nature of judicial sentencing decisions requires that a support system provides accurate and up-to-date data and is compatible with the professional working experience of a judge. The difficulties caused by mobility and the data dependence of the decision-making process are addressed by an Internet-based architecture for collecting and distributing system data. We describe an approach to dictionary-based data compression and the structure of an information system that makes use of this technology.

1 Introduction

Over the last decade, information systems (IS) have developed to encompass Internet technology and the advantages that this paradigm provides for co-operation between decision-makers. More recent developments have resulted in progressive reduction of the form-factor of the kinds of hardware needed to underpin IS. This has coincided with the spread of IS technology to mobile users. The professional activities of such users require them to operate in sites away from the typical centralised provision of technical support that has underpinned conventional concepts of IS. Laptop computers have helped to provide technological support in this kind of working environment. The next stage in the miniaturisation of computer systems is the personal digital assistant (PDA). Such systems represent many benefits for mobile users in business environments however miniaturisation necessitates the use of small and relatively slow processors as well as limited random access memory. Whilst the increasing density of integrated circuits will undoubtedly result in improvements in processor and memory performance, the dependence of miniaturised systems on battery power is likely to remain a constraint on small form factor technology. Data compression can be used to mitigate some of these problems if it can be arranged that the subsequent processing of such data does not require extensive on-line use of decompression. This paper describes the development of a mobile information system to support judicial decision making and the compression strategy needed to ensure that operation of the system is compatible with the working environment of the target user group.

A taxonomy of mobile working environments provides a useful framework for understanding mobile information systems. We classify working environments as either static or peripatetic following the work of Dahibom and Ljungberg [2]. The peripatetic subtype can be further classified as deterministic, non-deterministic or dynamic. Deterministic mobility is characterised as taking place where there are fixed working locations and the worker has to travel between these locations. Information technology support is typically provided by desktop systems in the various locations. Non-deterministic mobility is defined by working activities in which the worker is expected to visit different locations but these locations can not be predicted. The location would typically provide some support for the working environment and a laptop computer would be an appropriate platform for meeting information technology needs. In dynamic mobility, there is no prior determination of the location in which work takes place and no provision for a conventional working environment. In an environment such as this, a PDA represents a useful platform for information technology support. Many professional activities involve different classes of mobility. Whilst formal interactions may take place in static or deterministic modes, the nature of professional work suggests that the process is often carried out in non-deterministic or dynamic modes. This is particularly true of some of the processes that contribute to judicial decisions. Whilst some of the work is carried out in static or deterministic modes, non-deterministic and dynamic work is also carried out within and outside the locations where justice is formally dispensed. Given this pattern, a laptop computer is appropriate where the judge is working in a defined location and a PDA provides the best platform for supporting dynamically mobile aspects of professional activity. A further factor that may influence the choice of platforms is the social acceptability of computer usage. A laptop computer is acceptable in a formal working environment. By contrast, a PDA can be used without intrusion in business meetings and other locations. As a consequence of our analysis of the mobility of our user group, the initial target platform chosen was a laptop computer. Subsequent developments of PDA technology have opened the possibility of providing support for dynamic mobility.

1.1 Judicial Sentencing Decisions

Judges tend to enjoy very wide discression in the manner in which individual cases are dealt with. There are many factors that may be taken into account by a judge during the sentencing process. Most jurisdictions provide a defined maximum penalty for any offence, but beyond that there is little statutory guidance. Similarly, the overall aim of the sentencing process is ill-defined. Deterrence, rehabilitation, protection of the public and retribution are all identifiable as valid aims but in reality, a particular sentence may well be informed by a combination of these factors. Given the emphasis on the individualised nature of the sentencing process, it is not surprising that disparity in sentencing practice emerges from time-to-time as an issue for public concern. Public expectations of consistency in sentencing are reflected in media response to sentences that appear to be unusually lenient or severe although there is often no clear concensus on what could be termed 'normal' in any particular set of circumstances. The focus of this paper is on the technical support that can be used to provide a judge with an overview of sentencing patterns for cognate offences.

Decision support for sentencing has been investigated in a number of jurisdictions. The courts in New South Wales provide access to first instance sentences as well as to sentencing law and appeal court judgements [6]. The system operates by allowing the user to specify the act and section that relate to the offence. Characteristics of the offender may be specified by the user and sentencing patterns are displayed to show the distribution of particular types of sentence. The data is centralised and can be accessed over a wide area network from remote sites. An alternative approach to providing computer support for sentencing is to use a knowledge-based system to guide sentencing decisions. Murbach and Nonn [5] describe a prototype sentencing DSS limited to fraud cases. Discussion with the judiciary was used to establish a sentencing model and subsequently to construct a knowledge-based system to incorporate the reasoning process.

The requirement for our system is to provide a means whereby a judge may retrieve previous examples of sentencing behaviour. The judge is able to control the level of abstraction used to retrieve data. Given the mobile nature of a judge's working experience, it is necessary to provide this support in a flexible way using different platforms. Off-line compression of data presents a useful way of enabling rapid transfer of the database to a PDA-based system therby supporting the dynamically mobile working environment of our user group. The initial system design was based on a model of deterministic mobility. We provide support for this by the use of laptop computers. The additional implementation effort of data compression is not essential in the latter environment.

2 Architecture

Data compression is useful for underpinning the operation of the PDA-based platform since it helps to conserve memory and battery power. Conventional main-memory databases represent data items as strings [3] [4] although work is reported on the use of fixed length pointers to replace domain values [7]. Our strategy is to mimimise the size of the tokens used to represent data by basing token size on the entropy of the domain to be represented. Our method of compression enables us to compress the data off-line and resolve queries by de-compressing only the output data [1].

2.1 Dictionary-Based Data Compression

The minimum entropy approach to data compression requires that each domain in a database is represented by a code with a minimum number of bits. The

NAME	START YEAR	SERVICE INTERVAL
Corolla	1980	6000
Carina	1984	10000
Camry	1983	10000
Celica	1985	10000
Supra	1980	6000
Space Cruiser	1985	10000

Fig. 1. MODEL relation

Table 1. Field lengths and tuple sizes for the MODEL relation

NAME	13
START YEAR	4
SERVICE INTERVAL	5
Tuple size	22

relation MODEL (Figure 1) represents data as it would be stored in an uncompressed database.

This data would typically be stored in tables with fixed length fields in which case the field lengths and associated tuple size in bytes would be as shown in Table 1 Since the relation MODEL contains six tuples, the size of the relation would be 6 * 22 * 8 = 1056 bits Inspection of the table suggests that it would be possible to represent the information content in a more compact form by using codes to represent the domain values rather than using the domain values themselves in the relation. The attribute NAME contains six different values therefore in its most compact form, it could be represented as a three bit integer. Since there are only two values in the SERVICE INTERVAL attribute, it could be represented as a one bit integer. The compressed integer representation of the relation MODEL is shown in Table 2.

Table 2. Compression of MODEL

	Raw		Compressed
Corolla	1980	6000	000 00 0
Carina	1984	10000	001 10 1
Camry	1983	10000	010 01 1
Celica	1985	10000	011 11 1
Supra	1980	6000	100 00 0
Space Cruiser	1985	10000	101 11 1

NAME
Corolla
Carina
Camry
Celica
Supra
Space Cruiser

START YEAR
1980
1983
1984
1985

SERVICE INTERVAL
6000
10000

Fig. 2. Dictionaries for MODEL

NAME	ENGINE SIZE	ENGINE STYLE
Corolla	1290	OHV
Corolla	1587	OHV
Carina	1587	OHC
Carina	1974	OHC
Camry	1839	OHC
Camry	1974	OHC

Fig. 3. ENGINE relation

The effect of representing data in this entropy-encoded format is to reduce the space occupied by MODEL to 36 bits. To this it is necessary to add the dictionary that allows the tokens to be converted to their string equivalents and for the reverse process to take place (Figure 2). Dictionaries can be represented as lists of domain values. In the case of all non-key attributes the number of entries in the dictionary will be less than the number of tuples in the relation.

Suppose that we have a second relation, ENGINE, that specifies the engines fitted to various models (Figure 3). The domain from which the values in the NAME attribute of ENGINE are drawn is a sub-domain of that used in the MODEL relation. Since there are 3 models listed, first order compression of the column would require the use of 2 bit integers. This however would entail the establishment of a new dictionary to handle the values in the NAME attribute for the MODEL relation. In the case of a primary key, the size of such a dictionary is almost certain to be greater than the total number of bits required to encode the column.

Our objective is to minimise the size of the total database. It therefore makes sense to determine the columns in the database that can share dictionaries. These are the columns that contain values belonging to the same domain. An advantage of a tokenised architecture is that it can accelerate the evaluation of queries. If a query initially expressed in terms of string pattern matches, is compressed, its new expression is in terms of integer comparisons. These are inherently faster because the amount of data that has to be moved into the CPU and compared for each selection operation is significantly reduced. Clearly the final answer has to be converted from the abstract to the concrete representation. This involves

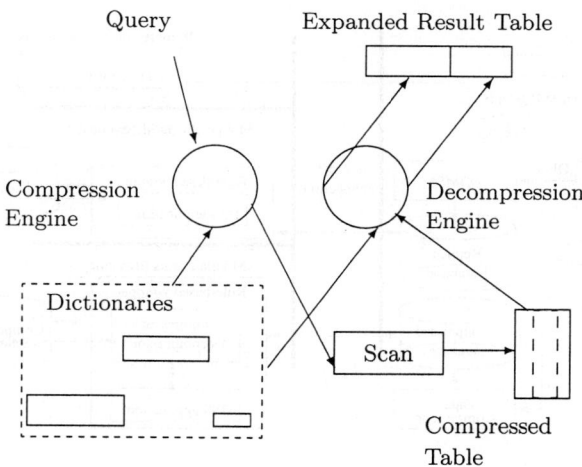

Fig. 4. Querying a database in the compressed form

a decompression phase in which the field codes are mapped to their associated keywords. The computational cost of this will be borne only on the tuples that are returned as a result. Since this phase is dominated by output delays in the screen handling software, the perceived cost of this decompression is likely to be minimal.

The purpose of the information system is to provide judges with a means of retrieving previous examples of sentencing behaviour. The compression strategy we have developed can be used to enable this function to be provided in small form-factor systems. The architecture is shown diagrammatically in Figure 5. This structure has evolved over a period of eight years since the start of the project. There are three main elements in the structure: a non-mobile element that is used by clerical staff to carry out the functions of data entry and data quality control, a server that acts as a means of collating and distributing updates and a number of mobile client systems. As far as the end users of the system are concerned, the data we provide is read-only. This means that the compression needed to support the PDA architecture can be carried out off-line. In general we are able to arrange our compression system so that it can handle updates but in the case of this application it is not necessary. Instead, updates are made to the conventional representation of the data and the compression is carried out off-line so as to generate a new distribution of the database.

Database inserts can be carried out from any convenient workstation in the High Court buildings distributed round the country. These buildings all provide wide area network facilities and clerks are familiar with the use of web browsers. Passwords are used to identify data entered with particular clerks (in case of consistent misunderstandings about the taxonomy of offence details). It is also simpler if data is entered directly into the consolidated database rather than

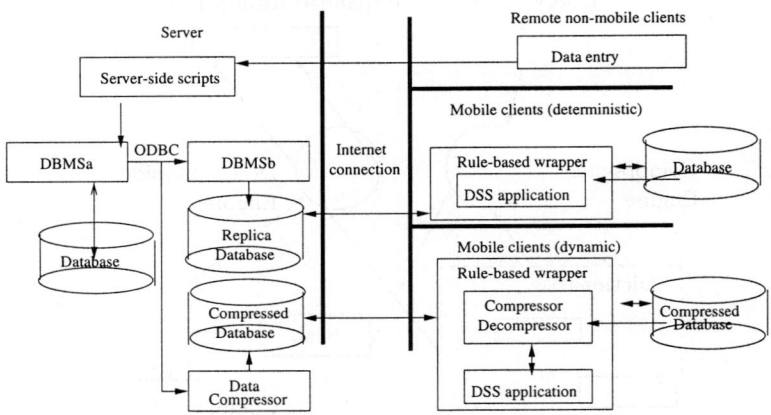

Fig. 5. Architecture for a mobile data-intensive information system

stored locally for forwarding and consolidation at a later date. The advantages of a browser-based solution to this problem are considerable. As well as familiarity and controlled access, the code and the underlying data of the data entry system remains accessible for maintenance purposes. In this particular case, CGI scripts were used since this environment was familiar to development staff, however other server-side scripting technologies would be equally acceptable.

The server requires a number of database management systems to solve licensing problems in a multi-operating system environment. The data entry scripts and the main database are resident on a Unix system but the mobile clients run on versions of MS Windows. To resolve this problem, an ODBC link is used to replicate the consolidated database into the proprietary system that is appropriate for the laptop clients.

On each client system, a wrapper is used to contain the data retrieval system. The purpose of the wrapper is to update the database if a newer version is available on the server than that present on the client. In many cases it will be inappropriate to carry out the copying process that would be necessary to transfer the replica database from the server to the client. The wrapper contains a number of rules that enable it to determine whether it is appropriate to carry out the update.

The application operates by allowing the judge to select cases that match some of the criteria of the case under consideration. We directly involved the user community in the design of the interface and in the development of a taxonomy for the cases to be entered into the system. Early in this process it became clear that the focus of the system was the retrieval of cases appropriate to a particular decision. We considered and rejected a knowledge-based approach that could have been used to suggest an appropriate course of action in a given set of circumstances. One of the challenges of the design process was to ensure that data was aggregated in such a way as to provide a substantial number of cases that would help with any specific decision. There are about one thousand serious criminal convictions in Scotland every year. The bulk of these are assaults and robberies however our user group was able to identify fifteen different categories of criminal activity. Associated with each category are a variable number of attributes of both the offender and the offence.

The data can be considered as a multi-dimensional cube with each dimension being one of the indexed attributes. The cells within the matrix contain aggregations of the cases that correspond to the index values on each dimension. The sparsity of the matrix is the proportion of non-zero elements. The retrieval of data by specifying values along each dimension quickly reveals the curse of dimensionality. Judges retrieving cases from a small pool of data by specifying many dimensions are likely to find only small numbers of matches.

A detailed analysis of the judges needs to search the database on a relatively large number of attributes results in a data cube with a sparsity of 0.14%. The effect of this is that users are unlikely to be able to retrieve interesting cases if they specify values for all or most of the indexed attributes. We use two approaches to counteract this problem. Allowing the user to define the attributes used to index data permits aggregations to be constructed over fewer dimensions, thereby reducing the sparsity. During the user training, we emphasise that the most productive use of the system is achieved by specifying only the most important criteria in the first instance. The user is left to decide which attributes are of importance in a particular case. It is quite easy to gauge whether there is sufficient data to support queries with greater specificity. This approach implies that the system responds rapidly enough to be searched on an interactive basis. As an alternative approach to the problem, the users developed a second taxonomy that could be used to group cases on an holistic basis. This approach lost some of the detail from individual cases but the coarser grouping provided larger aggregations for each cell in the resulting matrix. Using this approach, the sparsity of the data structure was 11.25%.

We provided a facility that allows the user to drill down into the aggregations produced by the top-level query. Drill down provides progressively more information about each aggregate and at the lowest level, users are able to view the details of specific cases.

3 Implementation

The implementation of the compression algorithm is based on the use of a string pool to store the lexemes (the uncompressed representation of attribute values). The tokens are represented by integers that give the indices of offsets of the lexemes in the string pool. This approach ensures that the tokens are of minimal length. Off-line data compression is carried out by hashing the tokens to discover the entry point in the offset table. If the hash value is pointing at a vacant entry in the table (after handling overflows) then the lexeme is inserted into the dictionary and the offset stored in the appropriate cell. The hash value is then stored in the data structure that represents the relation. On the retrieval side, tokens recovered from the database can be converted into lexemes by retrieving the offset and using that as an entry point into the string pool.

We used this strategy to compress the data collected for the information system and overall were able to reduce the volume of the data to 13% of the initial representation as stored in a conventional database system. This represents a useful benefit for the PDA version of the information system. The data can be stored in an optimally compacted form without prejudicing the performance of queries on the system. In addition, since the database file is now represented in minimal space, updated files can be transferred from the server to the mobile client with optimal efficiency.

Table 3. Comparison of conventional and compressed storage for sentencing data

	Conventional Storage S_p (Mb)	Compressed Storage S_c (Mb)	Compressed to Conventional $\frac{S_c}{S_p}$
relation1	1.9	0.23	12%
relation2	0.35	0.03	9%
relation3	0.34	0.05	15%
relation4	0.18	0.03	17%
relation5	0.05	0.02	40%
Cumulative	2.82	0.36	13%

We used a direct manipulation interface to the system since our user group was initially unfamiliar with the concept of using computer support for sentencing decisions. Figure 6 shows the appearance of the laptop version of the interface. To arrive at this point, the user has first to set a number of characteristics of the offence. The chart presents the aggregations of cases in each category of sentence and these can be explored further by drilling down into the respective bars. The PDA interface uses dynamic queries to achieve the same result. The text entries at the foot of the screen (Figure 7) represent cascading menus that allow the user to make choices about the details of the cases to be displayed. Each time a choice is made, the distribution chart is updated to show the aggregation of cases that match the currently selected criteria. The bars in the chart can be drilled in a similar manner to the laptop based system. The direct manipulation interface was well received and judges found that they were rapidly able to construct meaningful queries and retrieve appropriate data despite having limited prior experience of computer use.

A preliminary evaluation of the laptop based system was carried out with two cohorts of users each consisting of four users. Users were assigned to cohorts in a random manner. Restrictions caused by administration of the project allowed monitoring to be carried out over twelve weeks for the first cohort and five weeks

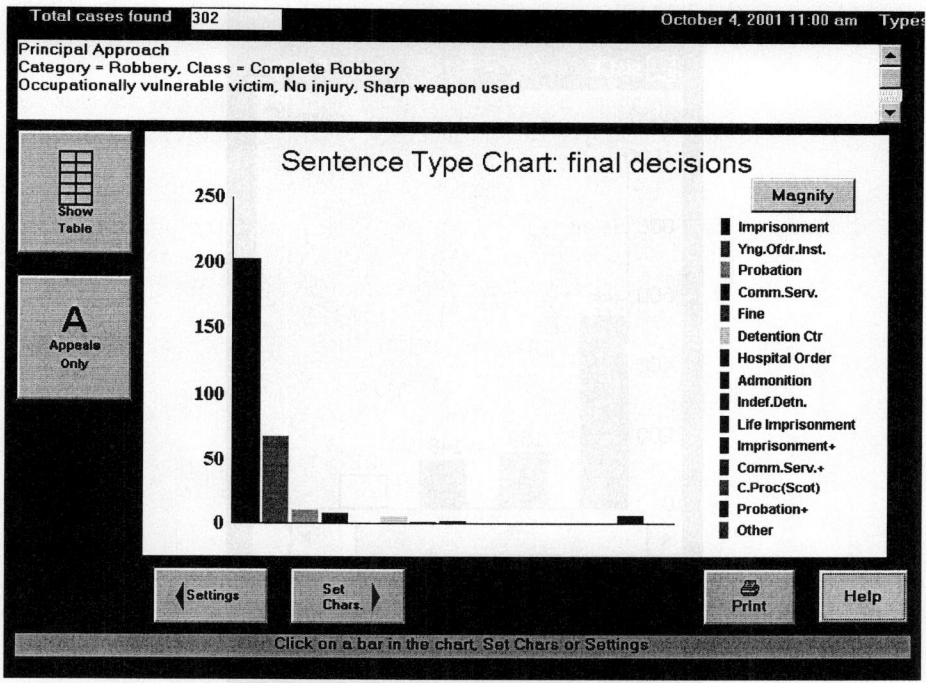

Fig. 6. Laptop interface to the information system

for the second cohort. The results for system usage are shown in Figure 8. There is a clear novelty aspect to the system usage pattern for the first cohort in the first week of the trial but thereafter, usage settled down at a much lower level. The second cohort did not show the same novelty peak but subsequent usage reflected a similar pattern to the first cohort.

4 Conclusion

Judges claim, with justification, that each sentencing decision is made on the merits of the specific case. Within this constraint, it is recognised by all the participants in our project that sentencing decisions can profit from contextualisation within the patterns set by precedent. The challenge is how to reconcile the need to make each decision unique with the benefits of contextualisation. Our solution to this conflict is to build a system that supports the decision makers and is compatible with their mobile working environment. Data compression makes a significant contribution to the provision of this support by facilitating the use of non-intrusive systems. The small form factor of the PDA allows quick and easy access to sentencing patterns. Data compression presents an opportunity to

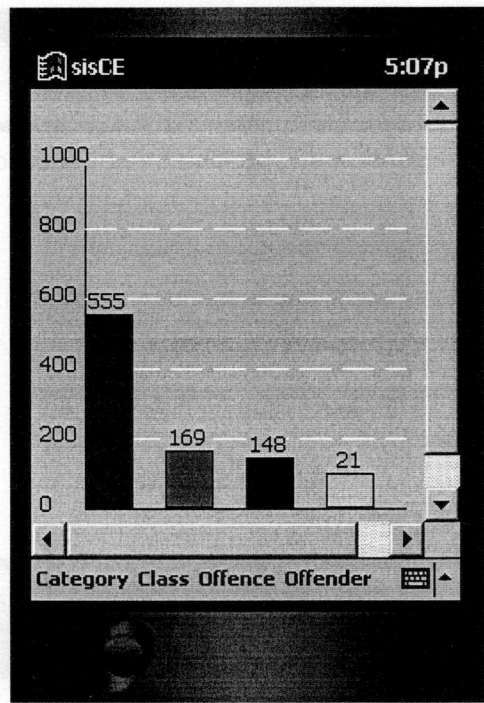

Fig. 7. PDA interface to the information system

reduce response times as well as the on-line time needed to update the system. We intend to use wireless technology to support updates. Data compression will accelerate wireless updates and reduce the power consumption of the process.

The laptop-based system we have developed has been in use by some of the judges in Scotland for three years and has proved robust and useful. We are currently extending the provision to all the judges in the jurisdiction and installing the support architecture. The PDA-based system we are developing provides a step in the direction of support for dynamic mobility and opens up a number of technical issues. Current PDA technology is at a relatively early stage of development. Memory sizes and processor speeds need to be increased in order to make even medium-scale data intensive applications feasible on such platforms. The approach that we have developed of using data compression to optimise the storage of data on the PDA makes the best possible use of the memory and processing capability that is available in these small form factor devices.

The support for sentencing that we are providing is limited to statistical information on sentencing patterns. Our users are interested in increasing the textual content of the system both to enable the storage and retrieval of narrative

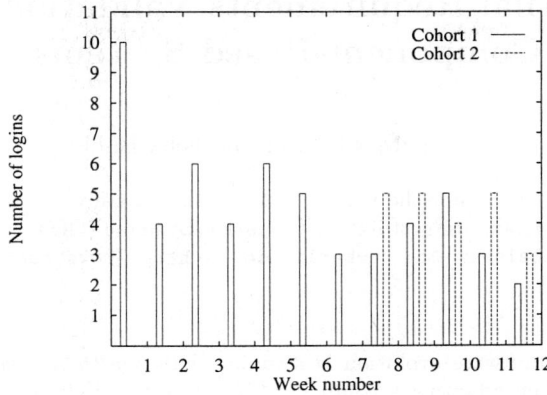

Fig. 8. System usage in the pilot deployment

descriptions of particular cases and also to enable them to search databases of case law. The provision of mobile access to this kind of Intranet data remains a challenge for database systems.

References

1. W.P. Cockshott, D.R. McGregor, and J.N. Wilson. High performance operations using a compressed database architecture. *Computer Journal*, 41(5):283–296, 1998.
2. B. Dahlbom and F. Ljungberg. Mobile informatics. *Scandinavian Journal of Information Systems*, 10(1):227–234, 1999.
3. H. Garcia-Molina and K. Salem. Main memory database systems: an overview. *IEEE Transactions on Knowledge and Data Engineering*, 4:6:509516, 1992.
4. T. Lehman, E. Shekita, and L. Cabrera. An evaluation of starburst's memory resident storage component. *IEEE Transactions Knowledge and Data Engineering*, 4:6, 1992.
5. R. Murbach and E. Nonn. Similarity in harder cases. *Proceedings of the 4th International Conference on Artificial Intelligence and Law Amsterdam, June,*, pages 236–244, 1993.
6. I. Potas, D. David Ash, M. Sagi, S. Cumines, and N. Marsic. Informing the discretion: The sentencing information system of the Judicial Commission of New South Wales. *International Journal of Law and Information Technology*, 6:99, 1998.
7. P. Pucheral, J. Thevenin, and P. Valduriez. Efficient main memory data management using dbgraph storage model. *Proceedings of the 16th VLDB Conference,Brisbane*, pages 683–695, 1990.

External Requirements Validation for Component-Based Systems

Andreas Leicher and Felix Bübl

Technische Universität Berlin, Germany
Computergestützte InformationsSysteme (CIS)
{fbuebl|aleicher}@cs.tu-berlin.de — http://www.cocons.org

Abstract. Software evolution is a major challenge to software development. When adapting a component-based system to new, altered or deleted requirements, existing requirements should not accidentally be violated. Invariant conditions are usually specified via constraint languages like OCL on a high precision level close to source code. On the contrary, this paper uses a new constraint mechanism. One *context-based constraint* (CoCon) specifies one requirement for a group of *indirectly associated* components that share a context. This paper proposes a 'Rule Manager' approach to monitor a system's compliance with requirements automatically at runtime. The approach is compatible with modern middleware technologies and allows the transparent integration of requirement validation in legacy systems or COTS.

1 Introduction

1.1 Continuous Software Engineering

The context for which a software system was designed continuously changes throughout its lifetime. *Continuous software engineering* is a paradigm discussed in [22] to keep track of the ongoing changes and to adapt legacy systems to altered requirements. Only component-based systems are addressed in the KONTENG[1] project, because this rearrangeable software architecture is best suited for continuous software engineering.

1.2 The Notion of 'External Requirements Validation'

Some requirements should be reflected during the design phase, some during deployment and some at runtime. This paper focuses on requirements validation at runtime. We propose to monitor a system's compliance with requirement specifications at runtime. Requirements tend to change quite often. The new approach

---

[1] This work was supported by the German Federal Ministry of Education and Research as part of the research project KONTENG (Kontinuierliches Engineering für evolutionäre IuK-Infrastrukturen) under grant 01 IS 901 C

presented in this paper suggests *not* to implement requirements validation *into* any of the components involved. Instead, conformity with requirements is enforced *externally* of the components. Hence, the system can be *transparently* adapted to changed or new requirements via connector refinement without modifying the components directly. Furthermore, legacy components or components 'off the shelf' can be forced to comply with requirements that are not taken into consideration by the components themselves.

2 Context-Based Constraints (CoCons)

This section explains the concept of 'context' used in this paper and introduces how to specify requirements via 'context-based constraints'.

2.1 The New Constraint Technique 'CoCons' in Brief

This article is an overview on the new constraint technique – much more details are provided in the corresponding technical report ([3]). The basic concept can be explained in just a few sentences.

1. Yellow sticky notes are stuck to the components. They are called 'context properties', because meta-information describing their component's context is written on them.
2. A new constraint mechanism refers to this meta-information for identifying the part of the system where the constraint applies. Only those components whose meta-information fits the constraint's 'context condition' must fulfil the constraint. Up to now, no constraint technique exists that selects the constrained components according to their meta-information.
3. Via the new constraint technique a requirement for a group of components that share a context can be automatically protected.

2.2 Introducing Context Properties

The term 'context' is used an various senses. When using context-based constraints, 'context' refers to the state, situation or environment of a component. The context is expressed by assigning context properties to components. A **context property** has a name and a set of values as illustrated in figure 2. One set of values can be assigned to a single component c for each context property cp. This set is called $ConPropVals^{cp,c}$. If a context property value is associated with a component, it describes how or where this component is used – this meta-information describes the 'context' of this component. Each context property is only useful if a requirement must be specified for a *part* of the system that can be identified by this context property. This paper discusses only the context property **'Personal Data'**. It signals whether a component handles data of private nature. Its values associated with a component are defined manually.

On the contrary, **system properties**, like 'the current User' or 'the current IP Address', can be automatically queried from the middleware platform during configuration or at runtime. Each middleware technology enables certain system properties to be queried, but it's beyond the scope of this paper how the various technologies query the system property values.

Many techniques for writing down metainformation exist. The notion of context or container properties is well established in component runtime infrastructures such as COM+, EJB, or .NET. The primary benefit of enriching components with context properties is revealed in next section, where such properties are used to specify requirements.

2.3 A New Notion of Invariants

One requirement can affect several components that do not invoke each other directly or even do not run on the same platform. A **context-based constraint** (CoCon) specifies a requirement for a group of components that share a context. The shared context is identified via the context property values assigned to these components. If these values comply with the CoCon's context condition then their components share the same context. The metamodel in figure 1 shows the metamodel for CoCons. This metamodel resembles a UML 1.4 ([14]) profile if you rename the metaclass 'Component' to 'ModelElement', 'Context Property' to 'TagDefinition' and 'Context Property Value' to 'TaggedValue' in figure 1. However, this paper focuses on using CoCons at runtime. Thus, integration in UML is not discussed. CoCons should be preserved and considered in model modifications, during deployment, at runtime and when specifying another – possibly contradictory – CoCon. Thus, a CoCon is an *invariant*. It describes which parts of the system must be protected. If a requirement is written down via a CoCon, its violation can be detected *automatically*.

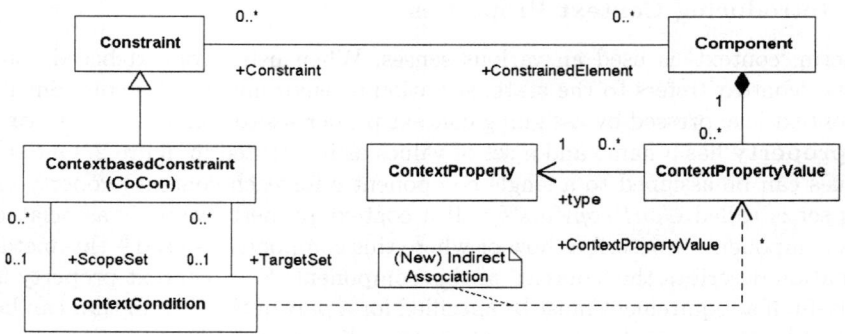

Fig. 1. The CoCon Metamodel

The context property 'Personal Data' is described section 2.2. Either its value 'True' or 'False' is associated with a component. Thus, a CoCon can state that *"components where 'Personal Data' has the value 'True'* must be inaccessible by the component 'SalesMgr'"(**Example A**). This constraint is based on the context property values of the components – it is a context-based constraint or CoCon. The shared context is expressed via a **'context condition'** which selects components via their context property values. It describes a (possibly empty) *set* of components. In example A, the part in italics represents the context condition that selects the **'target set'**.

In Example A, the *scope* of the CoCon is a single component: the component 'SalesMgr'. But the scope can be a set containing any number of components, as illustrated in **example B**: *"The component 'SalesMgr' must be inaccessible by any component that is currently used by a 'Controller' who is not located in 'Frankfurt'"*. Users of the system have the role 'controller' if they check the financial transactions of accountancy. Both example A and B are explained in section 3.2. The **'scope set'** contains those components, where the elements of the target set must meet the constraint. In Example B, the scope set contains all the components used by a controller not located in Frankfurt. Both target set elements and scope set elements can be specified either directly or indirectly:

...directly: Set elements can be specified by directly naming the component(s) involved. In Example A, the CoCon is associated directly with the 'SalesMgr' component. This unambiguously identifies the only element of the scope set.
...indirectly: The indirect association of a constraint to its constrained elements is the key new concept of context-based constraints. Set elements can be indirectly selected via a context condition. The scope set in Example B contains all the components where the context property 'Current User Role' has the value 'Controller' and 'Current Caller Location' does not equal 'Frankfurt'. These scope set elements are anonymous. They are not directly named, but described indirectly via their context properties. If no component fulfils the context condition, the set is empty. This simply means that the CoCon does not apply to any component.

A CoCon **attribute** can define details of its CoCon. This paper only discusses the attribute **Action**. It defines what to do in case of a CoCon violation. More Details on CoCons are introduced in [4].

2.4 A Textual Language for CoCon Specification

This section introduces a textual language for specifying context-based constraints. The standard technique for defining the syntax of a language is the Backus-Naur Form (BNF), where "::=" stands for the definition, "Text" for a nonterminal symbol and "**TEXT**" for a terminal symbol.

The **C**ontext-based **C**onstraint **L**anguage *CCL for components* ([3]) consists of different CoCon types. However, this paper only discussed one CoCon type. For a complete syntax definition please refer to the implementation of the 'CCL plugin for ArgoUML' described in section 6.1. All rules concerning the separator (',' ; 'AND'or 'OR') are abbreviated. For instance, "Rule {'OR' Rule }*" is abbreviated "(Rule)+^{OR}". This is the BNF Syntax for CoCons of the InaccessibleBy Type:

```
InaccessibleByCoCon ::= (ElementSelection)+^OR 'MUST BE Inac-
                         cessibleBy' (ElementSelection)+^OR Attribute
ElementSelection    ::= ContextCondition | DirectSelection
DirectSelection     ::= ('THE COMPONENT' CompName) | 'THIS'
ContextCondition    ::= 'ALL        COMPONENTS        WHERE'
                         ContextQuery+^AND or OR
ContextQuery        ::= ContextPropertyName Condition
                         (ContextPropertyValue | SetOfConPropValues)
SetOfConPropValues  ::= ('{' (ContextPropertyValue)+^Comma '}') |
                         ContextPropertyName
Condition           ::= 'CONTAINS' | 'DOES NOT CONTAIN' |
                         '=' | '!=' | '<' | '>' | '<=' | '>='
Attribute           ::= 'WITH ACTION =' ('Abort' | 'Redirect' |
                         'Filter')
```

An example is given in section 3.2. The ContextCondition rule allows for the *indirect* selection of the elements involved. In contrast, the ElementName rule *directly* selects elements by naming them. The ContextQuery describes (one or more) set(s) of *RequiredValues^{cp}*. A context condition selects the component c if for each context property cp used in the context condition the *RequiredValues^{cp}* $\subseteq$ *ConPropVals^{cp,c}*. Besides **'CONTAINS'** ($\subseteq$), this paper suggests other expressions like '!=' (does not equal) and **'DOES NOT CONTAIN'** ($\not\subseteq$). Only simple comparisons (inclusion, equality,...) are used in order to keep CoCons comprehensible. Future research might reveal the benefits of using complex logical expression, such as temporal logic.

2.5 Comparing OCL to Context-Based Constraints

Typically, the *Object Constraint Language OCL* summarized in [21] is used for the constraint specification of object-oriented models. One OCL constraint refers to (normally one) *directly identified* element, while a context-based constraint can refer both to directly identified and to (normally many) indirectly identified, *anonymous and unrelated* elements. A CoCon can select the elements involved according to their meta-information. In the UML, tagged values are a mechanism similar to context properties for expressing meta-information. There is no concept of selecting the constrained elements via their tagged values in OCL or any other existing formal constraint language.

An OCL constraint can only refer to elements that are directly linked to its scope. On the contrary, a CoCon scope is not restricted. It can refer to elements that are not necessarily associated with each other or even belong to different models. When specifying an OCL constraint it is not possible to consider elements that are unknown at specification time. In contrast, an element becomes involved in one context-based constraint simply by having the matching context property value(s). Hence, the target elements and the scope elements can change without modifying the CoCon specification.

Before discussing another distinction, the OMG meta-level terminology will be explained briefly. Four levels exist: Level 'M_0' refers to a system's objects at runtime, 'M_1' refers to a system's model or schema, such as a UML model, 'M_2' refers to a metamodel, such as the UML metamodel, and 'M_3' refers to a meta-metamodel, such as the Meta-Object Facility (MOF). If an OCL constraint is associated with a model element on level M_i, then it refers the instances of this model element on level M_{i-1} — in OCL, the 'context' [6] of an invariant is an *instance* of the associated model element. If specified in a system model on M_1 level, an OCL constraint refers to *runtime* instances of the associated model element on level M_0. In order to refer to M_1 level, OCL constraints must be defined at M2 level (e.g. within a stereotype). On the contrary, a CoCon can be verified automatically on the *same* meta-level where it is specified. All CoCons discussed in this paper are specified *and* verified on M_0 level because this paper focuses on checking them at runtime.

3 Applying Context-Based Constraints at Runtime

Today, abstract constraints, like CoCons, are generally not supported by modern component technologies, like Enterprise JavaBeans [7] or Microsoft *.NET*. They have to be implemented manually into components. In fact, finalized components have to be extended and modified by additional logic. They require a programmatic extension that reduces the system's maintainability. This complicates the programming, the handling and the evolution of components. This paper, therefore, proposes to specify constraints declaratively. Most contemporary middleware systems only allow for the specification of constraints for well-defined tasks such as security and transactional behaviour at the time of deployment. Beyond that, the approach presented allows CoCons to be specified and monitored *dynamically* at runtime.

3.1 Main Objectives

The main objective is the transparent integration of a mechanism for monitoring CoCons into modern middleware technologies. This brings the advantage that modifying components is not longer necessary when adapting the system to new or changed requirements expressed via CCL CoCons. In addition, the transparent integration as well as the separation of the requirements specification support the evolution of systems. Requirements are encapsulated as separate aspects of the application logic and are treated separately. Therefore, the approach facilitates the integration with legacy systems, which can be enforced even at runtime to conform to new or changed constraints without modifying the legacy components themselves. Furthermore, components 'of the shelf ' (COTS) can be transparently complemented by additional constraints for the same reasons.

Their standard functionality can be restricted by the approach presented without modifying themselves.

3.2 Scenario

The following example describes a trading system of a company located in New York(main office), Tokyo(branch office) and Frankfurt(branch office). The systems main components are shown in figure 2. They are associated with appropriate context property values. An identical configuration of the system will be deployed and installed at each location. Personal data of local users is stored at the user's location whereas a global user schema exists for the whole system. The following context properties are shown in figure 2:

System.Location: Specifies the installation place of the component

System.UserRole: Describes user groups: In our example, an user is either a Trader or a Controller. Controllers are able to check personal data on all transactions.

In this paper only one requirement is discussed: *"Controllers who are not located in Frankfurt must not be able to access Frankfurt's personal data"*. The system must comply with this requirement due to German federal law. The corresponding CoCon specification is defined as follows:

```
ALL COMPONENTS WHERE 'Personal Data' = 'True'
AND System.Location = 'Frankfurt'
MUST BE InaccessibleBy
ALL COMPONENTS WHERE System.Location != 'Frankfurt' AND
System.UserRole = 'Controller'
WITH ACTION = 'Abort'
```

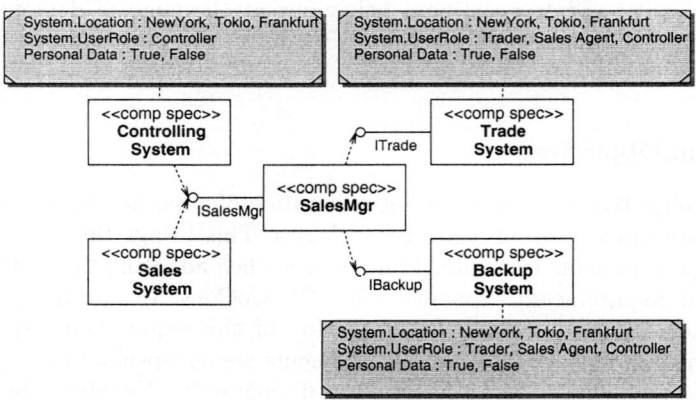

Fig. 2. Trader System Scenario

3.3 Runtime Realisation

The example requirement is checked at runtime since it refers to dynamically changing context properties values. The components in question may not be changed because transparent monitoring is strived for. Rather, the communication of the components involved must be intercepted. Hence, monitoring points (Points of Interception) are installed in the communication paths of the components. For this, we use as the technical foundation the proxy pattern[8]. Most middleware technologies use a kind of this standard communication method to realize local and distributed communication.

Figure 3 shows the example scenario once more. This time a J2EE application server is used as the starting point. Requests to the system are routed via the controlling system component to the sales management component. The point of interception is placed, in front of the sales management component. Each incoming call is monitored, for whether it complies with the specified CoCon. In the case a violation against a CoCon, predefined actions are executed.

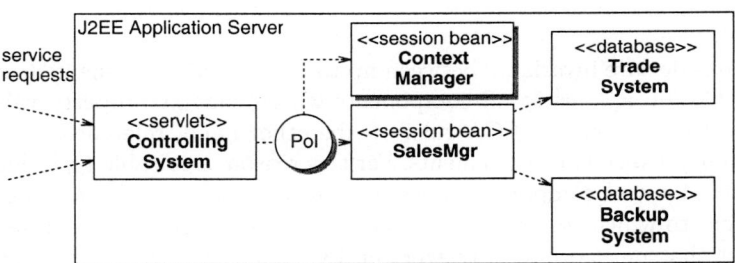

Fig. 3. Point of Interception

4 Rule Manager Approach

Our approach is based on two well-known concepts. On the one hand, it uses Event Condition Action (ECA) rules. They are typically applied in active databases [24], where ECA rules are used to check for basic database operations and where additional actions are triggered when specified conditions are met. On the other hand, middleware systems are integrated via a proxy mechanism. It allows for transparent integration in common technologies by intercepting communication between components. The proxy mechanism is extended by the needed monitoring functionality. Thus, it becomes possible to place interception points between components. The extended proxy can be seen as a *connector*, which facilitates requirement protection. Consequently, a connector is treated as a *first-class entity*[19], which has to be carefully designed.

4.1 ECA Rules

The approach presented uses ECA rules to monitor CoCons at runtime. ECA rules are based on a formal specification language and have a syntax depicted in figure 4. A rule consists of four parts: a *type clause*, an *event clause*, a *conditional clause* and an *action clause*[2]. One of the main tasks of this approach is to translate a CoCon into ECA rule definitions.

```
declare rule rule_name
  proxy typeclause
  on eventclause
  if conditionalclause
  do actionclause
end rule
```

Fig. 4. Rule Definition

```
declare rule security_example
  proxy type(SalesMgt)
  on request(true)
  if context('PersonalData', 'True') AND
     ¬(context(System.Location, 'Frankfurt')) AND
     context(System.UserRole, 'Controller')
  do abort
end rule
```

Fig. 5. Example Rule

CoCons declare invariants between up to two sets of components (see section 2). One CoCon applies to all components whose context property values fulfil its context condition. An ECA rule, on the other hand, references a particular connection between two components. For this reason, a suitable *type clause* must be declared for *each* component affected by the CoCon. A *type clause* specifies the component to which communication has to be filtered. An *event clause* specifies the event that must occur to trigger the ECA rule. An event can be related to a specific, or to several services.

Different types of CoCons exist (though, in this paper only one type relevant to runtime is discussed). These types determine the *conditional clause*. If the constraint is to be evaluated at runtime, as in figure 5, the *conditional clause* contains *context clauses* that determines the matching context property values at runtime. A *context clause* is related to the Context Manager, which provides the context property values of a component. The context manager detects this information through technology-specific functions. Every message (or procedure call) to a certain proxy is checked by an ECA rule at runtime. In case of a conditional match, there are many possible actions. These can be stated in the *actions clause*. Actions are managed in an *action template* repository that contains some predicates with platform specific mappings.

4.2 Actions

The specification of a runtime CoCon includes the action that must be taken in the case where a CoCon is violated. There are many possible actions. A selection of typical actions follows without claiming to be complete:

---

[2] In the following, clauses are stated as predicates

Abort Action The communication is prevented specifically. This can be realized by sending back an exception to the calling client. This is totally transparent to the application components.

Redirect Action: The communication, which is normally initiated between components $A \rightarrow B$, will be redirected to an available and fully compatible component C $(A \rightarrow C)$. Component C has to fulfil the contract of component B with A.

Filter Action: The data transferred in communication calls have to be modified. Therefore, the exact knowledge of the format used for the submitting information is necessary.

Context-Aware Service: Besides normal communication, additional actions will be executed. For example, log-entries or some kind of analysis could be transparently integrated into communication.

4.3 Calculating the Points of Interception

The monitoring of CoCons at runtime requires that monitoring points (interception points) be determined. As a starting point of the calculation, there are both a component specification model as known from Cheesman/Daniels[5] and an abstract requirements (CoCon) specification. The component specification model has been enriched by context properties. The following problems arise in the context of the calculation:

- CoCons can specify requirements for sets of components. Thus, a large number of ECA rules can result from a single CoCon. Because of the nature of CoCons components can be directly or transitively associated. The resulting ECA rules must be installed at each possible connection path between the sets of components. This ensures that the communication between components can be suitable monitored.
- Interception points between components that are not connected directly can be installed in different places. The problem therefore arises to localize the best suitable point.

In the following possible solutions to these problems are discussed briefly.

Invocation Path Calculation The component specification model (which shows dependencies between components) can be used to calculate all invocation paths of the system. A sequence of components that are directly connected with each other is referred as an invocation path. Figure 6 shows a part of the component specification diagram from the scenario, including context properties. Additionally, a CoCon is indicated. CoCons are build up out of two sets, the target set and the scope set. All components, which belong to one of these sets, are involved in the current CoCon. In order to determine the interception points, all of the invocation paths between these components must be identified. Therefore, direct and transitive dependencies between all the components in each set have to be calculated. As a result. all invocation paths have to fulfil the following predicates: They start with an element of the scope set, they end with an element of the target set, and all elements between them are connected directly via invocation dependencies.

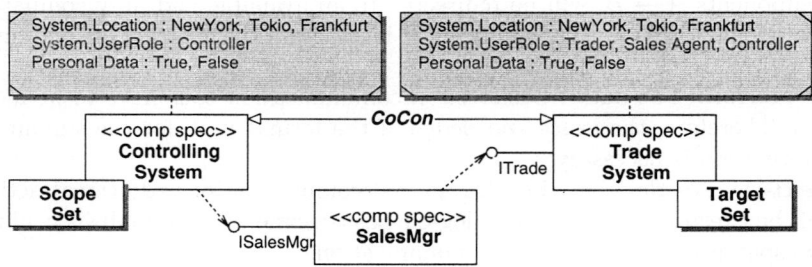

Fig. 6. Invocation path Calculation

Identifying the Interception Point An interception point has to be determined for each invocation path. This is a complicated task because the integrity and the performance of the system have to be maintained. Currently, we follow the heuristic to place the interception point in front of the serving component (service provider). This has the advantage of guaranteeing that all communication calls can be intercepted. In this way, we maintain the integrity of the system but haven't optimised the intercepting mechanism.

4.4 System Structure

As explained above, CoCons must be translated into ECA rules that have to be assigned to appropriate proxies. These tasks are reflected in the structure of the Rule Engine (see figure 7), which consists primarily of two parts:

The Rule Compiler translates CCL constraints into formal ECA rule specifications for each proxy involved. Context information as well as *context-templates* assist the compiler in translating the CCL constraint. Context-templates enable the necessary information to be determined at runtime. In order to install the ECA rules at proxies, they are compiled to executable Java code called *plug-ins* and dynamically uploaded to corresponding proxies. Proxies are enabled to update and execute these plug-ins.

The Rule Manager is the central management component of the engine. It manages the ECA rules in a repository and is responsible for updating the proxies in case of changes. The rule manager registers all proxies in the repository and transmits applicable ECA rules only to the components concerned.

The main problem of this approach arises from the determination of the context property values of the components involved in the checked communication call.

Current values can be extracted from the call protocol in question, from the environment (e.g. the application server) or even from the client. The context manager(see figure 3) serves as a central repository that provides the current context property values of each component.

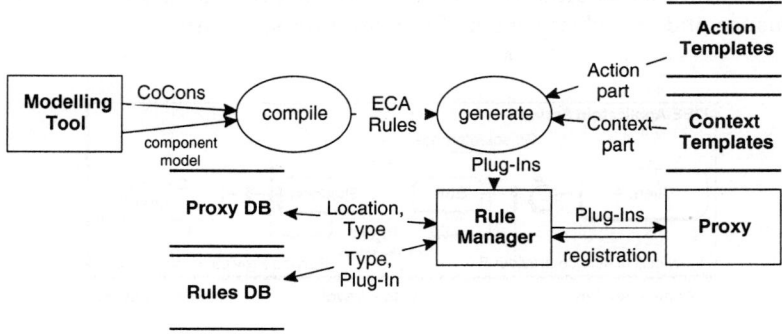

Fig. 7. System Structure Overview

5 Integration Approach

The integration of a CoCon monitoring mechanism into middleware systems can be realized through different concepts. The main difficulty is the incorporation of the extended proxy mechanism into existing wiring standards of middleware technologies.

5.1 System-Level Integration

The underlying middleware technology is transparently modified via the extension mechanism proposed. Therefore, the middleware's source code, especially of the proxy mechanism, has to be modified. At a minimum, the interception call has to be inserted into the code, but also the whole extension mechanism can be integrated, as well. Figure 8 shows the intended basic concept. The RPC/RMI functionality of the J2EE Application Server is thereby enlarged. Obviously, components at the application level communicate directly with each other. At the system level, however, communication is controlled by a proxy mechanism, which realizes remote connection and services like transactionality and security. Proxies are currently examined in various scientific works such as [2,18,17]. To customize transparent integration, some middleware platforms offer *callback* functions to modify standard behaviour. The JBoss Server ([15]), for example, supports a callback interface to intercept method calls to Enterprise JavaBeans. Such extensions simplify setting up integration approaches. The BEA WebLogic Server [1], for example, supports a callback interface in order to specify customized load balancing. In addition, Microsoft offers several integration techniques that easily and transparently allow adding intercepting functions to existing software. For example, so-called *Hooks* can be used to monitor relevant events and to call declared functions to handle these events ([9]). At the moment, a prototype based on JBoss is being developed. It cannot fulfil all advantages due to limited interception interfaces. However, we hope to achieve conclusions regarding the performance and the effectiveness of system-level integration.

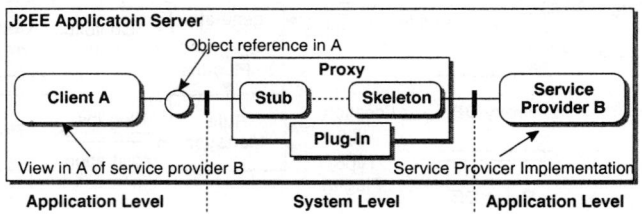

Fig. 8. Proxy Mechanism

5.2 Application-Level Integration

At the application level, there are several possibilities for obtaining the needed monitoring functionality. Most techniques are based on a wrapping concept for integrating additional functionality to existing concepts. Some wrapping concepts are represented in illustration 9. The standard approach is shown as variant 1. It is based on a proxy component, which is put in front of the service provider component. The advantage of this approach is that application level components do not have to be modified. It is a transparent integration approach. In contrast to the same principle on the system level, however the control is limited. For example, the Self problem (disclosure of the component's identity)[23] cannot be fully prevented and even worse, not all contexts can be evaluated. The second variant shows the inheritance of the application level component. This means that the source code of the component is needed and has to be extended to contain monitoring functionality. This approach has not been investigated further at this time. The third variant shows an aggregation approach. It is similar to the first approach, but merges the proxy and application component. Therefore, changing the source code is normally needed here, as well. In contrast to the second version, however, the component's classes could be repacked in Java without directly modifying the code. At present, we also use this concept in our research.

An alternative technology comparable to wrapping is not shown in the figure: Aspect-oriented programming[10]. Aspects cleanly encapsulate crosscutting concerns. Consequently, the extended proxy mechanism could be declared as an aspect and precompiled into the components involved.

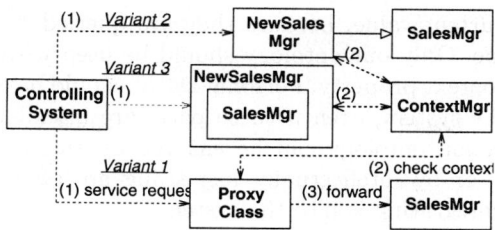

Fig. 9. Integration Variants

6 Conclusion

6.1 Applying CCL in Different Development Levels

This paper focuses on checking CCL CoCons at runtime. However, in this section the application of CCL throughout the software development process is outlined.

During requirements analysis the business experts must be asked specific questions in order to find out useful context properties and CoCons. Currently a CCL-aware method for requirements analysis is being developed at the Technical University (TU) of Berlin in cooperation with Eurocontrol, Paris.

The benefits of considering both requirements and architecture throughout the **design phase** are discussed in [13]. The application of CLL during design is currently being evaluated in a case study being carried out in cooperation with the ISST Fraunhofer Institute, the TU Berlin and the insurance company Schwäbisch Hall. In winter term 2001/02 a 'CCL plugin' for the open source UML editor 'ArgoUML' has been implemented at the TU Berlin to automatically protect CCL specifications during design. It is available for download at ccl-plugin.berlios.de.

The people who want to enforce a new requirement often don't know the details of every part of the system, and neither do they have access to the complete source code. By using CoCons, developers don't have to understand every detail ('glass box view') or modify autonomous parts of the system in order to enforce a new requirement on them. Instead, context properties can be assigned *externally* to an autonomous component, and the communication with this component can be monitored *externally* for whether it complies with the CoCon specification **at runtime**. A prototypical rule manager framework as described in this paper currently is integrated into an application server at application level in cooperation of the TU of Berlin with BEA Systems and the Fraunhofer ISST. Thus, legacy components or components 'off the shelf' can be forced to comply with new requirements.

6.2 Limitations of Context-Based Constraints

Regarding only the context properties of a component bears some risks. It is crucial that theses values are always up-to-date. System properties, however, always have the current value, because they are queried from the middleware platform at runtime. Only one ontology should be used within a single system. For example, the context property 'Personal Data' should have exactly this name in every part of the system, even if these parts are manufactured by different companies. A common ontology can be ensured by either demanding it from the manufacturers or by intellectually inspecting an 'off the shelf' or legacy component when integrating it into the system.

6.3 Benefits of Context-Based Constraints

Similar to context properties, [16] suggest assigning metadata to components in order to use it for different tasks throughout the software engineering lifecycle. Likewise, [20] annotate components in order to perform dependency analysis over these descriptions. Other concepts for considering metadata exist, but none of them writes down *constraints that reflect this metadata* as introduced here. Key requirements can now be expressed according to the system's context. They can be specified in an easily comprehensible, straightforward language.

Maintenance is a key issue in *continuous software engineering* ([12]). CoCons facilitate consistency in system evolution. They assist in detecting when software or context modifications compromise intended functionality. Requirements tend to change quite often. The Rule Manager approach enables a system to be adapted to changed to new requirements via connector refinement without modifying the components. Thus, legacy components or 'off the shelf' components can be forced to comply with requirements that are not taken into consideration by the components themselves. The adaptability of a system is improved by enforcing conformity with meta-information. This meta-information can be easily adapted, whenever the context of a component changes. Furthermore, CoCon specifications themselves can be modified, as well, if the requirements change. Each deleted, modified or added CoCon can be automatically enforced, and resulting conflicts can be identified automatically as described in [3]. It is changing contexts that drive evolution. CoCons are context-based and are therefore easily adapted if the contexts, the requirements or the configuration changes. The compliance of a system with requirements can now verified automatically. According to [11], automated support for software evolution is central to solving some very important technical problems in current day software engineering.

References

1. BEA Systems, Inc. *BEA WebLogic Server, Using WebLogic Server Clusters*, March 2001.
2. Marko Boger, Toby Baier, Frank Wienberg, and Winfried Lamersdorf. Structuring QoS-supporting services with smart proxies. In *Extreme Programming and Flexible Processes in Software Engineering - XP2000*, Reading, 2000. Addison-Wesley.
3. Felix Bübl. The context-based constraint language CCL for component. Technical report, Technical University Berlin, available at www.CoCons.org, 2002.

4. Felix Bübl. Introducing context-based constraints. In Herbert Weber and Ralf-Detlef Kutsche, editors, *Fundamental Approaches to Software Engineering (FASE '02), Grenoble, France*. Springer, April 2002.
5. John Cheesman and John Daniels. *UML Components*. Addison-Wesley, 2000.
6. Steve Cook, Anneke Kleppe, Richard Mitchell, Jos Warmer, and Alan Wills. Defining the context of OCL expressions. In B.Rumpe and R.B.France, editors, *2nd International Conference on the Unified Modeling Language, Colorado, USA*, volume 1723 of *LNCS*. Springer, 1999.
7. Linda G. DeMichiel, L. Umit Yalcinalp, and Sanjeev Krishnan. *Enterprise JavaBeans Specification*. Sun Microsystems, Inc., 901 San Antonio Road, Palo Alto, California 94303, U.S.A., April 2001. Proposed Final Draft.
8. Erich Gamma, Richard Helm, Ralph Johnson, and John Vlissides. *Design Patterns, Elements of Reusable Object-Oriented Software*. Addison-Wesley, 1995.
9. Yariv Kaplan. API spying techniques for windows 9x, NT and 2000. http://www.internals.com/articles/apispy/apispy.htm, 2001.
10. G. Kiczales, J. Lamping, A. Menhdhekar, C. Maeda, C. Lopes, J. Loingtier, and J. Irwin. Aspect-oriented programming. In Mehmet Akşit and Satoshi Matsuoka, editors, *ECOOP '97 — Object-Oriented Programming 11th European Conference, Jyväskylä, Finland*, volume 1241, pages 220–242. Springer, New York, 1997.
11. Tom Mens and Theo D'Hondt. Automating support for software evolution in UML. *Automated Software Engineering*, 7(1):39–59, 2000.
12. Hausi Müller and Herber Weber, editors. *Continuous Engineering of Industrial Scale Software Systems*, Dagstuhl Seminar #98092, Report No. 203, IBFI, Schloss Dagstuhl, March 2-6 1998.
13. Bashar Nuseibeh. Weaving the software development process between requirements and architecture. In *Proceedings of ICSE-2001 International Workshop: From Software Requirements to Architectures (STRAW-01) Toronto, Canada*, 2001.
14. OMG. UML specification v1.4 (ad/01-02-14), 2001.
15. JBoss Organization. Jboss website. http://www.jboss.org, December 2001.
16. Alessandro Orso, Mary Jean Harrold, and David Rosenblum. Component metadata for software engineering tasks. In Wolfgang Emmerich and Stefan Tai, editors, *Engineering Distributed Objects (EDO 2000)*, volume 1999 of *LNCS*, Berlin, November 2000. Springer.
17. G. S. Reddy and R. K. Joshi. Filter objects for distributed object systems. *Journal of Object Oriented Programming*, 13(9):12–17, January 2001.
18. E. F. Robert, S. Barret, D. D. Lee, and T. Linden. Inserting ilities by controlling communications. *Communications of the ACM*, 45(1):116–122, January 2002.
19. Mary Shaw and David Garlan. *Software Architecture*. Prentice-Hall, 1996.
20. Judith A. Stafford and Alexander L. Wolf. Annotating components to support component-based static analyses of software systems. In *Grace Hopper Celebration of Women in Computing, Hyannis, Massachusetts*, September 2000.
21. Jos B. Warmer and Anneke G. Kleppe. *Object Constraint Language – Precise modeling with UML*. Addison-Wesley, Reading, 1999.
22. Herbert Weber. Continuous engineering of information and communication infrastructures (extended abstract). In Jean-Pierre Finance, editor, *Fundamental Approaches to Software Engineering FASE'99 Amsterdam Proceedings*, volume 1577 of *LNCS*, pages 22–29, Berlin, March 22-28 1999. Springer.
23. Ian Welch and Robert J. Stroud. From Dalang to Kava - the evolution of a reflective java extension. In *Reflection*, pages 2–21, 1999.
24. Jennifer Widom and Umeshwar Dayal. *A Guide To Active Databases*. Morgan-Kaufmann, 1993.

Using Business Rules in EXtreme Requirements

Maria Carmen Leonardi[1] and Julio Cesar Sampaio do Prado Leite[2]

[1] INTIA- UNCPBA - Tandil, Buenos Aires-Republica Argentina
cleonard@exa.unicen.edu.ar
[2] Pontifícia Universidade Católica do Rio de Janeiro — PUC-Rio
Rua Marquês de São Vicente 255, 22451-041 Gávea-RJ
Rio de Janeiro, Brasil
julio@inf.puc-rio.br

Abstract. Extreme Requirements (XR) is a proposal that tries to improve the quality of Extreme Programming (XP). XP is a well known agile method for software production. XP key elements are: little documentation, simplicity, analysis as constant activity, evolutionary design, integration and daily test. XR defines a requirements strategy that can be coupled with XP. In this article, we present an XR business rules based process. Our process is oriented to the customer, based on natural language, facilitating construction and validation. One of the strongest aspects of our proposed process is communication with customers, making them active participants in the software production process.

1 Introduction

Extreme Programming (XP) [1] is a development method that falls into the category of agile method, whose two main characteristics are to be adaptative and people oriented [2]. XP is based on oral communication, continuous testing and a code communication structure. XP uses descriptions, User-Stories, to register the desired system functionality. User-Stories are used in all XP cycles: requirements, design and test.

Research on software evolution [3] has convinced us that change is intrinsic to the task of software construction, so we need better processes to address change. We see Extreme Programming as a way of dealing with constant change. Because of this and due to its growing insertion on object-Oriented developments, we believe, from Requirements Engineering perspective, that it is important to adapt requirements strategies to enhance XP without altering its principles.

This paper is an extension of [4] where one of us proposes XR, a family of requirements processes based on scenarios. This article extends XR with the incorporation of a business rule model and a set of heuristics to derive CRCs cards [5].

In XP, customers[1] have an active role in the process, working in close contact with the engineers [2], providing business experience in which the software engineer will be able to trust and to consider it as the basis for the development. For this reason, we believe that it is fundamental to provide a customer-Oriented process to be used in the context of XP.

XR proposes the use of scenarios [6] and the Lexicon model (LEL) [7] to elicit and model requirements. LEL represents the language of the Universe of Discourse($UofD$)[2], allowing a natural communication with clients. In this paper, we extend this approach to incorporate a business rule model [8]. Business rules are part of the heart of any organisation, modelling the policies and constraints that guide and govern the structure and behaviour of an organisation [9]. As XP deals with change, we think it is important to incorporate a Business rules based process, since it reflects how an organisation should behave and it is easily updated due to its granularity level. We also propose a set of heuristics to derive CRC cards[3]. Although more documents are added to the process, and one of XP goals is to try to reduce documentation, we consider it is useful to add an initial model for requirements with the objective of favouring communication with the customer. This documentation is obtained in a fast and easy way, with little overhead, without altering XP working philosophy and contributing to the clarity of the first stages of development by providing better communication with customers.

2 An Introduction to XP

Extreme Programming [1] is an agile method for small to medium software teams. It is a method designed for situations where the requirements are vague. Its key elements are: little documentation, simplicity, analysis as a constant activity, evolutionary design, integration and daily tests. It eliminates over documentation and focuses on small releases which are quickly implemented and tested. Therefore, the system grows together with the client's new knowledge and its new necessities. Figure 1 (http://www.extremeprogramming.org/map/project.html) shows the general process of XP.

In this work, we will focus on the first stages of XP. Nowhere in the XP process is there a mention to a requirements document, but the term requirements is used several times in the book [1]. XP uses User-Stories and CRCs[4] in the first stages of development, and we assume that these models are its requirements and design models.

---

[1] Despite the fact that XP refers to one customer (on-site customer), we understand that there is more than one customer, so we use the term customers (see Section 4.1).

[2] The Universe of Discourse is the overall context in which the software will be developed and operated [10].

[3] CRC (Class Responsibilities Collaborators) is an exploratory technique used in several object oriented methods during the design task. It is based on index cards that register the name of the class, its responsibilities and its collaborators. The CRC card was proposed by Beck and Cunningham [5], and used by the Responsibility Driven Design [11] and by the Fusion method [12] among others.

[4] Although CRC cards are not mentioned in the original XP proposal [1] they are referred to on the XP site [www.extremeprogramming.org] as product of the XP design process.

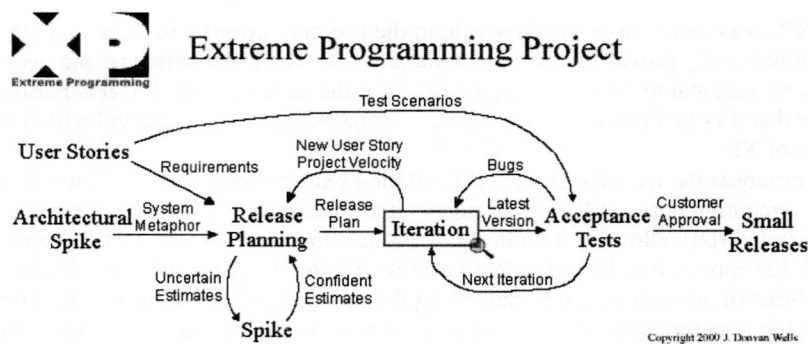

Fig. 1. XP Project (http://www.extremeprogramming.org/map/project.html)

The User-Stories or stories are written by the customer and report the tasks the system should perform. Its construction depends mainly on the ability of the client to define them. They are written in natural language, without a predetermined format, not exceeding some few text lines. Stories guide the construction towards the acceptance tests, key elements in XP, and they are used to estimate development time. In this sense, they only provide enough details to make a reasonable estimation. In the iteration planning, User-Stories are split up into tasks; the next step is a quick design session.

CRC cards [5] were proposed in order to document collaborative design decisions. The cards represent the responsibilities and collaborators of a particular class, focussing on the motivation for collaboration by representing many messages as a phrase of a text. XP uses CRC cards during design without imposing any particular discipline. Developers, managers, and users move the cards around making it easy to describe how classes work and interact. XP does not save the cards. The classes themselves are the documentation of the design: they represent what the system really is . In section 4.1 we describe some problems related to XP requirements and our proposal to deal with them. XR proposes the use of scenarios instead of User-Stories. Scenarios model improves the XP User-Stories techniques in several ways, but mainly due to its well established construction process [13]. We also supplement the XP requirements phase with client-Guided models and a simple construction process. Therefore, we improve communication with customers without altering the method principle of simplicity.

3 Natural Language Oriented Requirements Models

In this section, the models used in XR are briefly described. These models are exemplified in Section 5.

3.1 Language Extended Lexicon

The Language Extended Lexicon, LEL [7] is a structure that allows the representation of significant terms of the *UofD (Universe of Discourse)*. The purpose of the lexicon is to help the understanding of the application vocabulary and its semantics, leaving the comprehension of the problem for a future step. It unifies the language allowing communication with customers. . LEL is composed by a set of symbols which represents the basis of an application language. Symbols are, in general, words or phrases that customers repeat or emphasise. The lexicon is a series of symbols with the following structure: *symbol name:* word or phrase and set of synonyms, *notions* that describe the denotation of the symbol and *behavioural responses or impacts,* describing the symbol connotation. In the description of notions and impacts there are two basic rules that must be followed simultaneously: the "closure principle" that encourages the use of LEL symbols in other LEL symbols, thus forming a graph, and the "minimum vocabulary principle " where the use of symbols external to the application language is minimised, and the ones used should refer to a very small and well accepted general core. LEL terms define objects, subjects, verbal phrases and states.

The purpose of constructing a lexicon is not only to enable good communication and agreement between the customers and the engineering team but also to bootstrap the scenario and business rules construction process and to help in their description. The use of the symbols of the lexicon in the scenarios and business rules makes it possible for these symbols to be a natural hyperlink between these three representation structures, a fundamental characteristic of our Requirements Baseline concept [10]. The construction process is carried out by means of two elicitation techniques: interviews and reading. The first interviews are non-Structured and aim at collecting candidate symbols. Reading documents related to the application is also a way of finding symbols. After the first interviews and readings a list of symbols is defined, with the most frequently used words. Next, these symbols are classified according to a general classification. The following stage is the description of each symbol, consisting in determining its notions and behavioural responses, which then will be validated with customers. As a result of the validation interviews, we have the first LEL version, which will be polished to unify the syntax in order to attain a consistent and homogeneous LEL.

3.2 Scenario Model

A scenario describes *UofD* situations [6]. Scenarios use natural language as their basic representation. They are naturally connected to LEL. Figure 2 describes the components of a scenario.

Notions of *Constraint* and *Exception* are added to some of the components of a scenario. A *constraint* refers to non-Functional requirements and may be applied to context, resources or episodes. An *exception,* applied to episodes, causes serious disruptions in the scenario, asking for a different set of actions which may be described separately as an exception scenario.

The scenario construction process [13] starts from the application lexicon, producing a first version of the scenarios derived exclusively from the LEL. These scenarios are improved using other sources of information and organised in order to obtain a consistent set of scenarios that represents the application.. During or after these activities, the scenarios are verified and validated with the clients/users to detect Discrepancies, Errors and Omissions (DEO). The process is composed of five activities.

> *Title:* identifies a scenario. In the case of a sub-scenario, the title is the same as the sentence containing the episode.
> *Objective:* describes the purpose of the scenario.
> *Context:* defines geographical and temporal locations and preconditions.
> *Resources:* identify passive entities with which actors work.
> *Actors:* detail entities actively involved in the scenario, generally a person or an organization.
> *Set of episodes:* each episode represents an action performed by actors using resources. An episode may be explained as a scenario; this enables a scenario to be split into sub-scenarios.

Fig. 2. Scenario Components

1. The Derive activity aims at generating the derived candidate scenarios from the information of the LEL using the scenario model and applying the derivation heuristics. The derivation process consists in three steps: identifying the actors of the *UofD*, identifying candidate scenarios and creating them using the lexicon.
2. The Describe activity aims at improving the candidate scenarios by adding information from the *UofD* using the scenario model, the lexicon symbols in the descriptions and applying the description heuristics. The result is a set of fully described scenarios. This activity should be planned and usually relies on structured interviews, observations and document reading.
3. The Organise activity is the most complex and more systematised one in our scenario construction process. Its root is the idea of *integration scenarios*, "artificial" descriptions with the sole purpose of making the set of scenarios more understandable and manageable. Integration scenarios give a global vision of the application. Each integration scenario episode corresponds to a scenario.
4. The Verify activity is performed at least twice during the scenario building process, the first one over the fully described scenario set and the second after the Organise activity. This is done following a checklist with verification heuristics. As a consequence of this activity, two DEO lists are produced, one used at Describe and the other used during the LEL construction process. The verification is divided in intra scenarios, inter scenarios and against the LEL. Using the verification DEO lists, the scenarios and the LEL are modified. If major corrections were needed, a new verification could be required.
5. Finally, scenarios are validated with stakeholders usually by performing structured interviews or meetings.

3.3 Business Rule Model

We define business rules as statements about the enterprise's way of doing Business [8]. Organisations have policies in order to: satisfy the business objectives, satisfy customers, make good use of resources, and conform to laws or general business conventions. The business rule model distinguishes between functional rules and non-Functional rules as shown in Figure 3.

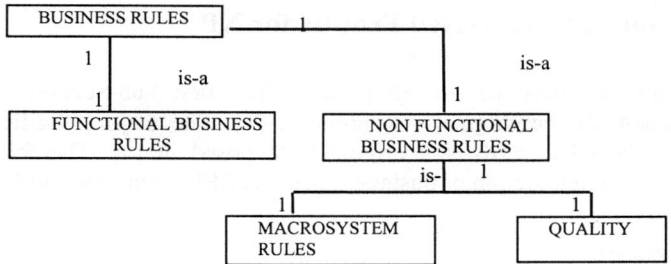

Fig. 3. Business rule Taxonomy

Functional rules are general policies regarding the organisation functionality. *Macrosystem rules* describe policies that constraint the behaviour and structure of the organisation. *Quality rules* are demands of the organisation on the characteristics of its processes or products. They usually reflect general policies related to quality standards or expectations of the organisation. We can follow some syntax patterns to build the rules, in which case their main components may be an LEL entry.

The business rules construction process [14] begins with the identification of the sources of information. Organisation documents, such as ISO required documents [15] and organisational models [16] [17] are generally the best sources. If the company does not have any documentation, other techniques such as observation, interviews and meetings should be used to acquire the information.

We categorise the sentences that appear in the sources considering their purpose in the organisation. We try to distinguish sentences referring to: limits, responsibilities and rights. To decide if a sentence is a business rule, we analyse if it is determined by a decision of the organisation (for internal or external reasons) or if it is an inherent sentence to the functionality of the *UofD* (in which case it is not considered a rule).

Taking the concept of stability [18] we determine the stability of each sentence. We use the degree of stability of a sentence not only to determine if it is a rule, but also to attach that information to the rule. Information regarding stability will help the construction of a change oriented architecture. Business rules are classified and documented following syntax patterns, connecting them with the corresponding LEL symbols. After documentation, the model is verified against the set of scenarios and the LEL.

For the verification process we use a set of questions of the type: a) for a given rule: Which is the context of the organisation in which this rule is applied? What is the associated behaviour? Which are the consequences produced by the application of the rule? b) for a particular scenario: Are there any policies that can modify the behaviour of the episodes?

Finally, the model is validated with customers to detect elicitation errors or organisational conflicts. It is an informal validation with the help of a syntactic-Oriented procedure that identifies subsets of related rules given by the use of LEL symbols [19].

4 A Business Rules Based Process for XP

In this section we describe the XR process. The first Sub-Section describes the updated version of the original XR proposal [4]. The major modification is the inclusion of the CRC cards, not originally proposed in [4]. The following Sub-Sections detail the integration of business rules, the LEL, scenarios and CRCs cards.

4.1 XR for XP

As we mentioned in Section 2, XP carries out its requirements definition process through the continuous construction of stories, tests, new stories and so on, where the client has an active participation to define the scope and priorities of each release. XR is a family of processes based on client-Guided requirements models, easy to build and to understand, that facilitates communication with clients without altering the basic philosophy of XP. Although it generates more documentation, this is easy to obtain and maintain. XR tries to solve some problems that XP presents related to Requirements Process [4] and summarised below:

Problem 1: The assumption that, in the planning game, business could be represented by just one customer
Problem 2: The lack of consideration of non-Functional requirements from the standpoint of business
Problem 3: The lack of explicit links between stories, tasks cards and CRCs to the code
Problem 4: The lack of a process to produce functional tests
Problem 5: The lack of a process to produce stories, tasks and CRCs

XR proposes to mitigate these problems with a simplified requirements process based on LEL and scenarios. In this work, we extend XR with the incorporation of the business rules model. Business rules guide the elaboration of simplified versions of the scenarios, and help priority determination for each release. The rules are also key to evolution, since, as the organisation changes, rules will change and thus the changes will propagate to scenarios and CRC cards. Following the XP philosophy, XR simplifies the requirements models construction process. Despite this, the XR process improves the construction of the models in an organised way, resolving the problems pointed above.

Considering the XP iteration philosophy through the releases, XR proposes the construction of business rules and the LEL as a prior activity since the business rules describe an organisation entirely independent of the existence of a software system. We follow the general idea that rules do not imply any technical implementation since they are statements that define or constraint some aspect of the business [20]. Scenarios depend on each release, they can be defined based on the selected rules, as the client can determine priorities and decide to define only scenarios related to a particular set of business rules. Based on the selected scenarios, the CRCs are defined for each release.

4.2 Business Rules and LEL Construction

The strategies for building the LEL and the business rule model, briefly described in Section 3, have been simplified in order to work in the context of XP.

As business rule model discovery and validation require knowledge of the business processes, this model may be obtained starting with interviews or collaborative workshops with customers following the idea presented in [21]. Customers usually express organisational aspects in terms of *limits, rights* and *responsibilities* of the parts involved in the *UofD*. What responsibilities do the actors of the system have? What limits and rights? Why is an activity carried out in a certain way? Does external legislation affect the business directly or indirectly?

In the XP spirit, it is not necessary to follow the writing patterns strictly, instead, engineers and business customers collaborate to create a business rule template that is expressed in natural language, based on common sense and which is directly relevant to the business customer[9]. It is useful to identify which the symbol responsible for each rule is and the other involved terms. Generally, for each functional rule there will be several associate non-Functional rules. Starting from the group of rules defined by the customer, the engineer completes them by carrying out questions that help the customer to raise aspects that have not been clear.

In these interviews or collaborative workshops, characteristic terms of the *UofD* denoting a resource, a process, a person or a sector are identified. LEL is constructed to define the vocabulary, to eliminate any type of ambiguity or wrong usage of the terms.

For each symbol, the notions and behavioural responses are defined and the term is classified as Subject, Object, Verbal Phrase or State. The LEL, at the same time as it facilitates communication with the customer, is also used as a simple mechanism for traceability, since it relates all the models obtained in this and later stages by the use of a restricted language. Therefore, XR implements traceability by means of common terms (LEL) and by the name spacing process that enforces scenarios and CRCs to use LEL symbols, offering a solution for *problem 3* described in Section 4.1. The name spacing process aims to guarantee that the names in the lexicon are preserved in the stories and will be the same names used in the code. That is, the *coding standards* must have a explicit rule on naming the operators and operands with the same names present in the lexicon. In the context of XP, we do not need a complete LEL to start with, but just a list of the important symbols, since the definitions will be added from the continuous feedback of the XP process.

4.3 Building Scenarios Using Business Rules

We propose the use of scenarios instead of User-Stories. Scenario is a description technique that enhances understandability of task related descriptions and communicability among stakeholders. Our scenario description language is very easy to learn and easy to use. In order to integrate our description language to XP, some minor adaptations were necessary. One of them was to focus scenarios not on the actual situation of the *UofD*, but on the desired situation with the presence of the software. The XP task cards may be taken from sub-scenarios.

The use of scenarios allows representing non-Functional aspects, solving *problem 2* described in 4.1. The *Constraint* component of the scenario language allows engineers to represent non-Functional aspects. To mitigate *problem 4*, we propose to write derived situations from the scenario, with the goal of making the system fail.

Related to *problem 5*, we propose the strategy for producing scenarios, briefly described in Section 3.2. Because of the XP spirit, heuristics to derive the scenarios are simplified and we incorporate the use of the business rules model throughout the construction process in order to reflect the organisational policies. In XR, the focus is on getting a very first cut of scenarios, such that they can be a reasonable basis for producing the functional tests and guiding the CRC design process.

The Derive process is concerned with eliciting the information and is performed by Business using the LEL. We use the business rules model to select a set of scenarios to derive CRCs for each release. Business rules are the organisational policies, therefore it is easy for the customer to identify priorities in this model: what functionality does he prefer to implement in each release? Customers select the most representative business rules they want to implement and through the trace mechanism it is possible to identify related scenarios. The Describe process details the scenarios as well as the functional test cases. We add the use of business rules to complete the description. As scenarios are described from one point of view, business rules allow them to represent general behaviour related to the situation but not derived directly with the *on-Site* customer who is used for this particular scenario description. In this way, we mitigate *problem 1*. The Validate activity is performed by Business through the process of sharing viewpoints or viewpoint resolution [22], also mitigating *problem 1*. Verify will be performed by the XP team during the activities of *testing* and *listening*. Note that the Validate sub-Process is not the XP practice *testing*, here we are just making sure that the scenarios and the functional tests express the overall viewpoint of Business.

4.4 CRCs Construction Process

Taking into account the XP spirit, we propose a meeting for CRCs construction. But we also propose a simple construction process to build them, a very simplified version of [19]. We derived CRCs from LEL and Scenarios through a set of heuristics. Since business rules were considered in the scenario construction, CRC cards will model the organisational policies.

Subject LEL Symbols are Candidates to be Modeled as CRCs:

We have to consider Subject symbols that appear in the selected scenarios of each release. When considering limits of the software, we have two options depending on what our automation policy is:

- If the Subject represents an important abstraction for the future system (taking into account related business rules), the symbol becomes a CRC card representing the behaviour the subject performs in the real world or representing a record of this behaviour. The responsibilities of each CRC are defined taking into account the behavioural responses of the corresponding LEL symbol.

- If the symbol ought to be an external entity, then its behavioural responses become system input/outputs managed by other classes. In order to do this, it is analysed who the receptor/generator of the data is. It is important to use scenarios to understand the moment and the precise form of communication of the system with the external entity.

Analyse LEL Symbols that Appear in Previous CRCs Responsibilities (Collaborators):

A list with the terms representing objects, verbal phrases and states that appear in the previous responsibilities is built. These new classes are collaborators of the previous ones. Each one of these symbols is analysed to determine if they will be modelled as a class.

The *Object* is modelled as a class if it has significant behaviour for the system, since it defines an important behaviour that can be modelled as a necessary independent abstraction to collaborate with other classes. To discard it as a class it should be analysed if the impacts of the symbols are not describing similar actions of some primitive class, that is to say that although it is an abstraction characteristic of the system, in terms of objects, it does not justify to be a new class. If the symbol is a *Verbal Phrase, it* can be modelled as A class or A responsibility. It is represented as a class when it has characteristics that cannot be assigned to other classes. If this is the case, it is modelled as a class, otherwise, it becomes one or more responsibilities of the involved classes. Finally, we have to treat the symbols of type state. Each symbol will be modelled as a class if it is not possible to include it on an already existing class, that is, if the state has impacts that can be modelled as independent responsibilities.

For each class, the responsibilities are defined by analysing the impacts of the corresponding LEL symbol. It is necessary to keep in mind the category of the symbol since, as it is the category, it changes the sense of the impacts being able to, in some cases, add responsibilities to other classes.

Modelling Business Rules as CRCs:

There are some cases in which it is possible to model a group of rules as classes, to isolate policies in a single object or because the rules affect different objects and it is not possible to associate them in a particular class. Business rules as classes improve the understanding of the policies that govern the system SINCE they are described explicitly as separate classes and they are not absorbed in any other class of the system. They also improve the maintenance of the system since, if a rule changes, it is easy to propagate the change into the associate rules encapsulated in the same class. Also, it can be specialised independently from the classes it affects. Finally, it is possible to have an activation mechanism in the same object to reflect the dynamism of the rules without affecting the involved conceptual objects [18]. The disadvantage of modelling business rules as classes is that, by adding more classes and their relationships, the complexity of the system increases.

Validate CRC Model through the Scenarios:

The resulting CRCs are evaluated as proposed in [23]. Each scenario is "executed" determining if the involved CRCs and their responsibilities can carry out the actions.

The responsibilities can be refined adding the necessary functionality to satisfy each scenario. As scenarios have been completed with business rules, the resulting CRCs will contain all the functionality defined by the rules.

5   A Case Study: Potatoes

Don Juan is a small agricultural business with 17 employees. In this example we show some aspects of potatoes commercialisation. The elicitation was conducted by interviews with the commercial area. In this Section, we show some examples of the models generated by the strategy. [5] Interviews for business rules elicitation were conducted by simple questions: Who are Don Juan clients? Are all types of clients the same? Is there any price policy ?
  Some examples of business rules elicited from Don Juan:

1. Don Juan sells to Wholesalers, Consignees and Production Plants (FR)
2. The Plant carries out discounts and allowances on the price settled down in the contract starting from the result of the samples. (NFR)
3. The degree of quality is defined by the Plant in the contract (FR)
4. If the Plant rejects trucks, Don Juan fulfils the contract with merchandise bought outside or own. (NFR)
5. The Plant accepts or rejects the product according to the degree of quality obtained in the sample. (NFR)
6. Don Juan uses the result of the samples, carried out by the Plant, to make decisions, as for that of potato production and for selection, to carry out in his next shipment. (RF)
7. According to the financial state, the product stock or convenience of the market, Don Juan sells to Wholesalers or Consignees, choosing them for their commercial characteristics (NFR)
8. When a demand is done, it is analysed if it suits to satisfy it for market prices and for commercial characteristics.
9. If it is not possible to satisfy several clients' demands, it is prioritised for commercial characteristics (NFR)

  LEL symbols (underlined in the above rules) were defined during the interviews. Figure 4 shows some examples of the defined symbols.
  Taking into account the business rules, we select, for the first release, all the scenarios related to the Plant, the most important client for Don Juan (see rules 1-6). Figure 5 shows an example of a scenario built from Product Delivery point of view (from Behavioural Responses of Don Juan's LEL symbol). During the Describe activity, this scenario was completed according to the business rules model to reflect the delivery aspects with the commercial aspects: episode 4 appears as a consequence of Rule 2 and episode 5 is included to reflect rule 4. In this way, we mitigate problem 1 of Section 4.1

---

[5] Please, note that all the examples were written in Spanish and were *freely* translated to English

Production Plant / Plant
Notions
- Don Juan's Customer who processes the potatoes obtaining frozen French fried potatoes

Behavioural Responses
- It carries out contracts with Don Juan to establish the requirements and conditions for the acquisition of each variety of the product
- It receives the shipment of the product in one or more trips
- It takes samples of each load of the trucks sent by Don Juan
- It can reject some or all of the trucks of a reception according to the degree of quality specified in the contract/s
- It carries out discounts and bonuses according to the degree of quality of the sent products
- Every year, it defines the degree of quality

Contract /Contract of Acquisition and production of potatoes
Notions
- it is a document; one is signed by a responsible for the Plant and the other by Don Juan that establishes the production conditions, purchases, delivery terms and payment of the product.
- One should be made by each marketed variety per year.
- It contains the conditions of product delivery and the classification procedure
- It contains the definition of the degree of quality
- It describes the price to pay and the bonus

Behavioral Responses
- It is used as base in the event of non-fulfillment of the payments
- It is used as base in the event of non-execution of Don Juan
- It is used as base for the rejection or acceptance of the product

Fig.4. LEL examples

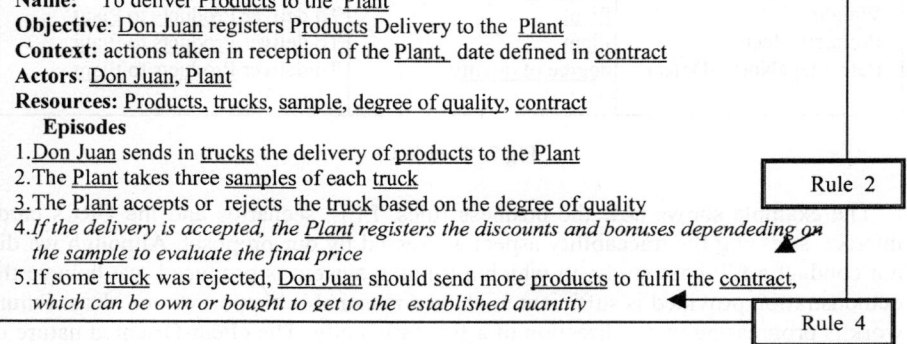

Name: To deliver Products to the Plant
Objective: Don Juan registers Products Delivery to the Plant
Context: actions taken in reception of the Plant, date defined in contract
Actors: Don Juan, Plant
Resources: Products, trucks, sample, degree of quality, contract
Episodes
1. Don Juan sends in trucks the delivery of products to the Plant
2. The Plant takes three samples of each truck
3. The Plant accepts or rejects the truck based on the degree of quality
4. If the delivery is accepted, the Plant registers the discounts and bonuses depending on the sample to evaluate the final price
5. If some truck was rejected, Don Juan should send more products to fulfil the contract, which can be own or bought to get to the established quantity

Fig. 5. Example of Scenario

Finally, CRCs are built taking into account the selected scenarios. Figure 6 shows an example derived from a Subject LEL. The use of scenarios and underlined terms representing LEL symbols enhance traceability.

name: Plant		
Responsibilities	**Collaborations**	**Scenarios**
To carry out <u>Contracts</u>	<u>Contracts</u> <u>DonJuan</u>	To carry out <u>Contracts</u>
To receive shipment	trip, driver	To deliver <u>Products</u> to <u>Plant</u>
To take <u>sample</u>	<u>sample</u>	To deliver <u>Products</u> to <u>Plant</u>
To reject <u>Truck</u>	sample,	To deliver <u>Products</u> to <u>Plant</u>
	degree of quality	
To carry out discounts/bonuses	contract, invoice	To deliver <u>Products</u> to <u>Plant</u>
	degree of quality	
To <u>define</u> discounts/bonuses	degree of quality,	To carry out <u>Contracts</u>
	Don Juan, Contract	
To define <u>degree of quality</u>	degree of quality,	To carry out <u>Contracts</u>
	Contracts	

Fig.6. CRC card of the Plant

The following CRC corresponds to a Sample. Although the sample is carried out by the Plant, it is necessary to define a class that reflects it, since, as defined in rule 6, it is Don Juan's interest to control each sample. It was also suggested that they should register samples of their production and of the one bought to the producers to fulfil the requirements and to do a statistical analysis through different seasons.

Name: Sample		
Responsibilities	**Collaborators**	**Scenarios**
Origin	producer	
Weight	Plant	To deliver <u>Products</u> to <u>Plant</u>
ProductDefects	Plant	To deliver <u>Products</u> to <u>Plant</u>
PercentageNotFulDefect	degree of quality	To deliver <u>Products</u> to <u>Plant</u>

Fig.7. Sample CRC

The example shows how the business rules, LEL, scenarios and the CRCs cards interact, stressing the traceability aspect addressed by our proposal. Although we did not conduct a full case study, in which a running system is produced, we believe the demonstration provided is sufficient to show a reasonable support of our ideas. Future work is progressing in the direction of a full case study. The client-Oriented nature of the proposed process facilitates and encourages the participation of the customer, in this case, the actor in charge of Don Juan's commercial sector. Each CRC is derived from LEL and scenarios, keeping the trace to its origin, and since scenarios were constructed following the business rules model, we can assert that the CRC model reflects the organisational policies.

6 Conclusion

Our proposal integrates well with the XP philosophy. Requirements evolution [3] has been a major concern in our research and we see XP as a possible paradigm to transfer to practice our evolution ideas. As such, we propose in this paper a first step in this direction that is how to substantiate the XP process with a requirements focus based on business rules. We do not discuss the applicability of XP, nor its successes or failures. We have just analysed the requirements part and we have proposed an add-on which we do believe has high cohesion with the XP proposal.

XP does not propose an explicit requirement strategy, it presents several problems in its informal way of dealing with requirements, as we described in Section 4.1. We consider that the use of natural language oriented requirements models fits well in the spirit of XP, since they allow engineers to represent the organisation through a set of models that are easily validated with customers. As Kotonya and Sommerville suggest in [24] and Sommerville et Sawyer describe in Rule 8.8. *"Paraphrase System Models"* [25] is fundamental to have a natural language oriented model to allow the participation of customers.

Our strategy favours the adaptative, customer-Oriented and incremental vision of XP, in particular: LEL unifies the vocabulary allowing communication with the customer. Scenarios improve User-Stories techniques through their representation, construction and inspection process. Business rules describe the knowledge from a simple and close way of the form in which customers perceive the organisation. They also guide in the releases definition by allowing the client to identify his priorities from this declarative model. Since there are no explicit heuristics to derive CRC, we think that our proposal shows how to derive CRC cards directly from the requirements models enhancing traceability and reflecting the real requirements and organizacional policies. The requirements models are adaptable to changes: A change in the organisation can affect the policies, invalidating or generating new business rules. The customer identifies the changes easily and how they impact in the rules, since these are defined in his own language.

On the other hand, some of the controls we have defined in [13] are not used in favour of an agile development. Of course it will impact the overall quality of the scenarios, but here we sustain, without data, that the results reported by the XP community are a strong argument to relax these controls. Due to the increasing popularity of this kind of methods [26], known as agile[www.agilemodeling.com], and the explosion of customer-Oriented Internet applications, which may need different production techniques[27], we believe that the requirement engineering area has to research and propose simple requirements models and strategies to be used in this context. Our proposal to this challenge is based on our experience in requirements, and in the idea that natural oriented requirements models fit in with the XP philosophy. Experience on the integration of XR is essential. We hope to have the opportunity to implement these ideas and gather data on their use. We also see this proposal as a way of exposing to the object oriented community what the role of requirements in a programming centered paradigm is.

References

1. Beck, K., Extreme Programming Explained Embrace Change, Addison Wesley Longman, Inc., (2000)
2. Fowler Martin "New Methodology", http://martinfowler.com/articles/newMethodology.html
3. Leite, J.C.S.P., Scenario Evolution. Dagstuhl-Seminar-Report; 199, Schloss Dagstuhl, Internationales Begegnungs-und Forschungszentrum Fur Informatik, Bui, Carrol and Jarke (editors), Alemanha, (1998) 13-14
4. Leite J.C.S.P "Extreme Requirements (XR)", Jornadas de Ingeniería de Requisitos Aplicada. Sevilla, 11 y 12 de Junio (2001)
5. Beck K., Cunningham W, "A Laboratory For Teaching Object-Oriented Thinking:" From the OOPSLA'89 Conference Proceedings October 1-6 (1989) 1-6
6. Leite, J.C.S.P., Rossi, G., Maiorana, V., Balaguer, F., Kaplan, G., Hadad, G., Oliversos, A. Enhancing a Requirements Baseline with Scenarios, Proceedings of the Third International Symposium on Requirements Engineering, IEEE Computer Society Press (1997) 44-53
7. Leite, J.C.S.P., Anchoring the Requirements Process on Vocabulary, Requirements Capture, Documentation and Validation, Dagstuhl Seminar Report – 241 (1999). www.dagstuhl.de/DATA/Reports/99241
8. Leite J.C.S.P, Leonardi Ma. Carmen, "Business rules as organizational Policies", IEEE IWSSD9: Ninth International Workshop on Software Specification and Design, IEEE Computer Society Press (1998) 68-76
9. Gottesdiener "Business RULES Show, Power, Promise", Application Development Trends, Vol 4, nro. 3 (1997) http://www.ebgconsulting.com/
10. Leite J.C.S.P, Oliveira A. Pádua Albuquerque. "A Customer Oriented Requirements Baseline", Proceedings of the Second IEEE International Symposium on Requirements Engineering , IEEE Computer Society Press (1995) 108-115
11. R.Wirfs-Brock, B. Wilkerson, and L. Wiener Designing Object-Oriented Software, Prentice Hall International, Englewood Cliffs, NJ, (1990)
12. Coleman et al., Object-Oriented Development The Fusion Method, Prentice Hall, Englewood Cliffs, NJ, (1994
13. Leite J, Hadad G, Doorn J, Kaplan G., "A Scenario Construction Process" Requirements Engineering Journal, Springer-Verlag. Vol.5 N1 (2000) 38-61
14. Leonardi Carmen, Leite J.C.S.P, Rossi G., "Estrategias para la identificación de Reglas de Negocio", Proceeding de Sbes98 "Simposio Brasilero de Engenharia de Software" Sociedad Brasilera de Computacao, Brasil, 14-16 de Octubre (1998) 53-67
15. Schmauch, Ch., ISO 9000 for software Developers, revised Edition, ASQC, Quality Press (1995)
16. Fiorini, S., Leite, J.C.S.P., Macedo-Soares, T., "Integrando Processos de Negocio a Elicitacao de Requisitos" Revista de Informática Teorica e Aplicada, Instituto de Informática da Universidade Federal do Rio Grande do Sul, Vol. IV, N. I. 7-48

17. Yu E., Modelling Strategic Relationships for Process Reingeneering, PhD Thesis, University of Toronto (1995)
18. Diaz, O., Iturrioz, J., Piattine, M., "Promoting business policies in object-oriented methods" Sesión Trabajos ya publicados: publicado en The Journal of Systems and Software, 1998. Actas de II Jornadas de Ingeniería de Software, JIS97, Dpto. de Informática , Universidad del país Vasco, San Sebastián, España (1997) 384-400
19. Leonardi Carmen, Una Estrategia de Modelado Conceptual de Objetos basada en Modelos de Requisitos en Lenguaje Natural. Tesis de Magister en Ingeniería de Software, Dpto. de Informática de la Universidad Nacional de La Plata (2001)
20. Guide Business Rules Project, "Defining Business Rules - What are they are really", (1996) www.guide.org/pubs.htm
21. Gottesdiener Ellen "Business Rules as Requirements" Software Development. Volume 7, No. 12. December (1999) http://www.ebgconsulting.com/
22. Leite, J.C.S.P, Freeman, P. A. "Requirements Validation Through Viewpoint Resolution" IEEE Transactions on Software Engineering: Vol. 17, N. 1 (1991) 1253 - 1269
23. Cockburn Alistair "Responsibility-based Modeling", Technical Memo HaT TR-99.02. http://members/aol.com/humansandt/techniques/responsabilities.htm.
24. Kotonya G, Sommerville I., Requirements Engineering, J. Wiley and Sons, (1998)
25. Sommerville I, Sawyer P "Requirements Engineering: A good practice guide" J. Wiley and Sons (1997)
26. Highsmith Jim and Cockburn Alistair " Agile Software Development: The Business of Innovation". IEEE Computer, V.24, N.8. 120-122
27. Brokat Advisor TM "Ruling a Self-Service World" http://www.brokat.com/brwhitepapers/advisor_selfservice.pdf

Evaluating CM³: Problem Management

Mira Kajko-Mattsson

Dept. of Computer and Systems Sciences, IT University, Forum 100,
SE-16440, Kista, Sweden
mira@dsv.su.se

Abstract. *CM³: Problem Management* is a detailed problem management process model to be utilised within corrective maintenance. It has been developed at ABB and evaluated for its industrial relevance within 17 non-ABB organisations. In this paper, we present the evaluation results of *CM³: Problem Management*. Our primary goal is to confirm its industrial relevance. Our secondary goal is to establish current state of problem management practice in the industry in order to provide a basic reference point from which the desperately needed research into software maintenance can proceed.

1 Introduction

Software problem management process is one of the most important processes within corrective maintenance. It not only manages software problems, but also provides a basis for quantitative feedback important for assessing product quality and reliability, crucial for continuous process analysis and improvement, essential for defect prevention and for making different kinds of decisions. Mature problem management process is a prerequisite for achieving CMM Level 5 [1].

Corrective Maintenance Maturity Model (CM³): Problem Management is a detailed problem management process model. It has been developed at ABB and evaluated for its industrial relevance within 17 non-ABB organisations. In this paper, we have chosen some of the process requirements inherent in *CM³: Problem Management* and matched them against the state of practice in software organisations. Our primary goal is to confirm the industrial relevance of *CM³: Problem Management*, that is, to find out whether our model is realistic, down-to-earth, and whether it properly reflects current industrial practice. Our secondary goal is to establish current state of problem management practice in the industry to provide a basic reference point from which the desperately needed future research into software maintenance can proceed.

2 Methodology

CM³: Problem Management was developed at two ABB organisations: *ABB Automation Products* (ABB APR) and *ABB Robotics (ABB ROP)*. Due to the scarcity of relevant literature about this domain, it is entirely based on our empirical study of industrial processes.

Table 1. Organisations contributing to the evaluation of CM^3: Problem Management

Name	No of employees	Products/Services	Software size
Ericsson Radio Systems	14 000	Base stations	Impossible to assess
Ericsson Telecom AB	300 (75 maintainers)	Telecommunication systems	ca 100 000 LOC
Ericsson Global IT Services	900 (5 maintainers)	Telecommunication products	ca 120 000 LOC
Ericsson Infotech	600	Sw processes and tools	Impossible to access
Ericsson AB	26 000	platform for AXE switches	400 blocks
ABB Automation Products	1400	Process control systems	Impossible to assess
ABB Robotics	600	Industrial robot systems	3 000 000 LOC
European Space Agency	3-4 maintainers/interviewed departm.	Space robot arm	250 000 LOC
SAAB AEROSPACE	6000 (400 maintainers)	Software for military aircraft	Impossible to assess
Nexus	300	Embedded systems	10000-1000000 LOC.
Postgirot Bank AB	3200 (170 maintainers)	Financial systems	6000 programs in 168 different systems
eumetrix Financial Solutions	55	Financial Systems	500 000 LOC
Navigera Business Consulting	47	Business systems	No size provided
Foyer Consulting AB	1	Various types of systems	Strongly varying
On, Line	20	Administration systems	700 000 LOC
Sema Group Infodata	300 (17 maintainers)	Information systems	142 programs
VM Data Public Partner	70 maintainers/depart.	Financial systems	Impossible to assess
Försvarets Radio Anstalt	ca 1000	Support systems	Impossible to assess
Tele2	6000	Support systems	250 000 LOC /interv. dep.

CM^3: *Problem Management* was evaluated both within and outside ABB. Seventeen non-ABB organisations agreed to expose their process models to our study. When choosing them, we have attempted to cover the wide spectrum of the today's IT state. Deliberately, we have chosen different sizes and different types of software organisations. The types of products maintained by these organisations varies from financial systems, business systems, embedded real-time systems, consulting services, administrative systems, and different types of support systems. The evaluation organisations are presented in Table 1.

The evaluation was conducted against a specific evaluation model presented in Appendix A. This model consists of the interview questions reflecting all the process steps inherent in CM^3: *Problem Management*. For learning about our process model, we advice our reader to study [2].

The fine-grained nature of our questions makes our interview results highly sensitive. Our results reveal the detailed state of practice of the organisations studied. To ensure the anonymity of the organisations studied, we have grouped the results with no references to a particular organisation.

It is not easy to evaluate a process model within the industry. Many industrial processes are still too coarse-grained. They have not implemented all the process steps suggested by our model. When evaluating CM^3: *Problem Management*, we first checked whether a certain process step was fully implemented by the industrial processes. If not, then we checked whether this step was logically followed. This sufficed to fully defend its implementation.

3 Evaluation Results

Seventeen non-ABB organisations exposed their processes to our evaluation. One of these organisations was a consultant company evaluating our problem management process within about ten organisations. Since no exact quantitative feedback could be provided for these ten organisations, we have excluded them from our quantitative analysis. These organisations are however included in our qualitative analysis.

Our two ABB organisations are also involved in our evaluation. Presently, ABB APR is in the process of changing its problem management process, but the old process is in use as well. For this reason, we treat the two ABB APR processes as two separate ones. When presenting their results, we refer to them as to two separate organisations. Summing up, nineteen processes are involved in the quantitative evaluation of CM^3: *Problem Management* (three ABB and 16 non-ABB processes; one non-ABB organisation was excluded from our quantitative study) and thirty processes are involved in the qualitative one.

Due to the fact that our model is very comprehensive, we cannot present the evaluation results for all process steps. We have chosen only a subset of them. We have also excluded all kinds of motivations for choosing CM^3 process steps. Instead, we advise our reader to study [2]. Each process step presented below has a numerical reference to the interview question(s) listed in Appendix A. Our evaluation results are presented in Sections 3.1-3.11.

3.1 Process Definition and Process Visibility

We have checked whether the organisations studied have defined and documented their problem management processes, whether they have divided them into process phases, whether they have recorded the results of these process phases, and finally, whether they record additional activities that have not been predetermined by their defined problem management processes.

Problem Management Process Definition (see I:Q.1): Sixteen out of 19 organisations have defined and documented their problem management process. The interviewees from two of the three remaining organisations claim that they have defined a problem management process but they have not documented it as yet. Finally, the third organisation has no process model defined at all. Maintainers in this organisation use their own personal methodology based on the experience gained.

Process Visibility (see I:Q.2 and I:Q.3): Sixteen out of 19 organisations divide their problem management processes into several phases. This division however, is coarse-grained. Usually, it consists of the following phases: *Problem Reporting, Problem Analysis,* and *Problem Resolution*. Only four of these 16 organisations further divide these phases into sub-phases and activities. These four organisations have also defined process models for the major problem management activities such as *Problem Investigation, Problem Cause Identification, Modification Design* and *Modification Implementation*. These process models are usually represented in the form of process guidelines. Six other (out of 16) organisations have expressed a strong wish for process models for each major problem management activity. Two of these six are presently working on fine-graining their problem management processes and on defining process models for major activities.

Recording the Results of Process Phases (see I: Q.4.1 and Q.4.3): Fifteen out of 19 organisations record process data concerning the results of the process phases. This data is however very coarse-grained. Usually, it encompasses the combined results of the following group of major activities: *Problem Investigation, Problem Cause Identification, Modification Design,* and *Modification Implementation*. The information being recorded varies. Usually, it covers effort, resources, modification size, impact, and experience gained. Only two of the 15 organisations record the results of each individual process activity.

Recording Additional Activities Not Predefined by the Problem Management Process (see I: Q.4.2): Four out of 19 organisations record the additional activities that have not been predetermined by their problem management process. Only major additional activities are recorded such as a visit to a customer site.

3.2 Process Analysis and Control

In this section, we report on the types of activities that are conducted in order to analyse and control the problem management process. We have checked the following: (1) measurement of the problem management progress, (2) rules for recording problems in problem reports, (3) management of duplicate problem reports, (4) control of the correctness of the problem report data, (5) distinguishing between internal and external problem reports, (6) categorisation of maintenance requests, and finally, (7) comparison of plans to the actual results.

Progress of Problem Management (see II: Q.1): Sixteen out of 19 organisations measure the progress of problem management process using status values and the dates when these status values change. This information is primarily used for monitoring the problem resolution process and workload of individual engineers. It is also used for controlling the amount of corrective work that remains to be done for a certain release.

Rules for Recording Problems in Problem Reports (see II: Q.2 and Q.3): Sixteen out of 19 organisations studied identify all maintenance requests (problem reports in our case) by assigning a unique identifier to each reported problem. Thirteen out of 19 organisations describe one problem in one and only one problem report. If a problem report communicates several problems or if an analysis of a problem reveals several underlying problems, then all these problems get reported anew in separate problem reports. The six remaining organisations sometimes report on several problems in one problem report. Usually, these problems are somewhat related. The interviewees coming from these organisations admit that this practice is clumsy, severely obstructing problem management.

Management of Duplicate Problem Reports (see II: Q.4, Q.5, and Q.6): Sixteen out of 19 organisations distinguish between unique and duplicate problems. If several problem reports relate to the same problem, then usually one report becomes a master report containing all information about the unique characteristics of the problem. This master report is continuously updated with relevant information from the duplicate problem reports. The duplicate problem reports get closed, but remain related to the master report.

Two of the organisations simultaneously attend to all the duplicate problem reports in a group. They do so with the motivation that these reports come from different customers and hence may contain information that differs from customer to customer, that they wish to keep in separate problem reports.

All the sixteen organisations continuously revise the uniqueness of the problems throughout the process. One of the interviewees has mentioned that sometimes as late as during the modification implementation, the maintainers may discover that the problem being attended to is a duplicate problem.

Control of the Correctness of the Problem Report Data (see II: Q.2 and Q.3): Seventeen out of 19 organisations continuously check the correctness of the problem report data throughout the whole problem management life cycle. Eighteen out of 19 organisations check the quality of the reported data before assigning the problem report to the maintenance team. This is usually conducted by a role corresponding to CM^3 *Problem Report Administrator*, CM^3 *Problem Report Owner*, or a CM^3: *CCB*.

Distinguishing between Internal and External Problems (see II: Q.9 in Appendix A): Ten out of 19 organisations studied actively classify problem reports as internal or external. This information is utilised for different purposes such as statistics, planning, evaluation of customer satisfaction, and measurement of effort. Five of the remaining nine organisations may record this information, but they do not use it for any particular purpose. For one of the remaining four organisations, this information is not relevant. They only maintain internal support systems.

Identifying Maintenance Category (see II: Q.10, Q.11, and Q.12): All the organisations studied identify a maintenance category for each maintenance request. In our context, this means that all software problems are classified as corrective maintenance, to be distinguished from perfective and adaptive categories. Seven of 19 organisations studied conduct some form of preventive maintenance. By this, they mainly mean restructuring some parts of the software system. Sixteen of the 19 organisations studied continuously revise the maintenance category during the problem management life cycle.

Comparing Plans to Actual Results (see II: Q.18): Eleven out of 19 organisations compare the plans to the actual results. They do it for learning lessons and for providing feedback for process improvement. The maintainers within the remaining seven organisations do not make any comparisons at all.

3.3 Managing Software Products

In this section, we report on the mechanism used for identifying the software products affected by the reported problems, utilisation of the information on the product environment at both the customers and maintainers' sites, recording practice of the problem occurrence date, and finally, the designation of releases in which problems will be investigated and in which problem solutions will be implemented.

Identifying Software Products (see III: Q.1, Q.1.1, Q.1.2, and Q.1.3): All the organisations studied identify the products in which software problems are encountered. They usually report the *Release Id* or *Article ID*, a name which is then translated into the *Release Id* by the maintenance organisation.

The identification of the software systems is not always so straightforward when reporting on external software problems. Some systems are very complex. They may be real-time embedded systems, integrated with other systems, and these systems may not always be produced by one and the same organisation. In such a case, it is not always easy to identify the system and its release at the problem encounter. The organisations possessing such systems have chosen a special procedure for system identification. Usually, representatives from different systems have a meeting or a series of meetings during which they attempt to analyse the problem and localise it within such a complex system.

Only in twelve organisations out of 19, external submitters are able to identify the software product on a more detailed level than its *Release ID*. Usually, they may identify some major functionality or sub-component. In the remaining processes, more detailed identification of the product cannot be made by the external submitters.

Concerning the reporting of software problems internally, problems may be reported on as detailed level as module- and/or even module line level in most of the organisations studied. This, however, depends on the problem nature and on the individual problem submitter.

Identifying Product Environment (see III: Q.2, Q.2.1, and Q.2.2): Eighteen out of 19 organisations studied have access to the data on the environment of their customers. They either have this information available at the maintenance execution level or they are provided with it by the upfront maintenance level (support). We have not checked, however, whether this information is easily available at upfront maintenance. Due to the specific nature of their product, the remaining 19th organisation contacts its customers for finding out this information, when necessary.

Date and Time when the Problem was Encountered (see III: Q3 and Q3.1): Ten out of 19 organisations record the date and time when the problem was encountered. This value may also be easily recreated from log files. Only two of the organisations studied use this value in the reliability measurements. Primarily, the organisations studied use this value to learn about the problem, for instance, to find out whether it was time related. Some organisations use this value to study the log files before the problem was encountered in search of problem symptoms.

Designating Software Releases in which the Problem is Investigated (see III: Q.5 and Q.5.1): Thirteen out of 19 organisations carefully choose the versions in which the software problem is to be investigated. First, they usually recreate the problem in the version of the product in which the customer encountered the problem. Second, they choose the release(s) in which it is relevant to identify the reported software problem. This choice is usually determined by many varying factors such as the number of releases being presently utilised by the customers, customer status and business criticality, the severity of the problem, and so on.

In the remaining six out of the 19 organisations, the designation of the appropriate version is not an issue. These organisations usually attend to software problems in the latest releases. Therefore, they investigate the software problem first in the release in which the software problem was encountered (irrespective of its age) and the latest release in order to find out whether the problem still exists. It may happen that the problem has disappeared due to changes in the earlier releases.

Designating Software Releases in which the Problem Solution will be Implemented (see III:Q.4, Q.4.1, and Q.4.2): Thirteen out of 19 organisations designate versions of the software system in which the problem will be implemented. Usually, more than one release may be designated for this purpose. These organisations also continuously revise the designation of these software releases. The continuous revising is necessary for a meaningful planning and prioritisation of problems as new software problems (with higher severity and priority) are reported or as maintenance engineers gain better understanding of the problem.

Five of these thirteen organisations make patches. They do so mainly in cases when it is urgent to solve a problem. These patches, however, are soon transformed to new releases. In the remaining six out of 19 organisations, the choice of the version in which the problem will be implemented is not relevant. This is because they either have only one customer or they have a policy that they never do changes in the older releases. If their customers have encountered a problem in some older release, then they must simply upgrade their systems if they want the problem to be solved.

3.4 Recording Problem Reports (see IV: Q.4 and Q.4.1)

Sixteen out of 19 organisations studied record all their problems in an organisation-wide problem report repository and tracking systems. The remaining three organisations do it partially. Some problems internally encountered may never get reported in these three organisations. They may be communicated orally via the telephone or email. The first of these three organisations does not record minor problems of the cosmetic type. In the second organisation, recording discipline depends on the individual maintenance engineer. In the third organisation, the problems that are usually reported via the mailing tool do not get stored in the organisation-wide repository. In this organisation, all problem reports disappear as soon as they get resolved. Hence, no historical data may be extracted. Finally, the consultant organisation not included in our quantitative analysis claims that there are still organisations that record their problem reports in a paper form.

3.5 Describing Software Problems

We have checked whether the organisations studied provide guidance (templates) to their problem submitters on how to describe software problems when reporting them, whether the organisations submit reports on problems encountered during maintenance work, and, whether the organisations continuously revise the descriptions of software problems during the problem management process.

Templates for Describing Software Problems (see V: Q.1, Q.1.1-1.8, and Q.2): Sixteen out of the 19 organisations studied provide a template for problem descriptions. This template, however, differs in the number and choice of predefined constituent data fields. The following data fields are provided:

General problem description: All the organisations studied allow their submitters to provide a general description of a software problem.

Problem effects and consequences: Nine out of 19 organisations studied provide a predetermined data field in a problem report for describing problem effects and consequences. In the remaining ten organisations, this information may be communicated as part of the general problem description.

Problem symptoms: Only three out of 19 organisations actively collect information on the problem symptoms using a predetermined data field in a problem report. Four other organisations treat symptoms as consequences. The remaining twelve organisations may communicate them as part of the general problem description. The information on symptoms is utilised for problem investigation. Symptom information provides important feedback when finding out what exactly happened before the problem occurred. Symptom information is also used as a checklist for the identification of duplicate problems. Identification of duplicate reports using the symptom information is conducted manually by the organisations studied.

Problem conditions: Five out of 19 organisations provide predetermined fields for describing problem conditions. One of those five organisations provides a combination of several predetermined fields utilised for the purpose of describing problem conditions. The remaining 14 organisations may or may not collect this information as part the general problem description on a case to case basis. By problem conditions, the organisations studied mean the specific date and time of the problem occurrence (e.g., a year shift, or peak time), a combination of applications active during the problem occurrence, cargo, weather conditions, exact position of the product (if embedded product), and other things.

Problem Reproduction: Ten out of 19 organisations provide a predefined field for a description of how to reproduce the reported software problem. This field is also utilised for describing alternative execution path(s) to the problem. Out of these ten organisations, five classify problems as reproducible and irreproducible. The remaining nine organisations may provide this information as part of the general problem description. One out of these remaining nine organisations provides a predetermined field for classifying whether the problem is reproducible or not.

Attachments: Sixteen out of 19 organisations manage attachments such as log files, application programs, error messages, screen dumps, data base contents. Only one of these 16 organisations manages attachments manually, whereas the remaining 15 do it electronically.

Submitting Additional Problem Reports (see V:Q.6): Twelve out of 19 organisations always report on additional problems encountered during the problem management process. In these organisations, the engineers are not allowed to attend to problems without first reporting on them, even if these problems imply trivial changes. Three out of the seven remaining organisations never report on software problems encountered internally. They attend to these problems without reporting them. At most, this information may be visible in the release documentation. One of these organisations admits that it is a bad habit. They feel that they must change it, because they cannot get the whole picture of the changes in their systems. Also, if a new problem is encountered, then they cannot see whether it has already been resolved. In the remaining four out of seven organisations, reporting on additional software problems varies as follows:

If the encountered problem is not related to the problem that is currently being managed, then a new problem report is created. Otherwise, it is described in the problem report being currently attended to. The organisation admits that this practice creates difficulties especially in cases when the problem substantially expands. It then becomes difficult to manage and control.

If a similar problem is discovered during attendance to some problem, and it implies very little change, then it is not reported but corrected under the umbrella of the attended problem. All other similar problems must be reported in separate problem reports.

Revising Problem Report Data (see V:Q.5): Seventeen out of 19 organisations continuously revise the problem report data as they gain more understanding about the problem. This step however is usually not an explicit part of the maintenance methodology of the organisations studied. Concerning the two remaining organisations, this step is up to each individual maintainer. The interviewees from these organisations agree that an explicit statement of this step is essential for increasing productivity and making problem validation and verification effective.

3.6 Problem Investigation

We have checked whether the main activities within the *Problem Investigation* phase have been implemented. They are (1) study of a problem report, (2) study of a software system, and (3) recreation of the problem.

Study of Problem Report (see VI: Q.1, Q.1.1): All the organisations studied include studying of a problem report as the first step within the *Problem Investigation* phase. The duration of this step varies from half an hour to several months. The longer time usually arises when the maintainer must complement the problem report with additional data by contacting the problem submitter. Please observe that many of the organisations studied contact problem submitters via the upfront maintenance (support) process.

Study of Software System (see VI: Q.2, Q.2.1, Q.2.2): All interviewees claim that their maintenance engineers study the software system when investigating the problem. Twelve of the interviewees claim that their maintainers fully understand the part of the software system they are maintaining. However, most of them have no process feedback for supporting this statement. The remaining seven interviewees admit that their maintainers have problems with understanding the software systems. In one of them, the second root cause to the externally reported software problems is lack of maintainers' knowledge of a software product.

Lack of knowledge may arise in cases when the system has been developed by a third party (another organisation), or the system is so complex that even a limited set of components can be difficult to understand. In one organisation, the maintainers only learn the parts of the product required for understanding the problem and for infusing changes without acquiring the knowledge of its remaining parts.

To study a software system may take time. The time span required for conducting this process step varies from half a day to several months. In cases when it takes a longer time, the maintainer is a novice, or she must study several releases of the same product and identify their differences, or the nature of a problem is such that it requires a meticulous study of a software system, for instance, in embedded systems when one must check all the interfaces to hardware, or there is inadequate documentation so that reverse engineering needs to be performed.

Recreating Problems (see VI: Q.3, Q.3.1): When recreating software problems, the organisations may follow problem descriptions, simulate software, or define test cases and test software. Seventeen out of 19 organisations studied define test cases when investigating software problems. All except two of those 17 organisations document these test cases. The remaining two organisations (out of 19) do not create any test cases. They just follow the problem descriptions when recreating problems.

3.7 Problem Cause Identification

We have checked whether the main activities within the *Problem Cause Identification* phase have been implemented. They are (1) identification and recording of defects, and (2) classification of defects.

Identification and Recording of Problem Causes (see VII: Q.2, Q.2.1, Q.2.2, Q.2.3): When identifying causes, all the organisations studied prescribe a study of the pertinent documentation items and a control of their correctness. Sixteen of them record all the documentation items in which defects were found. Usually, these documentation items are identified on a module granularity level. Only three of those 16 organisations record defects on the software code line level. One of the three remaining organisations (out of 19) only records this information for problems whose defects are difficult to identify. The remaining two organisations do not implement this process step at all.

Classification of Defects (Problem Causes) (see VII: Q.3, Q.4, Q.5): Eleven of the 19 organisations studied classify the defects (problem causes). This information is used for planning future work and for different types of statistical analyses. Five out of these eleven organisations use it for identifying deficiencies (root causes) in the organisational processes.

3.8 Root Cause Analysis (see VIII: Q1, Q.2, Q.3, Q.4)

We have checked whether the organisations studied attempt to identify deficiencies in the process leading to the defects. Only five out of 19 organisations studied conduct root cause analysis. However, they do not do it on every software problem. The candidates for root cause analysis are either external software problems, very serious internal and/or external ones, or groups of very frequently encountered problems.

3.9 Modification Design

We have checked whether the organisations studied create mental pictures of problem solutions in the early phases of the problem management process, whether the organisations create suggestions for problem solutions before implementing them, whether they evaluate and inspect/review these suggestions, and whether they plan for implementing them.

Mental Pictures of Problem Solutions (result of questions see IX: Q.1, Q.2, Q.3): Design of problem solutions should start as soon as the problem gets reported to the maintenance organisation irrespective of how much detail is provided about it. All organisations except for one (18 organisations), create a mental picture of what a problem solution might look like. This mental picture provides an important feedback for making important decisions through the problem management process. It is also continuously revised as more understanding is gained about the problem solution. Only two of those 18 organisations document the mental pictures of problem solutions.

Suggestions for Problem Solutions (see IX: Q.1, Q.2, Q.3): Fifteen out of 19 organisations may create one or several modification designs (problem solutions) for resolving a problem. Usually, these organisations create one problem solution. Several alternative problem solutions are only created for major and/or more severe problems, especially for those implying expensive changes. Four of these 15 organisations always attempt to create several problem solutions, if possible. But, only one suggestion is recorded in the problem report repository and tracking system.

The remaining four organisations only create one problem solution. One of them has a time constraint to deliver a problem solution as quickly as possible. From the time when the problem cause (defect) has been identified, the clock starts ticking and the maintainers have only 48 hours to resolve the problem. Hence, there is no time for creating alternative solutions.

Evaluating Problem Solutions (see IX: Q.4, Q.5, Q.6): Within 18 out of the 19 organisations, maintainers evaluate their own suggestions for problem solutions. When evaluating them, they consider these factors: modification size, change impact, ripple effect, effect on customers, effort and resources required for solving the problem, the feasibility of solving the problem, and the benefits and drawbacks of solving the problem.

Inspecting and/or Reviewing Suggestions for Problem Solutions (see IX: Q.7, Q.8): Before being presented to the CCB, the suggestions for problem solutions should be inspected and/or informally reviewed. Within 15 out of 19 organisations, inspections and/or informal reviews are being conducted. The four remaining organisations neither inspect nor review their suggestions for problem solutions.

The level of formality varies in the 15 organisations depending on the size, severity and complexity of the software problem. Usually, major problems are formally inspected and minor problems are only informally reviewed. It may also happen that suggestions for solutions of minor problems are not reviewed at all. In four out of the 15 organisations, all suggestions, even those for trivial changes, are always inspected and/or informally reviewed.

Planning for Implementing Problem Solutions (see IX: Q.9, Q.10): Eighteen out of 19 organisations make plans for implementing problem solutions, but only 16 out of those 18 record these plans. The remaining 19th organisation does not make any plans at all (time is ticking and the organisation must resolve the problem as soon as possible).

For one of the 18 organisations, planning means designating the date when the problem solution should be ready. In the remaining 17 organisations, the plans encompass time schedule, designation of the versions of the software system in which problem solutions will be implemented, effort and resources required such as person-hours and equipment to be available during a certain period of time, prerequisites for implementing the solution such as closure of the system for a certain period of time, and a time schedule.

3.10 Modification Decision

We have checked whether the organisations studied have institutionalised a practice for making decisions on all corrective changes in the software product. Two types of decision making have been identified: (1) management decision where the maintenance engineers' closest managers are involved in following the problem management process and in making intermediate decisions important for its further progress, and (2) CCB decisions where *Change Control Board* members make the most important decisions on changes to software systems.

Management Decision (see X: Q.1, Q.2, Q.6): Within 15 out of 19 organisations, the maintainers report on the results of major problem management phases to some authority for control and for decision making on the future progress of the problem. Usually, correspondences to the CM^3 role *"Problem Report Engineer"* report to the correspondences to the CM^3 role *"Problem Report Owner"*. This reporting is however scarcely documented. It is mainly managed orally. At the most, its results may be visible in the change of the problem report status values, their dates, and some comments. Within four remaining organisations (out of 19), this reporting does not take place at all. Maintainers are allowed to make their own decisions during the problem management process.

CCB Decision (see X: Q3-Q.6): Within 16 out of 19 organisations, the most important decisions are made by a *Change Control Board*. These decisions concern the progress of serious problems and changes to software. In 14 organisations (out of 16) all changes must be permitted by the CCB. In two organisations (out of 16), only major problems are paid heed to. CCB chooses a suggestion for a problem solution on the basis of the evaluation results conducted by maintainers themselves, inspectors/reviewers, and the CCB itself. Fifteen out of these 16 organisations document the decisions made by the CCB and their motivations, but only within eleven organisations are these decisions visible via the problem report repository and tracking system.

3.11 Modification Implementation

We have checked whether the organisations studied record all the changes made to software systems, whether they implement these changes according to some documentation standard, and whether the organisations inspect/review the changes made.

Recording Changes to Software (see XI: Q.1, Q.1.1): All the organisations studied record the changes made to the system. These changes are either visible in the problem report repository and tracking system, release documentation, or in the code - in its comment part.

The granularity level of recording the changes is usually on a module level (the identification of a module that has been changed). Finer granularity level such as the identification of the lines being changed due to a particular problem can be achieved manually either via a *"diff"* command in a version management tool or by reading comments in the modules identifying the lines that have been changed.

Rules for Documentation Standard (see XI: Q.3): Fifteen out of 19 organisations have defined rules for how to write software code and documentation. The interviewees from these organisations claim that they follow these rules. The remaining four organisations have not defined such rules at all.

Inspecting/Reviewing Changes (adapted from IX: Q.7): The practice of inspecting/reviewing changes is followed by the same organisations as the practice of inspecting/reviewing suggestions for problem solutions: 15 out of 19 organisations conduct inspections and/or informal reviews on all changes made; four do not.

4 Conclusions

Problem management process is one of the most important processes within software engineering. Its main role is to manage software problems in a formal and disciplined way. Its other role is to help us look back in time and analyse our earlier processes (either development or other maintenance process) in order to identify their weak and strong points. These points are an important feedback for continuous process assessment and improvement, and for piloting innovations exploiting the best engineering practices [1]. For this reason, we need to achieve maximal visibility into problem management process and all other development and maintenance processes.

The problem management process visibility equips us with data providing an important basis for assessing product quality and reliability, crucial for continuous process analysis and improvement, and essential for defect prevention. Good insight into the process helps us make sound decisions. Mature problem management process is a prerequisite for achieving CMM Level 5 [1].

CM^3: *Problem Management* is a very detailed problem management process model. It has been developed at ABB and evaluated for its industrial relevance within 17 non-ABB organisations. In this paper, we have presented our evaluation results of CM^3: *Problem Management*.

Our evaluation results show, that all the process steps of our model have been either explicitly or implicitly implemented by the majority of the organisations studied. This proves that CM^3: *Problem Management* is realistic and down-to-earth, and correctly represents current industrial practice. The state of implementing our process steps varies across the organisations studied. Some of them implemented most of our process steps, whereas other have hardly defined any problem management process. By delineating the strong and weak points in the industrial processes studied, we hope that we have been able to better visualise the current state of problem management practice within corrective maintenance, and thereby, to provide a basic reference point from which the desperately needed research into software maintenance can proceed.

Acknowledgements

I would like to thank all the software engineers at ABB who co-operated with me personally. They are: Ulf Westblom from ABB Corporate Research; Sari Ebarasi, Margaretha Holmgren, Bengt Kelvinius, Bengt Jönsson, Mats Medin, Ulf Olsson and Stefan Törnqvist from ABB APR; Stefan Forssander, Gunnar Andersson, Tord Fahlgren, Elisabet de Waal, Gunilla Sundelius, Sven-Erik Johansson and Pär Andersson from ABB Robotics, and finally Lars-Olof Tjerngren from ABB Service.

I appreciate the contributions of the practitioners who participated in the evaluation of our model. They are Jan-Eric Claesson from Nexus; Håkan Andersskär from Ericsson Infotech, Leif Thedvall from Postgirot Bank; Jan Lindviken from Ericsson Global IT Services; Birgitta Ervik from Ericsson AB, Claes Ericsson from eumetrix Financial Solutions; Jordanis Caracolias from Ericsson Telecom; Åsa Gustafson from Navigera Business Consulting; Per Foyer from Foyer Consulting; Göran Näsman from On Line; Helena Lindström from Sema Group Infodata; Bo Andersson from WM Data Public Partner; Jorge Amador Monteverde from European Space Agency; Conny Axeus and Per Simonsson from Ericsson Radio Systems; Tore Isacsson from Försvarets Radioanstallt; Jan-Ola Kruger, Kjell Alm and Mats Rundqvist from SAAB Aerospace; and finally, Toni Baknor from Tele2.

Let me thank the Swedish National Board for Industrial and Technical Development (Nutek). This study has been made possible thanks to their recognition of the importance of unifying academia with industry in Sweden. Thanks to its support, the impossible research has been made possible.

Finally, I would like to thank Telefonaktiebolaget LM Ericssons Stiftelse for their financial support allowing us to validate our model within Ericsson Group.

References

1. Carnegie Mellon University, Software Engineering Institute, *The Capability Maturity Model: Guidelines for Improving the Software Process*, Addison-Wesley, 1994.
2. Kajko-Mattsson M, Corrective Maintenance Maturity Model: Problem Management, PhD thesis, ISBN Nr 91-7265-311-6, ISSN 1101-8526, ISRN SU-KTH/DSV/R--01/15, Department of Computer and Systems Sciences (DSV), Stockholm University and Royal Institute of Technology, 2001.

5 Appendix A.1 : Our Questionnaire, Part I

I. Process Definition and Process Visibility
Q.1: Have you defined a model for problem management?
Q.2: Do you divide your problem management process into phases?
Q.2.1: What do they look like?
Q.2.2: Have you defined process models for the following activities: (1) Problem investigation, (2) Problem cause identification, (3) Modification design, (4) Root cause analysis, (5) Modification implementation?
Q.3: Are the problem management phases further divided into activities/tasks?
Q.4: For each problem reporting phase/activity/task:
Q.4.1: Do you record the date and time when the problem report was in this phase/activity/task?
Q.4.2: Do you identify and record additional activities/tasks performed during this phase?
Q.4.3: Do you record the effort and resources of each phase/activity/task?

II. Process Analysis and Control
Q.1: Do you measure the progress? How?
Q.2: Are all problems uniquely identified?
Q.3: How many problems do you describe in one problem report?
Q.4: Do you identify the unique problems?
Q.5: How do you manage unique and duplicate problems?
Q.6: Do you revise the uniqueness of the problem throughout the problem management process?
Q.7: Do you continuously check the correctness of the problem report data?
Q.8: Do you check the quality of the reported data before assigning the problem report to some maintenance team?
Q.9: Do you classify problem reports into external and internal ones?
Q.9.1: If yes, what do you use this classification for?
Q.10: Do you identify a maintenance category for each software problem?
Q.11: Do you revise the maintenance category continuously during the problem management process?
Q.12: What types of maintenance categories do you distinguish?
Q.13: Do you record severity and priority of the problem?
Q.14: Do you separate the submitter's and maintainer's judgement of severity and priority?
Q.15: What do you use these values for?
Q.16: Do you identify the activity during which the problem was encountered?
Q.16.1: If yes, what do you use this for?
Q.17: Do you record the date and time when the problem was reported?
Q.18: Do you compare the plans to the actual results in order to improve the process?

III. Managing Software Products
Q.1: Do you identify the product in which the problem was encountered?
Q.1.1: Do you identify the product and its release ID in which the problem was encountered?
Q.1.2: Do you identify the product component/function in which the problem was encountered?
Q.1.3: What is the lowest granularity level in which you identify the product in which the problem was encountered?
Q.2: Do you identify the environment of the product in which the problem was encountered?
Q.2.1: What do you mean by the product environment?
Q.2.2: Do you consider information on the customer environment when investigating the problem? Does it help in recreating the problem?
Q.3: Do you record the date and time when the problem was encountered?
Q.3.1: If yes, what do you use this value for?
Q.4: Do you designate the version(s) of the software product in which the problem solution will be implemented?
Q.4.1: What criteria do you use when choosing the versions in which the software product will be investigated?
Q.4.2: Do you continuously revise the designation of) the version(s) of the software product in which the problem solution will be implemented?
Q.5: Do you designate (an) appropriate version(s) of the software product in which the problem will be investigated?
Q.5.1: What criteria do you use when choosing the versions in which the software product will be investigated?
Q.6: Do you ensure the traceability of the modified documentation item to the other (modified and unmodified) documentation items within the system?
Q.6.1: On what granularity level do you achieve this traceability?
Q.7: Do you ensure the traceability of change?
Q.7.1: On what granularity level do you achieve this traceability?

IV. Resource Management
Q.1: Do you identify the problem submitter?
Q.1.1: If it is an external problem submitter, do you have his/her/submitter organisation's identification data easily available?
Q.1.2: Do you often use the submitter's identification data? What for?
Q.1.3: In what situations do you contact problem submitters?
Q.2: Do you allow problem submitters to describe (a) work around(s), that is, a list of a set of steps describing how to avoid the problem?
Q.2.1: What do you use it for?
Q.3: Do you allow problem submitters to describe suggestions for how to solve software problems?
Q.3.1: What do you use it for?
Q.4: Do you record problem reports into the organisation-wide problem report repository and tracking system?
Q.4.1: Do you record all software problems in the repository?
Q.5: Do you assign the problem report to the maintenance team for attendance?
Q.5.1: According to what rules do you choose the maintenance team?
Q.5.2: What is this team responsible for?
Q.6: Exactly what roles are involved in the management of software problems and what exactly do they do?
Q.6.1 Who attends to the reported problems (1) anybody, (2) a specially dedicated maintenance team ?

6 Appendix A.2: Our Questionnaire, Part 2

V. Describing and Reporting Software Problems
Q.1: How do you describe the problem?
Q.1.1: Do you provide a template on how to describe software problems?
Q.1.2: Do you give a general textual description of the problem?
Q.1.3: Do you describe the problem effect(s) and consequence(s)?
Q.1.4: Do you describe the symptoms of the problem?
Q.1.5: How do you use the information on symptoms?
Q.1.6: Do you describe the problem conditions?
Q.1.7: Do you describe how to reproduce the problem?
Q.1.7.1: Do you classify the problem as reproducible or non-reproducible?
Q.1.7.2: Do you indicate the repeatability of the problem (once, several, repeatable)?
Q.1.7.3: Do you describe how to reproduce the problem?
Q.1.8: Do you describe alternative execution path(s) to the problem?
Q.2: Do you attach relevant file(s) for visualising/confirming the problem?
Q.3: Do you identify the type of a problem, for instance, requirement problem, design problem, software code problem, etc.?
Q.3.1: If yes, what does your classification look like?
Q.3.2: What do you use this classification for?
Q.4: Do you identify problems related to the reported problem, if any?
Q.5: Do you revise the software problem report data continuously during the problem management process as you gain more understanding about the problem?
Q.6: Do you submit additional problems encountered during the problem management process?

VI. Problem Investigation
Q.1: Do you study the problem report?
Q.1.1: Do you encounter any problems/difficulties during this step?
Q.2: Do you study the software system?
Q.2.1: Do you spend enough time for studying the software system?
Q.2.2: Do you fully understand the software system?
Q.3: Do you define a set of test cases required for the recreation of some problems or do you just recreate the problem in an ad hoc manner?
Q.3.1: Do you document these test cases?
Q.4: What exactly do you document during problem investigation?
Q.5: What else do you do when investigating problems?

VII. Problem Cause Identification
Q1: Do you study the results of the activity "*Problem Investigation*" in order to get acquainted (with (if another Problem Report Engineer) or get reacquainted with the problem?
Q.2: When identifying the problem causes, what exactly do you do?
Q.2.1: Do you study the pertinent documentation items and check their correctness?
Q.2.2: Do you identify and record the documentation items containing the defect(s)?
Q.2.3: On what granularity level do you record the problem causes (component/line level)?
Q.3: Do you classify the identified problem cause(s)/(defect(s))?

Q.4: What do you use this classification for?
Q.5: What exactly do you document during this activity?

VIII. Root Cause Analysis
Q.1: Do you identify the process activities/tasks during which the problem cause (defect) was introduced?
Q.2: Do you identify the root causes for the defect by analysing the process steps during which the problem cause/(defect) was introduced? How do you do it?
Q.3: Do you classify the root cause(s)?
Q.4: Why do you conduct root cause analysis?

IX. Modification Design
Q.1: How many suggestions for problem solution do you make?
Q.2: Do you record all these suggestions?
Q.3: What exactly is recorded: (1) a general description of what a problem solution should look like, (2) a specification of measures to be conducted in order to solve the problem?
Q.4: Do you evaluate the problem solution?
Q.5: What is exactly evaluated: (1) a general description of what a problem solution should look like, (2) a specification of measures to be conducted in order to solve the problem?
Q.6: When evaluating problem solutions, what exactly do you consider (1) modification size, (2) impact of the modification, ripple effect, effect on customer, (3) the effort and resources required for solving the problem, (4) the feasibility of solving the problem, (5) the benefits and drawbacks of solving the problem?
Q.7: Do you inspect/review the modification designs?
Q.8: Who does the inspection/reviewing?
Q.9: Do you make an implementation plan for each problem solution?
Q.10: What exactly do you plan?
Q.11: When at the earliest do you start designing problem solutions?
Q.12: Do you evaluate the early preliminary problem solutions?

X. Modification Decision (Stage 4)
Q.1: Do you report the results of the major process activity to some authority?
Q.2: Do you make decisions whether to proceed with the problem resolution after each major process activity?
Q.3: Do you have a Change Control Board (CCB)?
Q.4: What kinds of decisions does CCB make?
Q.5: When making decisions on the choice of modification designs, what exactly does the CCB do?
Q.6: Do you record all the decisions made (1) after each major process phase, (2) decisions made for all solutions?

XI. Modification Implementation (Stage 5)
Q.1: Do you record all the changes made to the software product?
Q.1.1: On what granularity level?
Q.2: Do you unit test these changes?
Q.3: Do you modify the product according to some documentation standard?
Q.4: For each change, do you record the following: (1) reason for the changes, (2) modification size, (3)effort and resources, (4) ripple effect, (5) feasibility, (6) drawbacks and benefits?
Q4.1: Do you record this information for the whole modification effort or for each individual measure specified in problem solution?

Database Schema Matching
Using Machine Learning with Feature Selection

Jacob Berlin and Amihai Motro

Information and Software Engineering Department
George Mason University, Fairfax, VA 22030
{jberlin,ami}@gmu.edu

Abstract. Schema matching, the problem of finding mappings between the attributes of two semantically related database schemas, is an important aspect of many database applications such as schema integration, data warehousing, and electronic commerce. Unfortunately, schema matching remains largely a manual, labor-intensive process. Furthermore, the effort required is typically linear in the number of schemas to be matched; the next pair of schemas to match is not any easier than the previous pair. In this paper we describe a system, called Automatch, that uses machine learning techniques to automate schema matching. Based primarily on Bayesian learning, the system acquires probabilistic knowledge from examples that have been provided by domain experts. This knowledge is stored in a knowledge base called the *attribute dictionary*. When presented with a pair of new schemas that need to be matched (and their corresponding database instances), Automatch uses the attribute dictionary to find an optimal matching. We also report initial results from the Automatch project.

1 Introduction

Schema matching is the problem of finding mappings between the attributes of two semantically related database schemas. The schema matching problem is an important, current issue for many database applications such as schema integration, data warehousing, and electronic commerce [12,15]. Unfortunately, schema matching remains largely a manual, labor-intensive process. Furthermore, the effort required is typically linear in the number of schemas to be matched; the next pair of schemas to match is not any easier than the previous pair. Thus, database applications that require schema matching are limited to environments in which the set of member information sources is small and stable. These applications would scale-up to much larger communities of member sources if the schema matching "bottleneck" was broken by automating the matching process.

In this paper we discuss such a system, called Automatch, for automating the schema matching process. Based primarily on Bayesian learning, the system acquires probabilistic knowledge from examples of schemas that have been "mapped" by domain experts into a knowledge base of database attributes called the *attribute dictionary*. Roughly speaking, this dictionary characterizes different attributes by means of their *possible values* and the *probability estimates* of these values. Furthermore, the dictionary may be extended to contain any attribute metadata that has a probabilistic interpretation (e.g. attribute names or string patterns).

When presented with a pair of "client" schemas that need to be matched (and their corresponding database instances), Automatch matches them "through" its dictionary. Using probabilistic methods, an attempt is made to match every attribute of one client schema with every attribute of the other client schema, resulting in individual "scores." An optimization process based on a Minimum Cost Maximum Flow network algorithm finds the overall optimal matching between the two client schemas, with respect to the sum of the individual attribute matching scores.

To overcome the problem of very large dictionaries caused by very large attribute domains, Automatch employs statistical *feature selection* techniques to learn an efficient representation of the examples. That is, each attribute is represented with a minimal set of most informative values. Thus the attribute dictionary is made human understandable through aggressive reduction in the number of values. Although the example schemas may contain many thousands of values, we are able to focus learning on a very small subset, consisting of as few as 10% of the initial values.

The results of our initial experimentation with Automatch are encouraging as they show performance that exceeds 70% (measured as the harmonic mean of the soundness and the completeness of the matching process). Although the attribute dictionary was built for Automatch, we conjecture that it could be employed as a knowledge asset in other schema matching systems.

The remainder of this paper is organized as follows. Section 3 describes the basic methodology of Automatch; in particular, the probabilistic information in the acquired knowledge base and how it is used to infer optimal matchings between "client" schemas. Section 4 describes alternative methods for reducing the size of the knowledge base through feature selection. Section 5 explains the experiment and its conclusions. Section 6 summarizes the contributions and suggests future research directions. We begin with a brief discussion of other published approaches and how they are related to Automatch.

2 Related Work

A thorough discussion of schema matching techniques and implementations can be found in [6,11,15]. Here we mention two such approaches and compare them to Automatch. Automated schema matching can be classified as rule based and learner based [6].

The Artemis system [5] is a rule-based approach for schema integration. This system determines the *affinity* of attributes from two schemas in a pair-wise fashion. Affinity is based on comparisons of attribute names, structure, and domain types and is scored on a [0,1] interval. The process relies on thesauri to determine semantic relationships. The system uses hierarchical clustering based on affinity values to group together related attributes. Finally, a set of unification rules are employed to interactively guide a user through the construction of an integrated schema. In contrast with Automatch, Artemis considers schema information; Automatch considers instance information. Furthermore, knowledge in Artemis is "pre-coded" in the thesaurus and unification rules; knowledge in Automatch is learned from examples.

SemInt [9,10] is a learner-based system that uses neural networks to identify similar attributes from different schemas. This system uses a combination of schema and instance information. Schema information includes such information as data types, field length, and constraint information. Instance information includes such information as value distributions, character ratios, numeric mean and variance.

For each type of information the system exploits, it determines a numerical value on a $[0, 1]$ interval. A tuple of these numerical values for one attribute is the *signature* of the attribute. The system uses these signatures to cluster similar attributes within the same schema. The system then uses the signatures of the cluster centers to train a neural network to output an attribute category based on the input signatures. Given a new schema, the system determines the signature of each schema attribute using the same type of schema and instance information used for training. These signatures are then applied to the neural network to determine the category of the respective attributes. In contrast with Automatch, SemInt uses a fixed set of features for learning; Automatch combines feature selection with learning to find an optimal set of features for a given problem domain. Furthermore, SemInt discovers matches to attribute clusters; Automatch discovers matches to individual attributes.

3 Methodology

This section describes the basic methodology of Automatch, providing details of its data structures and algorithms. It begins with an intuitive description of the approach and a formal description of the problem.

3.1 The Overall Approach

Automatch is based on a knowledge base about schema attributes which is constructed from examples. When presented with two new "client" schemas that need to be matched (and their corresponding database instances), Automatch checks every client attribute against its attribute dictionary, obtaining individual "matching scores" for each pair of client attribute and dictionary attribute.

These client-dictionary attribute scores are combined to generate client-client attribute scores. To illustrate, assume B is an attribute of one client scheme, C is an attribute of the other client scheme, and A is an attribute of the dictionary, and assume that the matching of B to A is scored w_1 and the matching of C to A is scored w_2; then the matching $B \leftrightarrow C$ receives the score $w_1 + w_2$.[1]

---

[1] We combine the individual scores by their sum, but other combinations are also possible; for example, their product.

In turn, these individual client-client attribute scores are combined to generate overall schema-schema matching scores. To illustrate, assume schemas $R_1 = \{B_1, B_2\}$ and $R_2 = \{C_1, C_2\}$ and assume the client-client attribute scores: $w_1 : B_1 \leftrightarrow C_1$, $w_2 : B_1 \leftrightarrow C_2$, $w_3 : B_2 \leftrightarrow C_1$, and $w_4 : B_2 \leftrightarrow C_2$. The schema matching $\{B_1 \leftrightarrow C_2, B_2 \leftrightarrow C_1\}$ is then scored $w_2 + w_3$. Other schema matchings are scored similarly.

In a subsequent optimization process, Automatch finds the schema matching with the highest schema-schema score.

3.2 Formalization of the Problem

Our formalization is based on the relational model. However, we are confident that the methods can be extended to other models, such as the object-oriented or the semi-structured models. A *database schema* is simply a finite set of *attributes* $\{A_1, \ldots, A_n\}$. Given two database schemas $R_1 = \{B_1, \ldots, B_p\}$ and $R_2 = \{C_1, \ldots, C_q\}$, a *matching* is a mapping between a subset of R_1 and a subset of R_2.

We assume a knowledge base about database attributes, called the *attribute dictionary* and denoted D. In this knowledge base, each attribute is characterized by a select set of possible values and their probability estimates.

In addition, we assume a *scoring function* f that, given (1) the attribute dictionary D, (2) a pair of database schemas R_1 and R_2, (3) a pair of corresponding database instances r_1 and r_2, and (4) a matching between R_1 and R_2, issues a value (a real number), that indicates the "goodness" of the matching.

The problem is then to find the *best* matching for two given schemas R_1 and R_2. This abstract description leaves two major issues to be discussed in detail:

1. The nature of the attribute dictionary D and the scoring function f.
2. The optimization of f (i.e., finding the best schema matching).

These two issues are discussed in the next two subsections.

3.3 The Attribute Dictionary and the Scoring Function

The attribute dictionary D consists of a finite set of schema *attributes* $\{A_1, \ldots, A_r\}$. Each attribute in the attribute dictionary is characterized by a set of *possible values* and their *probability estimates*. The attribute dictionary serves as a knowledge base that accumulates information about attributes. All attempts to match attributes of client schemas refer to this knowledge base. We use Bayesian learning to populate the attribute dictionary with example values provided by domain experts.

Recall from the intuitive description in Section 3.1 that the first task is to determine client-dictionary attribute scores.

Let X be a client attribute, let A denote a dictionary attribute, and let V denote a set of values that are observed in X (these values are derived from the instance of the client schema to which X belongs).

Let $P(A)$ be the *prior* probability that X maps to A (before observing any values of X), let $P(V)$ represent the unconditional probability of observing values V in X, and let $P(V|A)$ represent the conditional probability of observing the values V, given that X maps to A. Bayes Theorem states that

$$P(A|V) = \frac{P(V|A) \cdot P(A)}{P(V)}. \tag{1}$$

$P(A|V)$ is referred to as the *posterior* probability that X maps to A, because it reflects the probability that a mapping of X to A holds *after* the values V have been observed. This posterior probability serves as the score of the client attribute X and the dictionary attribute A.

Letting V be a sequence of values $(v_1, \ldots, v_n)$, and assuming *conditional independence* of values given the mapping, the client-dictionary attribute score is

$$M(X, A) = \frac{P(A)}{P(V)} \cdot \prod_{k=1}^{n} P(v_k|A). \tag{2}$$

Although the attribute values may not be conditionally independent, such an assumption has been shown to be an acceptable approach, aimed at reducing the number of probabilities to a tractable amount while not sacrificing optimality [7,8,13].

To build the attribute dictionary for each attribute A we must learn and store the probability estimates $P(A)$, $P(\neg A)$, $P(v|A)$, and $P(v|\neg A)$ for all dictionary attributes A and values v. Note that we do not need to learn $P(V)$ because this term is determined by the requirement that $M(X, A) + M(X, \neg A) = 1$.

$P(A)$, the probability that a client attribute X maps to A, is estimated by the proportion of examples provided by the domain expert that have been mapped to A. $P(v|A)$, the probability that attribute value v occurs given that a mapping to A holds, is estimated by counting the occurrences of v in the set of examples provided by the domain expert. The remaining terms are learned in a similar fashion. For numeric data values, we assume a normal distribution and use the normal probability density function to estimate the conditional probabilities. A thorough discussion of the algorithms for estimating these terms is reported in [4]. A critical selection process that reduces the number of values v that are maintained for each attribute A is discussed in Section 4.

3.4 Optimal Schema Matching

Assume now two given schemas R_1 and R_2 with their corresponding instances r_1 and r_2, and let D denote the attribute dictionary.

The scores $M(X, A)$ from Equation 2 are calculated for each attribute X in the given schema and for each attribute A of the dictionary. A threshold is then adopted, and scores that are below this threshold are interpreted as evidence that X should not be mapped to A. These results may be represented in a weighted tripartite graph in which nodes correspond to attributes, edges correspond to matches, and edge weights correspond to the posterior probabilities.

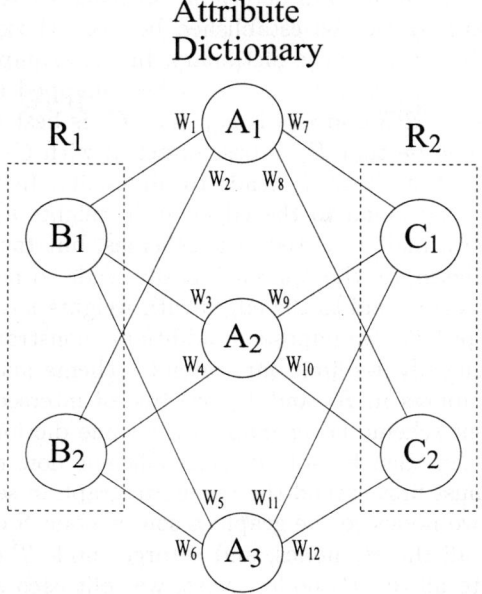

Fig. 1. Weighted tripartite graph for representing individual attribute-attribute scores

Figure 1 shows such a graph for a simple case in which $R_1 = \{B_1, B_2\}$, $R_2 = \{C_1, C_2\}$, and $D = \{A_1, A_2, A_3\}$. This example shows a *full* tripartite graph (every node in the left or right partitions is connected to every node in the center partition), but the use of a threshold implies that in general the graph need not be full.

Recall from the intuitive description in Section 3.1, that the client-dictionary attribute scores w_i are combined to generate client-client attribute scores. Note, however, that every two client attributes may be matched through every dictionary attribute. In the example, B_1 and C_1 may be matched through A_1 (with score $w_1 + w_7$), through A_2 (with score $w_3 + w_9$) and through A_3 (with score $w_5 + w_{11}$). Note that associating a dictionary attribute with every attribute match is like providing a *common type* for the matching attribute pair.

In turn, client-client attribute scores are used in generating overall schema-schema scores. In the example, the schema matching comprising of $B_1 \stackrel{A_1}{\leftrightarrow} C_2$ and $B_2 \stackrel{A_3}{\leftrightarrow} C_1$ receives the score $w_1 + w_8 + w_6 + w_{11}$. Obviously, the number of possible matchings between R_1 and R_2 is too high for a simple process that enumerates all the matchings and scores each.

One obvious approach for matching R_1 and R_2 is to choose for each client attribute the most probable dictionary attribute. For instance, in the example, the highest of w_1, w_3 and w_5 will determine whether B_1 is mapped to A_1, A_2 or A_3. Then a mapping can be established between those schema attributes that share a node in the attribute dictionary. In the example, assume that the highest of w_1, w_3 and w_5 is w_3; (i.e., B_1 is best mapped to A_2), and assume that the highest of w_8, w_{10} and w_{12} is w_{10} (i.e., C_2 is best mapped to A_2); the conclusion would then be that B_1 is best matched with C_2. The problem with such an approach is that it easily leads to ambiguity. In the example, if the optimal mappings correspond to the edges with weights w_3, w_4, w_9 and w_{10}, we have established a match between the schemas, but the attribute mapping is ambiguous. Furthermore, the approach easily leads to no match; e.g., if the optimal mappings correspond to the edges with weights w_1, w_6, w_9, and w_{10}.

To avoid these pitfalls, we impose an additional constraint on the matching of R_1 and R_2. Specifically, we limit our search to schema mappings in which the paths between attributes in R_1 and R_2 are free of intersections. That is, two attributes of a client scheme never map to the same dictionary attribute. The resulting problem can then be solved using efficient flow network techniques. Towards this, we must first extend the tripartite graph in several ways.

First, we add two nodes to the graph: a source node S on the left, which is then connected to all the R_1 nodes, and a target node T on the right, which is then connected to all the R_2 nodes. Next, we split each attribute dictionary node A into two nodes, A^{in} and A^{out}. Each A_i^{in} is connected to its corresponding A_i^{out} node. Next, we reconnect the edges from R_1 and R_2 to the appropriate A_{in} or A_{out} node. Finally, each edge is given direction, capacity, and cost. All edges are directed away from the source node S and towards the target node T. The capacity for each edge is 1 (thus, the flow through an edge will be either 0 or 1). The cost of each of the new edges added to the graph is 0. The cost of each of the old edges is the negation of the edge weight. Figure 2 shows the new graph for the example of Figure 1. Edge capacities and costs were omitted for clarity.

The reason for the negation of the weights is that we will be using an algorithm that searches for a minimum when we actually wish to find the maximum (finding a maximum is equivalent to finding the minimum of the negation). With these modifications, we can now find a matching between the schemas R_1 and R_2 that conforms to our constraints by using a Minimum Cost Maximum Flow network algorithm [1]. In the current implementation of Automatch, we use the LEDA software package for this purpose [2].

Specifically for Figure 2, since the source has two outgoing edges of capacity 1 and the target has two incoming edges of capacity 1 (i.e., two attributes are matched on each side), the maximum flow is 2. Thus, we seek to find the edges in the graph that have the minimum cost while supporting a maximum flow of 2. The edges in this set correspond to the optimal mapping of attributes of R_1 to R_2.

Note that when the client schemas do not have the same number of attributes, some of the attributes of the larger schema will be matchless. Moreover, since the tripartite is not necessarily full, the optimal matching may leave attributes

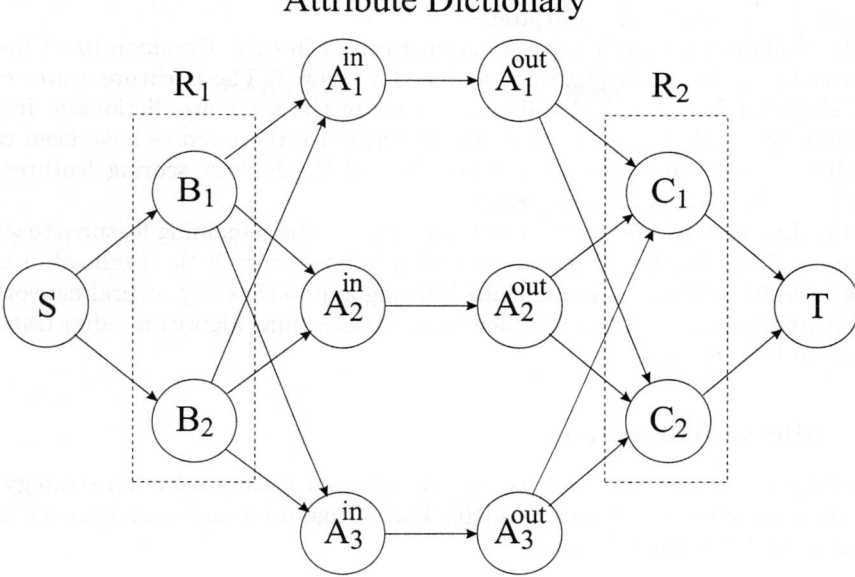

Fig. 2. Minimum-Cost-Maximum-Flow graph for finding optimal schema matching

in the *smaller* schema matchless as well. This is not an undesirable consequence, as it simply indicates that the client schemas include attributes that are unique to their schemas.

4 Optimal Selection of Dictionary Values

Recall that the attribute dictionary of Automatch represents each attribute with a set of possible values and their probability estimates. For schema attributes that contain text, the number of needed probabilities is proportional to the number of unique values of this attribute. An attribute such as *CustomerName* could assume thousands of values, thus imposing considerable space and processing requirements. Furthermore, not all of these probabilities are equally informative. Indeed, many of them are either uninformative (irrelevant) or misleading (noise).

A critical consideration in our methods is to reduce the dictionary representation of attributes while retaining the most informative values. In machine learning terminology these values are called *features* and the reduction process is called *feature selection*. To reduce the size of the Automatch dictionary, we have tested and compared three statistical feature selection strategies: Mutual Information, Information Gain, and Likelihood Ratio. The former two strategies are commonly used for feature selection; to our knowledge the latter strategy has not been used for this purpose.

We will discuss each feature selection strategy in turn. Common to all these approaches is that each feature is assigned a "score." These feature scores can be calculated from the probability estimates in the attribute dictionary. In all of these approaches, higher scores are better. Once these scores have been calculated for a given approach, a percentage of the highest scoring features is retained with ties broken arbitrarily.

Finally, we must normalize the probabilities of the remaining features to sum to unity. Thus, statistical feature selection imposes very little overhead in our approach. In contrast, other machine learning approaches (e.g. neural networks, rule learners, etc.) must execute their respective learning algorithms after feature selection is completed.

4.1 Mutual Information

Mutual information has been used previously as a feature selection strategy in information retrieval tasks such as [16]. The mutual information of a value v and an attribute A is defined as

$$MI(v, A) = \log \frac{P(v \wedge A)}{P(v) \cdot P(A)} . \qquad (3)$$

When v and A are independent, the mutual information of v and A is zero. Intuitively, $P(v)$ is a measure of the event that a value v occurs in the client attribute X, and $P(A)$ is a measure of the event the client attribute X is mapped to the dictionary attribute A. Hence, $MI(v, A)$ is a measure of the *co-occurrence* of these two events. For example, if the events are independent (their co-occurrence is unbiased), then the mutual information is 0.

For the purpose of characterizing dictionary attributes, we wish to retain the values that have the greatest score regardless of whether they favor A or $\neg A$. Therefore, we score values in the MI approach using this formula:

$$MI_{max}(v, A) = \max \left\{ \log \frac{P(v \wedge A)}{P(v) \cdot P(A)}, \log \frac{P(v \wedge \neg A)}{P(v) \cdot P(\neg A)} \right\} . \qquad (4)$$

The values v with the highest $MI_{max}(v, A)$ are chosen as the characterization of attribute A. The actual number of values chosen is discussed in Section 5.2.

4.2 Information Gain

Information gain is often used in machine learning to determine the value of a particular feature [13]. Given a client attribute X and a dictionary attribute A, the issue is whether X maps to A or not. This issue may be formatted as a binary *message*: 1 if yes, 0 if no.

Denote $P(A)$ the probability that X maps to A. Assume first that our only knowledge is the proportion of attributes that are mapped to A (how "popular" A is as a target of mappings). The entropy (information content) of the message is then

$$H = -(P(A) \cdot \log P(A) + P(\neg A) \cdot \log P(\neg A)) . \qquad (5)$$

Assume now that we know a new fact: $v \in X$. The new entropy (information content) of the message is

$$H_1 = -(P(A \mid v) \cdot \log P(A \mid v) + P(\neg A \mid v) \cdot \log P(\neg A \mid v)) . \qquad (6)$$

Assume now that we know an alternative fact: $v \notin X$. The new entropy (information content) of the message is

$$H_2 = -(P(A \mid \neg v) \cdot \log P(A \mid \neg v) + P(\neg A \mid \neg v) \cdot \log P(\neg A \mid \neg v)) . \qquad (7)$$

H_1 and H_2 may be combined using $P(v)$, the probability that v is in X. Then the entropy (information content) of the message is

$$H' = P(v) \cdot H_1 + p(\neg v) \cdot H_2 . \qquad (8)$$

The *information gained* by knowing the presence or absence of v is

$$IG(v, A) = H - H' . \qquad (9)$$

4.3 Likelihood Ratio

The likelihood ratio for a value v and attribute A, defined as $P(v|A)/P(v|\neg A)$, measures the *retrospective* support given to A by the occurrence of v [14]. The likelihood ratio produces scores on the interval $(0, \infty)$. It has a value of 1 if the feature provides no support. Likelihood ratios greater than 1 indicate that the feature supports A; likelihood ratios less than 1 indicate that the feature supports $\neg A$.

For the task at hand, we wish to retain the features that provide the most support regardless of whether they favor A or $\neg A$. The features that favor A are on the interval $(1, \infty)$, with higher values indicating stronger support, whereas the features that favor $\neg A$ are on the interval $(0, 1)$, with lower values indicating stronger support. Consequently, it is difficult to use the likelihood ratio as defined, because higher scores are not necessarily better. For this reason, we use an adjustment that inverts the likelihood ratios that support $\neg A$, placing them on the same scale as likelihood ratios that support A, and then choose the stronger of the supports:

$$LR(v, A) = \max \left\{ \frac{P(v|A)}{P(v|\neg A)}, \frac{P(v|\neg A)}{P(v|A)} \right\} . \qquad (10)$$

This strategy produces scores on the interval $(1, \infty)$ and higher scores are always better.

5 Experimentation

5.1 Setting Up the Experiment

To experiment with the methods discussed in this paper, we built an attribute dictionary for computer retail information with the following attributes: *DesktopManufacturer, MonitorManufacturer, PrinterManufacturer, DesktopModel, MonitorModel, PrinterModel, DesktopCost, PeripheralCost, Inventory.*

Data for this experiment was taken from the web sites of 15 different computer retailers (e.g. Gateway, Outpost, etc). A total of 22 relations were extracted. The data was collected off-line from HTML web pages and imported into relational database tables accessible through the ODBC protocol.

To experiment with this data, we used a procedure from data mining called *stratified cross-validation* which we briefly describe (see [17] for a complete description). Each of the 22 schemas was manually mapped into our attribute dictionary. We then partitioned these 22 schemas into three *folds* of approximately equal size. Using two folds for learning and one fold for testing, we repeated the experiment for the three possible combinations of folds. For the test fold, we chose two schemas at a time (for all possible combinations) and used Automatch to match the schemas. We used the manually constructed mappings to judge the mappings which Automatch concluded.

5.2 Measuring Performance

To measure performance, each schema-matching result was interpreted as set of mapping decisions for pairs of schema attributes $\langle R_1(B_i), R_2(C_j)\rangle$, where i ranges over all the attributes of R_1 and j ranges over all the attributes of R_2. Each of these attribute mapping decisions falls into one of four sets, A, B, C, and D, where

A = True Positives (decision to map $R_1(B_i)$ to $R_2(C_j)$ is correct).
B = False Negatives (decision to not map $R_1(B_i)$ to $R_2(C_j)$ is incorrect).
C = False Positives (decision to map $R_1(B_i)$ to $R_2(C_j)$ is incorrect).
D = True Negatives (decision to not map $R_1(B_i)$ to $R_2(C_j)$ is correct).

The ratio $|A|/(|A|+|C|)$ is the proportion of true positives among the cases thought to be positive; i.e., it measures the accuracy of Automatch when it decides *True*. The ratio $|A|/(|A|+|B|)$ is the proportion of positives detected by Automatch among the complete set of positives; i.e., it measures the ability to detect positives. Specifically to our application, the former ratio measures the *soundness* of the discovery process, and the latter ratio measures its *completeness*. These two ratios are known from the field of information retrieval as *precision* and *recall*, but we shall refer to them here as the soundness and completeness of the schema matching process.

To simplify the comparison of the three feature selection approaches, we combined soundness and completeness into a single performance measure using their *harmonic mean*. The harmonic mean of precision and recall is often used in information retrieval whenever a single performance measure is preferred [3]. The harmonic mean for our mapping problem is calculated as

$$F(x) = 2 \cdot \frac{S(x) \cdot C(x)}{S(x) + C(x)} \qquad (11)$$

where $S(x)$ and $C(x)$ are the soundness and completeness of the discovery process at a given percent reduction x in the feature space. The harmonic mean assumes high values only when both soundness and completeness are high. Thus, maximizing the harmonic mean can be thought of as the best compromise between soundness and completeness.

To measure the performance of each of the feature selection strategies that were discussed in Section 4, we determine the harmonic mean of soundness and completeness for each strategy as we increase the percentage of the feature space that is discarded. We reduce the feature space in increments of 5 percent until 95 percent of the feature space has been discarded.

5.3 Interpreting the Results

First we measured the performance of Automatch without any attempt at optimizing the dictionary through feature selection; that is, we use the Bayesian approach to score matches (Section 3.3) and the flow graph approach to optimize matches (Section 3.4). Using cross validation, we achieved a performance of 66% (measured as the harmonic mean of soundness and completeness). In a separate experiment, we used random guessing to match the same schemas and achieved a performance of 10%.

Next, we compared the three feature selection strategies of Section 4 and assessed their impact on schema matching. Figure 3 shows the performance for schema matching for each of the feature selection strategies. The x-axis is the percentage of low-scoring features that have been discarded, and the y-axis is the performance, measured as the harmonic mean of soundness and completeness. The leftmost point in the graph corresponds to our first experiment with no feature selection.

Initially, with 5% feature reduction, all the feature selection strategies improve performance by at least 6%. The strategies then perform comparably up to 60% reduction. At levels of reduction over 80%, IG and LR continue to produce improved matching performance (relative to no feature selection) while MI falls below performance with no feature selection.

All three feature selection strategies improve performance when compared to the initial performance with no feature selection (though the level to which they sustain this improvement varies). This observation indicates that *all* of these approaches are acceptable for reducing the feature space. Furthermore, if we are seeking the most ambitious reduction in the feature space, LR is preferable to IG which is preferable to MI.

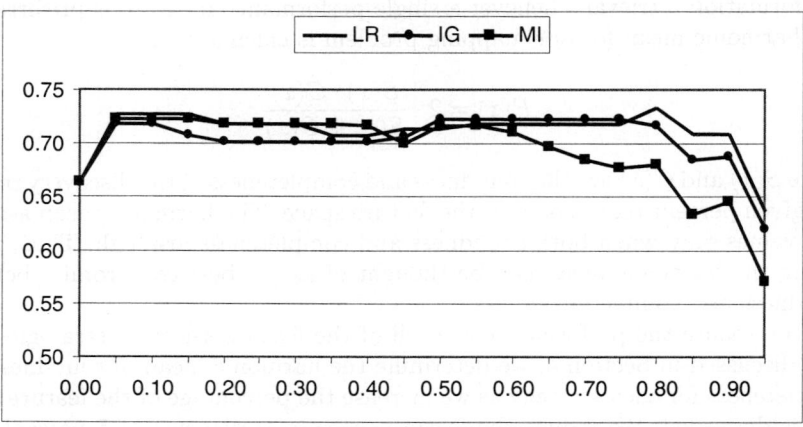

Fig. 3. Harmonic mean of soundness and completeness (y-axis) as the feature set is reduced in increments of 5 percent (x-axis)

6 Conclusion

In this paper we described an automated solution for the well-known problem of database schema matching. Our approach uses Bayesian machine learning, statistical feature selection, and the Minimum Cost Maximum Flow network algorithm to find an optimal matching of attributes between two semantically related schemas.

Our significant findings and contributions in this paper were:

- The Automatch system is a new and viable approach to eliminate the schema-matching bottleneck present in modern database applications. Our results are encouraging as they show performance that exceeds 70% (measured as the harmonic mean of the soundness and the completeness of the attribute matching process).
- Statistical feature selection can be used to improve the performance of Automatch. The improvement is in three areas: (1) in the *storage requirements* for the auxiliary knowledge base, (2) in the *computational costs* of the matching algorithm, and (3) in the *quality* (soundness and completeness) of the results. We estimate that statistical feature selection can be used to improve the performance of other automated schema-matching approaches (such as [6,10]) that must deal with high-dimensional feature spaces.
- Statistical feature selection incurs little overhead in Automatch since we are using a probabilistic learning approach. Learning after feature selection consists simply of normalizing the probabilities of the remaining features. In contrast, other machine learning approaches (e.g. neural networks, rule learners, etc.) must execute their respective learning algorithms after feature selection is completed.

While the performance of 70% in these experiments is promising, user interaction is still necessary to complete the matching process. In our future research, we plan on building a user interface that allows a domain expert to adjust the attribute mappings that have been proposed by Automatch. Furthermore, the interface will allow for iterative adjustment (i.e., after the user adjusts some of the mappings, we can re-apply Automatch for the remaining unmapped attributes).

An important benefit of user interaction in Automatch is that the system will be able to learn continuously. As new matches are provided through the user interface, the learner will be able to combine this information with what has already been learned. Note that this is significantly different than re-executing the entire learning algorithm. Such continuous learning is possible due to the statistical nature of the learning algorithm. As new matches are validated by a user, we can learn from these additional examples by updating the frequency counts of the features.

Finally, while this initial experimentation is encouraging, it is admittedly of a limited scale. Additional experimentation is planned to validate these preliminary conclusions.

Acknowledgement

The authors wish to thank Joseph (Seffi) Naor for his important suggestions in the area of network flows.

References

1. Ravindra K. Ahuja, Thomas L. Magnanti, and James B. Orlin. *Network Flows: Theory, Algorithms, and Applications*. Prentice Hall, 1993.
2. Algorithmic Solutions. *The LEDA Users Manual (Version 4.2.1)*, 2001.
3. Ricardo Baeza-Yates and Berthier Ribeiro-Neto. *Modern Information Retrieval*. ACM Press, 1999.
4. Jacob Berlin and Amihai Motro. Autoplex: Automated discovery of content for virtual databases. In *Proceedings of the Ninth International Conference on Cooperative Information Systems*, pages 108–122, 2001.
5. Silvana Castano and Valeria De Antonellis. A schema analysis and reconciliation tool environment for heterogeneous databases. In *Proceedings of the International Database Engineering and Applications Symposium*, pages 53–62, 1999.
6. AnHai Doan, Pedro Domingos, and Alon Y. Halevy. Reconciling schemas of disparate data sources: A machine-learning approach. In *Proceedings ACM Special Interest Group for the Management of Data (SIGMOD)*, 2001.
7. Pedro Domingos and Michael Pazzani. Conditions for the optimality of the simple bayesian classifier. In *Proceedings of the 13th International Conference on Machine Learning*, pages 105–112, 1996.
8. Pat Langley, Wayne Iba, and Kevin Thompson. An analysis of bayesian classifiers. In *Proceedings of the Tenth National Conference on Artificial Intelligence*, pages 223–228, 1992.

9. Wen-Syan Li and Chris Clifton. Semantic integration in heterogeneous databases using neural networks. In *Proceedings of 20th International Conference on Very Large Data Bases*, pages 1–12, 1994.
10. Wen-Syan Li and Chris Clifton. Semint: A tool for identifying attribute correspondences in heterogeneous databases using neural networks. *Data & Knowledge Engineering*, 33(1):49–84, 2000.
11. Jayant Madhavan, Philip A. Bernstein, and Erhard Rahm. Generic schema matching with cupid. In *Proceedings of the 27th International Conferences on Very Large Databases*, pages 49–58, 2001.
12. Renée Miller, Laura Haas, and Mauricio Hernández. Schema mapping as query discovery. In *Proceedings of the 26th International Conferences on Very Large Databases*, pages 77–88, 2000.
13. Tom Mitchell. *Machine Learning*. McGraw-Hill, 1997.
14. Judea Pearl. *Probabilistic Reasoning in Intelligent Systems: Networks of Plausible Inference*. Morgan Kaufmann, 1988.
15. Erhard Rahm and Philip Bernstein. On matching schemas automatically. Technical Report MSR-TR-2001-17, Microsoft, Redmond, WA, February 2001.
16. Mehran Sahami, Susan Dumais, David Heckerman, and Eric Horvitz. A bayesian approach to filtering junk e-mail. *AAAI-98 Workshop on Learning for Text Categorization*, 1998.
17. Ian H. Witten and Eibe Frank. *Data Mining: Practical Machine Learning Tools and Techniques with Java Implementations*. Morgan Kaufmann, 2000.

Evolving Partitions in Conceptual Schemas in the UML

Cristina Gómez and Antoni Olivé

Departament de Llenguatges i Sistemes Informàtics,
Universitat Politècnica Catalunya,
Jordi Girona 1-3 E08034 Barcelona (Catalonia)
{cristina,olive}@lsi.upc.es

Abstract. The evolution of information systems from their conceptual schemas is an important research area in information systems engineering. In this paper, we aim at contributing to the area by focusing on a particular conceptual modeling construct, the partitions. We analyze the evolution of partitions in conceptual schemas of information systems. We deal with conceptual models with multiple specialization and classification, and consider whether entity types are base or derived. We provide a list of possible schema changes and, for each of them, we give its preconditions, and its effects on the schema, taking into account the state of the information base. In this paper, we deal with conceptual schemas in the UML. However, the results reported here should be applicable to most conceptual modeling languages and also to object-oriented database schemas.

1 Introduction

The evolution of information systems is one of the most important problems in the field of information systems engineering. For several reasons, many organizations need to change very often their activities, and this usually requires an evolution of the information system that supports those activities. The evolution must be done always efficiently, and often quickly and without interrupting critical services [2]. Automated support for information system evolution becomes central to satisfy these evolution requirements [12].

Ideally, the evolution of information systems should follow the strategy called 'forward information system maintenance' in [8]: changes should be applied directly to the conceptual schema, and from here they should propagate automatically down to the database logical schema(s) and application programs. If needed, the database extension(s) should be also converted automatically. This strategy implies that the conceptual schema is the only description to be defined, and the basis for the specification of the evolution. All the others are internal to the system.

Many past and current research efforts aim directly or indirectly at that ideal. Most of them have been done in the database field and, more precisely, in the subfield that deals with the problem of schema evolution. The problem has two aspects: the semantics of changes (i.e. their effects on the schema) and the change propagation (i.e. the propagation of the schema changes to the underlying existing instances) [18]. Both aspects have been studied extensively for the relational and the object-oriented data models, in the temporal and the non-temporal variants [19]. The results have been often incorporated into commercial or prototype database systems (e.g., Orion [3], O$_2$ [26], Cocoon [24], F2 [1] and Tigukat [7]).

More recently, in the software engineering field, the problem of software evolution is being dealt with a refactoring approach [16]. A refactoring is a parameterized behavior-preserving program transformation that automatically updates an application's design and source code. Design refactoring deals with design constructs rather than code, and therefore it can be applied also to models in the UML [22]. The approaches in the databases and software engineering fields are similar, because database schema evolution transformations have their parallels in refactoring transformations [23].

In this paper, we aim at contributing to the general field of information systems evolution from conceptual schemas. We extend the work reported in [10] by dealing with a particular conceptual modeling construct, partitions, and analyze, the possible changes and their effects at the schema and instance levels.

Partitions are well-known constructs, used in conceptual modeling, object-oriented software design and object-oriented database schemas. A partition of an entity type like, for example, *Person* into entity types *Man* and *Woman* states that *Man* and *Woman* are subtypes of *Person*, that *Man* and *Woman* are disjoint, and that the population of *Person* is exactly the union of that of *Man* and *Woman*. The interest of partitions lies in their simplicity, expressiveness and generality (since specializations and generalizations can be transformed into partitions). Often it is easier to develop, analyze and reason about conceptual schemas, when only partitions are considered [21, 4, 25, 13].

However, partitions have not been studied in the literature on schema evolution. Since the early works of Orion [3], there has been a lot of work related to the evolution of specializations (or generalizations or subclass/superclass relationships) but, as far as we know, there are not published results on the evolution of partitions. The work most similar to ours is [5], which takes into account disjointness and completeness constraints between entity types, but partitions are not considered schema objects, and the context is restricted to object-oriented databases.

The main contribution of our paper is the analysis of the evolution of partitions in conceptual schemas of information systems. We deal with conceptual models with multiple specialization and classification, and consider whether entity types are base or derived (with different kinds of derivability). We show that derivability has an important influence on the evolution of partitions. We provide a list of possible schema changes (related to partitions and derivability) and, for each of them, we give its preconditions, and its effects on the schema, taking into account the state of the information base.

In this paper, we deal with conceptual schemas expressed in the UML. We hope that, we ease the application of our results to industrial projects, and the integration with other ongoing projects. However, the results reported here should be applicable to most conceptual modeling languages and also to object-oriented database schemas. In particular, the results can be adapted to the logic-based language used in [10].

The rest of the paper is structured as follows. Section 2 reviews the concept of taxonomic constraints, partitions, derived types and constraint satisfaction. In Section 3, we propose an UML Profile for Partitions in Conceptual Modeling. This profile is an extension to the UML, using the standard mechanisms provided by the language. We explain that the profile is needed to represent partitions, taxonomic constraints and different kinds of derived types in the UML. In Sections 4 and 5, we present the operations that we propose to evolve partitions and derivability, respectively. For each operation, we give a description and an intuitive explanation of its pre and postconditions. Due to space limitations, we can include the formal specification in the OCL of only one operation. The full details of the profile and operations can be found in [6]. Finally, Section 6 gives the conclusions and points out future work.

2 Partitions

In this section, we review briefly the basic concepts and the terminology that will be used throughout the paper, taken mainly from [14].

2.1 Taxonomic Constraints and Partitions

A taxonomy consists of a set of entity types and their specialization relationships. There are also taxonomies of relationship types, but these will not be studied in this paper. We call taxonomic constraints the set of specialization, disjointness and covering constraints defined in a schema.

A *specialization* constraint between entity types E' (the subtype) and E (the supertype) means that if an entity e is instance of E', then it must be instance of E.

A *disjointness* constraint between entity types E_1 and E_2 means that the populations of E_1 and E_2 are disjoint.

Finally, a *covering* constraint between an entity type E and a set of entity types $\{E_1,...,E_n\}$, means that if e is instance of E, it must be also instance of at least one E_i.

A generalization corresponds to a set of specialization constraints between E_i and E, for $i = 1,..,n$, with a common supertype E. A generalization is *disjoint* if their subtypes are mutually disjoint; otherwise, it is *overlapping*. A generalization is *complete* if the supertype E is covered by the subtypes $E_1,...,E_n$; otherwise it is *incomplete*.

A partition is a conceptual modeling construct that allows us to define in a succinct way a set of taxonomic constraints. A *partition* is a generalization that is both disjoint and complete. A partition of E into $E_1,...,E_n$ is semantically equivalent to:

- A set of n specializations constraints between E_i and E, for $i = 1,..,n$
- A covering constraint of E by $\{E_1,...,E_n\}$
- A set of $n(n-1)/2$ disjointness constraints between E_i and E_j, for $i,j = 1,..,n$, $i > j$.

2.2 Derived Types

The entity types involved in a partition can be base or derived. We will see that this aspect has a strong influence on the satisfaction of taxonomic constraints related to a partition. An entity type E is derived when the population of E can be obtained from

the facts in the information base, using a derivation rule. Derived entity types can be classified depending on the form of their derivation rule. We give a special treatment to the following classes:
- Derived by *specialization*. Entity type E is derived by specialization of entity types $E_1, ..., E_n$, with $n \geq 1$, if the population of E is the subset of the intersection of the populations of $E_1, ..., E_n$, that satisfy some condition. For example, *Young* may be defined as a specialization of *Person*, with the condition "age less than 18 years".
- Derived by *exclusion*. This is a particular case of specialization. Entity type E is derived by exclusion if its population corresponds to the population of an entity type E', excluding those entities that belong also to some entity types $E_1, ..., E_n$, with $n \geq 1$. For instance, *Unmarried* may be defined as specialization of *Person*, excluding *Married*.
- Derived by *union*. Entity type E is derived by union if its population is the union of the populations of several entity types $E_1, ..., E_n$, with $n \geq 1$. For instance, *Person* may be defined as the union of *Man* and *Woman*.

2.3 Satisfaction of Partition Taxonomic Constraints

In general, satisfaction of integrity constraints can be ensured by the schema or by enforcement. A constraint *IC* is satisfied *by the schema* when the schema entails *IC*. That is, the derivation rules and the (other) constraints defined in the schema imply *IC* or, in other words, *IC* is a logical consequence of the schema. In this case no particular action must be taken at runtime to ensure the satisfaction of *IC*.

A constraint *IC* is satisfied *by enforcement* when it is not satisfied by the schema, but it is entailed by the information base. That is, *IC* is a condition true in the information base. In this case, the system has to enforce *IC* by means of checking and corrective actions (database checks, assertions, triggers, or transaction pre/post-conditions), to be executed whenever the information base is updated.

An analysis of the taxonomic constraints satisfied by a schema is presented in [14]. We restructure and summarize the conclusions presented there as follows:

- - A specialization constraint between E_i and E is satisfied by a schema when:
    - E_i is derived by specialization of E.
    - E_i is derived and E is base.
    - E is derived by union of a set of types that includes E_i.
- - A covering constraint between E and $\{E_1,...,E_n\}$ is satisfied by a schema when:
    - E is derived by union of $\{E_1,...,E_n\}$.
    - There is an $E_i \in \{E_1,...,E_n\}$ derived by specialization of E and exclusion of $\{E_1,...,E_n\} - \{E_i\}$.
    - There is a partition P with supertype E and subtypes $\{E_1,...,E_n\}$ and such that all subtypes are derived by specialization of E.
- -A disjointness constraint between E_i and E_j is satisfied by a schema when:
    - There is a partition P with supertype E and subtypes $\{E_1,...,E_n\}$, with $E_i, E_j \in \{E_1,...,E_n\}$ and such that all subtypes are derived by specialization of E.
    - E_i is base and E_j is derived.
    - E_i is derived by specialization of some E and exclusion of a set of entity types that includes E_j.

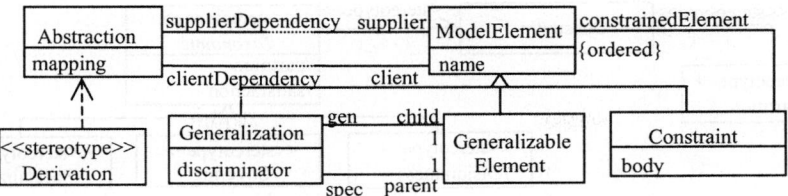

Fig. 1. Fragment of UML metamodel

These relationships allow us to determine which taxonomic constraints are satisfied by the schema and, complementarily, which ones need to be enforced. The distinction is very important when efficiency is a concern, as it is the case in this paper.

For example, if *Person* is derived by union of *Man* and *Woman*, then the specialization constraints between *Man* and *Person*, and between *Woman* and *Person* are satisfied by the schema. Similarly, the covering constraint between *Person* and *{Man, Woman}* is satisfied by the schema. Note that, in this case, the disjointness constraint between *Man* and *Woman* must be enforced.

3 Uml Profile for Partitions

In this section, we justify the need to extend the UML in order to deal with partitions, derived types and their associated concepts. We use the standard extension mechanisms provided by the UML [20], and define a UML Profile for Partitions in Conceptual Modeling. This profile could be integrated into a larger one for conceptual modeling. We explain below the main elements of the profile. The complete details of the stereotypes, constraints and additional operations (and their formalization in the OCL), tag definitions and tagged values of the profile can be found in [6].

3.1 Constraints

In the UML metamodel a *Generalization* is a taxonomic relationship between two *GeneralizableElements*: *child* and *parent* (Fig 1). In this paper we only deal with *GeneralizableElements* that are entity types, which we represent as classes with the standard stereotype <<type>> [15]. Sets of *Generalizations* sharing a given parent can be distinguished using the *Discriminator*.

A *Constraint* is an assertion (defined in the *body*) on a set of *ModelElements* that must be true in the information base (Fig 1). The UML has only a few predefined constraints. Among them, there are *complete* and *disjoint*.

Therefore, in the UML, a partition is represented by a set of *Generalizations* having the same parent and the same discriminator, and two predefined constraints (complete and disjoint) that have, as *constrainedElement*, those generalizations. However, it is convenient to have a single schema object representing a partition, to which we can attach properties and several rules. On the other hand, we need to have subtypes of *Constraint* corresponding to the taxonomic constraints, to which we can attach also properties and rules. To this end, we define in our profile the five stereotypes of *Constraint* shown in Fig 2.

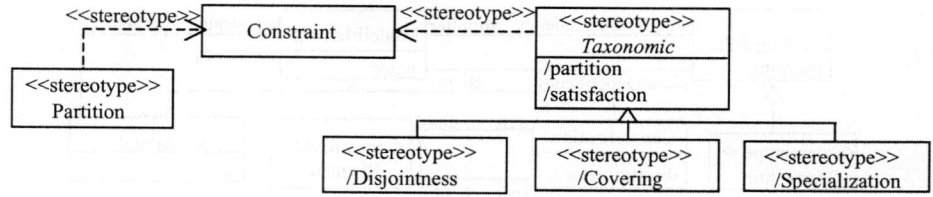

Fig. 2. Stereotypes of Constraint in the profile

The most important stereotype is <<partition>>. A single instance of a constraint with this stereotype will correspond to a partition in the conceptual schema. Graphically, this constraint will appear as shown in the examples of Fig 5.

The *constrainedElements* of a <<partition>> constraint must be a set of *Generalizations*. This is an example of a meta schema integrity constraint, also called "Well-Formedness Rules" in the UML metamodel, or invariants in database schema evolution [3]. The rules are expressed as constraints attached to stereotypes. In this case, we attach the constraint to *Partition*, and define it formally in the OCL:

context Partition **inv**: --The constrained elements are Generalizations
self.constrainedElement -> forAll(g | g.oclIsTypeOf(Generalization))

The other main constraints attached to *Partition* are (we only give their description):
- A partition has one or more generalizations.
- All generalizations belonging to the same partition must have the same parent and discriminator.
- All generalizations with the same parent and discriminator belong to the same partition.
- The generalizableElements of generalizations belonging to a partition are Types.
- A partition cannot have two generalizations with the same child.
- Two partitions with the same parent cannot have a generalization with the same child.

The *body* of a *Partition* will be empty and, therefore, it is not a real constraint. We will translate automatically a partition into the set of taxonomic constraints semantically equivalent to it. These constraints will be instances of the stereotypes <<disjointness>>, <<covering>> and <<specialization>>, shown in Fig 2. Instances of these stereotypes are constraints that must be satisfied in the information base, like any other instance of *Constraint*. The *body* of these constraints will be derived automatically, as shown in Section 3.3.

The constraint stereotype <<taxonomic>> is abstract, and serves only to define two common derived tags: *partition* and *satisfaction*. Unsurprisingly, *partition* gives the partition corresponding to the constraint; its value is defined when the instances are generated. *Satisfaction* can be *BySchema* or *Enforced*; its value is defined by a derivation rule explained in Section 3.3.

We define the stereotypes *Disjointness*, *Covering* and *Specialization* as derived, because their instances can be obtained automatically from the *Partitions* and their *Generalizations*. In the UML metamodel, *ModelElements* have a tag called *derived*. A true value indicates that it can be derived from other *ModelElements*. The details of derivation are given in an *Abstraction* dependency, with the standard stereotype <<derive>>, and name of the stereotype class Derivation [15]. A derivation dependency specifies that the client can be computed from the supplier. A derivation rule is an instance of *Derivation*. The expression of the rule is defined in the attribute *Mapping* (Fig 1). The expression can be defined formally in the OCL.

The expression corresponding to *Covering* would be:

Partition.allInstances -> forAll(p:Partition | Covering.allInstances→one(cov:Covering | cov.partition = p and cov.constrainedElement = Sequence {p}))

The rule defines that for each *Partition p* there must be one (and only one) instance *cov* of *Covering* such that its *partition* tag has the value *p*, and its *constrainedElements* is the sequence consisting in only *p*. The derivation rules for *Disjointness* and *Specialization* are similar.

3.2 Derived Types

We need to distinguish between the three classes of derived entity types defined in Section 2.2, and therefore we define in our profile the three stereotypes of *Abstraction* shown in Fig 3: <<DerivedUnion>>, <<DerivedSpec>> and <<DerivedExcl>>. The first two are subtype of the standard *Derivation* (Fig 1), and the third one subtype of *DerivedSpec*. In the three cases, the client is the derived entity type.

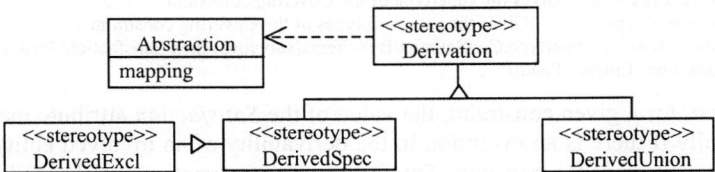

Fig. 3. Stereotypes of Abstraction dependency in the profile

The profile includes several meta schema integrity constraints concerning derived types and partitions. The main constraints attached to *DerivedUnion* are:
- A derived by union dependency must have at least one supplier.
- In a derived by union dependency, the client cannot be one of its direct or indirect suppliers.
- The suppliers of a derived by union dependency cannot be direct or indirect suppliers of themselves.
- The main constraints attached to *DerivedSpec* are:
- A derived by specialization dependency must have at least one supplier.
- In a derived by specialization dependency, the client cannot be one of its direct or indirect suppliers.
- The suppliers of a specialization dependency cannot be direct or indirect suppliers of themselves.
- The main constraint attached to *DerivedExcl* is:
- A derived by exclusion dependency must have at least two suppliers.

3.3 Satisfaction of Constraints

In Section 2.3, we have seen that some constraints are satisfied by the schema. The relationships between the derivability and schema satisfaction, are formalized by three OCL operations on *Type*, that are used in several parts of the profile and in the operations. The names, parameters and (short) description of the operations are:

Type::SpecSatisfiedBySchema (subtype:Type):Boolean
- True if the specialization constraint between subtype and self is satisfied by the schema.

Type::CovSatisfiedBySchema (subs:Set(Type)):Boolean
- True if the covering constraint between self and subs is satisfied by the schema.

Type::DisjSatisfiedBySchema (type:Type):Boolean
- True if the disjointness constraint between self and type is satisfied by the schema.

We have seen (Fig 2), that the instances of *Disjointness*, *Covering* and *Specialization* have a derived tag called *Satisfaction*, with values *BySchema* and *Enforced*. We define a derivation rule for *Satisfaction* in each of the three stereotypes. The rules can be expressed easily using the above operations. As an example, the rule for *Satisfaction* in *Covering* is:

```
context Covering:
  let supertype:Type = .... -- Gives the supertype of the Covering constraint
  let subtypes:Set(Type) = .... -- Gives the set of subtypes of the Covering constraint
  in self.Satisfaction = if supertype.CovSatisfiedBySchema(subtypes) then Satisfaction::BySchema
     else Satisfaction::Enforced endif
```

Note that, for a given constraint, the value of the *Satisfaction* attribute may change automatically if there is an evolution in the derivability of an involved entity type, or in the composition of the partition. This is one of the advantages of derived attributes of schema objects: The operations need not to be concerned with the effect of changes on them. The effects are defined declaratively in a single place of the profile.

We take a similar approach for the definition of the *body*. Fig 2 shows that the instances of *Disjointness*, *Covering* and *Specialization* are *Constraints* and, therefore, have the attribute *body*. The value of this attribute is an OCL expression corresponding to the constraint that must be satisfied by the information base. We define a derivation rule for *body* in each of the three stereotypes. The rules can be defined easily using the above operations.

The generated expression is tailored to each particular constraint, so that its evaluation can be performed efficiently. We distinguish between constraints satisfied by the schema and those to be enforced. The former have an empty *body*, because they need not to be enforced at runtime. The body for the latter is the specific constraint that must be enforced. For example the covering constraint between *Person* and *{Woman, Man}* not satisfied by the schema, would have for the *body* the value:

"Woman.allInstances -> union(Man.allInstances) -> includesAll(Person.allInstances)"

which means that the population of *Person* must be included in the union of populations of *Woman* and *Man*.

4 Evolving Partitions

In this section, we present the operations that we need to evolve partitions. We adopt the classical framework with the reflective architecture [9, 11, 17, 10] shown in Fig 4. In our case, the meta conceptual schema is the UML metamodel and the Profile presented in the previous section. The meta external events are the operations presented in this section and in the following one. The effects of these operations are a changed meta information base (conceptual schema or UML model) and, if required, a changed information base. The framework is very general and it allows an easy adaptation to an implementation environment in which both processors are integrated or tightly coupled, or which both information bases are integrated.

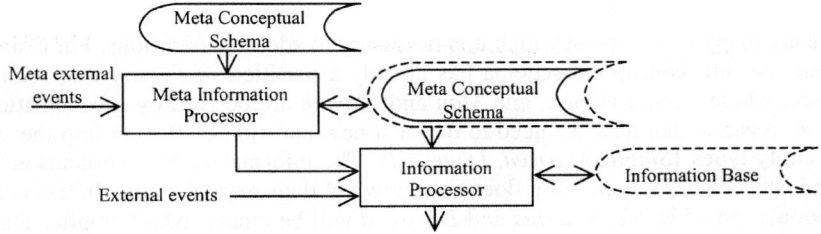

Fig. 4. Framework for the evolution

4.1 Changes to Partitions

The list of evolution operations of partitions is as follows:

1. Creating a partition: allows the designer to define a new partition in the UML schema with one supertype, a set of subtypes and a discriminator.
2. Adding a subtype to a partition: allows the designer to add an empty entity type as a subtype of an existing partition.
3. Removing a subtype from a partition: allows the designer to remove an empty entity type as a subtype of an existing partition.
4. Replacing subtypes: allows the designer to replace a set of subtypes of a given partition by another one.
5. Resizing a partition: allows the designer to add (to remove) a non empty subtype to (from) a partition where the supertype is derived by union of its subtypes.
6. Removing a partition: allows the designer to remove an existing partition.

In the next subsections we describe and justify each of the above operations, and give an intuitive explanation of their pre and postconditions. Preconditions are conditions that must be satisfied when an invocation of the operation occurs. Postconditions define the conditions that are satisfied when the operation finishes. Additionally, and implicitly, the execution of the operations:

- must maintain the meta schema integrity constraints defined in the stereotypes, and
- may induce effects on the schema and/or the information base defined by the derivation rules attached to the stereotypes.

Due to space limitations, we include the formal specification of only one operation.

4.2 Creating Partitions

The operation *AddPartition* allows the designer to define a new partition of existing entity types in a conceptual schema. The parameters are the supertype, a set of one or more subtypes and a discriminator.

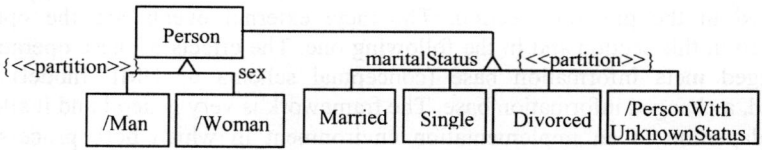

Fig. 5. Two examples of partitions

There are many situations in which it is necessary to add new partitions. For example, assume that our conceptual schema has already a partition of *Person* into *Man* and *Woman*, where *Person* is base, and *Man* and *Woman* are derived by specialization of *Person*. Assume that now we need to define a new partition of *Person* into the set of base entity types {*Single, Married, Divorced*}. The information base contains already some instances of *Person*, but it does not know yet their marital status. Initially, then, the population of *Single*, *Married* and *Divorced* will be empty, which implies that the partition is not possible. We decide then to include a fourth, temporary entity type in the partition, that we call *PersonWithUnknownStatus*, and that we define as derived by specialization of *Person* with the exclusion of *Single, Married* and *Divorced* (Fig. 5). The idea is to have initially all persons automatically instance of *PersonWithUnknownStatus*, and ask the users to enter progressively the marital status. The preconditions must ensure that the taxonomic constraints equivalent to the partition will be satisfied in the information base after the operation is executed. Otherwise, the information base would enter in an inconsistent state. The main preconditions are:

- *SpecAreSatisfied*: The instances of each subtype must be a subset of the instances of the supertype.
- *DisjAreSatisfied*: The instances of the subtypes must be mutually disjoint.
- *CovIsSatisfied*: The instances of the supertype must be covered by the union of the instances of the subtypes.

In fact, it is not necessary to test all the taxonomic constraints, but only those that are not satisfied by the schema.

In the example, we will only need to check that *Single, Married* and *Divorced* are subsets of *Person*, and that they are mutually disjoint. These checks are performed by querying the information base. In our framework (Fig. 4) this means that the meta information processor issues a query to the information processor, which is the only one that can access the information base. In the example, the checks will be very easy because the population of *Single, Married* and *Divorced* is initially empty.

The postconditions guarantee that a new partition will be created, a generalization will be created for each subtype, and the constrained elements of the partition will be the set of generalizations just created. The OCL definition of the operation is:

```
context Partition::AddPartition (discriminator:Name, super:Type, subs:Set(Type))
  pre: subs -> notEmpty() -- There must be at least one subtype
  pre SpecAreSatisfied:
   subs -> forAll(sub:Type | not super.SpecSatisfiedBySchema(sub) implies
   super.allInstances -> includesAll (sub.allInstances))
  pre DisjAreSatisfied: -- Pairs of types in subs must be mutually disjoint. We avoid duplicate checks.
   let subsSeq:Sequence(Type) = subs -> asSequence()
   let numberSubtypes:Integer = subs -> size()
   in Sequence {1..numberSubtypes} ->
   forAll (i, j:Integer | i > j and not subsSeq->at(i).DisjSatisfiedBySchema(subsSeq->at(j))
   implies
   subsSeq -> at(i).allInstances -> excludesAll (subsSeq -> at(j).allInstances))

  pre CovIsSatisfied:
   not super.CovSatisfiedBySchema(subs) implies
   subs -> iterate(sub:Type; acc:Set(Type) = Set{} | acc->union(sub.allInstances))->
   includesAll(super.allInstances)
  post:
  p. oclIsNew() and p.oclIsTypeOf(Partition) -A new partition is created
  and -- Create a generalization for each subtype
  subs -> forAll(sub:Type | ge.oclIsNew() and ge.oclIsTypeOf(Generalization))
  and ge.discriminator = discriminator and ge.child = sub
  and ge.parent = super and p.constrainedElement -> includes(ge))
```

In addition to the effects defined by the postconditions, the execution of the operation induces other effects on the schema, as defined by the Profile derivation rules. In this operation, the induced effects are:

- For each *Generalization* created by the operation, an instance of *Specialization* is created as well.
- For each pair of subtypes of the new partition, an instance of *Disjointness* is created as well.
- A new instance of *Covering* is created.
- In the three cases, the new instances are associated to the *ModelElements* that they constrain and to the partition that originates them. The attribute *body* has as value an OCL expression corresponding to the constraint that must be satisfied by the information base, and the tag *satisfaction* has as value *BySchema* or *Enforced*, depending on whether the constraint is already satisfied by the schema, or needs to be enforced.

4.3 Adding a Subtype to a Partition

The operation *AddSubtype* allows the designer to add an empty entity type as a subtype of an existing partition. The parameters are the partition and the subtype.

There are many situations in which it is necessary to add a subtype to an existing partition. In the example of the partition of *Person* by *maritalStatus*, shown in Fig 5, we may be interested now in other marital status such as, for instance, *Widower*. We define then a new entity type and add it to the partition.

The main precondition of the operation is that the new subtype has no instances and, therefore, the new taxonomic constraints equivalent to the changed partition will be necessarily satisfied in the information base after the operation has been executed. The postconditions guarantee that a new generalization will be created, and that it will be added to the constrained elements of the partition.

4.4 Removing a Subtype from a Partition

The operation *RemoveSubtype* allows the designer to remove an empty entity type as a subtype of an existing partition. The parameters are the partition and the subtype.

This operation is the inverse of the previous one. In the example of the partition of *Person* by *maritalStatus*, shown in Fig 5, we may already know the marital status of each person and, therefore, *PersonWithUnknownStatus* is automatically empty. We can then remove it from the partition.

The main precondition of the operation is that the subtype to be removed has no instances and, therefore, the new taxonomic constraints equivalent to the changed partition will be necessarily satisfied in the information base after the operation has been executed. The postconditions guarantee that the corresponding generalization will be deleted, and that it will be removed from the constrained elements of the partition.

4.5 Replacing Subtypes

The operation *ReplaceSubtypes* allows the designer to replace a set of subtypes of a given partition by another one. The parameters are the partition, the old set, and the new set. There are several situations in which the designer may need to evolve a partition using this operation. We explain one of them in our example. Assume that we have in the schema the partition of *Person* by *maritalStatus*, but now we need to group the subtypes *Single*, *Divorced* and *Widower* into a new entity type *Unmarried*, and want also to change the original partition to one with only two subtypes: *Married* and *Unmarried* (see Fig 6).

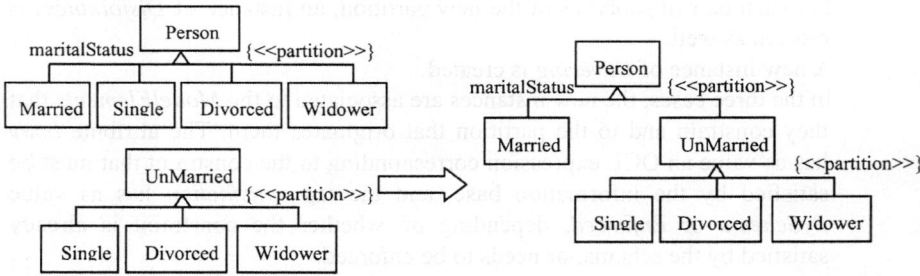

Fig. 6. Example of the Replacing operation: In the partition of *Person* by *maritalStatus*, the set {*Single, Divorced, Widower*} is replaced by {*UnMarried*}

This operation must satisfy two main preconditions in order to ensure that, after the operation has been executed, the taxonomic constraints equivalent to the partition remain satisfied:

- The instances of the set of new subtypes must be mutually disjoint.
- The union of the populations of the set of old subtypes must be the same as the union of the new subtypes. This condition preserves the covering constraint, as well as the disjointness with the unaffected subtypes.

When the old set and the new set are the super and the subtypes of an existing partition preconditions need not to be checked, because they are already guaranteed.

The postconditions guarantee that the old generalizations are removed, the new ones created, and the constrained elements of the partition have the new value.

4.6 Resizing a Partition

The operations of *Adding*, *Removing* and *Replacing* subtypes allow us to restructure a partition provided that the population of the supertype remains unchanged. However, there are cases in which we need to restructure a partition with the effect of increasing or decreasing the population of the supertype.

Assume, for example, a library that loans books and journals. The library has also audio CD, but they cannot be loaned. The corresponding conceptual schema (Fig 7) includes the base entity types *Book*, *Journal*, *AudioCD* and *ItemOnLoan*. Entity type *Book* is partitioned into *LoanableBook* and *NonLoanableBook*, both of which are derived. Entity type *LoanableItem* is defined as the union of *LoanableBook* and *Journal*. There is also a partition of *LoanableItem* into *ItemOnLoan* and *AvailableItem*. This latter is defined as derived by specialization of LoanableItem with the exclusion of *ItemOnLoan*.

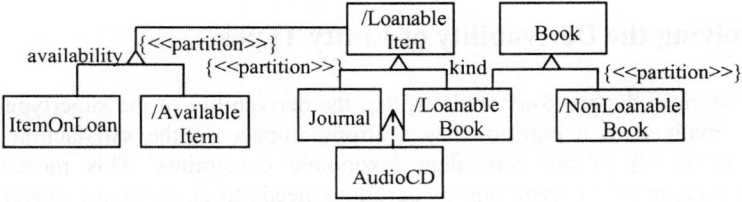

Fig. 7. Example of Resizing partition

Now, the policy of the library changes, and it allows loans of *AudioCD*. Therefore, we have to evolve the existing partition, but this cannot be done with the *Adding* operation, because the population of *AudioCD* is not empty. The operation *Resize* allows us to do that in a controlled manner.

The operation *Resize* can be applied only to partitions whose supertype is derived by union of its subtypes. The operation allows the designer to add or to remove a subtype, and to change simultaneously the derivation rule of the supertype. The overall effect is that the population of the supertype has been expanded or contracted. The operation has two parameters: the partition and the non-empty subtype to be added to or removed from it.

The are two non-trivial preconditions for this operation. The first is that if the partition is being expanded, the new subtype must be disjoint with the population of the existing supertype. The specialization and covering constraints are already guaranteed by the derivation rule (union) of the supertype. In the example, this means checking that *AudioCD* is disjoint with the existing population of *LoanableItem*.

The execution of the operation changes (adds or reduces) the population of the supertype. In general, such change could affect other constraints, which can be or not taxonomic. We, therefore, only allow resizing a partition if the resulting change cannot affect any other constraint. We check this in the second precondition. In the example, this could happen, for instance, if *LoanableItem* is a subtype in another partition (the disjointness or the specialization constraints could be violated) or if it is a supertype of other partitions (the covering constraint could be violated). Fig 7 shows that *LoanableItem* is the supertype of another partition into *ItemOnLoan* and *AvailableItem*, but no constraint is affected in this case because *AvailableItem* is derived by exclusion. The existing audios CD become initially, and automatically, available items.

The postconditions ensure that a generalization has been created (deleted), the constrained elements of the partitions have the new value, and that the derivation rule of the supertype has been changed.

4.7 Removing a Partition

The operation *Remove* allows the designer to remove an existing partition. The parameter is the partition. The operation has no preconditions. The postconditions ensure that the generalizations corresponding to a partition are deleted, as well as the partition itself.

5 Evolving the Derivability of Entity Types

We have seen, in the previous sections, that the derivability of the supertype and the subtypes involved in a partition has a strong impact on the satisfaction (by the schema, enforced) of the equivalent taxonomic constraints. This means that a complete account of the evolution of partitions needs to consider the operations for the evolution of derivability. In this respect, we define two operations: one that changes the derivability to base, and one that changes it to derived.

5.1 Changing Derivability to Base

The operation *ChangeDerivabilityToBase* allows the designer to change the derivability of a derived entity type to base. The only parameter of the operation is the entity type.

The only precondition of this operation is that the entity type must not be base. The main problem with this operation lies in its postconditions; more precisely, in what happens to the population of the changed entity type. Several strategies are possible in this respect. One strategy that seems appropriate in the context of partitions is to assume that the population will not change.

The implementation of this postcondition in our framework (Fig 4) requires that the meta information processor issues an event to the information processor, with the intended effect of materializing the population existing at the moment the operation is executed.

5.2 Changing Derivability to Derived

The operation *ChangeDerivabilityToDerived* allows the designer to define a base entity type as derived, or to change the derivation rule of a derived entity type. We are in the context of partitions, and we need to ensure that initially the population remains unchanged. To check this with our preconditions, we require two entity types: the one that has to be changed, E, and another one, E', that we call the model, with the derivation rule that we want to assign to E. The parameters of the operation are the affected entity type (E) and the model (E').

The preconditions must ensure that the population of both entity types are initially the same. The postconditions guarantee that the affected entity type will have the desired derivation rule (that is, the one that the model has).

6 Conclusions

The evolution of information systems from their conceptual schemas is one of the important research areas in information systems engineering. In this paper, we aim at contributing to the area by focusing on a particular conceptual modeling construct, the partitions. We have determined the possible evolutions of partitions in a conceptual schema, and we have defined, for each of them, the preconditions that must be satisfied, and the resulting postconditions. We take into account the state of, and the impact on, both the conceptual schema and the information base.

We have dealt with conceptual schemas in the UML. The choice of the language has been based on its industrial diffusion and the current (and future) availability of CASE tools. However, our results could be adapted easily to other conceptual modeling languages.

We have needed to extend the UML to deal with partitions and their evolution. We have done so using the standard extension mechanisms provided by the language itself. We have adhered strictly to the standard, and we have defined a UML Profile for Partitions in Conceptual Modeling. The profile allows us to define partitions in conceptual schemas, the taxonomic constraints equivalent to them, and the way how they can be satisfied. We hope that the approach we have taken to define particular classes of constraints, and the automatic derivation of schema objects and their attributes may be useful in future developments of UML Profiles.

We have dealt with partitions in conceptual models that include derived types (with different kinds of derivability), multiple specialization and multiple classification. We have taken into account all these elements in our evolution operations. However, the operations could be adapted (and, hopefully, be useful) to more restrictive contexts, such as those of object-oriented database schemas.

The work reported here can be continued in several directions. We mention three of them here. The first could be to define operations to evolve taxonomies in general. In this paper, we have focused on partitions only, due to their special characteristics that have not been studied before. The inclusion of other well known operations related to taxonomies (add/remove an entity type, add/remove a generalization, etc.) should not be difficult. Compound operations could be defined also. The second continuation could be to extend the profile with other known conceptual modeling constructs, with the aim of developing a complete UML Profile for Conceptual Modeling. The corresponding evolution operations could be defined as well, in the line of the ones described here. The third continuation could be to take into account the temporal aspects of conceptual schemas [10], and to develop a UML Profile for Temporal Conceptual Modeling.

Acknowledgments

We would like to thank Juan Ramon López, Dolors Costal, Maria Ribera Sancho and Ernest Teniente for his useful comments. This work has been partly supported by CICYT program project TIC99-1048-C02-1.

References

1. Al-Jadir, L.; Léonard, M. "Multiobjects to Ease Schema Evolution in an OODBMS", Proc. ER'98, Singapore, LNCS 1507, Springer, pp. 316-333.
2. Andrade, L.F.; Fiadeiro, J.L. "Coordination Technologies for Managing Information System Evolution", CAiSE 2001, LNCS 2068, pp. 374-387.
3. Banerjee, J.; Chou, H-T.; Garza, J.F.; Kim, W.; Woelk, D.; Ballou, N. "Data Model Issues for Object-Oriented Applications". ACM TOIS Vol. 5, No. 1, January, pp. 3-26.
4. de Champeaux, D.; Lea, D.; Faure, P. "Object-Oriented System Development", Addison-Wesley Pub. Co.
5. Franconi, E.; Grandi, F.; Mandreoli, F. "Schema Evolution and Versioning: A Logical and Computational Characterisation", In Balsters, H.; de Brock, B.; Conrad, S. (eds.) "Database Schema Evolution and Meta-Modeling", LNCS 2065, pp. 85-99.
6. Gómez, C., Olivé A; "Evolving Partitions in Conceptual Schemas in the UML (Extended Version)",Technical Report UPC, LSI-02-15-R.
7. Goralwalla, I.; Szafron, D.; Özsu, T.; Peters, R. "A Temporal Approach to Managing Schema Evolution in Object Database Systems". Data&Knowledge Eng. 28(1), October, pp. 73-105.
8. Hainaut, J-L.; Englebert, V.; Henrard, J.; Hick, J-M.; Roland, D. "Database Evolution: the DB-MAIN Approach". 13th. Intl. Conf. on the Entity-Relationship Approach - ER'94, LNCS 881, Springer-Verlag, pp. 112-131.
9. ISO/TC97/SC5/WG3. "Concepts and Terminology for the Conceptual Schema and Information Base", J.J. van Griethuysen (ed.), March.
10. López, J-R.; Olivé, A. "A Framework for the Evolution of Temporal Conceptual Schemas of Information Systems", CAiSE 2000, LNCS 1789, pp. 369-386.
11. Manthey, R. "Beyond Data Dictionaries: Towards a Reflective Architecture of Intelligent Database Systems", DOOD'93, Springer-Verlag, pp. 328-339.
12. Mens, T.; D'Hondt, T. "Automating Support for Software Evolution in UML", Automated Software Engineering, 7, pp. 39-59.
13. Olivé, A.; Costal, D.; Sancho, M-R. "Entity Evolution in ISA Hierarchies", ER'99, LNCS 1728, pp. 62-80.
14. Olivé, A. "Taxonomies and Derivation Rules in Conceptual Modelling", CAiSE 2001, LNCS 2068, pp. 417-432.
15. OMG. "Unified Modeling Language Specification", Version 1.4, September 2001.
16. Opdyke, W.F. "Refactoring object-oriented frameworks", PhD thesis, University of Illinois.

17. Peters, R.J.; Özsu, T. "Reflection in a Uniform Behavioral Object Model". Proc. ER'93, Arlington, LNCS 823, Springer-Verlag, pp. 34-45.
18. Peters, R.J., Özsu, M.T. "An Axiomatic Model of Dynamic Schema Evolution in Objectbase Systems", ACM TODS, 22(1), pp. 75-114.
19. Roddick, J.F. "A Survey of Schema Versioning Issues for Database Systems", Inf. Softw. Technol, 37(7), pp. 383-393.
20. Rumbaugh, J.; Jacobson, I.; Booch, G. "The Unified Modeling Language Reference Manual", Addison-Wesley, 550 p.
21. Smith, J.M.; Smith, D.C.P. "Database Abstractions: Aggregation and Generalization". ACM TODS, 2,2, pp. 105-133.
22. Sunyé, G.; Pennaneac'h, F.; Ho, W-M.; Le Guennec, Al.; Jézéquel, J-M. "Using UML Action Semantics for Executable Modeling and Beyond", CAiSE 2001, LNCS 2068, pp. 433-447.
23. Tokuda, L.; Batory, D. "Evolving Object-Oriented Designs with Refactorings", Automated Software Engineering, 8, pp. 89-120.339
24. Tresch, M.; Scholl, M.H. "Meta Object Management and its Application to Database Evolution", 11th. Intl. Conf. on the Entity-Relationship Approach - ER'92, LNCS 645, Springer-Verlag, pp. 299-321.
25. Wieringa, R.; de Jonge, W.; Spruit, P. "Using Dynamic Classes and Role Classes to Model Object Migration", TPOS, Vol 1(1), pp. 61-83.
26. Zicari, R. "A Framework for Schema Updates in Object-Oriented Database System", in Bancilhon,F.; Delobel,C.; Kanellakis, P. (ed.) "Building an Object-Oriented Database System - The Story of O2", Morgan Kaufmann Pub., pp. 146-182.

Schema Evolution in Heterogeneous Database Architectures, A Schema Transformation Approach

Peter McBrien[1] and Alexandra Poulovassilis[2]

[1] Dept. of Computing, Imperial College,
180 Queen's Gate, London SW7 2BZ, pjm@doc.ic.ac.uk
[2] Dept. of Computer Science, Birkbeck College, University of London,
Malet Street, London WC1E 7HX, ap@dcs.bbk.ac.uk

Abstract. This paper presents a new approach to schema evolution, which combines the activities of schema integration and schema evolution into one framework. In previous work we have developed a general framework to support schema transformation and integration in heterogeneous database architectures. Here we show how this framework also readily supports *evolution of source schemas*, allowing the global schema and the query translation pathways to be easily repaired, as opposed to having to be regenerated, after changes to source schemas.

1 Introduction

Common to many methods for integrating heterogeneous data sources is the requirement for *logical integration* [21, 9] of the data, due to variations in schema design for the same universe of discourse. Logical integration requires facilities for transforming and integrating a set of source schemas into a global schema, and for translating queries posed on the global schema to queries over the source schemas. In previous work [14, 15, 19, 17, 16] we have developed a general framework which provides these facilities. In this paper we consider the problem of evolving the global schema, and repairing the query translation pathways, as source schemas evolve.

Other heterogeneous database systems, such as TSIMMIS [6], InterViso [22], IM [13], and Garlic [20], are what may be termed *query-oriented*. They provide mechanisms by which users define global schema constructs as views over source schema constructs (or vice versa in the case of IM). More recent work on automatic wrapper generation [23, 7, 2, 8] and agent-based mediation [3] is also query-oriented. In contrast, our approach is *schema transformation-oriented*. We provide a flexible framework by which transformations on schemas can be specified. These transformations are then used to automate the translation of queries between global and source schemas. Clio [18] also fits into this category, using the specification of correspondences between constructs as a basis for translating data. However it is limited in the range of transformations it can perform.

Our transformation-oriented approach provides a set of primitive schema transformations each of which makes a 'delta' change to the schema, adding, deleting or renaming just one schema construct. These primitive transformations are incrementally composed into more complex schema transformations. As we will see below, an advantage of our approach over query-oriented approaches is that it allows systematic repair of global schemas as source schemas evolve.

Much of the previous work on schema evolution has presented approaches in terms of just one data model e.g. [1, 4, 5, 11]. In contrast, we represent higher-level data modelling languages in terms of an underlying hypergraph-based data model [17]. Thus, the techniques for handling source schema evolutions that we propose in this paper can be applied to any of the common data modelling languages. In [12] it was argued that a uniform approach to schema evolution and schema integration is both desirable and possible, and this is our view also. The higher-order logic language *SchemaLog* was used to define the relationship between schemas, contrasting with our approach which uses a simple set of schema transformation primitives augmented with a first-order query language. A particular advantage of our approach is that we clearly distinguish between equivalent and non-equivalent constructs in different schemas, and hence are able to distinguish between queries that can and cannot be translated between the two schemas. This ability to specify *capacity-augmentations* is also present in the approach of [4], but that work is specific to object-oriented schemas and not readily transferable to other data models.

The remainder of this paper is as follows. Section 2 reviews the hypergraph data model that underpins our approach. Section 3 shows how global schemas and global query translation can be repaired in the face of source schema evolution, considering in particular the evolution of a source schema into a semantically equivalent, semantically contracted, or semantically expanded schema. Section 4 shows how the same approach can be used to repair global schemas defined using higher-level modelling languages. Section 5 gives our conclusions.

2 Review of Our Framework

A **schema** in the **hypergraph data model** (HDM) is a triple $\langle Nodes, Edges, Constraints \rangle$. *Nodes* and *Edges* define a labelled, directed, nested hypergraph. It is 'nested' in the sense that edges may link any number of both nodes and other edges (necessary in order to support higher-level constructs such as composite attributes and attributes on relations [19]). It is a directed hypergraph because edges link sequences of nodes or edges. A **query** q **over a schema** $S = \langle Nodes, Edges, Constraints \rangle$ is an expression whose variables are members of $Nodes \cup Edges$. *Constraints* is a set of boolean-valued queries over S. Nodes have unique names. Edges and constraints have an optional name associated with them. The nodes and edges of a schema are identified by their **scheme**. For a node this is of the form $\langle\!\langle nodeName \rangle\!\rangle$ and for an edge it is of the form $\langle\!\langle edgeName, scheme_1, scheme_2, \ldots, scheme_n \rangle\!\rangle$.

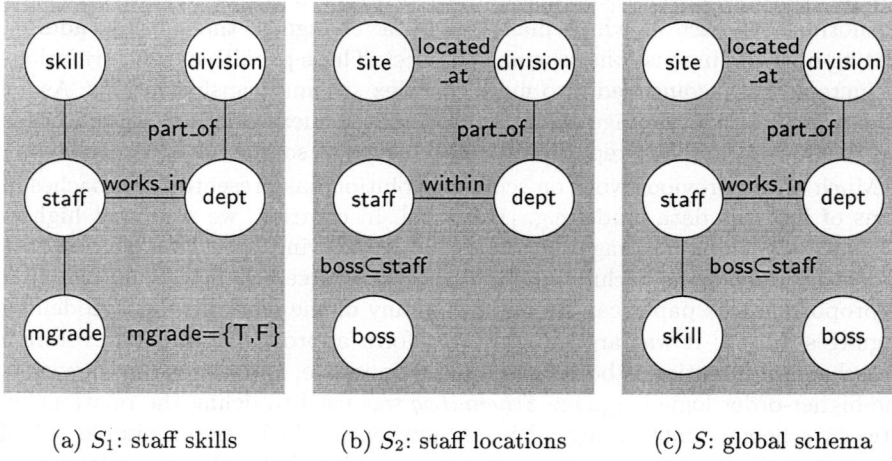

Fig. 1. Two HDM source schemas, and a global schema

Figure 1 illustrates three HDM schemas that we will use as a running example in this paper. Schema S_1 contains information about staff, whether or not they are of manager grade, the skills of each member of staff, and the department in which they work. Each department belongs to a division. The node mgrade is constrained to have a two-valued extent $\{T, F\}$. Instances of $\langle\!\langle \text{staff} \rangle\!\rangle$ who are managers are linked to T by an instance of $\langle\!\langle \_, \text{staff}, \text{mgrade} \rangle\!\rangle$ while other staff are linked to F. (The underscore means the edge has no name).

Schema S_2 is drawn from the same domain, and contains information about staff, their departments, and the division that each department belongs to. However, S_2 differs from S_1 in several ways: the edge between $\langle\!\langle \text{staff} \rangle\!\rangle$ and $\langle\!\langle \text{dept} \rangle\!\rangle$ has a different name in the two schemas, although its 'real-world' semantics are the same; S_2 does not contain information about staff skills; S_2 contains information about the site that each division is located at; S_2 represents the information about managers in a different manner to S_1, using a node $\langle\!\langle \text{boss} \rangle\!\rangle$ to hold instances of staff which are managers, together with a constraint that states that all instances of manager are also instances of staff.

Schema S is an integration of S_1 and S_2, with the edge within of S_2 having been renamed to works_in, and the node boss of S_2 being used to record information about which staff members are managers, rather than the node mgrade of S_1. We will shortly see how S_1 and S_2 are integrated into S using our framework.

The HDM is equipped with a set of **primitive transformations** on schemas. Three primitive transformations are available for adding a node n, edge e, or constraint c to an HDM schema, S: addNode(n, q), addEdge(e, q), and addCons(c). Here, q is a query on S which defines the extent of a new node or edge in terms of the extents of the existing constructs of S (so adding this new construct does not change the information content of the schema). Similarly, the following primitive transformations delete a node, edge or constraint: delNode(n,q), delEdge(e,q), and delCons(c). Here, q is a query on S which defines how the extent of the deleted construct can be reconstructed from the extents of the remaining schema constructs (so deleting this construct does not change the information content of the schema). There are also two primitive transformations for renaming a node or an edge: renNode($\langle\!\langle n\rangle\!\rangle, \langle\!\langle n^{new}\rangle\!\rangle$) and renEdge($\langle\!\langle n, s_1, \ldots, s_m\rangle\!\rangle, \langle\!\langle n^{new}\rangle\!\rangle$) (where $s_1, \ldots, s_m$ are the schemes linked by edge n).

In [16] we defined four more low-level transformations to also allow transformations between semantically overlapping schemas rather than just between semantically equivalent schemas: extendNode(n) is equivalent to addNode($n, void$), where the *void* query component indicates that the new node cannot be derived from the existing schema constructs; extendEdge(e) is similarly equivalent to addEdge($e, void$); contractNode(n) is equivalent to delNode($n, void$), where the *void* query component indicates that the removed node cannot be derived from the remaining schema constructs; and contractEdge(e) is similarly equivalent to delEdge($e, void$).

Example 1 Building the global schema S. Schemas S_1 and S_2 are transformed into S by the two composite transformations listed below.

In step ①, the query $\{x \mid x \in \langle\!\langle \text{staff}\rangle\!\rangle; \langle x, \mathsf{T}\rangle \in \langle\!\langle \_,\text{staff},\text{mgrade}\rangle\!\rangle\}$ states how to populate the extent of the new node $\langle\!\langle \text{boss}\rangle\!\rangle$ from the extents of the existing schema constructs (indicating that $\langle\!\langle \text{boss}\rangle\!\rangle$ adds no new information to the schema). In particular, the extent of $\langle\!\langle \text{boss}\rangle\!\rangle$ is those instances of $\langle\!\langle \text{staff}\rangle\!\rangle$ linked to the value T of $\langle\!\langle \text{mgrade}\rangle\!\rangle$ by an instance of the $\langle\!\langle \_,\text{staff},\text{mgrade}\rangle\!\rangle$ edge.

In ③, the query $\{x, \mathsf{T} \mid x \in \langle\!\langle \text{boss}\rangle\!\rangle\} \cup \{x, \mathsf{F} \mid x \in \langle\!\langle \text{staff}\rangle\!\rangle - \langle\!\langle \text{boss}\rangle\!\rangle\}$ states how the extent of the deleted edge $\langle\!\langle \_,\text{staff},\text{mgrade}\rangle\!\rangle$ can be recovered from the remaining schema constructs (indicating that this edge is a redundant construct). In particular, an instance $\langle x, \mathsf{T}\rangle$ is created for each manager x and an instance $\langle x, \mathsf{F}\rangle$ is created for each staff member x who is not a manager.

In ⑤, the query $\{\mathsf{T}, \mathsf{F}\}$ states how the extent of the deleted node mgrade can be recovered, in this case by a simple enumeration of its two values.

The rest of the steps are straight-forward:

transformation $S_1 \to S$
① *addNode* $\langle\!\langle \text{boss}\rangle\!\rangle$ $\{x \mid \langle x, \mathsf{T}\rangle \in \langle\!\langle \_,\text{staff},\text{mgrade}\rangle\!\rangle\}$
② *addCons* $\langle\!\langle \text{boss}\rangle\!\rangle \subseteq \langle\!\langle \text{staff}\rangle\!\rangle$
③ *delEdge* $\langle\!\langle \_,\text{staff},\text{mgrade}\rangle\!\rangle$ $\{x, \mathsf{T} \mid x \in \langle\!\langle \text{boss}\rangle\!\rangle\} \cup \{x, \mathsf{F} \mid x \in \langle\!\langle \text{staff}\rangle\!\rangle - \langle\!\langle \text{boss}\rangle\!\rangle\}$
④ *delCons* $\langle\!\langle \text{mgrade}\rangle\!\rangle = \{\mathsf{T}, \mathsf{F}\}$
⑤ *delNode* $\langle\!\langle \text{mgrade}\rangle\!\rangle$ $\{\mathsf{T}, \mathsf{F}\}$
⑥ *extendNode* $\langle\!\langle \text{site}\rangle\!\rangle$
⑦ *extendEdge* $\langle\!\langle \text{located\_at},\text{division},\text{site}\rangle\!\rangle$

transformation $S_2 \to S$
⑧ *renEdge* $\langle\!\langle \text{within},\text{staff},\text{dept}\rangle\!\rangle$ works_in
⑨ *extendNode* $\langle\!\langle \text{skill}\rangle\!\rangle$
⑩ *extendEdge* $\langle\!\langle \_,\text{staff},\text{skill}\rangle\!\rangle$

Schema transformations defined on the HDM, or on higher-level modelling languages defined in terms of the HDM, are *automatically reversible* [16]. In particular, every add transformation step is reversible by a del transformation with the same arguments. For example, the reverse transformations from S to S_1 and from S to S_2 are automatically generated from the two transformations given in Example 1 and are as follows, where each step $\bar{t}$ is the reverse of step t in Example 1:

transformation $S \rightarrow S_1$
⑦ *contractEdge* ⟪located_at,division,site⟫
⑥ *contractNode* ⟪site⟫
⑤ *addNode* ⟪mgrade⟫ {T, F}
④ *addCons* ⟪mgrade⟫ = {T, F}
③ *addEdge* ⟪_,staff,mgrade⟫ $\{x, \mathsf{T} \mid x \in \langle\!\langle \mathsf{boss}\rangle\!\rangle\} \cup \{x, \mathsf{F} \mid x \in \langle\!\langle \mathsf{staff}\rangle\!\rangle - \langle\!\langle \mathsf{boss}\rangle\!\rangle\}$
② *delCons* ⟪boss⟫ ⊆ ⟪staff⟫
① *delNode* ⟪boss⟫ $\{x \mid \langle x, \mathsf{T}\rangle \in \langle\!\langle \_,\mathsf{staff},\mathsf{mgrade}\rangle\!\rangle\}$

transformation $S \rightarrow S_2$
⑩ *contractEdge* ⟪_,staff,skill⟫
⑨ *contractNode* ⟪skill⟫
⑧ *renEdge* ⟪works_in,staff,dept⟫ within

In [16] we show how this reversibility of schema transformations allows automatic query translation between schemas. In particular, if a schema S is transformed to a schema S' by a single primitive transformation step, the only cases that need to be considered in order to translate a query Q posed on S to a query Q' posed on S' are ren transformations, in which case the renaming needs to be applied in reverse, and del transformations, in which case occurrences in Q of the deleted construct need to be substituted by the query q specified in the transformation. For sequences of primitive transformations, these substitutions are successively applied in order to obtain the final translated query Q'.

This translation scheme can be applied to each of the constructs of a global schema in order to obtain the possible derivations of each construct from the set of source schemas. These derivations can then be substituted into any query over the global schema in order to obtain an equivalent query over the source schemas [10]. To illustrate, consider the following query on schema S, which finds the skills of staff members working within divisions based at the London site:
$\{sk \mid \langle s, sk\rangle \in \langle\!\langle \_,\mathsf{staff},\mathsf{skill}\rangle\!\rangle;\ \langle s, dep\rangle \in \langle\!\langle \mathsf{works\_in},\mathsf{staff},\mathsf{dept}\rangle\!\rangle;$
   $\langle dep, div\rangle \in \langle\!\langle \mathsf{part\_of},\mathsf{dept},\mathsf{division}\rangle\!\rangle;$
   $\langle div, \text{'London'}\rangle \in \langle\!\langle \mathsf{located\_at},\mathsf{division},\mathsf{site}\rangle\!\rangle\}$
Applying our translation scheme to this query, gives the following query over the constructs of S_1 and S_2, where we distinguish the constructs of these schemas by the suffixing them by 1 or 2, respectively:
$\{sk \mid \langle s, sk\rangle \in \langle\!\langle \_,\mathsf{staff},\mathsf{skill}\rangle\!\rangle_1 \cup void;$
   $\langle s, dep\rangle \in \langle\!\langle \mathsf{works\_in},\mathsf{staff},\mathsf{dept}\rangle\!\rangle_1 \cup \langle\!\langle \mathsf{within},\mathsf{staff},\mathsf{dept}\rangle\!\rangle_2;$
   $\langle dep, div\rangle \in \langle\!\langle \mathsf{part\_of},\mathsf{dept},\mathsf{division}\rangle\!\rangle_1 \cup \langle\!\langle \mathsf{part\_of},\mathsf{dept},\mathsf{division}\rangle\!\rangle_2;$
   $\langle div, \text{'London'}\rangle \in void \cup \langle\!\langle \mathsf{located\_at},\mathsf{division},\mathsf{site}\rangle\!\rangle_2\}$

The first line of the query indicates that $\langle s, sk \rangle$ may only be retrieved from the $\langle\!\langle \_, \text{staff}, \text{skill}\rangle\!\rangle$ edge in S_1, the second line indicates that $\langle s, dep \rangle$ may be retrieved from either $\langle\!\langle \text{works\_in}, \text{staff}, \text{dept}\rangle\!\rangle$ in S_1 or from $\langle\!\langle \text{within}, \text{staff}, \text{dept}\rangle\!\rangle$ in S_2, the third line that $\langle dep, div \rangle$ may be retrieved from $\langle\!\langle \text{part\_of}, \text{dept}, \text{division}\rangle\!\rangle$ in S_1 or S_2, and the last line that $\langle div, \text{'London'} \rangle$ may be retrieved from $\langle\!\langle \text{located\_at}, \text{division}, \text{site}\rangle\!\rangle$ in S_2. Standard optimisation techniques can now be applied to this translated query, in order to generate a reasonable query plan for execution.

3 Handling Evolution of Source Schemas

We turn now to the main theme of this paper, namely how global schemas can be repaired (as opposed to regenerated) in order to reflect changes in source schemas, and how query translation operates over the repaired global schema. Although our examples assume HDM schemas and queries/constraints expressed in a comprehension language, the treatment is fully general and applies to higher-level schema constructs and other query formalisms. We discuss this issue further in Section 4, by illustrating the approach applied to UML models.

Let us suppose then that there are n source schemas $S_1, ..., S_n$ which have been transformed and integrated into a global schema S. There are thus available n transformations $T_1 : S_1 \to S, ..., T_n : S_n \to S$. From these, the reverse transformations $\overline{T_1} : S \to S_1, ..., \overline{T_n} : S \to S_n$ are automatically generated and can be used to translate queries posed on S to queries on $S_1, ..., S_n$.

The source schema evolution problem that we consider is illustrated in Figure 2 and is as follows: if some source schema S_i evolves, to S'_i say, how should S be repaired to reflect this change and how should queries on the repaired S now be translated in order to operate on S'_i rather than on S_i?

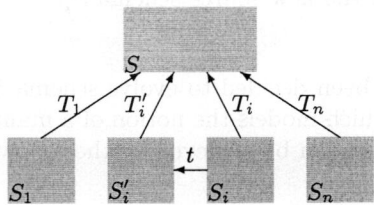

Fig. 2. Evolution of a source schema S_i

The first step is to specify the change from S_i to S'_i by a transformation. The second step is to analyse this transformation. Without loss of generality, we need only consider changes on S_i that consist of a *single* primitive transformation step t being applied to give S'_i, since changes that are composite transformations can be handled as a sequence of primitive transformations. A new transformation pathway T'_i from S'_i to S can be automatically generated as $T'_i = \bar{t}; T_i$ (and so

$\overline{T_i'}$ from S to S_i' is $\overline{T_i'} = \overline{T_i}; t$). How we now handle T_i' depends on what type of transformation t was:

1. If t was an add, delete or rename transformation, then the new schema S_i' will be equivalent S_i. In this case, all information in the global schema S that was derivable from S_i may now be derived from S_i', and no changes are required to S. Section 3.1 illustrates such an equivalence preserving transformation for our example. The only issue is that T_i' might be simplifiable, which we consider in Section 3.2.
2. If t was a contract transformation, then there will be some information which used to be present in S_i that will no longer be available from S_i'. In Section 3.3 we discuss the circumstances in which this will require S to also be contracted.
3. If t was an expand transformation, then the relationship of the new construct with what is already present in S needs to be investigated, and we discuss this in Section 3.4.

A final point to note is that this treatment also covers the case where a new schema S_{n+1} is added to the set of source schemas from which S is derived, in that the original schema S_{n+1} can be regarded as an empty schema which is successively expanded with new constructs. Similarly, our treatment covers the removal of a source schema S_i, since its constructs can be successively contracted to leave an empty schema.

3.1 Equivalence-preserving transformations

Suppose that t is an equivalence-preserving transformation, so that S_i' is equivalent to S_i. Then T_i' and $\overline{T_i'}$ as defined above provide a new automatic translation pathway between S and the new source schema S_i'.

Example 2

Suppose that it has been decided to evolve schema S_1 in Figure 1 to a new equivalent schema S_1^a which models the notion of a manager in the same way as S_2 (see Figure 3(a)). This can be achieved by the following composite transformation:

transformation $S_1 \to S_1^a$
⑪ addNode ⟨⟨boss⟩⟩ $\{x \mid \langle x, \mathsf{T}\rangle \in \langle\langle \_, \mathsf{staff}, \mathsf{mgrade}\rangle\rangle\}$
⑫ addCons ⟨⟨boss⟩⟩ $\subseteq$ ⟨⟨staff⟩⟩
⑬ delEdge ⟨⟨_,staff,mgrade⟩⟩ $\{x, \mathsf{T} \mid x \in \langle\langle \mathsf{boss}\rangle\rangle\} \cup \{x, \mathsf{F} \mid x \in \langle\langle \mathsf{staff}\rangle\rangle - \langle\langle \mathsf{boss}\rangle\rangle\}$
⑭ delCons ⟨⟨mgrade⟩⟩= $\{\mathsf{T}, \mathsf{F}\}$
⑮ delNode ⟨⟨mgrade⟩⟩ $\{\mathsf{T}, \mathsf{F}\}$

The reverse transformation, ⑮, ⑭, ⑬, ⑫, ⑪, from S_1^a to S_1 is automatically generated. This is prefixed to the transformation $S_1 \to S$ of Example 1 to give the new transformation from S_1^a to S:

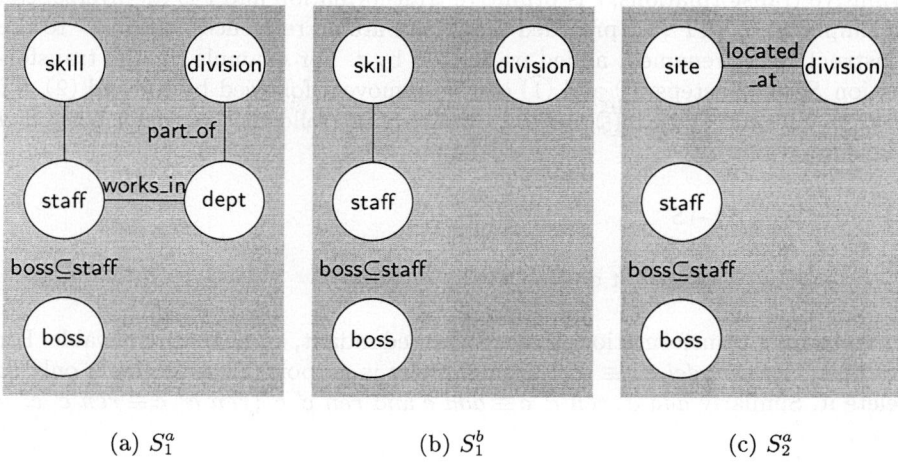

Fig. 3. Evolution of source schemas

transformation $S_1^a \to S$
⑮ *addNode* ⟨⟨mgrade⟩⟩ {T, F}
⑭ *addCons* ⟨⟨mgrade⟩⟩ = {T, F}
⑬ *addEdge* ⟨⟨_,staff,mgrade⟩⟩ {x, T | $x \in$ ⟨⟨boss⟩⟩} ∪ {x, F | $x \in$ ⟨⟨staff⟩⟩ − ⟨⟨boss⟩⟩}
⑫ *delCons* ⟨⟨boss⟩⟩ ⊆ ⟨⟨staff⟩⟩
⑪ *delNode* ⟨⟨boss⟩⟩ {x | ⟨x, T⟩ ∈ ⟨⟨_,staff,mgrade⟩⟩}
① *addNode* ⟨⟨boss⟩⟩ {x | ⟨x, T⟩ ∈ ⟨⟨_,staff,mgrade⟩⟩}
② *addCons* ⟨⟨boss⟩⟩ ⊆ ⟨⟨staff⟩⟩
③ *delEdge* ⟨⟨_,staff,mgrade⟩⟩ {x, T | $x \in$ ⟨⟨boss⟩⟩} ∪ {x, F | $x \in$ ⟨⟨staff⟩⟩ − ⟨⟨boss⟩⟩}
④ *delCons* ⟨⟨mgrade⟩⟩ = {T, F}
⑤ *delNode* ⟨⟨mgrade⟩⟩ {T, F}
⑥ *extendNode* ⟨⟨site⟩⟩
⑦ *extendEdge* ⟨⟨located_at,division,site⟩⟩

Conversely, the new transformation from S to S_1^a is automatically obtained by appending steps ⑪–⑮ to the transformation $S \to S_1$ of Example 1. This new transformation can now be used to automatically translate queries posed on S to queries on S_1^a rather than on S_1.

3.2 Removing redundant transformation steps

In composite transformations such as those above there may be pairs of primitive transformation steps which are inverses of each other and which can be removed without altering the overall effect of the transformation. In particular, a composite transformation $T; t; T'; \bar{t}; T''$, where T, T', T'' are arbitrary sequences of primitive transformations, t is primitive transformation and $\bar{t}$ is its inverse, can be simplified to $T; T'; T''$ provided that there are no references within T' to the construct being renamed, added or deleted by t. For example, in the transformation $S_1^a \to S$, steps ⑪ and ① can be removed, followed by ⑫ and ②, ⑬ and ③, ⑭ and ④, and ⑮ and ⑤, obtaining the following expected simplified transformation:

transformation $S_1^a \to S$
⑥ extendNode ⟪site⟫
⑦ extendEdge ⟪located_at,division,site⟫

Renaming transformations may also be redundant, and hence removable. For example, $ren\ c\ c'; del\ c' \equiv del\ c$, since there is no point in renaming c only to delete it. Similarly $add\ c'; ren\ c'\ c \equiv add\ c$ and $ren\ c'\ c''; ren\ c''\ c \equiv ren\ c'\ c$.

3.3 Contraction transformations

Suppose S_i is transformed to S_i' by a primitive transformation t of the form *contract c*. The new transformation pathway from S to S_i' is $\overline{T_i}$; *contract c*. Any sub-queries over S that translate to the construct c of S_i will now correctly be replaced by the value *void* over S_i'.

However, after a series of contractions on source schemas, the global schema S may eventually contain constructs that are no longer supported by *any* source schema. How can S be repaired so that it no longer contains such unsupported constructs? One way is by *dynamic repair* during query processing: if a sub-query posed on a construct of S returns *void* for all possible local sub-queries, then that construct can be removed from S. Note that if this construct participates in any edges in S, then these must be removed first (if the construct has already been removed from all the source schemas, then so must any edges that it participated in there, and so such edges will also be redundant in S).

Another way to repair S if it contains constructs that are no longer supported by any source schema is by *static repair*. With this approach, we can first use T_i to trace how the removed construct c of S_i is represented in S — call this global representation $global(c)$. The transformations $\overline{T_j}\ j \neq i$ can be used to trace how $global(c)$ is represented in all the other source schemas S_j, $j \neq i$. If all of these source constructs have *void* extents, then $global(c)$ can be removed from S (again taking care to precede the removal of a construct by removal of any edges that it participates in).

Example 3 illustrates how the removal of a construct from one source schema may or may not still allow the construct to be derived from another source schema.

Example 3 Contractions of source schemas.
Suppose the owner of schema S_1^a has decided not to export information about departments. Schema S_1^b illustrated in Figure 3(b) is derived from S_1^a as follows:

transformation $S_1^a \rightarrow S_1^b$
⑯ contractEdge ⟨⟨within,staff,dept⟩⟩
⑰ contractEdge ⟨⟨part_of,dept,division⟩⟩
⑱ contractNode ⟨⟨dept⟩⟩

Adopting a static repair approach to repairing S involves checking the transformation paths of the contracted constructs dept, works_in and part_of from S to S_1^b and S_2, and would discover that all of them still map to a non-*void* extent in S_2. Thus, S would not be changed. With a dynamic repair approach, it would be found that queries on S over dept, works_in or part_of can still be posed on S_2 and so S would again not be changed.

Suppose now that S_2 is also transformed in a similar manner, resulting in S_2^a illustrated in Figure 3(c):

transformation $S_2 \rightarrow S_2^a$
⑲ contractEdge ⟨⟨within,staff,dept⟩⟩
⑳ contractEdge ⟨⟨part_of,dept,division⟩⟩
㉑ contractNode ⟨⟨dept⟩⟩

At this stage the transformations from S to S_1^b and S_2^a are as follows:

transformation $S \rightarrow S_1^b$
⑦ contractEdge ⟨⟨located_at,division,site⟩⟩
⑥ contractNode ⟨⟨site⟩⟩
⑯ contractEdge ⟨⟨works_in,staff,dept⟩⟩
⑰ contractEdge ⟨⟨part_of,dept,division⟩⟩
⑱ contractNode ⟨⟨dept⟩⟩

transformation $S \rightarrow S_2^a$
⑩ contractEdge ⟨⟨_,staff,skill⟩⟩
⑨ contractNode ⟨⟨skill⟩⟩
⑧ renEdge ⟨⟨works_in,staff,dept⟩⟩ within
⑲ contractEdge ⟨⟨within,staff,dept⟩⟩
⑳ contractEdge ⟨⟨part_of,dept,division⟩⟩
㉑ contractNode ⟨⟨dept⟩⟩

Adopting a static repair approach again means checking the transformation paths of the contracted constructs dept, works_in and part_of from S to S_1^b and S_2^a. In this case all three of them map to a *void* extent in both source schemas. Thus, they are removed from S, obtaining the schema S^a illustrated in Figure 4. The corresponding *contract* steps are also removed, as are any prior renamings of these constructs, from the transformations from S^a to the source schemas S_1^b and S_2^a (in the reverse transformations the corresponding *extend* steps would be removed). With a dynamic repair approach, it would be found that queries over dept, works_in and part_of on S translate to *void* on all source schemas, and the same actions would be taken. With both approaches, the resulting transformation from S^a to S_1^b is ⑦, ⑥ and from S^a to S_2^a is ⑩, ⑨.

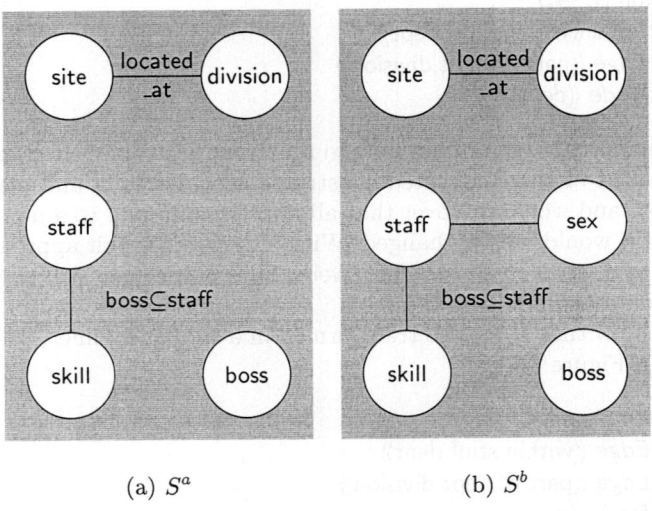

Fig. 4. Global schema following evolution of source schemas

We note that it is not actually *wrong* in our framework for a construct from a global schema to map to a *void* extent in all source schemas — for example, a new source schema may later be added that does support an extent for this construct, and this is likely to be a common situation in mediator architectures. Sub-queries over such constructs would merely translate to *void*.

3.4 Extension transformations

Suppose S_i is transformed to S'_i by a primitive transformation t of the form *extend c*, meaning that a new construct c is now supported by S'_i that is not derivable from S_i. Naively, the new transformation pathway from S to S'_i is $\overline{T_i}$; *extend c*. However, this may be incorrect and there are four alternatives to be considered:

1. c does not appear in S but can be derived from S by some transformation T.
   In this case, S is transformed to a new global schema S' that contains c by appending T to the transformation from each local schema to the original S. The transformation pathway from S' to S'_i then simplifies to just $\overline{T_i}$ i.e. $\overline{T}$ and *extend c* are inverses of each other and can be removed.
2. c does not appear in S, and cannot be derived from S.
   In this case, S is transformed to a new global schema S' that contains c by appending the step *extend c* to the transformation from each local schema to the original S. The reverse transformation from S' to S'_i thus consists of an initial *contract c* step. This matches up with the newly appended *extend c*

step. This pair of steps must be removed in order for the new extent of c in S'_i to be usable by queries posed on S'.
3. c appears in S and has the same semantics as the newly added c in S'_i.
   In this case there must be a transformation step *contract* c in the original transformation from S to S_i. This matches up with the newly appended *extend* c in the transformation from S to S'_i. This pair of steps must be removed in order for the new extent of c in S'_i to be usable by queries posed on S.
4. c appears in S but has different semantics to the newly added c in S'_i.
   In this case there must again be a transformation step *contract* c in the original transformation from S to S_i. Now, the new construct c in S'_i needs to be renamed to some name that does not appear in S, c', say. The resulting transformation from S to S'_i is $\overline{T_i}; extend\ c'; ren\ c'c$, and the situation reverts to case 2 above.

In 1 to 4 above, determining whether the new construct c can or cannot be derived from the existing constructs of S requires domain knowledge (as does specifying the transformation T in 1) e.g. from a human expert or a domain ontology. After this is determined, the repair steps on S and the transformation pathways can be performed automatically.

By analogy to our remark at the end of Section 3.3 (that it is not compulsory to repair the global schema after a series of contractions have left a global schema construct unsupported by any source schema), it is similarly not compulsory to extend the global schema after a new construct is added to a source schema in cases 2 and 4 above. If this is the choice, then the *extend* c step is not appended to the transformations from the source schemas to the global schema, and the final *extend* c step remains in the transformation from S to S'_i.

Example 4 Extensions of source schemas.
Suppose that the owner of S_2^a (Figure 3(c)) has decided to extend it into a new schema S_2^b containing information about staff members' skills and their sex. This can be achieved by the following transformation:

transformation $S_2^a \to S_2^b$
㉒ extendNode ⟨⟨skill⟩⟩
㉓ extendEdge ⟨⟨_,staff,skill⟩⟩
㉔ extendNode ⟨⟨sex⟩⟩
㉕ extendEdge ⟨⟨_,staff,sex⟩⟩

Comparing S_2^b with S^a (Figure 4(a)), it is apparent that the constructs introduced by ㉒ and ㉓ already appear in S^a. For these two constructs a choice must be made between cases 3 and 4 above. Let us suppose that both constructs have the same semantics in S^a and S_2^b, so that case 3 holds. Examining the transformations $S^a \to S_2^a$ and $S_2^a \to S_2^b$, the redundant pair ⑨ and ㉒ can be eliminated, as can the redundant pair ⑩ and ㉓. This results in the following transformation from S^a to S_2^b:

transformation $S^a \rightarrow S_2^b$
㉔ *extendNode* ⟨⟨sex⟩⟩
㉕ *extendEdge* ⟨⟨_,staff,sex⟩⟩

Suppose now that the constructs introduced by ㉔ and ㉕ are entirely new ones, so that case 2 above applies. Then S^a is extended to S^b using these same two extend steps. The two redundant contract/extend pairs are then removed from the transformation $S^b \rightarrow S_2^b$, giving the expected identity transformation from S_2^b and S^b.

4 Handling Higher-Level Modelling Languages

In [17] we showed how higher-level modelling languages L can be expressed using the HDM, representing each construct c in L as a set of constructs $c_1, \ldots, c_n$ in the HDM. We then showed how *add*, *del* and *ren* primitive transformations on c can be automatically derived as sequences of primitive HDM transformations on $c_1, \ldots, c_n$. In particular, we showed how primitive transformations for UML schemas such as *addClass, delClass, addAttribute, delAttribute, addAssociation, delAssociation, addGeneralisation, delGeneralisation,* are defined in terms of the set of primitive transformations on HDM schemas presented in Section 2. Thus, the schema evolution methodology presented in Section 3 transfers directly to this higher semantic level.

To illustrate this, Figure 5(a) shows a UML class diagram U_1 which is semantically equivalent to the HDM schema S_1 of Figure 1(a). The nodes ⟨⟨staff⟩⟩, ⟨⟨dept⟩⟩ and ⟨⟨division⟩⟩ are represented as classes, and ⟨⟨mgrade⟩⟩ and ⟨⟨skill⟩⟩ as attributes of **staff**. The ⟨⟨works_in,staff,dept⟩⟩ and ⟨⟨part_of,dept,division⟩⟩ edges are represented as associations. Figure 5(d) shows a UML class diagram U which is semantically equivalent to the HDM schema S of Figure 1(c). The node ⟨⟨boss⟩⟩ from S is represented as a class in U, and the constraint **boss** ⊆ **staff** is represented by the generalisation hierarchy between **staff** and **boss**. Transforming U_1 to U may be achieved by the following steps:

transformation $U_1 \rightarrow U$
①' *addClass* boss $\{x \mid x \in$ staff$; \langle x, \mathsf{T}\rangle \in$ staff.mgrade$\}$
②' *addGeneralisation* (staff,boss)
③' *delAttribute* staff.mgrade $\{x, \mathsf{T} \mid x \in$ boss$\} \cup \{x, \mathsf{F} \mid x \in$ staff$; x \notin$ boss$\}$
④' *extendAttribute* division.site

Note that each of the steps in $U_1 \rightarrow U$ equates with one or more of the steps in $S_1 \rightarrow S$. In particular, ①' adding UML class **boss** is equivalent to ①, ②' adding the UML generalisation is equivalent to ②, ③' deleting a UML attribute is equivalent to ③ and ④, and ④' extending the UML schema with an attribute is equivalent to ⑥ and ⑦.

Figure 5(b) shows a schema U_1^a which is semantically equivalent to S_1^a. The following is an equivalence-preserving transformation from U_1 to U_1^a (again, the steps in this transformation can be equated with those in $S_1 \rightarrow S_1^a$):

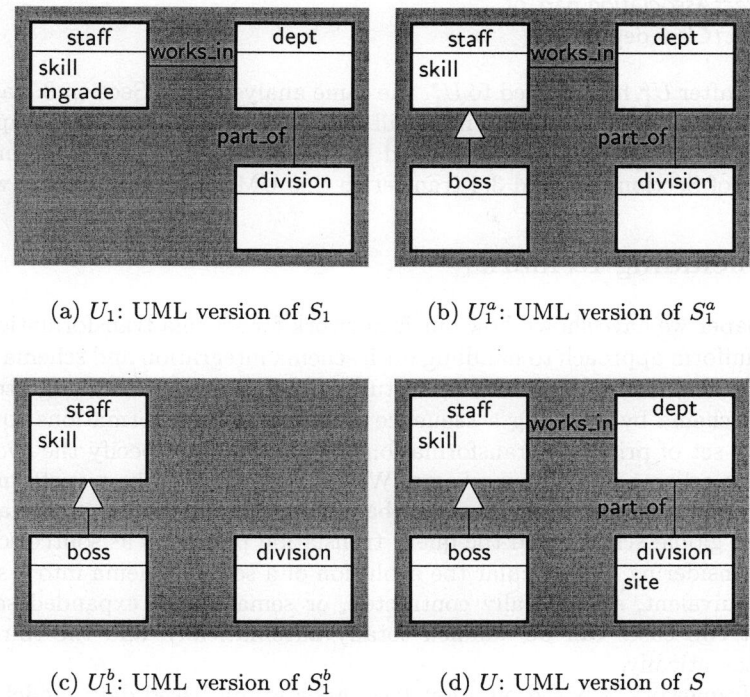

Fig. 5. Transformations on UML class diagrams

transformation $U_1 \rightarrow U_1^a$
Ⓤ5 *addClass* boss $\{x \mid x \in \text{staff}; \langle x, \mathsf{T} \rangle \in \text{staff.mgrade}\}$
Ⓤ6 *addGeneralisation* (staff,boss)
Ⓤ7 *delAttribute* staff.mgrade $\{x, \mathsf{T} \mid x \in \text{boss}\} \cup \{x, \mathsf{F} \mid x \in \text{staff}; x \notin \text{boss}\}$

Since all UML schema transformations are equivalent to some HDM schema transformation, our analysis from Section 3 can be applied to the evolution of source schemas expressed in UML. For example, since $U_1 \rightarrow U_1^a$ is an equivalence-preserving transformation, then the steps of $U_1 \rightarrow U_1^a$ allow any query on U that used to execute on U_1 to instead execute on U_1^a using the transformation pathway $U \rightarrow U_1; U_1 \rightarrow U_1^a =$ Ⓤ4, Ⓤ3, Ⓤ2, Ⓤ1, Ⓤ5, Ⓤ6, Ⓤ7. Applying the removal of redundant pairs of transformations in Section 3.2 to the higher level of UML simplifies $U \rightarrow U_1^a$ to just Ⓤ4.

Our analysis of contraction and extension of HDM source schemas can also be applied at the UML level in the obvious way. For example, the following UML contraction from U_1^a to U_1^b is equivalent to the HDM contraction $S_1^a \rightarrow S_1^b$:

transformation $U_1^a \rightarrow U_1^b$
Ⓤ8 *contractAssociation* works_in

⑨ contractAssociation part_of
⑩ contractClass dept

Thus, after U_1^a has evolved to U_1^b, the same analysis as in Section 3.3 applies, where dept, works_in and part_of in U will map to *void* in U_1^b, but still map to an non-*void* extent in U_2 (the unillustrated UML equivalent of S_2). The remaining examples of Sections 3.3 and 3.4 transfer to this UML level in a similar way.

5 Concluding Remarks

In this paper we have shown how our framework for schema transformation provides a uniform approach to handling both schema integration and schema evolution in heterogeneous database architectures. Source schemas are integrated into a global schema by applying a sequence of primitive transformations to them. The same set of primitive transformations can be used to specify the evolution of a source schema into a new schema. We have shown how the transformations between the source schemas and the global schema can be used to systematically repair the global schema and the query translation pathways as source schemas evolve, considering in particular the evolution of a source schema into a semantically equivalent, semantically contracted, or semantically expanded schema. The first two cases can be handled totally automatically, and the third case semi-automatically.

Our framework is based on a low-level hypergraph-based data model whose primitive constructs are nodes, edges, and constraints. In previous work we have shown how this HDM supports the representation and transformation of a wide variety of higher-level data modelling languages. Our use of the relatively simple HDM means that our approach to schema evolution is straightforward to analyse while at the same time being applicable to real-world modelling situations using more complex data models for database schemas. We are currently implementing the schema transformation, integration and evolution functionality described here within the AutoMed project (http://www.doc.ic.ac.uk/automed/).

References

1. J. Andany, M. Leonard, and C. Palisser. Management of schema evolution in databases. In *Proceedings of VLDB'91*. Morgan-Kaufman, 1991.
2. N. Ashish and C.A. Knoblock. Wrapper generation for semi-structured internet sources. *SIGMOD Record*, 26(4):8–15, December 1997.
3. R.J. Bayardo et al. InfoSleuth: Agent-based semantic integration of information in open and dynamic environments. *SIGMOD Record*, 26(2):195–206, June 1997.
4. Z. Bellahsene. View mechanism for schema evolution in object-oriented dbms. In *Advances in Databases: 14th British National Conference on Databases, BNCOD14*, volume 1094, pages 18–35. Springer-Verlag, 1996.
5. B. Benatallah. A unified framework for supporting dynamic schema evolution in object databases. In *Proceedings of ER99*, LNCS, pages 16–30. Springer-Verlag, 1999.

6. S.S. Chawathe, H. Garcia-Molina, J. Hammer, K. Ireland, Y. Papakonstantinou, J.D. Ullman, and J. Widom. The TSIMMIS project: Integration of heterogeneous information sources. In *Proceedings of the 10th Meeting of the Information Processing Society of Japan*, pages 7–18, October 1994.
7. T. Critchlow, M. Ganesh, and R. Musick. Automatic generation of warehouse mediators using an ontology engine. In *Proceedings of the 5th International Workshop on Knowledge Represenation Meets Databases (KRDB '98)*, volume 10. CEUR Workshop Proceedings, 1998.
8. J. Hammer, H. Garcia-Molina, S. Nestorov, R. Yerneni, M. Breunig, and V. Vassalos. Template-based wrappers in the TSIMMIS system. *SIGMOD Record*, 26(2):532–535, June 1997.
9. R. Hull. Managing sematic heterogeneity in databases: A theoretical perspective. In *Proceedings of PODS*, 1997.
10. E. Jasper. Query translation in heterogeneous database environments. MSc thesis, Birkbeck College, September 2001.
11. M. Kradolfer and A. Geppert. Dynamic workflow schema evolution based on workflow type versioning and workflow migration. In *Proceedings of CoopIS 1999*, pages 104–114, 1999.
12. L.V.S. Lakshmanan, F. Sadri, and I.N. Subramanian. On the logical foundations of schema integration and evolution in heterogeneous database systems. In *Proceedings of DOOD'93*, pages 81–100, Phoenix, AZ, December 1993.
13. A. Levy, A. Rajamaran, and J.Ordille. Querying heterogeneous information sources using source description. In *Proc 22nd VLDB*, pages 252–262, 1996.
14. P.J. McBrien and A. Poulovassilis. A formal framework for ER schema transformation. In *Proceedings of ER'97*, volume 1331 of *LNCS*, pages 408–421, 1997.
15. P.J. McBrien and A. Poulovassilis. A formalisation of semantic schema integration. *Information Systems*, 23(5):307–334, 1998.
16. P.J. McBrien and A. Poulovassilis. Automatic migration and wrapping of database applications — a schema transformation approach. In *Proceedings of ER99*, volume 1728 of *LNCS*, pages 96–113. Springer-Verlag, 1999.
17. P.J. McBrien and A. Poulovassilis. A uniform approach to inter-model transformations. In *Advanced Information Systems Engineering, 11th International Conference CAiSE'99*, volume 1626 of *LNCS*, pages 333–348. Springer-Verlag, 1999.
18. R.J. Miller, M.A. Hernández, L.M. Haas, L.-L. Yan, C.T.H. Ho, R. Fagin, and L. Popa. The Clio project: Managing heterogeneity. *SIGMOD Record*, 30(1):78–83, 2001.
19. A. Poulovassilis and P.J. McBrien. A general formal framework for schema transformation. *Data and Knowledge Engineering*, 28(1):47–71, 1998.
20. M.T. Roth and P. Schwarz. Don't scrap it, wrap it! A wrapper architecture for data sources. In *Proceedings of the 23rd VLDB Conference*, pages 266–275, Athens, Greece, 1997.
21. A. Sheth and J. Larson. Federated database systems. *ACM Computing Surveys*, 22(3):183–236, 1990.
22. M. Templeton, H.Henley, E.Maros, and D.J. Van Buer. InterViso: Dealing with the complexity of federated database access. *The VLDB Journal*, 4(2):287–317, April 1995.
23. M.E. Vidal, L. Raschid, and J-R. Gruser. A meta-wrapper for scaling up to multiple autonomous distributed information sources. In *Proceedings of the 3rd IFCIS International Conference on Cooperative Information Systems (CoopIS98)*, pages 148–157. IEEE-CS Press, 1998.

Serviceflow Beyond Workflow?
Concepts and Architectures for Supporting Inter-organizational Service Processes

Ingrid Wetzel and Ralf Klischewski

Hamburg University, Department for Informatics
Vogt-Koelln-Str. 30, 22527 Hamburg, Germany
{wetzel,klischewski}@informatik.uni-hamburg.de

Abstract. With Serviceflow Management we put the service nature of inter-organizational processes into the center of modeling, design and architectures. The underlying conceptual distinction between the serviceflow, the portion of the process where the customer's concern is evaluated and cared for, and background processes, guides in (1) providers as well as designers to focus on service design and delivery, (2) to provide support for serviceflows with enhanced flexibility and service configuration and (3) to design service points where service workers and customers "meet". By this, the original workflow metaphor, which directs the design of process support from a mass production point of view, is questioned and replaced by a more suitable concept, which considers social and quality aspects in service delivery. Instance-based XML process representations and generic components and architectures for their exchange and for the provision of service tasks are presented, discussed, and exemplified by an e-health process.

1 Introduction

As different authors [11] [19] suggest, we are entering an advanced phase of Internet usage. The internet having become a key medium for global marketing in 1995 (known as brochureware), e-commerce initiatives started from 1997 upwards, e-business projects boomed among business partners since 1999 and we are now in the phase of e-enterprises [12], or virtual organizing [4], or business networking [21]. The overall idea is to apply *process orientation*, implemented in the 90s within organizations, to inter-organizational processes [21]. Furthermore, the aim is to create added-value by *converging e-commerce*, i.e. interacting with the customer in single transactions, and *customer relationship management*, i.e. comprehensive customer care over time, and *supply chain management*, i.e. in-time ordering of supplies, in order to provide an overall *comprehensive service*. Intended applications are, e.g. process portals as successors of web-portals, through which services and goods, often supplied by different providers, are offered by a single provider (the service integrator) in a personalized and configurable way. Moreover, and this is the special focus of this paper, the customer should be guided through the corresponding inter-organizational service process. This kind of system support has to overcome the still existing product-oriented manner in service delivery as it is visible e.g. in buying real estate [21], planning a move [5], undergoing an operation [17]. Efforts should be made to relieve the customer from being forced to become an expert in the process (over time) and being involved in coordination work.

Furthermore, support has to offer a configurable and flexible service, where the customer concern may *change* processes over time and the customer's *satisfaction* is determined by a multitude of factors [7]. Quality in service delivery, as we will see, will certainly go *beyond* mere *efficiency* and requires new approaches, which *go beyond familiar ways of systems design*. We argue accordingly.

Section 2 is centered around characteristics of inter-organizational service processes, illustrated by means of a healthcare example, and it discusses the limitations of available technology in the light of the given demands. Section 3 presents the overall concept and modeling approach of Serviceflow Management. Section 4 describes the use of different stages of realization among provider organizations, from XML-process representations to the provision of different generic components, to the configuration of different network architectures. After presenting Serviceflow Management, section 5 discusses whether we meet our claim to go beyond workflow or not. In doing this, we compare our approach with others found in the literature. Finally, section 6 will summarize the main results.

2 Characteristics of Inter-Organizational Service Processes and Limits in Available Technology

Taking a typical example from the healthcare domain for illustration – the description of similar cases are found in [17] [3] – we consider the process of the preparation for, performance and aftercare of an inpatient surgical operation [13].

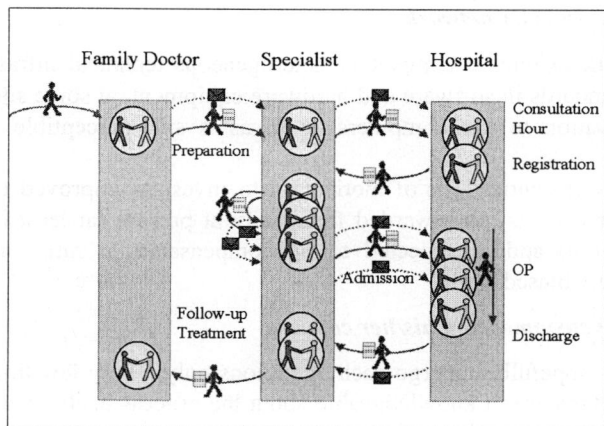

Fig. 1. Service example: preparation, performance and aftercare of an operation

Based on our analysis in cooperation with a German clinic specialized in bone surgery and endoprothetic, the presented scenario describes a standard procedure for hip replacements. In this process, the patient usually moves back and forth between different physicians/specialists and a clinic to receive an in-depth diagnosis as well as appropriate medical care and treatment. A patient typically starts with consulting a family doctor, is directed to a specialist, chooses a hospital, goes through consultation and registration at the hospital with a schedule for further preparation, passes through all stages of preparation, stays in the hospital where the operation is performed, all of which is followed by aftercare treatment at specialists (see figure 1). In the course of this process, various documents have to be exchanged, some of which are delivered by the patient while others are sent by mail or fax.

The performance of this sample composite service exhibits a number of characteristics.

Concerning the process

- *Process Responsibility and Flexibility.* There is a lack of overall responsibility for either the process or its planning. Rather, the process seems to rely on the ability of individual providers to flexibly shape the service according to their special insights about the patient's case (which is why they are called in). Furthermore, the patient's status and hence his concern, continually influence the provider's actions/services over time.
- *Rules about Conducting the Service.* A further problem relates to the exchange of documents. At present, there are no clear rules. It is neither obvious in which way documents are to be delivered nor which kind of documents should be exchanged at all.
- *Monitoring Process Status.* Providers involved do not receive a complete picture of the process, its current status or development. They often lack information about deviations from tacitly assumed ways to proceed, or are unable to obtain this knowledge.

Concerning the provider network

- The network exhibits a completely heterogeneous technical infrastructure, with missing standards in software and hardware equipment, at some sites paired with poor motivation to use computers at all as is still perceptible among health providers.
- There is a substantial lack of motivation to invest in improved cooperation as articulation work is not rewarded financially at present (at least in the German health system) and is expected to be compensated in future in a probably unfortunately biased form.

Concerning the customer and his/her concern

- As patients hopefully undergo such operations only a very few times throughout their lives, they aren't knowledgeable about the process itself, even though some of the coordination tasks are left to them. However, over time, they learn about the process themselves in order to intercept some of the lack of coordination.

- The patient usually expects the networking providers to adjust their actions according to actual findings, needs and changes as they evolve over time. Consequently, a high quality service can only be delivered if the different providers act in a coherent and constantly adapting way.
- The success of a delivered service can sometimes be evaluated instantly but more often only with a certain time-lag to the actual treatment.
- These characteristics result in manifold requirements regarding the software support for inter-organizational services. They certainly depend on the kind of service process in question, as is clearly discussed in [1], and on the focus of support (e.g. [5][6][8][18]). To simplify matters, we structure the requirements in three dimensions (see figure 2):

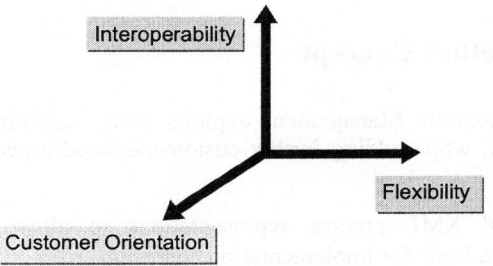

Fig. 2. Requirements for the support of inter-organizational processes

- *Flexibility Support.* The process underlying the comprehensive service delivery is a main object to be supported. Support has to provide flexibility and dynamic selection and configuration of services as the process moves on. Furthermore, the steps of the process need to be transparent to the parties involved including the customer in order to support adjustment and service coherence.
- *Interoperability.* The underlying software systems of providers need to be able to communicate. This includes the exchange of information, may include the remote execution of software components or the sharing of (meta-) knowledge (e.g. about service templates) or services (including cooperation support tools).
- *Customer Orientation.* Service delivery has to consider the possibly changing customer concern and the subtleties in customer satisfaction. This goes beyond efficiency criteria of underlying processes and has to do with understanding the customer concern and with service customization, with the nurturing of personal relationships [9], the mutual adjustment of subservices, possibly the ubiquitous availability of services, and many more [7].

Currently, widespread approaches and tools only match these requirements in a limited way.

Regarding *workflow management,* the overall idea of executable process models comes to its limits. Being based on a central workflow engine that controls a case's execution according to a predefined process, it does not comply with the required flexibility. Although being criticized for the strictness of their execution over the years, it is only today that their former proponents admit this clearly by speaking about the ill-suitedness of conventional "bulk-based" workflow management with regard to ad-hoc flexibility [2]. Likewise, the centralized workflow engine is not suitable with respect to *interoperability* [1].

Internet technology, on the other hand, still lacks supporting processes. However, it makes major contributions towards interoperability. Whether it is the ubiquitous cost-effective network with its standard http-protocol or recently established standards such as XML and, based on it, SOAP or WSDL, these techniques allow for an exchange of standardized/typed messages, also in remote method calls.

As a consequence, recent efforts have been based on combining the two technologies. The respective approaches are called inter-organizational workflow, or composite e-services, e.g. [1][5], see also section 5.

3 The Serviceflow Concept

Accordingly, Serviceflow Management exploits both, workflow management and Internet technology, while adding further customer-related aspects. The overall idea is to

- use case-based XML process representations to allow for flexibility and adaptability as a basis for implementation concepts,
- supply middleware components for delivery and handling of these representations to achieve interoperability,
- conceptually distinguish customer-near parts of the service process from background processes in order to guarantee improved customer orientation and care.

In particular, a serviceflow is defined in terms of service points. A service always creates some social situation, it needs "places" [11] which frame the situation where service tasks are carried out in an individual way. These places we call service points, and the successive interrelation of a number of service points is a serviceflow.

However, from the service provider's point of view, the challenge is to look for recurrent serviceflow patterns. In order to define these patterns, both the sequence of service points and the service at each service point have to be modeled. The sequence of service points for our example is shown in figure 3. Each service point captures specific service tasks to be carried out (forming a very flexible sort of subprocess) and their respective pre- and postconditions from the provider's point of view. The pre- and postconditions represent the contract for interrelating the service points. Service tasks are modeled as UML use cases with each use case being further linked to a rich description, a scenario, and a use case picture. Cooperation pictures can augment the serviceflow representation to further illustrate cooperation among the actors involved, for more detail see [15]. Background processes may be modeled or not. As long as they are captured in some sort of interface description, as pointed out in [1], these interface specifications may suffice as a basis of agreement. In our approach, the formulation of pre- and postconditions serves for this purpose.

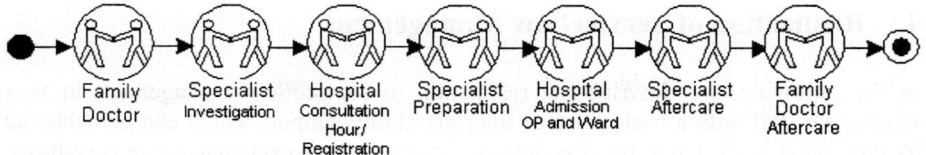

Fig. 3. Serviceflow model for the healthcare service example (s. section 2)

Thus, we combine social "places" and individualized serviceflows for customer concern and care with serviceflow patterns in order to support the efficient organization of mass-service delivery between providers. The overall concept for serviceflow management is now centered around the technical representations of the modeled process patterns that lead to the notion of service float and service point script. Service floats are sent from service point to service point and capture personalized, always up-to-date process knowledge, whereas service point scripts support and document the standard and adaptable activities at each service point (see figure 4).

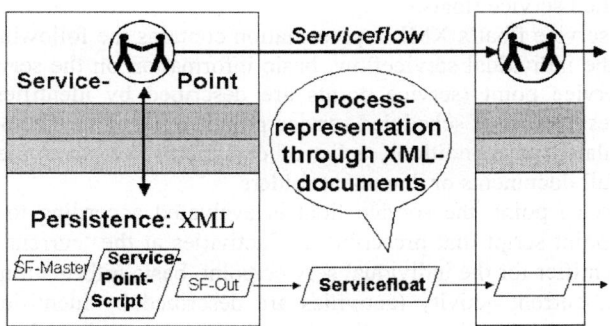

Fig. 4. Service floats and service point scripts

Overall, the approach bears the following potential:

- Initializing a service float by copying (and possibly adapting) a standard serviceflow pattern guides each provider as to how to deliver the service.
- Enabling providers to access and update the process representations (as material) allows for flexibility and instant realization of changes.
- Documenting "the history" enables a service provider to be informed about deviations from the standard and their reasons.
- The update of the current and setting of the next service points forms a basis for automating the delivery of service floats to the next provider.
- The design of service points with flexible support of customer interaction and service delivery.

Note: Serviceflow Management requires agreements on the content of the modeled serviceflow pattern and on the handling of these representations during exchange.

4 Realization of Serviceflow Management

In the following, we describe the realization of serviceflow management in four stages. We start with a basic form of interoperability support which can be achieved by specifying XML-based process representations that are exchanged on a case-basis. Further stages will provide generic components in order to support the exchange of process information, to perform service tasks at service points and to provide suitable interfaces. The components are designed in such a way that they are configurable into decentralized, half-centralized and centralized architectures.

4.1 XML Representation

Basic interoperability can be achieved by exchanging process representations between providers on the condition that providers are able to interpret these representations in a uniform manner and guarantee certain rules for their handling. Following major improvements in standardization, we represent serviceflows technically as XML documents, called service floats.

In detail, a service float's XML representation contains the following elements: an identifier for the individual serviceflow, basic information on the serviceflow client, the current service point (service points are described by identifier, name, type, provider, address), a list of scheduled service points, a list of service points passed, a list of accumulated postconditions, a list of documents, i.e. short message texts or references to full documents or document folders.

At each service point, the service float is evaluated according to the respective XML service point script that prescribes the activities at the 'current service point', which is an identifier for the individual service point, basic information on the service point provider, current activity (activities are described by identifier, name, type, task), a list of scheduled activities, a list of passed activities, a list of preconditions for the set of activities at this service point, and a list of documents.

To use XML-based service floats for interoperability requires from

- the provider network
  - to distribute the XML-DTD/schema for service floats and service point scripts and other shared data structures (e.g. forms, patient data, patient record),
  - to agree upon XML "master"-documents for service floats and service point scripts according to different serviceflow types,
- each provider
  - to meet a set of rules on how to manipulate and share those XML documents
  - to provide a technical infrastructure for enabling the rules.

Summing up, this "stage 0" realization is based on process representations and methods for their handling. Although it enables interoperability between heterogeneous systems of different organizations it leaves open how each provider enables the actual system support. (This proved to be successful in providing the postal vote application service through www.hamburg.de [14][16]).

4.2 Component-Based Architectures

Beyond basic interoperability, the serviceflow management approach aims at providing suitable components which may be distributed to different sites in order to ease the effort of joining networks. We distinguish three stages which provide additional components for handling the service float, the servicepointscript and the interaction (s. figure 5).

- Stage 1 offers a component which enables the swap-in and swap-out of service floats including the routing and the update.
- Stage 2 provides additional support for processing the tasks at each servicepoint (s. below).
- Stage 3 builds on the underlying stages and provides a web-interface for service providers or customers to be integrated in a process portal.

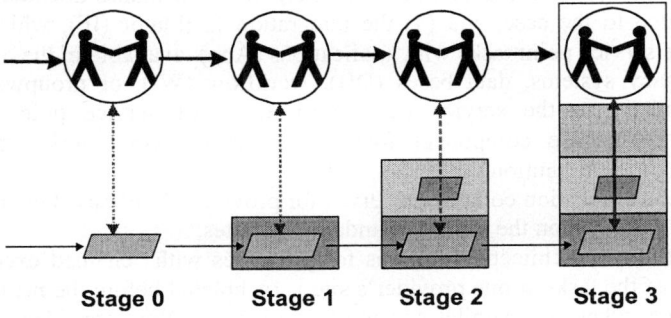

Fig. 5. Stages 0 to 3 in serviceflow management support

Note that the same components can be configured in different architectures ranging from a decentralized, to a partly centralized, to a fully centralized architecture as discussed in the following.

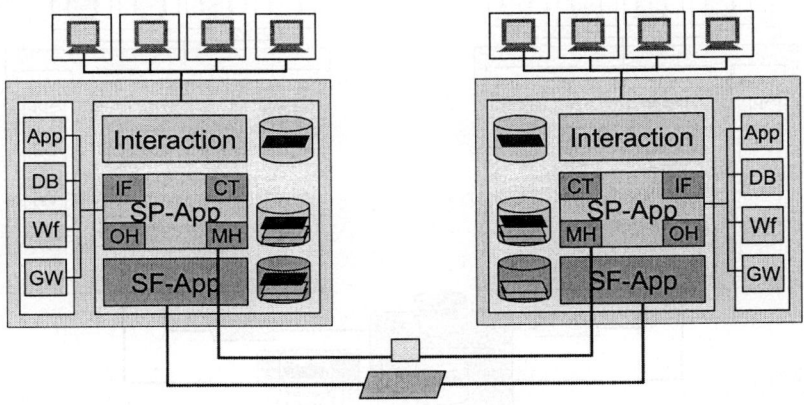

Fig. 6. A decentralized architecture for serviceflow management

The *decentralized architecture* is given in figure 6 and shows two organizations both of which apply to stage 3. The exchange of service floats is accomplished by the service float application (SF-App) at each site, which apart from the routing support offers methods to update and query a service float. Furthermore, it comprises a storage component where the service float masters are stored (at the starting node in the network) and each incoming and outgoing service float can be documented for statistical reasons or for error handling. In this sense, the architecture is completely decentralized.

The service point application (SP-App) captures at least four subcomponents, (1) a message handler (MH), which receives incoming or delivers outgoing messages carrying information, e.g. about the completion of a background process or the availability of further information, (2) a condition trigger (CT), which compares messages with preconditions of a service point and informs workers about a changed status if necessary, (3) the object handler (OH), which manages documents or other objects related to the case, and (4) the integration facilitator (IF), which serves to integrate the service point tasks with applications (App) available in the organization, such as legacy systems, data bases (DB), workflow (Wf), or groupware systems (GW). Similarly to the service float application, the service point application comprises a database component for storing service point script masters and documenting their execution.

Finally, the interaction component serves for providing html-based client interfaces and can be structured on the basis of standard templates.

A decentralized architecture suffices for processes with "chained execution" [1], where each of the tasks at one provider's site is completed before the next provider is in charge, i.e. where no parallel execution is required. Now consider our example case. A patient may be part of two serviceflows in parallel, in which case different providers may share documents across serviceflows. Likewise, a specialist may need to add a delayed result of an examination to a service float which has already been sent to the next provider. Here, a partially centralized architecture may be more suitable in order to provide the required infrastructure.

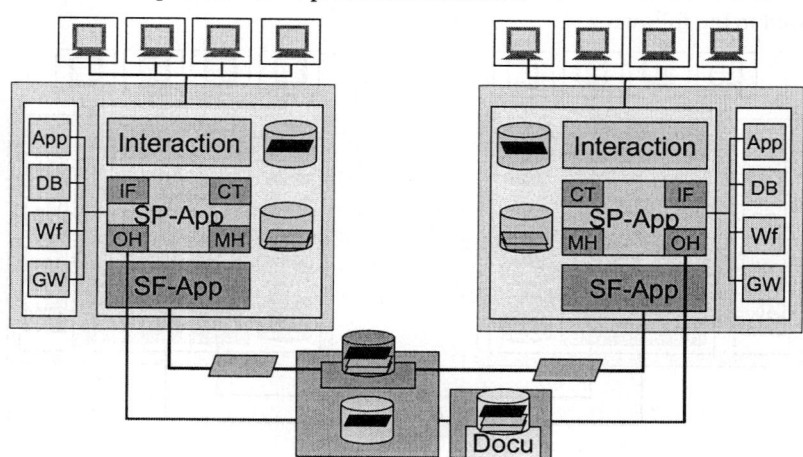

Fig. 7. A partly centralized architecture for serviceflow management

Figure 7 indicates a partially centralized architecture with a central server for documents, assuming that the documents are no longer part of the service floats. In this case they will be sharable among different serviceflows and updateable after a service point has ceased to be active (in which case an additional message has to be sent in order to provide awareness information to the next provider or the whole network, signaling that additional information is available and should be considered immediately).

In this architecture, a second central server can be installed. It may provide a centralized routing support, which eases the serviceflow application in that each provider must send service floats to this centralized server only and routing information is kept in one hand. Additionally, service float masters can be stored at this server. Furthermore, the centralized documentation of the in- and out-serviceflows at each provider's site allows for comprehensive queries regarding the actual state of a particular flow, statistical evaluation, or error handling. Finally, the centralized storage of service point script masters provides the means for standardization of service delivery at service points across different providers in the same network.

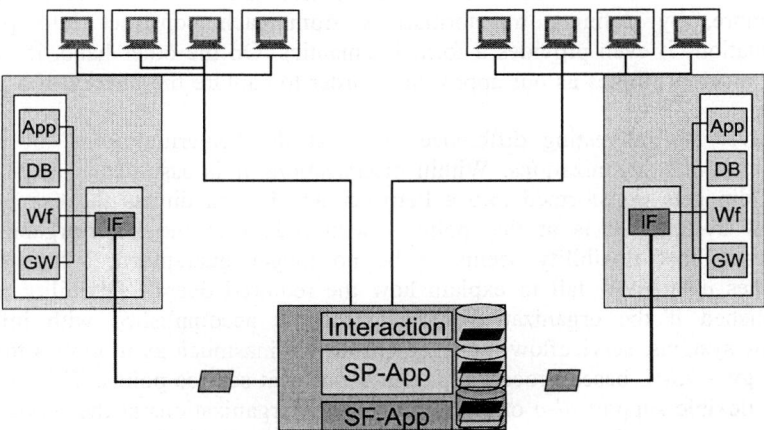

Fig. 8. A centralized architecture for serviceflow management

A further step is made if all architectural serviceflow components are united at one central provider/server leading to a fully centralized architecture, possibly managed by an application service provider in charge. This scenario, as indicated in figure 8, has the advantage of providing direct Web connection to clients/service points for service workers and the customers themselves without requiring any extra software equipment at the provider's site. However, the main difficulty with such a scenario lies in the integration effort "behind" the central component. As discussed in [23] the handling might be very complex. Still, we depart from their approach in that we assign (again) an integration facilitator within each provider organization for hiding details of server connections. This allows for a further level of abstraction which is necessary both because changes in a provider's infrastructure should not jeopardize the functioning of the provider network and because dynamic joining in and out of the provider network should be as easy as possible.

5 Discussion: Serviceflow beyond Workflow

In the following, we compare our approach with other approaches and e-platforms in order to underline and summarize its specifics along the three dimensions given in section 2.

5.1 Flexibility and Interoperability

Like other recent approaches [17] [3] [23] which aim at combining workflow and internet technology in order to support interorganizational processes, we use XML based process representations that are exchanged among providers. As we have seen, this allows for (1) interoperability by using XML standard and Internet-based communication and (2) flexibility of service delivery on the basis of *instance-based* process "execution".

Further, we have to mention that the underlying extensible routing language XRL [3] is in some aspects more sophisticated than our routing language as it provides XML elements for each workflow modeling construct (and thus concurrent branches). Furthermore, by defining transformations from each construct into petri-net representations it even provides a formal semantics. On the other hand, it may not offer as much attributes as our approach in order to capture the history of a process instance.

However, an interesting difference arises at the "entering point" of process descriptions into organizations. Within organizations it is assumed in [3] that the routing slip gets transformed into a Petri-net which then directs the execution of workflow systems. It is at this point – with regard to the inner-organizational processes – that flexibility seems to be no longer guaranteed. Whereas these approaches up to now fail to explain how the required overall flexibility may be accomplished if the organization-internal work is accomplished with inflexible workflow systems, serviceflow management differs inasmuch as it applies the same technology – XML-based process representations – at service points. This allows to provide flexible support *also* or *mainly* within the organizations at the servicepoints where customers and service workers meet and thus individual customer care takes place.

At the same time, applying XML-based process representations at service points bears the potential of standardizing these subprocesses either within the organization or across service providers. The latter also contributes to the dynamic configuration and contracting of service processes which, on the basis of these templates, eases switching in of providers into the network and enables the implementation of future service and process brokers. Admittedly, this requires a quite sophisticated service point application, which is still under development.

Brief mention should be made of further work on e-service platforms for managing the dynamic configuration of e-services in inter-organization processes, which addresses a wide spectrum of support. Aspects taken are e.g. the provision of templates [6], the distinction between service and method nodes, and the introduction of migration support [5], the support of matchmaking and contract completion based on service monitoring, flexible change control, and transaction models [8], and the support of catalogues, guarantees, measurements and multimedia cooperation [18].

Apart from the correlation discussed above to other current approaches which already go beyond typical workflow management in allowing ad-hoc flexibility and interoperability, we want to underline another general difference from (former) workflow approaches we perceive. This relates to the exchange of service history (as captured by service floats) among providers and potential consequences.

For this let us briefly consider typical execution environments in workflow management systems. Originating in the area of mass production, these approaches saw an advantage in equipping a worker with only the one particular bit of the overall process knowledge which seemed sufficient for him/her to perform the specialized task at hand. The traditional division in analysis and production (Taylorism) made analysts responsible for knowing and (re)designing efficient processes that were carried out by a highly specialized work force [20]. Accordingly, neither in workflow management literature nor in workflow products was the user interface of much interests, and it seldom provided more than a simple list of work tasks at a first glance.

Instead, serviceflow management aims at explicitly equipping the service workers involved with access to process patterns (standard plans) and individual histories (based on enhanced user interfaces) with possibly far reaching consequences. As pointed out in [10] service delivery requires "empowered" employees responsible for both decision making and execution. Improved support in information technology may, thus, contribute to lessening the de-skilling tendency of encounter based service delivery in general.

Or to put it this way, comprehensive service understanding at delivery time goes beyond workflow assumptions of separating plans and actions in order to certainly improve situatedness and decision making [24], adding to an overall service quality.

5.2 Customer Orientation

Apart from supporting the aspects of flexibility/situatedness and a sharing of service history, each of which already contributes to quality in service delivery, with the concept of serviceflow management we pursue a further step in customer orientation. An example will make this clear.

In his article "Process-oriented Architectures for Electronic Commerce and Interorganizational Workflow" [1], van der Aalst distinguishes different kinds of interorganizational processes in order to select suitable architectures[1]. For a process type called "loosely coupled", which allows a process to be split up into parts and be executed in parallel, he gives the following example of an ordering process, s. figure 9. Briefly, the customer orders an item which causes the producer to order two sub-items from two suppliers, then the producer assembles the product and delivers it. The figure is presented in the usual way, exhibiting an *overall process* with *subprocesses*.

Now consider the following in the context of this sample process: in serviceflow management we are mainly interested in those parts of the process which interact with

---

[1] Referring to the work of the WfMC van der Aalst argues: "These interoperability standards address the technical issues but not the content of the coordination structure. It is our belief that possible conceptual architectures for truly supporting interorganizational workflows should be explored before solving the technical issues (mainly syntactical)".

the customer. Accordingly, we distinguish conceptually between customer contact and support processes as indicated in figure 9.

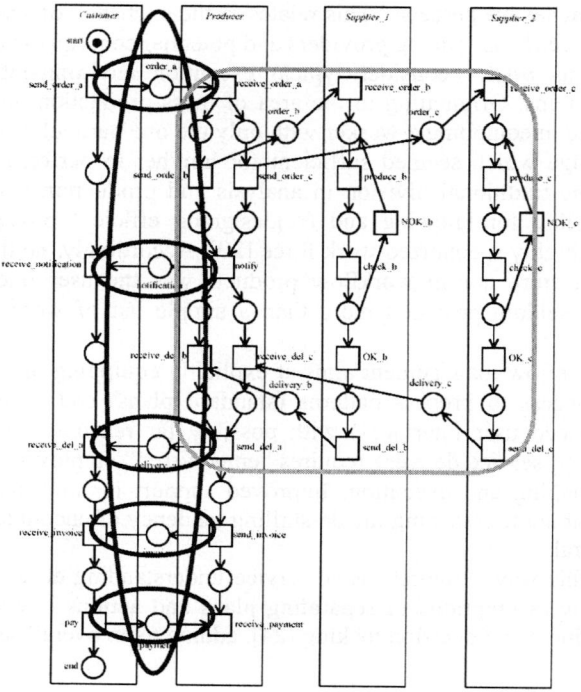

Fig. 9. A conceptual distinction supporting customer orientation (process example from [1])

This allows for differences in their support and has several consequences:

1. It allows for prioritizing the serviceflow over subprocesses. In their book "The Brave New Service Strategy" [10] the authors discuss an actual case which can be seen as an instance of the given example. Under the perspective of service quality they summarize the following process situation. A customer orders a computer on the Internet. However, shortly afterwards he or she has to cancel the order for whatever reason. Although trying different media to reach the provider – e-mail, phone, fax – the customer fails to succeed. Some days later he/she finally gets some response indicating that the best way of handling the situation is to "simply" have the computer delivered as planned and then send it right back. Two things are remarkable in our context. Obviously, a service point for canceling an order was missing – either intentionally or unintentionally. Secondly, the background process seems to direct the interaction with the customer. Thus, with *prioritizing* the serviceflow over the background processes we argue *for carefully designing service points* as well as their interaction with background processes. This leads to the next aspect.

2. With conceptually distinguishing a serviceflow from other processes we revalorize customer contact in service points. As an important by-product, the simple concept of service points brings the customer orientation to each actor/stakeholder involved by providing a concept and language. More often than not, organizations *get stuck* in focusing on their *internal processes* instead of *designing customer contact points*. Furthermore, the metaphor may also be applied in order to redesign or design new electronic services by carefully deciding which of the service points may get transferred into e-service points. This structured approaching was applied in an e-government project in the city state of Hamburg (Germany) supporting the postal vote application through the city's web portal on the basis on serviceflow management (see [14][16]). Considering the healthcare example, it seems difficult to impossible to introduce e-services as most of the time the patient has to be physically present to undergo examinations, care or treatment. However, the first service point may be a candidate for a virtual consultation. The patient could describe the problems and receive a referral slip while being helped to choose from different specialists to consult. Also, an additional e-service point may be added to the existing scenario. For choosing among hospitals, the patient may consider detailed information about possible hospitals over the Internet at home and then again consult a specialist in order to make the decision.
3. The conceptual distinction also helps to discern differences in the software support of serviceflow and background processes according to *their distinctive nature in cooperation*. E.g. coordinating the work of specialists seems to require much more flexibility than the ordering of an implant which can be performed by workflow support.

6 Summary and Further Work

With serviceflow management we contribute to supporting inter-organizational service processes and applications. Having exemplified typical requirements for a healthcare service, we state three main requirements: flexibility in process execution, interoperability, and customer orientation.

The concept of serviceflow management corresponds with recent research in inter-organizational processes in that we apply XML-process representations in order to exchange case/instance based process knowledge among providers. This enables flexibility as well as interoperability and thus *goes beyond* former "bulk"-based *workflow* execution. Sharing process history even allows for empowerment of highly functional specialized work places in service delivery. Applying the same technology (XML-process representation) in order to allow for flexible process execution at service points, we contribute to a set of aspects such as flexible service delivery within organizations, standardization, future template-based contracting and dynamic configuration of services within a provider network.

Furthermore, the conceptual distinction between a serviceflow and background processes together with a revalorization of service points and their design contribute to a *customer orientation beyond a mere process orientation*. The latter is still found in several recent publications and can be traced to business process redesign where efficiency aspects were considered sufficient tokens of customer orientation.

Future work needs to address several aspects. Applying serviceflow management to different service processes will provide further insight into what are suitable architectures. Exploring spreading technology will lead to the rebuilding and extending of existing components, in respect to stage 0: extending the serviceflow representation, to stages 1-3: redesigning existing components, and to stage 3: extending generic interfaces for service points.

To sum up: if inter-organizational processes are designed to converge e-commerce, customer relationship management and supply chain management and thus to enable comprehensive service processes, we argue for serviceflow management for clearly focusing on the customer and his/her concern. This asks for metaphors, concepts and architectures beyond traditional workflow management as presented to serve an (e-) service-based economy.

References

1. van der Aalst, W.M.P.: Process-oriented Architectures for Electronic Commerce and Interorganizational Workflow. In: Information Systems, 24 (8), (2000) pp. 639-671
2. van der Aalst, W.M.P., Jablonski, S.: Dealing with Workflow Change: Identification of Issues and Solutions. International Journal of Computer Systems, Science, and Engineering 15 (5), (2000) pp. 267-276
3. van der Aalst, W.M.P. and Kumar, A.: XML Based Schema Definition for Support of Inter-organizational Workflow. University of Colorado and Eindhoven University of Technology Report. (2001) http://spot.colorado.edu/~akhil/pubs.html
4. Alt, R., Puschmann, T., Reichmayr, C.: Strategies for Business Networking. In: Hubert Österle, Elgar Fleisch, Rainer Alt (eds): Business Networking – Schaping Collaboration Between Enterprises, Springer-Verlag. (2001) pp. 89-11
5. Casati, F., Ilnicki, S., Jin, L.-J., Krishnamoorthy, V., Shan, M.-C.: eFlow: a Platform for Developing and Managing Composite e-Services. HP Labs Technical Reports HPL-2000-36 (2000) www.hpl.hp.com/techreports/2000
6. Christophide, V., Hull, R., Kumar, A., Simeon, J.: Workflow Mediation using VorteXML, Data Engineering 24 (1), March (2001)
7. Gabbot, M., Hogg, G.: Consumers and Services, John Wiley & Sons, Chicester, (1998)
8. Grefen, P., Aberer, K., Ludwig, H., Hoffner, Y.: CrossFlow: Cross-Organizational Workflow Management for Service Outsourcing in Dynamic Virtual Enterprises. Data Engineering, Vol. 24, No. 1, March (2001)
9. Gutek, B., The Dynamics of Service, Jossey-Bass Publishers, San Francisco (1995)
10. Gutek, B., Welsh, T.: The Brave New Service Strategy: Aligning Customer Relationships, Market Strategies, and Business Structures, Amacom, (2000)

11. Harrison, S., Dourish, P.: Re-Place-ing Space: The Roles of Place and Space in Collaborative Systems, Proceedings CSCW'96, pp. 67-76 (1996)
12. Hoque, F.: e-Enterprise – Business Models, Architecture, and Components. Cambridge University Press (2001)
13. Klischewski, R., Wetzel, I.: Serviceflow Management for Health Provider Networks. Information Age Economy. Proceedings 5th International Conference Wirtschaftsinformatik (Business Information Systems). Physica, Heidelberg, (2001) pp. 161-174
14. Klischewski, Ralf; Wetzel, Ingrid, XML-based Process Representation for e-Government Serviceflows, Schmid, B., et al. (ed.): Towards the E-Society: E-commerce, E-business, and E-government (I3E 2001, IFIP). Dordrecht: Kluwer, 2001, pp. 789-802, (2001)
15. Klischewski, R., Wetzel, I., Bahrami, A.: Modeling Serviceflow. In print: Proc. of the 1st International Conference on Information Systems Technology and its Applications (ISTA). Kharkiv, Ukraine, June, (2001)
16. Klischewski, R., Wetzel, I.: Serviceflow Management: Caring for the Citizen's Concern in Designing E-Government Transaction Processes, to appear in HICSS'35 (Hawaii International Conference on Systems Sciences), (2002)
17. Kumar, A., Zhao, J.L.: Workflow Support for Electronic Commerce Applications, http://spot.colorado.edu/~akhil/ (1999)
18. Lazcano, A., Alonso, G., Schuldt, H., Schuler, C.: The WISE approach to Electronic Commerce. International Journal of Computer Systems Science & Engineering, special issue on Flexible Workflow Technology Driving the Networked Economy, Vol. 15, No. 5, September (2000)
19. Merz, M.: E- Commerce und E- Business. Marktmodelle, Anwendungen und Technologien, Springer Verlag, (1999)
20. Mintzberg, H.: The Structuring of Organizations, Prentice-Hall, (1979)
21. Österle, H., Fleisch, E., Alt, R. (eds): Business Networking – Shaping Collaboration Between Enterprises. Springer-Verlag (2001)
22. Schmid, R.E., Bach, V., Österle, H.: Mit customer Relationship Management zum Prozessportal. In: Bach, V., Österle, H. (eds), Customer Relationship Management in der Praxis. Springer (2000)
23. Shegalov, G., Gillmann, M., Weikum, G.: XML-enabled Workflow Management for E-Services across Heterogeneous Platforms. VLDB Journal 10 (1), (2001) pp. 91-103
24. Suchman, L.: Plans and Situated Actions. The Problem of Human-Machine Communication. Cambridge (NY), Cambridge University Press (1987)

Design for Change: Evolving Workflow Specifications in ULTRAflow

Alfred Fent, Herbert Reiter, and Burkhard Freitag*

University of Passau, Department of Computer Science
94030 Passau, Germany
Tel. (+49) 851 509 3131, Fax (+49) 851 509 3182
{fent,reiter,freitag}@fmi.uni-passau.de

Abstract. Updating the specification of workflows on the fly in a workflow management system is currently considered an important topic in research as well as application. Yet, most approaches are either very simplistic, allowing only newly started workflows to take advantage of updated specifications, or they are complex, trying to transfer every active workflow from the old to the new schema.

In the workflow management system ULTRAflow, updates to workflow specifications are handled by using a multi-version concurrency control protocol. This is facilitated by the specification language for workflows, which is rule based and therefore provides a natural partitioning of specifications into smaller units. The proposed method allows active, running workflows to partly use new specifications if this does not conflict with already executed sub-workflows. Moreover, an architecture which is also applicable in a distributed system is presented.

While the method to update the specifications is discussed in the context of a workflow management system, it can also be applied in CORBA or EJB applications, or the now ubiquitous electronic services.

1 Introduction

Updating the specification of workflows in a workflow management system (WfMS) is currently considered an important topic in research as well as application. Of special interest are procedures to perform these updates on the fly, i.e., without disturbing the execution of active workflows in the system. However, many approaches, especially those applied in commercial systems, are very simplistic, allowing only newly started workflows to take advantage of the updated specification, while active workflows still use the original one; other approaches that try to transfer every running workflow instance from the old to the new schema often are complex and complicated [26].

The way our workflow management system ULTRAflow [10,11,12] handles evolving workflow specifications lies between these two extremes. A multi-version concurrency control protocol is employed to control access to the changed parts

---

* The work described in this paper has been funded by the German Research Agency (DFG) under contract number Fr 1021/3-3.

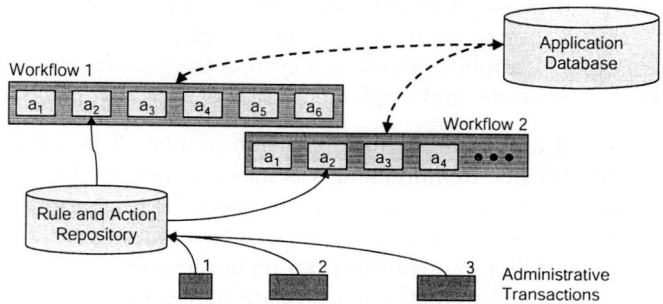

Fig. 1. Changes of specifications are also considered transactions

of a workflow specification. This is facilitated by the specification language of ULTRAflow, which is rule based [13,27,28] and therefore provides a natural partitioning of specifications into smaller units. The proposed method allows active, running workflows to partly use new specifications if this does not conflict with sub-workflows or basic operations already executed. This is not possible in known versioning schemes where a "snapshot" is taken at the beginning of the workflow. It is also applicable in a distributed environment.

The general situation is depicted in Fig. 1: several workflows are running concurrently, each consisting of steps $a_1, a_2, \ldots$ which can be basic operations or sub-workflows that are again defined in the ULTRAflow language. While a workflow is executing – which typically takes some non-negligible time, i.e. several hours, days, or weeks – it retrieves the specifications of its steps from a repository for rules and actions. In the meantime, some of the specifications of steps are updated in the repository by administrative transactions to account for new technologies, changes in business rules, new processes, etc. Access to the rule- and action repository is handled through a multi-version concurrency control protocol. This protocol protects the retrieval of steps by workflows from updates of the steps by administrative transactions and controls which of the workflows can use an updated specification, and which has to stick to the old one. This way, it eliminates the "dynamic change bug" [9,26], i.e., errors introduced by changing specifications of active workflows.

Within the transactions formed by the workflows each step can execute arbitrary actions (represented by dotted lines in the figure) on, e.g., an application database. Correctness of these actions with several workflows running concurrently is ensured by techniques well-known from databases [1] but not in the scope of this paper.

A solution for the dynamic change bug must meet the following requirements:

1. No errors or failures of active workflows are caused due to the change
2. If a new specification for a workflow is provided, other workflows that use it as a sub-workflow do not have to be modified to continue functioning

3. Updating a specification does not cause the WfMS to stop execution of running workflows, nor to delay starting new ones
4. The solution must be applicable within a system that isolates workflows with some kind of transactions and implements recovery by compensation [17]

Requirements 1 and 2 are derived from [9], while number 3 is more than reasonable in a real-life WfMS. Requirement 4 is mainly motivated by our specific setting, as ULTRAflow uses compensation for recovery, i.e., it performs semantically reverse actions to undo the effects of aborted transactions. In systems that do not rely on compensation, our solution can be implemented even more easily.

Although in this paper the method to update and control access to specifications is presented in the context of a WfMS, it can also be applied in other situations where parts of a (possibly long running) program have to be exchanged on the fly. This happens in application servers for, e.g., CORBA [20] or Enterprise Java Bean (EJB) applications [25], when new versions of the program code are deployed and integrated into the system. This is frequently referred to as "hot deployment". We performed some tests with Apache/Tomcat [2] which can be seen as a minimal application server. Today, this combination detects new versions of code, however it then delays new requests until all instances of the old code which are still active are finished, loads the new code, and continues handling requests with the new version then. The delay could be eliminated with our method. The full-fledged EJB application server Orion [21] behaved similarly in our tests; it even exchanged definitions used several times within still active transactions, thus stumbling directly into the dynamic change bug [9].

Also, the now ubiquitous electronic services (e-services) [22] can profit from our method. In e-services, it is usually assumed that at the beginning of an application the necessary services are searched and decided upon, and that they are used throughout the application. Yet, this may impose rather long setup times at the start of the application or at the first invocation of a service if the search is delayed until this moment. So, systems will begin to "cache" this information and reuse the same e-service for several applications, providing some kind of "e-service application server" which will run into the same issues as described above.

The rest of the paper is organized as follows: we start with overviews of related work and the ULTRAflow system in Sect. 2 and 3, before we detail on updating specifications in Sect. 4 and ensuring correctness in Sect. 5. Practical aspects of our architecture are presented in Sect. 6. The paper is concluded with a summary in Sect. 7.

2 Related Work

Modification of workflow specifications has been quite frequently addressed in recent research, so we will only mention a selection of the related work here. Many other articles concerning adaptive workflows can be found e.g. in [3,16].

The so-called "dynamic change bug" was introduced in [9], where also correctness criteria for workflow evolution were proposed; however, the paper does not discuss what to do with instances that do not meet these criteria. This is done in [6], where primitive operations on workflow specifications are defined. The paper also discusses "progressive policies" dependent on the state of active instances which can either continue with the initial specification, be migrated to the new one under certain conditions, migrated to an ad hoc workflow, or be aborted. Our solution is in fact a mixture of the first two policies: parts of the workflow are migrated, and parts continue with the old version.

"Ad hoc changes", i.e., changes performed as part of the workflow itself, are the topic within ADEPT$_{\text{flex}}$ [23]. While this is important, our work deals with an evolution of the specifications driven from outside the running workflow instances. This is the typical case for planned workflows that are specified and installed by a workflow administrator. Approaches to transform running instances of an old to instances of a new specification are discussed in [8,19], and an infrastructure based on language reflection that supports such transformations is presented in [7]. Our approach, in contrast, is not based on explicit transformation, but uses new specifications automatically if they do not conflict with those already used by the workflow.

The determination of a so-called "change region", i.e., the part of a workflow that is affected by an update, is the topic of [26]. Workflow instances whose executions are currently not within this region immediately use an updated specification, while the updates are postponed for other instances until they leave the region. However, the algorithm of [26] to compute the change region has a complexity in $O(n^4(n!)^2)$, where n is the number of nodes of the workflow. Moreover, if compensation is used the change region may include the rest of the workflow, such that the anticipated advantage of minimizing the number of versions is not achieved.

Work on handling exceptions and using compensation [15] is related to our approach in so far as we also use compensation in the workflows within ULTRAflow. Yet, changes to workflow specifications or basic operations are not addressed in [15].

3 The ULTRAflow System

ULTRAflow [10,11,12] is a WfMS which is based on a rule-based specification language. It is implemented as a prototype that is integrated into a web-server as a lightweight component, thus leveraging the access to the system from almost arbitrary client systems, having HTML as the least common denominator. The overall architecture is shown in Fig. 2. Actors, i.e., usually humans interacting with the WfMS, can access the system from within a company intranet or from the internet, where in the latter case either some kind of virtual private network (VPN) or the authorization and authentication features of the web-server are used to restrict admission to the system. Part of the ULTRAflow system is the rule engine [13,27,28], which executes the workflow specifications. These specifications also include information about task assignment to different actors or access to other systems (like organisation information or production data, but

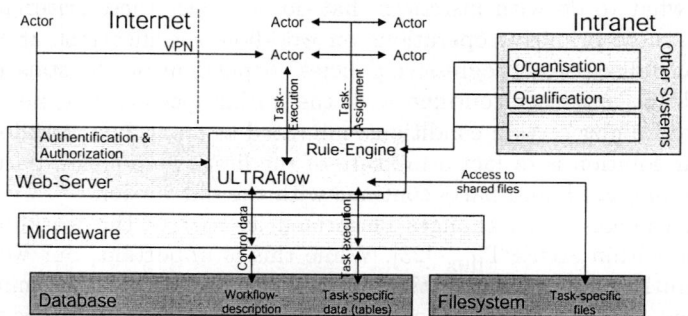

Fig. 2. The overall architecture of the ULTRAflow system

also databases etc.). General control data, as well as task-specific data (information about work progress, status, etc.) are accessed through a middleware layer. Moreover, files stored in a filesystem can be integrated into the workflow execution.

Although actors usually are human workers, other systems calling a service provided by ULTRAflow are also supported, such that the WfMS can be integrated into, e.g., an e-service infrastructure [24]. However, in this case methods for authentication and authorization specifically developed for e-services may be more appropriate [22].

The rule engine works on workflow specifications that are expressed in the action language of ULTRAflow, which itself is an instance of the general ULTRA framework [27,28]. Basic operations, like calls to other applications, posts on user- or role-specific blackboards, etc., can be composed into more complex specifications, which then can be reused in other rules. The rule language is expressive enough to describe most patterns that arise in workflow specification [10]. Features like handling of sub-workflows are inherent to the language, and formal methods known for rule languages can be applied. For instance, the dependency graph [18] reflects the workflow/sub-workflow relation.

During the execution of a workflow in the ULTRAflow system, the rules defining the workflow are "expanded" on demand in resolution-like steps [13,18]. This is in contrast to many other WfMSs where the complete workflow specification is instantiated (e.g., in the form of a graph or Petri net) when a new instance of a workflow is started.

Example 1. As an example for rule resolution, look at the following part of a simple workflow specified in the rule language of ULTRAflow:

$send(P, D, B) \leftarrow prepare\_shipment(P) : [ship(P, D) \mid send\_bill(B)]$.
$prepare\_shipment(X) \leftarrow collect\_items(X) : package(X)$.

The program describes sending a parcel P to delivery address D and billing address B. In ULTRAflow, a colon (":") denotes sequential composition, while concurrent execution is denoted by a vertical bar ("|"); where necessary, brackets "[" and "]" indicate precedence. As usual in logic programming, variables are denoted by capital letters. To send the parcel, first the sub-workflow *prepare_shipment* is executed, then the parcel is *ship*ped to the delivery address, while concurrently the bill is sent to the billing address. The specification of sub-workflow *prepare_shipment* for a parcel X consists of the activities to *collect_items* for X that are to be sent, and to *package* them together.

If this workflow is executed, the system proceeds just as described above. For every subgoal on the right hand side of a rule, the adequate definition is looked up, which either yields another rule (like in *prepare_shipment*) or a class in Java, the implementation language of ULTRAflow, in case of a basic operation.

When errors occur during the execution of a workflow, like logical failure in rule evaluation [18], transactional conflicts, etc., compensation [17] is used to rollback the execution state to the last existing choice point. The existence of a compensation method is mandatory for basic operations and optional for rules defining sub-workflows.

In the architecture of Fig. 2 there is only one block called ULTRAflow; however, this block can be implemented as a distributed system which spreads the load of workflow execution over several nodes according to some schema based on availability of resources, physical proximity, or other distribution aspects. Whether a rule specifying a sub-workflow is executed at the same or a remote system is transparent to the caller.

4 Updating Workflow Specifications

Before we analyze how a system might evolve, we first describe workflow specifications in more detail.

4.1 Components of a Workflow Specification

As ULTRAflow uses a rule based specification language, every workflow and sub-workflow specification is represented by a number of rules. An entire workflow instance is started by issuing a (top-level) query, whereas the start of a sub-workflow is caused by a sub-query within the specification of the superordinate workflow. The call to a sub-workflow and also to a basic operation is just a name and a number of arguments. However, the WfMS itself needs additional information to be able to call the sub-workflow and to ensure correctness of the execution in the application level sense. All this information can be divided into the following parts:

Syntactic Information includes everything the WfMS needs to identify the specific basic operation or workflow which is called. In the ULTRAflow system, this is currently just the name, but additional information like name spaces or module names may be present, too.

Interface Definition describes the arguments of the sub-workflow or basic operation, their number and types, etc.

Semantical Context covers everything that the WfMS needs to ensure correctness during the execution. In the ULTRAflow system, this includes a compatibility matrix, a description of transactional features (e.g., support for two phase commit [4,5,14]), and recovery aspects for basic operations. For complex workflows, the semantical context may also contain recovery data (name of a compensating workflow), estimated execution times for sub-workflows and actions, etc. In other words, the semantical context of a step comprises all the meta data available to the WfMS.

Program Code is called when the operation or workflow is executed, i.e., it is the actual implementation. For basic operations the program code is given by the name of a Java class (cf. Sect. 6). As compensation [17] is used for recovery (see requirement 4 in Sect. 1), this class must provide forward (do) and backward (undo) methods. For complex (sub-)workflows, the program code consists of the defining rules for the predicate corresponding to the workflow; providing an undo-workflow is optional, as the effects can always be removed by compensating the basic operations. So, in short, "program code" includes everything that is needed to perform the step or to remove its effects in case of (transactional) failure.

Definition 1. *A (specification of a) step is a tuple $a = (N, I, S, C)$ consisting of name N, interface I, semantical context S, and code C. A step can be a basic operation or a sub-workflow that is defined by a rule in the ULTRAflow language. The set of all steps known to the system is called P.*

Example 2. The specification of step *prepare_shipment* of Ex. 1 is the tuple

$$N = \text{"prepare\_shipment"}$$
$$I = X \text{ plus adequate type information}$$
$$S = \text{representation of semantical context}$$
$$C = \{collect\_items(X) : package(X)\}$$

The set of all steps is as follows, with tuples abbreviated to their names:

$$P = \{(\text{"send"}, \ldots), (\text{"prepare\_shipment"}, \ldots), (\text{"ship"}, \ldots),$$
$$(\text{"send\_bill"}, \ldots), (\text{"collect\_items"}, \ldots), (\text{"package"}, \ldots)\}$$

4.2 Adding New Specifications

Adding new specifications to the system is relatively easy from the theoretical point of view and poses only engineering issues. We can simply define

Definition 2. *A step $a' = (N', I', S', C')$ is new (in P) if its name is not contained in P, i.e., $\forall a = (N, I, S, C) \in P : N \neq N'$. Adding a new step a' to P is done by insertion, i.e., $P' = P \cup \{a'\}$ where P' is the new set of steps.*

This definition which is used in the ULTRAflow system only relies on the name of the operation. Alternatively it would be possible to also take the interface definition into account like in object-oriented languages and define a' as new if $\forall a = (N, I, S, C) \in P : (N \neq N' \wedge I \neq I')$. Yet, it does not make a difference in the following presentation which is why we stick to the simple definition based only on the names of predicates.

In the following, we identify the step $a = (N, I, S, C)$ with its name N.

4.3 Deleting an Existing Specification

It may also happen that the specification of a step is removed from the system. However, we do not discuss this here for a simple reason: requirements 1 and 2 of Sect. 1 said that the specifications of other workflows in the system must not be altered because of an update, and that no errors may occur due to it. Now, if we removed a step that is used in another workflow, this other workflow will no longer work, i.e., it will cause runtime errors. So our requirements would be violated. If, on the other hand, the step to delete is not used in any other workflow specification, it is only "dead code" and therefore can be removed, anyway.

4.4 Updating an Existing Specification

As described in the previous sections, adding new and deleting existing steps are more or less straightforward and do not pose a lot of problems. This is no longer the case when we consider updating the specification of an existing step. We then have to analyze three cases, as three parts of the step can be changed: interface, code, and semantical context.

Changing the Interface As mentioned in Def. 2 of Sect. 4.2, the interface is not used to identify the step itself, but only the predicate name. So it is possible to provide a new version with a changed interface. Yet, as one of our basic requirements is that the specifications of workflows using the updated step have to remain unchanged (see Sect. 1) this precludes a change to the interface; otherwise, runtime errors would occur. If a changed step really needs other arguments, mappings from the old to the new interface have to be provided within the implementation code, such that the visible interface stays unchanged. Otherwise, a new step with the new interface has to be added to the system.

Changing the Implementation This is the most frequent case: the overall syntactical and semantical appearance of the step stays the same, but its code is updated to reflect some change in the environment, to provide an optimized or corrected version of the implementation, etc. Recall from Sect. 4.1 that the code includes do- and undo-methods.

Formally, changing the specification of step $a = (N, I, S, C)$ to the new code C' corresponds to replacing P with the new set $P' = P \cup \{(N, I, S, C')\} \setminus \{a\}$.

The notion of "code" here does not necessarily imply some kind of programming, binary data, or compiled executable. In WfMS, for example, it is quite frequent that applications like word processors or spreadsheets are started for the user. If now a company changes its corporate design and therefore replaces the standard style sheets, letter heads, etc. of the word processor, this must also be seen as a change to the implementation code of the corresponding operation "call word processor".

Changing Semantical Information Besides the code itself, there may be additional semantical information that is provided to the system. In ULTRAflow, this information mainly covers compatibility information to facilitate scheduling operations of concurrent workflows. In other systems semantical information may comprise arbitrary data necessary for the correct execution of workflows.

Like above, changing the specification of step $a = (N, I, S, C)$ to the new semantical information S' corresponds to replacing P with the new set $P' = P \cup \{(N, I, S', C)\} \setminus \{a\}$.

5 Ensuring Correctness

The previous section analyzed the types of changes that can occur within a running WfMS. From the various possibilities (adding, deleting, and changing any of the four components a step consists of) several were ruled out because they violate the requirements of Sect. 1. Adding and deleting steps were already described, such that we are now left with the two most interesting (and challenging) cases: changing program code and changing semantical information.

5.1 Updating Implementation Code

Updates to and usage of specifications have to be synchronized, especially if (part of) the specification of an active workflow is to be updated. This obviously resembles the classical and well-known case of concurrent access to data items in a database system, except that we do not access data, but code and rules. In fact, in ULTRAflow we reuse serializability theory [4,5,14] to ensure that changes to specifications of steps do not have negative effects on active workflows. Therefore, we will introduce – in addition to transactions that the system already may use – a second layer of transactions that protect access to the specifications of steps. In other words, we consider the implementation code as the data objects that are either read or written.

To avoid having to reinvent all the definitions and theorems from database concurrency control, we observe that the execution of a workflow only reads its steps, while changes to the specification only write to it. Due to the rule based specification language of ULTRAflow we consider a workflow specification as a structured object with each rule (step) being accessible separately. This allows us to treat the execution of a workflow as a sequence of accesses to its steps.

Definition 3. *A workflow execution which executes the steps $a_1, a_2, \ldots, a_n$ is a transaction T_i which only reads these specifications, denoted by $r_i(a_1) \; r_i(a_2) \ldots r_i(a_n)$.*

An administrative transactions that updates the steps $b_1, b_2, \ldots, b_m$ is a transaction T_j which only writes to the specifications, denoted by $w_j(b_1) \; w_j(b_2) \ldots w_j(b_m)$.

With these definitions, we can now easily distinguish the "productive" workflows which only read and execute the steps from the administrative transactions that update them. Note that we talk about changes and updates to the steps here, i.e., we see the set P as the database and the elements of P as data items (recall Fig. 1: P corresponds to the rule and action repository). This is independent from the read and write access that the basic operations actually perform on an application database containing production data. In other words, a workflow is a sequence of reads from P but can also write data to the application database. However, it must not write to P.

Example 3. Recall the setting of Ex. 1 and that we identify the step $a = (N, I, S, C)$ with its name N. The execution of an instance of the top-level workflow *send* corresponds to the following transaction T_i (the numbers denote times and are used for reference later):

$$
\begin{aligned}
&1: \quad r_i(send) \\
&2: \quad r_i(prepare\_shipment) \\
&3: \quad r_i(collect\_items) \\
&4: \quad r_i(package) \\
&5: \quad r_i(ship) \\
&6: \quad r_i(send\_bill)
\end{aligned}
$$

Note that after each read of the specification of a step the workflow executes it. For steps like *prepare_shipment* which are defined by a rule this results in further read operations (reads of *collect_items* and *package*). Execution of basic operations like *ship* can involve access to the application database, e.g., to record the shipment.

In database concurrency control, an interleaved execution of transactions is considered correct if it has the same effects as some serial, i.e., non-interleaved, execution of these transactions (serializability, cf. [4,5,14]). We adopt this notion here and define correctness of specification changes as follows:

Definition 4. *An interleaved execution of instances of a workflow specification and updates of its steps is correct, if it is equivalent to some serial, non-interleaved execution.*

Now that we mapped the execution of workflows and changes to their steps to classical database concurrency control, we can reuse the protocols developed there.

The most frequently used concurrency control protocols are those based on locking, with two phase locking as the most prominent representative [4,5,14]. However, locking protocols have the inherent property that they may block the execution of transactions, and if this happens to one of the productive workflows, it violates requirement 3 of Sect. 1. So locking protocols cannot be used in our context.

Optimistic protocols [4,5,14] avoid blocking, but they also cannot be used here: incorrect executions are only detected at a transaction's commit time;

erroneous transactions then are aborted and restarted. In a WfMS, this is clearly unacceptable, as all the work done within the workflow, which can be worth several weeks, would be lost.

The most suitable protocols to choose in the specific situation are in fact the multi-version concurrency control protocols [4,5]. The different versions of the data object in database theory correspond to the different implementation versions in our WfMS setting. Moreover, we can exploit a simple property that is valid in this specific setting where modification of specifications is concerned: there are only two kinds of transactions, namely the productive workflows which only read the steps, and the administrative transactions that only write them. So we have only "queries" and "updaters" (in the terminology of [4]) in the system. In this case, it is possible to use a mixture of two protocols: multi-version timestamp ordering is used to synchronize queries, i.e., access to the steps, and strict two phase locking to synchronize updaters, viz., changes of the steps. This mixed protocol, which is described and analyzed in detail in [4, Chap. 5.5] and [5, Chap. 6.6], especially has the property that a query is never forced to wait for updaters and never causes updaters to wait. The scheduler can always process a query's read without delay, i.e., execution of a workflow instance is never blocked by an update of the specification. To make this paper self contained, we repeat the protocol here:

Definition 5 (Multi-version Mixed Concurrency Control with Commit Lists [4]).
When a query begins executing, a list of all the committed update transactions is associated with it, called the commit list. *The query attaches the commit list to every read that it sends to the scheduler, essentially treating the list like a timestamp. When the scheduler receives $r_i(x)$ for a query transaction T_i, it finds the most recently committed version of x whose transaction identifier is in T_i's copy of the commit list.*

Updaters use strict two phase locking, so two transactions may not concurrently create new versions of the same data item and the order of a data item's versions (and hence the version list) is well defined.

Given this organization of versions, to process $r_i(x)$ for a query transaction T_i, the scheduler scans the version list of x until it finds a version written by a transaction that appears in the commit list associated with T_i.

So, while using concurrency control to protect access to the code guarantees that requirement 1 of Sect. 1 is fulfilled, the selection of the specific concurrency control protocol also satisfies requirement 3.

Moreover, the protocol is also implementable efficiently in distributed systems. This is important in our setting, as execution of a workflow can span several systems, either by distribution of the workflow (several concurrent parts run on different systems), or by migration from one system to another (execution is transferred to another system). Using the distributed version of the protocol, we can ensure that no matter on which system a part of a workflow is executed, it always uses the correct version of its steps.

However, the protocol of Def. 5 has a disadvantage: the starting time of a query transaction fully determines all the versions that the program sees, as the commit list is generated at this time. While this is acceptable for normal database transactions, an application to updating workflow specifications would yield the simple versioning schema that is also employed in many commercial systems [26], as it corresponds to taking a snapshot at the beginning of each workflow. However, we want active workflows also to use changes to their steps that happen after their start, if they do not conflict with the work executed *so far*.

Example 4. Recall the setting of Ex. 3 and assume that *ship* is updated by a transaction T_j between times 3 and 4. Then the history reads like this:

	T_i	T_j
	...	
3 :	$r_i(collect\_items)$	
3.1 :		$w_j(ship)$
3.2 :		$commit_j$
4 :	$r_i(package)$	
5 :	$r_i(ship)$	

This update can be caused by implementing a new shipment procedure that is more efficient than the old one. Now we would like the active workflow T_i to take advantage of this new, improved *ship* definition. However, as the commit list of T_i was built at its starting time, it does not contain transaction T_j, and consequently the read of step *ship* at time 5 will return the old version instead of the updated one.

Therefore, we use the following extension of the protocol of Def. 5 in ULTRAflow:

Definition 6 (Multi-version Mixed Concurrency Control with Dynamic Commit Lists). *When a query begins executing, a list of all the committed update transactions is associated with it, called the* commit list. *It attaches the commit list to every read that it sends to the scheduler. When the scheduler receives $r_i(x)$ for a query transaction T_i, it finds the most recently committed version of x whose transaction id is in T_i's commit list. Moreover, a mark is set on data item x which records the read access of T_i. We denote the set of all data items which are marked at time t by transaction T_i as $mark(t, T_i)$.*

Updater transactions use strict two phase locking, so two transactions may not concurrently create new versions of the same data item and the order of a data item's versions (and hence the version list) is well defined. We denote the set of all data items that are written by a transaction T_j as $write(T_j)$. Whenever an updater commits, its transaction id is added to the commit lists of all query transactions T_i for which $mark(c, T_i) \cap write(T_j) = \emptyset$, where c denotes commit time of T_j.

In other words, the modified protocol is like the original one, only whenever an updater commits, its transaction id is added to the commit lists of all those query transactions, which did not yet read any data item that the updater wrote.

528   Alfred Fent et al.

The procedures to purge old versions and to keep the commit list short that are shown in [4] can also be applied to our modified protocol. Moreover, as updater transactions do only write and not read data (i.e., implementation code), the issues of the original protocol in a distributed environment cannot arise here.

Proposition 1. *The protocol of Def. 6 creates only multi-version serializable histories.*

Proof. A formal proof of the proposition can be found in [12]. Intuitively, Def. 6 extends the protocol of Def. 5 in one respect: the commit lists are not determined and kept unmodified during the whole lifetime of a query transaction, but may grow whenever an updating transaction commits. We have to distinguish two cases:

First, for query transactions whose commit list is not modified the protocol is correct, as it then coincides with the one of Def. 5 which is known to be correct.

Second, a query transactions T_i whose commit list is modified did not read any of the data that was written by the committed updater transaction T_j up to commit time of T_j. This is the condition for the commit list to be changed. So the interleaved execution of T_i and T_j is obviously equivalent to a serial execution of T_j before the start of T_i. In the serial case, T_j would be in the commit list of T_i. So adding it in the interleaved case is allowed, too.

Note that the argumentation relies heavily on the fact that query transactions only read data, while updater transactions only write it. This precludes workflows that modify their own specification as they are investigated, e.g., in ADEPT$_{\text{flex}}$ [23].

If there are n queries and m committed updaters, $O(nm)$ modifications of commit lists are performed. However, $O(n)$ accesses are necessary even in the original protocol (Def. 5) to initially create the commit lists. As we can assume that the workflows always outnumber the administrative transactions by far, m is small in comparison to n, and the induced overhead is acceptable.

The marks set during read operations are *not* read locks and consequently do not block writes from updating transactions. They only record access to the definitions and can be used at commit time of an updater transaction to determine the commit lists to be changed: recall that updaters use strict two phase locking. When now the locks on updated data items (i.e., specifications) are released, an *exclusion list* is built containing all ids of query transactions that marked these data items. The id of the committed updater is added to the commit lists of all query transactions not in the exclusion list. As updaters usually consist of only a few writes, the exclusion list can be built efficiently.

As a side effect, the exclusion list can also be used to support workflows that must stick to the old version of a step, e.g., for legal reasons or because usage of this old version is demanded in a contract: it suffices to add the transaction ids of such workflows to the exclusion lists and they will never use a new version during their runtime.

The protocol of Def. 6 ensures correctness, but allows some committed modifications to be visible to query transactions even after their start. In our workflow context this enables active workflows to take advantage of updates to steps they did not yet use.

Example 5. Recall Ex. 4. At the time when T_j commits T_i has not yet read the new version of *ship*. So, using the new protocol T_j is added to T_i's commit list at time 3.2, and T_i will use the new version of *ship* at time 5.

Let again T_i be a productive workflow, and T_j be the administrative transaction which now additionally updates the step *package*. Let T_h be another workflow.

	T_i	T_j	T_h
	...		...
3:	$r_i(collect\_items)$		
3.1:			$r_h(collect\_items)$
3.2:		$w_j(ship)$	
3.3:		$w_j(package)$	
4:	$r_i(package)$		
4.1:		$commit_j$	
4.2:			$r_h(package)$
4.3:			$r_h(ship)$
5:	$r_i(ship)$		

Although *ship* is again read by T_i after the commit of T_j, this time it will return the old version, because T_i already used the old version of *package* (the new version was not yet committed at this time), and consequently T_j will not be added to T_i's commit list at time 4.1. So, the erroneous situation where the old version of *package* and the new version of *ship* are combined is avoided.

However, workflow T_h can use the new definitions, as it did not access any of the updated steps before T_j's commit, and so T_j was added to T_h's commit list at time 4.1. That is, although T_i read the step *ship* after T_h it will correctly see the old version, while T_h already gets the new one.

An additional problem arises through the use of compensation [17] to rollback workflows in case of failures (cf. [15]). As backward operations heavily depend on the forward operations they have to undo, it must be ensured that the correct version is selected even if the steps have been updated between the time the forward and backward operation are called. In ULTRAflow, this is achieved by packaging forward and backward operations together. This is reflected in the set P of all steps because it does not contain special elements for the undo operations, i.e., there is no $ship^{-1}$ or $send^{-1}$. Instead, the Java objects that represent the steps in the implementation always have to provide methods for the forward and backward actions (cf. Sect. 4.1). However, from the administrative transaction's point of view these can only be changed together. The call to a compensating backward operation appears as read access to the specification for the forward operation, and consequently the multi-version concurrency control protocol ensures that the correct version of the implementation is accessed.

Table 1. Compatibility matrices before (a) and after (b) updating semantical information

a)

	a	b
a	+	+
b	+	−

b)

	a	b
a	+	−
b	−	−

5.2 Updating Semantical Information

In the previous section, we described that a multi-version concurrency control protocol can be used to change specifications of steps. Yet there is a subtlety that has to be observed when not only the implementation code but also additional semantical information are changed. Although the latter usually is associated with one specific step, its proposition may involve several steps. Compatibility information as described below is one representative of this phenomenon, but it occurs with other step-related information as well: changing its average duration may have ramifications for other steps if an overall deadline is to be met, new access rights can influence following steps, etc.

In ULTRAflow, every basic operation class contains not only the code for the forward and backward implementation, but also a compatibility matrix as semantical information to facilitate scheduling of concurrent workflows using a nested transaction approach [1,13]. The effects of changes to this matrix can even be shown using standard database conflict serialization theory [4,5,14]. Consider the following example:

Example 6. We assume two transactions T_1, T_2 executing basic operations a and b with a compatibility matrix as shown in Tab. 1a. Note that the matrix is arbitrarily chosen for the sake of the example. The history a_1 b_2 b_1 a_2 $commit_1$ $commit_2$ obviously is serializable as the only operations in conflict are b_2 and b_1.

Now suppose the definition of b has been changed by another transaction. We write $\mu(b)$ to denote this event and get the new history a_1 b_2 $\mu(b)$ b_1 a_2 $commit_1$ $commit_2$. With our concurrency control protocol of Def. 6 transaction T_1 uses the new version of b, while T_2 uses the old one. Still, the overall execution is correct.

But what if the change of the code of b affects its compatibility behavior, i.e., if it implies a new matrix like Tab. 1b? The history a_1 b_2 $\mu(b)$ b_1 a_2 $commit_1$ $commit_2$ is no longer serializable, as after the update b_2 and b_1 imply the order $T_2 < T_1$, while b_1 and a_2 imply $T_1 < T_2$. However, all our correctness criteria state that the history is correct.

Apparently, the change made in the compatibility matrix of b implicitly changed also the matrix of a, and consequently the history should contain modifications of both, a and b, and look like a_1 b_2 $\mu(a,b)$ b_1 a_2 $commit_1$ $commit_2$. In this case it is obvious that T_1 has to execute the old version of b before the change. Then the original compatibility matrix (Tab. 1a) is used, and the history is serializable and thus correct.

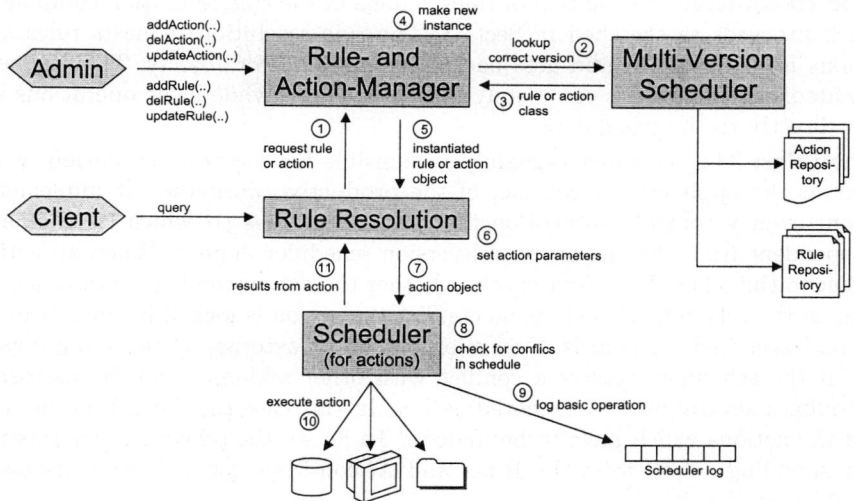

Fig. 3. Ensuring safe modification of operations by using an additional scheduler

The essence of this example is that changes of the semantical information may have effects on more than one operation and that they have to be accounted for adequately. In the case of **ULTRAflow**, it is enough to ensure that a change to semantical information is performed on *every* affected operation. In other systems that require other semantical information the effects of changing semantical information have to be analyzed, too.

6 Implementation within ULTRAflow: An Architecture

The architecture of Fig. 3 incorporates the multi-version scheduling for administrative transactions. The main components are as follows:

Rule- and Action-Manager: The central component of our architecture is the Rule- and Action-Manager (RAM). It manages the registered complex specifications and basic operations in a Rule- and an Action-Repository, resp., which map an action name to the appropriate implementation code (a class file). Each time a request for a rule or action is sent to the RAM, it gets the implementation of the rule or action from the repositories and then creates a new instance. Since the implementation can be changed at any time the RAM accesses the repositories not directly, but through the separate multi-version scheduler. The repositories correspond to the set P of Def. 1.

Multi-version Scheduler: This component implements the protocol as described in Sect. 5 and controls access to the Action and Rule Repositories. As required by the multi-version protocol, older implementations are kept in the repositories, too.

Rule Resolution: Evaluation of rules is done in the rule resolution component which proceeds as sketched in Sect. 3. The rule resolution requests rules and actions from the RAM and gets back instantiated Java objects. This happens repeatedly until a rule is completely resolved [13,18], while basic operations are sent directly to the scheduler.

Scheduler: The scheduler is mainly responsible for a correct execution of actions at the application level, i.e., of the productive workflows. It implements a concurrency control protocol on the basic operations [1] which is in general independent from the one the multi-version scheduler applies. When an action is sent to the scheduler it first checks whether the action conflicts with other actions in the schedule. If there is no conflict the action is logged in the scheduler log and executed afterwards. Execution can affect external systems, databases, etc. If the scheduler detects a conflict with other actions it can be necessary to rollback several actions executed earlier. In this case the log will be used to find the actions which have to be undone. To do so, the scheduler requests the corresponding action from the Rule- and Action-Manager and compensates it using its *undo* method.

Client: Clients are workflow instances that correspond to queries against the workflow rule base and are sent to the Rule Resolution (see below).

Admin: In the diagram, "Admin" stands for administrative tools that update workflow specifications and basic operations, i.e., steps. In the terminology of Sect. 5 these are the updater transactions, while the clients are the query transactions.

The chronological sequence of workflow execution is as follows: assume that a client workflow is started. This corresponds to a query "$\leftarrow q$" which is sent to the Rule Resolution. This component first requests an action or rule object from the RAM by giving the name (1), e.g., "*ship*". The RAM resolves the name and accesses the repository (2, 3) through the multi-version scheduler which returns the correct version of the requested rule or action. It then creates a new instance of the corresponding class (4) and returns this instance to the Rule Resolution (5). The Rule Resolution initializes the object by setting the calling parameters (6) that are bound during the resolution process. Complex sub-workflows are iteratively resolved, i.e., steps (1) to (6) are repeated.

Basic operations are passed to the scheduler (7). Before executing the action the scheduler checks for conflicts with other actions in the schedule (8) and makes an entry in its log (9). Provided the scheduler did not detect any conflicts the action is executed (10). This may cause for example access to a database, the file system or popup a message on the screen. Finally, results are returned to the Rule Resolution through the action object (11) which is given back after the execution.

7 Conclusion

Updating workflow specifications is an important topic in research as well as in practice. We showed how workflow specifications can evolve safely by defining additional administrative transactions which are scheduled using a multi-version concurrency control protocol. This new protocol allows active workflows to use new specifications that were updated even after its start. Furthermore, we showed how this solution is implemented in our WfMS ULTRAflow. The proposed solution can also be applied to application servers and e-services.

Further work includes application of the schema to so-called "scientific workflows" that are only partly specified, as well as tuning of the rule resolution component and its interaction with the rule and action manager. In particular, a prefetching schema for steps is under investigation that can improve the reaction time of the system when a step in a workflow is finished and the next one is to be retrieved.

References

1. G. Alonso, D. Agrawal, A. E. Abbadi, M. Kamath, R. Günthör, and C. Mohan. Advanced transaction models in workflow contexts. In *Proc. 12th Int. Conf. on Data Engineering*, pages 574–583, 1996.
2. Apache Software Foundation. *The Apache HTTP daemon*, 2001. http://www.apache.org.
3. A. Bernstein, C. Dellarocas, and M. Klein. Towards adaptive workflow systems (CSCW-98 workshop report). *ACM SIGMOD Record*, 28(3), 1999.
4. P. A. Bernstein, V. Hadzilacos, and N. Goodman. *Concurrency control and recovery in database systems*. Addison-Wesley, 1987.
5. P. A. Bernstein and E. Newcomer. *Principles of Transaction Processing*. Morgan Kaufmann, 1997.
6. F. Casati, S. Ceri, B. Pernici, and G. Pozzi. Workflow evolution. *Data and Knowledge Engineering*, 24(3):211–238, 1998.
7. D. Edmond and A. H. M. ter Hofstede. A reflective infrastructure for workflow adaptability. *Data and Knowledge Engineering*, 34(3):271–304, 2000.
8. C. Ellis and K. Keddara. ML-DEWS: Modeling language to support dynamic evolution within workflow systems. *Computer Supported Cooperative Work*, 9(3/4):293–333, 2000.
9. C. Ellis, K. Keddara, and G. Rozenberg. Dynamic change within workflow systems. In *Proc. Conf. on Organizational Computing Systems*, pages 10–22, 1995.
10. A. Fent and B. Freitag. ULTRAflow – a lightweight workflow management system. In *Proc. Int. Workshop on Functional and (Constraint) Logic Programming (WFLP2001), Kiel, Germany*, pages 375–378, 2001.
11. A. Fent and B. Freitag. ULTRAflow – Ein regelbasiertes Workflow Management System. In *Innovations-Workshop im Rahmen der Stuttgarter E-Business Innovationstage, 5.-8. November 2001, Stuttgart*. Fraunhofer IAO, 2001.
12. A. Fent, H. Reiter, and B. Freitag. Design for change: Evolving workflow specifications in ULTRAflow. Technical Report MIP-0104, University of Passau (FMI), 2001. http://daisy.fmi.uni-passau.de/papers/.
13. A. Fent, C.-A. Wichert, and B. Freitag. Logical update queries as open nested transactions. In *Transactions and Database Dynamics*, volume 1773 of *LNCS*, pages 45–66. Springer, 2000.
14. J. Gray and A. Reuter. *Transaction Processing: Concepts and Techniques*. Morgan Kaufmann, 1993.

15. C. Hagen and G. Alonso. Exception handling in workflow management systems. *IEEE Transactions on Software Engineering*, 26(10):943–958, 2000.
16. M. Klein, C. Dellarocas, and A. Bernstein. Special issue on adaptive workflow systems. *Computer Supported Cooperative Work*, 9(3/4), 2000.
17. H. F. Korth, E. Levy, and A. Silberschatz. A formal approach to recovery by compensating transactions. In V. Kumar and M. Hsu, editors, *Recovery mechanisms in database systems*, chapter 15, pages 444–465. Prentice Hall, 1998.
18. J. W. Lloyd. *Foundations of Logic Programming*. Springer, 1987.
19. N. C. Narendra. Adaptive workflow management - an integrated approach and system architecture. In *Proc. 2000 ACM Symposium on Applied Computing, Villa Olmo, Italy*, volume 2, pages 858–865, 2000.
20. Object Management Group. *The Common Object Request Broker Architecture, v2.0*, 1997. http://www.omg.org.
21. Orion Software. *The Orion J2EE Server*, 2001. http://www.orionserver.org.
22. T. Pilioura and A. Tsalgatidou. E-Services: Current technology and open issues. In *Proc. 2nd Int. Workshop on Technologies for E-Services (TES), Rome*, volume 2193 of *LNCS*, pages 1–15. Springer, 2001.
23. M. Reichert and P. Dadam. $ADEPT_{flex}$ – supporting dynamic changes of workflows without losing control. *Journal of Intelligent Information Systems*, 10:93–129, 1998.
24. G. Shegalov, M. Gillmann, and G. Weikum. XML-enabled workflow management for e-services across heterogeneous platforms. *VLDB-Journal*, 10(1):91–103, 2001.
25. Sun Microsystems. *Enterprise Java Beans*, 2001. http://www.javasoft.com/ejb.
26. W. van der Aalst. Exterminating the dynamic change bug. A concrete approach to support workflow change. *Information Systems Frontiers*, 3(3):297–317, 2001.
27. C.-A. Wichert. *ULTRA – A logic transaction programming language*. PhD thesis, University of Passau, 2000.
28. C.-A. Wichert, A. Fent, and B. Freitag. A logical framework for the specification of transactions (extended version). Technical Report MIP-0102, University of Passau (FMI), 2001. http://daisy.fmi.uni-passau.de/papers/.

An Alternative Way to Analyze Workflow Graphs

W. M. P. van der Aalst, A. Hirnschall, and H. M. W. Verbeek

Eindhoven University of Technology, Faculty of Technology and Management
Department of Information and Technology
P.O. ox 513, NL-5600 MB, Eindhoven, The Netherlands
w.m.p.v.d.aalst@tm.tue.nl

Abstract. At the CAiSE conference in Heidelberg in 1999, Wasim Sadiq and Maria Orlowska presented an algorithm to verify workflow graphs [19]. The algorithm uses a set of reduction rules to detect structural conflicts. This paper shows that the set of reduction rules presented in [19] is not complete and proposes an alternative algorithm. The algorithm translates workflow graphs into so-called WF-nets. WF-nets are a class of Petri nets tailored towards workflow analysis. As a result, Petri-net theory and tools can be used to verify workflow graphs. In particular, our workflow verification tool Woflan [21] can be used to detect design errors. It is shown that the absence of structural conflicts, i.e., deadlocks and lack of synchronization, conforms to soundness of the corresponding WF-net [2]. In contrast to the algorithm presented in [19], the algorithm presented in this paper is complete. Moreover, the complexity of this alternative algorithm is given.

1 Introduction

Business processes can be formally defined by process models that need to be correct in order to not directly affect business objectives negatively. Proper definition, analysis, verification, and refinement of these models is indispensable before enacting the process model using a workflow management system. There are several aspects of a process model including process structure, data flow, roles, application interface, temporal constraints, and others. The techniques used in this paper, i.e., workflow graphs [19,20] and workflow nets [2], focus on the process structure. The structure of a workflow defines the way of execution, scheduling, and coordination of workflow tasks.

Various approaches to workflow modeling can be found in literature [2,4,7,9,12,13,16,18,19]. Most workflow management systems use a proprietary workflow language. Despite the standardization efforts of the Workflow Management Coalition [13] a "lingua franca" is still missing. The specification of Interface 1/WPDL is ambiguous (no formal semantics is given) and its expressive power is limited. Moreover, the languages of many existing tools and Interface 1/WPDL do not provide starting point for workflow analysis. Therefore, techniques such as workflow graphs [19,20] and workflow nets [2] have been proposed. Workflow nets are based on Petri nets and the application of these nets has been explored by many authors [1,7]. Workflow graphs have been introduced by Wasim Sadiq and Maria Orlowska as a more direct way of modeling workflow processes [19,20].

The design of large workflow specifications can result in hidden errors, which may lead to undesirable execution of some or all possible instances of a workflow. These problems should be corrected during the design phase rather than after deploying the workflow application. Only limited work in literature covers workflow verification. Some issues of workflow structure verification have been examined in [9] together with complexity evaluations. In [18] the issue of correctness in workflow modeling has been identified.

This paper shows that the set of reduction rules for the detection of structural conflicts presented by Wasim Sadiq and Maria Orlowska in [19] is not complete. Instead an alternative algorithm is presented that translates workflow graphs into workflow nets. Workflow nets are a subclass of Petri nets tailored toward workflow analysis [2]. Through this translation it is possible to verify workflow graphs using Petri-net-based analysis tools such as Woflan [21]. In contrast to the technique described in [19], the algorithm presented in this paper is complete. Moreover, the computational complexity of our approach is at least as good as other analysis techniques specifically tailored towards workflow graphs [14].

In this paper we first present the definition of a workflow graph together with its consistency and correctness criteria. A counter example showing that the reduction rules in [19] are not complete and an alternative algorithm and its complexity [14], are presented in Section 3. Section 4 defines Petri nets, workflow nets, and verification criteria. Section 5 outlines an algorithm for mapping workflow graphs onto workflow nets. Woflan, a tool for analyzing workflow process definitions specified in terms of Petri nets is described in Section 6. Section 7 draws the conclusion that the algorithm presented in this paper is complete, efficient, and allows for more advanced constructs such as arbitrary cycles.

2 Workflow Graphs

Figure 1 shows process modeling objects that may be *nodes* or *edges*. The *control flow relation* links two nodes in a graph and shows the execution order. A *node* can either be a *task* or a *choice/merge coordinator*. A *task* stands for work required to reach an objective and is used to build *forks* and *synchronizers*. *Choice/merge coordinators* are represented by a circle. In a workflow graph two nodes are linked together by a control flow relation represented by a directed edge. It shows the execution order between *start tasks* and *end tasks* of a workflow graph.

A *sequence* consists of a node that has an incoming and an outgoing arc.

A *fork* node allows independent execution between concurrent paths within a workflow graph and is modeled by connecting two or more outgoing control flow relations to a task.

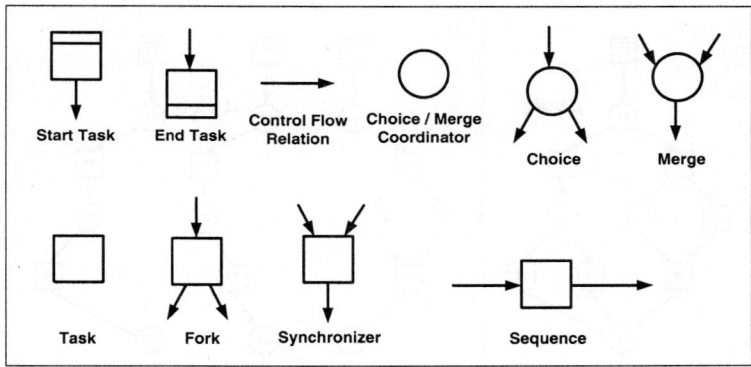

Fig. 1. Process modeling objects

A *synchronizer* node with more than one incoming control flow relation is applied to synchronize such concurrent paths. A synchronizer waits until all incoming control flow relations have lead into the task.

A *choice* node has two or more outgoing control flow relations resulting in mutually exclusive alternative paths. This ensures that only one alternative outgoing control flow relation is selected at run-time.

A *merge* node is the counterpart of the choice node and has two or more incoming control flow relations. It joins mutually exclusive alternative paths into one path.

Definition 1 (Workflow graph). *A workflow graph is a tuple $WG = (N, T, T^S, T^E, C, F)$:*

- *N is a finite set of nodes,*
- *$T \subseteq N$ is a finite set of tasks,*
- *$T^S \subseteq T$ is a finite set of start tasks,*
- *$T^E \subseteq T$ is a finite set of end tasks,*
- *$C \subseteq N$ is a finite set of choice/merge coordinators,*
- *$N = T \cup C$, and*
- *$F \subseteq N \times N$ is the control flow relation.*

The relation F defines a directed graph with nodes N and arcs F. In this directed graph, we can define the input nodes and the output nodes of a given node. $\bullet x = \{y \in N \mid Fx\}$ is the set of input nodes of $x \in N$ and $x \bullet = \{y \in N \mid Fy\}$ is the set of output nodes of x.

Figure 2 shows a workflow graph in the left column. The nodes are represented by rectangles and circles where the first stand for tasks and the latter for choice/merge coordinators. *C1* and *C2* are choice coordinators. *C3* is a merge coordinator. The start and end tasks of the workflow graph are marked as *T1* and *T9* respectively. Control flow relations are modeled as arcs between the nodes.

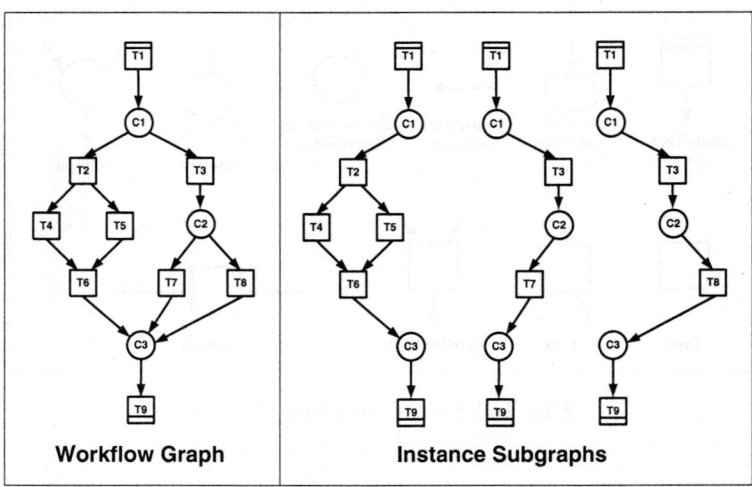

Fig. 2. A workflow graph (left) and its three instance subgraphs (right)

Task *T2* serves as an input node for *T4* while the latter task represents an output node of *T2*.

Definition 2 allows for graphs which are unconnected, without start/end tasks, tasks without any input and output, etc. Therefore we need to restrict the definition to consistent workflow graphs.

Definition 2 (Consistent). *A workflow graph* $WG = (N, T, T^S, T^E, C, F)$ *is consistent if:*

- *for all $t \in T$: $\bullet t = \emptyset$ if and only if $t \in T^S$,*
- *for all $t \in T$: $t \bullet = \emptyset$ if and only if $t \in T^E$,*
- *(N, F) is a directed acyclic graph, and*
- *every node is on a path from some start task to some end task, i.e., for all $n \in N$: there is a $t^s \in T^S$ and a $t^e \in T^E$ such that $t^s F^* n$ and $n F^* t^e$.*

In the remainder we only consider consistent workflow graphs. Moreover, without loosing generality we assume that both T^S and T^E are singletons, i.e., $T^S = \{t^s\}$ and $T^E = \{t^e\}$.

We need to define the concept of instance subgraphs before presenting the correctness criteria for workflow graphs. The right column of Figure 2 shows which possible paths the execution of the workflow graph in the left column might take. Choice coordinator *C1* can lead a token to the fork *T2* or to task *T3*. In the latter case the choice coordinator *C2* leads to the creation of two possible paths of workflow instances. Thus, each of these instance subgraphs represents a subset of workflow tasks that may be executed for a particular instance of a workflow. They can be generated by visiting a workflow graph's

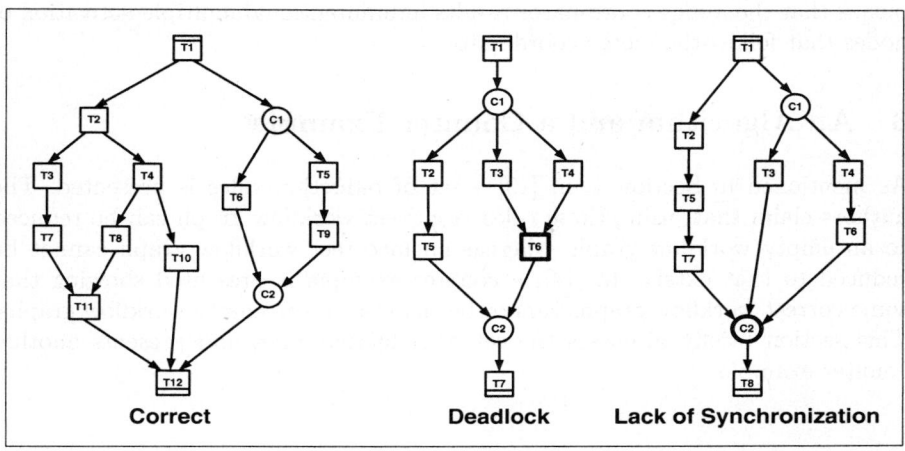

Fig. 3. A correct workflow graph and two incorrect ones exhibiting deadlock and lack of synchronization

nodes on the semantic basis of underlying modeling structures. The subgraph representing the visited nodes and flows forms an instance subgraph.

The semantics of a workflow graph are given by the set of instance subgraphs. Note that instance subgraphs correspond to the concept of runs/occurrence graphs of Petri nets [17]. The concept of instance subgraphs allows us to define the following notion of correctness.

Definition 3 (Correctness criteria). *A workflow graph is correct if and only if there are no structural conflicts:*

- *Correctness criterion 1*
  Deadlock free workflow graphs: A workflow graph is free of deadlock structural conflicts if it does not generate an instance subgraph that contains only a proper subset of the incoming nodes of an and-join node (i.e., synchronizer).
- *Correctness criterion 2*
  Lack of synchronization free workflow graphs: A workflow graph is free of lack of synchronization structural conflicts if it does not generate an instance subgraph that contains more than one incoming node of an or-join node (e.g., a merge).

It has been mentioned that all split structures introduced after a start task must be closed through a join structure before reaching the final structure. Thus, a synchronizer is used for joining fork-split paths and a merge for choice coordinator-split paths. Figure 3 shows examples for a *deadlock error* and *lack of synchronization*. Joining the choice coordinator *C1* with the synchronizer *T6* leads to a deadlock. Similarly, joining the multiple paths leaving start task *T1* with the merge coordinator *C2* introduces a lack of synchronization conflict. It means that the merge coordinator results in unintentional multiple activation of nodes that follow the merge coordinator.

3 An Algorithm and a Counter Example

As mentioned in Section 1, in [19] a set of reduction rules is presented. The authors claim that, using these rules, a correct workflow graph can be reduced to an empty workflow graph, whereas an incorrect workflow graph cannot be reduced to that extent. In [14], a counter example is presented showing that some correct workflow graphs cannot be reduced to the empty workflow graphs. This section briefly discusses the set of reduction rules and presents another counter example.

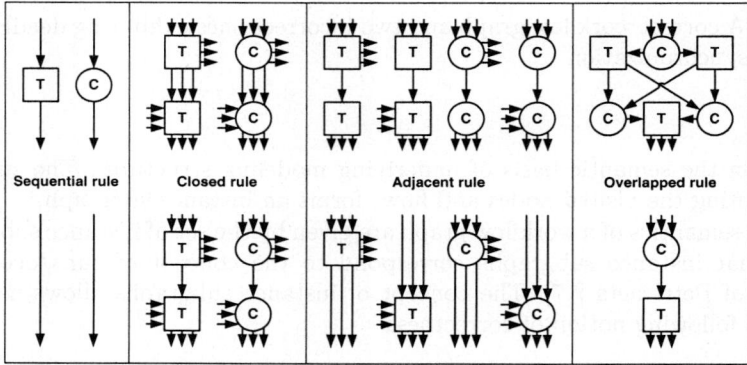

Fig. 4. Reduction rules of [19]

The set of reduction rules as presented in [19] consist of four rules: the *sequential* rule, the *adjacent* rule, the *closed* rule, and the *overlapped* rule. [20] claims that the complexity of applying these four rules is $O(n^2)$, where $n = |N| + |F|$.

- The sequential rule reduces sequential nodes, that is, nodes that have exactly one input node and one output node. A sequential node is reduced by removing it from the graph and adding an arc from its input node to its output node.
- The closed rule collapses multiple arcs between nodes of the same type to a single arc. Note that this rule is slightly out of the ordinary, because in a workflow graph (which is basically a directed acyclic graph [19]) multiple arcs cannot exist. Evidently, in a *reduced* workflow graph multiple arcs are allowed to exist.
- The adjacent rule reduces adjacent nodes, that is, nodes that have exactly one input node or one output node, and where the input node or output

node is of the same type. An adjacent node is reduced by removing it from the graph and adding arcs connecting all its input nodes to all its output nodes.
- The overlapped rule reduces a subgraph in between a coordinator and a task, provided that the coordinator has only tasks as output nodes, the task has only coordinators as input nodes, every input node of the task is an output node for every output node of the coordinator, and every output node of the coordinator is an input node of the task. This subgraph is reduced by removing all output nodes of the coordinator and all input nodes of the task from the graph and adding an arc from the coordinator to the task.

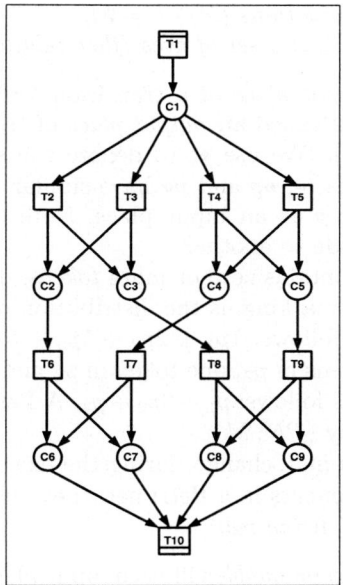

Fig. 5. Counter Example

Figure 4 visualizes the reduction rules proposed by [19]. The upper row shows workflow graph constructs before the application of a particular reduction rule. The lower row displays the results while the columns separate the different rules.

Although [19] claims otherwise, these rules are not complete. Figure 5 shows a correct workflow graph that cannot be reduced by the rules. This incompleteness was already signaled in [14], where another counter example is presented. [14] introduces three additional rules for replacing the overlapped rule, and claims that using the six remaining rules (i) the set of reduction rules is complete, and (ii) the complexity is $O(n^2.m^2)$, where $n = |N| + |F|$ and $m = |N|$. Whereas the counter example shown in [14] only needs two of the three replacement rules (leaving the third rule a bit as a surprise), our counter example needs all three replacement rules to reduce the workflow graph to the empty graph.

4 Workflow Nets

The classical Petri net is a directed bipartite graph with two node types called *places* and *transitions*. The nodes are connected via directed *arcs*. Connections between two nodes of the same type are not allowed. Places are represented by circles and transitions by rectangles.

Definition 4 (Petri net). *A Petri net is a triple* (P, T, F):

- P *is a finite set of places,*
- T *is a finite set of transitions* $(P \cap T = \emptyset)$,
- $F \subseteq (P \times T) \cup (T \times P)$ *is a set of arcs (flow relation)*

A place p is called an *input place* of a transition t iff there exists a directed arc from p to t. Place p is called an *output place* of transition t iff there exists a directed arc from t to p. We use $\bullet t$ to denote the set of input places for a transition t. The notations $t\bullet$, $\bullet p$ and $p\bullet$ have similar meanings, e.g., $p\bullet$ is the set of transitions sharing p as an input place. Note that we do not consider multiple arcs from one node to another.

At any time a place contains zero or more *tokens*, drawn as black dots. The *state*, often referred to as marking, is the distribution of tokens over places. We will represent a state as follows: $1p_1 + 2p_2 + 1p_3 + 0p_4$ is the state with one token in place p_1, two tokens in p_2, one token in p_3 and no tokens in p_4. We can also represent this state as follows: $p_1 + 2p_2 + p_3$. A Petri net PN and its initial marking M are denoted by (PN, M).

The number of tokens may change during the execution of the net. Transitions are the active components in a Petri net: they change the state of the net according to the following *firing rule*:

(1) A transition t is said to be *enabled* iff each input place p of t contains at least one token.
(2) An enabled transition may *fire*. If transition t fires, then t *consumes* one token from each input place p of t and *produces* one token for each output place p of t.

The firing rule specifies how a Petri net can move from one state to the next one. If at any time multiple transitions are enabled, a non-deterministic choice is made. A firing sequence $\sigma = t_1 t_2 \ldots t_n$ is enabled if, starting from the initial marking, it is possible to subsequently fire $t_1, t_2, \ldots t_n$. A marking M is reachable from the initial marking if there exists a enabled firing sequence resulting in M. Using these notions we define some standard properties for Petri nets.

Definition 5 (Live). *A Petri net* (PN, M) *is live iff, for every reachable state* M' *and every transition* t *there is a state* M'' *reachable from* M' *which enables* t.

Definition 6 (Bounded, safe). *A Petri net (PN, M) is bounded iff for each place p there is a natural number n such that for every reachable state the number of tokens in p is less than n. The net is safe iff for each place the maximum number of tokens does not exceed 1.*

Definition 7 (Strongly connected). *A Petri net is strongly connected iff, for every pair of nodes (i.e., places and transitions) x and y, there is a path leading from x to y.*

Free-choice nets from an important subclass of Petri nets for which strong theoretical results exist. In a free-choice net choice and synchronization are separated.

Definition 8 (Free-choice). *A Petri net is a free-choice Petri net iff, for every two transitions t_1 and t_2, $\bullet t_1 \cap \bullet t_2 \neq \emptyset$ implies $\bullet t_1 = \bullet t_2$.*

A Petri net which models the control-flow dimension of a workflow, is called a *WorkFlow net* (WF-net). It should be noted that a WF-net specifies the dynamic behavior of a single case in isolation.

Definition 9 (WF-net). *A Petri net $PN = (P, T, F)$ is a WF-net (Workflow net) if and only if:*

(i) There is one source place $i \in P$ such that $\bullet i = \emptyset$.
(ii) There is one sink place $o \in P$ such that $o \bullet = \emptyset$.
(iii) Every node $x \in P \cup T$ is on a path from i to o.

A WF-net has one input place (i) and one output place (o) because any case handled by the procedure represented by the WF-net is created when it enters the workflow management system and is deleted once it is completely handled by the workflow management system, i.e., the WF-net specifies the life-cycle of a case. The third requirement in Definition 9 has been added to avoid 'dangling tasks and/or conditions', i.e., tasks and conditions which do not contribute to the processing of cases.

The three requirements stated in Definition 9 can be verified statically, i.e., they only relate to the structure of the Petri net. However, there is another requirement which should be satisfied:

> For any case, the procedure will terminate eventually and the moment the procedure terminates there is a token in place o and all the other places are empty.

Moreover, there should be no dead tasks, i.e., it should be possible to execute an arbitrary task by following the appropriate route though the WF-net. These two additional requirements correspond to the so-called *soundness property*.

Definition 10 (Sound). *A procedure modeled by a WF-net $PN = (P, T, F)$ is sound if and only if:*

(i) For every state M reachable from state i, there exists a firing sequence leading from state M to state o.

(ii) State o is the only state reachable from state i with at least one token in place o.
(iii) There are no dead transitions in (PN, i).

Note that the soundness property relates to the dynamics of a WF-net. The first requirement in Definition 10 states that starting from the initial state (state i), it is always possible to reach the state with one token in place o (state o). If we assume a strong notion of fairness, then the first requirement implies that eventually state o is reached. Strong fairness means in every infinite firing sequence, each transition fires infinitely often. The fairness assumption is reasonable in the context of workflow management: All choices are made (implicitly or explicitly) by applications, humans or external actors. Clearly, they should not introduce an infinite loop. Note that the traditional notions of fairness (i.e., weaker forms of fairness with just local conditions, e.g., if a transition is enabled infinitely often, it will fire eventually) are not sufficient. See [2,11] for more details. The second requirement states that the moment a token is put in place o, all the other places should be empty. The third requirement rules out dead parts.

Given a WF-net $PN = (P, T, F)$, we want to decide whether PN is sound. In [1] we have shown that soundness corresponds to liveness and boundedness. To link soundness to liveness and boundedness, we define an extended net $\overline{PN} = (\overline{P}, \overline{T}, \overline{F})$. $\overline{PN}$ is the Petri net obtained by adding an extra transition t^* which connects o and i. The extended Petri net $\overline{PN} = (\overline{P}, \overline{T}, \overline{F})$ is defined as follows: $\overline{P} = P$, $\overline{T} = T \cup \{t^*\}$, and $\overline{F} = F \cup \{\langle o, t^* \rangle, \langle t^*, i \rangle\}$. In the remainder we will call such an extended net the *short-circuited* net of PN. The short-circuited net allows for the formulation of the following theorem. Note that $\overline{PN}$ is strongly connected.

Theorem 1. *A WF-net PN is sound if and only if $(\overline{PN}, i)$ is live and bounded.*

Proof. See [1]. □

This theorem shows that standard Petri-net-based analysis techniques can be used to verify soundness.

For a complex WF-net it may be intractable to decide soundness. (For arbitrary WF-nets liveness and boundedness are decidable but also EXPSPACE-hard, cf. Cheng, Esparza and Palsberg [5].)

Free-choice Petri nets have been studied extensively (cf. Best [3], Desel and Esparza [6], Hack [8]) because they seem to be a good compromise between expressive power and analyzability (cf. Definition 8). It is a class of Petri nets for which strong theoretical results and efficient analysis techniques exist. For example, the well-known Rank Theorem (Desel and Esparza [6]) enables us to formulate the following corollary.

Corollary 1. *The following problem can be solved in polynomial time.*
Given a free-choice WF-net, to decide if it is sound.

Proof. Let PN be a free-choice WF-net. The short-circuited net $\overline{PN}$ is also free-choice. Therefore, the problem of deciding whether $(\overline{PN}, i)$ is live and bounded can be solved in polynomial time (Rank Theorem [6]). By Theorem 1, this corresponds to soundness. □

Corollary 1 shows that, for free-choice nets, there are efficient algorithms to decide soundness.

5 Mapping Workflow Graphs onto WF-Nets

In this section we introduce an approach that maps workflow graphs onto WF-nets. This way Petri-net-based analysis techniques can be used to verify workflow graphs. Figure 6 visualizes the algorithm for mapping workflow graphs to Petri nets. Tasks are mapped onto transitions and choice/merge coordinators are mapped onto places. In row a) of Figure 6 the easiest case of mapping a workflow net to a Petri net can be seen. Whenever a task is directly followed by a choice/merge coordinator then no mapping adjustments are required. In Row b) a place has to be put between two directly connected tasks. It is marked with p and the task labels in brackets.

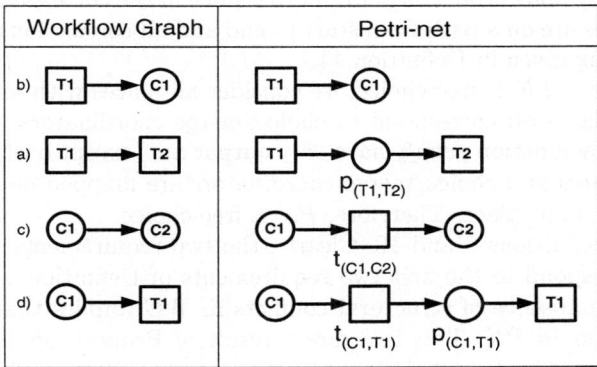

Fig. 6. Mapping workflow graphs to Petri nets

If two choice/merge coordinators are connected to each other as in row c) of Figure 6 then a transition must be put between the corresponding places. The place labels refer to the names of both coordinators. Row d) of the workflow graph column shows a coordinator connected to a task. In order to achieve Petri net mapping, an additional transition and place have to be added. Since the choice is made in the coordinator, a silent transition needs to be introduced. The following definition formatices the mapping of workflow graphs onto Petri nets.

Definition 11 (Petrify). *Let $WG = (N, T, T^S, T^E, C, F)$ be a consistent workflow graph with a unique source and sink node. The function petrify maps a workflow graph onto a Petri net $PN = (P', T', F')$ where:*

- $P' = C \cup \{i, o\} \cup \{p_{(x,y)} \mid Fy \wedge \in T\}$,
- $T' = T \cup \{t_{(x,y)} \mid Fy \wedge \in C\}$,
- $F' = \{(i,t) \mid \in T^S\} \cup \{(t,o) \mid \in T^E\} \cup \{(t,c) \mid Fc \wedge \in T \wedge \in C\} \cup$
  $\bigcup\{\{(c, t_{(c,t)}), (t_{(c,t)}, p_{(c,t)}), (p_{(c,t)}, t)\} \mid Ft \wedge \in C \wedge \in T\} \cup$
  $\bigcup\{\{(c, t_{(c,c')}), (t_{(c,c')}, c')\} \mid Fc' \wedge \in C \wedge' \in C\} \cup$
  $\bigcup\{\{(t, p_{(t,t')}), (p_{(t,t')}, t')\} \mid Ft' \wedge \in T \wedge' \in T\}$

Function *petrify* results in a Petri net satisfying a number of properties as mentioned by the following theorem.

Theorem 2. *Let WG be a consistent workflow graph and petrify(WG) = PN.*

- *PN is a WF-net,*
- *PN is free-choice,*
- *PN is sound if and only if WG has no structural conflicts.*

Proof. It is easy to show that *PN* is a WF-net. There is one source place i and one sink place o. These places are explicitly added by the function *petrify*. Moreover, every node is on a path from i to o since in the corresponding workflow graph all nodes are on a path from start to end and all connections are preserved by the mapping given in Definition 11.

To show that *PN* is free-choice, we consider all places with multiple output arcs. These places all correspond to choice/merge coordinators. All additional places added by function *petrify* have only output arc (except o which has none). All outgoing arcs of a choice/merge coordinators are mapped onto a transition with only one input place. Therefore, *PN* is free-choice.

Consider definitions 3 and 10. Clearly, the two requirements stated in Definition 3 correspond to the first two requirements of Definition 10. Remains to prove that the absence of structural conflicts in *WG* implies that there are no dead transitions in *PN*. This is a direct result of Proposition 13 in [1] which demonstrates that for free-choice nets the first two requirements imply the third one. □

Corollary 2. *The following problem can be solved in polynomial time. Given a consistent workflow graph, to decide if it is correct.*

Proof. For free-choice WF-nets, soundness can be checked in polynomial time (Corollary 1). The mapping given in Definition 11 can also be done in polynomial time. Therefore, correctness of a consistent workflow graph can be verified in polynomial time. □

The complexity of the algorithm presented by Sadiq and Orlowska is $O(n^2)$ where $n = |N| + |F|$ [20]. However, this algorithm does not reduce all workflow graphs without structural conflicts as indicated in Section 3. Lin, Zhao, Li, and Chen [14] claim to have solved this problem. The complexity of the algorithm presented in [14] is $O(n^2 \cdot m^2)$ where $n = |N| + |F|$ and $m = |N|$.

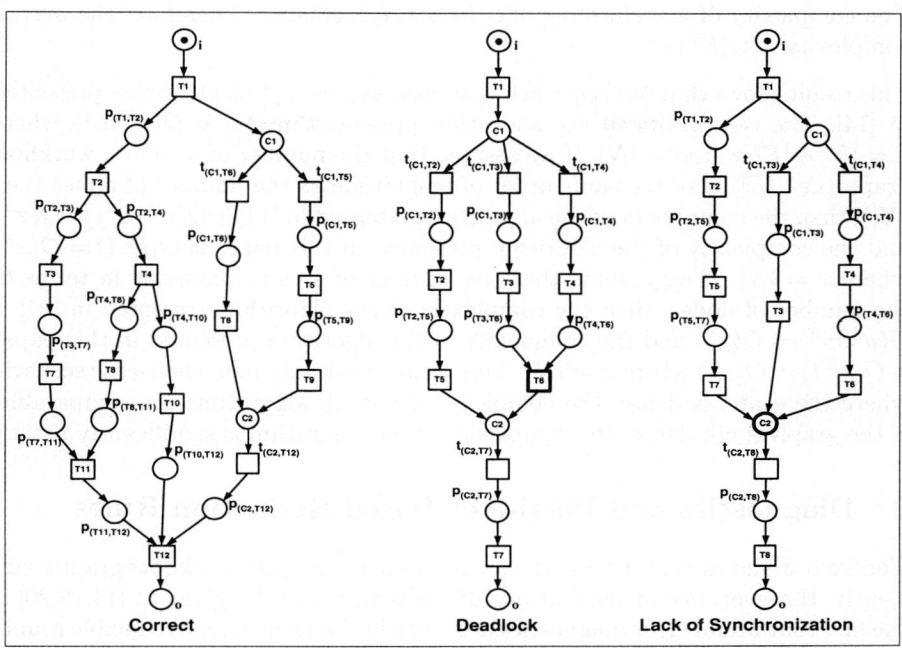

Fig. 7. Three WF-nets corresponding to the three workflow graphs shown in Figure 3

In [10] an algorithm is given which decides whether a strongly-connected free-choice net is live and bounded. The complexity of this algorithm is $O(p^2.t)$ where p is the number of places and t the number of transitions. This algorithm is an improvement of the approach based on the Rank theorem and uses state-machine decomposability by computing a sufficient set of minimal deadlocks to cover the net. This result can be used to analyze workflow graphs efficiently as indicated by the following theorem.

Theorem 3. *Let $WG = (N, T, T^S, T^E, C, F)$ be a consistent workflow graph. An upper bound for the complexity of checking whether WG has no structural conflicts through the construction of the corresponding WF-net and verifying whether the short-circuited net is live and bounded is $O(k^2.l)$ where $k = |C|+|F|$ and $l = |T|+|F|$.*

Proof. $petrify(WG) = PN = (P', T', F')$. The number of places in the short-circuited net is $|P'| < |C| + 2 + |F|$. The number of transitions is $|T'| < |T| + |F| + 1$. The complexity of the algorithm presented in [10] is $O(p^2.t)$ where p is the number of places and t the number of transitions. Hence, deciding whether PN is sound has a complexity of $O(k^2.l)$ where $k = |C| + |F|$ and $l = |T| + |F|$.

The complexity of transforming WG into PN is smaller. Therefore, the overall complexity is $O(k^2.l)$. □

This result shows that our approach is at least as good as the algorithm presented in [14]. The complexity of the algorithm presented in [14] is $O(n^2.m^2)$ where $n = |N| + |F|$ and $m = |N|$. If we assume that the number of arcs in a workflow graph (i.e., $|F|$) is of the same order of magnitude as the number of nodes (i.e., $|N|$), then the complexity of the algorithm presented in [14] is $O(n^2.m^2) = O(x^4)$ and the complexity of the algorithm presented in this paper is $O(k^2.l) = O(x^3)$ where $x = |N|$. If we assume that the number of arcs is quadratic in terms of the number of nodes, then the complexity of the algorithm presented in [14] is $O(n^2.m^2) = O(x^6)$ and the complexity of the algorithm presented in this paper is $O(k^2.l) = O(x^6)$ where $x = |N|$. This means that only in a worst-case scenario where the graph is dense, the complexities of both algorithms are comparable. If the graph is not dense, the complexity of our algorithm is significantly better.

6 Diagnostics and Petri-Net-Based Reduction Rules

Theorem 3 shows that Petri-net can be used to analyze workflow graphs efficiently. However, one of the features of the reduction rules given in [14,19,20] is the fact that useful error diagnostics are given in the form of an irreducible graph. In this section, we briefly discuss the diagnostics provided by our Petri-net-based verification tool Woflan. Moreover, we also provide pointers to Petri-net-based reduction rules. These reduction rules are more powerful than the rules given in [14,19,20].

Woflan (WOrkFLow ANalyzer) has been designed to verify process definitions which are downloaded from a workflow management system [21]. At the moment there are several workflow tools that can interface with Woflan, among which Staffware (Staffware plc., Berkshire, UK) and COSA (COSA Solutions/ Software-Ley, Pullheim, Germany) are the most prominent ones. The BPR tool Protos (Pallas Athena, Plasmolen, The Netherlands) can also interface with Woflan. If the workflow process definition is not sound, Woflan guides the user in finding and correcting the error. Since a detailed description of the functionality of Woflan is beyond the scope of this paper, we will use the example WF-nets shown in Figure 7 and the WF-net shown in Figure 8, which corresponds to the counter example shown in Figure 5, to illustrate the features of Woflan. For the *Deadlock* WF-net, Woflan gives the following diagnostics:

- The net is a WF-net, but is not coverable by so called S-components [6]. Because we know that the WF-net is (by construction) free-choice, we deduce (see [21]) that the WF-net is not sound, and thus that the corresponding workflow graph (see Figure 3) is not correct.
- Woflan points out the fact that a PT-handle exists in the WF-net: Starting from place $C1$ there exist two mutual disjoint paths to transition $T6$. This clearly indicates the source of the error.

The *Lack of Synchronization* WF-net is diagnosed by Woflan as follows:

- This net is also a WF-net, and like the *Deadlock* WF-net, it cannot be covered by S-component. Hence, this WF-net is also not sound.
- In this net, a TP-handle exists: Starting from transition *T1* there exists mutual disjoint paths to the place *C2*. Once more, this clearly indicates the source of the error.

Finally, both the correct WF-net shown in Figure 7 and the WF-net shown in Figure 8 are diagnosed as follows:

- These nets are WF-nets, *and* they can be covered by S-components. As a result, no unbounded places exist and these WF-nets can still be sound.
- All transitions are live, hence the WF-nets are sound.

Note that the WF-net shown in Figure 8 corresponds to the workflow graph shown in Figure 5, i.e., the counter example. This graph can not be reduced by the technique presented in [19,20]. However, it can be analyzed by Woflan.

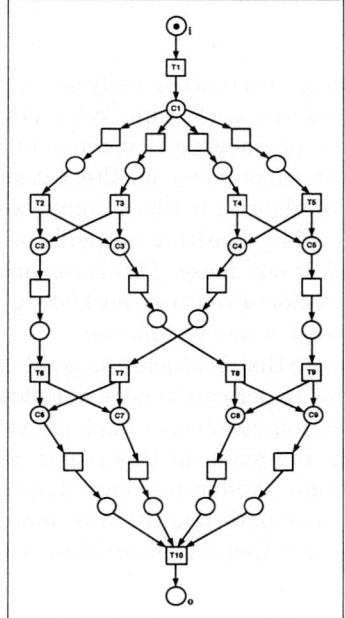

Fig. 8. Counter example mapped to workflow net

Woflan also supports a set of reduction rules. Before the analysis of soundness starts, the reduction rules presented in [15] can be used to reduce the size of the WF-net. These rules have be added to improve the analysis of large models. Note that the set of rules described in [15] is not complete. Therefore, there are sound WF-nets that cannot be reduced to the "empty net". However, for live and bounded free-choice net there is a complete set of reductions rules $\{\phi_A, \phi_S, \phi_T\}$, cf. citedeselesparza. Rule ϕ_A is an abstraction rule which replaces place/transition pairs by arcs. Rules ϕ_S and ϕ_T are linear dependency rules which remove redundant places respectively transitions. As is shown in [6] these rules can be used to reduce any live and bounded free-choice net into a net consisting of one place and one transition. This means that the short-circuited Petri-net representation of any correct workflow graph can be reduced into a net $PN = (\{p\}, \{t\}, \{\langle p,t \rangle, \langle t,p \rangle\})$ in polynomial time. If the workflow graph is not correct, the reduction will stop before reaching the net consisting of one place and one transition. This will provide similar diagnostics as in [14,19,20]. However, (1) only three reduction rules are needed (instead of seven), (2) the reduction applies to a larger class of workflow processes (e.g., having loops), and (3) the rules are more compact and their correctness can be verified using standard Petri-net theory. Currently we are investigating if we can map the seven rules of [14] onto $\{\phi_A, \phi_S, \phi_T\}$.

7 Conclusion

In this paper, we presented an alternative analysis technique for the verification of workflow graphs as introduced by Wasim Sadiq and Maria Orlowska [19,20]. We presented a counter example showing that the reduction rules given in [19,20] cannot be applied. Moreover, we provided an alternative approach for identifying structural conflicts with an algorithm who's complexity is $O(k^2.l)$ where $k = |C| + |F|$ and $l = |T| + |F|$. This algorithm outperforms the algorithm presented in [14] if the workflow graph is not dense. This is remarkable since the techniques presented in [19,20,14] are tailored towards workflow graphs while our approach is based on standard Petri-net-based techniques.

Within a complexity range that is at least as good as the approach presented in [14], the algorithm in this paper can handle workflow graphs with cycles and more advanced synchronization constructs (as long as they correspond to free-choice nets). The mapping presented in this paper, allows for the verification using our analysis tool Woflan. Woflan provides high-quality diagnostics in case of an error and allows for a smooth transition to more expressive models, e.g., workflow languages having non-free choice constructs.

References

1. W. M. P. van der Aalst. Verification of Workflow Nets. In P. Azéma and G. Balbo, editors, *Application and Theory of Petri Nets 1997*, volume 1248 of *Lecture Notes in Computer Science*, pages 407–426. Springer-Verlag, Berlin, 1997.
2. W. M. P. van der Aalst. The Application of Petri Nets to Workflow Management. *The Journal of Circuits, Systems and Computers*, 8(1):21–66, 1998.

3. E. Best. Structure Theory of Petri Nets: the Free Choice Hiatus. In W. Brauer, W. Reisig, and G. Rozenberg, editors, *Advances in Petri Nets 1986 Part I: Petri Nets, central models and their properties*, volume 254 of *Lecture Notes in Computer Science*, pages 168–206. Springer-Verlag, Berlin, 1987.
4. F. Casati, F. S. Ceri B. Pernici, and G. Pozzi. Conceptual Modeling of Workflows. In M.P. Papazoglou, editor, *Proceedings of the 14th International Object-Oriented and Entity-Relationship Modeling Conference*, volume 1021 of *Lecture Notes in Computer Science*, pages 341–354. Springer-Verlag, Berlin, 1998.
5. A. Cheng, J. Esparza, and J. Palsberg. Complexity results for 1-safe nets. In R.K. Shyamasundar, editor, *Foundations of software technology and theoretical computer science*, volume 761 of *Lecture Notes in Computer Science*, pages 326–337. Springer-Verlag, Berlin, 1993.
6. J. Desel and J. Esparza. *Free Choice Petri Nets*, volume 40 of *Cambridge Tracts in Theoretical Computer Science*. Cambridge University Press, Cambridge, UK, 1995.
7. C. A. Ellis and G. J. Nutt. Modelling and Enactment of Workflow Systems. In M. Ajmone Marsan, editor, *Application and Theory of Petri Nets 1993*, volume 691 of *Lecture Notes in Computer Science*, pages 1–16. Springer-Verlag, Berlin, 1993.
8. M. H. T. Hack. Analysis production schemata by Petri nets. Master's thesis, Massachusetts Institute of Technology, Cambridge, Mass., 1972.
9. A. H. M. ter Hofstede, M. E. Orlowska, and J. Rajapakse. Verification Problems in Conceptual Workflow Specifications. *Data and Knowledge Engineering*, 24(3):239–256, 1998.
10. P. Kemper. Linear Time Algorithm to Find a Minimal Deadlock in a Strongly Connected Free-Choice Net. In M. Ajmone Marsan, editor, *Application and Theory of Petri Nets 1993*, volume 691 of *Lecture Notes in Computer Science*, pages 319–338. Springer-Verlag, Berlin, 1993.
11. E. Kindler and W. M. P. van der Aalst. Liveness, Fairness, and Recurrence. *Information Processing Letters*, 70(6):269–274, June 1999.
12. D. Kuo, M. Lawley, C. Liu, and M. E. Orlowska. A General Model for Nested Transactional Workflows. In *Proceedings of the International Workshop on Advanced Transaction Models and Architecture (ATMA '96)*, pages 18–35, Bombay, India, 1996.
13. P. Lawrence, editor. *Workflow Handbook 1997, Workflow Management Coalition*. John Wiley and Sons, New York, 1997.
14. H. Lin, Z. Zhao, H. Li, and Z. Chen. A Novel Graph Reduction Algorithm to Identify Structural Conflicts. In *Proceedings of the Thirty-Fourth Annual Hawaii International Conference on System Science (HICSS-35)*. IEEE Computer Society Press, 2002.
15. T. Murata. Petri Nets: Properties, Analysis and Applications. *Proceedings of the IEEE*, 77(4):541–580, April 1989.
16. M. Reichert and P. Dadam. ADEPTflex: Supporting Dynamic Changes of Workflow without Loosing Control. *Journal of Intelligent Information Systems*, 10(2):93–129, 1998.
17. W. Reisig and G. Rozenberg, editors. *Lectures on Petri Nets I: Basic Models*, volume 1491 of *Lecture Notes in Computer Science*. Springer-Verlag, Berlin, 1998.
18. W. Sadiq and M. E. Orlowska. On Correctness Issues in Conceptual Modeling of Workflows. In *Proceedings of the 5th European Conference on Information Systems (ECIS '97)*, pages 19–21, Cork, Ireland, 1997.

19. W. Sadiq and M. E. Orlowska. Applying Graph Reduction Techniques for Identifying Structural Conflicts in Process Models. In M. Jarke and A. Oberweis, editors, *Proceedings of the 11th International Conference on Advanced Information Systems Engineering (CAiSE '99)*, volume 1626 of *Lecture Notes in Computer Science*, pages 195–209. Springer-Verlag, Berlin, 1999.
20. W. Sadiq and M. E. Orlowska. Analyzing Process Models using Graph Reduction Techniques. *Information Systems*, 25(2):117–134, 2000.
21. H. M. W. Verbeek, T. Basten, and W.M.P. van der Aalst. Diagnosing Workflow Processes using Woflan. *The Computer Journal*, 44(4):246–279, 2001.

Auditing Interval-Based Inference*

Yingjiu Li, Lingyu Wang, X. Sean Wang, and Sushil Jajodia

Center for Secure Information Systems, George Mason University
Fairfax VA 22030-4444, USA
{yli2,lwang3,xywang,jajodia}@gmu.edu

Abstract. In this paper we study the feasibility of auditing *interval-based inference*. Sensitive information about individuals is said to be compromised if an accurate enough interval, called *inference interval*, is obtained into which the value of the sensitive information must fall. Compared with auditing exact inference that is traditionally studied, auditing interval-based inference is more complicated. Existing auditing methods such as audit expert do not apply to this case. Our result shows that it is intractable to audit interval-based inference for bounded integer values; while for bounded real values, the auditing problem is polynomial yet involves complicated computation of mathematical programming. To further examine the practicability of auditing interval-based inference, we classify various auditing methods into three categories: exact auditing, optimistic auditing, and pessimistic auditing. We analyze the trade-offs that can be achieved by these methods among various auditing objectives: inference security, database usability, and auditing complexity.

1 Introduction

Conflicts exist between individual rights to privacy and society's needs to know and process information [24]. In many applications, from census data through statistical databases to data mining and data warehousing, only aggregated information is allowed to be released while sensitive (private) information about individuals must be protected. However, *inference problem* exists because sensitive information could be inferred from the results of aggregation queries.

Depending on what is exactly inferred from the queries about aggregated information, various types of inference problem have been identified and studied. See surveys [10,1,14,12]. Most existing works deal with either the inference of exact values, referred to as *exact inference* (or exact disclosure), or statistical estimators, referred to as *statistical inference* (or partial disclosure).

Interval-Based Inference We study another type of inference. Consider a relation with attributes (*model*, *sale*) where attribute *model* is public and attribute *sale* is sensitive. Assume that a user issues two sum queries and that the correct answers are given as following: (1) The summed sales of model A

---

* This work was partially supported by the National Science Foundation under grant CCR-0113515.

and model C are 200; (2) The summed sales of model A and model B are 4200. Clearly, from those two queries, the user cannot infer any exact value of *sale*. However, due to the fact that attribute *sale* is positive, first the user is able to determine from query (1) that both the sales of model A and the sales of model C are between zero and 200, and then from query (2) that the sales of model B are between 4000 and 4200. The length of interval [4000, 4200], which is the maximum error of user's estimation of the sales of model B, is less than 5% of actual sales of that model. This certainly can be regarded as a disclosure of sensitive information about model B.

The above example indicates that a database attacker is able to infer an accurate enough interval when he or she may not infer an exact value of the sensitive attribute. We call this type of inference *interval-based inference* and the interval *inference interval*.

Interval-based inference poses a different threat to individual privacy in comparison with exact inference and statistical inference. On one hand, exact inference can be regarded as a special case of interval-based inference where the length of inference interval is equal to zero. This means that exact inference certainly leads to interval-based inference while interval-based inference may still occur in the absence of exact inference. On the other hand, the statistical inference is studied in the context that random perturbation, i.e., noise, is added to sensitive individual data. If the variance of the noise that is added is no less than a predetermined threshold, then the perturbed database is considered "safe" in terms of statistical inference. Because the perturbation is probabilistic, it is possible – no matter how large the variance of the noise is – that some perturbed values are close enough to the unperturbed ones, leading to interval-based inference.

Inference Control Techniques For controlling exact inference, many restriction based techniques have been studied (in the statistical database literature) which include restricting the size of a *query set* (i.e., the entities that satisfy a single query) [17,13], controlling the overlap of query sets [15], suppressing sensitive data cells in a released table of statistics (i.e., query results) [9], partitioning data into mutually exclusive chunks and restricting each query set to some undivided data chunks [6,7], and (closer to our concerns in this paper) auditing all queries in order to determine whether inference is possible [8,5,20,23]. For controlling statistical inference, some perturbation based techniques have been studied which include adding noise to source data [27,28], changing output results [2], altering database structure [25], or sampling data to answer queries[11].

Auditing We study the auditing approach in this paper. By auditing, all queries made by each user are logged and checked for possible inference before the results of new queries are released. For auditing exact inference of arbitrary queries with real-valued data, one of the best results was given by Chin and Özsoyoglu [8] in a system called *audit expert*. Audit expert uses a binary matrix to efficiently describe the knowledge about the sensitive attributes (e.g., *sale*), where each row of the matrix represents a query; each column, a database record; and each element, whether the record is involved in the query. Audit expert transforms the matrix by elementary row operations to a standard form and concludes that exact inference exists iff at least one row contains all zeros except one column. It has been shown that it takes audit expert no more than $O(n^2)$ time to process a new query where n is the number of individuals or database records, and no more than $O(mn^2)$ time to process a set of m queries. Recall that audit expert deals with exact inference; one may ask natural questions about interval-based inference: *Is it possible to adapt audit expert to audit interval-based inference?* If not: *Is it tractable to audit interval-based inference?* Answering these questions will shed new lights on auditing and inference control studies.

As pointed out in [20], most of works in this area, including audit expert, assume that the confidential data are real-valued and essentially unbounded. In real world applications, however, data may have maximum or minimum values that are fixed a priori and attainable. In such a case, traditional auditing methods such as audit expert are inadequate, especially for protecting databases against interval-based inference. One reason is that such methods do not take the boundary information into account, which has a significant impact on the inference. To illustrate this, consider a single sum query with each response represented by $\sum_{i=1}^{n} a_i x_i = b$, where a_i is either one or zero, and each real variable x_i is bounded: $l_i \leq x_i \leq r_i$, $1 \leq i \leq n$, then the k-th variable x_k must fall into the following interval I_k:

$$I_k = \begin{cases} [max(l_k, b - \sum_{i \neq k}^{n} a_i r_i), min(r_k, b - \sum_{i \neq k}^{n} a_i l_i)] & \text{, if } a_k = 1 \\ [l_k, r_k] & \text{, if } a_k = 0 \end{cases}$$

For example, given $x_1 + x_2 = 5$ and $1 \leq x_1, x_2 \leq 3$, we have $2 \leq x_1, x_2 \leq 3$ and $I_1 = I_2 = [2,3]$. If the length of the interval I_k is less than a predetermined value (e.g., 5% of the actual value of x_k), then variable x_k can be considered as compromised in terms of interval-based inference. This shows that even a single sum query of multiple variables may be vulnerable to interval-based inference, while audit expert will indicate "safe" in this case.

Another reason is the impact of data types. Recall that audit expert deals with real-valued data. In fact, discrete-valued data (Boolean data or integer data) make the auditing problem more difficult. For example, regarding exact inference, Kleinberg et al. [20] recently proved that auditing Boolean attributes is a NP-hard problem. Hence, as for the problem of auditing interval-based inference, an interesting question is: *What is the complexity for auditing interval-based inference with different types of data?*

Our study answers the above questions. In section 2, we define interval-based inference and formulate the problem of auditing interval-based inference. In section 3, we investigate the particular challenges presented by interval-based inference, boundary information, and different data types. Our result shows that it is intractable to audit the interval-based inference for bounded integer values; whereas for bounded real values, the auditing problem is polynomial yet involves complicated computation of mathematical programming. In section 4, we further examine the practicability of auditing interval-based inference. First we classify various auditing systems into three categories: exact auditing system, optimistic auditing system, and pessimistic auditing system. Then we analyze the trade-offs that can be achieved by these auditing systems among different auditing objectives: inference security, database usability, and auditing complexity. Finally we point out some promising future directions based on our discussions.

2 Problem Formulation

In this section, we formulate the auditing problem. Consider an attribute with n individual values $x_1^*, \ldots, x_n^*$ stored in a database. Denote $x^* = (x_1^* \ldots x_n^*)^T$. A *sum query* (or *query* for short) is defined to be a subset of the individual values in vector x^* and the *query response* the sum of the values in the specified subset.

From the point of view of database users, each individual value x_i^* is secret and thus a variable (to be inferred), denoted by x_i. Let $x = (x_1 \ldots x_n)^T$. To model that database users or attackers may have a priori knowledge about variable bounds, we assume that $l_i \leq x_i \leq r_i$, where l_i, r_i are the lower bound and upper bound of x_i, respectively (l_i and/or r_i can be infinite). We use $l \leq x \leq r$ to denote the boundary information $\{l_i \leq x_i \leq r_i | 1 \leq i \leq n\}$.

By above notation, *each query with its response w.r.t. x^** can be expressed by a linear equation $a_i^T x = b_i$, where a_i is an n-dimensional vector whose component is either one or zero, and b_i is a scalar that equals to $a_i^T x^*$. Similarly, *a set of m queries with responses w.r.t. x^** can be expressed by a system of linear equations $Ax = b$, where A is an $m \times n$ matrix whose element is either one or zero, and b is an m-dimensional vector that equals to Ax^*.

Given a set of queries with responses w.r.t. x^*, $Ax = b$, and the boundary information $l \leq x \leq r$, exact inference and interval-based inference can be defined as follows.

Definition 2.1. (Exact Inference of x_k) In all the solutions for x that satisfy $Ax = b$ and $l \leq x \leq r$, variable x_k has the same value x_k^*.

Definition 2.2. (Interval-Based Inference of x_k) There exists an interval $I_k = [x_k^{min}, x_k^{max}]$ such that (i) the length of the interval I_k, $|I_k| = x_k^{max} - x_k^{min}$, satisfies $|I_k| < \epsilon_k$; (ii) in all the solutions for x that satisfy both $Ax = b$ and $l \leq x \leq r$, variable x_k has values in the interval I_k; (iii) x_k^{min}, x_k^{max} and x_k^* are three of these values (in the interval I_k), where ϵ_k is a predefined threshold called *tolerance level*.

In the above definition, tolerance level ϵ_k (usually $\epsilon_k \ll r_k - l_k$, $k = 1, \ldots, n$) is used to indicate whether variable x_k is compromised in terms of interval-based inference. For example, we may set $\epsilon_k = 5\% \times x_k^*$. Denote $\epsilon = (\epsilon_1 \ldots \epsilon_n)^T$. Interval $I_k = [x_k^{min}, x_k^{max}]$ is called the *k-th inference interval* (or *inference interval* for short). The endpoints x_k^{min} and x_k^{max} of I_k can be derived as the optimal objective values of the following mathematical programming problems (MPs) $\mathcal{P}^{min}[k]$ and $\mathcal{P}^{max}[k]$, respectively:

$\mathcal{P}^{min}[k]$:	minimize	x_k	$\mathcal{P}^{max}[k]$:	maximize	x_k
	subject to	$Ax = b$		subject to	$Ax = b$
		$l \leq x \leq r$			$l \leq x \leq r$

Due to the fact that the feasible set $P = \{x | Ax = b, l \leq x \leq r\}$ of the above MPs is a nonempty bounded polyhedron (note x^* must be in P), the values x_k^{min} and x_k^{max} must exist uniquely.

In the case of $\epsilon_k = 0$, variable x_k has the same value x_k^* in all the solutions that satisfy $Ax = b$ and $l \leq x \leq r$. Therefore, interval-based inference is more general than exact inference.

Problem of Auditing Interval-Based Inference Given a set of queries with responses w.r.t. x^*, $Ax = b$, boundary information $l \leq x \leq r$, and tolerance level ϵ, show there is no interval-based inference for any variable x_k (that is, $|I_k| \geq \epsilon_k$). Specifically, we study the following two problems:

1. *Auditing integer variables*, where x, l, r, b are restricted to be integer vectors. In this case, the corresponding MPs $\mathcal{P}^{min}[k]$ and $\mathcal{P}^{max}[k]$ ($1 \leq k \leq n$) are integer programmings (IPs).
2. *Auditing real variables*, where x, l, r, b are real vectors. In this case, the MPs $\mathcal{P}^{min}[k]$ and $\mathcal{P}^{max}[k]$ ($1 \leq k \leq n$) are linear programmings (LPs).

3 Auditing Interval-Based Inference

We study the complexity of auditing interval-based inference. The complexity results are given with respect to the number of queries (m) and the number of database records (n). By default, we consider arbitrary queries ($Ax = b$) w.r.t. a single sensitive attribute[1] (x^*). For auditing integer variables, we also consider one-dimensional range queries.

Proposition 3.1. *Auditing integer variables is NP-hard.*

Proof: Our proof is based on the result that *auditing exact inference of Boolean variables*[2] is NP-hard [20]. Auditing integer variables is NP-hard due to restriction to the problem of auditing exact inference of Boolean variables by allowing only instances in which $l = (0, \ldots, 0)^T$, $r = (1, \ldots, 1)^T$, and $\epsilon_k = 0$ ($k = 1, \ldots, n$). □

Proposition 3.1 indicates that it is intractable for auditing integer variables of arbitrary queries. This also implies that solving each IP $\mathcal{P}^{min}[k]$ or $\mathcal{P}^{max}[k]$ is NP-hard (Note that the NP-hardness of $\mathcal{P}^{min}[k]$ and $\mathcal{P}^{max}[k]$ cannot be derived directly from the fact that general IP is NP-hard since $\mathcal{P}^{min}[k]$ and $\mathcal{P}^{max}[k]$

---

[1] The setting may involve multiple nonsensitive attributes since they are known to database users. It can also be extended to the queries that even involve multiple sensitive attributes if the auditing system treats them independently; that is, each time a single sensitive attribute is audited while the others are treated as "nonsensitive." We do not consider inferring information using other database features such as schema constraints and functional dependencies. The reader is referred to [4,3] for the study in this aspect.

[2] Auditing exact inference of Boolean variables can be described as follows: Given n 0-1 variables $\{x_1, \ldots, x_n\}$ and a set of sum queries $Ax = b$, show there is no variable x_k ($1 \leq k \leq n$) such that in all 0-1 solutions of $Ax = b$, variable x_k has the same value.

are special IP problems) in that (i) all $\mathcal{P}^{min}[k]$ and $\mathcal{P}^{max}[k]$ ($k = 1, \ldots, n$) are equivalent problems; (ii) if anyone of them can be solved in polynomial time, then all can be solved in polynomial time; therefore, all inference intervals I_k ($k = 1, \ldots, n$) can be computed in polynomial time, which is a contradiction to proposition 3.1.

Although proposition 3.1 indicates that it is theoretically difficult (i.e., NP-hard) to audit integer variables, it does not necessarily mean that the problem is practically unsolvable. People have developed various methods such as branch-and-bound, cutting planes, and heuristics (see, e.g., [19]) to solve IP problems in practice. Such methods can be used in auditing. On the other hand, proposition 3.1 holds in the case of arbitrary queries, the following result shows that it is polynomial in the case of *one-dimensional range queries*. A set of one-dimensional range queries with responses w.r.t. x^* can be defined as $Ax = b$, where the matrix A holds the *consecutive ones property* (i.e., the ones in each row must be consecutive) and $b = Ax^*$.

Proposition 3.2. *For one-dimensional range queries, auditing integer variables is polynomial.*

Proof: We first prove that every vertex $\hat{x}$ of polyhedron $P = \{x|Ax = b, l \leq x \leq r\}$ is an integer vector. By the definition of vertex, there are n linearly independent constraints[3] that are active[4] at $\hat{x}$ (certainly all equality constraints $Ax = b$ must be active). Let $A'x = b'$ denote the active constraints. We know that vertex $\hat{x}$ satisfies the constraints $\hat{x} = (A')^{-1}b'$ and $l \leq \hat{x} \leq r$ and that $n \times n$ matrix A' has the consecutive ones property. Since any nonsingular matrix with the consecutive ones property has determinants $+1$ or -1 [26], the matrix inverse A^{-1} is an integer matrix. Therefore, vertex $\hat{x}$ is an integer vector.

Next we show that the optimal objective value of each LP $\mathcal{P}^{min}[k]$ (actually $\mathcal{P}^{min}[k]$ is IP but we consider its LP relaxation here) is an integer. We know that if a LP has nonempty feasible set and finite optimal objective, then there exists a vertex in its feasible set which is its optimal solution. Let x^{min} denote this vertex of $\mathcal{P}^{min}[k]$. The vertex x^{min} is an integer vector since every vertex of polyhedron P is an integer vector. Therefore, the optimal objective of $\mathcal{P}^{min}[k]$ must be an integer. The same conclusion also holds for LP $\mathcal{P}^{max}[k]$. Hence, inference interval I_k can be computed by any polynomial-time algorithm for LPs $\mathcal{P}^{min}[k]$ and $\mathcal{P}^{max}[k]$ (note that $\mathcal{P}^{min}[k]$ and $\mathcal{P}^{max}[k]$ are actually IPs). □

Regarding to the problem of auditing real variables, we have the following result.

Proposition 3.3. *Auditing real variables is polynomial.*

Proof: The proof is straightforward due to the fact that LP problems can be solved in polynomial time. □

---

[3] A set of linear equality or inequality constraints is said to be *linearly independent* if the corresponding vectors a_i are linearly independent.
[4] Given a linear equality or inequality constraint $a_i^T x \geq b_i$ or $a_i^T x \leq b_i$ or $a_i^T x = b_i$, the constraint is said to be *active* at $\hat{x}$ if $\hat{x}$ satisfies $a_i^T \hat{x} = b_i$.

One of the most efficient algorithms for solving those LPs is Karmarkar's algorithm[19], whose time complexity is $O(mn^{4.5})$ (strictly speaking, the complexity is $O(n^{3.5}L)$ where L is the number of bits required to store each LP $\mathcal{P}^{min}[k]$ or $\mathcal{P}^{max}[k]$ in computer). Therefore, if we solve those LPs $\mathcal{P}^{min}[k]$ and $\mathcal{P}^{max}[k]$ by the Karmarkar's algorithm, the complexity of auditing real variables (or equivalently, auditing integer variables in the case of one-dimensional queries) is $O(mn^{5.5})$ (note that we need to solve $2n$ LPs), which is worse than the complexity result $O(mn^2)$ of audit expert[8] in the case of auditing exact inference.

Because the feasible set $P = \{x|Ax = b, l \leq x \leq r\}$ of LPs $\mathcal{P}^{min}[k]$ and $\mathcal{P}^{max}[k]$ is a convex set, for any $x_k \in I_k$ there exists a solution $x' \in \{x|Ax = b, l \leq x \leq r\}$ such that $x'_k = x_k$. This means that a database attacker cannot obtain any strict subset of I_k without extra knowledge.

4 Auditing Systems with Different Auditing Policies

In the previous section, we studied the problem of auditing interval-based inference. Specifically, we proved the following results: (i) auditing integer variables is NP-hard; (ii) auditing integer variables in the case of one-dimensional queries or auditing real variables is polynomial (w.r.t. the number of queries and the number of database records). In this section, we study various auditing systems that enforce different auditing policies. An *auditing policy* determines under which condition a set of queries are "safe" or "unsafe", and an *auditing system* checks user queries and enforces a particular auditing policy. We analyze the trade-offs among inference security, database usability, and auditing complexity in various auditing systems.

4.1 Auditing System State

We first define *auditing system state* for the purpose of describing auditing systems. The auditing system state consists of three components: *inference security*, *database usability*, and *auditing complexity*, each of which is defined as a lattice.

Definition 4.1. (Inference Security) *Inference security is defined as a lattice* $\langle S, \subseteq_s \rangle$, *where* S *is the power set of* n *variables* $x_1, \ldots, x_n$, *and* $\subseteq_s$ *is subset relationship* $\subseteq$ *on* S.

For each pair $s_1, s_2 \in S$, the least upper bound is $s_1 \cup s_2$ and the greatest lower bound is $s_1 \cap s_2$. Each element $s \in S$ describes an auditing system which *guarantees no interval-based inference (in any set of queries) for any variable in* s. Given $s_1, s_2 \in S$, if $s_1 \subseteq_s s_2$, then the auditing system described by s_2 is safer than the one described by s_1. Particularly, $s = \{x_1, \ldots, x_n\}$ indicates no interval-based inference, and $s = \emptyset$ gives no guarantee on interval-based inference.

Definition 4.2. (Database Usability) *Database usability is defined as a lattice $\langle U, \subseteq_u \rangle$, where U is the power set of the power set of all the queries, and $\subseteq_u$ is subset relationship $\subseteq$ on U.*

Each element $u \in U$ describes an auditing system in which the sets of answerable queries are given by u. For example, if $u = \{\{\{x_2, x_3\}\}, \{\{x_1, x_2\}, \{x_1, x_3\}\}\}$, it means that the auditing system can answer the query $\{x_2, x_3\}$, or any subset of the queries $\{\{x_1, x_2\}, \{x_1, x_3\}\}$. Given $u_1, u_2 \in U$, if $u_1 \subseteq_u u_2$, then the auditing system described by u_2 is more accessible than the one described by u_1. We say that an auditing system described by $u \in U$ provides (i) *appropriate restriction* (on database usability) if $u = u_{approp}$ and u_{approp} contains all the sets of queries except exactly the sets of queries which lead to interval-based inferences; (ii) *strong restriction* if $u = u_{strong}$ and $u_{strong} \subset u_{approp}$; (iii) *weak restriction* if $u = u_{weak}$ and $u_{weak} \supset u_{approp}$; and (iv) *inappropriate restriction* if the system provides neither appropriate nor strong nor weak restriction. An auditing system that provides appropriate or strong restriction is free of interval-based inference, while the one that provides weak or inappropriate restriction gives no such guarantee.

Definition 4.3. (Auditing Complexity) *Given an arbitrary set of m queries on n variables, auditing complexity is defined as a lattice $\langle C, \subseteq_c \rangle$, where $C = \{NP\text{-}hard^5\} \cup \{m^i n^j : i, j \geq 0\}$, and $\subseteq_c$ is a binary relationship on C: (i) for each $c = m^i n^j$ in C we have $NP\text{-}hard \subseteq_c c$; (ii) for each pair $c_1 = m^{i_1} n^{j_1}$ and $c_2 = m^{i_2} n^{j_2}$ in C we have $c_1 \subseteq_c c_2$ iff $i_1 \geq i_2$ and $j_1 \geq j_2$.*

Auditing complexity $\langle C, \subseteq_c \rangle$ is a lattice with infinite number of elements. The lattice is used to classify sets of auditing problems that fall in the appropriate complexity class. For each pair $c_1 = m^{i_1} n^{j_1}$ and $c_2 = m^{i_2} n^{j_2}$ in C, the least upper bound is $m^{min(i_1, i_2)} n^{min(j_1, j_2)}$, and the greatest lower bound is $m^{max(i_1, i_2)} n^{max(j_1, j_2)}$. If $c_1 = m^i n^j$ and $c_2 = NP\text{-}hard$, then the least upper bound is $m^i n^j$, and the greatest lower bound is $NP\text{-}hard$. If $c_1 = c_2 = NP\text{-}hard$, then both the least upper bound and the greatest lower bound are $NP\text{-}hard$. If $c = m^i n^j$, it means that auditing interval based inference will take $\Theta(m^i n^j)$ time (we may also interpret it in terms of space). Similarly, $c = NP\text{-}hard$ indicates that the auditing problem is NP-hard. We use $O(m^i n^j)$ to denote those c satisfying $m^i n^j \subseteq_c c$, and $\Omega(m^i n^j)$ those c satisfying $c \subseteq_c m^i n^j$.

Definition 4.4. (Auditing System State) *The space of auditing system states $\langle \mathcal{O}, \subseteq_o \rangle$ is defined as the product lattice of the three underlying lattices: inference security $\langle S, \subseteq_s \rangle$, database usability $\langle U, \subseteq_u \rangle$, and auditing complexity $\langle C, \subseteq_c \rangle$. The auditing system state of an auditing system is an element $o \in \mathcal{O}$, denoted as a triple $o = \langle s, u, c \rangle$ where $s \in S$, $u \in U$, and $c \in C$.*

---

[5] Note that we assume $NP \neq P$ in definition 4.3. If $NP = P$, the node of "$NP\text{-}hard$" can be simply removed from the lattice $\langle C, \subseteq_c \rangle$ without affecting its validity.

Auditing policy	Auditing result "safe"	Auditing result "unsafe"
Exact auditing "safe"$\Leftrightarrow s = \{x_1,\ldots,x_n\}$	No inference	Presence of inference
Optimistic auditing "safe"$\Leftarrow s = \{x_1,\ldots,x_n\}$	Possible presence of inference (false negatives)	Presence of inference
Pessimistic auditing "safe"$\Rightarrow s = \{x_1,\ldots,x_n\}$	No inference	Possible no inference (false positives or alarms)

Fig. 1. Definition of different auditing policies

4.2 Auditing Policies

Now we define different auditing policies for the purpose of classifying various auditing systems. Given a set of queries, an auditing policy stipulates that under which condition the auditing result "safe" or "unsafe" is given. The auditing result "safe" means that the given set of queries is answerable and that response "unsafe" means unanswerable. Either "safe" or "unsafe" must be given as an auditing result. We define three types of auditing policies given a set of queries:

Exact Auditing The auditing result "safe" is given *iff* no interval-based inference exists; that is, "safe"$\Leftrightarrow s = \{x_1,\ldots,x_n\}$. We denote the auditing system state for exact auditing (policy) as $o_{exact} = \langle s_{exact}, u_{exact}, c_{exact}\rangle$.

Optimistic Auditing The auditing result "safe" is given *if* no interval-based inference exists; that is, "safe"$\Leftarrow s = \{x_1,\ldots,x_n\}$. We denote the auditing system state for optimistic auditing (policy) as $o_{opti} = \langle s_{opti}, u_{opti}, c_{opti}\rangle$.

Pessimistic Auditing The auditing result "safe" is given *only if* there is no interval-based inference; that is, "safe"$\Rightarrow s = \{x_1,\ldots,x_n\}$. We denote the auditing system state for pessimistic auditing (policy) as $o_{pessi} = \langle s_{pessi}, u_{pessi}, c_{pessi}\rangle$.

The definition of the auditing policies is summarized in figure 1. We classify various auditing systems into three categories according to the auditing policies they enforce: *exact auditing system, optimistic auditing system* and *pessimistic auditing system*. The characteristics of these auditing systems can be described in terms of *soundness* and *completeness*. An auditing system is *sound* means that if the auditing system says that there is an interval-based inference, then an inference exists. An auditing system is *complete* means that if there exists an interval-based inference, then the system will say so. In terms of soundness and completeness, exact auditing system is both sound and complete; optimistic auditing system is sound but may not be complete; and pessimistic auditing system is complete but not necessarily sound. In other words, optimistic auditing system may produce false negatives (i.e., some inference may not be detected) but no false positives (false alarms); on the contrary, the pessimistic auditing system may produce false positives but no false negatives. Exact auditing system produces neither false negatives nor false positives.

4.3 Auditing Systems

Now we study the auditing systems that enforce auditing policies. We focus on the trade-offs among the three components of auditing system state $o = \langle s, u, c \rangle$ that can be achieved by various auditing systems. To enforce the optimistic auditing policy, certain interval-based inference can be tolerated if only it is "hard" for database attackers to obtain it. To enforce pessimistic auditing policy, even some restrictions on "safe" queries can be allowed if its impact on database usability is negligible. In both cases, auditing complexity is balanced against inference security and/or database usability.

Exact Auditing System Exact auditing system is defined as an auditing system that enforces exact auditing policy. Exact auditing system can be described as follows: (i) it guarantees no interval-based inference on inference security ($s_{exact} = \{x_1, \ldots, x_n\}$); (ii) it imposes an appropriate restriction on database usability ($u_{exact} = u_{approp}$); (iii) its auditing complexity is NP-hard for interval variables ($c_{exact} = NP\text{-}hard$) and polynomial for real variables or for integer variables in the case of one-dimensional range queries ($c_{exact} \supseteq_c mn^{5.5}$).

Exact auditing system requires that the length of each inference interval $|I_k|$ ($1 \leq k \leq n$) be exactly computed; that is, the *exact* optimal solutions to IPs/LPs $\mathcal{P}^{min}[k]$ and $\mathcal{P}^{max}[k]$ must be obtained. Due to the fast development of computing techniques, these IP problems (for auditing integer variables) can be commonly solved in hundreds or thousands of variables and constraints, so do the LP problems (for auditing real variables) with tens or hundreds of thousands of variables[18]. As a result, exact auditing system can be implemented for small or medium size auditing problems. However, database attackers benefit more from this than auditing systems do. To compromise sensitive information, a database attacker can use dedicate computing resources for a single set of queries. In comparison, to detect all possible inferences, an auditing system must perform the computation for all potential attackers (database users). It is thus impractical in a large auditing system with many users, especially in an on-line environment.

Optimistic Auditing System Optimistic auditing system is defined as an auditing system that enforces optimistic auditing policy. Optimistic auditing system is based on the belief that if it is computationally infeasible to audit an interval-based inference in a set of queries, it is also infeasible for a database attacker to compromise the sensitive information in the same set of queries even though the information is actually revealed in principle. Compared with exact auditing system, we have (i) $s_{opti} \subseteq_s s_{exact}$, (ii) $u_{opti} \not\subseteq_u u_{exact}$[6], and usually we require that $c_{opti} \supseteq_c c_{exact}$. In other words, optimistic auditing system seeks to improve database usability and/or auditing complexity at the expense of inference security. We illustrate this through the following case studies.

---

[6] As to database usability, optimistic auditing resorts to weak restriction or inappropriate restriction. Note that inappropriate restriction can always be transferred to weak restriction by updating database usability $u = u_{opti} \cup u_{approp}$ while at the same time keeping inference security $s = s_{opti}$ unchanged.

Case study 4.1. (Optimistic auditing: auditing by LP relaxation) Consider auditing integer variables by solving the IPs $\mathcal{P}^{min}[k]$ and $\mathcal{P}^{max}[k]$ ($1 \leq k \leq n$). It is NP-hard to solve those IPs under exact auditing policy. However, optimistic auditing policy allows us to compute each "inference interval" by solving LP relaxations of those IPs rather than the IPs themselves (the length of the "inference interval" computed this way is greater than its true value – leading to false negatives). Consequently, auditing complexity is improved from NP-hard to polynomial. □

Case study 4.2. (Optimistic auditing: auditing with relaxed bounds) Consider using relaxed bounds $l' \leq x \leq r'$ in stead of $l \leq x \leq r$ in solving the MPs $\mathcal{P}^{min}[k]$ and $\mathcal{P}^{max}[k]$ ($1 \leq k \leq n$), where $l' \leq l$ and $r' \geq r$. By doing so, the length of the "inference interval" computed is greater than its true value – leading to false negatives, and database usability is improved compared with exact auditing system. □

Optimistic auditing system might be impractical in some applications since it is usually difficult to decide when it is infeasible for a database attacker to compromise the sensitive information that is actually released. Therefore, the implementation of optimistic auditing could be "dangerous" due to the presence of false negatives. This inspires the study of pessimistic auditing system.

Pessimistic Auditing System Pessimistic auditing system is defined as an auditing system that enforces pessimistic auditing policy. Compared with exact auditing system, we have (i) $s_{pessi} = s_{exact}$, (ii) $u_{pessi} \subseteq_u u_{exact}$, and usually we require that $c_{pessi} \supseteq_c c_{exact}$. In other words, pessimistic auditing system ensures no inference on inference security. It seeks to achieve a better result on auditing complexity by imposing strong restriction on database usability. We examine pessimistic auditing system through the following case studies.

Case study 4.3. (Pessimistic auditing: auditing by trace) Given a set of sum queries $a_k x = b_k$, $1 \leq k \leq n$ (or $Ax = b$) w.r.t. $x^* = (x_1^* \ldots x_n^*)^T$, we define the *trace* $\tau(x_i^*)$ of value x_i^* as the set $\{k | a_{ki} = 1, 1 \leq k \leq n\}$. Auditing by trace is based on the following observation: If for each value x_i^*, there exists a value x_j^* such that $|x_i^* - x_j^*| \geq \epsilon$ and $\tau(x_i^*) = \tau(x_j^*)$, then no interval-based inference exists, where ϵ is the tolerance level. The observation is true because a database attacker can never discriminate between variable x_i and x_j.

To implement auditing by trace, we maintain a graph whose vertex set is the collection of the variables. We join variables x_i and x_j by an edge if $|x_i^* - x_j^*| \geq \epsilon$ and $\tau(x_i^*) = \tau(x_j^*)$. Before any set of queries has been presented, we have $\tau(x_i^*) = \tau(x_j^*) = \emptyset$ for any two different variables x_i and x_j. Define the k-th query set as $Q_k = \{i | a_{ki} = 1, 1 \leq i \leq n\}$, $k = 1, \ldots, n$. With each query set Q_k, we delete the edge (x_i, x_j) iff $|Q_k \cap \{i, j\}| = 1$. As long as the graph has no isolated nodes, no inference exists. It is easy to know that the complexity of such implementation is $O(mn^2)$, and that the complexity of checking whether a new query can be answered is $O(n^2)$ – similar to the complexity result of audit expert in the case of auditing exact inference. □

Case study 4.4. (Pessimistic auditing: auditing by approximation) Auditing by approximation seeks to obtain each inference interval with its length smaller than its true value. To achieve this, we solve the MPs $\mathcal{P}^{min}[k]$ and $\mathcal{P}^{max}[k]$ ($1 \leq k \leq n$) using approximate algorithms rather than exact algorithms, as long as these approximate algorithms stop at feasible solutions of the original MPs. In mathematical programming literature, many approximate algorithms provide feasible solutions and have better time complexity compared with corresponding exact algorithms. □

Case study 4.5. (Pessimistic auditing: auditing by feasible solution) Auditing by feasible solution seeks the same objective as auditing by approximation; however, it directly uses the exact algorithms of the MPs and stop in the middle as long as feasible solutions are obtained. If the exact algorithms search the optimal solutions within feasible sets (actually most exact algorithms do so), we can always achieve polynomial time complexity since we can stop the algorithms at any time (it should be balanced against database usability requirement). □

Case study 4.6. (Pessimistic auditing: auditing with enhanced bounds) Consider using enhanced bounds $l' \leq x \leq r'$ in stead of $l \leq x \leq r$ in solving the MPs $\mathcal{P}^{min}[k]$ and $\mathcal{P}^{max}[k]$ ($1 \leq k \leq n$), where $l' \geq l$ and $r' \leq r$. By doing so, the length of the "inference interval" computed is less than its true value – leading to false alarms, and database usability is decreased compared with exact auditing system. □

Integrated Auditing Systems In practice, there might exist many different ways to implement pessimistic auditing (or optimistic auditing). Each way can be considered as an independent auditing system, called *pessimistic (or optimistic) auditing unit*. A number of such auditing units can be integrated into a generic framework, called *integrated pessimistic (or optimistic) auditing system*. In the following discussion, we focus on integrated pessimistic auditing system; while the extension to integrated optimistic auditing system is trivial.

Integrated pessimistic auditing system is shown in figure 2. For convenience, denote the auditing system state of unit i using $o_i = \langle s_i, u_i, c_i \rangle$ and the integrated system using $o_{sys} = \langle s_{sys}, u_{sys}, c_{sys} \rangle$. In figure 2, when a unit receives its input, it first determines whether it is applicable for the input. If not, it hands over the input to the next unit (if available); otherwise, it audits the input. If the auditing result is "safe", the whole auditing process is terminated with result "safe" (due to that pessimistic auditing produces no false negatives); otherwise, the input is handed over to the next unit (if available). When the last unit outputs "unsafe", the whole auditing process is terminated with the result "unsafe" (though it is still possible the input is "safe" – false alarm).

Briefly speaking, integrated pessimistic auditing system responses "safe" iff one of its unit answers "safe". It is clear that the integrated system enforces pessimistic auditing policy; we have (i) $s_{sys} = \cap_i s_i$ ($s_{sys} = s_{exact} = \{x_1, \ldots, x_n\}$), (ii) $u_{sys} = \cup_i u_i$ ($u_{sys} \subseteq_u u_{exact}$), and (iii) c_{sys} is no worse than the greatest lower bound of those c_i in the auditing complexity lattice (see definition 4.3). Note

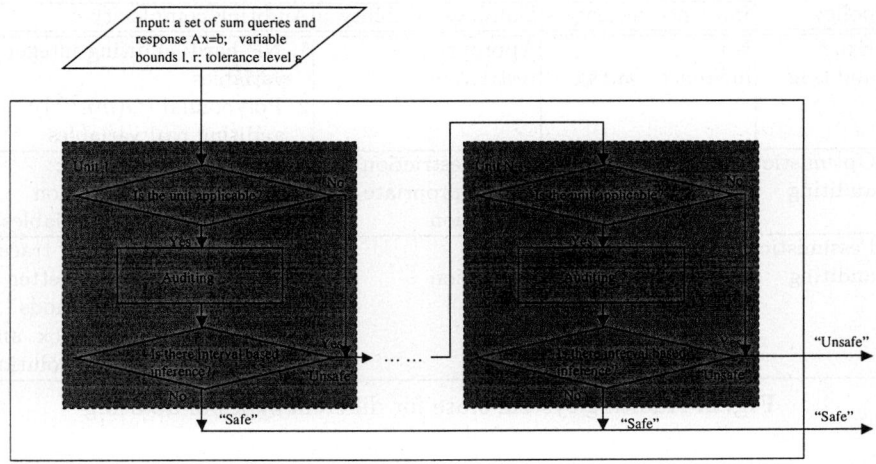

Fig. 2. Integrated pessimistic auditing system

that sorting the units in certain orders may help improve auditing complexity of the system; however, we do not address this issue in this paper.

For integrated optimistic auditing system, our purpose is to increase the auditing security at the expense of database usability and/or the auditing complexity. The system responses "safe" iff all (or many) its units response "safe". In this case, we have (i) $s_{sys} = \cup_i s_i$, (ii) $u_{sys} = \cap_i u_i$, and (iii) c_{sys} is no worse than the greatest lower bound of those c_i in the auditing complexity lattice.

Finally, the auditing system state for various types of auditing discussed in this paper is summarized in figure 3.

5 Conclusion and Future Directions

In this paper, we pointed out the significance to investigate interval based inference and formulated the auditing problem formally. Our study showed that: (1) The auditing problem invalidates existing methods (e.g., audit expert) designed for auditing exact inference. (2) Auditing interval-based inference is possible; however, it involves complicated computation of mathematical programming. The complexity of auditing integer variables is NP-hard, while auditing real variables is polynomial. (3) Under different auditing policies, various auditing systems can be classified into three categories: exact auditing, optimistic auditing, and pessimistic auditing. Trade-offs can be achieved by different auditing systems among inference security, database usability and auditing complexity.

Auditing policy	auditing system state $o = \langle s, u, c \rangle$		
	Inference security s	Database usability u	Auditing complexity c
Exact auditing	No inference	Appropriate restriction	1. NP-hard: auditing integer variables 2. Polynomial ($O(mn^{5.5})$): auditing real variables
Optimistic auditing	Possible presence of some inferences	Weak restriction or inappropriate restriction	Polynomial ($O(mn^{5.5})$): auditing by LP relaxation for auditing integer variables
Pessimistic auditing	No inference	Strong restriction	1. $O(mn^2)$: auditing by trace 2. Possible to achieve better results by other methods e.g. auditing by approx. and auditing by feasible solution

Fig. 3. Auditing system state for different types of auditing

For practical auditing systems, we believe that the optimistic auditing and pessimistic auditing are promising. Also, observe that many real world applications, such as OLAP, restrict user queries to specific meaningful forms; we may take advantage of such restrictions to build efficient audit systems for such applications. It would also be interesting to reconsider other inference control methods such as microaggregation (see, e.g., [16,22]) and random data perturbation (RDP) techniques for interval-based inference [21]. Although such techniques would provide users imprecise (perturbed) query responses rather than exact responses, the upper side is that no restrictions are imposed on user queries and that the complexity for perturbing data is low.

6 Acknowledgments

We thank the anonymous referees for their valuable comments.

References

1. N.R. Adam and J.C. Wortmann. Security-control methods for statistical databases: a comparative study. *ACM Computing Surveys*, 21(4):515–556, 1989.
2. L.L. Beck. A security mechanism for statistical databases. *ACM Trans. on Database Systems*, 5(3):316–338, 1980.
3. A. Brodsky, C. Farkas, and S. Jajodia. Secure databases: Constraints, inference channels, and monitoring disclosures. *IEEE Trans. Knowledge and Data Engineering*, 12(6):900–919, 2000.
4. A. Brodsky, C. Farkas, D. Wijesekera, and X.S. Wang. Constraints, inference channels and secure databases. In *the 6th International Conference on Principles and Practice of Constraint Programming*, pages 98–113, 2000.
5. F.Y. Chin, P. Kossowski, and S.C. Loh. Efficient inference control for range sum queries. *Theoretical Computer Science*, 32:77–86, 1984.

6. F.Y. Chin and G. Özsoyoglu. Security in partitioned dynamic statistical databases. In *Proc. of IEEE COMPSAC*, pages 594–601, 1979.
7. F.Y. Chin and G. Özsoyoglu. Statistical database design. *ACM Trans. on Database Systems*, 6(1):113–139, 1981.
8. F.Y. Chin and G. Özsoyoglu. Auditing and inference control in statistical databases. *IEEE Trans. on Software Engineering*, 8(6):574–582, 1982.
9. L.H. Cox. Suppression methodology and statistical disclosure control. *Journal of American Statistic Association*, 75(370):377–385, 1980.
10. D.E. Denning. Are statistical data bases secure? In *AFIPS conference proceedings*, volume 47, pages 199–204, 1978.
11. D.E. Denning. Secure statistical databases with random sample queries. *ACM Trans. on Database Systems*, 5(3):291–315, 1980.
12. D.E. Denning and P.J. Denning. Data security. *ACM computing surveys*, 11(3):227–249, 1979.
13. D.E. Denning, P.J. Denning, and M.D. Schwartz. The tracker: A threat to statistical database security. *ACM Trans. on Database Systems*, 4(1):76–96, 1979.
14. D.E. Denning and J. Schlörer. Inference controls for statistical databases. *IEEE Computer*, 16(7):69–82, 1983.
15. D. Dobkin, A.K. Jones, and R.J. Lipton. Secure databases: protection against user influence. *ACM Trans. on Database Systems*, 4(1):97–106, 1979.
16. J. Domingo-Ferrer and J. M. Mateo-Sanz. Practical data-oriented microaggregation for statistical disclosure control. *IEEE Trans. Knowledge and Data Engineering (to appear)*.
17. L.P. Fellegi. On the qestion of statistical confidentiality. *Journal of American Statistic Association*, 67(337):7–18, 1972.
18. R. Fourer. Linear programming frequently asked questions. Optimization Technology Center of Northwestern University and Argonne National Laboratory, 2001. http://www-unix.mcs.anl.gov/otc/Guide/faq/linear-programming-faq.html.
19. J.P. Ignizio and T.M. Cavalier. *Linear Programming*. Prentice Hall, 1994.
20. J. Kleinberg, C. Papadimitriou, and P. Raghavan. Auditing boolean attributes. In *Proc. of the 9th ACM SIGMOD-SIGACT-SIGART Symposium on Principles of Database Systems*, pages 86–91, 2000.
21. Y. Li, L. Wang, and S. Jajodia. Preventing interval-based inference by random data perturbation. In *Workshop on Privacy Enhancing Technologies (to appear)*.
22. Y. Li, S. Zhu, L. Wang, and S. Jajodia. A privacy-enhanced microaggregation method. In *Proc. of the 2nd International Symposium on Foundations of Information and Knowledge Systems*, pages 148–159, 2002.
23. F.M. Malvestuto and M. Moscarini. Computational issues connected with the protection of sensetive statistics by auditing sum-queries. In *Proc. of IEEE Scientific and Statistical Database Management*, pages 134–144, 1998.
24. M.A. Palley. Security of statistical databases compromise through attribute correlational modeling. In *Proc. of IEEE Conference on Data Engineering*, pages 67–74, 1986.
25. J. Schlörer. Security of statistical databases: multidimensional transformation. *ACM Trans. on Database Systems*, 6(1):95–112, 1981.
26. A. Schrijver. *Theory of Linear and Integer Programming*. Wiley, 1986.
27. J.F. Traub, Y. Yemini, and H. Woźnaikowski. The statistical security of a statistical database. *ACM Trans. on Database Systems*, 9(4):672–679, 1984.
28. S.L. Warner. A survey technique for eliminating evasive answer bias. *Journal of American Statistic Association*, 60(309):63–69, 1965.

A Logical Foundation for XML

Mengchi Liu

School of Computer Science, Carleton University
Ottawa, Ontario, Canada K1S 5B6
mengchi@scs.carleton.ca

Abstract. XML is fast emerging as the dominant standard for data representation and exchange on the World Wide Web. How to view an XML document, i.e., XML data model, and how to query XML documents are two primary research issues for XML. The purpose of this paper is twofold. First, we propose a novel data model for XML that allows us to view XML data in a way similar to complex object data models. Based on this data model, we then investigate how rule-based paradigm can be used to query XML documents and what benefits it brings over existing XML query languages. To this end, we present a rule-based query language called XML-RL, in which we treat existing XML documents as extensional databases, and the queries and functions expressed in rules as intensional databases as in deductive databases. We show that the querying part and result constructing part in XML-RL are strictly separated, the rule body is used to query XML documents and bind variables while the rule head is used to construct the resulting XML document. As several rules can be used for the same query, complex queries can be expressed in XML-RL in a simple and natural way as in logic programming. Also, rules provide a uniform framework for both functions/methods and queries and support recursion in a natural way. Finally, rule-based framework has a formal logic foundation that is lacking in other query languages.

1 Introduction

XML is fast emerging as the dominant standard for data representation and exchange on the World Wide Web. Unlike HTML in which tags are mainly used to describe how to display data, XML tags describe the data itself so that XML data is self-describing. Therefore, a program receiving an XML document can interpret it in multiple ways, can extract, synthesize, and analyze its contents, and restructure it to suit the application's needs.

How to view an XML document, i.e., XML data model, and how to query XML documents are two primary research issues for XML. There are several data models proposed for XML, such as DOM [1], XSL data model [4], XML information set [11], and XML Query Data Model [14]. However, they are low-level data models using nodes and trees and are primarily for machine representation of XML documents.

There are also several query languages proposed for extracting and restructuring the XML contents, such as Lorel [3], XML-GL [7], XPath [10], XML-QL [12], XSL [4], XQuery [9], XML Query Algebra [13], etc. Some of them are in the tradition of database query languages, others more closely inspired by XML. The XML Query Working Group has recently published XML Query Requirements for XML query languages [8]. The discussion is going on within the World Wide Web Consortium, within many academic forums and within IT industry, with XQuery been selected as the basis for an official W3C query language for XML. In our view, the main problem with existing query languages, including XQuery, is that the query part and the result constructing part are intermixed, an inherent problem inherited from SQL and OQL [6]. For example, XQuery uses a FOR-LET-WHERE-RETURN (FLWR) construct similar to SQL. The FOR clause plays the same role as the FROM clause in SQL, the LET clause binds a variable to an entire expression, the WHERE clause functions the same as in SQL, and the RETURN clause is analogous to SELECT used to construct/restructure the query results. Like SQL and OQL, simple FLWR construct cannot express complex queries and construct/restructure query results so that the FLWR construct has to be nested in the RETURN clause, and thus makes queries complicated to comprehend.

Also, current work on XML lacks logic foundation to account for various features introduced.

In this paper, we first propose a novel data model for XML that allows us to view XML data in a way similar to complex object data models [2]. Based on this data model, we then investigate how rule-based paradigm can be used to query XML documents and what benefits it brings over existing XML query languages. To this end, we present a rule-based query language called XML-RL, in which we treat existing XML documents as extensional databases, and the queries and functions expressed in rules as intensional databases as in deductive databases. We show that the querying part and result constructing part in XML-RL are strictly separated, the rule body is used to query XML documents and bind variables while the rule head is used to construct the resulting XML document. As several rules can be used for the same query, complex queries can be expressed in XML-RL in a simple and natural way as in logic programming. Also, rules provide a uniform framework for both functions/methods and queries and support recursion in a natural way. Finally, rule-based framework has a formal logic foundation that is lacking in other query languages.

The rest of the paper is organized as follows. Section 2 introduces our data model for XML. Section 3 defines our rule-based query language for XML. Section 4 summarizes and points out further research issues.

2 Data Model for XML

In this section, we introduce our data model for XML. We assume the existence of a set $\mathcal{U}$ of URLs, a set $\mathcal{C}$ of constants, and the symbol *null*.

Definition 1. The notion of *objects* is defined as follows:

(1) null is an *empty* object.
(2) Let $c \in \mathcal{C}$ be a constant. Then c is a *lexical* object.
(3) Let $o_1, ..., o_n$ be objects with $n \geq 0$. Then $\langle o_1, ..., o_n \rangle$ is a *list* object.
(4) Let $a \in \mathcal{C}$ be a constant, and o a lexical object or a list of lexical objects. Then @$a : o$ is an *attribute* object and o is the *value* of the attribute a.
(5) Let @$a_1 : o_1$,...,@$a_m : o_m$ be attribute objects, $p_1, ..., p_n$ be element, lexical, or empty objects with $m \geq 0, n > 0$. Then $o = $ (@$a_1 : o_1, ...,$ @$a_m : o_m, p_1, ..., p_n$) is a *tuple* object, with two components: attribute component and content component and can be written as $o = $ @$(a_1 : o_1, ..., a_m : o_m)(p_1, ..., p_n)$. When $m = 0$, it is a *pure content* tuple object and can be written as $o = (p_1, ..., p_n)$. When $n = 1$ and p_1 is either *null* or a lexical object, we can also write it as $o = $ @$(a_1 : o_1, ..., a_m : o_m)p_1$.
(6) Let $o = (o_1, ..., o_i, ..., o_n)$ be a tuple object. If o_i is an attribute/element object with a list value, i.e, $o_i = l_i : \langle p_1, ..., p_m \rangle$ with $n \geq 1$, then we can replace it in o with m sequential attribute/element objects as $(o_1, ..., l_i : p_1, ..., l_i : p_m, ..., o_n)$ and vice versa. If every such attribute/element object is replaced in this way, then the resulting tuple object is *flat*. If none of such attribute/element objects are replaced in this way, then o is *normalized*.
(7) Let $e \in \mathcal{C}$ be a constant, and o a tuple object. Then $e : o$ is an *element* object.

The following are examples of objects:

Lexical objects: Computer Science, Database Systems
List objects: ⟨John, Mary⟩, ⟨o123, o234⟩
Attribute objects: @id: o123, @year: 1995, @children: ⟨o123,o234⟩
Tuple object: (@id:o123, @children:⟨o123, o234⟩, title:XML)
Element objects: address:null, title:XML, name:(First:Smith, Last:John)

Lexical objects correspond to character data and attribute values in XML, list objects are used to represent the multiple values of the same attributes or elements, attribute objects to represent attribute-value pairs in XML, tuple objects to represent the relationship among attributes and elements in XML, and element objects to represent element-data pairs, Like other proposals for XML, we use the symbol @ in front of attributes to differ them from elements in tuple objects.

Note that a tuple object in our data model can have several different views: flat view, normalized view and their various mixtures based on Item (6) in Definition 1. The following examples demonstrate their difference:

(@children : o123, @children : o234, title : XML, author : John, author : Tony)
(@children : ⟨o123, o234⟩, title : XML, author : ⟨John, Tony⟩)
(@children : ⟨o123, o234⟩, title : XML, author : John, author : Tony)

The first view is flat as it does not show any list objects. The second view is normalized as it only uses list objects. The last view only shows list objects for attribute objects but not for element objects and is much closer to XML presentation of data. In the rule-based query language introduced in Section 3, we use the flat view when we have individual variables and use the normalized view when we have list variables.

Conversion between XML and our model is straightforward using the following tranformation operator T:

(1) Let s be a character string or a quoted character string. Then $T(s) = s$.
(2) Let $s = "s_1...s_n"$ be a list of quoted character strings separated by the white space. Then $T(s) = \langle T(s_1), ..., T(s_n) \rangle$.
(3) Let E be a null element: $E = \langle e\ A_1...A_m/ \rangle$ or $E = \langle e\ A_1...A_m \rangle \langle /e \rangle$ with $m \geq 0$. Then $T(E) = e : (T(A_1), ..., T(A_m))null$.
(4) Let E be a children or mixed element: $E = \langle e\ A_1...A_m \rangle E_1...E_n \langle /e \rangle$ with $m \geq 0$ and $m > 0$. Then $T(E) = e : (T(A_1), ..., T(A_m), T(E_1), ..., T(E_n))$.

The following are several simple examples:

$T(\text{John}) = \text{John}$	by (1)
$T("\text{John}") = \text{John}$	by (1)
$T("\text{o123 o234}") = \langle \text{o123,o234} \rangle$	by (2)
$T(\langle \text{person id}="\text{o123}"/ \rangle) = \text{person: (@id:o123) null}$	by (3)
$T(\langle \text{name} \rangle \text{John} \langle /\text{name} \rangle) = \text{name: John}$	by (4)
$T(\langle \text{person id}="\text{o123}" \rangle \langle \text{name} \rangle \text{John} \langle /\text{name} \rangle \langle /\text{person} \rangle)$	
$= \text{person: (@id: o123, name: John)}$	by (4)
$T(\langle \text{person id}="\text{o234}" \rangle \text{Tony} \langle /\text{person} \rangle) = \text{person: (@id: o123) Tony}$	by (4)

Example 1. Consider the following XML document:

```
<chapter>
    <title>Data Model</title>
    <section>
        <title> Syntax For Data Model</title>
    </section>
    <section>
        <title>XML</title>
        <section>
            <title>Basic Syntax</title>
        </section>
        <section>
            <title> XML and Semistructured Data</title>
        </section>
    </section>
</chapter>
```

It is transformed into our data model as the following attribute object:

```
chapter: (title: Data Model,
         section: (title: Syntax For Data Model),
         section: (title: XML,
                   section: (title: Basic Syntax),
                   section: (title: XML and Semestructured Data)))
```

Example 2. Consider another example:

```
<bib>
   <book year="1995">
     <title> Introduction to DBMS </title>
     <author> <last> Date </last> <first> C. </first></author>
     <publisher> <name> Addison-Wesley </name > </publisher>
   </book>
   <book year="1998">
     <title> Foundation for ORDB</title>
     <author> <last> Date </last> <first> C. </first></author>
     <author> <last> Darwen </last> <first> D. </first></author>
     <publisher> <name> Addison-Wesley </name > </publisher>
   </book>
   <book></book>
</bib>
```

It is transformed into our data model as follows:

```
bib: (book: (@year:1995,
             title: Introduction to DBMS,
             author: (last: Date, first: C.),
             publisher: (name: Addison-Wesley)),
      book: (@year:1998,
             title: Foundation for ORDB,
             author: (last: Date, first: C.),
             author: (last: Darwen, first: D.),
             publisher: (name: Addison-Wesley))
      book: null)
```

Note here that the element object is in flat form.

Example 3. Consider the following DTD and the corresponding XML document with ID, IDREF and IDREFS attributes:

```
<!ELEMENT people (person+)>
<!ELEMENT person (name)>
<!ELEMENT name (#PCDATA)>
<!ATTLIST  person
           id ID #REQUIRD
           mother IDREF #IMPLIED
           children IDREFS #IMPLIED>
```

```
<people>
  <person id="o123">
    <name>Jane</name>
  </person>
  <person id="o234" mother="o456">
    <name>John</name>
  </person>
  <person id="o456" children ="o123 o234">
    <name>Mary</name>
  </person>
</people>
```

It is transformed into our data model as follows:

people: (person: (@id:o123, name: Jane),
         person: (@id:o234, @mother: o456, name: John),
         person: (@id:o456, @children: ⟨o123,o234⟩, name: Mary))

The following example demonstrate how to represent XML document with mixed content in our data model.

Example 4. Consider the following example:

```
<Address>
John lives on
<Street>Main St</Street>
with house number
<Number>123</Number>
in
<City>Ottawa</City>
<Country>Canada</Country>
</Address>
```

It is transformed into our data model as follows:

Address:(John lives on,
         Street: Main St,
         with house number,
         Number: 123,
         in,
         City: Ottawa,
         Country: Canada)

A well formed XML document over the Web has a URL and exactly one root element. We therefore introduce the following notion to represent it in our data model.

Definition 2. Let u be a URL and e be an element object. Then $(u)/e$ is an XML object.

Suppose the XML document shown in Example 3 is found at the URL www.abc.com/people.xml. Then we can represent it as an XML object as follows:

```
(www.abc.com/people.xml)
/people: (person: (@id:o123, name: Jane),
         person: (@id:o234, @mother: o456, name: John),
         person: (@id:o456, @children: ⟨o123,o234⟩, name: Mary))
```

3 Rule-Based Query Language for XML

In this section, we present a rule-based language based on our data model called XML-RL (XML Rule-based Language) to query XML documents. First, we define the syntax. Then we give some examples. Finally, we define the semantics.

3.1 Syntax of XML-RL

Besides the set $\mathcal{U}$ of URLs and the set $\mathcal{C}$ of constants in the data model, XML-RL uses a set $\mathcal{V}$ of variables that is partitioned into two kinds: single-valued variables started with '$' followed by a string and '$' itself is an anonymous variable, and list-valued variables started with '#' followed by a string.

Definition 3. The *terms* are defined recursively as follows:

(1) null is an *empty* term.
(2) Let $c \in \mathcal{C}$ be a constant. Then c is a *lexical* term.
(3) A list value or a list-valued variable is a *list* term.
(4) Let X be a constant or a single-valued variable, and Y a term. Then $@X : Y$ is an *attribute* term, and Y denotes the value of the attribute that X denotes.
(5) Let $X_1, ..., X_n$ be a set of terms with $n \geq 1$. Then $@(X_1, ..., X_n)$ is a *tuple* term.
(6) Let X be a non-anonymous variable and $X_1, ..., X_n, (n \geq 1)$ be a set of attribute terms and element terms. Then $X(X_1, ..., X_n)$ is a *tuple selection* term. When $n = 1$, we can simply use X/X_1 instead.
(7) Let X be a constant or a variable, and Y a term. Then $X : Y$ is an *element* term, and Y denotes the content of the element that X denotes. If Y is an attribute term $X' : Y'$ or a tuple term $(X' : Y')$, then we can simply use $X/X' : Y'$. The case for Y' is the same.
(8) Let X be a single valued variable, Then $\{X\}$ is a *grouping* term.
(9) A single-valued variable is either an *empty* term, *lexical* term, an *attribute* term, an *element* term, or a *tuple* term depending on the context.

The grouping term is used solely to construct query results. The list term is used to manipulate list values. In a tuple selection term $\$t(X_1,...,X_n)$, $\$t$ is used to denote a tuple and $X_1,...,X_n$ are used to specify conditions that the tuple $\$t$ must satisfy.

The following are examples of terms:

Lexical terms:	Computer Science, Database Systems, $Name
List terms:	⟨⟩, ⟨John, Mary⟩, ⟨o123, o234⟩, #s
Attribute terms:	@Id:o123, @Id:$x, @year:$y, @$y:1995, @$x:$y
Tuple terms:	(@Id : $x, author : $a), (Title : $t, author : ⟨John⟩), $t
Tuple Selection terms:	$t(publisher : Springer), $t/Title : XML
Element terms:	name:$n, book/author:$a, bib/book: ⟨$b⟩, $x:$y,
Grouping terms:	{title: $t}, {(title : $t, {author : $a})},

A term is *ground* if it has no variables.

Definition 4. The *expressions* are defined as follows:

(1) Let U be a url or a single-valued variable and T an element term. Then $(U)/T$ is a *positive expression*.
(2) If P is a positive expression, then $\neg P$ is a *negative expression*.
(3) Arithmetic, logical, string, and list expressions are defined using terms in the usual way.

The following are several examples of expressions:

Positive exp: (http://www.abc.com/bib.xml)/people: $p
Negative exp: ¬($url)/people/person: (name: John)
Other exp: $a = $b × 2, count(#authors) > 2, first(#authors) = John

The positive expression above is equivalent to the following XQuery expression:

FOR $p IN document("http://www.abc.com/bib.xml")/people

Definition 5. A *rule* has the form $A \Leftarrow L_1,...,L_n$ and A is the *head* and $L_1,...,L_n$ is the *body* of the rule, where A is a positive expression, and each L_i is a positive expression, a negative expression, or an arithmetic, logical, string, list expression and only A can contain grouping terms.

The rule body is used to query data in XML documents while the rule head is used to construct the resulting XML document.

We require the variables in the head of the rule to be covered or limited as defined in [5,15,16]. An anonymous variable '$' may appear several times in a rule and their different appearances in general stand for different variables. It cannot appear in the head of a rule.

Definition 6. A *query* is a set of rules.

In order to make queries easier, we adopt XPath abbreviation in rules. That is, if there is a rule: $A \Leftarrow ..., (U)//X, ...$ where $//$ means any number of levels down, then this rule stand for the following rules:

- $A \Leftarrow ..., (U)/X, ...$
- $A \Leftarrow ..., (U)/X_1/X, ...$
- ...

If there are several such Xpath abbreviations in a rule, then it stands for their various combinations as outlined above. Also, if we have $X : ...\$t..., \$t(Y_1, ..., Y_n)$ in the body of a rule, then we can simply use $X : ...\$t(Y_1, ..., Y_n)...$ instead.

If URL U in the head $(U)/T$ is the default one, such as standard output, then we can omit it and use $/T$ instead.

3.2 Query Examples

The following queries are based on the XML documents shown in the last section.

(Q_1) List book elements for books published by Addison-Wesley after 1991.

    (file:///home/users/xml/result.xml)
    /results/book: $b
    $\Leftarrow$
    (http://www.abc.com/bib.xml)
    /bib/book: $b(publisher/name: Springer, year: $y, title: $t), $y > 1991

Since there are a number (list) of book elements in the XML document, variable $b matches one book element (a tuple) and tuple selection term specifies the condition that $b should satisfy. The result is a list of book elements under the root element *results*.

If we simply want to display the result on the screen, then we can simply use the following instead:

    /results/book: $b $\Leftarrow$
    (http://www.abc.com/bib.xml)
    /bib/book: $b(publisher/name: Springer, year: $y, title: $t), $y > 1991

(Q_2). Create a flat list of all the title-author pairs, with each pair enclosed in a "result" element.

    (file:///home/users/xml/result.xml)
    /results/result: (title: $t, author: $a)
    $\Leftarrow$
    (http://www.abc.com/bib.xml)
    /bib/book : (title: $t, author : $a)

Note here the variable $a in the body matches one author at a time.

(Q_3). For each author in the bibliography, list the author's name and the titles of all books by that author, grouped inside a "result" element.

>(file:///home/users/xml/result.xml)
>/results/result: (author: $a, {title: $t})
>⇐
>(http://www.abc.com/bib.xml)
>/bib/book : (title: $t, author: $a)

The grouping term {title: $t} in the head is used to group the titles of all books by author $a.

(Q_4). For each book that has at least two authors, list the title and first two authors.

>(file:///home/users/xml/result.xml)
>/results/result : (title: $t, {author: $a})
>⇐
>(http://www.abc.com/bib.xml)
>/bib/book : (title: $t, author: #a), count(#a) > 2, $a ∈ first_two(#a)

Note here the variables #a is a list-valued variable that match a list of authors.

(Q_5). For each person, list his/her ancestors IDs.

>(file:///home/users/xml/result.xml)
>/results/result : (@id: $c, {ancestors: $p})
>⇐
>(http://www.abc.com/people.xml)
>/people/person : (@id: $p, children: #c), $c ∈ #c

>(file:///home/users/xml/result.xml)
>/results/result : (@id: $c, {ancestors: $p})
>⇐
>(file:///home/users/xml/result.xml)
>/results/result : (@id: $c, ancestors: $a),
>(http://www.abc.com/people.xml)
>/people/person : (@id: $p, children: #c), $a ∈ #c

The first rule says for each person identified by $p, if $c is a child, then $p is an ancestor of $c. The second rule says if $a is an ancestor of $c, and $a is a child of $p, then $p is also an ancestor of $c. Note here the second rule is recursively defined.

In practice, we can simplify the above query by following Prolog convention to combine the two rules with the same head using ';' as follows:

(file:///home/users/xml/result.xml)
/results/result : (@id: $c, {ancestors: $p})
⇐
(http://www.abc.com/people.xml)
/people/person : (@id: $p, children: #c), $c ∈ #c;
(file:///home/users/xml/result.xml)
/results/result : (@id: $c, ancestors: $a),
(http://www.abc.com/people.xml)
/people/person : (@id: $p, children: #c), $a ∈ #c

3.3 Semantics of XML-RL

In this section, we define the Herbrand-like logical semantics for XML-RL queries.

Definition 7. The *Herbrand universe* U of XML-RL is the set of all ground terms that can be formed.

Definition 8. The *Herbrand base* B of XML-RL is the set of all XML positive expressions that can be formed using terms in U.

Definition 9. An *XML database* XDB is a set of XML objects.

Definition 10. A *ground substitution* θ is a mapping from the set of variables $\mathcal{V} - \{\$\}$ to $U \cup 2^U$. It maps a single-valued variable to an element in U and a list-valued variable to an element in 2^U.

The use of anonymous variables allows us to simply our query rules as demonstrated in the examples above. However, when we deal with semantics, we disallow anonymous variables. We assume that each appearance of anonymous variable is replaced by another variable that never occur in the query rules. This is why we do not map anonymous variable '$' to any object in the above definition.

Given a set of XML documents, our queries just select part of them. Thus, we introduce the following auxiliary notions in order to define the semantics.

Definition 11. A ground term o is *part-of* of another ground term o', denoted by $o \preceq o'$, if and only if one of the following hold:

(1) both are lexical or list objects and $o = o'$;
(2) both are attribute terms or element terms: $o \equiv l : o_i$ and $o' \equiv l : o'_i$ such that $o_i \preceq o'_i$;
(3) both are list terms and $o = o'$;
(4) both are tuple terms: $o \equiv (X_1 : o_1, ..., X_m : o_m)$ and $o' \equiv (X_1 : o'_1, ..., X_n : o'_n)$ with $m \leq n$ such that $o_i \preceq o'_i$ for $1 \leq i \leq m$.

A Logical Foundation for XML   579

The part-of relationship between o and o' captures the fact that o is part of o'. We need this notion because query results are always based on part of one or more XML documents.

The following are several examples:

John $\preceq$ John
author: (first: John) $\preceq$ author: (first: John, last: Mary)
(title:XML, author:John) $\preceq$ (title:XML, author:John, author:Mary)

Definition 12. Let $O = (u)/t$, $O' = (u')/t'$ be two XML objects. Then O is *part-of* O', denoted by $O \preceq O'$, if and only if $u = u'$ and $t \preceq t'$.

Definition 13. Let XDB and XDB' be two XML databases. Then XDB is *part-of* XDB', denoted by $XDB \preceq XDB'$, if and only if for each $O \in XDB - XDB'$, there exists $O' \in XDB' - XDB$ such that $O \preceq O'$.

Definition 14. Let XDB be an XML database. The notion of satisfaction (denoted by $\models$) and its negation (denoted by $\not\models$) based on XDB are defined as follows.

(1) For a ground positive expression $(u)/t$, $XDB \models (u)/t$ if and only if there exists $(u)/t' \in XDB$ such that $t \preceq t'$.
(2) For a ground negative expression $\neg(u)/t$, $XDB \models \neg(u)/t$ if and only if $XDB \not\models (u)/t$
(3) For a ground arithmetic, logical, string, or list expression ψ, $XDB \models \psi$ (or $XDB \models \neg\psi$) if and only if ψ is true (or false) in the usual sense.
(4) For a ground tuple selection term $X(Y_1, ..., Y_n)$. $XDB \models X(Y_1, ..., Y_n)$ if and only if Y_i is satisfied in X for $1 \leq i \leq n$.
(5) For a rule r of the form $A \Leftarrow L_1, ..., L_n$, $XDB \models r$ if and only if for every ground substitution θ, $XDB \models \theta L_1, ..., XDB \models \theta L_n$ implies $XDB \models \theta A$

For example, let XDB denote the XML objects in Example 3. Then we have

$XDB \models$ (www.abc.com/people.xml)/people/person : (@id : o123, name : Jane)
$XDB \models \neg$(www.abc.com/people.xml)/people/person : (name : Tony)
$XDB \models$ count($\langle$John, Mary$\rangle$) > 1, first_one($\langle$John, Mary$\rangle$) = John, 6 = 3 * 2
$XDB \models$ (@id : o123, name : Jane)(name : Jane)
$XDB \not\models$ (@id : o123, name : Jane)(name : Tony)

Definition 15. Let Q be a query. A *model* M of Q is a web database that satisfies Q. A model M of Q is *minimal* if and only if for each model N of Q, $M \preceq N$.

Definition 16. Let XDB be an XML database and Q a set of query rules. The *immediate logical consequence* operator T_Q over XDB is defined as follows:

$$T_Q(XDB) = \langle \theta A \mid A \Leftarrow L_1, ..., L_n \in Q \text{ and } \exists \text{ a ground substitution} \theta$$
$$\text{such that } XDB \models \theta L_1, ..., XDB \models \theta L_n \}$$

Example 5. Consider query Q_3 in Section 3.2. Then

$T_{Q_3}(DB) =$
⟨(resultURL)/results/result:(author:(last:Date, first: C.),
⟨Title:Introduction to DBMS⟩),
(resultURL)/results/result:(author:(last:Date, first: C.),
⟨Title:Foundation for ORDB⟩),
(resultURL)/results/result:(author:(last:Darwen, first: D.),
⟨Title: Foundation for ORDB ⟩)⟩

where $resultURL \equiv file:///home/users/xml/result.xml$.

Note that the operator T_Q does not perform result construction. Therefore, we introduce the following notions.

Definition 17. Two ground terms o and o' are *compatible* if and only if one of the following holds:

(1) both are constants and are equal;
(2) $o \equiv a : o_i$ and $o' \equiv a : o'_i$ such that o_i and o'_i are compatible;
(3) both are grouping terms;
(4) $o \equiv (X_1, ..., X_n)$ and $o' \equiv (X'_1, ..., X'_n)$ such that X_i and X'_i are compatible for $1 \leq i \leq m$.

For example, the following pairs are compatible:

John and John
Author:(last:Date, first: C.) and Author:(last:Date, first: C.)
⟨Title : Databases⟩ and ⟨Title : XML⟩
(author:(last:Date, first: C.), ⟨Title: Database⟩) and
(author:(last:Date, first: C.), ⟨Title: Foundation for ORDB⟩)

Definition 18. Two ground positive expression $(u)/o$ and $(u')/o'$ are *compatible* if and only if $u = u'$ and o and o' are compatible. A set of ground positive expressions are *compatible* if and only if each pair of them are compatible.

For example, the set of ground positive expressions in Example 5 are compatible.

Definition 19. Let S be a set of ground positive expressions (terms) and S' a compatible subset of S. Then S' is a *maximal* compatible set in S if there does not exist a ground positive expressions (terms) $o \in S - S'$ that is compatible with each element in S'.

Definition 20. Let S be a list of ground terms and ⊎ list concatenation operator. Then the *constructing* operator C is defined recursively on S as follows:

(1) If S is partitioned into n maximal compatible sets: $S = S_1 \uplus ... \uplus S_n$ with $n > 1$, then $C(S) = \langle C(S_1), ..., C(S_n) \rangle$.

(2) $S = \langle o \rangle$ then $C(S) = o$.
(3) If S is a compatible set of attribute terms or element terms: $S = \langle a : o_1, ..., a : o_n \rangle$, then $C(S) = a : C(\langle o_1, ..., o_n \rangle)$.
(4) Let $S = \langle \langle X_1 \rangle, ..., \langle X_n \rangle \rangle$ be a set of grouping terms of attribute or element objects. If $n = 1$, then $C(S) = C(X_1)$. Otherwise, $C(S) = (C(X_1), ..., C(X_n))$.
(5) Let S be a set of compatible tuples $S = \langle (X_1, ..., X_m, Y_1), ...(X_1, ..., X_m, Y_n) \rangle$ where $X_1, ..., X_m$ are non-grouping terms and $Y_1, ..., Y_n$ are grouping terms. Then $C(S) = (C(X_1), ..., C(X_m), C(Y_1), ..., C(Y_n))$.

The following is an constructing example:

$C(\langle$bib: $\langle$book: (Title: Web)$\rangle$,
     bib: $\langle$book: (Title: Databases)$\rangle$,
     bib: $\langle$Journal: (Title: XML)$\rangle\rangle)$
$=$ bib : $C(\langle\langle$book: (Title: Web)$\rangle$,
              $\langle$book: (Title: Databases)$\rangle$,
              $\langle$Journal: (Title: XML)$\rangle\rangle)$ by (3)
$=$ bib : (book: (Title: Web),
          book: (Title: Databases),
          Journal: (Title: XML))   by (4)

We extend the constructing operator to a list of ground positive expressions as follows: if S is a compatible list of objects of the form $(u)/o_1, ..., (u)/o_n$, then $C(S) = (u)/C(\langle o_1, ..., o_n \rangle)$. Otherwise, C is not defined.

Definition 21. The *powers* of the operation T_Q over the XML database XDB are defined as follows:

$T_Q \uparrow 0(DB) = DB$
$T_Q \uparrow n(DB) = T_Q(C(T_Q \uparrow n-1(DB))) \cup T_Q \uparrow n-1(DB)$ if C is defined
$T_Q \uparrow \omega(DB) = \cup_{n=0}^{\infty} T_Q \uparrow n(DB) - DB$ if $T_Q \uparrow n(DB)$ is defined

Continue with Example 5, we have

$C(T_{Q_3} \uparrow \omega(DB))$
$= C(\langle\langle$(resultURL)/results/result :(author : (last : Date, first : C.),
                                         $\langle$Title : IntroductiontoDBMS$\rangle$),
      (resultURL)/results/result : (author : (last : Date, first : C.),
                                         $\langle$Title : FoundationforORDB$\rangle$),
      (resultURL)/results/result : (author : (last : Darwen, first : D.),
                                         $\langle$Title : FoundationforORDB$\rangle\rangle)\rangle)$
$=$(resultURL)/results : $C(\langle$result : (author :(last : Date, first : C.),
                                         $\langle$Title : IntroductiontoDBMS$\rangle$),
                     result :(author :(last : Date, first : C.),
                                         $\langle$Title : FoundationforORDB$\rangle$),
                     result :(author :(last : Darwen, first : D.),
                                         $\langle$Title : FoundationforORDB$\rangle\rangle)\rangle)$ by (3)

=(resultURL)/results : $(C(\langle$result:(author :(last:Date, first: C.),
                      $\langle$Title : IntroductiontoDBMS$\rangle)),$
              result : (author :(last:Date, first: C.),
                      $\langle$Title : Foundation for ORDB$\rangle)\rangle),$
          $C(\langle$result : (author :(last:Darwen, first: D.),
                      $\langle$Title : Foundation for ORDB$\rangle)\rangle)))$ by (1)
=(resultURL)/results:(result : $C(\langle\langle$author :(last:Date, first: C.),
                      $\langle$Title : Introduction to DBMS$\rangle)),$
                 (author :(last:Date, first: C.),
                      $\langle$Title : Foundation for ORDB$\rangle)\rangle),$
              result : $C(\langle\langle$author :(last:Darwen, first: D.),
                      $\langle$Title : Foundation for ORDB$\rangle)\rangle)))$ by (3)
=(resultURL)/results : [result : (author :(last:Date, first: C.),
                      Title : Introduction to DBMS,
                      Title : Foundation for ORDB)),
              result : (author :(last:Darwen, first: D.),
                      Title : Foundation for ORDB))   by (5)

Theorem 1. Let XDB be a web database and Q a set of query rules. Then $C(T_Q \uparrow \omega(XDB))$ is a minimal model of Q.

Definition 22. Let XDB be an XML database and Q a set of query rules. Then the *semantics* of Q under XDB is given by $C(T_Q \uparrow \omega(XDB))$.

4 Conclusion

In this paper, we have proposed a novel data model for XML that is able to represent XML documents in a natural and direct way. It establishes relationship between XML and complex object data models. Using this data model, we can easily comprehend XML from database point of view.

We have also presented a rule-based query language based on the data model proposed. Formal syntax and logic-based declarative semantics of XML-RL are presented. XML-RL provides a simple but very powerful way to query XML documents and to construct/restructure the query results. As defined, XML-RL is capable of handling (recursive) queries that make use of partial information of the given XML documents. A number of XML-RL queries are included in the paper to demonstrate the usefulness of XML-RL.

The main novel features that make XML-RL simple to use is the introduction of grouping terms and the corresponding constructing operator so that the querying part and the result constructing part can be strictly separated. More importantly, we have provided a formal logic foundation that is lacking in other XML query languages.

Indeed, other kinds of database query languages, such as calculus-based, can also be developed based on our data model and the work done in the database community for nested-relational and complex object databases.

We have implemented XML-RL using Java. The system will soon be available from the Web site at http://www.scs.carleton.ca/~mengchi/XML-RL/ after further testing and debugging.

The language presented here is not a full-fledge one as our primary focus is on the formal foundation. However, many other features can be added. We leave it as our future work.

References

1. Document Object Model (DOM). *http://www.w3.org/DOM/*.
2. S. Abiteboul, R. Hull, and V. Vianu. *Foundations of Databases*. Addison Wesley, 1995.
3. S. Abiteboul, D. Quass, J. McHugh, J. Widom, and J. L. Wiener. The Lorel Query Language for Semistructured Data. *Intl. Journal of Digital Libraries*, 1(1):68–88, 1997.
4. S. Adler, A. Berglund, J. Caruso, S. Deach, P. Grosso, E. Gutentag, A. Milowski, S. Parnell, J. Richman, and S. Zillies. Extensible Stylesheet Language (XSL) Version 1.0. *http://www.w3.org/TR/2000/CR-xsl-20001121*, November 2001.
5. C. Beeri, S. Naqvi, O. Shmueli, and S. Tsur. Set Construction in a Logic Database Language. *Journal of Logic Programming*, 10(3,4):181–232, 1991.
6. R. G. G. Cattell and D. Barry, editors. *The Object Database Standard: ODMG 2.0*. Morgan Kaufmann, Los Altos, CA, 1997.
7. S. Ceri, S. Comai, E. Damiani, P. Fraternali, S. Paraboschi, and L. Tanca. XML-GL: a Graphical Language for Querying and Restructuring WWW data. In *Proceedings of the 8th International World Wide Web Conference*, Toronto, Canada, 1999.
8. D. Chamberlin, P. Fankhauser, M. Marchiori, and J. Robie. XML Query Requirements. *http://www.w3.org/TR/2001/WD-xmlquery-req-20010215*, February 2001.
9. D. Chamberlin, D. Florescu, J. Robie, J. Siméon, and M. Stefanescu. XQuery: A Query Languge for XML. *http://www.w3.org/TR/2001/WD-xquery-20010215*, February 2001.
10. J. Clark and S. DeRose. XML Path Language (XPath) Version 1.0. *http://www.w3.org/TR/1999/REC-xpath-19991116*, November 2001.
11. J. Cowan and R. Tobin. XML Information Set Data Model. *http://www.w3.org/TR/xml-infoset*, May 2001.
12. A. Deutsch, M. Fernandez, D. Florescu, A. Levy, and D. Suciu. XML-QL: A Query Language for XML. *http://www.w3.org/TR/1998/Note-xml-ql-19980819*, August 1998.
13. P. Fankhauser, M. Fernández, A. Malhotra, M. Rys, J. Siméon, and P. Wadler. The XML Query Algebra. *http://www.w3.org/TR/2001/WD-Query-algebra-20010215*, February 2001.
14. M. Fernandez and J. Robie. XML Query Data Model. *http://www.w3.org/TR/2001/WD-Query-datamodel-20010215*, February 2001.
15. M. Liu. Relationlog: A Typed Extension to Datalog with Sets and Tuples. *Journal of Logic Programming*, 36(3):271–299, 1998.
16. J. D. Ullman. *Principles of Database and Knowledge-Base Systems*, volume 1. Computer Science Press, 1988.

Providing the Semantic Layer for WIS Design

Richard Vdovjak and Geert-Jan Houben

Eindhoven University of Technology
POBox 513, 5600 MB Eindhoven, The Netherlands
{r.vdovjak,g.j.houben}@tue.nl

Abstract. Designing Web-based information systems requires the use of a thorough design methodology. Particularly, when the content of the system is gathered from different information sources available via the Web, the specification of how data is to be retrieved requires appropriate design tools. Concretely, a solution to the problem of how to facilitate the design of integrating heterogeneous information sources is needed, in order to be able to provide a uniform access to data gathered from different sources. In this paper we propose the use of the Hera methodology extended with the Semantic Layer, which concentrates on the integration aspect. The presented integration framework provides a coherent and meaningful (with respect to a given conceptual model) view of the integrated heterogeneous information sources.

1 Introduction and Related Work

The WWW has become one of the most popular information channels of today. This results into an ever-growing demand for new Web applications. The Web is, however, becoming a victim of its own success. Ad hoc hacking without a prior design, using no rigorous methodology is currently the common Web development practice. This approach fails to meet the demand for high quality data-driven Web applications such as Web-based Information Systems (WIS).

WIS applications use Web technologies to fulfill the needs of professional information systems. The specific role of modern WIS asks for a highly structured and controlled approach to Web engineering [1]. Many WIS have a data-driven nature, that requires a process of automatically generating hypermedia or multimedia (Web) presentations for the data to be output.

To facilitate the engineering of these data-driven Web applications there is an obvious need for a design framework. This framework should allow designers to specify and reason about WIS in an appropriate level of abstraction depending on the different stages of the engineering project (requirements analysis, design, and implementation), but also on the different dimensions of the problem area (e.g. ata integration and modeling, hyperspace navigation, user/platform adaptation, layout design etc.).

The specification of artifacts (models) of the different stages of the design process can benefit a lot from technologies like RDF(S)[2,3], introduced with the Semantic Web initiative [4], where the main idea is to allow for the data that resides on the WWW to be targeted not only for humans but to become also machine-understandable. The goal is to achieve semantic interoperability, which would facilitate creation of new services such as smart search engines, automated information integration and exchange, presentation generation, etc. We argue that semantic interoperability will have a positive impact on the design and use of WIS, especially those constructed from several heterogeneous sources.

Existing methodologies for designing Web applications, such as RMM[5], OOHDM[6], WebML[7], do not explicitly cover the integration phase. We believe that the integration issues (Conceptual Model design, Schema integration, and Data integration) should be taken into consideration during the design of those data-driven Web applications, for which the content is coming from heterogeneous data sources.

In previous work [8,9] we suggested a methodology inspired by RMM for the design of automatically generated data-driven Web presentations for ad-hoc user queries. This paper is a follow-up extending the methodology with the Semantic Layer, so that it can be used as a basis for engineering WIS-like applications. We focus on designing those WIS that are built from collections of heterogeneous information sources. The paper addresses problems of information integration (both schema and data), such as syntactic and semantic reconciliation of different sources.

The rest of the paper is structured as follows. Section 2 presents the different steps of our design methodology and the underlying software suite that provides the means for executing the specifications resulting from the design process. In section 3 we focus on the Semantic Layer and we cover in detail the issues regarding the design of the models that create the foundation of this layer. Section 4 introduces a software architecture that implements the Semantic Layer. We conclude the paper by section 5 with a short summary and future work.

2 Hera Design Methodology

The Hera design methodology has its origins in RMM[5]. Similarly to RMM, it distinguishes several steps to be followed during the design process of a Web application[1]. Each design step produces as its outcome a specification with a certain level of abstraction based on the separation-of-concerns principle. The sequence of the main steps is depicted in figure 1.[2]

The first step, the Requirements Analysis clarifies and captures the needs and demands that the client has for the future application, into a requirements document, which serves as a "wish list" that has to be fulfilled by the designer(s) and as a "check list" for testing, once the application is developed.

---

[1] Although the methodology is general and can be applied to many (types of) Web applications, here we primarily concentrate on data-driven Web applications of the typical WIS nature.
[2] Note that the arrows in the picture denote only the general flow; it is possible to have feedback loops in the process.

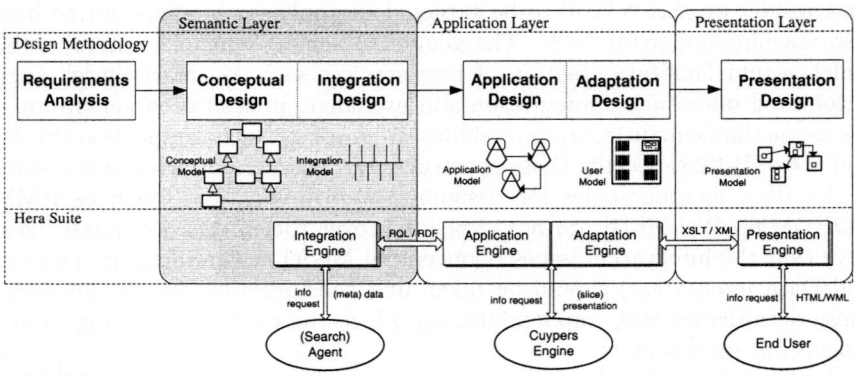

Fig. 1. Design Methodology, and underlying set of data-processing engines

In the Conceptual Design step the application domain is captured into a Conceptual Model (CM) consisting of a hierarchy of concepts, their properties, and relations. Within an information system one usually distinguishes a data repository, which contains the data that is available for querying: each answer to a query results in the generation of a (Web) presentation. The purpose of the CM is to describe which information is available inside this data repository.

Note that if the data is coming from different (possibly heterogeneous) sources, the data repository can be virtual (not materialized). In this case an Integration Model (IM) must be introduced, which selects sources and articulates (translates) the relevant concepts from them into the CM. It is evident that the design of CM influences the creation[3] of IM (IM mappings depend on the CM), but the dependency here is mutual. There is not much use of introducing concepts into the CM if they cannot be populated with data instances if we do not have appropriate data sources for them in the IM. So, it is often the case that the CM design and IM creation are intertwined and accomplished in an iterative manner.

In the Application Design step, the concepts from the CM are transformed into slices. In analogy to RMM, we use the notions of slice and slice relationship to model how the concepts from the CM will be presented. While the CM gives a *semantic description* of the information that is available, the Application Model (AM) [9] gives a *navigational description* of that information. Having in mind that Web presentations will be generated for queries against this information, the navigational description specifies (a blueprint for) the hypermedia nature of those presentations. The AM does not yet include all the rendering details covered in the next steps of the methodology, but it does allow for a first, logical sketch of the presentation to be generated. This implies the translation of

---

[3] We make a distinction between "creating" and "designing" in a sense that the first can be to a large extent automated while the second is more "human dependent".

concepts into "pages" and the establishing of a navigational structure between those pages.

The era of "one size fits all" Web applications seems to be vanishing and personalization and adaptation (one-to-one content delivery) is becoming an issue for an increasing number of applications. A User Adaptation Model (UAM) supporting the adaptation is built during Adaptation Design; in line with the AHAM reference model [10] this UAM includes the specification of a user model and adaptation rules. The design of UAM is intertwined and associated with the Application Design, just like in the case of IM creation and CM design.

The Presentation Design step introduces a rendering independent Presentation Model (PM)[9], which focuses on layout, hyperlinking, timing and synchronization issues. The Presentation Design elaborates on the Application Design and bridges it with the actual code generation for the desired platform, e.g. TML, WML, SMIL etc.

The Hera suite (the lower part of figure 1) is a collection of engines (software programs), which can interpret the specifications (or models) provided by the designer during the different phases of the design process.

The suite is split into several layers each of them processing a different model and thus reflecting a different design phase.

- The Semantic Layer, which is the primary focus of this paper, integrates the data that is available in a collection of heterogeneous external data sources into one Conceptual Model (CM) with well-understood semantics. The Mediator as a main component of this layer, provides mediation services for the Application Layers and offers also a connectivity for the "outside world" of software agents.
- The Application Layer provides the logical functionality of the application, in the sense that it exploits the structure of the CM to lay a foundation for the hypermedia nature of the output in the form of the AM. The Application Engine and the Adaptation engine are two main components of this layer: the first generates a relevant (depending on the given query) "subset" of the AM, which is then populated with data coming from the Semantic Layer; the second interprets the adaptation rules and updates the UAM accordingly.
- The Presentation Layer of the framework is responsible for the transformation of the Application Model (possible including the User Adaptation Model) into a chosen rendering platform (e.g. TML, WML or SMIL). In order to achieve this, the Presentation Engine uses a relevant part (again depending on the given query) of the implementation independent Presentation Model provided by the designer, which is populated with data coming from the previous layer. This is then transformed by means of XSLT [11] to a chosen rendering platform.

3 Designing the Semantic Layer

As already suggested in the previous section, the main purpose of the Semantic Layer is to provide a semantically unified interface for querying (selected) heterogeneous information sources. We do not aim at merging all possible sources together to provide a cumulated view of all attributes. We argue that such an approach offers weak semantics, where the understanding of the semantic structure of all integrated sources is effectively left up to the user who is issuing the query against such a view. Instead, we chose to provide the user with a semantic entry point in terms of the CM, which is interconnected with the underlying sources by means of the IM.

Because of the Web nature of our target applications in combination with the dynamically changing data in the underlying sources, we chose to base our integration framework on the lazy retrieval paradigm [12] assuring that the delivered data is always up-to-date. To provide support for interoperability we combine this retrieval with the technologies introduced with the Semantic Web initiative, namely RDF(S)[3,2]. There are several reasons why we decided to use RDF(S):

- Compared to a traditional database schema, it deals better with the semi-structured nature of Web data.
- RDF(S), a W3C standard for metadata, and its extensions such as DC[13], CC/PP[14], RSS[15] etc. bring us closer to interoperability at least as far as descriptive metadata is concerned.
- On top of RDF(S) high level ontology languages (e.g. AML+OIL[16]) are (becoming) available, which allow for expressing axioms and rules about the described classes giving the designer a tool with larger expressive power. Choosing RDF(S) as the foundation for describing the CM, enables a smooth transition in this direction.

When looking at integration as a (design) process, the following two principal phases can be distinguished: designing the Conceptual Model and designing/deriving the Integration Model. Further on, we detail these phases.

3.1 Conceptual Model Design

The Conceptual Model (CM) provides a uniform interface to access the data integrated within a given Web application. It corresponds to a mediated schema that is filled with data during query resolution. The application user is assumed to be familiar with the semantics of terms within his field of interest, and the function of the CM is to offer the user a uniform semantic view over the different sources, that usually use different terms and/or different semantics.

The CM consists of hierarchies of concepts relevant within the given domain, their properties, and relations. As already mentioned above it is expressed in RDF(S).

Although RDF(S) seems to be a promising modeling tool it does not provide all modeling primitives we demand. Namely, the notion of cardinality and inverse relationship is missing and there is also a lack of basic types. There are more ways how to approach this problem, for example, in [17] it is shown how to combine the data semantics, expressed in RDF(S), with the data constraints, modeled in XML Schema [18]. As there is no clear W3C Recommendation on this subject yet, we chose for the purist approach, i.e. to model both data constraints and data semantics in RDF(S) itself, by extending it with the mentioned modeling primitives (the extensions are recognizable in the actual encoding with the abbreviated namespace prefix "*sys:*").

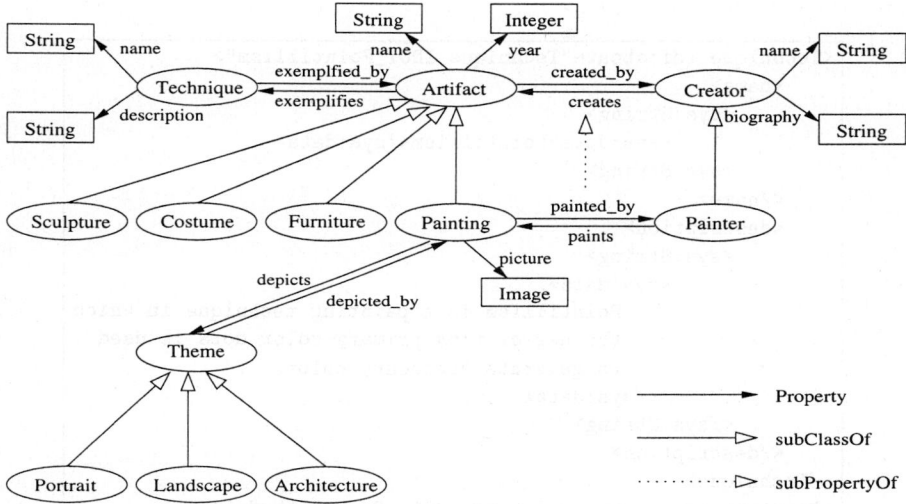

Fig. 2. Conceptual Model

The running example that we use throughout the paper describes the design of a virtual museum Web information system, which allows visitors to choose (query) their favorite artist(s) and/or pieces, and to browse exhibitions (Web presentations) assembled from exhibits coming from different (online) museums and art galleries, and possibly annotated with relevant descriptions from an online art encyclopedia. All this data is offered from a single entry point, semantically represented by a CM. In order to create a good CM it usually requires both the domain expertise and modeling know-how. In this example, we let ourselves be inspired by an existing CM. The Conceptual Model of our application roughly corresponds to the actual museum catalog of the Rijksmuseum in Amsterdam[4].

A part of this CM is depicted in a graphical notation in figure 2:

– Concepts are depicted as ovals; the more abstract ones such as *Artifact* and *Creator* are on the top part of the model. From those, more concrete concepts are inherited, e.g. *Painting* and *Painter*.
– Relationships are denoted with full arrows and are modeled as RDF properties. Similarly to concepts there are abstract relationships (properties) such

---

[4] www.rijksmuseum.nl

as *created_by*, *creates* and their more concrete subrelationships (subproperties) *painted_by* and *paints*.
– Attributes, e.g. *Creator.name: String*, are treated as properties having as its domain a concept, e.g. *Creator*, and as its range a basic type, e.g. *String* (indicated with the rectangle).

```
<Technique rdf:about="Technique_ID01_Pointillism">
    <name>
        <sys:String>
            <sys:data>Pointillism</sys:data>
        <sys:String>
    </name>
    <description>
        <sys:String>
            <sys:data>
                Pointillism is a painting technique in which
                the use of tiny primary-color dots is used
                to generate secondary colors...
            </sys:data>
        </sys:String>
    </description>
</Technique>
<Painting rdf:about="Painting_ID01_ BanksoftheSeine ">
    <name>
        <sys:String>
            <sys:data>Banks of the Seine</sys:data>
        <sys:String>
    </name>
    <year>
        <sys:Integer>
            <data>1887</data>
        </sys:Integer>
    </year>
    <exemplifies rdf:resource="#Technique_ID01_Pointillism"/>
    <painted_by rdf:resource="#Painter_ID01_VincentvanGogh"/>
</Painting>
```

Fig. 3. Examples of RDF instances of the CM

Note that the graphical notation of the CM directly corresponds to an RDF(S) graph. RDF(S) as such has not only graphical but also a textual (XML) syntax. This XML-RDF(s) serialization is used in our software prototype to represent the CM.

During the actual run-time process of presentation generation the CM is on request populated with instances (RDF statements), which represent the query result coming from the Application Layer. Note that the source data generally comes from different (heterogeneous) sources and that the actual instance retrieval is performed by the Integration Engine. Figure 3 presents in a XML-RDF(S) syntax a concrete example of generated instances adhering to our CM, as a response to the given query which propagated from the Application Layer.

3.2 Integration Model Design/Creation

The task of building the Integration Model is rather complex. It includes steps like finding relevant information sources, parsing, understanding and articulating the relevant parts of their schemas in terms of the CM. An articulation that connects the CM with a concrete source is implemented as a set of mappings, which relate (express) concepts from the source to (in terms of) concepts in the CM. These articulations are then used during the data integration step to provide the actual data response to a given query. Some of the above steps can be automated, some still need a human interaction. In the following, we look at them in more detail.

Source Discovery As it usually takes the human insight of the designer(s) to create a (good) CM, finding relevant sources to populate the CM with data is currently also mostly done by humans. When creating the CM, the designer can be helped by available ontology engineering tools, which allow for export in the RDF/S format. However, in the search for suitable sources the designer is currently left alone in the vast space of the World Wide Web. We envision that when the idea of the Semantic Web becomes reality (i.e. hen most of the Web sources would provide a machine understandable semantics of their data and services), search agents and information brokers will be capable of finding (recommending) suitable sources to populate the CM.

Schema Integration An essential prerequisite to achieve interoperability is to be able to identify and link together semantically similar data coming from different sources. To fully automate this task is very difficult, especially in the context of the semistructured Web sources. Even in the more structured database world, this has been recognized as a not always solvable problem [19]. We try to split this problem into two. The first one, easier to solve, deals with syntactical issues. The second, more complicated one, deals with the reconciliation of semantic discrepancies.

- Syntactic issues
  Unlike the case of database integration, where the schemas of integrated sources are assumed to be known explicitly, in the Web environment we often have to do the pre-integration schema discovery. In other words, it is needed to identify and make explicit what classes/concepts are provided by the integrated sources. In the ideal world of semantically annotated sources,

which export their schemas in RDF/S, this would be a question of parsing an RDF file, so it can be fully automated.

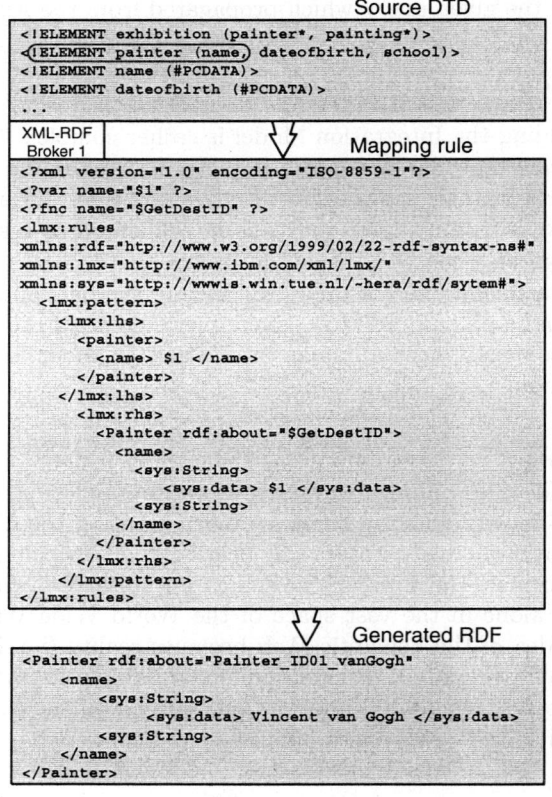

Fig. 4: The concept extraction from a DTD and its corresponding mapping to the CM

At the present however, most of the Web sources do not provide more than an XML description of their content. In the following we consider sources having at least this capability[5].

Even if the sources are encoded in XML, assuming no particular XML structure, it is still difficult to automatically recognize concepts and in order to do so, the insight of an application designer is often needed. The difficulty here varies based on the way in which the sources are encoded in XML.

---

[5] In case of HTML-only sources, a wrapping process is required to extract the source's content to an XML form.

Source DTD/XML

```
<?xml version="1.0" encoding="UTF-8"?>
<!DOCTYPE results [
    <!ELEMENT results (entity-class*)>
    <!ELEMENT entity-class (entity-instance)*>
    <!ATTLIST entity-class name CDATA #REQUIRED >
    <!ELEMENT entity-instance (attr)*>
    <!ATTLIST entity-instance ID ID #REQUIRED >
    <!ELEMENT attr (#PCDATA)>
    <!ATTLIST attr attrID ID #REQUIRED >
]>
<results>
    <entity-class name = "Technique">
        <entity-instance ID="TechniqueInst1">
            <attr attrID= "Name">
                Pointillism
            </attr>
            <attr attrID= "Describtion">
                Pointillism is a painting technique in which
                the use of tiny primary-color dots is used
                to generate secondary colors...
            </attr>
        </entity-instance>
    </entity-class>
</results>
```

XML-RDF Broker 2

Mapping rule

```
<?xml version="1.0" encoding="ISO-8859-1"?>
<?var name="$1" ?>
<?var name="$2" ?>
<?fnc name="$GetSrcID" ?>
<lmx:rules xmlns:lmx="http://www.ibm.com/xml/lmx/"
    xmlns:rdf="htp://www.w3.org/1999/02/22-rdf-syntax-ns#"
    xmlns:sys="http://wwwis.win.tue.nl/~hera/rdf/sytem#">
<lmx:pattern>
    <lmx:lhs>
        <results>
            <entity-class name="Technique">
                <entity-instance ID="$GetSrcID">
                    <attr attrID="Name"> $1 </attr>
                    <attr attrID="Describtion">  $2 </attr>
                </entity-instance>
            </entity-class>
        </results>
    </lmx:lhs>
    <lmx:rhs>
        <Technique rdf:about="$GetDestID">
            <name>
                <sys:String>
                    <sys:data>$1</sys:data>
                <sys:String>
            </name>
            <description>
                <sys:String>
                    <sys:data> $2 </sys:data>
                </sys:String>
            </description>
        </Technique>
    </lmx:rhs>
</lmx:pattern>
</lmx:rules>
```

Fig. 5: The concept extraction from XML data and its corresponding mapping to the CM

For example, assume that one of the online galleries that we integrate in our virtual museum provides a description of the available data in the form of a DTD, a part of which is shown in figure 4 (top). The designer can conclude directly from this DTD that the element *painter* together with its subelement *name* is to be extracted as a relevant concept and mapped to our CM. However, looking only at DTDs (XMLSchemas) is sometimes not enough. Assume for instance that an online art encyclopedia encodes its concepts as XML attribute values, providing only a general DTD as shown in figure 5 (top). In this case, the designer must also examine the actual XML data to conclude that the encyclopedia offers a concept called *Technique*, which is to be linked to our CM.

– Semantic issues

After reconstructing the source schemas, the main problem is to choose the right concepts occurring in the source schemas and to relate them to the concepts from the CM (recall that unlike in classical database schema integration, we do not integrate all concepts from sources, but rather select the relevant ones with respect to the defined CM).

The problem of relating concepts form the source schemas to the ones from the CM can be mapped to the problem of merging or aligning ontologies. The approaches to solve the problem are usually based on lexical matches, relying mostly on dictionaries to determine synonyms and hyponyms; this is however often not enough to yield good results.

In [20] the structure of ontologies is also taken into account when searching for corresponding concepts. Neither of these approaches, however, delivers satisfactory results especially if ontologies are constructed differently, e.g. having a very different structure or differing in the depth of the class hierarchy. This is often the case in uncoordinated development of ontologies across the Web and that is why ontology aligning is currently mostly a manual process, where a domain expert identifies the concepts that are similar and records the mappings between them. In our framework, we also currently rely on the designer who provides such mappings[6].

As mentioned above an articulation is implemented as a set of mappings, which relate concepts from a source to the concepts from the CM. In case of integrating an RDF source the mappings are mostly straightforward and usually they are also expressible in RDF. However, if we want to integrate an XML source we need something that transforms the source's XML to the RDF(S) of the CM. For this kind of transformation we use mapping rules that extract the relevant portions of information [7] from the (XML) sources and relate them to the CM.

These mappings are expressed in the form of LMX[8][21] rules consisting of a left-hand side, the *"from* part", and the right-hand side, the *"to* part". The data that is to be transferred is specified by positioning variables denoted as $x. These are declared at the beginning as processing instructions

---

[6] We intend to re-address this issue in the future by providing the designer with a tool, which would suggest initial correlations.

[7] It is often the case that only some attributes from the source concept are linked to a concept from the CM.

[8] Language for Mapping XML documents.

(together with functions such as *GetDestId*, which is used for a coordinated assignment of IDs) to make the application aware of them. In figure 4 we present an example of such a mapping rule together with the RDF instances it yields. Another example is presented in figure 5; this rule maps the *Technique* element coming from the online art encyclopedia to the corresponding concept in our CM. The result (an RDF instance) of this mapping is shown in figure 3 (top). Given the mappings, the semantic reconciliation is performed by the XML2RDF brokers described in section 4.

Data Integration Once the relevant high level sources have been identified and mappings to the CM established, the user can ask a query. The integration system must reformulate it into a query that refers directly to the source schemas taking into account the source query capabilities. Then the results are collected and presented to the user. Note that sometimes it is also the case that different sources provide information about the same real world entities but refer to these entities differently; this is also called a designation conflict. The integration system has to determine such cases and consider them adequately.

The query processing, and the composition of results is a task performed by the mediator described in section 4.

4 Implementing the Semantic Layer

The notion of mediator as introduced in [22] laid the foundation for building mediating architectures that have the ambition to overcome the semantic heterogeneity and facilitate a seamless access to data coming from many heterogeneous sources. In order to provide the Semantic Layer, our prototype implements such a mediating architecture. To address the issues mentioned in the previous sections, the architecture is split from software point of view into separate independent (sub)layers (figure 6), each them responsible for a different task and together creating a well-knit integration framework. We describe each of the layers further.

- Source Layer
  The Source Layer contains external data sources such as relational or object databases, HTML pages, XML repositories, or possibly RDF (ontology) based sources. This layer provides the content to be integrated. Our target applications can be built from fairly general sources that can be distributed across the Web. As already mentioned, we assume that the sources have the capability of exporting their data in XML serialization. However, due to heterogeneity, we do not impose any particular structure the XML data sources should comply to. This allows us to leave the XML wrapping process for the source providers.
  Note that by choosing RDF(S) as the foundation for the CM and by exporting it via the mediator to the outside world, one instance of our framework

can qualify as a resource for another framework, hence providing composability [9].

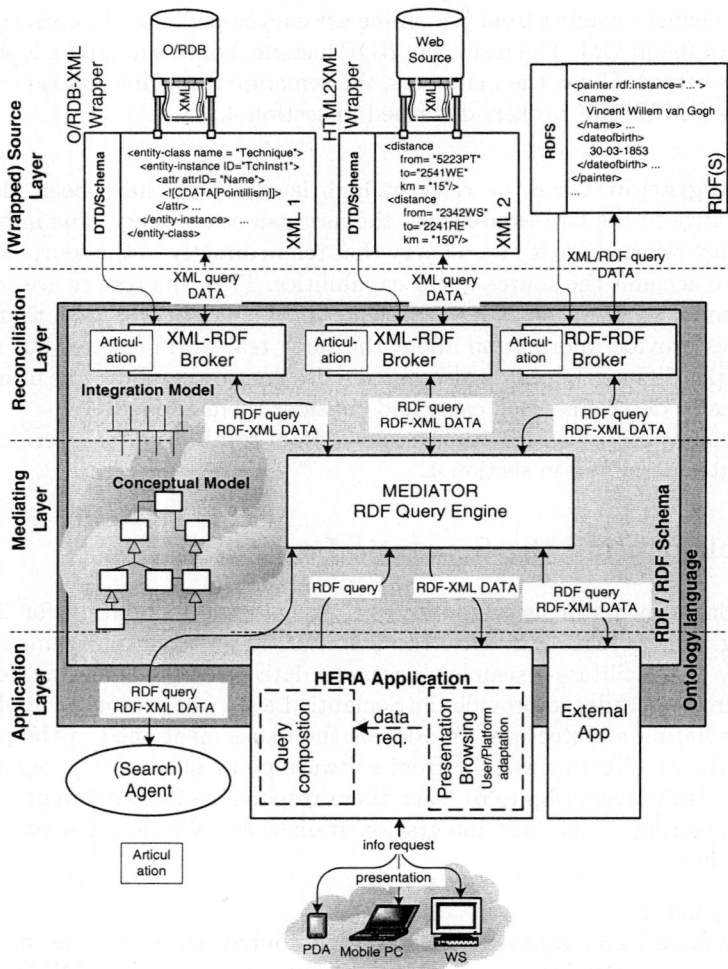

Fig. 6: Architecture facilitating semantic integration of heterogeneous information sources

– Reconciliation Layer

---

[9] We acknowledge that implementing our architecture on newly appearing middleware standards such as J2EE from Sun Microsystems could bring composability and interoperability even further.

This layer is responsible for the semantic reconciliation of the sources with respect to the CM and consists of XML2RDF brokers, which provide the bridge between the XML instances from the previous layer and the mediator. The designer tailors each XML2RDF broker to its source by specifying an articulation that maps XML sources to the underlying CM. This articulation is implemented as a set of mapping rules, which are used by the XML2RDF broker while resolving a query coming from the mediator. Providing the actual response to a mediator's query requires the broker to poll the source for data and to create RDF statements, that is riplets (*subject*, textitpredicate, textitobject).

- Mediating Layer
  This layer is responsible for the query services and data integration, its central component being the mediator. The mediator can be considered as a secondary source which does not have a data repository; instead, it maintains the CM. From the technical point of view the mediator contains a query decomposition module and an RDF query engine [23]. After the mediator receives a query from the Application Layer it proceeds as follows.
  First, it decomposes the query into subqueries [24] and distributes them among the brokers trying to push the processing of the query as much as possible on the sources, while taking into account the source query capabilities. The actual querying is triggered by a navigation request coming from the Application Layer.
  Then it collects the data from the brokers, applies a field matching algorithm citeAEMCPE:96 to resolve possible designation conflicts, constructs the response and sends it to the Application Layer.
- Application Layer
  The Application Layer utilizes the Mediating Layer by asking queries against the CM. For the Application Layer, the Mediating Layer is actually the front-end of the Semantic Layer introduced in section 2. From the mediating point of view it is not important whether the application generates (Web) presentations for the end-user (e.g. s the Hera suite does) or it only processes the pure information provided by this layer (e.g. s a search agent does): both cases are served in the same manner by answering queries from the CM.

5 Conclusions and Future Work

Creating Web-based information systems requires the use of a thorough design methodology. Specially, when the content of the system is gathered from different information sources available via the Web, the specification of how data is retrieved requires appropriate design tools. Concretely, a solution to the problem of integrating heterogeneous information sources is needed in order to be able to provide a uniform access to data gathered from the different sources. In this paper we have extended the Hera design methodology with the Semantic Layer concentrating on its integration aspect. The proposed integration framework combines semantic metadata with on-demand retrieval. It offers a composable semantic interface for (dynamic) access to heterogeneous information sources.

In terms of the software, on-going experiments in the context of the Hera project are verifying our ideas about integration specification with an implementation of the framework's prototype. In the future we would like to extend our framework with an algorithm that would deliver starting correlations between source concepts and the concepts from the CM, which can be then improved by the designer. Next, we also intend to extend the conceptual model with a high level ontology language allowing for expressing inference rules.

References

1. Deshpande, Y., Ginige, A., Hansen, S., Murugesan, S.: Web Engineering: A New Discipline for Web-Based System Development. Proc. of the First ICSE Workshop on Web Engineering, ACM, 1999
2. Lassila, O., Swick, R. R.: Resource Description Framework (RDF) Model and Syntax Specification. W3C Recommendation, 1999 http://www.w3.org/TR/1999/REC-rdf-syntax-19990222
3. Brickley, D., Guha, R. V.: Resource Description Framework (RDF) Schema Specification 1.0. W3C Candidate Recommendation, 2000 http://www.w3.org/TR/2000/CR-rdf-schema-20000327
4. Berners-Lee, T., Hendler, J., Lassila, O.: The Semantic Web. Scientific American, 2001 May, http://www.scientificamerican.com/2001/0501issue/0501berners-lee.html
5. Balasubramanian, P., Isakowitz, T., Stohr, E. A.: RMM: A Methodology for Structured Hypermedia Design. Communications of the ACM, Vol. 38, No. 8, 1995
6. Barbosa, S. D. J., Rossi, G., Schwabe, D.: Systematic Hypermedia Application Design with OOHDM. Proc. of the Seventh ACM Conference on Hypertext, 1996
7. Bongio, A., Ceri, S., Fraternali, P.: Web Modeling Language (WebML): a modeling language for designing Web sites. Proc. of the Nineth International World Wide Web Conference (WWW9), Elsevier, 2000
8. De Bra, P., Houben, G. J.: Automatic Hypermedia Generation for ad hoc Queries on Semi-Structured Data. Proc. of the Fifth ACM Conference on Digital Libraries, ACM, 2000
9. Frasincar, F., Houben, G. J., Vdovjak, R.: An RMM-Based Methodology for Hypermedia Presentation Design. Proc. of the Fifth East-European Conference on Advances in Databases and Information Systems (ADBIS '01), Springer-Verlag, 2001
10. De Bra, P., Houben, G. J., Wu, H.: AHAM: A Dexter-based Reference Model for Adaptive Hypermedia. Proc. of the 10th ACM Conference on Hypertext and Hypermedia (Hypertext '99), ACM, 1999
11. Clark, J.: XSL Transformations (XSLT) Version 1.0. W3C Recommandation, 1999 http://www.w3.org/TR/xslt
12. Ludscher, B., Papakonstantinou, Y., Velikhov, P.: A Framework for Navigation-Driven Lazy Mediators. Proc. of ACM Workshop on the Web and Databases, ACM,1999
13. Dublin Core Metadata Element Set, Version 1.1: Reference Description. DCMI, 1999 http://dublincore.org/documents/1999/07/02/dces/
14. Klyne, G., Ohto, H., Reynolds, F., Woodrow, C.: Composite Capability/Preference Profiles (CC/PP): Structure and Vocabularies. W3C Working Draft, 2001 http://www.w3c.org/TR/CCPP-struct-vocab/

15. Beged-Dov, G., Brickley, D., Dornfest, R., Davis, I., Dodds, L., Eisenzopf, J., Galbraith, D., Guha, R. V., MacLeod, K., Miller, E., Aaron Swartz, A., van der Vlist, E.: RDF Site Summary (RSS) 1.0. RSS-DEV, 2001 http://purl.org/rss/1.0/spec
16. Connolly, D., van Harmelen, F., Horrocks, I., McGuinness, D. L., Patel-Schneider, P. F., Stein, L. A.: DAML+OIL (March 2001) Reference Description. W3C Note, 2001 http://www.w3.org/TR/daml+oil-reference
17. Hunter, J., Lagoze, C.: Combining RDF and XML Schemas to Enhance Interoperability Between Metadata Application Profiles. Proc. of the Tenth International World Wide Web Conference (WWW10), ACM, 2001
18. Biron, P. V., Malhotra, A.: XML Schema Part 2: Datatypes. W3C Recommandation, 2001 http://www.w3.org/TR/xmlschema-2
19. Kashyap, V., Sheth, A.: Schema Correspondences between Objects with Semantic Proximity. Technical report DCS-TR-301, Department of Computer Science Rutgers University, 1993, October
20. Mark, A. M., Noy, N. F.: Anchor-PROMPT: Using Non-Local Context for Semantic Matching. Proc. of the Workshop on Ontologies and Information Sharing at the Seventeenth International Joint Conference on Artificial Intelligence, 2001
21. Maruyama, H., Tamura, K., Tamuran, K., Uramoto, N.: In: XML and Java, LMX: Sample Nontrivial Application. Addison-Wesley, 1999, 97–142
22. Wiederhold, G.: Mediators in the Architecture of Future Information Systems. Computer Magazine of the Computer Group News of the IEEE Computer Group Society, Vol. 25. IEEE, 1992, 38–49
23. Alexaki, S., Christophides, V., Karvounarakis, G., Plexousakis, D.: The RDFSuite: Managing Voluminous RDF Description Bases. Proc. of the Second International Workshop on the Semantic Web (SemWeb '01),WWW10, 2001
24. Duschka, O. M., Genesereth, M. R., Levy, A. Y.: Recursive Query Plans for Data Integration. Journal of Logic Programming, Vol. 43, No. 1, 2000, 49–73
25. Elkan, C. P., Monge, A. E.: The field matching problem: Algorithms and applications. Proc. of the Second International Conference on Knowledge Discovery and Data Mining, AAAI Press, 1996

Towards a Framework for Comparing Process Modelling Languages

Eva Söderström[1], Birger Andersson[2], Paul Johannesson[2], Erik Perjons[2], and Benkt Wangler[1]

[1] Department of Computer Science, University of Skövde
Box 408, 541 28 Skövde, Sweden
{eva.soderstrom,benkt.wangler}@ida.his.se
[2] Department of Computer and Systems Sciences
Stockholm University/Royal Institute of Technology
Electrum 230, 164 40 Kista, Sweden
{ba,pajo,perjons}@dsv.su.se

Abstract. The increasing interest in process engineering and application integration has resulted in the appearance of various new process modelling languages. Understanding and comparing such languages has therefore become a major problem in information systems research and development. We suggest a framework to solve this problem involving several instruments: a general process meta-model with a table, an analysis of the event concept, and a classification of concepts according to the interrogative pronouns: what, how, why, who, when, and where. This framework can be used for several purposes, such as translating between languages or verifying that relevant organisational aspects have been captured. To validate the framework, three different process modelling languages have been compared: Business Modelling Language (BML), Event-driven Process Chains (EPC) and UML State Diagrams.

1 Introduction

Business Process Modelling has become a major focus of attention in Information Systems Engineering, in order to create efficiency, quality and customer satisfaction. Process models can be used for planning, design, simulation and automatic execution of business processes, e.g. in Workflow Management Systems and Process Brokers [1, 2]. Furthermore, methods like Total Quality Management and Business Process Reengineering, and software packages like SAP R/3 and Baan ERP all have put the business processes in the centre of analysis. As a result, several different process modelling languages have been developed, e.g. Business Modelling Language, Event-driven Process Chains, and UML Activity and State Diagrams. However, these languages often define and use concepts in different and sometimes ambiguous ways, which makes comparisons between and integration of process models difficult.

Language comparison can be made easier by using e.g. a meta-model. The reason is that the meta-model provides a graphical illustration of the basic concepts and their relations that is easy to grasp even for non-experts on process modelling languages. The purpose of this paper is to suggest a framework that aims at making comparisons between business process modelling languages easier to perform. The framework consists of several instruments: a general process meta-model, an analysis of the event concept, and a classification of concepts according to the interrogative pronouns: what, how, why, who, when, and where. The intended users of the framework are IS/IT-managers, business people and other stakeholders involved in business process management in different domains. The framework must therefore: firstly, be easy to understand for people not familiar with process modelling; secondly, include basic business concepts that are central to business process management (e.g. activity, event, actor, location, resource and time); and thirdly, be extensible to enable users to complement it with concepts of interest to a certain business domain.

The paper is structured as follows: Related research in Chapter 2 presents approaches such as meta-modelling and ontology analysis for comparing and evaluating process modelling languages. Chapter 3 presents a process meta-model, an analysis of the event concept and a classification of the concepts according to the interrogative pronouns. Chapter 4 introduces three process modelling languages: EPC, UML State diagram and BML. In chapter 5, the meta-model is used to compare the three such languages, and the result is presented in a in a table (referred to as a "comparison matrix"). Chapter 6 contains conclusions and directions for further research.

2 Related Research

Meta-models, ontologies and conceptual models are often used to describe and analyse the relations between concepts. A model is an abstraction of phenomena in the real world, and a meta-model is yet another abstraction highlighting properties of the model itself [3]. *Meta-modelling* is closely related to, and to some extent overlapping, ontology analysis and conceptual modelling.

Ontology is a philosophical discipline where the nature of the real world is studied. Some ontologies attempt to define basic concepts in a certain domain, e.g. medicine or automobile manufacturing, while others try to be more domain independent. The Bunge, Wand and Weber (BWW) ontology [4, 5] is domain independent. Wand and Weber [5, 6] have used the BWW ontology to provide a theoretical foundation for the evaluation of information systems models. They assume that an information system (IS) represents a real world system, and that it is built to manage information process functions in this real world. They present a set of basic real world concepts that IS models should be able to express. By mapping the concepts (e.g. thing, state, event and system) to concepts in different languages, Wand and Weber discuss strengths and weaknesses in these languages. However, some concepts in this ontology are difficult for non-experts to map to concepts in everyday process modelling languages.

Examples of *models of process concepts* are the Workflow Management Coalition WfMC reference model [7] and the FRISCO report [8]. In the WfMC reference model, terminology, structure, components and interfaces for workflow management systems and languages are defined. The FRISCO report also defines central concepts in the IS area (e.g. process, state and action), but its definitions of are different from those given by WfMC. None of these models show how concepts from different types of process modelling languages, e.g. activity-oriented, state-oriented and communication-oriented languages, relate to one another. Activity-oriented languages primarily describe which activities follow and precede another in a process. Examples of such languages are UML Activity Diagram [9], Task Structures [10], and Event-driven Process Chain (EPC) [11, 12]. State-oriented languages, for instance UML State Diagram [9], describe which states follow and precede another in a process. SDL [13] and Business Modeling Language (BML) [2, 14] are examples of communication-oriented languages that focus on the interaction between people and systems, and between systems.

The basic grammar of most process modelling languages derives from Petri nets [15], which provide both a graphical description and formal definition of processes. Researchers [16, 10] have mapped EPC and Task Structures to Petri nets to give the languages formal semantics, and hence to verify the correctness (soundness) of the process definitions. This approach could be used to compare different process modelling languages, but Petri net analysis are for method experts and cannot easily work as a platform for communication between business people. Furthermore, a process modelling language for business process management must include more concepts than just places, transitions and tokens that are present in classical Petri nets.

We have grouped the meta-model concepts according to a set of interrogative pronouns to clarify what aspects of processes that different concepts represent. Other researchers that use interrogative pronouns to structure their analysis are Zachman [17] who uses them to classify a descriptive representation of an enterprise with focus on managing and developing an enterprise's system and Bunge [18] who uses the pronouns to understand and separate basic types of domain-dependent problems.

3 The Framework

The framework will be explained starting with the basic concepts, before the meta-model is introduced. Finally, we explain how and why the interrogative pronouns have been used in the meta-model.

3.1 Basic Concepts

Most process modelling languages include at least four basic concepts: time point, activity, state and event, i.e. these four concepts are the common denominators of process modelling languages. Intuitively, a *time point* is an instant in time, not further decomposable. An *activity* is a performance of some sort, possibly changing some thing's *state,* i.e. its set of properties. An *event* is a noteworthy occurrence. Usually, one is interested in particular events associated with changes of state, i.e. activities are involved in some way. Activities, states and the running of time can be thought of as existing regardless of an observer but events are some facts about a thing that an observer notice and records by some means.

Most process modelling languages agree on the general meaning of these concepts and their definitions are usually precise but differ in some respects. The greatest differences between the languages lie in the understanding of the relations between the concepts. We claim that it is useful to consider an event as a connector that connects states and activities in time as is schematically illustrated by the lines from event to the other three concepts in Fig.1. One reason why languages differ is that activities, states and time can be connected in many ways and this suggests that the relations between the concepts are best understood by analysing the event concept.

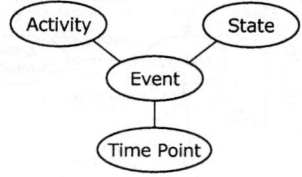

Fig. 1. The intuitive relation between the event concept and other basic concepts

The following event types were identified in an analysis of the event concept from the languages BML, UML State Diagram, and EPC:

- Events can either record a certain point in time (*time point events*) or record the time between two time points (*time duration events*).
- Events can either record the start of an activity (*pre-activity events*) or record the end of an activity (*post-activity events*).
- Events may record the change of a state (*state change events*) or not.

Using the event types described above in a language analysis, some conclusions can be drawn about the languages and their use of the event concept. Firstly, the languages define an event as non-similar combinations of the above mentioned event types. For example, one language defines an event as a combination of post-activity and state change events, i.e. the completion of an activity always leads to a change of the process' state. Other languages define event as a combination of time point and pre-activity events, and so on. Secondly, some languages do not recognise differences between event types as they are presented above, e.g. by not distinguishing between pre-activity and post-activity events.

3.2 The Meta-model

Figure 2 shows the meta-model, which is divided into two levels: type and instance. On the type level, we find activity, resource, role and logical dependencies between activities. On the instance level, we find event, state, actor, and temporal dependencies between events. Thus, the meta-model includes some additional concepts besides the basic ones to make it more useful in a business setting.

A process is modelled on a type level as a structure of logical dependencies between activities. These activities use one or more resources as input, and produces one or more resources as output. One specific type of resource, the role, is regarded to be responsible for that one or more activities will be performed.

The execution of a process is regarded to be a time-bound series of events, caused by an actor. These events may result in a state change for a resource. An actor who causes an event always has an intention with his/her actions to achieve a specific state for a resource. The state can be either different from the resource's current state, or it can be the same state as the current one.

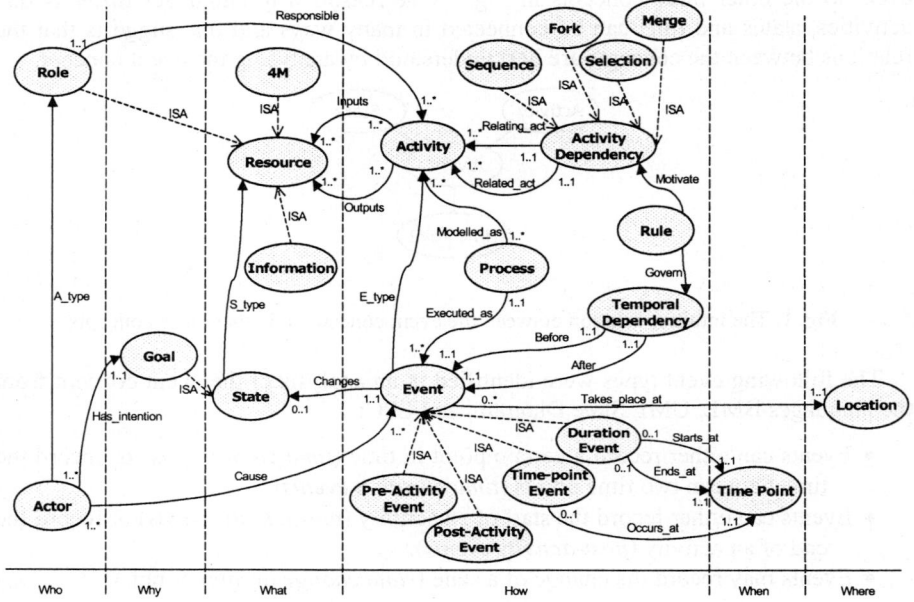

Fig. 2. The meta-model

An actor is regarded to be an instantiation of a role, a state is viewed as an instance of a resource, and an event is an instance of an activity. In the latter case, our perception of an activity is through the event that initiates and/or terminates it. An event always occurs at a certain time point or between two time points on a certain location.

3.3 Interrogative Pronouns

The interrogative pronouns: where, who, how, when, what and why, have been inserted into the meta-model to enhance readability and understandability. They provide an easy-to-grasp classification of the concepts according to various aspects, and also give an intuitive meaning to the abstract concepts.

This classification can help organisations to ask questions about their processes and process models, and to aid organisations in selecting the process modelling language appropriate to their business. For example, an organisation for which actors are central can exclude languages that do not model actors, i.e. languages that disregard from the "who" aspect.

4 Process Modelling Languages

EPC, UML State Diagram and BML represent different types of process modelling languages: an activity-oriented, a state-oriented, and a communication-oriented (see section 2). The three languages are considered to be representative of their respective category, which motivates their presence in this paper. Following are a short presentation of the languages, and a description of how the event concept is used in respective language. This section includes as an example a very short snippet of a manufacturing process to show language symbols and how they are used.

4.1 Event-Driven Process Chains (EPC)

Event-driven Process Chains (EPC) [11] is used for instance to describe business processes in the SAP/R3 enterprise system. The EPC diagrams are also embedded and used in the process view of the Architecture of Integrated Information System (ARIS) framework that integrates five different perspectives or views (data, function, organisation, output and process) of an organisation [12].

EPC is a graph with active nodes, called functions (soft rectangles), and passive nodes, called events (hexagons), see Fig. 3 (left). In EPC, a process is considered to be a chain of business functions to be executed, and of events describing the situation before and after each function. EPC does not explicitly use the state concept. The logical relationships and dependencies between functions and events are described using logical connectors (circles including the logical AND, OR and XOR) and control flow (arrows). The EPC diagram of Fig. 3 shows that two events, *Order received* and *Production date arrived* must occur before the business function *Manufacturing* can take place. When the function is completed, two additional events must occur: *Product in store* and *Order executed*. The function nodes can be connected to information, material, product and services and responsible organisational unit, by adding the other views of the ARIS framework. This is not included in Fig. 3.

EPC explicitly uses the following event types:

- Pre-activity events (i.e. the events before the functions in the EPC diagram).
- Post-activity events (i.e. the events after the functions in the EPC diagram).

EPC does not use the following event types:

- State change events (because EPC does not explicit use the concept state)

EPC does not explicitly distinguish between following event types:

- Time point events and Time duration events

Note that EPC does not explicitly combine any event types.

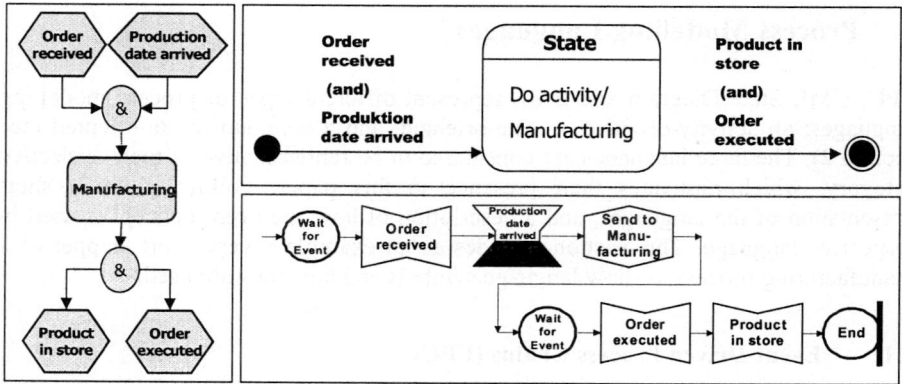

Fig. 3. Three different modelling languages: EPC (left), UML State Diagram (top, right) and BML (down, right)

4.2   UML State Diagram (SD)

The Unified Modelling Language (UML) [19] is an industry standard maintained by the Object Management Group (OMG) [9]. The state – or state-chart – diagram (SD) is one of several diagram types in UML. SD is a graphical representation of a state machine and visualises how and under what circumstances a modelled element, e.g. a UML class, a system or a business process, changes its state. SD is also used to show which activities that are executed as a result of events. The SD graph uses symbols for states (soft rectangles), transitions (arrows), events (text labels), and activities (text labels), and always includes a start state (solid circle) and one or more final states ("bulls-eye"), see Fig. 3 (right, top).

A state consists three components: name, variables (describing local variables like counters and timers), and activities; where all but the name component is optional. The state symbol is divided into three compartments to illustrate this division. The difference between an action and an activity is that an action is non-divisible and non-interruptible, and that an activity can contain several actions. There are three different types of actions/activities associated with the state of a modelled element: *entry action* (performed when entering the state); *exit action* (performed when exiting the state), and *do activity* (performed while in the state). Fig. 3 only shows the *do activity* Manufacturing. A state that does not contain any activities is called a wait state.

State changes are called transitions (arrows connecting the states). A transition occurs if an event occurs and aborts an ongoing do activity, or if a do activity has been completed and triggered a completion event. However, before a transition can occur, an optional condition called "guard" must be evaluated. If the guard evaluates to true, the transition occurs, otherwise it will not. During a transition certain actions can be performed. A SD considers events to occur instantaneously, while states have duration, but UML does not hinder modellers to redefine events to have duration and states to have no duration. Some additional event types from UML state diagrams are omitted in this paper for the sake of brevity.

SD explicitly uses the following simple or combined event types:

- Post-activity events (i.e. an event occurs, which aborts an ongoing do activity, but does not trigger a transition since a guard is evaluated to false).
- Post-activity events and State change events (i.e. an event occurs, which both aborts an ongoing do activity and triggers a transition).
- Post-activity events, and Pre-activity events (i.e. an event occurs, which both aborts an ongoing do activity and initiates the exit action, but does not trigger a transition because a guard is evaluated false).
- Post-activity events, Pre-activity events and State change events (i.e. an event occurs, which both aborts an ongoing do activity, initiates an optional exit action, triggers a transition, triggers some optional actions while in transition, and initiates optional entry action and do activities in the next state).
- State change events (i.e. an event occurs, and the state is a wait state, and the event triggers a transition).
- Pre-activity events (i.e. an event occurs, and the state is a wait state, and the event initiates an exit action, but does not trigger a transition because a guard is evaluated to false).
- Pre-activity events, and State change events (i.e. an event occurs, and the state is a wait state, and the event both initiates an optional exit action, triggers a transition, trigger some optional actions while in transition, and initiates optional entry action and do activities in the next state).

SD does not explicitly distinguish between the following event types:

- Time point events and Time duration events

4.3 Business Modelling Language (BML)

The Business Modelling Language (BML) is used in a Process Broker [2], the Visuera Process Manager [14]. BML focuses on describing interactions between systems through the sending and receiving of messages. The language has similarities to SDL (Specification and Description Language) [13], but is more adapted to application integration. One important feature of BML is that it can be used for business specification and design as well as for the execution of systems.

BML describes structure and behaviour of a system by using two kinds of diagrams. The Business Process Integration (BPI) diagram shows the system structure in terms of its logical decomposition into parts and the communication taking place between the system and its environment, i.e. external applications and human agents. The communication metaphor is sending and receiving messages through a channel. The Business Integration Application (BIA) diagrams describe the dynamic behaviour of the system, visualising when the system sends and receives messages, the rules for handling messages and what activities to perform depending on the messages' contents.

The BML symbols in the process diagram (BIA), some of which are presented in Fig. 2 (right, down), are: Receive message (concave box), Send message (convex box), and State (circle). Further BML symbols are: Start timer (hourglass "full of time"), Expire timer (hourglass "out of time"), Business activity (rectangle, not shown), and Automated business decision (rhombus, not shown), which shows what paths should be taken through the process according to business rules. BIA always includes a start state (circle without name) and one or more End states (circle with the label "End"). A BIA can visualise to which application, human agent or process that a message is sent to or received from, by using labels (or icons) above the diagram's send and receive symbols (not shown in Fig. 2).

An instance of a BIA can either be in a state or in transition from one state to another. A transition is initiated when a message is received or when a timer is expired. Activities that may occur during the transition, e.g. Send message and Start timer, are considered to happen instantaneously.

BML explicitly uses the following combined event types:

- Time point events, Pre-activity events and State change events (i.e. a Receive Message or Expire Timer triggers one or several activities, i.e. Send message, Start timer and/or, Business activity, and a transition.)
- Time point events and State change events, (i.e. a Receive Message or BML Expire Timer triggers a BML transition, but not an activity.)

BML does not explicitly use the following event types:

- Post-activity events
- Time duration events

5 Language Comparison

Results from comparing process modelling language using the meta-model is presented in Table 1. The table provides a structured overview of defined concepts, and clearly indicates some differences between the languages. For example, empty boxes in the table illustrate that a particular language does not explicity express this concept. Anyone creating and using the table for language selection is made aware of this fact and can eliminate a language that cannot express desired concepts or extend it with the missing concept. Furthermore, the table makes differences in definitions between the languages explicit, which enables organisations to discover languages which defines and uses concepts in ways similar to the organisation itself. Creating the table may also provide an opportunity for organisations to reflect about the way they define their own concepts and consider alternative definitions.

6 Summary and Further Research

The framework presented in this paper consists of a meta-model of process concepts with a comparison matrix, a classification of the concepts according to interrogative pronouns, and an analysis of the event concept. It aims at making comparisons between various process modelling languages easier. In this summary, we will highlight contributions and strengths of both the parts, and of the framework as a whole. Since the parts provide slightly different views of the same phenomenon, some of their contributions will be the same.

Table 1. Comparison of EPC, BML and UML SD

Concept	EPC	BML	SD
Time Point			
Event	Uses two simple events types: 1) Pre-activity events 2) Post-activity events	Uses two combinations of event types: 1) Time point+ Pre-activity+State change events. 2) Time point+State change events. Both correspond to the BML concepts "Receive Message" and "Expire Timer"	Uses seven simple or combined event types, see section 4.2.
State		Corresponds to the BML concept "Wait for Event"	Corresponds to the SD concepts "State" and "Wait State"
Activity	Corresponds to EPC concept "Function"	Corresponds to the BML concepts "Business activity", "Send message" and "Start timer"	Corresponds to the SD concepts "entry action", "do activity" and "exit action"
Process	Corresponds to a partially ordered set of logically dependent "functions"	Corresponds to a partially ordered set of logically dependent "business activities"	Corresponds to a partially ordered set of logically dependent "actions/activities"
Rules	Corresponds to a set of pre- and post conditions ("events") that must be true before and after an "function"	Corresponds the BML concept "Automated business decisions"	Corresponds to a set of conditions on the "transitions"
Resource	Corresponds to the EPC concept "Resource".	Corresponds to the BML concept "BIA"	Corresponds to the SD concept "Class"
Actor		Corresponds to the BML concepts "BIA", "application", and human agent, capable of sending "messages" at a time point.	Corresponds to the SD concept "Object" capable of producing an "event".
Location			

Starting with the *meta-model*, one contribution is that it explores basic definitions of concepts used in various process modelling languages. Furthermore, the meta-model is extensible and can thus be adapted to different business domains. It also enables organisations to cover many different organisational aspects through the use of the *interrogative pronouns*. These pronouns provide understandability, readability, and an easy-to-grasp classification of concepts. The meta-model still needs some work, however, such as a deeper exploration into all the meta-model concepts, and real life cases through which the extensibility of the meta-model can be shown.

By using a *comparison matrix* (or table) to present the results from applying the meta-model, several contributions can be identified. The matrix provides a structured overview of defined concepts, and an explicit illustration of definitional differences between the languages. This enables organisations to identify the language that best suits the organisation's own definitions and intentions. Should an organisation lack explicit definitions of its concepts, the matrix can provide a basis for creating such definitions.

By analysing the *event* concept, we have highlighted that some major differences between the languages lie in how they use this concept. However, the other basic concepts (activity and state) also need to be analysed to enhance the usefulness of the framework, as do the concepts in the complete meta-model (rule, resource, actor, and goal).

The *framework as a whole* was validated by comparing three different process modelling languages: BML, EPC and UML SD. The comparison shows that the framework can be used for several purposes, many of them already described in this chapter. Different process modelling languages can be compared with respect to their concepts definitions, concept relationships, and correspondences of concepts between languages. The result provides a basis for selecting the process modelling language that best suites the organisational needs. The framework can also be used as a translation instrument between process modelling languages, and to identify what organisational aspects that the languages cover. As mentioned, the framework still needs some work: a method for using the framework, including step-by-step guidelines for how to perform e.g. language comparisons, needs to be developed. Furthermore, more formal definitions of the basic concepts are needed, as are experiences from real life case studies where the framework is applied, validated and verified.

References

1. Linthicum, D.: Enterprise Application Intergration, Addison-Wesley (2000).
2. Johannesson, P., Perjons, E.: Design Principles for process modelling in enterprise application integration, Information Systems, 26:165-184 (2001)
3. van Gigch, J. P (1991) System Design Modeling and Metamodeling. Plenum Press, New York. ISBN 0-306-43740-6
4. Bunge, M.: Treatise on Basic Philosophy Vol 3, Ontology I: The Furniture of the World, Reidel, Dordrecht, Boston (1977)
5. Wand, Y.: Ontology as a Foudation for Meta-modelling and method engineering, In: Information and Software Technology 38 (1996), 281-287
6. Wand, Y., Weber, R.: An Ontological Model of an Information System, In: IEEE Transactions on Software Engineering, 11 (1990), p 1282-1290

7. Reference Model - The Workflow Reference Model, WFMC-TC-1003, 19-Jan-95 (1995), 1.1, and Terminology & Glossary, WFMC-TC-1011, Feb-1999, 3.0 (1999). Available at: http://www.aiim.org/wfmc/mainframe.htm
8. The FRISCO Report, A Framework of Information System Concept, IFIP (1998), available at: http://www.liacs.nl/~verrynst/frisco.html
9. OMG Unified Modelling Language Specification, Version 1.3. (1999), available at: http://www.oml.org
10. van der Aalst, W. M. P, Ter Hofstede, A. H. M.: Verification of Workflow Task Structures: A Petri-net-based Approach, Information Systems, vol. 25, no. 1 (2000)
11. Keller, G., Nüttgens, M. , Scheer, A.W.: Semantische Processmodellierung auf der Grundlage Ereignisgesteuerter Processketten (EPK). Veröffentlichungen des Instituts für Wirtschaftsinformatik, Heft 89, University of Saarland, Saarbrücken (1992)
12. Sheer, A.: ARIS-Business Process Modelling. Springer-Verlag, Berlin (1998)
13. Belina, F., Hogrefe, D., Amardeo, S.: SDL with Applications from Protocol Specification. Carl Hanser Verlag and Prentice Hall International, UK (1991)
14. Wåhlander, C., Nilsson, M., Törnebohm, J.: Visuera PM Introduction, Copyright Visuera AB (2001)
15. Reisig, W.: Petri Nets: an introduction. Springer-Verlag, Berlin (1985)
16. van der Aalst, W. M. P: Formalization and Verification of Event-driven Process Chains, In: Information and Software Technology, 41(10):639-650, (1999)
17. Zachman, J.: Enterprise Architecture: The Issue of the Century In: Zifa Framwork Articles (1996), available at: http://www.zifa.com
18. Bunge, M.: Scientific Research I, Springer-Verlag, (1967)
19. Rumbaugh, J., Jacobson, I., Booch, G.: The unified modeling language reference manual, Addison Wesley Longman Inc. (1999)

Generic Models for Engineering Methods of Diverse Domains

N. Prakash[1] and M. P. S. Bhatia[2]

[1]JIIT A10, Sector 62 NOIDA 201307, India
praknav@hotmail.com
[2]NSIT Sector 3, Dwarka, New Delhi 110045, India
bhatia_mps@hotmail.com

Abstract. The 3-layer architecture for methods consisting of the generic model, meta-model, and method layers is considered and the advantages of introducing the generic layer are brought out. It is argued that this layer helps in method selection, construction of methods in diverse domains and has the potential of rapidly engineering methods. A generic model is introduced and then instantiated from meta-models from the Information Systems and Robotics and Project Planning domains. Thereafter methods are produced by an instantiation of these meta-models. Computer based support for the 3-layer architecture is considered and notion of a generic-CASE tool is introduced.

1 Introduction

A number of meta-models (Gro97, Pra97a, Pra97b, Pra99a, Pra99b, Rol95, Sou91) have been developed in the last decade for a range of uses

- Understanding conceptual models of the 1970s and 1980s
- Identifying commonalties between models
- Representing product and process aspects of methods
- Understanding process models
- Representing quality aspects of methods
- Developing techniques for Requirements Engineering
- Investigating Data Warehouses

Indeed meta-models have emerged as a principal means to understanding the activities seen in the area of Information Systems. Meta-modelling has been used in the development of CASE tools including those for Requirements Engineering. It has also been used for Method Engineering and more specifically, in the development of CAME tools.

In method engineering, meta-models provide an abstraction of method concepts, inter-relationships between these, and constraints binding these together into a coherent system that forms a method. However, as noted in (Pra97a), whereas meta-models provide useful abstractions of methods, they do not clearly articulate the *essential* nature of the methods they deal with and do not address the critical issue of what *is* a method. Consequently, the class of methods being modelled in a meta-model determines the nature of methods assumed by the meta-model. Thus, in their early period, meta-models emphasised only the product aspects of methods. Later, the dichotomy of product and process aspects was modelled or the process aspects were emphasised.

A comprehensive 3-layer framework was proposed (Pra99a) in which the highest layer is the generic layer where the nature of a method is articulated, the middle layer is the meta-model layer and, finally, the lowest layer is the method layer. The successive layers were seen as instantiations of their immediately higher layer. This framework was illustrated with a generic model whose instantiation resulted in a meta-model of a method that, in turn, was instantiated as a method. Subsequently, the method engineering activity to support this and an associated CAME tool called MERU (Gup01), have been developed.

In this paper, we focus on the generic layer and raise two questions. The first is concerning the usefulness of the generic layer itself: What does it achieve? what does it get for us? As indicated earlier, we believe that the generic layer deals with the essential nature of methods and makes explicit the domain of these methods. It helps in the following ways:

Since it makes explicit the nature of the domain, it promotes the development of methods and processes specific to that domain. We expect this to lead to greater method acceptability among application engineers.

Again, by making explicit the nature of domain, it helps us in understanding and comparing different domains.

It helps in meta-method engineering. A meta-model can be checked out for consistency and completeness under the generic view. This can be facilitated by constructing Generic-CAME tools.

A Generic tool can be developed to produce CASE tools directly from domain specific models thus speeding up the construction of domain specific tools.

The generic approach can also be used for simulating real process and real systems before they are actually implemented. For example, in the Robotics domain, the entire robot can be conceptualised, and a method produced. Using CASE support, application processes can be built to check that the robot does, in fact, handle the proposed range of tasks. If not then the robot can be re-conceptualised. Thus, before constructing the real robot, its viability can be fully established.

The second question we raise here is regarding the generic model inhabiting the generic layer. What is the system of concepts that makes the generic model truly generic? In other words, can the generic model be used for methods of a wide range of domains, not just the IS domain? Indeed, if such a generic model can be found then the domain of IS would contribute significantly to other domains.

In this paper we first present a generic model. Thereafter we consider three meta-models, one in the domain of Information Systems, Robotics and Project Planning. We show that these could be defined by instantiating the generic model. We then consider the method level for the Information Systems, the Robotics and the Project Management domains by instantiating the meta-models. The advantages of these approaches in the three cases are then brought out.

The layout of the papers is as follows. In the next section, the generic model is presented. Thereafter in sections 3, 4 and 5 respectively the Information Systems, Robotics and Project Planning meta-models are presented. Also, an instantiation of these to yield methods is considered in these sections. The differences between the meta-models of the three domains are highlighted. In section 5 we outline the nature of the computer support that can be provided. Generic-CASE tools at higher level of abstraction then the meta-CASE tools of today. The generic-CASE tool is at two levels.

2 The Generic Model

The Generic View of a method (Pra99b) is based on the view of a method as an artifact that provides the capability to construct a product. A method has two aspects to it, its static and dynamic properties. Static properties of interest, from a modeling point of view, are those that describe the holistic structure of the artifact, identify the component parts of the artifact, and bring out the inter-relationships between these components. The dynamic properties of artifacts are those that describe the interaction of the artifact with its environment. This interaction may be viewed in holistic terms, as the interaction of the entire artifact, or in terms of its components.

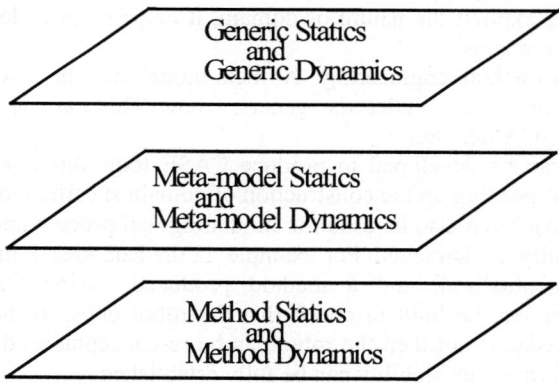

Fig. 1: The Three-Layered Architecture

As shown in Fig. 1 a method is organised in three layers, the generic layer, the meta-model, and the method layer. Each lower layer is an instantiation of its immediately higher layer.

In the *generic* view, the interest is on the intrinsic notion of a method, namely, (a) what it is, (b) what it can do, (c) how this capability is achieved, (d) what kinds of methods exist and what are their inter-relationships. Thus, the generic view looks at methods in meta-model independent terms and seeks to uncover their very essence. In this paper, we will deal with method statics: generic, meta-model, and method. The genericity of method dynamics is the subject of another paper.

Generic Method Statics

In this section we provide an overview of generic method statics. Details can be found in (Pra97a) and (Par97b).

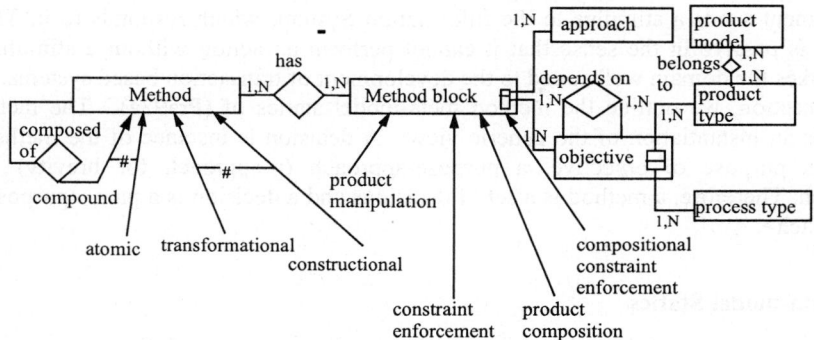

Fig. 2: Generic Method Statics

As shown in Fig. 2, there are two kinds of methods, *transformational* and *constructional*. A *transformational* method is used for transforming a product, expressed in one or more product models, into a product of other product model(s). In contrast, a *constructional* method is used whenever a new product, expressed in one or more product models, is to be constructed.

Any method can be *atomic* or compound. An *atomic* method deals only with those products, which are expressed, in exactly one product model. A *constructional* method, which builds products for the ER model, is *atomic* since the product is expressed in exactly one model. Similarly, the transformational method for converting an ER product into a relational product is atomic since each of the products is expressed in exactly one product model. On the other hand, as shown in Fig. 2, a compound method is composed out of other simpler methods. For example, the *constructional atomic* methods to construct the OM, the FM, and the DM products of OMT, compose the *constructional compound* method of OMT.

We view a method (Fig. 2) as a set of *method blocks*. When expressed in terms of method blocks, *compound* methods are composed of *method blocks*, which belong to several methods whereas all *method blocks* of an *atomic* method belong to the *atomic* method only. A method block is a pair, <objective, approach>. The objective of a method block tells us what the block tries to achieve. The approach tells us the technique that can be used to achieve the objective of the block. An objective itself is a pair <product type, process type>.

As shown in the figure, product types belong to a product model. For each product type of the product model, the process types that act upon it are associated with it to yield the objectives of the method. Method blocks do not exist independently of one another. Instead they exhibit dependencies among themselves. In (Pra97a) we have postulated four kinds of dependencies. Details can be found there.

3 The Information Systems Meta-model

The Information Systems domain aims to build teleological systems that mirror the real world. This domain deals with passive systems embedded in an environment. The environment sends a stimulus to the Information System, which responds to it. The domain is passive in the sense that it cannot perform an action without a stimulus. This makes the domain well suited to the development of transaction based systems.

In this section, we outline the method meta-model statics of (Pra97a). The meta-model is an instantiation of the generic view. A decision is instance of the method block, a purpose of objective, a purpose-approach (p-approach for brevity) of approach. Therefore, a method is a set of decisions and a decision is a pair, <purpose, p-approach>.

3.1 Meta-model Statics

There are two kinds of product types: conceptual structures and fixed structures. Similarly there are two kinds of process types, production manipulation which operates on the former and quality enforcement for manipulating the latter. These have been dealt with in (Pra97a) and (Pra99b) respectively.

As shown in Fig 3, conceptual structures can be partitioned into two clusters. The first cluster classifies them as either simple or complex. The second cluster partitions conceptual structures into disjoint classes of structures called constraint, definitional, constructional, link, and collection of concepts respectively.

A simple conceptual structure cannot be broken up into any components. It is atomic. Complex conceptual structures are constructed out of others which may themselves be complex or simple.

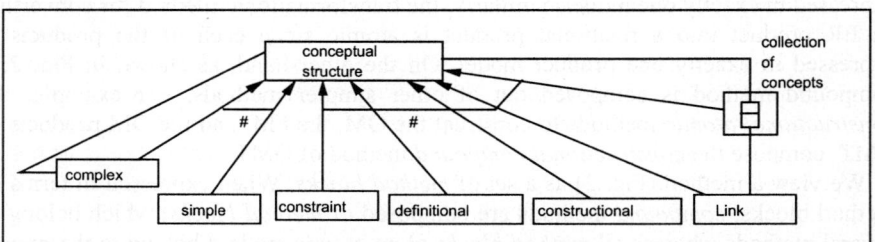

Fig. 3: The Conceptual Structure

There are five kinds of conceptual structures:

- Constructional: Constructional structures are used to represent the architecture of the product. For example, in order to display a conceptual schema expressed in ER terms, Chen uses the notions of entity and relationship respectively.
- Link: Product models use links extensively. For example, ISA links and aggregation links.
- Collection of Concepts: These are constructed whenever structures are connected by links. Aggregations, specialisation hierarchies, and subtype hierarchies are examples of such collections.

- Definitional: They define the properties of conceptual structures.
- Constraint: Constraints impose application-related integrity constraints on conceptual structures. For example, such a constraint could say that the ages of employees should be less than 65 years.

3.1.1 Fixed Structures

Fixed structures (Pra99a) are those which cannot be created or destroyed by application engineers. They identify the criteria that must be met by a good quality product. There are four kinds of fixed structures as shown in Fig. 4.

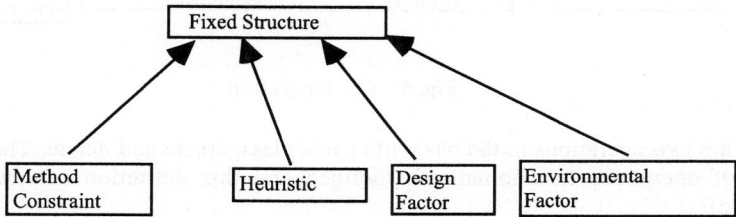

Fig. 4: The Fixed Structure

Environmental factors are fixed structures that specify the properties of the product as part of the environment in which it is embedded. These factors look after the various 'ilities' of software engineering, reliability, maintainability, usability, re-usability etc.

Design factors define method aims that are integral to method use. When translated into products, the resulting product is good because it meets method aims. For example, modularity is essential in object-oriented models and therefore is a design factor for such models. Heuristics are defined in methods to control the quality of the product. They provide rules of the thumb for good quality products and identify the bounds/criteria for acceptable products under the method.

Method constraints (Pra97a) deal with the restrictions that make conceptual structures well defined and well formed. There are four kinds of method constraints, completeness, conformity, fidelity, and consistency constraints.

3.1.2 The Operation

Operations identify the set of process types that operate upon product types to provide product manipulation and quality checking capability to application engineers. Operations are classified into two four classes (Fig. 5)

- Basic Life Cycle : for the creation and deletion of instance of structures
- Relational: for establishing relationships between concepts
- Integration: for building constructional/transformational products.
- Fixed Structure Enforcement: for quality enforcement

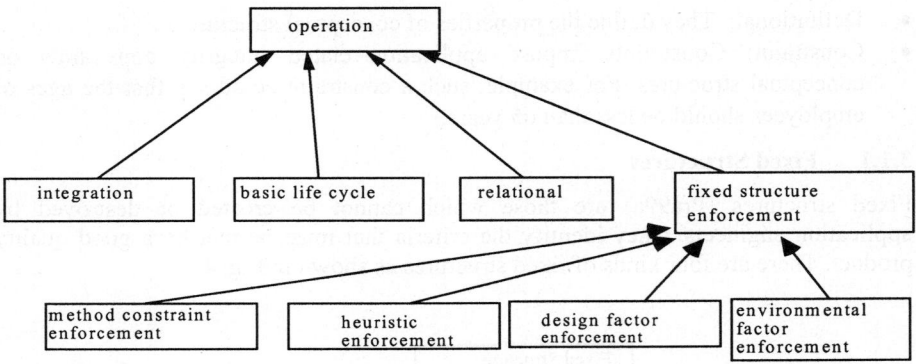

Fig. 5: The Operation

There are two operations in the basic life cycle class, create and delete. The relational class of operations is axiomatically defined and this definition can be found in (Pra97a).

3.1.3 Defining Decisions

A decision is an instance of a method block. In the meta-model, a decision has two components to it, the purpose and the p-approach. The purpose of the decision is a statement of what the decision wants to achieve. There can be many ways of achieving the purpose and this aspect is embodied in the p-approach. Thus,

Decision = < Purpose, P-approach >

A purpose is an instance of the objective of the generic model. It is a pair

Purpose = <structure, operation>

Thus, the following are purposes

<simple constructional structure, create>
<simple constructional structure, simple constructional structure, ISA link, relate>

3.2 Validating the Information System Meta-model

The validity of the foregoing meta-model has been established in (Gup01) and we only outline this here. Consider a method having the following concepts:

Cardinality, functionality, attributes, primary key, entity, relationship.

An instantiation of the meta-model is as follows

- Simple definitional concepts: cardinality, functionality
- Complex definitional concepts: attribute, primary key
- Simple constructional concepts: entity
- Complex constructional concept: relationship

A part of the total set of purposes is given below. The full set of purposes can be found in (Gup01).

<attribute, create>
<entity, create>
<relationship, create>
<entity, attribute, attach>
<entity, relationship, associate>

4 The Robotics Meta-model

In this section we consider building methods for the domain of Robotics. Unlike the Information Systems domain that we term as passive, we view the Robotics domain as active. Information systems are transaction-based and respond to stimuli from their environments. In contrast, robots perform specific tasks spontaneously and are programmed with the method to carry out these tasks. It is in this sense that the Robotics domain is active.

A robot can behave differently depending on the process that it is programmed to carry out. However, a robot addresses a class of tasks, and processes can be defined that fall into this class. Robots are similar to models like ER: just as a number of processes can be defined to build ER schemata so also a number of processes can be defined for a robot to carry out specific tasks. This is shown in the bottom row of Table 1. Just as it is possible to build meta-models that are an abstraction of the methods in the Information Systems domain, it is possible to build meta-models for robots that abstract their essential features into meta-models. This correspondence is shown in Table 1. Finally, the common properties of meta-models are abstracted out into the generic model of section 2.

Table 1. Correspondence between IS and Robotics Domains

Information Systems	Robotics
Generic Model	Generic Model
Information Systems Meta-models	Robotic Meta-models
IS Method like ER, SHM	Robot like Mitsubishi Industrial Robot

Our Robotics meta-model is presented in Figs. 6 to 7. In the rest of this section we show that this meta-model itself is an instantiation of the generic model and by doing so, we establish the genericity of the generic model. Thereafter, we instantiate the meta-model with the Mitsubishi Industrial Micro Robot System RV-IV (Mitsu) to show that the meta-model is valid.

The instantiation of the generic model is shown in Table 2.

Table 2. : The Instantiation of the Generic Method

Generic Concept	Robotics Meta-model Concept
Product type	Object
Process type	Action
Objective	Ability

The notion of an object is elaborated in Fig. 6. As shown, an object can be either an Operator or a Product. Operator refers to a component of a robot that has to be controlled, for example, its arm. Product is the object on which the operator acts. It is the real object which is to be manipulated by the operator, for example, a physical thing that has to be picked up, a screw that is to be tightened etc. Fig. 6 also shows that Object has attributes. Attributes capture the different properties that Operator/Product may have. For example, an operator which is the arm of a Robot may have as attributes the speed and direction of movement.

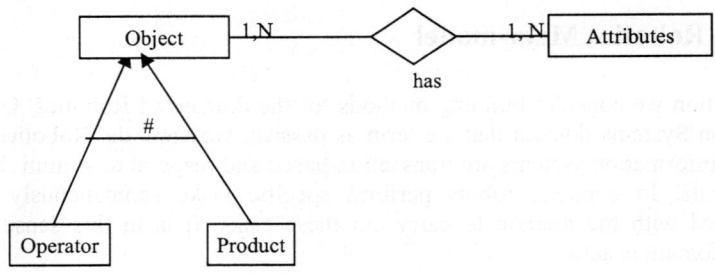

Fig. 6: The Object Meta-Concept

The notion of Action is shown in Fig. 7. There are two kinds of action, primitive and compound. Primitive actions cannot be decomposed into simpler ones whereas a compound action is built of other simpler actions. An example of an action is Move Robot Arm.

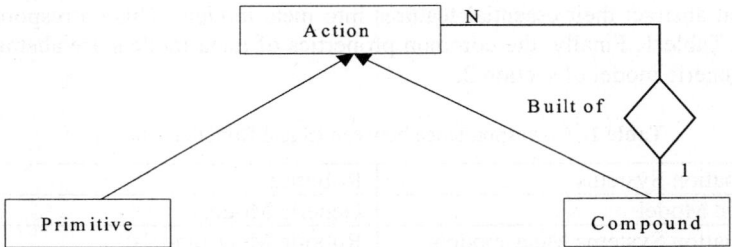

Fig. 7. The Action meta-concept

As shown in Table 2, an ability is an instantiation of objective. It is a pair, <object, action>.

4.1 Validating the Meta-model

The Mitsubishi Industrial Micro Robot System RV-IV robot can be integrated with a PC and can be used to pick and place physical objects. It is possible to control the robot through parameters like speed of movement and direction etc. The arm of this robot is an instance of Operator. It has the attributes speed, gripper_status, and pressure. Product is any item that has to be picked up and placed in some position by the robot. The instantiation of the Robotic meta-model is given in Table 3. We have listed out only some of the primitive and compound actions of this robot. Full details can be found in (Mitsu).

Table 3. Instantiation of the Robotic Meta-model

Meta-model concepts	Concepts of Robot System
Operator	Robot arm
Product	Item (to be picked)
Attribute	Speed, gripper_status, pressure
Primitive Action	MP(Move Position), MS(Move Straight), MT(Move Tool), GC(Grip Close), GO(Grip Open), GP(Grip Pressure)
Compound Action	Movemaster program

The set of abilities defines the full instruction set of the robot and can be used to simulate the behaviour of the robot. In this sense the abilities are a specification of the functionality of the robot. A partial set of abilities of the robot is given below.

<Robot arm, MP>
<Robot arm, MS>
<Robot arm, GC>
<Robot arm, GO>
<Item, MT>
<Item, GP>

5 Project Planning Meta-model

To establish the genericity of the generic model, we now consider another passive domain, that of project planning and management. Project planning involves the completion of numerous activities (project components) by various resources-men materials, machines, money, and time –so that a project on paper is translated into concrete reality.

As for the other two domains, we will adopt the three-layer architecture for methods. At the highest level is the generic model. Below this is the meta-model that, in this case, will abstract out the common properties of project planning methods. At the lowest level, are the methods themselves that are instantiations of the project planning meta-model. The instantiation of the generic view with a project planning meta-model is shown in Table 4.

Table 4. The Instantiation of the Generic Method

Generic Concept	Project Planning Meta-model Concept
Product type	Project Concept
Process type	Operation
Objective	Capability

The Project Planning meta-model is shown in Fig. 8 and 9. There are two kinds of project concepts, components and constraints. Constraints are similar to method constraints and impose restrictions on well-formedness and well-definedness of the project plan. Components are concepts that are used in the representation of the project plan. These can be activities or events. Activities are long-duration actions that are triggered by events. The Figure shows that components have attributes. Thus, for example, an activity has a cost, a start time and an end time.

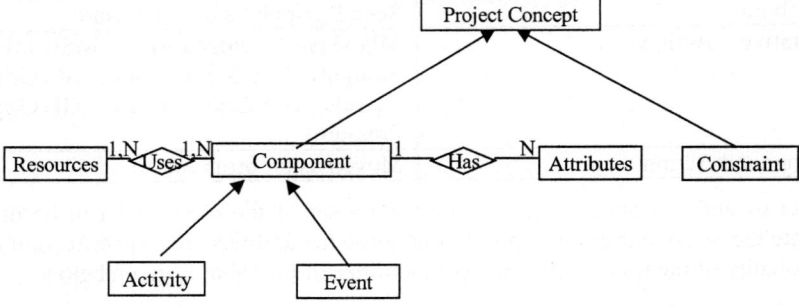

Fig. 8. The Project Concept of the Meta-model

The operations that can be performed on project concepts are shown in Fig. 9. There are two kinds of operations, those that enforce constraints and those for manipulating components. The latter are partitioned into basic life cycle and combinational classes of operations. Basic life cycle operations are used for creating/deleting components whereas combinational operations allow components to be related to one another. For example, the start event of an activity can be associated with it by a combinational operation.

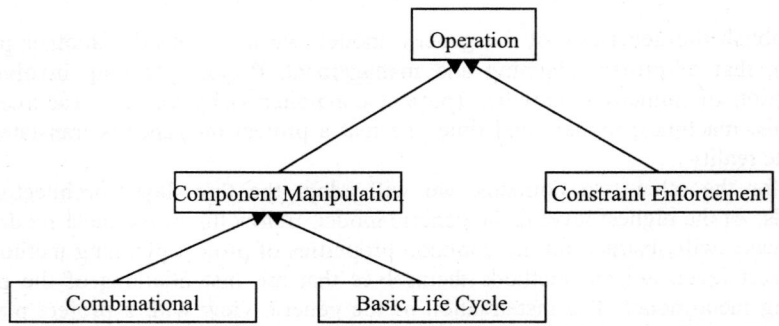

Fig. 9: Operations of the Project Planning Meta-Model

5.1 Validating the Meta-model

The activities of a project have inter-relationships arising from physical, technical, and other considerations. For proper planning, scheduling, and control of activities, network techniques have been found quite useful. We consider the construction of such networks here. There are two basic network techniques: PERT and CPM. The orientation of PERT is 'probabilistic' and CPM is ' deterministic'. A project in both these can be broken into a well defined set of jobs or activities. The common characteristics of both these techniques are the imposition of an ordering on the activities that can be performed. The instantiation of the project planning meta-model for network construction is shown in Table 5.

Table 5. : Instantiation of the Project Planning Meta-model

Meta-model concepts	Project Planning Method Concepts
Constraint	1. Precedence/succession constraint: For every action there is a preceding and succeeding event. 2. No loops are allowed. 3. Not more than one activity can have the same Proceeding and succeding events.
Activity	Activity
Event	Event
Attribute	Cost
Resource	Person
Combinational Operation	Attach attribute to project component Associate resource with project component Relate a start event and an end event with Activity
Basic Life Cycle Operation	Create event/activity Delete event/activity

Some of the capabilities of the project planning, method are as follows:

<activity, create>   <activity, cost, attach>
<activity, delete>   <activity, person, associate>
<event, create>   <activity, event, event, relate>
<event, delete>
<person, create>

6 Providing Computer Support

In this section we outline the manner in which computer assistance can be provided in the task of constructing methods of any domain. Our proposal is to raise the level of meta-CASE tools/CASE shells to generic CASE tools. These tools have the property that they can generate methods for diverse domains: Information Systems as well as others like the Robotics and Project Planning domains.

Method engineering has relied on the notion of meta-models to build CAME tools. Meta-CASE tools or CASE shells have a CAME tool as their front-end and a CASE generator as a back-end. Given that the generic view of section 2 has the capability to deal with a range of domains, we are in the process of designing Generic-CASE shells with a generic part added in front of the CAME part. This part is used to instantiate the generic model, possibly, with the meta-model of the domain of interest. Thus, for example, the Generic tool can be used to instantiate the generic model with the Robotics meta-model of section 4. This capability can be used to develop generic-CASE that can produce methods and associated CASE tools of any domain.

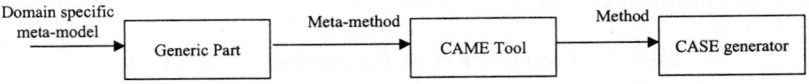

Fig. 10. The Three Stages of the Generic-CASE Tool

Fig. 10 shows that the Generic tool takes the specification of a domain specific meta-model as input and outputs the meta-method in terms of the set of abilities. This set is the definition of the full capability available with the meta-model and therefore with the meta-method. The meta-method is then given to the CAME tool from which the method is produced. Whereas the meta-method is domain-dependent, the method is dependent on the meta-method itself. The CASE generator produces a tool that makes the method usable.

The first step in the construction of the generic-CASE is a language in which meta-models can be defined. This language, the Generic Specification Language (GSL), expresses the meta-concepts and the generic concept to which they correspond. The interpretation system behind this language generates the set of objectives that form part of the meta-method.

7 Concluding Remarks

We have shown that the generic layer can help in instantiating meta-models of diverse domains. Of course, the generic layer can be used for different meta-models of a given domain as well. Thus, for the Information Systems domain, it can be used to instantiate process meta-models or integrated process-product meta-models. This genericity can be viewed as replacing meta-model dependence with generic model dependence.

Dependence of methods on meta-models implies that the features and limitations of meta-models get carried over to methods. In this sense, meta-model dependence constrains methods. The introduction of the generic layer and generic-CASE tools is an attempt at reducing the effect of this meta-model dependence. First, with generic-CASE tools, it shall be possible to build meta-models faster. This will encourage the development of meta-models that are tailor-made to produce the needed methods. Second, it shall be possible to take the output of the generic part of the generic-CASE, experiment with it and determine whether or not the meta-model provides the features that it was supposed to provide. Thus, we see the generic-CASE tool as providing a comprehensive structure for situational method engineering.

We shall observe similar effects in domains other than Information Systems. Thus, for example in the Robotics domain, the robot engineer has to first determine the nature of the robot to be produced and then construct the robot. Use of the generic-CASE tool here helps in a number of ways (a) it makes the robot engineer concentrate on the task of defining robot characteristic and not its construction (b) it is possible to check out the usefulness of the robot meta-model before committing to a robot (c) once the functionality of a specific robot has been output by the tool, then it is possible to check out the robot before actually proceeding to construct it. Thus, the generic-CASE shall help in designing the needed robot.

We are now working on the generic-CASE tool itself. A draft generic specification language that will be input to the generic part of the tool has been designed and is under test. Thereafter, the actual task of generic-tool construction shall be undertaken. We shall use the meta-CASE MERU as the back-end of the generic-CASE.

References

(Cha95)   Chandra P., Projects Planning, Analysis, Selection, Implementation and Review. Tata McGraw-Hill
(Gro97)   Grosz G., *et al*. Modelling and Engineering the Requirements Engineering Process: An Overview of the NATURE approach. Requirement Engineering Journal, 2(3): 115-131
(Gup01)   Gupta D., and Prakash N., Engineering Methods From Their Requirements Specification, Requirements Engineering Journal, 6, 3, 133-160
(Mitsu)   Industrial Micro-Robot System model RV-M1 MovemasterEX manual, Mitsubishi
(Pra94)   Prakash N., A Process View of Methodologies, in Advanced Information Systems Engineering, Wijers, Brinkkemper, and Wasserman(eds.), LNCS 811, Springer Verlag, 339-352
(Pra96a) Prakash N., and Sabharwal S., Building CASE tools for Methods Represented as Abstract Data Types, OOIS'96, Patel, Sun, and Patel (eds.), Springer, 357-369
(Pra96b) Prakash N., Domain Based Abstraction for Method Modelling, Ingénierie Des Systèmes d'Information, AFCET/HERMES 4(6), 745-767
(Pra97a) Prakash N., Towards a Formal Definition of Methods, Requirements Engineering Journal, Springer, 2, 1, 23-50
(Pra97b) Prakash N., and Sibal R., Computer Assisted Quality Engineering: A CASE for Building Quality Products, Proc. First Intl. Workshop on The Many Facets of Process Engineering, Gammarth, Tunisia, 25-35
(Pra99a) Prakash N., and Sibal R., Modelling Method Heuristics for Better Quality Products, Advanced Information Systems Engineering, Jarke M. and Oberweis A. (eds.), 429-433
(Pra99b) Prakash N., On Method Statics and Dynamics, Information Systems Journal, Vol. 24, No.8, 613-637
(Rol95)   Rolland C., Souveyet C., and Moreno M., An Approach for Defining Ways of Working, Information System Journal, 20, 4, 337-359
(Sou91)   Souveyet C.: Validation des Specifications Conceptuelles d'un Systeme d'information, Ph.D. Thesis, Universite de Paris VI

Role of Model Transformation in Method Engineering

Motoshi Saeki

Dept. of Computer Science, Tokyo Institute of Technology
Ookayama 2-12-1, Meguro-ku, Tokyo 152, Japan
saeki@cs.titech.ac.jp

Abstract. This paper discusses two applications of model transformation to method engineering; one is method assembly of diagram based methods and formal methods and the other one is providing formal semantics with meta models by means of the transformation of the meta model descriptions into the formal descriptions. We use Class Diagram to define the meta models, and the models following the meta model can be represented with instance graphs. Thus our model transformation is based on graph grammars. To show and clarify the benefits of model transformation in method engineering, we illustrate the transformation rules and how to transform models. We use two examples; one is a method assembly of Class Diagram and Z and the other one is defining formal semantics of the meta model of Class Diagram.

1 Introduction

As information systems to be developed become larger and more complex, modeling methods such as object-oriented analysis and design methods (simply, methods) are being one of the key technologies to develop them with high quality. Modern methods such as RUP[9] adopt the techniques from multiple viewpoints. For example, UML[17], which is used in these methods, has nine diagrams that can depict functional aspects, structure, behavior, collaboration and implementation ones of the system. In this situation, transformation on these models from different views, we call it model transformation, has played an important role as follows;

1. Checking consistency : transforming into a common notation the different descriptions that have overlaps with each other[13]. For example, a data flow diagram and a state diagram in OMT are transformed into logical formulas in order to check if the behavior specified with the state diagram is consistent with the data flow diagram[3].
2. Changing different notations : In Rational Rose, a CASE tool for UML, a sequence diagram can be automatically transformed into a collaboration diagram and vice versa, because these diagrams represent the same view of the system, i.e. collaboration of objects.

3. Providing formal semantics with diagrams : Diagrams such as UML are called semi-formal because they have no rigorous formal semantics in detail level yet. Some studies are related to the techniques of transforming UML diagrams to formal descriptions, e.g. class diagrams to algebraic descriptions[5], state diagrams to LOTOS[22] and so on.
4. Generating a program from a design model : Model descriptions in a design level are translated into an executable model such as a state transition machine. The executable model sometimes is too abstract, and in this case, it is refined further into a more concrete description such as a program by using a stepwise refinement technique adopted in model-based formal description techniques like Z[14] and VDM[11]. In DAIDA project[10], an object-oriented design model of an information system written in TaxisDL language is translated to an abstract state machine which can be refined into an implementation.

In this paper, we discuss two potentials for the other roles of model transformation as the techniques of method engineering for information systems development. According to Sjaak Brinkkemper[7], Method Engineering can be defined as an engineering discipline to investigate how to construct and to adapt methods which are suitable for the situation of development projects. One of the ways to construct suitable methods is method assembly, where we selects method fragments (reusable parts of methods) and assemble them into the suitable methods. In [8,15], method fragments stored in a method base (data base of methods and/or method fragments) are defined as meta models, and method assembly is performed by means of manipulating these meta models. At first this paper suggests another technique for method assembly based on model transformation and this is one of the roles that we will discuss in the paper. Another role is concerned with the way to provide formal semantics with meta models. Some researchers investigated and proposed meta-modeling techniques based on Entity Relationship Model[6], Object-Oriented Model (MOF)[2], Predicate Logic (including Object Z)[18] and attribute grammars[20]. They successfully defined just the structure of the artifacts that were produced in a development project following a method, i.e. *abstract* syntax of the artifacts in a sense, but did not specify the semantics of the artifacts. We apply a model transformation technique to providing formal semantics with meta models.

The rest of the paper is organized as follows. Section 2 sketches the transformation technique based on graph grammars, which we have used in this paper. In section 3, we discuss method assembly of a diagram based method and a formal method, more concretely a class diagram and a formal method Z[14]. In section 4, as another application of model transformation, we discuss the formal semantics of these meta models by providing a set of the transformation rules that can generate a formal description of an instance of a meta model.

2 Graph Rewriting System

A graph rewriting system converts a graph into another graph or a set of graphs following pre-defined rewriting rules. There are several graph rewriting systems such as PROGRESS[19] and AGG[21]. We use the definition of the AGG system. A graph consists of nodes and edges, and type names can be associated with them. Nodes can have attribute values depending on their type. Figure 1(a) is a simple example of rewriting rules. A rule consists of a left-hand (graph B1) and a right-hand (graph B2) which are separated with "::=". A rectangle stands for a node of a graph and it is separated into two parts with a dashed lines. Type name of a node appears in the upper part, while the lower part contains its attribute values. In the figure, the node of "TypeA" in B1 has the attribute "val" and its value is represented with the variable "x". Numerals are used for identifying a node between the left-hand graph and the right-hand graph. For example, the numeral "1" in the node of "TypeA" in B1 means that the node is identical to the node of "TypeA" having "1" in B2. A graph labeled with NAC (Negative Application Condition) appearing in the left-hand controls the application of the rule. If a graph includes the NAC graph, the rule cannot be applied to the graph. The procedure of graph rewriting is as follows ;

1. Extracting the part of the graph that structurally matches to the left-hand of the rule. If the type names are attached with nodes and/or edges, these names should also match during this process. The variables appearing in attributes of the nodes are assigned.
2. Replacing the extracted part with the right-hand of the rule and embedding the result to the original graph, if none of the part which structurally matches a graph of NAC appears. New attribute values are calculated and assigned to the attributes.

Figure 1(b) illustrates rewriting the graph G into the graph H. The triangle part of the graph G is replaced with the rectangular sub graph that is derived from the right-hand of the rule. The attribute values 5 and 2 are assigned to x and y respectively, and those of the two instance nodes of "TypeD" result in 7 (x+y) and 3 (x−y). The other parts of G are not changed in this rewriting process. On the other hand, since the graph I includes the node of "TypeD", the NAC graph of this rule, it cannot be transformed by the rule. In addition, we attach the priority of rule-application with the rules. If we have more than one applicable rule to a graph, we select some of them by their priority and rewrite the graph by using the selected rules at first.

3 Method Assembly of Diagram Based Methods and FDTs

3.1 Method Assembly Based on Transformation

Various kinds of formal description technique (simply, FDT) such as LOTOS, Estelle, SDL, Z[14], and VDM[11] have been developed to specify software systems formally and are putting into practice. The benefits of using FDTs result

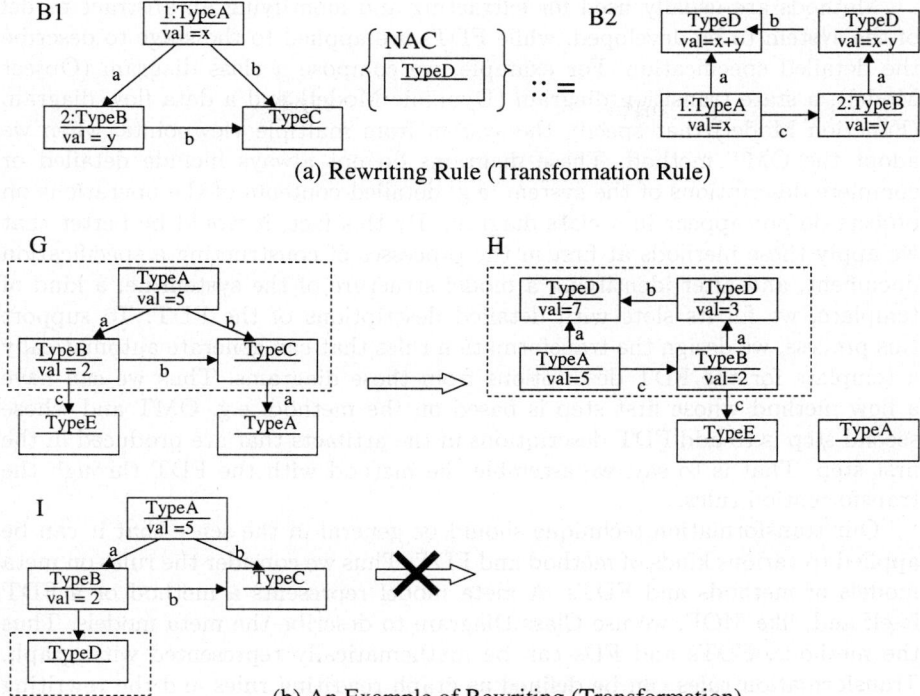

Fig. 1. Graph Rewriting Rule and Rewriting Process

from their rigorous and formal semantics based on mathematics. Software developers can use formal descriptions (FDs) as communication tools, and can verify some properties of them such as consistency and correctness. Furthermore some of the FDs such as LOTOS can be executed as prototype.

However it is difficult for developers to understand documents written in a FDT and to construct a specification in the FDT without learning and training it, because it has specific syntax and semantic rules based on mathematics such as set theory, algebra and mathematical logic. Furthermore no sufficient methods for guiding how to construct formal specifications are embedded to a FDT. Methods such as SA/SD, OMT[16] and RUP[9] guide developers to construct the models of an information system step by step. And almost of them produce diagrams as specifications that are easy for the developers to understand. The methods are one of key factors to efficiently construct the specification of high quality. Method assembly is one of the techniques to combine the methods with FDTs and several case studies have been reported[12,4], even in industries. We assemble an existing method and a FDT into a new method by using transformation rules. More concretely, we transform some artifacts that are developed following the method into the descriptions written in FDT.

Methods are usually used for extracting and identifying an abstract model of the system to be developed, while FDTs are applied to the stage to describe the detailed specification. For example, we compose a class diagram (Object Model), a state transition diagram (Dynamic Model) and a data flow diagram (Function Model) that specify the system from multiple viewpoints, when we adopt the OMT method. These diagrams do not always include detailed or complete descriptions of the system, e.g. detailed contents of the operations on objects do not appear in a class diagram. By this fact, it would be better that we apply these methods at first in the processes of constructing a specification document, and after identifying a model structure of the system i.e. a kind of template, we fill its slots with detailed descriptions of the FDT. To support this process, we design the transformation rules that can generate automatically a template for the FDT descriptions from these diagrams. Thus we can have a new method whose first step is based on the method, e.g. OMT and whose second step is to add FDT descriptions in the artifacts that are produced in the first step. That is to say, we assemble the method with the FDT through the transformation rules.

Our transformation technique should be general in the sense that it can be applied to various kinds of method and FDT. Thus we consider the rules on meta models of methods and FDTs. A meta model represents a method or a FDT itself and, like MOF, we use Class Diagram to describe the meta models. Thus the methods, FDTs and FDs can be mathematically represented with graph. Transformation rules can be defined as graph rewriting rules and the rewriting system can execute the transformation automatically. Furthermore connecting CASE tools for the method with the rewriting system allows us to have an integrated tool supporting seamlessly the processes to construct a FD by using methods.

This process can be summarized as follows;

1. Following the method, we construct a model description, e.g. class diagrams, data flow diagrams, etc., of the system to be developed.
2. From the model description, we get the graph form of the description, called instance graph, based on the meta model of the method.
3. We transform the instance graph into the instance graph for the FDT (i.e. the graph-representation form of a FD) by using the graph rewriting rules.
4. The template of the FD is automatically generated from the FDT instance graph.
5. We describe the detailed parts that are slots in the template.

The details will be discussed in the next section by using an example. Figure 2 sketches the above process.

3.2 Method Assembly Example

In this subsection, we illustrate the method assembly of class diagrams and formal method Z, which is based on ZF set theory and predicate logic. Figure 3 depicts a part of the meta models of class diagrams and of Z.

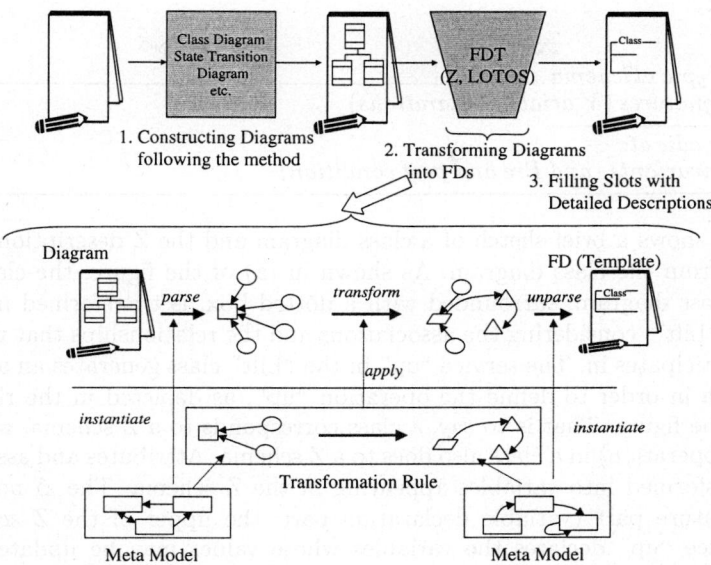

Fig. 2. Method Assembly and Transformation Process

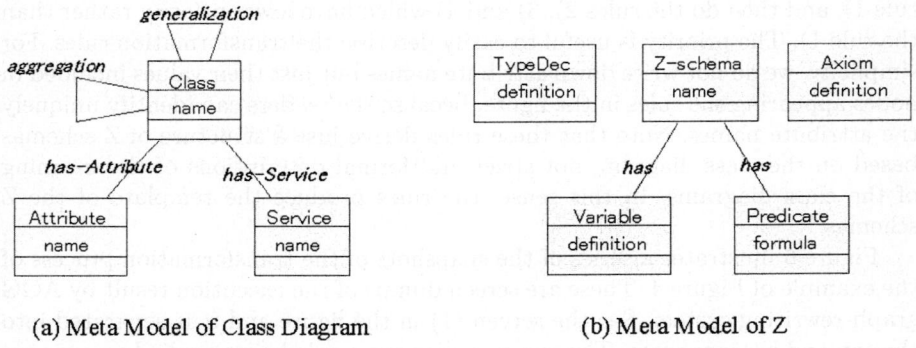

Fig. 3. A Meta Model of Class Diagrams and Z

We must note briefly the conventions on Z notation. The Z schema defines variables and constraints on them with predicate logical formulas in the following style;

TypicalSchema
Signatures (*Variable Declarations*)

Pr edic ate
(*Invariants, and Pre and post condition*)

Figure 4 shows a brief sketch of a class diagram and the Z description which is derived from the class diagram. As shown in (a) of the figure, the class "Lift" in the class diagram, surrounded with a dotted box, is transformed into the Z schema "Lift", considering the associations and the relationships that the "Lift" class participates in. The service "up" in the "Lift" class generates an additional Z schema in order to define the operation "up", as depicted in the right-hand side in the figure. That is to say, a class corresponds to a Z schema, while each service (operation) in a class also does to a Z schema. Attributes and associations are transformed into variables appearing in the Z schema. The Δ notation in the signature part (variable declaration part: the upper of the Z schema) of the service "up" declares the variables whose values may be updated by the operation. The variables with the prime (') decoration represent the values after the operation is executed, while the variables that are not decorated represent the values before the operation. Graph-representation forms of Figure 4(a) following the meta models of Figure 3 (a) are depicted in the figure (b).

Transformation rules of a class diagram into a Z description can be defined as a graph grammar in straightforward way as shown in Figure 5. The rules have the priority, for example, the rule 1) has the priority of 1, the highest one. This rule should be applied at first. After no rules with higher priority are applicable, we can use the rules of the next lower priority. In the figure, we should apply the rule 1), and then do the rules 2), 3) and 4) which have lower priority rather than the rule 1). The priority is useful to easily describe the transformation rules. For simplicity, we do not write down attribute names but just their values included in nodes appearing the rules in the figure, because the readers can identify uniquely the attribute names. Note that these rules derive just a structure of Z schemas based on the class diagram, not strict and formal descriptions of the meaning of the class diagrams. In this sense, the rules produce the template of the Z schemas.

Figure 6 illustrates a series of the snapshots of the transformation process of the example of Figure 4. These are screen dumps of the execution result by AGG graph-rewriting system. See the screen (1) in the figure and it is separated into the top and bottom areas. The top area displays a rule being applied to a graph, which the graph to be rewritten is in the bottom area. Furthermore the top area consists of two or three areas from left to right. These display a NAC, a left-hand side of the rule and a right-hand side respectively. By repeatedly applying the rule 1), for each class appearing in a graph, a node of the corresponding Z

Role of Model Transformation in Method Engineering   633

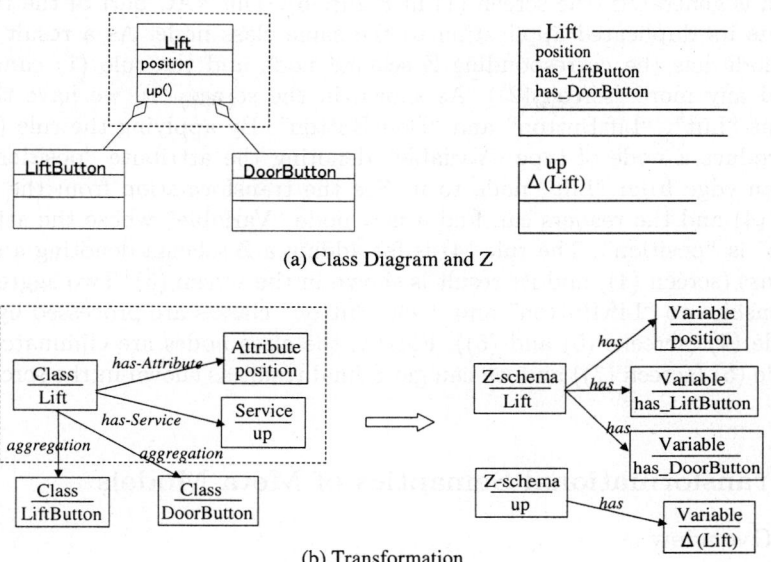

Fig. 4. Transformation of Class Diagrams

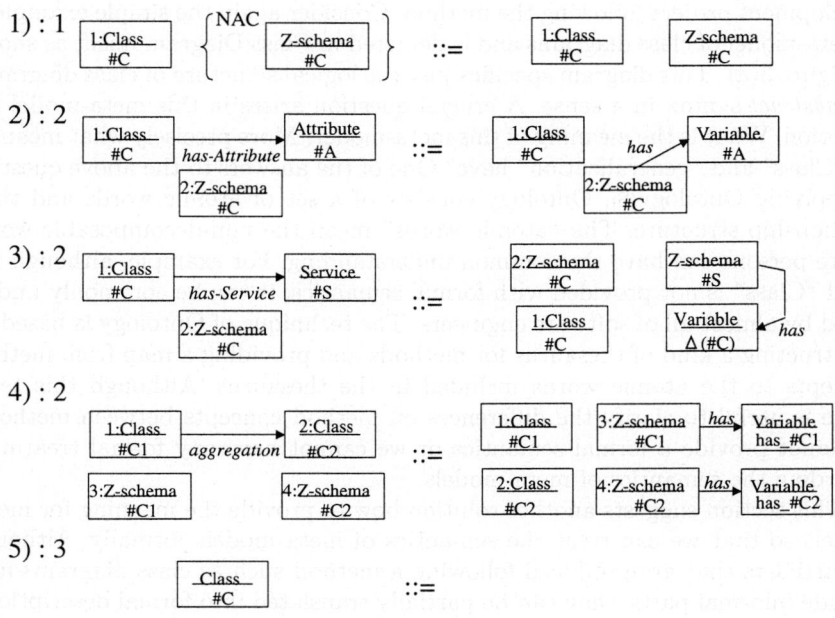

Fig. 5. A Part of Transformation Rules for Method Assembly

schema is generated (the screen (1) in Figure 6). The NAC part of the rule (1) prevents its duplicated application to the same class node. As a result, every class node has the corresponding Z schema node and the rule (1) cannot be applied any more (screen (2)). As shown in the screen (2), we have three Z schemas "Lift", "LiftButton" and "DoorButton". By applying the rule (2), we can produce a node of type "Variable" denoting the attribute "position" and draw an edge from "Lift" node to it. See the transformation from the screen (3) to (4) and the readers can find a new node "Variable" whose the attribute "name" is "position". The rule (4) is for adding a Z schema denoting a service of a class (screen (4)) and its result is shown in the screen (5). Two aggregation relationships to "LiftButton" and "DoorButton" classes are processed by using the rule (4) (screens (5) and (6)). Finally, the class nodes are eliminated with the rule (5) (screen (7)) and we can get a final result as shown in the screen (8).

4 Transformational Semantics of Meta Models

4.1 Overview

Some researchers investigated and proposed meta-modeling techniques based on Entity Relationship Model[8], Predicate Logic (including UML/OCL)[9,18], attribute grammars[20] and MOF[2], in order to define precisely methods. They successfully defined just the structure of the artifacts that were produced in a development project following the method. Consider again the simple example of a meta-model of class diagrams and is depicted in Class Diagram itself, as shown in Figure 3(a). This diagram specifies just the logical structure of class diagrams, i.e. *abstract* syntax in a sense. A crucial question arises in this meta-model description. What is the meaning of this meta-model? More precisely what meaning do "Class" and "generalization" have? One of the answers to the above question is applying Ontology[8]. Ontology consists of a set of atomic words and their relationship structure. The "atomic words" mean the non-decomposable words where persons can have the common understanding. For example, although the word "Class" is not provided with formal semantics, it can be commonly understood by almost all of software engineers. The technique of Ontology is based on constructing a kind of thesaurus for methods and providing a map from method concepts to the atomic words included in the thesaurus. Although this technique is useful to clarify the differences on method concepts between methods, it cannot provide a formal semantics or we cannot have any formal treatment regarding the semantics of meta models.

This section suggests another solution how to provide the meaning for metamodels so that we can treat the semantics of meta models formally. Although the artifacts that are produced following a method such as class diagrams may include informal parts, they can be partially translated into formal descriptions, and the parts that can be translated can have formal semantics. We capture the semantics of a meta-model as the rules that generate the formal specification (Z description) of a real system when we specify the system following the

Role of Model Transformation in Method Engineering 635

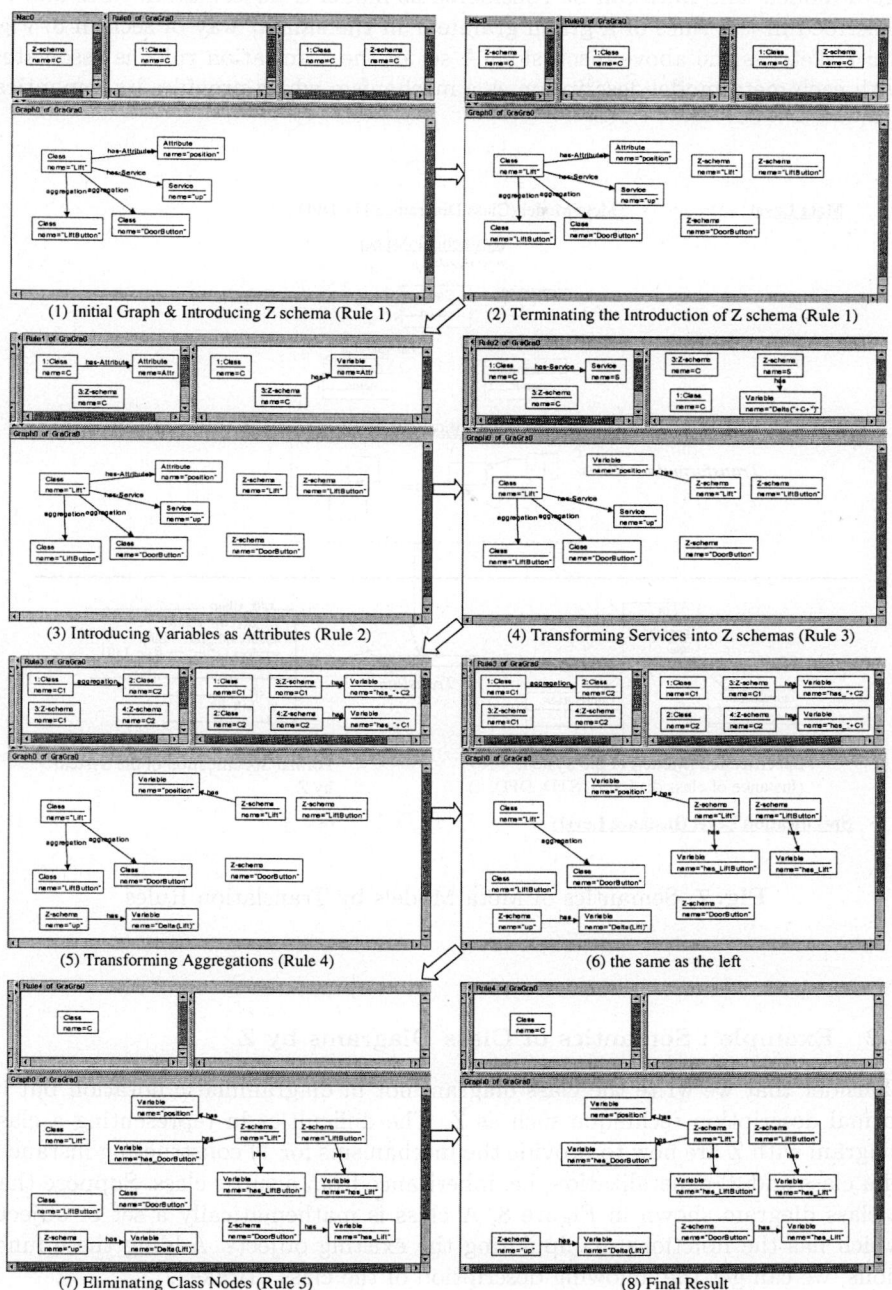

Fig. 6. A Snapshot of A Transformation Process

meta-model. The rules can be considered as model transformation rules and be described in the rules of a graph grammar in the similar way of section 3. Figure 7 sketches the above discussion. A set of the translation rules is associated with each meta-model description as a mechanism which provides its semantics.

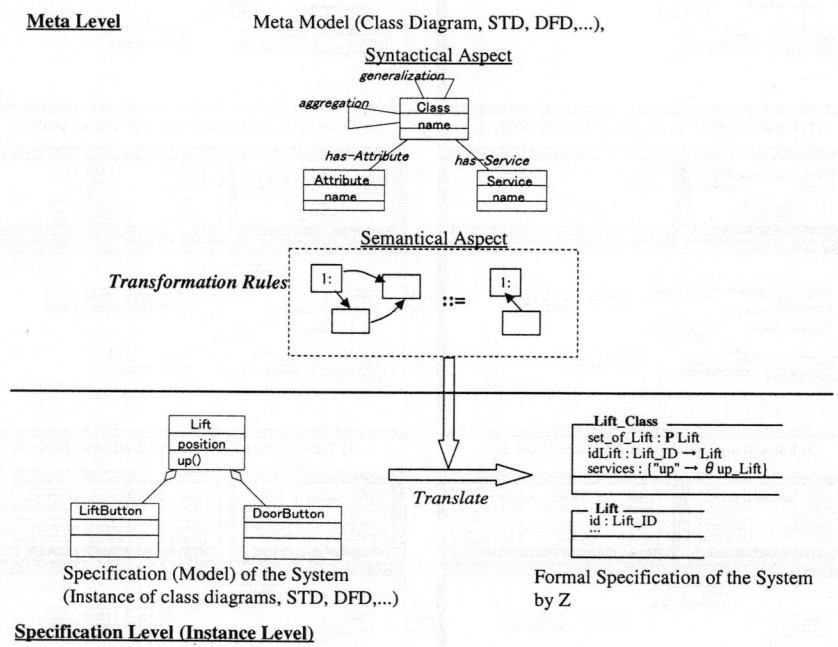

Fig. 7. Semantics of Meta Models by Translation Rules

4.2 Example : Semantics of Class Diagrams by Z

Consider that we write the class diagram not in diagrammatic notation but in formal description technique such as Z. The difficulties in representing a class diagram with Z are how to provide the mechanisms for 1) constructing instances of a class and 2) generalization, i.e. inheritance from a super class. Suppose that a class diagram shown in Figure 8. A class is mathematically a set of objects which has the functions manipulating the existing objects. Adding these functions, we can get the following description of the class "Brake".

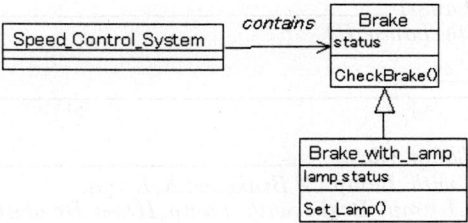

Fig. 8. An Example of A Class Diagram

$[Brake\_ID]$

---Brake--------------------------------
$id : Brake\_ID$
$status :$
$contains\_destination : SpeedControl\_System\_ID$

---Brake_Class----------------------------
$set\_of\_Brake : \mathbb{P}\ Brake$
$idBrake : Brake\_ID \twoheadrightarrow Brake$
$services: \{\text{``CheckBrake''} \mapsto \theta CheckBrake\_Brake\}$

$idBrake = \{x : set\_of\_Brake \bullet x.id \mapsto x\}$

---CheckBrake_Brake-----------------------
$\Delta(Brake)$
$\ldots$

$id' = id$
$\ldots$

---Brake_new------------------------------
$\Delta Brake\_Class$
$new\_Brake! : Brake$

$\neg(new\_Brake.id \in \text{dom } set\_of\_Brake)$
$set\_of\_Brake' = set\_of\_Brake \cup \{new\_Brake!\}$

$[Brake\_with\_Lamp\_ID]$

$Brake\_with\_Lamp\_ID \subseteq Brake\_ID$

---Brake_with_Lamp------------------------
$Brake \leftarrowtail Brake\_with\_Lamp!$

$\begin{array}{|l}\hline \_\_Brake\_with\_Lamp1_____\\ id : Brake\_with\_Lamp\_ID \\ lamp\_status : \\ \hline \end{array}$

$\begin{array}{|l}\hline \_\_Brake\_with\_Lamp\_Class_____\\ set\_of\_Brake\_with\_Lamp : \mathbb{P}\ Brake\_with\_L\ amp \\ idBrake\_with\_L\ amp: Brake\_with\_Lamp\_ID \twoheadrightarrow Br\ ake\_with\_L\ amp \\ services : Brake\_Class.servic\ es \leftarrow\!\!\!\!\!\!\!\!\!\!\!\!-\!\!\!\!\!\!\!\!\!\!\!\!-\!\!\!\!\!\!\!\!\!\!\!\!p \\ \quad \{ \text{``}Set\_L\ amp\text{''} \mapsto \theta Set\_L\ amp\_Brake\_with\_L\ amp\} \\ \hline idBrake\_with\_L\ amp = \\ \quad \{x : Br\ ake\_with\_L\ amp \bullet x.id \mapsto x\} \\ \hline \end{array}$

$\begin{array}{|l}\hline \_\_Brake\_with\_Lamp\_new_____\\ \Delta Brake\_with\_L\ amp\_Class \\ new\_Brake\_with\_Lamp! : Brake\_with\_L\ amp \\ \hline \neg(new\_Br\ ake\_with\_Lamp!.id \in \mathrm{dom}\ set\_of\_Brake\_with\_Lamp) \\ set\_of\_Brake\_with\_Lamp' = \\ \quad set\_of\_Brake\_with\_L\ amp \cup \{new\_Brake\_with\_Lamp!\} \\ \hline \end{array}$

$\begin{array}{|l}\hline \_\_Set\_Lamp\_Brake\_with\_Lamp_____\\ \hline \end{array}$

$\begin{array}{|l}\hline \_\_Sp\ eedControl\_System_____\\ id : Sp\ eedControl\_System\_ID \\ contains\_sour\ ce: \mathbb{P}\ Br\ ake\_ID \\ \hline \end{array}$

$\begin{array}{|l}\hline \_\_Sp\ eedControl\_System\_Class_____\\ \hline \end{array}$

The Z schemas "*Brake*" and "*Brake_Class*" define a brake object and its class respectively. The "*Brake_Class*" has the variable "*set_of_Brake*" which holds the information on which brake objects currently exist, i.e. have been already created by its constructor. The map "*idBrake*" in "*Brake_Class*" is for accessing brake objects with their identifiers. Since it is defined as a function, a unique identifier should be attached to a brake object, i.e. their identifiers are different if the objects are different. The operation "*Brake_new*", a constructor for brake objects, adds a newly generated object "*new_Brake!*" into the set "*set_of_Brake*" and returns it as a result of the operation. The first line of the predicate part of "*Brake_new*" says that the identifier of the newly generated object is not equal to any identifiers of the existing objects. When translating a class diagram into a Z description, we should add the Z schemas for holding the existing objects and for defining constructors, as mentioned above. In addition, the variable "*services*" included in the schema "*Brake_Class*" has the information on which services the schema has. When the name of a service is specified with the variable, say *services* ("*CheckBrake*"), we can get the specification of the service defined with Z schema. We use the operator θ for specifying the Z schema itself.

Association and aggregation relationships between classes can be formally and simply specified by means of introducing into the Z schemas the variables that hold the relationship information. In the example, we define the variable "*contains_destination*" in the schema "*Brake*", through which the Brake objects are linked to the "*Speed_Control_System*" objects. It is the same technique as introducing the variables like "*has_LiftButton*" in the section 3.2 in order to specify the aggregation relationships.

Inheritance (generalization-specialization) relationships would be more complicated. Mathematically, an object of a sub class is also an object of its super class, and the formula $Brake\_with\_Lamp\_ID \subseteq Brake\_ID$ specifies this mathematical property of set-inclusion. Since the definition of a subclass overrides that of its super class, we use an override operator $\oplus$ on Z schema. Suppose that A is a map. In this case, $(A \oplus \{x \mapsto y\})(z) = y$ if $z = x$, otherwise the resulting value is $A(z)$. In the case that A is a Z schema, $(A \oplus [a : new\_domain]).x$ returns the value of new_domain if $a = x$, otherwise it follows the definition of the schema A. For simplicity, we define the modified version of the override operator $\oplus$ as $A \hookleftarrow B = (A \oplus B) \cup B$. The newly defined operator $\hookleftarrow$ can play a role on keeping the definitions included in B. By using $\hookleftarrow$, we can formally and separately define the override mechanism of attributes and services of classes.

Turn back the example to clarify how to translate inheritance mechanism of super-sub classes. In the example, "*Brake_with_Lamp*" is a sub class of "*Brake*" and its instance has a lamp indicator for notifying pushing the brake. We generate an auxiliary schema "*Brake_with_Lamp1*" which has newly defined variables only, i.e. "*lamp_status*" in addition to its identifier *id*. To get the Z schema of the subclass, we connect this schema to the Z schema of super class with the override operator "$\hookleftarrow$", and we can have the schema "*Brake_with_Lamp*" which has both variables of "*Brake*" and of "*Brake_with_Lamp*". It is the definition of the instances of the subclass "*Brake_with_Lamp*". As for the schema "*Brake_with_Lamp_Class*", we just override the variable "*services*" in order to add the services that are newly defined in the sub class.

The above formal description of the class diagram has the strict meaning that is provided by the semantics of Z, i.e. set theory and predicate logic. In other words, if we can have some translation rules of diagrammatic representations to a formal description, the rules define the meaning of the diagrammatic representations. It suggests that the semantics of the meta-models can be defined as the translation rules from the meta-models to Z descriptions, as shown in Figure 7. The rules generate the formal description of the system when the system is specified following a method, i.e. when its meta-model is instantiated with the system specification.

A part of the translation rules of class diagrams into Z as graph rewriting ones can be designed in Figure 9 and these can be considered as formal semantics of the meta model of Figure 3(a).

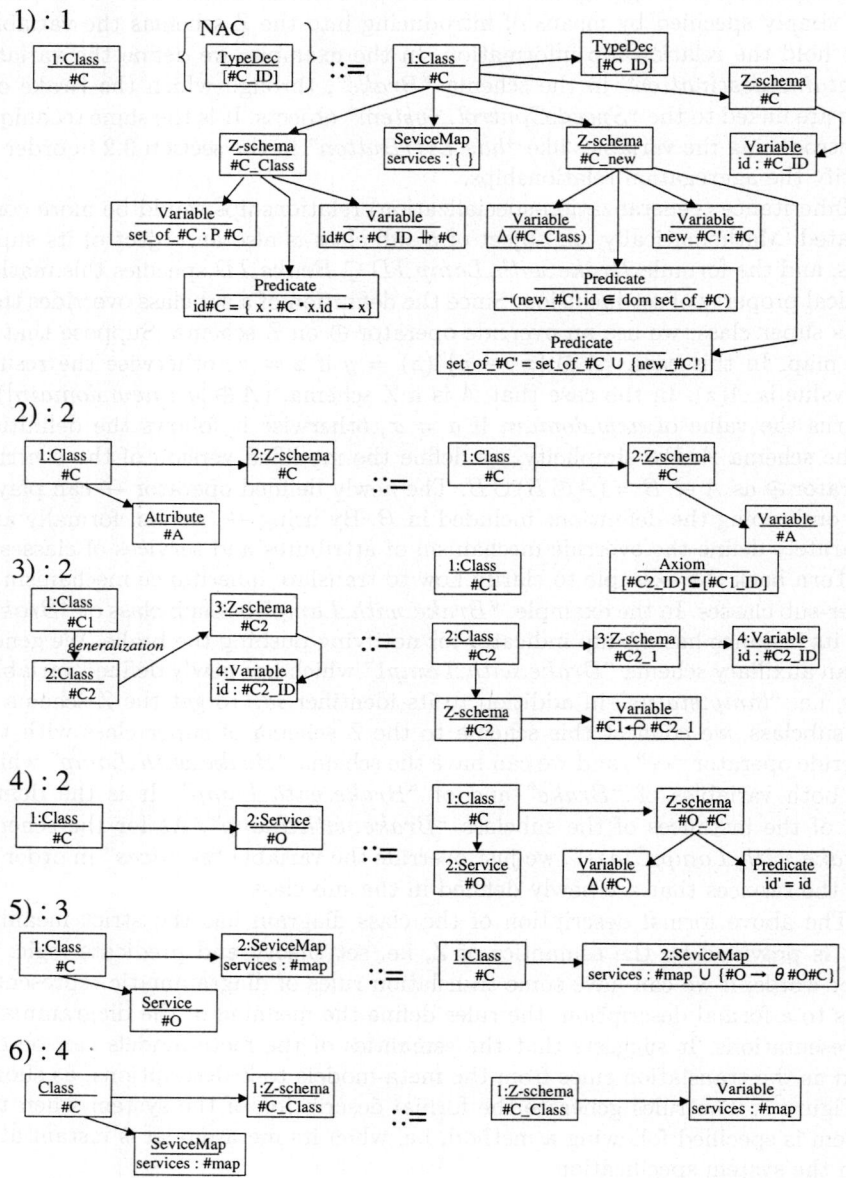

Fig. 9. Transformation Rules for Semantics of Class Diagrams

5 Conclusion and Research Agenda

In this paper, we discuss the roles of model transformation based on meta models in method engineering. The one role that we discussed was transformational approach to method assembly and the other one was formal semantics of meta-model descriptions. The semantics is provided by the rules which transform any model following the meta-model into a formal description. The transformation is defined with a graph grammar and its graph rewriting system can execute automatically the transformation. We also illustrated method assembly of class diagrams and Z, and the formal semantics of the meta model of class diagrams by means of Z. We have developed 12 transformation rules for the method assembly example and 20 rules for providing the example semantics.

In this paper, we have selected Z to provide formal semantics with the artifacts that have been produced following methods. There are several other formal description techniques (FDTs) such as VDM, LOTOS and algebraic specification languages for Abstract Data Type. In particular, some excellent studies to provide formal semantics with the diagrams of OMT exist [5,22]. Although the aim of these researches are the verification and/or consistency checking of specifications written with OMT diagrams, we can apply these techniques to our approach if we select their formal methods such as LOTOS and algebraic languages as a semantic basis on meta-models. We should explore which FDT is suitable for the semantics of meta-models.

The transformation rules are defined with graph grammars. To describe them, as well as meta models and models, with high portability, adopting XML techniques[1] are one of the significant topics. Although the AGG system holds graphs in the form of XML documents, its format is specific and some kind of converter is necessary to combine a method engineering tool.

References

1. XML : eXtensible Markup Language. *ftp://ftp.omg.org/pub/docs/ad/*, 1996.
2. Meta Object Facility (MOF) Speicication. *ftp://ftp.omg.org/pub/docs/ad/*, 2000.
3. T. Aoki and T. Katayama. Unification and Consistency Verification of Object-Oriented Analysis Models. In *Proc. of 5th Asia-Pacific Softwrae Engineering Conference (APSEC'98)*, pages 296–303, 1997.
4. D. Berry and M. Weber. A Pragmatic, Rigorous Integration of Structural and Behavioral Modeling Notations. In *Proc. of 1st International Conference on Formal Engineering Methods*, pages 38–48, 1997.
5. R. Bourdeau and B. Cheng. A Formal Semantics for Object Model Diagrams. *IEEE Trans. on Software Engineering*, 21(10):799 – 821, 1995.
6. S. Brinkkemper. *Formalisation of Information Systems Modelling*. Thesis Publisher, 1990.
7. S. Brinkkemper. Method Engineering : Engineering of Information Systems Development Methods and Tools. *Information and Software Technology*, 37(11), 1995.
8. S. Brinkkemper, M. Saeki, and F. Harmsen. Meta-Modelling Based Assembly Techniques for Situational Method Engineering. *Information Systems*, 24(3):209 –228, 1999.

9. I. Jacobson, G. Booch, and J. Rumbaugh. *The Unified Software Development Process*. Addison Wesley, 1999.
10. M. Jarke, J. Mylopoulos, J. Schmidt, and Y. Vassiliou. DAIDA : An Environment for Evolving Information Systems. *ACM Trans. on Information Systems*, 10(1):1–50, 1992.
11. C. B. Jones. *Systematic Software Development Using VDM*. Prentice Hall, 1986.
12. K. Kronlöf, editor. *Method Integration – Concepts and Case Studies*. Wiley, 1993.
13. C. Pons, R. Giandini, and G. Baum. Dependency Relations Between Models in the Unified Process. In *Proc. of 10th International Workshop on Software Specification and Design (IWSSD-10)*, pages 149–158, 2000.
14. B. Potter, J. Sinclair, and D. Till. *An Introduction to Formal Specification and Z*. Prentice Hall, 1996.
15. J. Ralyte and C. Rolland. An Assembly Process Model for Method Engineering. In *Lecture Notes in Comupter Science (CAiSE'01)*, volume 1626, pages 267–283, 2001.
16. J. Rumbaugh, M. Blaha, W. Premerlani, F. Eddy, and W. Lonrensen. *Object-Oriented Modeling and Design*. Prentice-Hall, 1991.
17. J. Rumbaugh, I. Jacobson, and G. Booch. *The Unified Modeling Language Reference Manual*. Addison Wesley, 1999.
18. M. Saeki and K. Wenyin. Specifying Software Specification & Design Methods. In *Lecture Notes in Computer Science (CAiSE'94)*, pages 353–366. Springer-Verlag, 1994.
19. A. Schurr. Developing Graphical (Software Engineering) Tools with PROGRES. In *Proc. of 19th International Conference on Software Engineering (ICSE'97)*, pages 618–619, 1997.
20. X. Song and L. J. Osterweil. Experience with an Approach to Comparing Software Design Methodologies. *IEEE Trans. on Soft. Eng.*, 20(5):364–384, 1994.
21. G. Taentzer, O. Runge, B. Melamed, M. Rudorf, T. Schultzke, and S. Gruner. AGG : The Attributed Graph Grammar System. *http://tfs.cs.tu-berlin.de/agg/*, 2001.
22. E. Wang, H. Richer, and B. Cheng. Formalizing and Integrating the Dynamic Model within OMT*. In *Proc. of 19th International Conference on Software Engineering*, pages 45 – 55, 1997.

A Generic Role Model for Dynamic Objects

Mohamed Dahchour[1], Alain Pirotte[1], and Esteban Zimányi[2]

[1] University of Louvain, IAG School of Management, Information Systems Unit
(ISYS)
1 Place des Doyens, 1348 Louvain-la-Neuve, Belgium
dahchour@isys.ucl.ac.be
pirotte@info.ucl.ac.be
[2] University of Brussels, Informatics Department
50 Av. F. Roosevelt, C.P. 165, 1050 Brussels, Belgium
ezimanyi@ulb.ac.be

Abstract. The *role* generic relationship for conceptual modeling relates a class of objects (e.g., persons) and classes of roles (e.g., students, employees) for those objects. The relationship is meant to capture temporal aspects of real-world objects while the common generalization relationship deals with their more static aspects. This paper presents a generic role model, where the semantics of roles is defined at both the class and the instance levels. The paper also discusses the interaction between the role relationship and generalization, and it attempts to clarify some of their similarities and differences.

Keywords: Information modeling, role model, object technology

1 Introduction

Object models represent real-world applications as a collection of objects and classes. Objects model real-world entities while classes represent sets of similar objects. The *classification/instantiation* relationship relates a class to its instances. Classes are organized in *generalization/specialization* hierarchies where subclasses inherit structure and behavior from their superclasses.

Most object models assume that an object cannot be an instance of more than one class at the same time (except in the presence of generalization) and that an object cannot change its class. Those assumptions are not well suited to modeling some dynamic situations from the real world. Consider class **Person** specialized into classes **Student** and **Employee**. If **John** is created as an instance of **Student**, it also becomes an instance of **Person**. But **John** cannot be created as an instance of **Person** and later become in addition an instance of **Student**. Neither can student **John** change its class to become, say, an employee.

Some models accept *overlapping* generalizations with, e.g., subclasses **Student** and **Employee** of **Person** sharing instances. This leads to multiple classification, which is discussed later.

An alternative is to allow *multiple inheritance* with *intersection classes*. Thus, for example, an intersection class **StudentEmployee** could be created as a common subclass of Student and Employee. Multiple inheritance may lead to a combinatorial explosion in the number of subclasses. Also, an instance of StudentEmployee cannot be viewed as only a student or only an employee. Such a context-dependent access to properties is not supported by generalization [12].

Multiple classification [5] allows an object to be a direct instance of more than one class (e.g., John as an instance of both Student and Employee). Although multiple classification avoids the combinatorial explosion of multiple inheritance, it does not allow a context-dependent access to object properties: the attributes of an object comprise all the attributes of its classes. It is thus not possible, e.g., to view John either as a Student or as an Employee.

Another problem pointed out in, e.g., [12,20,24,25] is the impossibility of representing the same real-world object as more than one instance of the same class. For example, John could be a student at two universities, say ULB and UCL, with, in each of them, a student number and a registration in a number of courses. A possible modeling of such a situation requires three classes: two subclasses ULB_Students and UCL_Students of Student, and an intersection class ULB_UCL_Students as a subclass of both ULB_Students and UCL_Students. Such a solution is heavy and impractical.

The role relationship [2,7,10,12,19,24,25] was proposed as a way to overcome those limitations of classical object models. It captures evolutionary aspects of real-world objects that cannot be modeled by time-dependent attribute values and that are not well captured by the generalization relationship.

The rest of the paper is organized as follows. Section 2 presents a comprehensive semantics for our role model. Section 3 addresses some issues about object identity and role identity. Section 4 explores similarities and differences between the role and generalization relationships. Section 5 introduces two concepts for specifying role control: *meaningful combinations* of role classes, used for monitoring membership in several role classes, and *transition predicates*, used for specifying when objects may evolve by gaining and/or losing roles. Section 6 summarizes the class- and instance-level semantics of our role relationship. Section 7 discusses related work and suggests criteria to account for the variety of approaches for role modeling. Section 8 summarizes and concludes the paper.

2 Our Role Model: General Structure

This section presents the general structure of our role model. We will sometimes simply say "role-of" for the role relationship of our model.

Role-of (of pattern ObjectClass⊙←RoleClass) relates a class, called *object class*[1], and another class, called *role class*, that describes dynamic roles for the object class. Figure 1 shows two role relationships relating the Person object class to role classes Student and Employee. We say that instances of the object class gain roles (also that they *play* roles), which are instances of the role class. The

---

[1] The *object class* of a role relationship has sometimes been called *root type*, *base class*, *player class*, *base role*, *natural type*, or *role model*.

object class defines permanent properties of objects over their lifetime, while each role class defines some of their transient properties. When the context is clear, instances of object classes will be called *objects* while instances of role classes will be called *roles*.

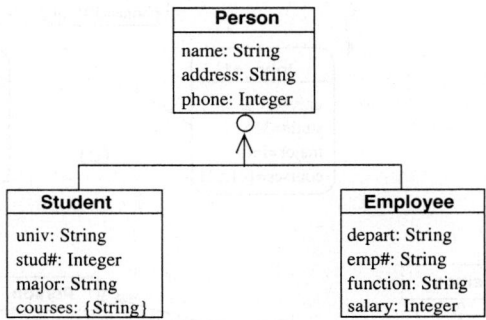

Fig. 1. An example of role relationship

The role concept addresses three main issues arising when modeling evolving entities with traditional object models:

(1) **Dynamic change of class**, i.e., objects changing their classification. If the object undergoing the transition remains an instance of the source class, the transition is called an **extension**. Otherwise, it is called an **evolution**.
(2) **Multiple instantiation of the same class**, i.e., an object becoming an instance more than once of the same class, while losing or retaining its previous membership. For example, a student may be registered in two different universities.
(3) **Context-dependent access**, i.e., the ability to view a multi-faceted object in a particular perspective. For example, person John can be viewed separately either as an employee or as a member of the golf club.

A role can be viewed as a possible state for an object. An evolving object is represented by an instance of an object class and by a set of instances of role classes. The basic idea is that the set of instances of role classes for the object can evolve easily over time. Still, some state changes are naturally modeled as changes of attribute values rather than as roles. The idea is that roles concern new responsibilities, facets, or aspects. For example, a salary raise could be naturally modeled as the change of an attribute value, while an employee becoming a member of a golf club could be naturally modeled as a new role for the employee.

Some versions of the entity-relationship (ER) model associate a notion of role with relationships. An entity involved in a relationship is said to play a role. Most often those roles are little more than an alternative name for the relationship, emphasizing the viewpoint of one participating entity. According to [7], a role

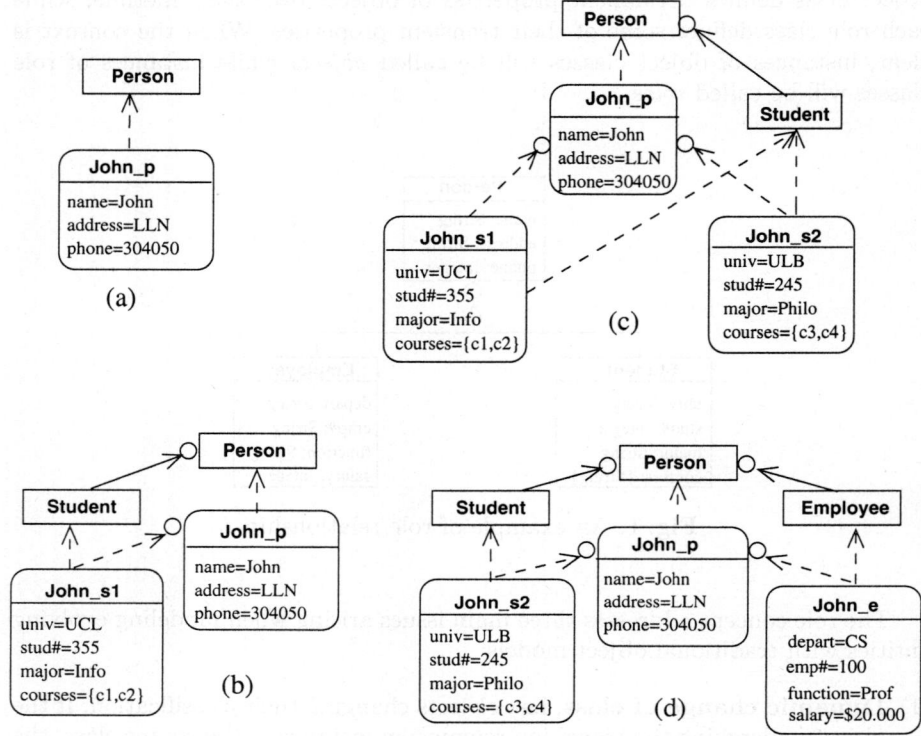

Fig. 2. Various roles for an object

class $\mathcal{R}_1$ related to an object class $\mathcal{O}$ (i.e., $\mathcal{R}_1 \rightarrow \circ \mathcal{O}$) necessarily participates as a role (in the sense of ER model) in a specific relationship. For example, the intuition behind the roles of Figure 1 is that persons may play the role of students, registered in some universities, and of employees, working in some departments. Thus, classes Student and Employee can be viewed as role classes in relationships Student$\xrightarrow{registers}$University and Employee$\xrightarrow{works}$Department, respectively. Of course, the semantics underlying the role concept of relationship role-of cannot be wholly captured by the role concept of the ER model.

Figure 2[2] shows on some instances of the schema of Figure 1 how persons may evolve by gaining and/or losing roles. In Figure 2(a), John_p is created as instance of Person. Figure 2(b) shows an instance John_s1 of Student, related to John_p by the role relationship, expressing that John_p has become a stu-

---

[2] We draw classes as rectangular boxes and instances as boxes with rounded corners. Classification links appear as dashed arrows and generalization links as solid arrows. Role-of relationships at the class level are drawn as solid oriented links with a circle on the side of the object class. Role-of links at the instance level are drawn as dashed oriented links with a circle on the side of the object instance.

dent. Both instances John_p and John_s1 coexist with different identifiers (see Section 3). If John ceases to be a student, then instance John_s1 will just be removed. Figure 2(c) shows another instance of Student, John_s2, modeling that John has registered at another university (ULB). Figure 2(d) shows John having left the UCL, become an employee (John_e), while still being a student at the ULB university.

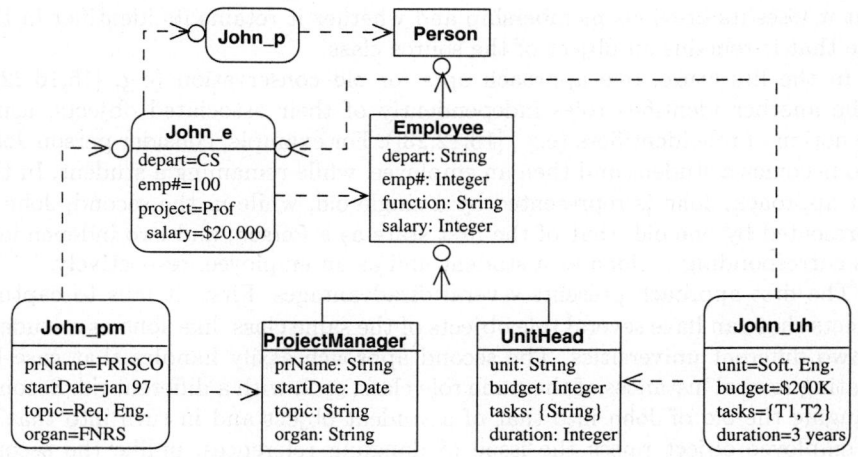

Fig. 3. Composition of roles

Role relationships can be composed in hierarchies, where the role class of one role relationship is also the object class of another role relationship, like Employee in Figure 3, which is a role class for class Person and an object class for role classes ProjectManager and UnitHead. Persons can be ProjectManager only if they play the role of Employee. Figure 3 also shows John_e of Figure 2(d) as an object with a new role John_pm, instance of ProjectManager. If John is promoted as head of the software-engineering unit at the CS department, this role is represented as an instance (John_uh) of UnitHead. John_e is thus a role for John_p, and an object for John_pm and John_uh.

3 Object Identity versus Role Identity

The concept of object identity has a long history in programming languages [13]. It is more recent in database management [14]. In a model with object identity, an object has an existence which is independent of its attribute values. Hence identity (twice the same object) is not the same thing as equality (objects with the same attribute values)[3].

A related concept called *role identity* (rid) is introduced and compared to object identity in [23]. The need for both oid and rid is motivated in [24] as follows:

assume that Passenger is a subclass of Person (in the sense of generalization) and consider persons who migrate to Passenger, say, by boarding a bus. A bus may carry 500 passengers during one day, but these passengers may actually be only 100 different persons, if a person may board the bus several times. Hence the necessity of two ways of counting passengers.

The migration of an object from a source class to target class(es), with the object losing or retaining its previous membership, introduces the issue of object-identity conservation, i.e., whether the object changes its identifier in the case that it loses its previous membership and whether it retains its identifier in the case that it remains an object of the source class.

In the literature, one approach opts for oid conservation (e.g, [15,16,22]), while another identifies roles independently of their associated objects, using the notion of role identifiers (e.g., [10,12,23]). For example, consider person John who becomes a student and then an employee, while remaining a student. In the first approach, John is represented by a single oid, while in the second, John is represented by one oid, that of the first state as a Person, and two independent rids corresponding to John as a student and as an employee, respectively.

The first approach presents several disadvantages. First, it fails to capture objects that can have several role objects of the same class, like John as a student at two different universities. The second approach easily handles that case by creating several instances of the same role class, each with a different rid. Second, changing the oid of John into that of a student object and in turn into that of an employee object raises the issue of dangling references, unlike the second approach, which represents each new role instance with its own rid. Thirdly, the first approach does not permit to represent historical information as the history of oids is lost. For those reasons, our model follows the second approach.

4 Roles versus Generalization

This section compares the role and generalization relationships. Section 4.1 examines how generalization alone approaches object dynamics. Section 4.2 discusses some differences between the relationships and Section 4.3 presents various cases where a class may be involved in both generalization and role relationships.

4.1 Dealing with Object Dynamics with Generalization Alone

Dealing with object dynamics with generalization is heavy and impractical [1], as illustrated by the following examples, where the role relationships Student→∘Person∘←Employee of Figure 4 (a) are modeled as generalization Student—▷Person◁—Employee. Then:

- *how do persons become students?* If John is an instance of Person, establishing it as an instance of Student requires replacing instance John by a new instance John_s of Student and changing the references to John into references to John_s.

- *how can persons be both students and employees at the same time?* A common subclass of **Student** and **Employee** is needed (with multiple inheritance). Anticipating each meaningful combination of classes is impractical.
- *how can persons be employees at more than one department?* To represent John as an employee at two departments, three subclasses of **Employee** are needed, one for each of the departments and a common intersection class.

4.2 Differences between Generalization and the Role Relationship

This section points out some differences between generalization and the role relationship, illustrated in Figure 4. Some of these differences are discussed in [24].

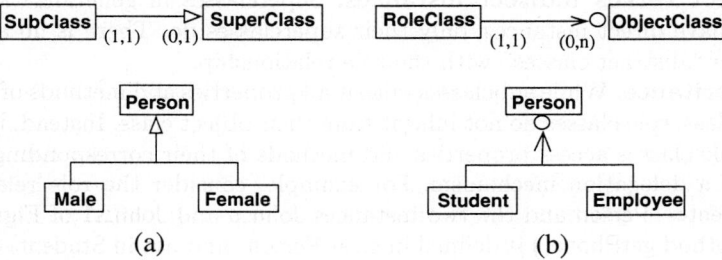

Fig. 4. Generalization (a) versus role relationship (b)

- **Cardinalities.** Each instance of a subclass (e.g., Male) is related to exactly one instance of its superclass (e.g., Person) and each instance of the superclass is related to at most one instance of its subclasses. Each instance of a role class (e.g., Student) is related to exactly one instance of its object class (e.g., Person) but, unlike generalization, each instance of the object class can be related to any number of instances of the role class (given by the maximal cardinality n at the side of the object class).
- **Object identity.** An instance of a subclass has the same object identifier oid as the associated instance of the superclass (it is the same object viewed differently). Each instance of a role class has its own role identifier rid, different from that of all other instances of the role class. For example, the identity of student John is different from that of person John. If John is registered at two universities, there is one person instance with its oid and two student instances each with their rid.
- **Change of classes.** In most object models, an instance of superclass A that is not an instance of subclass B cannot later become an instance of B. Instead, an instance of object class A can later become or cease to be an instance of role class B. For example, an instance of Person that is not a Student can become a Student.

- **Change of subclasses.** An instance of a subclass in a partition of the superclass cannot later become an instance of another subclass of the same partition. For example, in Figure 4(a), an instance of Male cannot change to an instance of Female. Instead, an instance of a given role class in the partition of the object class can become an instance of another role class of the partition. For example, in Figure 4(b), an instance of Student can become an instance of Employee.
- **Set of instances.** When a subclass changes the set of its instances by creating new objects, then its superclass also changes its instances. For example, the creation of a Male also creates a Person. Instead, when a role class creates a new role, then the related object class does not change its instances. For example, the creation of a new role for person John (e.g., John becomes an employee or registers at a university) does not affect the instances of Person.
- **Direct versus indirect instances.** Superclasses in generalizations need not have direct instances, only their superclasses do. There is no analog to those "abstract classes" with the role relationship.
- **Inheritance.** While subclasses inherit all properties and methods of their superclass, role classes do not inherit from their object class. Instead, instances of role classes access properties and methods of their corresponding objects with a delegation mechanism. For example, consider the role relationship Student∘←Person and the two instances John_p and John_s1 of Figure 2(b). If method getPhone() is defined in class Person (and not in Student) to access the value of the phone attribute, then the message John_s1→getPhone() sent to student John_s1 will be delegated to object John_p.

4.3 Combination of Generalization and Role-of

A role class $\mathcal{R}_1$ can be subclassed by other role classes $\mathcal{R}_2$ and $\mathcal{R}_3$ (i.e., $\mathcal{R}_2 \rightarrow \triangleright \mathcal{R}_1 \triangleleft \leftarrow \mathcal{R}_3$), with the usual semantics of generalization (e.g., an instance of $\mathcal{R}_2/\mathcal{R}_3$ is also an instance of $\mathcal{R}_1$, an instance of $\mathcal{R}_2$ cannot become an instance of $\mathcal{R}_3$). Instead, for role relationships $\mathcal{R}_2 \rightarrow \circ \mathcal{R}_1 \circ \leftarrow \mathcal{R}_3$, an instance of $\mathcal{R}_2$ is not an instance of $\mathcal{R}_1$ and an instance of $\mathcal{R}_2$ can become an instance of $\mathcal{R}_3$.

Two derivation rules are associated with the combination of generalization and role-of:

(1) if $\mathcal{R}_1$ is a role class of $\mathcal{O}$ and $\mathcal{R}_2$ is a role subclass of $\mathcal{R}_1$, then $\mathcal{R}_2$ is also a role class of $\mathcal{O}$ (i.e., $\mathcal{R}_2 \rightarrow \triangleright \mathcal{R}_1 \rightarrow \circ \mathcal{O} \Rightarrow \mathcal{R}_2 \rightarrow \circ \mathcal{O}$);
(2) if $\mathcal{R}_1$ is a role class of $\mathcal{O}_1$ and $\mathcal{O}_1$ is a subclass of $\mathcal{O}_2$, then $\mathcal{R}_1$ is a role class of $\mathcal{O}_2$ (i.e., $\mathcal{R}_1 \rightarrow \circ \mathcal{O}_1 \rightarrow \triangleright \mathcal{O}_2 \Rightarrow \mathcal{R}_1 \rightarrow \circ \mathcal{O}_2$).

Figure 5 illustrates interactions between generalization and role relationships. Class Person is subclassed by classes Male and Female. Class Male has a role class Draftee accounting for military duties. According to rule (2) above, Draftee is also a role class of Person. Class Person is refined by two role classes Student and Employee. Student is subclassed by role classes ForeignStudent and CountryStudent (an instance of ForeignStudent cannot become an instance of CountryStudent nor conversely). According to rule (1), ForeignStudent and CountryStudent in turn become role classes of class Person. Class Employee has two role classes, Professor and UnitHead. This is an example of compositions of roles.

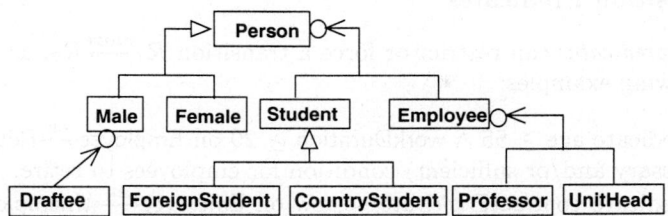

Fig. 5. Hierarchies of is-a and role-of

5 Role-Control Specification

An object can be related to several roles. This section introduces *meaningful combinations* of roles, for monitoring membership in various role classes, and *transition predicates*, for controlling how objects may gain and/or lose roles.

5.1 Meaningful Combinations of Roles Classes

When an object class $\mathcal{O}$ is related to role classes $\mathcal{R}_1, \ldots, \mathcal{R}_n$, not all combinations of roles are permitted for $\mathcal{O}$ objects. For example, if Person has roles Employee and Retired, only employees can acquire the role of retirees, but not the converse.

The notion of *meaningful combination* of role classes helps characterize the legal combinations of roles for an object. We define four types of *role combinations*:

- **Evolution**, noted $\mathcal{R}_1 \xrightarrow{ev} \mathcal{R}_2$ for role classes $\mathcal{R}_1$ and $\mathcal{R}_2$, states that an object with role r_1 of $\mathcal{R}_1$ may lose r_1 and gain a new role r_2 of $\mathcal{R}_2$, with $\mathcal{R}_1 \neq \mathcal{R}_2$. Evolutions may be bidirectional (e.g., Employee$\xleftrightarrow{ev}$Unemployed) or unidirectional (e.g., Employee$\xrightarrow{ev}$Retired), depending on whether the lost role of $\mathcal{R}_1$ may be recovered later.
- **Extension**, noted $\mathcal{R}_1 \xrightarrow{ext} \mathcal{R}_2$, with $\mathcal{R}_1$ not necessarily different from $\mathcal{R}_2$, states that an object with role r_1 of $\mathcal{R}_1$ may gain a new role r_2 of $\mathcal{R}_2$, while retaining r_1. Examples include Professor$\xrightarrow{ext}$DepartHead and Student$\xrightarrow{ext}$Student, the latter for a person allowed to register more than once as a student, for example in two different universities.
- **Acquisition**, noted $\rightarrow \mathcal{R}$, states that an object may freely acquire a role of $\mathcal{R}$, if it does not have one. For example, $\rightarrow$Student means that persons can become students. Notice that $\rightarrow$Student could be noted as Person$\xrightarrow{ext}$Student, where Person is the object class of role class Student.

- **Loss**, noted $\mathcal{R} \rightarrow$, specifies that an object may freely lose roles of $\mathcal{R}$. For example, Student$\rightarrow$ means that students may cease to be students. Student$\rightarrow$ could be noted as Student$\xrightarrow{ev}$Person.

5.2 Transition Predicates

Transition predicates can restrict or force a transition $\mathcal{R}_1 \xrightarrow{mode} \mathcal{R}_2$, as illustrated in the following examples:

- The predicate age $\geq$ 55 $\land$ workDuration $\geq$ 20 on Employee$\xrightarrow{ev}$Retired states a (necessary and/or sufficient) condition for employees to retire.
- The predicate contractExpirDate $\leq$ now on Employee$\xleftarrow{ev}$Unemployed specifies that employees whose contract has expired automatically become unemployed. Another predicate could state that unemployed persons with a new contract automatically become employees.
- The predicate grade $\geq$ min and funding = OK on Master$\xrightarrow{ext}$PhD specifies a condition for master students to be allowed to register as PhD students.
- The predicate nbProgs $\leq$ max on Student$\xrightarrow{ext}$Student states that the number of registrations for a student is limited by some maximum.
- The predicate age $\geq$ 18 on $\rightarrow$ Employee states that only adults can become employees.

6 Summary of Role Semantics

Like most generic relationships [8,9], the semantics of role-of concerns both the class and the instance levels. In the literature, these levels have mostly been considered as a whole, which has resulted in unwarranted complexity in the semantic definition and implementation of roles.

6.1 Class-Level Semantics

- An object class can have several role classes.
- A role class has exactly one object class.
- An object class has an arbitrary cardinality (c_{min}, c_{max}) regarding each of its role classes.
- Each role class has cardinality (1,1) regarding its object class.
- A role class can have other role classes.
- Meaningful combinations of role classes can be associated with object classes to provide what we have called *role control*.
- A predicate can be associated with object/role classes to describe constraints on how objects may evolve, as well as on how objects may or must automatically gain and lose roles.

6.2 Instance-Level Semantics

- A role r is not identical to an object o with that role, but it is a state in which object o can be.
- A role inherits properties and methods from its associated object by delegation.
- An object can gain several roles of the same role class or of different role classes.
- For each role, there is only one object with that role.
- Roles can be acquired and lost independently of each other.
- A role has its own identifier that is different from that of the object with the role.
- Roles evolve independently from each other or under the control of specified transition predicates.
- If an object class $\mathcal{O}$ has two role classes $\mathcal{R}_1$ and $\mathcal{R}_2$ and o is an instance of $\mathcal{O}$ with role r1 of $\mathcal{R}_1$, then r1 can only evolve as an instance of $\mathcal{R}_1$ or $\mathcal{R}_2$.
- In a composition of role-of, say $\mathcal{R}_1 \to \circ \mathcal{R}_2 \to \circ \mathcal{O}$, an object of $\mathcal{O}$ can acquire a role of $\mathcal{R}_1$ unless it already holds a role of $\mathcal{R}_2$.

7 Related Work

The interest for capturing the roles of an object goes back to the late 70's [4]. Since then, various approaches to role modeling have been proposed. We suggest the following criteria to account for the variety of those approaches.

Generalization and role-of. Various extensions to generalization were defined to deal with evolving objects (e.g., [15,16,17]). In [16], each class is considered as a particular *perspective* for its instances and the class itself denotes a role for its instances. Classes are endowed with special methods to manage roles: add a new role for an existing object, remove an existing role, etc. In [15], the concepts of *base class* and *residential class* denote, respectively, the class where an object is initially created and the class where the object currently resides; they correspond, respectively, to the *object class* and the *role class* of our model. The role model of [17] deals with evolving objects as follows. Classes are organized along the generalization hierarchy assumed to be static. If an instance of class C evolves to another class D, then D must necessarily be created dynamically as a subclass or superclass of C. D is referred to as a *role-defining* class. As a result, the application schema can be seen as composed of a static generalization hierarchy and a collections of dynamic ones.

The role model of [2] defines a single hierarchy of *role types* along the subtyping relationship, where a role subtype can have several supertypes. Thus, all classes are viewed as potentially dynamic, in that their instances may evolve over time. In that model an object is not manipulated directly but only through its roles. The answer of an object to a message depends on the role that receives it: an object does not exist on its own but is incarnated in a particular role.

In other approaches, both generalization and a specific role relationship coexist with orthogonal semantics [12,22,24,25]. In [24], the relationship between a role class and the root class (called object class) is called *played-by* (i.e., our role relationship). Role classes in turn can be refined as other role classes, and so on. The model of [12] supports both hierarchies under the names of *class hierarchy* and *role hierarchy*. A role type and its direct ancestor in the role hierarchy are linked by a relationship called *role-of*. In the DOOR model of [25], the role hierarchy is organized along the *player* relationship. The model of [22] also supports both hierarchies called *type hierarchy* and *role hierarchy*. The type hierarchy is composed of the so-called *natural* types (i.e., our object types) organized along the *subtype/supertype* relationship. The role hierarchy is composed of the so-called *roles* (i.e., our role classes) organized along the *subrole/superrole* relationship. The *role-filler* relationship (i.e., our role relationship) is defined between natural types and roles.

Preserving the oid. The issue here is whether an object that evolves over time by gaining new roles maintains its identity (i.e., oid) or acquires other identities. As mentioned in Section 3, one approach consists in preserving the single object identity regardless of how objects evolve. It is adopted by models such as [2,15,16,17] that clearly distinguish generalization and roles. Another approach argues that identifying "ordinary" objects and identifying roles raise distinct issues. As seen in Section 3, we may count one person where we count five passengers at different times of the day, which corresponds to various states of the same person. This approach has been adopted by most models, such as [10,12,24], that clearly distinguish generalization and role-of hierarchies. The approach of [25] differs from [12,23] in that roles are identified by the names of their role classes as well as their values, instead of using globally unique object/role identifiers.

Inheritance versus delegation. In addition to structure and behavior supplied by role classes, roles have to access the properties of their objects. Here again, two approaches coexist: attribute inheritance via generalization (class-based inheritance) and value propagation by delegation (instance-based inheritance). Approaches that do not clearly separate generalization and the role-of hierarchies retain attribute inheritance (e.g., [2,15,16,17]), while those that clearly distinguish them (e.g., [10,12,22,24]) mainly use delegation. Systems that follow a prototype-based paradigm (e.g., [21]) systematically use delegation.

Several roles of the same class per object. This possibility (e.g., of the same person being a student at two different universities at the same time), is easily handled in [12,24] thanks to the coexistence of both object identity (oid) and role identity (rid). Models that use the unique-oid mechanism to identify both objects and their roles (e.g., [2,15,16,17]) do not support that possibility. The model of [25] that represents roles differently than [12,24] also fails here, whereas models such as [18,20] provide the facility, although they do not introduce an explicit rid.

Context-dependent access. This means the ability to view a multi-faceted object in each role separately. For example, person John can be viewed as an employee or as a student. Most role models provide this ability. A remarkable exception is Iris [11], which allows an object to belong to several types, and to gain or lose type memberships over time, but requires the structure and methods of all the types of an object to be visible in every context. As a side effect, the name of attributes and methods must be unique across all roles.

Vertical versus horizontal role possession. This issue concerns models where role support is integrated with generalization. With vertical role possession (e.g., [17]), an object can possess roles only within the direct or indirect subclasses or superclasses of its defining class. With horizontal role possession, objects are also allowed to gain roles in so-called *sibling* or *cousin* classes (e.g., [16]). Two sibling classes are not related by a subclassing relationship nor do they have a common subclass.

Composition of roles. This refers to the possibility for a role class to serve as object class for other role classes. It holds for all models (e.g., [12,22,24,25]) that clearly separate generalization and role-of hierarchies, but not for models where the distinction is less sharp (e.g., [2,15,16,17,18]).

Role compatibility. This is the ability to explicitly control the compatibility of role possessions. For example, persons may evolve from being employees to being retirees but cannot be employees and retirees at the same time. Few models provide such a facility. The concept of *player qualification* of a role class is introduced in [25] to specify a set of classes whose instances are qualified to possess roles of the class. The concepts of *independent roles* and *coordinated roles* are introduced in [18]. Coordinating between various roles of an object is achieved through rules. The concept of *disjoint predicate* is introduced in [16] to specify that no object may be member of more than one class from a specified collection of role classes at the same time. For example, the predicate disjoint(Child, Employee, Retired) can be attached to class Person. Migration control is proposed in [15] through so-called *migration permissions*, like *relocation* (e.g., <Single, Married, relocation>) and *propagation* (e.g., <Professor, Consultant, propagation>). Relocation and propagation permissions correspond to our modes of role possession, *evolution* and *extension*, respectively. Our role-control mechanism was inspired from the migration control of [15] and enriched by the transition predicates, not supported in [15].

Transition predicates. They specify when objects may explicitly or automatically gain or lose roles from given classes. This is achieved through rules in [18]. The population of the predicate classes of [6] is governed by membership predicates for the instances of the classes. Role classes can be created in [17] by means of predicates called *role-generating* conditions, but there are no transition predicates. For example, two predicate-based classes HighlyPaidAcademic and ModeratelyPaidAcademic can be defined as subclasses of Academic by associating the predicate "Academic.salary $\geq$ 100K" to the first class and "100K >Academic.salary > 50K" to the second class. However, there is no way to define a transition predicate $\mathcal{P}$ that would control the migration from ModeratelyPaidAcademic to HighlyPaidAcademic.

The concept of *category class* was introduced in [16] to control the *implicit* or *explicit* membership in a class with a predicate. The concept of transition predicates was inspired from [16]. However, our transition predicates have different semantics concerning the predicates associated with category classes. Given a meaningful combination of roles $\mathcal{R}_1 \xrightarrow{mode} \mathcal{R}_2$, a predicate specifies when an object with a role of $\mathcal{R}_1$ may or must automatically acquire a role of $\mathcal{R}_2$, depending on *mode*. For role relationships Teenager→∘Person∘←Adult, if predicate "age$\geq$18" is associated with the role class Adult, then Adult becomes a category class in the sense of [16], meaning that the membership in Adult depends on satisfying "age$\geq$18". We would rather associate the transition predicate "age$\geq$18" with the evolution (i.e., role combination) Teenager$\xrightarrow{ev}$Adult.

8 Conclusion

This paper has presented a generic model for roles that builds upon existing models (mostly [12,24]) and extends them in several respects (like role-control support). It clearly distinguishes between generalization and role hierarchies and supports their interaction. It also features the following characteristics:

- the possibility for roles themselves to gain roles
- the coexistence of object identifiers and roles identifiers
- a context-dependent access to objects with several roles
- the ability for an object to possess several roles of the same class
- the ability for an object to gain a role in any role class, provided the role is declared as a valid destination for the evolving object
- the coexistence of class-based inheritance (via generalization) and instance-based inheritance (delegation)
- vertical and horizontal role possession
- the control of role compatibility, through the concepts of meaningful combinations of roles and transition predicates.

References

1. L. Al-Jadir and M. Léonard. If we refuse the inheritance... In T.J.M. Bench-Capon, G. Soda, and A.M. Tjoa, editors, *Proc. of the 10th Int. Conf. on Database and Expert Systems Applications, DEXA'99*, LNCS 1677, Florence, Italy, 1999. Springer-Verlag.
2. A. Albano, R. Bergamini, G. Ghelli, and R. Orsini. An object data model with roles. In R. Agrawal, S. Baker, and D. Bel, editors, *Proc. of the 19th Int. Conf. on Very Large Data Bases, VLDB'93*, pages 39–51, Dublin, Ireland, 1993. Morgan Kaufmann.

3. M. Atkinson, F. Bancilhon, D. Dewitt, K. Dittrich, D. Maier, and S. Zdonik. The object-oriented database system manifesto. In W. Kim, J.-M. Nicolas, and S. Nishi, editors, *Proc. of the 1st Int. Conf. on Deductive and Object-Oriented Databases, DOOD'89*, pages 223–240, Kyoto, Japan, 1991. North-Holland. Reprinted in the O2 Book, pp. 3–20.
4. C. W. Bachman and M. Daya. The role concept in data models. In *Proc. of the 3rd Int. Conf. on Very Large Data Bases, VLDB'77*, pages 464–476, Tokyo, Japan, 1977. IEEE Computer Society and ACM SIGMOD Record 9(4).
5. E. Bertino and G. Guerrini. Objects with multiple most specific classes. In W.G. Olthoff, editor, *Proc. of the 9th European Conf. on Object-Oriented Programming, ECOOP'95*, LNCS 952, pages 102–126, Aarhus, Denmark, 1995. Springer-Verlag.
6. C. Chambers. Predicate classes. In O. Nierstrasz, editor, *Proc. of the 7th European Conf. on Object-Oriented Programming, ECOOP'93*, LNCS 707, pages 268–296, Kaiserslautern, Germany, 1993. Springer-Verlag.
7. W. W. Chu and G. Zhang. Associations and roles in object-oriented modeling. In D.W. Embley and R.C. Goldstein, editors, *Proc. of the 16th Int. Conf. on Conceptual Modeling, ER'97*, LNCS 1331, pages 257–270, Los Angeles, California, 1997. Springer-Verlag.
8. M. Dahchour. *Integrating Generic Relationships into Object Models Using Metaclasses*. PhD thesis, Department of Computing Science and Engineering , University of Louvain, Belgium, March 2001.
9. M. Dahchour, A. Pirotte, and E. Zimányi. Materialization and its metaclass implementation. Technical Report YEROOS TR-9901, IAG-QANT, Université catholique de Louvain, Belgium, February 1999. To be published in IEEE Transactions on Knowledge and Data Engineering.
10. N. Edelweiss, J. Palazzo de Oliveira, J. Volkmer de Castilho, E. Peressi, A. Montanari, and B. Pernici. T-ORM: Temporal aspects in objects and roles. In *Proc. of the 1st Int. Conf. on Object Role Modeling, ORM-1*, 1994.
11. D. H. Fishman, D. Beech, H. P. Cate, E. C. Chow, T. Connors, J. W. Davis, N. Derrett, C.G. Hoch, W. Kent, P. Lyngbæk, B. Mahbod, M-A. Neimat, T. A. Ryan, and M-C. Shan. IRIS: An object-oriented database management system. *ACM Trans. on Office Information Systems*, 5(1):48–69, 1987. Also in *Readings in Object-Oriented Database Systems*, Morgan-Kaufmann, 1990.
12. G. Gottlob, M. Schrefl, and B. Röck. Extending object-oriented systems with roles. *ACM Trans. on Office Information Systems*, 14(3):268–296, 1996.
13. W. Kent. A rigorous model of object reference, identity, and existence. *Journal of Object-Oriented Programming*, 4(3):28–36, June 1991.
14. S. N. Khoshafian and G. P. Copeland. Object identity. In N.K. Meyrowitz, editor, *Proc. of the Conf. on Object-Oriented Programming Systems, Languages and Applications, OOPSLA'86*, pages 406–416, Portland, Oregon, 1986. ACM SIGPLAN Notices 21(11), 1986.
15. Q. Li and G. Dong. A framework for object migration in object-oriented databases. *Data & Knowledge Engineering*, 13(3):221–242, 1994.
16. E. Odberg. Category classes: Flexible classification and evolution in object-oriented databases. In G. Wijers, S. Brinkkemper, and T. Wasserman, editors, *Proc. of the 6th Int. Conf. on Advanced Information Systems Engineering, CAiSE'94*, LNCS 811, pages 406–420, Utrecht, The Netherlands, 1994. Springer-Verlag.
17. M. P. Papazoglou and B. J. Krämer. A database model for object dynamics. *Very Large Data Bases Journal*, 6:73–96, 1997.
18. B. Pernici. Objects with roles. In *Proc. of the Conf. on Office Information Systems*, pages 205–215, Cambridge, MA, 1990.

19. D. W. Renouf and B. Henderson-Sellers. Incorporating roles into MOSES. In C. Mingins and B. Meyer, editors, *Proc. of the 15th Conf. on Technology of Object-Oriented Languages and Systems, TOOLS 15*, pages 71–82, 1995.
20. J. Richardson and P. Schwarz. Aspects: Extending objects to support multiple, independent roles. In J. Clifford and R. King, editors, *Proc. of the ACM SIGMOD Int. Conf. on Management of Data, SIGMOD'91*, pages 298–307, Denver, Colorado, 1991. SIGMOD Record 20(2).
21. E. Sciore. Object specialization. *ACM Trans. on Office Information Systems*, 7(2):103–122, 1989.
22. F. Steimann. On the representation of roles in object-oriented and conceptual modeling. *Data & Knowledge Engineering*, 35(1):83–106, October 2000.
23. R. J. Wieringa and W. de Jonge. The identification of objects and roles: Object identifiers revisited. Technical Report IR-267, Faculty of Mathematics and Computer Science, Vrije Universiteit, Amsterdam, December 1991.
24. R. J. Wieringa, W. De Jonge, and P. Spruit. Using dynamic classes and role classes to model object migration. *Theory and Practice of Object Systems*, 1(1):61–83, 1995.
25. R. K. Wong, H. L. Chau, and F.H. Lochovsky. A data model and semantics of objects with dynamic roles. In A. Gray and P.-A. Larson, editors, *Proc. of the 13th Int. Conf. on Data Engineering, ICDE'97*, pages 402–411, Birmingham, UK, 1997. IEEE Computer Society.

Understanding Redundancy in UML Models for Object-Oriented Analysis

Dolors Costal, Maria-Ribera Sancho, and Ernest Teniente

Universitat Politècnica de Catalunya
Dept. Llenguatges i Sistemes Informàtics
Jordi Girona 1-3, 08034 Barcelona (Catalonia)
{dolors,ribera,teniente}@lsi.upc.es

Abstract. A phenomenon that frequently appears when designers define analysis specifications is that of redundancy between models. A correct and deep understanding of this phenomenon is necessary to help the task of the designer. In this paper, we study the problem of redundancy in UML Models for Object-Oriented Analysis. In this context, we identify different kinds of redundancies that may arise. We evaluate the impact of redundancy in specifications from the point of view of their desirable properties. We also propose how to obtain a canonical analysis model, which does not include any of the identified redundancies, and we sketch the possibility of having redundant views of some aspects of the canonical model.

1 Introduction

In this paper we study the problem of having redundant specifications at the analysis level. This is done for the particular case of object-oriented models, written in the UML. To the best of our knowledge, redundancy in object-oriented analysis models has not been considered before.

We say that an analysis model has redundancy when an aspect of the specified system is defined more than once. We think that identifying the different kinds of redundancy that may appear at the analysis level helps to fully understand the artifacts that are used in that stage. Furthermore, having (or not having) redundancy in a given specification has a great impact on their desirable properties, such as, understandability, modifiability, consistency and ease of design and implementation. Being aware of this impact helps the designer to define better and more comprehensible analysis models. Understanding redundancy also contributes to obtain better design models since it makes easier to decide the responsibilities of each software component.

In the context of the UML notation [RJB99], the most well-known proposal of software development process is the Unified Process (UP) [JBR99]. The Unified Process must be understood as a framework that encompasses the best development practices and not just as a strict universal process. The main strengths of the UP are to be use-case driven, architecture-centric, iterative and incremental.

One of the main difficulties that arise during software development is that of establishing a clear frontier between the analysis and design phases [Kai99]. We think, following the most accepted practices for software development [Rum96, Pres97] that this deserves special attention because the analysis model constitutes a permanent model of the reality in itself. In the UP (or in object-orientation in general) this is even more difficult due to the iterative process, the use of the same models in both phases and to the different criteria used by different authors.

As far as analysis is concerned, the UP admits a certain degree of freedom with respect to the way to view and employ the models or artifacts generated during this stage. In this sense, an interesting proposal is that of Larman [Lar98] because it provides good criteria to define the boundary between analysis and design and it proposes how UML artifacts have to be used acording to that criteria. Our work takes this proposal as starting point.

In this context, we study the already mentioned problem of having redundant specifications at the analysis level. One of the main points of this paper is to identify which kind of redundancies may arise. Moreover, we evaluate the impact of redundancy in specifications from the point of view of their desirable properties.

We advocate also for avoiding redundancy in the analysis models. In this sense, we propose how to obtain a canonical model which does not include any of the identified redundancies. Moreover, we sketch the possibility of having redundant views of some aspects of the analysis model to help the designer in his task. In this way, he may take advantage of having redundant and non-redundant models altogether.

This paper is structured as follows. Next section reviews the main UML models used during the Analysis phase according to Larman's proposal. Section 3 is devoted to identify different kinds of redundancy that may appear in that phase. Section 4 discusses the issue of redundancy: advantages and inconveniences and provides a set of guidelines to avoid the identified redundancies. Finally, we present our conclusions in section 5.

2 UML Models for Analysis

In this section, we will briefly describe the UML models used during the analysis phase following the main lines of Larman's proposal [Lar98]: the Analysis Use Case Model, the Conceptual Model, the System Behaviour Model and the Analysis State Model.

In Larman's work, analysis is characterized by emphasizing static and dynamic information about a system. Therefore, a static model describes structural properties of the system while a dynamic one describes the behavioural ones. Larman's main contribution relies on proposing to define the system behaviour as a 'black box' before proceeding to a logical design of how a software application will work. The main idea behind this solution has also been sketched in [Boo96, FS97, Mul97, Dou98, RV00].

This has a clear impact, during analysis, on the sequence diagrams definition and on the assignment of operations to classes. Sequence diagrams are considered as *system sequence diagrams* that show the events that external actors generate; their order and the system response to those events. On the other hand, operations responding to those external events are not assigned to particular classes since they are recorded in an artificial type named *system*. In this way, responsibilities are not assigned to objects during analysis.

We believe this is a good criteria to define the boundary between analysis and design. We should mention that some difficulties may arise when trying to develop these models along this direction. The overcoming of those situations is out of the scope of this paper.

In the following, we will use a simple example that is aimed to model the assignments of employees to departments in a certain company to illustrate the Analysis Models.

2.1 Use Case Model

In the plan and elaborate phase, high-level use cases are identified. They are defined very briefly, usually several sentences that describe a process. The Analysis Use Case Model consists of the definition of expanded use cases which are longer and more detailed than high-level use cases, in order to describe the course of events that occur as a result of actor actions and the system responses to them. In our example, we need a use case to fire employees. This use case is described in Figure 2.1.

Use Case: Fire employee
Actors: Director (initiator), Adm-Staff.
Overview: Fires an employee.
Type: Primary and essential.
Typical Course of Events:

Actor Action	System Response
1. The use case begins when the director decides to fire an employee.	
2. An administrative staff introduces the employee identifier.	
	3. The system removes the employee and all her/his assignments, if this can be done.

Figure 2.1

2.2 The Conceptual Model

The Conceptual Model conforms the static part of the analysis and, consequently describes the structural properties of the objects that model concepts of the problem domain. It is illustrated with a set of static structure diagrams (a class diagram) in which no operations are defined.

For example, Figure 2.2 shows a static structure diagram. Object classes Employee, Department and Date are linked with the Is-assigned-to association. An occurrence of the association indicates that a particular employee has been assigned to a particular department at a given date. The corresponding association class named Assignment has an attribute to indicate the duration of this assignment. The diagram is complemented with textual constraints, which cannot be expressed graphically in the UML.

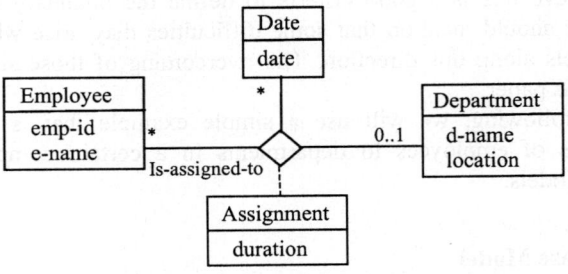

Textual Constraints:
- Class identifiers: (Employee, emp-id); (Date, date); (Department, d-name)
- An employee may not have two overlapping assignements.

Figure 2.2

2.3 The System Behaviour Model

The System Behaviour Model describes dynamic aspects of the system. As mentioned in the introduction of this section, the system behaviour is defined as a 'black box' in the Analysis phase and it is illustrated through system sequence diagrams and the contracts of the corresponding operations.

A system sequence diagram shows, for a particular course of events within a use case, the external actors that interact directly with the system, the system as a 'black box', and the system events that the actors generate. The following sequence diagram corresponds to the use case of Figure 2.1:

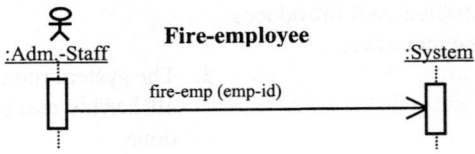

Figure 2.3

A system operation is an operation that the system executes in response to a system event. Therefore, there is a one to one correspondence between events and operations and we will refer to them as events or operations, indistinctly. It is defined by means of a contract that includes the signature of the operation, its semantics, a set of conditions that are guaranteed to be true when the operation is executed (its precondition) and the set of conditions that hold after the operation execution (its postcondition). The contract of the previous operation *fire-emp* looks as follows:

Operation: fire-emp (emp-id)
Precondition:
Semantics: Fire an employee.
Postcondition:
1. If the employee emp-id does not exist then the operation is invalid.
2. Otherwise, the operation is valid and
   2.1. The employee identified by emp-id is deleted.
   2.2. All the assignments of this employee are deleted.

Figure 2.4

2.4 The Analysis State Model

Finally, the Analysis State Model consists of a set of state diagrams that illustrate the interesting events and states of objects, and the behaviour of those objects in reaction to an event. An example of analysis state model will be shown in Section 3.3.

3 Identifying Redundancy in the UML Analysis Model

Each one of the models explained so far shows different perspectives of a software system: the static one, the behavioural one, etc. It usually happens that a certain aspect of the system can be viewed from different models. We say that an analysis model has redundancy when an aspect is specified in more than one of its models.

In this section we identify several redundancies that may arise among the UML analysis models.

3.1 Conceptual Model and System Behaviour Model

The Analysis Conceptual Model allows to express several constraints about the information that it defines. In general, we may consider three different kinds of constraints: *graphical*, *textual* and *structural*.

Graphical constraints (like multiplicity, generalization constraints, subset, xor, etc.) can be directly represented by means of a graphical symbol in the UML. Textual constraints define conditions that the conceptual model must satisfy but that can not be graphically represented. They will usually be specified in the OCL language [WK99]. Structural constraints are implicit in the Conceptual Model and, thus, they are not represented neither graphically nor textually. For instance, each association (associative class) implies a structural constraint stating that there may not exist two instances of an association linking the same objects.

On the other hand, the System Behaviour Model includes Operation Contracts that describe the effect of the operations upon the system and, in particular, how the information of the Conceptual Model will be updated.

It is not difficult to see that an update may lead to a violation of a certain constraint. In this sense, it may happen that the post-condition of a certain operation contract checks a constraint that is already entailed by the conceptual model.

Example 3.1: consider the following Conceptual Model, which is aimed to model the Enrolments of Students into Subjects, during Academic Courses. Subjects may be offered during academic courses. An offered subject can be open or closed. When an offered subject is closed, no new students can be enrolled in it.

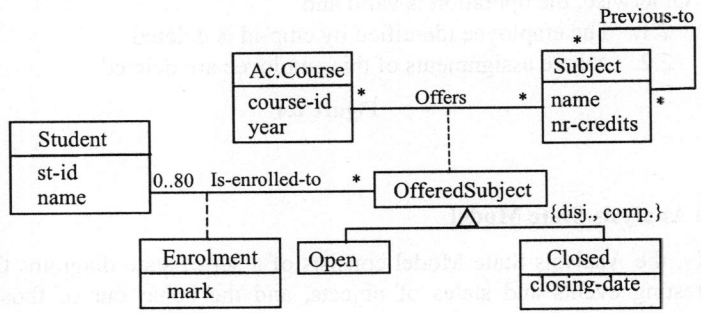

Textual Constraints:
- Class identifiers: (Student, st-id); (Ac.Course, course-id); (Subject, name)
- A student may not be enrolled in a subject if s/he had a mark greater than 5 in a previous enrolment of that subject.
- A student may not be enrolled in a subject if s/he does not have a mark greater than 5 in all its previous subjects.
- A student must be enroled at most in five subjects during an academic course.
- The association Previous-to is transitive.
- A subject may not be previous to itself.

Figure 3.1

The previous Conceptual Model specifies several constraints. In particular, regarding the enrolments of students into subjects, it entails that:

An offered subject is defined by a subject and an academic course (structural constraint). Two different assertions are deduced from this constraint. First, it guarantees that two different instances of offered subject may not be linking the same instances of subject and academic course. Second, if an offered subject exists, it is guaranteed that the subject and the academic course also exist.

An instance of the association *Is-enrolled-to* is defined by a student and an offered subject (structural constraint). Two different assertions are deduced from this constraint. First, it guarantees that two different instances of enrolment may not be linking the same instances of student and offered subject. Second, if an instance of the association exists, it is guaranteed that the student and the offered subject also exist.

a) An offered subject must have at most 80 enrolled students (graphical).
b) An offered subject may not be open and closed at the same time (graphical).
c) A student may not be enrolled in a subject if s/he had a mark greater than 5 in a previous enrolment of this subject (textual).

d) A student may not be enrolled in a subject if s/he does not have a mark greater than 5 in all its previous subjects (textual).
e) A student must be enrolled at most into 5 subjects during an academic course (textual).

There are at least four operations that may violate some of the previous integrity constraints: to offer a subject in an academic course, to enrol a student, to change the enrolment of a student and to close an offered subject. We will illustrate this issue in the context of the operation that enrols a student in a subject offered in an academic course which could be specified by means of the following contract:

Operation: enrol-1 (course-id, subject-name, st-id)
Precondition:
Semantics: To enrol a student into a subject offered in an academic course.
Postcondition:

1. If the student st-id or the course course-id or the subject subject-name do not exist, then the operation is invalid.
2. If the subject subject-name is not offered in course course-id, then the operation is invalid.
3. If the student st-id is already enrolled into subject subject-name for the course course-id, then the operation is invalid.
4. If the student st-id has already five enrolments corresponding to academic course course-id, then the operation is invalid.
5. If the student st-id has already an enrolment into subject subject-id with a mark greater than 5, then the operation is invalid.
6. If the offered subject corresponding to course-id and subject-name is closed, then the operation is invalid
7. Otherwise, the operation is valid, and
    7.1   An instance of the association Is-enrolled-to, defined by the corresponding Student, Subject and Academic Course is created.

Figure 3.2

Clearly, the postconditions 4 and 5 and the integrity constraints g) and e) are redundant. Also, postconditions 1, 2 and 3 are redundant with the structural constraints a) and b). In this latter case, it is not difficult to see that structural constraints guarantee that an enrolment of a student in an offered subject can only be performed if the student is not already enrolled on that offered subject and if the student and the offered subject exist. Similarly, if an offered subject exists, the academic course and the subject also exist.

On the other hand, if we had specified the contract of Figure 3.3 for enrolments, the previous redundancy would not appear since the postconditions of this operation do not include the checking of the previous constraints.

Note that the existence of redundancy between the operation and the conceptual model does not imply that all constraints of the conceptual model that affect the operation are included in its postconditions. As an example, enrol-1 does not check constraints c) and f) although they can be violated by enrolling a student into an offered course.

Operation: enrol-2 (course-id, subject-name, st-id)
Precondition:
Semantics: To enrol a student into a subject offered in an academic course.
Postcondition:

1. If the offered subject corresponding to course-id and subject-name is closed, then the operation is invalid
2. An instance of the association Is-enrolled-to, defined by the corresponding Student, Subject and Academic Course is created.

Figure 3.3

Therefore, in addition to the conditions already implied by its postconditions, an operation will also be invalid if any of the constraints entailed by the conceptual model is violated. For instance, operation enrol-2 will be invalid if any of the constraints entailed by the conceptual model is violated due to its postcondition.

In general, it is very difficult to ensure that an operation contract guarantees all constraints specified in a conceptual model. For this reason, whenever we talk about redundancy in this paper we will be referring to relative redundancy since absolute redundancy (in the sense that operation contracts specify all the aspects of the software system that can be affected by operation execution) is as difficult to achieve as non-redundancy.

3.2 Redundancy inside the System Behaviour Model

In addition to the Operation Contracts, the System Behaviour Model includes System Sequence Diagrams that specify the external events generated by actors in the context of a use case, its order, and the system operations that respond to those events.

Since, at the analysis level, there is a one-to-one correspondence between external events and system operations, the system sequence diagram already guarantees that the operations are handled in a specific order. Consequently, a certain operation is only executed when all previous operations have been handled satisfactorily. Therefore, it is guaranteed that the postconditions of its precedent operations in the sequence diagram are already satisfied.

A System Sequence Diagram and an Operation Contract would be redundant if the contract checks aspects already guaranteed by the sequencing entailed by the sequence diagram.

Example 3.2: assume that there is a use case that, at the beginning of an academic course, offers a new subject and enrols some students to that subject. The system sequence diagram of this use case could look as follows:

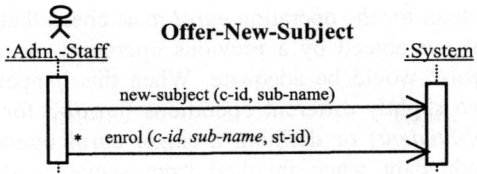

Figure 3.4

The operations *new-subject* and *enrol* should be specified by means of the corresponding contracts. The first operation, *new-subject*, is aimed to add the subject as an offered subject of the given academic course. This offered subject is specialised to open. The second operation, *enrol*, will perform individual enrolments of students for that subject into that course.

Note that, in a non-redundant analysis model, the contract of the operation *enrol* does not need to check none of the conditions that are entailed by *new-subject*. In this sense, part of the postconditions of *new-subject* become preconditions of *enrol* and, thus, they must not necessarily be specified again in its contract.

In particular, postcondition 1 stating that the offered subject must be open is not necessary. Then, the corresponding contract enrol-3 would be:

Operation: enrol-3 (course-id, subject-name, st-id)
Precondition:
Semantics: To enrol a student into a subject offered in an academic course.
Postcondition:

1. An instance of the association Is-enrolled-to, defined by the corresponding Student, Subject and Academic Course is created.

Figure 3.5

In some cases, it is very difficult to avoid redundancy completely among sequence diagrams and operations contracts. This will happen when a certain event (operation) may appear in several sequence diagrams since the events previously invoked will differ from diagram to diagram. In such cases, it is not possible to ensure that the conditions that are already satisfied are always the same and we have to choose between considering a different operation contract in each case or considering a single operation contract that may be redundant for a certain sequence diagram.

As an example, assume an additional use case that enrols a student in a subject. The system sequence diagram of this use case could look as follows:

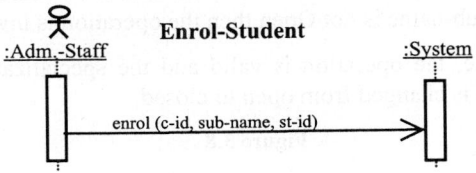

Figure 3.6

In this case, the contract for the operation *enrol* must check that the offered subject is open since it is not guaranteed by a previous operation. As a consequence, the operation contract enrol-2 would be adequate. When this happens, we may choose between specifying two slightly different operations (*enrol-3* for *Offer-New-Subject* and *enrol-2* for *Enrol-Student*) or defining a single enrol operation (*enrol-2*) that would be partially redundant when invoked from sequence diagram *Offer-New-Subject*.

3.3 Analysis State Model and System Behaviour Model

An Analysis State Diagram shows the life-cycle of an object, the events that affect it, its transitions and the states it is in between these events. In this sense, it shows the behaviour of an object in reaction to events.

Each state transition specified in the diagram defines changes on an object that are caused by the invocation of a certain event (operation) on that object. An object may only suffer a certain transition if its state is the one required for the transition when the event is invoked.

An Operation Contract and a State Diagram are redundant if the contract checks conditions about the state of the objects that are already entailed by the state diagram transitions.

As an example, assume the following Analysis State Diagram for offered subjects:

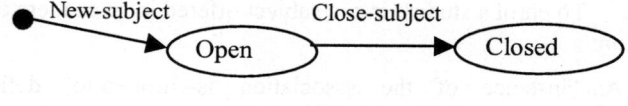

Figure 3.7

This state diagram specifies that the event *new-subject* is the creation event for offered subjects and that the event *close-subject* can only be applied to open offered subjects. Therefore, it would be redundant to specify this information in the contracts of the corresponding operations. The designer could easily specify the following contract to close an offered subject:

Operation: Close-subject (sub-name, course-id)
Precondition:
Semantics: To close a subject of an academic course.
Postcondition:

1. If the offered subject o defined by the academic course course-id and the subject sub-name is not Open then the operation is invalid.

2. Otherwise, the operation is valid and the specialization of the offered subject o is changed from open to closed.

Figure 3.8

The postcondition 1 of the previous contract is redundant since it specifies an aspect already defined in the state diagram for offered subjects defined in Figure 3.7.

4 Dealing with Redundancy in the UML Analysis Model

In this section we discuss about the advantages and inconveniences of considering non-redundant UML Analysis Models. We propose some guidelines to avoid redundancy and we define the semantics of the execution of a sequence diagram in this case. We finally show the advantages that could provide a tool able to generate (redundant) views of a non-redundant model.

4.1 Discussion about the Advantages of Non-redundant Analysis Models

We think that a non-redundant analysis model presents the following advantages as far as software development is concerned:

1. It contributes to desirable properties of a software system specification

Modifiability and consistency are some of the properties that must be achieved to obtain a well-written specification [Dav93].

Usually, a software system is under continuous evolution. A specification is *modifiable* if changes to the requirements can be made easily, completely and consistently. It is not difficult to see that, if a certain redundant aspect evolves, we need to modify it in all the models where it is specified. On the contrary, this does not happen in a non-redundant specification.

For instance, if it happens that the requirement about the maximum number of subjects a student may be enrolled in during an academic course changes from five to seven, it will be more difficult to modify the analysis model if we consider the operation contract enrol-1 (see Figure 3.2) than with the operation contract enrol-3 (see Figure 3.5).

On the other hand, a specification is *consistent* if no subset of requirements stated therein conflict. Again, in a redundant specification, it is easier to define inconsistent requirements because, since a single aspect is specified several times and in several models, it is difficult to guarantee that it is always specified in the same way.

For instance, it will be more difficult to keep the specification consistent with the operation contract enrol-1 since we could easily have specified in it that the maximum number of subjects for a student into an academic course is three, which would clearly enter in contradiction with the information provided by the conceptual model.

2. It facilitates software design and implementation

Redundancies at the analysis level will be easily propagated to the following stages of software development, i.e. to design and implementation, causing in general a significant reduction in the efficiency of the final system. For instance, a certain aspect could be designed and implemented twice, also in two different ways, if the designer or the programmer do not realise that it is redundantly specified.

Consider again the conceptual model of Figure 3.1. If we are implementing it in a relational database, we will probably obtain a (partial) logical schema with the following tables (primary key attributes are underlined):

Ac-course (<u>course-id</u>, year)
Subject (<u>s-name</u>, nr-credits)
Offered-course (<u>course-id</u>, <u>s-name</u>)
       {course-id} is a foreign key that references Ac-course
       {s-name} is a foreign key that references Subject
Student (<u>st-id</u>, name)
Enrolment (course-id, s-name, st-id)
       {course-id, s-name} is a foreign key that references Offered-course
       {st-id} is a foreign key that references Student

If we directly design the transaction corresponding to the operation contract enrol-1 (see Figure 3.2), the transaction will include a check for each of the validation postconditions of the operation contract. In particular, it will verify that (postconditions 1, 2 and 3):

- Student st-id, course course-id and subject subject-name exist.
- Course-id is offered in course course-id.
- Student st-id is not enrolled into subject subject-name for the course course-id.

However, it is not difficult to see that due to primary and foreign keys the database alone will already guarantee that these postconditions are satisfied, (and thus, that they must not be implemented inside the transaction).

In a similar way, we could implement the checking of the constraints e) and g) directly into the database management system by means of triggers or stored procedures. Again, the transaction corresponding to enrol-1 would probably also unnecessarily include a check to guarantee that these constraints are not violated by the transaction.

Although it can be argued that this drawback can be prevented if software design includes a first initial step to remove redundancy between the different models, we believe that this would enter into a contradiction with the way in which we do analysis since we would first redundantly specify an aspect into different models to remove the same redundancy afterwards.

4.2 Defining a Canonical (Non-redundant) Analysis Model

As we have seen in the previous section, non-redundant analysis models present several advantages over the redundant ones. Therefore, we need some criteria to define non-redundant models. We call *canonical analysis model* the non-redundant analysis model resulting from applying the criteria proposed in this section.

Removing redundancy between the graphical and structural constraints of the conceptual model and the operation contracts can only be done by avoiding the definition of the corresponding postconditions in the operation contracts since they cannot be removed from the conceptual model.

In a similar way, redundancy between sequence diagrams or the state model and the operation contracts can only be done by avoiding the definition of the corresponding postconditions in the operation contracts. One could argue that it could also be removed from the sequence diagram or the state model but this would imply not to define them at all. Nevertheless, since the utility of these UML diagrams is doubtless, we believe that this alternative is not realistic.

To remove redundancy between textual constraints in the conceptual model and the postconditions of the operation contracts, we could choose to specify either the constraints or the postconditions. In the first case, if we just specify textual constraints, we would increase the localization of the information definition since we would specify a constraint a single time in the conceptual model rather than distributed among all the operations that may affect it. Since localization is an important issue regarding the construction, understanding and changeability of analysis models [Oli86, CSO+97], we think that this is the best alternative to obtain the canonical model.

For instance, we increase the localization of the information definition if the constraint that at most 80 students can be enrolled into an offered course is specified only once in the conceptual model instead of several times in the contracts of the operations to enrol a student, to change the enrolment of a student, to offer a new subject, etc., i.e. once for each operation that may violate this constraint.

The canonical model of our example of section 3 would contain the conceptual model of Figure 3.1, the sequence diagram of Figure 3.4, the state diagram of Figure 3.7 and the operation contracts of enrol-3 (Figure 3.5) and close-subject (Figure 3.8, without the postcondition 1).

As a conclusion, we can see that the canonical analysis model keeps away from redundancy by avoiding it in the definition of the postconditions of the operation contracts. This is not surprising since we can observe that operation contracts are involved in all different types of redundancy that we have identified. Moreover, an aspect specified into a certain model (other than the contracts), may be affected in general by several operations. Therefore, to increase localization, it is more reasonable to specify it in only one place.

Furthermore, this proposal leads to postconditions with only dynamic constraints (all the static ones are specified in the conceptual model). As a side effect, this results in an emphasis of dynamic constraints that improves their understandability.

Finally, in the canonical model, since only the operation contracts are textual descriptions, a certain aspect is specified graphically whenever possible. This results also in a more comprehensive analysis model.

4.3 Semantics of Sequence Diagrams Execution

When we consider non-redundant operation contracts, its execution semantics depend on the rest of the analysis models. Therefore, an operation postcondition must be understood as something that is performed as a necessary, but not always sufficient, condition to execute the corresponding operation. In this sense, it is not guaranteed that an operation will be executed satisfactorily if its postcondition succeeds, since its execution may lead to a violation of a constraint specified somewhere else.

As a consequence, the semantics of the execution of a system sequence diagram has to be defined as follows:

- The conditions entailed by a State Diagram must be satisfied before the execution of each operation appearing in the system sequence diagram.
- The conditions entailed by the Conceptual Model must be satisfied after the execution of all the operations that appear in a system sequence diagram.
- For each operation of the system sequence diagram, its postconditions do not lead to an invalid execution of the operation.
- If any of the previous three conditions does not hold, then all the operations are rejected and the information base is not updated at all.

Note that this semantics is required not only for non-redundant models but also for any relative redundant model. Therefore, in practice, as absolute redundancy is almost never achieved, the semantics stated here should be the usual one.

4.4 Redundant Views of a Canonical Analysis Model

The whole idea of analysis models is to foster understanding and this may sometimes require to isolate certain aspects from other aspects. Since many aspects participate in multiple views, one could argue that this redundancy is unavoidable and, in this way, disagree with the guideline that suggests not to have redundancy in the analysis model. However, the use of a canonical model does not prevent the designer having redundant views of the analysis model.

In fact, the use of a graphical language like the UML is based on the assumption that we will be using computer-based tools and not 'paper and pencil' or mere semantics-free drawing tools. Therefore, we think that such a CASE tool should store explicitly only the canonical model and should be able to reason about it to identify redundancy that could appear in the operation contracts and to keep consistency among them. Moreover, a tool of this kind could also be able to generate a skeleton of an operation contract that includes all aspects already specified in other models. This would clearly help the work of the designer since he would have a more complete view of the impact of each decision taken. The definition of such a CASE tool is far beyond the scope of this paper and it is left for further research.

For instance, if we had the conceptual model of Figure 3.1, we could think of a CASE tool that would automatically generate the following absolute redundant skeleton of a contract for the operation to enrol a student into an academic course. Note that this skeleton includes the checking of all constraints specified in the conceptual model.

Operation: enrol (course-id, subject-name, st-id)
Precondition:
Semantics: To enrol a student into a subject offered in an academic course.
Postcondition:

1. If the student st-id or the course course-id or the subject subject-name do not exist, then the operation is invalid.
2. If the subject subject-name is not offered in course course-id, then the operation is invalid.
3. If the student st-id is already enrolled into subject subject-name for the course course-id, then the operation is invalid.
4. If the student st-id has already five enrolments corresponding to academic course course-id, then the operation is invalid.
5. If the student st-id has already an enrolment into subject subject-id with a mark greater than 5, then the operation is invalid.
6. If the offered course defined by subject subject-name and academic course course-id has 80 enrolments already, then the operation is invalid.
7. If, for any of the subjects previous to subject-name, the student st-id does not have a mark greater than five into some enrolment in that subject, then the operation is invalid.

Figure 4.1

Even if such a CASE tool does not exist yet, we believe that the advantages we have discussed in section 3 justify putting the effort to generate a canonical model rather than falling into redundancy. Moreover, the inexistence of such a CASE tool alone does not justify the preference for redundant analysis models since, as we have seen, it is as difficult to define an absolute redundant analysis model (the only way we can get rid of all interactions between multiple views) by hand than a canonical one.

5 Conclusions

In this paper, we have studied the problem of redundancy in the context of the UML Analysis Models. First, we have identified redundancies that may arise and we have classified them in three different types: redundancy between the Conceptual Model and Operation Contracts, redundancy between System Sequence Diagrams and Operation Contracts and redundancy between Analysis State Diagrams and Operation Contracts. We think that being aware of these different kinds of redundancy helps the designer to fully understand the relationships that exist among different parts of an specification.

We have also justified the advantages of non-redundant analysis models in terms of desirable properties of software specifications and ease of design and implementation. We have defined a canonical model that avoids redundancy by not including already entailed checkings in the postcondition of operation contracts. We have described several advantages that our canonical model presents over alternative ways of avoiding redundancy. We have provided an adequate semantics of Sequence Diagrams execution in order to define the correct behaviour of non-redundant operations. This semantics should also be applied in case of having not fully redundant operations. Finally, since redundancy may be useful in some cases to permit the isolate use of certain parts of an specification, we have sketched the possibility of having redundant views of some aspects of the analysis model.

Acknowledgements

We would like to thank Antoni Olivé, Cristina Gómez and the anonymous referees for their useful comments. This work has been partially supported by the CICYT program project TIC99-1048-C02-01.

References

[Boo96] G.Booch. "Object Solutions: Managing the Object-Oriented Project", Addison-Wesley, 1996.
[CSO+97] D.Costal; M.R.Sancho; A.Olivé; M.Barceló; P.Costa; C.Quer and A.Roselló. "The Cause-Effect Rules of ROSES", Proc. of the First East-European Symposium on Advances in Databases and Information Systems (ADBIS'97), St. Petersburg, September 1997, pp. 399-405.
[Dav93] A.M. Davis "Software Requirements. Objects, Functions and States", Prentice-Hall, 1993.
[Dou98] B.Douglass. "Real-time UML: Developing Efficient Objects for Embedded Systems", Addison-Wesley, 1998.
[FS97] M.Fowler and K.Scott. "UML Distilled", Addison-Wesley, 1997.
[JBR99] I.Jacobson; G.Booch and J.Rumbaugh. "The Unified Software Development Process", Addison-Wesley, 1999.
[Kai99] H.Kaindl. "Difficulties in the Transition From OO Analysis to Design". IEEE Software, Sept./Oct. 99, pp. 94-102
[Lar98] C.Larman. "Applying UML and Patterns", Prentice Hall, 1998.
[Mul97] P.A.Muller. "Modélisation Object avec UML" (in french), Éditions Eyrolles, 1997.
[Oli86] A.Olivé. "A comparison of the operational and deductive approaches to conceptual information systems modelling", Proc. IFIP-86, North-Holland, Dublin, 1986, pp. 91-96.
[Pre97] R.Pressman. "Software Engineering: A Practitioner's Approach", McGraw-Hill, 1997.
[RJB99] J.Rumbaugh; I.Jacobson and G.Booch. "The Unified Modeling Language Reference Manual", Addison-Wesley, 1999.
[Rum96] J.Rumbaugh; et al. "Object Oriented Modeling and Design", Prentice-Hall, 1996.
[RV00] P.Roques and F.Vallée. "UML en action" (in french), Éditions Eyrolles, 2000.
[WK99] J.Warmer and A.Kleppe. "The Object Constraint Language", Addison-Wesley, 1999.

Representation of Generic Relationship Types in Conceptual Modeling

Antoni Olivé

Departament de Llenguatges i Sistemes Informàtics
Universitat Politècnica de Catalunya
08034 Barcelona (Catalonia)
olive@lsi.upc.es

Abstract. A generic relationship type is a relationship type that may have several realizations in a domain. Typical examples are *IsPartOf*, *IsMemberOf* or *Materializes*, but there are many others. The use of generic relationship types offers several important benefits. However, the achievement of these benefits requires an adequate representation method of the generic relationship types, and their realizations, in the conceptual schemas. In this paper, we propose two new alternative methods for this representation; we describe the contexts in which one or the other is more appropriate, and show their advantages over the current methods. We also explain the adaptation of the methods to the UML.

1 Introduction

A significant amount of research work, in the conceptual modeling field, has focussed on the identification, analysis, representation and implementation of generic relationship types. A generic relationship type is a relationship type that may have several realizations in a domain. A realization is a particular combination of the participant entity types, and can be seen as a specific relationship type [Dach98, PiZD98]. The most prominent generic relationship type is the *IsPartOf* [Mots93, WaSW99], which, in a particular domain, may have realizations such as *Division-Company*, *Company-Company* or *Office-Building*. All other combinations (like *Company-Division*) are not allowed. Generic relationship types are also known sometimes as *semantic* [Stor93] relationship types.

Among other generic relationship types that have been studied in detail there are: *MemberOf*, with example realizations *TennisPlayer-TennisClub*, *Person-ProjectTeam* or *Person-Committee* [MoSt95]; *Materializes*, with example realizations *Car-CarModel*, *Performance-Play* or *Volume-Book* [PZMY94]; and *Owns*, with example realizations *Person-Building*, *Bank-Mortgage* or *Person-Car* [YHGP94].

From a conceptual modeling point of view, generic relationship types offer the following benefits: (1) They ease the definition of realizations, because their common aspects are predefined. Generic relationship types foster the reuse of conceptual schemas [PiZD98]; (2) They allow the definition of general knowledge, in the form of derived entity types, attributes or relationship types, and of integrity constraints, which can be included in libraries, and 'imported' by conceptual schemas when needed [Matt88]; and (3) They facilitate automated schema design tools that help the designers to develop, verify, validate and implement conceptual schemas [Stor93].

In broad domains, there are many generic relationship types. The top-level categories of general ontologies [Cyco97, Sowa00] include many of them. If the conceptual schema for a particular domain is embedded within a general ontology, then many domain specific relationship types are realizations of generic ones. Given the benefits, some authors recommend that all relationship types should be defined as realizations of generic ones [PiZD98].

However, the achievement of these benefits requires an adequate representation method of the generic relationship types, and their realizations, in the conceptual schemas. Surprisingly, the current methods do not represent the generic relationship type explicitly in the schema, but only its realizations. The consequence is that the benefits cannot be achieved in their full extent. Some methods, mainly based on Telos [MBJK90], define the common aspects of the realizations at the metalevel, which are then 'inherited' by the realizations, but again -with very few exceptions- they do not represent the generic relationship type explicitly in the schema.

In this paper, we argue that the achievement of the above benefits requires that generic relationship types be represented explicitly in the schema. We propose two new alternative methods for this representation, and describe the contexts in which one or the other is more appropriate. Our methods can be integrated with existing conceptual modeling languages. In particular, we show their adaptation to the UML.

The structure of the paper is as follows. Section 2 defines the terminology and the notation that will be used in the paper. In Section 3 we describe our first method for the representation of generic relationship types in conceptual schemas. We show that the method can be adapted to the UML. We analyze also the possibilities the method offers to define additional knowledge and comment some possible extensions. Section 4 does the same for the second method. Section 5 analyzes the properties of both methods, and compares them with the current ones. Finally, in Section 6 we give the conclusions.

2 Terminology and Notation

In this paper, we deal with entities, relationships, entity types, relationship types and meta entity types. We take a temporal view, and assume that entities, relationships and entity types are instance of their types at particular time points, which are expressed in a common base time unit such as second or day. We make this assumption for the sake of generality, but our work is also applicable when a temporal view is not needed.

We represent by $In(e_1, e^1{}_1, t)$ the fact that entity e_1 is instance of entity type $e^1{}_1$ at time t. We assume multiple classification, and allow an entity to be direct instance of several entity types. An entity type is also an entity, which is instance of a meta entity type. Therefore, we represent also by $In(e^1{}_1, e^2{}_1, t)$ the fact that entity type $e^1{}_1$ is instance of meta entity type e^2_1 at time t. We use predicate *In* as a shorthand for *IsInstanceOf*. Also, we use the convention that constants are capitalized, variables start with a lowercase letter, variables denoting entity types have the superscript *1*, and those denoting meta entity types have the superscript *2*.

A relationship type has a name and a set of n participants, with $n \geq 2$. A *participant* is an entity type that plays a certain role in the relationship type. $R(p_1:E_1,...,p_n:E_n)$ denotes a relationship type named R with entity type participants $E_1,...,E_n$ playing the roles $p_1,...,p_n$, respectively. We say that $R(p_1:E_1,...,p_n:E_n)$ is the *schema* of the relationship type and that $p_1:E_1, ..., p_n:E_n$ are their participants. When the role name is omitted, it is assumed to be the same as the corresponding entity type. In this paper, attributes will be considered as ordinary binary relationship types.

We represent by $R(e_1,...,e_n,t)$ the fact that entities $e_1,...,e_n$ participate in an instance of R at time t. We also say that $(e_1,...,e_n)$ is an instance of R at t. The usual referential integrity constraint associated with R guarantees that $e_1, ..., e_n$ are instance of their corresponding entity types $E_1,...,E_n$:

$$R(e_1,...,e_n,t) \rightarrow In(e_1,E_1,t) \wedge ... \wedge In(e_n,E_n,t)$$

In the formulas, we assume that the free variables are universally quantified in the front.

A *class relationship type* is an ordinary relationship type but where some or all of its participants are meta entity types. We distinguish between class relationship type and meta relationship type. Instances of the former are facts, while instances of the latter are relationship types. In the UML, a class relationship type is an association having one or more association ends with the value *Classifier* for the attribute *targetScope* [OMG01, p. 2-23]. An example of class relationship type could be:

CanBeExpressedIn (QuantityType, Unit)

where *QuantityType* is a meta entity type, and *Unit* is an entity type.

In this paper, we only deal with class relationship types where *all* participants are meta entity types. An example could be:

InstancesAreFruitOf (FruitType, TreeType)

with the meaning that "The instances of FruitType <ft> are fruit of some instance of TreeType <tt>". Example instances are the facts:

InstancesAreFruitOf (Apple, AppleTree,_),

InstancesAreFruitOf (Orange, OrangeTree,_)

Note the difference with the relationship type:

IsFruitOf (Fruit, Tree)

whose instances are the relationships between particular fruits and their corresponding trees.

A generic relationship type R is an ordinary relationship type $R(p_1:E_1,...,p_n:E_n)$ with a set of m realizations, $m \geq 0$, and a realization constraint. A realization i is a set $\{p_1:E_{1,i},...,p_n:E_{n,i}\}$. We will assume that the entity types of the realizations $E_{j,i}$ are direct or indirect subtypes of the corresponding participant E_j in the generic relationship type R. For example, the generic relationship type:

$$\text{IsPartOf (part:Entity, whole:Entity)}$$

where *Entity* is the direct or indirect supertype of all entity types in a schema, could have two realizations:

$$\{\text{part:Division, whole:Company}\}, \{\text{part:Company, whole:Company}\}$$

The *realization constraint* of a generic relationship R with m realizations ensures that:

- if entities $e_1,...,e_n$ participate in an instance of R, then
- they are instance of a set $E_{1,i},...,E_{n,i}$ of corresponding types, such that
- $\{p_1:E_{1,i},...,p_n:E_{n,i}\}$ is a realization.

The general form of the realization constraint of a generic relationship type R with m realizations $\{p_1:E_{1,i},...,p_n:E_{n,i}\}, i = 1...m$, is:

$$R(e_1,...,e_n,t) \rightarrow [(\text{In}(e_1,E_{1,1},t) \wedge ... \wedge \text{In}(e_n,E_{n,1},t)) \vee ... \vee \\ (\text{In}(e_1,E_{1,m},t) \wedge ... \wedge \text{In}(e_n,E_{n,m},t))]$$

3 Realizations as Subtypes

In this section, we describe our first method for the representation of generic relationship types in conceptual schemas. For presentation purposes, we structure the description in two parts: the basic idea of the method and its possible extensions. We show that the method can be adapted to the UML. We analyze also the possibilities that this method offers to define additional knowledge.

3.1 The Method

The basic idea of our first method is very simple: A generic relationship type $R(p_1:E_1,...,p_n:E_n)$ with m realizations ($m \geq 0$) is represented in the conceptual schema by $m+1$ relationship types:

- The generic relationship type R itself.
- A relationship type $R_i(p_1:E_{1,i},...,p_n:E_{n,i})$ for each realization, $i = 1...m$, with the same number (n) and name (p_i) of roles as in R.

The relationship type R is defined as derived by union of the R_i. Therefore, its derivation rule has the general form:

$$R(e_1,...,e_n,t) \leftrightarrow R_1(e_1,...,e_n,t) \vee ... \vee R_m(e_1,...,e_n,t)$$

The R_i are then subtypes of R. We call them *realization subtypes* of R. The realization subtypes may be base or derived.

Note that, in this method, there is a relationship type R whose population comprises all the instances of the generic relationship type. The existence of this relationship type allows us to centralize the definition of the knowledge common to all those instances. The centralization of that knowledge is one of the main differences of our methods with respect to the current ones. We call our first method *Realizations as Subtypes* (RS), because the realizations are defined as subtypes.

As an example, consider the generic relationship type:

MemberOf (member:Member, group:Group)

and the three realizations:

{member:Person, group:ProjectTeam}
{member:Person, group:Committee}
{member:Manager, group:BoardOfDirectors}

Their representation in the conceptual schema using the RS method would comprise the generic relationship type and three realization subtypes. The common relationship type is the *MemberOf* itself, that we would define with the schema:

MemberOf (member:Member, group:Group)

with the meaning:

Member <m> is a direct member of Group <g>

and with general integrity constraints such as, for example, "An entity cannot be member of itself". The instances of *MemberOf* give all the groups of all members. In the RS method, there is a *single* relationship type such that its instances are all the groups of all members. The other three relationship types are the realization subtypes:

PersonMemberOfTeam (member:Person, group:ProjectTeam)
PersonMemberOfComm (member:Person, group:Committee)
ManagerMemberOfBoard (member:Manager, group:BoardOfDirectors)

In general, the meaning and general descriptions of these relationship types are essentially the same as that of *MemberOf*, because they are the same concept.

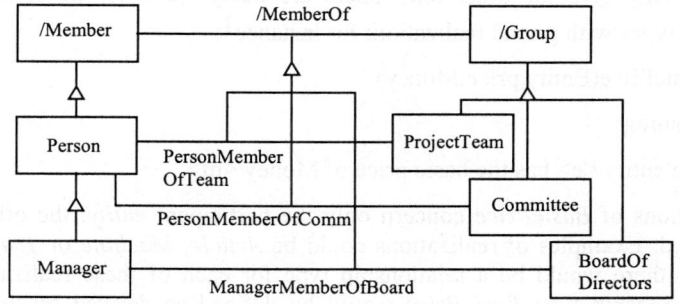

Figure 1. Representation in UML of the generic relationship type *MemberOf* in the RS method.

In the RS method, it is not necessary to define explicitly the realization constraint in the conceptual schema. The constraint is implicit in the fact that each realization has its own relationship type, and that the generic relationship type is derived by union of the realization subtypes.

As we have explained in Section 2, we assume that the entity types of the realizations are direct or indirect subtypes of the corresponding participant entity types in the generic relationship type *R*. In the example, this means that *Person* and *Manager* are subtypes of *Member*, and that *ProjectTeam*, *Committee* and *BoardOfDirectors* are subtypes of *Group*. This fact ensures that the realizations conform to the referential integrity constraint of *MemberOf*.

On the other hand, it may be convenient to define the participant entity types of *R* as derived by union [Oliv01] of the corresponding entity types of the realizations. In the example, we could define that *Group* is derived by union of *ProjectTeam*, *Committee* and *BoardOfDirectors*. In this way, we prevent the occurrence of undesirable instances of *Group*. Moreover, we can then define easily constraints that must be satisfied for all instances of *Group*.

3.2   Adaptation to the UML

The RS method can be adapted easily to conceptual schemas in the UML. Figure 1 illustrates this adaptation with its application to the example. The generic relationship type (associations in the UML) *MemberOf* is defined as derived. Its derivation rule can be expressed formally using the OCL.

3.3   Extensions

The basic idea of the RS method can be extended in several ways. We describe briefly here one extension that we find useful: "generic relationship types with partial realizations".

A generic relationship type with partial realizations $R(p_1:E_1,...,p_n:E_n)$ is one such that only *j* of the participants are realized, with $j > 0$ and $j < n$; the other ones $(n - j)$ remain fixed. In the binary case, this means that one participant is fixed, and the realizations only give the other one. There are many examples of binary generic relationship types with partial realization; for instance[1]:

BasicPrice(Entity,price:Money)

with the meaning:

The entity <e> has the basic price of Money <m>

The realizations of *BasicPrice* concern only the participant *entity*; the other (*price*) remains fixed. Examples of realizations could be *Article*, *Machine* or *Travel*. In the RS method, there would be a relationship type for each of these realizations. The generic relationship type *BasicPrice* would be defined as derived by union of its subtypes. Once defined in the conceptual schema, *BasicPrice* can be combined with other elements to infer additional knowledge.

---

[1] This relationship type corresponds to predicate #$basicPrice : <#$Individual> <#$Money> of the CYC Ontology. See [Cyco97] for details.

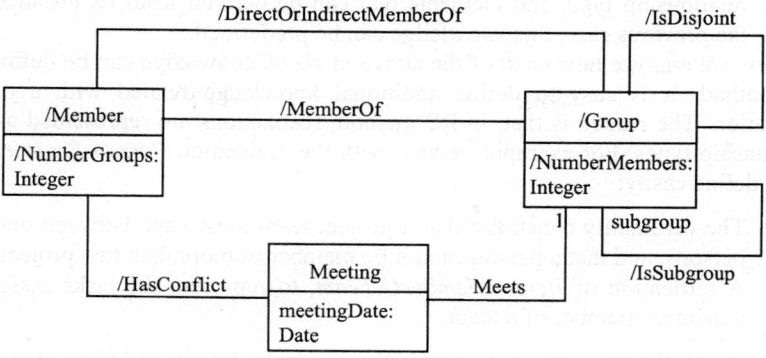

Figure 2. Example of additional knowledge at the level of the generic relationship type *MemberOf*.

3.4 Definition of Additional Knowledge

We have seen the representation of a generic relationship type *R* and its realizations, in the RS method. Now, we analyze how we can define additional knowledge related to *R* or to its realizations. This aspect is very important to evaluate the method, and to compare it with others. We distinguish among three kinds of additional knowledge:

- Related to a *particular* realization. This includes integrity constraints that must be satisfied only by the instances of *R* corresponding to that particular realization, new elements (entity types, attributes, relationship types) that can be defined related to the realization, and elements that can be derived from those instances. For example, we may need to define that, in a particular realization of *MemberOf*, a person cannot be member of more than three project teams.
- Related to *each* realization. This includes integrity constraints that must be satisfied by the instances of *R* corresponding to each realization, independently from the others, new elements that can be defined for each realization, and elements that can be derived from those instances. For example, for each realization of *MemberOf* we may wish to define a relationship type:
- MaximumNumberOfMembers (group:E_2, maximum:Natural) and the integrity constraint that the current number of members of the corresponding group is not greater than the maximum (a time-varying number given by the users). This knowledge can be predefined, and be part of a library of conceptual schema fragments, or of an ontology.
- Related to the *generic* relationship type. This includes integrity constraints whose evaluation requires the knowledge of all instances of the generic relationship type. For instance the constraint that a person cannot be member of more than five groups, which can be of any type (*ProjectTeam*, etc.). It includes also new elements that can be defined related to the generic

relationship type, and elements that can be derived from its instances. As in the previous case, this knowledge can be predefined.

Now, we analyze how each of the above kinds of knowledge can be defined in the RS method. It is easy to define additional knowledge related with a *particular* realization. The reason is that, in RS method, realizations are represented as explicit relationship types. For example, related with the realization *Person-ProjectTeam* we could define easily:

- The cardinality constraint that a project team must have between one and ten persons, and that a person cannot be member of more than two project teams.
- A reification of *PersonMemberOfTeam*, to represent the tasks assigned to a person as member of a team.

In general, the RS method does not allow a single definition of knowledge related to each realization. It must be defined explicitly in each realization.
Contrary to this, the RS method allows defining easily knowledge related with the generic relationship type. In our example, among the useful elements that we could relate to *MemberOf* there are:

- The derived relationship type *DirectOrIndirectMemberOf*.
- The integrity constraint that no entity can be direct or indirect member of itself.
- The derived attribute *NumberOfMembers* of a group.
- The derived attribute *NumberOfGroups* of a member.
- The derived relationship types *IsSubgroup* and *IsDisjoint* between groups.
- The relationship type *Meets*, between a group and a meeting.
- The derived relationship type *HasConflict* between a member and a meeting, stating that a member has another meeting with the same meeting date.
- and many others. Figure 2 shows the graphical definition of the above elements in the UML.

4 Metalevel-Governed Representation

In this section, we describe our second method for the representation of generic relationship types in conceptual schemas. For presentation purposes, we also structure here the description in two parts: the basic idea of the method and its possible extensions. We show that the method can be adapted to the UML. We analyze also the possibilities that this method offers to define additional knowledge.

4.1 The Method

The basic idea of our second method is also very simple: For each generic relationship type $R(p_1:E_1,...,p_n:E_n)$ we define two base relationship types in the conceptual schema:

- The generic relationship type R itself.
- A class relationship type $GovR(p_1:E_1,...,p_n:E_n)$, with the same number ($n$) and name ($p_i$) of roles as in R. The instances of $GovR$ are the realizations of R, and

therefore $E_1,...,E_n$ are metaentity types. We say that *GovR* is the *governing relationship type* of *R*, because the instances of *GovR* govern (constrain) the instances of *R* in the realization constraint. The name *GovR* is a mere notational convention. It is obtained by prefixing *R* with *Gov* (for governing).

As in the RS method, this method defines also in the conceptual schema a relationship type *R* whose population comprises all the instances of the generic relationship type. We call this method *Metalevel-Governed* (MG), because the instances of *R* are governed by instances of a class relationship type.

The basic idea of the MG method is similar to the one used in [Fowl97, p. 24+] to handle schema complexity, suggesting the introduction of two levels, called knowledge and operational, such that "instances in the knowledge level *govern* the configuration of instances in the operational level".

We illustrate the MG method with the same generic relationship example as before. Its representation in the conceptual schema will comprise the relationship types *MemberOf* and *GovMemberOf*. The instances of *MemberOf* (*member:Member, group:Group*) give all groups of all members. Note again that, in the MG method, there is also a *single* relationship type to represent the members of all groups. All characteristics of *MemberOf* are defined only once, in a single place.

The governing relationship type of *MemberOf* is:

GovMemberOf(member:MemberType, group:GroupType)

where *MemberType* and *GroupType* are metaentity types, whose instances are entity types of members and of groups, respectively. The meaning of *GovMemberOf* is:

Instances of MemberType <memType> may be member of
instances of GroupType <grType>

The realizations of *MemberOf* would then be defined as instances of *GovMemberOf* in the knowledge base. For example, the realizations (we omit the time arguments):

GovMemberOf(Person, ProjectTeam, _)
GovMemberOf (Person, Committee, _)
GovMemberOf (Manager, BoardOfDirectors, _)

Note that in the MG method, the realizations are explicit in the knowledge base. This allows the system to answer easily queries like "Who may be member of a ProjectTeam group?"

We define both *R* and *GovR* as base relationship types. In the section 4.4 we describe an extension in which *R* has a base and a derived part. The instances of *R* are constrained by the realization constraint. In the MG method, the general form of this constraint is:

$$R(e_1,...,e_n,t) \rightarrow \exists e^1_1,...,e^1_n \, (In(e_1,e^1_1,t) \wedge ... \wedge In(e_n,e^1_n,t) \wedge GovR(e^1_1,..., e^1_n,t))$$

The constraint requires that entities $e_1,...,e_n$ participating in an instance of *R* at *t*, must be instance of a combination of entity types $e^1_1,..., e^1_n$, respectively, such that the combination is one of the realizations of *R*. The adaptation of the general form of the realization constraint to *MemberOf* gives:

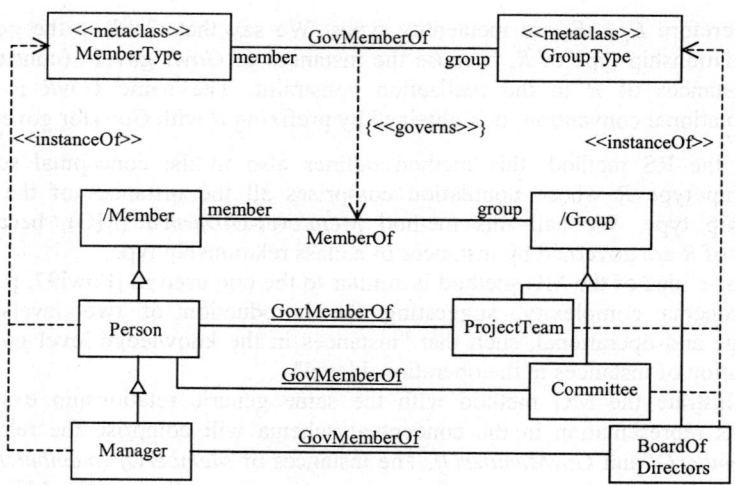

Figure 3. Representation in UML of the generic relationship type *MemberOf* in the MG method.

$$\text{MemberOf (mem,gr,t)} \rightarrow$$
$$\exists e^1{}_1, e^1{}_2 \ (\text{In}(mem, e^1{}_1, t) \land \text{In}(gr, e^1{}_2, t) \land \text{GovMemberOf}(e^1{}_1, e^1{}_2, t))$$

The constraint ensures that the two participating instances (*mem,gr*) in *MemberOf* have a pair of types ($e^1{}_1, e^1{}_2$) defined as a realization in *GovMemberOf*. This constraint would be defined in the conceptual schema, as any other integrity constraint. Note that if, at some time *t*, the population of *GovMemberOf* is empty then *MemberOf* cannot have any instance at *t*. Note also that our realization constraint does not change when a realization is removed from (or added to) *GovR*.

4.2 Adaptation to the UML

We now show how the MG method can be adapted to conceptual schemas represented in the UML. Figure 3 illustrates this adaptation with its application to the example. The generic *R* and the governing *GovR* relationship types can be represented as ordinary associations in UML. See *MemberOf* and *GovMemberOf* in Figure 3. The participants of *GovR* are defined with the predefined stereotype <<metaclass>> [OMG01, p.2-29] because their instances are classes (types). Realizations of *R* are defined as instances (links) of *GovR*.

Figure 3 shows three instances of *GovMemberOf*, which correspond to the three realizations of *MemberOf*. (Note that in the UML the association name is underlined to indicate an instance).

The entity types Person, Manager (resp., ProjectTeam, Committee, BoardOfDirectors) are defined as:

- direct or indirect subtypes of *Member* (resp., *Group*), and as instance of *MemberType* (resp., *GroupType*), shown as a dashed arrow with its tail in the entity type and its head on the metaentity type. The arrow has the standard keyword <<instanceOf>> [OMG01, p.3-93].

Ideally, the realization constraint would be predefined, like the constraints *complete* or *xor*, but this would require extending the UML metamodel. A more practical alternative is to use the extension mechanisms provided by the UML, particularly the stereotypes. We define a stereotype of *Constraint*, called <<governs>>, that constraints two associations: *GovR* and *R*. Graphically, an instance of this constraint is shown as a dashed arrow from *GovR* to *R*, labeled by <<governs>> in braces [OMG01, p. 3-27]. See the example in Figure 3.

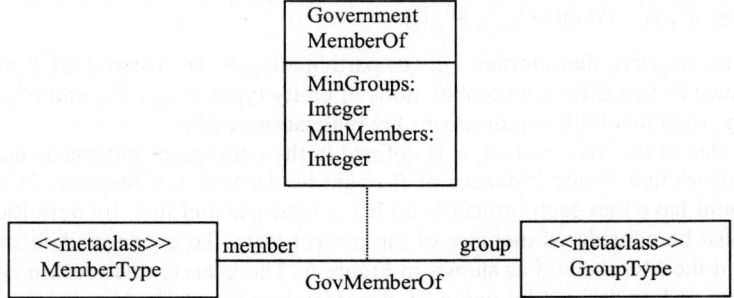

Figure 4. The reification of *GovMemberOf* allows an additional level of government of *MemberOf*.

4.3 Extensions

The MG method admits several extensions. One interesting extension is the reification [Oliv99] of the governing relationship type, *GovR*. This allows us to define details of realizations, which can be used to provide an additional level of automatic government of the generic relationship type.

We illustrate this extension with its application to the example. Figure 4 shows the reification of *GovMemberOf* into entity type *GovernmentMemberOf*. We have included two attributes in this entity type: *MinGroups* and *MinMembers*, which define the minimum cardinalities of the corresponding realizations. Thus, if we have *MinGroups* = 0 and *MinMembers* = 1 in the realization *Manager - BoardOfDirectors*, the meaning could be that not all managers must be members of a board, and that a board must have at least one manager as member. Many other attributes and relationship types could be included in *GovernmentMemberOf*.

The interest of the extension is that now we can define general integrity constraints on *MemberOf* to ensure that their instances conform to the 'details' given in the corresponding instance of *GovernmentMemberOf*. In the example of Figure 4, we would define two integrity constraints.

Another possibility this extension offers is to generate automatically specific integrity constraints and/or attributes and/or relationship types when a new realization is defined (in the example, when *GovMemberOf* and *GovernmentMemberOf* are instantiated).

In some cases, this extension requires that realizations satisfy what we call the *realization exclusivity* constraint. This constraint may be needed to prevent that an instance of *MemberOf* has a member and a group such that they conform to two realizations. In some cases, this may not be acceptable because then there could be an ambiguity as to which realization applies.

The general form of the realization exclusivity constraint is:

$$(R(e_1,...,e_n,t) \wedge In(e_1,e^1{}_1,t) \wedge ... \wedge In(e_n,e^1{}_n,t) \wedge GovR(e^1{}_1,..., e^1{}_n,t) \to$$
$$\neg \exists e^{'1}{}_1,..., e^{'1}{}_n ((e^1{}_1 \neq e^{'1}{}_1 \vee ... \vee e^1{}_n \neq e^{'1}{}_n) \wedge In(e_1,e^{'1}{}_1,t) \wedge ... \wedge$$
$$In(e_n,e^{'1}{}_n,t) \wedge GovR(e^{'1}{}_1,..., e^{'1}{}_n,t))$$

The constraint requires that entities $e_1,...,e_n$ participating in an instance of R at t, cannot be instance of two different combinations of entity types $e^1{}_1,..., e^1{}_n$, and $e^{'1}{}_1,..., e^{'1}{}_n$ respectively, such that both combinations are realizations of R.

In the basic idea of the MG method, R is defined in the conceptual schema as base. This is overly restrictive. Some instances of R might be derived. For instance, in our example we could have that each project team has a manager and that, by definition, the manager must be considered member of the project team. To accommodate such cases, we extend the MG method as shown in Figure 5. The generic relationship type *MemberOf* is defined as derived by union of *BaseMemberOf* and *DerMemberOf*. As their name suggests, *BaseMemberOf* is base and *DerMemberOf* is derived. The designer would define the derivation rule of *DerMemberOf*.

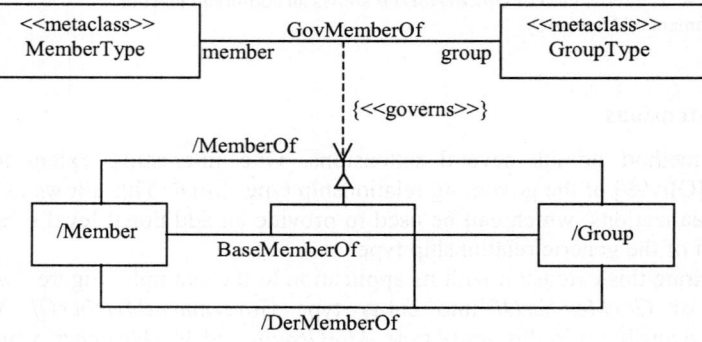

Figure 5. Extension of the MG method, in which the generic relationship type has a base and a derived part.

4.4 Definition of Additional Knowledge

Now we analyze how each of the three kinds of knowledge described in Section 3.4 can be defined in the MG method. It is not easy to define knowledge related with a *particular* realization. The reason is that, in the MG method, realizations are not represented as explicit relationship types. If needed, additional knowledge particular to a realization must be defined as refinement of the generic relationship type.

For example, assume that we want to define that *Committee* groups have at least two members. In the OCL this would be defined as:

context Group **inv** CommitteesHaveTwoOrMoreMembers:
self.oclIsKindOf(Committee) **implies** self.member ->size() > 1.

As we have seen, the reification of the governing relationship type eases the definition of knowledge related to *each* realization.

As in the RS method, the fact that we define only one relationship type for all instances of a generic relationship type R, allows us to define easily knowledge related to R.

5 Analysis and Evaluation

In this section, we analyze some of the properties of our two methods, and discuss the contexts in which their use may be appropriate. We do so by means of a comparison with the current methods. The comparison takes into account the following aspects:

- The definition of knowledge related to a generic relationship type, to each realization and to a particular realization.
- The knowledge of the existing realizations in a conceptual schema.
- The definition of new realizations.
- The simplicity of the representation.

5.1 RS vs. MG

The RS and the MG methods are equivalent with respect to the definition of knowledge related with a generic relationship type. The reason is that, as we have seen, both methods define explicitly the generic relationship type. The MG method, extended with the reification of the governing relationship type, allows an easy definition of knowledge related to each realization. In the RS method, that knowledge must be repeated in each realization. The methods differ also with respect to the definition of knowledge related with a particular realization. The RS method provides greater flexibility, since each realization has its own relationship type. In the MG method, that knowledge must be defined as refinement of the generic relationship type. Both methods allow querying the schema about the defined realizations.

The definition of new realizations is easier in the MG method: it is just a new instantiation of the governing relationship type. In the RS method, a new realization requires a new relationship type, and its definition as a subtype of the generic one.

With respect to the simplicity of the representations, we must distinguish between the structural and the behavioral parts of a schema. Structurally, we tend to consider both methods alike. For each realization relationship type in the RS method we have an instance of the governing relationship type in the MG method. Instead of the subtype relationships in the RS method, we have <<instanceOf>> relationships between entity and metaentity types in the MG method, and the {governs} constraint (compare Figures 1 and 3). Behaviorally, however, the MG method is simpler, because updates (insertions, deletions) and their effects are defined in a single place:

the generic relationship type. In the RS method, there must be a different definition for each realization, since in each case the updated relationship type is different.

Therefore, we conclude that both methods can be useful, depending on the generic relationship type and its realizations. In one extreme, with many realizations but without the need to define particular knowledge related to them, the MG method seems clearly better. In another extreme, with few realizations and with the need to define much specific knowledge in each of them, the RS method seems more appropriate.

5.2   One Relationship Type for Each Realization

We now analyze the current methods, starting with the simplest one, and the one most widely used in practice (with a few exceptions, presented below). The method consists in defining a different relationship type for each realization. The relationship types thus defined are not related each other, nor have a common root. The application of this method to our *MemberOf* example, with three realizations, would give only three relationship types:

- PersonMemberOfTeam (Person, ProjectTeam)
- PersonMemberOfComm (Person, Committee)
- ManagerMemberOfBoard (Manager, BoardOfDirectors)

The definition of a new realization is easy: just define a new relationship type. Note that these relationship types are like any other in the schema and, thus, there is no formal way to detect that they are realizations of some generic relationship type. Therefore, this representation method does not allow querying the schema about the defined realizations.

In this method, the knowledge related to a generic relationship type or to each realization must be repeated in each realization that requires it. The lack of an explicit generic relationship type makes the definition of that knowledge very complex. In contrast, the definition of knowledge related with a particular realization is very easy.

The representations obtained by this method are simple, provided that there are no too many realizations and that does not make extensive use of additional knowledge. Otherwise, the representations tend to be large and redundant.

In conclusion, the advantage of this method is its simplicity and the ease of definition of knowledge specific with a realization. This makes it very appropriate for conceptual schemas with only one realization of a generic relationship type, or when there are several realizations of a generic relationship type, but there is no need of additional knowledge related to it or to each realization, and there is no need to query the schema about the realizations of a generic relationship type.

5.3   One Marked Relationship Type for Each Realization

This is the most widely used method in practice for *some* generic relationship types. The idea is to define a relationship type for each realization, as in the previous method, but now all realizations of the same generic relationship type have a mark, which distinguishes them from the others. The real effect of such mark on the conceptual schema is predefined, and may consist of some implicit static and/or dynamic integrity constraints.

The best example is the generic relationship type *PartOf*. The UML distinguishes two variants of it: aggregation and composition. Aggregation associations are marked graphically with a hollow diamond, attached to the whole entity type. The "only real semantics is that the chain of aggregate links may not form cycles" [RuJB99, p. 148]. Composition associations are marked graphically with a solid-filled diamond. Conceptually, a composition has "the additional constraint that an entity may be part of only one composite at any time ... " [RuJB99, p. 226]. Note that this knowledge is implicit and, therefore, it cannot be integrated with the rest of the knowledge defined in the conceptual schema. In the UML, the only predefined generic relationship types are the aggregation and the composition. Others may be added using the stereotyping extension mechanism.

The analysis of this method (one marked relationship type for each realization) reveals that it improves always the previous one in the following aspects:

- Some general knowledge, mainly in the form of integrity constraints, is attached automatically and implicitly to the realizations. However, the amount of knowledge that can be attached automatically is rather limited.
- The schema can be queried about the realizations of a generic relationship type that have been defined.

Therefore, our evaluation is that the advantage of this method is its simplicity, the ease of definition of knowledge specific with a realization and the availability of some level of predefined general knowledge. This makes it very appropriate for conceptual schemas with only one realization of a generic relationship type, or when there are several realizations of a generic relationship type, but there is no need of general knowledge related to it or to each realization, besides the implicit one.

5.4 Metaclass

This is the preferred method in research works and in advanced information systems. The idea is to define a meta relationship type for each generic relationship type, which is instantiated for each realization. Thus, we have, as in the previous methods, a relationship type for each realization, but now all realizations of the same generic relationship type are instance of the same meta relationship type.

In the literature, this representation method is usually associated with the Telos language, although other languages could serve as well (see, for instance [KaSc95]). [Mots93] describes the application of the method to the *PartOf*; and [MoSt95] does the same for *MemberOf*. [Dach98] describes an application of the same method for *Materializes*, which is, however, apparently similar to our MG method, but the overall idea is quite different.

From a conceptual modeling point of view, this method is always better than the previous one, because the knowledge related with a realization is now explicitly defined in the meta relationship type. However, as we have explained above, the amount of knowledge that can be defined at the level of the meta relationship type has its limits.

Therefore, our evaluation is that the advantage of this method is its simplicity of use, the ease of definition of knowledge specific to a realization, and of the knowledge related to each realization. This makes it very appropriate for conceptual schemas with only one realization of the generic relationship type, or when there are several realizations of the generic relationship type, but there is no need of additional knowledge related to it.

6 Conclusions

This paper has focused on the representation of generic relationship types in conceptual schemas. We have proposed two new methods for this representation, called the RS and the MG methods. We have seen that both methods can be useful, depending on the generic relationship type and its realizations. The RS method is appropriate when many realizations require the definition of particular knowledge related to them, different from one realization to the other, whereas the MG method is more appropriate when realizations are similar one another. We have explained in detail the adaptation of our methods to the UML. The adaptation to other conceptual modeling languages should also be possible.

We have compared the proposed methods with the current ones. We have seen that the main difference is that we define explicitly the generic relationship type in the schema, while the current methods define only its realizations. The current methods are then very appropriate when there is not the need to define knowledge at the generic level. When such a need do exist, then our methods could be more appropriate.

The need for knowledge related to a generic relationship type exists in large information systems, in generic information systems that can be adapted to several specific domains, or in information systems with advanced reasoning capabilities. This knowledge can be predefined and be part of a library of conceptual schema fragments, or part of a general ontology. On the other hand, in those contexts there are many generic relationship types, and many specific ones can be considered as realizations of some generic one. We hope then that our methods will be especially useful in those contexts.

Acknowledgements

The author wishes to thank Dolors Costal, Cristina Gómez, Juan Ramón López, Maria-Ribera Sancho, Ernest Teniente, Toni Urpí and the anonymous referees for their useful comments. This work has been partially supported by CICYT program project TIC99-1048-C02-01.

7 References

[Cyco97] Cycorp. " CYC® Ontology Guide", http://www.cyc.com/cyc-2-1/toc.html.
[Dach98] Dahchour, M. "Formalizing Materialization Using a Metaclass Approach", CAiSE 1998, LNCS 1413, pp. 401-421.
[Fowl97] Fowler, M. "Analysis Patterns: Reusable Object Models", Addison-Wesley, 357 p.
[KaSc95] Klass, W.; Schrefl, M. "Metaclasses and Their Application", LNCS 943.
[Matt88] Mattos, N.M. "Abstraction Concepts: The Basis for Data and Knowledge Modeling", ER 1988, pp. 473-492
[MBJK90] Mylopoulos, J.; Borgida, A.; Jarke, M.; Koubarakis, M. "Telos: Representing Knowledge About Information Systems", TOIS 8(4), pp. 325-362.
[MoSt95] Motschnig-Pitrik, R.; Storey, V.C. "Modelling of set Membership: The Notion and the Issues", DKE 16(2), pp. 147-185.
[Mots93] Motschnig-Pitrik, R. "The Semantics of Parts Versus Aggregates in Data/Knowledge Modelling", CAiSE 1993, LNCS 685, pp. 352-373.
[Oliv01] Olivé, A. "Taxonomies and Derivation Rules in Conceptual Modelling", CAiSE 2001, LNCS 2068, pp. 417-432.
[Oliv99] Olivé, A. "Relationship Reification: A Temporal View", CAiSE 1999, LNCS 1626, pp. 396-410.
[OMG01] OMG. "Unified Modeling Language Specification", Version 1.4, September 2001, http://www.omg.org/technology/documents/formal/uml.htm
[PiZD98] Pirotte, A.; Zimányi, E.; Dahchour, M. "Generic relationships in information modeling", Technical Report TR-98/09, IAG-QANT, Université catholique de Louvain, Belgium, December.
[PZMY94] Pirotte, A.; Zimányi, E.; Massart, D.; Yakusheva, T. "Materialization: A Powerful and Ubiquitous Abstraction Pattern", VLDB 1994, pp. 630-641.
[RuJB99] Rumbaugh, J.; Jacobson, I.; Booch, G. "The Unified Modeling Language Reference Manual", Addison-Wesley, 550 p.
[Sowa00] Sowa, J. "Knowledge Representation. Logical, Philosophical and Computational Foundations", Brooks/Cole, 594 p.
[Stor93] Storey, V.C. "Understanding Semantic Relationships", VLDB Journal 2(4), pp. 455-488.
[WaSW99] Wand, Y.; Storey, V.C.; Weber, R. "An Ontological Analysis of the Relationship Construct in Conceptual Modeling", ACM TODS, 24(4), pp. 494-528.
[YHGP94] Yang, O.; Halper, M.; Geller, J.; Perl, Y. "The OODB Ownership Relationship", OOIS 1994, pp. 278-291.

Building Spatio-Temporal Presentations Warehouses from Heterogeneous Multimedia Web Servers

Michel Adiba and José-Luis Zechinelli-Martini*

LSR-IMAG, University of Grenoble
BP 72 38402 Saint-Martin d'Hères, France
Michel.Adiba@imag.fr
zechinel@ifi.unizh.ch

Abstract. Building warehouses from existing data sources is one of the main challenges of future information systems. Over the last three years, we defined and experienced an infrastructure called JAGUAR (model, language, architecture, and prototype SMIL/JMF) to configure presentations warehouse(s) managers. Such managers provide means to play and query multimedia presentations stored in a warehouse. This paper summarizes the main results that we obtained.

1 Introduction

This paper presents JAGUAR, an infrastructure for configuring and generating multimedia Presentations Warehouse Managers (PWM) [Zec01, ZA01]. Having several multimedia distributed servers (text, image, audio, video), JAGUAR builds a PWM that can (1) retrieve specific objects coming from heterogeneous multimedia servers accessible through the Web; and (2) synchronize them and organize them spatially (on a screen) for building so called multimedia presentations (scenarios or multimedia documents). These presentations are themselves considered and stored as database objects and associated with specific spatio-temporal knowledge. Objects in these presentations are either referenced through their URL (*on-demand*) or copied into the presentations warehouse (*in-advance*), allowing static or dynamic links with the data sources.

Dealing with multimedia data brings new challenges because of their specific nature. Large volume of data; temporal and spatial attributes of respectively videos and images; continuous nature of video and audio data requiring specific QoS (Quality of Service) in order to be delivered to the user without alteration, are examples of these challenges. There exist many standards for multimedia data. The W3C proposes several (meta) languages for multimedia data exchange (XML family [W3C98]) and for specifying synchronization when

---

* J. L. Zechinelli-Martini was supported by a fellowship SFERE-CONACyT. He is currently working at the Information Technology Department of the University of Zurich, Wintertuhrerstr. 190, 8057, Zurich, Switzerland.

presenting different objects (SMIL). Also, in the Java context, JMF [SI] is a proposal for implementing synchronization between objects coming from different sources (URL).

Multimedia DBMS [Vaz96, Jag96] have concentrated on extending traditional DBMS (e.g., relational, object) for storing and retrieving multimedia data. Querying support for retrieving multimedia data and building presentations has received particular attention [WML98, ASS00]. Yet, the problem of integrating different multimedia data sources is not fully addressed. Finally, mediation infrastructures have been proposed for integrating heterogeneous sources through mediators. However, very few approaches such as [MIKS00] address directly problems associated to multimedia data and classical data integration.

The remainder of this paper is organized as follows. Section 2 gives an overview of JAGUAR our infrastructure for configuring PWM. Section 3 shows how our approach and prototype have been used for implementing a presentations warehouse for a forecast weather application. Finally, Section 4 concludes and introduces some research perspectives.

2 Jaguar Infrastructure for Presentations Warehouses

A Presentations Warehouse (PW) is a collection of spatio-temporal presentations of multimedia objects. JAGUAR provides means to configure and generate what we call PWM (see Figure 1).

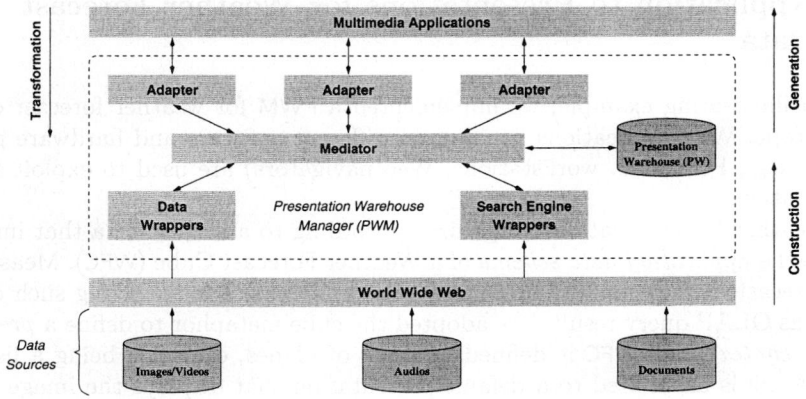

Fig. 1. General architecture of a PWM

Warehouse manager specification For specifying a PWM using JAGUAR, a developer specifies (1) an *application data schema* that defines the data types to be used by applications (i.e., image, text, video, audio, document, etc.); (2) a *presentation context* to be used by applications that specifies how to present (visualize) each data type of the *application data schema*; and (3) for each application and source, its interaction with the PWM[1].

Warehouse manager generation Using this information JAGUAR associates each object type in the *application data schema* with a default presentation given in the *presentation context*. According to interaction rules, it configures the PWM for using specific wrappers to retrieve objects from sources. Transformation and generation rules specify how to configure adapters so that applications can communicate with the PWM.

Presentations warehouse manager It enables programmers to build and manage warehouses by gathering multimedia data over the Web and integrating functions provided by different standards and systems. It is a middleware configured for interacting with sources through wrappers and managing (defines, builds, stores, formats) data presentations used by several applications. Client applications can then use traditional browsers augmented with specific capabilities (CGI, Java, etc.) to deal with a very large spectrum of data. For defining their presentations (according to a predefined schema), applications interact with the PWM through adapters. Specifications are transformed into an OQLiST[2] expression that the PWM mediator understands. The mediator evaluates specifications with a PW to retrieve the whole presentation or part of it. Only missing parts are then retrieved from sources through wrappers. Supported by a presentation model [Zec01, ZA01], the mediator integrates results into a presentation and returns it to an adapter. The latter transforms it into a format understood by the client (e.g., a SMIL program).

3 Application to Presentations for Weather Forecast Data

As an illustrating example, we implemented a PWM for weather forecast data in Europe. Web applications running on different software and hardware platforms (e.g., PDA, PC, workstations, Web navigators) are used to exploit such information.

Weather forecast data are organized according to a star schema that implements the *application data schema* of a Weather Forecast Cube (WFC). Measures are forecast facts organized by Season, Year, and Zone. For analyzing such data given as OLAP query results, we adopted the cube metaphor to define a *presentation context*. The WFC is defined as a list of planes, each one being a list of cells. A cell is associated to a default presentation that displays the image of a zone with the a season average temperature in its center. Planes are presented as a table of cells with the name of the season at the upper left corner of the

---
[1] Interaction is defined by interaction, transformation and generation rules. In our prototype, these rules are of the form Condition/Action and expressed in Java.
[2] OQLiST stands for "Object Query Language integrating Spatial and Temporal aspects". It is an extension of OQL with specific constructors for spatial and temporal attributes.

first cell in each row. The default presentation of a cube displays a set of planes, one in front of the other with an offset corresponding to half of the cell length.

Using JAGUAR we generated a PWM for manipulating the WFC at different aggregation levels associated to dimensions. This is done using querying operators such as SLICE-N-DICE, ROLL-UP, PIVOT, etc. that we specified using OQLiST and that are supported by the generated PWM.

4 Conclusion

This paper addressed multimedia warehouse construction through the JAGUAR infrastructure. JAGUAR enables the specification and implementation of PWM that integrate heterogeneous and distributed data sources (Web, image databases, etc.). One of the main contributions of our work consists of offering flexible PWM for multimedia presentations enabling the integration and reuse of several existing objects. Two main aspects can be highlighted. First, our approach takes into account spatial and temporal characteristics that can be found in existing standards (e.g., SMIL). Second, the possibility of configuring PWM according to application needs (specification of types and their associated visualization) and data sources characteristics. Our approach is being used in a real application for medical data. The objective is to gather information from several (relational) databases and build a presentation warehouse showing how some diseases are distributed over geographical regions. This implies that we integrate data sources and geographical information systems, but also for analyzing medical data (statistic).

References

[ASS00] S. Adali, M. L. Sapino, and V. S. Subrahmanian. An algebra for creating and querying multimedia presentations. *Multimedia Systems*, 7, 2000. Also in Special Issue on Multimedia Authoring and Presentation Techniques, 8(3).

[Jag96] H. V. Jagadish. Indexing for retrieval by similarity. In V. S. Subrahmanian and Sushil Jajodia, editors, *Multimedia Database Systems. Issues and Research Directions*. Springer-Verlag, 1996.

[MIKS00] E. Mena, A. Illarramendi, V. Kashyap, and A. P. Sheth. Observer: An approach for query processing in global information systems based on interoperation across pre-existing ontologies. *Distributed and Parallel Databases*, 8(2), 2000.

[SI] Sun Microsystems Inc. and IBM. Java Media Framework 2.0 API. http://java.sun.com/products/java-media/jmf.

[Vaz96] M. Vazirgiannis. An object-oriented modeling of multimedia database objects and applications. In K. Nowsu, B. Thuraisingham, and B. Berra, editors, *Multimedia Database Management Systems. Design and Implementation Strategies*, chapter 8. Kluwer Academic Publishers, 1996.

[W3C98] Synchronized Multimedia Integration Language (SMIL). Recommendation REC-smil-19980615, World Wide Web Consortium (W3C), 1998. http://www.w3.org/TR/REC-smil.

[WML98] C-H. Wu, R. J. Miller, and M.T Lui. Querying multimedia presentations. *Computer Communications Journal*, 21(14), September 1998.
[ZA01]   J. L. Zechinelli-Martini and M. Adiba. Spatio-temporal multimedia presentations as database objects. In *Proc. of ENC'01, Encuentro International de Computación*, Aguas Calientes - Mexico, September 2001.
[Zec01] J. L. Zechinelli-Martini. *Construction et manipulation de présentations spatio-temporelles multimédias à partir de serveurs d'objets répartis : applications aux données sur le Web*. PhD thesis, Université Joseph Fourier, Grenoble - France, avril 2001.

A Practical Agent-Based Method to Extract Semantic Information from the Web*

J. L. Arjona, R. Corchuelo, A. Ruiz, and M. Toro

Escuela Técnica Superior de Ingeniería Informática de la Universidad de Sevilla
Departamento de Lenguajes y Sistemas Informáticos
Avda. de la Reina Mercedes, s/n, Sevilla, Spain
{arjona,corchu,aruiz,mtoro}@lsi.us.es

Abstract. The semantic Web will bring meaning to the Internet, making it possible for web agents to understand the information it contains. However, current trends seem to suggest that it is not likely to be adopted in the forthcoming years. In this sense, meaningful information extraction from the web becomes a handicap for web agents. In this article, we present a framework for automatic extraction of semantically-meaningful information from the current web. Separating the extraction process from the business logic of an agent enhances modularity, adaptability, and maintainability. Our approach is novel in that it combines different technologies to extract information, surf the web and automatically adapt to some changes.

1 Introduction

In recent years, the web has consolidated as one of the most important knowledge repositories. Furthermore, the technology has evolved to a point in which sophisticated new generation web agents proliferate. They enable efficient, precise, and comprehensive retrieval and extraction of information from the vast web information repository. A major challenge for these agents has become sifting through an unwieldy amount of data to extract meaningful information. The following important factors contribute to these difficulties:

- Most web pages are available in human-readable forms, and they lack a description of the structure or the semantics associated with their data.
- The layout and the aspect of a web page may change unexpectedly. This changes may invalidate the automatic extraction methods used so far.
- The access to the page that contains the information in which we are interested may involve navigating through a series of intermediate pages, such as login or index pages.

Several authors have worked on techniques for extracting information from the web, and inductive wrappers are amongst the most popular ones [2,6,7,9,10].

---
* The work reported in this article was supported by the Spanish Inter-ministerial Commission on Science and Technology under grant TIC2000-1106-C02-01

They are components that use a number of extraction rules generated by means of automated learning techniques such as inductive logic programming, statistical methods, and inductive grammars. Although induction wrappers are suited, they do not associate semantics with the data they extract.

There are also some related proposals in the field of databases, e.g., TSIM-MIS [5] and ARANEUS [8]. Their goal is to integrate heterogeneous information sources such as traditional databases and web pages so that the user can work on them as if they were a homogeneous information source. However, these proposals lack a systematic way to extract information from the web because extraction rules need to be implemented manually, which makes them not scalable and unable to recover from unexpected changes on the web.

In this article, we present a proposal that achieves a complete separation between the logic an agent encapsulates, the navigation path to the page that contains the information it needs, and way to extract it. Giving the necessary mechanisms to associate semantics with the extracted information and to adapt automatically to some changes on the web.

2 Our Proposal

Our proposal aims at providing agent developers with a framework in which they can have access to semantically-meaningful data that resides on heterogeneous, user-friendly web pages. It relies on using a number of agents that we call information channels or IC for short. They allow to separate the extraction of information from the logic of an agent, and offer agent developers a good degree of flexibility. In order to allow for semantic interoperability, the information they extract references a number of concepts in a given application domain that are described by means of ontologies.

2.1 The Architecture

Figure 1 sketches the architecture of our proposal. As we mentioned above, information channels are at its core because they specialise in extracting information from different sources, and are able to react to information inquiries (reactivity) from other agents (social ability). They act in the background proactively according to a predefined schedule to extract information and to maintain the extraction rules updated.

Each information channel uses several inductive wrappers to extract information so that they can detect inconsistencies amongst the data they extract. If such inconsistencies are found, they then use a voting algorithm to decide whether to use the data extracted by most wrappers or regenerate the set of extraction rules on the fly. This may happen because of an unexpected change to the structure of the web page that invalidates the extraction rules used so far.

There is also an agent broker for information extraction that acts as a trader between the agents that need information from the web and the set of available information channels. When an agent needs some information, it contacts the

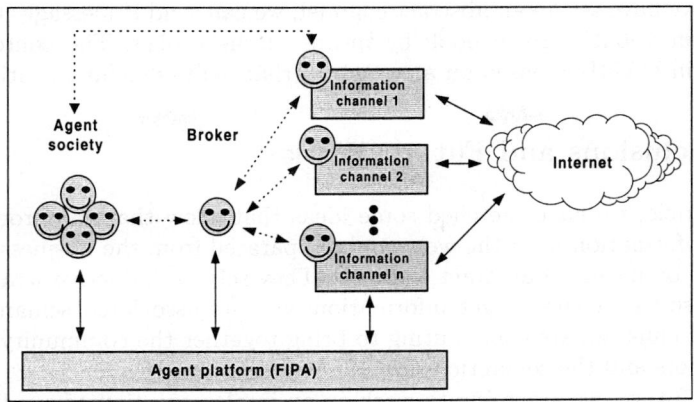

Fig. 1. Proposed architecture

broker, which redirects the request to the appropriate information channel, if possible. This way, agents need not be aware of the existence of different ICs, which can thus be adapted, created or removed from the system transparently (yellow pages).

2.2 Information Channels

. An information channel is characterised by the following features: a set of ontologies, a set of extraction rules, and a navigational document.

- *The Ontologies.* The ontologies [3] associated with an IC describe the concepts that define the semantics associated with the information we are going to extract from a high-level, abstract point of view. An ontology allows to define a common vocabulary by means of which different agents may interoperate semantically.
- *The Extraction Rules.* The extraction rules allow to define how to have access to the information in which we are interested. To generate them, we need a set of sample pages containing test data on which we use inductive techniques. To endow the sample pages with semantics, we also need to annotate them with DAML [1] tags that associate the concepts that appear in them with their ontologies. Once the sample pages have been annotated, we can generate the extraction rules using a tool called *wrapper generator*.
- *The Navigational Document.* A navigational document defines the path to intermediate pages, such as login or index pages, we need to visit in order to have access to the page that contains the information in which we are interested. Roughly speaking, a navigational document may be viewed as a state machine in which each state is a web page, and the transitions between states may be viewed as the navigation from the page associated with the initial state to the page associated with the destination state.

Once we have set up an abstract channel, we can send it messages to retrieve information about a given book by means of the broker. The content of the messages in DAML is based on an ontology that defines communication [4].

3 Conclusions and Future Work

In this article, we have sketched some ideas that show that the process of extracting information from the web can be separated from the business logic of a web agent by means of abstract channels. They rely on inductive wrappers and can analyse web pages to get information with its associated semantics automatically. Thus, we are contributing to bring together the community of agents programmers and the semantic web.

In the future, we are going to work on an implementation of our framework in which data sources can be more heterogeneous (databases, news servers, mail servers, and so on). Extraction of information from multimedia sources such as videos, images, or sound files will be also paid much attention.

References

1. DARPA (Defense Advanced Research Projects Agency). The darpa agent mark up language (daml). http://www.daml.org, 2000.
2. W. W. Cohen and L. S. Jensen. A structured wrapper induction system for extracting information from semi-structured documents. In Workshop on Adaptive Text Extraction and Mining (IJCAI-2001), 2001.
3. O. Corcho and A. Gómez-Pérez. A road map on ontology specification languages. In Workshop on Applications of Ontologies and Problem solving methods. 14th European Conference on Artificial Intelligence (ECAI'00), 2000.
4. S. Cranefield and M. Purvis. Generating ontology-specific content languages. In Proceedings of Ontologies in Agent Systems Workshop (Agents 2001), pages 29–35, 2000.
5. H. García-Molina, J. Hammer, K. Ireland, Y. Papakonstantinou, J. Ullman, and J. Widom. Integrating and accessing heterogeneous information sources in TSIMMIS. In The AAAI Symposium on Information Gathering, pages 61–64, March 1995.
6. C. A. Knoblock. Accurately and reliably extracting data from the web: A machine learning approach. Bulletin of the IEEE Computer Society Technical Com-mittee on Data Engineering, 2000.
7. N. Kushmerick. Wrapper induction: Efficiency and expressiveness. Artificial Intelligence, 118(2000):15–68, 1999.
8. G. Mecca, P. Merialdo, and P. Atzeni. ARANEUS in the era of XML. Data Engineering Bullettin, Special Issue on XML, September 1999.
9. I. Muslea, S. Minton, and C. Knoblock. Wrapper induction for semistructured, web-based information sources. In Proceedings of the Conference on Automated Learning and Discovery (CONALD), 1998.
10. S. Soderland. Learning information extraction rules for semi-structured and free text. Machine Learning, pages 1–44, 1999.

Process Inheritance

Christoph Bussler

Oracle Corporation
Redwood Shores, CA 94065, U. S. A.
Chris.Bussler@Oracle.com

Abstract. In large process deployments where an enterprise has to model and maintain a large number of processes that are specializations of each other it is advantageous to provide formal support for process specialization called process inheritance. A process inheritance model definition is introduced as well as a process definition language construct for defining process specialization.

1 Introduction

A very naïve but very pragmatic way to achieve the specialization of processes is to copy the most relevant process definition and modify the copy until it implements the desired behavior. Maintenance of processes becomes very difficult this way since changes that have to be applied to the original and all of its copies have to be updated manually (let alone the copies of the copy, etc.). Furthermore, the differences between the modified copy and the original are not explicitly stated. Anyone who would like to understand the difference has to compare the definitions.

A much more elegant and useful approach is to achieve public process specialization through process inheritance. In the following first a definition of "process" is given followed by the definition of "process inheritance".

2 Process Definition

A process definition consists of several different process aspects [2] [3] [4]:
- **Functional aspect**. The functional aspect provides constructs to define process types and process steps. A process type is the topmost entity that is decomposed into several process steps. Process steps are the unit of work a human or an executable program has to fulfill. Subprocesses are process steps that are themselves further decomposed. Through this mechanism an abstraction hierarchy of arbitrary depth can be defined.

    Process types as well as process steps have input and output parameters. Parameters are used to communicate data values to process steps or obtain results from process step execution.

- **Control flow aspect**. The control flow aspect provides constructs to define the sequencing between process steps. The most important constructs are sequence, parallel branching, conditional branching as well as looping.
- **Data and data flow aspect**. Process types as well as process steps have to access data in order to execute the business logic. Process data are stored locally as local variables in the scope of process types. Data flow constructs connect process data with the input parameters and output parameters of process steps. Data flow constructs define which process data are connected to which process steps in order to define which process step can read or write which process data. Data flow makes explicit which process step reads or writes to which process data.
- **Organizational aspect**. The organizational aspect defines which human user is responsible for executing a process step. If a process step is to be executed automatically, it is an automatic process step without any human user assignment.
- **Operational aspect**. The operational aspect defines the binding of process steps to executable programs. These programs can be productivity tools for human users or executables for automatic process steps.

3 Process Inheritance Definition

A process that inherits from another process is called a subprocess class. The process it inherits from is called the superprocess class. A subprocess class has to have a unique name amongst all processes. If no changes are applied to the subprocess class its instances at execution time behave exactly the same way than instances of the superprocess class. If changes are applied, the changes dictate the new behavior. Changes to subprocess classes can be of two fundamental types, process element overwrite and process element addition.

- **Process element overwrite**. A process element overwrite replaces a process element as defined in the superprocess class with another element. The overwrite takes place in the subprocess class. For example, if two process steps have a sequence control flow construct between them in the superprocess class, the control flow construct can be overwritten by a parallel branching construct in the subprocess class. This would allow the two process steps to be executed in parallel in any instance of the subprocess class. All process aspects as introduced earlier can be subject to overwrite.
- **Process element addition**. A subprocess class does not necessarily have to only overwrite process elements of its superprocess class. It is possible that in the subprocess class new process elements are added. An example for this type of change is the addition of a logging process step that explicitly logs data from the data flow. All process aspects as introduced above can be added.

These two fundamental types of changes that can be applied to subprocess classes at the same time define the concept of public process inheritance.

Related work in process inheritance that requires explicit discussion at this point can be found in [1]. While the above definition targets at a pragmatic and complete approach addressing all process aspects, [1] targets an abstract and theoretical definition of process inheritance. [1] abstracts in its discussion from the data flow aspect, from subworkflows in the functional aspect, from the organizational aspect and from the operational aspect. Since these process aspects are not addressed, no definition of their inheritance semantics is provided. Furthermore, it reduces the process definition to a specific class of Petri-Nets.

4 Process Language

In the following the process definition language (similar to the one defined in [3]) is taken as the basis for adding constructs for specialization. Due to the space limitations, only a short and abstract example is given.

```
WORKFLOW_CLASS S /* SEND */
    (IN message: send_message) /* step sending a message */
END_WORKFLOW_CLASS

WORKFLOW_CLASS R /* RECEIVE */
    (OUT message: received_message) /* step receiving a message */
END_WORKFLOW_CLASS
```

Based on these two steps, a process called R/R (for request/reply) is defined. After declaring two steps the control flow definition "cf_1" between the two steps follows. They are executed in strict sequence without any branching or parallelism. Then the data flow definitions "df_1" and "df_2" follow. Two local variables are defined that are going to store the two messages that are sent or received. Two types of message are necessary: "out_message" and "in_message". The data flow section defines which steps set or read the local variables. The organizational aspect definitions "o_1" and "o_2" define that the process steps are executed automatically.

```
WORKFLOW_CLASS R/R
    SUBWORKFLOWS
    S: send_step;
    R: receive_step;
    END_SUBWORKFLOWS
    CONTROL_FLOW
    cf_1: sequence(send_step, receive_step);
    END_CONTROL_FLOW
    WORKFLOW_DATA
    Message: out_message;
    Message: in_message;
    END_WORKFLOW_DATA
    DATA_FLOW
    df_1: out_message -> send_step.send_message;
    df_2: receive_step.received_message -> in_message;
    END_DATA_FLOW
    ORGANIZATION
        o_1: send_step: automatic;
        o_2: receive_step: automatic;
    END_ORGANIZATION
END_WORKFLOW_CLASS
```

5 "subclass_of" Construct

In order to denote process inheritance the "subclass_of" construct is introduced to the process language. Local variables, steps, subworkflows, control flow, data flow, the organizational aspect as well as the operational aspect can be extended and/or overwritten in the subclass by introducing new ones or referring to the name of these constructs in the superclass.

In the following the concept of process inheritance is applied to the R/R example. In this example acknowledgements are added to confirm the receipt of messages or to receive the receipt of a sent message.

```
WORKFLOW_CLASS R/R_ACK
   SUBCLASS_OF R/R
   SUBWORKFLOWS
     S: send_acknowledgment;
     R: receive_acknowledgment;
   END_SUBWORKFLOWS
   CONTROL_FLOW
     cf_1: sequence(send_step, receive_acknowledgment);
     cf_2: sequence(receive_acknowledgment, receive_step);
     cf_3: sequence(receive_step, send_acknowledgment);
   END_CONTROL_FLOW
   WORKFLOW_DATA
     Message: in_acknowledgment;
     Message: out_acknowledgment;
   END_WORKFLOW_DATA
   DATA_FLOW
     df_3: receive_acknowledgment.received_message ->
     in_acknowledgment;
     df_4: out_acknowledgment -> send_acknowledgment.send_message;
   END_DATA_FLOW
   ORGANIZATION
     o_3: send_acknowledgment: automatic;
     o_4: receive_acknowledgment: automatic;
   END_ORGANIZATION
END_WORKFLOW_CLASS
```

Two steps are added to send and to receive the acknowledgements. "cf_1" is overwritten in order to add the "receive_acknowledgment" step after the "send_step". Data and data flow is added to store the acknowledgements and to pass them to the correct steps. Organization definitions are added for the two additional steps indicating their automatic execution.

References

1. Aalst, W. M. P. van der; Basten, T.: *Inheritance of Workflows - An approach to tackling problems related to change.* Computing Science Reports 99/06, Eindhoven University of Technology, Eindhoven, 1999
2. Aalst, W. M. P. van der; Hee, Kees van: *Workflow Management. Models, Methods, and Systems.* The MIT Press, 2002

3. Jablonski, S.; Bussler, C.: *Workflow Management. Concepts, Architecture and Implementation*. International Thomson Publisher, 1995
4. Leymann, F.; Roller, D.: *Production Workflow. Concepts and Techniques*. Prentice Hall PTR, 2000

Addressing Performance Requirements Using a Goal and Scenario-Oriented Approach

Zhiming Cai[1] and Eric Yu[2]

[1] Department of Computer Science, University of Toronto, Canada
zmcai@cs.toronto.edu
[2] Faculty of Information Studies, University of Toronto, Canada
yu@fis.utoronto.ca

Abstract. Performance requirements should be addressed as early as possible during requirements analysis and architectural design. This paper presents a goal-oriented and scenario-oriented approach for qualitatively addressing and refining performance requirements. The goal-oriented language GRL[1] is used to represent the refinement of performance goals from abstract to concrete ones, eventually operationalizing them into design alternatives. The Use Case Maps (UCM)[4] notation is used to represent system operations at a high level of abstraction using scenarios.

1 Introduction

Performance requirements and performance evaluation can have a global impact on alternatives for target system [2]. The goal of performance modelling is to address performance requirements and make the performance of system more predictable. Performance modelling of the whole system at the requirements analysis and high-level design stages can provide feedback into the decision-making process prior to detailed design and implementation.

Group Communication Server (GCS) system described in [3] is a multi-user system for document management. An approach called PERFECT in [3] quantitatively evaluates the different proposals for concurrency architecture by "virtual implementations". An important challenge is to qualitatively address performance of different architectures without implementation. Quantitative metrics and qualitative treatments are complementary for performance modelling.

This paper proposes an approach "PeGU" for performance modelling by using GRL (Goal oriented Requirement Language) and UCM (Use Case Map). The modeler uses PeGU to qualitatively evaluate each of architectures over each possible technology choice decision at an early stage. PeGU treats performance requirements as softgoals and goals of GRL. GRL is a modelling language proposed at University of Toronto for supporting goal-oriented modelling and reasoning of requirements. Modelling both goals and scenarios is complementary and goal-scenario coupling may aid in identifying further goals, additional scenarios and scenario steps. Use Case

Maps is used for representation of scenarios. The structure and the behavior can be described in the same UCM diagram. The paths of execution are represented against the background of the system components.

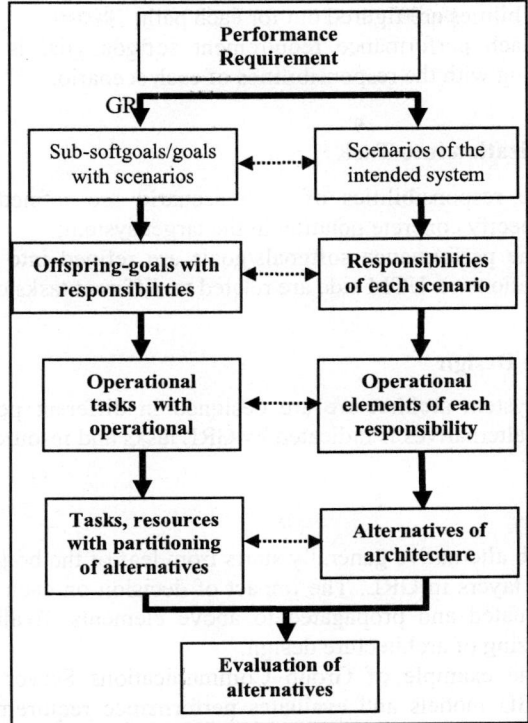

Fig.1. Overview of PeGU

2 Overview of PeGU

2.1 High-Level Performance Requirement

The high-level performance requirements are qualitatively specified as GRL softgoals and goals. The UCM and GRL modeling method are employed alternately in the following steps. (see Fig.1.)

2.2 Scenario

UCM side – The scenarios of the intended system are outlined in large-grained behaviour pattern according to system requirements;

GRL side – The high-level performance softgoals and goals are distributed to sub-softgoals (goals) for different scenarios.

2.3 Responsibility and Offspring-Softgoals/Goals

UCM side – Along each scenario path, some localized actions which the system must perform are viewed as responsibilities. With analyzing the paths of execution for the scenarios, responsibilities are figured out for each path;

GRL side – Each performance requirement softgoal/goal is decomposed into offspring, correlating with the responsibilities of each scenario.

2.4 Operationalization into Task

UCM side – The responsibilities of each scenario are refined into operational elements, which specify concrete notation in the target system;

GRL side – The performance softgoals/goals are refined into operational tasks. The different operations on UCM side are related to different tasks on GRL side.

2.5 Architecture Design

Alternatives for system architecture are designed in different possible ways. The partitioning of the alternatives is indicated by GRL tasks and resources.

2.6 Evaluation

Evaluation for each alternative generally starts from leaf of the bottom layer and then up through higher layers in GRL. The impact of decision on each operation of each alternative is evaluated and propagated to above elements. Evaluation may result change and optimizing of architecture design.

We will use the example of Group Communications Server (GCS) in [3] to illustrate how PeGU models and evaluates performance requirements qualitatively and deals with trade-offs among a number of factors.

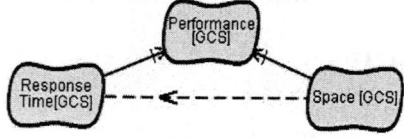

Fig.2. High-level performance requirements of GCS

3 PeGU Methodology - Applying to GCS

1. We define *Performance[GCS]* softgoal as a top level requirement of GCS. The contributing factors to overall performance are response time and space usage. *Performance[GCS]* is thus refined into two sub-softgoals: *ResponseTime[GCS]* and *Space[GCS]* as shown in Fig.2. in GRL graphical notation. *ResponseTime[...]* means seeking decreased or low response time for specific user requests; *Space[...]* means decreased or low space usage. Here, *Performance[GCS]* and its subgoals are related by an *AND* "contribution" link.

The *Space[GCS]* has correlation-link with *ResponseTime[GCS]* because the relationship between ResponseTime and Space is not an explicit desire, but is a side-effect.

2. Fig.3 shows scenarios of GCS in UCM notation: *Update Document, Notification, Send New Document, Subscription, UnSubscription* and *Get New Document*. The responsibilities *upd, noti, new, sub, uns* and *get* specify the actions for each scenario. The timestamp points *Tarr, Tupd, Tnot, Tnew, Tsub, Tuns* and *Tget*, represent the start and end points for response-time requirement of each scenario.

   The high-level performance softgoals in GRL are distributed to sub-softgoals on the scenarios, as in Fig.4. *ReponseTime[upd]* Softgoal means good response time for scenario *update*. Other softgoals are similar for other scenarios.

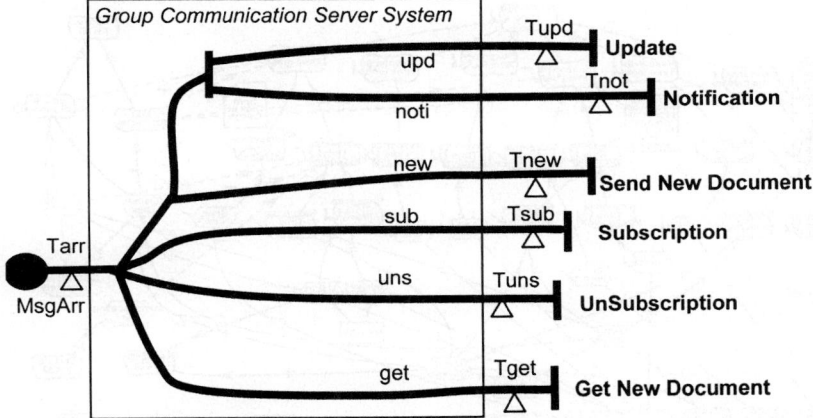

Fig.3. Scenarios of GCS

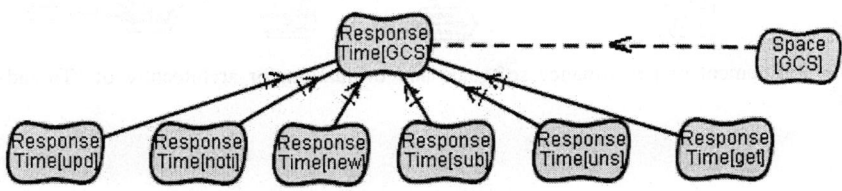

Fig.4. GCS performance softgoals on the scenarios

3. The execution of each path can be considered as several segments or activities in UCM. Some concrete behaviours can be extracted from the abstract responsibilities. The performance requirement for each scenario can be refined further in GRL, correlating with segments and activities of each path in UCM.
4. As the operational elements for the responsibilities of each scenario become concrete in UCM, the operationalization of each performance softgoal and goal can be made in GRL. The tasks and resources are exploited and connected to the softgoals.

5. After the concrete operational elements are worked out both in UCM and GRL, the different architectural design options can be considered. The partitions of each alternative are coupled with related tasks for different softgoals.
6. Fig.5 shows the softgoal refinement after (3)(4)(5) and evaluation of response-time for the concurrent architecture of "Thread-per-disk" in GRL notation. The labels of the softgoals connected to labeled tasks are propagated from bottom to up. For instance, *ResponseTime[upd]* is undecided as *ResponseTime[PreMsgUpd]* is undecided though *ResponseTime[WriteDisk(upd)]* is satisfied, but with And-contribution. *ResponseTime[GCS]* softgoal is eventually considered as undecided since response-time on most (4/6) scenarios are undecided after the propagating. The designs and evaluations for other architectures can be done in a similar way.

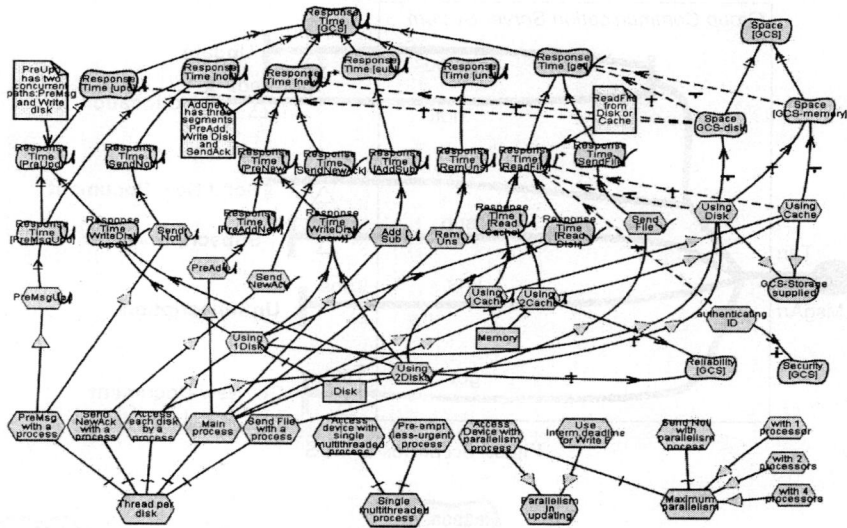

Fig.5. Refinement of performance softgoals and evaluation for architecture of "Thread-per-disk"

References

1. GRL On-line at: http://www.cs.toronto.edu/km/GRL/
2. Nixon, B.A., Management of Performance Requirements for Information System. *IEEE Transactions on SE*, 26(12): 1122-1146,2000
3. Scratchley, W.C. and Woodside, C.M., Evaluating Concurrency Options in Software Specifications. *Seventh International Symposium on Modelling, Analysis and Simulation*, College Park Maryland, USA, 1999.
4. UCM On-line at: http://www.usecasemaps.org/pub/UCMtutorial/

Querying Data with Multiple Temporal Dimensions

Carlo Combi[1] and Angelo Montanari[2]

[1] Dipartimento di Informatica, Università degli Studi di Verona
Ca' Vignal 2, strada le Grazie, 15, I-37134 Verona, Italy
combi@sci.univr.it

[2] Dipartimento di Matematica e Informatica, Università degli Studi di Udine
Via delle Scienze, 206, I-33100 Udine, Italy
montana@dimi.uniud.it

Abstract. This paper focuses on the problem of designing a query language for data models with multiple temporal dimensions.

1 Data Models with Multiple Temporal Dimensions

Valid and transaction times are commonly recognized as the basic (orthogonal) temporal dimensions for data [2], and a variety of issues related these two dimensions have been systematically explored in the literature [3]. In parallel, a considerable effort has been devoted to understand whether or not valid and transaction times suffice to capture all relevant temporal aspects in a natural and efficient way. In [1] we defined a new conceptual data model with four temporal dimensions that refines and extends a number of previous proposals. Besides valid and transaction times, such a model includes event and availability times. The *event times* of a fact are the occurrence times of the events that respectively initiate and terminate its validity interval. The *availability time* of a fact is the time interval during which the fact is available to and believed correct by the information system (such an interval does not necessarily coincide with the transaction time interval of the fact). In this paper, we focus on basic problems involved in querying data with multiple temporal dimensions. The outcome is the identification of the *general requirements* that a query language must satisfy to allow one to manage multiple temporal dimensions.

2 Querying Data with Multiple Temporal Dimensions

The management of multiple temporal dimensions has an impact on many components of query languages. In this section, we restrict our attention to those aspects specifically related to queries involving the four temporal dimensions. To exemplify the features of the query language, we will consider (a portion of) a clinical database, consisting of two tables, namely, *pat_sympt* and *pat_ther*, which contain data on patients' symptoms and therapies, respectively. Table schema is as follows:

pat_sympt(P_id, symptom, VT, ET_i, ET_t, AT, TT)
pat_ther(P_id, therapy, VT, ET_i, ET_t, AT, TT)
where the attributes VT, ET_i, ET_t, AT, and TT respectively denote the valid time, the initiating event time, the terminating event time, the availability time, and the transaction time of stored facts.

WHERE and WHEN clauses. Comparisons between temporal dimensions can be supported in two alternative ways [3]: the first one is to deal with temporal and non-temporal data in the WHERE clause; the second one is to constrain purely temporal conditions to appear in an ad-hoc WHEN clause. Obviously, to make it possible to check conditions mixing temporal and non-temporal data, we must allow temporal dimensions to occur, whenever necessary, in the WHERE clause, no matters what option we choose. In case we opt for the second alternative (this allows one to exploit specific tools to manage temporal data, at logical and physical levels), another design issue is the specification of the temporal dimensions we can refer to in the WHEN clause. The most general option is to allow all the four temporal dimensions to be used in the WHEN clause. According to this choice, a query that returns all and only the patient's symptoms that appeared no later than 3 days after their initiating event can be formulated as follows:

```
SELECT symptom
FROM pat_sympt S
WHEN BEGIN(VALID(S)) - INITIATING_ET(S) ≤ 3
```
where INITIATING_ET(·), VALID(·), and BEGIN(·) are functions that return the initiating event time of a tuple, the valid time interval of a tuple, and the starting point of a given interval, respectively.

Querying past states. By default, a query is evaluated with respect to the current state of the database (and thus to the knowledge currently available to the information system). However, there must be the possibility of evaluating a query over both the current and the past states of the database and/or of the information system. If we are interested in querying the database about its past states, we can use the well-known AS OF clause. We add an AS KNOWN clause that allows the user to query the database about the knowledge which was available to the information system at given time points in the past. We may also need to jointly use both clauses. As an example, the following query determines which data was available to the physician on October 18, according to the database contents on October 20:

```
SELECT *
FROM pat_sympt S
AS OF 97Oct20
AS KNOWN 97Oct18
```

Temporal joins. Some issues arise when more than one relation comes into play in a query. For example, we have to assign a proper meaning to the cartesian product of the relations that appear in the FROM clause. A possible choice is to impose that temporal tuples of different relations can be associated only when both their transaction times and their availability times overlap. Even though this solution seems meaningful, it does not allow the users to formulate some queries, such as, for instance, hypothetical queries where information available at different times has to be considered. In general, the language should allow the user to choose among different ways of executing the cartesian product between temporal relations (one can even opt for the usual cartesian product of relations, where the temporal attributes are treated as the standard ones).

Furthermore, besides the standard (atemporal) join, the language should support some forms of temporal join, where the join condition allows the user to join tuples taking into account different temporal features. As an example, consider a scenario where the physician wants to determine the symptoms of patients for which the valid time intervals of symptoms and therapies intersect. The query can be formulated as follows:

```
SELECT symptom, S.P_id
FROM pat_sympt S, pat_ther T
WHEN NOT(VALID(S) BEFORE VALID(T)) AND
   NOT(VALID(T) BEFORE VALID(S))
WHERE S.P_id = T.P_id
```

The WHEN and WHERE clauses can actually be replaced by a suitable join in the FROM clause, as shown by the following equivalent formulation of the query:

```
SELECT symptom, S.P_id
FROM pat_sympt S TJOIN pat_ther T ON S.P_id = T.P_id AND
   NOT(VALID(S) BEFORE VALID(T)) AND NOT(VALID(T) BEFORE VALID(S))
```

where we used the keyword TJOIN in the SELECT clause to point out that the join involves the temporal dimensions of information.

Further complex temporal queries can be defined when the different temporal dimensions have to be considered together. For example, for any given patient and symptom, the following query determines the therapies decided after that the information system became aware of the symptom and started before the end of the symptom:

```
SELECT S.P_id, therapy, symptom
FROM pat_sympt S JOIN pat_ther T ON S.P_id = T.P_id
WHEN INITIATING_ET(T) AFTER BEGIN(AVAILABLE(S)) AND
    BEGIN(VALID(T)) BEFORE END(VALID(S))
```

where AVAILABLE(·) returns the availability time of the considered tuple.

Defining temporal dimensions of query results. When several temporal relations are involved in a query, the language must provide some mechanisms to allow the user to obtain a consistent result, that is, a temporal relation endowed with valid, transaction, event, and availability times[1].

---

[1] In this paper, we consider only temporal databases where each relation has all the four temporal dimensions. As in the case of valid and transaction databases, one can

While transaction and availability times of the resulting relation can be obtained (according to the standard definition of the cartesian product given above) as the intersection of the transaction times and the availability times of the considered tuples, respectively, valid and event times are often explicitly defined by the user. In order to properly evaluate a query, however, some default criteria must be specified to determine the values of the valid and event times of the resulting relation, whenever the user does not provide any explicit rule. As an example, the valid time of each tuple belonging to the resulting relation can be defined as the intersection of the valid times of the corresponding tuples belonging to the relations that occur in the FROM clause, while its initiating and terminating event times can be defined as the maximum of the initiating and terminating event times of the corresponding tuples, respectively. However, we expect that, in most cases, the user explicitly defines the way in which the valid and event times of the resulting relation must be computed, taking into account the meaning he/she assigns to the query and the relative data. As an example, in the following query the user assigns to the valid and event times of the resulting relation the values that these attributes have in the *pat_sympt* relation:

```
SELECT symptom, S.P_id WITH VALID(S) AS VALID, INITIATING_ET(S)
    AS INITIATING, TERMINATING_ET(S) AS TERMINATING
FROM pat_sympt S TJOIN pat_ther T ON S.P_id = T.P_id AND
    NOT(VALID(S) BEFORE VALID(T)) AND NOT(VALID(T) BEFORE VALID(S))
```

3 Conclusions

This paper focused on the design of a query language for temporal databases with multiple temporal dimensions. Even though we can debate whether or not a database system needs to provide a special support, at the logical/physical level, to manage multiple temporal dimensions, it is not controversial that these dimensions must be taken into consideration at the level of requirements engineering applied to the design of information systems.

References

1. C. Combi and A. Montanari. Data Models with Multiple Temporal Dimensions: Completing the Picture. In K. R. Dittrich, A. Geppert, M. C. Norrie (eds.), Advanced Information Systems Engineering, 13th International Conference, (CAiSE 2001). LNCS 2068, Springer, Berlin Heidelberg, 187–202, 2001.
2. C. Jensen, C. Dyreson (Eds.) et al. The Consensus Glossary of Temporal Database Concepts - February 1998 Version. In *Temporal Databases - Research and Practice*, LNCS 1399, Springer, Berlin Heidelberg, 367–405, 1998.
3. G. Özsoyoglu and R. T. Snodgrass. Temporal and Real-Time Databases: A Survey. *IEEE Transactions on Knowledge and Data Engineering*, 7(4): 513–532, 1995.

---

provide suitable clauses and/or keywords to allow the user to obtain relations with a proper subset of temporal dimensions.

Query Explorativeness for Integrated Search in Heterogeneous Data Sources

Ruxandra Domenig and Klaus R. Dittrich

Department of Information Technology, University of Zurich
{domenig,dittrich}@ifi.unizh.ch

Abstract. We consider query systems which allow imprecise queries and define a new property called *query explorativeness*. This property characterizes the transformations performed by a system in order to answer imprecise queries, i.e. the system's "work" for mapping input queries into more precise target queries.

1 Introduction

Query systems today, for example Web search engines, had to learn to deal with the rapid increase of volume and diversity of on-line information and continuous changes in the number, content, and location of data sources. Several more or less suitable solutions for these problems have been proposed in recent years. One important property characterizes search engines, namely the simplicity of formulating queries. These are mostly specified by simply typing in keywords and the search engine finds the documents that may fulfill the given information need. We call such queries *fuzzy* queries. However, the price for this simplicity of querying is the quality of answers. WWW search tools often return too many results and, at the same time, results which are relevant to users are not returned.

Modern database management systems (DBMS) do a good job in managing and providing access to a large volume of record-oriented data. They store data together with its structure, which is used when formulating queries. We say that users formulate *exact* queries. The main advantage of this approach is the high quality of answers. In other words, the price for relevant results has to be payed by users through the involved formulation of queries.

These examples are the two extremes for the spectrum of sources which are available today for querying data. Systems which allow fuzzy queries are suitable for new requirements, i.e. huge amount of on-line data and of different users which want to query this data. On the other hand, there are a lot of applications which require specific, exact portions of the available data (for example financial applications), and for this reason, systems which return just relevant results of a query are still needed. In this paper, we characterize the difference between these two types of query systems through a property which we call *query explorativeness*. A system which allows fuzzy queries needs to find the meaning of such a query, i.e. to find out what users are looking for in terms of an "equivalent" set of precise queries. For this reason, query explorativeness characterizes the special query transformation steps performed by the system in order to "explore" the query and the available data. The main aim of this extended abstract is to show the importance of systems with high explorativeness and the way it can be implemented.

2 Query Explorativeness

We consider a query system S which returns a collection of *data units* as an answer to a query and which allows fuzzy queries. This means that users may get results which do not necessary fulfill their information need. Such a system is said to expose *answer fuzziness*. For S and a query q, we use the notation Q_q for the set of data units which are an answer to q and U_q for the set of data units which the system returns for q.

Definition 1. *A query system S exposes answer fuzziness, if*

$$\exists q : (Q_q \cup U_q) \setminus (Q_q \cap U_q) \neq 0.$$

In other words, query systems expose answer fuzziness if exists a query for which the system does not return all data units that are an answer or it returns some data units that are not an answer.

Obviously, a query systems exposing answer fuzziness has to internally perform some processing steps which translate the input query into one or more *target queries*. These transformations characterize what we call *query explorativeness*. We call the intermediate queries generated during the transformation process *working queries*.

Definition 2. *We consider a query system S with answer fuzziness. For a query q, query explorativeness is the number of working queries generated for answering q.*

Query explorativeness and retrieval effectiveness. Query explorativeness and retrieval effectiveness[1] are ortogonal to each other, since there are systems which offer a high explorativeness, but the retrieval effectiveness is low. Since the purpose of a query system is to offer a high retrieval effectiveness, the main question is when to choose systems with a high query explorativeness. In our opinion, a system with a high query explorativeness should be used if the users' information need is not well defined, i.e. users need to "explore" for themselves the data available for querying, or to receive hints as to where and how to search in order to fulfill their information need. As we discussed in Section 1, for several applications, query systems today should allow users to formulate queries on the fly,

---

[1] Retrieval effectiveness "is the ability to retrieve what the user wants to see" [Sch97]. The most well-known measures for effectiveness are *recall* and *precision*. They estimate the percentage of relevant documents which have been retrieved from the given document collection and the percentage of retrieved documents which are relevant.

i.e. they should be able to issue queries without knowing the structure, location or existence of requested data. Consequently, in this case, systems with a high query explorativeness are suitable.

Query explorativeness and users feedback. A system with a high query explorativeness may generate queries that lower the retrieval effectiveness. Since retrieval effectiveness is dependent on a subject, i.e. a user, a good solution for this problem is to involve users in the evaluation of queries, through user feedback. The traditional way of user feedback in an information retrieval system is to evaluate the initial query, present the results, and give users the possibility to classify the results as right or wrong. Then, using the initial query and the user's feedback specification, the system can reevaluate the initial query. This method is known in information retrieval as "relevance feedback". However, for a system with a high query explorativeness, it makes sense to offer users the possibility to give their feedback already during the process of query transformation, so they can choose the right working and target queries which should be evaluated.

Query explorativeness for integrated heterogeneous query systems. Query explorativeness has a different meaning for integrated heterogeneous query systems, i.e. for systems which offer users the possibility to query data from a network of heterogeneous data sources in an unified way. In this case, queries entered into the system are first preprocessed, then transformed as in traditional DBMS and finally they are split into subqueries for the underlying data sources. An integrated query system which offers a high query explorativeness implements during query preprocessing algorithms and heuristics which translate the (fuzzy) input query into equivalent target queries. This translation is necessary, since users did not formulate the respective target queries, because they did not take into consideration the structure and query capabilities of the underlying sources. Consequently, one can also say that an integrated query system with high explorativeness in a first step searches for queries, instead for searching directly for data.

SINGAPORE, a system for integrated search in heterogeneous data sources. We have developed a system called SINGAPORE (**SING**le **A**ccess **PO**int for heterogeneous data **RE**positories) which can be used for querying data sources which are *structurally heterogeneous*, i.e. they contain structured, semistructured and/or unstructured data. Its main focus is on offering a unified query language, so that retrieving information can be supported by the traditional task of database querying, but also by a more vague or "fuzzy" way to query, as in information retrieval systems. Additionally the system allows on-the-fly registration of new sources, making new information available for querying at run-time.

The query language of SINGAPORE, SOQL, is an extention of OQL [Cat00], with features for unstructured and semistructured data, and for integrating data. For example, we introduced the operator **contains**, which takes as arguments keywords and searches for them in the data sources specified in the **FROM** part of the query. Another example is the operator **LIKE**, which allows to formulate queries using the structure of the data, even if this is not fully known.

Since the system allows the formulation of fuzzy queries, it also offers a high query explorativeness. We have implemented query explorativeness during the preprocessing step. When a query is submitted to SINGAPORE, a parse tree is generated and the syntax is checked. The semantical check contains three special steps:

1. Handling of the special operators defined in the query language (for example contains, **LIKE**).
2. Generation of paths for structural specifications in the query.
3. Generation of consistent queries, eliminating inconsistencies in queries which might have been introduced during the previous steps.

For a detailed presentation of the system and the implementation of the explorativeness see [DD00, DD01a, DD01b].

3 Conclusions

We have identified a new property, query explorativeness, which characterizes query systems and which is of high importance for querying large amounts of data in a flexible way, i.e. without knowing the structure, location or existence of requested data. Query explorativeness characterizes the transformations performed by the query system in order to "explore" the query and the available data.

Even if there is no direct relationship between query explorativeness and retrieval effectiveness, we believe that systems which implement high query explorativeness are needed today, since they offer users the ability to formulate queries on the fly, in the sense that they "explore" for themselves the data available for querying, or they receive hints as to where and how to search.

References

[Cat00] R. G. G. Cattell, editor. *The Object Database Standard: ODMG 3.0*. Morgan Kaufmann, 2000.

[DD00] Ruxandra Domenig and Klaus R. Dittrich. A query based approach for integrating heterogeneous data sources. *Proc. 9th International Conference on Information and Knowledge Management, Washington, DC*, November 2000.

[DD01a] Ruxandra Domenig and Klaus R. Dittrich. Query preprocessing for integrated search in heterogeneous data sources. *Proc. Datenbanksysteme in Buero, Technik und Wissenschaft, Oldenburg, Germany*, 2001.

[DD01b] Ruxandra Domenig and Klaus R. Dittrich. SINGAPORE: A system for querying heterogeneous data sources. *Proc. International Conference on Data Engineering, ICDE (demo session), Heidelberg, Germany*, 2001.

[Sch97] Peter Schäuble. *Multimedia Information Retrieval*. Kluwer Academic Publishers, 1997.

Using Nested Tables for Representing and Querying Semistructured Web Data*

Irna M.R. Evangelista Filha[1], Altigran S. da Silva[1,**], Alberto H. F. Laender[1], and David W. Embley[2]

[1] Department of Computer Science, Federal University of Minas Gerais
31270-901 Belo Horizonte MG Brazil
{imre,alti,laender}@dcc.ufmg.br
[2] Department of Computer Science, Brigham Young University
Provo, Utah 84602 USA
embley@cs.byu.edu

Abstract. This paper proposes an approach for representing and querying semistructured Web data, which is based on nested tables allowing internal nested structural variations. Our motivation is to reduce the complexity found in typical query languages for semistructured data and to provide users with an alternative for quickly querying data obtained from multiple-record Web pages. We show the feasibility of our proposal by developing a prototype for a graphical query interface called QSByE (*Querying Semistructured data By Example*), which implements a set of QBE-like operations that extends typical nested-relational-algebra operations to handle semistructured data.

1 Introduction

In recent years, the demand for technologies to manage data available on the Web has increased considerably. Motivated by such a demand, several researchers have proposed adapting database techniques to efficiently and flexibly deal with the particularities of semistructured Web data. Unfortunately, the inherent freedom common in semistructured data (e.g., XML) inhibits the deployment of metaphors and paradigms like the ones that have been used extensively in typical data management tasks.

We propose in this paper the use of nested tables for representing and querying semistructured Web data. We show that nested tables can be nicely adapted for this kind of data and can provide a simple and intuitive representation close to record-based database representations, since they naturally accommodate hierarchical data. The distinction, and main contribution, of our proposal is that it

---

* This work was partially supported by Project SIAM (MCT/CNPq/PRONEX grant number 76.97.1016.00) and by CNPq (grant number 467775/00-1). The first and second authors are supported by scholarships from CAPES. The fourth author is supported by NSF (grant number IIS-0083127).
** On leave from the University of Amazonas, Brazil.

also allows the representation of variations and irregularities typical of semistructured data.

We also introduce a set of query operations for semistructured data represented as an internally varying nested table and describe QSByE (*Querying Semistructured data By Example*) [3], a query interface that implements such operations. QSByE combines features of QBE (*Query By Example*) [6] with typical features of query languages for semistructured data, such as type coercion and path expressions [1]. Particularly, QSByE makes it possible to handle data extracted from Web pages by a tool called DEByE (*Data Extraction By Example*) [4].

2 Nested Tables with Structural Variants

In this section we propose a generalization of regular nested tables in which we allow a column to have two or more distinct substructures called *variants*.

As an example, consider the nested table illustrated in Figure 1, which contains data extracted from an Amazon.com Web page that shows products related to Paul McCartney available in several "stores". To simplify our example, we consider only the stores *Popular Music, Books*, and *Auctions*. Observe that the information about products from each store is different. The information consists of Title, Artist, and AudioType for popular music; Title, Authors, and BookType for books; and Item, Bid, and Time for auctions. As a consequence, the internal structures of the data in the column Info are distinct for each of the rows.

Store	Info		
	Title	Artist	AudioType
Popular Music	*Wingspan (Hits & History)*	*Paul McCartney*	*Audio CD*
	...	...	...
	Title	Authors	BookType
Books	*Blackbird Singing ...*	*Paul McCartney Adrian Mitchell*	*HardCover*
	...	...	...
	Item	Bid	Time
Auctions	*PAUL MCCARTNEY At ...*	*$ 26.99*	*1 days, 20:15:57*
	...	...	...

Fig. 1. Example of a Nested Table Allowing Structural Variants

Despite the relative simplicity of dealing with semistructured data in the form of nested tables, it is easy to see that such a representation is not as expressive as general semistructured data models or XML. However, in this work we are mainly concerned with representing data extracted from a specific type of Web page that is said to be a *data rich, ontological narrow, multiple-record* Web page. Examples of such pages are found in Web sites such as bookstores, electronic catalogs, travel agencies, and classified ads and include pages composed of data whose overall structure is naturally hierarchical, but exhibits a modest degree of variation [4].

3 Query Operations and the QSByE Interface

In this section we present a set of operations for querying semistructured data represented as nested tables, which extends the operations proposed by Colby [2]. We also illustrate how these operations work in the QSByE interface. These operations, selection, projection, nest and unnest, are briefly described in what follows.

The *selection* operation allows selection conditions to be specified at any level of nesting. A selection condition is a boolean expression defined over the value in a column or over the existence of a column in an internal subtable (i.e., a *structural condition*). The *projection* operation is similar to the projection operation defined in the relational algebra. We can say that this operation horizontally reduces a table by keeping only the columns specified by the user. Similar to what was proposed by Thomas and Fischer [5], the *nest* operation has two distinct semantics. When applied to a single column, this operation groups the values in the column that are associated with equal values occurring in other columns. Otherwise, it creates a new internal table that groups the values of these columns and, consequently, generates a new level of nesting in the table. The *unnest* operation is the inverse of the nest operation. It also has two distinct semantics, according to [5], and it is only valid for columns containing list of atoms or an internal table. If it is applied to a list of atoms, it will "ungroup" its elements, i.e., it will split them into different rows of the table. Otherwise, if it is applied to an internal table it will eliminate a level of nesting.

These operations were implemented in QSByE (*Querying Semistructured data By Example*) [3], a query interface that adopts a variation of the QBE paradigm [6] to provide a suitable environment for casual users to query semistructured Web data. We illustrate how queries are formulated with QSByE by means of an example of a query over the data in the nested table of Figure 1.

Suppose a user is interested in issuing the following query: *List the title and the type of the books written by John Grisham. Rearrange the result by nesting the values of the column BookType.* To formulate this query, the user first selects a repository (resultant from a data extraction using DEByE) containing the data of interest. This immediately provides the structure of the stored data in the form of a nested skeleton, as illustrated in Figure 2(a). Then, the user specifies the selection conditions on the columns **Store** and **Authors** to retrieve only books written by John Grisham. This is shown in Figure 2(a). Notice that the condition on **Authors** has been specified using the ~ operator that denotes approximate comparison by pattern matching. To show only the title and type of the books, the user specifies a projection operation by clicking on the header of the corresponding columns. This is also shown in Figure 2(a). Figure 2(b) shows an excerpt of the query result.

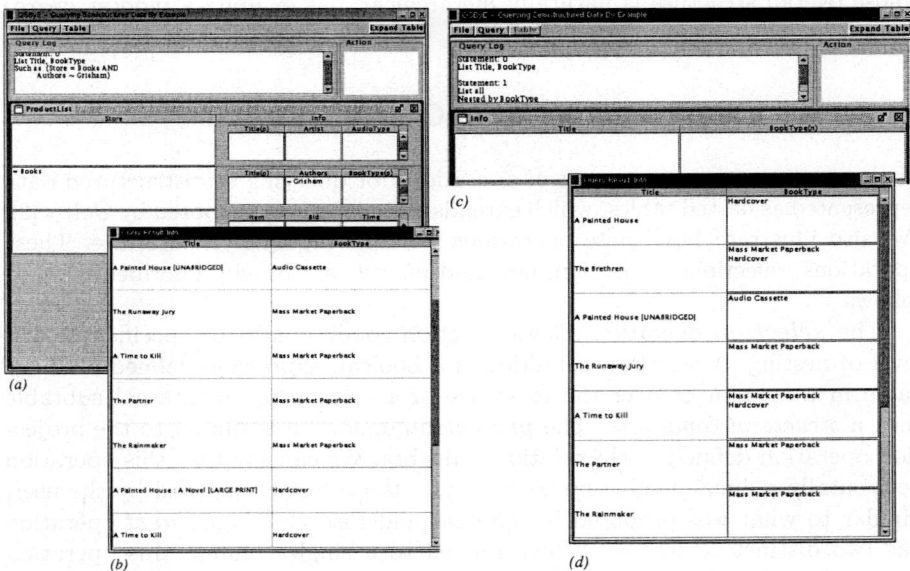

Fig. 2. Specification and Result of the Example Query

To satisfy the query specification, it is necessary to rearrange the result table of Figure 2(b), by nesting the values of the column **BookType**. This is accomplished as follows. By clicking on the "Query" button (Figure 2(a)), the user makes QSByE to replace the current skeleton table by the skeleton of the result table of Figure 2(b), as shown in Figure 2(c). Then, the user clicks on the "Table" button, selects the nest operation and clicks on the column **BookType**. QSByE then marks the header of this column with an "(n)" (see Figure 2(c)). The table resulting from this operation is shown in Figure 2(d).

4 Conclusions

We have presented a generalization of nested tables for semistructured data in which distinct rows are allowed to contain data with distinct structures. We have shown that these nested tables can be used to represent and query semistructured data extracted from the Web. We extended nested relational algebra operations to manage the variable nestings we defined, and we implemented QSByE to allow a user to issue queries in a QBE-like manner. Preliminary experimentations with QSByE have demonstrated that with a small amount of training even unskilled users can use the interface to query semistructured data extracted from Web pages.

References

1. Abiteboul, S., Quass, D., McHugh, J., Widom, J., and Wiener, J. The Lorel Query Language for Semistructured Data. *International Journal on Digital Libraries 1*, 1 (1997), 68–88.
2. Colby, L. S. A Recursive Algebra and Query Optimization for Nested Relations. In *Proceedings of the 1989 ACM SIGMOD International Conference on Management of Data* (Portland, Oregon, 1989), pp. 273–283.
3. Evangelista-Filha, I. M. R., Laender, A. H. F., and Silva, A. S. Querying Semistructured Data By Example: The QSByE Interface. In *Proceedings of the International Workshop on Information Integration on the Web* (Rio de Janeiro, Brazil, 2001), pp. 156–163.
4. Laender, A. H. F., Ribeiro-Neto, B., and da Silva., A. S. DEByE – Data Extraction by Bxample. *Data and Knowledge Engineering 40*, 2 (2002), 121–154.
5. Thomas, S. J., and Fischer, P. C. Nested Relational Structures. *Advances in Computing Research 3* (1986), 269–307.
6. Zloof, M. M. Query-by-Example: A Data Base Language. *IBM Systems Journal 16*, 4 (1977), 324–343.

Defining and Validating Measures for Conceptual Data Model Quality

Marcela Genero[1], Geert Poels[2], and Mario Piattini[1]

[1]ALARCOS Research Group, Department of Computer Science
University of Castilla-La Mancha
Paseo de la Universidad, 4 - 13071 - Ciudad Real (Spain)
{mgenero,mpiattin}@inf-cr.uclm.es
[2]Dept. Business Administration, University of Sciences and Arts
Koningsstraat, 336, 1030 Brussels (Belgium)
gpoels@vlekho.wenk.be

Abstract. For assessing conceptual data model quality it is useful to have quantitative and objective measurement instruments. The scarcity of such measurement instruments leaded us to define a set of measures for structural complexity, an internal quality attribute of conceptual data models, with the idea that it is related to the external quality of such models. In order to gather empirical evidence that the proposed measures could be early quality indicators of conceptual data models, we carried out a controlled experiment. The aim of the experiment was to investigate the relation between the structural complexity of conceptual data models and maintainability sub-characteristics such as understandability and modifiability.

1 Introduction

Given that conceptual data models lay the foundation of all later design work their quality has a significant impact on the quality of the database which is ultimately implemented. However, before evaluating and if necessary improving the quality of a conceptual data model, it is necessary to assess it in an objective way. It is in this context that measurement can help database designers to make better decisions during design activities. Even though several quality frameworks for conceptual data models have been proposed, most of them lack valid quantitative measures to evaluate the quality of conceptual data models in an objective way. Papers referring to measures for conceptual data models are scarce. Kesh [4] and Moody [5] have proposed some measures to measure different quality characteristics of ERDs, but their utility in practice has not been demonstrated.

The scarcity of measures that are well-defined and also theoretically and empirically validated leaded us to define a set of measures to quantify various aspects related to one particular, but highly important internal quality attribute of conceptual data models, i.e. their structural complexity. As Whitmire remarked [7] complexity is believed to be an indicator of external quality attributes such as understandability, modifiability, etc., but the empirical evidence supporting these relationships is scarce and suspect.

In [3] we have defined and theoretically validated a set of measures for the structural complexity of Entity Relationship Diagrams (ERDs) (see table 1), following the DISTANCE framework [6].

Table 1. Measures for the structural complexity of ERDs

MEASURE	DEFINITION
NE	The total number of entities within an ERD.
NA	The total number of attributes within an ERD.
NDA	The total number of derived attributes within an ERD.
NCA	The total number of composite attributes within an ERD.
NMVA	The total number of multivalued attributes within an ERD.
NR	The total number of relationships within an ERD.
NM:NR	The total number of M:N relationships within an ERD.
N1:NR	The total number of 1:N relationships (including also 1:1 relationships) within an ERD.
NBinaryR	The total number of binary relationships within an ERD.
NIS_AR	The total number of IS_A relationships (generalisation/ specialisation) within an ERD. In this case, we consider one relationship for each child-parent pair within the IS_A relationship.
NRefR	defined as the total number of reflexive relationships within an ERD.
NRR	defined as the number of relationships that are redundant in an ERD.

The aim of this paper is to present a controlled experiment we carried out to gather empirical evidence that the proposed measures could be early quality indicators of ERDs.

2 A Controlled Experiment

The aim of the experiment is to investigate the relationship between the structural complexity of ERDs and two important components of maintainability: understandability and modifiability. The subjects were forty students enrolled in the third year of Computer Science in the Department of Computer Science at the University of Castilla-La Mancha in Spain. The experimental material consisted of a guide explaining the ER notation, and four ERDs (all the experimental material is available at http://alarcos.inf-cr.uclm.es). These diagrams are related to different universes of discourse that are general enough to be easily understood by each of the subjects. The structural complexity of each diagram is different, because the values of the measures are different for each diagram.

Each diagram had a test enclosed which includes two parts:

- Part 1. A questionnaire in order to evaluate if the subjects really understand the content of the ERD. Each questionnaire contained exactly the same number of

questions (five) and the questions were conceptually similar and in identical order. Each subject had to write down the time spent answering the questionnaire, by recording the initial time and final time. The difference between the two is what we call the understandability time (expressed in minutes).
- Part 2. Two new requirements for the ERD. The subjects had to modify the ERD according to these new requirements, again writing down the initial time and the final time. The difference between these two times is what we called modifiability time, which includes both the time spent analysing what modifications had to be done and the time needed to perform them.

We selected a within-subject design experiment, i.e. all the tests (i.e. experimental tasks) had to be solved by each of the subjects. The subjects were given the tests in different order. We allowed one hour to do all the tests. Each subject had to work alone. In case of doubt, they could only consult the supervisor who organised the experiment. We collected all the tests controlling if they were complete and the responses were correct. We discarded the tests of 9 subjects, because they included an incorrect answer or a required modification that was done incorrectly. Therefore, we take into account the responses of 31 subjects.

To analyse the data, we first applied the Kolmogorov-Smirnov test to ascertain if the distribution of the data collected was normal or not. As the data was normal we decided to use a parametric test like Pearson's correlation coefficient, with a level of significance $\alpha = 0.05$, which means the level of confidence is 95% (i.e. the probability that we reject H_0 when H_0 is false is at least 95%, which is statistically acceptable). Using Pearson's correlation coefficient, each of the measures was correlated separately to the understandability and the modifiability time (see table 2).

Table 2. Pearson's correlation coefficients between the measures and the understandability and modifiability time (all values are significant)

	NE	NA	NR	NBinaryR	N1:RN	NM:NR
Understandability time	0.7168	0.5588	0.7168	0.7168	0.7168	0.7168
Modifiability time	0.7246	0.5508	0.7246	0.7246	0.7246	0.7246

3 Conclusions

Analysing the Pearson's correlation coefficients shown in table 2, we can conclude that there is a high correlation between the understandability time and the modifiability time and the measures NE, NA, NR, N1:NR, NM:NR, NBinaryR because the correlation coefficient is greater than 0.5, which is a common threshold to evaluate correlation values. Only the NA measure seems to be less correlated to the understandability and modifiability time than the other measures (though the correlation value is still greater than 0.5).

The results obtained in this experiment corroborate, at some extent, the results obtained in a previous similar experiment [2] and the results obtained in a case study using data extracted from 5 real projects [1].

In spite of this we are aware that it is necessary to replicate the experiment and to carry out new ones in order to confirm our results. Also it is necessary to apply these measures to data obtained from "real projects".

Acknowledgements

This research is part of the DOLMEN project supported by CICYT (TIC 2000-1673-C06-06).

References

1. Genero, M., Piattini, M., Calero, C.: An Approach To Evaluate The Complexity Of Conceptual Database Models. 3nd European Software Measurement Conference - FESMA 2000, Madrid (2000).
2. Genero, M., Olivas, J., Piattini M., Romero, F.: Knowledge Discovery For Predicting Entity Relationship Diagram Maintainability, SEKE 2001, Argentina, Proceedings, Knowledge Systems Institute, (2001) 203-211.
3. Genero, M.: Defining and Validating Metrics for Conceptual Models, Ph.D. thesis, University of Castilla-La Mancha. (2002).
4. Kesh, S.: Evaluating the Quality of Entity Relationship Models, Information and Software Technology, Vol. 37 N° 12, (1995) 681-689.
5. Moody, L.: Metrics for Evaluating the Quality of Entity Relationship Models, Proceedings of the Seventeenth International Conference on Conceptual Modelling (E/R '98), Singapore, November 16-19, (1998) 213-225.
6. Poels, G., Dedene, G.: Distance-based software measurement: necessary and sufficient properties for software measures, Information and Software Technology, Vol. 42 N° 1, (2000) 35-46.
7. Whitmire, S.: Object Oriented Design Measurement, John Wiley & Sons, Inc. (1997).

An Architecture for Building Multi-device Thin-Client Web User Interfaces

John Grundy and Wenjing Zou

Department of Computer Science, University of Auckland
Private Bag 92019, Auckland, New Zealand
john-g@cs.auckland.ac.nz

Abstract. We describe a new approach to providing adaptable thin client interfaces for web-based information systems. Developers specify web-based interfaces using a high-level mark-up language based on the logical structure of the user interface. At run-time this single interface description is used to automatically provide an interface for multiple web devices e.g. desk-top HTML and mobile WML-based systems, as well as highlight, hide or disable interface elements depending on the current user and user task. Our approach allows developers to much more easily construct and maintain adaptable web-based user interfaces than other current approaches.

1 Introduction

Many web-based information systems require degrees of adaptation of the system's user interfaces to different client devices, users and user tasks [11, 8]. Interfaces need to be provided for conventional web browsers as well as wireless PDAs, mobile phones and pagers [8, 7, 12]. Adapting to different user and user tasks is required [4, 6, 11], such as hiding "Update" and "Delete" buttons if the user is a customer or a staff member doing an information retrieval task.
Building such interfaces using current technologies is difficult, time-consuming and systems are hard-to-maintain. Various approaches have been developed to support forms of user interface adaptation. Proxies such as Web Clipping™ and Portal-to-go services automatically convert e.g. HTML content to WML content for wireless devices [8, 7, 11, 9]. Typically these produce poor interfaces as the conversion is difficult for all but simple web interfaces. Some systems take XML-described interface content and transform it into different HTML or WML formats depending on the requesting device information [8, 11]. The degree of adaptation supported is generally limited, and each interface type requires complex scripting. Intelligent, adaptive and component-based user interfaces often support user and task adaptation [6]. Most existing approaches only provide thick-client interfaces (i.e. that run in the client device, not the server), and most provide no device adaptation capabilities. Some recent proposals for multi-device user interfaces [11, 7] use generic, device-

independent user interface descriptions, but most do not typically support user and task adaptation and many are application-specific.

2 Our Approach

Many organisations want to leverage the increasingly wide-spread access of their staff (and customers) to thin-client user interfaces on desktop, laptop and mobile (PDA, phone, pager etc) devices [1, 8] but without developing versions of every user interface for every possible device, user and user task comnination possible. To support this our user interfaces are specified using a device-independent mark-up language describing screen elements and layout, along with any required dynamic content (currently using embedded Java code, or "scriptlets"). Screen element descriptions may include annotations indicating which user(s) and user task(s) the elements are relevant to. We call this Adaptive User Interface Technology (AUIT). Our systems adopt the four-tier software architecture illustrated in Fig. 1.

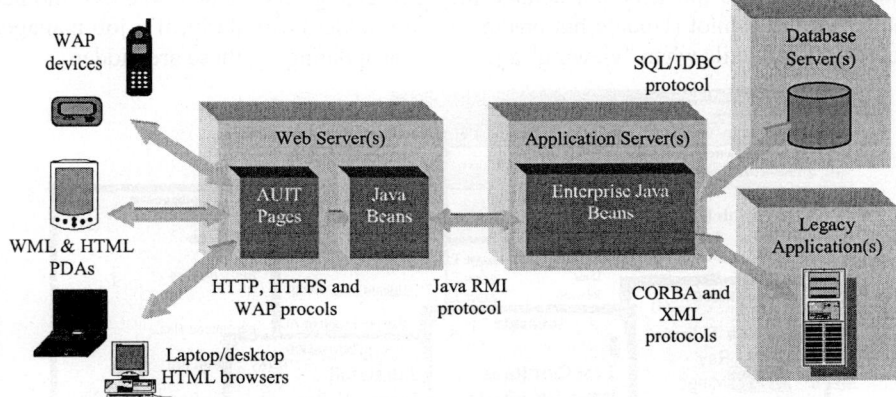

Fig. 1. Our 4-tier web-based information system software architecture

The AUIT pages are implemented by Java Server Pages (JSPs) containing a special mark-up language independent of device-specific rendering languages like HTML and WML but that contain descriptions of screen elements, layout and user/task relevance. Developers implement their thin-client web screens using this mark-up language, specifying in a device, user and task-independent way each screen for their application i.e. only M screens, despite the N combinations of user, user task and display device combinations possible for each screen. At run-time, accessed AUIT pages determine the requesting display device type, current user and current user task. A display mark-up language suitable for the device is generated, taking into account the user and user task. Dynamic page content is via JavaBeans, connected to Enterprise JavaBeans accessing databases and possibly legacy systems.

3 An Example of AUIT in Use

We illustrate the use of our AUIT system used to build some adaptable, web-based user interfaces for a collaborative job maintenance system. Fig. 2 shows examples of a job listing screen being displayed for the same user in a desktop web browser (1), mobile PDA device (2 and 3) and mobile WAP phone (4-6). The web browser can show all jobs (rows) and job details (columns). It can also use colour to highlight information and hypertext links. The PDA device can not show all job detail columns, and so additional job details are split across a set of screens. The user accesses these additional details by using the hypertext links added to the sides of the screen. This interface splitting is done automatically by our AUIT tag implementation and uses the logical structure of screens to ensure a sensible re-organisation. The WAP phone similarly can't display all columns and rows, and links are added to access these. In addition, the WAP phone doesn't provide the degree of mark-up and scripting the PDA and web browser can, so buttons, links, colour and client-side scripts are not used. The user accesses other pages via a text-based menu listing. If a customer job manager accesses job lists and details, they can change the details whereas another staff member cannot (Update buttons/menus are hidden). Similarly, if a job manager accesses job details when "viewing" a job (versus updating it), these are hidden.

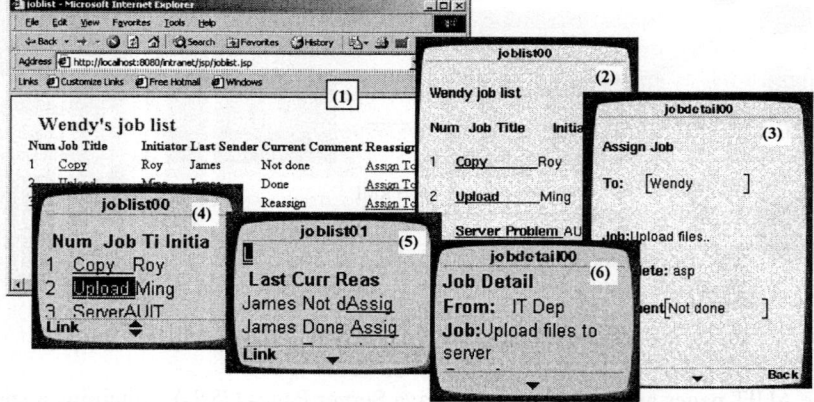

Fig. 2. (a) Examples of job listing screen running on multiple devices

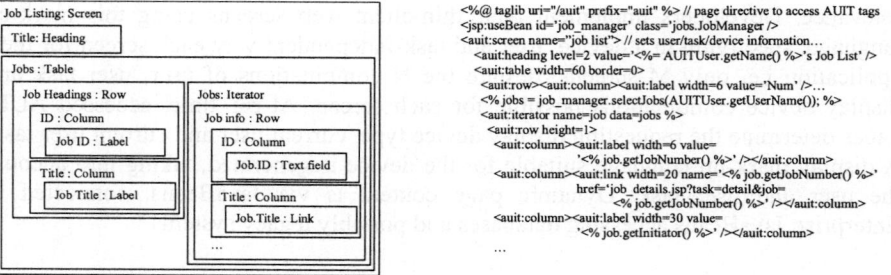

Fig. 3. (a) Logical structure of and (b) example AUIT description parts of the job listing screen

Fig. 3 (a) shows the logical structure of the job listing screen using our AUIT custom tags. The screen is comprised of a heading and list of jobs. The first table row displays column headings, the subsequent rows are generated by iterating over a list of job objects returned by a Java Bean. Fig. 3 (b) shows part of the AUIT Java Server Page that specifies this interface. These AUIT tags generate HTML or WML mark-up as output, adapting the layout, use of graphics and highlighting, available buttons and menu items, data fields shown and so on to the requesting device, user and user task information supplied when the page is accessed. Use of a logical structure for web-based interfaces is essential to this approach, as in related approaches [3, 11].

We have carried out an empirical evaluation of both the AUIT tag library by experienced web developers and the AUIT-generated user interfaces, comparing them to interfaces from custom-written JSPs. Results have been very encouraging with developers able to build quite sophisticated web-based information systems whose interfaces suitably adapt to a variety of display devices, users and user tasks. We are continuing to refine and extend the custom tags and their properties to allow more complex layout, highlighting and client-side scripting to be adapted.

References

1. Amoroso, D.L. and Brancheau, J. Moving the Organization to Convergent Technologies: e-Business and Wireless, Proc. 34th Annual Hawaii International Conference on System Sciences, Maui, Hawaii, Jan 3-6 2001, IEEE CS Press.
2. Bonifati, A., Ceri, S., Fraternali, P., Maurino, A. Building multi-device, content-centric applications using WebML and the W3I3 Tool Suite, Proc. Conceptual Modelling for E-Business and the Web, LNCS 1921, pp. 64-75.
3. Ceri, S., Fraternali, P., Bongio, A. Web modelling Language (WebML): a modelling language for designing web sites, Computer Networks 33 (1-6), 2000.
4. Eisenstein, J. and Puerta, A. Adaptation in automated user-interface design, Proc. 2000 Conference on Intelligent User Interfaces, New Orleans, 9-12 January 2000, ACM Press, pp. 74-81.
5. Fox, A., Gribble, S. Chawathe, Y., and Brewer, E. Adapting to Network and Client Variation Using Infrastructural Proxies: lessons and perspectives, IEEE Personal Communications 5 (4), (1998), 10-19.
6. Grundy, J.C. and Hosking, J.G. Developing Adaptable User Interfaces for Component-based Systems, to appear in Interacting with Computers, Elsevier (2001).
7. Han, R., Perret, V., and Naghshineh, M. WebSplitter: A unified XML framework for multi-device collaborative web browsing, Proc. CSCW 2000, Philadelphia, Dec 2-6 2000.
8. Marsic, I. Adaptive Collaboration for Wired and Wireless Platforms, IEEE Internet Computing (July/August 2001), 26-35.
9. Palm Corp. Web Clipping services, www.palm.com (2001).
10. Rossel M. Adaptive support: the Intelligent Tour Guide. Proc. 1999 International Conference on Intelligent User Interfaces. ACM Press.

11. Van der Donckt, J., Limbourg, Q., Florins, M., Oger, F., and Macq, B. Synchronised, model-based design of multiple user interfaces, Proc. 2001 Workshop on Multiple User Interfaces over the Internet, HCI-IHM'2001, 10-14 September 2001 Lille, France.
12. Zarikas, V., Papatzanis, G., and Stephanidis, C. An architecture for a self-adapting information system for tourists, Proc. 2001 Workshop on Multiple User Interfaces over the Internet, HCI-IHM'2001, 10-14 September 2001 Lille, France.

A Framework for Tool–Independent Modeling of Data Acquisition Processes for Data Warehousing

Arne Harren and Heiko Tapken

Oldenburg Research and Development Institute for Computer Science Tools and Systems (OFFIS)
Escherweg 2, 26121 Oldenburg, Germany
{arne.harren,heiko.tapken}@offis.de
http://www.offis.de

Abstract. Due to their integrated and unified view over data of various operational and external systems, data warehouse systems nowadays are well established to serve as a technical fundament for strategic data analyses. Unfortunately, data acquisition which is responsible for introducing new or changed data from source systems into the data warehouse is not static and new requirements may be identified as time walks by. Therefore, comprehensibility and maintainability of data acquisition processes are crucial to the long-time success of a data warehouse.
Within the scope of this paper we sketch some aspects of our framework for tool-independent data acquisition design including the framework's architecture, the underlying design process model, and the management of metadata.

1 Introduction

Data warehouses which usually integrate cleansed data from operational and external data sources, provide a reliable platform for decision support. Besides the data warehouse database, enterprise-wide data warehouse environments typically comprise multitudes of components which store data, e.g. data sources, staging areas, operational data stores, and online analytical processing systems. Often, these environments contain more than one physical data warehouse or data mart that are fed by the source systems. For further complexity, these components may be spread across various platforms and may store their metadata in vendor-dependent repositories.

With regard to the overall coordination of the data flow, maintainability and comprehensibility are key factors for sound data acquisition. Therefore, our research project TODAY (Toolsuite for Managing a Data Warehouse's Data Supply) aims at providing a framework that supports an iterative definition of data acquisition processes from data sources to target systems, enforces a clear separation of process descriptions from their corresponding, optimized implementations, and employs commercial extraction, transformation and loading tools for process execution.

2 Architecture

The framework enables modeling of the overall data flow within data acquisition processes on an extensible, tool-independent *design layer* that permits hiding tool-specific details of process implementations. After process design is done, (semi-)automatic derivation of optimized, tool-specific implementations is provided by the framework's optimization component in conjunction with tool-dependent deployment components. Thus, processes on the design layer may be modeled intuitively and do not necessarily have to be specified in an optimized way from a tool's point of view. This enables easy adoption of new functionality within a process without having the designer worrying about the impacts on later optimization.

Subsequent to the deployment of process implementations into the tools' proprietary metadata repositories, data acquisition processes can be set to production at the *execution layer*. At this layer, process execution is scheduled and monitored by a dedicated controller component.

Figure 1 sketches the framework's architecture and the relationship between the design layer and execution layer.

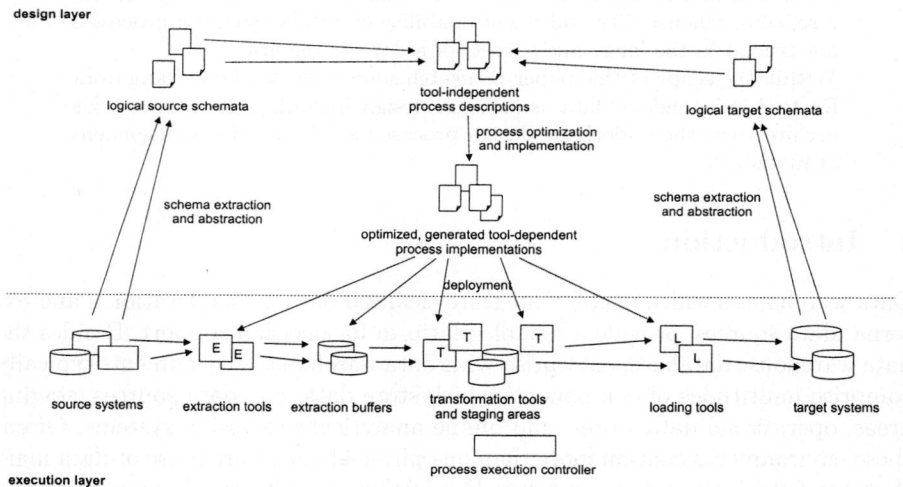

Fig. 1. Framework architecture

3 Design Process Model

For process design at the design layer, we have developed a process model which allows simple, flexible, comprehensive design of data acquisition [3]. This process model comprises the following six phases which are traversed iteratively:

1. As a prerequisite for tool-independent modeling, counterparts of physical source and target schemata have to be described on the basis of our framework's logical data model. These logical schemata hide details of the corresponding data structures, e.g. relational databases or XML files.
2. Data transformations can be modeled by means of data flow graphs in which each node describes a data processing step. Each step is associated with an operator, e.g. for providing data from a source system, deriving new attribute values, or filtering data streams. Data can be manipulated using our tool-independent transformation language TL^2.
3. In order to be able to generate process implementations in subsequent phases, appropriate tools have to be selected from a given set of available tools.
4. As a first part of process optimization, processes are partitioned and restructured based on tool capabilities and operator dependencies.
5. The previous phase results in process segments consisting of unary and binary operators that are now converted to tool-dependent operators. As a second part of process optimization, each segment is locally optimized with regard to the specific tool.
6. All generated, optimized, tool-dependent process segments are now deployed into the tools' private repositories using the required, vendor specific metadata format. Functions for data manipulation described in TL^2 are mapped to equivalent functions in tool-specific programming languages.

4 Metadata Management

Within our framework we are using a hybrid metadata architecture (cp. [1,4]). Therefore, each software component involved in the environment may use its own repository for local metadata while shared metadata are primarily stored in a central repository.

For central metadata storage, we have developed the prototyped, extensible repository system TOY (TODAY Open Repository) [2] which is capable of handling metadata based on metadata structures using the Meta Object Facility (MOF) [6]. We implemented the Common Warehouse Metamodel (CWM) [5] and use extensions to it in order to meet all needs at the design and execution layer. Access to a repository instance is possible using the system's object-oriented API or using text streams which comply to the metadata interchange format XMI [7]. By combining API and stream-based metadata exchange with XSL [8] and additional wrappers for accessing proprietary repository systems, we can reduce time and effort which needs to be spent for developing mappings between different metadata repositories.

5 Current Status and Future Work

We are currently implementing a prototype system of our framework. In this prototype we support a set of base operators for data transformations (cp. [3]) and integrate a commercial tool for extraction, transformation, and loading of data.

Completing the prototype shall show the soundness of our concepts. Evaluation will be done in cooperation with an enterprise within the telecommunication industry.

References

1. H. H. Do, and E. Rahm: *On Metadata Interoperability in Data Warehouses*, Technical report 1-2000, Institute for Informatics, University of Leipzig, 2000.
2. A. Harren, H. Tapken: *TODAY Open Repository: An Extensible, MOF-Based Metadata Repository System*, technical report, Oldenburg Research and Development Institute for Computer Science Tools and Systems (OFFIS), 2001.
3. A. Harren, H. Tapken: *A Process Model for Enterprise-Wide Design of Data Acquisition for Data Warehousing*, Proc. of the 4th Intl. Conference on Enterprise Information Systems, Ciudad Real, Spain, ICEIS Press, 2002.
4. D. Marco: *Building and Managing the Meta Data Repository, A Full Lifecycle Guide*, Wiley Computer Publishing, 2000.
5. Object Management Group: *Common Warehouse Metamodel (CWM) Specification. Version 1.0*, 2001.
6. Object Management Group: *OMG Meta Object Facility (MOF), Specification, Version 1.3*, 1999.
7. Object Management Group: *OMG XML Metadata Interchange (XMI) Specification, Version 1.1*, 2000.
8. World Wide Web Consortium: *Extensible Stylesheet Language (XSL) Version 1.0*, W3C Recommendation, 2001.

Managing Complexity of Designing Routing Protocols Using a Middleware Approach

Cosmina Ivan[1], Vasile Dadarlat[2], and Kalman Pusztai[3]

[1] Department of Computer Science & Information Systems
University of Limerick, Ireland
cosmina.ivan@ul.ie
[2] Department of Electronics & Computer Engineering
University of Limerick, Ireland
vasile.dadarlat@ul.ie
[3] Department of Computer Science
Technical University of Cluj, Romania
kalman.pusztai@cs.utcluj.ro

Abstract. Designing and architecting new routing protocols is an expensive task, because they are complex systems managing distributed network state, in order to create and maintain the routing databases. Existing routing protocol implementations are compact, bundling together a database, an optimal path calculation algorithm and a network state distribution mechanism. The aim of this paper is to present a middleware-based approach for designing and managing routing protocols based on the idea of decomposing routing protocols into fundamental building blocks and identifying the role of each component, and also to propose a framework for composing dynamically new routing protocols making use of a distributed object platform.

1 A New Approach for Designing Protocols

A routing protocol allows the communication nodes of different networks to exchange information in order to update and maintain routing tables. Well known examples of routing protocols are: RIP, IGRP, EIGRP, and OSPF. The routers are capable to support multiple independent routing protocols and maintain forwarding tables for several routed protocols [3].

Traditionally, the term middleware was applied to software that facilitates remote database access and systems transactions, some common middleware categories may include: TPs, DCE or RPC systems, various ORBs. In newer accepts, the role of middleware would be to manage the complexity and heterogeneity of distributed infrastructures, providing simpler programming environments for distributed-application developers and new communication services. Well-known platforms offering middleware solutions for programming various distributed objects systems are OMG's CORBA and Microsoft's DCOM [9], [10].

As a general observation, the existing routing protocols are developed and implemented in a compact, monolithic manner, and they are highly integrated into each vendor's equipment, or even specific to each vendor. This approach obstructs the dynamic introduction of new routing protocols and services into the Internet. Making use of distributed objects technologies, it is possible to design a *binding model*, used by the programmable objects to construct the traditional services, as well as a design solution for new routing services. [2], [6].

On making use of OO-distributed technologies one must design the routing protocol implementations based on separating the routing database, the routing information announcement and the optimal path calculation. This technique would allow protocol developers to create various routing architectures in a modular fashion and to be able to introduce new routing services in a dynamic way, as a basis for the programmability of routing protocols [2], [10].

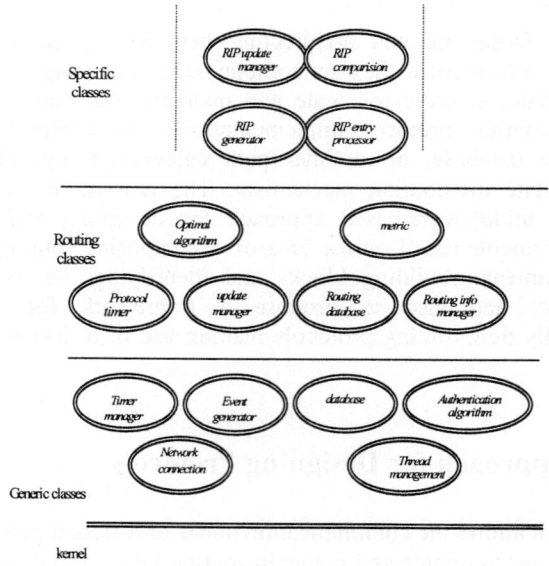

Fig. 1. RIP class hierarchy

2 Design and Implementation Considerations

We propose a binding model for characterizing each routing protocol used for decomposing the protocol into fundamental blocks and a hierarchy of classes, which reflects the general structure of any routing protocol implementations. The most important components of *the binding model* are:

- *Access interfaces*, acting above the operating system's kernel
- *RI manager* managing the routing information in the network
- *Event generator*, controls internally the transmission of routing information for the database updating, or the calculus of the optimal paths
- *Database object*, used for maintaining the distributed routing state of nodes, and *update manager object*, which updates the database when new routing information is received
- *Optimal path algorithms*, are components which operate on the contents of the database to calculate forwarding tables

By introducing standard interfaces between these routing components, code reuse could be enabled assuring the independency of the specific routing protocols and being fully programmable. By allowing components to create bindings at run-time, we enable the dynamic introduction of new routing services into networks.

To realize the binding model was designed a routing SDK named RP-ware, consisting of a hierarchy of base class's implemented using Java and making use of CORBA services. The prototype implements a set of three groups of classes: generic classes which offers basic functionality, a middleware layer containing routing component classes and the lower layer which contains the protocol specific classes. (Figure 1).

A short presentation of the functionality for some of these classes is made below a *database class* supports generic methods for creating new databases. The *network connection class* provides the mechanisms used at the interface with the system level, for transmitting routing messages to the network. A range of communication mechanisms will be supported, including TCP and UDP socket management or remote method invocations (RMI)[8]. Because many routing protocols are multithreaded, a *thread management class* will wrap operating system specific methods. Routing component classes are defined or derived to allow the construction of different routing architectures. A *routing database* extends the generic *database* class, encapsulating all the route entries available at a network node and will provide information about the network nodes and their associated paths. Protocol specific classes are used to describe the objects that participate in a specific routing protocol implementation.

The components of a programmable RIP implementation are shown in Figure 2. The component that directly communicates with the network is the *network connection* object (based on UDP sockets, or remote method invocations). In the case of sockets, a *RIP packet processor* object is involved, reading routing protocol specific headers from the received packets. Once a packet has been examined and verified, a route entry is extracted and sent to the *RIP entry processor* object. The *RIP update manager* object is then invoked, which exchanges information with the *metric* object, the *RIP route comparison* object, and the *routing database*. Following this, the *RIP route comparison* object inputs the two entries and produces the comparison result based on a specified set of metrics. If the received entry is better than the existing one, the *routing database* object is used to replace the existing entry. For this purpose the *RIP event generator* initiates a RIP triggered update, issued by the *RIP update manager*. Updated entries are finally transmitted to the neighboring routers via the *routing info manager* and *network connection* objects. Regular RIP updates are periodically initiated, also using a *routing info manager* object.

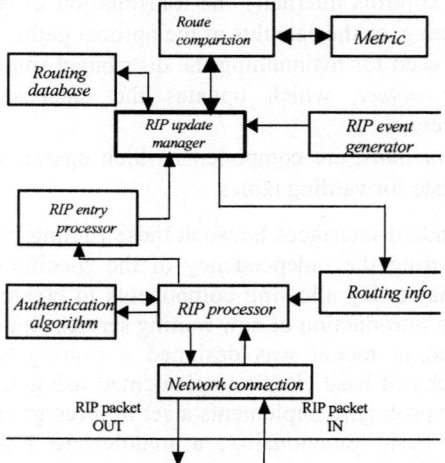

Fig. 2. The programmable RIP

The interfaces were written using Interface Definition Language (IDL)[8] and compiled using Orbacus 4.1.1 over NT platform. Since the functions of a router are over a wide range, we have provided interfaces for the following modules: the retrieval of information about host and interfaces, and IP route additions and deletions which result in kernel routing table updates. We also intend to extend our project to offer support for other routing protocols covering BGP, OSPF. An extract from the idle definition file for the RIP update manager:

```
struct rip_interface
{
/* RIP is enabled on this interface. */
   int enable_network;
   int enable_interface;
   /* RIP is running on this interface. */
   int running;
   /* RIP version control. */
   int ri_send;
   int ri_receive;
};
interface rip_interface
{
void rip_interface_clean ();
void rip_interface_reset ();
}
```

3 Conclusions

In our work, we have identified similarities between a numbers of routing protocols and designed a routing development kit and middleware for programming routing protocols. We have argued for the construction of routing protocols by extending and combining a set of components, hierarchically organized. This leads to an open programmable design that can greatly facilitate the design and deployment of new routing architectures. We have proposed a set of components and have outlined their interaction in order to construct a routing protocol. By being able to dynamically program routing protocols we can evaluate and change their structure in a dynamic manner, as is needed.

References

1. Lazar, A.A., : Programming Telecommunication Networks, *IEEE Network,* vol.11, no.5, September/October 1997.
2. Yemini, Y., and Da Silva, S, "Towards Programmable Networks", *IFIP/IEEE International Workshop on Distributed Systems: Operations and Management*, L'Aquila, Italy, October,(1996)
3. Malkin, M. ,:IP version 2- IETF Network Working Group RFC 1723, (1994.)
4. Merwe J. et al., "The Tempest: A Practical Framework for Network Programmability", *IEEE Network Magazine, 12(3)*, (1998)
5. Merit GateD Consortium, http://www.gated.net
6. Moy, J.,:OSPF version 2- IETF Network Working Group RFC 2328, April 1998
7. Staccatos, V., Kounavis, E., Campbell, A.,: Sphere- A binding model and middleware for routing protocols, *OPENARCH' 01*, Alaska, April 27-28, 2001.
8. www.omg.org
9. Vinoski, S. "CORBA: Integrating Diverse Applications Within Distributed Heterogeneous Environments," *IEEE Communications Magazine*, vol. 14, February 1997.

Deferred Incremental Refresh of XML Materialized Views*

Hyunchul Kang and JaeGuk Lim**

Dept. of Computer Science and Engineering, Chung-Ang University
Seoul, 156-756, Korea
{hckang,jglim}@dblab.cse.cau.ac.kr

Abstract. The view mechanism can provide the user with an appropriate portion of database through data filtering and integration. In the Web era where information proliferates, the view concept is also useful for XML documents in a Web-based information system. Views are often materialized for query performance, and in that case, their consistency needs to be maintained against the updates of the underlying data. They can be either recomputed or incrementally refreshed by reflecting only the relevant updates. In this paper, we address the issues in deferred incremental refresh of XML materialized views.

1 Introduction

In database systems, the view concept has been a useful and effective mechanism in accessing and controlling data. It is related to many aspects of data management and database design. Among others, one of the most important applications of the view is information filtering and integration, functionality which is getting even more crucial for information engineering in today's Web-based computing environment where vast amount of heterogeneous information proliferates every day.

Since XML emerged as a standard for Web documents, many research issues in XML data management have been investigated. The view concept is also useful for XML data [2][4][5]. For the frequently submitted query against XML documents, its expression can be defined as an XML view for later convenient and efficient reuse. For example, the frequently accessed portions out of huge collection of XML documents in the XML warehouse could be defined as views and possibly maintained as the materialized ones for query performance. Recently, a dynamic large-scale warehouse for XML documents of Web, out of Xyleme project [8] at INRIA, France, which provides sophisticated database-like services like querying, update control, and data integration has already been in commercial service [9].

---

* This work was supported by grant No. R01-2000-00272 from the Basic Research Program of the Korea Science & Engineering Foundation.
** Current address: R&D center, Tong Yang Systems Corp., Seoul, 138-130, Korea.

This paper address the issues involved in management of XML materialized views. When XML views are materialized, their consistency needs to be maintained against the updates of the underlying documents either by recomputing or by incrementally refreshing the outdated portion of the materialization. The latter can be done either immediately after the source document update occurs or in a deferred way. In this paper, we focus on deferred incremental refresh of XML materialized views.

The problem of incremental refresh of materialized views received much attention in relational database systems [3]. The same problem was investigated for the views over semistructured data [1][10][7] in the context of semistructured DBMS. In this paper, we investigate the problem with the XML repository built on top of a relational or an object-relational DBMS instead of the semistructured one. Such an approach deserves thorough investigation because of its pragmatic importance.

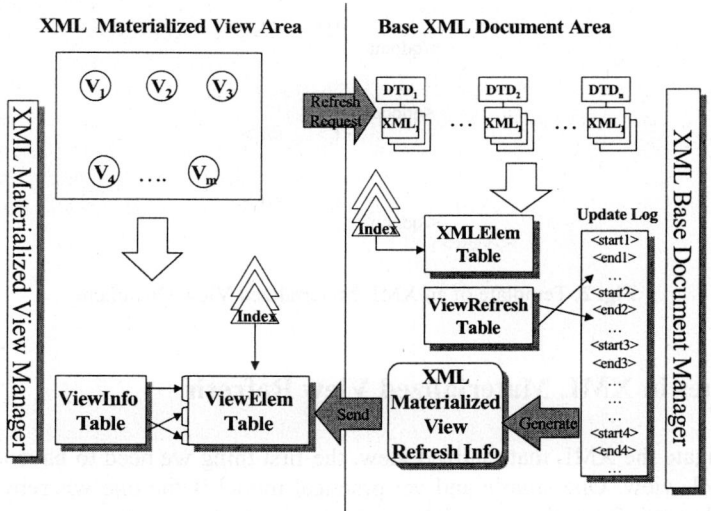

Fig. 1. Framework of XML Materialized View Refresh

2   Framework of XML Materialized View Refresh

Fig. 1 shows a framework of deferred incremental refresh of XML materialized views using a DBMS. The XML repository consists of two areas: the underlying base XML document area and the XML materialized view area. The former is managed by the base document manager, and the latter by the view manager. In the base document area, the DTDs and the XML documents conforming to them are stored. Document indexing is provided for fast access to them. In the view area, the materialized views and the information on the views such as their definition are stored. Indexing is also provided for fast retrieval and refresh of the materialized views. Each update done to the base XML documents is recorded in the update log chronologically for deferred incremental refresh of materialized views. View refresh is done when the view is requested by an application. That is, the updates are neither immediately nor periodically propagated to the relevant views. Such a materialized view access model is the one employed in [6]. The scenario for retrieval of an XML materialized view is as follows: When view V is requested, the view manager requests the document manager to send it the information necessary for V's refresh. Then, the document manager examines the update log to figure out which updates done to the base documents thus far are relevant to V, generates the view refresh information, and sends it to the view manager. Now the view manager refreshes V as directed by the received view refresh information, and then provides up-to-date V.

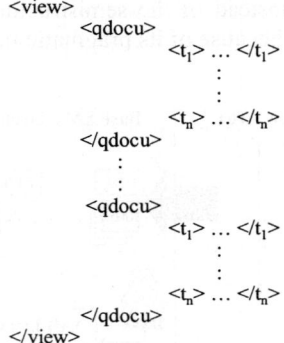

Fig. 2. Template of an XML Materialized View Document

3 Issues in XML Materialized View Refresh

To investigate the XML materialized view, the first thing we need to have is a model of the XML view. One simple and yet practical model is the one whereby an XML view is derived from the base XML documents that conform to the same (and therefore, a single) DTD, and defined by an XML query language expression. The components of XML view definition include the filtering condition, the elements against which the condition is specified, the target elements, and the information for query result restructuring. Complexity of XML view definition allowed directly affects the process of view refresh. Complex views require more work than simpler ones both in checking an update's relevance to them and in generating their refresh information. For deferred incremental refresh of views to be effective, it is desirable to perform both of the above-mentioned tasks with no or least access to the source data. The next thing we need to have is a scheme for representation of XML view materialization. One scheme is to represent the XML materialized view as an XML document. Fig. 2 shows the template of an XML materialized view document. Each element 'qdocu' which stands for 'the base document qualified for the view' is for a base document that satisfies the view's filtering condition, and its subelements 't_i', $i = 1, ..., n$, are the target elements of the view retrieved from that particular base document.

Further issues to be resolved based on the model of XML materialized views such as the one described above include the following: First, the database schema for storing not just XML documents but materialized views and other information for their refresh needs to be designed. Secondly, the post optimization in generating the view refresh information with the deferred view refresh policy needs to be considered. Once the view refresh information is generated by scanning the update log, it could be optimized by merging the related refresh information. For example, if an element of a newly inserted document is modified later, then their refresh information can be merged so that the modified value may be inserted instead of the original one. Thirdly, a scheme for efficient logging of updates needs to be devised. Especially, we need to avoid the log records of very large size when inserting a large document or modifying a large element. The logged values of elements are redundantly stored in the corresponding base documents. As such, some referencing mechanism where a log record points to its relevant portion of the base document, is desirable. The penalty for that is on the process of checking the update's relevance to a view, which inevitably requires access to the base documents. Finally and most importantly, the efficient algorithms to check relevance between an update and a view, to generate view refresh information for the relevant pairs, and to reflect the refresh information to the view materialization should be carefully devised. The complexity of these algorithms depends on the granularity of XML document updates as well as on the complexity of view definition allowed.

4 Concluding Remarks

We are currently working on development of an XML repository system that supports XML materialized views using an object-relational DBMS. The performance of the deferred incremental refresh scheme is compared with that of view recomputation. One of the most influencing performance parameters is the amount of logged updates to be examined for deferred incremental refresh. The preliminary results show that for a large collection of XML documents of moderate size and a practical view, the deferred incremental refresh scheme outperforms the recomputation counterpart as long as the proportion of the base XML document updates is less than about 30%.

References

1. S. Abiteboul et al., "Incremental Maintenance for Materialized Views over Semistructured Data," *Proc. Int'l Conf. on VLDB*, 1998, pp. 38-49.
2. S. Abiteboul, "On Views and XML," *Proc. ACM Symp. on Principles of Database System*, 1999, pp. 1-9.
3. A. Gupta and I. Mumick, "Maintenance of Materialized Views: Problems, Techniques, and Applications," *IEEE Data Eng. Bulletin*, Vol. 18, No. 2, Jun. 1995, pp. 3-18.
4. S. Kim and H. Kang, "XML Query Processing Using Materialized Views," *Proc. Int'l Conf. on Internet Computing*, Jun. 2001, pp. 111-117.

5. Y. Papakonstantinou and V. Vianu, "DTD Inference for Views of XML Data," *Proc. of 19th ACM SIGACT-SIGMOD-SIGART Symp. on PODS*, 2000.
6. N. Roussopoulos, "An Incremental Access Method for ViewCache: Concept, Algorithms, and Cost Analysis," *ACM Trans. on Database Systems*, Vol. 16, No. 3, Sep. 1991, pp. 535-563.
7. D. Suciu, "Query Decomposition and View Maintenance for Query Languages for Unstructured Data," *Proc. Int'l Conf. on VLDB*, 1996, pp. 227-238.
8. L. Xyleme, "A Dynamic Warehouse for XML Data of the Web," *IEEE Data Engineering Bulletin*, Vo. 24, No. 2, Sep. 2001, pp. 40-47.
9. Xyleme Home Page, *http://www.xyleme.com*.
10. Y. Zhuge and H. Garcia-Molina, "Graph Structured Views and Their Incremental Maintenance," *Proc. Int'l Conf. on Data Engineering*, 1998, pp. 116-125.

Requirements for Hypermedia Development Methods: A Survey of Outstanding Methods

Susana Montero, Paloma Díaz, and Ignacio Aedo

Laboratorio DEI. Dpto. de Informática, Universidad Carlos III de Madrid
Avda. de la Universidad 30. 28911 Leganés, Spain
smontero@inf.uc3m.es
pdp@inf.uc3m.es
aedo@ia.uc3m.es
http://www.dei.inf.uc3m.es

Abstract. The aim of this paper is to present a framework of requirements to survey design methods for hypermedia systems. Such requirements are taken from software engineering as well as from hypermedia engineering fields. Finally, these requirements are applied to a set of outstanding design methods in order to identify both their good qualities and their lacks.

1 Introduction

Hypermedia systems, and specially web applications, have been extremely and ungently demanded in different areas. The rush to develop applications has led most developers to skip the conceptual design phase and directly go to the implementation stage, producing applications of poor quality, usability and maintainability.

Such tools do not pay attention to intrinsic features of hypermedia systems such as sophisticated navigational structures, interactive behaviours and multimedia compositions. Moreover, another feature which should be taken into account is security, since hypermedia applications are accessed by different users with different purposes [4].

Many research and development groups have proposed a series of methods which are used as a guideline during the design process.

In this paper, we analyse some of these methods such as HDM, RMM, OOHDM, WSDM, Autoweb, WebML and OO-H method. This survey starts defining a framework of requirements to cover the modeling space of design methods for hypermedia systems from the literature and the experience of our group in the design of this kind of systems [4,5]. On the basis of this framework, the methods previously mentioned have been evaluated to assess their modeling capabilities. This survey can be also useful for novice hypermedia developers to choose the most suitable method according to their needs.

2 A Framework for Hypermedia System Design Methods

To analyse different design methods, it is necessary to establish a framework that determines what elements, activities and design views must be taken into account by a method. In our case, this framework is determined by a set of requirements gathered both from the software and hypermedia engineering fields.

2.1 Requirements Derived from Software Engineering

The experience gained in years of research in the software field about modeling techniques, methods and methodologies can help to improve hypermedia development [11]. We borrow some features from this area, but do not consider issues such as project planning or project management since our survey will be centred on the design of hypermedia systems. According to [1,15], any design software method must:

- Describe a formal process to guide the development of a software application.
- Contain a model to describe the real world and transfer it to a physical system.
- Provide the designer with products to specify functional, non-functional and usability requirements.
- Include validation rules for each design product.
- Maintain relations of integrity among the different design products.
- Allow design reuse.
- Count on software support tools to help in the development process.

2.2 Requirements Derived from Hypermedia Technology

It is necessary to stress the following requirements took from hypermedia engineering [3,13]:

- Allow to describe the problem domain in terms of hypermedia components: nodes, contents, links and anchors.
- Provide tasks to model the navigation structure, both the links structure and the navigation tools (visual maps, active indexes, guided tours, marks, footprints and backtracking mechanisms).
- Organize and harmonize multimedia contents.
- Model the different types of users.
- Provide conceptual tools to formalize security policies.
- Allow to describe the interactive behaviour of hypermedia systems.
- Allow a bottom-up design.
- Make possible the evaluation of the system utility.

3 Methods under Consideration

It is difficult to find a hypermedia design method that is appropriated for the development of any hypermedia system due to rapid change in this technology and the mix of different techniques and fields (database, object oriented, hypermedia, web, ...) which have to be applied. However, the methods here presented are a proof of the concern about covering process modeling of hypermedia systems. Those methods are HDM [8], RMM [10], OOHDM [14], WSDM [6], Autoweb [7], WebML [2], (OO-H) method [9].

Table 1 presents the summary of analysis of these methods performed using the framework. The left part enumerates the software and hypermedia requirements and on the right side their rate of performance is shown for each method. Three kinds of notations have been used: C, if the method fulfills the whole of requirement; P, if the method allows it partially; and N when the requirement are not dealt by the method.

Table 1. Comparison between requirements and methods

Requirements for design methods of hypermedia systems	HDM	RMM	OOHDM	WSDM	Autoweb	WebML	OO-H
process modeling	P	C	C	C	C	C	P
based on a model	C	C	P	P	C	P	P
functional, no-functional and usability requirements	P	P	P	P	P	P	P
validation rules for each product	N	N	N	N	N	P	N
integrity relationships among phases	N	N	N	N	N	N	N
design reuse	C	N	C	N	N	P	C
software support tools	C	P	P	N	C	C	C
hypermedia components	C	C	C	P	C	C	C
navigation structure	C	C	C	P	C	C	C
organization and harmonization of multimedia contents	C	P	P	N	P	P	N
user modeling	N	N	C	C	N	C	N
formalization of security policies	N	N	N	N	N	N	N
description of interactive behaviour	C	N	C	N	N	C	C
bottom-up design	C	C	N	N	N	N	N
evaluation of system utility	C	C	N	N	N	N	N

From this table, the following conclusions can be observed. On the one hand, all of these methods are making an effort to establish the steps and techniques to get a scalable, maintainable and usable application. They contain a model to represent the essence of the design using hypermedia components and navigation structures in a automatic way. Moreover, methods mention the interactive behaviour, although they do not make clear how to specify or use it.

Some weak points are also revealed during this survey including:

- **No-functional and usability characteristics**. These kinds of characteristics could improve the quality and efficiency of the system.
- **Validation and integrity rules**. This kind of rules help determine the correctness and the completeness of design and the integrity of the designed elements.
- **Design reuse**. Interface and structure patterns, as well as design components allow us to reuse designers' experience.

- **Content modeling.** It allows us to represent different data views in addition to handling aesthetic aspects with synchronization and alignment of contents.
- **User modeling.** This modeling allows us to handle system adaptability in a conceptual way.
- **Security modeling.** This characteristic allows us to define security constraints and apply access control mechanisms to different system users.
- **Bottom-up design.** This design way together with a top-down design allow a better feedback among stages [12].
- **Evaluation stage.** This stage could help improve the utility and usability of the application and make possible a development more incremental and iterative.

4 Conclusions

This work is a glance into process modeling of hypermedia systems in order to observe and measure the current state of this area. Some ideas can be taken from it to identify new research directions. HDM is the method that covers more requirements, in spite of being the oldest one. So, designers should have it as a basis for their researches. Moreover, both hypermedia and web methods should put more stress on characteristics such as multimedia compositions, user adaptability, security politicies and evaluation mechanisms which are more particular of hypermedia systems.

Finally, the requirements here presented can be used as a framework to compare hypermedia methods.

Acknowledgements

This work is supported by "Dirección General de Investigación del Ministerio de Ciencia y Tecnología" (TIC2000-0402)."

References

1. Avison, D.E. and Fitzgerald, G. *Information systems development: techniques and tools*. Blackwell Scientific Publications, Oxford, 1995.
2. Ceri, S., Fraternali, P. and Bongio, A. Web modeling language (WebML): a modeling language for designing web sites. *WWW9 / Computer Networks*, 33(1-6):137–157, 2000.
3. Díaz, P., Aedo, I. and Montero, S. Ariadne, a development method for hypermedia. In *proceedings of Dexa 2001*, volume 2113 of *Lecture Notes in Computer Science*, pages 764–774, 2001.
4. Díaz, P., Aedo, I. and Panetsos, F. Modelling security policies in hypermedia and web-based applications. In *Web Engineering: Managing diversity and complexity of web application development*, volume 2016, pages 90–104. Springer, 2001.

5. Díaz, P., Aedo, I. and Panetsos, F. Modelling the dynamic behaviour of hypermedia applications. *IEEE Transactions on Software Engineering*, 27(6):550–572, June 2001.
6. De Troyer, O. and Leune, C. WSDM: a user centered design method for web sites. In *Proceedings of the 7th International World-Wide Web Conference*, 1998.
7. Fraternali, P. and Paolini, P. Model-driven development of web applications: the autoweb system. *ACM Transactions on Office Information Systems*, 18(4):323–282, 2000.
8. Garzotto, F., Paolini, P. and Schwbe, D. HDM- a model-based approach to hypertext application design. *ACM Transactions on Information Systems*, 11(1):1–26, 1993.
9. Gómez, J. Cachero, C. and Pastor, O. Conceptual modeling of device-independent web applications. *IEEE MultiMedia*, 8(2):26–39, 2001.
10. Isakowitz, T. and Kamis, A. and Koufaris, M. The extended RMM methodology for web publishing. Technical Report IS98 -18, Center for Research on Information Systems, 1998.
11. Lowe, D. and Webby, R. The impact process modelling project work in progress. In *1st International Workshop on Hypermedia Development Held in conjunction with Hypertext'98*, Pittsburgh, PA, USA, June 20-24 1998.
12. Nanard, J. and Nanard, M. Hypertext design environments and the hypertext design process. *Comm. of the ACM*, 38(8):49–56, 1995.
13. Retschitzegger, W. and Schwinger, W. Towards modeling of dataweb applications - a requirements' perspective. In *Proc. of the Americas Conferenc on Information Systems (AMCIS) Long Beach California*, volume 1, 2000.
14. Schwabe, D. and Rossi, G. An object oriented approach to web-based application design. *Theory and practice of object systems*, 4(4):207–225, 1998.
15. Sommerville, I. and Sawyer, P. *Requirements engineering: a good practice guide*. Wiley, Chichester, 1997.

An Approach for Synergically Carrying out Intensional and Extensional Integration of Data Sources Having Different Formats

Luigi Pontieri[1], Domenico Ursino[2], and Ester Zumpano[3]

[1] ISI, Consiglio Nazionale delle Ricerche
Via Pietro Bucci, 87036 Rende (CS), Italy
pontieri@si.deis.unical.it
[2] DIMET, Università di Reggio Calabria
Via Graziella, 89060 Reggio Calabria, Italy
ursino@ing.unirc.it
[3] DEIS, Università della Calabria
Via Pietro Bucci, 87036 Rende (CS), Italy
zumpano@si.deis.unical.it

Abstract. In this paper we propose a data source integration approach capable of uniformly handling different source formats, ranging from databases to XML documents and other semi-structured data. The proposed approach consists of two components, performing intensional and extensional integration, respectively; these are strictly coupled, since they use related models for representing intensional and extensional information and are synergic in their behaviour.

1 Introduction

The activity of integrating different data sources involves two different levels, namely the intensional and the extensional ones. As a matter of fact, these two forms of integration consider two different, yet complementary, aspects of the problem. In more detail, *Intensional Integration* [1,4,5] concerns with the activity of combining *schemes* of involved data sources for obtaining a global scheme representing all of them. *Extensional Integration* [2,3] is the activity of producing (either virtual or materialized) data representing all *instances* present in the involved data sources. In [5] an *intensional integration* technique, based on a model, called *SDR-Network* [6], capable of uniformly handling data sources with different representation formats, has been presented. In this paper we propose a technique for carrying out *extensional integration* of data sources with different formats. In order to uniformly represent and handle instances of involved data sources, our technique exploits a logic model, called *E-SDR-Network*, which is the counterpart, at the extensional level, of the SDR-Network conceptual model. The definition of an extensional integration technique, whose behaviour and reference model are strictly related to those ones relative to the intensional integration technique proposed in [5], allows us to obtain, in the whole, an approach consisting of two components, synergically carrying out the intensional and the extensional integration, respectively. Interestingly enough, our extensional integration technique is also capable of handling null or unknown values. In addition, it is able to reconstruct, at the extensional level, the information sources which an integrated E-SDR-Network has been derived from; this important feature is directly inherited from the specific properties of the E-SDR-Network model. Last, but not the least, our technique is capable of producing consistent query answers from inconsistent data.

2 The E-SDR-Network Logic Model

The E-SDR-Network logic model extends, at the extensional level, the SDR-Network conceptual model [6], conceived to operate at the intensional one. An E-SDR-Network $E\_Net(DS)$ representing, at the extensional level, a data source DS, is a rooted directed labeled graph:

$$E\_Net(DS) = \langle E\_NS(DS), E\_AS(DS)\rangle = \langle E\_NS_A(DS) \cup E\_NS_C(DS), E\_AS(DS)\rangle$$

Here, $E\_NS(DS)$ is a set of nodes, each representing an instance of a concept of DS. Nodes in $E\_NS(DS)$ are subdivided in two subsets, namely, the set of *atomic nodes* $E\_NS_A(DS)$ and the set of *complex nodes* $E\_NS_C(DS)$. A node is atomic if it has no outgoing arcs, complex otherwise. Each atomic node $N_A \in E\_NS_A(DS)$ is an instance of an atomic node of the corresponding SDR-Network and represents a value; it is identified by a pair $[N, V]$, where N is the name of the SDR-Network node which N_A is an instance of, and V is the value which N_A represents. Each complex node $N_C \in E\_NS_C(DS)$ is an instance of a complex node in the corresponding SDR-Network; it is identified by a pair $[N, I]$, where N is the name of the SDR-Network node which N_C is an instance of, and I is an identifier allowing to uniquely single out N_C among all nodes of $E\_NS_C(DS)$.

$E\_AS(DS)$ denotes a set of arcs; an E-SDR-Network arc represents a relationship between two E-SDR-Network nodes; in addition, it is an instance of an SDR-Network arc. An E-SDR-Network arc A from S to T, labeled L_{ST} and denoted by $\langle S, T, L_{ST}\rangle$, indicates that the instance represented by S is related to the instance denoted by T. S is called the *source node* of A whereas T represents its *target node*. At most one arc may exist from S to T. The label L_{ST} of A has been conceived for supporting the integration task. In particular, L_{ST} is a set; if $E\_Net(DS)$ does not derive from an integration task then L_{ST} is equal to $\{E\_Net(DS)\}$. Vice versa, if $E\_Net(DS)$ has been obtained from the integration of some E-SDR-Networks, then A derives from the merge of some E-SDR-Network arcs, each belonging to one of the E-SDR-Networks that have been integrated[1]; in this case L_{ST} is equal to the set of E-SDR-Networks containing the arcs which have been merged to obtain A. L_{ST} plays a relevant role in the integration task since it stores information about the original sources of

---

[1] Observe that, for some of these E-SDR-Networks, it could not exist an arc taking part to the construction of A.

integrated data. It provides the extensional integration technique with the capability of reconstructing the original contents of data sources involved in the integration task; as we pointed out in the Introduction, this is one of the most interesting features of our technique.

Observe that any data source can be generally represented, at the extensional level, as a set of instances and a set of relationships among instances. Since E-SDR-Network nodes and arcs are well suited to represent both instances and their relationships, the E-SDR-Network can be used to uniformly model, at the extensional level, most existing data sources.

3 Extensional Integration Algorithm

Our Extensional Integration Algorithm takes in input: *(i)* a global SDR-Network SDR_G, obtained by applying the Intensional Integration Algorithm, described in [5], on two SDR-Networks SDR_1 and SDR_2;*(ii)* two E-SDR-Networks $ESDR_1$ and $ESDR_2$ such that $ESDR_1$ (resp., $ESDR_2$) is an E-SDR-Network corresponding to SDR_1 (resp. SDR_2). It returns a global E-SDR-Network $ESDR_G$ which corresponds, at the extensional level, to the global SDR-Network SDR_G. The algorithm first examines all SDR_G nodes; let N_G be one of them. If N_G derives from the merge of two nodes N_1 of SDR_1 and N_2 of SDR_2, the algorithm determines the set of nodes $ENSet_1$ of $ESDR_1$ and $ENSet_2$ of $ESDR_2$ corresponding, at the extensional level, to N_1 and N_2; then it transforms all nodes of $ENSet_1$ and $ENSet_2$ so that they become instances of N_G in $ESDR_G$. If there exist two nodes $EN_1 \in ENSet_1$ and $EN_2 \in ENSet_2$ representing the same real world instance, they are merged for obtaining a unique $ESDR_G$ node EN_G being an instance of the SDR_G node N_G; arcs incoming to and outgoing from EN_1 and EN_2 are transferred to EN_G. If N_G derives from only one node N of either SDR_1 or SDR_2, the algorithm determines the set of nodes $ENSet$ corresponding, at the extensional level, to N and transforms each node $EN_i \in ENSet$ so that it becomes an instance EN_G of N_G in $ESDR_G$. Arcs incoming to and outgoing from EN_i are transferred to EN_G. By applying these operations to all SDR_G nodes, the algorithm constructs all nodes and arcs of $ESDR_G$. After these operations, it could be possible that two arcs exist in $ESDR_G$ from a node EN_S to a node EN_T; if this happens, they must be merged. The Extensional Integration Algorithm can be encoded as follows:

Algorithm for the Extensional Integration of two data sources
Input: a global SDR-Network SDR_G, obtained from the integration of two
  SDR-Networks SDR_1 and SDR_2; two E-SDR-Networks $ESDR_1$ and
  $ESDR_2$ corresponding to SDR_1 and SDR_2, resp.;
Output: a global E-SDR-Network $ESDR_G$;
var
  $NSet$: a set of SDR-Network nodes; N_G: an SDR-Network node;
  $ENSet$: a set of E-SDR-Network nodes;
  EN_S, EN_T: an E-SDR-Network node;
  $EASet$: a set of E-SDR-Network arcs; A_1, A_2: an SDR-Network arc;

```
begin
    NSet := Get_Nodes(SDR_G);
    for each N_G ∈ NSet do
        Construct_Node_Instances(N_G, ESDR_1, ESDR_2, ESDR_G);
    ENSet := E_Get_Nodes(ESDR_G);
    for each EN_S ∈ ENSet do
        for each EN_T ∈ ENSet do begin
            EASet := E_Get_Arcs(EN_S, EN_T);
            if (EASet = {A_1, A_2}) then E_Merge_Arcs(A_1, A_2, ESDR_G)
        end
end
```

The presence of arc labels in the E-SDR-Network logic model provides our algorithm with the capability to reconstruct, at the extensional level, the information sources which an integrated E-SDR-Network has been derived from. This is an important feature "per se", but it becomes even more relevant in that it allows to produce consistent query answers from inconsistent data. Indeed, the user can be requested to associate a reliability degree with each data source; whenever she/he poses a query involving inconsistent data, derived from different sources, those coming from the source which she/he has considered more reliable are taken. Finally, our algorithm is capable to handle null or unknown values. Indeed, whenever two complex instances, say EN_1 and EN_2, relative to two E-SDR-Networks $ESDR_1$ and $ESDR_2$, and representing the same real world instance, are merged for obtaining a global instance EN_G of $ESDR_G$, if EN_1 (resp., EN_2) has a property, say P, having a null or unknown value, and EN_2 (resp., EN_1) has a specific value, say V, for P, then V will appear as the value assumed by P into EN_G. Interestingly enough, our technique allows to substitute the null or unknown value, which P had in EN_1 (resp., EN_2), with the value V, which P assumed in EN_2 (resp., EN_1). In this way it is able to restore the missing information relative to a given source taking part to the integration task.

References

1. S. Castano, V. De Antonellis, and S. De Capitani di Vimercati. Global viewing of heterogeneous data sources. *Transactions on Data and Knowledge Engineering*, 13(2), 2001.
2. Y. Kanza, W. Nutt, and Y. Sagiv. Queries with incomplete answers over semistructured data. In *Proc. of Symposium on Principles of Database Systems*, pages 227–236.
3. M. Liu, T.W. Ling, and T. Guang. Integration of semistructured data with partial and inconsistent information. In *Proc. of International Database Engineering and Applications Symposium*, pages 44–52.
4. J. Madhavan, P.A. Bernstein, and E. Rahm. Generic schema matching with cupid. In *Proc. of International Conference on Very Large Data Bases*, pages 49–58.
5. D. Rosaci, G. Terracina, and D. Ursino. A semi-automatic technique for constructing a global representation of information sources having different formats and structures. In *Proc. of International Conference on Database and Expert Systems Applications*, pages 734–743.

6. G. Terracina and D. Ursino. Deriving synonymies and homonymies of object classes in semi-structured information sources. In *Proc. of International Conference on Management of Data*, pages 21–32.

DSQL – An SQL for Structured Documents
Extended Abstract

Arijit Sengupta[1] and Mehmet Dalkilic[2]

[1] Department of A&IS, Kelley School of Business, Indiana University
Bloomington, IN 47405, USA
asengupt@indiana.edu
http://www.kelley.iu.edu/asengupt/
[2] School of Informatics, Indiana University
Bloomington, IN 47405, USA
dalkilic@indiana.edu

Abstract. SQL has been the result of years of query language research, and has many desirable properties. We introduce DSQL - a language that is based on a theoretical foundation of a declarative language (document calculus) and an equivalent procedural language (document algebra). The outcome of this design is a language that looks and feels like SQL, yet is powerful enough to perform a vast range of queries on structured documents (currently focused on XML). The design of the language is independent of document formats, so the capability of the language will not change if the underlying markup language were changed. In spite of its familiarity and simplicity, we show that this language has many desirable properties, and is a good candidate for a viable query language for XML. This paper presents a canonical form of DSQL, showing only the properties of the language that affect the complexity of the language. Remarkably, SQL = core DSQL for flat input and outputs.

1 Introduction

We propose an extension of SQL called the Document SQL (DSQL) as a query language for XML. Interestingly, DSQL maintains its "roots" by being able to perform its role as SQL on flat structures that represent tables. DSQL possesses a number of important elements. DSQL, like SQL, gives data independence, freeing users from having to write procedural components. DSQL, like SQL, is simple. And since SQL is the *de facto* standard, learning DSQL requires substantially less effort than learning an entirely new language. DSQL has the potential to be optimized–a benefit of SQL that has made it so commercially popular. Lastly, DSQL is based on formal design principles which means its semantics is well-understood.

There is a precedence for using SQL, *e.g.*, [1], demonstrating various levels of success in their respective fields by relying on the familiarity of SQL. One of the most well-known examples is OQL (Object Query Language) [2], a query language for Object-Oriented database systems that is extension of SQL capable of handling the nuances of the Object-Oriented database model.

There are a number of converging design objectives for an XML query language in this paper. We briefly describe three here. First is a language that is based on a well-known, well-accepted formal semantics. Second is a language that does not rely on the underlying data structure, thus exhibiting data independence. Third, is the applicability of well-known query language design principles like low complexity, closure, and non-Turing completeness.

2 DSQL Specification

W3C (http://www.w3.org) is currently involved in an effort towards the query language XQuery which has been presented through a series of related W3C recommendations. XML has been widely recognized as the next generation of markup language for the Internet. There is necessarily a need for querying XML. We now describe the language characteristics of DSQL. DSQL is different from SQL primarily in DSQL's ability to search along paths and restructure data. Most omitted features are exactly the same as standard SQL. The basic syntax and an example of a DSQL query are shown below.

```
SELECT  output_structure
FROM    input_specification          SELECT  result<B.title>
WHERE   conditions                   FROM    bibdb..book B
grouping_specs                       WHERE   B.title = 'Extending SQL'
ordering_specs
```

As in SQL, only the SELECT and the FROM clauses are required. The other clauses are optional. Also, multiple SELECT queries can be combined using the standard set operations (Union, Intersect, Minus). The SELECT clause allows the creation of structures with arbitrary levels of nesting. The FROM clause utilizes XPath to retrieve trees, subtrees, *etc.*. The WHERE conditions in DSQL are similar to those in SQL. The main difference in semantics is due to paths, *i.e.*, all expressions in DSQL are path expressions, so operators are often set operators.

3 Comparative Examples

The language proposed in this paper is capable of performing most of the queries in the W3C XQuery use case that are independent of XML-specific issues such as namespaces. We show three pairwise equivalent queries to compare the two languages, XQuery (left) and DSQL (right).

Query 1. List books published by Addison-Wesley after 1991, including their year and title.

```
<bib>
{ FOR $b IN                                  SELECT  bib<B.title>
   document("http://www.bn.com")/bib/book    FROM    BN.bib.book  B
  WHERE $b/publisher = "Addison-Wesley"      WHERE   B.publisher =
     AND $b/@year > 1991                             "Addision-Wesley"
  RETURN                                     AND     B.attval(year) > 1991
    <book year={$b/@year}>{$b/title}</book>
}</bib>
```

Query 2 . Create a flat list of all the title-author pairs, with each pair enclosed in a "result" element.

```
<results>
{ FOR $b IN
    document("http://www.bn.com")/bib/book,
  $t IN $b/title,                    SELECT results<B.title,
  $a IN $b/author                            B.author>
  RETURN                             FROM    BN.bib.book
  <result> { $t } { $a } </result>
} </results>
```

Query 3. For each book in the bibliography, list the title and authors, grouped inside a "result" element.

```
<results>
{ FOR $b IN
    document("http://www.bn.com")/bib/book
  RETURN                             SELECT   result<B.title,
    <result>                                  B.author>
      { $b/title }                   FROM     BN.bib.book
      { FOR $a IN $b/author          GROUP BY B.title
        RETURN $a }
    </result>
} </results>
```

4 Important Observations and Contributions

DSQL is derived from a calculus (DC) and has an equivalent algebra (DA) that are analogous to the Relational calculus and algebra for SQL. Among the more important properties of DC and DA are: (i) the calculus and algebra are semantically equivalent; (ii) they are safe and (iii) they are in PTIME.

The primary contribution of this work is based on our results of semantic and syntactic equivalence of DSQL with SQL. This implies any SQL query would run unchanged on the structured equivalent of the tabular data, and thus systems capable of processing SQL can seamlessly integrate DSQL (and hence structured querying) into the existing infrastructure. Although many languages have been proposed for XML, no language to our knowledge has this property. A summary of all the results from the language are presented below.

1. **DSQL properties** Because of the equivalence with the calculus and algebra, DSQL is implicitly safe, closed, and in PTIME.
2. **DSQL Macros** DSQL can be augmented with macros that allow structuring operations that do not change any complexity, such as decision and link traversal. IF-ELSE queries can be implemented using `union`, and finite link traversal can be performed using `exists`.
3. **No ordering ambiguity** The sequential nature of documents is built into DSQL. A single document is always sequential, but a document is fragmented using a path expression creates unordered elements (since the result of a path expression is a set).

4. **Set-Atom ambiguity** All non-atomic expressions (queries and path expressions) in DSQL are set expressions, so there is no ambiguity in comparison of different expressions.
5. **Similarity with Relational domain** Because of the analogous nature of DSQL with SQL, most of the language processing methods work unchanged. For example, all the optimization equalities hold in DSQL, which indicates that the same optimization principles will be applicable in processing DSQL queries.
6. **DSQL=SQL for flat structures** For flat structures as input, and intended flat structures as output, DSQL queries are exactly the same as the corresponding SQL queries.
7. **Merging relational and document databases** DSQL can easily support queries which include local documents, remote documents via a URL, and relational tables all in the same FROM clause. This is an easy yet elegant technique for incorporating distributed heterogeneous databases in this query language.
8. **Implementation architecture** We built a prototype implementation of DSQL in DocBase[3] that also demonstrates the applicability of the concepts described here.

5 Future Research Issues

A number of issues need to be handled in order to apply DSQL in XML. Specific XML features (such as namespaces, attributes, etc.) are not included in DSQL because of its markup-independent design. XML-specific features can easily be added on to the language in order to satisfy all the W3C XML Query requirements. DSQL does not support recursion, and we have no intention of supporting direct unbounded recursion in the language. Similar to SQL, DSQL can be embedded in a host language or a 4GL-type language for such language features. We are also in the process of performing an empirical study comparing DSQL with XQuery based on a human-factors analysis involving users. See [4] for a full version of this paper.

References

1. Mendelzon, A., Mihaila, G., Milo, T.: Querying the world wide web. International Journal of Digital Libraries **1** (1997) 68–88
2. Cluet, S.: Designing OQL: Allowing objects to be queried. Information Systems **23** (1998) 279–305
3. Sengupta, A.: DocBase - A Database Environment for Structured Documents. PhD thesis, Indiana University (1997)
4. Sengupta, A., Dalkilic, M.: DSQL - an SQL for structured documents (http://www.kelley.iu.edu/ardennis/wp/tr108-1.pdf). Technical Report TR108-1, Indiana University (2001)

A Comparative Study of Ontology Languages and Tools

Xiaomeng Su* and Lars Ilebrekke

Norwegian University of Science and Technology (NTNU)
N-7491, Trondheim, Norway
xiaomeng@idi.ntnu.no
ilebrekk@stud.ntnu.no

Abstract. There are many languages and tools for constructing ontologies. In this paper we survey and compare different ontology languages and tools by the aid of an evaluation framework. A semiotic framework is adopted to aid the evaluation.We hope the evluation results can be used in helping user to choose suitable language and tool in the task of onotloy building.

1 Introduction

The word "ontology" becomes a buzzword nowadays in computer science.In spite of varying interests in research and the use of ontologies, constructing good ontologies is of common interest. The available languages and tools to aid this work are many. In this paper we will survey and compare a selection of languages and tools by the aid of an evaluation framework. The evaluation framework is originated in information system community and we apply it for ontology analysis since as far as we can see, the current meaning of "ontology" is synonymous with conceptual model.

We will start by presenting the framework for evaluating language and model quality, then we survey the languages and evaluate them in section 3. In section 4 we evaluate the tools using the framework.

2 Quality Evaluation Framework

A semiotic framework is adopted to aid the evaluation. It will be used both for discussing the quality of ontologies (related to tools and underlying methodology), and for evaluating the quality of ontology languages. The framework is described in[2]. This paper gives a short adjusted description of the framework. The framework is based on the following concepts: domain knowledge is represented in an ontology expressed in an ontology language. The ontology is subject to audience interpretation, which includes both human actors and technical actors (tools). The stakeholders that contribute to modeling are called participants.

---

* Part of the research has been supported by Accenture, Norway

They reflect their participant knowledge of that domain in the ontology. Relationships between these concepts give a framework for understanding quality related to ontology.

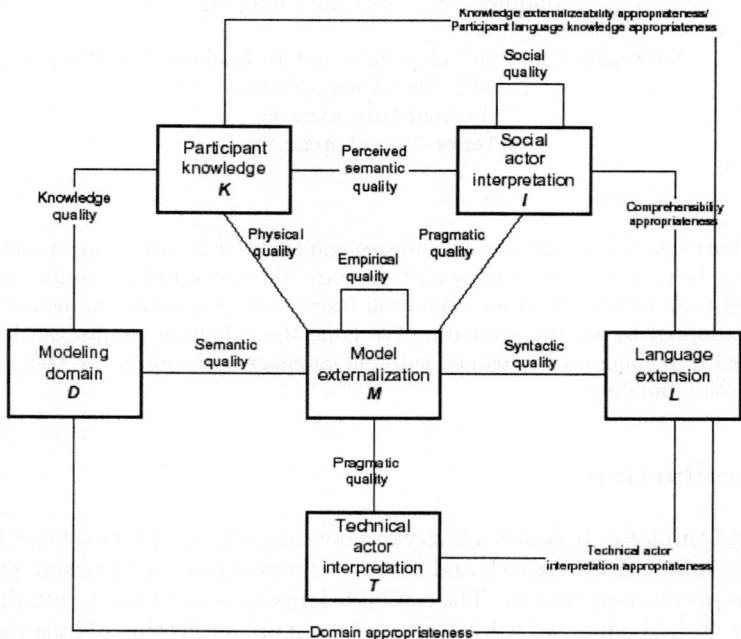

Fig. 1. A framework for discussing quality of conceptual models

3 Survey and Evaluation of Languages

Figure 2 depicts the candidate languages and how they are related to each other. The categorization is adopted from a former evaluation of languages in[1].

The evaluation results are summarized in table 1. The languages are evaluated according to three of the quality aspects mentioned in the evaluation framework. *domain appropriateness, comprehensibility appropriateness* and *technical actor interpretation appropriatness.*

Domain Appropriateness Domain appropriateness is divided into *expressive power*, and *perspectives*.Most of the languages have good expressive power, while Ontolingua and CycL supersede the others.Another important aspect to examine domain appropriateness is to check the coverage of seven modeling perspectives (structural (S), functional (F), behavioral (B), rule (R), object (O), communication (C) and actor-role (AR)).As we can see from the table, most of the ontology

A Comparative Study of Ontology Languages and Tools   763

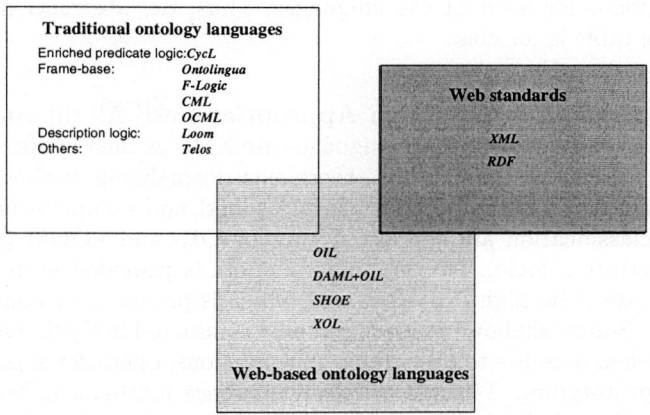

Fig. 2. Classification of language

Table 1. Evaluation of ontology languages

		CycL	Ontolingua	F-Logic	OCML	LOOM	Telos	RDF(S)	OIL	DAML+OIL	XOL	SHOE
Domain appropriateness	Expressive Power	High	High	Medium	Medium+	Medium	High	Medium-	Medium-	Medium+	Medium	Medium
	Perspectives	S,O-,R	S,O+,R	S,O+,R	S-,O,R,F,	S,O+,R,	S,O,R+ F,AR-	S,O,R-	S,O,R-	S,O,R-	S,O,R-	S,O,R
Comprehensibility appropriateness	Number of Constructs	Large	Large	Medium	Medium+	Medium	Medium+	Small	Small	Medium-	Medium	Small
	Abstraction Mechanism	Cla Gen+ Agg Ass	Cla Gen+ Agg Ass	Cla Gen+ Agg Ass	Cla Gen+ Agg Ass	Cla Gen+ Agg Ass	Cla Gen+ Agg Ass	Cla Gen- Agg- Ass	Cla Gen Agg- Ass	Cla Gen- Agg- Ass	Cla Gen- Agg- Ass	Cla Gen- Agg- Ass
Technical actor interpretation appropriateness	Formal Syntax	Yes	Yes	Yes	Yes	Yes	Yes	Yes	Yes	Yes	Yes	Yes
	Formal Semantics	Yes	Yes	Yes	Yes	Yes	Yes	Yes-	Yes	Yes-	No	Yes-
	Inference Engine	Weak	No	Good+	Good	Good+	Good	No	Good+	Possible	No	Good
	Constraint Checking	Good	Good	Good	Good	Good	Good	Weak	Weak	Weak	Weak-	Weak

languages are more focused on describing static information, where taxonomy is at the centre, and dynamic information can not be easily described.

Comprehensibility Appropriateness To make the language comprehensible to the social actor, it requires that the number of the phenomena should be reasonable and they should be organized hierarchically. These are the two criteria we use her to measure comprehensibility appropriateness. The abstraction mechanisms are classification (Cla), generalization (Gen), aggregation (Agg) and association (Ass).As we can see from the table, most of the web-based languages have smaller number of constructs and this is one of the reasons why they claim they are simple and easy to use.Besides SHOE and XOL, which don't support slot hierarchy, all the other languages provide abstraction mechanisms for both class and relations. It is not surprising that the abstraction mechanism for class is more at focus for most of the languages. Thus, the abstraction mechanism listed in the table is for class.

Technical Actor Interpretation Appropriateness All the languages have formal syntax and the web-based languages use XML as their syntax base. When it comes to semantics, except XOL, there exist formalizing methods for all the other languages. F-Logic and OIL provide sound and complete inference and automatic classification are supported only by OIL and LOOM (due to their root in description logic). No reasoning support is provided with Ontolingua, largely because of its high express power, which is provided without any means to control it. Some "shallow" reasoning can be conducted in CycL. OCML exceed the others when it comes to executable specifications, operational semantics and automatic prototyping. Telos provides an inference mechanism, but it has not been used in knowledge bases, which use Telos as their underlining knowledge model, and the reason is its inefficiency. RDF(s) and XOL have no inference support and DAML+OIL can use OIL's inference system, because they are quite similar.

Fig. 3. Evaluation of ontology tools

			Ontolingua	WebOnto	WebODE	Protégé	OntoEdit	OilEd
Physical Quality	Meta-model adapt.	Expr. power	High	Medium+	Medium+	Medium-	Medium-	Medium
		Perspective	S, O, R	S, O, R, B, F, C, AR	S, O, R	S, O, R	S, O, R	S, O, R
		Persistency	Server storage	Server storage	Server storage	Local storage	Local storage	Local storage
	Availability	Web-based	Yes	Yes	Yes	No	No	No
		Export	KIF, Loom, OKBC	No	XML, RDF(S), OIL	RDF(S)	F-logic, DAML-OIL	OIL, DAML-OIL, RDF(S)
Empirical quality			Weak	Good-	Good	Good-	Good-	Good-
Syntactic quality			Error detection	Error prevention	Error prevention	Error detection	Error prevention	Weak
Semantic quality	Consistency checking		Weak+	Weak+	Good-	Weak+	Good-	Good
	Model reuse		Library & integration	Library	Library & integration	Integration	No	No
Perceived semantic quality	Tutorial		Yes	Yes-	Yes-	Yes	Yes-	Yes-
	Tool tips		No	No	Yes-	Yes	Yes	Yes
Pragmatic quality	Visualization		Weak+	Good-	Good	Good-	Good-	Good-
	Filtration		Weak+	Good-	Good-	Good-	Good-	Good-
	Explanation		Weak+	Weak+	Good	Good	Weak+	Good-
	Execution		No	Yes	No	No	No	No
Social quality			Model integration	Weak	Model integration	Model integration	Weak	Weak

4 Evaluation of Tools

Tools suitable for ontology development are emphasized, and six tools have been found most relevant: *Ontolingua, WebOnto, WebODE, Protégé-2000, OntoEdit* and *OilEd*.

The evaluation results are given in table 2. Physical quality is discussed according to: *meta-model adaption, persistency* and *availability*. Semantic quality is discussed according to: *consistency checking* and *model reuse*, and perceived pragmatic quality according to: *tutorial* and *tool tips*. Pragmatic quality is discussed according to: *visualization, filtration, explanation* and *execution*. The other three quality types are: *empirical, syntactic* and *social quality*.

References

1. O. Corcho and A. Gomez-Prez. A roadmap to ontology specification languages. In *Proceedings of EKAW'00, France*, 2000.
2. O. I. Lindland, G. Sindre, and Soelvberg A. Understanding quality in conceptual modeling. *IEEE software*, 11(2):42–49, 1995.

Life Cycle Based Approach for Knowledge Management: A Knowledge Organization Case Study

Vijayan Sugumaran and Mohan Tanniru

Department of Decision and Information Sciences
School of Business Administration
Oakland University
Rochester, MI 48309
{Sugumara,Tanniru}@oakland.edu

Abstract. Knowledge Management (KM) is emerging as one of the management tools to gain competitive advantage. Though several organizations have reported successful KM projects, there are a large number failures due to a variety of reasons including the incongruence between strategic and KM objectives, as well as lack of a sound framework and architecture that supports KM activities. This paper presents a knowledge management framework that takes into account the different levels of knowledge that exists within an organization, and an architecture for a KM environment that incorporates enabling technologies such as intelligent agents and XML. A proof-of-concept prototype is currently under development.

1 Introduction

Knowledge Management (KM) concepts and techniques are permeating the corporate world and organizations such as Chevron, Xerox, AT&T, Hewlett-Packard, FinnAir, and 3M have successfully implemented KM initiatives and reported tremendous benefits [3]. While several organizations have successfully implemented KM initiatives, there are many reported cases of unsuccessful KM projects [1], [5]. Some of the pitfalls of KM projects [4] include lack of congruence between strategic objectives and KM objectives, identification and standard representation of knowledge assets to be managed, routine processes to support KM life cycle, and infrastructure to support access. Fahey and Prusak [5] also point out that the fundamental purpose of managing knowledge is to create a shared context between individuals, which is not always achieved.

Hence, the objective of this research is to develop a knowledge management framework for systematically capturing, manipulating and disseminating knowledge using systems life-cycle concepts and discuss an architecture to implement this framework using enabling technologies such as intelligent agents and XML. A case study is used throughout to illustrate both the development and implementation of this framework.

2 Knowledge Management Framework

Probst et al. [7] identify processes such as identification, acquisition, development, utilization, distribution and retention for knowledge management. However, these processes are defined from the perspective of knowledge worker (an *application* or stakeholder view). A firm has to ensure that the knowledge gathered and managed is *aligned* with its knowledge goals to effectively articulate and develop individual performance measures. The successful development of a KM system requires a design phase, where both the logical and physical model of the knowledge is developed prior to its implementation, which is the primary focus of this research.

The first step in developing the logical knowledge model is to *acquire* various pieces of knowledge that are known about a specific problem domain and are needed to meet both the alignment and application needs. We will refer to this knowledge as "logical knowledge model – Level 0." While acquisition forms the basis for gathering instances of various problem case scenarios, one needs to *abstract* broad generalizations across various dimensions to support their potential reuse. This abstraction process, using appropriate techniques such as qualitative synthesis and machine learning, will lead to the development of "logical knowledge model – level 1."

The knowledge, abstracted from internal experiences, has to be validated and refined using knowledge acquired from various outside sources. In other words, knowledge in level 1 may be *augmented* with external knowledge (theories, proven methodologies, etc.) to ensure that an organization can fully leverage its access to all its available sources. The knowledge, thus appended, will form the basis for "logical knowledge model - level 2." Thus, the design of a KM system calls for the extraction of a logical knowledge model at levels 0, 1 and 2 using three major steps: acquire, abstract and augment. Next section will use a case to illustrate these three steps.

3 Example Logical Knowledge Model – A Case Study

A project-based organization, which completes *"corporate projects,"* is used to illustrate the derivation of the logical knowledge model. At the time of this report, the organization has completed over 200 corporate projects with over 40 corporations.

Acquisition. The project team meets with the corporate clients and gathers project related information, which becomes part of the "project definition document". The team generates a project plan and estimate of resources needed. In addition, weekly status reports and presentations are created. The firm also documents each project on various characteristics such as the system development phase the project addresses, functional area it supports, primary technologies used, experience level of team and the project type. All of this information becomes part of the project knowledge repository. Much of this knowledge is available for future extraction. However, there is no effective way to relate this knowledge to a new project that is not exactly similar. In other words, generalizations are needed from specific instances of these projects so they can be used in new situations. This leads to the *abstraction* phase.

Abstraction. Three possible means of abstraction or generalization are used here and others may be possible. A project may use some standard techniques that have been already used elsewhere and references to such techniques may be available in the project document. Secondly, the project coordinator may see similarities in projects with respect to the approaches used, complexity, level of coordination or technology support necessary, team experience, etc. Thirdly, some of the project data may be fed directly to algorithms (statistical or artificial intelligence) to help the organization establish factors that are contributing to project success. Thus, the acquired project knowledge is used to generate three levels of abstraction: *established procedures*, *references from external sources*, and *new abstractions* created through knowledge manager's intervention, or by the application of algorithms.

Augmentation. The greater reliance the organization can put on its knowledge artifacts, the greater the chance of their utilization. Deployment of specific knowledge elements, which have been abstracted from "project instances," can only be effective if it is augmented with external data or research. For example, in this case study, several training projects involving ERP or large systems were completed and through this experience, a few factors for determining training success were extracted. However, these observations were augmented with research on "training enablers" and a full-training model was developed.

4 Design and Implementation of KM Environment

Based on the knowledge activities discussed in the previous section, we propose the KM environment shown in Figure 1. This environment distinguishes between three levels of knowledge: 'level 0,' 'level 1,' and 'level 2.' 'Level 0' knowledge deals with project details and characteristics whereas 'level 1' knowledge captures higher-level abstractions derived from a group of similar projects. 'Level 2' knowledge relates to application domain knowledge derived from internal and external sources. This environment also emphasizes easy access to these different levels of knowledge for all the stakeholders and has a feedback mechanism between the different levels of knowledge. It provides facilities for aligning the knowledge repository with strategic objectives by specifying what type of knowledge to gather and how to utilize it.

A proof-of-concept portal prototype, which uses three-tier client-server architecture, is currently under development. The client is the basic web browser that the stakeholders use to carryout different tasks. For example, students use the portal to create and store project related artifacts. The sponsors use the portal to monitor the progress of the projects as well as gaining insights from the application domain knowledge. The server side consists of the KM application, which facilitates knowledge alignment, deriving the knowledge models, and populating the knowledge repositories. The server-side features are supported by the following agents: a) interface agent, b) acquisition agent, c) abstraction agent, and d) augmentation agent. These agents are being implemented using JADE [2], and their reasoning capabilities implemented through JESS [6]. The project knowledge and the application domain knowledge are stored using XML with appropriate DTDs.

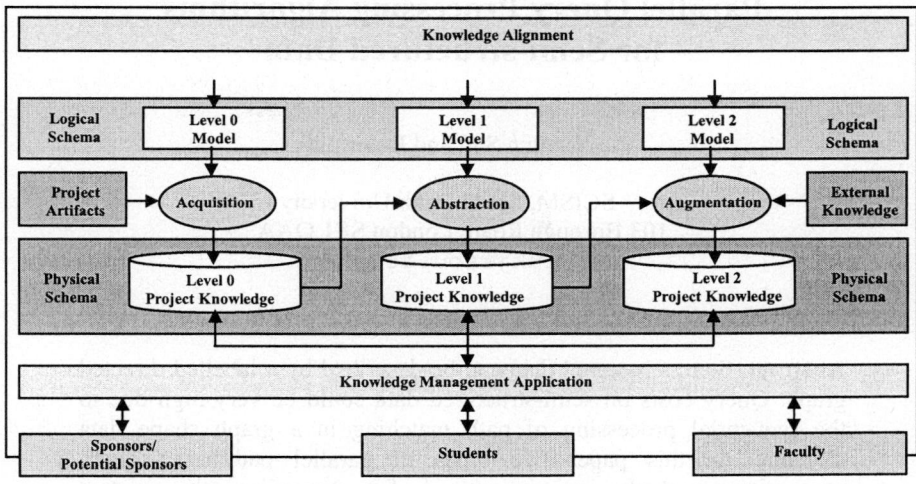

Fig. 1. Knowledge Management Environment

5 Summary

This paper has presented a KM framework that takes into account different levels of knowledge that exists within an organization. Drawing from system development principles, this framework differentiates between the logical and physical knowledge models and provides a phased approach for knowledge creation (acquisition, abstraction, and augmentation), storage and utilization. It also emphasizes the need for the alignment between the strategic and knowledge management objectives. A proof-of-concept prototype is currently under development, which uses a client-server architecture that integrates enabling technologies such as intelligent-agent and XML.

References

1. Barth, S.: KM Horror Stories. Knowledge Management, Vol. 3, No. 10, (2000) pp. 36-40
2. Bellifemine, F., Poggi,, A., and Rimassa, G.: JADE - A FIPA-compliant agent framework. Proceedings of PAAM'99, London, April (1999) pp.97-108
3. CIO Magazine: The Means to an Edge: Knowledge Management Key to Innovation. CIO Special Advertising Supplement, (1999) Sep 15.
4. Davenport, T.H.: Known Evils: The Common Pitfalls of Knowledge Management. CIO Magazine, June 15 (1997)
5. Fahey, L. and Prusak, L.: The Eleven Deadliest Sins of Knowledge Management. California Management Review, Vol. 40, No. 3, (1998) pp. 265-276
6. Friedman-Hill, E.: Jess, the Expert System Shell. Sandia National Laboratories, Livermore, CA. (2002) URL: http://herzberg.ca.sandia.gov/jess
7. Probst, G., Raub, S., Romhardt, K.: Managing Knowledge: Building Blocks for Success. Chichester: John Wiley & Sons (2000)

Parallel Query Processing Algorithms for Semi-structured Data

Wenjun Sun and Kevin Lü

SCISM, South Bank University
103 Borough Road, London SE1 OAA
lukj@sbu.ac.uk

Abstract. Semi-structured data can be described by a labelled directed graph. Query costs on semi-structured data could be very high due to the sequential processing of path matching in a graph shape data structure. In this paper two types of parallel path-based query processing methods are introduced for improving the system performance. The first type includes three parallel version of pointer chasing methods based on the principle of message-driven computation. In the second type of method, the pre-fetch technique is used to achieve a low communication cost and a high degree of parallelisation.

Keywords: Path-based query, Parallel processing, Semi-structured data.

1 Introduction

Queries on semi-structured data depend not only on the contents of the data sets but also on the data schema. A number of methods for query processing and query optimisation have been introduced [1, 2]. These investigations are all based on an assumption that the platform used for query processing is a serial processing environment. The query cost could be very high due to the sequential processing of path matching in a graph shape data structure, in particular, when complex queries (including join operations and multiple path expressions) are involved.

One promising solution is using parallel techniques to improve overall system performance. Parallelism has been employed in both relational and object-oriented databases to improve the system throughput and respond time. To our knowledge, the issues of applying parallel techniques for path expression queries for semi-structured databases have not yet been investigated. Although the data models [3, 4] used to describe semi-structured data are similar to object oriented data models which are graph based models, there are significant differences between them. Because of the features of semi-structured data, the methods used for parallel query processing in traditional database applications will not be suitable, and it poses new challenges to existing data processing technologies.

In this paper, we are going to introduce four newly designed parallel query process algorithms for semi-structured data. The major contribution of this work is that only massage (not data objects, or part of data objects) passing amongst *processing elements (PEs)* during query evaluation. The organisation of the rest of the paper is as follows. Section 2 and 3 describe four parallel query process algorithms. In section 4 presents a summary.

2 Passage Driven Parallel Methods

In this section three new parallel algorithms are introduced for processing semi-structured data. They are the parallel versions of the serial *top-down, bottom-up* and *hybrid methods* [5], namely, Parallel Top-down Query Processing Strategy (PTDQ), Parallel Bottom-up Query Processing Strategy (PBUQ) and Parallel Hybrid Query Processing Strategy (PHQ). These algorithms are designed to explore the possible ways to utilise the resources of a shared-nothing architecture and maximise the degree of parallelisation.

2.1 Parallel Top-Down Query Processing Strategy (PTDQ)

The top-down strategy is a natural way for evaluating a path expression. It follows the path from the root to the target collections using the depth first graph traversal algorithm. It processes the path expression by navigating through object references following the order of the collections in path expressions. If there are multiple references from one object to the objects in the next collection, the navigation follows the depth first order.

2.2 Parallel Bottom-Up Query Processing Strategy (PBUQ)

The parallel bottom-up strategy starts with identifying all objects via the last edge in the input path and check if the objects satisfying the predicate, then traverses backwards through the path, going from children to parents. Similar to the top-down strategy, if it finds that the next object is in another *PE*, it will send an *search instruction* (*SI*) to it. The advantage of this approach is that it starts with objects guaranteed to satisfy at least part of the predicate, and it does not need examine the path any further if the path does not satisfy the predicate.

2.3 Parallel Hybrid Query Processing Strategy (PHQ)

The PHQ strategy start to evaluate a query from both top down and bottom up directions at the same time, and processes from both directions will meet somewhere in the middle. This will increase the degree of paralleisation for query processing. On the direction of top down, the PHQ uses the PTDQ algorithm to create a temporary result which satisfying the predicate so far. Meanwhile, on the other hand, this algorithm traverses up from the bottom vertex using the PBUQ algorithm and reaches the same point as the top-down thread does. A join between the two temporary results yields the complete set of satisfying paths. The detailed algorithms can be found [6].

3   Parallel Partial Match Query Processing Strategy (PPMQ)

The algorithms introduced in Section 3 have provided solutions for processing path expression query in parallel. However, these three algorithms require messages to be passed amongst processing nodes. In addition, a *SI* queue may be built up at a *PE* if it is busy, and it will require further waiting time. To transfer data amongst *PEs* is much more expensive compare other data operations, it should be kept as less as possible.

To overcome these drawbacks, a parallel partial match query processing strategy is introduced. The basic idea of PPMQ is that every *BPE* searches the paths in parallel. When they find an object in a path which is not in their local *PEs*, they will keep records of the identication of the *PE* in which the target object is located rather than send messages to that the descendant *PEs* immediately (where in PTDQ, PBUQ and PHQ, such a message will be sent out). After all possible *partial matched routes* (which will be defined below) have been generated, these *routes* will be sent to one of these *PEs*. In this *PE*, all of *partial matched routes* are merged together and a check is carried out to see if it matches the predicate path expression. During this process, no object (data) or message is required to be transferred between PEs before the finaly merge. This approach could cost less compare to other three approaches, if the operation cost for message passing during the query process in the other three approaches is higher than the cost of final merge in PPMQ, and that in fact it is very much of the case for processing complex queries.

4   Summary

Observing the four algorithms introduced in this paper, it can be found that the key factors that influence the efficiency of these algorithms are the serial fragments and the coefficient of the parallel fragments. The first three methods has two drawbacks: the first drawback is that a large number of communications between PEs may required; the second drawback is when the PEs spinning due to excessive coherence traffic on the communication line causes additional waiting time. As in some cases, PEs must wait for messages from other PEs. This requires synchronisation between PEs and consequently it decreases the degree of parallelisation. The fourth method has been proposed for solving the above drawbacks of first three methods. The main purpose of this strategy is to reduce both communication time and waiting time. However, the price is that it sometimes may need more merging time compare with the other three methods. A linear speed up along with the number of processor could be achieved for the first three algorithms if the waiting time and communication time are considerably low. For the fourth algorithm, a linear speed up could also be possible if there are quite few of number of elements need to be merged. The first three algorithms have a linear speed up apart from the waiting time and communication time. The partial match algorithm also has linear speed up apart from the optimisation time and final merging time.

These algorithms have been coded in C programming language and the system runs under Lunix operating system in a cluster computer system environment. Presently, only a small number of tests have been conducted. In the future, we will test them under different data sets, query sets with different frequency, to understand more about these algorithms and to find the possible ways to improve them. We also intend to extend the current cost models for these algorithms with additional functions (such as estimate the selectivity, queue waiting time) to develop a set of performance estimation tools for parallel semi-structure data management systems.

References

1. Z.G.Ives, A.Y. Levy, D. S. Weld, Efficient Evaluation of Regular Path Expressions on Streaming XML Data , *UW CS&E Technical Reports by Date* UW-CSE-00-05-02.PS.Z , 2000
2. Curtis E. Dyreson, Michael H. Bohlen, Chriatian S. Jensen, Capturing and Querying Multiple Aspects of Semi-structured Data, *Proc. of the 25th International Conference on Very Large Databases*, Edinburgh, Scotland, 1999.
3. Y.Papakonstantinou, H.Garcia-molina, and Jennifer Widom, Object Exchange Across Heterogeneous Information Sources, in *Proceedings of the Eleventh International Conference on Data Engineering*, PP.251-260, Taipei, Taiwan, March 1995.
4. Document Object Model, *W3C Technical Report*, Nov. 2000, http://www.w3.org/TR/2000/REC-DOM-Level-2-Core-20001113.
5. Jason McHugh, Jennifer Widom, Query Optimization for XML, *Proceedings of the Twenty-Fifth International Conference on Very Large Data Bases*, Edinburgh, Edinburgh, Scotland, 1999.
6. Y. Zhu, W. Sun, K. J. Lü. Parallel Query Processing for Semi-structured Data. Technique report 02-01-KL, SCIMS South Bank University, 2001

Domain-Specific Instance Models in UML

Marco Torchiano[1] and Giorgio Bruno[2]

[1]Computer and Information Science Department (IDI) NTNU
Sem Sælands vei 7-9, N-7491 Trondheim, Norway,
Phone: +47 7359 4485 Fax: +47 7359 4466
Marco.Torchiano@idi.ntnu.no
[2]Dip.Automatica e Informatica, Politecnico di Torino
C.so Duca degli Abruzzi, 24, I-10129 Torino, Italy
Phone: +39 011 564 7003 Fax: +39 011 564 7099
bruno@polito.it

Abstract. UML is a widespread software modeling language. It can be a good candidate for modeling non-software systems, such as enterprise systems. While several proposals have been formulated, they are either incomplete or complex. In this paper we propose a modeling approach that is based on the basic object-orientation concepts. In particular we stress the use of instance models as a key concept.

1 Introduction

In the development of enterprise information systems, more time is spent in analyzing business needs than in coding [1]. Thus programming will increasingly deal with concepts at the application-domain level. Typical development will be relegated to small portions where it is unavoidable. It is important to find out if the Unified Modeling Language (UML) [4] (possibly extended) is suitable to satisfy modeling needs of users which are not software developers, e.g. process engineers.

Here we will present a solution for modeling complex enterprise systems that do not use the standard UML extension mechanism. Object-orientation offers a set of concepts, which could be effectively exploited without the need of extension mechanisms. In particular the proposed approach emphasizes the importance of instance-level models. We will take into consideration UML 1.3 since it is, at the time of this writing, the most widely know version. Much attention will be paid to supporting tools.

In section 2 we presents an assessment of UML capabilities, and in section 3 we analyze issues related to instance models. Then in section 3 we outline our proposal, and finally in section 5 we draw some conclusions.

2 Assessment of UML Capabilities

UML was not designed to model the enterprise domain, therefore it is important to to assess its capabilities in this area.

The organization of an enterprise can be modeled by means of the UML standard profile for business modeling. This profile defines a stereotype, named Organization Unit, which extends the Subsystem concept to represent the organization units of an enterprise. An example of organization model is shown in Fig. 1.

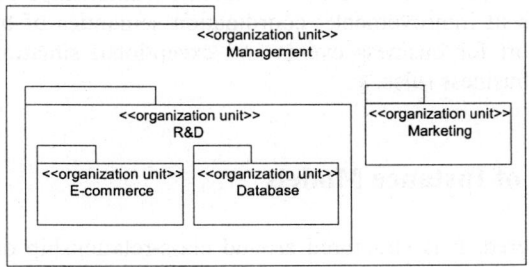

Fig. 1. Organization

In this example there is a top-level unit, *Management*, which contains two subunits, *R&D* and *Marketing*; the former contains units *E-commerce* and *Database*. This graphical representation in current tools does not have any semantics; it is a mere arrangement of shapes.

UML activity diagrams can be used to describe business processes. An example of a business process described with an activity diagrams is presented in Fig. 2.

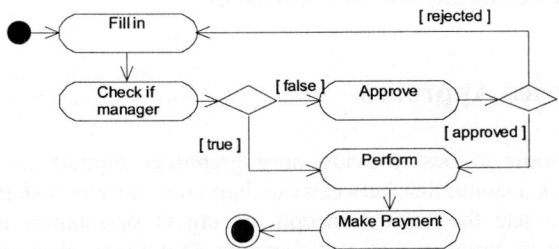

Fig. 2. Business Process

This is a simplified purchasing business process. After the purchase request has been filled in, if the requester is not a manager an approval is required, then the purchase can be performed and finally payment can be done. This diagram is not disciplined in any way and its business semantics is left largely unspecified.

A first and simple approach to enterprise modeling has been defined in the UML specification itself [4] by applying the UML Standard Profile for Business Modeling. It doesn't provide any support for business process modeling.

The UML profile for Enterprise Application Integration (EAI) [3] needs a part of business process modeling in order to set a base for integration. The models presented in reply to the initial OMG RFP are based on the existing UML modeling concepts and define a set of new modeling elements and relationships between them.

None of the previous works addresses in a satisfying way the description of business processes. In fact the OMG issued a request for proposal related to a UML Extensions for Workflow Process Definition [5].

According to [2] many of the useful business concepts are dispersed across different UML views and it is not easy to establish relationships between them. The following are areas of improvement: coordination semantics of business processes (e.g. explicit support for business events and exceptional situations), semantics of business roles and business rules.

3 Discussion of Instance Models

UML is class-centered. It is structured around class-relationship diagrams. Instance models are treated as second order entities; they are used only to show examples of data structures or to describe the behavior in particular scenarios

According to UML an object diagram is a graph of instances, including objects and data values. It shows a snapshot of the detailed state of a system at a point in time. The notation guide states that tools don't need to support a separate format for object diagrams. Class diagrams can contain objects, so a class diagram with objects and no classes is an "object diagram".

In many tools it is not possible to place an object in class diagrams, thus the only viable way to draw objects and links is to use a collaboration diagram, which is intended to model behavior and not static structure. Thus what we have is only a graphical diagram lacking any semantic foundation.

4 The Proposed Approach

Available UML tools at best provide only graphical support to model business concepts. They lack a sound link between the diagrams and a well-defined semantics.

We propose to use the basic concepts of object orientation to represent the modeling concepts required in different domains. Our proposal is intended to be an alternative to the approaches described in the section 2. The difference is mainly in the modeling mechanisms rather than in the semantics of the models.

The basic object-oriented concepts are classes and objects. Classes pertain to the level of problem domain, while objects pertain to the level of system domain. In the case of business models we can say that *process*, *activity* and *organization unit* are classes, while *MakePayment* is an object, i.e. an instance of a class (in particular of class Activity). Two sequential modeling activities are needed: domain modeling and system modeling.

The purpose of domain modeling is to analyze the problem domain in order to identify the main concepts (classes) and their relationships. The classes are abstract building blocks to be used in system modeling, while the relationships define the rules for how concrete building blocks (objects) can be connected to each other. In addition classes define attributes, i.e. they specify what kind of information can be stored into the concrete building blocks.

The aim of system modeling is to build a model of the intended system as a composition of building blocks, i.e. instances of the classes defined in the domain model. Connections between instances are regulated by the relationships between the corresponding classes.

Domain modeling and system modeling involve different roles. First, domain experts analyze the problem domain and, with the help a modeling expert, define a sort of modeling vocabulary (the domain model). Then, problem experts will use such a new "language" to build a model of the actual system.

A complex domain can present different features, which in most cases can be modeled separately. Therefore the domain model will result in a number of submodels that we call *schemas*. A schema is mapped into a UML package acting as a container of classes and relationships.

5 Conclusions

In the intention of UML creators, UML extension mechanism should be used in those cases when the basic expressive power of the language is not sufficient, and additional semantic information should be provided in order to provide modeling concepts at a higher abstraction level.

Several extensions in the field of enterprise model have been proposed or are the subject of ongoing efforts. None of them addresses the issue of a broad integrated enterprise model, which could provide the high level vocabulary to model enterprise systems.

We proposed an approach is easier to understand since it is based on the fundamental concepts of object orientation.

References

1. B. Bloom, J. Russell, J. Vlissides, M. Wegman. "High-Level Program Development", Dr. Dobb's Special Report December 2000
2. Cooperative Research Centre for Enterprise Distributed Systems Technology (DSTC). "UML Profile for EAI", document ad/00-08-07, August 2000.
3. Joint Submission "UML Profile for EAI", OMG document ad/00-08-05, August 2000
4. OMG. "Unified Modeling Language Specification" version 1.3, June 1999.
5. OMG, "UML Extensions for Workflow Process Definition - Request For Proposal" OMG Document: bom/2000-12-11

Extended Faceted Ontologies

Yannis Tzitzikas[1,2], Nicolas Spyratos[3], Panos Constantopoulos[1,2], and Anastasia Analyti[2]

[1] Department of Computer Science, University of Crete, Greece
[2] Institute of Computer Science, ICS-FORTH
{tzitzik, panos, analyti}@csi.forth.gr
[3] Laboratoire de Recherche en Informatique, Universite de Paris-Sud, France
spyratos@lri.fr

Abstract. A faceted ontology consists of a set of facets, where each facet consists of a predefined set of terms structured by a subsumption relation. We propose two extensions of faceted ontologies, which allow inferring conjunctions of terms that are valid in the underlying domain. We give a model-theoretic interpretation to these extended faceted ontologies and we provide mechanisms for inferring the valid conjunctions of terms. This inference service can be exploited for preventing errors during the indexing process and for deriving navigation trees that are suitable for browsing. The proposed scheme has several advantages by comparison to the hierarchical classification schemes that are currently used, namely: *conceptual clarity*: it is easier to understand, *compactness*: it takes less space, and *scalability*: the update operations can be formulated easier and be performed more efficiently.

1 Introduction - Motivation

Faceted classification schemes ([1]), hereafter *faceted ontologies*, seem to be superior to hierarchical classification schemes with regard to comprehensibility, storage requirements and scalability ([2]). They are also better suited for indexing collections that are subject to continuous expansion and change.

However, in a faceted ontology *invalid* conjunctions of terms coming from different facets may occur. A conjunction of terms is considered invalid if it cannot be applied to any of the objects of the domain. For example, in a tourist information application, the conjunction Crete.WinterSports, where Crete belongs to a facet Location and WinterSports to a facet Sports (e.g. see Figure 1.(a)), is invalid because there is not enough snow in Crete. In contrast, the conjunction Crete.SeaSports is certainly valid. Figure 1.(b) enumerates the set of valid and the set of invalid conjunctions (descriptions) that consist of one term from each facet. The inability to infer the valid conjunctions of terms may give rise to problems in the indexing of the objects (laborious and may erroneous indexing), and in browsing (an invalid conjunction of terms will yield no objects).

Being able to infer the validity of a conjunction in a faceted ontology would be very useful for aiding the indexer and for preventing indexing errors. Such an aid is especially important in cases where the indexing is done by many people. For example, the indexing of Web pages in the Open Directory[1] is done

[1] http://dmoz.org

by more than 20.000 volunteer human editors (indexers). Moreover, if we could infer the valid conjunctions of terms in a faceted ontology then we would be able to generate navigation trees on the fly, which consist of nodes that correspond to valid conjunctions of terms. However, defining manually the set of valid descriptions even for facets of relatively small size, would be a formidable task for the designer.

In this paper we present two extensions of faceted ontologies in the context of which one can infer valid or invalid conjunctions of terms through an inference mechanism. The designer simply declares a small set of valid or invalid conjunctions and other (valid or invalid) conjunctions are then inferred by the proposed mechanism. A full version of this paper can be found in [7].

2 Faceted Ontologies

Roughly, a *faceted ontology* consists of a finite set of facets. Each facet is designed separately, and models a distinct aspect of the domain. For instance, the faceted ontology for the domain of UNIX tools, presented in [2], consists of four facets, namely, "ByAction", "ByObject", "ByDataStructure" and "BySystem". Each *facet* consists of a *terminology*, i.e. a finite set of names or *terms*, structured by a *subsumption* relation. Examples of faceted ontologies can be found in [3], [8], [5], [2]. Below we define precisely what we call ontology, faceted ontology and then we give a semantic interpretation to a faceted ontology.

Def. 1. An *ontology* is a pair $(T, \preceq)$ where T is a *terminology*, i.e. a finite set of names, or *terms*, and $\preceq$ is a *subsumption* relation over T, i.e. a reflexive and transitive relation over T.

Def. 2. A *faceted ontology* is a finite set $\mathcal{F} = \{F_1, ..., F_k\}$ of *ontologies* in which each $F_i = (T_i, \preceq_i)$ is called a *facet*.

Let Obj denote the set of objects of the domain (e.g. the set of all Web pages). Given a terminology T, we call *interpretation* of T over Obj any function $I : T \to 2^{Obj}$.

Def. 3. An interpretation I of T is a *model* of the ontology $(T, \preceq)$ if for all $t, t' \in T$, if $t \preceq t'$ then $I(t) \subseteq I(t')$.

Given a faceted ontology $\mathcal{F} = \{F_1, ..., F_k\}$ let $\mathcal{T} = T_1 \cup ... \cup T_k$ and $\preceq = \preceq_1 \cup ... \cup \preceq_k$. We shall call $(\mathcal{T}, \preceq)$ *the* ontology of $\mathcal{F}$. Now, an interpretation I of $\mathcal{T}$ is a *model* of $\mathcal{F}$, if it is a model of the ontology $(\mathcal{T}, \preceq)$.

Now, a *description* (conjunction) d over $\mathcal{F}$ is either a term $t \in \mathcal{T}$ or a sequence of terms separated by "·", i.e. any string derived by the following grammar $d ::= d \cdot t \mid t$. Let D denote the set of all descriptions. An interpretation I of $\mathcal{T}$ can be extended to an interpretation of D as follows: for any description $d = t_1 \cdot t_2 \cdot ... \cdot t_k$ in D we define $I(d) = I(t_1) \cap I(t_2) \cap ... \cap I(t_k)$.

Now, we define semantically what we shall call valid and invalid description. A description d is *valid* in $\mathcal{F}$ if $I(d) \neq \emptyset$ in every model I of $\mathcal{F}$. A description d is *invalid* in $\mathcal{F}$ if $I(d) = \emptyset$ in every model I of $\mathcal{F}$. In the following section we propose two different extensions of an ontology that allows us to infer valid or invalid descriptions from other descriptions that have been declared as valid or invalid by the designer of the faceted ontology.

3 Extended Faceted Ontologies

Def. 4. A *Positive Extended Faceted Ontology*, or *PEFO* for short, is a pair $<\mathcal{F}, P>$ where $\mathcal{F}$ is a faceted ontology and P is a set of descriptions over $\mathcal{T}$. An interpretation I of $\mathcal{T}$ is a *model* of $<\mathcal{F}, P>$ if:
(a) I is a model of $\mathcal{F}$, and
(b) for each $d \in P$, $I(d) \neq \emptyset$.
Now, the set of valid descriptions VD of a $PEFO <\mathcal{F}, P>$ is defined as follows: $VD = \{d \in D \mid I(d) \neq \emptyset$ in every model I of $<\mathcal{F}, P>\}$. This means that a description d is valid in $<\mathcal{F},P>$ if there is a description $p \in P$ such that $<\mathcal{F},P> \models p \preceq d$ [2]. If a description is not an element of the set VD, then it is considered invalid (thus we adopt a closed world assumption).

Def. 5. A *Negative Extended Faceted Ontology*, or *NEFO* for short, is a pair $<\mathcal{F}, N>$ where $\mathcal{F}$ is a faceted ontology and N is a set of descriptions over $\mathcal{T}$. An interpretation I of $\mathcal{F}$ is a *model* of $<\mathcal{F}, N>$ if:
(a) I is a model of $\mathcal{F}$, and
(b) for each $d \in N$, $I(d) = \emptyset$.
Now, the set of invalid descriptions ID of a $NEFO <\mathcal{F}, N>$ is defined as follows: $ID = \{d \in D \mid I(d) = \emptyset$ in every model I of $<\mathcal{F}, N>\}$. This means that a description d is *invalid* in $<\mathcal{F},N>$ if there is an $n \in N$ such that $<\mathcal{F},N> \models d \preceq n$. If a description is not an element of the set ID, then it is considered valid, i.e. $VD = D \setminus ID$ (thus we adopt a closed world assumption).

Checking description validity requires performing $|P|$ subsumption checks in the case of a *PEFO*, and $|N|$ in the case of a *NEFO*. In both cases, subsumption checking can be performed by the inference mechanism described in [6].

Figures 1.(c) and 1.(d) show how we can specify the valid descriptions of the faceted ontology of Figure 1.(a) (i.e. the sets "Valid Descriptions" and "Invalid Descriptions" as enumerated in Figure 1.(b)) by employing a *PEFO* and a *NEFO* respectively.

The designer can employ a *PEFO* or a *NEFO* depending on the faceted ontology of the application. If the majority of the descriptions are valid then it is better to employ a *NEFO*, so as to specify only the invalid descriptions. Concerning the methodology for defining the set N, it is more efficient for the designer to put in N "short" descriptions that consist of "broad" terms. The reason is that from such descriptions a large number of new invalid descriptions can be inferred. For example in the hypothetical case that we want to specify that all descriptions over the faceted ontology of Figure 1.(a) are invalid, it suffices to put in N one description, i.e. the description Sports.Location.

Conversely, if the majority of the descriptions are invalid, then it is better to employ a *PEFO* so as to specify only the valid ones. Concerning the methodology for defining the set P, it is more efficient for the designer to put in P "long" descriptions that consist of "narrow" terms, since from such descriptions a large number of new valid descriptions can be inferred. For example in the hypothetical case that we want to specify that all descriptions over the faceted ontology of Figure 1.(a) are valid, it suffices to put in P just the following description: SeaSports.WinterSports.Crete.Pilio.Olympus.

---

[2] We write $<\mathcal{F},P> \models d \preceq d'$ if $I(d) \subseteq I(d')$ in every model I of $<\mathcal{F},P>$.

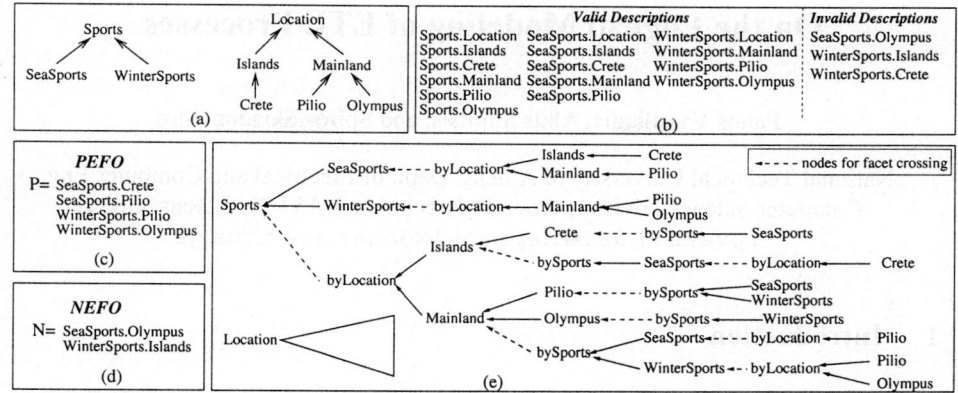

Fig. 1. Our running example

4 Conclusion

We presented a novel approach for indexing and retrieving objects based on multiple aspects or facets. Although even thesauri ([4]) may have facets that group the terms of the thesaurus in classes, our work is original since we described a faceted scheme enriched with a method for specifying the combinations of terms that are valid. Having a *PEFO* or a *NEFO* we can derive *dynamically* a navigation tree such as the one shown in Figure 1.(e), i.e. a tree with nodes that correspond to valid terms only (and nodes for "facet crossing"). Our approach can be used for developing Web catalogs which offer complete navigation trees, require less storage space, and are more comprehensive and scalable.

References

1. Amanda Maple. "Faceted Access: A Review of the Literature", 1995. http://theme.music.indiana.edu/tech_s/mla/facacc.rev.
2. Ruben Prieto-Diaz. "Implementing Faceted Classification for Software Reuse". *Communications of the ACM*, 34(5), 1991.
3. S. R. Ranganathan. "The Colon Classification". In Susan Artandi, editor, *Vol IV of the Rutgers Series on Systems for the Intellectual Organization of Information*. New Brunswick, NJ: Graduate School of Library Science, Rutgers University, 1965.
4. International Organization For Standardization. "Documentation - Guidelines for the establishment and development of monolingual thesauri", 1988. Ref. No ISO 2788-1986.
5. J. H. Sugarman. *"The development of a classification system for information storage and retrieval purposes based upon a model of scientific knowledge generation"*. PhD thesis, School of Education, Boston University, 1981.
6. Yannis Tzitzikas, Nicolas Spyratos, and Panos Constantopoulos. "Deriving Valid Expressions from Ontology Definitions". In *11th European-Japanese Conference on Information Modelling and Knowledge Bases*, Maribor, Slovenia, May 2001.
7. Yannis Tzitzikas, Nicolas Spyratos, and Panos Constantopoulos. "Faceted Ontologies for Web Portals". Technical Report TR-293, Institute of Computer Science-FORTH, October 2001.
8. B. C. Vickery. "Knowledge Representation: A Brief Review". *Journal of Documentation*, 42(3):145–159, 1986.

On the Logical Modeling of ETL Processes

Panos Vassiliadis, Alkis Simitsis, and Spiros Skiadopoulos

National Technical University of Athens, Dept. of Electrical and Computer Eng.
Computer Science Division, Iroon Polytechniou 9, 157 73, Athens, Greece
{pvassil,asimi,spiros}@dbnet.ece.ntua.gr

1 Introduction

Extraction-Transformation-Loading (ETL) tools are pieces of software responsible for the extraction of data from several sources, their cleansing, customization and insertion into a data warehouse. Research has only recently dealt with the above problem and provided few models, tools and techniques to address the issues around the ETL environment [1,2,3,5]. In this paper, we present a logical model for ETL processes. The proposed model is characterized by several templates, representing frequently used ETL activities along with their semantics and their interconnection. In the full version of the paper [4] we present more details on the aforementioned issues and complement them with results on the characterization of the content of the involved data stores after the execution of an ETL scenario and impact-analysis results in the presence of changes.

2 Logical Model

Our logical model abstracts from the technicalities of monitoring, scheduling and logging while it concentrates (a) on the flow of data from the sources towards the data warehouse and (b) on the composition of the activities and the derived semantics.

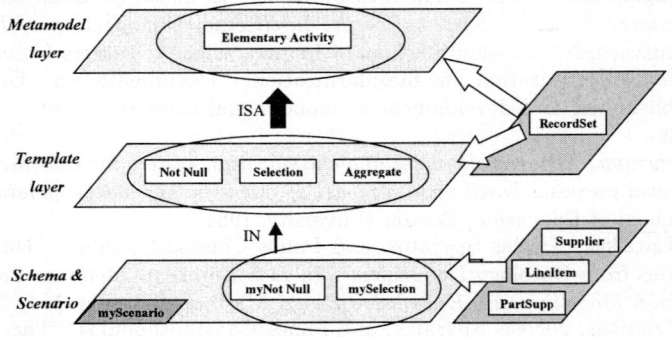

Fig. 1 The metamodel for the logical entities of the ETL environment

Activities are the backbone of the structure of any information system. In our framework, activities are logical abstractions representing parts, or full modules of code. We distinguish between three layers of instantiation/specialization for the logical model of ETL activities, as depicted in Fig.1: *Metamodel, Template,* and *Custom Layers*.

Metamodel Layer. The most generic type of an activity forms the upper level of instantiation (*Metamodel layer* in Fig. 1), covering the most general case of an atomic execution entity within the ETL context.

In Fig. 2 one can see the high level abstraction of the operation of an elementary binary activity. Data coming from the two inputs are propagated to the output, while the rejections are dumped to the Rejected Rows file. The operation is tuned through a set of parameters. Activities are depicted with triangles. The annotated edges characterize the data consumer/provider semantics. The + symbol denotes that data are appended to the Output; the ! symbol denotes that the rejected rows are propagated towards the Rejected Rows file, whose contents they overwrite; the → symbol denotes that data are simply read from Input 1; and the − symbol denotes that the data from Input 2 that match the criteria of the activity are deleted from Input 2, once they have been read by the activity.

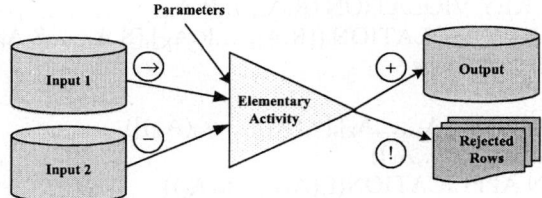

Fig. 2 The basic idea behind the mechanism of Elementary Activities

An *Elementary Activity* is formally described by the following elements:

- *Name*: a unique identifier for the activity.
- *Input Schemata*: a finite set of one or more input schemata that receive data from the data providers of the activity.
- *Output Schema*: the schema that describes the placeholder for the rows that pass the check performed from the activity.
- *Rejections Schema*: a schema that describes the placeholder for certain rows that do not pass the check performed by the activity.
- *Parameter List*: a set of pairs (name and schema) which act as regulators for the functionality of the activity.
- *Output Operational Semantics*: an SQL statement describing the content passed to the output of the operation, with respect to its input.
- *Rejection Operational Semantics*: an SQL statement describing the rejected records.
- *Data Provider/Consumer Semantics*: a modality of each schema which defines (a) whether the data are simply read (symbol → in Fig. 2) or read and subsequently deleted from the data provider (symbol − in Fig. 2 and (b) whether

the data are appended to the data consumer (symbol + in Fig. 2) or the contents of the data consumer are overwritten from the output of the operation (symbol ! in Fig. 2).

Template Layer. Providing a single metaclass for all the possible activities of an ETL environment is not really enough for the designer of the overall process. A richer "language" should be available, in order to describe the structure of the process and facilitate its construction. To this end, we provide a set of *Template Activities* (*Template Layer* in Fig. 1), which are specializations of the generic metamodel class. We have already pursued this goal in a previous effort [5]; in this paper, we extend this set of template objects and deal with the semantics of their combination (see [4] for more details).

Filters

SELECTION ($\varphi(A_{n+1},\ldots,A_{n+k})$)
UNIQUE VALUE (R.A)
NOT NULL (R.A)
DOMAIN MISMATCH (R.A,x_{low},x_{high})
PRIMARY KEY VIOLATION (R.A_1,...,R.A_K)
FOREIGN KEY VIOLATION ([R.A_1,...,R.A_K],[S.A_1,...,S.A_K])

Unary Transformations

PUSH
AGGREGATION ([A_1,...,A_k],[$\gamma_1(A_1)$,...,$\gamma_m(A_m)$])
PROJECTION([A_1,...,A_k])
FUNCTION APPLICATION($f_1(A_1)$,...,$f_k(A_k)$)
SURROGATE KEY ASSIGNMENT (R.PRODKEY,S.SKEY,x)
TUPLE NORMALIZATION (R.A_{n+1},...,R.A_{n+k},A_{CODE},A_{VALUE},h)
TUPLE DENORMALIZATION (A_{CODE},A_{VALUE},R.A_{n+1},...,R.A_{n+k},h')

Binary Transformations

UNION(R,S)
JOIN(R,S,[(A_1,B_1),...,(A_k,B_k)])
DIFF(R,S,[(A_1,B_1),...,(A_k,B_k)])

Fig. 3 Template Activities grouped by category

As one can see in Fig. 3, we group the template activities in three major groups. The first group, named *Filters*, provides checks for the respect of a certain condition by the rows of a certain condition. The semantics of these filters are the obvious (starting from a generic selection condition and proceeding to the check of *value uniqueness*, *primary or foreign key violation*, etc.). The second group of template activities is called *Unary Transformations* and except for the most generic *Push* activity (which simply propagates data from the provider to the consumer) consists of the classical *aggregation* and *function application* operations along with three data warehouse specific transformations (*surrogate key assignment, normalization* and *denormalization*). The third group consists of classical *Binary Operations*, such as *union*, *join* and *difference* with the last being a special case of the classic relational operator.

Custom Layer. The instantiation and the reuse of template activities are also allowed in our framework. The activities that stem from the composition of other activities are called *composite activities*, whereas the instantiations of template activities will be grouped under the general name of *custom activities* (*Custom Layer* in Fig. 1). Custom activities are applied over the specific recordsets of an ETL environment. Moreover, they also involve the construction of ad-hoc, user tailored elementary activities by the designer.

3 Exploitation of the Model

In order to perform operations like zooming in/out, consistency checking and what-if analysis, each scenario is modeled as a graph, which we call the *Architecture Graph* (see [4] from more details). Activities, data stores and attributes are modeled as nodes and their relationships as edges.

Zooming in and out the architecture graph. We can zoom in and out the architecture graph, in order to eliminate the information overflow, which can be caused by the vast number of involved attributes in a scenario. In a different kind of zooming, we can follow the major flow of data from sources to the targets.

Consistency Checks. We can perform several consistency checks on the architecture graph, like the detection of activities having input attributes without data providers, the detection of non-source tables having attributes without data providers, or the detection of useless source attributes.

What-if analysis. We can identify possible impacts in the case of a change, by modeling changes as additions, removals or renaming of edges and nodes. Still, out of the several alternatives, only the *drop node* operation seems to have interesting side effects. Moreover, even if atomic operations are of no significance by themselves, they are important when they are considered in the case of composite operation transitions.

References

1. H. Galhardas, D. Florescu, D. Shasha and E. Simon. Ajax: An Extensible Data Cleaning Tool. In Proc. ACM SIGMOD Intl. Conf. On the Management of Data, pp. 590, Dallas, Texas, (2000).
2. V. Raman, J. Hellerstein. Potters Wheel: An Interactive Framework for Data Cleaning and Transformation. Technical Report University of California at Berkeley, Computer Science Division, 2000. Available at http://www.cs.berkeley.edu/~rshankar/papers/pwheel.pdf
3. S. Sarawagi. Special Issue on Data Cleaning (ed.). IEEE Computer Society, Bulletin of the Technical Committee on Data Engineering, **23**(4), (2000).

4. P. Vassiliadis, A. Simitsis, S. Skiadopoulos. On the Conceptual and Logical Modeling of ETL Processes. Available at http://www.dbnet.ece.ntua.gr/~pvassil/publications/VaSS_TR.pdf
5. P. Vassiliadis, Z. Vagena, S. Skiadopoulos, N. Karayannidis, T. Sellis. Arktos: Towards the modeling, design, control and execution of ETL processes. Information Systems, 26(8), pp. 537-561, December 2001, Elsevier Science Ltd.

Intelligent Agent Supported Flexible Workflow Monitoring System

Minhong Wang and Huaiqing Wang

Department of Information Systems, City University of Hong Kong
Kowloon, Hong Kong
{iswmh,iswang}@is.cityu.edu.hk

Abstract. The unpredictability of business process requires workflow systems to support workflow monitoring functions with the ability to flexibly adapt to the changing environment. Traditional approaches to handling this problem have fallen short, providing little support for monitoring flexibility. In this paper, we will describe a flexible workflow monitoring system, in which a society of intelligent agents work together to perform flexible monitoring processes based on various monitoring requests.

1 Intelligent Agent Assistance

With the rising tide of unexpected output of tasks, events or exceptions due to changing environment to be met with during the whole life of an organization, the reinforcement of workflow adaptability has become crucial to cater for these deviations [1]. It is important for exception management to have the ability to detect an actual exception or the possibility of an exception as well as improve the ability of participant to react and recover. However, present workflow systems provide only a few built-in monitoring functions, not allowed changes of monitoring specifications [2]. Our proposed monitoring system is to develop a flexible monitoring application, in which various monitors can execute respective monitoring tasks by submitting their monitoring requests on workflow management. It is our belief that intelligent agents are well suited to dealing with problems of flexible monitoring in an autonomous and collaborative fashion. By utilizing a society of intelligent agents, each charged with carrying out a different function autonomously, such as monitoring request processing, monitoring scheming, data searching and diagnosing, our workflow monitoring system can be applied to perform monitoring tasks in a flexible way.

Intelligent agents, which used to denote software-based computer systems that enjoy such properties as autonomy, co-operativity, reactivity, pro-activity and mobility [3], are well suited to dealing with flexible monitoring in our system. The proposed system consists of a number of agents, which operate autonomously and cooperate with each other to perform their tasks. The taxonomy of intelligent agents with specific behaviours is shown in Fig.1. In our system, intelligent agents can be classified into the following five sub-classes in terms of their functions.

User Agent. User Agent assists monitors to input various monitoring requests, receive monitoring results and communicate with other monitors for further decision.

Monitoring Scheming Agent. This agent is charged to process monitors' requests, generate respective monitoring schemes, and send them to Searching Agents and Diagnostic Agent to perform data searching and diagnosing respectively.

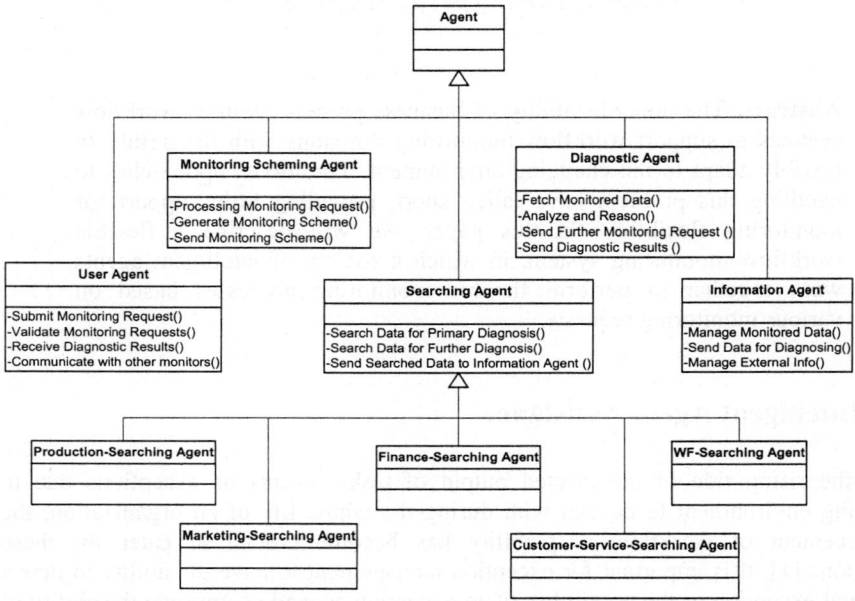

Fig.1. A class diagram of intelligent agents in the workflow monitoring system

Searching Agent. There are various searching agents in our system, such as Workflow Searching Agent, Production Searching Agent, Marketing Searching Agent, and so on, which may be located distributedly. Each assists to collect monitored data in workflow systems or other application systems for various monitoring schemes.

Diagnostic Agent. The role of this agent is to make analysis for various monitoring schemes, and then distribute diagnostic results such as warning messages or workflow adjustment indications to monitors or a workflow system. Diagnoses are made on the basis of diagnostic rules specialized in monitoring schemes, as well as diagnostic policies stored in Diagnostic Agent as meta level knowledge for diagnosis.

Information Agent. This agent is responsible for information relative management for monitoring processes, such as information store, retrieval or filtration on monitored data, monitoring reports, other monitors' information, industry information or other useful information supporting monitoring.

2   System Architecture

Based on the above taxonomy of intelligent agents, we present the architecture of our intelligent agents based workflow monitoring system in Fig.2. This framework provides the conceptual basis for thinking about the overall monitoring system.

As an independent monitoring system, our system contains two kinds of interactions with outside. First, various monitors interact with the monitoring system via User

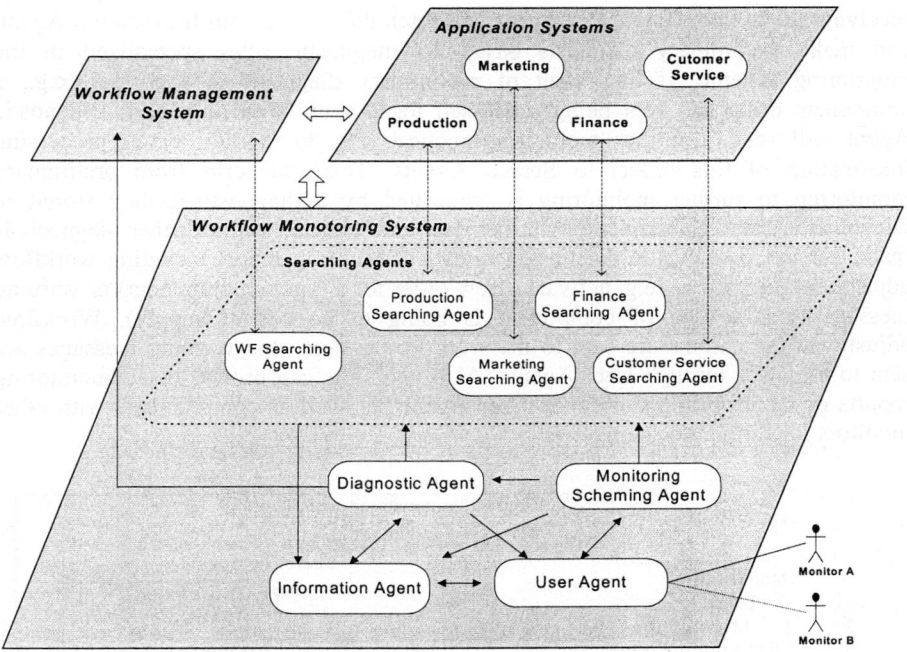

Fig.2. An architecture of intelligent agents based workflow monitoring system

Agents to search available monitored data lists, submit monitoring requests, receive warning messages, browse monitoring reports, as well as communicate with other monitors for further decision. Second, our monitoring system interacts with a workflow system or other application systems of an organization to collect necessary information for monitoring as well as perform adjustments on the workflow system. The operation inside the monitoring system is described in the following section.

3   System Operation

In order to evaluate the effectiveness of our proposed workflow monitoring system, we will describe its operation (see Fig.3) based on an example of a monitoring process to demonstrate how these intelligent agents work together.

For example, a monitor is to monitor components supply for current production. He submits his monitoring request including monitored data list (e.g. order status, available time, quantity in storage) and diagnostic rules (e.g. order status rule, minimum storage rule) via User Agent to Monitoring Scheming Agent. Then, Monitoring Agent transforms this monitoring request into a monitoring scheme after interpretation and validity checking on it, and sends the monitoring scheme to relative Searching Agents and Diagnostic Agent. After receiving the monitoring scheme, Search Agents will collect relative data for preliminary diagnosis, and send them to Information Agent as well as send a data-available notice to Diagnostic Agent. Once receiving the notice, Diagnostic Agent will fetch those data from Information Agent, and make preliminary diagnosis based on diagnostic rules specialized in the monitoring scheme. If the result of preliminary diagnosis is abnormal (e.g., a component order has kept being processed for 2 hours with no reply), Diagnostic Agent will send a further monitoring request (e.g. to monitor detail processing information of this order) to Search Agents. This transform from preliminary monitoring to further monitoring is controlled by a diagnostic policy stored in Diagnostic Agent. Subsequently, further data are collected and a further diagnosis is made. At last, Diagnostic Agent generates a monitoring report including workflow adjustment indications (e.g. activate a new order for a type of component) or warning message (e.g. a type of component is going to be out of supply). Workflow adjustment indications are sent to the workflow system, and warning messages are sent to monitors through User Agents. Also, monitors can browse detail monitoring reports or monitoring histories via User Agents, as well as communicate with other monitors for further decision.

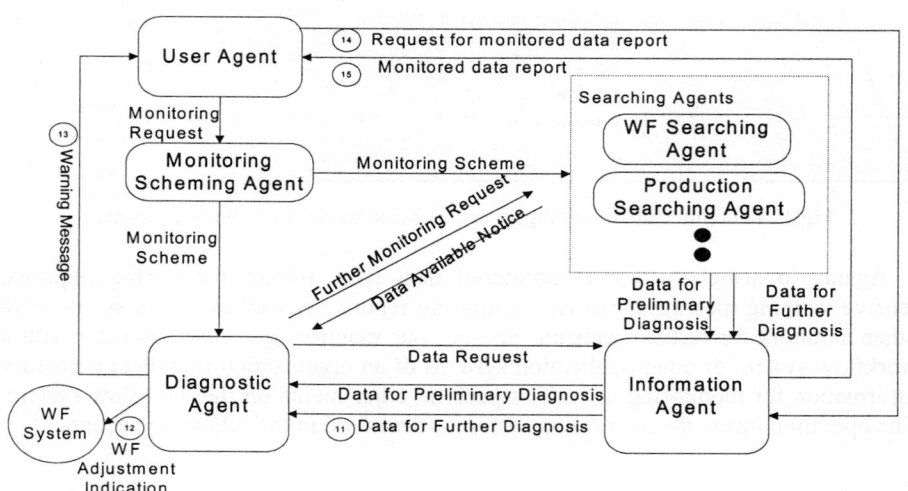

Fig.3. Intelligent agents based flexible monitoring operation

References

1. Kammer, P.J., Bolcer, G.A., Taylor, R.N., Hitomi, A.S., Bergman, M., Techniques for Supporting Dynamic and Adaptive Workflow, Computer Supported Cooperative Work (CSCW), November 2000, pp.269-292.
2. Baker, D.; Georgakopoulos, D.; Schuster, H.; Cassandra, A.; Cichocki, A., Providing customized process and situation awareness in the collaboration management infrastructure, Cooperative Information Systems, 1999. CoopIS '99. Proceedings. 1999 IFCIS International Conference on, 1999, pp.79 –91.
3. Wang, H., "Intelligent Agent Assisted Decision Support Systems: Integration of Knowledge Discovery, Knowledge Analysis, and Group Decision Support", Expert Systems with Applications, 1997, Vol. 12, No. 3, pp.323-335.

A Meeting Scheduling System Based on Open Constraint Programming

Kenny Qili Zhu and Andrew E. Santosa

Department of Computer Science, National University of Singapore
S16, 3 Science Drive 2, Singapore 117543, Republic of Singapore
{kzhu,andrews}@comp.nus.edu.sg

Abstract. In this paper, we introduce a meeting scheduling system based on open constraint programming (OCP) paradigm. OCP is an extension to constraint logic programming (CLP), where a server capable of executing constraint logic programs acts as a mediator of communicating reactive agents. A meeting among several users can be scheduled automatically by a constraint logic program in the server based on the meeting participants' preferences. Flexible user preferences can be programmed using the OCP reactors language. CLP is suitable to be used in meeting scheduling which is a combinatorial problem. Its declarative programmability is more amenable to changes.

1 Introduction

Commercial calendars such as Outlook are not flexible enough to adapt to different working environments. On the other hand, building custom software is often costly and does not cater for frequent changes in corporate management.

In this paper, we present a meeting scheduling system based on *Open Constraint Programming* (*OCP*) paradigm [3]. OCP extends CLP with *reactivity* and *openness*. OCP is a concurrent programming framework which allows special queries that react to internal and external events, hence the reactivity. The queries can be submitted by concurrently running, distributed client programs that can be written in any language, hence the openness. These queries, a.k.a. *reactors*, are written using a simple language with synchronization and time-out capabilities. Our system stands out from the rest due to this *declarative programmability* of scheduling constraints.

The system consist of a constraint store in the form of a constraint logic program, a CLP($\mathcal{R}$) solver, an OCP server, and a web-based CGI user interface. The store contains global and user data, integrity and user constraints and other rules that govern the behavior of the system. The users may send a query by clicking buttons on the user interface. These are translated into OCP reactors and sent to the server. Some of the reactors can be delayed in the server and triggered later when some condition is satisfied.

In the next section we will explain the knowledge base which is a part of the constraint logic program. We will thus elaborate on the triggering mechanism in Section 3. We will describe some related works in Section 4 before concluding our paper in Section 5.

2 Knowledge Base

We assume an organization consisting of research groups, as in universities. A research group itself consists of a principal researcher, and co-researchers. A principal researcher often needs to call for a meeting by announcing it to the potential participants. The participants thus reply to the announcement by stating their preferences on the timing. These concepts are captured by the following components of the constraint store:

- **Users.** There are three *roles* in the system, namely *normal users* (or *participants*), *hosts*, and *administrator*. A user assumes at least one of the role, and can have multiple roles at the same time.
- **User preferences.** All the preferences are real numbers between 0 and 1, where 0 represent "blackout" for that slot and 1 shows a free slot. For example:
  pref(kenny, pingpongmatch, [1.0, 1.0, 0.5, ..., 0.3, 1.0]).
- **Public resources.** Resources required for the meetings like space and equipment.
- **Public meetings.** Each is defined as having a *title*, *proposed participants*, *required resources*, *deadline of submission*, and *schedule time window*.
- **Bundles.** Bundles are collections of time slots with practical meaning to a user or a group of users, e.g. "all mornings", "every Tuesday afternoon", "lunch time", etc.
- **Optimization rules and integrity constraints.** The optimization rules aim at maximizing the combined weighted preferences of all participants of a meeting, and the integrity constraints ensure that no conflicts such as one resource being used in two locations will occur.

The CLP($\mathcal{R}$) solver is used to solve the *static event scheduling problem:* Given a set of variable constraints on participants, resources and meeting time window, produce a schedule of events that achieve collective satisfaction among all the participants before pre-defined deadlines. When there are a number of events to be scheduled together, this becomes a combinatorial optimization problem. The constraint solving based on CLP($\mathcal{R}$) allows a good, if not optimal, solution.

User-defined constraints and their preferences can be added, removed or changed dynamically. For example, as a user adds more meetings to attend to his calendar, the addition will be automatically translated into changed preferences. Each such change will trigger a constraint solving procedure.

3 User Reactors

OCP is a framework which generalizes constraint stores and their interactions [3]. The essential model consists of a shared constraint store, concurrent programmable agents, which are independent of the store, and a notion of reactor, which provides synchronization and atomicity of operations against the store. A reactor follows this syntax:

$$\textbf{wait } \langle cond_1 \rangle \Rightarrow \langle action \rangle$$
$$\textbf{unless } \langle cond_2 \rangle$$

The reactor would be suspended in the OCP server until the *sustain condition* $\langle cond_1 \rangle$ becomes true and remains true during the execution of $\langle action \rangle$. At any point, any query or suspended query will be aborted when the *timeout condition* $\langle cond_2 \rangle$ is satisfied.

Next we introduce the workings of the system by using sample reactors.

User's calendar consists of time slots. Priority states how much the user prefers to attend that meeting in the time slot. The reverse of this priority which we call *preference* is defined as $preference(time, user) = 1 - priority(time, user)/10$. The following is the reactor triggered if a user is invited to a meeting:

wait $\texttt{invited}(meeting, participants), user \in participants$
$\Rightarrow \texttt{update\_pref}(user, preferences), \texttt{update\_cons}(user, constraints)$
unless $\texttt{false}$

A normal user may manually change their preferences in the calendar, and re-submit it. Some other meetings added to the system may also automatically change his or her preferences. When a tentative schedule has been computed, it is marked on the user's calendar. We have the reactors:

wait $\texttt{true}$
$\Rightarrow \texttt{set\_pref}(user, preferences),$
$\quad \texttt{set\_cons}(user, constraints)$
unless $\texttt{false}$

wait $\texttt{tentative\_schedule}(meeting, time)$
$\Rightarrow \texttt{mark\_calendar}(meeting, time)$
unless $\texttt{deadline}(meeting, d), clock?d$

The host is a special user proposing a meeting:
wait $\texttt{true} \Rightarrow \texttt{propose}(meeting, timewindow, participants, resources)$
unless $\texttt{false}$

The host has the right to favor certain participants by giving their preferences higher priority, so that their weighted preferences are higher.

After all participants have submitted their preferences and constraints, the solver will present to the host the average preferences of all the time slot within the time window, along with the best solutions, in the form of a preferences table. The host may thus choose one of the time slot for the meeting. The host also reserves the right to cancel the meeting if it is no longer needed, or if the schedule produced by the system is not satisfactory. However, the host may not tamper with other user's preferences to make a particular time slot more favorable. As user preferences change over time, the server computes new average preferences. The host thus may change the meeting's schedule accordingly. The host can also submit constraints to bias the solutions computed by the server since the system is very flexible to cope with changes in such requirements. By entering different constraints using the user interface, the behavior of the system can be altered easily.

The following reactor is used by the host to notify the participants of a new solution to meeting schedule:

wait $\texttt{new\_schedule}(meetings, times), meeting \in meetings, time \in times$
$\Rightarrow \texttt{tentative\_schedule}(meeting, time)$
unless $\texttt{false}$

The administrator is in charge of scheduling for all meetings whenever any user preferences, constraints or required resources are updated. The following reactor sustains on such changes:

wait (change_resource(r), $r \in resources$;
 change_preferences($user, preferences$), $user \in participants$);
 change_constraints($user, constraints$), $user \in participants$)
$\Rightarrow$ re_schedule($open\_meetings, times$)
unless deadline($meeting, d$), $meeting \in open\_meetings$, $clock?d$

The administrator also controls the availability of public resources:
wait true $\Rightarrow$ update_resource($resource, newschedule$)
unless false

4 Related Work

In the paper [6], the authors stated that 88% of the users of calendar system said that they use calendars to schedule meetings. This justifies an integrated approach to calendar and meeting scheduling system. As in our system, in [1] the meeting scheduling system is integrated with users' calendar. User specifies the events that they want to attend, and the priority of the event. Users calendars are combined to find an appropriate time slot for a meeting. However, negotiation is done manually through exchanging of email messages. Our system can be seen as providing additional automated negotiation feature.

The paper [7] describes a formal framework for analyzing distributed meeting scheduling systems in terms of quantitative predictions. The aspects analyzed are announcement strategies, bidding strategies and commitment strategies. Interesting analyses are presented in the paper, including probability of time slots being available.

Groupware toolkits [2,5,4] provide APIs for building groupware applications. The APIs often provide user configurability as a limited fashion to cope with changes in user requirements. However, toolkits are intended solely to be used by the developers, but our system is intended to be programmable by the users as well as developers.

5 Conclusion

In this paper we have presented a meeting scheduling system. The system consists of a single open constraint programming (OCP) server and a number of client calendars UI. The OCP server provides synchronization, concurrency control, and a knowledge base. The constraint solving capability at the server aims at maximizing user satisfaction in terms of preferences. We have presented a set of reactors functioning to schedule meetings that can be submitted from the client UI. In future, more advanced topics such as scalability, fault tolerance and communication efficiency, as well as actual usability of the system will be addressed.

References

1. D. Beard, M. Palaniappan, A. Humm, D. Banks, A. Nair, and Y.-P. Shan. A visual calendar for scheduling group meetings. In *Proceedings of the CSCW '90 Conference on Computer-Supported Cooperative Work*, pages 279–290. ACM Press, 1990.
2. S. Greenberg and M. Roseman. Groupware toolkit for synchronous work. In M. Beaudoin-Lafon, editor, *Computer-Supported Cooperative Work*, volume 7 of *Trends in Software*, chapter 6, pages 135–168. John Wiley & Sons, Ltd, 1999.
3. J. Jaffar and R. H. C. Yap. Open constraint programming. In *Principles and Practice of Constraint Programming – CP'98, 4th International Conference, Pisa, Italy*, volume 1520 of *Lecture Notes in Computer Science*, page 1. Springer, 1998.
4. Lotus Corp. *Lotus Notes Developer's Guide Version 4.0*. Cambridge, MA, USA, 1995.
5. I. Marsic. A framework for multimodal collaboration in heterogeneous environments. *ACM Computing Surveys*, (4), June 1999.
6. L. Palen. Social, individual, and technological issues for groupware calendar systems. In *Proceedings of the CHI '99 Conference on Human Factors in Computing Systems*, pages 17–24. ACM Press, 1999.
7. S. Sen and E. H. Durfee. A formal study of distributed meeting scheduling. *Group Decision and Negotiation*, 7:265–289, 1998.

Author Index

Aalst, W. M. P. van der 535
Adiba, M. 692
Aedo, I. 747
Analyti, A. 778
Andersson, B. 600
Aoumeur, N. 296
Arjona, J. L. 697

Benatallah, B. 344
Benerecetti, M. 311
Berlin, J. 452
Bhatia, M. P. S. 612
Brasethvik, T. 167
Brodie, M. L. 1
Bruno, G. 774
Bübl, F. 404
Bussler, C. 701

Cai, Z. 706
Calì, A. 262
Calvanese, D. 262
Cohen, M. A. 52
Combi, C. 711
Constantopoulos, P. 778
Corchuelo, R. 697
Costal, D. 659
Curson, J. 100
Cymerman, S. G. 67

Dadarlat, V. 737
Dahchour, M. 643
Dalkilic, M. 757
Dew, P. 100
Dittrich, K. R. 715
Domenig, R. 715
Díaz, P. 747

Eder, J. 83
Embley, D. W. 719

Fent, A. 516
Filha, I.M.R. E. 719
Fox, M. S. 230
Freitag, B. 516

Gans, G. 328
Genero, M. 724
Gergatsoulis, M. 183
Giacomo, G. De 262
Gómez, C. 467
Grundy, J. 728
Gulla, J. A. 167

Hamadi, R. 344
Harren, A. 733
Hirnschall, A. 535
Hoover, H. J. 151
Hou, D. 151
Houben, G.-J. 584
Huisman, M. 134

Iivari, J. 134
Ilebrekke, L. 761
Ivan, C. 737

Jajodia, S. 553
Jarke, M. 2, 4, 328
Johannesson, P. 600

Kajko-Mattsson, M. 436
Kang, H. 742
Kim, H. M. 230
Klamma, R. 4
Klischewski, R. 500
Koncilia, C. 83
Kwon, D. 377

Laender, A. H. F. 719
Lakemeyer, G. 328
Lee, S. 377

Author Index

Lee, S. 377
Leicher, A. 404
Leite, J. C. S. do Prado 420
Lenzerini, M. 262
Leonardi, M. C. 420
Li, Y. 553
Lim, J. G. 742
Lipson, H. F. 216
Liu, L. 37
Liu, M. 568
Liu, P. 100
Lu, J. 361
Lü, K. 770

McBrien, P. 484
Mead, N. R. 216
Mendelzon, A. O. 67
Mohan, R. 52
Montanari, A. 711
Montero, S. 747
Moore, A. P. 216
Morzy, T. 83
Motro, A. 452

Norrie, M. C. 245

Olivé, A. 467, 675

Päivärinta, T. 117
Paik, H.-Y. 344
Palinginis, A. 245
Panti, M. 311
Papadopoulos, N. 200
Papazoglou, M.. P. 21
Perjons, E. 600
Piattini, M. 724
Pirotte, A. 643
Plexousakis, D. 200
Poels, G. 724
Pontieri, L. 752
Poulovassilis, A. 484
Prakash, N. 612
Pusztai, K. 737

Reiter, H. 516
Ruaro, W. 67
Ruiz, A. 697

Saake, G. 296
Saeki, M. 626
Sancho, M.-R. 659
Santosa, A. E. 792
Schiefer, J. 52
Sengupta, A. 757
Silva, A. S. da 719
Simitsis, A. 782
Skiadopoulos, S. 782
Smolander, K. 117
Söderström, E. 600
Spalazzi, L. 311
Spyratos, N. 778
Stavrakas, Y. 183
Stroulia, E. 151, 280
Su, X. 761
Sugumaran, V. 766
Sun, W. 770

Tacconi, S. 311
Tanniru, M. 766
Tapken, H. 733
Teniente, E. 659
Torchiano, M. 774
Toro, M. 697
Tzitzikas, Y. 778

Ursino, D. 752

Vaisman, A. A. 67
Vassiliadis, P. 782
Vdovjak, R. 584
Verbeek, H. M. W. 535
Vits, T. 328

Wang, H. 787
Wang, L. 553
Wang, M. 787
Wang, X. S. 553
Wangler, B. 600
Welty, C. 3

Wetzel, I. 500	Zechinelli-Martini, J.-L. 692
Wilson, J. N. 392	Zhang, H. 280
	Zhu, K. Q. 792
	Zimányi, E. 643
Yang, J. 21	Zou, W. 728
Yu, E. 37, 706	Zumpano, E. 752

Lecture Notes in Computer Science

For information about Vols. 1–2269
please contact your bookseller or Springer-Verlag

Vol. 2270: M. Pflanz, On-line Error Detection and Fast Recover Techniques for Dependable Embedded Processors. XII, 126 pages. 2002.

Vol. 2271: B. Preneel (Ed.), Topics in Cryptology – CT-RSA 2002. Proceedings, 2002. X, 311 pages. 2002.

Vol. 2272: D. Bert, J.P. Bowen, M.C. Henson, K. Robinson (Eds.), ZB 2002: Formal Specification and Development in Z and B. Proceedings, 2002. XII, 535 pages. 2002.

Vol. 2273: A.R. Coden, E.W. Brown, S. Srinivasan (Eds.), Information Retrieval Techniques for Speech Applications. XI, 109 pages. 2002.

Vol. 2274: D. Naccache, P. Paillier (Eds.), Public Key Cryptography. Proceedings, 2002. XI, 385 pages. 2002.

Vol. 2275: N.R. Pal, M. Sugeno (Eds.), Advances in Soft Computing – AFSS 2002. Proceedings, 2002. XVI, 536 pages. 2002. (Subseries LNAI).

Vol. 2276: A. Gelbukh (Ed.), Computational Linguistics and Intelligent Text Processing. Proceedings, 2002. XIII, 444 pages. 2002.

Vol. 2277: P. Callaghan, Z. Luo, J. McKinna, R. Pollack (Eds.), Types for Proofs and Programs. Proceedings, 2000. VIII, 243 pages. 2002.

Vol. 2278: J.A. Foster, E. Lutton, J. Miller, C. Ryan, A.G.B. Tettamanzi (Eds.), Genetic Programming. Proceedings, 2002. XI, 337 pages. 2002.

Vol. 2279: S. Cagnoni, J. Gottlieb, E. Hart, M. Middendorf, G.R. Raidl (Eds.), Applications of Evolutionary Computing. Proceedings, 2002. XIII, 344 pages. 2002.

Vol. 2280: J.P. Katoen, P. Stevens (Eds.), Tools and Algorithms for the Construction and Analysis of Systems. Proceedings, 2002. XIII, 482 pages. 2002.

Vol. 2281: S. Arikawa, A. Shinohara (Eds.), Progress in Discovery Science. XIV, 684 pages. 2002. (Subseries LNAI).

Vol. 2282: D. Ursino, Extraction and Exploitation of Intensional Knowledge from Heterogeneous Information Sources. XXVI, 289 pages. 2002.

Vol. 2283: T. Nipkow, L.C. Paulson, M. Wenzel, Isabelle/HOL. XIII, 218 pages. 2002.

Vol. 2284: T. Eiter, K.-D. Schewe (Eds.), Foundations of Information and Knowledge Systems. Proceedings, 2002. X, 289 pages. 2002.

Vol. 2285: H. Alt, A. Ferreira (Eds.), STACS 2002. Proceedings, 2002. XIV, 660 pages. 2002.

Vol. 2286: S. Rajsbaum (Ed.), LATIN 2002: Theoretical Informatics. Proceedings, 2002. XIII, 630 pages. 2002.

Vol. 2287: C.S. Jensen, K.G. Jeffery, J. Pokorny, Saltenis, E. Bertino, K. Böhm, M. Jarke (Eds.), Advances in Database Technology – EDBT 2002. Proceedings, 2002. XVI, 776 pages. 2002.

Vol. 2288: K. Kim (Ed.), Information Security and Cryptology – ICISC 2001. Proceedings, 2001. XIII, 457 pages. 2002.

Vol. 2289: C.J. Tomlin, M.R. Greenstreet (Eds.), Hybrid Systems: Computation and Control. Proceedings, 2002. XIII, 480 pages. 2002.

Vol. 2290: F. van der Linden (Ed.), Software Product-Family Engineering. Proceedings, 2001. X, 417 pages. 2002.

Vol. 2291: F. Crestani, M. Girolami, C.J. van Rijsbergen (Eds.), Advances in Information Retrieval. Proceedings, 2002. XIII, 363 pages. 2002.

Vol. 2292: G.B. Khosrovshahi, A. Shokoufandeh, A. Shokrollahi (Eds.), Theoretical Aspects of Computer Science. IX, 221 pages. 2002.

Vol. 2293: J. Renz, Qualitative Spatial Reasoning with Topological Information. XVI, 207 pages. 2002. (Subseries LNAI).

Vol. 2294: A. Cortesi (Ed.), Verification, Model Checking, and Abstract Interpretation. Proceedings, 2002. VIII, 331 pages. 2002.

Vol. 2295: W. Kuich, G. Rozenberg, A. Salomaa (Eds.), Developments in Language Theory. Proceedings, 2001. IX, 389 pages. 2002.

Vol. 2296: B. Dunin-Kęplicz, E. Nawarecki (Eds.), From Theory to Practice in Multi-Agent Systems. Proceedings, 2001. IX, 341 pages. 2002. (Subseries LNAI).

Vol. 2297: R. Backhouse, R. Crole, J. Gibbons (Eds.), Algebraic and Coalgebraic Methods in the Mathematics of Program Construction. Proceedings, 2000. XIV, 387 pages. 2002.

Vol. 2298: I. Wachsmuth, T. Sowa (Eds.), Gesture and Language in Human-Computer Interaction. Proceedings, 2001. XI, 323 pages. 2002. (Subseries LNAI).

Vol. 2299: H. Schmeck, T. Ungerer, L. Wolf (Eds.), Trends in Network and Pervasive Computing – ARCS 2002. Proceedings, 2002. XIV, 287 pages. 2002.

Vol. 2300: W. Brauer, H. Ehrig, J. Karhumäki, A. Salomaa (Eds.), Formal and Natural Computing. XXXVI, 431 pages. 2002.

Vol. 2301: A. Braquelaire, J.-O. Lachaud, A. Vialard (Eds.), Discrete Geometry for Computer Imagery. Proceedings, 2002. XI, 439 pages. 2002.

Vol. 2302: C. Schulte, Programming Constraint Services. XII, 176 pages. 2002. (Subseries LNAI).

Vol. 2303: M. Nielsen, U. Engberg (Eds.), Foundations of Software Science and Computation Structures. Proceedings, 2002. XIII, 435 pages. 2002.

Vol. 2304: R.N. Horspool (Ed.), Compiler Construction. Proceedings, 2002. XI, 343 pages. 2002.

Vol. 2305: D. Le Métayer (Ed.), Programming Languages and Systems. Proceedings, 2002. XII, 331 pages. 2002.

Vol. 2306: R.-D. Kutsche, H. Weber (Eds.), Fundamental Approaches to Software Engineering. Proceedings, 2002. XIII, 341 pages. 2002.

Vol. 2307: C. Zhang, S. Zhang, Association Rule Mining. XII, 238 pages. 2002. (Subseries LNAI).

Vol. 2308: I.P. Vlahavas, C.D. Spyropoulos (Eds.), Methods and Applications of Artificial Intelligence. Proceedings, 2002. XIV, 514 pages. 2002. (Subseries LNAI).

Vol. 2309: A. Armando (Ed.), Frontiers of Combining Systems. Proceedings, 2002. VIII, 255 pages. 2002. (Subseries LNAI).

Vol. 2310: P. Collet, C. Fonlupt, J.-K. Hao, E. Lutton, M. Schoenauer (Eds.), Artificial Evolution. Proceedings, 2001. XI, 375 pages. 2002.

Vol. 2311: D. Bustard, W. Liu, R. Sterritt (Eds.), Soft-Ware 2002: Computing in an Imperfect World. Proceedings, 2002. XI, 359 pages. 2002.

Vol. 2312: T. Arts, M. Mohnen (Eds.), Implementation of Functional Languages. Proceedings, 2001. VII, 187 pages. 2002.

Vol. 2313: C.A. Coello Coello, A. de Albornoz, L.E. Sucar, O.Cairó Battistutti (Eds.), MICAI 2002: Advances in Artificial Intelligence. Proceedings, 2002. XIII, 548 pages. 2002. (Subseries LNAI).

Vol. 2314: S.-K. Chang, Z. Chen, S.-Y. Lee (Eds.), Recent Advances in Visual Information Systems. Proceedings, 2002. XI, 323 pages. 2002.

Vol. 2315: F. Arhab, C. Talcott (Eds.), Coordination Models and Languages. Proceedings, 2002. XI, 406 pages. 2002.

Vol. 2316: J. Domingo-Ferrer (Ed.), Inference Control in Statistical Databases. VIII, 231 pages. 2002.

Vol. 2317: M. Hegarty, B. Meyer, N. Hari Narayanan (Eds.), Diagrammatic Representation and Inference. Proceedings, 2002. XIV, 362 pages. 2002. (Subseries LNAI).

Vol. 2318: D. Bošnački, S. Leue (Eds.), Model Checking Software. Proceedings, 2002. X, 259 pages. 2002.

Vol. 2319: C. Gacek (Ed.), Software Reuse: Methods, Techniques, and Tools. Proceedings, 2002. XI, 353 pages. 2002.

Vol.2320: T. Sander (Ed.), Security and Privacy in Digital Rights Management. Proceedings, 2001. X, 245 pages. 2002.

Vol. 2322: V. Mařík, O. Štěpánková, H. Krautwurmová, M. Luck (Eds.), Multi-Agent Systems and Applications II. Proceedings, 2001. XII, 377 pages. 2002. (Subseries LNAI).

Vol. 2323: À. Frohner (Ed.), Object-Oriented Technology. Proceedings, 2001. IX, 225 pages. 2002.

Vol. 2324: T. Field, P.G. Harrison, J. Bradley, U. Harder (Eds.), Computer Performance Evaluation. Proceedings, 2002. XI, 349 pages. 2002.

Vol 2326: D. Grigoras, A. Nicolau, B. Toursel, B. Folliot (Eds.), Advanced Environments, Tools, and Applications for Cluster Computing. Proceedings, 2001. XIII, 321 pages. 2002.

Vol. 2327: H.P. Zima, K. Joe, M. Sato, Y. Seo, M. Shimasaki (Eds.), High Performance Computing. Proceedings, 2002. XV, 564 pages. 2002.

Vol. 2329: P.M.A. Sloot, C.J.K. Tan, J.J. Dongarra, A.G. Hoekstra (Eds.), Computational Science – ICCS 2002. Proceedings, Part I. XLI, 1095 pages. 2002.

Vol. 2330: P.M.A. Sloot, C.J.K. Tan, J.J. Dongarra, A.G. Hoekstra (Eds.), Computational Science – ICCS 2002. Proceedings, Part II. XLI, 1115 pages. 2002.

Vol. 2331: P.M.A. Sloot, C.J.K. Tan, J.J. Dongarra, A.G. Hoekstra (Eds.), Computational Science – ICCS 2002. Proceedings, Part III. XLI, 1227 pages. 2002.

Vol. 2332: L. Knudsen (Ed.), Advances in Cryptology – EUROCRYPT 2002. Proceedings, 2002. XII, 547 pages. 2002.

Vol. 2334: G. Carle, M. Zitterbart (Eds.), Protocols for High Speed Networks. Proceedings, 2002. X, 267 pages. 2002.

Vol. 2335: M. Butler, L. Petre, K. Sere (Eds.), Integrated Formal Methods. Proceedings, 2002. X, 401 pages. 2002.

Vol. 2336: M.-S. Chen, P.S. Yu, B. Liu (Eds.), Advances in Knowledge Discovery and Data Mining. Proceedings, 2002. XIII, 568 pages. 2002. (Subseries LNAI).

Vol. 2337: W.J. Cook, A.S. Schulz (Eds.), Integer Programming and Combinatorial Optimization. Proceedings, 2002. XI, 487 pages. 2002.

Vol. 2338: R. Cohen, B. Spencer (Eds.), Advances in Artificial Intelligence. Proceedings, 2002. X, 197 pages. 2002. (Subseries LNAI).

Vol. 2342: I. Horrocks, J. Hendler (Eds.), The Semantic Web – ISCW 2002. Proceedings, 2002. XVI, 476 pages. 2002.

Vol. 2345: E. Gregori, M. Conti, A.T. Campbell, G. Omidyar, M. Zukerman (Eds.), NETWORKING 2002. Proceedings, 2002. XXVI, 1256 pages. 2002.

Vol. 2347: P. De Bra, P. Brusilovsky, R. Conejo (Eds.), Adaptive Hypermedia and Adaptive Web-Based Systems. Proceedings, 2002. XV, 615 pages. 2002.

Vol. 2348: A. Banks Pidduck, J. Mylopoulos, C.C. Woo, M. Tamer Ozsu (Eds.), Advanced Information Systems Engineering. Proceedings, 2002. XIV, 799 pages. 2002.

Vol. 2349: J. Kontio, R. Conradi (Eds.), Software Quality – ECSQ 2002. Proceedings, 2002. XIV, 363 pages. 2002.

Vol. 2350: A. Heyden, G. Sparr, M. Nielsen, P. Johansen (Eds.), Computer Vision – ECCV 2002. Proceedings, Part I. XXVIII, 817 pages. 2002.

Vol. 2351: A. Heyden, G. Sparr, M. Nielsen, P. Johansen (Eds.), Computer Vision – ECCV 2002. Proceedings, Part II. XXVIII, 903 pages. 2002.

Vol. 2352: A. Heyden, G. Sparr, M. Nielsen, P. Johansen (Eds.), Computer Vision – ECCV 2002. Proceedings, Part III. XXVIII, 919 pages. 2002.

Vol. 2353: A. Heyden, G. Sparr, M. Nielsen, P. Johansen (Eds.), Computer Vision – ECCV 2002. Proceedings, Part IV. XXVIII, 841 pages. 2002.

Vol. 2359: M. Tistarelli, J. Bigun, A.K. Jain (Eds.), Biometric Authentication. Proceedings, 2002. XII, 373 pages. 2002.